Psychology
A Journey 4e

Psychology

A Journey 4e

Dennis Coon

John O. Mitterer
Brock University

WADSWORTH
CENGAGE Learning

Australia • Brazil • Japan • Korea • Mexico • Singapore • Spain • United Kingdom • United States

WADSWORTH
CENGAGE Learning

Psychology: A Journey, Fourth Edition
Dennis Coon and John O. Mitterer

Senior Publisher: Linda Schreiber

Executive Editor, Psychology: Jon-David Hague

Senior Sponsoring Psychology Editor: Jane Potter

Managing Development Editor: Jeremy Judson

Senior Assistant Editor: Rebecca Rosenberg

Editorial Assistant: Alicia McLaughlin

Media Editor: Lauren Keyes

Marketing Manager: Tierra Morgan

Marketing Assistant: Molly Felz

Executive Marketing Communications Manager: Talia Wise

Senior Content Project Manager: Pat Waldo

Creative Director: Rob Hugel

Senior Art Director: Vernon Boes

Print Buyer: Karen Hunt

Rights Acquisitions Account Manager, Text: Margaret Chamberlain-Gaston

Rights Acquisitions Account Manager, Image: Don Schlotman

Photo Researcher: Kathleen Olson

Production Service: Dan Fitzgerald, Graphic World Inc.

Text Designer: Jeanne Calabrese

Cover Designer: Jeanne Calabrese

Cover Image: Dave & Les Jacobs/Getty Images

Compositor: Graphic World Inc.

For product information and technology assistance, contact us at
Cengage Learning Customer & Sales Support, 1-800-354-9706
For permission to use material from this text or product,
submit all requests online at **www.cengage.com/permissions**
Further permissions questions can be e-mailed to
permissionrequest@cengage.com

Library of Congress Control Number: 2009935593

Student Edition:

ISBN-10: 0-495-81170-X

ISBN-13: 978-0-495-81170-1

Loose-leaf Edition:

ISBN-10: 0-495-81180-7

ISBN-13: 978-0-495-81180-0

Wadsworth
20 Davis Drive
Belmont, CA 94002-3098
USA

Cengage Learning is a leading provider of customized learning solutions with office locations around the globe, including Singapore, the United Kingdom, Australia, Mexico, Brazil, and Japan. Locate your local office at **www.cengage.com/global**

Cengage Learning products are represented in Canada by Nelson Education, Ltd.

To learn more about Wadsworth, visit **www.cengage.com/Wadsworth**

Purchase any of our products at your local college store or at our preferred online store **www.ichapters.com.**

Printed in the United States of America
1 2 3 4 5 6 7 13 12 11 10 09

For Justin

Dennis Coon After earning a doctorate in psychology from the University of Arizona, Dennis Coon taught for 22 years at Santa Barbara City College, California. Throughout his career, Dr. Coon has especially enjoyed the challenge of teaching introductory psychology. He and his wife, Sevren, have returned to Tucson, where he continues to teach, write, edit, and consult.

Dr. Coon is the author of *Introduction to Psychology* and *Psychology: Modules for Active Learning*, as well as *Psychology: A Journey*. Together, these texts have been used by more than 2 million students. Dr. Coon frequently serves as a reviewer and consultant to publishers, and he edited the best-selling trade book *Choices*. He also helped design modules for PsychNow! Wadsworth's interactive CD-ROM.

In his leisure hours, Dr. Coon enjoys hiking, photography, painting, woodworking, and music. He also designs, builds, and plays classical and steel string acoustic guitars. He has published articles on guitar design and occasionally offers lectures on this topic, in addition to his more frequent presentations on psychology.

John O. Mitterer was awarded his doctorate in cognitive psychology from McMaster University. Currently, Dr. Mitterer teaches at Brock University, where he has taught over 20,000 introductory psychology students. He is the recipient of the 2003 Brock University Distinguished Teaching Award, a 2003 Ontario Confederation of University Faculty Associations (OCUFA) Teaching Award, a 2004 National 3M Teaching Fellowship, and the 2005 Canadian Psychological Association Award for Distinguished Contributions to Education and Training in Psychology.

Dr. Mitterer's primary research focus is on basic cognitive processes in learning and teaching. While he has consulted for a variety of companies, such as Bell Northern Research, Unisys Corporation, IBM Canada, and computer-game developer Silicon Knights, he devotes most of his energy to applying cognitive principles to the improvement of undergraduate education. In support of his introductory psychology course, he has been involved in the creation of textbooks and ancillary materials such as CD-ROMs and websites for both students and instructors. Dr. Mitterer has published and lectured on undergraduate instruction throughout Canada and the United States.

In his spare time, Dr. Mitterer strives to become a better golfer and to attain his life goal of seeing all of the bird species in the world. To this end he recently traveled to the Galapagos Islands, Papua New Guinea, Brazil, Australia, and South Africa.

Introduction
Psychology for Your Life—Self-Reflective Learning 1

1 Discovering Psychology and Research Methods 14

2 Brain and Behavior 52

3 Human Development 87

4 Sensation and Perception 132

5 States of Consciousness 182

6 Conditioning and Learning 225

7 Memory 264

8 Intelligence, Cognition, Language, and Creativity 301

9 Motivation and Emotion 343

10 Personality 387

11 Health, Stress, and Coping 428

12 Psychological Disorders 469

13 Therapies 509

14 Social Behavior 549

Appendix
Behavioral Statistics 593

Glossary G-1
References R-1
Name Index N-1
Subject Index S-1

CONTENTS

>Introduction Psychology for Your Life—Self-Reflective Learning 1

Hi There! 1
Self-Reflective Reading—How to Tame a Textbook 1
How to Use *Psychology: A Journey* 3
Self-Reflective Note Taking—LISAN Up! 4
    Using and Reviewing Your Notes 5
Self-Reflective Study Strategies—Making a Habit of Success 5
Self-Regulated Learning—Academic All-Stars 6

Procrastination—Avoiding the Last-Minute Blues 7
    Time Management 8
    Goal Setting 8
    Make Learning an Adventure 8
Self-Reflective Test Taking—Are You "Test Wise"? 8
    General Test-Taking Skills 9
Using Digital Media—Netting New Knowledge 10
    The Book Companion Website 10
    CengageNOW 11
    Cengage's Psychology Resource Center 11
    Psychology Websites 11
    A Final Word 12
    Web Resources 13
    Interactive Learning 13

>1 Discovering Psychology and Research Methods 14

Journey into Psychology: Wondering about Human Behavior 14
Psychology—Focus on Behavior 15
    Seeking Empirical Evidence 15
    Psychological Research 16
    Research Specialties 16
    Psychology's Goals 17
Critical Thinking—Take It with a Grain of Salt 19
    Thinking About Behavior 19
Pseudopsychologies—Palms, Planets, and Personality 20
    Problems in the Stars 21
Scientific Research—How to Think Like a Psychologist 23
    The Scientific Method 23
A Brief History of Psychology—Psychology's Family Album 26
    Structuralism 26
    Functionalism 26
    Behaviorism 27
    Gestalt Psychology 27
    Psychoanalytic Psychology 28

    Humanistic Psychology 28
    The Role of Diversity in Psychology's Early Days 29
Psychology Today—Three Complementary Perspectives on Behavior 30
    The Biological Perspective 31
    The Psychological Perspective 31
    The Sociocultural Perspective 31
Psychologists—Guaranteed Not to Shrink 33
    Other Mental Health Professionals 35
    Specialties in Psychology 35
The Psychology Experiment—Where Cause Meets Effect 36
    Variables and Groups 37
Double Blind—On Placebos and Self-Fulfilling Prophecies 38
    Research Participant Bias 39
    Researcher Bias 39
Nonexperimental Research Methods—Different Strokes 41
    Naturalistic Observation 41
    Correlational Studies 42
    The Clinical Method 43
    Survey Method 44
Psychology in Action: Psychology in the Media—Separating Fact from Fiction 46

BOXED FEATURES IN CHAPTER 1
Discovering Psychology: Is a Career in Psychology Right for You? 35

>2 Brain and Behavior 52

Journey into Psychology: Finding Music in Walnut-Grapefruit Tofu 52

Neurons—Building a "Biocomputer" 53
- Parts of a Neuron 53
- The Nerve Impulse 53
- Synapses and Neurotransmitters 56
- Neural Networks 57

The Nervous System—Wired for Action 58
- The Peripheral Nervous System 59
- The Spinal Cord 59

Research Methods—Charting the Brain's Inner Realms 61
- Mapping Brain Structure 61
- Exploring Brain Function 62

The Cerebral Cortex—My, What a Big Brain You Have! 65
- Cerebral Hemispheres 66
- Hemispheric Specialization 67
- Lobes of the Cerebral Cortex 69

The Subcortex—At the Core of the (Brain) Matter 73
- The Hindbrain 73
- The Forebrain 74
- The Magnificent Brain 75

The Endocrine System—My Hormones Made Me Do It 76

Psychology in Action: Handedness—Are You Sinister or Dexterous? 79

BOXED FEATURES IN CHAPTER 2
Discovering Psychology: You Can Change Your Mind, But Can You Change Your Brain? 58
Critical Thinking: Repairing Your Brain 61
Human Diversity: His and Her Brains? 72

>3 Human Development 87

Journey into Psychology: It's a Girl! 87

Nature and Nurture—It Takes Two to Tango 88
- Heredity 88
- Environment 90
- Reciprocal Influences 92

The Newborn—More Than Meets the Eye 93
- Perceptual and Cognitive Development 94
- Motor Development 96
- Emotional Development 97

Social Development—Baby, I'm Stuck on You 99
- Attachment 99
- Day Care 100
- Attachment and Affectional Needs 101

Parental Influences—Life with Mom and Dad 101
- Parenting Styles 101
- Maternal and Paternal Influences 102
- Ethnic Differences: Four Flavors of Parenting 102

Language Development—Who Talks Baby Talk? 104
- Language and the Terrible Twos 105
- The Roots of Language 105

Cognitive Development—Think Like a Child 108
- Piaget's Theory of Cognitive Development 108
- Piaget Today 111
- Vygotsky's Sociocultural Theory 113

Adolescence and Young Adulthood—The Best of Times, the Worst of Times 115
- Puberty 115
- The Search for Identity 116
- The Transition to Adulthood 117

Moral Development—Growing a Conscience 117
- Levels of Moral Development 118

The Story of a Lifetime—Rocky Road or Garden Path? 119
- Erikson's Psychosocial Theory 119

Middle and Late Adulthood: Will You Still Need Me When I'm 64? 122
- A Midlife Crisis? 122
- Old Age 122

Psychology in Action: Effective Parenting—Raising Healthy Children 124

BOXED FEATURES IN CHAPTER 3
Discovering Psychology: What's Your Attachment Style? 100
Human Diversity: Ethnic Diversity and Identity 116
Critical Thinking: The Twixters 117

>4 Sensation and Perception 132

Journey into Psychology: Dancing the Two-Step 132
Sensory Systems—The First Step 133
   Selection 133
   Sensory Coding 134
Vision—Catching Some Rays 135
   Structure of the Eye 135
   Rods and Cones 136
   Color Vision 138
   Dark Adapting to Dim Light 140
Hearing—Good Vibrations 142
   How We Hear Sounds 142
Smell and Taste—The Nose Knows When the Tongue
   Can't Tell 145
   The Sense of Smell 145
   Taste and Flavors 146
The Somesthetic Senses—Flying by the Seat of Your Pants 148
   The Skin Senses 148
   The Vestibular System 149

Adaptation, Attention, and Gating—Tuning In and Tuning
   Out 150
   Sensory Adaptation 150
   Selective Attention 151
   Sensory Gating 151
Perception—That Second Step 154
   Bottom-up and Top-down Processing 155
   Gestalt Organizing Principles 156
   Perceptual Constancies 158
Depth Perception—What If the World Were Flat? 160
   Binocular Depth Cues 161
   Monocular Depth Cues 162
Perceptual Learning—Perception from the Top Down 168
   Perceptual Expectancies 168
   Motives, Emotions, and Perception 169
   Perceptual Learning 169
Extrasensory Perception—Do You Believe in Magic? 171
   An Appraisal of ESP 172
Psychology in Action: Becoming a Better Eyewitness to Life 175

BOXED FEATURES IN CHAPTER 4
Discovering Psychology: Are You Color-Blind? 140
Brain Waves: The Matrix: Do Phantoms Live Here? 152
Clinical File: Staying in Touch with Reality 156
Human Diversity: Do They See What We See? 169

>5 States of Consciousness 182

Journey into Psychology: Bending Your Mind 182
States of Consciousness—The Many Faces of Awareness 183
   Altered States of Consciousness 183
Sleep—Catching a Few ZZZ's 183
   The Need for Sleep 184
   Sleep Patterns 185
Stages of Sleep—The Nightly Roller-Coaster 186
   Sleep Stages 186
   The Dual Process Hypothesis of Sleep 187
Sleep Disturbances—Showing Nightly: Sleep Wars! 190
   Insomnia 190
   Sleepwalking, Sleeptalking, and Sleepsex 192
   Nightmares and Night Terrors 193
   Sleep Apnea 193

Dreams—A Separate Reality? 194
   REM Sleep Revisited 194
   Dream Theories 194
   Dream Worlds 196
Hypnosis—Look into My Eyes 197
   Theories of Hypnosis 197
   The Reality of Hypnosis 197
   Stage Hypnosis 199
Meditation and Sensory Deprivation—Chilling, the Healthy
   Way 200
   Meditation 201
   Sensory Deprivation 202
   Positive Psychology: Mindfulness and Well-Being 202
Drug-Altered Consciousness—The High and Low of It 203
   Drug Dependence 205
   Patterns of Abuse 205
Uppers—Amphetamines, Cocaine, MDMA, Caffeine,
   Nicotine 206
   Cocaine 208
   MDMA ("Ecstasy") 209

Caffeine **209**

Nicotine **210**

Downers—Sedatives, Tranquilizers, and Alcohol **211**

Barbiturates **212**

GHB **212**

Tranquilizers **212**

Alcohol **213**

Hallucinogens—Tripping the Light Fantastic **215**

LSD and PCP **215**

Marijuana **216**

A Look Ahead **217**

>6 Conditioning and Learning **225**

Journey into Psychology: Rats! **225**

What Is Learning—Does Practice Make Perfect? **226**

Types of Learning **226**

Classical Conditioning—Does the Name Pavlov Ring a Bell? **227**

Pavlov's Experiment **228**

Principles of Classical Conditioning—Here's Johnny **229**

Acquisition **229**

Expectancies **230**

Extinction and Spontaneous Recovery **230**

Generalization **230**

Discrimination **231**

Classical Conditioning in Humans—An Emotional Topic **231**

Conditioned Emotional Responses **232**

Vicarious, or Secondhand, Conditioning **233**

Operant Conditioning—Can Pigeons Play Ping-Pong? **234**

Positive Reinforcement **234**

Acquiring an Operant Response **234**

The Timing of Reinforcement **235**

Shaping **237**

Operant Extinction **237**

Negative Reinforcement **238**

Punishment **238**

Psychology in Action: Exploring and Using Dreams **218**

BOXED FEATURES IN CHAPTER 5

Human Diversity: Consciousness and Culture **184**

Clinical File: They Came from Outer Space? **189**

Discovering Psychology: Swinging Suggestions **198**

Brain Waves: How Psychoactive Drugs Affect the Brain **204**

Operant Reinforcers—What's Your Pleasure? **239**

Primary Reinforcers **239**

Secondary Reinforcers **239**

Feedback **241**

Partial Reinforcement—Las Vegas, a Human Skinner Box? **243**

Schedules of Partial Reinforcement **244**

Stimulus Control—Red Light, Green Light **246**

Punishment—Putting the Brakes on Behavior **248**

Variables Affecting Punishment **248**

The Downside of Punishment **249**

Using Punishment Wisely **249**

Cognitive Learning—Beyond Conditioning **252**

Cognitive Maps **252**

Latent Learning **252**

Modeling—Do as I Do, Not as I Say **254**

Observational Learning **254**

Modeling and the Media **255**

Psychology in Action: Behavioral Self-Management— A Rewarding Project **258**

BOXED FEATURES IN CHAPTER 6

Clinical File: Coping with Chemo **229**

Brain Waves: Tickling Your Own Fancy **239**

Discovering Psychology: Learning and Conservation **241**

Critical Thinking: Are Animals Stuck in Time? **245**

Critical Thinking: You Mean Video Games Might Be Bad for Me? **256**

>7 Memory 264

Journey into Psychology: Fuhgeddaboudit 264
Stages of Memory—Do You Have a Mind Like a Sieve? 265
   Sensory Memory 265
   Short-Term Memory 266
   Long-Term Memory 266
Short-Term Memory—Do You Know the Magic Number? 268
   Chunking 268
   Rehearsing Information 269
Long-Term Memory—A Blast from the Past 269
   Constructing Memories 270
   Organizing Memories 271
   Skill Memory and Fact Memory 273
Measuring Memory—The Answer Is on the Tip of My Tongue 275
   Recalling Information 275
   Recognizing Information 275
   Relearning Information 276
   Explicit and Implicit Memories 277

Forgetting in LTM—Why We, Uh, Let's See; Why We, Uh. . . . Forget! 278
   When Encoding Fails 279
   When Memory Storage Fails 280
   When Retrieval Fails 281
   Interference 282
Memory and the Brain—Some "Shocking" Findings 284
   Consolidation 285
   Long-Term Memory and the Brain 286
Exceptional Memory—Wizards of Recall 287
   Eidetic Imagery 288
   A Case of Photographic Memory 289
   Memory Champions 289
Improving Memory—Keys to the Memory Bank 290
   Encoding Strategies 290
   Retrieval Strategies 292
   A Look Ahead 293
Psychology in Action: Mnemonics—Memory Magic 294

BOXED FEATURES IN CHAPTER 7
Critical Thinking: Do You Like Jam with Your Memory? 271
Critical Thinking: Telling Wrong from Right in Forensic Memory 272
Discovering Psychology: Card Magic! 280
Clinical File: The Recovered Memory/False Memory Debate 284

>8 Intelligence, Cognition, Language, and Creativity 301

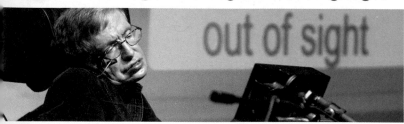

Journey into Psychology: Homo sapiens 301
Human Intelligence—The IQ and You 302
   Defining Intelligence 302
   Measuring Intelligence 302
   The Wechsler Tests 303
   Intelligence Quotients 304
   Group Tests 305
   Artificial Intelligence 305
Variations in Intelligence—Curved Like a Bell 306
   The Mentally Gifted 306
   Intellectual Disability 308

Questioning Intelligence—How Intelligent Is the Idea of Intelligence? 309
   Culture and Intelligence 309
   Multiple Intelligences 310
   IQ and Heredity 311
What Is Thinking?—Brains over Brawn 314
   Some Basic Units of Thought 314
Mental Imagery—Does a Frog Have Lips? 315
   The Nature of Mental Images 315
Concepts—I'm Positive, It's a Whatchamacallit 317
   Forming Concepts 317
   Types of Concepts 317
Language—Don't Leave Home Without It 319
   The Structure of Language 320
   Animal Language 322
Problem Solving—Getting an Answer in Sight 324
   Mechanical Solutions 324
   Solutions by Understanding 325
   Heuristics 325

Insightful Solutions **326**

Common Barriers to Problem Solving **328**

Creative Thinking—Down Roads Less Traveled 329

Tests of Creativity **330**

Stages of Creative Thought **330**

Positive Psychology: The Creative Personality **332**

Intuitive Thought—Mental Shortcut? Or Dangerous Detour? 332

Intuition **333**

Wisdom **335**

Psychology in Action: Enhancing Creativity—Brainstorms 336

BOXED FEATURES IN CHAPTER 8

Clinical File: Meet the Rain Man **308**

Human Diversity: Intelligence—How Would a Fool Do It? **310**

Critical Thinking: You Mean Video Games Might Be Good for Me? **313**

Human Diversity: Bilingualism—*Si o No, Oui ou Non,* Yes or No? **320**

Critical Thinking: Have You Ever Thin-Sliced Your Teacher? **333**

>9 Motivation and Emotion 343

Journey into Psychology: Are You Moved by the Music of Life? 343

Motivation—Push Me, Pull Me 344

A Model of Motivation **344**

Biological Motives and Homeostasis **345**

Circadian Rhythms **345**

Hunger—Pardon Me, My Hypothalamus Is Growling 347

Internal Factors in Hunger **347**

External Factors in Hunger and Obesity **349**

Dieting **350**

Eating Disorders **352**

Biological Motives Revisited—Thirst, Pain, and Sex 354

Thirst **354**

Pain **354**

The Sex Drive **355**

Sexual Behavior—Mapping the Erogenous Zones 355

Sexual Arousal **356**

Human Sexual Response **356**

Sexual Scripts **358**

Sexual Orientation—Who Do You Love? **358**

Healthy Sexual Relationships **359**

Sexual Problems—When Pleasure Fades **360**

Stimulus Motives—Monkey Business 361

Arousal Theory **361**

Sensation Seekers **361**

Levels of Arousal **362**

Coping with Test Anxiety **362**

Learned Motives—The Pursuit of Excellence 363

The Need for Achievement **363**

The Key to Success **364**

Motives in Perspective—The View from the Pyramid 365

Intrinsic and Extrinsic Motivation **366**

Turning Play into Work **367**

Inside an Emotion—How Do You Feel? 368

Primary Emotions **369**

Emotion and the Brain **369**

Physiology and Emotion—Arousal, Sudden Death, and Lying 370

Fight or Flight **371**

Lie Detectors **372**

Expressing Emotions—Making Faces and Talking Bodies 374

Facial Expressions **375**

Body Language **376**

Theories of Emotion—Several Ways to Fear a Bear 376

The James-Lange Theory **376**

The Cannon-Bard Theory **377**

Schachter's Cognitive Theory of Emotion **377**

Emotional Appraisal **378**

The Facial Feedback Hypothesis **379**

A Contemporary Model of Emotion **380**

Psychology in Action: Emotional Intelligence—The Fine Art of Self-Control 381

BOXED FEATURES IN CHAPTER 9

Brain Waves: Your Brain's "Fat Point" **349**

Discovering Psychology: Behavioral Dieting **351**

Human Diversity: What's Love Got to Do with It? **359**

Clinical File: Suppressing Emotion—Don't Turn the Music Off **380**

> 10 Personality 387

Journey into Psychology: The Hidden Essence 387
The Psychology of Personality—Do You Have Personality? 388
  Traits **388**
  Types **389**
  Self-Concept **389**
  Personality Theories **390**
The Trait Approach—Describe Yourself in 18,000 Words or Less 391
  Predicting Behavior **392**
  Classifying Traits **392**
  The Big Five **393**
Psychoanalytic Theory—Id Came to Me in a Dream 396
  The Structure of Personality **396**
  The Dynamics of Personality **397**
  Personality Development **398**
Learning Theories of Personality—Habit I Seen You Before? 401
  How Situations Affect Behavior **401**
  Personality=Behavior **402**
  Social Learning Theory **402**
  Behavioristic View of Development **403**
  Personality and Gender **404**

Humanistic Theory—Peak Experiences and Personal Growth 407
  Maslow and Self-Actualization **407**
  Carl Rogers' Self Theory **409**
  Humanistic View of Development **410**
Traits and Situations—The Great Debate 411
  Do We Inherit Personality? **411**
  Is Personality Affected by Situations? **413**
  Traits, Consistency, and Situations **413**
  Overview and Comparison of Personality Theories **414**
Personality Assessment—Psychological Yardsticks 415
  The Interview **416**
  Direct Observation and Rating Scales **416**
  Personality Questionnaires **418**
  Projective Tests of Personality **420**
Psychology in Action: Barriers and Bridges—Understanding Shyness 422

BOXED FEATURES IN CHAPTER 10
Human Diversity: Self-Esteem and Culture—Hotshot or Team Player?! **390**
Discovering Psychology: What's Your Musical Personality? **392**
Discovering Psychology: Which Personality Are You (and Which Is Best)? **394**
Clinical File: Telling Stories About Ourselves **410**
Critical Thinking: Amazing Twins **412**

> 11 Health, Stress, and Coping 428

Journey into Psychology: Jennifer's Amazing Race 428
Health Psychology—Here's to Your Good Health 429
  Behavioral Risk Factors **429**
  Health-Promoting Behaviors **431**
  Early Prevention **431**
  Community Health **433**
  Positive Psychology: Wellness **433**
STDs and Safer Sex—Choice, Risk, and Responsibility 434
  Sexually Transmitted Diseases **434**
  HIV/AIDS **434**
  Behavioral Risk Factors **435**

Stress—Threat or Thrill? 436
  General Adaptation Syndrome **437**
  Stress, Illness, and Your Immune System **437**
  When Is Stress a Strain? **438**
  Appraising Stressors **439**
  Coping with Threat **440**
Frustration—Blind Alleys and Lead Balloons 440
  Reactions to Frustration **442**
  Coping with Frustration **443**
Conflict—Yes, No, Yes, No, Yes, No, Well, Maybe 443
  Managing Conflicts **445**
Psychological Defense—Mental Karate? 447
Learned Helplessness—Is There Hope? 449
  Depression **451**
  Depression: Why Students Get the Blues **451**
  Coping with Depression **452**

Stress and Health—Unmasking a Hidden Killer 453
    Life Events and Stress 453
    Psychosomatic Disorders 456
    Biofeedback 456
    The Cardiac Personality 457
    Hardy Personality 459
Psychology in Action; Stress Management—Winning the Stress Game 460

BOXED FEATURES IN CHAPTER 11
Discovering Psychology: Unhealthy Birds of a Feather 432
Clinical File: Coping with Traumatic Stress 441
Human Diversity: Acculturative Stress—Stranger in a Strange Land 455
Critical Thinking: It's All in Your Mind 456

>12 Psychological Disorders 469

Journey into Psychology: Beware the Helicopters 469
Normality—What's Normal? 470
    Core Features of Disordered Behavior 471
    Insanity 472
Classifying Mental Disorders—Problems by the Book 472
    An Overview of Psychological Disorders 473
    General Risk Factors 475
Psychotic Disorders—The Dark Side of the Moon 477
    The Nature of Psychosis 477
Delusional Disorders—An Enemy Behind Every Tree 479
    Paranoid Psychosis 480
Schizophrenia—Shattered Reality 480
    Disorganized Schizophrenia 481
    Catatonic Schizophrenia 481
    Paranoid Schizophrenia 482
    The Causes of Schizophrenia 482
    Implications 486
Mood Disorders—Peaks and Valleys 487
    Major Mood Disorders 487
    What Causes Mood Disorders? 488

Anxiety-Based Disorders—When Anxiety Rules 490
    Adjustment Disorders 490
    Anxiety Disorders 491
    Obsessive-Compulsive Disorder 493
    Stress Disorders 493
    Dissociative Disorders 494
    Somatoform Disorders 494
Anxiety and Disorder—Four Pathways to Trouble 496
    Psychodynamic Approach 496
    Humanistic-Existential Approaches 496
    Behavioral Approach 497
    Cognitive Approach 497
Personality Disorders—Blueprints for Maladjustment 498
    Maladaptive Personality Patterns 498
    Antisocial Personality 498
Disorders in Perspective—Psychiatric Labeling 499
    Social Stigma 500
    A Look Ahead 500
Psychology in Action: Suicide—Lives on the Brink 501

BOXED FEATURES IN CHAPTER 12
Discovering Psychology: Crazy for a Day 471
Human Diversity: Running Amok with Cultural Maladies 474
Brain Waves: The Schizophrenic Brain 485
Clinical File: Sick of Being Sick 495
Human Diversity: A Disease Called Freedom 500

>13 Therapies 509

Journey into Psychology: The Duck Syndrome 509
Psychotherapy—The Talking Cure 510
    Dimensions of Therapy 510

Origins of Therapy—Bored Out of Your Skull 511
Psychoanalysis—Expedition into the Unconscious 512
    Psychoanalysis Today 513
Humanistic Therapies—Restoring Human Potential 514
    Client-Centered Therapy 514
    Existential Therapy 515
    Gestalt Therapy 515
Therapy at a Distance—Psych Jockeys and Cybertherapy 516
    Media Psychologists 516
    Telephone and Internet Therapists 517

Behavior Therapy—Healing by Learning 518
    Aversion Therapy **519**
    Desensitization **520**
Operant Therapies—All the World Is a Skinner Box? 523
    Nonreinforcement and Extinction **524**
    Reinforcement and Token Economies **525**
Cognitive Therapy—Think Positive! 526
    Cognitive Therapy for Depression **526**
    Rational-Emotive Behavior Therapy **527**
Group Therapy—People Who Need People 529
    Psychodrama **530**
    Family and Couples Therapy **530**
    Group Awareness Training **530**
Psychotherapy—An Overview 531
    Core Features of Psychotherapy **532**
    The Future of Psychotherapy **532**
    Basic Counseling Skills **533**

Medical Therapies—Psychiatric Care 535
    Drug Therapies **535**
    Electrical Stimulation Therapy **536**
    Psychosurgery **537**
    Hospitalization **537**
    Community Mental Health Programs **538**
Psychology in Action: Self-Management and Seeking Professional Help 539

BOXED FEATURES IN CHAPTER 13
Discovering Psychology: Feeling a Little Tense? Relax! **521**
Discovering Psychology: Ten Irrational Beliefs—Which Do You Hold? **527**
Clinical File: Overcoming the Gambler's Fallacy **528**
Critical Thinking: How Do We Know Therapy Actually Works? **531**
Human Diversity: Therapy and Culture—A Bad Case of "Ifufunyane" **534**

> 14 Social Behavior 549

Journey into Psychology: Love and Hate 549
Affiliation and Attraction—Come Together 550
    Social Comparison Theory **550**
    Interpersonal Attraction **550**
    Self-Disclosure **552**
Liking and Loving—Dating, Rating, Mating 552
    Evolution and Mate Selection **553**
Humans in a Social Context—People, People, Everywhere 555
    Group Structure, Cohesion, and Norms **556**
    Making Attributions **557**
Social Influence—Follow the Leader 558
    Mere Presence **558**
    Conformity **558**
Compliance—A Foot in the Door 561
Obedience—Would You Electrocute a Stranger? 562
    Milgram's Obedience Studies **562**
Coercion—Brainwashing and Cults 564
    Brainwashing **565**
    Cults **565**
Assertiveness Training—Standing Up for Your Rights 566

Attitudes—Belief + Emotion + Action 568
    Forming Attitudes **569**
    Attitudes and Behavior **569**
Attitude Change—Meet the "Seekers" 570
    Persuasion **570**
    Cognitive Dissonance Theory **571**
Prejudice—Attitudes that Injure 573
    Becoming Prejudiced **573**
    The Prejudiced Personality **574**
Intergroup Conflict—The Roots of Prejudice 574
    Experiments in Prejudice **576**
Aggression—The World's Most Dangerous Animal 579
    Instincts **579**
    Biology **580**
    Frustration **580**
    Preventing Aggression **582**
Prosocial Behavior—Helping Others 583
    Bystander Intervention **584**
    Who Will Help Whom? **585**
Psychology in Action: Multiculturalism—Living with Diversity 586

BOXED FEATURES IN CHAPTER 14
Critical Thinking: Groupthink—Agreement at Any Cost **559**
Discovering Psychology: Quack Like a Duck **563**
Human Diversity: Choking on Stereotypes **575**
Critical Thinking: Is America Purple? **577**

> Appendix Behavioral Statistics 593

Journey into Psychology: Statistics from "Heads" to "Tails" 593

Descriptive Statistics—Psychology by the Numbers 594

Graphical Statistics 594

Measures of Central Tendency 594

Measures of Variability 596

Standard Scores 597

The Normal Curve 597

Correlation—Rating Relationships 599

Relationships 599

The Correlation Coefficient 600

Inferential Statistics—Significant Numbers 602

Samples and Populations 602

Significant Differences 603

Glossary G-1

References R-1

Name Index N-1

Subject Index S-1

Preface

To the Student—The Journey Begins

Greetings from your authors. We are delighted to be your guides as you explore the exciting field of psychology. We hope you will find that psychology is at once familiar, exotic, surprising, and challenging. What, really, could be more intriguing than our evolving understanding of human behavior?

Psychology is about each of us. It asks us to adopt a self-reflective attitude as we inquire, "How can we step outside of ourselves to look objectively at how we live, think, feel, and act?" Psychologists believe the answer is through careful thought, observation, and inquiry. As simple as that may seem, thoughtful reflection takes practice to develop. It is the guiding light for all that follows.

Please view this book as a long letter from your authors to you. It is, in a very real sense, written about you, for you, and to you. We sincerely hope you will find human behavior as fascinating as we do. In the pages that follow, we have done all that we could imagine to make your first journey through psychology enjoyable and worthwhile.

Getting Started

None of us likes to start a new adventure by reading a manual. We just want to get right into a new computer game, step off the airplane and begin our vacation, or just start using our new camera or cell phone. You might be similarly tempted to just start reading this textbook.

Please be patient. Successfully learning psychology depends on how you study this book, as well as how you read it. *Psychology: A Journey* is your passport to an active adventure in learning, not just passive reading. To help you get off to a good start, we strongly encourage you to read our short *Introduction,* which precedes Chapter 1. The Introduction describes study skills, including the self-reflective SQ4R method, which you can use to get the most out of this text and your psychology course. It also tells how you can explore psychology through the Internet, electronic databases, and interactive CDs.

Each chapter of this book will take you into a different realm of psychology, such as personality, abnormal behavior, memory, consciousness, or human development. Each realm is complex and fascinating in its own right, with many pathways, landmarks, and interesting detours to discover. The title of this book, *Psychology: A Journey,* reflects the fact that learning is an adventure. Like any journey of discovery, your "tour" of psychology will help you to better understand yourself, others, and the world around you. It's definitely a trip worth taking.

To the Instructor—A Concise Survey of Psychology

Thank you for choosing this book for your students and your course. Marcel Proust wrote, "The real voyage of discovery consists not in seeing new landscapes but in having new eyes." It is in this spirit that we encourage you to use this book's special features to help you change the way your students see human behavior. Accordingly, we have written this book to promote an interest in human behavior, including an appreciation of the practical applications of psychology, the richness of human diversity, and the field of positive psychology. At the same time, we have structured this book to help students learn efficiently and apply critical-thinking skills. Without such skills, students cannot easily go, as Jerome Bruner put it, "beyond the information given" (Bruner, 1973).

Psychology: A Journey was written to provide a concise, but complete, first course in psychology. It is organized into 14 chapters so that the entire field can be covered in a single term, at a pace of one chapter per week. *Journey's* brevity prompted us to select only the very "best" material from the many topics that could be presented. Nevertheless, *Journey* covers not only the heart of psychology, but also many topics at the cutting edge of current knowledge. New information, anecdotes, perspectives, and narratives appear throughout the fourth edition. The result is a concise text that is readable, manageable, informative, and motivating.

Readability and Narrative Emphasis

Selecting a textbook is half the battle in teaching a successful course. When a book overwhelms students or cools their interest, teaching and learning suffer. A good text does much of the work of imparting information to your students. This frees class time for your discussion, extra topics, or media presentations. It also leaves students asking for more.

Many introductory psychology students are reluctant readers. No matter how interesting a text may be, its value is lost if students fail to read it. That's why we've worked hard to make this a clear, readable, and engaging text. We want students to read this book with genuine interest and enthusiasm, not merely as an obligation.

To encourage students to read, we made a special effort to weave narrative threads through every chapter. Everyone loves a good story, and the story of psychology is among the most compelling to be told. Throughout *Psychology: A Journey,* we have used intriguing anecdotes and examples to propel reading and sustain interest. As students explore concepts, they are encouraged to think about ideas and relate them to their own experiences.

Practical Applications

Psychology: A Journey is designed to give students a clear grasp of major concepts without burying them in details. At the same time, it offers a broad overview that reflects psychology's rich heritage of ideas. We think students will find this book informative and intellectually stimulating. Moreover, we have emphasized the many ways that psychology relates to practical problems in daily life.

A major feature of this book is the *Psychology in Action* section found at the end of each chapter. These high-interest discussions bridge the gap between theory and practical application. We believe it is fair for students to ask, "Does this mean anything to me? Can I use it? Why should I learn it if I can't?" The Psychology in Action features show students how to solve problems and manage their own behavior. This allows them to see the benefits of adopting new ideas, and it breathes life into psychology's concepts.

An Integrated Study Guide

The chapters of this text are divided into short segments by special sections called *Study Breaks.* These "mini–study guides" challenge students to think critically about the principles they are learning, to relate concepts to their own experiences, and to quiz themselves. For this edition, we have reorganized the Study Breaks into *Recite* and *Reflect* sections, to better mirror the self-reflective SQ4R method. *Recite* quizzes are somewhat easier than in-class test questions and are designed to provide immediate feedback to students. *Reflect* questions come in two "flavors." *Critical Thinking* questions encourage critical reflection and come with answers. *Relate* questions are open-ended invitations to students to elaborate just-read material by relating it to their personal experiences.

In addition, each chapter concludes with a self-assessment called *Test Your Knowledge.* The multiple-choice questions in Test Your Knowledge provide a way for students to judge how well they are doing in their studies, by taking a sample test. These tests now include 20 questions that are comparable in difficulty to in-class exams.

If students would like even more feedback and practice, a traditional *Study Guide* is available, and students can use a web-based course-management tool called *WebTutor*™ to take online quizzes or practice with electronic flash cards.

Electronic Resources

To encourage further exploration, students will find a section called *Web Resources* at the end of each chapter. The websites described there offer a wealth of information on topics related to psychology. Students are also directed to relevant articles in *InfoTrac® College Edition,* Wadsworth's exclusive online college library.

Human Diversity

Today's students reflect the multicultural, multifaceted nature of contemporary society. In *Psychology: A Journey,* students will find numerous discussions of human diversity, including differences in race, ethnicity, culture, gender, abilities, sexual orientation, and age. Too often, such differences needlessly divide people into opposing groups. Our aim throughout this text is to discourage stereotyping, prejudice, discrimination, and intolerance. We've tried to make this book gender neutral and sensitive to diversity issues. All pronouns and examples involving females and males are equally divided by gender. In artwork, photographs, and examples, we have tried to portray the rich diversity of humanity. In addition, a boxed feature, *Human Diversity,* appears throughout the book, providing students with examples of how to be more self-reflective about human diversity. In short, many topics and examples in this book encourage students to appreciate social, physical, and cultural differences and to accept them as a natural part of being human (see ● Table 1 and ● Table 2 for specific diversity and gender topics).

Positive Psychology

In January 2000, Martin Seligman and Mihaly Csikszentmihalyi co-edited a special issue of *American Psychologist* devoted to optimal functioning, happiness, and "positive psychology." Over the past 100 years, psychologists have paid ample attention to the negative side of human behavior. This is easy to understand because we urgently need to find remedies for human problems. However, Seligman and Csikszentmihalyi have urged us to also study positive psychology. What do we know, for instance, about love, happiness, creativity, well-being, self-confidence, and achievement? Throughout this book, we have attempted to answer such questions for students. Our hope is that students who read this book will gain an appreciation for the potential we all have for optimal functioning. Also, of course, we hope that they will leave introductory psychology with emotional and intellectual tools they can use to enhance their lives (see ● Table 3 for specific positive psychology topics).

How Chapter Features Support Active Learning

Psychology: A Journey uses *self-reflective SQ4R,* an active-learning format, to make studying psychology a rewarding experience. Notice how the steps of the self-reflective SQ4R method—survey, question, read, recite, reflect, and review—are incorporated into the chapter design:

Survey   Features at the beginning of each chapter help students build cognitive maps of upcoming topics, thus serving as advance organizers. A short *Journey into Psychology* opening vignette arouses interest, gives an overview of the chapter, and focuses attention on the task at hand. Next, a list of *Survey Questions* provides a focused overview of the chapter. These same Survey Questions appear in the main body of the chapter to help students structure their learning. Later, the Survey Questions are used to organize the chapter Summary, and they also appear in the *Study Guide.* In this way, students are given a consistent framework for studying and learning. These chapter-opening features invite students to read with a purpose and actively process information.

● Table 1 Human Diversity and Culture in *Psychology: A Journey*

CHAPTER 1: DISCOVERING PSYCHOLOGY AND RESEARCH METHODS

- Cultural psychology
- Human diversity, appreciating social and cultural differences
- The impact of culture
- Cultural relativity
- A broader view of diversity
- Human diversity and representative samples

CHAPTER 2: BRAIN AND BEHAVIOR

- Spinal cord and brain repair
- Hypopituitary dwarfism
- Handedness and laterality
- Computer aids for people with total paralysis

CHAPTER 3: HUMAN DEVELOPMENT

- Ethnic differences in child rearing
- The relationship between culture and babbling
- Parentese in different cultures
- Piagetian stages and cultural influences
- Sociocultural influences on cognitive development (Vygotsky)
- Adolescent status and culture
- Diversity and the adolescent search for identity
- Ethnicity and personal identity
- Culture and moral reasoning
- 20-somethings and emerging adulthood
- Ageism and myths about the elderly

CHAPTER 4: SENSATION AND PERCEPTION

- The "other race" effect in facial recognition
- Culture and the recognition of pictorial depth cues
- Culture and the Müller-Lyer illusion
- Cross-racial perceptions (eyewitness accuracy)
- Cultural differences in perception

CHAPTER 5: STATES OF CONSCIOUSNESS

- States of consciousness and culture
- Meditation traditions
- The cultural context of drug use

CHAPTER 6: CONDITIONING AND LEARNING

- Comparing U.S. television content with cultures that limit televised violence

CHAPTER 7: MEMORY

- Aging and memory
- Cultural influences on memory
- Eyewitnesses and cross-racial recognition
- Labeling and the ability to remember people from other social groups

CHAPTER 8: INTELLIGENCE, COGNITION, LANGUAGE, AND CREATIVITY

- Cultural barriers to problem solving
- Age and IQ
- The developmentally disabled
- Race, culture, ethnicity, and intelligence
- Cultural differences in intelligence (as taught to children)
- Culture-fair intelligence testing
- Social stereotypes and cognition
- The effects of unconscious prejudice on word recognition
- Linguistic misunderstandings between cultures
- The pros and cons of bilingualism
- Cultural differences in the use of phonemes
- The deaf community and gestural languages
- Bias in the use of IQ tests for educational placement

CHAPTER 9: MOTIVATION AND EMOTION

- Cultural values and food preferences
- Culture, ethnicity, and dieting
- Pain avoidance and cultural conditioning
- The influence of culture on emotional expressions
- Cultural differences in the occurrence of emotion
- Cultural differences in facial expressions
- Cultural learning and body language

CHAPTER 10: PERSONALITY

- Personality, character, and culture
- Self-esteem and culture
- Personality and music
- Gender development and culture

CHAPTER 11: HEALTH, STRESS, AND COPING

- Scapegoating of ethnic group members
- Culture shock and acculturative stress

CHAPTER 12: PSYCHOLOGICAL DISORDERS

- How culture affects judgments of psychopathology
- Culture-specific psychological "disorders"
- Ethnic group differences in psychopathology

CHAPTER 13: THERAPIES

- Cultural issues in counseling and psychotherapy
- Culturally aware therapists

CHAPTER 14: SOCIAL BEHAVIOR

- Gendered friendships
- Male–female differences in mate preferences
- Evolutionary perspectives on male and female mate selection
- Aggression and culture
- Stereotyping, discrimination, and prejudice
- Multiculturalism

Table 2 Gender in *Psychology: A Journey*

CHAPTER 1: DISCOVERING PSYCHOLOGY AND RESEARCH METHODS
- The psychology of gender
- Women in psychology
- A broader view of diversity

CHAPTER 2: BRAIN AND BEHAVIOR
- Differences between men's and women's brains
- Differences between men's and women's endocrine systems
- Oversecretion of sex hormones (and virilism and prepuberty)

CHAPTER 3: HUMAN DEVELOPMENT
- Motherhood, prenatally and postnatally
- Parenting styles and gender role development
- Comparing male and female mid-life transitions
- Gender and happiness

CHAPTER 4: SENSATION AND PERCEPTION
- Color blindness

CHAPTER 5: STATES OF CONSCIOUSNESS
- Sexual arousal during dreams
- Specific effects of some drugs (e.g., caffeine) on women
- Metabolism of alcohol
- Effects of alcohol on sexual performance
- Sexual effects of Ecstasy

CHAPTER 6: CONDITIONING AND LEARNING
- Effects of television on children's perceptions of sex roles
- Effects of television on children's level of aggression

CHAPTER 8: INTELLIGENCE, COGNITION, LANGUAGE, AND CREATIVITY
- Sex and IQ
- Gender and genetic mutations

CHAPTER 9: MOTIVATION AND EMOTION
- Eating disorders in men and women
- How hormones affect sex drive
- Sexual arousal and response in men and women
- Sexual orientation
- Sexual problems in men and women
- Gender differences in emotion

CHAPTER 10: PERSONALITY
- Freudian views of men and women (and critique)
- Social learning of male and female traits
- Gender stereotypes and androgyny

CHAPTER 12: PSYCHOLOGICAL DISORDERS
- How gender affects judgments of psychopathology
- Gender differences in rates of anxiety disorders
- Gender differences in rates of clinical depression
- Gender differences in suicide (attempt and completion)

CHAPTER 14: SOCIAL BEHAVIOR
- Double standards for male and female performance
- Influence of physical attractiveness
- Male–female differences in mate preferences
- Gendered friendships
- Male–female differences in loving and liking
- Evolutionary perspectives on male and female mate selection

Table 3 Positive Psychology in *Psychology: A Journey*

Appreciating human diversity (Ch. 1)
Characteristics of the gifted (Ch. 8)
Constructive child discipline (Ch. 3)
Dreams and creativity (Ch. 5)
Elements of positive mental health (Ch. 11)
Emotional intelligence (Ch. 9)
Enhancing creativity (Ch. 8)
Enriching early development (Ch. 3)
Ethical research (Ch. 1)
Exceptional memory (Ch. 7)
Facilitating cognitive development (Ch. 3)
Friendship and attraction (Ch. 14)
Fully functioning person (Ch. 10)
Hardiness and happiness (Ch. 11)
Health-promoting behaviors (Ch. 11)

Health-promoting conditions in therapy (Ch. 13)
High achievers (Ch. 9)
Hope (Ch. 11)
Humanistic psychology (Chs. 1, 9, 10, 13)
Improving memory (Ch. 7)
Intrinsic motivation and creativity (Ch. 9)
Loving and liking (Ch. 14)
Meditation (Ch. 11)
Meta-needs (Ch. 9)
Moral behavior (Ch. 3)
Multiple intelligences (Ch. 8)
Optimal caregiving (Ch. 3)
Peak performance (Ch. 9)

Perceptual awareness (Ch. 4)
Positive states of consciousness (Ch. 5)
Promoting secure attachment (Ch. 3)
Promoting self-esteem in children (Ch. 3)
Quality day care (Ch. 3)
Repair of brain damage (Ch. 2)
Self-actualization (Chs. 1, 9, 10)
Self-efficacy (Ch. 10)
Self-confidence (Ch. 10)
Self-esteem (Ch. 10)
Self-regulated learning (Introduction)
Successful aging (Ch. 3)
Wellness (Ch. 11)
Well-being and happiness (Ch. 3)

Question Throughout each chapter, frequent italicized *Guide Questions* also serve as advance organizers. That is, Guide Questions prompt students to look for important ideas as they read, and thus promote active learning. They also establish a dialogue in which the questions and reactions of students are anticipated. This clarifies difficult points—in a lively give-and-take between questions and responses.

Read We've made every effort to make this a clear, readable text. To further aid comprehension, we've used a full array of traditional learning aids. These include boldface terms (with phonetic pronunciations), bullet summaries, a robust illustration program, summary tables, a name index, a subject index, and a detailed glossary.

An *Integrated Glossary* aids reading comprehension by providing precise definitions directly in context. When important terms first appear, they are immediately defined. In this way, students get clear definitions when and where they need them—in the general text itself. In addition, a parallel *Running Glossary* defines key terms in the margins of pages. The Running Glossary makes it easier for students to find, study, and review important terms.

Recite Every few pages, a *Study Break* gives students a chance to test their recall and understanding of preceding topics. As mentioned earlier, the Study Breaks include a Recite section (a short, noncomprehensive quiz), which helps students actively process information and assess their progress. Recite questions are not as difficult as in-class tests, and they are just a sample of what students could be asked about various topics. Students who miss any items are asked to backtrack and clarify their understanding before reading more. Completing Recite questions serves as a form of recitation to enhance learning.

Reflect Cognitive psychology tells us that elaboration, the self-reflective processing of new information, is one of the best ways to foster understanding and form lasting memories (Anderson, 2005; Gadzella, 1995; Goldstein, 2008). The more students elaborate ideas as they read and study, the richer their understanding will be and the better they will remember new concepts.

Self-reference, a particularly powerful form of elaboration, makes new information more meaningful by relating it to what is already known (Klein & Kihlstrom, 1986). *Discovering Psychology* boxes in this edition are "try-it" demonstrations that enable students to observe interesting facets of their own behavior or do self-assessment exercises. In this way, students can link new information to concrete experiences.

To help students further elaborate their new understanding, each Study Break includes a series of *Relate* questions that encourage students to associate new concepts with personal experiences and prior knowledge.

A course in psychology also naturally contributes to deeper forms of reflection, such as the development of critical-thinking abilities. To further facilitate reflection, each Study Break also includes one or more *Critical-Thinking Questions*. These stimulating questions challenge students to think critically and analytically about psychology. Each is followed by a brief answer with which students can compare their own thoughts. Many of these answers are based on research and are informative in their own right.

In addition, several boxed highlights encourage other forms of self-reflective thought. The *Critical Thinking* boxes model a reflective approach to the theoretical and empirical foundations of critical thinking in psychology. In addition, *Human Diversity* boxes encourage reflection on the variability of the human experience, *The Clinical File* boxes encourage reflection on the clinical applications of psychology, and *Brain Waves* boxes, which are new to this edition, encourage reflection on brain mechanisms that underlie psychological phenomena.

Review As noted previously, all important terms appear in a Running Glossary throughout the book, which aids review. As also noted, a Psychology in Action section shows students how psychological concepts relate to practical problems, including problems in their own lives. The information found in Psychology in Action helps reinforce learning by illustrating psychology's practicality.

To help students consolidate their learning, the Chapter in Review section restates all of the major ideas presented earlier in the chapter. This section begins with a list of *Major Points* that summarize the "take home" concepts every student should be able to remember 10 years after reading this text. Next, a point-by-point *Summary* provides a detailed synopsis of the chapter. As mentioned before, the Summary is organized around the same Survey Questions found at the beginning of the chapter. This brings the self-reflective SQ4R process full-circle and reinforces the learning objectives for the chapter. Every chapter concludes with *Test Your Knowledge,* the brief multiple-choice test described earlier. Students who miss any questions on this test are urged to review further, using various supplements available with this text.

Critical Thinking

The active, questioning nature of the self-reflective SQ4R method is, in itself, an inducement to think critically. Many of the Guide Questions that introduce topics in the text act as models of critical thinking. So do the Critical Thinking, Human Diversity, Discovering Psychology, The Clinical File, and Brain Waves boxed highlights. Further, Chapter 1 contains a discussion of critical thinking skills and a rational appraisal of pseudo-psychologies. In addition, the discussion of research methods in Chapter 1 is actually a short course on how to think clearly about behavior. It is augmented by suggestions about how to critically evaluate claims in the popular media. Chapter 8, which covers intelligence, cognition, language, and creativity, includes many topics related to critical thinking. Throughout the text, many boxed highlights promote critical thinking about specific topics that students should approach with healthy skepticism. As mentioned earlier, every Study Break includes Critical Thinking questions. Taken together, these features will help students gain thinking skills of lasting value.

Psychology: A Journey—What's New in the Fourth Edition?

Thanks to psychology's vitality and suggestions from professors, this text is improved in many ways. The fourth edition of *Psychology: A Journey* features some of the most recent and interesting information in psychology, plus fully updated references and statistics. The following annotations highlight some of the new topics and features that appear in this edition.

Introduction: Psychology for Your Life— Self-Reflective Learning

The SQ4R framework has again been updated and is now referred to as "self-reflective SQ4R." Our intent is to combine the comprehension-boosting power of critical-thinking approaches with the memory-boosting power of the traditional SQ4R method. As in the previous edition, the traditional SQ4R term "Relate" has been replaced by the term "Reflect." Study Breaks have been restructured so that students can more easily see the connection with the self-reflective SQ4R method. Specifically, *Learning Check* questions are now *Recite* questions. A new section titled *Reflect* now includes *Relate* questions and *Critical Thinking* questions. This combination makes it clearer that relating new information to personal experiences and thinking critically about new information are both forms of self-reflective cognition.

The *Introduction,* which we recommend that you ask students to read, offers updated information on how to read effectively, study more efficiently, take good notes, prepare for tests, perform well on various types of tests, create study schedules, and avoid procrastination.

Chapter 1: Discovering Psychology and Research Methods

The chapter title has been changed to better reflect our deliberate focus on critical-thinking skills. The chapter has been rewritten and reorganized beginning with a new chapter-opening vignette. The material on critical thinking and pseudo-psychology has been moved nearer to the front of the chapter and followed immediately by a discussion of the scientific method. This permits a tighter link to be drawn between critical thinking and scientific research. The section on placebo effects and the experimenter effect has been upgraded to discuss research participant bias (with placebo effects being one variant). The material on case studies, surveys, correlations, and natural observation has been gathered under one major heading following the section on the experimental method.

Chapter 2: Brain and Behavior

This chapter has been lengthened to reflect the growing importance of neuroscience to psychology. The chapter-opening vignette has been updated. A new Discovering Psychology feature invites students to explore self-directed neuroplasticity. A new Critical Thinking feature entitled *Repairing Your Brain* has also been added. A new section on saltatory conduction has also been added. The section on exploring brain function has been reorganized; ESB, ablation, and deep lesioning are now treated in that order. The section on fMRI has been enhanced with the inclusion of a discussion of lie detection (including a new figure). The section on lobes of the cerebral cortex has been reorganized. The order of coverage has been changed and the treatment of association areas and primary sensory areas sharpened. In particular, the section on association areas has been incorporated into the four sections on lobes.

Chapter 3: Human Development

The opening discussion of nature–nurture has been reworked. Readiness is now discussed in the first major section under *Genetics,* as is maturation. We correct the now outdated assumption that human evolution has not progressed since our caveman days. Sensitive periods are now treated after prenatal influences. Temperament is now treated in an expanded section on reciprocal influences. The section on Piaget has been reorganized (for example, the early description of conservation failure has been more appropriately situated later in the section. In addition, conservation is given more weight). A new major section on *Adolescence and Young Adulthood* has been created. Previous material on puberty and identity has been expanded and moved to this new section. *Middle and Late Adulthood* is now a major section, and a short piece on middle age has been added.

Chapter 4: Sensation and Perception

The new opening vignette more clearly stresses the two-step nature of the sensation–perception sequence. The core point that sensation is about transduction is brought to the fore right away in the first major section. In the section on vision, the eye–camera comparison is updated to an eye–digital camera comparison. The major sections on perception have been broadly reorganized. The notion of perception as a construction is brought to the fore. This allows an immediate discussion of perceptual misconstruction, illusions, and reality testing. The notion of perception as a top-down–bottom-up interaction also is presented earlier. Gestalt organizing principles are now discussed before constancies. A Human Diversity feature, *Do They See What We See?* has been added.

Chapter 5: States of Consciousness

Theories of sleep and dreaming have been updated. The hypothesis that sleep involves dual processes introduces newer explanations of the functions of REM and NREM sleep. The section on sleepwalking and sleeptalking now includes a discussion of sexsomnia. The section on dream theories adds a discussion of neurocognitive dream theory to the existing discussions of psychodynamic dream theory and the activation-synthesis hypothesis. The terms "manifest content" and "latent content" are now included in the discussion of psychodynamic dream theory. The section on hypnosis has been reorganized, with material on stage hypnosis now appearing at the end of the section. A new section on mindfulness and well-being has been added, as has a new Brain Waves feature, *How Psychoactive Drugs Affect the Brain.* A new section on polydrug abuse highlights drug interactions. The first study to examine the long-term effects of Ecstasy is discussed.

Chapter 6: Conditioning and Learning

A new chapter-opening vignette better highlights the various forms of learning covered in the chapter. The treatment of conditioning and cognitive learning has been rebalanced. The opening headings have now been reworked (as has the entire chapter) to better highlight the distinction between associative and cognitive learning. The section on feedback has been rewritten. Feedback is now distinguished from knowledge of results (which is one simpler form of feedback). A new Critical Thinking feature asks *Are Animals Stuck in Time?*

Chapter 7: Memory

The chapter-opening vignette has been updated. The chapter reverses the order in which the Atkinson-Schiffrin model (now identified as such), and the terms "encoding," "storage," and "retrieval" are introduced. The phrase "elaborative rehearsal" has been changed to "elaborative encoding." This change ties elaboration back to encoding, one of the three memory processes introduced early in the chapter. In general, the three memory processes play a greater organizing role in the chapter. A new Critical Thinking feature, *Do You Like Jam with Your Memory?* offers an interesting and current example of constructive processing. Material on flashbulb memories has been moved to a new section on memory and emotion and better linked to a discussion of memory and the brain. Material on exceptional memory has been relocated and reorganized.

Chapter 8: Intelligence, Cognition, Language, and Creativity

A new chapter-opening vignette now features Steven Hawking. The remarkable Kim Peek, who was the focus of the previous vignette, is now discussed in a new Clinical File feature, *Meet the Rain Man.* Artificial Intelligence is now treated as another approach to defining intelligence. The Human Diversity feature, *Intelligence—How Would a Fool Do It?* has been moved to the section on controversies about intelligence. The Wechsler IQ tests are now presented immediately following the discussion of the Stanford-Binet. The outdated term "mentally retarded" has been changed to "intellectually disabled."

Chapter 9: Motivation and Emotion

The section on eating disorders has been expanded to include eating disorders in men. A broader set of reasons why people develop eating disorders is explored. A new Human Diversity feature, *What's Love Got to Do with It?* explores new, more casual sexual scripts. The section on sexual orientation now more firmly stresses the role of genetic/biological factors and presents the prenatal hormone theory. The role of the amygdala in emotional experience is more clearly presented. The three fundamental types of motives are now referred to as biological, stimulus, and learned motives. Sections on cultural differences in expressing emotions, gender and emotion, theories of emotion, and emotional intelligence have all been reorganized.

Chapter 10: Personality

This chapter has been extensively reorganized. A new Clinical File feature, *Telling Stories About Ourselves,* about narrative psychology and personality change, and a new Discovering Psychology feature, *Which Personality Are You (and Which Is Best)?* have been added. Material about the role of heredity and environment in personality has been moved to a later section entitled *Traits and Situations—The Great Debate.* As a consequence, students now encounter theories of personality earlier in the chapter. The material on the role of gender and the treatment of androgyny has also been reworked.

Chapter 11: Health, Stress, and Coping

This chapter has been extensively reorganized. Material on sexually transmitted diseases is now covered early in the chapter, as an example of the kind of health issues tackled by health psychology. The section on stress management is now covered in the chapter-ending Psychology in Action section. A new Discovering Psychology feature entitled *Unhealthy Birds of a Feather,* which discusses social factors in health, has been added, along with a new Critical Thinking feature, *It's All in Your Mind.* A new table summarizes the top sources of stress at work.

Chapter 12: Psychological Disorders

Mental disorders are presented in a revised order. Psychotic disorders are now covered first, followed by mood disorders, anxiety disorders, and personality disorders. A new Clinical File feature, *Sick of Being Sick,* on Munchausen syndrome by proxy, has been added. Incidence statistics and some case study examples of the major disorders have been updated. The legal concept of insanity is now discussed nearer to the front of the chapter. The treatment of dementias now includes a discussion of organic dementia and Alzheimer's disease. A new section discusses the upcoming DSM-V and some issues about adding and deleting disorders.

Chapter 13: Therapies

This chapter has been updated for greater clarity. The basic aspects of therapy identified at the beginning of the chapter now better align with the dimensions presented in Table 13.2. The same dimensions are more consistently used throughout the chapter. The material on distance therapies and the role of digital media has been updated. A new Clinical File feature, *Overcoming the Gambler's Fallacy,* addresses gambling addiction among young people. A new Critical Thinking feature, *How Do We Know Therapy Actually Works?* has also been added. The material on medical therapies has been updated and a new section on *Interpersonal Therapy* has been added.

Chapter 14: Social Behavior

The chapter-opening vignette has been revised, and the order of coverage of material in the chapter has been adjusted accordingly. Robert Sternberg's triarchic theory of love is now discussed. The section on social influence has been expanded to include coverage of the effects of mere presence. Brainwashing and cults are treated as forms of coercion, the most extreme type of social influence. A new Human Diversity box, *Choking on Stereotypes,* presents the idea of stereotype threat.

A Complete Course—Teaching and Learning Supplements

A rich array of supplements accompanies *Psychology: A Journey,* including several that make use of the latest technologies. These supplements are designed to make teaching and learning more effective. Many are available free to professors or students. Others can be packaged with this text at a discount. For more information on any of the listed resources, please call Cengage Learning's Customer Service at 1-800-874-2383; technical support questions may be sent to www.cengage.com/support.

Student Support Materials

Introductory students must learn a multitude of abstract concepts, which can make a first course in psychology difficult. The materials listed here will greatly improve students' chances for success.

Practice Exams with Visual Guides   Now included as easy-to-follow pull-out cards in the back of the book, the Visual Guides present important topics from each chapter in an easy-to-use flow chart. Each chapter has its own card, which includes the Visual Guides to help students connect ideas and build cognitive maps of key concepts, as well as short practice tests. The Practice Exams, written by Shawn Talbot of Kellogg Community College, consist of 20 multiple-choice questions that students can use to evaluate their understanding and prepare for classroom tests.

Study Guide (to facilitate learning)   The Study Guide provides abundant opportunities for practice, self-testing, and rehearsal. The Study Guide is structured around the self-reflective SQ4R method and is closely coordinated with this text. Each chapter includes the following sections: Chapter Overview (a concise chapter summary), Learning Objectives (a detailed list of what students need to know), Recite and Review (a survey of major terms and concepts), Connections (matching items), Check Your Memory (true–false items), Final Survey and Review (fill-in-the-blank questions), and a Mastery Test (multiple-choice questions similar to in-class test items). The Study Guide also includes a Language Development Guide. For some students, language and culture can be major barriers to comprehension. The Language Development Guide helps clarify idioms and special phrases, cultural and historical allusions, and tricky vocabulary. All terms and phrases in the manual are page referenced to the text and are followed by concise definitions. (Study Guide, by Danielle Gagne of Alfred University, ISBN: 0-8400-3222-6.)

Careers in Psychology: Opportunities in a Changing World   This informative new booklet, written by Tara L. Kuther, is a Wadsworth exclusive. The pamphlet describes the field of psychology, as well as how to prepare for a career in psychology. Career options and resources are also discussed. *Careers in Psychology* can be packaged with this text at no additional cost to students (ISBN 0-495-60074-1).

Multimedia CD-ROM

Interactive CD-ROMs make it possible for students to directly experience some of the phenomena they are studying. The following CD from Wadsworth provides a wealth of engaging modules and exercises.

Psyk.trek™ 3.0: A Multimedia Introduction to Psychology   This student tutorial, available on CD-ROM or online, contains 150 concept checks as well as new tests, critical-thinking questions, and learning objectives, and provides an intuitive landscape to any introductory psychology course. Available to accompany all introductory textbooks (ISBN 0-495-09035-2).

Internet Resources

The Internet is providing new ways to exchange information and enhance education. In psychology, Wadsworth is at the forefront in making use of this exciting technology.

Book Companion Website   As users of this text, you and your students will have access to the book companion website for *Psychology: A Journey,* www.cengage.com/psychology/coon. The site includes learning objectives, a glossary, flash cards, crossword puzzles, and extensive web links. It also offers chapter quizzing—multiple-choice and essay questions.

CengageNOW   CengageNOW is an online teaching and learning resource that gives you more control in less time and delivers better outcomes—NOW. Not only is CengageNOW a valuable course management and timesaving tool for you, it also offers many features that provide students with efficient ways to study for success in your course. CengageNOW includes diagnostic pretests and posttests, with resulting personalized study plans. For every chapter, your students' Personalized Study Plans enable them to focus on what they need to learn and select the activities that best match their learning styles. CengageNOW includes an integrated eBook, videos, simulations, and animations—all designed to help students gain a deeper understanding of important concepts.

WebTutor Jump-start your course with customizable, rich, text-specific content within your Course Management System. Whether you want to web-enable your class or put an entire course online, WebTutor™ delivers. WebTutor offers a wide array of resources, including videos, animations, simulations, learning modules, chapter-by-chapter quizzing, pretests and posttests, and more! Visit webtutor.cengage.com to learn more.

Essential Teaching Resources

As every professor knows, teaching an introductory psychology course is a tremendous amount of work. The supplements listed here should not only make life easier for you, but also make it possible for you to concentrate on the more creative and rewarding facets of teaching.

Instructor's Resource Manual The Instructor's Resource Manual (ISBN: 0-8400-3214-5) was prepared by Wanda McCarthy of the University of Cincinnati. For every chapter in the text, this manual includes: learning objectives and detailed chapter outlines; discussion topics, classroom activities, and hand-outs; web links; and video suggestions. The manual also includes a detailed Resource Integration Guide that shows, at a glance, how each of this text's supplements correlates to each chapter of the text.

Test Bank The Test Bank was prepared by Jeannette Murphey of Meridian Community College. It includes over 4,000 multiple-choice questions organized by chapter and by learning objectives. All items, which are classified as factual, conceptual, or applied, include correct answers and page references from the text. Every chapter of the Test Bank also includes 35–40 fill-in-the-blank and 20 essay questions that tie into the learning objectives (ISBN-10: 0-495-90946-7/ISBN-13: 978-0-495-90946-0).

PowerLecture This one-stop lecture and class preparation tool contains ready-to-use PowerPoint® slides that allow you to assemble, edit, publish, and present custom lectures for your course. PowerLecture lets you bring together text-specific lecture outlines and art from Coon & Mitterer's text along with videos or your own materials, culminating in a powerful, personalized media-enhanced presentation.

The DVD also includes the JoinIn™ Student Response System that lets you pose topic-specific polling questions, video polling questions, and book-specific questions and display students' answers seamlessly within the PowerPoint slides of your own lecture in conjunction with the "clicker" hardware of your choice, as well as the ExamView® assessment and tutorial system, which guides you step-by-step through the process of creating tests.

Videotapes and Films

Wadsworth offers a variety of videotapes and films to enhance classroom presentations. Many video segments in the Wadsworth collection pertain directly to major topics in this text, making them excellent lecture supplements.

Wadsworth Film and Video Library for Introductory Psychology Adopters can select from a variety of continually updated film and video options. The Wadsworth Film and Video Library includes selections from the Discovering Psychology series, the Annenberg series, and Films for Humanities. Contact your local sales representative or Wadsworth Marketing at 877-999-2350 for details.

ABC® Videos for Introductory Psychology ABC Videos feature short, high-interest clips from current news events as well as historic raw footage going back 40 years. Perfect for discussion starters or to enrich your lectures and spark interest in the material in the text, these brief videos provide students with a new lens through which to view the past and present, one that will greatly enhance their knowledge and understanding of significant events and open up to them new dimensions in learning. Clips are drawn from such programs as *World News Tonight, Good Morning America, This Week, PrimeTime Live, 20/20,* and *Nightline,* as well as numerous ABC News specials and material from the Associated Press Television News and British Movietone News collections. VHS also available on request.

Research in Action DVD, Vols. I & II Research in Action features the work of research psychologists to give students an opportunity to learn about cutting-edge research—not just who is doing it, but also how it is done, and how and where the results are being used. By taking students into the laboratories of both established and up-and-coming researchers, and by showing research results being applied outside of the laboratory, these videos offer insight into both the research process and the many ways in which real people's lives are affected by research in the fields of psychology and neuroscience.

PSYCH IN FILM® DVD Psych in Film contains 35 clips from Universal Studios films illustrating key concepts in psychology. Clips from *Schindler's List, Snow Falling on Cedars,* and many other films are combined with commentary and discussion questions to help bring psychology alive for students and demonstrate its relevance to contemporary life and culture. Teaching tips are correlated to specific text chapters and concepts, and are available on the instructor website.

Supplementary Books

No text can cover all of the topics that might be included in an introductory psychology course. If you would like to enrich your course, or make it more challenging, the Wadsworth titles listed here may be of interest.

Critical Thinking in Psychology: Separating Sense from Nonsense, Second Edition

The second edition of *Critical Thinking in Psychology: Separating Sense from Nonsense* (ISBN: 0-534-63459-1) provides the tools to distinguish between the true science of human thought and behavior from pop psychology. John Ruscio's book provides a tangible and compelling framework for making that distinction. Because we are inundated with "scientific" claims, the author does not merely differentiate science and pseudoscience, but goes further to teach the fundamentals of scientific reasoning on which students can base their evaluation of information.

Challenging Your Preconceptions: Thinking Critically About Psychology, Second Edition

This paperbound book (ISBN: 0-534-26739-4), written by Randolph Smith, helps students strengthen their critical-thinking skills. Psychological issues such as hypnosis and repressed memory, statistical seduction, and the validity of pop psychology, among other topics, are used to illustrate the principles of critical thinking.

Writing Papers in Psychology: A Student Guide

The eighth edition of *Writing Papers in Psychology* (ISBN: 0-495-50956-6), by Ralph and Mimi Rosnow, is a valuable "how to" manual for writing term papers and research reports. This new edition has been updated to reflect the latest APA guidelines. The book covers each task with examples, hints, and two complete writing samples. Citation ethics, how to locate information, and new research technologies are also covered.

Your Guide to College Success: Strategies for Achieving Your Goals, Concise Edition (with Instant Access Code-CengageNOW™)

Authored by John Santrock, a prominent developmental psychologist, and Jane Halonen, an educational leader in critical thinking, this fourth edition (ISBN: 1-413-02073-9) emphasizes student self-awareness in the pursuit of college success goals, as well as active learning strategies.

College Survival Guide: Hints and References to Aid College Students

This fourth edition of Bruce Rowe's *College Survival Guide* (ISBN: 0-534-35569-2) is designed to help students succeed. Rowe provides valuable tips on how to finance an education, how to manage time, how to study for and take exams, and more. Other sections focus on maintaining concentration, credit by examination, use of the credit/no-credit option, cooperative education programs, and the importance of a liberal arts education.

Cross-Cultural Perspectives in Psychology

How well do the concepts of psychology apply to various cultures? What can we learn about human behavior from cultures different from our own? These questions lie behind a collection of original articles written by William F. Price and Rich Crapo. The fourth edition of *Cross-Cultural Perspectives in Psychology* (ISBN: 0-534-54653-6) contains articles on North American ethnic groups as well as cultures from around the world.

Wadsworth Quick Guide for Career Planning

This quick guide (ISBN: 1-413-02264-2) provides highly useful tools for students needing step-by-step advice on career planning.

Wadsworth Quick Guide to Our Diverse World

This booklet (ISBN: 1-413-02259-6) tackles the topic of diversity, including how to fight the natural tendency to stereotype, discriminate, and hold prejudicial views of others.

Culture and Psychology: People Around the World, Third Edition

David Matsumoto and Linda Juang's unique book (ISBN: 0-534-53591-7) discusses similarities and differences in research findings in the United States and other cultures. By doing so, it helps students see psychology and their own behavior from a broader, more culturally aware perspective.

College Success Internet at a Glance (Trifold Brochure)

This handy one-page laminated reference (ISBN: 0-534-56411-9) for students has a host of URL addresses related to college success—to give you a guided tour of the Internet!

Summary

We sincerely hope that teachers and students will consider this book and its supporting materials a refreshing change from the ordinary. Creating it has been quite an adventure. In the pages that follow, we think students will find an attractive blend of the theoretical and the practical, plus many of the most exciting ideas in psychology. Most of all, we hope that students using this book will discover that reading a college textbook can be entertaining and enjoyable.

Acknowledgments

Chad Graham, Meridian Community College
Jeannette Murphey, Meridian Community College
Anna S. Napier, Hazard Community and Technical School
Liz L. Nelson, American River College
Sara Jane Overstreet, Mercer University
Jim Previte, Victor Valley College
Nancy Zombro, Cape Cod Community College

Psychology is a cooperative effort requiring the talents and energies of a large community of scholars, teachers, researchers, and students. Like most endeavors in psychology, this book reflects the efforts of many people. We deeply appreciate the contributions of all those who have supported this text's evolution, including the following psychologists:

Jean Brown, Cambrian College
Anice Bullock, Tomball College
Lisa Clark, Clark Atlanta University
Eric Comstock, Heald College, Concord
David Das, Elgin Community College
Michael Gardner, California State University, Northridge
Dorothy Gomez, Bunker Hill Community College
Frank Hager, Allegany College of Maryland
John Haworth, Florida Community College at Jacksonville
John S. Klein, Castleton State College
Patricia Lanzon, Henry Ford Community College
Denis Laplante, Lambton College
Laura Madson, New Mexico State University
Errol Magidson, Richard J. Daley College
Horace Marchant, Westfield State College
Richard Mascolo, El Camino Community College
Shawn Mikulay, Elgin Community College
Pike Nelson, Chicago State University
Alysia Ritter, Murray State University
Moises Salinas, Central Connecticut State University
Matthew Westra, Longview Community College

We especially wish to thank the following professors, whose sage advice helped improve the third edition of *Psychology: A Journey:*

Dana Albright, Clovis Community College
Saundra Ciccarelli, Gulf Coast Community College
Ellen Cotter, Georgia Southwestern State University
Keith Davis, University of South Carolina
Mary Ellen Dello Stritto, Ball State University
Mylo Egipciaco, Los Angeles Pierce College
Richard Epro, Nassau County Community College
Sabra Jacobs, Prestonsburg Community College
Thuy Karafa, Ferris State University
Jimi Leopold, Tarleton State University
Feleccia Moore-Davis, Houston Community College
Todd Nelson, California State University, Stanislaus
Randall Osborne, Southwest Texas State University
Sandra Phipps, Hazard Community College
Robert Wellman, Fitchburg State College
Matthew Zagumny, Tennessee Tech University

Producing *Psychology: A Journey* and its supplements was a formidable task. We are especially indebted to each of the following individuals for supporting this book:

Sean Wakely
Michelle Julet
Linda Schreiber
Jon-David Hague

We also wish to thank the individuals at Cengage Learning who so generously shared their knowledge and talents over the past year. These are the people who made it happen:

Vernon Boes
Tierra Morgan
Pat Waldo
Jeremy Judson
Rebecca Rosenberg
Lauren Keyes
Jane Potter
Kathleen Olson

We would especially like to express our deepest gratitude to our publisher, Linda Schreiber, who has actively supported our efforts, and our editor, Jane Potter, for helping us define a new vision for *Journey* and make this book the best it can possibly be. Their guidance will make life easier for professors and students who use this book. Dan Fitzgerald from Graphic World was more than very helpful in getting this book to press. We also owe a profound debt to Jeremy Judson, whose brilliant assistance and wonderful friendship has been utterly invaluable.

At home, Barbara Kushmier and Kayleigh Hagerman helped with several aspects of the preparation of this book. Last of all, we would like to thank our wives, Sevren and Heather, for making the journey worthwhile.

Psychology for Your Life— Self-Reflective Learning

Hi There!

You're actually reading this! As your authors, we're glad. Too often, students just jump in and plough through a textbook from the first assigned chapter to the last. That's a shame because it's far better to study a textbook, not just read it. Think about it: How much do you typically remember after you've read straight through a whole chapter? If the answer is "nada," "zilch," or simply "not enough," it may be because reading is not the same as studying. Even if you're an excellent student, you may be able to improve your study skills. Students who get good grades tend to work smarter, not just longer or harder (Santrock & Halonen, 2007). They also tend to understand and remember more of what they've learned long after their exams are over. Psychology is for their lives, not just for their exams. To help you get a good start, let's look at several ways to improve studying.

Self-Reflective Reading— How to Tame a Textbook

What's the difference between reading a textbook and studying it? Have you ever spent an evening mindlessly watching television? Psychologist Donald Norman (1993) notes that our thinking tends to be hazy when we just passively take in experiences. He calls this

"I'm too busy going to college to study."

experiential cognition, and as you may have noticed after watching TV, your memory for such experiences is usually not very good.

In contrast, suppose you watch a TV special about global warming and it really gets you thinking. You might wonder how global warming will affect your own future. Perhaps you are skeptical about some of the program's predictions. Didn't you read something different recently? Now you are reacting "mindfully" and "going beyond the information given" (Bruner, 1973). This is **reflective cognition** (Norman, 1993). Rather than just having an experience, you *actively think* about it. Similarly, you will learn more from a textbook if you mindfully reflect on what you read. Reflective thinking can help you remember details about an experience in the future. This is especially true if you are *self-reflective.*

How can I be more self-reflective while reading? One straightforward way to be more self-reflective is through **self-reference.** As you read, you should relate new facts, terms, and concepts to your own experiences and information you already know well. Doing so will make new ideas more personally meaningful and easier to remember. In Chapter 7 you will find out more about why self-reference is an effective way to improve memory. Critical thinking is another powerful way to be more self-reflective. **Critical thinkers** pause to evaluate, compare, analyze, critique, and synthesize what they are reading. You should, too. In Chapter 1 we will learn how to think critically about psychology.

These ways to improve learning can be combined into the **Self-reflective SQ4R method.** SQ4R stands for *survey, question, read, recite, reflect,* and *review.* These six steps can help you study more effectively:

S = *Survey.* Skim through a chapter before you begin reading it. Start by looking at topic headings, figure captions, and summaries. Try to get an overall picture of what lies ahead. Because this book is organized into short sections, you can survey just one section at a time if you prefer.

Q = *Question.* As you read, turn each topic heading into one or more questions. For example, when you read the heading "Stages of Sleep," you might ask: "Is there more than one stage of sleep?" "What are the stages of sleep?" "How do they differ?" Asking questions prepares you to read with a purpose.

R1 = *Read.* The first R in SQ4R stands for read. As you read, look for answers to the questions you asked. Read in short "bites," from one topic heading to the next, then stop. For difficult material, you may want to read only a paragraph or two at a time.

R2 = *Recite.* After reading a small amount, you should pause and recite or rehearse. Try to mentally answer your questions. Better yet, summarize what you just read in brief notes. Making notes will reveal what you know and don't know, so you can fill gaps in your knowledge (Peverly et al., 2003).

If you can't summarize the main ideas, skim over each section again. Until you can understand and remember what you just read, there's little point to reading more. After you've studied a short "bite" of text, turn the next topic heading into questions. Then read to the following heading. Remember to look for answers as you read and to recite or take notes before moving on. Ask yourself repeatedly, "What is the main idea here?" Repeat the question–read–recite cycle until you've finished an entire chapter (or just from one Study Break to the next, if you want to read shorter units).

R3 = *Reflect.* As you read, self-reflect on what you are reading. As stated earlier, two powerful ways to do this are self-reference and critical thinking. This is the most important step in the self-reflective SQ4R method. The more mindfulness and genuine interest you can bring to your reading, the more you will learn (Hartlep & Forsyth, 2000).

Experiential cognition Style of thinking arising during passive experience.

Reflective cognition Style of thinking arising while actively thinking about an experience.

Self-reference The practice of relating of new information to prior life experience.

Critical thinking An ability to evaluate, compare, analyze, critique, and synthesize information.

Self-reflective SQ4R method An active study-reading technique based on these steps: survey, question, read, recite, reflect, and review.

◀◀ **FIGURE I.1** The Self-reflective SQ4R method promotes active learning and information processing. You should begin with a survey of the chapter or a shorter section, depending on how much you plan to read. Then, you should proceed through cycles of questioning, reading, reciting, and reflecting, and conclude with a review of the section or the entire chapter.

R4 = *Review.* When you're done reading, skim back over a section or the entire chapter, or read your notes. Then check your memory by reciting and quizzing yourself again. Try to make frequent, active review a standard part of your study habits. (See ▶▶ Figure I.1.)

Does this really work? You bet! Using a self-reflective reading strategy improves learning and course grades (Taraban, Rynearson, & Kerr, 2000). It also results in enhanced long-term understanding. Simply reading straight through a chapter can give you "intellectual indigestion." That's why it's better to stop often to think, question, recite, self-reflect, review, and "digest" information as you read.

How to Use *Psychology: A Journey*

You can apply the self-reflective SQ4R method to any text. However, we have specifically designed this textbook to help you actively learn psychology.

Survey

Each chapter opens with a *Preview* called *Journey into Psychology* and a list of *Survey Questions* to help you identify important ideas as you begin reading. The Previews should help you get interested in the topics you will be reading about, and Survey Questions are a good guide to the kinds of information you should look for as you read. After you've studied these features, take a few minutes to do your own survey of the chapter, including the figure captions and chapter-ending material. Doing so will help you build a "mental map" of upcoming topics.

Question

How can I use the self-reflective SQ4R method to make reading more interesting and effective? One of the key steps is to ask yourself a lot of questions while you read. The Survey Questions are repeated throughout each chapter to help you identify key topics. In addition, dialogue questions like the one that began this paragraph appear throughout each chapter. They are similar to questions that students like you ask themselves as they read this book. Try to anticipate these questions. Even better, be sure to ask your own questions. Try to actively interact with your textbooks as you read.

Read

As an aid to reading, important terms are printed in **boldface type** and defined where they first appear. (Some are followed by pronunciations — capital letters show which syllables are accented.) You'll also find a *running glossary* in the lower right-hand corner of pages you are reading, so you never have to guess about the meaning of technical terms. If you want to look up a term from a lecture or another chapter, check the main *Glossary*. This "mini-dictionary" is located near the end of the book. Perhaps you should take a moment to find it now. In addition, many figures and tables will help you quickly grasp important concepts.

Recite and Reflect

To help you study in smaller "bites," this book is divided into short sections ending with *Study Breaks,* which make good stopping points. By using *Recite* questions in the Study Breaks you can check how well you remember what you just read. Additionally, *Critical*

● Table I.1 Using the
Self-Reflective SQ4R Method

SURVEY

- Preview
- Survey Questions
- Figure Captions
- Chapter in Review

QUESTION

- Topic Headings
- Survey Questions
- In-Text Dialogue Questions

READ

- Topic Headings
- Boldface Terms
- Running Glossary (in margins)
- Figures and Tables

RECITE

- Recite Questions (in Study Breaks)
- Practice Quizzes (online)
- Notes (make them while reading)

REFLECT

- Reflect Questions (in Study Breaks); including Critical Thinking Questions and Relate Questions
- Boxed Features (throughout the text)

REVIEW

- Chapter in Review
- Boldface Terms
- Running Glossary (in margins)
- Tables
- Test Your Knowledge
- Practice Quizzes (online)
- Study Guide

thinking questions invite you to think more deeply, and *Relate questions* will help you connect new ideas to your own life. (Don't forget to also take notes or recite and self-reflect on your own.)

This book provides many other opportunities for you to self-reflect more deeply about what you are reading. Each chapter ends with a *Psychology in Action* section. These discussions are filled with practical ideas you can relate to your own life. In many chapters, *Discovering Psychology* boxes also invite you to relate psychology to your own behavior. *Critical Thinking* boxes present intriguing questions you can use to sharpen your critical thinking skills. In addition, *Human Diversity* boxes encourage you to self-reflect on the rich variety of human experience; *Brainwaves* boxes show how the brain relates to psychology; and in *The Clinical File* boxes, we will see how psychology can be applied to treat clinical problems.

Review

Each chapter concludes with a detailed *Chapter in Review*, to help you identify key ideas to remember. Each Chapter in Review begins with a list of *Major Points* that make up the most important concepts or "big ideas" of the chapter. Then, a point-by-point *Summary* reviews the chapter in greater detail. These summaries are organized around the same Survey Questions you read at the beginning of the chapter. You can also return to the glossary items throughout each chapter for further review.

On the last page of every chapter you will find a brief quiz called *Test Your Knowledge*. You can use this quiz to get a preliminary idea about how well you remember ideas and concepts from your reading. But don't stop studying just because you do well on one of these quizzes. Additional review and practice will add greatly to your understanding—not to mention your test scores.

● Table I.1 summarizes how this text helps you apply the self-reflective SQ4R method. Even with all this help, there is still much more you can do on your own.

Self-Reflective Note Taking—LISAN Up!

Self-reflective reading strategies may be good for studying, but what about taking notes in class? Sometimes it's hard to know what's important. Just as studying a textbook is best done self-reflectively, so too is learning in class (Norman, 1993). Like effective reading, good notes come from actively seeking information. People who are **active listeners** avoid distractions and skillfully gather ideas. Here's a listening/note-taking plan that works for many students. The letters LISAN, pronounced like the word *listen,* will help you remember the steps:

L = *Lead. Don't follow.* Read assigned materials before coming to class. Try to anticipate what your teacher will say by asking yourself questions. If your teacher provides course notes or PowerPoint overheads before lectures, review them before coming to class. Self-reflective questions can come from those materials or from study guides, reading assignments, or your own curiosity.

I = *Ideas.* Every lecture is based on a core of ideas. Usually, an idea is followed by examples or explanations. Ask yourself often, "What is the main idea now? What ideas support it?"

S = *Signal words.* Listen for words that tell you what direction the instructor is taking. For instance, here are some signal words:

There are three reasons why. . . .	Here come ideas
Most important is. . . .	Main idea
On the contrary. . . .	Opposite idea
As an example. . . .	Support for main idea
Therefore. . . .	Conclusion

Active listener A person who knows how to maintain attention, avoid distractions, and actively gather information from lectures.

A = *Actively listen.* Sit where you can get involved and ask questions. Bring questions you want answered from the last lecture or from your text. Raise your hand at the beginning of class or approach your professor before the lecture. Do anything that helps you stay active, alert, and engaged.

N = *Note taking.* Students who take accurate lecture notes tend to do well on tests (Williams & Eggert, 2002). However, don't try to be a tape recorder. Listen to everything, but be selective and write down only key points. If you are too busy writing, you may not grasp what your professor is saying. When you're taking notes, it might help to think of yourself as a reporter who is trying to get a good story (Ryan, 2001).

Actually, most students take reasonably good notes—and then don't use them! Many students wait until just before exams to review. By then, their notes have lost much of their meaning. If you don't want your notes to seem like "chicken scratches," it pays to review them daily (Rowe, 2007).

Using and Reviewing Your Notes

When you review, you will learn more if you take the extra steps listed here (Knaus & Ellis, 2002; Rowe, 2007; Santrock & Halonen, 2007):

- As soon as you can, self-reflectively improve your notes by filling in gaps, completing thoughts, and looking for connections among ideas.
- Remember to link new ideas to what you already know.
- Summarize your notes. Boil them down and *organize* them.
- After each class session, write down several major ideas, definitions, or details that are likely to become test questions. Then, make up questions from your notes and be sure you can answer them.

Summary

The letters LISAN are a guide to active listening, but listening and good note taking are not enough. You must also review, organize, self-reflect, extend, and think about new ideas. Use active listening to get involved in your classes and you will undoubtedly learn more (Rowe, 2007).

Self-Reflective Study Strategies— Making a Habit of Success

Grades depend as much on effort as they do on "intelligence." However, don't forget that good students work more *efficiently,* not just harder. Many study practices are notoriously unreflective, such as recopying lecture notes, studying class notes but not the textbook (or the textbook but not class notes), outlining chapters, answering study questions with the book open, and "group study" (which often becomes a party). The best students emphasize *quality:* They study their books and notes in depth and attend classes regularly. It's a mistake to blame poor grades on events "beyond your control." Students who are motivated to succeed usually get better grades (Perry et al., 2001). Let's consider a few more things you can do to improve your study habits.

Study in a Specific Place

Ideally, you should study in a quiet, well-lit area free of distractions. If possible, you should also have at least one place where you *only study.* Do nothing else there: Keep magazines, MP3 players, friends, cell phones, pets, posters, video games, puzzles, food, lovers, sports cars, elephants, pianos, televisions, YouTube, and other distractions out of the area. In this way, the habit of studying will become strongly linked with one specific place. Then, rather than trying to force yourself to study, all you have to do is go to your study area. Once there, you'll find it is relatively easy to get started.

Use Spaced Study Sessions

It is reasonable to review intensely before an exam. However, you're taking a big risk if you are only "cramming" (learning new information at the last minute). Spaced practice is much more efficient (Anderson, 2005). **Spaced practice** consists of a large number of relatively short study sessions. Long, uninterrupted study sessions are called **massed practice.** (If you "massed up" your studying, you probably messed it up too.)

Cramming places a big burden on memory. Usually, you shouldn't try to learn anything new about a subject during the last day before a test. It is far better to learn small amounts every day and review frequently (Anderson, 2005).

Try Mnemonics

Mnemonics make new information more familiar and memorable. Forming an image of a duck wearing a pot for a hat might help you remember that *pato* is the Spanish word for duck.

Learning has to start somewhere, and memorizing is often the first step. Many of the best ways to improve memory are covered in Chapter 7. Let's consider just one technique here.

A **mnemonic** (nee-MON-ik) is a memory aid. There are many ways to create mnemonics. Most mnemonics link new information to ideas or images that are easy to remember. For example, what if you want to remember that the Spanish word for duck is *pato*, pronounced POT-oh? To use a mnemonic, you could picture a duck in a pot or a duck wearing a pot for a hat. Likewise, to remember that the cerebellum controls coordination, you might picture someone named "Sarah Bellum" who is very coordinated. For best results, make your mnemonic images exaggerated or bizarre, vivid, and interactive (Macklin & McDaniel, 2005).

Test Yourself

A great way to improve grades is to take practice tests before the real one in class. In other words, studying should include **self-testing,** in which you pose questions to yourself. You can use flash cards, *Study Break* "Recite" questions, end-of-chapter "Test Your Knowledge" questions, online quizzes, a study guide, or other means. As you study, ask many questions and be sure you can answer them. Studying without self-testing is like practicing for a basketball game without shooting any baskets.

For more convenient self-testing, your professor may make a *Study Guide* or a separate booklet of *Practice Quizzes* available. You can use either to review for tests. Practice quizzes are also available on the book companion website, as described later. However, don't use practice quizzes as a substitute for studying your textbook and lecture notes. Trying to learn from quizzes alone will probably *lower* your grades. It is best to use quizzes to find out what topics you need to study more (Brothen & Wambach, 2001).

Overlearn

Many students *underprepare* for exams, and most *overestimate* how well they will do. A solution to both problems is **overlearning,** in which you continue studying beyond your initial mastery of a topic. In other words, plan to do extra study and review *after* you think you are prepared for a test. One way to overlearn is to approach all tests as if they will be essays. That way, you will learn more completely, so you really "know your stuff."

Spaced practice Practice spread over many relatively short study sessions.

Massed practice Practice done in a long, uninterrupted study session.

Mnemonic A memory aid or strategy.

Self-testing Evaluating learning by posing questions to yourself.

Overlearning Continuing to study and learn after you first think you've mastered a topic.

Self-Regulated Learning—Academic All-Stars

Think of a topic you are highly interested in, such as music, sports, fashion, cars, cooking, politics, or movies. Whatever the topic, you have probably learned a lot about it—painlessly. How could you make your college work more like voluntary learning? An approach called self-regulated learning might be a good start. **Self-regulated learning** is deliberately self-reflective and active self-guided study (Hofer & Yu, 2003). Here's how you can change passive studying into goal-oriented learning:

1. *Set specific, objective learning goals.* Try to begin each learning session with specific goals in mind. What knowledge or skills are you trying to master? What do you hope to accomplish (Knaus & Ellis, 2002)?

2. *Plan a learning strategy.* How will you accomplish your goals? Make daily, weekly, and monthly plans for learning. Then put them into action.

3. *Be your own teacher.* Effective learners silently give themselves guidance and ask themselves questions. For example, as you are learning, you might ask yourself, "What are the important ideas here? What do I remember? What don't I understand? What do I need to review? What should I do next?"

4. *Monitor your progress.* Self-regulated learning depends on self-monitoring. Exceptional learners keep records of their progress toward learning goals (pages read, hours of studying, assignments completed, and so forth). They quiz themselves, use study guides, make sure they follow the self-reflective SQ4R system, and find other ways to check their understanding while learning.

5. *Reward yourself.* When you meet your daily, weekly, or monthly goals, reward your efforts in some way, such as going to a movie or downloading some new music. Be aware that self-praise also rewards learning. Being able to say, "Hey, I did it!" or "Good work!" and know that you deserve it can be very rewarding. In the long run, success, self-improvement, and personal satisfaction are the real payoffs for learning.

6. *Evaluate your progress and goals.* It is a good idea to frequently evaluate your performance records and goals. Are there specific areas of your work that need improvement? If you are not making good progress toward long-range goals, do you need to revise your short-term targets?

7. *Take corrective action.* If you fall short of your goals you may need to adjust how you budget your time. You may also need to change your learning environment, to deal with distractions such as watching TV, daydreaming, talking to friends, or testing the structural integrity of the walls with your stereo system.

If you discover that you lack necessary knowledge or skills, ask for help, take advantage of tutoring programs, or look for information beyond your courses and textbooks. Knowing how to regulate and control learning can be a key to lifelong enrichment and personal empowerment.

Procrastination—Avoiding the Last-Minute Blues

All these study techniques are fine. But what can I do about procrastination? A tendency to procrastinate is almost universal. (When campus workshops on procrastination are offered, many students never get around to signing up!) Even when procrastination doesn't lead to failure, it can cause much suffering. Procrastinators work only under pressure, skip classes, give false reasons for late work, and feel ashamed of their last-minute efforts. They also tend to feel frustrated, bored, and guilty more often (Blunt & Pychyl, 2005).

Why do so many students procrastinate? Many students equate grades with their *personal worth.* That is, they act as if grades tell whether they are good, smart people who will succeed in life. By procrastinating, they can blame poor work on a late start, rather than a lack of ability (Beck, Koons, & Milgrim, 2000). After all, it wasn't their best effort, was it? Perfectionism is a related problem. If you expect the impossible, it's hard to start an assignment. Students with high standards often end up with all-or-nothing work habits (Onwuegbuzie, 2000).

Self-regulated learning Deliberately self-reflective and active self-guided study.

Time Management

Most procrastinators must eventually face the self-worth issue. Nevertheless, most can improve by learning study skills and better time management. We have already discussed general study skills, so let's consider time management in a little more detail.

A **weekly time schedule** is a written plan that allocates time for study, work, and leisure activities. To prepare your schedule, make a chart showing all the hours in each day of the week. Then fill in times that are already committed: sleep, meals, classes, work, team practices, lessons, appointments, and so forth. Next, fill in times when you will study for various classes. Finally, label the remaining hours as open or free times.

Each day, you can use your schedule as a checklist. That way you'll know at a glance which tasks are done and which still need attention (Knaus & Ellis, 2002).

You may also find it valuable to make a **term schedule** that lists the dates of all quizzes, tests, reports, papers, and other major assignments for each class.

The beauty of sticking to a schedule is that you know you are making an honest effort. It will also help you avoid feeling bored while you are working or guilty when you play.

Be sure to treat your study times as serious commitments, but respect your free times, too. And remember, students who study hard and practice time management *do* get better grades (Rau & Durand, 2000).

Goal Setting

As mentioned earlier, students who are self-reflective, active learners set **specific goals** for studying. Such goals should be clear-cut and measurable (Knaus & Ellis, 2002). If you find it hard to stay motivated, try setting goals for the semester, the week, the day, and even for single study sessions. Also, be aware that more effort early in a course can greatly reduce the "pain" and stress you will experience later. If your professors don't give frequent assignments, set your own day-by-day goals. That way, you can turn big assignments into a series of smaller tasks that you can actually complete (Ariely & Wertenbroch, 2002). An example would be reading, studying, and reviewing 8 pages a day to complete a 40-page chapter in 5 days. For this textbook, reading from one Study Break to the next each day might be a good pace. Remember, many small steps can add up to an impressive journey.

Make Learning an Adventure

A final point to remember is that you are most likely to procrastinate if you think a task will be unpleasant (Pychyl et al., 2000). Learning can be hard work. Nevertheless, many students find ways to make schoolwork interesting and enjoyable. Try to approach your schoolwork as if it were a game, a sport, an adventure, or simply a way to become a better person. The best educational experiences are challenging, yet fun (Ferrari & Scher, 2000).

Virtually every topic is interesting to someone, somewhere. You may not be particularly interested in the sex life of South American tree frogs. However, a biologist might be fascinated. (Another tree frog might be, too.) If you wait for teachers to "make" their courses interesting, you are missing the point. Interest is a matter of *your attitude*. (See ▶▶ Figure I.2 for a summary of study skills.)

Study Skills Checklist

Time Management
- [ ] Make formal schedule
- [ ] Set specific goals

Study Habits
- [ ] Study in specific area
- [ ] Pace study and review
- [ ] Create memory aids
- [ ] Test yourself
- [ ] Overlearn

Reading
- [ ] Use reflective SQ4R method
- [ ] Study while reading
- [ ] Review frequently

Note Taking
- [ ] Listen actively
- [ ] Use LISAN method
- [ ] Review notes frequently

▲ **FIGURE I.2** Study skills checklist.

Weekly time schedule A written plan that allocates time for study, work, and leisure activities during a one-week period.

Term schedule A written plan that lists the dates of all major assignments for each of your classes for an entire semester or quarter.

Specific goal A goal with a clearly defined and measurable outcome.

Self-Reflective Test Taking—Are You "Test Wise"?

If I read and study effectively, is there anything else I can do to improve my grades? You must also be able to show what you know on tests. Here are some ways to improve your test-taking skills:

General Test-Taking Skills

You'll do better on all types of tests if you observe the following guidelines (Wood & Willoughby, 1995):

1. Read all directions and questions carefully. They may give you good advice or clues.
2. Quickly survey the test before you begin.
3. Answer easy questions before spending time on more difficult ones.
4. Be sure to answer all questions.
5. Use your time wisely.
6. Ask for clarification when necessary.

Objective Tests

Several additional strategies can help you do better on objective tests. Objective tests (multiple-choice and true–false items) require you to recognize a correct answer among wrong ones or a true statement versus a false one. Here are some strategies for taking objective tests:

1. First, relate the question to what you know about the topic. Then, read the alternatives. Does one match the answer you expected to find? If none match, re-examine the choices and look for a *partial* match.
2. Read *all* the choices for each question before you make a decision. Here's why: If you immediately think that *a* is correct and stop reading, you might miss seeing a better answer like "both *a* and *d.*"
3. Read rapidly and skip items you are unsure about. You may find "free information" in later questions that will help you answer difficult items.
4. Eliminate certain alternatives. With a four-choice multiple-choice test, you have one chance in four of guessing right. If you can eliminate two alternatives, your guessing odds improve to 50-50.
5. Unless there is a penalty for guessing, be sure to answer any skipped items. Even if you are not sure of the answer, you may be right. If you leave a question blank, it is automatically wrong. When you are forced to guess, don't choose the longest answer or the letter you've used the least. Both strategies lower scores more than random guessing does.
6. There is a bit of folk wisdom that says: "Don't change your answers on a multiple-choice test. Your first choice is usually right." This is *false.* If you change answers, you are more likely to gain points than to lose them. This is especially true if you are uncertain of your first choice or it was a hunch and if your second choice is more self-reflective (Higham & Gerrard, 2005).
7. Remember, you are searching for the one *best* answer to each question. Some answers may be partly true yet flawed in some way. If you are uncertain, try rating each multiple-choice alternative on a 1–10 scale. The answer with the highest rating is the one you are looking for.
8. Few circumstances are *always* or *never* present. Answers that include superlatives such as *most, least, best, worst, largest,* or *smallest* are often false.

Essay Tests

Essay questions are a weak spot for students who lack organization, don't support their ideas, or don't directly answer the question (Rowe, 2007). When you take an essay exam, try the following:

1. Read the question carefully. Be sure to note key words, such as *compare, contrast, discuss, evaluate, analyze,* and *describe.* These words all demand a certain emphasis in your answer.
2. Answer the question. If the question asks for a definition and an example, make sure you provide both. Providing just a definition or just an example will get you half marks. Giving three examples instead of the one asked for will not earn you any extra marks.

3. Self-reflect on your answer for a few minutes and list the main points you want to make. Just write them as they come to mind. Then rearrange the ideas in a logical order and begin writing. Elaborate plans or outlines are not necessary.
4. Don't beat around the bush or pad your answer. Be direct. Make a point and support it. Get your list of ideas into words.
5. Look over your essay for errors in spelling and grammar. Save this for last. Your *ideas* are of central importance. You can work on spelling and grammar separately if they affect your grades.

Short-Answer Tests

Tests that ask you to fill in a blank, define a term, or list specific items can be difficult. Usually, the questions themselves contain little information. If you don't know the answer, you won't get much help from the questions.

The best way to prepare for short-answer tests is to overlearn the details of the course. As you study, pay special attention to lists of related terms.

Again, it is best to start with the questions whose answers you're sure you know. Follow that by completing the questions whose answers you think you *probably* know. Questions whose answers you have no idea about can be left blank.

Again, for your convenience, ▶▶ Figure I.2 provides a checklist summary of the main study skills we have covered.

Using Digital Media—Netting New Knowledge

Digital media offer another way to be more self-reflective. Search the Internet for any psychological term, from *amnesia* to *zoophobia*, and you will find a vast array of information. Websites range from the authoritative, like the one provided by the American Psychological Association, to Wikipedia entries and personal blogs. However, be aware that information on the Internet is not always accurate. It is wise to approach all websites with a healthy dose of skepticism.

The Book Companion Website

How can I find reliable information about psychology on the Internet? Your first stop on the Internet should be the website for this book. Here's some of what you'll find there:

Web Links. This area is a "launching pad" that will take you to other psychology-related sites on the Internet selected by your authors.

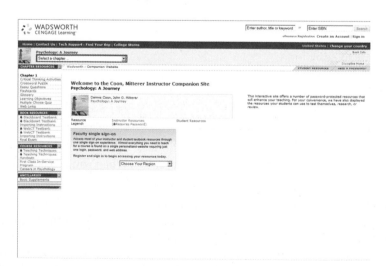

The book companion website gives you online access to a variety of valuable learning aids and interesting materials.

Quizzes. You can use these chapter-by-chapter multiple-choice and true–false quizzes to practice for tests and check your understanding.

Flashcards. These online flashcards allow you to practice terms and concepts interactively.

Crossword Puzzles. Crosswords are a fun way to check your knowledge of key terms and their definitions.

The book companion website is located at **www.cengage .com/psychology/coon.** Be sure to visit this site for valuable information about how to improve your grades and enhance your appreciation of psychology.

CengageNOW

Students can also make use of *CengageNOW for Coon/Mitterer's Psychology: A Journey 4e.* *CengageNOW* is a web-based, personalized study system that provides a pretest and a posttest for each chapter. You'll find it at academic.cengage.com/login. *CengageNOW* also creates personalized study plans, which include media such as videos, animations, learning modules, and links to the eBook. These materials can help you master the topics you need to study most (▶▶ Figure I.3).

Cengage's Psychology Resource Center

Do you like videos, simulations, and animations? Do you learn best when you get actively involved in psychology? The Cengage Psychology Resource Center brings psychology to life with a full library of original and classic video clips plus interactive learning modules tied to all of the topics covered in your introductory psychology course. Log in at **www.cengage.com/login** to visit the resource center.

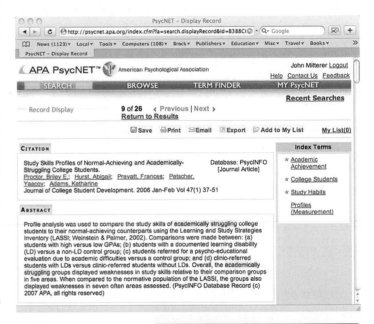

Psychology Websites

You'll find the titles of interesting websites you may want to explore at the end of each chapter in this book, including this one. The best way to reach these sites is through the book companion website. We have not included website addresses in the book because they often change or may become inactive. At the book companion site you'll find up-to-date links for websites listed in this book. The sites we've listed are generally of high quality.

PsycINFO

Psychological knowledge can also be found through specialized online databases. One of the best is PsycINFO, offered by the American Psychological Association (APA). **PsycINFO** provides summaries of the scientific and scholarly literature in psychology. Each record in PsycINFO consists of an abstract (short summary), plus notes about the author, title, source, and other details (▶▶ Figure I.4). All entries are indexed using key terms. Thus, you can search for various topics by entering words such as *drug abuse, postpartum depression,* or *creativity.*

Almost every college and university subscribes to PsycINFO. If this is the case, you can usually search PsycINFO from a terminal in your college library or computer center—for free. PsycINFO can also be directly accessed (for a fee) through the Internet via APA's PsycINFO Direct service. For more information on how to gain access to PsycINFO, check this website: **www.apa.org/psycinfo.**

PsycINFO A searchable online database that provides brief summaries of the scientific and scholarly literature in psychology.

The APA Website

The APA also maintains an online library of general interest articles on aging, anger, children and families, depression, divorce, emotional health, kids and the media, sexuality, stress, testing issues, women and men, and other topics. They are well worth consulting when you have questions about psychological issues. You'll find them at **www.apa.org.** For links to recent articles in newspapers and magazines, be sure to check the APA's PsycPORT page at **www.psycport.com.**

Please do take some of the "digital journeys" described here. You might be surprised by the fascinating information that awaits you. Investigating psychology on your own is one of the best ways to enrich an already valuable course.

A Final Word

There is a distinction in Zen between "live words" and "dead words." Live words come from personal experience; dead words are "about" a subject. This book can only be a collection of dead words unless you accept the challenge of taking an intellectual journey. You will find many helpful, useful, and exciting ideas in the pages that follow. To make them yours, you must set out to *actively* and *self-reflectively* learn as much as you can. The ideas presented here should get you off to a good start. Good luck!

For more information, consult any of the following books:

Hettich, P. I. (2005). *Connect college to career: Student guide to work and life transition.* Belmont, CA: Wadsworth.

Knaus, W. J., & Ellis, A. (2002). *The procrastination workbook: Your personalized program for breaking free from the patterns that hold you back.* Oakland, CA: New Harbinger Press.

Rosnow, R. L. (2006). *Writing papers in psychology: A student guide to research papers, essays, proposals, posters, and handouts* (7th ed.). Belmont, CA: Wadsworth.

Rowe, B. (2007). *College awareness guide: What students need to know to succeed in college.* Upper Saddle River, NJ: Prentice Hall.

Santrock, J. W. & Halonen, J. S. (2007). *Connections to college success.* Belmont, CA: Wadsworth.

study break
Study Skills

RECITE

1. The four Rs in self-reflective SQ4R stand for "read, recite, reflect, and review." T or F?
2. When using the LISAN method, students try to write down as much of a lecture as possible so that their notes are complete. T or F?
3. Spaced study sessions are usually superior to massed practice. T or F?
4. According to research, you should almost always stick with your first answer on multiple-choice tests. T or F?
5. To use the technique known as overlearning, you should continue to study after you feel you have begun to master a topic. T or F?
6. Setting learning goals and monitoring your progress are important parts of _____ learning.
7. Procrastination is related to seeking perfection and equating self-worth with grades. T or F?

REFLECT
Critical Thinking

8. How are the self-reflective SQ4R method and the LISAN method related?

Relate

Which study skills do you think would help you the most? Which techniques do you already use? Which do you think you should try? To what extent do you already engage in self-regulated learning? What additional steps could you take to become a more active, goal-oriented learner?

ANSWERS

1. T 2. F 3. T 4. F 5. T 6. self-regulated 7. T 8. Both encourage people to actively seek information as a way of learning more effectively.

Web Resources

For an up-to-date list of direct links to interesting sites, including those listed here, visit the student companion site for this book at www.cengage.com/psychology/coon

How to Succeed as a Student Advice on how to be a college student. Topics from studying to housing to preparation for work are included.

Library Research in Psychology Hints on how to do library research in psychology.

Psychology Glossary You can use this glossary to get additional definitions for common psychological terms.

Study Skills More information on SQ4R, taking tests, note taking, and time management.

Interactive Learning

PSYCHOLOGY: A JOURNEY BOOK COMPANION WEBSITE
WWW.CENGAGE.COM/PSYCHOLOGY/COON
Visit your book companion website, where you will find flash cards, practice quizzes, web links, and more to help you study.

JUST WHAT YOU NEED TO KNOW NOW! CENGAGENOW™
Spend time on what you need to master rather than on information you already have learned. Take a pretest for this chapter, and CengageNOW will generate a personalized study plan based on your results. The study plan will identify the topics you need to review and direct you to online resources to help you master those topics. You can then take a posttest to help you determine the concepts you have mastered and what you will need to work on. Try it out! Go to www.cengage.com/login to sign in with an access code or to purchase access to this product.

Discovering Psychology and Research Methods

Journey into Psychology: Wondering about Human Behavior

Near the end of every summer, a remote stretch of Nevada desert hosts Burning Man, an eclectic weeklong festival attended by tens of thousands of, well, unusual folks. It's hard to explain just what this unique event is about except to say that attendees are encouraged to openly express themselves in any way they see fit. (Feel free to unleash your imagination on this one.) Revelers participate in a riotous cultural experience that climaxes with the burning of a giant wicker man. Old hippies mix with self-described rednecks, performance artists, musicians, sun worshippers, and individualists of every stripe.

Why, you might wonder, do people go to Burning Man, some of them year after year? But then again, you might equally wonder why people join the army, or get married, or travel to different countries, or become suicide bombers, or live out their lives in monasteries, or go to school. You might even wonder, at least sometimes, why *you* do what you do. In other words, just like your authors, the odds are you are curious about human behavior. That may even be a part of the reason you are taking a course in psychology and reading this book.

Psychology is an ever-changing panorama of people and ideas. You really can't call yourself educated without knowing something about it. And although we might envy those who have walked on the moon or explored the ocean's depths, the ultimate frontier lies much closer to home. Psychology can help you better understand yourself and others. This book is a guided tour of human behavior. We hope you enjoy the journey.

Psychology—Focus on Behavior

What is psychology and what are its goals?

People have always been curious about human behavior. The word *psychology* itself is thousands of years old, coming from the ancient Greek roots *psyche*, which means "mind," and *logos*, meaning "knowledge or study." However, have you ever actually seen or touched a "mind"? Because the mind can't be studied directly, **psychology** is now defined as the scientific study of behavior and mental processes.

To what does behavior refer in the definition of psychology? Anything you do—eating, hanging out, sleeping, talking, or sneezing—is a behavior. So are studying, snowboarding, gambling, watching television, tying your shoelaces, giving someone a gift, learning Spanish, and reading this book. Naturally, we are interested in *overt behaviors* (directly observable actions and responses). But psychologists also study *covert behaviors*. These are private, internal activities, such as thinking, dreaming, remembering, and other mental events (Jackson, 2008).

Today, psychology is both a *science* and a *profession*. As scientists, some psychologists do research to discover new knowledge. Others are teachers who share their knowledge with students. Still others apply psychology to solve problems in mental health, education, business, sports, law, and medicine (Coolican et al., 2007). Later we will return to the profession of psychology. For now, let's focus on how knowledge is created. Whether they work in a classroom, a lab, or a clinic, all psychologists rely on critical thinking and information gained from scientific research.

Survey Questions

- What is psychology and what are its goals?
- What is critical thinking?
- How does psychology differ from false explanations of behavior?
- How is the scientific method applied in psychological research?
- How did the field of psychology emerge?
- What are the current perspectives in psychology?
- What are the major specialties in psychology?
- How is an experiment performed?
- What is a double-blind experiment?
- What nonexperimental research methods do psychologists use?
- How good is psychological information found in the popular media?

Seeking Empirical Evidence

Many people regard themselves as expert "people watchers" and form their own "commonsense" theories of behavior. However, you may be surprised to learn how often self-appointed authorities and long-held commonsense beliefs about human behavior are wrong. For example, have you ever heard that people who are blind have an amazingly accurate sense of touch? Or that the more motivated you are, the better you will do at solving a complex problem? It turns out that these widely held beliefs, and many others, are wrong (Landau & Bavaria, 2003).

Because common sense is flawed, psychologists have a special respect for **scientific observation,** which is based on gathering *empirical evidence* (information gained from direct observation). Unlike our everyday personal experiences, scientific observation is *systematic*, or carefully planned. Scientific observations are also *intersubjective*, which means they can be confirmed by more than one observer. Basically, the empirical approach says, "Let's take a more objective look" (Stanovich, 2007). Psychologists study behavior directly and collect data (observed facts) so they can draw valid conclusions. Would you say it's true, for instance, that "Absence makes the heart grow fonder"? Why argue about it? As psychologists, we would simply get some people who are separated ("absent hearts") and some who see each other every day ("present hearts") and find out who is fonder of their loved ones!

Here's an example of gathering empirical evidence: Have you ever wondered if people become more hostile when it's boiling hot outside? John Simister and Cary Cooper (2005) decided to find out. They obtained data on temperatures and criminal activity in Los Angeles over a 4-year period. When they graphed air temperature and the frequency of aggravated assaults, a clear relationship emerged (see ▶▶ Figure 1.1). Assaults and temperatures rise and fall more or less in parallel (so there may be something to the phrase "hot under the collar").

Picture Partners/Alamy

Psychologists are highly trained professionals. In addition to the psychological knowledge they possess, psychologists learn specialized skills in counseling and therapy, measurement and testing, research and experimentation, statistics, diagnosis, treatment, and many other areas.

Psychology The scientific study of behavior and mental processes.

Scientific observation An empirical investigation structured to answer questions about the world in a systematic and intersubjective fashion (observations can be reliably confirmed by multiple observers).

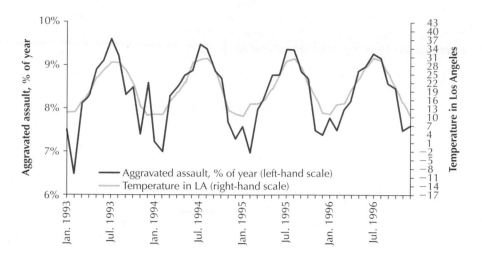

▶▶ **FIGURE 1.1** Results of an empirical study. The graph shows that aggravated assaults in Los Angeles become more likely as air temperature increases. This suggests that physical discomfort is associated with interpersonal hostility. (Data from Simister & Cooper, 2005.)

The scientific study of dreaming was made possible by use of the EEG, a device that records the tiny electrical signals generated by the brain as a person sleeps. The EEG converts these electrical signals into a written record of brain activity. Certain shifts in brain activity, coupled with the presence of rapid eye movements, are strongly related to dreaming. (See Chapter 5 for more information.)

Isn't the outcome of this study fairly predictable? Not if you started out believing otherwise. Sometimes the results of studies match our personal observations and commonsense beliefs and sometimes they come as a surprise. In this instance, you may have guessed the outcome. Your suspicions were confirmed by scientific observation. However, hostile actions that require more extreme physical exertion, such as fistfights, might become *less* likely at very high temperatures. Without systematically gathering data, we wouldn't know for sure if overheated Angelenos become sluggish or more aggressive when it gets hot.

Psychological Research

Many fields, such as history, law, art, and business, are also interested in human behavior. How is psychology different? Psychology's great strength is that it uses scientific observation to systematically answer questions about behavior (Stanovich, 2007). Of course, studying some topics may be impractical or unethical. More often, questions go unanswered for lack of a suitable **research method** (a systematic process for answering scientific questions). In the past, for example, we had to take the word of people who say they never dream. Then the EEG (electroencephalograph, or brain-wave machine) was invented. Certain EEG patterns, and the presence of eye movements, can reveal that a person is dreaming. People who "never dream," it turns out, dream frequently. If they are awakened during a dream, they vividly remember it. Thus, the EEG helped make the study of dreaming more scientific.

Research Specialties

What kinds of topics do psychologists study? Here's a sample of what various psychologists might say about their work:

"I'm a *personality theorist.* I study personality traits, motivation, and individual differences. I am especially interested in the personality profiles of highly creative college students."

"In general, *developmental psychologists* study the course of human growth and development, from conception until death. I'm especially interested in transitions from the teenage years to early adulthood."

"Like other *learning theorists,* I study how and why learning occurs in humans and animals. Right now I'm investigating how patterns of punishment affect learning."

"As a *sensation and perception psychologist,* I investigate how we discern the world through our senses. I am using a perceptual theory to study how we are able to recognize faces in a crowd."

"*Comparative psychologists* study and compare the behavior of different species, especially animals. Personally, I'm fascinated by the communication abilities of porpoises."

"*Cognitive psychologists* are primarily interested in thinking. I want to know how reasoning, problem solving, memory, and other mental processes relate to computer game playing."

Research method A systematic approach to answering scientific questions.

"*Biopsychologists* are interested in how behavior relates to biological processes, especially activities in the nervous system. I've been doing some exciting research on how the brain controls hunger."

"*Gender psychologists* study differences between females and males. I want to understand how gender differences are influenced by biology, child rearing, education, and stereotypes."

"*Social psychologists* explore human social behavior, such as attitudes, persuasion, riots, conformity, leadership, racism, and friendship. My own interest is interpersonal attraction. I place two strangers in a room and analyze how strongly they are attracted to each other."

"*Evolutionary psychologists* investigate how our behavior is guided by patterns that evolved during the long history of humankind. I am studying some interesting trends in male and female mating choices."

"*Cultural psychologists* study the ways in which culture affects human behavior. The language you speak, the foods you eat, how your parents disciplined you, what laws you obey, who you regard as 'family,' whether you eat with a spoon or your fingers—these and countless other details of behavior are strongly influenced by culture."

"*Forensic psychologists* apply psychological principles to legal issues. I am interested in improving the reliability of eyewitness testimony during trials."

This small sample should give you an idea of the diversity of psychological research. It also hints at some of the information we will explore in this book.

Animals and Psychology

Research involving animals was mentioned in some of the preceding examples. Why is that? You may be surprised to learn that psychologists are interested in the behavior of *any* living creature—from flatworms to humans. Indeed, some comparative psychologists spend their entire careers studying rats, cats, dogs, parrots, or chimpanzees.

Although only a small percentage of psychological studies involve animals, they include many different types of research (Ord et al., 2005). Some psychologists use **animal models** to discover principles that apply to humans. For instance, animal studies have helped us understand stress, learning, obesity, aging, sleep, and many other topics. Psychology also benefits animals. For example, caring for domestic animals, as well as endangered species in zoos, relies on behavioral studies.

Psychology's Goals

What do psychologists hope to achieve? As scientists, our ultimate goal is to benefit humanity (O'Neill, 2005). Specifically, the goals of psychology are to *describe, understand, predict,* and *control* behavior. What do psychology's goals mean in practice? Let's see.

Description

Answering psychological questions often begins with a careful description of behavior. **Description,** or naming and classifying, is typically based on making a detailed record of scientific observations.

But a description doesn't explain anything, does it? Right. Useful knowledge begins with accurate description, but descriptions fail to answer the important "why" questions. *Why* do more women attempt suicide, and *why* do more men complete it? *Why* are people more aggressive when they are uncomfortable? *Why* are bystanders often unwilling to help in an emergency?

Understanding

We have met psychology's second goal when we can explain an event. That is, **understanding** usually means we can state the causes of a behavior. For example, research on "bystander apathy" reveals that people often fail to help when *other* possible helpers are nearby. Why? Because a "diffusion of responsibility" occurs. Basically, no one feels personally obligated to pitch in. As a result, the more potential helpers there are, the less likely it is that anyone will help (Darley, 2000; Darley & Latané, 1968). Now we can explain a perplexing problem.

Ron Cohn/The Gorilla Foundation

Some of the most interesting research with animals has focused on attempts to teach primates to communicate with sign language. Psychologist Penny Patterson has spent 25 years teaching Koko more than 1,000 signs. One of Koko's favorite signs ("stink") is shown here. (For more, Google "The Gorilla Foundation.") Such research has led to a better understanding of the origins of language. (See Chapter 8 for more information.)

Animal model In research, an animal whose behavior is used to derive principles that may apply to human behavior.

Description In scientific research, the process of naming and classifying.

Understanding In psychology, understanding is achieved when the causes of a behavior can be stated.

Prediction

Psychology's third goal, **prediction,** is the ability to forecast behavior accurately. Notice that our explanation of bystander apathy makes a prediction about the chances of getting help. If you've ever been stranded on a busy freeway with car trouble, you'll recognize the accuracy of this prediction: Having many potential helpers nearby is no guarantee that anyone will stop to help.

Control

Description, explanation, and prediction seem reasonable, but is control a valid goal? Control may seem like a threat to personal freedom. However, to a psychologist, **control** simply refers to altering conditions that affect behavior. If a clinical psychologist helps a person overcome a terrible fear of spiders, control is involved. If you suggest changes in a classroom that help students learn better, you have exerted control. Control is also involved in designing automobiles to keep drivers from making fatal errors. Clearly, psychological control must be used wisely and humanely.

In summary, psychology's goals are a natural outgrowth of our desire to understand behavior. Basically, they boil down to asking the following questions:

What is the nature of this behavior? (description)

Why does it occur? (understanding and explanation)

Can we forecast when it will occur? (prediction)

What conditions affect it? (control)

Some psychologists specialize in administering, scoring, and interpreting psychological tests, such as tests of intelligence, creativity, personality, or aptitude. This specialty, which is called psychometrics, is an example of using psychology to predict future behavior.

Flash! Light/Stock, Boston

Prediction An ability to accurately forecast behavior.

Control Altering conditions that influence behavior.

---

study break
The Science of Psychology

RECITE

To check your memory, see if you can answer these questions. If you miss any, skim over the preceding material before continuing, to make sure you understand what you just read.

1. Psychology is the _____ study of _____ and _____ processes.
2. The best psychological information is typically based on
   a. proven theories
   b. opinions of experts and authorities
   c. anthropomorphic measurements
   d. empirical evidence
3. In psychological research, animal _____ may be used to discover principles that apply to human behavior.
4. Which of the following questions relates most directly to the goal of *understanding* behavior?
   a. Do the scores of men and women differ on tests of thinking abilities?
   b. Why does a blow to the head cause memory loss?
   c. Will productivity in a business office increase if room temperature is raised or lowered?
   d. What percentage of college students suffer from test anxiety?

Match the following research areas with the topics they cover.

_____	5. Developmental psychology	A. Attitudes, groups, leadership
_____	6. Learning	B. Conditioning, memory
_____	7. Personality	C. The psychology of law
_____	8. Sensation and perception	D. Brain and nervous system
_____	9. Biopsychology	E. Child psychology
_____	10. Social psychology	F. Individual differences, motivation
_____	11. Comparative psychology	G. Animal behavior
		H. Processing sensory information

REFLECT
Critical Thinking

12. All sciences are interested in controlling the phenomena they study. True or false?

Relate

At first, many students think that psychology is primarily about abnormal behavior and psychotherapy. Did you? How would you describe the field now?

ANSWERS

1. scientific, behavior, mental 2. d 3. models 4. b 5. E 6. B 7. F 8. H 9. D 10. A 11. C 12. False. Astronomy and archaeology are examples of sciences that do not share psychology's fourth goal.

Critical Thinking—Take It with a Grain of Salt

What is critical thinking?

How does critical thinking play a role in psychology? Most of us would be skeptical when offered a "genuine" Rolex watch or expensive designer sunglasses for just a few dollars on eBay. Likewise, most of us easily accept our ignorance of subatomic physics. But because we deal with human behavior every day, we tend to think that we already know what is true in psychology. All too often, we are tempted to "buy" commonsense beliefs and even outrageous claims about psychics "channeling" dead people, the powers of "healing" crystals, "miraculous" herbal remedies, astrology, and so forth.

For this and many more reasons, learning to think critically is one of the lasting benefits of a college education. **Critical thinking** refers to an ability to reflect on, evaluate, compare, analyze, critique, and synthesize information. Critical thinkers are willing to challenge conventional wisdom by asking the hard questions. For example, everyone knows that women are more talkative than men, right? Critical thinkers might immediately ask: "How do we know that women talk more than men? Is there any empirical evidence that supports this 'wisdom' "? (Be on the lookout later in this chapter for some evidence concerning this belief.) What could we do to find out for ourselves?

Thinking About Behavior

The heart of critical thinking is a willingness to actively *reflect* on ideas. Critical thinkers evaluate ideas by analyzing the evidence supporting their beliefs and probe for weaknesses in their reasoning. They question assumptions and look for alternate conclusions. True knowledge, they recognize, comes from constantly revising our understanding of the world. They are not afraid to admit they were wrong. As Susan Blackmore (2001) said when her studies caused her to abandon some long-held beliefs, "Admitting you are wrong is always hard—even though it's a skill that every psychologist has to learn."

Critical thinking relies on the following basic principles (Elder, 2006; Kida, 2006):

1. *Few "truths" transcend the need for empirical testing.* While religious beliefs and personal values may be held as matters of faith, without supporting evidence, most other ideas can be evaluated by applying the rules of logic, evidence, and the scientific method.
2. *Judging the quality of evidence is crucial.* Imagine that you are a juror in a courtroom, judging claims made by two battling lawyers. To decide correctly, you can't just weigh the amount of evidence. You must also critically evaluate the *quality* of the evidence. Then you can give greater weight to the most credible facts.
3. *Authority or claimed expertise does not automatically make an idea true.* Just because a teacher, guru, celebrity, or authority is convinced or sincere doesn't mean you should automatically believe that person. It is unscientific and self-demeaning to just take the word of an "expert" without asking, "What evidence convinced her or him? How good is it? Is there a better explanation?"
4. *Critical thinking requires an open mind.* Be prepared to consider daring departures and go wherever the evidence leads. However, don't become so "open-minded" that you are simply gullible. As astronomer Carl Sagan once noted, "It seems to me that what is called for is an exquisite balance between two conflicting needs: the most skeptical scrutiny of all hypotheses that are served up to us and at the same time a great openness to new ideas" (Kida, 2006, p. 51).

To put these principles into action, here are some questions to ask over and over again as you evaluate new information (Browne & Keeley, 2007; Elder, 2006):

1. What claims are being made? What are their implications?
2. What tests (if any) of these claims has been made? What was the nature and quality of the tests? Are they credible? Can they be repeated?

Critical thinking An ability to reflect on, evaluate, compare, analyze, critique, and synthesize information.

3. How good is the evidence? (In general, scientific observations provide the highest-quality evidence.)
4. Who did the tests? How reliable and trustworthy were the investigators? Do they have conflicts of interest? Do their findings appear to be objective? Has any other independent researcher duplicated the findings?
5. Finally, how much credibility can the claim be given? High, medium, low, provisional?

A course in psychology naturally enriches thinking skills. In this book, all upcoming chapters include Critical Thinking questions like the ones you have seen here. Take the time to tackle these questions. The effort will sharpen your thinking abilities and make learning more lively. For an immediate thinking challenge, let's take a critical look at several nonscientific systems that claim to explain behavior.

Pseudopsychologies—Palms, Planets, and Personality

How does psychology differ from false explanations of behavior?

A **pseudopsychology** (SUE-doe-psychology) is any unfounded system that resembles psychology. Many pseudopsychologies give the appearance of science but are actually false. (*Pseudo* means "false.") Pseudopsychologies change little over time because followers seek evidence that appears to confirm their beliefs and avoid evidence that contradicts them. Scientists, in contrast, actively look for contradictions as a way to advance knowledge. They are skeptical critics of their own theories (Schick & Vaughn, 2004).

Can you give some examples of false psychologies? One early pseudopsychology, known as *phrenology,* was popularized in the nineteenth century by Franz Gall, a German anatomy teacher. Phrenology claimed that personality traits are revealed by the shape of the skull. Modern research has long since shown that bumps on the head have nothing to do with talents or abilities. In fact, the phrenologists were so far off that they listed the part of the brain that controls hearing as a center for "combativeness"! *Palmistry* is a similar false system that claims that lines on the hand reveal personality traits and predict the future. Despite the overwhelming evidence against this, palmists can still be found separating the gullible from their money in many cities.

At first glance, a pseudopsychology called *graphology* might seem more reasonable. Some graphologists claim that personality traits are revealed by handwriting. Based on such claims, some companies use graphologists to select job candidates. This is troubling because graphologists score close to zero on tests of accuracy in rating personality (Furnham, Chamorro-Premuzic, & Callahan, 2003). In fact, graphologists do no better than untrained college students in rating personality and job performance (Neter & Ben-Shakhar, 1989). Even a graphological society recommends that handwriting analysis should not be used to select people for jobs (Simner & Goffin, 2003). (By the way, graphology's failure at revealing personality should be separated from its value for detecting forgeries.)

Graphology might seem harmless enough. However, imagine being denied a job because a graphologist didn't like your handwriting. This false system has been used to determine who is hired, given bank credit, or selected for juries. In these and similar situations, pseudopsychologies do, in fact, harm people.

If pseudopsychologies have no scientific basis, how do they survive and why are they popular? There are several reasons, all of which can be illustrated by a critique of astrology.

Phrenology was an attempt to assess personality characteristics by examining various areas of the skull. Phrenologists used charts such as the one shown here as guides. Like other pseudopsychologists, phrenologists made no attempt to empirically verify their concepts.

Would you hire this man? Here's a sample of your author's handwriting. What do you think it reveals? Your interpretations are likely to be as accurate (or inaccurate) as those of a graphologist.

Pseudopsychology Any false and unscientific system of beliefs and practices that is offered as an explanation of behavior.

Problems in the Stars

Astrology is arguably the most popular pseudopsychology. Astrology holds that the positions of the stars and planets at the time of one's birth determine personality traits and affect behavior. Like other pseudopsychologies, astrology has repeatedly been shown to have no scientific validity. The objections to astrology are numerous and devastating (Kelly, 1999):

1. A study of more than 3,000 predictions by famous astrologers found that only a small percentage were fulfilled. These "successful" predictions tended to be vague ("There will be a tragedy somewhere in the east in the spring") or easily guessed from current events (Culver & Ianna, 1988).
2. If astrologers are asked to match people with their horoscopes, they do no better than would be expected by chance. In one famous test, astrologers could not even use horoscopes to distinguish murderers from law-abiding people (Gauquelin, 1970).
3. There is no connection between people's astrological signs and their intelligence or personality traits (Hartmann, Reuter, & Nyborg, 2006). There is also no connection between the "compatibility" of couples' astrological signs and their marriage and divorce rates or between astrological signs and leadership, physical characteristics, or career choices (Martens & Trachet, 1998).
4. Astrologers have failed to explain why the moment of birth should be more important than, say, the moment of conception. (Perhaps it is because it is relatively easy to figure out the moment of birth and much trickier and touchy to determine the moment of conception.) Besides, the zodiac has shifted in the sky by one full constellation since astrology was first set up. (In other words, if astrology calls you a Scorpio, you are really a Libra, and so forth.) However, most astrologers simply ignore this shift (Martens & Trachet, 1998).

In short, astrology doesn't work.

Then why does astrology often seem to work? The following discussion explains why.

Uncritical Acceptance

Even daily horoscopes printed in newspapers can seem uncannily accurate. However, such perceptions are typically based on **uncritical acceptance** (the tendency to believe positive or flattering descriptions of yourself). Horoscopes are generally made up of mostly flattering traits. Naturally, when your personality is described in *desirable* terms, it is hard to deny that the description has the "ring of truth." How much acceptance would astrology receive if a birth sign read like this:

> **Virgo:** You are the logical type and hate disorder. Your nitpicking is unbearable to your friends. You are cold, unemotional, and usually fall asleep while making love. Virgos make good doorstops.

Positive Instances

Even when an astrological description contains a mixture of good and bad traits, it may seem accurate. To find out why, read the following personality description.

> **Your Personality Profile**
> You have a strong need for other people to like you and for them to admire you. You have a tendency to be critical of yourself. You have a great deal of unused energy that you have not turned to your advantage. While you have some personality weaknesses, you are generally able to compensate for them. Your sexual adjustment has presented some problems for you. Disciplined and controlled on the outside, you tend to be worrisome and insecure inside. At times you have serious doubts as to whether you have made the right decision or done the right thing. You prefer a certain amount of change and variety and become dissatisfied when hemmed in by restrictions and limitations. You pride yourself on being an independent thinker and do not accept other opinions without satisfactory proof. You have found it unwise to be too frank in revealing yourself to others. At times you are extroverted, affable, sociable, while at other times you are introverted, wary, and reserved. Some of your aspirations tend to be pretty unrealistic.*

*Reproduced with permission of authors and publisher from: Ulrich, R. E., Stachnik, T. J., & Stainton, N. R. "Student Acceptance of Generalized Personality Interpretations." Psychological Reports, 1963, 13, 831–834. © Southern Universities Press 1963.

Uncritical acceptance The tendency to believe generally positive or flattering descriptions of oneself.

Non Sequitur

Does this describe your personality? A psychologist read this summary individually to college students who had taken a personality test. Only 5 students out of 79 felt that the description was inaccurate. Another classic study found that people rated this "personality profile" as more accurate than their actual horoscopes (French et al., 1991).

Reread the description and you will see that it contains both sides of several personality dimensions ("At times you are extroverted. . . . while at other times you are introverted"). Its apparent accuracy is an illusion based on the **fallacy of positive instances,** in which we remember or notice things that confirm our expectations and forget the rest. The pseudo-psychologies thrive on this effect. For example, you can always find "Aquarius characteristics" in an Aquarius. If you looked, however, you could also find "Gemini characteristics," "Scorpio characteristics," or whatever. Perhaps this explains why, in an ironic twist, 94 percent of those sent the full 10-page horoscope of a famous mass murderer accepted it as their own (Gauquelin, 1970).

The fallacy of positive instances is also used by various "psychic mediums" who pretend to communicate with the deceased friends and relatives of audience members. An analysis shows that the number of "hits" (correct statements) made by these fakes tends to be very low. Nevertheless, many viewers are impressed because of the natural tendency to remember apparent hits and ignore misses. Of course, embarrassing misses are often edited out before such shows appear on television (Nickell, 2001).

The Barnum Effect

Pseudopsychologies also take advantage of the **Barnum effect,** which is a tendency to consider personal descriptions accurate if they are stated in general terms (Kida, 2006). P. T. Barnum, the famed circus showman, had a formula for success: "Always have a little something for everybody." Like the all-purpose personality profile, palm readings, fortunes, horoscopes, and other products of pseudopsychology are stated in such general terms that they can hardly miss. There is always "a little something for everybody." To observe the Barnum effect, read *all 12* of the daily horoscopes found in newspapers for several days. You will find that predictions for other signs fit events as well as do those for your own sign. Try giving a friend the wrong horoscope sometime. Your friend may still be quite impressed with the "accuracy" of the horoscope.

Astrology's popularity shows that many people have difficulty separating valid psychology from systems that seem valid but are not. The goal of this discussion, then, has been to make you a more critical observer of human behavior and to clarify what is, and what is not, psychology. Here is what the "stars" say about your future:

> Emphasis now on education and personal improvement. A learning experience of lasting value awaits you. Take care of scholastic responsibilities before engaging in recreation. The word *psychology* figures prominently in your future.

Pseudopsychologies may seem like no more than a nuisance, but they can do harm. For instance, people seeking treatment for psychological disorders may become the victims of self-appointed "experts" who offer ineffective, pseudoscientific "therapies" (Kida, 2006; Lilienfeld et al., 2005). Valid psychological principles are based on scientific observation and evidence, not fads, opinions, or wishful thinking.

Fallacy of positive instances The tendency to remember or notice information that fits one's expectations, while forgetting discrepancies.

Barnum effect The tendency to consider a personal description accurate if it is stated in very general terms.

Scientific Research—How to Think Like a Psychologist

How is the scientific method applied in psychological research?

Suppose that your friend marries someone just like her. What do people say? "Ah. . . . birds of a feather flock together." And what do they say if she gets divorced soon after? "Well, she should have known that opposites attract." Let's examine another *commonsense* statement. It is frequently said that "every cloud has a silver lining." With this in mind, you use your lover's worrisome absences as a chance to spend more time with your family. You take comfort in this "silver lining" until a family member comments, "Where there's smoke, there's fire"! Much of what passes for common sense is equally vague and inconsistent. Notice also that most of these B.S. statements work best after the fact. (B.S., of course, stands for *Before Science.*)

Systematically recording facts and events is the heart of all sciences. To be *scientific,* our observations must be *systematic,* so that they reveal something about behavior (Stanovich, 2007). To use an earlier example, if you are interested in heat and aggression, you will learn little by driving around and making haphazard observations of aggressive behavior. To be of value, your observations must be planned and systematic.

The Scientific Method

Good to know

The **scientific method** is a form of critical thinking based on careful collection of evidence, accurate description and measurement, precise definition, controlled observation, and repeatable results (Jackson, 2008). In its ideal form, the scientific method has six elements:

1. Making observations
2. Defining a problem
3. Proposing a hypothesis
4. Gathering evidence/testing the hypothesis
5. Publishing results
6. Theory building

Let's take a closer look at some elements of the scientific method. All the basic elements of the scientific method are found in the example that follows.

Observation

Many people believe that women are more chatty than men. Is there any truth to this belief? University of Arizona psychologist Mathias Mehl and his colleagues observed that the results of a few published reports do seem to support this stereotype.

Defining a Problem

However, the researchers noticed that none of the studies had actually recorded men's and women's normal conversations over long time periods. Thus, they defined their problem as, "How can we record natural conversations without bothering people and perhaps biasing our observations?"

Proposing a Hypothesis

What exactly is a "hypothesis"? A **hypothesis** (hi-POTH-eh-sis) is a tentative statement about, or explanation of, an event or relationship. In common terms, a hypothesis is a *testable* hunch or educated guess about behavior. For example, you might hypothesize: "Frus-

Applying the scientific method to the study of behavior requires careful observation. Here, a psychologist videotapes a session in which a child's thinking abilities are being tested.

Dan McCoy/Rainbow

Scientific method A form of critical thinking based on careful measurement and controlled observation.

Hypothesis The predicted outcome of an experiment or an educated guess about the relationship between variables.

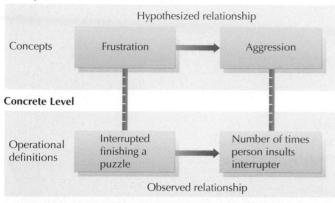

Conceptual Level

Hypothesized relationship

Concepts | Frustration → Aggression

Concrete Level

Operational definitions | Interrupted finishing a puzzle → Number of times person insults interrupter

Observed relationship

⬆ FIGURE 1.2 Operational definitions are used to link concepts with concrete observations. Do you think the examples given are reasonable operational definitions of frustration and aggression? Operational definitions vary in how well they represent concepts. For this reason, many different experiments may be necessary to draw clear conclusions about hypothesized relationships in psychology.

tration encourages aggression." How could you test this hypothesis? First you would have to decide how you are going to frustrate people. (This part might be fun.) Then you will need to find a way to measure whether or not they become more aggressive. (Not so much fun if you plan to be nearby.) Your observations would then provide evidence to confirm or disconfirm the hypothesis.

Because we cannot see or touch frustration, we must define it operationally. An **operational definition** states the exact procedures used to represent a concept. Operational definitions allow unobservable ideas, such as covert behaviors, to be tested in real-world terms (see ▶▶ Figure 1.2). For example, since you can't measure frustration directly, you might define frustration as "interrupting an adult before he or she can finish a puzzle and win an iPhone." And aggression might be defined as "the number of times a frustrated individual insults the person who prevented work on the puzzle." In other words, covert behaviors are operationally defined in terms of overt behavior so they can be observed and studied scientifically.

Gathering Evidence/Testing the Hypothesis

Now let's return to the question of whether women talk more than men do. To gather data, researchers used an electronically activated recorder to track people's conversations. This device recorded sounds for 30 seconds every 12.5 minutes. Participants could not tell when they were being recorded, so they acted and spoke normally. The number of words spoken when the recorder was on was counted and used to estimate the total number of words spoken each day. On average, women spoke 16,215 words a day, with men close behind at 15,699. This difference is too small to be meaningful, so we can conclude, as Mehl did, that there is no evidence that women talk more than men do (Mehl et al., 2007).

Theory Building

What about theory building? In research, a **theory** acts as a map of knowledge. Good theories summarize observations, explain them, and guide further research (▶▶ Figure 1.3). Without theories of forgetting, personality, stress, mental illness, and the like, psychologists would drown in a sea of disconnected facts (Stanovich, 2007).

While Mehl and his colleagues did not present a theory of why humans talk more or less, they did discuss how their findings might affect such a theory. For instance, they pointed out that they studied only university students and that older men and women might differ in how much they talk each day. Such findings invite others to study talkativeness in other age groups and to propose theories to explain any differences that might be observed.

Operational definition Defining a scientific concept by stating the specific actions or procedures used to measure it. For example, "hunger" might be defined as "the number of hours of food deprivation."

Theory A system of ideas designed to interrelate concepts and facts in a way that summarizes existing data and predicts future observations.

▶▶ FIGURE 1.3 Psychologists use the logic of science to answer questions about behavior. Specific hypotheses can be tested in a variety of ways, including naturalistic observation, correlational studies, controlled experiments, clinical studies, and the survey method. Psychologists revise their theories to reflect the evidence they gather. New or revised theories then lead to new observations, problems, and hypotheses.

Observation → Define problem → Propose hypothesis → Gather evidence Test hypothesis → Reject hypothesis / Retain hypothesis → Publish results → Theory building

Publishing Results

Scientific information must always be *publicly available.* That way, other researchers can read about the results and make their own observations if they doubt the study's findings. If others are able to *replicate* (repeat) the results of a study, those results become more credible.

The results of psychological studies are usually published in professional journals (see ● Table 1.1). That way, anyone willing to make appropriate observations can see whether or not a claim is true (Jackson, 2008). In a scholarly article published in the journal *Science*, Mehl and his colleagues (2007) describe the question they investigated, the methods they used, and the results of their study on male and female talkativeness.

● Table 1.1 Outline of a Research Report

- *Abstract* Research reports begin with a very brief summary of the study and its findings. The abstract allows you to get an overview without reading the entire article.
- *Introduction* The introduction describes the question to be investigated. It also provides background information by reviewing prior studies on the same or related topics.
- *Method* This section tells how and why observations were made. It also describes the specific procedures used to gather data. That way, other researchers can repeat the study to see if they get the same results.
- *Results* The outcome of the investigation is presented. Data may be graphed, summarized in tables, or statistically analyzed.
- *Discussion* The results of the study are discussed in relation to the original question. Implications of the study are explored and further studies may be proposed.

RECITE

1. The fallacy of positive instances refers to graphology's accepted value for the detection of forgeries. T or F?
2. Personality descriptions provided by pseudopsychologies are stated in general terms, which provide "a little something for everybody." This fact is the basis of the
   a. palmist's fallacy
   b. uncritical acceptance pattern
   c. fallacy of positive instances
   d. Barnum effect
3. Most of psychology can rightfully be called common sense because psychologists prefer informal observation to systematic observation. T or F?
4. A psychologist does a study to see if exercising increases sense of well-being. In the study, he will be testing an
   a. experimental hypothesis
   b. operational definition
   c. empirical definition
   d. anthropomorphic theory
5. _____ behaviors are operationally defined in terms of _____ behavior
   a. Overt, covert
   b. Observable, overt
   c. Covert, overt
   d. Covert, abstract

study break
Critical Thinking and the Scientific Method in Psychology

REFLECT
Critical Thinking

6. Can you think of some "commonsense" statements that contradict each other?
7. Each New Year's Day, phony "psychics" make predictions about events that will occur during the coming year. The vast majority of these predictions are wrong, but the practice continues each year. Can you explain why?

Relate

It is nearly impossible to get through a day without encountering people who believe in pseudopsychologies or who make unscientific or unfounded statements. How stringently do you evaluate your own beliefs and the claims made by others?

How might you scientifically test the old saw that you can't teach an old dog new tricks? Follow the steps of the scientific method to propose a testable hypothesis and decide how you would gather evidence. (Well, OK, you don't have to publish your results.)

ANSWERS

1. F 2. d 3. F 4. a 5. c 6. There are many examples. Here are a few more to add to the ones you thought of: "He (or she) who hesitates is lost" versus "Haste makes waste." "Never too old to learn" versus "You can't teach an old dog new tricks." 7. Because of the fallacy of positive instances, people remember only predictions that seemed to come true and forget all of the errors. Incidentally, "predictions" that appear to be accurate are usually easily deduced from current events or are stated in very general terms to take advantage of the Barnum effect.

A Brief History of Psychology— Psychology's Family Album

How did the field of psychology emerge?

Wilhelm Wundt, 1832–1920. Wundt is credited with making psychology an independent science, separate from philosophy. Wundt's original training was in medicine, but he became deeply interested in psychology. In his laboratory, Wundt investigated how sensations, images, and feelings combine to make up personal experience.

As we noted previously, people have been informally observing human behavior and philosophizing about it for thousands of years. In contrast, psychology's history as a science dates back only about 130 years to Leipzig, Germany. There, Wilhelm Wundt (VILL-helm Voont), the "father of psychology," set up a laboratory in 1879 to study conscious experience.

What happens, Wundt wondered, when we experience sensations, images, and feelings? To find out, he systematically observed and measured stimuli of various kinds (lights, sounds, weights). A **stimulus** is any physical energy that affects a person and evokes a response (stimulus: singular; stimuli [STIM-you-lie]: plural). Wundt then used **introspection,** or "looking inward," to probe his reactions to various stimuli. (Stop reading, close your eyes, carefully examine your thoughts, feelings, and sensations, and you will be introspecting.)

Over the years, Wundt studied vision, hearing, taste, touch, memory, time perception, and many other topics. By insisting on systematic observation and measurement, he asked some interesting questions and got psychology off to a good start (Schultz & Schultz, 2008).

Structuralism

Wundt's ideas were carried to the United States by Edward Titchener (TICH-in-er). Titchener called Wundt's ideas **structuralism** and tried to analyze the structure of mental life into basic "elements" or "building blocks."

How could he do that? You can't analyze experience like a chemical compound, can you? Perhaps not, but the structuralists tried, mostly by using introspection. For instance, an observer might heft an apple and decide that she had experienced the elements "hue" (color), "roundness," and "weight." Another example of a question that might have interested a structuralist is, What basic tastes mix together to create complex flavors as different as broccoli, lime, bacon, and strawberry cheesecake?

Introspection proved to be a poor way to answer most questions (Benjamin, 2009). Why? Because no matter how systematic the observations, the structuralists frequently *disagreed.* And when they did, there was no way to settle differences. Think about it. If you and a friend both introspect on your perceptions of an apple and end up listing different basic elements, who would be right? Despite such limitations, "looking inward" is still used as one source of insight in studies of hypnosis, meditation, problem solving, moods, and many other topics.

William James, 1842–1910. William James was the son of philosopher Henry James, Sr., and the brother of novelist Henry James. During his long academic career, James taught anatomy, physiology, psychology, and philosophy at Harvard University. James believed strongly that ideas should be judged in terms of their practical consequences for human conduct.

Functionalism

American scholar William James broadened psychology to include animal behavior, religious experience, abnormal behavior, and other interesting topics. James's brilliant first book, *Principles of Psychology* (1890), helped establish the field as a separate discipline (Hergenhahn, 2009).

The term **functionalism** comes from James's interest in how the mind functions to help us adapt to the environment. James regarded consciousness as an ever-changing stream or flow of images and sensations—not a set of lifeless building blocks, as the structuralists claimed.

The functionalists admired Charles Darwin, who deduced that creatures evolve in ways that favor survival. According to Darwin's principle of **natural selection,** physical features that help animals adapt to their environments are retained in evolution. Similarly, the functionalists wanted to find out how the mind, perception, habits, and emotions help us adapt and survive.

Stimulus Any physical energy sensed by an organism.

Introspection To look within; to examine one's own thoughts, feelings, or sensations.

Structuralism The school of thought concerned with analyzing sensations and personal experience into basic elements.

Functionalism The school of psychology concerned with how behavior and mental abilities help people adapt to their environments.

Natural selection Darwin's theory that evolution favors those plants and animals best suited to their living conditions.

Behaviorism

Functionalism and structuralism were soon challenged by **behaviorism,** the study of observable behavior. Behaviorist John B. Watson objected strongly to the study of the "mind" or "conscious experience." He believed that introspection is unscientific because there is no way to settle disagreements between observers. Watson realized that he could study the overt behavior of animals even though he couldn't ask them questions or know what they were thinking (Watson, 1913/1994). He simply observed the relationship between stimuli (events in the environment) and an animal's **responses** (any muscular action, glandular activity, or other identifiable behavior). These observations were *objective* because they did not involve introspecting on *subjective* experience. Why not, he asked, apply the same objectivity to human behavior?

Watson soon adopted Russian physiologist Ivan Pavlov's (ee-VAHN PAV-lahv) concept of *conditioning* to explain most behavior. (A *conditioned response* is a learned reaction to a particular stimulus.) Watson claimed, "Give me a dozen healthy infants, well-formed, and my own special world to bring them up in and I'll guarantee to take any one at random and train him to become any type of specialist I might select—doctor, lawyer, artist, merchant-chief, and yes, beggarman and thief" (Watson, 1913/1994).

Would most psychologists agree with Watson's claim? No, today it is regarded as an overstatement. Just the same, behaviorism helped make psychology a natural science, rather than a branch of philosophy (Benjamin, 2009).

Radical Behaviorism

The best-known behaviorist, B. F. Skinner (1904–1990), believed that our actions are controlled by rewards and punishments. To study learning, Skinner created his famous conditioning chamber, or "Skinner box." With it, he could present stimuli to animals and record their responses. Many of Skinner's ideas about learning grew out of work with rats and pigeons. Nevertheless, he believed that the same laws of behavior apply to humans. As a "radical behaviorist," Skinner also believed that mental events, such as thinking, are not needed to explain behavior (Schultz & Schultz, 2008).

Skinner was convinced that a "designed culture" based on positive reinforcement could encourage desirable behavior. (Skinner opposed the use of punishment because it doesn't teach correct responses.) Too often, he believed, misguided rewards lead to destructive actions that create problems such as overpopulation, pollution, and war.

Gestalt Psychology

Imagine that you just played "Happy Birthday" on a low-pitched tuba. Next, you play it on a high-pitched flute. The flute duplicates none of the tuba's sounds. Yet we notice something interesting: The melody is still recognizable—as long as the *relationship* between notes remains the same.

Now, what would happen if you played the notes of "Happy Birthday" in the correct order, but at a rate of one per hour? What would we have? Nothing! The separate notes would no longer be a melody. Perceptually, the melody is somehow more than the individual notes that define it.

It was observations like these that launched the Gestalt school of thought. German psychologist Max Wertheimer (VERT-hi-mer) was the first to advance the Gestalt viewpoint. It is inaccurate, he said, to analyze psychological events into pieces, or "elements," as the structuralists did. Accordingly, **Gestalt psychologists** studied thinking, learning, and perception

John B. Watson, 1878–1958. Watson's intense interest in observable behavior began with his doctoral studies in biology and neurology. Watson became a psychology professor at Johns Hopkins University in 1908 and advanced his theory of behaviorism. He remained at Johns Hopkins until 1920 when he left for a career in the advertising industry!

Archives of the History of American Psychology, University of Akron

B. F. Skinner, 1904–1990. Skinner studied simple behaviors under carefully controlled conditions. The "Skinner box" has been widely used to study learning in simplified animal experiments. In addition to advancing psychology, Skinner hoped that his radical brand of behaviorism would improve human life.

Yvonne Hemsey/Getty Images

Max Wertheimer, 1880–1941. Wertheimer first proposed the Gestalt viewpoint to help explain perceptual illusions. He later promoted Gestalt psychology as a way to understand not only perception, problem solving, thinking, and social behavior, but also art, logic, philosophy, and politics.

Archives of the History of American Psychology, University of Akron

Behaviorism The school of psychology that emphasizes the study of overt, observable behavior.

Response Any muscular action, glandular activity, or other identifiable aspect of behavior.

Gestalt psychology A school of psychology emphasizing the study of thinking, learning, and perception in whole units, not by analysis into parts.

▶▶ **FIGURE 1.4** The design you see here is entirely made up of broken circles. However, as the Gestalt psychologists discovered, our perceptions have a powerful tendency to form meaningful patterns. Because of this tendency, you will probably see a triangle in this design, even though it is only an illusion. Your whole perceptual experience exceeds the sum of its parts.

as whole units, not by analyzing experiences into parts. Their slogan was, "The whole is greater than the sum of its parts." (See ▶▶ Figure 1.4.) In fact the German word *Gestalt* means "form, pattern, or whole."

Like a melody, many experiences cannot be broken into smaller units, as the structuralists proposed. For this reason, studies of perception and personality have been especially influenced by the Gestalt viewpoint. Gestalt psychology also inspired a type of psychotherapy.

Sigmund Freud, 1856–1939. For more than 50 years, Freud probed the unconscious mind. In doing so, he altered modern views of human nature. His early experimentation with a "talking cure" for hysteria is regarded as the beginning of psychoanalysis. Through psychoanalysis, Freud added psychological treatment methods to psychiatry.

Hulton Archive/Getty Images

Psychoanalytic Psychology

As American psychology grew more scientific, an Austrian doctor named Sigmund Freud was developing radically different ideas that opened new horizons in art, literature, and history, as well as psychology (Jacobs, 2003). Freud believed that mental life is like an iceberg: Only a small part is exposed to view. He called the area of the mind that lies outside of personal awareness the **unconscious.** According to Freud, our behavior is deeply influenced by unconscious thoughts, impulses, and desires—especially those concerning sex and aggression.

Freud theorized that many unconscious thoughts are *repressed* (held out of awareness) because they are threatening. But sometimes, he said, they are revealed by dreams, emotions, or slips of the tongue. ("Freudian slips" are often humorous, as when a student who is late for class says, "I'm sorry I couldn't get here any later.")

Freud believed that all thoughts, emotions, and actions are *determined.* In other words, nothing is an accident: If we probe deeply enough we will find the causes of every thought or action. Freud was also among the first to appreciate that childhood affects adult personality ("The child is father to the man"). Most of all, perhaps, Freud is known for creating **psychoanalysis,** the first fully developed psychotherapy or "talking cure." Freudian psychotherapy explores unconscious conflicts and emotional problems (see Chapter 13). Today, his ideas have been altered so much that few strictly psychoanalytic psychologists are left. However, Freud's legacy is still evident in various **psychodynamic theories,** which continue to emphasize internal motives, conflicts, and unconscious forces (Gedo, 2002).

Abraham Maslow, 1908–1970. As a founder of humanistic psychology, Maslow was interested in studying people of exceptional mental health. Such self-actualized people, he believed, make full use of their talents and abilities. Maslow offered his positive view of human potential as an alternative to the schools of behaviorism and psychoanalysis.

Bettmann/Corbis

Humanistic Psychology

Humanism is a view that focuses on subjective human experience. Humanistic psychologists are interested in human potentials, ideals, and problems.

How is the humanistic approach different from others? Carl Rogers, Abraham Maslow, and other humanists rejected the Freudian idea that we are ruled by unconscious forces. They were also uncomfortable with the behaviorist emphasis on conditioning. Both views have a strong undercurrent of **determinism** (the idea that behavior is determined by forces beyond our control). In contrast, the humanists stress **free will,** our ability to make voluntary choices. Of course, past experiences do affect us. Nevertheless, humanists believe that people can freely *choose* to live more creative, meaningful, and satisfying lives.

Humanists are interested in psychological needs for love, self-esteem, belonging, self-expression, creativity, and spirituality. Such needs, they believe, are as important as our biological urges for food and water. For example, newborn infants deprived of human love may die just as surely as they would if deprived of food.

Unconscious Contents of the mind that are beyond awareness, especially impulses and desires not directly known to a person.

Psychoanalysis A Freudian approach to psychotherapy emphasizing the exploration of unconscious conflicts.

Psychodynamic theory Any theory of behavior that emphasizes internal conflicts, motives, and unconscious forces.

Humanism An approach to psychology that focuses on human experience, problems, potentials, and ideals.

Determinism The idea that all behavior has prior causes that would completely explain one's choices and actions if all such causes were known.

Free will The idea that human beings are capable of freely making choices or decisions.

Maslow's concept of self-actualization is a key feature of humanism. **Self-actualization** refers to developing one's potential fully and becoming the best person possible. According to humanists, everyone has this potential. Humanists seek ways to help it emerge.

How scientific is the humanistic approach? Initially, humanists were less interested in treating psychology as a science. They stressed subjective factors, such as one's self-image, self-evaluation, and frame of reference. (*Self-image* is your perception of your own body, personality, and capabilities. *Self-evaluation* refers to appraising yourself as good or bad. A *frame of reference* is a mental perspective used to interpret events.) Today, humanists still seek to understand how we perceive ourselves and experience the world. However, most now do research to test their ideas, just as other psychologists do (Schneider, Bugental, & Pierson, 2001). (● Table 1.2 presents a summary of psychology's early development.)

Margaret Washburn, 1871–1939.

Francis Cecil Sumner, 1895–1954.

The Role of Diversity in Psychology's Early Days

Were all the early psychologists Caucasian men? Even though most of the earliest psychologists were men of European descent, women and ethnic minorities have long contributed to psychology (Minton, 2000). The first woman to be awarded a Ph.D. in psychology was Margaret Washburn, in 1894. By 1906 in America, about 1 psychologist in 10 was a woman. In 1908 Margaret Washburn published an influential textbook on animal behavior, titled *The Animal Mind*. In 1920, Francis Cecil Sumner became the first African American to earn a doctoral degree in psychology. Inez Beverly Prosser, the first African-American female psychologist, was awarded her Ph.D. in 1933.

Since 2000, over 70 percent of all undergraduate and graduate degrees in psychology have been awarded to women (APA, 2003a). Similarly, one quarter of all undergraduate degrees and 16 percent of doctorates in psychology were awarded to persons of color (APA, 2003b). Increasingly, psychology has come to reflect the rich diversity of humanity (Hyde, 2004).

Inez Beverly Prosser, ca. 1895–1934.

● Table 1.2 The Early Development of Psychology

PERSPECTIVE	DATE	NOTABLE EVENTS
Experimental psychology	1875	• First psychology course offered by William James
	1878	• First American Ph.D. in psychology awarded
	1879	• Wilhelm Wundt opens first psychology laboratory in Germany
	1883	• First American psychology lab founded at Johns Hopkins University
	1886	• First American psychology textbook written by John Dewey
Structuralism	1898	• Edward Titchener advances psychology based on introspection
Functionalism	1890	• William James publishes *Principles of Psychology*
	1892	• American Psychological Association founded
Psychodynamic psychology	1895	• Sigmund Freud publishes first studies
	1900	• Freud publishes *The Interpretation of Dreams*
Behaviorism	1906	• Ivan Pavlov reports his research on conditioned reflexes
	1913	• John Watson presents behaviorist view
Gestalt psychology	1912	• Max Wertheimer and others advance Gestalt viewpoint
Humanistic psychology	1942	• Carl Rogers publishes *Counseling and Psychotherapy*
	1943	• Abraham Maslow publishes "A Theory of Human Motivation"

Self-actualization The ongoing process of fully developing one's personal potential.

Psychology Today—Three Complementary Perspectives on Behavior

What are the current perspectives in psychology?

At one time, loyalty to each school of thought was fierce, and clashes were common. Now, some early systems, such as structuralism, have disappeared entirely, while new ones have gained prominence. Also, viewpoints such as functionalism and Gestalt psychology have blended into newer, broader perspectives. Certainly, loyalties and specialties still exist. But today, many psychologists realize that a single perspective is unlikely to fully explain complex human behavior. As a result, they are *eclectic* (ek-LEK-tik) and draw insights from a variety of perspectives. The three broad views that shape modern psychology are the *biological, psychological,* and *sociocultural* perspectives (● Table 1.3). As we will see, insights from one perspective often complement insights from the others.

● Table 1.3 Contemporary Ways to Look at Behavior

Biological Perspective

Biopsychological View
Key Idea: *Human and animal behavior is the result of internal physical, chemical, and biological processes.*
Seeks to explain behavior through activity of the brain and nervous system, physiology, genetics, the endocrine system, and biochemistry; neutral, reductionistic, mechanistic view of human nature.

Evolutionary View
Key Idea: *Human and animal behavior is the result of the process of evolution.*
Seeks to explain behavior through evolutionary principles based on natural selection; neutral, reductionistic, mechanistic view of human nature.

Psychological Perspective

Behavioristic View
Key Idea: *Behavior is shaped and controlled by one's environment.*
Emphasizes the study of observable behavior and the effects of learning; stresses the influence of external rewards and punishments; neutral, scientific, somewhat mechanistic view of human nature.

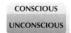

Cognitive View
Key Idea: *Much human behavior can be understood in terms of the mental processing of information.*
Concerned with thinking, knowing, perception, understanding, memory, decision making, and judgment; explains behavior in terms of information processing; neutral, somewhat computer-like view of human nature.

Psychodynamic View
Key Idea: *Behavior is directed by forces within one's personality that are often hidden or unconscious.*
Emphasizes internal impulses, desires, and conflicts—especially those that are unconscious; views behavior as the result of clashing forces within personality; somewhat negative, pessimistic view of human nature.

Humanistic View
Key Idea: *Behavior is guided by one's self-image, by subjective perceptions of the world, and by needs for personal growth.*
Focuses on subjective, conscious experience, human problems, potentials, and ideals; emphasizes self-image and self-actualization to explain behavior; positive, philosophical view of human nature.

Sociocultural Perspective

Sociocultural View
Key Idea: *Behavior is influenced by one's social and cultural context.*
Emphasizes that behavior is related to the social and cultural environment within which a person is born, grows up, and lives from day to day; neutral, interactionist view of human nature.

The Biological Perspective

The **biological perspective** seeks to explain our behavior in terms of biological principles such as brain processes, evolution, and genetics. By using new techniques, *biopsychologists* are producing exciting insights about how the brain relates to thinking, feelings, perception, abnormal behavior, and other topics. Biopsychologists and others who study the brain and nervous system, such as biologists and biochemists, are part of the broader field of *neuroscience*. As mentioned earlier, *evolutionary psychologists* look at how human evolution and genetics might explain our current behavior.

The Psychological Perspective

The **psychological perspective** views behavior as the result of psychological processes within each person. This view continues to emphasize objective observation, just as the early behaviorists did. However, the psychological perspective now includes cognitive psychology, which seeks to explain how mental processes affect our thoughts, actions, and feelings. Cognitive psychology has gained prominence in recent years as researchers have devised ways to objectively study covert behaviors, such as thinking, memory, language, perception, problem solving, consciousness, and creativity. With a renewed interest in thinking, it can be said that psychology has finally "regained consciousness" (Robins, Gosling, & Craik, 1998).

Freudian psychoanalysis continues to evolve into the broader *psychodynamic view*. Although many of Freud's ideas have been challenged or refuted, psychodynamic psychologists continue to trace our behavior to unconscious mental activity. They also seek to develop therapies to help people lead happier, fuller lives. The same is true of humanistic psychologists, although they stress subjective, conscious experience and the positive side of human nature, rather than unconscious processes.

Positive Psychology

Psychologists have always paid attention to the negative side of human behavior. This is easy to understand because of the pressing need to solve human problems. However, more and more psychologists, some of them inspired by the humanists, have begun to ask, What do we know about love, happiness, creativity, well-being, self-confidence, and achievement? Together, such topics make up **positive psychology,** the study of human strengths, virtues, and optimal behavior (Compton, 2005; Seligman & Csikszentmihalyi, 2000). Many topics from positive psychology can be found in this book. Ideally, they will help make your own life more positive and fulfilling (Simonton & Baumeister, 2005).

The Sociocultural Perspective

As you can see, it is helpful to view human behavior from more than one perspective. This is also true in another sense. The **sociocultural perspective** stresses the impact that social and cultural contexts have on our behavior. We are rapidly becoming a multicultural society, made up of people from many different nations. How has this affected psychology? Let us introduce you to Jerry, who is Japanese American and is married to an Irish-Catholic American. Here is what Jerry, his wife, and their children did one New Year's Day:

> We woke up in the morning and went to Mass at St. Brigid's, which has a black gospel choir. . . . Then we went to the Japanese-American Community Center for the Oshogatsu New Year's program and saw Buddhist archers shoot arrows to ward off evil spirits for the year. Next, we ate traditional rice cakes as part of the New Year's service and listened to a young Japanese-American storyteller. On the way home, we stopped in Chinatown and after that we ate Mexican food at a taco stand. (Njeri, 1991)

Jerry and his family reflect a new social reality: Cultural diversity is becoming the norm. Over 100 million Americans are now African American, Hispanic, Asian American, Native

Biological perspective The attempt to explain behavior in terms of underlying biological principles.

Psychological perspective The traditional view that behavior is shaped by psychological processes occurring at the level of the individual.

Positive psychology The study of human strengths, virtues, and effective functioning.

Sociocultural perspective The focus on the importance of social and cultural contexts in influencing the behavior of individuals.

As shown by this photo from the inauguration of President Barack Obama, America is becoming more diverse. To fully understand human behavior, personal differences based on age, race, culture, ethnicity, gender, and sexual orientation must be taken into account.

American, or Pacific Islander (U.S. Bureau of Census, 2007). In some large cities "minority" groups are already the majority.

In the past, psychology was based mostly on the cultures of North America and Europe. Now, we must ask, Do the principles of Western psychology apply to people in all cultures? Are some psychological concepts invalid in other cultures? Are any universal? As psychologists have probed such questions, one thing has become clear: Most of what we think, feel, and do is influenced in one way or another by the social and cultural worlds in which we live (Lehman, Chiu, & Schaller, 2004).

Cultural Relativity

Imagine that you are a psychologist. Your client, Linda, who is a Native American, tells you that spirits live in the trees near her home. Is Linda suffering from a delusion? Is she abnormal? Obviously, you will misjudge Linda's mental health if you fail to take her cultural beliefs into account. **Cultural relativity** (the idea that behavior must be judged relative to the values of the culture in which it occurs) can greatly affect the diagnosis and treatment of mental disorders (Draguns, Gielen, & Fish, 2004). Cases like Linda's teach us to be wary of using narrow standards when judging others or comparing groups.

A Broader View of Diversity

In addition to cultural differences, age, ethnicity, gender, religion, disability, and sexual orientation all affect the **social norms** that guide behavior. Social norms are rules that define acceptable and expected behavior for members of various groups. All too often, the unstated standard for judging what is "average," "normal," or "correct" has been the behavior of white, middle-class males (Reid, 2002). To fully understand human behavior, psychologists need to know how people differ, as well as the ways in which we are all alike. To be effective, psychologists must be sensitive to people who are ethnically and culturally different from themselves (APA, 2003c). For the same reason, an appreciation of human diversity can enrich your life, as well as your understanding of psychology (Denmark, Rabinowitz, & Sechzer, 2005).

In a moment we will further explore what psychologists do. First, here are some questions to enhance your learning.

Cultural relativity The idea that behavior must be judged relative to the values of the culture in which it occurs.

Social norms Rules that define acceptable and expected behavior for members of a group.

RECITE

Match:

_____ 1. Philosophy
_____ 2. Wundt
_____ 3. Structuralism
_____ 4. Functionalism
_____ 5. Behaviorism
_____ 5. Behaviorism
_____ 6. Gestalt
_____ 7. Psychodynamic
_____ 8. Humanistic
_____ 9. Cognitive
__F__ 10. Washburn
_____ 11. Biopsychology

A. Against analysis; studied whole experiences
B. "Mental chemistry" and introspection
C. Emphasizes self-actualization and personal growth
D. Interested in unconscious causes of behavior
E. Interested in how the mind aids survival
F. First woman Ph.D. in psychology
G. Studied stimuli and responses, conditioning
H. Part of psychology's "long past"
I. Concerned with thinking, language, problem solving
J. Used introspection and careful measurement
K. Relates behavior to the brain, physiology, and genetics
L. Also known as engineering psychology

12. Universal norms exist for judging the behavior of people in various cultural and social groups. T or F?

REFLECT

Critical Thinking

13. Modern sciences like psychology are built on observations that can be verified by two or more independent observers. Did structuralism meet this standard? Why or why not?

Relate

Which school of thought most closely matches your own view of behavior? Do you think any of the early schools offers a complete explanation of why we behave as we do? What about the three broad contemporary perspectives? Can you explain why so many psychologists are eclectic?

ANSWERS

1. H 2. J 3. B 4. E 5. G 6. A 7. D 8. C 9. I 10. F 11. K 12. F 13. No, it did not. The downfall of structuralism was that each observer examined the contents of his or her own mind—which is something that no other person can observe.

Psychologists—Guaranteed Not to Shrink

Psychologist A person highly trained in the methods, factual knowledge, and theories of psychology.

What are the major specialties in psychology?

Psychologists are all shrinks, right? Nope. "Shrinks" (a slang term derived from "head shrinkers") are *psychiatrists,* a different type of mental health professional. A **psychologist** is highly trained in the methods, knowledge, and theories of psychology. Psychologists usually have a master's degree or a doctorate. These degrees typically require several years of postgraduate training.

Psychologists are often inaccurately portrayed in the media. Some films have featured psychologists who are more disturbed than their patients (such as Jack Nicholson's character in *Anger Management*) or psychologists who are bumbling buffoons (such as Billy Crystal's character in *Analyze This*). In the movie comedy *Prime* a therapist listens to a patient describe intimate details of her relationship with a man but fails to tell the patient that the man is her son. Such characters may be dramatic and entertaining, but they seriously distort public perceptions of responsible and hardworking psychologists (Schultz, 2004). Real psychologists follow an ethical code that stresses respect for people's privacy, dignity, confidentiality, and welfare (APA, 2002).

Even without media distortions, misconceptions about psychologists are common. For instance, most psychologists are not therapists in private practice. Instead, they are employed by schools, businesses, and social agencies. Likewise, only 12 percent work in clinics or hospitals.

© Mike Baldwin / Cornered

BALDWIN

"Thanks to you, Doc, I'm beginning to feel a lot more normal."

● Table 1.4 Kinds of Psychologists and What They Do

SPECIALTY		TYPICAL ACTIVITIES
Biopsychology	B*	Does research on the brain, nervous system, and other physical origins of behavior
Clinical	A	Does psychotherapy; investigates clinical problems; develops methods of treatment
Cognitive	B	Studies human thinking and information processing abilities
Community	A	Promotes community-wide mental health through research, prevention, education, and consultation
Comparative	B	Studies and compares the behavior of different species, especially animals
Consumer	A	Researches packaging, advertising, marketing methods, and characteristics of consumers
Counseling	A	Does psychotherapy and personal counseling; researches emotional disturbances and counseling methods
Cultural	B	Studies the ways in which culture, subculture, and ethnic group membership affect behavior
Developmental	A, B	Conducts research on infant, child, adolescent, and adult development; does clinical work with disturbed children; acts as consultant to parents and schools
Educational	A	Investigates classroom dynamics, teaching styles, and learning; develops educational tests, evaluates educational programs
Engineering	A	Does applied research on the design of machinery, computers, airlines, automobiles, and so on, for business, industry, and the military
Environmental	A, B	Studies the effects of urban noise, crowding, attitudes toward the environment, and human use of space; acts as a consultant on environmental issues
Forensic	A	Studies problems of crime and crime prevention, rehabilitation programs, prisons, courtroom dynamics; selects candidates for police work
Gender	B	Does research on differences between males and females, the acquisition of gender identity, and the role of gender throughout life
Health	A, B	Studies the relationship between behavior and health; uses psychological principles to promote health and prevent illness
Industrial-organizational	A	Selects job applicants, does skills analysis, evaluates on-the-job training, improves work environments and human relations in organizations and work settings
Learning	B	Studies how and why learning occurs; develops theories of learning
Medical	A	Applies psychology to manage medical problems, such as the emotional impact of illness, self-screening for cancer, compliance in taking medicine
Personality	B	Studies personality traits and dynamics; develops theories of personality and tests for assessing personality traits
School	A	Does psychological testing, referrals, emotional and vocational counseling of students; detects and treats learning disabilities; improves classroom learning
Sensation and perception	B	Studies the sense organs and the process of perception; investigates the mechanisms of sensation and develops theories about how perception occurs
Social	B	Investigates human social behavior, including attitudes, conformity, persuasion, prejudice, friendship, aggression, helping, and so forth

*Research in this area is typically applied (A), basic (B), or both (A, B).

One perception of psychologists is accurate: Most do help people in one way or another. Psychologists interested in emotional problems specialize in clinical or counseling psychology (see ● Table 1.4). **Clinical psychologists** treat psychological problems or do research on therapies and mental disorders. In contrast, **counseling psychologists** tend to treat milder problems, such as troubles at work or school. However, such differences are fading, and many counseling psychologists now work full time as therapists.

To enter the profession of psychology, it is best to have a doctorate (Ph.D., Psy.D., or Ed.D.). Most clinical psychologists have a Ph.D. degree and follow a scientist-practitioner model. That is, they are trained to do either research or therapy. Many do both. Other clinicians earn the Psy.D. (Doctor of Psychology) degree, which emphasizes therapy skills rather than research (Peterson, 2001).

Have you ever wondered what it takes to become a psychologist? See "Is a Career in Psychology Right for You?"

Clinical psychologist A psychologist who specializes in the treatment of psychological and behavioral disturbances or who does research on such disturbances.

Counseling psychologist A psychologist who specializes in the treatment of milder emotional and behavioral disturbances.

Is a Career in Psychology Right for You?

As you read this book we encourage you to frequently reflect on new ideas by relating them to your own life in order to better understand and remember them. "Discovering Psychology" boxes like this one are designed to help you be more reflective about how psychology relates to your own life. Answer the following questions to explore whether you would enjoy becoming a psychologist:

1. I have a strong interest in human behavior. True or False?

2. I am good at recognizing patterns, evaluating evidence, and drawing conclusions. True or False?

3. I am emotionally stable. True or False?

4. I have good communication skills. True or False?

5. I find theories and ideas challenging and stimulating. True or False?

6. My friends regard me as especially sensitive to the feelings of others. True or False?

7. I enjoy planning and carrying out complex projects and activities. True or False?

8. Programs and popular books about psychology interest me. True or False?

9. I enjoy working with other people. True or False?

10. Clear thinking, objectivity, and keen observation appeal to me. True or False?

If you answered "True" to most of these questions, a career in psychology might be a good choice. And remember that many psychology majors also succeed in occupations such as management, public affairs, social services, business, sales, and education.

Other Mental Health Professionals

Clinical psychologists are not the only people who work in the field of mental health. Often they coordinate their efforts with other specially trained professionals. What are the differences among psychologists, psychiatrists, psychoanalysts, counselors, and other mental health professionals? Certainly, they're not all "shrinks." Each has a specific blend of training and skills.

A **psychiatrist** is a medical doctor who treats mental disorders, usually by doing psychotherapy. Psychiatrists can also prescribe drugs, which is something psychologists usually cannot do. However, this is changing. Psychologists in New Mexico and Louisiana can now legally prescribe drugs. It will be interesting to see whether other states grant similar privileges (Munsey, 2008).

To be a psychoanalyst, you must have a moustache and goatee, spectacles, a German accent, and a well-padded couch—or so the media stereotype goes. Actually, to become a **psychoanalyst,** you must have an M.D. or Ph.D. degree plus further training in Freudian psychoanalysis. In other words, either a physician or a psychologist may become an analyst by learning a specific type of psychotherapy.

In many states, counselors also do mental health work. A **counselor** is an adviser who helps solve problems with marriage, career, school, work, or the like. To be a licensed counselor (such as a marriage and family counselor, a child counselor, or a school counselor) typically requires a master's degree plus 1 or 2 years of full-time supervised counseling experience. Counselors learn practical helping skills and do not treat serious mental disorders.

Psychiatric social workers play an important role in many mental health programs where they apply social science principles to help patients in clinics and hospitals. Most hold an M.S.W. (Master of Social Work) degree. Often, they assist psychologists and psychiatrists as part of a team. Their typical duties include evaluating patients and families, conducting group therapy, or visiting a patient's home, school, or job to alleviate problems.

Specialties in Psychology

Do all psychologists do therapy and treat abnormal behavior? No. Only about 59 percent are clinical and counseling psychologists. The rest are found in other specialties. At present, the American Psychological Association (APA) consists of more than 50 divisions, each reflecting special skills or areas of interest. Some of the major specialties are listed in ● Table 1.4 (also see ►► Figure 1.5). Thirty percent of all psychologists are employed full-time at colleges or universities, where they teach and do research, consulting, or therapy. Some do *basic research,* in which they seek knowledge for its own sake. For example, a psychologist might study memory simply to understand how it works. Others do *applied research* to solve immediate practical problems, such as finding ways to improve athletic performance. Some do both types of research.

In a moment we'll take a closer look at how research is done. Before that, here's a chance to do a little research on how much you've learned.

Psychiatrist A medical doctor with additional training in the diagnosis and treatment of mental and emotional disorders.

Psychoanalyst A mental health professional (usually a medical doctor) trained to practice psychoanalysis.

Counselor A mental health professional who specializes in helping people with problems not involving serious mental disorder; for example, marriage counselors, career counselors, or school counselors.

Psychiatric social worker A mental health professional trained to apply social science principles to help patients in clinics and hospitals.

(a) Specialties in Psychology

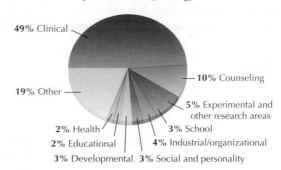

49% Clinical
19% Other
10% Counseling
5% Experimental and other research areas
2% Health
2% Educational
3% Developmental
3% Social and personality
3% School
4% Industrial/organizational

▶▶ **FIGURE 1.5** *(a)* Specialties in psychology. Percentages are approximate. *(b)* Where psychologists work. *(c)* This chart shows the main activities psychologists do at work. Any particular psychologist might do several of these activities during a work week. As you can see, most psychologists specialize in applied areas and work in applied settings (APA, 2007).

(b) Where Psychologists Work

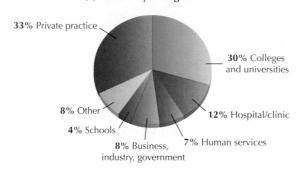

33% Private practice
30% Colleges and universities
8% Other
4% Schools
8% Business, industry, government
7% Human services
12% Hospital/clinic

(c) What Psychologists Do (Primary Activity)

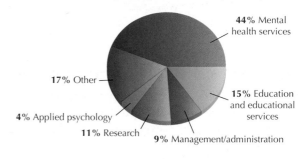

44% Mental health services
17% Other
4% Applied psychology
11% Research
9% Management/administration
15% Education and educational services

---

study break

Psychologists and Their Specialties

RECITE

1. Which of the following can prescribe drugs?
   a. a psychologist   b. a psychiatrist
   c. a psychotherapist   d. a counselor
2. A psychologist who specializes in treating human emotional difficulties is called a _____ psychologist.
3. Roughly 40 percent of psychologists specialize in counseling psychology. T or F?

4. Who among the following would most likely be involved in the detection of learning disabilities?
   a. a consumer psychologist   b. a forensic psychologist
   c. an experimental psychologist   d. a school psychologist

REFLECT

Critical Thinking

5. If many psychologists work in applied settings, why is basic research still of great importance?

Relate

Which specialty in psychology is most interesting to you? What is it about that specialty that most attracts you?

ANSWERS

1. b 2. clinical or counseling 3. F 4. d 5. Because practitioners benefit from basic psychological research in the same way that physicians benefit from basic research in biology. Discoveries in basic science form the knowledge base that leads to useful applications.

The Psychology Experiment— Where Cause Meets Effect

How is an experiment performed?

To get beyond description and fully understand behavior, psychologists must be able to explain *why* we act the way we do. To discover the *causes* of behavior, we must usually conduct an **experiment.** An experiment is a formal trial undertaken to confirm or disconfirm a hypothesis about the causes of behavior. (Sometimes, naturalistic observation or correla-

Experiment A formal trial undertaken to confirm or disconfirm a fact or principle.

tions can also reveal causes, as explained later.) Experiments allow psychologists to carefully control conditions and bring cause-and-effect relationships into sharp focus. Hence, they are generally accepted as the most powerful scientific research tool. To perform an experiment you would do the following:

1. Directly vary a condition you think might affect behavior.
2. Create two or more groups of subjects. These groups should be alike in all ways *except* the condition you are varying.
3. Record whether varying the condition has any effect on behavior.

Suppose you want to find out if using cell phones while driving a car affects the likelihood of having an accident. First, you would form two groups of people. Then you could give the members of one group a test of driving ability while they are using a cell phone. The second group would take the same test without using a cell phone. By comparing average driving ability scores for the two groups, you could tell if cell phone use affects driving ability.

As you can see, the simplest psychological experiment is based on two groups of *experimental subjects* (animals or people whose behavior is investigated; human subjects are also called *participants*). One group is called the *experimental group;* the other becomes the *control group.* The control group and the experimental group are treated exactly alike except for the condition you intentionally vary. This condition is called the *independent variable.*

Variables and Groups

A *variable* is any condition that can change and that might affect the outcome of the experiment. Identifying causes and effects in an experiment involves three types of variables:

1. **Independent variables** are conditions altered or varied by the experimenter, who sets their size, amount, or value. Independent variables are suspected *causes* for differences in behavior.
2. **Dependent variables** measure the results of the experiment. That is, they reveal the *effects* that independent variables have on *behavior.* Such effects are often revealed by measures of performance, such as test scores.
3. **Extraneous variables** are conditions that a researcher wishes to prevent from affecting the outcome of the experiment.

We can apply these terms to our cell phone/driving experiment in this way: Cell phone use is the independent variable—we want to know if talking on a cell phone affects driving ability. Driving ability (defined by scores achieved on a test of driving ability) is the dependent variable—we want to know if the ability to drive well depends on whether a person is using a cell phone. All other variables that could affect driving ability are extraneous. Examples of extraneous variables are the number of hours slept the night before the test, driving experience, and familiarity with the car used in the experiment. (You might be interested to know that people using cell phones drive no better than people who are legally drunk [Strayer, Drews, & Crouch, 2006].)

As you can see, an **experimental group** consists of participants exposed to the independent variable (cell phone use in the preceding example). Members of the **control group** are exposed to all conditions except the independent variable.

Let's examine another simple experiment. Suppose you notice that you seem to study better while listening to your iPod. This suggests the hypothesis that music improves learning. We could test this idea by forming an experimental group that studies with music. A control group would study without music. Then we could compare their scores on a test.

Is a control group really needed? Can't people just study while listening to their iPods to see if they do better? Better than what? The control group provides a *point of reference* for comparison with the scores in the experimental group. Without a control group it would be impossible to tell if music had any effect on learning. If the average test score of the experimental group is higher than the average of the control group, we can conclude that music improves learning. If there is no difference, it's obvious that the independent variable had no effect on learning.

Independent variable In an experiment, the condition being investigated as a possible cause of some change in behavior. The values that this variable takes are chosen by the experimenter.

Dependent variable In an experiment, the condition (usually a behavior) that is affected by the independent variable.

Extraneous variables Conditions or factors excluded from influencing the outcome of an experiment.

Experimental group In a controlled experiment, the group of subjects exposed to the independent variable or experimental condition.

Control group In a controlled experiment, the group of subjects exposed to all experimental conditions or variables *except* the independent variable.

FIGURE 1.6 Elements of a simple psychological experiment to assess the effects of music during study on test scores.

Dependent Variable

Experimental Group   Control Group

☐ Extraneous Variables
☐ Independent Variable

FIGURE 1.7 Experimental control is achieved by balancing extraneous variables for the experimental group and the control group. For example, the average age (A), education (B), and intelligence (C) of group members could be made the same for both groups. Then we could apply the independent variable to the experimental group. If their behavior (the dependent variable) changes (in comparison with the control group), the change must be caused by the independent variable.

Random assignment The use of chance (for example, flipping a coin) to assign subjects to experimental and control groups.

In this experiment, the amount learned (indicated by scores on the test) is the *dependent variable.* We are asking, Does the independent variable *affect* the dependent variable? (Does music affect or influence learning?)

Experimental Control

How do we know that the people in one group aren't more intelligent than those in the other group? It's true that personal differences might affect the experiment. However, they can be controlled by randomly assigning people to groups. **Random assignment** means that a participant has an equal chance of being in either the experimental group or the control group. Randomization evenly balances personal differences in the two groups. In our musical experiment, this could be done by simply flipping a coin for each participant: Heads, and the participant is in the experimental group; tails, it's the control group. This would result in few average differences in the number of people in each group who are women or men, geniuses or dunces, hungry, hungover, tall, music lovers, or whatever.

Other *extraneous,* or outside, variables—such as the amount of study time, the temperature in the room, the time of day, the amount of light, and so forth—must also be prevented from affecting the outcome of an experiment. But how? Usually this is done by making all conditions (except the independent variable) *exactly* alike for both groups. When all conditions are the same for both groups—*except* the presence or absence of music—then any difference in the amount learned *must* be caused by the music (▶▶ Figure 1.6).

Cause and Effect

Now let's summarize. In an experiment two or more groups of subjects are treated differently with respect to the independent variable. In all other ways they are treated the same. That is, extraneous variables are equated for all groups. The effect of the independent variable (or variables) on some behavior (the dependent variable) is then measured. In a carefully controlled experiment, the independent variable is the only possible *cause* for any *effect* noted in the dependent variable. This allows clear cause-and-effect connections to be identified (▶▶ Figure 1.7).

Double Blind—On Placebos and Self-Fulfilling Prophecies

What is a double-blind experiment?

Suppose a researcher hypothesizes that the drug amphetamine (a stimulant) improves learning. She explains her hypothesis to her participants and gives experimental group participants an amphetamine pill before they begin studying. Control group members get nothing. Later, she assesses how much each participant learned. Does this experiment seem valid? Actually, it is seriously flawed for several reasons.

Why? The experimental group took the drug and the control group didn't. Differences in the amount they learned must have been caused by the drug, right? No, because the drug wasn't the only difference between the groups. For a start, because of what they were told, participants in the experimental group likely *expected* to learn more. Any observed differences between groups then may reflect differences in expectation, not the actual effect of the drug.

Research Participant Bias

In a well-designed experiment, you must be careful about what you tell participants. Small bits of information might create **research participant bias,** or changes in participants' behavior caused by the influence of their expectations. Notice also that experimental group participants swallowed a pill, and control participants did not. This is another form of research participant bias. It could be that those who swallowed a pill unconsciously *expected* to do better. After all, pills are medicine, aren't they? This alone might have created a **placebo** (plah-SEE-bo) **effect** (changes in behavior caused by belief that one has taken a drug). Suppose the researcher had not given the experimental group an amphetamine pill and instead had given them a placebo, or fake drug. Inactive substances such as sugar pills and saline (saltwater) injections are commonly used as placebos. If a placebo has any effect, it must be based on suggestion, rather than chemistry (Thompson, 2005).

Placebo effects can be quite powerful. For instance, a saline injection is 70 percent as effective as morphine in reducing pain. That's why doctors sometimes prescribe placebos—especially for complaints that seem to have no physical basis. Placebos have been shown to affect pain, anxiety, depression, alertness, tension, sexual arousal, cravings for alcohol, and many other processes (Wampold et al., 2005).

How could an inert substance have any effect? Placebos alter our expectations, both conscious and unconscious, about our own emotional and physical reactions. Because we associate taking medicine with feeling better, we expect placebos to make us feel better, too (Stewart-Williams, 2004). After a person takes a placebo, there is a reduction in brain activity linked with pain, so the effect is not imaginary (Wager et al., 2004).

The placebo effect is a major factor in medical treatments. Would you also expect the placebo effect to occur in psychotherapy? (It does, which complicates studies on the effectiveness of new psychotherapies.)

Controlling Research Participant Bias

How can you avoid research participant bias? To control for research participant bias, we could use a **single-blind experiment.** In this case, participants do not know if they are in the experimental or the control group or if they are receiving a real drug or a placebo. All participants are given the same instructions and everyone gets a pill or injection. People in the experimental group get a real drug, and those in the control group get a placebo. Because participants are *blind* as to the hypothesis under investigation and whether they received the drug, their expectations (conscious *and* unconscious) are the same. Any difference in their behavior must be caused by the drug. However, even this arrangement is not enough, because researchers themselves sometimes affect experiments by influencing participants. Let's see how this occurs.

Researcher Bias

How could a researcher influence subjects? As we saw above, when the experimenter explained her hypothesis to the participants, she likely biased the results of the study. But even if a researcher uses a single-blind procedure to avoid deliberately biasing participants, **researcher bias** (changes in behavior caused by the unintended influence of a researcher) remains a problem. In essence, experimenters run the risk of finding what they expect to find. This occurs because humans are very sensitive to hints about what is expected of them (Rosenthal, 1994).

Researcher bias even applies outside the laboratory. Psychologist Robert Rosenthal (1973) reports an example of how expectations influence people: At the U.S. Air Force Academy Preparatory School, 100 airmen were randomly assigned to five different math classes. Their teachers did not know about this random placement. Instead, each teacher was told that his or her students had unusually high or low ability. Students in the classes labeled "high ability" improved much more in math scores than those in "low ability" classes. Yet, initially, all of the classes had students of equal ability.

Although the teachers were not conscious of any bias, apparently they subtly communicated their expectations to students. Most likely, they did this through tone of voice, body

Research participant bias Changes in the behavior of research participants caused by the unintended influence of their own expectations.

Placebo effect Changes in behavior due to a participant's expectations that a drug (or other treatment) will have some effect.

Single-blind experiment An arrangement in which participants remain unaware of whether they are in the experimental group or the control group.

Researcher bias Changes in participants' behavior caused by the unintended influence of a researcher's actions.

language, and by giving encouragement or criticism. Their "hints," in turn, created a self-fulfilling prophecy that affected the students. A **self-fulfilling prophecy** is a prediction that prompts people to act in ways that make the prediction come true. For instance, many teachers underestimate the abilities of ethnic minority children, which hurts the students' chances for success (Weinstein, Gregory, & Strambler, 2004). In short, people sometimes become what we prophesy for them. It is wise to remember that others tend to live *up* or *down* to our expectations for them (Jussim & Harber, 2005).

The Double-Blind Experiment

Because of research participant bias and researcher bias, it is common to keep both participants and researchers "blind." In a **double-blind experiment** neither subjects nor researchers know who is in the experimental group or the control group, including who received a drug and who took a placebo. Typically, someone else conducts the experiment, including preparing the pills or injections so that actual researchers don't know until after testing who got what. This not only controls for research participant bias, it also keeps researchers from unconsciously influencing participants.

Double-blind testing has shown that about 50 percent of the effectiveness of antidepressant drugs, such as the "wonder drug" Prozac, is due to the placebo effect (Kirsch & Sapirstein, 1998). Much of the popularity of herbal health remedies is also based on the placebo effect (Seidman, 2001).

Self-fulfilling prophecy A prediction that prompts people to act in ways that make the prediction come true.

Double-blind experiment An arrangement in which both participants and experimenters are unaware of whether participants are in the experimental group or the control group, including who might have been administered a drug or a placebo.

study break
The Psychology Experiment

RECITE

1. To understand cause and effect, a simple psychological experiment is based on creating two groups: the _____ group and the _____ group.
2. There are three types of variables to consider in an experiment: _____ variables (which are manipulated by the experimenter); _____ variables (which measure the outcome of the experiment); and _____ variables (factors to be excluded in a particular experiment).
3. A researcher performs an experiment to learn if room temperature affects the amount of aggression displayed by college students under crowded conditions in a simulated prison environment. In this experiment, the independent variable is which of the following?
   a. room temperature   b. the amount of aggression
   c. crowding   d. the simulated prison environment
4. A procedure used to control both research participant bias and researcher bias in drug experiments is the
   a. correlation method   b. extraneous prophecy
   c. double-blind technique   d. random assignment of subjects

REFLECT
Critical Thinking

5. There is a loophole in the statement "I've been taking vitamin C tablets, and I haven't had a cold all year. Vitamin C is great!" What is the loophole?
6. People who believe strongly in astrology have personality characteristics that actually match, to a degree, those predicted by their astrological signs. Can you explain why this occurs?

Relate

In a sense, we all conduct little experiments to detect cause-and-effect connections. If you are interested in cooking, for example, you might try adding a particular spice to a meal on one occasion but not another. The question then becomes, "Does the use of the spice (the independent variable) affect the appeal of the meal (the dependent variable)?" By comparing a spiced meal (the control group) with an unspiced meal (the experimental group), you could find out if that spice is worth using. Can you think of at least one informal experiment you've run in the last month? What were the variables? What was the outcome?

ANSWERS

1. experimental, control 2. independent, dependent, extraneous 3. a 4. c 5. The statement implies that vitamin C prevented colds. However, not getting a cold could just be a coincidence. A controlled experiment with a group given vitamin C and a control group not taking vitamin C would be needed to learn if vitamin C actually has any effect on susceptibility to colds. 6. Belief in astrology can create a self-fulfilling prophecy in which people alter their behaviors and self-concepts to match their astrological signs (van Rooij, 1994).

Nonexperimental Research Methods— Different Strokes

What nonexperimental research methods do psychologists use?

Determining cause-and-effect relationships between variables lies at the heart of explaining not just *what* we do, but *why* we do it. For this reason, psychologists place a special emphasis on controlled experimentation (**experimental method**). However, because it is not always possible to conduct experiments, psychologists gather evidence and test hypotheses in many other ways (Jackson, 2008). They observe behavior as it unfolds in natural settings *(naturalistic observation)*; they make measurements to discover relationships between events *(correlational method)*; they study psychological problems and therapies in clinical settings *(clinical method)*; and they use questionnaires to poll large groups of people *(survey method)*. Let's see how each of these is used to advance psychological knowledge.

Naturalistic Observation

Psychologists sometimes rely on **naturalistic observation,** the active observation of behavior in a *natural setting* (the typical environment in which a person or animal lives). For example, in 1960 Jane Goodall observed a chimpanzee use a grass stem as a tool to remove termites from a termite mound (Van Lawick-Goodall, 1971). Notice that naturalistic observation provides only *descriptions* of behavior. In order to *explain* observations we may need information from other research methods. Just the same, Goodall's discovery showed that humans are not the only tool-making animals (Nakamichi, 2004).

Chimpanzees in zoos use objects as tools. Doesn't that demonstrate the same thing? Not necessarily. Naturalistic observation allows us to study behavior that hasn't been tampered with or altered by outside influences. Only by observing chimps in their natural environment can we tell if they use tools without human interference.

Limitations

Doesn't the presence of human observers affect the animals' behavior? Yes. The observer effect is a major problem. The **observer effect** refers to changes in a subject's behavior caused by an awareness of being observed. Naturalists must be very careful to keep their distance and avoid "making friends" with the animals they are watching. Likewise, if you are interested in why automobile drivers have traffic accidents, you can't simply get in people's cars and start taking notes. As a stranger, your presence would probably change the drivers' behaviors. When possible, the observer effect can be minimized by concealing the observer.

Another solution is to use hidden recorders. One naturalistic study of traffic accidents was done with video cameras installed in 100 cars (Dingus et al., 2006). It turns out that most accidents are caused by failing to look at the traffic in front of the car (eyes forward!). Hidden stationary video cameras have also provided valuable observations of many animal species. As recording devices have become miniaturized, it has even become possible to attach "critter cams" directly to many species, allowing observations to be in a wide range of natural environments (▶▶ Figure 1.8). For example, zoologist Christian Rutz and his colleagues outfitted shy New Caledonian crows with "crow cams" to better understand their use of tools to forage for food (Rutz et al., 2007). Apparently, humans and other primates are not the only tool-using species.

Observer bias is a related problem in which observers see what they expect to see or record only selected details (Jackson, 2008). For instance, teachers in one classic study were told to watch normal elementary school children who had been labeled (for the study) as "learning disabled," "mentally retarded," "emotionally disturbed," or "normal." Sadly, teachers gave the children very different ratings, depending on the labels used (Foster & Ysseldyke, 1976). In some situations, observer bias can have serious consequences (Spano, 2005).

© Jolyon Troscianko 2006

▲ **FIGURE 1.8** New Caledonian crows wearing tiny "crow cams" barely half the weight of a silver dollar have been recorded using twigs to forage for food (Rutz et al., 2007).

Experimental method Investigating causes of behavior through controlled experimentation.

Naturalistic observation Observing behavior as it unfolds in natural settings.

Observer effect Changes in an organism's behavior brought about by an awareness of being observed.

Observer bias The tendency of an observer to distort observations or perceptions to match his or her expectations.

For example, a police officer expecting criminal behavior might shoot a person who is reaching for his wallet because he appears to be reaching for a gun.

A special mistake to avoid while observing animals is the **anthropomorphic** (AN-thro-po-MORE-fik) **error.** This is the error of attributing human thoughts, feelings, or motives to animals—especially as a way of explaining their behavior (Wynne, 2004). The temptation to assume that an animal is "angry," "jealous," "bored," or "guilty" can be strong. If you have pets at home, you probably already know how difficult it is to avoid anthropomorphizing. But it can lead to false conclusions. For example, if your dog growls at your date, you might assume the dog doesn't like your companion. But it's possible that your date is merely wearing a cologne or perfume that irritates the dog's nose.

Psychologists doing naturalistic studies make a special effort to minimize bias by keeping an *observational record,* or detailed summary of data and observations. As suggested by the study of traffic accidents and the use of "critter cams," video recording often provides the most objective record of all. Despite its problems, naturalistic observation can supply a wealth of information and raise many interesting questions. In most scientific research it is an excellent starting point.

Correlational Studies

Let's say a psychologist notes an association between the IQs of parents and their children, or between beauty and social popularity, or between anxiety and test performance, or even between crime and the weather. In each case, two observations or events are **correlated** (linked together in an orderly way). The Los Angeles study of crime and temperature mentioned earlier in this chapter is an example of a **correlational study.** First, two factors are measured. Then a statistical technique is used to find their degree of correlation. (See the Statistics Appendix near the end of this book for more information.) For example, we could find the correlation between the number of hours spent practicing and sports performance during competitions. If the correlation is large, knowing how much a person practices would allow us to predict his or her success in competition. Likewise, success in competition could be used to predict how much an athlete practiced.

Correlation Coefficients

How is the degree of correlation expressed? The strength and direction of a relationship can be expressed as a **coefficient of correlation.** This can be calculated as a number falling somewhere between +1.00 and −1.00 (see the Statistics Appendix). Drawing graphs of relationships can also help clarify their nature (see ▶▶ Figure 1.9). If the number is zero or close to zero, the association between two measures is weak or nonexistent (see ▶▶ Figure 1.9c). For example, the correlation between shoe size and intelligence is zero. (Sorry, size 12 readers.) If the correlation is +1.00, a perfect positive relationship exists (see ▶▶ Figure 1.9e); if it is −1.00, a perfect negative relationship has been discovered (see ▶▶ Figure 1.9a).

Correlations in psychology are rarely perfect. But the closer the coefficient is to +1.00 or −1.00, the stronger the relationship. For example, identical twins tend to have almost identical IQs. In contrast, the IQs of parents and their children are only generally similar. The correlation between the IQs of parents and children is .35; between identical twins it's .86.

What do the terms "positive" and "negative" correlation mean? A *positive correlation* shows that higher scores in one measure are matched by higher scores in the other. For example, there is a moderate positive correlation between high school grades and college grades; students who do well in high school tend to do well in college (and the reverse). (See ▶▶ Figure 1.9d.) In a *negative correlation,* higher scores in the first measure are associated with lower scores in the second. We might observe, for instance, a moderate negative correlation between the number of hours that students play computer games and grades. That is, more play is associated with lower grades. (This is the well-known computer-game-zombie effect.) (▶▶ Figure 1.9b)

Wouldn't that show that playing computer games too much causes lower grades? It might seem so, but as we saw previously, the best way to be confident that a cause-and-effect relationship exists is to perform a controlled experiment.

Anthropomorphic error The error of attributing human thoughts, feelings, or motives to animals, especially as a way of explaining their behavior.

Correlation The existence of a consistent, systematic relationship between two events, measures, or variables.

Correlational study A nonexperimental study designed to measure the degree of relationship (if any) between two or more events, measures, or variables.

Coefficient of correlation A statistical index ranging from −1.00 to +1.00 that indicates the direction and degree of correlation.

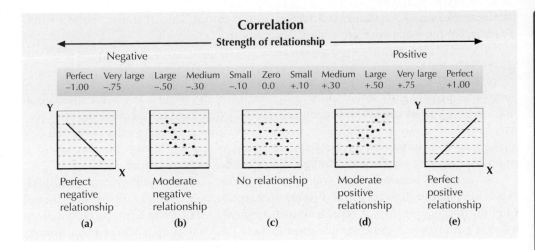

Correlation

Strength of relationship

← Negative   Positive →

Perfect	Very large	Large	Medium	Small	Zero	Small	Medium	Large	Very large	Perfect
−1.00	−.75	−.50	−.30	−.10	0.0	+.10	+.30	+.50	+.75	+1.00

(a)	(b)	(c)	(d)	(e)
Perfect negative relationship	Moderate negative relationship	No relationship	Moderate positive relationship	Perfect positive relationship

◄◄ FIGURE 1.9 The correlation coefficient tells how strongly two measures are related. These graphs show a range of relationships between two measures, A and B. If a correlation is negative, increases in one measure are associated with decreases in the other. (As B gets larger, A gets smaller.) In a positive correlation, increases in one measure are associated with increases in the other. (As B gets larger, A gets larger.) The center-left graph ("medium negative relationship") might result from comparing anxiety level (B) with test scores (A): Higher anxiety is associated with lower scores. The center graph ("no relationship") would result from plotting a person's shoe size (B) and his or her IQ (A). The center-right graph ("medium positive relationship") could be a plot of grades in high school (B) and grades in college (A) for a group of students: Higher grades in high school are associated with higher grades in college.

Correlation and Causation

Correlational studies help us discover relationships and make predictions. However, correlation *does not* demonstrate *causation* (a cause-effect relationship) (Elder, 2006). It could be, for instance, that students who aren't interested in their classes have more time for computer games. If so, then their lack of study and lower grades would *both* result from *disinterest,* not from excessive game playing. Just because one thing *appears* to be related to another does not mean that a cause-and-effect connection exists.

Here is another example of mistaking correlation for causation: What if a psychologist discovers that the blood of patients with schizophrenia contains a certain chemical not found in the general population? Does this show that the chemical *causes* schizophrenia? It may seem so, but schizophrenia could cause the chemical to form. Or, both schizophrenia and the chemical might be caused by some unknown third factor, such as the typical diet in mental hospitals. To reiterate, just because one thing *appears* to cause another does not *confirm* that it does. The best way to be confident that a cause-and-effect relationship exists is to perform a controlled experiment.

The Clinical Method

It may be impractical, unethical, or impossible to use the experimental method to study rare events, such as unusual mental disorders, childhood "genius," or "rampage" school shootings (Harding, Fox, & Mehta, 2002). In such instances, a **case study** (an in-depth focus on a single subject) may be the best source of information. Clinical psychologists rely heavily on case studies, especially as a way to investigate mental disorders, such as depression or psychosis. Also, case studies of psychotherapy have provided many useful ideas about how to treat emotional problems (Wedding & Corsini, 2005).

Case studies may sometimes be thought of as *natural clinical tests* (accidents or other natural events that provide psychological data). Gunshot wounds, brain tumors, accidental poisonings, and similar disasters have provided much information about the human brain. One remarkable case from the history of psychology is reported by Dr. J. M. Harlow (1868). Phineas Gage, a young foreman on a work crew, had a 13-pound steel rod blown through the front of his brain by a dynamite explosion (▶▶ Figure 1.10). Amazingly, he survived the accident. Within 2 months Gage could walk, talk, and move normally, but the injury forever changed his personality. Instead of the honest and dependable worker he had been before, Gage became a surly, foul-mouthed liar. Dr. Harlow carefully recorded all details of what was perhaps the first in-depth case study of an accidental frontal lobotomy (the destruction of front brain matter).

When a Los Angeles carpenter named Michael Melnick suffered a similar injury, he recovered completely, with no lasting ill effects. Melnick's very different reaction to a similar injury shows why psychologists prefer controlled experiments and often use lab animals for

⬆ FIGURE 1.10 Some of the earliest information on the effects of damage to frontal areas of the brain came from a case study of the accidental injury of Phineas Gage.

Case study An in-depth focus on all aspects of a single person.

studies of the brain. Case studies lack formal control groups. This, of course, limits the conclusions that can be drawn from clinical observations.

Survey Method

Sometimes psychologists would like to ask everyone in the world a few well-chosen questions: "Do you drink coffee? How often per week?" "What form of discipline did your parents use when you were a child?" "What is the most dishonest thing you've done?" Honest answers to such questions can reveal much about people's behavior. But, because it is impossible to question everyone, doing a survey is often more practical.

In the **survey method,** public polling techniques are used to answer psychological questions (Tourangeau, 2004). Typically, people in a representative sample are asked a series of carefully worded questions. A **representative sample** is a small group that accurately reflects a larger population. A good sample must include the same proportion of men, women, young, old, professionals, blue-collar workers, Republicans, Democrats, whites, African Americans, Native Americans, Latinos, Asians, and so on as found in the population as a whole.

A *population* is an entire group of animals or people belonging to a particular category (for example, all college students or all single women). Ultimately, we are interested in entire populations. But by selecting a smaller sample, we can draw conclusions about the larger group without polling each and every person. Representative samples are often obtained by *randomly* selecting who will be included (▶▶ Figure 1.11). (Notice that this is similar to randomly assigning participants to groups in an experiment.)

How accurate is the survey method? Modern surveys like the Gallup and Harris polls are quite accurate. The Gallup poll has erred in its election predictions by only 1.5 percent since 1954. However, if a survey is based on a biased sample, it may paint a false picture. A *biased sample* does not accurately reflect the population from which it was drawn. Surveys done by magazines, websites, and online information services can be quite biased. Surveys on the use of guns done by *O: The Oprah Magazine* and *Guns and Ammo* magazine would probably produce very different results—neither of which would represent the general population. That's why psychologists using the survey method go to great lengths to ensure that their samples are representative. Fortunately, people can often be polled by telephone, which makes it easier to obtain large samples. Even if one person out of three refuses to answer survey questions, the results are still likely to be valid (Hutchinson, 2004).

Internet Surveys

Recently, psychologists have started doing surveys and experiments on the Internet. Web-based research can be a cost-effective way to reach very large groups of people. Internet studies have provided interesting information about topics such as anger, decision making,

Survey method The use of public polling techniques to answer psychological questions.

Representative sample A small, randomly selected part of a larger population that accurately reflects characteristics of the whole population.

▶▶ **FIGURE 1.11** If you were conducting a survey in which a person's height might be an important variable, the upper, nonrandom sample would be very unrepresentative. The lower sample, selected using a table of random numbers, better represents the group as a whole.

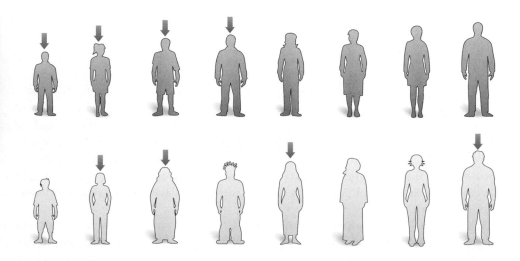

racial prejudice, what disgusts people, religion, sexual attitudes, and much more. Biased samples can limit web-based research (because it isn't easy to control who actually answers your online questionnaire), but psychologists are finding ways to gather valid information with it (Birnbaum, 2004; Whitaker, 2007).

Social Desirability

Even well-designed surveys may be limited by another problem. If a psychologist were to ask you detailed questions about your sexual history and current sexual behavior, how accurate would your replies be? Would you exaggerate? Would you be embarrassed? Replies to survey questions are not always accurate or truthful. Many people show a distinct *courtesy bias* (a tendency to give "polite" or socially desirable answers). For example, answers to questions concerning sex, drinking or drug use, income, and church attendance tend to be less than truthful. Likewise, the week after an election, more people will say they voted than actually did (Hutchinson, 2004).

Summary

Despite their limitations, surveys frequently produce valuable information. For instance, the survey method has been used to find out about the attitudes of Muslims in the Middle East toward U.S. policies in the region and to clarify the debate about Islam and violence that has arisen since the terrorist attacks of 9/11 (Haddad, 2003). To sum up, the survey method can be a powerful research tool. Like other methods, it has limitations, but new techniques and strategies are providing valuable information about our behavior (Kahneman et al., 2004).

Is so much emphasis on science really necessary in psychology? In a word, yes. As we have seen, science is a powerful way of asking questions about the world and getting trustworthy answers. (● Table 1.5 summarizes many of the important ideas we have covered.)

A Look Ahead

To help you get the most out of psychology, each chapter of this text includes a "Psychology in Action" section like the one that follows. There you will find ideas you can actually use, now or in the future. To complete the topics we have been discussing, let's take a critical look at information reported in the popular press. You should find this an interesting way to conclude our opening tour of psychology and its methods.

● Table 1.5 Comparison of Psychological Research Methods

	ADVANTAGES	DISADVANTAGES
Experimental Method	Clear cause-and-effect relationships can be identified; powerful controlled observations can be staged; no need to wait for natural event	May be somewhat artificial; some natural behavior not easily studied in laboratory (field experiments may avoid these objections)
Naturalistic Observation	Behavior is observed in a natural setting; much information is obtained, and hypotheses and questions for additional research are formed	Little or no control is possible; observed behavior may be altered by the presence of the observer; observations may be biased; causes cannot be conclusively identified
Correlational Method	Demonstrates the existence of relationships; allows prediction; can be used in lab, clinic, or natural setting	Little or no control is possible; relationships may be coincidental; cause-and-effect relationships cannot be confirmed
Clinical Method	Takes advantage of "natural clinical trials" and allows investigation of rare or unusual problems or events	Little or no control is possible; does not provide a control group for comparison, subjective interpretation is often necessary, a single case may be misleading or unrepresentative
Survey Method	Allows information about large numbers of people to be gathered; can address questions not answered by other approaches	Obtaining a representative sample is critical and can be difficult to do; answers may be inaccurate; people may not do what they say or say what they do

study break

Nonexperimental Research Methods

RECITE

1. Two major problems in naturalistic observation are the effects of the observer and observer bias. T or F?
2. The _____ fallacy involves attributing human feelings and motives to animals.
3. Correlation typically does not demonstrate causation. T or F?
4. Which correlation coefficient represents the strongest relationship?
   a. −0.86   b. +0.66   c. +0.10   d. +0.09
5. Case studies can often be thought of as natural tests and are frequently used by clinical psychologists. T or F?
6. For the survey method to be valid, a representative sample of people must be polled. T or F?
7. A problem with the survey method is that answers to questions may not always be _____ or _____.

REFLECT
Critical Thinking

8. A psychologist conducting a survey at a shopping mall (The Gallery of Wretched Excess) flips a coin before stopping passersby. If the coin shows heads, he interviews the person; if it shows tails, he skips that person. Has the psychologist obtained a random sample?
9. Is attributing mischievous motives to a car that is not working properly a thinking error similar to anthropomorphizing?

Relate

Google "critter cam" and find one you can watch. What species are you watching? What behaviors might you observe and record?

See if you can identify at least one positive correlation and one negative correlation that involves human behavior.

Have you ever known someone who suffered a brain injury or disease? How did his or her behavior change? Was the change clear-cut enough to serve as a natural clinical test?

Have you ever been asked to complete a survey? Did you do it or did you refuse? If you refused, do you think your refusal influenced the final results of the survey? What would it say about accuracy if lots of people refused to complete the survey? If you completed the survey, were you honest about your answers? What would it say about accuracy if lots of people refused to answer accurately?

ANSWERS

1. T 2. anthropomorphic 3. T 4. a 5. T 6. T 7. accurate, truthful 8. The psychologist's coin flips *might* produce a reasonably good sample of people at *the mall*. The real problem is that people who go to the mall may be mostly from one part of town, from upper income groups, or from some other nonrepresentative group. The psychologist's sample is likely to be seriously flawed. 9. Yes. It appears to be difficult for humans to resist thinking of other species and even machines in human terms.

psychology in action

Psychology in the Media—Separating Fact from Fiction

How good is psychological information found in the popular media?

Psychology is a popular topic in contemporary media. Unfortunately, much of what you will encounter is based on entertainment value rather than critical thinking or science. Here are some suggestions for separating high-quality information from misleading fiction:

Suggestion 1: Be skeptical. Have you ever played the game called "telephone" or "pass it down"? You know, one person whispers a sentence to someone else who, in turn, whispers it on down the line. Usually, when the person at the end of the line repeats the message, it has been humorously distorted. Similarly, modern media, and especially the Internet, function as a giant "echo chamber" awash with rumors, hoaxes, half-truths, and urban legends like the one about giant alligators living in New York sewers.

One of our all-time favorites was a story about the health department in Oregon seeking a Klingon interpreter for mental health patients who spoke only in the fictional language used on the *Star Trek* TV series. This tale started when a newspaper reported that Klingon was on a list of languages that some psychiatric patients claimed they could speak. The article specifically noted that "in reality, no patient has yet tried to communicate in Klingon." Nevertheless, as the story echoed around the Web, the idea that Oregon was looking for someone fluent in Klingon had become a "fact" (O'Neill, 2003).

Reports in the popular media tend to be made uncritically and with a definite bias toward reporting "astonishing" findings and telling interesting stories. Remember, saying, "That's incredible" means, "That's not believable"—which is often true.

Suggestion 2: Consider the source of information. It should come as no surprise that information used to sell a product often reflects a desire for profit rather than the objective truth. Here is a typical advertising claim: "Government tests prove that no sleep medicine is stronger or more effective than Coma." A statement like this usually means that there was *no difference* between Coma and the other products tested. No other sleep aid was stronger or more effective. But none was weaker either.

Keep the source in mind when reading the claims of makers of home biofeedback machines, sleep-learning devices, subliminal CDs, and the like. Remember that psychological services may be merchandised as well. Be wary of expensive courses that promise instant mental health and happiness, increased efficiency, memory, extrasensory perception (ESP) or psychic ability, control of the unconscious mind, an end to smoking, and so on. Usually they are promoted with a few testimonials and many unsupported claims (Lilienfeld et al., 2005).

Psychic claims should be viewed with special caution. Google magician James Randi's Million Dollar Challenge. Randi is offering $1,000,000 to anyone demonstrating such abilities under controlled conditions. Did you know that no one has even passed the preliminary tests yet?

Stage mentalists make a living by deceiving the public. Understandably, they are highly interested in promoting belief in their nonexistent powers. The same is true of the so-called psychic advisers promoted in TV commercials. These charlatans make use of the Barnum effect (the tendency to consider personal descriptions accurate if they are stated in general terms) to create an illusion that they know private information about the people who call them (Nickell, 2001).

Suggestion 3: Beware of oversimplifications, especially those motivated by monetary gain. Courses or programs that offer a "new personality in three sessions," "six steps to love and fulfillment in marriage," or some newly discovered "secret for unlocking the powers of the mind and the universe" should be immediately suspect.

An excellent example of oversimplification is provided by websites devoted to a video that promises to reveal "the secret to unlimited joy, health, money, relationships, love, youth: everything you have ever wanted." According to these sites, all you need to do is put your desires out to the universe and the universe must respond by granting your wishes. And all it will cost you is the price of ordering the video. (It's no secret that the promoters are the real winners in this game.)

Suggestion 4: Remember, "for example" is no proof. After reading this chapter you should be sensitive to the danger of selecting single examples. If you read, "Law student passes state bar exam using sleep-learning device," don't rush out to buy one. Systematic research showed long ago that these devices are of little or no value (Druckman & Bjork, 1994). A corollary to this suggestion is to ask, Are the reported observations important or widely applicable?

Examples, anecdotes, single cases, and testimonials are all potentially deceptive. According to numerous testimonials, believers in the power of the "secret" described above have been showered with money, success, and happiness immediately after viewing the video. Unfortunately, such *individual cases* (or even several) tell nothing about what is true *in general* (Stanovich, 2007). How many people *didn't* win the lottery after buying the video? Similarly, studies of large groups of people show that smoking increases the likelihood of lung cancer. It doesn't matter if you know a lifelong heavy smoker who is 95 years old. The general finding is the one to remember.

Suggestion 5: Ask yourself if there was a control group. The key importance of a control group in any experiment is frequently overlooked by the unsophisticated—an error to which you are no longer susceptible. The popular media are full of reports of "experiments" performed without control groups: "Talking to Plants Speeds Growth"; "Special Diet Controls Hyperactivity in Children"; "Graduates of Firewalking Seminar Risk Their Soles."

Firewalking is based on simple physics, not on any form of supernatural psychological control. The temperature of the coals may be as high as 1,200° F. However, coals are like the air in a hot oven: They are very inefficient at transferring heat during brief contact.

Consider the last example for a moment. Expensive commercial courses have long been promoted to teach people to walk barefoot on hot coals. (Why anyone would want to do this is itself an interesting question.) Firewalkers supposedly protect their feet with a technique called "neurolinguistic programming." Many people have paid good money to learn the technique, and most do manage a quick walk on the coals. But is the technique necessary? And is anything remarkable happening? We need a comparison group.

Fortunately, physicist Bernard Leikind has provided one. Leikind showed with volunteers that anyone (with reasonably callused feet) can walk over a bed of coals without being burned. The reason is that the coals, which are light, fluffy carbon, transmit little heat when touched. The principle involved is similar to briefly putting your hand in a hot oven. If you touch a pan, you will be burned because metal transfers heat efficiently. But if your hand stays in the heated air you'll be fine because air transmits little heat (Kida, 2006; Mitchell, 1987). Mystery solved.

Suggestion 6: Look for errors in distinguishing between correlation and causation. As you now know, it is dangerous to presume that one thing *caused* another just because they are correlated. In spite of this, you will see many claims based on questionable correlations. Here's an example of mistaking correlation for causation: Jeanne Dixon, a well-known astrologer, once answered a group of prominent scientists—who had declared that there is no scientific foundation for astrology—by saying, "They would do well to check the records at their local police stations, where they will learn that the rate of violent crime rises and falls with lunar cycles." Dixon, of course, believes that the moon affects human behavior.

If it is true that violent crime is more frequent at certain times of the month, doesn't that prove her point? Far from it. Increased crime could be due to darker nights, the fact that many people expect others to act crazier, or any number of similar factors. Besides, direct studies of the alleged "lunar effect" have shown that it doesn't occur (Dowling, 2005). Moonstruck criminals, influenced by "a bad moon rising," are a fiction (Iosif & Ballon, 2005).

Suggestion 7: Be sure to distinguish between observation and inference. If you see a person *crying,* is it correct to assume that she or he is *sad?* Although it seems reasonable to make this assumption, it is actually quite risky. We can observe objectively that the person is crying, but to *infer* sadness may be in error. It could be that the individual has just peeled 5 pounds of onions. Or maybe he or she just won a million-dollar lottery, or is trying contact lenses for the first time.

Psychologists, politicians, physicians, scientists, and other experts often go far beyond the available facts in their claims. This does not mean that their inferences, opinions, and interpretations have no value; the opinion of an expert on the causes of mental illness, criminal behavior, learning problems, or whatever can be revealing. But be careful to distinguish between fact and opinion.

Summary We are all bombarded daily with such a mass of new information that it is difficult to absorb it. The available knowledge, even in a limited area like psychology, biology, medicine, or contemporary hip-hop music, is so vast that no single person can completely know and comprehend it. With this situation in mind, it becomes increasingly important that you become a critical, selective, and informed consumer of information.

RECITE

1. Popular media reports usually stress objective accuracy. T or F?
2. Stage mentalists and psychics often use deception in their "acts." T or F?
3. Blaming the lunar cycle for variations in the rate of violent crime is an example of mistaking correlation for causation. T or F?
4. If a psychology student uses a sleep-learning device to pass a midterm exam, it proves that the device works. T or F?

REFLECT

Critical Thinking

5. Many parents believe that children become "hyperactive" when they eat too much sugar, and some early studies seemed to confirm this connection. However, we now know that eating sugar

rarely has any effect on children. Why do you think that sugar appears to cause hyperactivity?

Relate

How actively do you evaluate and question claims made by an authority or found in the media? Could you be a more critical consumer of information? *Should* you be a more critical consumer of information?

ANSWERS

1. F 2. T 3. T 4. F 5. This is another case of mistaking correlation for causation. Children who are hyperactive may eat more sugar (and other foods) to fuel their frenetic activity levels.

chapter in review

Major Points

- Psychology is the science of behavior and mental processes.
- Psychologists gather scientific data in order to describe, understand, predict, and control behavior.
- Critical thinking is central to the scientific method, to psychology, and to effective behavior in general.
- The scientific method consists of highly refined procedures for observing the natural world, testing hypotheses, and drawing valid conclusions.
- Psychologists use several specialized research methods. Each has strengths and weaknesses, so all are needed to fully investigate human behavior.
- Experimentation is the most powerful way to identify cause-and-effect relationships.
- The popular media are rife with inaccurate information. It is essential to critically evaluate information, no matter what its source may be.

Summary

What is psychology and what are its goals?

- Psychology is the scientific study of behavior and mental processes.
- Some major areas of research in psychology are comparative, learning, sensation, perception, personality, biopsychology, motivation and emotion, social, cognitive, developmental, the psychology of gender, cultural psychology, and evolutionary psychology.
- Psychologists may be directly interested in animal behavior, or they may study animals as models of human behavior.
- As a science, psychology's goals are to describe, understand, predict, and control behavior.

What is critical thinking?

- Critical thinking is the ability to evaluate, compare, analyze, critique, and synthesize information.
- To judge the validity of a claim, it is important to gather evidence *for* and *against* the claim and to evaluate the *quality* of the evidence.

How does psychology differ from false explanations of behavior?

- Unlike psychology, pseudopsychologies change little over time because followers seek evidence that appears to confirm their

beliefs and avoid evidence that contradicts their beliefs.
- Belief in pseudopsychologies is based in part on uncritical acceptance, the fallacy of positive instances, and the Barnum effect.

How is the scientific method applied in psychological research?

- Important elements of a scientific investigation include observing, defining a problem, proposing a hypothesis, gathering evidence/testing the hypothesis, publishing results, and forming a theory.
- Before they can be investigated, psychological concepts must be given operational definitions.

How did the field of psychology emerge?

- Historically, psychology is an outgrowth of philosophy.
- Wilhelm Wundt, who studied conscious experience, established the first psychological laboratory 130 years ago in Germany.
- The first school of thought in psychology was structuralism, a kind of "mental chemistry" based on introspection.
- Structuralism was followed by functionalism, behaviorism, and Gestalt psychology.
- Psychodynamic approaches, such as Freud's psychoanalytic theory, emphasize the unconscious origins of behavior.

- Humanistic psychology accentuates subjective experience, human potentials, and personal growth.

What are the current perspectives in psychology?

- Three complementary streams of thought in modern psychology are the biological perspective, including biopsychology and evolutionary psychology; the psychological perspective, including behaviorism, cognitive psychology, the psychodynamic approach, and humanism; and the sociocultural perspective.

What are the major specialties in psychology?

- Although psychologists, psychiatrists, psychoanalysts, and counselors all work in the field of mental health, their training and methods differ considerably.
- Clinical and counseling psychologists, who do psychotherapy, represent only two of dozens of specialties in psychology.
- Psychological research may be basic or applied.

How is an experiment performed?

- In an experiment, two or more groups of subjects are formed. These groups differ only with regard to the independent variable (condition of interest as a cause in the experiment).
- Effects on the dependent variable are then measured. All other conditions (extraneous variables) are held constant.

What is a double-blind experiment?

- Research participant bias arises when participants' expectations influence their

behavior in an experiment; the placebo effect is a source of research participant bias in experiments involving drugs.
- A related problem is researcher bias. Researcher expectations can create a self-fulfilling prophecy, in which a participant changes in the direction of the expectation.
- In a double-blind experiment, neither the research participants nor the researchers collecting data know who was in the experimental group or the control group, allowing valid conclusions to be drawn.

What nonexperimental research methods do psychologists use?

- Unlike controlled experiments, nonexperimental methods usually cannot demonstrate cause-and-effect relationships.
- Naturalistic observation is a starting place in many investigations.
- Three problems with naturalistic observation are the effects of the observer on the observed, observer bias, and an inability to explain observed behavior.
- In the correlational method, relationships between two traits, responses, or events are measured and a correlation coefficient is computed to gauge the strength of the relationship.
- Correlations allow prediction, but they do not demonstrate cause-and-effect connections.
- The clinical method employs case studies, which are in-depth records of a single subject. Case studies provide insights into human behavior that can't be gained by other methods.
- In the survey method, people in a representative sample are asked a series of carefully worded questions.

How good is psychological information found in the popular media?

- Information in the mass media varies greatly in quality and accuracy and should be approached with skepticism and caution.
- Problems in media reports are often related to biased or unreliable sources of information, uncontrolled observation, misleading correlations, false inferences, oversimplification, use of single examples, and unrepeatable results.

Web Resources

For an up-to-date list of direct links to interesting sites, including those listed here, visit the student companion site for this book at www.cengage.com/psychology/coon

What Is Psychology? Discusses psychology as a science, with links to other articles about various branches of psychology.

Critical Thinking in Everyday Life: 9 Strategies Some useful critical thinking strategies, along with many other articles on aspects of critical thinking.

Today in the History of Psychology Events in the history of psychology by the date, including podcasts.

Careers in Psychology Marky Lloyd's Careers in Psychology Page.

The Experimental Method An introduction to experimental research methods.

Psychological Research on the Net Find and complete a survey study.

That's Infotainment! Article about sensationalism in the news media.

Interactive Learning

PSYCHOLOGY: A JOURNEY BOOK COMPANION WEBSITE
WWW.CENGAGE.COM/PSYCHOLOGY/COON
Visit your book companion website, where you will find flash cards, practice quizzes, web links, and more to help you study.

JUST WHAT YOU NEED TO KNOW NOW! CENGAGENOW
Spend time on what you need to master rather than on information you already have learned. Take a pretest for this chapter, and CengageNOW will generate a personalized study plan based on your results. The study plan will identify the topics you need to review and direct you to online resources to help you master those topics. You can then take a posttest to help you determine the concepts you have mastered and what you will need to work on. Try it out! Go to www.cengage.com/login to sign in with an access code or to purchase access to this product.

test your knowledge

Psychology and Research Methods

For additional review, get more practice with *CengageNOW, WebTutor*, the *Practice Quizzes*, and/or the printed *Study Guide* available with this book.

1. Psychology is the _____ of _____ and mental processes.
   a. study, the mind
   b. knowledge, philosophy
   c. study, personality
   d. science, behavior

2. The best psychological information is typically based on
   a. proven theories
   b. opinions of experts and authorities
   c. anthropomorphic measurements
   d. empirical evidence

3. Who among the following is most interested in the growth of young children?
   a. learning theorist
   b. personality theorist
   c. comparative psychologist
   d. developmental psychologist

4. Research that can explain why people remember better if they relate new information to familiar ideas meets which of psychology's goals?
   a. describe
   b. understand
   c. predict
   d. control

5. Personality descriptions provided by pseudopsychologies are stated in general terms, which provide "a little something for everybody." This fact is the basis of the
   a. palmist's fallacy
   b. uncritical acceptance pattern
   c. fallacy of positive instances
   d. Barnum effect

6. Belief in astrology is based on the fallacy of positive instances, which is a failure to
   a. collect relevant correlations
   b. make use of introspection
   c. distinguish between observation and inference
   d. engage in critical thinking

7. A psychologist does a study to see if having control over difficult tasks reduces stress. In the study he will be testing an
   a. experimental hypothesis
   b. operational definition
   c. empirical definition
   d. anthropomorphic theory

8. After you identify an interesting problem or question about behavior, you will need to establish _____ of important variables before you begin to make controlled observations.
   a. correlations
   b. operational definitions
   c. double-blind controls
   d. a theory

9. The outcome of a psychology experiment is revealed by measuring changes in behavior. Such measures are the _____ variable of the experiment.
   a. independent
   b. correlational
   c. dependent
   d. extraneous

10. Double-blind experiments are designed to control for the
    a. placebo effect
    b. anthropomorphic fallacy
    c. unintended influence of operational definitions
    d. courtesy bias

11. Introspection was especially important to which school of thought in psychology?
    a. structuralism
    b. functionalism
    c. behaviorism
    d. Gestalt

12. Which two schools of thought have largely disappeared from contemporary psychology?
    a. behaviorism, Gestalt
    b. humanism, cognitive behaviorism
    c. functionalism, structuralism
    d. structuralism, humanism

13. Who among the following was a historic woman psychologist?
    a. Sumner   b. Wundt   c. Washburn   d. Watson

14. Who among the following is LEAST likely to treat serious behavioral and emotional disturbances?
    a. psychologist
    b. counselor
    c. psychiatrist
    d. psychoanalyst

15. A psychotherapist is working with a person from an ethnic group other than her own. She should be aware of how cultural relativity and _____ affect behavior.
    a. the anthropomorphic error
    b. operational definitions
    c. biased sampling
    d. social norms

16. Observer bias and the observer effect are problems in using
    a. naturalistic observation
    b. the correlational method
    c. the experimental method
    d. naturalistic experiments

17. Because correlation does not demonstrate causation, psychologists often use _____ to answer questions about behavior.
    a. experimentation
    b. naturalistic observation
    c. the survey method
    d. the clinical method

18. Case studies can often be thought of as natural tests and are frequently used by clinical psychologists. T or F?

19. Obtaining a representative sample is especially important in psychological research involving
    a. the placebo effect
    b. hypothesis testing
    c. the experimenter effect
    d. the survey method

20. An article in a magazine claims that "Special Diet Controls Hyperactivity in Children." This claim is meaningless unless
    a. the author is an authority on hyperactivity
    b. the diet has been tested empirically
    c. an animal model was used
    d. the author knows of a specific child who benefited from the diet

Answers   1. d 2. d 3. d 4. b 5. d 6. d 7. a 8. b 9. c 10. a 11. a 12. c 13. c 14. b 15. d 16. a 17. a 18. T 19. d 20. b

Brain and Behavior

Journey into Psychology: Finding Music in Walnut-Grapefruit Tofu

Your authors recently shared an evening together, watching some fiery Spanish flamenco. We both had brains on our minds. (Really!) The guitarist and dancer were passionate and brilliant. If they had been athletes, you would say they were "in the zone." Of course, in everything from classical to jazz to hip-hop, musicians regularly make music that no machine could duplicate. A virtual Coldplay? A mechanical Jennifer Hudson? We doubt it. That's why music is such a good example of the central role the brain plays in all that is human.

Your 3-pound brain is wrinkled like a walnut, the size of a grapefruit, and the texture of tofu. The next time you are in a market that sells beef brains, stop and have a look. What you will see is similar to your own brain, only smaller. How could such a squishy little blob of tissue allow us to make music of exquisite beauty? To seek a cure for cancer? To fall in love? Or read a book like this one?

Each of the billions of nerve cells in your brain is linked to thousands of others. The resulting network allows you to process immense amounts of information. In fact, there may be more *possible* pathways between the neurons in your brain than there are stars in the visible universe! Undeniably, the human brain is the most amazing of all computers.

Scientists use the power of the brain to study the brain. Yet, even now we must wonder if the brain will ever completely understand itself. Nevertheless, answers to many age-old questions about the mind, consciousness, and knowledge lie buried within the brain. Let's visit this fascinating realm.

Neurons—Building a "Biocomputer"

How do neurons operate and communicate?

Survey Questions

- How do neurons operate and communicate?
- What are the major parts of the nervous system?
- How is the brain studied?
- Why is the human cerebral cortex so important and what are its parts?
- What are the major parts of the subcortex?
- Does the glandular system affect behavior?
- In what ways do right- and left-handed individuals differ?

While they may seem far removed from your daily life, 100 billion tiny **neurons** (NOOR-ons: individual nerve cells) make up your brain. Neurons carry information from the senses to the brain, where they process it. They also activate muscles and glands. Yet, a single neuron is not very smart—it would take many just to make you blink. When a musician such as Bruce Springsteen plays a guitar riff, literally billions of neurons may be involved (Kalat, 2009).

Your brainpower arises because individual neurons link to one another in tight clumps and long "chains." Each neuron receives messages from many others and sends its own message on. Everything you think, feel, or do can be traced back to electrical impulses flashing through spidery networks of neurons. When neurons form vast networks, they produce intelligence and consciousness. Let's see how neurons operate and how the nervous system is "wired."

Parts of a Neuron

What does a neuron look like? What are its main parts? No two neurons are exactly alike, but most have four basic parts (▶▶ Figure 2.1). The **dendrites** (DEN-drytes), which look like tree roots, receive messages from other neurons. The **soma** (SOH-mah: cell body) does the same. In addition, the soma sends messages of its own (nerve impulses) down a thin fiber called the **axon** (AK-sahn).

Some axons are only 0.1 millimeter long. (That's about the width of a pencil line.) Others stretch up to a meter through the nervous system. (From the base of your spine to your big toe, for instance.) Like miniature cables, axons carry messages through the brain and nervous system. Altogether, your brain contains about 3 million miles of axons (Rosenzweig, Breedlove, & Watson, 2004).

Axons "branch out" into smaller fibers ending in bulb-shaped **axon terminals.** By forming connections with the dendrites and somas of other neurons, axon terminals allow information to pass from neuron to neuron.

Now let's summarize with a metaphor. Imagine that you are standing in a long line of people who are holding hands. A person on the far right end of the line wants to silently send a message to the person on the left end. She does this by pressing the hand of the person to her left, who presses the hand of the person to his left, and so on. The message arrives at your right hand (your dendrites). You decide whether to pass it on. (You are the soma.) The message goes out through your left arm (the axon). With your left hand (the axon terminals), you squeeze the hand of the person to your left, and the message moves on.

The Nerve Impulse   Q#4 Exam

Electrically charged molecules called *ions* (EYE-ons) are found inside each neuron (▶▶ Figure 2.2). Other ions lie outside the cell. Some ions have a positive electrical charge, and some are negative. When a neuron is inactive, more of these "plus" charges exist outside the neuron and more "minus" charges exist inside. As a result, the inside of each neuron in your brain has an electrical charge of about −70 millivolts. (A millivolt is one thousandth of a volt.) This charge allows each neuron in your brain to act like a tiny biological battery.

The electrical charge of an inactive neuron is called its **resting potential.** But neurons seldom get much rest: Messages arriving from other neurons raise and lower the resting potential. If the electrical charge rises to about −50 millivolts, the neuron will reach its *threshold,* or trigger point for firing (see Figure 2.2). It's as if the neuron says, "Ah-ha! It's time to send a message to my neighbors." When a neuron reaches threshold, an **action potential,** or nerve impulse, sweeps down the axon at up to 200 miles per hour

Neuron An individual nerve cell.

Dendrites Neuron fibers that receive incoming messages.

Soma The main body of a neuron or other cell.

Axon Fiber that carries information away from the cell body of a neuron.

Axon terminals Bulb-shaped structures at the ends of axons that form synapses with the dendrites and somas of other neurons.

Resting potential The electrical charge of a neuron at rest.

Action potential The nerve impulse.

FIGURE 2.1 A neuron, or nerve cell. In the right foreground you can see a nerve cell fiber in cross section. The upper left photo gives a more realistic picture of the shape of neurons. Nerve impulses usually travel from the dendrites and soma to the branching ends of the axon. The nerve cell shown here is a motor neuron. The axons of motor neurons stretch from the brain and spinal cord to muscles or glands of the body.

Synapse (see Figure 2.6 for an enlarged view)

Other neuron

Axon terminals

Nerve impulse

Myelin

Neurilemma

Nerve impulse

Soma (cell body)

Axon

Axon collateral (branch)

Nerve cell fiber

Myelin sheath

Axon

Dendrites

SEND INFO

RECEIVE

Membrane potential (in millivolts)

+30

0

−50

−70

Resting potential

Action potential

Negative after-potential

Threshold

Time

Axon

FIGURE 2.2 Electrical probes placed inside and outside an axon measure its activity. (The scale is exaggerated here. Such measurements require ultra-small electrodes, as described in this chapter.) The inside of an axon at rest is about 260 to 270 millivolts, compared with the outside. Electrochemical changes in a neuron generate an action potential. When sodium ions (Na^+) that have a positive charge rush into the cell, its interior briefly becomes positive. This is the action potential. After the action potential, positive potassium ions (K^+) flow out of the axon and restore its negative charge. (See ▶▶ Figure 2.3 for further explanation.)

1. In its <u>resting state</u>, the axon has a negatively charged <u>interior</u>.

2. During an action potential, positively charged atoms (ions) rush into the axon. This briefly changes the electrical charge inside the axon from negative to positive. Simultaneously, the charge outside the axon becomes negative.

3. The action potential advances as positive and negative charges reverse in a moving zone of electrical activity that sweeps down the axon.

4. After an action potential passes, positive ions rapidly flow out of the axon to quickly restore its negative charge. An outward flow of additional positive ions returns the axon to its resting state.

Axon

Action potential

Action potential

Action potential

◀◀ **FIGURE 2.3** The inside of an axon normally has a negative electrical charge. The fluid surrounding an axon is normally positive. As an action potential passes along the axon, these charges reverse so that the interior of the axon briefly becomes positive. This process is described in more detail in Figure 2.4.

Base how nervous system

(Figure 2.3). That may seem fast, but it still takes at least a split second to react. That's one reason why returning a 130-mile-per-hour professional tennis serve is so difficult.

What happens during an action potential? The axon membrane is pierced by tiny tunnels or "holes," called *ion channels*. Normally, these tiny openings are blocked by molecules that act like "gates" or "doors." During an action potential, the gates pop open. This allows sodium ions (Na+) to rush into the axon (Carlson, 2010). The channels first open near the soma. Then, gate after gate opens down the length of the axon as the action potential zips along (▶▶ Figure 2.4).

Each action potential is an *all-or-nothing event* (a nerve impulse occurs completely or not at all). You might find it helpful to picture the axon as a row of dominoes set on end. Tipping over the dominoes is an all-or-nothing act. Once the first domino drops, a wave of falling blocks will zip rapidly to the end of the line. Similarly, when a nerve impulse is triggered near the soma, a wave of activity (the action potential) travels down the length of the axon. This is what happens in long chains of neurons as a flamenco dancer's brain tells her feet what to do next, beat after beat.

After each nerve impulse, the cell briefly dips below its resting level and becomes less willing or ready to fire. This **negative after-potential** occurs because potassium ions (K^+) flow out of the neuron while the membrane gates are open (Figure 2.4). After a nerve impulse, ions flow both into and out of the axon, recharging it for more action. In our model, it takes an instant for the row of dominoes to be set up again. Soon, however, the axon is ready for another wave of activity.

▲ **FIGURE 2.4** The interior of an axon. The right end of the top axon is at rest. Thus, it has a negative charge inside. An action potential begins when ion channels open and sodium ions (Na^+) rush into the axon. In this drawing, the action potential would travel from left to right along the axon. In the lower axon, the action potential has moved to the right. After it passes, potassium ions (K^+) flow out of the axon. This quickly renews the negative charge inside the axon, so that it can fire again. Sodium ions that enter the axon during an action potential are pumped out more slowly. Removing them restores the original resting potential.

| **Negative after-potential** A drop in electrical charge below the resting potential.

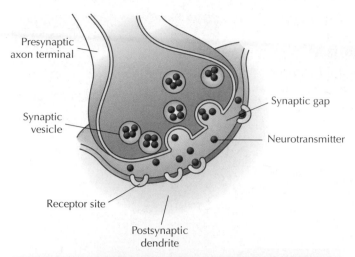

Presynaptic
axon terminal

Synaptic gap

Synaptic
vesicle

Neurotransmitter

Receptor site

Postsynaptic
dendrite

▲ FIGURE 2.5 A highly magnified view of a synapse. Neurotransmitters are stored in tiny sacs called synaptic vesicles (VES-ih-kels). When a nerve impulse reaches the end of an axon, the vesicles move to the surface and release neurotransmitters. These molecules cross the synaptic gap to affect the next neuron. The size of the gap is exaggerated here; it is actually only about one millionth of an inch. Some transmitter molecules excite the next neuron and some inhibit its activity.

Saltatory Conduction

The axons of some neurons (such as the one pictured in Figure 2.1) are coated with a fatty layer called *myelin* (MY-eh-lin). Small gaps in the myelin help nerve impulses move faster. Instead of passing down the entire length of the axon, the action potential leaps from gap to gap, a process called **saltatory conduction.** (The Latin word *saltare* means to hop or leap.) Without the added speed of saltatory action potentials, it would probably be impossible to brake in time to avoid many automobile accidents (or hit that professional tennis serve). When the myelin layer is damaged, a person may suffer from numbness, weakness, or paralysis. That, in fact, is what happens in multiple sclerosis, a disease that occurs when the immune system attacks and destroys the myelin in a person's body.

Synapses and Neurotransmitters

How does information move from one neuron to another? The nerve impulse is primarily electrical. That's why electrically stimulating the brain affects behavior. To prove the point, researcher José Delgado once entered a bullring with a cape and a radio transmitter. The bull charged. Delgado retreated. At the last instant the speeding bull stopped short. Why? Because Delgado had placed radio activated electrodes (metal wires) deep within the bull's brain. These, in turn, stimulated "control centers" that brought the bull to a halt (Horgan, 2005).

In contrast to the nerve impulse, communication between neurons is chemical. The microscopic space between two neurons, over which messages pass, is called a **synapse** (SIN-aps) (▶▶ Figure 2.5). When an action potential reaches the tips of the axon terminals, **neurotransmitters** (NOOR-oh-TRANS-mit-ers) are released into the synaptic gap. Neurotransmitters are chemicals that alter activity in neurons.

Exam Q# 4

Let's return to our metaphor of people standing in a line. To be more accurate, you and the others shouldn't be holding hands. Instead, each person should have a squirt gun in his or her left hand. To pass along a message, you would squirt the right hand of the person to your left. When that person notices this "message," he or she would squirt the right hand of the person to the left, and so on.

When chemical molecules cross over a synapse, they attach to special receiving areas on the next neuron (Figure 2.5). These tiny *receptor sites* on the cell membrane are sensitive to neurotransmitters. The sites are found in large numbers on nerve cell bodies and dendrites. Muscles and glands have receptor sites, too.

Do neurotransmitters always trigger an action potential in the next neuron? No, but they do change the likelihood of an action potential in the next neuron. Some transmitters *excite* the next neuron (move it closer to firing). Others *inhibit* it (make firing less likely).

More than 100 transmitter chemicals are found in the brain. Some examples are acetylcholine, epinephrine, norepinephrine, serotonin, dopamine, histamine, and various amino acids.

Why are there so many neurotransmitters? Good question. Some neurotransmitters are used by specific "pathways" that interlink regions of the brain. It is as if different pathways speak different languages. Perhaps this helps prevent confusing "crosstalk" or intermixing of messages. For example, the brain has a reward or "pleasure" system that mainly "speaks" dopamine (other neurotransmitters are also found in the system) (Salamone, 2007). (Keep an eye out for more about the pleasure system later in this chapter.)

Disturbances of any neurotransmitter can have serious consequences. Too much dopamine may cause schizophrenia (Di Forti, Lappin, & Murray, 2007). Too little serotonin may underlie depression (Merens et al., 2008).

Many drugs imitate, duplicate, or block neurotransmitters. For example, cocaine triggers an increase in dopamine and a drug "high" in the reward system (Briand et al., 2008).

Saltatory conduction The process by which nerve impulses conducted down the axons of neurons coated with myelin jump from gap to gap in the myelin layer.

Synapse The microscopic space between two neurons, over which messages pass.

Neurotransmitter Any chemical released by a neuron that alters activity in other neurons.

The overuse of recreational drugs like cocaine overstimulates the reward system and disturbs dopamine function, resulting in drug addiction (Volkow et al., 2007).

As another example, the drug curare (cue-RAH-ree) causes paralysis. Acetylcholine (ah-SEET-ul-KOH-leen) normally activates muscles. Without acetylcholine, our flamenco musicians couldn't even move, much less perform. By attaching to receptor sites on muscles, curare blocks acetylcholine, preventing the activation of muscle cells. As a result, a person or animal given curare cannot move—a fact known to South American Indians of the Amazon River Basin, who use curare as an arrow poison for hunting.

Neural Regulators

More subtle brain activities are affected by chemicals called **neuropeptides** (NOOR-oh-PEP-tides). Neuropeptides do not carry messages directly. Instead, they *regulate* the activity of other neurons. By doing so, they affect memory, pain, emotion, pleasure, moods, hunger, sexual behavior, and other basic processes. For example, when you touch something hot, you jerk your hand away. The messages for this action are carried by neurotransmitters. At the same time, pain may cause the brain to release *enkephalins* (en-KEF-ah-lins). These opiate-like neural regulators relieve pain and stress. Related chemicals called *endorphins* (en-DORF-ins) are released by the pituitary gland. Together, these chemicals reduce the pain so that it is not too disabling (Drolet et al., 2001).

Such discoveries help explain the painkilling effect of placebos (fake pills or injections), which raise endorphin levels (Stewart-Williams, 2004). A release of endorphins also seems to underlie "runner's high," masochism, acupuncture, and the euphoria sometimes associated with childbirth, painful initiation rites, and even sport parachuting (Janssen & Arntz, 2001). In each case, pain and stress cause the release of endorphins. These in turn induce feelings of pleasure or euphoria similar to being "high" on morphine. People who say they are "addicted" to running may be closer to the truth than they realize.

Ultimately, neural regulators may help explain depression, schizophrenia, drug addiction, and other puzzling topics. For example, women who suffer from severe premenstrual pain and distress have unusually low endorphin levels (Straneva et al., 2002).

Neural Networks

Let's put together what we now know about the nerve impulse and synaptic transmission to see how **neural networks** process information in our brains. ▶▶ Figure 2.6 shows a small part of a neural network. Five neurons synapse with a single neuron that, in turn, connects with three more neurons. At the point in time depicted in the diagram, the single neuron is receiving one stronger and two weaker excitatory messages (+) as well as two inhibitory ones (−). Does it fire an impulse? It depends: If enough "exciting" messages arrive close in time, the neuron will fire—but only if it doesn't get too many "inhibiting" messages that push it *away* from its trigger point. In this way, messages are *combined* before a neuron "decides" to fire its all-or-nothing action potential.

Let's try another metaphor. You are out shopping with five friends and find a pair of jeans you want to buy. Three of them think you should buy the jeans (your best friend is especially positive) and two think you shouldn't. Because, on balance, their input is positive, you go ahead and buy the jeans. Maybe you even tell some other friends they should buy those jeans as well. Similarly, any single neuron in a neural network "listens" to the neurons that synapse with it and combines that input into an output. At any instant, a single neuron may weigh hundreds or thousands of inputs to produce an outgoing message. After the neuron recovers from the resulting action potential, it again combines the inputs, which may have changed in the meantime, into another output, and another, and another.

▲ **FIGURE 2.6** A small neural network. Neuron A receives inputs from two weaker and one stronger excitatory connections (+) and two inhibitory connections (−) and combines the inputs into a "decision" to launch an action potential, which may help trigger further synaptic transmissions in other neurons.

Neuropeptides Brain chemicals, such as enkephalins and endorphins, that regulate the activity of neurons.

Neural networks Interlinked collections of neurons that process information in the brain.

You Can Change Your Mind, But Can You Change Your Brain?

You can always change your mind. But does that have anything to do with your brain? Philosophers have debated the relationship of the mind to the brain (and the rest of the body) for centuries. Biopsychologists believe that every mental event involves a brain event.

In one study, people suffering from spider phobias (an intense fear of spiders) could actually touch spiders after undergoing therapy (although they might not have been ready to appear on the TV program *Fear Factor*). Images of their brains

revealed reduced activity in brain areas related to the phobia (Paquette et al., 2003). Not only did they change their minds about spiders, they literally changed their brains.

Another study focused on patients with language difficulties caused by damage to the left sides of their brains. To aid their recovery, the patients were trained in language comprehension, which did, in fact, improve their ability to understand language. In addition, brain images revealed that the right sides of their brains had

become more active, to compensate for their left-brain damage (Musso et al., 1999). Again, a learning experience changed their brains.

Every time you learn something, you are reshaping your living brain. There is even a fancy phrase to describe what you are doing: *self-directed neuroplasticity*. Just think: As you study this psychology textbook, you are changing your mind—and your brain—about psychology.

In this way, each neuron in your brain functions as a tiny computer. Compared with the average laptop computer, a neuron is terribly simple and slow. But multiply these events by 100 billion neurons and 100 trillion synapses, all operating at the same time, and you have an amazing computer—one that could easily fit inside a shoebox.

Neuroplasticity

The neural networks in your brain constantly change. The term **neuroplasticity** refers to the capacity of our brains to change in response to experience. New synapses may form between neurons, or synaptic connections may grow stronger. (Figure 2.6 shows one particularly strong synapse—the large +.) Other synaptic connections may weaken and even die. Every new experience you have is reflected in changes in your brain. For example, rats raised in a complex environment have more synapses and longer dendrites in their brains than rats raised in a simpler environment (Kolb, Gibb, & Gorny, 2003). (See "You Can Change Your Mind, But Can You Change Your Brain?")

The Nervous System—Wired for Action

What are the major parts of the nervous system?

Harry and Maya are playing catch with a football. This may look fairly simple. However, to merely toss the football or catch it, a huge amount of information must be sensed, interpreted, and directed to countless muscle fibers. As they play, Harry's and Maya's neural circuits are ablaze with activity. Let's explore the "wiring diagram" that makes their game of catch possible.

As you can see in ▶▶ Figure 2.7, the **central nervous system (CNS)** consists of the brain and spinal cord. The brain carries out most of the "computing" in the nervous system. Harry must use his brain to anticipate when and where the football will arrive. Harry's brain communicates with the rest of his body through a large "cable" called the spinal cord. From there, messages flow through the **peripheral nervous system (PNS).** This intricate network of nerves carries information to and from the CNS.

Are neurons the same as nerves? No. Neurons are tiny cells. You would need a microscope to see one. **Nerves** are large bundles of neuron axons. You can easily see nerves without magnification.

Nerves in the peripheral nervous system can regrow if they are damaged. The axons of most neurons in nerves outside the brain and spinal cord are covered by a thin layer of cells called the *neurilemma* (NOOR-rih-LEM-ah). (Return to Figure 2.1.) The neurilemma forms a "tunnel" that damaged fibers can follow as they repair themselves. Because of this, patients can expect to regain some control over severed limbs once they have been reattached.

Neuroplasticity The capacity of the brain to change in response to experience.

Central nervous system (CNS) The brain and spinal cord.

Peripheral nervous system (PNS) All parts of the nervous system outside the brain and spinal cord.

Nerve A bundle of neuron axons.

Central nervous system — Brain, Spinal cord **(a)**

Peripheral nervous system — Somatic system, Autonomic system — Sympathetic system, Parasympathetic system **(b)**

The Peripheral Nervous System

The peripheral system can be divided into two major parts (see Figure 2.7). The **somatic nervous system (SNS)** carries messages to and from the sense organs and skeletal muscles. In general, it controls voluntary behavior, such as when Maya tosses the football or Tiger Woods hits a golf ball. In contrast, the **autonomic nervous system (ANS)** serves the internal organs and glands. The word *autonomic* means "self-governing." Activities governed by the autonomic nervous system are mostly "vegetative" or automatic, such as heart rate, digestion, and perspiration. Thus, messages carried by the somatic system can make your hand move, but they cannot cause your eyes to dilate. Likewise, messages carried by the ANS can stimulate digestion, but they cannot help you carry out a voluntary action, such as writing a letter. If Harry feels a flash of anger when he misses a catch, a brief burst of activity will spread through his autonomic system.

The ANS and SNS work together to coordinate the body's internal reactions to events in the world outside. For example, if a snarling dog lunges at you, the somatic system will control your leg muscles so that you can run. At the same time, the autonomic system will raise your blood pressure, quicken your heartbeat, and so forth. The ANS can be divided into the sympathetic and parasympathetic branches. Both are related to emotional responses, such as crying, sweating, heart rate, and other involuntary behavior (▶▶ Figure 2.8).

How do the branches of the autonomic system differ? The **sympathetic branch** is an "emergency" system. It prepares the body for "fight or flight" during times of danger or high emotion. In essence, it arouses the body for action.

In contrast, the **parasympathetic branch** quiets the body and returns it to a lower level of arousal. It is most active soon after an emotional event. The parasympathetic branch also helps keep vital processes such as heart rate, breathing, and digestion at moderate levels.

Of course, both branches of the ANS are always active. At any given moment, their combined activity determines if your body is more or less relaxed or aroused.

The Spinal Cord

As mentioned earlier, the spinal cord connects the brain to other parts of the body. If you were to cut through this "cable," you would see columns of *white matter* (bundles of axons covered with myelin). This tissue is made up of axons that eventually leave the spinal cord to form the peripheral nervous system nerves. Thirty-one *spinal nerves* carry sensory and

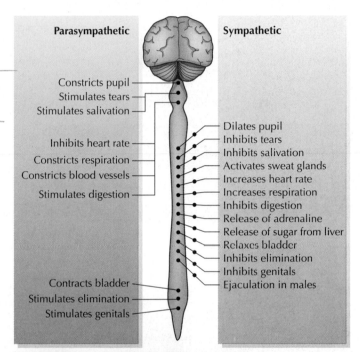

Parasympathetic
Constricts pupil
Stimulates tears
Stimulates salivation
Inhibits heart rate
Constricts respiration
Constricts blood vessels
Stimulates digestion
Contracts bladder
Stimulates elimination
Stimulates genitals

Sympathetic
Dilates pupil
Inhibits tears
Inhibits salivation
Activates sweat glands
Increases heart rate
Increases respiration
Inhibits digestion
Release of adrenaline
Release of sugar from liver
Relaxes bladder
Inhibits elimination
Inhibits genitals
Ejaculation in males

FIGURE 2.8 Sympathetic and parasympathetic branches of the autonomic nervous system. Both branches control involuntary actions. The sympathetic system generally activates the body. The parasympathetic system generally quiets it. The sympathetic branch relays its messages through clusters of nerve cells outside the spinal cord.

Somatic nervous system (SNS) The system of nerves linking the spinal cord with the body and sense organs.

Autonomic nervous system (ANS) The system of nerves carrying information to and from the internal organs and glands.

Sympathetic branch The branch of the ANS that arouses the body.

Parasympathetic branch The branch of the ANS that quiets the body.

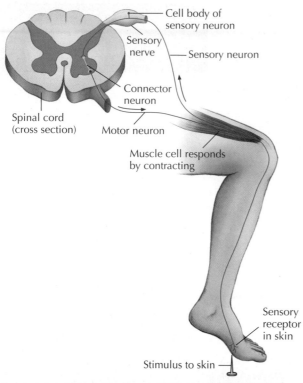

Cell body of sensory neuron

Sensory nerve

Sensory neuron

Connector neuron

Spinal cord (cross section)

Motor neuron

Muscle cell responds by contracting

Sensory receptor in skin

Stimulus to skin

⬆ FIGURE 2.9 A sensory-motor arc, or reflex, is set in motion by a stimulus to the skin (or other part of the body). The nerve impulse travels to the spinal cord and then back out to a muscle, which contracts. Such reflexes provide an "automatic" protective device for the body.

motor messages to and from the spinal cord. In addition, 12 pairs of *cranial nerves* leave the brain directly. Together, these nerves keep your entire body in communication with your brain.

Is the spinal cord's only function to connect the brain to the peripheral nervous system? Actually, the spinal cord can do some simple "computing" of its own. A **reflex arc** occurs when a stimulus provokes an automatic response. Such reflexes arise within the spinal cord, without any help from the brain (see ▶▶ Figure 2.9). Imagine that Maya steps on a thorn. (Yes, they're still playing catch.) Pain is detected in her foot by a *sensory neuron* (a nerve cell that carries messages from the senses toward the CNS). Instantly, the sensory neuron fires off a message to Maya's spinal cord.

Inside the spinal cord, the sensory neuron synapses with a *connector neuron* (a nerve cell that links two others). The connector neuron activates a *motor neuron* (a cell that carries commands from the CNS to muscles and glands). The muscle fibers are made up of *effector cells* (cells capable of producing a response). The muscle cells contract and cause Maya's foot to withdraw. Note that no brain activity is required for a reflex arc to occur. Maya's body will react automatically to protect itself.

In reality, even a simple reflex usually triggers more complex activity. For example, muscles of Maya's other leg must contract to support her as she shifts her weight. Even this can be done by the spinal cord, but it involves many more cells and several spinal nerves. Also, the spinal cord normally informs the brain of its actions. As her foot pulls away from the thorn, Maya will feel the pain and think, "Ouch, what was that?"

Perhaps you have realized how adaptive it is to have a spinal cord capable of responding on its own. Such automatic responses leave the brains of our football stars free to deal with more important information—such as the location of trees, lampposts, and attractive onlookers—as they take turns making grandstand catches.

While peripheral nerves can regrow, a serious injury to the brain or spinal cord is usually permanent. However, scientists are starting to make progress repairing damaged neurons in the CNS. For instance, they have partially repaired cut spinal cords in rats. First they close the gap with nerve fibers from outside the spinal cord. Then they biochemically coax the severed spinal nerve fibers to grow through the "tunnels" (neurilemma) provided by the implanted fibers. Within months, rats treated this way regain some use of their hind legs (Cheng, Cao, & Olson, 1996).

Similarly, medical researchers have already begun the first human trials in which nerve grafts will be used to repair damaged spinal cords (Féron et al., 2005). Imagine what that could mean to a person confined to a wheelchair. Although it is unwise to raise false hopes, solutions to such problems are beginning to emerge. Nevertheless, it is wise to take good care of your own CNS. That means using seat belts when you drive, wearing a helmet if you ride a motorcycle or bicycle, wearing protective gear for sports, and avoiding activities that pose a risk to your head or spinal cord.

Each year spinal cord injuries rob many thousands of people of the ability to move. Yet there is growing hope that nerve-grafting techniques may some-day make it possible for some of these people to walk again.

Blend Images/Jupiterimages

Can brain damage also be repaired? While we will be exploring the brain itself in more detail later in the chapter, we can, for now, answer with an optimistic but cautious yes. (See "Repairing Your Brain.")

Reflex arc The simplest behavior, in which a stimulus provokes an automatic response.

Repairing Your Brain

Until only a few years ago, it was widely believed that we are born with all the brain cells we will ever have. This led to the depressing idea that we all slowly go downhill, as the brain loses thousands of neurons every day. Rather than facing a steady decline, we now know that a healthy 75-year-old brain has just as many neurons as it did when it was careening through life in the body of a 25-year-old. Although it is true that the brain loses cells daily, it simultaneously grows new neurons to replace them. This process is called **neurogenesis** (noor-oh-JEN-uh-sis: the production of new brain cells) (Kempermann, 2005). Each day, thousands of new cells originate deep within the brain, move to the surface, and link up with other neurons to become part of the brain's circuitry. This was stunning news to brain scientists, who must now figure out what the new cells do. Most

likely they are involved in learning, memory, and our ability to adapt to changing circumstances (Gould & Gross, 2002).

Before neurogenesis was discovered, it was assumed that nerve cell transplants might be the only way to treat brain damage (Wong, Hodges, & Horsburgh, 2005). Imagine that a patient named Bobby M. has suffered a *stroke,* causing partial paralysis in his left arm. (A stroke occurs when an artery in the brain becomes blocked or bursts open. This interrupts blood flow and causes some brain tissue to die.) What could be done to help Bobby recover? One remedy involves injecting immature nerve cells into his damaged brain areas. This would allow the new cells to link up with existing neurons in order to repair Bobby's stroke damage (Borlongan, Sanberg, & Freeman, 1999; Zhang, Zhang, & Chopp, 2005).

The existence of neurogenesis in adult brains is leading to new treatments for some types of brain damage. For example, an approach called constraint-induced movement therapy could be used to speed Bobby M.'s recovery. In this case, Bobby's good right arm would be restrained, forcing his impaired left arm to be more active. By using his left arm, Bobby could increase neurogenesis in the damaged part of his brain (Taub, 2004). In another approach, drugs that speed up neurogenesis could be injected into the damaged area of Bobby's brain (Zhang, Zhang, & Chopp, 2005). Such techniques are beginning to offer new hope for people suffering from a variety of other disabilities, such as blindness and Parkinson's disease (Brinton & Wang, 2006; Burke et al., 2007).

In a few moments, we will probe more deeply into the brain. Before we do, it might be wise to explore some of the research tools biopsychologists use. Uncovering the brain's mysteries has not been easy. Let's consider some of the basics.

Research Methods—Charting the Brain's Inner Realms

How is the brain studied?

Biopsychology is the study of how biological processes, especially those occurring in the nervous system, relate to behavior. In their research, many biopsychologists try to learn which parts of the brain control particular mental or behavioral functions, such as being able to recognize faces or move your hands. That is, they try to learn where functions are localized (located) in the brain. Many techniques have been developed to help identify brain structures and the functions they control.

Mapping Brain Structure

Anatomists have learned much about brain structure by dissecting (cutting apart) autopsied human and animal brains and examining them under a microscope. Dissection reveals that the brain is made up of many anatomically distinct areas or "parts." Newer methods, such as the CT scan and the MRI scan, can be used to map brain structures in living brains.

CT Scan

Computerized scanning equipment has revolutionized the study of brain structures and made it easier to identify brain diseases and injuries. At best, conventional X-rays produce only shadowy images of the brain. **Computed tomographic (CT) scanning** is a specialized type of X-ray that does a much better job of making the brain visible. In a CT scan, X-rays taken from a number of different angles are collected by a computer and formed into an

Neurogenesis The production of new brain cells.

Computed tomographic scan (CT scan) A computer-enhanced X-ray image of the brain or body.

△ FIGURE 2.10 A colored MRI scan of the brain reveals many details. Can you identify any brain regions?

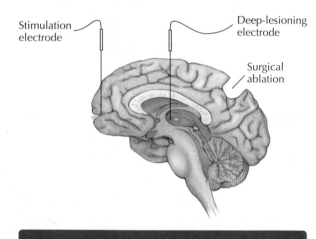

Stimulation electrode

Deep-lesioning electrode

Surgical ablation

△ FIGURE 2.11 The functions of brain structures are explored by selectively activating or removing them. Brain research is often based on electrical stimulation, but chemical stimulation is also used at times.

Magnetic resonance imaging (MRI) An imaging technique that results in a three-dimensional image of the brain or body, based on its response to a magnetic field.

Localization of function The research strategy of linking specific structures in the brain with specific psychological or behavioral functions.

Clinical case study A detailed investigation of a single person, especially one suffering from some injury or disease.

Electrical stimulation of the brain (ESB) Direct electrical stimulation and activation of brain tissue.

Electrode Any device (such as a wire, needle, or metal plate) used to electrically stimulate or destroy nerve tissue or to record its activity.

image of the brain. A CT scan can reveal the location of strokes, injuries, tumors, and other brain disorders.

MRI Scan

Magnetic resonance imaging (MRI) uses a very strong magnetic field, rather than X-rays, to produce an image of the body's interior. During an MRI scan, the body is placed inside a magnetic field. Processing by a computer then creates a three-dimensional model of the brain or body. Any two-dimensional plane, or slice, of the body can be selected and displayed as an image on a computer screen. MRI scans produce more detailed images than are possible with CT scans, allowing us to peer into the living brain almost as if it were transparent (▶▶ Figure 2.10).

Exploring Brain Function

How does the brain allow us to think, feel, perceive, or act? To answer questions like this, we must **localize function** by linking psychological or behavioral capacities with particular brain structures. In many instances, this has been done through **clinical case studies.** Such studies examine changes in personality, behavior, or sensory capacity caused by brain diseases or injuries. If damage to a particular part of the brain consistently leads to a particular loss of function, then we say the function is localized in that structure. Presumably, that part of the brain controls the same function in all of us.

Consider, for example, the story of Kate Adamson (Adamson, 2004). At the age of 33, she had a stroke that caused catastrophic damage to her brainstem. This event left her with *locked-in syndrome:* Just before the stroke she was fine, and the next moment she was totally paralyzed, trapped in her own body and barely able to breathe. As you can see, this clinical case suggests that our brainstems play a role in controlling vital life functions, such as movement and breathing.

But what happened to Kate? Oh, yes. Unable to move a muscle, but still fully awake and aware, Kate thought she was going to die. Her doctors, who thought she was *brain dead* (Laureys & Boly, 2007), did not administer painkillers as they inserted breathing and feeding tubes down her throat. However, in time Kate discovered that she could communicate by blinking her eyes. After a recovery that has been miraculous by any measure, she even went on to appear before the U.S. Congress.

Instead of relying on clinical studies, researchers have learned much from **electrical stimulation of the brain (ESB)** (▶▶ Figure 2.11). For example, the surface of the brain can be "turned on" by stimulating it with a mild electrical current delivered through a thin insulated wire called an **electrode.** When this is done during brain surgery, the patient can describe what effect the stimulation had. (The brain has no pain receptors, so surgery can be done while a patient is awake. Only local painkillers are used for the scalp and skull.) (Any volunteers?) Even structures below the surface of the brain can be activated by lowering a stimulating electrode, insulated except at the tip, into a target area inside the brain. ESB can call forth behavior with astonishing power. Instantly, it can bring about aggression, alertness, escape, eating, drinking, sleeping, movement, euphoria, memories, speech, tears, and more.

Could ESB be used to control a person against his or her will? It might seem that ESB could be used to control a person like a robot. But the details of emotions and behaviors elicited by ESB are modified by personality and circumstances. Sci-fi movies to the contrary, it would be impossible for a ruthless dictator to enslave people by "radio controlling" their brains.

An alternate approach is **ablation** (ab-LAY-shun: surgical removal) of parts of the brain (see Figure 2.11). When ablation causes changes in behavior or sensory capacity, we also gain insight into the purpose of the missing "part." By using a technique called **deep lesioning** (LEE-zhun-ing), structures below the surface of the brain can also be removed. In this case, an electrode is lowered into a target area inside the brain and a strong electric current is used to destroy a small amount of brain tissue (see Figure 2.11). Again, changes in behavior give clues about the function of the affected area.

By using ESB, ablation, and deep lesioning, researchers are creating a three-dimensional brain map. This "atlas" shows the sensory, motor, and emotional responses that can be elicited from various parts of the brain. It promises to be a valuable guide for medical treatment, as well as for exploring the brain (Kalat, 2009; Yoshida, 1993).

To find out what individual neurons are doing, we need to do a micro-electrode recording. A *microelectrode* is an extremely thin glass tube filled with a salty fluid. The tip of a microelectrode is small enough to detect the electrical activity of a *single* neuron. Watching the action potentials of just one neuron provides a fascinating glimpse into the true origins of behavior. (The action potential shown in Figure 2.2 was recorded with a microelectrode.)

Are any less invasive techniques available for studying brain function? Yes, several techniques allow us to observe the activity of parts of the brain without doing any damage at all. These include the EEG, PET scan, and fMRI. Such techniques allow biopsychologists to pinpoint areas in the brain responsible for thoughts, feelings, and actions.

▲ **FIGURE 2.12** An EEG recording.

EEG

Electroencephalography (ee-LEK-tro-in-SEF-ah-LOG-ruh-fee) measures the waves of electrical activity produced near the surface of the brain. Small disk-shaped metal plates are placed on a person's scalp. Electrical impulses from the brain are detected by these electrodes and sent to an **electroencephalograph (EEG).** The EEG amplifies these very weak signals (brain waves) and records them on a moving sheet of paper or a computer screen (▶▶ Figure 2.12). Various brain-wave patterns can identify the presence of tumors, epilepsy, and other diseases. The EEG also reveals changes in brain activity during sleep, daydreaming, hypnosis, and other mental states.

PET Scan

A newer technology, called **positron emission tomography (PET),** provides much more detailed images of activity both *near* the surface and *below* the surface of the brain. A PET scan detects positrons (subatomic particles) emitted by weakly radioactive glucose (sugar) as it is consumed by the brain. Because the brain runs on glucose, a PET scan shows which areas are using more energy. Higher energy use corresponds with higher activity. Thus, by placing positron detectors around the head and sending data to a computer, it is possible to create a moving, color picture of changes in brain activity. As you can see in ▶▶ Figure 2.13, PET scans reveal that very specific brain areas are active when you see, hear, speak, or think.

More active brains are good, right? Although we might assume that hardworking brains are smart brains, the reverse appears to be true. Using PET scans, psychologist Richard Haier and his colleagues found that the brains of people who perform well on a difficult reasoning test consume less energy than those of poor performers (Haier et al., 1988) (▶▶ Figure 2.14). Haier believes this shows that intelligence is related to brain efficiency: Less efficient brains work harder and still accomplish less (Haier, White, & Alkire, 2003). We've all had days like that!

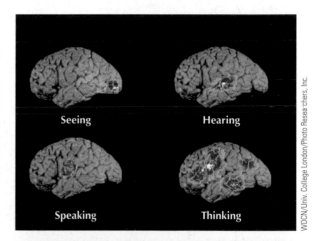

Seeing | Hearing
Speaking | Thinking

▲ **FIGURE 2.13** Colored PET scans reveal different patterns of brain activation when we engage in different tasks.

Ablation Surgical removal of tissue.

Deep lesioning Removal of tissue within the brain by use of an electrode.

Electroencephalograph (EEG) A device that detects, amplifies, and records electrical activity in the brain.

Positron emission tomography (PET) An imaging technique that results in a computer-generated image of brain activity, based on glucose consumption in the brain.

▶▶ **FIGURE 2.14** In the images you see here, red, orange, and yellow indicate high consumption of glucose; green, blue, and pink show areas of low glucose use. The PET scan of the brain on the left shows that a man who solved 11 out of 36 reasoning problems burned more glucose than the man on the right, who solved 33.

Is it true that most people use only 10 percent of their brain capacity? This is one of the lasting myths about the brain. Brain scans show that all parts of the brain are active during waking hours. Obviously, some people make better use of their innate brainpower than others do. Nevertheless, there are no great hidden or untapped reserves of mental capacity in a normally functioning brain.

fMRI

A **functional MRI (fMRI)** uses MRI technology to make brain activity visible. Like PET scans, fMRIs also provide images of activity throughout the brain. For example, if we scanned Carlos Santana while he played his guitar, areas of his brain that control his hands would be highlighted in an fMRI image.

Psychiatrist Daniel Langleben and his colleagues (2005) have even used fMRI images to tell if a person is lying. As ▶▶ Figure 2.15 shows, the front of the brain is more active when a person is lying, rather than telling the truth. This may occur because it takes extra effort to lie, and the resulting extra brain activity is detected with fMRI. Clearly, it is just a matter of time until even brighter beacons are flashed into the shadowy inner world of thought.

▶▶ **FIGURE 2.15** Participants were asked to tell the truth or to lie while fMRI images of their brains were taken. When compared with telling the truth (shown in green), areas toward the front of the brain were active during lying (shown in red). (Adapted from Langleben et al, HUMAN BRAIN MAPPING Copyright © 2005 Daniel Langleben. Reprinted by permission of John Wiley & Sons, Inc.)

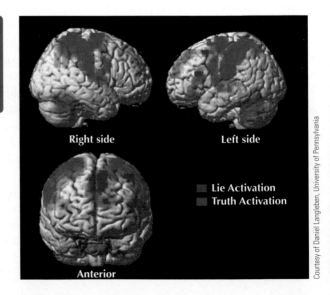

Functional MRI (fMRI) MRI technique that records brain activity.

RECITE

1. The _____ and _____ are receiving areas where information from other neurons is accepted.
2. Nerve impulses are carried down the _____ to the _____.
3. The _____ potential becomes a(n) _____ potential when a neuron passes the threshold for firing.
4. Neuropeptides are transmitter substances that help regulate the activity of neurons. T or F?
5. The somatic and autonomic systems are part of the _____ nervous system.
6. Sodium and potassium ions flow through ion channels in the synapse to trigger a nerve impulse in the receiving neuron. T or F?
7. The parasympathetic nervous system is most active during times of high emotion. T or F?
8. Which of the following research techniques has the most in common with clinical studies of the effects of brain injuries?
   a. EEG recording
   b. deep lesioning
   c. microelectrode recording
   d. PET scan
9. CT scans cannot determine which part of your brain plays a role in speech because CT scans
   a. use X-rays
   b. reveal brain structure, not brain activity
   c. reveal brain activity, not brain structure
   d. use magnetic fields

Neurons, the Nervous System, and Brain Research

REFLECT

Critical Thinking

10. What effect would you expect a drug to have if it blocked passage of neurotransmitters across the synapse?
11. Deep lesioning is used to ablate an area in the hypothalamus of a rat. After the operation, the rat seems to lose interest in food and eating. Why would it be a mistake to conclude that the ablated area is a "hunger center"?

Relate

To cope with all of the technical terms in this chapter, it might help to think of neurons as strange little creatures. How do they act? What excites them? How do they communicate? To remember the functions of major branches of the nervous system, think about what you *couldn't* do if each part were missing. How does a neural network differ from the central processing unit of a computer?

You suspect that a certain part of the brain is related to risk-taking. How could you use clinical studies, ablation, deep lesioning, and ESB to study the structure? You are interested in finding out how single neurons in the optic nerve respond when the eye is exposed to light. What technique will you use? You want to know which areas of the brain's surface are most active when a person sees a face. What methods will you use?

ANSWERS

1. dendrites, soma 2. axon, axon terminals 3. resting, action 4. T 5. peripheral 6. F 7. F 8. b 9. b 10. Such a drug could have wide-ranging effects. If the drug blocked excitatory synapses, it would depress brain activity. If it blocked inhibitory messages, it would act as a powerful stimulant. 11. Because other factors might explain the apparent loss of appetite, the taste or smell of food might be affected, or the rat might simply have difficulty swallowing. It is also possible that hunger originates elsewhere in the brain and the ablated area merely relays messages that cause the rat to eat.

The Cerebral Cortex—My, What a Big Brain You Have!

Why is the human cerebral cortex so important and what are its parts?

In many ways we are pretty unimpressive creatures. Animals surpass humans in almost every category of strength, speed, and sensory sensitivity. However, we do excel in intelligence.

Does that mean humans have the largest brains? Surprisingly, no. Elephant brains weigh 13 pounds, and whale brains, 19 pounds. At 3 pounds, the human brain seems puny—until we compare brain weight to body weight. We then find that an elephant's brain is 1/1,000 of its weight; the ratio for sperm whales is 1 to 10,000. The ratio for humans is 1 to 60. If someone tells you that you have a "whale of a brain," be sure to find out if they mean size or ratio!

So having a larger brain doesn't necessarily make a person smarter? That's right. While a small positive correlation exists between intelligence and brain size, overall size alone does not determine human intelligence (Johnson et al., 2008; Witelson, Beresh, & Kigar, 2006). In fact, many parts of your brain are surprisingly similar to corresponding brain areas in

Photographs of views of Einstein's brain: from the top *(A)*, left *(B)*, right *(C)*, bottom *(D)* and middle section *(E)*. Overall brain size was within normal limits. However, the parts of the brain necessary for spatial reasoning in the parietal lobe (see arrows in B & C) had a unique anatomy and were larger than in control brains (adapted from Witelson, Kigar & Harvey, *Lancet,* 1999, and reprinted with permission of S.F. Witelson).

lower animals, such as lizards. It is your larger **cerebral** (seh-REE-brel or ser-EH-brel) **cortex** that sets you apart.

The cerebral cortex, which looks a little like a giant, wrinkled walnut, consists of the two large hemispheres that cover the upper part of the brain. The two hemispheres are divided into smaller areas known as lobes. Parts of various lobes are responsible for the ability to see, hear, move, think, and speak. Thus, a map of the cerebral cortex is in some ways like a map of human behavior, as we shall see.

The cerebral cortex covers most of the brain with a mantle of *gray matter* (spongy tissue made up mostly of cell bodies). The cortex in lower animals is small and smooth. In humans it is twisted and folded, and it is the largest brain structure. (See ▶▶ Figure 2.16.) The fact that humans are more intelligent than other animals is related to this **corticalization** (KORE-tih-kal-ih-ZAY-shun), or increase in the size and wrinkling of the cortex.

Although the cortex is only 3 millimeters thick (one tenth of an inch), it contains 70 percent of the neurons in the central nervous system. It is largely responsible for our ability to use language, make tools, acquire complex skills, and live in complex social groups (Gibson, 2002). Without the cortex, we humans wouldn't be much smarter than toads.

Cerebral Hemispheres

The cortex is composed of two sides, or *cerebral hemispheres* (half-globes) connected by a thick band of fibers called the *corpus callosum* (KORE-pus kah-LOH-sum) (▶▶ Figure 2.17). The left side of the brain mainly controls the right side of the body. Likewise, the right brain mainly controls left body areas. When our friend Marge had a stroke, her right hemisphere suffered damage. In Marge's case, the stroke caused some paralysis and loss of sensation on the left side of her body. (Her paralysis was similar to what Bobby M. suffered, only more severe.)

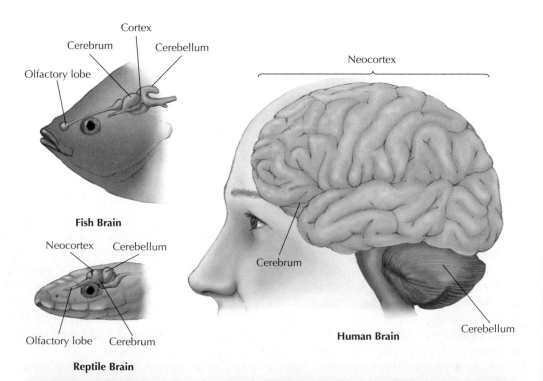

Cortex
Cerebrum
Cerebellum
Olfactory lobe

Fish Brain

Neocortex

Neocortex   Cerebellum

Olfactory lobe   Cerebrum

Reptile Brain

Cerebrum

Cerebellum

Human Brain

▲ **FIGURE 2.16**

Cerebral cortex The outer layer of the brain.

Corticalization An increase in the relative size of the cerebral cortex.

Damage to one hemisphere may also cause a curious problem called *spatial neglect*. A patient with right hemisphere damage may pay no attention to the left side of visual space. (See ▸▸ Figure 2.18.) Often, the patient will not eat food on the left side of a plate. Some even refuse to acknowledge a paralyzed left arm as their own (Hirstein, 2005). If you point to the "alien" arm, the patient is likely to say, "Oh, that's not my arm. It must belong to someone else."

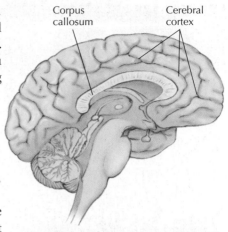

Hemispheric Specialization

In 1981, Roger Sperry (1914–1994) won a Nobel Prize for his remarkable discovery that the right and left brain hemispheres perform differently on tests of language, perception, music, and other capabilities.

How is it possible to test only one side of the brain? One way is to work with people who've had a **"split-brain" operation.** In this rare type of surgery, the corpus callosum is cut to control severe epilepsy. The result is essentially a person with two brains in one body (Gazzaniga, 2005). After the surgery, it is possible to send information to one hemisphere or the other (see ▸▸ Figure 2.19).

"Split Brains"

After the right and left brain are separated, each hemisphere will have its own separate perceptions, concepts, and impulses to act.

How does a split-brain person act after the operation? Having two "brains" in one body can create some interesting dilemmas. When one split-brain patient dressed himself, he sometimes pulled his pants up with one hand (*that* side of his brain wanted to get dressed. . . .) and down with the other (. . . . while *this* side didn't). Once, he grabbed his wife with his left hand and shook her violently. Gallantly, his right hand came to her aid and grabbed the aggressive left hand (Gazzaniga, 1970). However, such conflicts are actually rare. That's because both halves of the brain normally have about the same experience at the same time. Also, if a conflict arises, one hemisphere usually overrides the other.

Split-brain effects are easiest to see in specialized testing. For example, we could flash a dollar sign to the right brain and a question mark to the left brain of a patient named Tom. (Figure 2.19 shows how this is possible.) Next, Tom is asked to draw what he saw, using his left hand, out of sight. Tom's left hand draws a dollar sign. If Tom is then asked to point with his right hand to a picture of what his hidden left hand drew, he will point to a question mark (Sperry, 1968). In short, for the split-brain person, one hemisphere may not know what is happening in the other. This has to be the ultimate case of the "right hand not knowing what the left hand is doing"! ▸▸ Figure 2.20 provides another example of split-brain testing.

Right Brain/Left Brain

Earlier it was stated that the hemispheres differ in abilities. In what ways are they different? The brain divides its work in interesting ways. Roughly 95 percent of us use our left brain for language (speaking, writing, and understanding). In addition, the left hemisphere is superior at math, judging time and rhythm, and coordinating the order of complex movements, such as those needed for speech.

In contrast, the right hemisphere can produce only the simplest language and numbers. Working with the right brain is like talking to a child who can say only a dozen words or so. To answer questions, the right hemisphere must use nonverbal responses, such as pointing at objects (see Figure 2.20).

Although it is poor at producing language, the right brain is especially good at perceptual skills, such as recognizing patterns, faces, and melodies; putting together a puzzle; or

Model	Patient's copy

▲ FIGURE 2.18 Spatial neglect. A patient with right-hemisphere damage was asked to copy three model drawings. Notice the obvious neglect of the left side in his drawings. Similar instances of neglect occur in many patients with right-hemisphere damage. From *Left Brain, Right Brain,* 5th ed., by Sally P. Springer & Georg Deutsch. © 1981, 1985, 1989, 1993, 1998 by Sally P. Springer and Georg Deutsch. Used with permission of W. H. Freeman and Company.

"Split-brain" operation Cutting the corpus callosum.

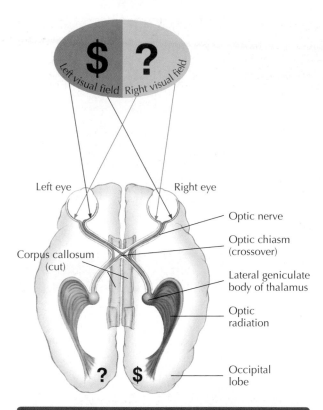

FIGURE 2.19 Basic nerve pathways of vision. Notice that the left portion of each eye connects only to the left half of the brain; likewise, the right portion of each eye connects to the right brain. When the corpus callosum is cut, a "split brain" results. Then visual information can be sent to just one hemisphere by flashing it in the right or left visual field as the person stares straight ahead.

drawing a picture. It also helps you express emotions and detect the emotions that other people are feeling (Borod et al., 2002; Stuss & Alexander, 2000).

One Brain, Two Styles

In general, the left hemisphere is involved mainly with *analysis* (breaking information into parts). It also processes information *sequentially* (in order, one item after the next). The right hemisphere appears to process information *simultaneously* and *holistically* (all at once) (Springer & Deutsch, 1998).

To summarize further, you could say that the right hemisphere is better at assembling pieces of the world into a coherent picture; it sees overall patterns and general connections. The left brain focuses on small details. (See ▶▶Figure 2.21.) The right brain sees the wide-angle view; the left zooms in on specifics. The focus of the left brain is local, the right is global (Hübner & Volberg, 2005).

Do people normally do puzzles or draw pictures with just the right hemisphere? Do they do other things with only the left? Numerous books have been written about how to use the right brain to manage, teach, draw, ride horses, learn, and even make love (Clark, Boutros, & Mendez, 2005). But such books drastically oversimplify right-brain and left-brain differences. People normally use both sides of the brain at all times. It's true that some tasks may make *more* use of one hemisphere or the other. But in most "real world" activities, the hemispheres share the work. Each does the parts it does best and shares information with the other side.

A smart brain is one that grasps both the details and the overall picture at the same time. For instance, during a concert a flamenco guitarist will use his left brain to judge time and rhythm and coordinate the order of his hand movements. At the same time, he will use his right brain to recognize and organize melodies.

Left Hemisphere   **Right Hemisphere**

FIGURE 2.20 A circle is flashed to the left brain of a split-brain patient and he is asked what he saw. He easily replies, "A circle." He can also pick out the circle by merely touching shapes with his right hand, out of sight behind a screen. However, his left hand can't identify the circle. If a triangle is flashed to the patient's right brain, he can't say what he saw (speech is controlled by the left hemisphere). He also can't identify the triangle by touch with the right hand. Now, however, the left hand has no difficulty picking out the triangle. In other tests, the hemispheres reveal distinct skills, as listed above the drawing.

Left hemisphere DETAILS		Right hemisphere OVERALL PATTERN
"A bunch of Ds"	D D D D DDDDD	"The letter L"
"It's about sewing."	**A stitch in time saves nine.**	"A small effort now saves time later."
"Dots and blobs"		"A dog"

Ronald C. James

Lobes of the Cerebral Cortex

Each of the two hemispheres of the cerebral cortex can be divided into several smaller *lobes*. Some of the lobes of the cerebral cortex are defined by larger fissures on the surface of the cortex. Others are regarded as separate areas because their functions are quite different. (See ▶▶ Figure 2.22.)

The Frontal Lobes

The **frontal lobes** are associated with higher mental abilities and play a role in your sense of self. This area is also responsible for the control of movement. Specifically, an arch of tissue at the rear of the frontal lobes, called the **primary motor area** (or **primary motor cortex**), directs the body's muscles. If this area is stimulated with an electrical current, various parts of the body will twitch or move. The drawing wrapped around the motor cortex in ▶▶ Figure 2.23 is out of proportion because it reflects the *dexterity* of body areas, not their size. The hands, for example, get more area than the feet. (See Figure 2.23.) If you've ever wondered why your hands are more skilled or agile than your feet, it's partly because more motor cortex is devoted to the hands. Incidentally, due to neuroplasticity, learning and experience can alter these "motor maps." For instance, violin, viola, and cello players have larger "hand maps" in the cortex (Hashimoto et al., 2004).

The rest of the frontal lobes are often referred to as *frontal association areas*. Only a small portion of the cerebral cortex (the primary areas) directly controls the body or receives information from the senses. All the surrounding areas, which are called **association areas** (or **association cortex**), combine and process information. For example, if you see a rose, association areas will help you connect your primary sensory impressions with memories, so that you can recognize the rose and name it. Some association areas also contribute to higher mental abilities, such as language. For example, a person with damage to association areas in the left hemisphere may suffer **aphasia** (ah-FAZE-yah: an impaired ability to use language).

One type of aphasia is related to **Broca's** (BRO-cahs) **area,** a "speech center" that is part of the left frontal association area (for 5 percent of all people, the area is part of the right frontal association area). Damage to Broca's area causes *motor (or expressive) aphasia,* a great difficulty in speaking or writing (Ward, 2006). Generally, the person knows what she or he wants to say but can't seem to fluently utter the words (Geschwind, 1979). Typically, a patient's grammar and pronunciation are poor and speech is slow and labored. For example, the person may say "bife" for bike, "seep" for sleep, or "zokaid" for zodiac.

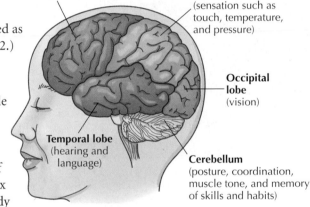

Frontal lobe
(sense of self, motor control, and higher mental abilities such as reasoning and planning)

Parietal lobe
(sensation such as touch, temperature, and pressure)

Occipital lobe
(vision)

Temporal lobe
(hearing and language)

Cerebellum
(posture, coordination, muscle tone, and memory of skills and habits)

▲ **FIGURE 2.22**

Frontal lobes A brain area associated with movement, the sense of self, and higher mental functions.

Primary motor area (primary motor cortex) A brain area associated with control of movement.

Association area (association cortex) All areas of the cerebral cortex that are not primarily sensory or motor in function.

Aphasia A speech disturbance resulting from brain damage.

Broca's area A language area related to grammar and pronunciation.

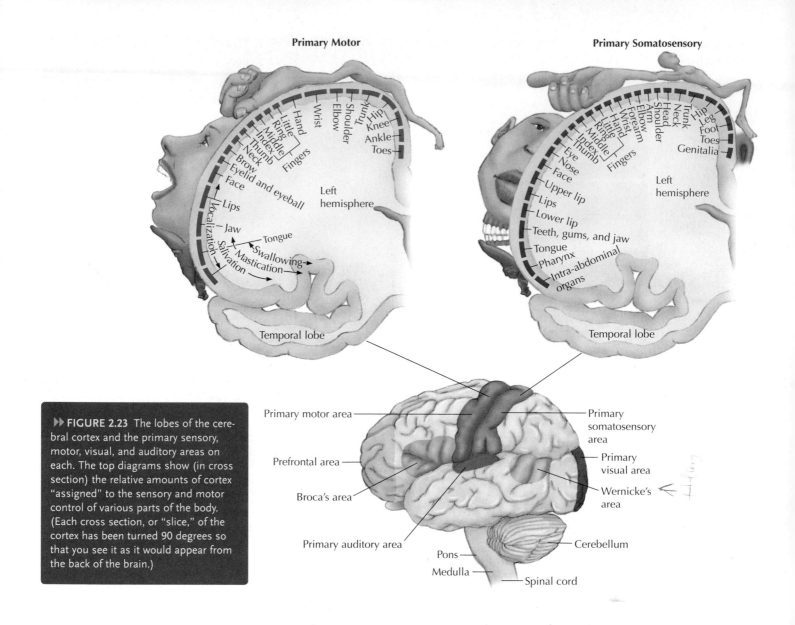

Primary Motor

Little
Ring
Middle
Index
Thumb
Neck
Brow
Eyelid and eyeball
Face
Lips
Vocalization
Jaw
Salivation
Mastication
Swallowing
Tongue
Hand
Wrist
Elbow
Shoulder
Trunk
Hip
Knee
Ankle
Toes
Fingers

Left
hemisphere

Temporal lobe

Primary Somatosensory

Trunk
Neck
Head
Arm
Elbow
Forearm
Shoulder
Hand
Little
Ring
Middle
Index
Thumb
Eye
Nose
Face
Upper lip
Lips
Lower lip
Teeth, gums, and jaw
Tongue
Pharynx
Intra-abdominal
organs
Hip
Leg
Foot
Toes
Genitalia
Fingers

Left
hemisphere

Temporal lobe

Primary motor area

Prefrontal area

Broca's area

Primary auditory area

Primary
somatosensory
area

Primary
visual
area

Wernicke's
area

Cerebellum

Pons

Medulla

Spinal cord

▶▶ **FIGURE 2.23** The lobes of the cerebral cortex and the primary sensory, motor, visual, and auditory areas on each. The top diagrams show (in cross section) the relative amounts of cortex "assigned" to the sensory and motor control of various parts of the body. (Each cross section, or "slice," of the cortex has been turned 90 degrees so that you see it as it would appear from the back of the brain.)

The very front of the frontal association region is known as the **prefrontal area** (or **prefrontal cortex**). This part of the brain is related to more complex behaviors. If the frontal lobes are damaged, a patient's personality and emotional life may change dramatically. Remember Phineas Gage, the railroad foreman described in Chapter 1? It's likely that Gage's personality changed after he suffered brain damage because the prefrontal cortex generates our sense of self, including an awareness of our current emotional state (Moran et al., 2006; Kawasaki et al., 2005).

Reasoning or planning may also be affected (Goel & Dolan, 2004). Patients with damage to the frontal lobes often get "stuck" on mental tasks and repeat the same wrong answers over and over (Stuss & Knight, 2002). PET scans suggest that much of what we call intelligence is related to increased activity in the frontal areas of the cortex (Duncan, 2005). Sadly, drug abuse can damage this important area of the brain (Liu et al., 1998).

The Parietal Lobes

Bodily sensations register in the **parietal** (puh-RYE-ih-tal) **lobes,** located just above the occipital lobes. Touch, temperature, pressure, and other somatic sensations flow into the **primary somatosensory** (SO-mat-oh-SEN-so-ree) **area** (or **primary somatosensory cortex**) of the parietal lobes. Again we find that the map of bodily sensations is distorted. In the case of somatosensory cortex, the drawing in Figure 2.23 reflects the *sensitivity* of body areas, not their size. For example, the lips are large in the drawing because of

Prefrontal area (prefrontal cortex) The very front of the frontal lobes; involved in sense of self, reasoning, and planning.

Parietal lobes Area of the brain where bodily sensations register.

Primary somatosensory area (primary somatosensory cortex) A receiving area for body sensations.

their great sensitivity, whereas the back and trunk, which are less sensitive, are much smaller. Notice that the hands are also large in the map of body sensitivity—which is obviously an aid to musicians, typists, watchmakers, massage therapists, lovers, and brain surgeons.

The Temporal Lobes

The **temporal lobes** are located on each side of the brain. Auditory information projects directly to the **primary auditory area,** making it the main site where hearing first registers. If we did a PET scan of your brain while you listened to your favorite MP3, your primary auditory area would be the first to light up, followed by association areas in your temporal lobes. Likewise, if we could electrically stimulate the primary auditory area of your temporal lobe, you would "hear" a series of sound sensations.

An association area called **Wernicke's** (VER-nick-ees) **area** (see Figure 2.23) lies on the left temporal lobe (again, for 5 percent of all people, the area is on the right temporal lobe). Wernicke's area also functions as a language site. If it is damaged, the result is a *receptive (or fluent) aphasia.* Although the person can hear speech, he or she has difficulty understanding the meaning of words. Thus, when shown a picture of a chair, someone with Broca's aphasia might say "tssair." In contrast, a Wernicke's patient might *fluently,* but incorrectly, identify the photo as "truck" (Ward, 2006).

The Occipital Lobes

At the back of the brain, we find the **occipital** (awk-SIP-ih-tal) **lobes,** the area of the cortex concerned with vision. Patients with tumors (cell growths that interfere with brain activity) in the **primary visual area,** the part of the cortex to first receive input from the eyes, experience blind spots in their vision.

Do the primary visual areas of the cortex correspond directly to what is seen? Images are mapped onto the cortex, but the map is greatly stretched and distorted (Carlson, 2010). That's why it's important to avoid thinking of the visual area as being like a little TV screen in the brain. Visual information creates complex patterns of activity in nerve cells; it does *not* make a TV-like image.

One of the most fascinating results of brain injury is **visual agnosia** (ag-KNOW-zyah), an inability to identify seen objects. Visual agnosia is often caused by damage to the association areas on the occipital lobes (Farah, 2004). This condition is sometimes referred to as "mindblindness." For example, if we show Alice, an agnosia patient, a candle, she can see it and can describe it as "a long narrow object that tapers at the top." Alice can even draw the candle accurately, but she cannot name it. However, if she is allowed to feel the candle, she will name it immediately. In short, Alice can still see color, size, and shape. She just can't form the associations necessary to perceive the meanings of objects.

Are agnosias limited to objects? No. A fascinating form of "mindblindness" is **facial agnosia,** an inability to perceive familiar faces (Farah, 2006). One patient with facial agnosia couldn't recognize her husband or mother when they visited her in the hospital, and she was unable to identify pictures of her children. However, as soon as visitors spoke, she knew them immediately by their voices.

Areas devoted to recognizing faces lie in association areas on the underside of the occipital lobes. These areas appear to have no other function. Why would part of the brain be set aside solely for identifying faces? From an evolutionary standpoint, it is not really so surprising. After all, we are social animals, for whom facial recognition is very important. This specialization is just one example of what a marvelous organ of consciousness we possess.

How much do individual brains differ? Could we find different specializations from brain to brain? Perhaps. "His and Her Brains?" explains why.

In summary, the bulk of our daily experience and all of our understanding of the world can be traced to the different areas of the cortex. The human brain is among the most advanced and sophisticated of the brain-bearing species on earth. This, of course, is no guarantee that our marvelous "biocomputer" will be put to full use. Still, we must stand in awe of the potential it represents.

Temporal lobes Areas that include the sites where hearing registers in the brain.

Primary auditory area Part of the temporal lobe where auditory information is first registered in the brain.

Wernicke's area A temporal lobe brain area related to language comprehension.

Occipital lobes Portion of the cerebral cortex where vision registers in the brain.

Primary visual area The part of occipital lobe that first receives input from the eyes

Visual agnosia Inability to identify seen objects.

Facial agnosia An inability to perceive familiar faces.

His and Her Brains?

As you read this book, you may be curious about the many ways people can differ from each other. "Human Diversity" boxes like this one are designed to help you be more reflective about the rich variety of humanity.

Are men's and women's brains specialized in different ways? In a word, yes (Cahill, 2006). Many physical differences between male and female brains have been found, although their effects remain to be better understood. In one series of studies, researchers observed brain activity while people did language tasks. Both men and women showed increased activity in Broca's area, on the left side of the brain, exactly as expected. Surprisingly, however, the left *and* the right brain were activated in more than half the women tested (Shaywitz et al., 1995; see ▶▶ Figure 2.24).

Using both sides of the brain for language may be a big advantage. When Broca's area is damaged, some women can use the right side of their brains to compensate for the loss, which allows them to resume speaking (Hochstenbach et al., 1998). A man with similar damage might be permanently impaired. Thus, when a man says, "I have half a mind to tell you what I think," he may be stating a curious truth. Despite this difference,

▲ **FIGURE 2.24** Language tasks activate both sides of the brain in many women *(left)* but only the left side in men *(right)*.

the two sexes performed equally well on a task that involved sounding out words (Shaywitz et al., 1995). The researchers concluded that nature has given the brain different routes to the same ability.

In a study of men and women with similar IQ scores, brain images revealed major differences in brain areas involved in intelligence (Haier et al., 2004). In general, the men had more gray matter (neuron cell bodies), while the women had more

white matter (axons coated in myelin). Further, the women had more gray and white matter concentrated in their frontal lobes than the men did. The men's gray matter was split between their frontal and parietal lobes, while their white matter was mostly in the temporal lobes. Whatever else these differences mean, they show that the human brain can be specialized in different ways to arrive at the same capabilities (Piefke et al., 2005).

study break
Hemispheres and Lobes of the Cerebral Cortex

RECITE

See if you can match the following.

K	1. Corpus callosum	A. Visual area
A	2. Occipital lobes	B. Language, speech, writing
H	3. Parietal lobes	C. Motor cortex and abstract thinking
M	4. Temporal lobes	D. Spatial skills, visualization, pattern recognition
C	5. Frontal lobes	E. Speech disturbances
L	6. Association cortex	F. Causes sleep
J	7. Aphasias	G. Increased ratio of cortex in brain
	8. Corticalization	H. Bodily sensations
B	9. Left hemisphere	I. Treatment for severe epilepsy
D	10. Right hemisphere	J. Inability to identify seen objects

I	11. "Split brain"	K. Fibers connecting the cerebral hemispheres
	12. Agnosia	L. Cortex that is not sensory or motor in function
		M. Hearing

REFLECT
Critical Thinking

13. If you wanted to increase the surface area of the cerebral cortex so that more would fit within the skull, how would you do it?
14. If your brain were removed, replaced by another, and moved to a new body, which would you consider to be yourself, your old body with the new brain, or your new body with the old brain?

Relate

Learning the functions of the brain lobes is like learning areas on a map. Try drawing a map of the cortex. Can you label all the different "countries" (lobes)? Can you name their functions? Where is the primary motor area? The somatosensory area? Broca's area? Keep redrawing the map until it becomes more detailed and you can do it easily.

ANSWERS

1. K 2. A 3. H 4. M 5. C 6. L 7. E 8. G 9. B 10. D 11. I 12. J 13. One solution would be to gather the surface of the cortex into folds, just as you might if you were trying to fit a large piece of cloth into a small box. This, in fact, is probably why the cortex is more convoluted (folded or wrinkled) in higher animals. 14. Although there is no "correct" answer to this question, your personality, knowledge, personal memories, and self-concept all derive from brain activity—which makes a strong case for your old brain in a new body being more nearly the "real you."

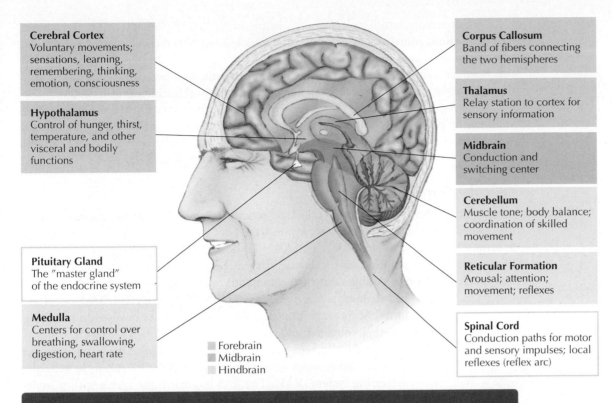

Cerebral Cortex
Voluntary movements; sensations, learning, remembering, thinking, emotion, consciousness

Hypothalamus
Control of hunger, thirst, temperature, and other visceral and bodily functions

Pituitary Gland
The "master gland" of the endocrine system

Medulla
Centers for control over breathing, swallowing, digestion, heart rate

Corpus Callosum
Band of fibers connecting the two hemispheres

Thalamus
Relay station to cortex for sensory information

Midbrain
Conduction and switching center

Cerebellum
Muscle tone; body balance; coordination of skilled movement

Reticular Formation
Arousal; attention; movement; reflexes

Spinal Cord
Conduction paths for motor and sensory impulses; local reflexes (reflex arc)

■ Forebrain
■ Midbrain
■ Hindbrain

▲ **FIGURE 2.25** This simplified drawing shows the main structures of the human brain and describes some of their most important features. (You can use the color code in the foreground to identify which areas are part of the forebrain, midbrain, and hindbrain.)

The Subcortex—At the Core of the (Brain) Matter

What are the major parts of the subcortex?

You could lose large portions of your cerebral cortex and still survive. Not so with the **subcortex,** the brain structures immediately below the cerebral cortex. Serious damage to the subcortex (lower brain) can be fatal. Hunger, thirst, sleep, attention, sex, breathing, and many other vital functions are controlled by parts of the subcortex. Let's take a quick tour of these brain areas, which can be divided into the brainstem (or hindbrain), the midbrain, and the forebrain. (The forebrain also includes the cerebral cortex, which we have already discussed because of its size and importance.) For our purposes the midbrain can be viewed as a link between the forebrain and the brainstem. Therefore, let us focus on the rest of the subcortex (see ▶▶ Figure 2.25).

The Hindbrain

Why are the lower brain areas so important? As the spinal cord joins the brain, it widens into the brainstem. The **brainstem** consists mainly of the medulla (meh-DUL-ah) and the cerebellum (ser-ah-BEL-uhm). The **medulla** contains centers important for the reflex control of vital life functions, including heart rate, breathing, swallowing, and the like. Various drugs, diseases, and injuries can disrupt the medulla and end or endanger life. That's why a karate chop to the back of the neck can be extremely dangerous.

The **pons,** which looks like a small bump on the brainstem, acts as a bridge between the medulla and other brain areas. In addition to connecting with many other locations, including the cerebellum, the pons influences sleep and arousal.

Subcortex All brain structures below the cerebral cortex.

Brainstem The lowest portions of the brain, including the cerebellum, medulla, pons, and reticular formation.

Medulla The structure that connects the brain with the spinal cord and controls vital life functions.

Pons An area on the brainstem that acts as a bridge between the medulla and other structures.

The cerebellum, which looks like a miniature cerebral cortex, lies at the base of the brain. The **cerebellum** primarily regulates posture, muscle tone, and muscular coordination. The cerebellum also stores memories related to skills and habits (Christian & Thompson, 2005). Again we see that experience shapes the brain: Musicians, who practice special motor skills throughout their lives, have larger than average cerebellums (Hutchinson et al., 2003).

What happens if the cerebellum is injured? Without the cerebellum, tasks like walking, running, or playing catch become impossible. The first symptoms of a crippling disease called *spinocerebellar degeneration* are tremor, dizziness, and muscular weakness. Eventually, victims have difficulty merely standing, walking, or feeding themselves.

Reticular Formation

A network of fibers and cell bodies called the **reticular** (reh-TICK-you-ler) **formation (RF)** lies inside the medulla and brainstem. As messages flow into the brain, the RF gives priority to some while turning others aside (Kalat, 2009). By doing so, the RF influences *attention*. The RF doesn't fully mature until adolescence, which may be why children have such short attention spans. The RF also modifies outgoing commands to the body. In this way the RF affects muscle tone, posture, and movements of the eyes, face, head, body, and limbs. At the same time, the RF controls reflexes involved in breathing, sneezing, coughing, and vomiting.

The RF also keeps us vigilant, alert, and awake. Incoming messages from the sense organs branch into a part of the RF called the **reticular activating system (RAS).** The RAS bombards the cortex with stimulation, keeping it active and alert. For instance, let's say a sleepy driver rounds a bend and sees a deer standing in the road. The driver snaps to attention and applies the brakes. She can thank her RAS for arousing the rest of her brain and averting an accident. If you're getting sleepy while reading this chapter, try pinching your ear—a little pain will cause the RAS to momentarily arouse your cortex.

The Forebrain

Like buried treasure, two of the most important parts of your body lie deep within your brain. The thalamus (THAL-uh-mus) and an area just below it called the hypothalamus (HI-po-THAL-uh-mus) are key parts of the forebrain (see Figure 2.25).

How could these be any more important than other areas already described? The **thalamus** acts as a final "switching station" for sensory messages on their way to the cortex. Vision, hearing, taste, and touch all pass through this small, football-shaped structure. Thus, injury to even small areas of the thalamus can cause deafness, blindness, or loss of any other sense, except smell.

The human hypothalamus is about the size of a small grape. Small as it may be, the **hypothalamus** is a kind of master control center for emotion and many basic motives (Carlson, 2010). The hypothalamus affects behaviors as diverse as sex, rage, body temperature, hormone release, eating and drinking, sleep, waking, and emotion. The hypothalamus is basically a "crossroads" that connects many areas of the brain. It is also the final pathway for many kinds of behavior. That is, the hypothalamus is the last place where many behaviors are organized or "decided on" before messages leave the brain, causing the body to react.

The Limbic System

As a group, the hypothalamus, parts of the thalamus, the amygdala, the hippocampus, and other structures make up the limbic system (▶▶ Figure 2.26). The **limbic system** has a major role in producing emotion and motivated behavior. Rage, fear, sexual response, and intense arousal can be localized to various points in the limbic system. Laughter, a delightful part of human social life, also has its origins in the limbic system (Cardoso, 2000).

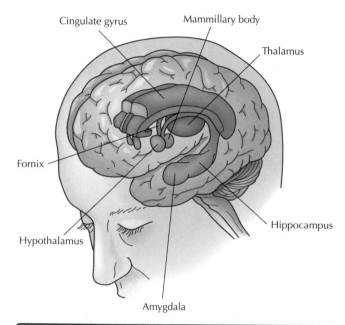

Cingulate gyrus
Mammillary body
Thalamus
Fornix
Hippocampus
Hypothalamus
Amygdala

⬆ **FIGURE 2.26** Parts of the limbic system. Although only one side is shown here, the hippocampus and the amygdala extend out into the temporal lobes at each side of the brain. The limbic system is a sort of "primitive core" of the brain strongly associated with emotion.

Cerebellum A brain structure that controls posture and coordination.

Reticular formation (RF) A network within the medulla and brainstem; associated with attention, alertness, and some reflexes.

Reticular activating system (RAS) A part of the reticular formation that activates the cerebral cortex.

Thalamus A brain structure that relays sensory information to the cerebral cortex.

Hypothalamus A small area of the brain that regulates emotional behaviors and motives.

Limbic system A system in the forebrain that is closely linked with emotional response.

During evolution, the limbic system was the earliest layer of the forebrain to develop. In lower animals, the limbic system helps organize basic survival responses: feeding, fleeing, fighting, and reproduction. In humans, a clear link to emotion remains. The **amygdala** (ah-MIG-dah-luh), in particular, is strongly related to fear.

The amygdala provides a primitive, "quick pathway" to the cortex. Like lower animals, we can be startled and, as such, are able to react to dangerous stimuli before we fully know what is going on. In situations where true danger exists, such as in military combat, the amygdala's rapid response may aid survival. However, disorders of the brain's fear system can be very disruptive. An example is the war veteran who involuntarily dives into the bushes when he hears a car backfire (Fellous & LeDoux, 2005; LaBar & LeDoux, 2002). The role of the amygdala in emotion may also explain why people who suffer from phobias and disabling anxiety often feel afraid without knowing why (LeDoux, 1999).

Some parts of the limbic system have taken on additional, higher-level functions. A part called the **hippocampus** (HIP-oh-CAMP-us) is important for forming lasting memories (Kumaran & Maguire, 2005). The hippocampus lies inside the temporal lobes, which is why stimulating the temporal lobes can produce memory-like or dream-like experiences. The hippocampus also helps us navigate through space. The right side of your hippocampus will become more active, for instance, if you mentally plan a drive across town (Maguire, Frackowiak, & Frith, 1997).

Psychologists have discovered that animals will learn to press a lever to deliver a dose of electrical stimulation to the limbic system. The animals act like the stimulation is satisfying or pleasurable. Indeed, several areas of the limbic system act as reward, or "pleasure," pathways. Many are found in the hypothalamus, where they overlap with areas that control thirst, sex, and hunger. Commonly abused drugs such as cocaine, amphetamine, heroin, nicotine, marijuana, and alcohol activate many of the same pleasure pathways. This appears to be part of the reason why these drugs are so powerfully rewarding (Kandel, Schwartz, & Jessell, 2003).

You might also be interested to know that music you would describe as "thrilling" activates pleasure systems in your brain. This may explain some of the appeal of music that can send shivers down your spine (Blood & Zatorre, 2001). (It may also explain why people will pay so much for concert tickets!)

Punishment, or "aversive," areas have also been found in the limbic system. When these locations are activated, animals show discomfort and will work hard to turn off the stimulation. Because much of our behavior is based on seeking pleasure and avoiding pain, these discoveries continue to fascinate psychologists.

The Magnificent Brain

We have seen that the human brain is an impressive assembly of billions of sensitive cells and nerve fibers. The brain controls vital bodily functions, keeps track of the external world, issues commands to the muscles and glands, responds to current needs, regulates its own behavior, and even creates the "mind" and the magic of consciousness—*all* at the same time.

A final note of caution is now in order. For the sake of simplicity, we have assigned functions to each "part" of the brain as if it were a computer. This is only a half-truth. In reality, the brain is a vast information-processing system. Incoming information scatters all over the brain and converges again as it goes out through the spinal cord, to muscles and glands. The overall system is much, much more complicated than our discussion of separate "parts" implies. In addition, the brain constantly revises its circuits in response to changing life experiences (Kolb & Whishaw, 2006).

We began our exploration of the brain with a virtuoso performance. Imagine the other extreme of being completely unable to move or speak. Even though you would remain alert and intelligent, you would be unable to communicate your simplest thoughts and feelings to others. Each year, this is the fate of thousands of people, like Kate Adamson, who are paralyzed by stroke, disease, or injury. In a very real sense, these people are *locked in,* prisoners in their own bodies (Smith & Delargy, 2005).

Aaron Horowitz/Photolibrary

The limbic system is responsible for many of our emotional responses. The amygdala, in particular, produces rapid fear, which can help protect us from danger. If you unexpectedly saw a striking rattlesnake, it is likely that you would instantly jump back in fear, without having to first think about whether you were in danger.

Amygdala A part of the limbic system associated with fear responses.

Hippocampus A part of the limbic system associated with storing memories.

What if they could "will" a computer to speak for them? Right on! Researchers have developed brain–computer interfaces that translate a patient's EEG recordings into commands that can be used to control a computer (Hinterberger et al., 2003) and even access the Internet (Karim et al., 2006).

The Endocrine System—My Hormones Made Me Do It

Does the glandular system affect behavior?

Our behavior is not solely a product of the nervous system. The endocrine (EN-duh-krin) glands form an equally important parallel communication system in the body. The **endocrine system** is made up of glands that secrete chemicals directly into the bloodstream or lymph system (see ▶▶ Figure 2.27). These chemicals, called **hormones,** are carried throughout the body, where they affect both internal activities and visible behavior. Hormones are related to neurotransmitters. Like other transmitter chemicals, hormones activate cells in the body. To respond, the cells must have receptor sites for the hormone. Hormones affect puberty, personality, dwarfism, jet lag, and much more.

How do hormones affect behavior? Although we are seldom directly aware of them, hormones affect us in many ways (Carlson, 2010). Here is a brief sample: Pregnancy and motherhood cause the release of hormones that lead to the dramatic changes involved in maternal behavior (Kingsley & Lambert, 2006). Hormone output from the adrenal glands rises

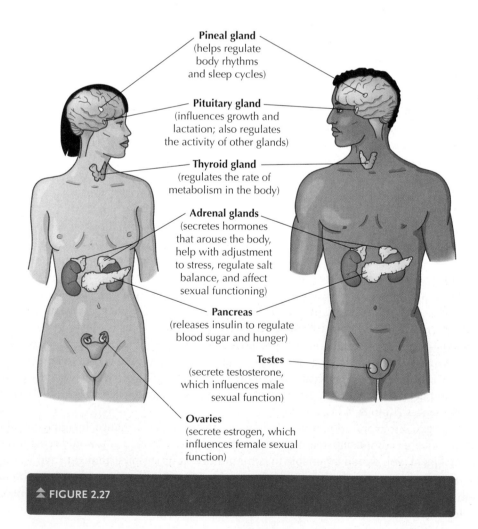

Pineal gland (helps regulate body rhythms and sleep cycles)

Pituitary gland (influences growth and lactation; also regulates the activity of other glands)

Thyroid gland (regulates the rate of metabolism in the body)

Adrenal glands (secretes hormones that arouse the body, help with adjustment to stress, regulate salt balance, and affect sexual functioning)

Pancreas (releases insulin to regulate blood sugar and hunger)

Testes (secrete testosterone, which influences male sexual function)

Ovaries (secrete estrogen, which influences female sexual function)

⌃ **FIGURE 2.27**

Endocrine system Glands whose secretions pass directly into the bloodstream or lymph system.

Hormone A glandular secretion that affects bodily functions or behavior.

during stressful situations; androgens ("male" hormones) are related to the sex drive in both males and females; hormones secreted during times of high emotion intensify memory formation; at least some of the emotional turmoil of adolescence is due to elevated hormone levels; and different hormones prevail when you are angry, rather than fearful. Even disturbing personality patterns may be linked to hormonal irregularities (Evardone, Alexander, & Morey, 2007).

In fact, something as routine as watching a movie can alter hormone levels. After watching violent scenes from *The Godfather,* men had higher levels of the male hormone testosterone. For both men and women, watching a romantic film boosted a hormone that's linked to relaxation and reproduction (Schultheiss, Wirth, & Stanton, 2004). Because these are just samples, let's consider some additional effects hormones have on the body and behavior.

The pituitary is a pea-sized globe hanging from the base of the brain (return to Figure 2.25). One of the pituitary's more important roles is to regulate growth. During childhood, the pituitary secretes a hormone that speeds body development. If too little **growth hormone** is released, a person may remain far smaller than average. If this condition is not treated, a child may be 6 to 12 inches shorter than age-mates. As adults, some will have *hypopituitary* (HI-po-pih-TU-ih-ter-ee) *dwarfism.* Such individuals are perfectly proportioned, but tiny. Regular injections of growth hormone can raise a hypopituitary child's height by several inches, usually to the short side of average.

Too much growth hormone produces *gigantism* (excessive bodily growth). Secretion of too much growth hormone late in the growth period causes *acromegaly* (AK-row-MEG-uh-lee), a condition in which the arms, hands, feet, and facial bones become enlarged. Acromegaly produces prominent facial features, which some people have used as a basis for careers as character actors, wrestlers, and the like.

The pituitary also governs the functioning of other glands (especially the thyroid, adrenal glands, and ovaries or testes). These glands in turn regulate such bodily processes as metabolism, responses to stress, and reproduction. In women, the pituitary controls milk output during breast-feeding.

The **pituitary** is often called the "master gland" because it influences other endocrine glands. But the master has a master: The pituitary is directed by the hypothalamus, which lies directly above it. In this way, the hypothalamus can affect glands throughout the body. This, then, is the major link between the brain and hormones (Kalat, 2009).

The pineal (pin-EE-ul) gland was once considered a useless remnant of evolution. In certain fishes, frogs, and lizards, the gland is associated with a well-developed light-sensitive organ, or so-called third eye. In humans, the function of the **pineal gland** is just now coming to light (so to speak). The pineal gland releases a hormone called **melatonin** (mel-ah-TONE-in) in response to daily variations in light. Melatonin levels in the bloodstream rise at dusk and peak around midnight and fall again as morning approaches. As far as the brain is concerned, it's bedtime when melatonin levels rise (Kennaway & Wright, 2002).

The **thyroid gland,** located in the neck, regulates metabolism. As you may remember from a biology course, *metabolism* is the rate at which energy is produced and expended in the body. By altering metabolism, the thyroid can have a sizable effect on personality. A person suffering from *hyperthyroidism* (an overactive thyroid) tends to be thin, tense, excitable, and nervous. An underactive thyroid (*hypothyroidism*) in an adult can cause inactivity, sleepiness, slowness, obesity, and depression (Joffe, 2006). In infancy, hypothyroidism limits development of the nervous system, leading to severe mental retardation.

Underactivity of the pituitary gland may produce a dwarf. Verne Troyer, best known for playing Mini-Me in the *Austin Powers* movies, has enjoyed an impressive career as an actor. Overactivity of the pituitary gland may produce a giant. Until his premature death in 2005, actor Matthew McGrory was best known for his role of Karl the Giant in the 2003 movie *Big Fish.*

Growth hormone A hormone, secreted by the pituitary gland, that promotes body growth.

Pituitary gland The "master gland" whose hormones influence other endocrine glands.

Pineal gland Gland in the brain that helps regulate body rhythms and sleep cycles.

Melatonin Hormone released by the pineal gland in response to daily cycles of light and dark.

Thyroid gland Endocrine gland that helps regulate the rate of metabolism.

When you are frightened or angry, some important reactions prepare your body for action: Your heart rate and blood pressure rise; stored sugar is released into the bloodstream for quick energy; your muscles tense and receive more blood; and your blood is prepared to clot more quickly in case of injury. As we discussed earlier, these changes are controlled by the autonomic nervous system. Specifically, the sympathetic branch of the ANS causes the hormones *epinephrine* and *norepinephrine* to be released by the adrenal glands. (Epinephrine is also known as adrenaline, which may be more familiar to you.) **Epinephrine** (ep-eh-NEF-rin), which is associated with fear, tends to arouse the body. **Norepinephrine** also tends to arouse the body, but it is linked with anger.

The **adrenal glands** are located just under the back of the rib cage, atop the kidneys. The *adrenal medulla,* or inner core of the adrenal glands, is the source of epinephrine and norepinephrine. The *adrenal cortex,* or outer "bark" of the adrenal glands, produces a set of hormones called *corticoids* (KOR-tih-coids). One of their jobs is to regulate salt balance in the body. A deficiency of certain corticoids can evoke a powerful craving for the taste of salt in humans. The corticoids also help the body adjust to stress, and they are a secondary source of sex hormones.

An oversecretion of the adrenal sex hormones can cause *virilism* (exaggerated male characteristics). For instance, a woman may grow a beard or a man's voice may become so low it is difficult to understand. Oversecretion early in life can cause *premature puberty* (full sexual development during childhood). One of the most remarkable cases on record is that of a 5-year-old Peruvian girl who gave birth to a son (Strange, 1965).

While we are on the topic of sex hormones, there is a related issue worth mentioning. One of the principal androgens, or "male" hormones, is testosterone, which is supplied in small amounts by the adrenal glands. (The testes are the main source of testosterone in males.) Perhaps you have heard about the use of anabolic steroids by athletes who want to "bulk up" or promote muscle growth. Most of these drugs are synthetic versions of testosterone.

Although there is some disagreement about whether steroids actually improve athletic performance, it is widely accepted that they may cause serious side effects. Problems include voice deepening or baldness in women and shrinkage of the testicles, sexual impotence, or breast enlargement in men (Millman & Ross, 2003). Dangerous increases in hostility and aggression ("roid rage") have also been linked with steroid use (Hartgens & Kuipers, 2004). Also common when steroids are used by younger adolescents are an increased risk of heart attack and stroke, liver damage, or stunted growth. Understandably, almost all major sports organizations ban the use of anabolic steroids.

In this brief discussion of the endocrine system, we have considered only a few of the more important glands. Nevertheless, this should give you an appreciation of how completely behavior and personality are tied to the ebb and flow of hormones in the body.

A Look Ahead

In the upcoming "Psychology in Action" section, we will return to the brain to see how hand preference relates to brain organization. You'll also find out if being right- or left-handed affects your chances of living to a ripe old age.

Epinephrine An adrenal hormone that tends to arouse the body; epinephrine is associated with fear. (Also known as adrenaline.)

Norepinephrine An adrenal hormone that tends to arouse the body; norepinephrine is associated with anger. (Also known as noradrenaline.)

Adrenal glands Endocrine glands that arouse the body, regulate salt balance, adjust the body to stress, and affect sexual functioning.

Subcortex and Endocrine System

CITE

Three major divisions of the brain are the brainstem or
_____, the _____, and the
_____.

Reflex centers for heartbeat and respiration are found in the
a. cerebellum   b. thalamus
c. medulla   d. RF

A portion of the reticular formation, known as the RAS, serves as
an _____ system in the brain.
a. activating   b. adrenal
c. adjustment   d. aversive

The _____ is a final relay, or "switching station," for
sensory information on its way to the cortex.

"Reward" and "punishment" areas are found throughout the
_____ system, which is also related to emotion.

Undersecretion from the thyroid can cause both
_____ and _____.
a. dwarfism   b. gigantism
c. obesity   d. mental retardation

The body's ability to resist stress is related to the action of the
adrenal _____.

REFLECT

Critical Thinking

8. Subcortical structures in humans are quite similar to corresponding lower brain areas in animals. Why would knowing this allow you to predict, in general terms, what functions are controlled by the subcortex?
9. Where in all the brain's "hardware" do you think the mind is found? What is the relationship between mind and brain?

Relate

If Mr. Medulla met Ms. Cerebellum at a party, what would they say their roles are in the brain? Would a marching band in a "reticular formation" look like a network? Would it get your attention? If you were standing in the final path for behavior leaving the brain, would you be in the thalamus? Or in the hy-**path**-alamus (please forgive the misspelling)? When you are emotional, do you wave your limbs around (and does your limbic system become more active)?

Name as many of the endocrine glands as you can. Which did you leave out? Can you summarize the functions of each of the glands?

ANSWERS

1. hindbrain, midbrain, forebrain   2. c   3. a   4. thalamus   5. limbic   6. c, d (in infancy)   7. cortex   8. Because the subcortex must be related to basic functions common to all higher animals: motives, emotions, sleep, attention, and vegetative functions, such as heartbeat, breathing, and temperature regulation. The subcortex also routes incoming information from the senses and outgoing commands to the muscles.   9. These questions, known as the mind-body problem, have challenged thinkers for centuries. One recent view is that mental states are "emergent properties" of brain activity. That is, brain activity forms complex patterns that are, in a sense, more than the sum of their parts. Or, to use a rough analogy, if the brain were a musical instrument, then mental activity would be like music played on that instrument.

---

psychology in action
Handedness—Are You Sinister or Dexterous?

In what ways do right- and left-handed individuals differ?

Around the world, left-handedness has been frowned upon. "Lefties" have often been characterized as clumsy, awkward, unlucky, or insincere. The Latin word for left is actually *sinister!* In contrast, right-handedness is the paragon of virtue. The Latin word for right is *dexter,* and "righties" are more likely to be referred to as dexterous, coordinated, skillful, and just. But is there any basis in fact for these attitudes?

What causes **handedness** (a preference for the right or left hand)? Why are there more right-handed than left-handed people? How do left-handed and right-handed people differ? Does being left-handed create any problems—or benefits? The answers to these questions lead us back to the brain, where handedness begins. Let's see what research has revealed about handedness, the brain, and you.

Handedness A preference for the right or left hand in most activities.

Assessing Handedness

Write your name on a sheet of paper, first using your right hand and then your left. You were probably much more comfortable writing with your dominant hand. This is interesting because there's no real difference in the strength or dexterity of the hands themselves. The agility of your dominant hand is an outward expression of superior motor control on one side of the brain. If you are right-handed, there is literally more area on the left side of your brain devoted to controlling your right hand. If you are left-handed, the reverse applies.

The preceding exercise implies that you are either entirely right- or left-handed. But handedness is a matter of degree. To better assess your handedness, complete a few questions adapted from the Waterloo Handedness Questionnaire (Brown et al., 2006) by circling an answer for each question. The more "Rights" you circle, the more right-handed you are.

Are You Right- or Left-Handed?

	RIGHT	LEFT	EITHER
1. Which hand would you use to spin a top?	✗		
2. With which hand would you hold a paintbrush to paint a wall?	✗		✗
3. Which hand would you use to pick up a book?	✗		
4. With which hand would you use a spoon to eat soup?	✗		
5. Which hand would you use to flip pancakes?			✗
6. Which hand would you use to pick up a piece of paper?		✗	
7. Which hand would you use to draw a picture?	✗		
8. Which hand would you use to insert and turn a key in a lock?	✗		
9. Which hand would you use to insert a plug into an electrical outlet?		✗	
10. Which hand would you use to throw a ball?	✗		

About 90 percent of all humans are right-handed; 10 percent are left-handed. Most people (about 75 percent) are strongly right- or left-handed. The rest show some inconsistency in hand preference. Which are you?

Is there such a thing as being left-footed? Excellent question. Do you have "two left feet"? **Sidedness** is often measured by assessing hand, foot, eye, *and* ear preference (Greenwood et al., 2006). We also generally prefer breathing through one nostril over the other and even have a preference for which direction we lean our head when kissing (Barrett, Greenwood, & McCullagh, 2006). (Do you kiss "right"?) Nevertheless, handedness remains the single most important behavioral indicator of sidedness.

If a person is strongly left-handed, does that mean the right hemisphere is dominant? Not necessarily. It's true that the right hemisphere controls the left hand, but a left-handed person's language-producing, **dominant hemisphere** may be on the opposite side of the brain.

Brain Dominance

About 97 percent of right-handers process speech in the left hemisphere and are left-brain dominant (▶▶ Figure 2.28). A good 68 percent of left-handers produce speech from the left hemisphere, just as right-handed people do. About 19 percent of all lefties and 3 percent of righties use their right brain for language. Some left-handers (approximately 12 percent) use both sides of the brain for language processing. All told, 94 percent of the population uses the left brain for language (Coren, 1992).

Is there any way for a person to tell which of his or her hemispheres is dominant? One classic clue is the way you write (see ▶▶ Figure 2.29). Right-handed individuals who write with a straight hand, and lefties who write with a hooked hand, are usually left-brain dominant for language. Left-handed people who write with their hand below the line, and righties who use a hooked position, are usually right-brain dominant (Levy & Reid, 1976). Another

Sidedness A combination of preference for hand, foot, eye, and ear.

Dominant hemisphere A term usually applied to the side of a person's brain that produces language.

Entire Population

Left 94%

Right 5%

Bilateral 1%

Right-handers

Left 97%

Right 3%

Left-handers

Left 68%

Right 19%

Bilateral 12%

⬆ **FIGURE 2.28** Language is controlled by the left side of the brain in the majority of right- and left-handers.

hint is provided by hand gestures. If you gesture mostly with your right hand as you talk, you probably process language in your left hemisphere. Gesturing with your left hand is associated with right-brain language processing (Hellige, 1993).

Are your friends right brained or left brained? Before you leap to any conclusions, be aware that writing position and gesture are not foolproof. The only sure way to check brain dominance is to do medical tests that involve assessing one cerebral hemisphere at a time (Kirveskari, Salmelin, & Hari, 2006).

Causes of Handedness

Is handedness inherited from parents? Yes, at least partly. Clear hand preferences are apparent even before birth, as can be seen in a fetal ultrasound image (▶▶ Figure 2.30). According to British psychologist Peter Hepper, prenatal handedness preferences persist for at least 10 years after birth (Hepper, Wells, & Lynch, 2005). This suggests that handedness cannot be dictated. Parents should never try to force a left-handed child to use the right hand. To do so may create speech or reading problems.

Studies of identical twins show that hand preferences are not directly inherited like eye color or skin color (Ooki, 2005; Reiss et al., 1999). Yet, two left-handed parents are more likely to have a left-handed child than two right-handed parents are (McKeever, 2000). The best evidence to date shows that handedness is influenced by a single gene on the X (female) chromosome (Jones & Martin, 2001).

Hooked Left   Straight Left   Straight Right   Hooked Right

⬆ **FIGURE 2.29** Research suggests that the hand position used in writing may indicate which brain hemisphere is used for language. (Redrawn from an illustration by M. E. Challinor.)

▲ **FIGURE 2.30** In this ultrasound image, a 4-month-old fetus sucks her right thumb. Research by British psychologist Peter Hepper suggests that she will continue to prefer her right hand long after she is born and that she will be right-handed as an adult.

On the other hand, environmental factors such as learning, birth traumas, and social pressure to use the right hand can also affect which hand you end up favoring (Bailey & McKeever, 2004; McKeever et al., 2000). In the past, many left-handed children were forced to use their right hand for writing, eating, and other skills. This is especially true in collectivist cultures like India and Japan, where left-handedness is viewed as especially negative. Not surprisingly, the proportion of left-handers in these societies is only about half that found in individualist cultures such as the United States and Canada (Ida & Mandal, 2003).

Advantage Right

Are there any drawbacks to being left-handed? A small minority of lefties owe their hand preference to birth traumas (such as prematurity, low birth weight, and breech birth). These individuals have higher rates of allergies, learning disorders, and other problems (Betancur et al., 1990). Similarly, people with inconsistent handedness (as opposed to consistent left-handers) may be at risk for more immune-related diseases (Bryden, Bruyn, & Fletcher, 2005).

Is it true that right-handed people live longer than left-handed people? It is true that there is a shortage of very old lefties. One possible explanation lies in the widespread finding that left-handers are more accident-prone (Dutta & Mandal, 2005). However, the supposed clumsiness of lefties may well be a result of living in a right-handed world. One study showed that left-handed locomotive engineers have higher accident rates and suggested that the cause was due to the design of locomotive controls (Bhushan & Khan, 2006). If it can be gripped, turned, or pulled, it's probably designed for the right hand. Even toilet handles are on the right side. On the other hand, the shortage of very old lefties may just reflect the fact that, in the past, more left-handed children were forced to become right-handed. That makes it look like many lefties don't survive to old age. In reality, they do, but many of them are masquerading as righties (Martin & Freitas, 2002)!

Advantage Left

Actually, there are some clear advantages to being left-handed. Throughout history a notable number of artists have been lefties, from Leonardo da Vinci and Michelangelo to Pablo Picasso and M. C. Escher. Conceivably, because the right hemisphere is superior at imagery and visual abilities, there is some advantage to using the left hand for drawing or painting (Springer & Deutsch, 1998). At the least, lefties are definitely better at visualizing three-dimensional objects. This may be why there are more left-handed architects, artists, and chess players than would be expected (Coren, 1992).

Similarly, being right-handed does not guarantee sports superiority, as you can see in ● Table 2.1.

● Table 2.1 Sports and Handedness

Sport	Handedness Advantage
Baseball	No overall left or right advantage
Boxing	Left
Fencing	Left
Basketball	Mixed and ambidextrous
Ice hockey	Mixed and ambidextrous
Field hockey	Mixed and ambidextrous
Tennis	Strong left or strong right
Squash	Strong left or strong right
Badminton	Strong left or strong right

Adapted with the permission of The Free Press, a Division of Simon & Schuster, Inc., from THE LEFT-HANDER SYNDROME by Stanley Coren. Copyright © 1992, 1993 by Stanley Coren. All rights reserved.

By the way, chalk up a few more for the left-handers, who have also done well in handball (Dane & Erzurumluoglu, 2003) and professional tennis (Holtzen, 2000).

Lateralization refers to specialization in the abilities of the brain hemispheres. One striking feature of lefties is that they are generally less lateralized than the right-handed. In fact, even the physical size and shape of their cerebral hemispheres are more alike. If you are a lefty, you can take pride in the fact that your brain is less lopsided than most! In general, left-handers are more symmetrical on almost everything, including eye dominance, fingerprints—even foot size (Polemikos & Papaeliou, 2000).

In some situations less lateralization may be a real advantage. For instance, individuals who are moderately left-handed or ambidextrous seem to have better than average pitch memory, which is a basic musical skill. Correspondingly, more musicians are ambidextrous than would normally be expected (Springer & Deutsch, 1998).

Math abilities may also benefit from fuller use of the right hemisphere. Students who are extremely gifted in math are much more likely to be left-handed or ambidextrous (Benbow, 1986). Even where ordinary arithmetic skills are concerned, lefties seem to excel (Annett, 2002; Annett & Manning, 1990).

The clearest advantage of being left-handed shows up when there is a brain injury. Because of their milder lateralization, left-handed individuals typically experience less language loss after damage to either brain hemisphere, and they recover more easily (Geschwind, 1979). Maybe having "two left feet" isn't so bad after all.

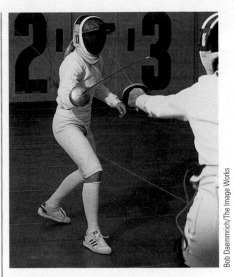

Bob Daemmrich/The Image Works

Left-handers have an advantage in sports such as fencing and boxing. Most likely, their movements are less familiar to opponents, who usually face right-handers (Coren, 1992).

Lateralization Differences between the two sides of the body; especially, differences in the abilities of the brain hemispheres.

RECITE

1. About 97 percent of left-handed people process language on the left side of the brain, the same as right-handed people do. T or F?
2. Left-handed individuals who write with their hand below the writing line are likely to be right-brain dominant. T or F?
3. People basically learn to be right- or left-handed. T or F?
4. In general, left-handed individuals show less lateralization in the brain and throughout the body. T or F?

REFLECT

Critical Thinking

5. News reports that left-handed people tend to die younger have been flawed in an important way: The average age of people in the left-handed group was younger than that of subjects in the right-handed group. Why would this make a difference in the conclusions drawn?

study break

Handedness and Brain Lateralization

Relate

Think for a moment about what you "knew" about handedness and left-handed people before you read this section. Which of your beliefs were correct? How has your knowledge about handedness changed?

ANSWERS

1. F 2. T 3. F 4. T 5. Because we can't tell if handedness or average age accounts for the difference in death rates. For example, if we start with a group of 20- to 30-year-old people, in which some die, the average age of death is a group of 30- to 40-year-old people, in which some die, the average age of death has to be between 30 and 40. Thus, the left-handed group might have an earlier average age at death simply because members of the group were younger to start with.

chapter in review

Major Points

- Biopsychologists study how processes in the body, brain, and nervous system relate to behavior.

- Ultimately, all behavior can be traced to the activity of nerve cells. Sensations, thoughts, feelings, motives, actions, memories, and all other human capacities are associated with brain activities and structures.

- To map the brain, researchers activate or disable specific areas and observe changes in behavior.

- Bioelectrical recordings and computer-generated images of brain activity provide further insights into the structure and function of the brain.

- Endocrine glands serve as a chemical communication system within the body. Behavior is greatly influenced by the ebb and flow of hormones in the bloodstream.

- Brain dominance and brain activity determine if you are right-handed, left-handed, or ambidextrous.

Summary

How do neurons operate and communicate?

- The firing of an action potential (nerve impulse) is basically an electrical event.
- Communication between neurons is chemical: Neurotransmitters cross the synapse, attach to receptor sites, and excite or inhibit the receiving cell.
- Chemicals called neuropeptides appear to regulate activity in the brain.
- By combining information, neurons act as simple computers, which become very powerful when they operate together as neural networks.
- The brain's circuitry is not static. The brain can "rewire" itself and even grow new nerve cells in response to changing environmental conditions.

What are the major parts of the nervous system?

- The nervous system can be divided into the central nervous system and the peripheral nervous system, which includes the somatic (bodily) and autonomic (involuntary) nervous systems.
- The brain carries out most of the "computing" in the nervous system.
- The spinal cord connects the brain to the peripheral nervous system and can process simple reflex arcs.
- The peripheral nervous system carries sensory information to the brain and motor commands to the body.
- "Vegetative" and automatic bodily processes are controlled by the autonomic nervous system, which has a sympathetic branch and a parasympathetic branch.
- Neurons and nerves in the peripheral nervous system can often regenerate. At present, damage in the central nervous system is usually permanent, although scientists are working on ways to repair damaged neural tissue.

How is the brain studied?

- Biopsychologists study how processes in the body, brain, and nervous system relate to behavior.
- Brain structure is investigated though dissection and less intrusive CT scans and MRI scans.
- Brain function is investigated through clinical case studies, electrical stimulation, ablation, deep lesioning, electrical recording, and microelectrode recording, as well as less intrusive EEG recording, PET scans, and fMRI scans.

Why is the human cerebral cortex so important and what are its parts?

- The human brain is marked by advanced corticalization, or enlargement of the cerebral cortex.
- The left cerebral hemisphere contains speech or language "centers" in most people. It also specializes in writing, calculating, judging time and rhythm, and ordering complex movements.
- The right hemisphere is largely nonverbal. It excels at spatial and perceptual skills, visualization, and recognition of patterns, faces, and melodies.
- "Split brains" can be created by cutting the corpus callosum. The split-brain individual shows a remarkable degree of independence between the right and left hemispheres.
- The most basic functions of the lobes of the cerebral cortex are as follows: frontal lobes—motor control, speech, abstract thought, and sense of self; parietal lobes—bodily sensation; temporal lobes—hearing and language; occipital lobes—vision. Damage to any of these areas will impair the named functions.
- Primary sensory and motor areas are found on the lobes of the cerebral cortex.
- Association areas on the cortex are neither sensory nor motor in function. They are related to more complex skills such as language, memory, recognition, and problem solving.
- Damage to either Broca's area or Wernicke's area causes speech and language problems known as aphasias.

What are the major parts of the subcortex?

- The brain can be subdivided into the forebrain, midbrain, and hindbrain. The subcortex includes hindbrain and midbrain structures as well as the lower parts of the forebrain, below the cortex.
- The medulla contains centers essential for reflex control of heart rate, breathing, and other "vegetative" functions.
- The cerebellum maintains coordination, posture, and muscle tone.
- The reticular formation directs sensory and motor messages, and part of it, known as the RAS, acts as an activating system for the cerebral cortex.
- The thalamus carries sensory information to the cortex.
- The hypothalamus exerts powerful control over eating, drinking, sleep cycles, body

temperature, and other basic motives and behaviors.

- The limbic system is strongly related to emotion. It also contains distinct reward and punishment areas and an area known as the hippocampus that is important for forming memories.

Does the glandular system affect behavior?

- Endocrine glands serve as a chemical communication system within the body. The ebb and flow of hormones from the endocrine glands entering the bloodstream affect behavior, moods, and personality.
- Many of the endocrine glands are influenced by the pituitary (the "master gland"), which is in turn influenced by the hypothalamus. Thus, the brain controls the body through the fast nervous system and the slower endocrine system.

In what ways do right- and left-handed individuals differ?

- The vast majority of people are right-handed and therefore left-brain dominant for motor skills. Over 90 percent of right-handed persons and about 70 percent of the left-handed also produce speech from the left hemisphere.
- Brain dominance and brain activity determine if you are right-handed, left-handed, or ambidextrous.
- Most people are strongly right-handed. A minority are strongly left-handed. A few have moderate or mixed hand preferences or they are ambidextrous. Thus, handedness is not a simple either/or trait.
- Left-handed people tend to be less strongly lateralized than right-handed people (their brain hemispheres are not as specialized).

Web Resources

For an up-to-date list of direct links to interesting sites, including those listed here, visit the student companion site for this book at www.cengage.com/psychology/coon

Neural Transmission View a series of animations about neural transmission illustrating the action potential and the resting potential.

Synaptic Transmission Read more detail about synaptic transmission or view an animation.

The Whole Brain Atlas View images of various parts of the brain.

Split Brain Consciousness Explore the cerebral hemispheres and what happens when they are split.

The Patient's Journey: Living With Locked-In Syndrome Meet Nick, who lives with locked-in syndrome after suffering brainstem damage.

Anabolic Steroid Abuse An article on steroids and steroid abuse from the National Institute on Drug Abuse.

What Is "Handedness"? Information about handedness and brain laterality, including a list of famous left handers.

Interactive Learning

PSYCHOLOGY: A JOURNEY BOOK COMPANION WEBSITE
WWW.CENGAGE.COM/PSYCHOLOGY/COON
Visit your book companion website, where you will find flash cards, practice quizzes, web links, and more to help you study.

JUST WHAT YOU NEED TO KNOW NOW! CENGAGENOW
Spend time on what you need to master rather than on information you already have learned. Take a pretest for this chapter, and CengageNOW will generate a personalized study plan based on your results. The study plan will identify the topics you need to review and direct you to online resources to help you master those topics. You can then take a posttest to help you determine the concepts you have mastered and what you will need to work on. Try it out! Go to www.cengage.com/login to sign in with an access code or to purchase access to this product.

test your knowledge

Brain and Behavior

For additional review, get more practice with *CengageNOW, WebTutor,* the *Practice Quizzes,* and/or the printed *Study Guide* available with this book.

1. The point at which information is passed from one neuron to another links the
   a. neurilemma and myelin
   b. soma and ion channels
   c. axon terminals and dendrites
   d. enkephalin and myelin

2. The activity of neurons is regulated by _____, which affect memory, pain, moods, hunger, and other processes.
   a. neuropeptides
   b. neurilemmas
   c. resting potentials
   d. dendrites

3. Muscles are activated by a transmitter substance called
   a. neuropeptide
   b. acetylcholine
   c. enkephalin
   d. endorphin

4. The brain grows new neurons to replace those that are lost. This process is known as
   a. neurogenesis
   b. neuileminal regeneration
   c. autonomic regeneration
   d. neuropeptosis

5. Nerves are made up of bundles of
   a. dendrites
   b. neurotransmitters
   c. synapses
   d. axons

6. The somatic nervous system is part of the
   a. PNS
   b. ANS
   c. sympathetic branch
   d. axon terminal

7. Quieting the body and returning it to a lower level of arousal after an emotional event is a specialty of the
   a. parasympathetic system
   b. peripheral nervous system
   c. spinal nerves
   d. effector cells

8. To record the electrical activity of a single neuron, you would need to use
   a. an EEG
   b. ESB
   c. a microelectrode
   d. surface ablation

9. Which research technique provides an image of ongoing brain activity?
   a. ESB
   b. deep lesioning
   c. PET
   d. surface ablation

10. Among animals and humans, greater corticalization is associated with increased
    a. muscular coordination
    b. intelligence
    c. fight-or-fight responses
    d. conduction speed in the axon

11. The left hemisphere of the brain processes information sequentially, and it is superior at
    a. recognizing patterns
    b. holistic thinking
    c. expressing and detecting emotions
    d. analysis

12. In a "split-brain" operation, the _____ is cut, thereby separating the two cerebral _____.
    a. corpus callosum, hemispheres
    b. chiasm, medullas
    c. motor cortex, lobes
    d. occipital region, reticulums

13. Impaired hearing could result from damage to the _____ lobes of the brain.
    a. frontal
    b. temporal
    c. occipital
    d. parietal

14. Damage to Broca's area causes
    a. a loss of coordination
    b. disturbed sleep patterns
    c. aphasia
    d. an inability to remember recent events

15. Structures in the brain that play a major role in producing emotion and motivating behavior are called the
    a. thalamic branch of the RAS
    b. cerebellar activating system
    c. medial brainstem
    d. limbic system

16. Which of the following parts of the brain is most involved in forming lasting memories?
    a. amygdala
    b. hippocampus
    c. thalamus
    d. hypothalamus

17. The endocrine gland that most influences the activities of other glands is the
    a. pituitary
    b. adrenal
    c. pineal
    d. thyroid

18. Dwarfism and gigantism can be caused by problems in the
    a. pituitary gland
    b. adrenal glands
    c. pineal gland
    d. thyroid gland

19. A majority of both right-handed and left-handed people produce speech from the
    a. right brain hemisphere
    b. corpus callosum
    c. left brain hemisphere
    d. hippocampus

20. One consistent finding about left-handed people is that they are
    a. less lateralized
    b. more likely to die at an early age
    c. unable to use the right brain to produce language
    d. usually also ambidextrous

Answers 1. c 2. a 3. b 4. a 5. d 6. a 7. a 8. c 9. c 10. b 11. d 12. a 13. b 14. c 15. d 16. b 17. a 18. a 19. c 20. a

Human Development

Journey into Psychology: It's a Girl!

With those words, Carol catches her first glimpse of Samantha, her tiny newborn baby. Frankly, at the moment Samantha looks something like a prune, with pudgy arms, stubby legs, and lots of wrinkles. Yet she looks so perfect—at least in her parents' eyes. As Carol and her husband, David, look at Samantha, they wonder, How will her life unfold? What kind of a person will she be? Will Samantha be a happy teenager? Will she marry, become a mother, find an interesting career? David and Carol can only hope that by the time Samantha is 83, she will have lived a full and satisfying life.

What if we could skip ahead through Samantha's life and observe her at various ages? What could we learn? Seeing the world through her eyes would be fascinating and instructive. For example, a child's viewpoint can make us more aware of things we take for granted. Younger children, in particular, are very literal in their use of language. When Samantha was 3, she thought her bath was too hot and said to David, "Make it warmer, Daddy." At first, David was confused. The bath was already fairly hot. But then he realized that what she really meant was, "Bring

the water closer to the temperature we call *warm*." It makes perfect sense if you look at it that way.

Research tells a fascinating story about human growth and development. Let's let Carol, David, and Samantha represent parents and children everywhere, as we see what psychology can tell us about the challenges of growing up, maturing, aging, and facing death. Tracing Samantha's development might even help you answer two very important questions: How did I become the person I am today? and Who will I become tomorrow?

Photodisc/Alamy

Survey Questions

- How do heredity and environment affect development?

- What can newborn babies do?

- Of what significance is a child's emotional bond with adults?

- How important are parenting styles?

- How do children acquire language?

- How do children learn to think?

- Why is the transition from adolescence to adulthood especially challenging?

- How do we develop morals and values?

- What are the typical tasks and dilemmas through the life span?

- What is involved in well-being during later adulthood?

- How do effective parents discipline and communicate with their children?

Nature and Nurture—It Takes Two to Tango

How do heredity and environment affect development?

When we think of development we naturally think of children "growing up" into adults. But even as adults we never really stop changing. **Developmental psychology,** the study of progressive changes in behavior and abilities, involves every stage of life from conception to death (or "the womb to the tomb"). Heredity and environment also affect us throughout life. Some events, such as Samantha's achieving sexual maturity, are governed mostly by heredity. Others, such as Samantha's learning to swim, read, or drive a car, are matters primarily of environment.

But which is more important, heredity or environment? Actually, neither. Biopsychologist Donald Hebb once offered a useful analogy: To define the area of a rectangle, what is more important, height or width? Of course, both dimensions are absolutely essential. If either is reduced to zero, there is no rectangle. Similarly, if Samantha grows up to become a prominent civil rights lawyer, her success will be due to both heredity and environment.

While heredity gives each of us a variety of potentials and limitations, these are, in turn, affected by environmental influences, such as learning, nutrition, disease, and culture. Ultimately, the person you are today reflects a continuous *interaction,* or interplay, between the forces of nature and nurture (Kalat, 2009). Let's look in more detail at this dance.

Heredity

Heredity ("nature") refers to the genetic transmission of physical and psychological characteristics from parents to their children. An incredible number of personal features are set at conception, when a sperm and an ovum (egg; *plural,* ova) unite.

How does heredity operate? The nucleus of every human cell contains **DNA,** deoxyribonucleic acid (dee-OX-see-RYE-bo-new-KLEE-ik). DNA is a long, ladder-like chain of pairs of chemical molecules (▸▸ Figure 3.1). The order of these molecules, or organic bases, acts as a code for genetic information. The DNA in each cell contains a record of all the instructions needed to make a human—with room left over to spare. In 2003, a major scientific milestone was reached when the Human Genome Project completed sequencing all 3 billion chemical base pairs in human DNA (U.S. Department of Energy Office of Science, 2005).

Human DNA is organized into 46 **chromosomes.** (The word *chromosome* means "colored body.") These thread-like structures hold the coded instructions of heredity (▸▸ Figure 3.2). Notable exceptions are sperm cells and ova, which contain only 23 chromosomes. Thus, Samantha received 23 chromosomes from Carol and 23 from David. This is her genetic heritage.

Developmental psychology The study of progressive changes in behavior and abilities from conception to death.

Heredity ("nature") The transmission of physical and psychological characteristics from parents to offspring through genes.

DNA Deoxyribonucleic acid, a molecular structure that contains coded genetic information.

Chromosomes Thread-like "colored bodies" in the nucleus of each cell that are made up of DNA.

Randi Berez/Getty Images

Identical twins. Twins who share identical genes (identical twins) demonstrate the powerful influence of heredity. Even when they are reared apart, identical twins are strikingly alike in motor skills, physical development, and appearance. At the same time, twins are less alike as adults than they were as children, which shows environmental influences are at work (Larsson, Larsson, & Lichtenstein, 2004).

Sugar-phosphate backbone

Organic bases

DNA

Cell

Nucleus

Chromosome

FIGURE 3.1 *(Top left)* Linked molecules (organic bases) make up the "rungs" on DNA's twisted "molecular ladder." The order of these molecules serves as a code for genetic information. The code provides a genetic blueprint that is unique for each individual (except identical twins). The drawing shows only a small section of a DNA strand. An entire strand of DNA is composed of billions of smaller molecules. *(Bottom left)* The nucleus of each cell in the body contains chromosomes made up of tightly wound coils of DNA. (Don't be misled by the drawing: Chromosomes are microscopic, and the chemical molecules that make up DNA are even smaller.)

Genes are small areas of DNA that affect a particular process or personal characteristic. Sometimes, a single gene is responsible for an inherited feature, such as Samantha's eye color. Genes may be dominant or recessive. When a gene is **dominant,** the feature it controls will appear every time the gene is present. When a gene is **recessive,** it must be paired with a second recessive gene before its effect will be expressed. For example, if Samantha got a blue-eye gene from David and a brown-eye gene from Carol, Samantha will be brown eyed, because brown-eye genes are dominant.

If brown-eye genes are dominant, why do two brown-eyed parents sometimes have a blue-eyed child? If one or both parents have two brown-eye genes, the couple's children can only be brown eyed. But what if each parent has one brown-eye gene and one blue-eye gene? In that case, both parents would have brown eyes. Yet, there is one chance in four that their children will get two blue-eye genes and have blue eyes (▶▶ Figure 3.3).

In actuality, few of our characteristics are controlled by single genes. Instead, most are **polygenic** (pol-ih-JEN-ik), or controlled by many genes working in combination. Through the expression of genes, heredity determines eye color, skin color, and susceptibility to some diseases. Also, genes can switch on (or off) at certain ages or developmental stages. In this way, heredity continues to exert a powerful influence throughout **maturation,** the physical growth and development of the body, brain, and nervous system. As the *human growth sequence* unfolds, genetic instructions influence body size and shape, height, intelligence, athletic potential, personality traits, sexual orientation, and a host of other details (Cummings, 2006). (See ● Table 3.1.)

Biophoto Associates/Photo Researchers, Inc.

FIGURE 3.2 This image, made with a scanning electron microscope, shows several pairs of human chromosomes. (Colors are artificial.)

Genes Specific areas on a strand of DNA that carry hereditary information.

Dominant gene A gene whose influence will be expressed each time the gene is present.

Recessive gene A gene whose influence will be expressed only when it is paired with a second recessive gene.

Polygenic characteristics Personal traits or physical properties that are influenced by many genes working in combination.

Maturation The physical growth and development of the body and nervous system.

Readiness A condition that exists when maturation has advanced enough to allow the rapid acquisition of a particular skill.

Readiness

At what ages will Samantha be ready to feed herself, to walk alone, or to say goodbye to diapers? Such milestones tend to be governed by a child's **readiness** for rapid learning. That is, minimum levels of maturation must occur before some skills can be learned. Parents are asking for failure when they try to force a child to learn skills too early (Schum et al., 2002).

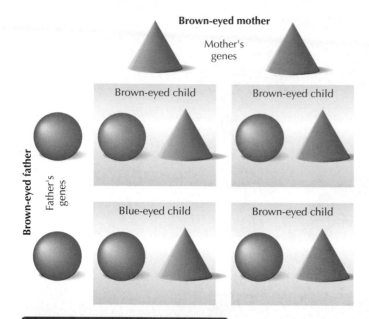

Brown-eyed mother

Mother's genes

Brown-eyed father / Father's genes

Brown-eyed child

Brown-eyed child

Blue-eyed child

Brown-eyed child

▲ **FIGURE 3.3** Gene patterns for children of brown-eyed parents, where each parent has one brown-eye gene and one blue-eye gene. Because the brown-eye gene is dominant, 1 child in 4 will be blue eyed. Thus, there is a significant chance that two brown-eyed parents will have a blue-eyed child.

It is impossible, for instance, to teach children to walk or use a toilet before they have matured enough to control their bodies.

Consider the eager parents who toilet-trained an 18-month-old child in 10 trying weeks of false alarms and "accidents." If they had waited until the child was 24 months old, they might have succeeded in just 3 weeks. Parents may control when toilet training starts, but maturation tends to dictate when it will be completed (Schum et al., 2002). The average age for *completed* toilet training is about 3 years (girls a little earlier, boys a little later) (Schum et al., 2001). So why fight nature? (The wet look is in.)

Environment

Our environment also exerts a profound influence on our development. **Environment ("nurture")** refers to the sum of all external conditions that affect a person. For example, the brain of a newborn baby has fewer *dendrites* (nerve cell branches) and *synapses* (connections between nerve cells) than an adult brain. However, the newborn brain is highly *plastic* (capable of being altered by experience). During the first 3 years of life, millions of new connections form in the brain every day. At the same time, unused connections disappear. As a result, early learning environments literally shape the developing brain, through "blooming and pruning" of synapses (Nelson, 1999).

Environment ("nurture") The sum of all external conditions affecting development, including especially the effects of learning.

● Table 3.1 Human Growth Sequence

PERIOD	DURATION	DESCRIPTIVE NAME
Prenatal Period	From conception to birth	Zygote
Germinal period	First 2 weeks after conception	Embryo
Embryonic period	2–8 weeks after conception	Fetus
Fetal period	From 8 weeks after conception to birth	Neonate
Neonatal Period	From birth to a few weeks after birth	Infant
Infancy	From a few weeks after birth until child is walking securely; some children walk securely at less than a year, while others may not be able to until age 17–18 months	
Early Childhood	From about 15–18 months until about 2-2½ years	Toddler
	From age 2–3 to about age 6	Preschool child
Middle Childhood	From about age 6 to age 12	School-age child
Pubescence	Period of about 2 years before puberty	Adolescent
Puberty	Point of development at which biological changes of pubescence reach a climax marked by sexual maturity	
Adolescence	From the beginning of pubescence until full social maturity is reached (difficult to fix duration of this period)	
Adulthood Young adulthood (19–25) Adulthood (26–40) Maturity (41 plus)	From adolescence to death; sometimes subdivided into other periods as shown at left	Adult
Senescence	No defined limit that would apply to all people; extremely variable; characterized by marked physiological and psychological deterioration	Adult (senile), "old age"

*Note: There is no exact beginning or ending point for various growth periods. The ages are approximate, and each period may be thought of as blending into the next. (Table courtesy of Tom Bond.)

Although human culture is accelerating the rate at which human DNA is evolving, modern humans are still genetically quite similar to cave dwellers who lived 30,000 years ago (Cochran & Harpending, 2009; Hawks et al., 2007). Nevertheless, a bright baby born today could learn to become almost anything—a ballet dancer, an engineer, a gangsta rapper, or a biochemist who likes to paint in watercolors. But an Upper Paleolithic baby could have become only a hunter or food gatherer.

Prenatal Influences

Environmental factors actually start influencing development before birth. Although the intrauterine environment (interior of the womb) is highly protected, environmental conditions can nevertheless affect the developing child. For example, when Carol was pregnant, Samantha's fetal heart rate and movements increased when loud sounds or vibrations penetrated the womb (Kisilevsky et al., 2004).

An 11-week old human fetus. Because of the rapid growth of basic structures, the developing fetus is sensitive to a variety of diseases, drugs, and sources of radiation. This is especially true during the first trimester (3 months) of gestation (pregnancy).

If during her pregnancy Carol's health or nutrition had been poor or if she had had German measles, syphilis, or HIV, had used drugs, or had been exposed to X-rays or radiation, Samantha's growth sequence might have been harmed. In such cases, babies can suffer from **congenital problems,** or "birth defects." These environmental problems affect the developing fetus and become apparent at birth. In contrast, **genetic disorders** are inherited from parents. Examples are sickle-cell anemia, hemophilia, cystic fibrosis, muscular dystrophy, albinism, and some types of mental retardation.

How is it possible for the embryo or the fetus to be harmed? No direct intermixing of blood takes place between a mother and her unborn child. Yet some substances—especially drugs—do reach the fetus. Anything capable of directly causing birth defects is called a **teratogen** (teh-RAT-uh-jen). Sometimes women are exposed to powerful teratogens, such as radiation, lead, pesticides, or polychlorinated biphenyls (PCBs), without knowing it. But pregnant women do have direct control over many teratogens. For example, a woman who takes cocaine runs a serious risk of injuring her fetus (Schuetze & Eiden, 2006). In short, when a pregnant woman takes drugs, her unborn child does too.

Some of the typical features of children suffering from fetal alcohol syndrome (FAS) include a small nonsymmetrical head, a short nose, a flattened area between the eyes, oddly shaped eyes, and a thin upper lip. Many of these features become less noticeable by adolescence. However, mental retardation and other problems commonly follow the FAS child into adulthood. The child shown here represents a moderate example of FAS.

Unfortunately, in the United States drugs are one of the greatest risk factors facing unborn children (Coles & Black, 2006). If a mother is addicted to morphine, heroin, or methadone, her baby may be born with an addiction. Repeated heavy drinking during pregnancy causes *fetal alcohol syndrome (FAS).* Affected infants have low birth weight, a small head, bodily defects, and facial malformations. Many also suffer from emotional, behavioral, and mental handicaps (Golden, 2005).

Tobacco is also harmful. Smoking during pregnancy greatly reduces oxygen to the fetus. Heavy smokers risk miscarrying or having premature, underweight babies who are more likely to die soon after birth. Children of smoking mothers score lower on tests of language and mental ability (Huijbregts et al., 2006). In other words, an unborn child's future can go "up in smoke." That goes for marijuana as well (Viveros et al., 2005).

Sensitive Periods

Early experiences can have particularly lasting effects. For example, children who are abused may suffer lifelong emotional problems (Goodwin, Fergusson, & Horwood, 2005). At the same time, extra care can sometimes reverse the effects of a poor start in life (Bornstein & Tamis-LeMonda, 2001). In short, environmental forces guide human development, for better or worse, throughout life.

Why do some experiences have more lasting effects than others? Part of the answer lies in **sensitive periods.** These are times when children are more susceptible to particular types of environmental influences. Events that occur during a sensitive period can permanently alter the course of development (Bruer, 2001). For example, forming a loving bond with a care-

Congenital problems Problems or defects that originate during prenatal development in the womb.

Genetic disorders Problems caused by defects in the genes or by inherited characteristics.

Teratogen Radiation, a drug, or other substance capable of altering fetal development in nonheritable ways that cause birth defects.

Sensitive period During development, a period of increased sensitivity to environmental influences. Also, a time during which certain events must take place for normal development to occur.

giver early in life seems to be crucial for optimal development. Likewise, babies who don't hear normal speech during their first year may have impaired language abilities (Thompson & Nelson, 2001).

Deprivation and Enrichment

Some environments can be described as *deprived* or *enriched*. **Deprivation** refers to a lack of normal nutrition, stimulation, comfort, or love. **Enrichment** exists when an environment is deliberately made more stimulating, loving, and so forth.

What happens when children suffer severe deprivation? Tragically, a few mistreated children have spent their first years in closets, attics, and other restricted environments. When first discovered, these children are usually mute, retarded, and emotionally damaged (Wilson, 2003). Fortunately, such extreme deprivation is unusual.

Nevertheless, milder perceptual, intellectual, or emotional deprivation occurs in many families, especially those that must cope with poverty. Poverty can affect the development of children in at least two ways (Sobolewski & Amato, 2005). First, poor parents may not be able to give their children needed resources such as nutritious meals, health care, or learning materials (Bradley & Corwyn, 2002). As a result, impoverished children tend to be sick more often, their mental development lags, and they do poorly at school. Second, the stresses of poverty can also be hard on parents, leading to marriage problems, less positive parenting, and poorer parent–child relationships. The resulting emotional turmoil can damage a child's socioemotional development. In the extreme, it may increase the risk of mental illness and delinquent behavior (Bradley & Corwyn, 2002).

Adults who grew up in poverty often remain trapped in a vicious cycle of continued poverty. Because one in seven American families fall below the poverty line, this grim reality plays itself out in millions of American homes every day (Sobolewski & Amato, 2005).

Can an improved environment enhance development? To answer this question, psychologists have created *enriched environments* that are especially novel, complex, and stimulating. Enriched environments may be the "soil" from which brighter children grow. To illustrate, let's consider the effects of raising rats in a sort of "rat wonderland." The walls of their cages were decorated with colorful patterns, and each cage was filled with platforms, ladders, and cubbyholes. As adults, these rats were superior at learning mazes. In addition, they had larger, heavier brains, with a thicker cortex (Benloucif, Bennett, & Rosenzweig, 1995). Of course, it's a long leap from rats to people, but an actual increase in brain size is impressive. If extra stimulation can enhance the "intelligence" of a lowly rat, it's likely that human infants also benefit from enrichment. Many studies have shown that enriched environments improve abilities or enhance development. It would be wise for David and Carol to make a point of nourishing Samantha's mind as well as her body (Beeber et al., 2007).

What can parents do to enrich a child's environment? They can encourage exploration and stimulating play by paying attention to what holds the baby's interest. It is better to "child-proof" a house than to strictly limit what a child can touch. There is also value in actively enriching sensory experiences. Infants are not vegetables. Babies should be surrounded by colors, music, people, and things to see, taste, smell, and touch. It makes perfect sense to take them outside, to hang mobiles over their cribs, to place mirrors nearby, to play music for them, or to rearrange their rooms now and then. Children progress most rapidly when they have responsive parents and stimulating play materials at home (Beeber et al., 2007). In light of this, it is wise to view all of childhood as a *relatively sensitive period* (Nelson, 1999).

Reciprocal Influences

Nurture often affects the expression of hereditary tendencies through ongoing reciprocal influences. A good example of such influences is the fact that growing infants influence their parents' behavior at the same time they are changed by it.

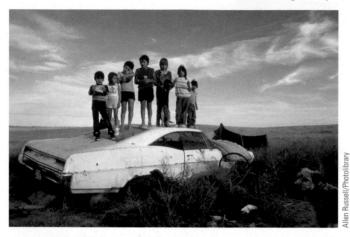

Children who grow up in poverty run a high risk of experiencing many forms of deprivation. There is evidence that lasting damage to social, emotional, and cognitive development occurs when children must cope with severe early deprivation.

Deprivation In development, the loss or withholding of normal stimulation, nutrition, comfort, love, and so forth; a condition of lacking.

Enrichment In development, deliberately making an environment more stimulating, nutritional, comforting, loving, and so forth.

Newborn babies differ noticeably in **temperament.** This is the inherited, physical core of personality. It includes sensitivity, irritability, distractibility, and typical mood (Kagan, 2004). About 40 percent of all newborns are *easy children* who are relaxed and agreeable. Ten percent are *difficult children* who are moody, intense, and easily angered. *Slow-to-warm-up children* (about 15 percent) are restrained, unexpressive, or shy. The remaining children do not fit neatly into a single category (Chess & Thomas, 1986).

Because of differences in temperament, some babies are more likely than others to smile, cry, vocalize, reach out, or pay attention. As a result, babies rapidly become active participants in their own development. For example, Samantha is an easy baby who smiles frequently and is easily fed. This encourages Carol to touch, feed, and sing to Samantha. Carol's affection rewards Samantha, causing her to smile more. Soon, a dynamic relationship blossoms between mother and child. Similarly, good parenting can reciprocally influence a very shy child who, in turn, becomes progressively less shy.

The reverse also occurs: Difficult children make parents unhappy and elicit more negative parenting (Parke, 2004). Alternately, negative parenting can turn a moderately shy child into a very shy one. This suggests that inherited temperaments are dynamically modified by learning (Kagan, 2005).

A person's **developmental level** is his or her current state of physical, emotional, and intellectual development. To summarize, three factors combine to determine your developmental level at any stage of life. These are *heredity, environment,* and your *own behavior,* each tightly interwoven with the others.

RECITE

1. Areas of the DNA molecule called genes are made up of dominant and recessive chromosomes. T or F?
2. Most inherited characteristics can be described as polygenic. T or F?
3. If one parent has one dominant brown-eye gene and one recessive blue-eye gene and the other parent has two dominant brown-eye genes, what is the chance that their child will have blue eyes?
   a. 25 percent
   b. 50 percent
   c. 0 percent
   d. 75 percent
4. The orderly sequence observed in the unfolding of many basic responses can be attributed to _____.
5. "Slow-to-warm-up" children can be described as restrained, unexpressive, or shy. T or F?
6. A _____ _____ is a time of increased sensitivity to environmental influences.
7. As a child develops, there is a continuous _____ between the forces of heredity and environment.

study break
The Interplay of Heredity and Environment

REFLECT
Critical Thinking

8. Environmental influences can interact with hereditary programming in an exceedingly direct way. Can you guess what it is?

Relate

Can you think of clear examples of some ways in which heredity and environmental forces have combined to affect your development?

How would maturation affect the chances of teaching an infant to eat with a spoon?

What kind of temperament did you have as an infant? How did it affect your relationship with your parents or caregivers?

ANSWERS

1. F 2. T 3. c 4. maturation 5. T 6. sensitive period 7. interaction 8. Environmental conditions sometimes turn specific genes on or off, thus directly affecting the expression of genetic tendencies (Gottlieb, 1998).

The Newborn—More Than Meets the Eye

What can newborn babies do?

At birth the human *neonate* (NEE-oh-NATE: newborn infant) will die if not cared for by adults. Newborn babies cannot lift their heads, turn over, or feed themselves. Does this mean they are inert and unfeeling? Definitely not! Contrary to common belief, newborn babies are

Temperament The physical core of personality, including emotional and perceptual sensitivity, energy levels, typical mood, and so forth.

Developmental level An individual's current state of physical, emotional, and intellectual development.

Newborn babies display a special interest in the human face. A preference for seeing their mother's face develops rapidly and encourages social interactions between mother and baby.

not oblivious to their surroundings. Infants have mental capacities that continue to surprise researchers and delight parents. The emergence of many of these capacities, as well as a baby's physical abilities, is closely related to maturation of the brain, nervous system, and body. Likewise, a baby's early emotional life unfolds on a timetable that is largely controlled by maturation.

Neonates like Samantha can see, hear, smell, taste, and respond to pain and touch. Although their senses are less acute, babies are very responsive. Samantha will follow a moving object with her eyes and will turn in the direction of sounds.

Samantha also has a number of adaptive infant reflexes (Siegler, DeLoache, & Eisenberg, 2006). To elicit the *grasping reflex,* press an object in the neonate's palm and she will grasp it with surprising strength. Many infants, in fact, can hang from a raised bar, like little trapeze artists. The grasping reflex aids survival by helping infants avoid falling. You can observe the *rooting reflex* (reflexive head turning and nursing) by touching Samantha's cheek. Immediately, she will turn toward your finger, as if searching for something.

How is such turning adaptive? The rooting reflex helps infants find a bottle or a breast. Then, when a nipple touches the infant's mouth, the *sucking reflex* (rhythmic nursing) helps her obtain needed food. Like other reflexes, this is a genetically programmed action. At the same time, food rewards nursing. Because of this, babies quickly learn to nurse more actively. Again, we see how the interplay of nature and nurture alters a baby's behavior.

The *Moro reflex* is also interesting. If Samantha's position is changed abruptly or if she is startled by a loud noise, she will make a hugging motion. This reaction has been compared to the movements baby monkeys use to cling to their mothers. (We leave it to the reader's imagination to decide if there is any connection.)

▲ **FIGURE 3.4** Infant imitation. In the top row of photos, Andrew Meltzoff makes facial gestures at an infant. The bottom row records the infant's responses. Videotapes of Meltzoff and of tested infants helped ensure objectivity.

Perceptual and Cognitive Development

Thirty years ago, many people thought of newborn babies as mere bundles of reflexes, like the ones just described. But infants are capable of much more. For example, psychologist Andrew Meltzoff (2005) has found that babies are born mimics. ▶▶ Figure 3.4 shows Meltzoff as he sticks out his tongue, opens his mouth, and purses his lips at a 20-day-old girl. Will she imitate him? Videotapes of babies confirm that they imitate adult facial gestures. As early as 9 months of age, infants can imitate actions a day after seeing them (Heimann & Meltzoff, 1996). Such mimicry obviously aids rapid learning in infancy.

How intelligent are neonates? Babies are smarter than many people think. From the earliest days of life, babies are learning how the world works. They immediately begin to look, touch, taste, and otherwise explore their surroundings. From an evolutionary perspective, a baby's mind is designed to soak up information, which it does at an amazing pace (Meltzoff & Prinz, 2002).

In the first months of life, babies are increasingly able to think, to learn from what they see, to make predictions, and to search for explanations. For example, Jerome Bruner (1983) observed that 3- to 8-week-old babies seem to understand that a person's voice and body should be connected. If a baby hears his mother's voice coming from where she is standing, the baby will remain calm. If her voice comes from a loudspeaker several feet away, the baby will become agitated and begin to cry.

Another look into the private world of infants can be drawn from testing their vision. However, such testing is a challenge because infants cannot talk. Robert Fantz invented a device called a *looking chamber* to find out what infants can see and what holds their attention (▶▶ Figure 3.5*a*). Imagine that Samantha is placed on her back inside the chamber, facing a lighted area above. Next, two objects are placed in the chamber. By observing the movements of Samantha's eyes and the images they reflect, we can tell what she is looking at. Such tests show that adult vision is about 30 times sharper, but babies can see large patterns, shapes, and edges.

Fantz found that 3-day-old babies prefer complex patterns, such as checkerboards and bull's-eyes, to simpler colored rectangles. Other researchers have learned that infants are excited by circles, curves, and bright lights (▶▶ Figure 3.5*b*) (Brown, 1990). Immediately after birth, Samantha will be aware of changes in the position of objects (Slater et al., 1991). When she is 6 months old, she will be able to recognize categories of objects that differ in shape or color. By 9 months of age she will be able to tell the difference between dogs and birds or other groups of animals (Mandler & McDonough, 1998). By 1 year of age, she will see as well as her parents (Sigelman & Rider, 2009). So, there really is a person inside that little body!

Neonates can most clearly see objects about a foot away from them. It is as if they are best prepared to see the people who love and care for them (Gopnik, Meltzoff, & Kuhl, 2000). Perhaps that's why babies have a special fascination with human faces. Just *hours* after they are born, babies begin to prefer seeing their mother's face, rather than a stranger's (Walton, Bower, & Bower, 1992). When babies are only 2 to 5 days old, they will pay more attention to a person who is gazing directly at them, rather than one who is looking away (Farroni et al., 2004) (▶▶ Figure 3.5*c*).

(a)

(b)

(c)

(d)

▲ **FIGURE 3.5** *(a)* Eye movements and fixation points of infants are observed in Fantz's "looking chamber." *(b)* Thirteen-week-old infants prefer concentric and curved patterns like those on the left to nonconcentric and straight-line patterns like those on the right. *(c)* When they are just days old, infants pay more attention to the faces of people who are gazing directly at them. *(d)* Infants look at the normal face longer than at the scrambled face and at both faces longer than at the design on the right. (Photo *a* courtesy of David Linton. Drawing by Alex Semenoick from "The Origin of Form Perception," by Robert L. Frantz, Copyright © 1961 by Scientific American, Inc. All rights reserved.)

In a looking chamber, most infants will spend more time looking at a human face pattern than a scrambled face or a colored oval (▶▶ Figure 3.5*d*). When real human faces are used, infants prefer familiar faces to unfamiliar faces. However, this reverses at about age 2. At that time, unusual objects begin to interest the child. For instance, in a classic study Jerome Kagan (1971) showed face masks to 2-year-olds. Kagan found that the toddlers were fascinated by a face with eyes on the chin and a nose in the middle of the forehead. He believes the babies' interest came from a need to understand why the scrambled face differed from what they had come to expect. Such behavior is further evidence that babies actively try to make sense of their surroundings (Gopnik, Meltzoff, & Kuhl, 2000).

Motor Development

As we noted previously, the emergence of many basic abilities is closely tied to *maturation,* which will be evident, for example, as Samantha learns motor skills, such as crawling and walking. Of course, the *rate* of maturation varies from child to child. Nevertheless, the *order* of maturation is almost universal. For instance, Samantha will be able to sit without support from David before she has matured enough to crawl. Indeed, infants around the world typically sit before they crawl, crawl before they stand, and stand before they walk (▶▶ Figure 3.6).

What about my weird cousin Emo who never crawled? Like cousin Emo, a few children substitute rolling, creeping, or shuffling for crawling. A very few move directly from sitting to standing and walking. Even so, their motor development is orderly. In general, muscular control spreads in a pattern that is *cephalocaudal* (SEF-eh-lo-KOD-ul:

1. Fetal posture (newborn)
2. Holds chin up (1 month)
3. Holds chest up (2 months)
4. Sits when supported (4 months)
5. Sits alone (7 months)
6. Stands holding furniture (9 months)
7. Crawls (10 months)
8. Walks if led (11 months)
9. Stands alone (11 months)
10. Walks alone (12 months)

▲ FIGURE 3.6 Motor development. Most infants follow an orderly pattern of motor development. Although the order in which children progress is similar, there are large individual differences in the ages at which each ability appears. The ages listed are averages for American children. It is not unusual for many of the skills to appear 1 or 2 months earlier than average or several months later (Harris & Liebert, 1991). Parents should not be alarmed if a child's behavior differs some from the average.

from head to toe) and *proximodistal* (PROK-seh-moe-DIS-tul: from the center of the body to the extremities). Even if cousin Emo flunked Elementary Crawling, his motor development followed the standard top-down, center-outward pattern (Piek, 2006).

Although maturation has a big impact, motor skills don't simply "emerge." Samantha must learn to control her actions. When babies are beginning to crawl or walk, they actively try new movements and select those that work. Samantha's first efforts may be flawed—a wobbly crawl or some shaky first steps. However, with practice, babies "tune" their movements to be smoother and more effective. Such learning is evident from the very first months of life (Piek, 2006; Thelen, 2000). (See ▶▶ Figure 3.7.)

Emotional Development

Although experts do not yet agree on exactly how quickly emotions unfold (Oster, 2005), early emotional development also follows a pattern closely tied to maturation (Panksepp & Pasqualini, 2005). Even the basic emotions of *anger, fear,* and *joy*—which appear to be unlearned—take time to develop. General *excitement* is the only emotion newborn infants clearly express. However, as David and Carol can tell you, a baby's emotional life blossoms rapidly. One researcher (Bridges, 1932) observed that all the basic human emotions appear before age 2. Bridges found that emotions appear in a consistent order and that the first basic split is between pleasant and unpleasant emotions (▶▶ Figure 3.8).

Psychologist Carroll Izard thinks that infants can express several basic emotions as early as 10 weeks of age. When Izard looks carefully at the faces of babies, he sees abundant signs of emotion. (See ▶▶ Figure 3.9.) The most common infant expression, he found, is not excitement, but *interest*—followed by *joy, anger,* and *sadness* (Izard et al., 1995).

If Izard is right, then emotions are "hardwired" by heredity and related to evolution. Perhaps that's why smiling is one of a baby's most common reactions. Smiling probably helps babies survive by inviting parents to care for them (Izard et al., 1995).

At first, a baby's smiling is haphazard. By the age of 8–12 months, however, infants smile more frequently when another person is nearby (Jones & Hong, 2001). This **social smile** is especially rewarding to parents. Infants can even use their social smile to communicate interest in an object, like the time Samantha smiled when her mother held up her favorite teddy bear (Venezia et al., 2004). On the other hand, when new parents see and hear a crying baby, they feel annoyed, irritated, disturbed, or unhappy. Babies the world over, it seems, rapidly become capable of letting others know what they like and dislike. (Prove this to yourself sometime by driving a baby buggy.)

With dazzling speed, human infants are transformed from helpless babies to independent persons. By her third year, Samantha will have a unique personality and she will be able to stand, walk, talk, and explore. At no other time after birth does development proceed more rapidly. During the same period, Samantha's relationships with other people will expand as well. Before we explore that topic, here's a chance to review what you've learned.

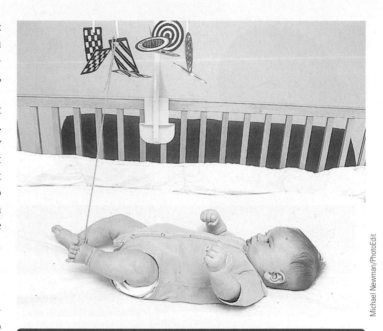

▲ **FIGURE 3.7** Psychologist Carolyn Rovee-Collier has shown that babies as young as 3 months old can learn to control their movements. In her experiments, babies lie on their backs under a colorful crib mobile. A ribbon is tied around the baby's ankle and connected to the mobile. Whenever babies spontaneously kick their legs, the mobile jiggles and rattles. Within a few minutes, infants learn to kick faster. Their reward for kicking is a chance to see the mobile move (Hayne & Rovee-Collier, 1995).

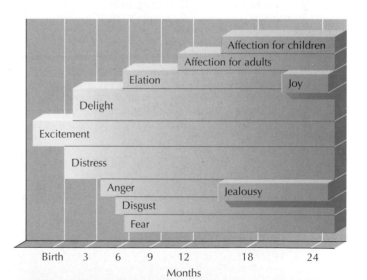

▲ **FIGURE 3.8** The traditional view of infancy holds that emotions are rapidly differentiated from an initial capacity for excitement. (After K. M. B. Bridges, 1932. Reprinted by permission of the Society for Research in Child Development, Inc.)

Social smile Smiling elicited by social stimuli, such as seeing a parent's face.

▶▶ **FIGURE 3.9** Infants display many of the same emotional expressions as adults do. Carroll Izard believes such expressions show that distinct emotions appear within the first months of life. Other theorists argue that specific emotions come into focus more gradually, as an infant's nervous system matures. Either way, parents can expect to see a full range of basic emotions by the end of a baby's first year.

study break
The Neonate and Early Maturation

RECITE

1. If an infant is startled, he or she will make movements similar to an embrace. This is known as the
   a. grasping reflex   b. rooting reflex
   c. Moro reflex   d. adaptive reflex
2. During infancy, a capacity for imitating others first becomes evident at about 9 months of age. T or F?
3. After age 2, infants tested in a looking chamber show a marked preference for familiar faces and simpler designs. T or F?
4. General excitement or interest is the clearest emotional response present in newborn infants, but meaningful expressions of delight and distress appear soon after. T or F?
5. Neonates display a social smile as early as 10 days after birth. T or F?

REFLECT
Critical Thinking

6. If you were going to test newborn infants to see if they prefer their own mother's face to that of a stranger, what precautions would you take?

Relate

What infant reflexes have you observed? Can you give an example of how heredity and environment interact during motor development?

To know what a baby is feeling, would it be more helpful to be able to detect delight and distress (Bridges) or joy, anger, and sadness (Izard)?

ANSWERS

1. c 2. F 3. F 4. T 5. F 6. In one study of the preferences of newborns, the hair color and complexion of strangers were matched to those of the mothers. Also, only the mother's or stranger's face was visible during testing. And finally, a scent was used to mask olfactory (smell) cues so that an infant's preference could not be based on the mother's familiar odor (Bushnell, Sai, & Mullin, 1989).

Social Development—Baby, I'm Stuck on You

Of what significance is a child's emotional bond with adults?

Like all humans, babies are social creatures. Their early **social development** lays a foundation for relationships with parents, siblings, friends, and relatives (Shaffer & Kipp, 2010). A first basic step into the social world involves becoming aware of oneself as a person. When you look in a mirror, you recognize the image staring back as your own—except, perhaps, early on Monday mornings. Like many such events, initial self-awareness depends on maturation of the nervous system. In a typical test of self-recognition, infants are shown images of themselves on a TV. Most infants have to be 18 months old before they recognize themselves (Nielsen & Dissanayake, 2004).

Attachment

The real core of social development is found in the **emotional attachment,** or close emotional bond, that babies form with their primary caregivers. There is a sensitive period (roughly the first year of life) during which this must occur for optimal development. Returning to Samantha's story, we find that attachment keeps her close to Carol, who provides safety, stimulation, and a secure "home base" from which Samantha can go exploring.

Mothers usually begin to feel attached to their baby before birth. For their part, as babies mature, they become more and more capable of bonding with their mothers. For the first few months, babies respond more or less equally to everyone. By 2 or 3 months, most babies prefer their mothers to strangers. By around 7 months, babies generally become truly attached to their mothers, crawling after them if they can. Shortly thereafter they begin to form attachments to other people as well, such as father, grandparents, or siblings (Sigelman & Rider, 2009).

A direct sign that an emotional bond has formed appears around 8 to 12 months of age. At that time Samantha will display **separation anxiety** (crying and signs of fear) when she is left alone or with a stranger. Mild separation anxiety is normal. When it is more intense, it may reveal a problem. At some point in their lives, about 1 in 20 children suffer from *separation anxiety disorder* (Dick-Niederhauser & Silverman, 2006). These children are miserable when they are separated from their parents, whom they cling to or constantly follow. Some fear that they will get lost and never see their parents again. Many refuse to go to school, which can be a serious handicap. Children tend to grow out of the disorder (Kearney et al., 2003), but if separation anxiety is intense or lasts for more than a month, parents should seek professional help for their child (Masi, Mucci, & Millepiedi, 2001).

Attachment Quality

According to psychologist Mary Ainsworth (1913–1999), the quality of attachment is revealed by how babies act when their mothers return after a brief separation. Infants who are **securely attached** have a stable and positive emo-

A sense of self, or self-awareness, develops at about age 18 months. Before children develop self-awareness, they do not recognize their own image in a mirror. Typically, they think they are looking at another child. Some children hug the child in the mirror or go behind it looking for the child they see there (Lewis, 1995).

Most parents are familiar with the storm of crying that sometimes occurs when babies are left alone at bedtime. Bedtime distress can be a mild form of separation anxiety. As many parents know, it is often eased by the presence of "security objects," such as a stuffed animal or favorite blanket (Donate-Bartfield & Passman, 2004).

Social development The development of self-awareness, attachment to parents or caregivers, and relationships with other children and adults.

Emotional attachment An especially close emotional bond that infants form with their parents, caregivers, or others.

Separation anxiety Distress displayed by infants when they are separated from their parents or principal caregivers.

Secure attachment A stable and positive emotional bond.

What's Your Attachment Style?

Do our first attachments continue to affect us as adults? Some psychologists believe they do, by influencing how we relate to friends and lovers (Bridges, 2003; Sroufe et al., 2005). Read the following statements and see which best describes your adult relationships.

Secure Attachment Style

In general, I think most other people are well intentioned and trustworthy.

I find it relatively easy to get close to others.

I am comfortable relying on others and having others depend on me.

I don't worry much about being abandoned by others.

I am comfortable when other people want to get close to me emotionally.

Avoidant Attachment Style

I tend to pull back when things don't go well in a relationship.

I am somewhat skeptical about the idea of true love.

I have difficulty trusting my partner in a romantic relationship.

Other people tend to be too eager to seek commitment from me.

I get a little nervous if anyone gets too close emotionally.

Ambivalent Attachment Style

I have often felt misunderstood and unappreciated in my romantic relationships.

My friends and lovers have been somewhat unreliable.

I love my romantic partner but I worry that she or he doesn't really love me.

I would like to be closer to my romantic partner, but I'm not sure I trust her or him.

Do any of the preceding statements sound familiar? If so, they may describe your adult attachment style. Most adults have a secure attachment style that is marked by caring, supportiveness, and understanding. However, it's not unusual to have an avoidant attachment style that reflects a tendency to resist intimacy and commitment to others (Collins et al., 2002). An ambivalent attachment style is marked by mixed feelings about love and friendship (Tidwell, Reis, & Shaver, 1996). Do you see any similarities between your present relationships and your attachment experiences as a child?

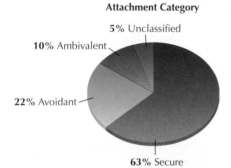

Attachment Category

5% Unclassified
10% Ambivalent
22% Avoidant
63% Secure

⬆ **FIGURE 3.10** In the United States, about two thirds of all children from middle-class families are securely attached. About 1 child in 3 is insecurely attached. (Percentages are approximate.) (From Kaplan, 1998.)

tional bond. They are upset by the mother's absence and seek to be near her when she returns. **Insecure-avoidant** infants have an anxious emotional bond. They tend to turn away from the mother when she returns. **Insecure-ambivalent attachment** is also an anxious emotional bond. In this case, babies have mixed feelings: They both seek to be near the returning mother and angrily resist contact with her. (See ▸▸ Figure 3.10.)

Attachment can have lasting effects. Infants who are securely attached at the age of 1 year show resiliency, curiosity, problem-solving ability, and social skill in preschool (Collins & Gunnar, 1990). In contrast, attachment failures can be quite damaging. Consider, for example, the plight of children raised in severely overcrowded Romanian orphanages (Wilson, 2003). These children got almost no attention from adults for the first year or two of their lives. Some have now been adopted by American and Canadian families, but many are poorly attached to their new parents. Some, for instance, will wander off with strangers, are anxious and remote, and don't like to be touched or to make eye contact with others (O'Conner et al., 2003). In short, for some children, a lack of affectionate care early in life leaves a lasting emotional impact well into adulthood. (See "What's Your Attachment Style?")

Promoting Secure Attachment

The key to secure attachment is a mother who is accepting and sensitive to her baby's signals and rhythms. Poor attachment occurs when a mother's actions are inappropriate, inadequate, intrusive, overstimulating, or rejecting. An example is the mother who tries to play with a drowsy infant or who ignores a baby who is looking at her and vocalizing. The link between sensitive caregiving and secure attachment appears to apply to all cultures (Posada et al., 2002).

What about attachment to fathers? Fathers of securely attached infants tend to be outgoing, agreeable, and happy in their marriage. In general, a warm family atmosphere—one that includes sensitive mothering *and* fathering—produces secure children (Belsky, 1996; Gomez & McLaren, 2007).

Day Care

Does commercial day care interfere with the quality of attachment? It depends on the quality of day care. Overall, *high-quality* day care does not adversely affect attachment to parents (NICHD, 1999). In fact, high-quality day care can actually improve children's social and

Insecure-avoidant attachment An anxious emotional bond marked by a tendency to avoid reunion with a parent or caregiver.

Insecure-ambivalent attachment An anxious emotional bond marked by both a desire to be with a parent or caregiver and some resistance to being reunited.

mental skills (Mercer, 2006). Children in high-quality day care tend to have better relationships with their mothers and fewer behavior problems. They also have better cognitive skills and language abilities (Burchinal et al., 2000; Vandell, 2004).

However, all the positive effects just noted are *reversed* for low-quality day care. Low-quality day care *is* risky and *may* weaken attachment. Poor-quality day care can even create behavior problems that didn't exist beforehand (Pierrehumbert et al., 2002). Parents are wise to carefully evaluate and monitor the quality of day care their children receive.

What should parents look for when they evaluate the quality of child care? Parents seeking quality should insist on *at least* the following: (1) a small number of children per caregiver, (2) small overall group size (12 to 15), (3) trained caregivers, (4) minimal staff turnover, and (5) stable, consistent care (Howes, 1997). (Also, avoid any child-care center with the words *zoo, menagerie,* or *stockade* in its name.)

Attachment and Affectional Needs

A baby's **affectional needs** (needs for love and affection) are every bit as important as more obvious needs for food, water, and physical care. All things considered, creating a bond of trust and affection between the infant and at least one other person is a key event during the first year of life. Parents are sometimes afraid of "spoiling" babies with too much attention, but for the first year or two this is nearly impossible. In fact, a later capacity to experience warm and loving relationships may depend on it.

Parental Influences—Life with Mom and Dad

How important are parenting styles?

From the first few years of life, when caregivers are the center of a child's world, through to adulthood, the style and quality of mothering and fathering are very important.

Parenting Styles

Psychologist Diana Baumrind (1991, 2005) has studied the effects of three major **parental styles,** which are identifiable patterns of parental caretaking and interaction with children. See if you recognize the styles she describes.

Authoritarian parents enforce rigid rules and demand strict obedience to authority. Typically they view children as having few rights but adult-like responsibilities. The child is expected to stay out of trouble and to accept, without question, what parents regard as right or wrong ("Do it because I say so"). The children of authoritarian parents are usually obedient and self-controlled. But they also tend to be emotionally stiff, withdrawn, apprehensive, and lacking in curiosity.

Overly permissive parents give little guidance, allow too much freedom, or don't hold children accountable for their actions. Typically, the child has rights similar to an adult's but few responsibilities. Rules are not enforced, and the child usually gets his or her way ("Do whatever you want"). Permissive parents tend to produce dependent, immature children who misbehave frequently. Such children are aimless and likely to "run amok."

Baumrind describes **authoritative parents** as those who supply firm and consistent guidance, combined with love and affection. Such parents balance their own rights with those of their children. They control their children's behavior in a caring, responsive, nonauthoritarian way ("Do it for this reason"). Effective parents are firm and consistent, not harsh or rigid. In general, they encourage the child to act responsibly, to think, and to make good decisions. This style produces children who are *resilient* (good at bouncing back after bad experiences) and develop the strengths they need to thrive even in difficult circumstances (Kim-Cohen et al., 2004; Masten, 2001). The children of authoritative parents are

Affectional needs Emotional needs for love and affection.

Parental styles Identifiable patterns of parental caretaking and interaction with children.

Authoritarian parents Parents who enforce rigid rules and demand strict obedience to authority.

Overly permissive parents Parents who give little guidance, allow too much freedom, or do not require the child to take responsibility.

Authoritative parents Parents who supply firm and consistent guidance combined with love and affection.

"All right now, give Mommy the super-glue."

competent, self-controlled, independent, assertive, and inquiring. They know how to manage their emotions and use positive coping skills (Eisenberg et al., 2003; Lynch et al., 2004). To read more about effective parenting, see this chapter's "Psychology in Action" section.

Maternal and Paternal Influences

Don't mothers and fathers parent differently? Yes. Although **maternal influences** (all the effects a mother has on her child) generally have a greater impact, fathers do make a unique contribution to parenting (Santrock, 2007). Although fathers are spending more time with their children, mothers still do most of the nurturing and caretaking, especially of young children (Craig, 2006).

Studies of **paternal influences** (the sum of all effects a father has on his child) reveal that fathers are more likely to play with their children and tell them stories. In contrast, mothers are typically responsible for the physical and emotional care of their children (▶▶ Figure 3.11).

It might seem that the father's role as a playmate makes him less important. Not so. Samantha's playtime with David is actually very valuable. From birth onward, fathers pay more visual attention to children than mothers do. Fathers are much more tactile (lifting, tickling, and handling the baby), more physically arousing (engaging in rough-and-tumble play), and more likely to engage in unusual play (imitating the baby, for example) (Crawley & Sherrod, 1984; Paquette et al., 2003). In comparison, mothers speak to infants more, play more conventional games (such as peekaboo), and, as noted, spend much more time in caregiving. Young children who spend a lot of time playing with their fathers tend to be more competent in many ways (Tamis-LeMonda, et al., 2004).

Overall, fathers can be as affectionate, sensitive, and responsive as mothers are. Nevertheless, infants and children tend to get very different views of males and females. Females, who offer comfort, nurturance, and verbal stimulation, tend to be close at hand. Males come and go, and when they are present, action, exploration, and risk-taking prevail. It's no wonder, then, that the parental styles of mothers and fathers have a major impact on children's gender role development (Lindsay, Mize, & Pettit, 1997; Videon, 2005).

▶▶ **FIGURE 3.11** Mother–child and father–child interactions. This graph shows what occurred on routine days in a sample of more than 1,400 Australian homes. Mothers spend about twice as long each day on child care, compared with fathers. Further, mothers spend more time on physical and emotional care (e.g., feeding, bathing, soothing) than on interactive care (e.g., playing, reading, activities); fathers show the reverse pattern. Finally, mothers spend more time on travel (e.g., driving children to sports or music lessons), communication (e.g., talking to teachers about their children), and passive care (e.g., supervising children while they play). (Adapted from Craig, 2006.)

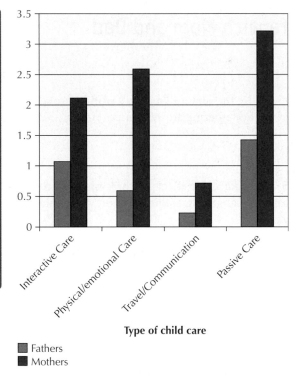

Type of child care

■ Fathers
■ Mothers

Ethnic Differences: Four Flavors of Parenting

Do ethnic differences in parenting affect children in distinctive ways? Diana Baumrind's work provides a good overall summary of the effects of parenting. However, her conclusions are probably most valid for families whose roots lie in Europe. Child rearing in other ethnic groups often reflects different customs and beliefs. Cultural differences are especially apparent with respect to the meaning attached to a child's behavior. Is a particular behavior "good" or "bad"? Should it be encouraged or discouraged? The answer will depend greatly on parents' cultural values (Leyendecker et al., 2005).

Maternal influences The aggregate of all psychological effects mothers have on their children.

Paternal influences The aggregate of all psychological effects fathers have on their children.

Making generalizations about groups of people is always risky. Nevertheless, some typical differences in child-rearing patterns have been observed in North American ethnic communities (Kaplan, 1998; Parke, 2004).

African-American Families

Traditional African-American values emphasize loyalty and interdependence among family members, security, developing a positive identity, and not giving up in the face of adversity. African-American parents typically stress obedience and respect for elders (Dixon, Graber, & Brooks-Gunn, 2008). Child discipline tends to be fairly strict (Parke, 2004), but many African-American parents see this as a necessity, especially if they live in urban areas where safety is a concern. Self-reliance, resourcefulness, and an ability to take care of oneself in difficult situations are also qualities that African-American parents seek to promote in their children.

Hispanic Families

Like African-American parents, Hispanic parents tend to have relatively strict standards of discipline (Dixon, Graber, & Brooks-Gunn, 2008). They also place a high value on family values, family pride, and loyalty. Hispanic families are typically affectionate and indulgent toward younger children. However, as children grow older, they are expected to learn social skills and to be calm, obedient, courteous, and respectful. In fact, such social skills may be valued more than cognitive skills (Delgado & Ford, 1998). In addition, Hispanic parents tend to stress cooperation more than competition. Such values can put Hispanic children at a disadvantage in highly competitive, European-American culture.

Asian-American Families

Asian cultures tend to be group oriented, and they emphasize interdependence among individuals. In contrast, Western cultures value individual effort and independence. This difference is often reflected in Asian-American child-rearing practices (Chao & Tseng, 2002). Asian-American children are taught that their behavior can bring either pride or shame to the family. Therefore, they are obliged to set aside their own desires when the greater good of the family is at stake (Parke, 2004). Parents tend to act as teachers who encourage hard work, moral behavior, and achievement. For the first few years, parenting is lenient and permissive. However, after about age 5, Asian-American parents begin to expect respect, obedience, self-control, and self-discipline from their children.

Arab-American Families

In Middle Eastern cultures, children are expected to be polite, obedient, disciplined, and conforming. Punishment generally consists of spankings, teasing, or shaming in front of others. Arab-American fathers tend to be strong authority figures who demand obedience so that the family will not be shamed by a child's bad behavior. Success, generosity, and hospitality are highly valued in Arab-American culture. The pursuit of family honor encourages hard work, thrift, conservatism, and educational achievement. The welfare of the family is emphasized over individual identity. Thus, Arab-American children are raised to respect their parents, members of their extended family, and other adults as well (Erickson & Al-Timimi, 2001; Medhus, 2001).

Implications

Child rearing is done in a remarkable variety of ways around the world. In fact, many of the things we do in North America, such as forcing young children to sleep alone, would be considered odd or wrong in other cultures. In the final analysis, parenting can be judged only if we know what culture or ethnic community a child is being prepared to enter (Leyendecker et al., 2005).

Fathering typically makes a contribution to early development that differs in emphasis from mothering.

In ethnic communities, norms for effective parenting often differ in subtle ways from parenting styles in Euro-American culture.

study break

Social Development in Childhood

RECITE

1. Clear signs of self-awareness or self-recognition are evident in most infants by the time they reach 8 months of age. T or F?
2. The development of separation anxiety in an infant corresponds to the formation of an attachment to parents. T or F?
3. High-quality day care can actually improve children's social and mental skills. T or F?
4. Fathers are more likely to act as playmates for their children rather than as caregivers. T or F?
5. According to Diana Baumrind's research, effective parents are authoritarian in their approach to their children's behavior. T or F?
6. Asian-American parents tend to be more individually oriented than parents whose ethnic roots are European. T or F?

REFLECT

Critical Thinking

7. Can you think of another way to tell if infants have self-awareness?
8. Can emotional bonding begin before birth?

Relate

Do you think that your experiences as a child, such as your early attachment pattern, really affect your life as an adult? Can you think of any examples from your own life?

Do you know any parents who have young children and who are authoritarian, permissive, or authoritative? What are their children like?

ANSWERS

1. F 2. T 3. T 4. T 5. F 6. F 7. Another successful method is to secretly rub a spot of rouge on an infant's nose. The child is then placed in front of a mirror. The question is, Will the child touch the red spot, showing recognition of the mirror image as his or her own? The probability that a child will do so jumps dramatically during the second year. 8. It certainly can for parents. When a pregnant woman begins to feel fetal movements, she becomes aware that a baby is coming to life inside of her. Likewise, prospective parents who hear a fetal heartbeat at the doctor's office or see an ultrasound image of the fetus begin to become emotionally attached to the unborn child (Santrock, 2007).

Language Development—Who Talks Baby Talk?

How do children acquire language?

There's something almost miraculous about a baby's first words. As infants, how did we manage to leap into the world of language? Even a quick survey like this one reveals that both maturation (nature) and social development (nurture) provide a foundation for language learning.

Language development is closely tied to maturation (Carroll, 2008; Gleason, 2005). As every parent knows, babies can cry from birth on. By 1 month of age they use crying to gain attention. Typically, parents can tell if an infant is hungry, angry, or in pain from the tone of the crying (Kaplan, 1998). Around 6 to 8 weeks of age, babies begin *cooing* (the repetition of vowel sounds such as "oo" and "ah").

By 7 months of age, Samantha's nervous system will mature enough to allow her to grasp objects, to smile, laugh, sit up, and *babble*. In the babbling stage, the consonants *b, d, m,* and *g* are combined with the vowel sounds to produce meaningless language sounds:

dadadadada or *bababa*. At first, babbling is the same around the world. But soon, the language spoken by parents begins to have an influence. That is, Japanese babies start to babble in a way that sounds like Japanese, Mexican babies babble in Spanish-like sounds, and so forth (Gopnik, Meltzoff, & Kuhl, 2000; Kuhl, 2004).

At about 1 year of age, children respond to real words such as *no* or *hi*. Soon afterward, the first connection between words and objects forms, and children may address their parents as "Mama" or "Dada." By age 18 months to 2 years, Samantha's vocabulary may include a hundred words or more. At first there is a *single-word stage,* during which children use one word at a time, such as "go," "juice," or "up." Soon after, words are arranged in simple two-word sentences called *telegraphic speech:* "Want-Teddy," "Mama-gone."

Language and the Terrible Twos

At about the same time that children begin to put two or three words together they become much more independent. Two-year-olds understand some of the commands parents make, but they are not always willing to carry them out. A child like Samantha may assert her independence by saying, "No drink," "Me do it," "My cup, my cup," and the like. It can be worse, of course. A 2-year-old may look at you intently, make eye contact, listen as you shout "No, no," and still pour her juice on the cat.

During their second year, children become increasingly capable of mischief and temper tantrums. Thus, calling this time "the terrible twos" is not entirely inappropriate. One-year-olds can do plenty of things parents don't want them to do. However, it's usually 2-year-olds who do things *because* you don't want them to (Gopnik, Meltzoff, & Kuhl, 2000). Perhaps parents can take some comfort in knowing that a stubborn, negative 2-year-old is simply becoming more independent. When Samantha is 2, Carol and David would be wise to remember: "This, too, shall pass."

After age 2, the child's comprehension and use of words takes a dramatic leap forward. From this point on, vocabulary and language skills grow at a phenomenal rate (Fernald, Perfors, & Marchman, 2006). By first grade, Samantha will be able to understand around 8,000 words and use about 4,000. She will have truly entered the world of language.

The Roots of Language

What accounts for this explosion of language development? Linguist Noam Chomsky (1975, 1986) has long claimed that humans have a **biological predisposition** or hereditary readiness to develop language. According to Chomsky, language patterns are inborn, much like a child's ability to coordinate walking. If such inborn language recognition does exist, it may explain why children around the world use a limited number of patterns in their first sentences. Typical patterns include (Mussen et al., 1979):

Identification:	"See kitty."
Nonexistence:	"Allgone milk."
Possession:	"My doll."
Agent-Action:	"Mama give."
Negation:	"Not ball."
Question:	"Where doggie?"

Does Chomsky's theory explain why language develops so rapidly? It is certainly part of the story. But many psychologists feel that Chomsky underestimates the importance of learning (Tomasello, 2003) and the social contexts that shape language development (Hoff, 2006). *Psycholinguists* (specialists in the psychology of language) have shown that imitation of adults and rewards for correctly using words (as when a child asks for a cookie) are important parts of language learning. Also, babies actively participate in language learning by asking questions, such as "What dis?" (Domingo & Goldstein-Alpern, 1999).

When a child makes a language error, parents typically repeat the child's sentence with needed corrections (Bohannon & Stanowicz, 1988; Hoff, 2006) or ask a clarifying question

Biological predisposition The presumed hereditary readiness of humans to learn certain skills, such as how to use language, or a readiness to behave in particular ways.

to draw the child's attention to the error (Saxton, Houston-Price, & Dawson, 2005). More important is the fact that parents and children begin to communicate long before the child can speak. A readiness to interact *socially* with parents may be as important as innate language recognition. The next section explains why.

Early Communication

How do parents communicate with infants before they can talk? Parents go to a great deal of trouble to get babies to smile and vocalize (▶▶ Figure 3.12). In doing so, they quickly learn to change their actions to keep the infant's attention, arousal, and activity at optimal levels. A familiar example is the "I'm-Going-to-Get-You" game. In it, the adult says, "I'm gonna getcha.... I'm gonna getcha.... I'm gonna getcha.... Gotcha!" Through such games, adults and babies come to share similar rhythms and expectations (Carroll, 2008). Soon a system of shared **signals** is created, including touching, vocalizing, gazing, and smiling. These help lay a foundation for later language use (Tamis-LeMonda, Bornstein, & Baumwell, 2001). Specifically, signals establish a pattern of "conversational" *turn-taking* (alternate sending and receiving of messages).

Carol	*Samantha*
"Oh what a nice little smile!"	(smiles)
"Yes, isn't that nice?"	
"There."	
"There's a nice little smile."	(burps)
"Well, pardon you!"	
"Yes, that's better, isn't it?"	
"Yes."	(vocalizes)
"Yes."	(smiles)
"What's so funny?"	

From the outside, such exchanges may look meaningless. In reality, they represent real communication. Samantha's vocalizations and attention provide a way of interacting emotionally with Carol and David. One study found that 6-week-old babies gaze at an adult's face in rhythm with the adult's speech (Crown et al., 2002). Infants as young as 4 months engage in vocal turn-taking with adults (Jaffe et al., 2001). The more children interact with parents, the faster they learn to talk and the faster they learn thinking abilities (Dickinson & Tabors, 2001; Hoff & Tian, 2005). Unmistakably, social relationships contribute to early language learning (Hoff, 2006).

▶▶ **FIGURE 3.12** Infant engagement scale. These samples from a 90-point scale show various levels of infant engagement, or attention. Babies participate in prelanguage "conversations" with parents by giving and withholding attention and by smiling, gazing, or vocalizing. (From Beebe et al., 1982.)

Signal In early language development, any behavior, such as touching, vocalizing, gazing, or smiling, that allows nonverbal interaction and turn-taking between parent and child.

85
Medium high positive

50
Neutral attention

20
Avert

Parentese

When they talk to infants, parents use an exaggerated pattern of speaking called **motherese** or **parentese.** Typically, they raise their tone of voice, use short, simple sentences, repeat themselves, and use frequent gestures (Gogate, Bahrick, & Watson, 2000). They also slow their rate of speaking and use exaggerated voice inflections: "Did Samantha eat it A-L-L UP?"

What is the purpose of such changes? Parents are apparently trying to help their children learn language (Soderstrom, 2007). When a baby is still babbling, parents tend to use long, adult-style sentences. But as soon as the baby says its first word, they switch to parentese. By the time babies are 4 months old, they prefer parentese over normal speech (Cooper et al., 1997).

In addition to being simpler, parentese has a distinct "musical" quality (Trainor & Desjardins, 2002). No matter what language mothers speak, the melodies, pauses, and inflections they use to comfort, praise, or give warning are universal. Psychologist Anne Fernald has found that mothers of all nations talk to their babies with similar changes in pitch. For instance, we praise babies with a rising, then falling pitch ("BRA-vo!" "GOOD girl!"). Warnings are delivered in a short, sharp rhythm ("Nein! Nein!" "Basta! Basta!" "Not! Dude!"). To give comfort, parents use low, smooth, drawn-out tones ("Oooh poor baaa-by." "Oooh pobrecito.") A high-pitched, rising melody is used to call attention to objects ("See the pretty BIRDIE?") (Fernald, 1989).

Parentese helps parents get babies' attention, communicate with them, and teach them language (Thiessen, Hill, & Saffran, 2005). Later, as a child's speaking improves, parents tend to adjust their speech to the child's language ability. Especially from 18 months to 4 years of age, parents seek to clarify what a child says and prompt the child to say more.

In summary, some elements of language are innate. Nevertheless, our inherited tendency to learn language does not determine if we will speak English or Vietnamese, Spanish or Russian. Environmental forces also influence whether a person develops simple or sophisticated language skills. The first 7 years of life are a sensitive period in language learning (Eliot, 1999). Clearly, a full flowering of speech requires careful cultivation.

Gary Conner/Photolibrary

As with motherese, parents use a distinctive style when singing to an infant. Even people who speak another language can tell if a tape-recorded song was sung to an infant or an adult. Likewise, lullabies remain recognizable when electronic filtering removes words (Trehub et al., 1993a, 1993b).

Motherese (or parentese) A pattern of speech used when talking to infants, marked by a higher-pitched voice; short, simple sentences; repetition, slower speech; and exaggerated voice inflections.

---

study break

Language Development in Childhood

RECITE

1. The development of speech and language usually occurs in which order?
   a. crying, cooing, babbling, telegraphic speech
   b. cooing, crying, babbling, telegraphic speech
   c. babbling, crying, cooing, telegraphic speech
   d. crying, babbling, cooing, identification
2. Simple two-word sentences are characteristic of _____ speech.
3. Noam _____ has advanced the idea that language acquisition is built on innate patterns.
4. Prelanguage turn-taking and social interactions would be of special interest to a psycholinguist. T or F?
5. The style of speaking known as _____ is higher in pitch and has a musical quality.

REFLECT

Critical Thinking

6. The children of professional parents hear more words per hour than the children of welfare parents, and they also tend to score higher on tests of mental abilities. How else could their higher scores be explained?

Relate

In order, see if you can name and imitate the language abilities you had as you progressed from birth to age 2 years. Now see if you can label and imitate some basic elements of parentese.

In your own words, state at least one argument for and against Chomsky's view of language acquisition.

You are going to spend a day with a person who speaks a different language than you do. Do you think you would be able to communicate with the other person? How does this relate to language acquisition?

ANSWERS

1. a 2. telegraphic 3. Chomsky 4. T 5. Parentese or motherese 6. Children in professional homes receive many educational benefits that are less common in welfare homes. Yet, even when such differences are taken into account, brighter children tend to come from richer language environments (Hart & Risley, 1999).

Cognitive Development—Think Like a Child

How do children learn to think?

Now that we have Samantha talking, let's move on to a broader view of intellectual development. Jean Piaget (Jahn pea-ah-ZHAY) provided some of the first great insights into how children develop thinking abilities.

How different is a child's understanding of the world from that of an adult? According to the Swiss psychologist and philosopher Jean Piaget (1951, 1952), their thinking is, generally speaking, less abstract. They tend to base their understanding on particular examples and objects they can see or touch. Also, children use fewer generalizations, categories, and principles.

Piaget's Theory of Cognitive Development

Jean Piaget—philosopher, psychologist, and keen observer of children.

#9 in exam (handwritten annotation)

Jean Piaget believed that all children mature through a series of distinct stages in intellectual development. Many of his ideas came from observing his own children as they solved various thought problems. (It is tempting to imagine that Piaget's illustrious career was launched one day when his wife said to him, "Watch the children for a while, will you, Jean?") Piaget's ideas have deeply affected our view of children (Feldman, 2004). The following is a brief summary of what he found.

Mental Processes

Piaget was convinced that intellect grows through processes he called assimilation and accommodation. **Assimilation** refers to using existing mental patterns in new situations. Let's say that Benjamin pounds on blocks with his favorite toy, a plastic hammer. For his birthday Benjamin gets an oversized toy wrench. If he uses the wrench for pounding, it has been assimilated to an existing knowledge structure.

In **accommodation,** existing ideas are modified to fit new requirements. For instance, a younger child might think that a dime is worth less than a (larger) nickel. However, as children begin to spend money, they must alter their ideas about what "more" and "less" mean. Thus, new situations are assimilated to existing ideas, and new ideas are created to accommodate new experiences.

The Sensorimotor Stage (0–2 Years)

Look up from this book until your attention is attracted to something else in the room. Now close your eyes. Is the book still there? How do you know? As an adult, you can keep an image of the object in your "mind's eye." According to Piaget, newborn babies cannot create *internal representations* such as mental images. As a result, they lack **object permanence,** an understanding that objects continue to exist when they are out of sight.

For this reason, in the first 2 years of life, Samantha's intellectual development will be largely nonintellectual and nonverbal. She will be concerned mainly with learning to coordinate information from her senses with her motor movements. But sometime during their first year, babies begin to actively pursue disappearing objects. By age 2, they can anticipate the movement of an object behind a screen. For example, when watching an electric train, Samantha will look ahead to the end of a tunnel, rather than staring at the spot where the train disappeared.

In general, developments in this stage indicate that the child's conceptions are becoming more *stable.* Objects cease to appear and disappear magically, and a more orderly and predictable world replaces the confusing and disconnected sensations of infancy.

Assimilation In Piaget's theory, the application of existing mental patterns to new situations (that is, the new situation is assimilated to existing mental schemes).

Accommodation In Piaget's theory, the modification of existing mental patterns to fit new demands (that is, mental schemes are changed to accommodate new information or experiences).

Sensorimotor stage Stage of intellectual development during which sensory input and motor responses become coordinated.

Object permanence Concept, gained in infancy, that objects continue to exist even when they are hidden from view.

The Preoperational Stage (2–7 Years)

Close your eyes again. Imagine the room you sleep in. What would it look like if you were perched on the ceiling and your bed were missing? You have now mentally operated on your image by *transforming* it. According to Piaget, even though preoperational children can form mental images or ideas, they are preoperational because they cannot easily **transform** those images or ideas in their minds.

This is why although children begin to think *symbolically* and use language before the age of 6 or 7, their thinking is still very concrete and **intuitive** (it makes little use of reasoning and logic). (Do you remember thinking as a child that the sun and the moon followed you when you took a walk?)

Let's visit Samantha at age 5: If you show her a short, wide glass full of milk and a taller, narrow glass full of milk, she will most likely tell you that the taller glass contains more milk (even if it doesn't). Samantha will tell you this even if she watches you pour milk from the short glass into an empty taller glass. Older children can easily mentally *reverse* the pouring of the milk to see that the shape of the container is irrelevant to the volume of milk it contains. But Samantha is preoperational; she cannot engage in the mental operation of transforming the tall, narrow glass of milk back into a short, wide glass. Thus she is not bothered by the fact that the milk appears to be transformed from a smaller to a larger amount. Instead, she responds only to the fact that *taller* seems to mean *more*. (See ▶▶ Figure 3.13.)

After about age 7, children are no longer fooled by this situation. Perhaps that's why 7 has been called the "age of reason." From age 7 on, we see a definite trend toward more logical, adult-like thought (Flavell, 1992).

During the preoperational stage, the child is also quite **egocentric** (unable to take the viewpoint of other people). The child's ego seems to stand at the center of his or her world. To illustrate, show Samantha a two-sided mirror. Then hold it between you and her, so she can see herself in it. If you ask her what she thinks *you* can see, she imagines that you see *her* face reflected in the mirror, instead of your own. She cannot mentally transform the view she sees into the view you must be seeing.

Such egocentrism explains why children can seem exasperatingly selfish or uncooperative at times. If Benjamin blocks your view by standing in front of the TV, he assumes that you can see it if he can. If you ask him to move so you can see better, he may move so that *he* can see better! Benjamin is not being selfish in the ordinary sense. He just doesn't realize that your view differs from his.

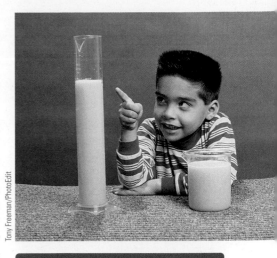

Tony Freeman/PhotoEdit

⮝ FIGURE 3.13 Children under age 7 intuitively assume that a volume of liquid increases when it is poured from a short, wide container into a taller, thinner one. This boy thinks the tall container holds more than the short one. Actually each holds the same amount of liquid. Children make such judgments based on the height of the liquid, not its volume.

Fogstock LLC/Photolibrary

Crossing a busy street can be dangerous for the preoperational child. Because their thinking is still egocentric, younger children cannot understand why the driver of a car can't see them if they can see the car. Children under the age of 7 also cannot consistently judge speeds and distances of oncoming cars. Adults can easily overestimate the "street smarts" of younger children. It is advisable to teach children to cross with a light, in crosswalks, or with assistance.

Preoperational stage Period of intellectual development during which children begin to use language and think symbolically, yet remain intuitive and egocentric in their thought.

Transformation The mental ability to change the shape or form of a substance (such as clay or water) and to perceive that its volume remains the same.

Intuitive thought Thinking that makes little or no use of reasoning and logic.

Egocentric thought Thought that is self-centered and fails to consider the viewpoints of others.

In addition, the child's use of language is not as sophisticated as it might seem. Children have a tendency to confuse words with the objects they represent. If Benjamin calls a toy block a "car" and you use the block to make a "house," he may be upset. To children, the name of an object is as much a part of the object as its size, shape, and color. This seems to underlie a preoccupation with name-calling. To the preoperational child, insulting words may really hurt. Samantha was once angered by her older brother. Searching for a way to retaliate against her larger and stronger foe, she settled on, "You panty-girdle!" It was the worst thing she could think of saying.

The Concrete Operational Stage (7–11 Years)

The hallmark of this stage is the ability to carry out mental operations such as *reversing* thoughts. A 4-year-old boy in the preoperational stage might have a conversation like this (showing what happens when a child's thinking *lacks* reversibility):

> "Do you have a brother?"
>
> "Yes."
>
> "What's his name?"
>
> "Sam."
>
> "Does Sam have a brother?"
>
> "No."

Reversibility of thought allows children in the concrete operational stage to recognize that if $4 \times 2 = 8$, then 2×4 does, too. Younger children must memorize each relationship separately. Thus, a preoperational child may know that $4 \times 9 = 36$, without being able to tell you what 9×4 equals.

The development of mental operations allows mastery of **conservation** (the concept that mass, weight, and volume remain unchanged when the shape of objects changes). Children have learned conservation when they understand that rolling a ball of clay into a "snake" does not increase the amount of clay. Likewise, pouring liquid from a tall, narrow glass into a shallow dish does not reduce the amount of liquid. In each case the volume remains the same despite changes in shape or appearance. The original amount is *conserved*. (See Figure 3.13.)

During the concrete operational stage, children begin to use concepts of time, space, and number. The child can think logically about very concrete objects or situations, categories, and principles. Such abilities help explain why children stop believing in Santa Claus when they reach this stage. Because they can conserve volume, they realize that Santa's sack couldn't possibly hold enough toys for millions of girls and boys.

The Formal Operations Stage (11 Years and Up)

After about the age of 11, children begin to break away from concrete objects and specific examples. Thinking is based more on abstract principles, such as "democracy," "honor," or "correlation." Children who reach this stage become self-reflective about their thoughts, and they become less egocentric. Older children and young adolescents also gradually become able to consider hypothetical possibilities (suppositions, guesses, or projections). For example, if you ask a younger child, "What do you think would happen if it suddenly became possible for people to fly?" the child might respond, "People can't fly." Older children are better able to consider such possibilities.

Full adult intellectual ability is attained during the stage of formal operations. Older adolescents are capable of inductive and deductive reasoning, and they can comprehend math, physics, philosophy, psychology, and other abstract systems. They can learn to test hypotheses in a scientific manner. Of course, not everyone reaches this level of thinking. Also, many adults can think formally about some topics, but their thinking becomes concrete when the topic is unfamiliar. This implies that formal thinking may be more a result of culture and learning than maturation. In any case, after late adolescence, improvements

Concrete operational stage Period of intellectual development during which children become able to use the concepts of time, space, volume, and number, but in ways that remain simplified and concrete, rather than abstract.

Conservation In Piaget's theory, mastery of the concept that the weight, mass, and volume of matter remains unchanged (is conserved) even when the shape or appearance of objects changes.

Formal operations stage Period of intellectual development characterized by thinking that includes abstract, theoretical, and hypothetical ideas.

in intellect are based on gaining specific knowledge, experience, and wisdom, rather than on any leaps in basic thinking capacity.

How can parents apply Piaget's ideas? Piaget's theory suggests that the ideal way to guide intellectual development is to provide experiences that are only slightly novel, unusual, or challenging. Remember, a child's intellect develops mainly through accommodation. It is usually best to follow a *one-step-ahead strategy,* in which your teaching efforts are aimed just beyond a child's current level of comprehension (Brainerd, 2003).

Parents should avoid *forced teaching,* or "hothousing," which is like trying to force plants to bloom prematurely. Forcing children to learn reading, math, gymnastics, swimming, or music at an accelerated pace can bore or oppress them. True intellectual enrichment respects the child's interests. It does not make the child feel pressured to perform (Alvino et al., 1996).

For your convenience, ● Table 3.2 briefly summarizes each Piagetian stage. To help you remember Piaget's theory, the table describes what would happen at each stage if we played a game of *Monopoly* with the child. You'll also find brief suggestions about how to relate to children in each stage.

Piaget Today

Piaget's theory is a valuable "road map" for understanding how children think. However, many psychologists are convinced that Piaget gave too little credit to the effects of the learning environment. For example, children who grow up in villages where pottery is made can correctly answer questions about the conservation of clay at an earlier age than Piaget would have predicted.

● Table 3.2 Piaget—A Guide for Parents

PIAGET	MONOPOLY GAME	GUIDELINES FOR PARENTS
Sensorimotor Stage (0–2 Years) The stage during which sensory input and motor responses become coordinated.	The child puts houses, hotels, and dice in her mouth and plays with "Chance" cards.	Active play with a child is most effective at this stage. Encourage explorations in touching, smelling, and manipulating objects. Peekaboo is a good way to establish the permanence of objects.
Preoperational Stage (2–7 Years) The period of cognitive development when children begin to use language and think symbolically, yet remain intuitive and egocentric.	The child plays Monopoly, but makes up her own rules and cannot understand instructions.	Specific examples and touching or seeing things continues to be more useful than verbal explanations. Learning the concept of conservation may be aided by demonstrations with liquids, beads, clay, and other substances.
Concrete Operational Stage (7–11 Years) The period of cognitive development during which children begin to use concepts of time, space, volume, and number, but in ways that remain simplified and concrete.	The child understands basic instructions and will play by the rules, but is not capable of hypothetical transactions dealing with mortgages, loans, and special pacts with other players.	Children are beginning to use generalizations, but they still require specific examples to grasp many ideas. Expect a degree of inconsistency in the child's ability to apply concepts of time, space, quantity, and volume to new situations.
Formal Operations Stage (11 Years and Up) The period of intellectual development marked by a capacity for abstract, theoretical, and hypothetical thinking.	The child no longer plays the game mechanically; complex and hypothetical transactions unique to each game are now possible.	It is now more effective to explain things verbally or symbolically and to help children master general rules and principles. Encourage the child to create hypotheses and to imagine how things could be.

3 to 6 years

7 to 15 years

16 to 20 years

◀◀ **FIGURE 3.14** Between the ages of 3 and 6 a tremendous wave of growth occurs in connections among neurons in the frontal areas of the brain. This corresponds to the time when children make rapid progress in their ability to think symbolically. Between ages 7 and 15, peak synaptic growth shifts to the temporal and parietal lobes. During this period children become increasingly adept at using language, a specialty of the temporal lobes. In the late teens, the brain actively destroys unneeded connections, especially in the frontal lobes. This pruning of synapses sharpens the brain's capacity for abstract thinking. (Courtesy of Dr. Paul Thompson, Laboratory of Neuro Imaging, UCLA School of Medicine.)

According to learning theorists, children continuously gain specific knowledge; they do not undergo stage-like leaps in general mental ability (Siegler, 2004). On the other hand, the growth in connections between brain cells occurs in waves that parallel some of Piaget's stages (see ▶▶ Figure 3.14). Thus, the truth may lie somewhere between Piaget's stage theory and modern learning theory.

On a broad scale, many of Piaget's *observations* have held up well. However, his *explanations* of childhood thinking abilities continue to be debated (Feldman, 2004). Where early infancy is concerned, even Piaget's observations may need updating. It looks like Piaget greatly underestimated the mental abilities of infants.

Infant Cognition

What evidence is there that Piaget underestimated infant abilities? Piaget believed that infants under the age of 1 year cannot think (use internal representations). Babies, he said, can have no memory of people and objects that are out of sight. Yet, we now know that infants begin forming representations of the world very early in life. For example, babies as young as 3 months of age appear to know that objects are solid and do not disappear when out of view (Baillargeon, 2004).

Why did Piaget fail to detect the thinking skills of infants? Most likely, he mistook babies' limited *physical* skills for *mental* incompetence. Piaget's tests required babies to search for objects or reach out and touch them. Newer, more sensitive methods are uncovering abilities Piaget missed. One such method takes advantage of the fact that babies, like adults, act surprised when they see something "impossible" or unexpected occur. To use this effect, psychologist Renee Baillargeon (1991, 2004) puts on little "magic shows" for infants. In her "theater," babies watch as possible and impossible events occur with toys or other objects. Some 3-month-old infants act surprised and gaze longer at impossible events. An example is seeing two solid objects appear to pass through each other. By the time they are 8 months old, babies can remember where objects are (or should be) for at least 1 minute (▶▶ Figure 3.15).

Piaget believed that abilities like those described in Figure 3.15 emerge only after a long period of sensorimotor development. However, it's clear that babies quickly acquire the capacity to form concepts about the world (Eimas, Quinn, & Cowan, 1994). It looks as if further study is likely to refine and amend the ideas that grew from Piaget's fateful decision to "watch the children for a while."

Another criticism of Piaget is that he underestimated the impact of culture on mental development. The next section tells how Samantha will master the intellectual tools valued by her culture.

"Young man, go to your room and stay there until your cerebral cortex matures."

▲ FIGURE 3.15 The panels on the left show a possible event, in which an infant watches as a toy is placed behind the right of two screens. After a delay of 70 seconds, the toy is brought into view from behind the right screen. In the two panels on the right, an impossible event occurs. The toy is placed behind the left screen and retrieved from behind the right. (A duplicate toy was hidden there before testing.) Eight-month-old infants react with surprise when they see the impossible event staged for them. Their reaction implies that they remember where the toy was hidden. Infants appear to have a capacity for memory and thinking that greatly exceeds what Piaget claimed is possible during the sensorimotor period. (Adapted from Baillargeon, R., De Vos, J., & Graber, M. "Location memory in 8-month-old infants in a non-search AB task." Cognitive Development, 4, 345–367. [Figure 1, p. 351]. Copyright © 1989, with permission from Elsevier.)

Vygotsky's Sociocultural Theory∗

While Piaget stressed the role of maturation in cognitive development, Russian scholar Lev Vygotsky (1896–1934) focused on the impact of sociocultural factors. Vygotsky's (1962, 1978) key insight is that children's thinking develops through dialogues with more capable persons.

How does that relate to intellectual growth? So far, no one has published *A Child's Guide to Life on Earth.* Instead, children must learn about life from various "tutors," such as parents, teachers, and older siblings. Even if *A Child's Guide to Life on Earth* did exist, we would need a separate version for every culture. It is not enough for children to learn how to think. They must also learn specific intellectual skills valued by their culture.

Like Piaget, Vygotsky believed that children actively seek to discover new principles. However, Vygotsky emphasized that many of a child's most important "discoveries" are guided by skillful tutors. Psychologists David Shaffer and Katherine Kipp (2010) offer the following example:

> Tonya, a 4-year-old, has just received her first jigsaw puzzle as a birthday present. She attempts to work the puzzle but gets nowhere until her father comes along, sits down beside her, and gives her some tips. He suggests that it would be a good idea to put together the corners first, points to the pink area at the edge of one corner piece, and says, "Let's look for another pink piece." When Tonya seems frustrated, he places two interlocking pieces near each other so that she will notice them, and when Tonya succeeds, he offers words of encouragement. As Tonya gradually gets the hang of it, he steps back and lets her work more and more independently. (p. 283)

Interactions like this are most helpful when they take place within a child's **zone of proximal development.**

What did Vygotsky mean by that? The word *proximal* means close or nearby. Vygotsky realized that, at any given time, some tasks are just beyond a child's reach. The child is close to having the mental skills needed to do the task, but it is a little too complex to be mastered alone. However, children working within this zone can make rapid progress if they receive sensitive guidance from a skilled partner (LeBlanc & Bearison, 2004). (Notice that this is similar to the one-step-ahead strategy described earlier.)

Zone of proximal development Refers to the range of tasks a child cannot yet master alone, but that she or he can accomplish with the guidance of a more capable partner.

Vygotsky also emphasized a process he called **scaffolding.** A scaffold is a framework or temporary support. Vygotsky believed that adults help children learn how to think by "scaffolding," or supporting, their attempts to solve problems or discover principles (Daniels, 2005). To be most effective, scaffolding must be responsive to a child's needs. For example, as Tonya's father helped her with the puzzle, he tailored his hints and guidance to match her evolving abilities. The two of them worked together, step by step, so that Tonya could better understand how to assemble a puzzle. In a sense, Tonya's father set up a series of temporary bridges that helped her move into new mental territory. As predicted by Vygotsky's theory, the reading skills of 8- to 10-year-old children are closely related to the amount of verbal scaffolding their mothers provided at ages 3 and 4 (Dieterich et al., 2006).

During their collaborations with others, children learn important cultural beliefs and values. For example, imagine that a boy wants to know how many baseball cards he has. His mother helps him stack and count the cards, moving each card to a new stack as they count it. She then shows him how to write the number on a slip of paper so he can remember it. This teaches the child not only about counting, but also that writing is valued in our culture. In other parts of the world, a child learning to count might be shown how to make notches on a stick or tie knots in a cord.

Implications

Scaffolding The process of adjusting instruction so that it is responsive to a beginner's behavior and supports the beginner's efforts to understand a problem or gain a mental skill.

Vygotsky saw that grown-ups play a crucial role in what children know. As they try to decipher the world, children rely on adults to help them understand how things work. Vygotsky further noticed that adults unconsciously adjust their behavior to give children the information they need to solve problems that interest the child. In this way, children use adults to learn about their culture and society (Gopnik, Meltzoff, & Kuhl, 2000; LeBlanc & Bearison, 2004).

study break
Cognitive Development in Childhood

RECITE

Match each item with one of the following stages.
A. Sensorimotor   B. Preoperational   C. Concrete operational
D. Formal operations

_____ 1. egocentric thought   _____ 2. abstract or hypothetical

_____ 3. purposeful movement   _____ 4. intuitive thought

_____ 5. conservation   _____ 6. reversibility thought

_____ 7. object permanence   _____ 8. nonverbal development

9. *Assimilation* refers to applying existing thought patterns or knowledge to new situations. T or F?
10. Newer methods for testing infant thinking abilities frequently make note of whether an infant is _____ by seemingly _____ events.
11. Vygotsky called the process of providing a temporary framework of supports for learning new mental abilities _____.

REFLECT
Critical Thinking

12. Using Piaget's theory as a guide, at what age would you expect a child to recognize that a Styrofoam cup has weight?

Relate

You are going to make cookies with children of various ages. See if you can name each of Piaget's stages and give an example of what a child in that stage might be expected to do.

You have been asked to help a child learn to use a pocket calculator to do simple addition. How would you go about identifying the child's zone of proximal development for this task? How would you scaffold the child's learning?

ANSWERS

1. B 2. D 3. A 4. B 5. C 6. C 7. A 8. A 9. T 10. surprised, impossible 11. scaffolding 12. Seventy-five percent of 4- to 6-year-olds say that a Styrofoam cup has no weight after lifting it! Most children judge weight intuitively (by the way an object feels) until they begin to move into the concrete operational stage (Smith, Carey, & Wiser, 1985).

Adolescence and Young Adulthood— The Best of Times, the Worst of Times

Why is the transition from adolescence to adulthood especially challenging?

Adolescence and young adulthood is a time of change, youthful exploration, and exuberance. It can also be a time of worry and problems, especially in today's world. It might even be fair to describe this period as "the best of times, the worst of times." During adolescence, a person's identity and moral values come into sharper focus even as the transition to adulthood is occurring at ever-later ages.

Adolescence is the culturally defined period between childhood and adulthood. Socially, the adolescent is no longer a child, yet not quite an adult. Almost all cultures recognize this transitional status. However, the length of adolescence varies greatly from culture to culture. For example, most 14-year-old girls in North America live at home and go to school. In contrast, many 14-year-old females in rural villages of many poorer countries are married and have children. In our culture, 14-year-olds are adolescents. In others, they may be adults.

Is marriage the primary criterion for adult status in North America? No, it's not even one of the top three criteria. Today, the most widely accepted standards are (1) taking responsibility for oneself, (2) making independent decisions, and (3) becoming financially independent. In practice, this typically means breaking away from parents by taking a job and setting up a separate residence (Arnett, 2001).

Puberty

Many people confuse adolescence with puberty. However, puberty is a *biological* event, not a social status. During **puberty,** hormonal changes promote rapid physical growth and sexual maturity. Biologically, most people reach reproductive maturity in the early teens. Social and intellectual maturity, however, may lie years ahead. Young adolescents often make decisions that affect their entire lives, even though they are immature mentally and socially. The tragically high rates of teenage pregnancy and drug abuse are prime examples. Despite such risks, most people do manage to weather adolescence without developing any serious psychological problems (Steinberg, 2001).

How much difference does the timing of puberty make? For boys, maturing early is generally beneficial. Typically, it enhances their self-image and gives them an advantage socially and athletically. Early-maturing boys tend to be more relaxed, dominant, self-assured, and popular. However, early puberty does carry some risks because early-maturing boys are also more likely to get into trouble with drugs, alcohol, and antisocial behavior (Steinberg, 2001).

For girls, the advantages of early maturation are less clear-cut. In elementary school, fast-maturing girls are *less* popular and have poorer self-images, perhaps because they are larger and heavier than their classmates (Deardorff et al, 2007). By junior high, however, early development includes sexual features. This leads to a more positive body image, *greater* peer prestige, and adult approval (Brooks-Gunn & Warren, 1988). Early-maturing girls tend to date sooner and are more independent and more active in school. However, like their male counterparts, they are also more often in trouble at school and more likely to engage in early sex (Flannery et al., 1993).

As you can see, there are costs and benefits associated with early puberty. One added cost of early maturation is that it may force premature identity formation. When Samantha is a teenager and she begins to look like an adult, she may be treated like an adult. Ideally, this change can encourage greater maturity and independence. However, if the search for identity ends too soon, it may leave Samantha with a distorted, poorly formed sense of self (▶▶ Figure 3.16).

Adolescence The culturally defined period between childhood and adulthood.

Puberty The biologically defined period during which a person matures sexually and becomes capable of reproduction.

Ethnic Diversity and Identity

Ethnic heritage can have a powerful influence on personal identity (Weisskirch, 2005). For adolescents of ethnic descent, the question is often not just "Who am I?" Rather, it is "Who am I at home? Who am I at school? Who am I with friends from my neighborhood?"

As ethnic minorities in America continue to grow in status and prominence, adolescents are less and less likely to feel rejected or excluded because of their ethnic heritage as they try to find their place in society. This is fortunate because ethnic adolescents have often faced degrading stereotypes concerning their intelligence, sexual-

ity, social status, manners, and so forth. The result can be lowered self-esteem and confusion about roles, values, and personal identity (de las Fuentes & Vasquez, 1999). At the same time, the increasingly multicultural nature of contemporary American society raises new questions for adolescents about what it means to be American (Schwartz, 2008).

In forming an identity, adolescents of ethnic descent face the question of how they should think of themselves. Is Lori an American or a Chinese American or both? Is Jaime a Latino, a Chi-

cano, or a Mexican American? The answer typically depends on how strongly adolescents identify with their family and ethnic community. Teens who take pride in their ethnic heritage have higher self-esteem, a better self-image, and a stronger sense of personal identity (Roberts et al., 1999; Tse, 1999). They are also less likely to engage in drug use (Marsiglia et al., 2004) or violent behavior (French, Kim, & Pillado, 2006).

Group pride, positive models, and a more tolerant society could do much to keep a broad range of options open to *all* adolescents.

▲ FIGURE 3.16 Dramatic differences in physical size and maturity are found in adolescents of the same age. The girls pictured are all 13, the boys 16. Maturation that occurs earlier or later than average can affect the "search for identity." (Adapted from "Growing Up" by J. M. Tanner. Copyright © September 1973 by Scientific American, Inc. All rights reserved.)

The Search for Identity

Identity formation is a key task of adolescence (Schwartz, 2008). Of course, problems of identity occur at other times too. But in a very real sense, puberty signals that it's time to begin forming a new, more mature self-image (Douvan, 1997). Many problems stem from unclear standards about the role adolescents should play within society. Are they adults or children? Should they be autonomous or dependent? Should they work or play? Such ambiguities make it difficult for young people to form clear images of themselves and of how they should act (Alsaker, 1995).

Answering the question "Who am I?" is also spurred by cognitive development. After adolescents have attained the stage of formal operations, they are better able to ask questions about their place in the world and about morals, values, politics, and social relationships. Then too, being able to think about hypothetical possibilities allows the adolescent to contemplate the future and ask more realistically, "Who will I be?" (Côté, 2006b). (See "Ethnic Diversity and Identity.")

The Twixters

Is becoming an adult strictly a biological event? Meet 22-year-old Kirsten:

"When our mothers were our age, they were engaged. . . . They at least had some idea what they were going to do with their lives. . . . I, on the other hand, will have a dual degree in majors that are ambiguous at best and impractical at worst (English and political science), no ring on my finger and no idea who I am, much less what I want to do. . . . I realize that having nothing ahead to count on means I now have to count on myself; that having no direction means forging one of my own." (Page, 1999).

Kirsten is a "twixter": twentysomething, still living at home, not yet married, with no children, and no settled career. In England, twixters are called "kippers" (Kids In Parents' Pockets Eroding Retirement Savings). In Australia they are "boomerang kids" (they always come back home). And in Germany they are "Nesthocker" (nest squatters). Are twixters adolescents who are taking longer to find their identity? Or are they young adults avoiding their need to enter the adult world? Are they self-indulgent individuals trapped in a "maturity gap" (Galambos, Barker, & Tilton-Weaver, 2003)? Or are they part of a new social status that could be called "emerging adulthood" (Arnett & Tanner, 2006)?

According to psychologist Jeffrey Arnett, emerging adulthood is increasingly common in affluent Westernized cultures that allow young people to take longer to settle into their adult roles (Arnett, 2000, 2004). However, in less affluent countries, as in poorer parts of America, most adolescents continue to "become adults" at much younger ages (Arnett & Galambos, 2003). Thus, words like *adolescent* or *adulthood* cannot be defined solely in terms of physical maturation. Sociocultural factors also play a role in defining when we stop being children or become adults (Arnett, 2004).

The Transition to Adulthood

Today the challenge of identity formation is further complicated by the fact that more and more young people are deferring young adulthood, preferring to prolong identity explorations into their twenties before they commit to long-term choices in love and work (Arnett, 2000, 2004; Arnett & Tanner, 2006). According to sociologist James Côté, Western industrialized societies, like the United States and Canada, are becoming increasingly tolerant of this period of extended adolescence (Côté, 2006a). (See "The Twixters.")

Samantha may live with Carol and David until her mid-twenties, delaying her transition to adulthood. Alternatively, she may make the transition to young adulthood during the traditional 18-to-21 period. Regardless, she will eventually face the primary adult issues of marriage, children, and career. How she manages, especially in her core relationships, will determine whether she feels a sense of intimacy or feels isolated from others.

In many ways adolescence and young adulthood are more emotionally turbulent than midlife or old age. One important aspect of the emotional turbulence of adolescence and young adulthood is the struggle with right and wrong—in other words, the need to develop moral values.

Moral Development—Growing a Conscience

How do we develop morals and values?

A person with a terminal illness is in great pain. She is pleading for death. Should extraordinary medical efforts be made to keep her alive? A friend of yours desperately needs to pass a test and asks you to help him cheat. Will you do it? These are *moral* questions, or questions of conscience.

Moral development starts in childhood and continues into adulthood (Turiel, 2006). Through this process, we acquire values, beliefs, and thinking patterns that guide responsible behavior. Moral values are especially likely to come into sharper focus during adolescence and the transition to adulthood, as capacities for self-control and abstract thinking increase (Hart & Carlo, 2005). Let's take a brief look at this interesting aspect of personal development.

Moral development The development of values, beliefs, and thinking abilities that act as a guide regarding what is acceptable behavior.

Levels of Moral Development

How are moral values acquired? In an influential account, psychologist Lawrence Kohlberg (1981) held that we learn moral values through thinking and reasoning. To study moral development, Kohlberg posed dilemmas to children of different ages. The following is one of the moral dilemmas he used (Kohlberg, 1969, adapted):

> A woman was near death from cancer and there was only one drug that might save her. It was discovered by a druggist who was charging 10 times what it cost to make the drug. The sick woman's husband could pay only $1,000, but the druggist wanted $2,000. He asked the druggist to sell it cheaper or to let him pay later. The druggist said no. So the husband became desperate and broke into the store to steal the drug for his wife. Should he have done that? Was it wrong or right? Why?

Each child was asked what action the husband should take. Kohlberg classified the reasons given for each choice and identified three levels of moral development. Each is based not so much on the choices made, but on the reasoning used to arrive at a choice.

At the lowest, **preconventional level,** moral thinking is guided by the consequences of actions (punishment, reward, or an exchange of favors). For example, a person at this level might reason: "The man shouldn't steal the drug because he could get caught and sent to jail" (avoiding punishment) or "It won't do him any good to steal the drug because his wife will probably die before he gets out of jail" (self-interest).

At the second, **conventional level,** reasoning is based on a desire to please others or to follow accepted authority, rules, and values. For example, a person at this intermediate level might say: "He shouldn't steal the drug because others will think he is a thief. His wife would not want to be saved by thievery" (avoiding disapproval) or "Although his wife needs the drug, he should not break the law to get it. Everyone has to obey the law. His wife's condition does not justify stealing" (traditional morality of authority).

At the highest, **postconventional level,** moral behavior is directed by self-chosen ethical principles that tend to be general, comprehensive, or universal. People at this level place high value on justice, dignity, and equality. For example, a highly principled person might say: "He should steal the drug and then inform the authorities that he has done so. He will have to face a penalty, but he will have saved a human life" (self-chosen ethical principles).

Does everyone eventually reach the highest level? People advance at different rates, and many fail to reach the postconventional level of moral reasoning. In fact, many do not even reach the conventional level. For instance, one English survey revealed that 11 percent of men and 3 percent of women would commit murder for $1 million if they could be sure of getting away with the crime ("They'd kill," 1991).

The preconventional level is most characteristic of young children and delinquents (Forney, Forney, & Crutsinger, 2005). Conventional, group-oriented morals are typical of older children and most adults. Kohlberg estimated that only about 20 percent of the adult population achieves postconventional morality, representing self-direction and higher principles. (It would appear that few of these people enter politics!)

Developing a "moral compass" is an important part of growing up. Many of the choices we make every day involve fundamental questions of right and wrong. Being able to think clearly about such questions is essential to becoming a responsible adult.

Preconventional moral reasoning Moral thinking based on the consequences of one's choices or actions (punishment, reward, or an exchange of favors).

Conventional moral reasoning Moral thinking based on a desire to please others or to follow accepted rules and values.

Postconventional moral reasoning Moral thinking based on carefully examined and self-chosen moral principles.

RECITE

1. In North America the primary criterion for the transition from adolescence to adulthood is marriage. T or F?
2. Identify formation is spurred by _____ and _____.
3. According to Jeffrey Arnett, the trend in affluent Westernized cultures towards allowing young people to take longer to settle into their adult roles is best referred to as
   a. emerging adulthood   b. hurried childhood
   c. a maturity gap   d. extended adolescence
4. According to Kohlberg, the conventional level of moral development is marked by a reliance on outside authority. T or F?
5. Self-interest and avoiding punishment are elements of postconventional morality. T or F?
6. About 80 percent of all adults function at the postconventional level of moral reasoning. T or F?

REFLECT

Critical Thinking

7. Are labels like "adolescent" or "young adult" reflective of heredity or environment?

Relate

To what extent does the concept of identity formation apply to your own experience during adolescence?

Do you know any twixters? (Are you one?) Do you think twixters are adolescents taking longer to find their identity or young adults avoiding their need to establish themselves in the world of adults?

At what stage of moral development do you think most terrorists function?

ANSWERS

1. F 2. puberty, cognitive development 3. a 4. T 5. F 6. F 7. Environment, rather than heredity, is the better answer. Even better, the meanings of terms like "adolescence" or "adult" vary considerably from culture to culture indicating that it is really a matter of definition (Côté, 2006a).

The Story of a Lifetime—Rocky Road or Garden Path?

What are the typical tasks and dilemmas through the life span?

[handwritten: Exam Q's II 11]

At the beginning of this chapter we noted that developmental psychologists are interested in every phase of life from the womb to the tomb. Thus far, we have concentrated on Samantha's early years because development during childhood can have a large impact on a person's life.

Every life is marked by a number of *developmental milestones*. These are notable events, markers, or turning points in personal development (Kail & Cavanaugh, 2010). Some examples include graduating from school, voting for the first time, getting married, watching a child leave home (or move back!), the death of a parent, becoming a grandparent, retirement, and one's own death. Thus far, we have traced Samantha's progress through childhood, adolescence, and young adulthood. What challenges lie ahead for her?

Erikson's Psychosocial Theory

[handwritten: social influences]

Perhaps the best way to get a preview of Samantha's life is to consider some of the major psychological challenges she is likely to encounter. Broad similarities can be found in the life stages of infancy, childhood, adolescence, young adulthood, middle adulthood, and old age. Each stage confronts a person with new **developmental tasks** that must be mastered for optimal development. Examples are learning to read in childhood, adjusting to sexual maturity in adolescence, and establishing a vocation as an adult.

Developmental task Any skill that must be mastered, or personal change that must take place, for optimal development.

Table 3.3 Erikson's Psychosocial Dilemmas

AGE	CHARACTERISTIC DILEMMA
Birth to 1 year	Trust versus mistrust
1 to 3 years	Autonomy versus shame and doubt
3 to 5 years	Initiative versus guilt
6 to 12 years	Industry versus inferiority
Adolescence	Identity versus role confusion
Young adulthood	Intimacy versus isolation
Middle adulthood	Generativity versus stagnation
Late adulthood	Integrity versus despair

In an influential book entitled *Childhood and Society,* personality theorist Erik Erikson (1903–1994) suggests that we face a specific *psychosocial dilemma,* or "crisis," at each stage of life. A **psychosocial dilemma** is a conflict between personal impulses and the social world. Resolving each dilemma creates a new balance between a person and society. A string of "successes" produces healthy development and a satisfying life. Unfavorable outcomes throw us off balance, making it harder to deal with later crises. Life becomes a "rocky road" and personal growth is stunted. ● Table 3.3 lists Erikson's (1963) dilemmas.

What are the major developmental tasks and life crises? A brief description of each psychosocial dilemma follows.

Personality theorist Erik Erikson (1903–1994) is best known for his life-stage theory of human development.

Stage One, First Year of Life: Trust Versus Mistrust

During the first year of life, children are completely dependent on others. Erikson believes that a basic attitude of trust or mistrust is formed at this time. **Trust** is established when babies are given warmth, touching, love, and physical care. **Mistrust** is caused by inadequate or unpredictable care and by parents who are cold, indifferent, or rejecting. Basic mistrust may later cause insecurity, suspiciousness, or an inability to relate to others. Notice that trust comes from the same conditions that help babies become securely attached to their parents.

Stage Two, 1–3 Years: Autonomy Versus Shame and Doubt

In stage two, children express their growing self-control by climbing, touching, exploring, and trying to do things for themselves. David and Carol fostered Samantha's sense of **autonomy** by encouraging her to try new skills. However, her first efforts were sometimes crude, involving spilling, falling, wetting, and other "accidents." If David and Carol had ridiculed or overprotected Samantha, they might have caused her to feel **shameful** about her actions and **doubt** her abilities.

Stage Three, 3–5 Years: Initiative Versus Guilt

In stage three, children move beyond simple self-control and begin to take initiative. Through play, children learn to make plans and carry out tasks. Parents reinforce **initiative** by giving children freedom to play, ask questions, use imagination, and choose activities. Feelings of **guilt** about initiating activities are formed if parents criticize severely, prevent play, or discourage a child's questions.

Stage Four, 6–12 Years: Industry Versus Inferiority

Many events of middle childhood are symbolized by that fateful day when you first entered school. With dizzying speed your world expanded beyond your family, and you faced a whole series of new challenges.

The elementary school years are a child's "entrance into life." In school, children begin to learn skills valued by society, and success or failure can affect a child's feelings of adequacy. Children learn a sense of **industry** if they win praise for productive activities, such as building, painting, cooking, reading, and studying. If a child's efforts are regarded as messy, childish, or inadequate, feelings of **inferiority** result. For the first time, teachers,

Psychosocial dilemma A conflict between personal impulses and the social world.

Trust versus mistrust A conflict early in life about learning to trust others and the world.

Autonomy versus shame and doubt A conflict created when growing self-control (autonomy) is pitted against feelings of shame and doubt.

Initiative versus guilt A conflict between learning to take initiative and overcoming feelings of guilt about doing so.

Industry versus inferiority A conflict in middle childhood centered around lack of support for industrious behavior, which can result in feelings of inferiority.

Sarah Putnam/Photolibrary

classmates, and adults outside the home become as important as parents in shaping attitudes toward oneself.

Stage Five, Adolescence: Identity Versus Role Confusion 11-17

As we have noted, adolescence is often a turbulent time. Erikson considers a need to answer the question "Who am I?" the primary task during this stage of life. As Samantha matures mentally and physically, she will have new feelings, a new body, and new attitudes. Like other adolescents, she will need to build a consistent **identity** out of her talents, values, life history, relationships, and the demands of her culture (Côté & Levine, 2002). Her conflicting experiences as a student, friend, athlete, worker, daughter, lover, and so forth must be integrated into a unified sense of self. Persons who fail to develop a sense of identity suffer from **role confusion,** an uncertainty about who they are and where they are going.

Stage Six, Young Adulthood: Intimacy Versus Isolation 18-40

What does Erikson believe is the major conflict in early adulthood? In stage six, the individual feels a need for *intimacy* in his or her life. After establishing a stable identity, a person is prepared to share meaningful love or deep friendship with others. By **intimacy,** Erikson means an ability to care about others and to share experiences with them. In line with Erikson's view, 75 percent of college-age men and women rank a good marriage and family life as important adult goals (Bachman & Johnson, 1979). And yet, marriage or sexual involvement is no guarantee of intimacy: Many adult relationships remain shallow and unfulfilling. Failure to establish intimacy with others leads to a deep sense of **isolation** (feeling alone and uncared for in life). This often sets the stage for later difficulties.

Stage Seven, Middle Adulthood: Generativity Versus Stagnation 40-60

According to Erikson, an interest in guiding the next generation provides emotional balance in mature adulthood. Erikson called this quality **generativity.** It is expressed by caring about oneself, one's children, and future generations. Generativity may be achieved by guiding one's own children or by helping other children (as a teacher or coach, for example). Productive or creative work can also express generativity. In any case, a person must broaden his or her concerns and energies to include the welfare of others and society as a whole. Failure to do this is marked by a **stagnant** concern with one's own needs and comforts. Life loses meaning, and the person feels bitter, dreary, and trapped (Friedman, 2004).

Stage Eight, Late Adulthood: Integrity Versus Despair 60-Death

What does Erikson see as the conflicts of old age? Old age is a time of reflection. According to Erikson, when Samantha grows old she must be able to look back over her life with acceptance and satisfaction. People who have lived richly and responsibly develop a sense of **integrity** (self-respect). This allows them to face aging and death with dignity. If previous life events are viewed with regret, the elderly person experiences **despair** (heartache and remorse). In this case, life seems like a series of missed opportunities. The person feels like a failure and knows it's too late to reverse what has been done. Aging and the threat of death then become sources of fear and depression.

The Life Span in Perspective

To squeeze a lifetime into a few pages, we had to ignore countless details. Although much is lost, the result is a clearer picture of an entire life cycle. Is Erikson's description, then, an exact map of Samantha's past and her future—or your own? Probably not. Still, psychosocial dilemmas are major events in many lives. Knowing about them may allow you to anticipate typical trouble spots in your own life. You may also be better prepared to understand the problems and feelings of friends and relatives at various points in the life cycle.

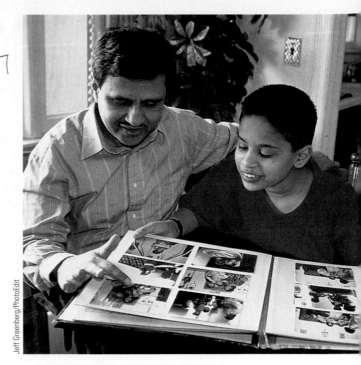

Jeff Greenberg/PhotoEdit

According to Erikson, an interest in future generations characterizes optimal adult development.

Identity versus role confusion A conflict of adolescence, involving the need to establish a personal identity.

Intimacy versus isolation The challenge of overcoming a sense of isolation by establishing intimacy with others.

Generativity versus stagnation A conflict of middle adulthood in which self-interest is countered by an interest in guiding the next generation.

Integrity versus despair A conflict in old age between feelings of integrity and the despair of viewing previous life events with regret.

Middle and Late Adulthood: Will You Still Need Me When I'm 64?

What is involved in well-being during later adulthood?

Although Erikson's dilemmas extend into adulthood, they are not the only challenges adults face. Others are all too familiar: marital strife, divorce, career difficulties, unemployment, health problems, financial pressures, legal conflicts, and personal tragedies—to name but a few. How do people maintain a state of well-being as they run the gauntlet of modern life? Psychologist Carol Ryff (1995; Ryff, Singer, & Palmersheim, 2004) believes that well-being during adulthood has six elements:

1. Self-acceptance
2. Positive relations with others
3. Autonomy (personal freedom)
4. Environmental mastery
5. A purpose in life
6. Continued personal growth

Ryff found that for many adults, age-related declines are offset by positive relationships and greater mastery of life's demands (Ryff & Keyes, 1995). Thus, sharing life's joys and sorrows with others, coupled with a better understanding of how the world works, can help carry people through midlife and into their later years (Ryff & Singer, 2000; Ryff, Singer, & Palmersheim, 2004). Despite the emphasis on youth in our culture, middle age and beyond can be a rich period of life in which people feel secure, happy, and self-confident (Rubenstein, 2002).

A Midlife Crisis?

But don't people face a "midlife crisis" at this point in their lives? Actually, it is more common to make a "midcourse correction," at midlife than it is to survive a "crisis" (Lachman, 2004). Only about a quarter of men and women believe they have experienced a midlife crisis (Wethington, Kessler, & Pixley, 2004). Ideally, the midlife transition involves reworking old identities, achieving valued goals, finding one's own truths, and preparing for old age. Taking stock may be especially valuable at midlife, but reviewing past choices to prepare for the future is helpful at any age (Lewchanin & Zubrod, 2001). For some people, difficult turning points in life can serve as "wake-up calls" that create opportunities for personal growth (Wethington, 2003).

Old Age

After the late fifties, personal development is complicated by physical aging. However, it is wrong to believe that most elderly people are sickly, infirm, or senile. (Nowadays, 60 is the new 40, an idea that both of your authors wholeheartedly agree with!) Only about 5 percent of those older than 65 are in nursing homes. Mentally, many elderly persons are at least as capable as the average young adult. On intellectual tests, top scorers over the age of 65 match the average for men younger than 35. What sets these silver-haired stars apart? Typically they are people who have continued to work and remain intellectually active (Salthouse, 2004). Gerontologist Warner Schaie (1994, 2005) found that you are most likely to stay mentally sharp in old age if:

1. You remain healthy.
2. You live in a favorable environment. (You are educated and have a stimulating occupation, an above-average income, and an intact family.)
3. You are involved in intellectually stimulating activities (reading, travel, cultural events, continuing education, clubs, professional associations).

4. You have a flexible personality.
5. You are married to a smart spouse.
6. You maintain your perceptual processing speed.
7. You were satisfied with your accomplishments in midlife.

A shorter summary of this list is "Those who live by their wit die with their wits."

Successful Aging

What are the keys to successful aging? They are not unlike the elements of well-being at midlife. Four psychological characteristics shared by the healthiest, happiest older people are (de Leon, 2005; Vaillant, 2002):

Optimism, hope, and an interest in the future

Gratitude and forgiveness; an ability to focus on what is good in life

Empathy; an ability to share the feelings of others and see the world through their eyes

Connection with others; an ability to reach out, to give and receive social support

Actually, these are excellent guidelines for well-being at any stage of adulthood.

In summary, enlightened views of aging call for an end to the forced obsolescence of the elderly. As a group, older people represent a valuable source of skill, knowledge, and energy that we can't afford to cast aside. As we face the challenges of this planet's uncertain future, we need all the help we can get!

At age 77, John Glenn became the oldest person to fly into space, in October 1998. Glenn was also the first American astronaut to orbit Earth, in 1962. As Glenn's space adventure shows, aging does not inevitably bring an end to engaging in challenging activities.

[handwritten margin note: 1. Stay out of sun 2. smoke/drink moderation]

Aging and Ageism

You have almost certainly encountered ageism in one way or another. **Ageism,** which refers to discrimination or prejudice based on age, can oppress the young as well as the old. For instance, a person applying for a job may just as well be told "You're too young" as "You're too old." In some societies, ageism is expressed as respect for the elderly. In Japan, for instance, aging is seen as positive, and greater age brings more status and respect. In most Western nations, however, ageism tends to have a negative impact on older individuals (Ng, 2002).

Ageism is often expressed through patronizing language. Older people are frequently spoken to in an overly polite, slow, loud, and simple way, implying that they are infirm, even when they are not (Nelson, 2005). Popular stereotypes of the "dirty old man," "meddling old woman," "senile old fool," and the like also help perpetuate myths about aging. But such stereotypes are clearly wrong: A tremendous diversity exists among the elderly—ranging from the infirm to aerobic-dancing grandmothers.

In many occupations, older workers perform well in jobs that require *both* speed and skill. Of course, people do experience a gradual loss of *fluid abilities* (those requiring speed or rapid learning) as they age but, often, this can be offset by many *crystallized abilities* (learned knowledge and skills), such as vocabulary and stored-up facts, which may actually improve—at least into the sixties (Schaie, 2005). Overall, very little loss of job performance occurs as workers grow older. In the professions, wisdom and expertise can usually more than compensate for any loss of mental quickness (Ericsson, 2000). Basing retirement solely on a person's age makes little sense.

Ageism Discrimination or prejudice based on a person's age.

study break

Challenges Across the Lifespan

RECITE

As a way to improve your memory, you might find it helpful to summarize Erikson's eight life stages. Complete this do-it-yourself summary and compare your answers with those given below.

Stage	Crisis	Favorable Outcome
First year of life	1. _____ vs.	Faith in the environment and in others
	2. _____	
Ages 1–3	Autonomy vs.	Feelings of self-control and adequacy
	3. _____	
Ages 3–5	4. _____ vs. guilt	Ability to begin one's own activities
Ages 6–12	Industry vs.	Confidence in productive skills, learning how to work
	5. _____	
Adolescence	6. _____ vs. role confusion	An integrated image of oneself as a unique person
Young adulthood	Intimacy vs. 7. _____	Ability to form bonds of love and friendship with others
Middle adulthood	Generativity vs. 8. _____	Concern for family, society, and future generations
Late adulthood	9. _____ vs. 10. _____	Sense of dignity and fulfillment, willingness to face death

11. After age 65, a large proportion of older people show significant signs of mental disability and most require special care. T or F?
12. Job performance tends to decline rapidly in older workers. T or F?

REFLECT

Critical Thinking

13. Trying to make generalizations about development throughout life is complicated by at least one major factor. What do you think it is?

Relate

See if you can think of a person you know who is facing one of Erikson's psychosocial dilemmas. Now see if you can think of specific people who seem to be coping with each of the other dilemmas.

See if you can describe three instances of ageism you have witnessed.

ANSWERS

1. Trust 2. mistrust 3. shame or doubt 4. Initiative 5. inferiority 6. Identity 7. isolation 8. stagnation 9. Integrity 10. despair 11. F 12. F 13. Different *cohorts* (groups of people born in various decades may have very different life experiences. People born in the same year) live in different historical times. This makes it difficult to identify universal patterns (Stewart & Ostrove, 1998).

psychology in action

Effective Parenting—Raising Healthy Children

How do effective parents discipline and communicate with their children?

Authoritative parents help their children grow up with a capacity for love, joy, fulfillment, responsibility, and self-control through *positive parent–child interactions*. Positive interactions occur when parents spend enjoyable time encouraging their children in a loving and mutually respectful fashion (Dinkmeyer, McKay, & Dinkmeyer, 1997).

As any parent can tell you, it is all well and good to talk about positive interactions until little Johnny misbehaves (and he will, count on it!). As children mature and become more independent, parents must find ways to control their children's behavior ("No, you may not smear banana pudding on Daddy's face"). When parents fail to provide *discipline* (guidance regarding acceptable behavior), children become antisocial, aggressive, and insecure. And yet, it is not easy to have a positive interaction while disciplining your child. This is one reason why overly permissive parents avoid disciplining their children.

Effective discipline is created through communication that is fair but loving, authoritative yet sensitive. It socializes a child without destroying the bond of love and trust between parent and child. Children should feel free to express their deepest feelings. However, this does not mean they can do whatever they please. Rather, the child is allowed to move freely within consistent, well-defined boundaries for acceptable behavior.

Effective Discipline

Parents typically discipline children in one of three ways. **Power assertion** refers to physical punishment or a show of force, such as taking away toys or privileges. As an alternative, some parents use **withdrawal of love** (withholding affection) by refusing to speak to a child, threatening to leave, rejecting the child, or otherwise acting as if the child is temporarily unlovable. **Management techniques** combine praise, recognition, approval, rules, reasoning, and the like to encourage desirable behavior. Each of these approaches can control a child's behavior, but their side effects differ considerably.

What are the side effects? Power-oriented techniques—particularly harsh or severe physical punishment—are associated with fear, hatred of parents, and a lack of spontaneity and warmth. Most children show no signs of long-term damage from spanking—*if* spanking is backed up by supportive parenting (Baumrind, Larzelere, & Cowan, 2002). However, emotional damage does occur if spankings are severe, frequent, or coupled with harsh parenting. In addition, frequent spanking tends to increase aggression, and it leads to *more* problem behaviors, not fewer (McLoyd & Smith, 2002). After reviewing many studies, psychologist Elizabeth Gershoff (2002) concludes that parents should minimize spanking or avoid it entirely.

Withdrawal of love produces children who tend to be self-disciplined. You could say that such children have developed a good conscience. Often, they are described as "model" children or as unusually "good." But as a side effect, they are also frequently anxious, insecure, and dependent on adults for approval.

Management techniques also have limitations. Most important is the need to carefully adjust to a child's level of understanding. Younger children don't always see the connection between rules, explanations, and their own behavior. Nevertheless, management techniques receive a big plus in another area: There is a direct connection between discipline and a child's self-esteem.

How does discipline affect self-esteem? If you regard yourself as a worthwhile person, you have **self-esteem.** High self-esteem is essential for good emotional health. In elementary school, children with high self-esteem tend to be more popular, cooperative, and successful in class. Children with low self-esteem are more withdrawn and tend to perform below average (Amato & Fowler, 2002).

Low self-esteem is related to physical punishment and the withholding of love. And why not? What message do children receive if a parent beats them or tells them they are not worthy of love? Thus, it is best to minimize physical punishment and avoid withdrawal of love. In contrast, high self-esteem is promoted by management techniques. Children who feel that their parents support them emotionally tend to have high self-esteem (Amato & Fowler, 2002; Nielsen & Metha, 1994).

Can self-esteem ever get too high? Yes it can. According to clinical psychologist Maggie Mamen, many modern parents try to "empower" their children by imposing few limits on behavior, making them feel special, and giving them everything they want (Mamen, 2004). But such good intentions can backfire, leaving parents with children who have developed an artificially high level of self-esteem and a sense of entitlement. That is, overly permissive parenting produces spoiled, self-indulgent children who have little self-control (Baumrind, 1991). Their sense of entitlement can lead them to bully other children to get their way or even to engage in criminal activity. As adults, such children may become addicted to seeking ways to enhance their self-esteem. For example, they may place excessive importance on being physically attractive, leading to stress, drug and alcohol use, and eating disorders (Crocker & Park, 2004).

Consistent Discipline

Individual parents choose limits on behavior that are more "strict" or less "strict." But this choice is less important than **consistency** (maintaining stable rules of conduct). Consistent discipline gives a child a sense of security and stability. Inconsistency makes the child's world seem insecure and unpredictable.

Power assertion The use of physical punishment or coercion to enforce child discipline.

Withdrawal of love Withholding affection to enforce child discipline.

Management techniques Combining praise, recognition, approval, rules, and reasoning to enforce child discipline.

Self-esteem Regarding oneself as a worthwhile person; a positive evaluation of oneself.

Consistency With respect to child discipline, the maintenance of stable rules of conduct.

What does consistent discipline mean in practice? To illustrate the errors parents often make, let's consider a few examples of inconsistency (Fontenelle, 1989). The following are mistakes to avoid:

Saying one thing and doing something else. You tell the child, "Bart, if you don't eat your brussels sprouts, you can't have any dessert." Then you feel guilty and offer him some dessert.

Making statements you don't mean. "If you don't quiet down, I'm going to stop the car and make you walk home."

Changing *no* to *yes,* especially to quiet a nagging child. A good example is the parent who first refuses to buy the child a toy and later gives in and buys it.

Responding differently to the same misbehavior. One day a child is sent to his room for fighting with his sister. The next day the fighting is overlooked.

Inconsistency makes children feel angry and confused because they cannot control the consequences of their own behavior. Inconsistency also gives children the message "Don't believe what I say because I usually don't mean it."

Using Discipline Constructively

At one time or another, most parents use power assertion, withdrawal of love, or management techniques to control their children. Each mode of discipline has its place. However, physical punishment and withdrawal of love should always be used with caution. Here are some guidelines:

1. Parents should separate disapproval of the act from disapproval of the child. Instead of saying, "I'm going to punish you because *you are bad,*" say, "I'm upset about *what you did.*"

2. State specifically what misbehavior you are punishing. Explain why you have set limits on this kind of conduct.

3. Punishment should never be harsh or injurious. Don't physically punish a child while you are angry. Also remember that the message "I don't love you right now" can be more painful and damaging than any spanking.

4. Punishment, such as a scolding or taking away privileges, is most effective when done immediately. This is especially true for younger children.

5. Spanking and other forms of physical punishment are not particularly effective for children younger than age 2. The child will only be confused and frightened. Spankings also become less effective after age 5 because they tend to humiliate the child and breed resentment.

6. As discussed earlier, many psychologists believe that children should never be spanked. If you do use physical punishment, reserve it for situations that pose an immediate danger to younger children; for example, when a child runs into the street.

7.   Remember, too, that it is usually more effective to reward children when they are being good than it is to punish them for misbehavior.

After age 5, management techniques are the most effective form of discipline, especially techniques that emphasize communication and the relationship between parent and child.

Communicating Effectively with Children

Creative communication is another important ingredient of successful child management (Bath, 1996). Child expert Haim Ginott (1965) believed that making a distinction between feelings and behavior is the key to clear communication. Because children (and parents, too) do not choose how they feel, it is important to allow free expression of feelings.

Accepting Feelings

The child who learns to regard some feelings as "bad," or unacceptable, is being asked to deny a very real part of his or her experience. Ginott encouraged parents to teach their children that all feelings are appropriate; it is only actions that are subject to disapproval. Consider this typical conversation excerpted from Ginott's (1965) classic book:

> *Son:* I am stupid, and I know it. Look at my grades in school.
> *Father:* You just have to work harder.
> *Son:* I already work harder and it doesn't help. I have no brains.
> *Father:* You are smart, I know.
> *Son:* I am stupid, I know.
> *Father:* (loudly) You are not stupid!
> *Son:* Yes, I am!
> *Father:* You are not stupid. Stupid!

By debating with the child, the father misses the point that his son *feels* stupid. It would be far more helpful for the father to encourage the boy to talk about his feelings. For instance, he might say, "You really feel that you are not as smart as others, don't you? Do you feel this way often?" In this way, the child is given a chance to express his emotions and to feel understood. The father might conclude by saying, "Look, son, in my eyes you are a fine person. But I understand how you feel. Everyone feels stupid at times." He might also offer some encouragement: "You're improving. Look at the progress you've made."

I-Messages

Child psychologist Thomas Gordon (2000) believes that parents should send *I-messages* to their children, rather than *you-messages.*

What's the difference? **You-messages** take the form of threats, name-calling, accusing, bossing, lecturing, or criticizing. Generally, you-messages tell children what's "wrong" with them. An **I-message** tells children what effect their behavior had on you. For example, after a hard day's work, Maria wants to sit down and rest awhile. She begins to relax with a newspaper when her 5-year-old daughter starts banging loudly on a toy drum. Many parents would respond with a you-message such as "You go play outside this instant" (bossing) or "Don't you ever make such a racket when someone is reading" (lecturing). Gordon suggests sending an I-message such as, "I am very tired, and I would like to read. I feel upset and can't read with so much noise." This forces the child to accept responsibility for the effects of her actions (Dinkmeyer, McKay, & Dinkmeyer, 1997).

Using Natural and Logical Consequences

Sometimes events automatically discourage misbehavior. For example, a child who refuses to eat dinner will get uncomfortably hungry. A child who throws a temper tantrum may gain nothing but a sore throat and a headache if the tantrum is ignored (Fontenelle, 1989). In such instances, a child's actions have **natural consequences** (intrinsic effects). In situations that don't produce natural consequences, parents can set up **logical consequences** (rational and reasonable effects). For example, a parent might say, "We'll go to the zoo when you've picked up all those toys," or "You can play with your dolls as soon as you've taken your bath," or "You two can stop arguing or leave the table until you're ready to join us."

You-message Threatening, accusing, bossing, lecturing, or criticizing another person.

I-message A message that states the effect someone else's behavior has on you.

Natural consequences The effects that naturally tend to follow a particular behavior.

Logical consequences Reasonable consequences that are defined by parents.

The concept of logical, parent-defined consequences can be combined with I-messages to handle many day-to-day instances of misbehavior. The key idea is to use an I-message to set up consequences and then give the child a choice to make: "Michelle, we're trying to watch TV. You can settle down and watch with us or go play elsewhere. You decide which you'd rather do" (Dinkmeyer, McKay, & Dinkmeyer, 1997).

How could Maria have dealt with her 5-year-old—the one who was banging on a drum? A response that combines an I-message with logical consequences would be, "I would like for you to stop banging on that drum; otherwise, please take it outside." If the child continues to bang on the drum inside the house, then she has caused the toy to be put away. If she takes it outside, she has made a decision to play with the drum in a way that respects her mother's wishes. In this way, both parent and child have been allowed to maintain a sense of self-respect, and a needless clash has been averted.

After you have stated consequences and let the child decide, be sure to respect the child's choice. If the child repeats the misbehavior, you can let the consequences remain in effect longer. But later, give the child another chance to cooperate.

With all child management techniques, remember to be firm, kind, consistent, respectful, and encouraging. And most of all, try every day to live the message you wish to communicate.

study break
Effective Parenting

RECITE

1. Effective discipline gives children freedom within a structure of consistent and well-defined limits. T or F?
2. One good way to maintain consistency in child management is to overstate the consequences for misbehavior. T or F?
3. Spankings and other physical punishments are most effective for children under the age of 2. T or F?
4. Giving recognition for progress and attempts to improve is an example of parental _____.
5. I-messages are a gentle way of accusing a child of misbehavior. T or F?
6. In situations where natural consequences are unavailable or do not discourage misbehavior, parents should define logical consequences for a child. T or F?

REFLECT
Critical Thinking

7. Several Scandinavian countries have made it illegal for parents to spank their own children. Does this infringe on the rights of parents?

Relate

What do you think are the best ways to discipline children? How would your approach be classified? What are its advantages and disadvantages?

Parents can probably never be completely consistent. Think of a time when your parents were inconsistent in disciplining you. How did it affect you?

Think of a you-message you have recently given a child, family member, roommate, or spouse. Can you change it into an I-message?

ANSWERS

1. T 2. F 3. T 4. encouragement 5. F 6. T 7. Such laws are based on the view that it should be illegal to physically assault any person, regardless of their age. Although parents may believe they have a "right" to spank their children, it can be argued that children need special protection because they are small, powerless, and dependent (Durrant & Janson, 2005).

chapter in review

Major Points

- You are a product of both your genetic heritage and the environments in which you have lived.

- Infant development is strongly influenced by heredity. However, environmental factors such as nutrition, parenting, and learning are also important.

- Forming an emotional bond with a caregiver is a crucial event during infancy.

- Studies suggest that parental styles have a substantial impact on emotional and intellectual development.

- Learning to use language is a cornerstone of early intellectual development.

- While Piaget's stage theory provides a valuable map of how thinking abilities unfold, Vygotsky's theory reminds us that a child's mind is shaped by culture and human relationships.

- Adolescents must form their identity and values at a time when they are also dealing with puberty and transition to adulthood is occurring at ever-later ages.

- As in other types of development, we develop morals and values as we grow through several levels.

- Erik Erikson identified a series of challenges that occur across the lifespan.

- Well-being during adulthood consists of six elements: self-acceptance, positive relations with others, autonomy, environmental mastery, having a purpose in life, and continued personal growth.

- Effective parental discipline is consistent, humane, encouraging, and based on respectful communication.

Summary

How do heredity and environment affect development?

- The chromosomes and genes in each cell of the body carry hereditary instructions. Most characteristics are polygenic and reflect the combined effects of dominant and recessive genes.
- Maturation of the body and nervous system underlies the orderly development of motor skills, cognitive abilities, emotions, and language.
- Many early skills are subject to the principle of readiness.
- Prenatal development is influenced by environmental factors, such as various teratogens, including diseases, drugs, and radiation, as well as the mother's diet, health, and emotions.
- During sensitive periods in development, infants are more sensitive to specific environmental influences.
- Early perceptual, intellectual, or emotional deprivation seriously retards development, whereas deliberate enrichment of the environment has a beneficial effect on infants.
- Temperament is hereditary. Most infants fall into one of three temperament categories: easy children, difficult children, and slow-to-warm-up children.
- A child's developmental level reflects heredity, environment, and the effects of the child's own behavior.

What can newborn babies do?

- The human neonate has a number of adaptive reflexes, including the grasping, rooting, sucking, and Moro reflexes. Neonates begin to learn immediately and they appear to be aware of the effects of their actions.
- Testing with a looking chamber reveals that neonates prefer bright lights and circular or curved designs.
- Infants prefer human face patterns, especially familiar faces. In later infancy, interest in the unfamiliar emerges.
- The rate of maturation varies from person to person. Also, learning contributes greatly to the development of basic motor skills.
- Emotions develop in a consistent order, starting with generalized excitement in newborn babies. Three of the basic emotions—fear, anger, and joy—may be unlearned.

Of what significance is a child's emotional bond with adults?

- Emotional attachment of human infants is a critical early event.
- Infant attachment is reflected by separation anxiety. The quality of attachment can be classified as secure, insecure-avoidant, or insecure-ambivalent.
- High-quality day care does not appear to harm children. Low-quality day care can be risky.
- Meeting a baby's affectional needs is as important as meeting needs for physical care.

How important are parental styles?

- Studies suggest that parental styles have a substantial impact on emotional and intellectual development.
- Three major parental styles are authoritarian, permissive, and authoritative (effective). Authoritative parenting appears to benefit children the most.
- Whereas mothers typically emphasize caregiving, fathers tend to function as playmates for infants.
- Parental styles vary across cultures.

How do children acquire language?

- Language development proceeds from crying to cooing, then babbling, the use of single words, and then to telegraphic speech.
- The underlying patterns of telegraphic speech suggest a biological predisposition to acquire language. This innate tendency is augmented by learning.
- Prelanguage communication between parent and child involves shared rhythms, nonverbal signals, and turn-taking.
- Motherese or parentese is a simplified, musical style of speaking that parents use to help their children learn language.

How do children learn to think?

- Jean Piaget theorized that intellectual growth occurs through a combination of assimilation and accommodation.
- Piaget also held that children go through a fixed series of cognitive stages. The stages and their approximate age ranges are sensorimotor (0–2), preoperational (2–7), concrete operational (7–11), and formal operations (11–adult).

- Learning principles provide an alternate explanation that assumes that cognitive development is continuous; it does not occur in stages.
- Recent studies of infants under the age of 1 year suggest that they are capable of thought well beyond that observed by Piaget.
- Lev Vygotsky's sociocultural theory emphasizes that a child's mental abilities are advanced by interactions with more competent partners. Mental growth takes place in a child's zone of proximal development, where a more skillful person may scaffold the child's progress.

Why is the transition from adolescence to adulthood especially challenging?

- Adolescents must form their identity and values at a time when they are also dealing with puberty and transition to adulthood is occurring at ever-later ages.
- Identity formation is even more challenging for adolescents of ethnic descent.
- In Western industrialized societies, the transition into adulthood is further complicated as it is increasingly delayed well into the twenties.

How do we develop morals and values?

- Lawrence Kohlberg identified preconventional, conventional, and postconventional levels of moral reasoning.
- Developing mature moral standards is also an important task of adolescence.
- Most people function at the conventional level of morality, but some never get beyond the selfish, preconventional level. Only a minority of people attain the highest, or postconventional, level of moral reasoning.

What are the typical tasks and dilemmas through the life span?

- Erik Erikson identified a series of specific psychosocial dilemmas that occur as we age. These range from a need to gain trust in infancy to the need to live with integrity in old age.
- Successful resolution of the dilemmas produces healthy development, whereas unsuccessful outcomes make it harder to deal with later crises.

What is involved in well-being during later adulthood?

- Physical aging starts early in adulthood. Every adult must find ways to successfully cope with aging.
- Only a minority of people have a midlife crisis, but midlife course corrections are more common.
- Intellectual declines associated with aging are limited, at least through one's seventies. This is especially true of individuals who remain mentally active.
- Successful lives are based on happiness, purpose, meaning, and integrity.
- Ageism refers to prejudice, discrimination, and stereotyping on the basis of age. It affects people of all ages but is especially damaging to older people. Most ageism is based on stereotypes, myths, and misinformation.

How do effective parents discipline and communicate with their children?

- Effective parental discipline tends to emphasize child management techniques (especially communication), rather than power assertion or withdrawal of love.

- Consistency is also an important aspect of effective parenting.
- Effective parents allow their children to express their feelings but place limits on their behavior.
- Much misbehavior can be managed by use of I-messages and the application of natural and logical consequences.

Web Resources

For an up-to-date list of direct links to interesting sites, including those listed here, visit the student companion site for this book at www.cengage.com/psychology/coon

Human Genome Project Learn more about your human genetic heritage.

Crack Babies A photostory by Ken Kobre.

Scaffolding as a Teaching Strategy Download a paper on the application of Vygotsky's idea of scaffolding to teaching.

A Positive Approach to Identity Formation of Biracial Children Join the debate about multi-ethnicity and identity formation.

Delayed Adulthood Read two articles about delayed adulthood.

Kohlberg Dilemmas Try your hand at answering several moral dilemmas.

Discipline: Logical & Natural Consequences Read about ways to effectively structure discipline.

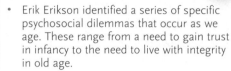

Interactive Learning

***PSYCHOLOGY: A JOURNEY* BOOK COMPANION WEBSITE**
WWW.CENGAGE.COM/PSYCHOLOGY/COON
Visit your book companion website, where you will find flash cards, practice quizzes, web links, and more to help you study.

JUST WHAT YOU NEED TO KNOW NOW! CENGAGENOW™
Spend time on what you need to master rather than on information you already have learned. Take a pretest for this chapter, and CengageNOW will generate a personalized study plan based on your results. The study plan will identify the topics you need to review and direct you to online resources to help you master those topics. You can then take a posttest to help you determine the concepts you have mastered and what you will need to work on. Try it out! Go to www.cengage.com/login to sign in with an access code or to purchase access to this product.

test your knowledge

Human Development

For additional review, get more practice with *CengageNOW, WebTutor,* the *Practice Quizzes,* and/or the printed *Study Guide* available with this book.

1. If a personal trait is controlled by a single dominant gene, the trait cannot be
   a. hereditary
   b. related to DNA sequences
   c. influenced by chromosomes
   d. polygenic

2. Early in life, the learning of basic skills is most effective when parents respect the
   a. Mozart effect
   b. value of reactive maternal involvement
   c. principle of readiness
   d. fact that babies cannot imitate adult actions until they are 18 months old

3. Deprivation has an especially strong impact on development during
   a. the reciprocal stage
   b. sensitive periods
   c. the polygenic stage
   d. the social play phase

4. According to research using a looking chamber, infants begin to show a preference for complex over simple patterns within _____ after birth.
   a. three months
   b. three years
   c. three days
   d. three weeks

5. Cephalocaudal and proximodistal patterns show the effects of _____ on motor development.
   a. enriched environments
   b. maturation
   c. scaffolding
   d. sensitive periods

6. A clear sign that infant attachment is beginning to occur is found in the presence of
   a. a social smile
   b. separation anxiety
   c. social scaffolding
   d. affectional needs

7. A baby who turns away from his mother when she returns after a brief separation shows signs of having which type of attachment?
   a. insecure-avoidant
   b. insecure-ambivalent
   c. solitary-ambivalent
   d. maternal-disaffectional

8. Psychologist Diana Baumrind describes parents who enforce rigid rules and demand strict obedience as
   a. authoritative
   b. permissive-repressive
   c. proactive-reactive
   d. authoritarian

9. Turn-taking with nonverbal signals is a first step toward
   a. secure attachment
   b. motor development
   c. using language
   d. an ability to make transformations

10. Parents talk to young children with a raised tone of voice and an exaggerated pattern of speaking that is called
   a. transformational grammar
   b. telegraphic speech
   c. signal switching
   d. parentese

11. Piaget believed that a child's understanding of the world grows through the mental processes of assimilation and
   a. intuition
   b. accommodation
   c. egocentrism
   d. reversibility

12. According to Piaget, a child's mastery of conservation occurs during the
   a. formal operations stage
   b. preoperational stage
   c. concrete operational stage
   d. sensorimotor stage

13. Vygotsky believed that adults help children learn how to think by using a process he called
   a. reversible thinking
   b. scaffolding
   c. accommodation
   d. moral reasoning

14. The phenomenon of delayed adulthood teaches us that terms like *adolescent* or *adulthood* cannot be defined solely in terms of
   a. identity formation
   b. emotional turbulence
   c. moral development
   d. physical maturation

15. According to Kohlberg, the highest level of moral development involves being guided by
   a. self-chosen universal ethical principles
   b. the consequences of actions
   c. a desire to follow accepted authority
   d. choosing right rather than wrong

16. In middle age, most adults experience
   a. a loss of crystallized abilities
   b. a midlife correction
   c. a midlife crisis
   d. ageism

17. According to Erikson, the dilemma faced by most 3- to 5-year-olds is
   a. autonomy versus shame and doubt
   b. initiative versus guilt
   c. trust versus mistrust
   d. industry versus inferiority

18. Erikson's theory states that mature adults are best able to avoid stagnation when they express
   a. integrity
   b. generativity
   c. intimacy
   d. preconventional moral reasoning

19. Which form of child discipline tends to make children insecure, anxious, and hungry for approval?
   a. withdrawal of love
   b. management techniques
   c. power assertion
   d. authoritative techniques

20. Which type of child discipline takes the form of threats, name-calling, accusing, bossing, lecturing, or criticizing?
   a. I-messages
   b. you-messages
   c. logical consequences
   d. natural consequences

Answers   1. d   2. c   3. b   4. c   5. b   6. b   7. a   8. d   9. c   10. d   11. b   12. c   13. b   14. d   15. a   16. c   17. b   18. b   19. a   20. b

>4

Sensation and Perception

Journey into Psychology: Dancing the Two-Step

Right now you are bathed in a kaleidoscope of electromagnetic radiation, heat, pressure, vibrations, molecules, and mechanical forces. Unless your senses translate these forces into a form your brain can understand, you will experience only a void of silence and darkness. Yet your senses do not give you a complete "picture" of reality.

One of your authors once stood at the mouth of a cave at dusk while a million bats streamed out. What did he hear? Even though every bat was "shouting," and listening for reflected echoes (to avoid colliding with other bats), he heard nothing. The bats were shouting at a pitch too high for humans to hear. To survive, we must collect sensory information,

while also limiting the amount bombarding the brain. Regardless, the next time you drink in the beauty of a sunset, a flower, or a friend, remember: Sensation makes it all possible. And that's just the first step in maintaining contact with the world.

Your other author was once approached in a supermarket by a young girl who screamed, "Help! Someone is killing my father." He followed her to another aisle and saw two men struggling violently. The guy on top had his victim by the throat. There was blood everywhere. It was a murder in progress! Soon, however, it turned out that the "guy on the bottom" had passed out, hit his head, and was bleeding. The "guy on top" saw the first man fall and

was loosening his collar. Obviously, the girl had misperceived what was happening to her father. Because of the dramatic influence of her words, so did your author. As this story shows, sensory information can be interpreted in various ways. That's step two in knowing the world.

We begin this chapter with the first step, a look at how the senses operate. Then we'll explore the second step, perception, when our brain assembles sensations into a meaningful "picture" of events. Our perceptions create faces, melodies, works of art, illusions, and occasionally, "murders" out of the raw material of sensation. Let's see how this takes place.

Sensory Systems—The First Step

In general, how do sensory systems function?

The primary function of the senses is to act as biological **transducers,** devices that convert one kind of energy into another (Fain, 2003). Each sense translates a specific type of external energy into patterns of activity (action potentials) in neurons. Then the brain processes these messages. Information arriving from the sense organs creates **sensations.** When the brain organizes sensations into meaningful patterns, we speak of **perception.** It is fascinating to realize that "seeing" and "hearing" take place in your brain, not in your eyes or ears.

Before we move on to perception, let's further explore sensation. Consider, for example, vision, which gives us amazingly wide access to the world. In one instant you can view a star light years away, and in the next, you can peer into the microscopic universe of a dewdrop. Yet, vision also narrows what we can possibly observe. Like the other senses, vision acts as a *data reduction system.* It selects and analyzes information in order to code and send to the brain only the most important data (Goldstein, 2010).

Selection

How does data reduction take place? Considerable selection occurs because sensory receptors do not transduce all of the energies they encounter. For example, a guitar transduces string vibrations into sound waves. Pluck a string and the guitar will produce a sound. However, stimuli that don't cause the string to move will have no effect. If you shine a light on the string, or pour cold water on it, the guitar will remain silent. (The owner of the guitar, however, might get quite loud at this point!) In a similar way, the eye transduces electromagnetic radiation, the ear transduces sound waves, and so on. Many other types of stimuli cannot be sensed directly because we lack sensory receptors to transduce their energy. For example, humans cannot sense the bioelectric fields of other living creatures, but sharks have special organs that can (Fields, 2007). (Do they *hear* the fields or *feel* them or what?)

Further, sense receptors transduce only part of their target energy range (Fain, 2003). For example, your eyes transduce only a tiny fraction of the entire range of electromagnetic energies—the part we call the *visible spectrum.* The eyes of honeybees can transduce, and therefore see, parts of the electromagnetic spectrum invisible to us humans. As described earlier, the ears of bats can transduce echoing sound waves that we humans can't hear. This ability, called *echolocation,* allows bats to fly in pitch darkness. As you can see, our rich sensory experiences are only a small part of what *could* be sensed and what some animals *can* sense.

Analysis

What we experience is also influenced by **sensory analysis.** As they process information, the senses divide the world into important **perceptual features** (basic stimulus patterns). The visual system, for example, has a set of *feature detectors* that are attuned to very specific stimuli, such as lines, shapes, edges, spots, colors, and other patterns (Hubel & Wiesel, 2005). Look at ▸▸ Figure 4.1 and notice how eye-catching the single vertical line is among a group of slanted lines. This effect, which is called *pop-out,* occurs because your visual system is highly sensitive to these perceptual features (Adler & Orprecio, 2006).

Similarly, frog eyes are highly sensitive to small, dark, moving spots. In other words, they are basically "tuned" to detect bugs flying nearby (Lettvin, 1961). But the insect (spot) must be moving, or the frog's "bug detectors" won't work. A frog could starve to death surrounded by dead flies.

Our sensitivity to perceptual features is an innate characteristic of the nervous system. Like other inborn capacities, this sensitivity is also influenced by experiences early in life. For instance, Colin Blakemore and Graham Cooper of Cambridge University raised kittens in a room with only vertical stripes on the walls. Another set of kittens saw only horizontal stripes. When returned to normal environments, the "horizontal" cats could easily jump onto a chair, but when walking on the floor, they bumped into chair legs. "Vertical" cats, on the other hand,

Survey Questions

- In general, how do sensory systems function?
- How does the visual system function?
- What are the mechanisms of hearing?
- How do the chemical senses operate?
- What are the somesthetic senses?
- Why are we more aware of some sensations than others?
- In general, how do we construct our perceptions?
- How is it possible to see depth and judge distance?
- How is perception altered by expectations, motives, emotions, and learning?
- Is extrasensory perception possible?
- How can I learn to perceive events more accurately?

Transducers Devices that convert one kind of energy into another

Sensation A sensory impression; also, the process of detecting physical energies with the sensory organs.

Perception The mental process of organizing sensations into meaningful patterns.

Sensory analysis Separation of sensory information into important elements.

Perceptual features Basic elements of a stimulus, such as lines, shapes, edges, or colors.

FIGURE 4.1 Visual pop-out. Pop-out is so basic that babies as young as 3 months respond to it. (Adapted from Adler & Orprecio, 2006).

easily avoided chair legs, but they missed when trying to jump to horizontal surfaces. The cats raised with vertical stripes were "blind" to horizontal lines, and the "horizontal" cats acted as if vertical lines were invisible (Blakemore & Cooper, 1970). Other experiments show that there is an actual decrease in brain cells tuned to the missing features (Grobstein & Chow, 1975).

Sensory Coding

As they select and analyze information, sensory systems *code* it. **Sensory coding** refers to converting important features of the world into neural messages understood by the brain (Hubel & Wiesel, 2005). To see coding at work, try closing your eyes for a moment. Then take your fingertips and press firmly on your eyelids. Apply enough pressure to "squash" your eyes slightly. Do this for about 30 seconds and observe what happens. (Readers with eye problems or contact lenses should not try this.)

Did you "see" stars, checkerboards, and flashes of color? These are called *phosphenes* (FOSS-feens: visual sensations caused by mechanical excitation of the retina). They occur because the eye's receptor cells, which normally respond to light, are also somewhat sensitive to pressure. Notice, though, that the eye is prepared to code stimulation—including pressure—only into visual features. As a result, you experience light sensations, not pressure. Also important in producing this effect is *sensory localization* in the brain.

Sensory localization means that the type of sensation you experience depends on which brain area is activated. Some brain areas receive visual information; others receive auditory information, and still others receive taste or touch (see Chapter 2). Knowing which brain areas are active tells us, in general, what kinds of sensations you are feeling.

Sensory localization may someday make it possible to artificially restore sight, hearing, or other senses. In fact, researchers have already used a miniature television camera to send electrical signals to the brain (▶▶ Figure 4.2) (Dobelle, 2000; Warren & Normann, 2005). In July 2006, a woman named Cheri Robinson became the 16th person in the world with an implant of this type. She can now "see" 100 dots of light. Like a sports scoreboard, these lights can be used to form crude letters (Dobelle, 2000). Eventually, a larger number of dots could make reading and "seeing" large objects, such as furniture and doorways, possible. Before we move on to discuss perception, let's look in more detail at our various senses, beginning with vision, the most magnificent sensory system of all.

▶▶ **FIGURE 4.2** An artificial visual system.

Actual image

Cameras

Visual cortex

Electrodes

Perceived image

Sensory coding Codes used by the sense organs to transmit information to the brain.

FIGURE 4.3 The visible spectrum.

INVISIBLE LONG WAVES   **VISIBLE LIGHT SPECTRUM**   **INVISIBLE SHORT WAVES**

Infrared rays
(beyond red)

Ultraviolet rays
(beyond violet)

1500 1000 700 600 500 400 300

| Radio | TV | Microwaves | Infra-red | | U-V | X-rays | Gamma rays | Cosmic rays |

Vision—Catching Some Rays

How does the visual system function?

What are the basic dimensions of light and vision? The *visible spectrum* (the spread of electromagnetic energies to which the eyes respond) is made up of a narrow range of wavelengths of electromagnetic radiation. Visible light starts at "short" wavelengths of 400 *nanometers* (nan-OM-et-er: one billionth of a meter), which we sense as purple or violet. Longer light waves produce blue, green, yellow, orange, and red, which has a wavelength of 700 nanometers (▶▶ Figure 4.3).

The term *hue* refers to the basic color categories of red, orange, yellow, green, blue, indigo, and violet. As just noted, various hues (or color sensations) correspond to the wavelength of the light that reaches our eyes (Mather, 2008). White light, in contrast, is a mixture of many wavelengths. Hues (colors) from a narrow band of wavelengths are very *saturated,* or "pure." (An intense "fire-engine" red is more saturated than a muddy "brick" red.) A third dimension of vision, *brightness,* corresponds roughly to the amplitude, or height, of light waves. Waves of greater amplitude are "taller," carry more energy, and cause the colors we see to appear brighter or more intense. For example, the same "brick" red would look bright under intense, high-energy illumination and drab under dim light.

Structure of the Eye

Although the visual system is much more complex than any digital camera, both cameras and eyes have a *lens* to focus images on a light-sensitive layer at the back of a closed space. In a camera, it is a layer of light-sensitive pixels in the digital image sensor. In the eye, it is a layer of *photoreceptors* (light-sensitive cells) in the **retina,** an area about the size and thickness of a postage stamp (▶▶ Figure 4.4).

How does the eye focus? Most focusing is done at the front of the eye by the *cornea,* a clear membrane that bends light inward. The lens makes additional, smaller adjustments. Your eye's focal point changes when muscles attached to the lens alter its shape. This process is called **accommodation.** In cameras, focusing is done more simply—by changing the distance between the lens and the image sensor.

Fovea

Blind spot

Optic nerve

Retinal arteries and veins

Ciliary muscle

Aqueous humor

Iris

Pupillary opening

Cornea

Lens

Retina

FIGURE 4.4 The human eye, a simplified view.

Retina The light-sensitive layer of cells at the back of the eye.

Accommodation Changes in the shape of the lens of the eye.

Point of focus   Distant point   Near point   Misshapen cornea

Misshapen lens

Part of image is focused; part is not

Concave lens   Convex lens   Nonsymmetrical lens

(a) Nearsighted Eye   **(b) Farsighted Eye**   **(c) Astigmatic Eye**

⯅ **FIGURE 4.5** Visual defects and corrective lenses: *(a)* A myopic (longer than usual) eye. The concave lens spreads light rays just enough to increase the eye's focal length. *(b)* A hyperopic (shorter than usual) eye. The convex lens increases refraction (bending), returning the point of focus to the retina. *(c)* An astigmatic (lens or cornea not symmetrical) eye. In astigmatism, parts of vision are sharp and parts are unfocused. Lenses to correct astigmatism are unsymmetrical.

Visual Problems

Focusing is also affected by the shape of the eye. If your eye is too short, nearby objects will be blurred, but distant objects will be sharp. This is called **hyperopia** (HI-per-OPE-ee-ah: farsightedness). If your eyeball is too long, images fall short of the retina and you won't be able to focus distant objects. This results in **myopia** (my-OPE-ee-ah: nearsightedness). When the cornea or the lens is misshapen, part of vision will be focused and part will be fuzzy. In this case, the eye has more than one focal point, a problem called **astigmatism** (ah-STIG-mah-tiz-em). All three visual defects can be corrected by placing glasses (or contact lenses) in front of the eye to change the path of light (▶▶ Figure 4.5).

As people age, the lens becomes less flexible and less able to accommodate. The result is **presbyopia** (prez-bee-OPE-ee-ah: old vision, or farsightedness due to aging). Perhaps you have seen a grandparent or older friend reading a newspaper at arm's length because of presbyopia. If you now wear glasses for nearsightedness, you may need bifocals as you age. (Just like your authors. Sigh.) Bifocal lenses correct near vision *and* distance vision.

Rods and Cones

The eye has two types of "image sensors," consisting of receptor cells called *rods* and *cones* (Mather, 2008). The 5 million **cones** in each eye work best in bright light. They also produce color sensations and fine details. In contrast, the **rods,** numbering about 120 million, can't detect colors (▶▶ Figure 4.6). Pure rod vision is black and white. However, the rods are much more sensitive to light than the cones are. The rods therefore allow us to see in very dim light.

Surprisingly, the retina has a "hole" in it: Each eye has a *blind spot* because there are no receptors where the optic nerve passes out of the eye and blood vessels enter (▶▶ Figure 4.7a). The blind spot shows that vision depends greatly on the brain. If you close one eye, part of what you see will fall on the blind spot of your open eye. Why isn't there a gap in your vision? The answer is that the visual cortex of the brain actively fills in the gap with patterns from surrounding areas (▶▶ Figure 4.7b). By closing one eye, you can visually "behead" other people by placing their images on your blind spot. (Just a hint

Hyperopia Difficulty focusing nearby objects (farsightedness).

Myopia Difficulty focusing distant objects (nearsightedness).

Astigmatism Defects in the cornea, lens, or eye that cause some areas of vision to be out of focus.

Presbyopia Farsightedness caused by aging.

Cones Visual receptors for colors and daylight visual acuity.

Rods Visual receptors for dim light that produce only black and white sensations.

Direction of light

Fibers of the optic nerve

Ganglion cell

Amacrine cell

Bipolar neuron

Horizontal cell

Direction of nerve impulses

Photoreceptor cells:
Cone
Rod

Pigment layer of retina

Choroid layer

Sclera

Retina

Optic nerve

Omnikron/Photo Researchers, Inc.

Retina

◀◀ **FIGURE 4.6** Anatomy of the retina. Note that light does not fall directly on the rods and cones. It must first pass through the cornea, the lens, the vitreous humor (a jelly-like substance that fills the eyeball), and the outer layers of the retina. Only about one half of the light at the front of the eye reaches the rods and cones—testimony to the retina's amazing sensitivity. The lower left photograph shows rods and cones as seen through an electron microscope. In the photograph the cones are colored green and the rods blue.

(a)

(b)

◀◀ **FIGURE 4.7** Experiencing the blind spot. *(a)* With your right eye closed, stare at the upper-right cross. Hold the book about 1 foot from your eye and slowly move it back and forth. You should be able to locate a position that causes the black spot to disappear. When it does, it has fallen on the blind spot. With a little practice, you can learn to make people or objects you dislike disappear too! *(b)* Repeat the procedure described, but stare at the lower cross. When the white space falls on the blind spot, the black lines will appear to be continuous. This may help you understand why you do not usually experience a blind spot in your visual field.

for some classroom fun.) The brain can also "erase" distracting information. Roll your eyes all the way to the right and then close your right eye. You should clearly see your nose in your left eye's field of vision. Now, open your right eye again and your nose will nearly disappear as your brain disregards its presence.

Visual Acuity

The rods and cones also affect **visual acuity,** or sharpness. The cones lie mainly at the center of the eye. In fact, the *fovea* (FOE-vee-ah: a small cup-shaped area in the middle of the retina) contains only cones—about 50,000 of them. Like high-resolution digital sensors made

Visual acuity The sharpness of visual perception.

of many small pixels, the tightly packed cones in the fovea produce the sharpest images. Normal acuity is designated as 20/20 vision: At 20 feet in distance, you can distinguish what the average person can see at 20 feet (▶▶ Figure 4.8). If your vision is 20/40, you can see at 20 feet only what the average person can see at 40 feet. If your vision is 20/200, everything is a blur and you need glasses! Vision that is 20/12 would mean that you can see at 20 feet what the average person must be 8 feet nearer to see, indicating better than average acuity. American astronaut Gordon Cooper, who claimed to see railroad lines in northern India from 100 miles above, had 20/12 vision.

Peripheral Vision

What is the purpose of the rest of the retina? Areas outside the fovea also get light, creating a large region of **peripheral** (side) **vision.** The rods are most numerous about 20 degrees from the center of the retina, so much of our peripheral vision is rod vision. Although rod vision is not very high resolution, the rods are quite sensitive to *movement* in peripheral vision. To experience this characteristic of the rods, look straight ahead and hold your hand beside your head, at about 90 degrees. Wiggle your finger and slowly move your hand forward until you can detect motion. You will become aware of the movement before you can actually "see" your finger. Seeing "out of the corner of the eye" is important for sports, driving, and walking down dark alleys. People who suffer from *tunnel vision* (a loss of peripheral vision) feel as if they are wearing blinders (Godnig, 2003).

The rods are also highly responsive to dim light. Because most rods are 20 degrees to each side of the fovea, the best night vision comes from looking *next to* an object you wish to see. Test this yourself some night by looking at, and next to, a very dim star.

Color Vision

How do the cones produce color sensations? The **trichromatic** (TRY-kro-MAT-ik) **theory** of color vision holds that there are three types of cones, each most sensitive to either red, green, or blue. Other colors result from combinations of these three.

A basic problem with the trichromatic theory is that four colors of light—red, green, blue, and yellow—seem to be primary (you can't get them by mixing other colors). Also, why is it impossible to have a reddish green or a yellowish blue? These problems led to the development of a second view, known as the **opponent-process theory,** which states that vision analyzes colors into "either-or" messages (Goldstein, 2010). That is, the visual system can produce messages for either red or green, yellow or blue, black or white. Coding one color in a pair (red, for instance) seems to block the opposite message (green) from coming through. As a result, a reddish green is impossible, but a yellowish red (orange) can occur.

According to opponent-process theory, fatigue caused by making one response produces an afterimage of the opposite color as the system recovers. *Afterimages* are visual sensations that persist after a stimulus is removed—like seeing a spot after a flashbulb goes off. To see an afterimage of the type predicted by opponent-process theory, look at ▶▶ Figure 4.9 and follow the instructions there.

Which color theory is correct? Both! The three-color theory applies to the retina, where three different types of *visual pigments* (light-sensitive chemicals) have been found in cones. As predicted, each pigment is most sensitive to light in roughly the red, green, or blue region. The three types of cones fire nerve impulses at different rates to produce various color sensations (▶▶ Figure 4.10).

In contrast, the opponent-process theory better explains what happens in optic pathways and the brain *after* information leaves the eye. For example, some nerve cells in the brain are excited by the color red and inhibited by the color green. So both theories are "correct." One explains what happens in the eye itself. The other explains how colors are analyzed after messages leave the eye (Gegenfurtner & Kiper, 2003).

Peripheral vision Vision at the edges of the visual field.

Trichromatic theory Theory of color vision based on three cone types: red, green, and blue.

Opponent-process theory Theory of color vision based on three coding systems (red or green, yellow or blue, black or white).

▲ **FIGURE 4.9** Negative afterimages. Stare at the dot near the middle of the flag for at least 30 seconds. Then look immediately at a plain sheet of white paper or a white wall. You will see the American flag in its normal colors. Reduced sensitivity to yellow, green, and black in the visual system, caused by prolonged staring, results in the appearance of complementary colors. Project the afterimage of the flag on other colored surfaces to get additional effects.

▲ **FIGURE 4.10** Firing rates of blue, green, and red cones in response to different colors. The taller the colored bar, the higher the firing rates for that type of cone. As you can see, colors are coded by differences in the activity of all three types of cones in the normal eye. (Adapted from Goldstein, 2010.)

Color Blindness and Color Weakness

Do you know anyone who regularly draws hoots of laughter by wearing clothes of wildly clashing colors? Or someone who sheepishly tries to avoid saying what color an object is? If so, you probably know someone who is color-blind.

What is it like to be color-blind? What causes color blindness? A person who is **color-blind** cannot perceive colors. It is as if the world were a black-and-white movie. The color-blind person either lacks cones or has cones that do not function normally (Deeb, 2004). Such total color blindness is rare. In **color weakness,** or partial color blindness, a person can't see certain colors. Approximately 8 percent of Caucasian males (but fewer Asian, African, and Native American males and less than 1 percent of women) are red-green color-blind (Delpero et al., 2005). These people see reds and greens as the same color, usually a yellowish brown (see ▶▶ Figure 4.11). Another type of color weakness, involving yellow and blue, is extremely rare (Hsia & Graham, 1997). (See "Are You Color-Blind?")

(a)   (b)   (c)

▲ **FIGURE 4.11** Color blindness and color weakness. *(a)* Photograph illustrates normal color vision. *(b)* Photograph is printed in blue and yellow and gives an impression of what a red-green color-blind person sees. *(c)* Photograph simulates total color blindness. If you are totally color-blind, all three photos will look nearly identical.

Color blindness A total inability to perceive colors.

Color weakness An inability to distinguish some colors.

Are You Color-Blind?

How can I tell if I am color-blind? Surprisingly, it is not as obvious as you might think; some of us reach adulthood without knowing. The *Ishihara test* is commonly used to measure color blindness and weakness. In the test, numbers and other designs made of dots are placed on a background also made of dots (▶▶ Figure 4.12). The background and the numbers are of different colors (red and green, for example). A person who is color-blind sees only a jumble of dots. If you have normal color vision, you can detect the numbers or designs (Mollon, Pokorny, & Knoblauch, 2003). The chart below Figure 4.12 lists what is seen by people with normal color vision and color blindness. Because this chart is just a replica, it is not a definitive test of color blindness. Nevertheless, if you can't see all of the embedded designs, you may be color-blind or color weak.

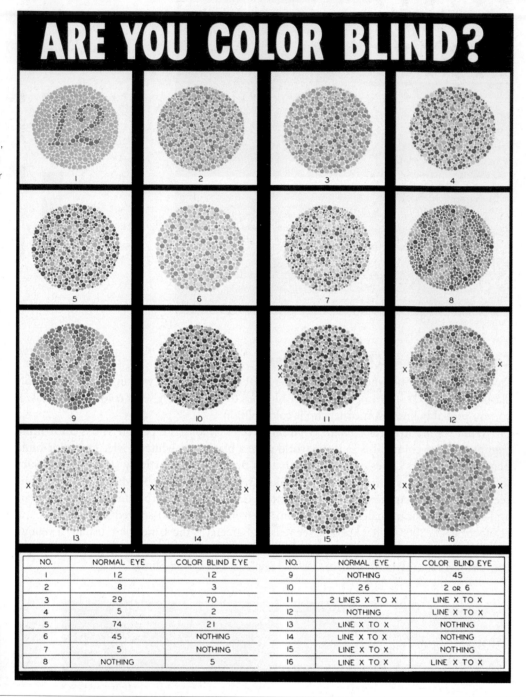

NO.	NORMAL EYE	COLOR BLIND EYE	NO.	NORMAL EYE	COLOR BLIND EYE
1	12	12	9	NOTHING	45
2	8	3	10	26	2 OR 6
3	29	70	11	2 LINES X TO X	LINE X TO X
4	5	2	12	NOTHING	LINE X TO X
5	74	21	13	LINE X TO X	NOTHING
6	45	NOTHING	14	LINE X TO X	NOTHING
7	5	NOTHING	15	LINE X TO X	NOTHING
8	NOTHING	5	16	LINE X TO X	LINE X TO X

▶▶ **FIGURE 4.12** A replica of the Ishihara test for color blindness.

How can color-blind individuals drive? Don't they have trouble with traffic lights? Red-green color-blind individuals have normal vision for yellow and blue, so the main problem is telling red lights from green. In practice, that's not difficult. The red light is always on top, and the green light is brighter than the red. Also, "red" traffic signals have yellow light mixed in with the red and a "green" light that is really blue-green.

Dark Adapting to Dim Light

What happens when the eyes adjust to a dark room? **Dark adaptation** is the dramatic increase in retinal sensitivity to light that occurs after a person enters the dark (Goldstein, 2010). Consider walking into a theater. If you enter from a brightly lighted lobby, you practically need to be led

Dark adaptation Increased retinal sensitivity to light.

to your seat. After a short time, however, you can see the entire room in detail (including the couple kissing over in the corner). It takes about 30 to 35 minutes of complete darkness to reach maximum visual sensitivity (▶▶ Figure 4.13). At that point, your eye will be 100,000 times more sensitive to light.

What causes dark adaptation? Like the cones, the rods contain a light-sensitive visual pigment. When struck by light, visual pigments *bleach,* or break down chemically. The afterimages you have seen after looking at a flashbulb are a result of this bleaching. In fact, a few seconds of exposure to bright white light can completely wipe out dark adaptation. That's why you should be sure to avoid looking at oncoming headlights when you are driving at night—especially the new bluish-white xenon lights. To restore light sensitivity, the visual pigments in the rods must recombine, which takes time.

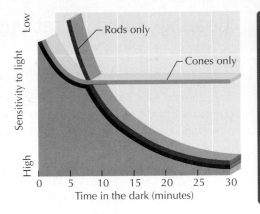

◀◀ FIGURE 4.13 Typical course of dark adaptation. The black line shows how the threshold for vision lowers as a person spends time in the dark. (A lower threshold means that less light is needed for vision.) The green line shows that the cones adapt first, but they soon cease adding to light sensitivity. Rods, shown by the red line, adapt more slowly. However, they continue to add to improved night vision long after the cones are fully adapted.

RECITE

1. Sensory receptors are biological _____, or devices for converting one type of energy to another.
2. Lettvin found that a frog's eyes are especially sensitive to phosphenes. T or F?
3. Important features of the environment are transmitted to the brain through a process known as
   a. phosphenation   b. coding
   c. detection   d. programming
4. Match:
   _____ Myopia   A. Farsightedness
   _____ Hyperopia   B. Elongated eye
   _____ Presbyopia   C. Farsightedness due to aging
   _____ Astigmatism   D. Lack of cones in the fovea
                    E. Misshapen cornea or lens
5. In dim light, vision depends mainly on the _____. In brighter light, color and fine detail are produced by the
   _____.
6. The fovea has the greatest visual acuity due to the large concentration of rods found there. T or F?
7. The eyes become more sensitive to light at night because of a process known as _____.

REFLECT

Critical Thinking

8. William James once said, "If a master surgeon were to cross the auditory and optic nerves, we would hear lightning and see thunder." Can you explain what James meant?
9. Sensory transduction in the eye takes place first in the cornea, then in the lens, then in the retina. True or false?

Relate

How does sensation affect what you are experiencing right now? What if data reduction didn't occur? What if you could transduce other energies? What if your senses were tuned to detect different perceptual features? How would the sensory world you live in change? What would it be like to be a bat?

Pretend you are a beam of light. What will happen to you at each step as you pass into the eye and land on the retina? What will happen if the eye is not perfectly shaped? How will the retina know you've arrived? How will it tell what color of light you are? What will it tell the brain about you?

ANSWERS

1. transducers 2. F 3. b 4. B, A, C, E 5. rods, cones 6. F 7. dark adaptation 8. The explanation is based on sensory localization: Even if a lightning flash caused rerouted messages from the eyes to activate auditory areas of the brain, we would nevertheless experience a sound sensation. Likewise, if the ears transduced a thunderclap, and sent impulses to the visual area, a sensation of light would occur. 9. False. The cornea and lens bend and focus light rays, but they do not change light to another form of energy. No change in the *type* of energy takes place until the retina converts light to nerve impulses.

What are the mechanisms of hearing?

Rock, classical, jazz, rap, country, hip-hop—whatever your musical taste, you have probably been moved by the riches of sound. Hearing also collects information from all around the body, such as detecting the approach of an unseen car (Yost, 2007). Vision, in all its glory, is limited to stimuli in front of the eyes (unless, of course, your "shades" have rearview mirrors attached).

What is the stimulus for hearing? If you throw a stone into a quiet pond, a circle of waves will spread in all directions. In much the same way, sound travels as a series of invisible waves of *compression* (peaks) and *rarefaction* (RARE-eh-fak-shun: valleys) in the air. Any vibrating object—a tuning fork, the string of a musical instrument, or the vocal cords—will produce sound waves (rhythmic movement of air molecules). Other materials, such as fluids or solids, can also carry sound. But sound does not travel in a vacuum or the airless realm of outer space. Movies that show characters reacting to the "roar" of alien starships or titanic battles in deep space do so solely for dramatic effect.

The *frequency* of sound waves (the number of waves per second) corresponds to the perceived *pitch* (higher or lower tone) of a sound. The *amplitude,* or physical "height," of a sound wave tells how much energy it contains. Psychologically, amplitude corresponds to sensed *loudness* (sound intensity) (▶▶ Figure 4.14).

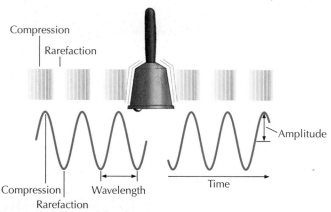

⏶ FIGURE 4.14 Waves of compression in the air, or vibrations, are the stimulus for hearing. The frequency of sound waves determines their pitch. The amplitude determines loudness.

How We Hear Sounds

How are sounds converted to nerve impulses? Hearing involves an elaborate chain of events that begins with the *pinna* (PIN-ah: the visible, external part of the ear). In addition to being a good place to hang earrings or balance pencils, the pinna acts like a funnel to concentrate sounds. After they are guided into the ear canal, sound waves collide with the *tympanic membrane* (eardrum), setting it in motion. This, in turn, causes three small bones (the *auditory ossicles*) (OSS-ih-kuls) to vibrate (▶▶ Figure 4.15). The ossicles are the malleus (MAL-ee-us), incus, and stapes (STAY-peas). Their common names are the hammer, anvil, and stirrup. The ossicles link the eardrum with the *cochlea* (KOCK-lee-ah: a snail-shaped organ that makes up the inner ear). The stapes is attached to a membrane on the cochlea called the *oval window.* As the oval window moves back and forth, it makes waves in a fluid inside the cochlea.

Inside the cochlea, tiny **hair cells** detect waves in the fluid. The hair cells are part of the **organ of Corti** (KOR-tee), which makes up the center part of the cochlea (▶▶ Figure 4.16). A set of *stereocilia* (STER-ee-oh-SIL-ih-ah), or "bristles," atop each hair cell brush against the tectorial membrane when waves ripple through the fluid surrounding the organ of Corti. As the stereocilia are bent, nerve impulses are triggered, which then flow to the brain.

How are higher and lower sounds detected? The **frequency theory** of hearing states that as pitch rises, nerve impulses of a corresponding frequency are fed into the auditory nerve. That is, an 800-hertz tone produces 800 nerve impulses per second. (*Hertz* refers to the number of vibrations per second.) This explains how sounds up to about 4,000 hertz reach the brain. But what about higher tones? **Place theory** states that higher and lower tones excite specific areas of the cochlea. High tones register most strongly at the base of the cochlea (near the oval window). Lower tones, on the other hand, mostly move hair cells near the narrow outer tip of the cochlea (▶▶ Figure 4.17). Pitch is signaled by the area of the cochlea most strongly activated. Place theory also explains why hunters sometimes lose hearing in a narrow pitch range. "Hunter's notch," as it is called, occurs when hair cells are damaged in the area affected by the pitch of gunfire.

Hair cells Receptor cells within the cochlea that transduce vibrations into nerve impulses.

Organ of Corti Center part of the cochlea, containing hair cells, canals, and membranes.

Frequency theory Holds that tones up to 4,000 hertz are converted to nerve impulses that match the frequency of each tone.

Place theory Theory that higher and lower tones excite specific areas of the cochlea.

External Ear
(air conduction)

Inner Ear
(fluid conduction)

(bone conduction
by ossicles)

Covers
movement;
body position

Auditory
canal

Incus

Malleus   Stapes

Vestibular
apparatus

Auditory
nerve

Pinna

Cochlea

Scala vestibuli
(with perilymph)

Cochlear
canal (with
endolymph)

Round
window

Oval
window

Tympanic
membrane
(eardrum)

Scala tympani
(with perilymph)

**Cochlea in
Cross Section**

Oval
window

Stapes

Cochlear
canal

Round
window

Cochlea "Unrolled"

Perilymph
(fluid inside cochlea)

Auditory nerve
fibers

Basilar
membrane

Hair cells

Organ of Corti

Stereocilia

Hair cells

Basilar membrane

FIGURE 4.15 Anatomy of the ear. The entire ear is a mechanism for transducing waves of air pressure into nerve impulses. The inset in the foreground ("Cochlea 'Unrolled'") shows that as the stapes moves the oval window, the round window bulges outward, allowing waves to ripple through fluid in the cochlea. The waves move membranes near the hair cells, causing cilia, or "bristles," on the tips of the cells to bend. The hair cells then generate nerve impulses carried to the brain. (See an enlarged cross section of cochlea in Figure 4.16.)

FIGURE 4.16 A closer view of the hair cells shows how movement of fluid in the cochlea causes the bristling "hairs" or cilia to bend, generating a nerve impulse.

Hearing Loss

What causes other types of hearing loss? The two most common types of hearing loss afflict some 278 million people worldwide (Tennesen, 2007). **Conductive hearing loss** occurs when the transfer of vibrations from the outer ear to the inner ear is weak. For example, the eardrums or ossicles may be damaged or immobilized by disease or injury. In many cases, conductive hearing loss can be overcome with a hearing aid, which makes sounds louder and clearer.

Conductive hearing loss Poor transfer of sounds from the eardrum to the inner ear.

► **FIGURE 4.17** Here we see a simplified side view of the cochlea "unrolled." Remember that the basilar membrane is the elastic "roof" of the lower chamber of the cochlea. The organ of Corti, with its sensitive hair cells, rests atop the basilar membrane. The colored line shows where waves in the cochlear fluid cause the greatest deflection of the basilar membrane. (The amount of movement is exaggerated in the drawing.) Hair cells respond most in the area of greatest movement, which helps identify sound frequency.

Dr. G. Oran Bredberg/SPL/Photo Researchers, Inc.

▲ **FIGURE 4.18** A highly magnified electron microscope photo of the cilia (orange bristles) on the top of human hair cells. (Colors are artificial.)

Sensorineural hearing loss results from damage to the inner ear hair cells or auditory nerve. Many jobs, hobbies, and pastimes can cause **noise-induced hearing loss,** a form of sensorineural hearing loss that occurs when very loud sounds damage hair cells (as in hunter's notch). The hair cells, which are about as thin as a cobweb, are very fragile (►► Figure 4.18). If you work in a noisy environment or enjoy loud music, motorcycling, snowmobiling, hunting, or similar pursuits, you may be risking noise-induced hearing loss. Dead hair cells are never replaced: When you abuse them, you lose them. By the time you are 65, more than 40 percent of them will be gone, mainly those that transduce high pitches (Chisolm, Willott, & Lister, 2003).

How loud must a sound be to be hazardous? Daily exposure to 85 decibels or more may cause permanent hearing loss (Mather, 2008). *Decibels* are a measure of sound intensity. Every 20 decibels increases the sound pressure by a factor of 10. In other words, a rock concert at 120 decibels is 1,000 times stronger than a voice at 60 decibels. Even short periods at 120 decibels can cause temporary hearing loss. Brief exposure to 150 decibels (a jet airplane nearby) may cause permanent hearing loss. You might find it interesting to check the decibel ratings of some of your activities in ►► Figure 4.19. Be aware that amplified musical concerts, iPod-style earbuds, and boombox car stereos can also damage your hearing.

Artificial Hearing

Hearing aids are of no help in cases of sensorineural hearing loss because auditory messages are blocked from reaching the brain. In many cases, however, the auditory nerve is actually intact. This finding has spurred the development of cochlear implants that bypass hair cells and stimulate the auditory nerves directly (►► Figure 4.20). Wires from a microphone carry electrical signals to an external coil. A matching coil under the skin picks up the signals and carries them to one or more areas of the cochlea. The latest implants make use of place theory to separate higher and lower tones. This has allowed some formerly deaf persons to hear human voices, music, and other higher-frequency sounds. About 60 percent of all multichannel implant patients can understand some spoken words and appreciate music (Leal et al., 2003; Tye-Murray, Spencer, & Woodworth, 1995). Some deaf children with implants learn to speak. Those who receive a cochlear implant before age 2 learn spoken language at a near normal rate (Dorman & Wilson, 2004).

At present, artificial hearing remains crude. All but the most successful cochlear implant patients describe the sound as "like a radio that isn't quite tuned in." In fact, 30 percent of all adults who have tried implants have given up on them. But cochlear implants are improving. And even now it is hard to argue with enthusiasts like Kristen Cloud. Shortly after Kristen received an implant, she was able to hear a siren and avoid being struck by a speeding car. She says simply, "The implant saved my life."

Sensorineural hearing loss Loss of hearing caused by damage to the inner ear hair cells or auditory nerve.

Noise-induced hearing loss Damage caused by exposing the hair cells to excessively loud sounds.

Typical Decibel Level	Dangerous Time Exposure	Examples

Extremely loud — 180, 170, 160, 150, 140, 130
Very loud — 120, 110, 100, 90, 80
Quiet — 70, 60, 50, 40
Very quiet — 30, 20, 10
Just audible — 0

Hearing loss certain
Any exposure dangerous
Immediate danger
Less than 8 hours
More than 8 hours

Space Shuttle launch
Shotgun blast
Jet airplane
Siren at 50 feet
Stereo headset (full volume)
Threshold of pain
Thunder, rock concert
Basketball or hockey crowd
Riveter
Factory noise, chain saw
Subway, tractor, power mower
Screaming child
Bus, motorcycle, snowmobile
Loud home stereo, food blender
Heavy traffic
Average automobile
Normal conversation
Quiet auto
Quiet office
Whisper at 5 feet
Broadcast studio when quiet
Studio for making sound pictures

◄◄ **FIGURE 4.19** The loudness of sound is measured in decibels. Zero decibels is the faintest sound most people can hear. Sounds of 110 decibels are uncomfortably loud. Prolonged exposure to sounds above 85 decibels may damage the inner ear. Rock music, which may be 120 decibels, has caused hearing loss in musicians and may affect audiences as well. Sounds of 130 decibels pose an immediate danger to hearing.

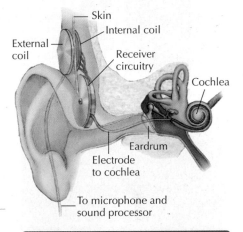

Skin
Internal coil
External coil
Receiver circuitry
Cochlea
Eardrum
Electrode to cochlea
To microphone and sound processor

▲ **FIGURE 4.20** A cochlear implant, or "artificial ear."

Smell and Taste—The Nose Knows When the Tongue Can't Tell

How do the chemical senses operate?

Unless you are a wine taster, a perfume blender, a chef, or a gourmet, you may think of **olfaction** (smell) and **gustation** (taste) as minor senses. Certainly you could survive without these *chemical senses* (receptors that respond to chemical molecules). But don't be deceived, life without these senses can be difficult (Drummond, Douglas, & Olver, 2007). One person, for instance, almost died because he couldn't smell the smoke when his apartment building caught fire. Besides, olfaction and gustation add pleasure to our lives. Let's see how they operate.

The Sense of Smell

Smell receptors respond to airborne molecules. As air enters the nose, it flows over roughly 5 million nerve fibers embedded in the lining of the upper nasal passages (▶▶ Figure 4.21). Receptor proteins on the surface of the fibers are sensitive to various airborne molecules. When a fiber is stimulated, it sends signals to the brain.

How are different odors produced? This is still an unfolding mystery. One hint comes from a type of *dysosmia* (dis-OZE-me-ah: defective smell), a sort of "smell blindness" for a single odor. Loss of sensitivity to specific types of odors suggests there are receptors for specific odors. Indeed, the molecules that produce a particular odor are quite similar in shape. Specific shapes produce the following types of odors: floral (flower-like), camphoric (camphor-like), musky (have you ever smelled a sweaty musk ox?), minty (mint-like), and etherish (like ether or cleaning fluid).

Does this mean that there are five different types of olfactory receptors? Actually, in humans, about 1,000 types of smell receptors are believed to exist (Bensafi et al., 2004). It appears that different-shaped "holes," or "pockets," exist on the surface of olfactory receptors. Like a piece fits in a puzzle, chemicals produce odors when part of a molecule matches a hole of the same shape. This is the **lock and key theory of olfaction.**

Olfaction The sense of smell.

Gustation The sense of taste.

Lock and key theory of olfaction Holds that odors are related to the shapes of chemical molecules.

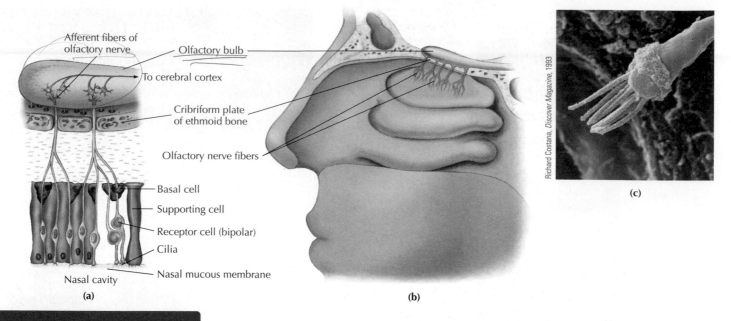

Afferent fibers of
olfactory nerve

Olfactory bulb

To cerebral cortex

Cribriform plate
of ethmoid bone

Olfactory nerve fibers

Basal cell

Supporting cell

Receptor cell (bipolar)

Cilia

Nasal mucous membrane

Nasal cavity

(a)

(b)

(c)

Richard Costana, *Discover Magazine*, 1993

▲ FIGURE 4.21 Receptors for the sense of smell (olfaction). *(a)* Olfactory nerve fibers respond to gaseous molecules. Receptor cells are shown in cross section to the left. *(b)* Olfactory receptors are located in the upper nasal cavity. *(c)* On the right, an extreme close-up of an olfactory receptor shows fibers that sense gaseous molecules of various shapes.

Further, molecules trigger activity in different *combinations* of odor receptors. Thus, humans can detect at least 10,000 different odors. Just as you can make many thousands of words from the 26 letters of the alphabet, many combinations of receptors are possible, resulting in many different odors. Scents are also identified, in part, by the *location* of the receptors in the nose that are activated by a particular odor. And finally, the *number of activated receptors* tells the brain how strong an odor is (Bensafi et al., 2004). The brain uses these distinctive patterns of messages it gets from the olfactory receptors to recognize particular scents (Laurent et al., 2001).

What causes dysosmia? Five people out of 100 experience some degree of dysosmia (Bramerson et al., 2004). Risks include infections, allergies, and blows to the head (which may tear the olfactory nerves). Exposure to chemicals such as ammonia, paints, solvents, and hairdressing potions can also cause dysosmia. If you value your sense of smell, be careful what you breathe (Drummond, Douglas, & Olver, 2007; Herz, 2001).

Taste and Flavors

There are at least four basic taste sensations: *sweet, salt, sour,* and *bitter.* We are most sensitive to bitter, less sensitive to sour, even less sensitive to salt, and least sensitive to sweet. This order may have helped prevent poisonings when most humans foraged for food, because bitter and sour foods are more likely to be inedible.

Most experts now believe that a fifth taste quality exists (Chandrashekar et al., 2006). The Japanese word *umami* (oo-MAH-me) describes a pleasant savory or "brothy" taste associated with certain amino acids in chicken soup, some meat extracts, kelp, tuna, human milk, cheese, and soybeans. The receptors for *umami* are sensitive to glutamate, a substance found in monosodium glutamate (MSG) (Sugimoto & Ninomiya, 2005).

If there are only four or five tastes, how can there be so many different flavors? Flavors seem more varied because we tend to include sensations of texture, temperature, smell, and even pain ("hot" chili peppers) along with taste. Smell is particularly important in determining flavor (Shepherd, 2006). If you plug your nose and eat small bits of apple, potato, and onion, they will "taste" almost exactly alike. So do gourmet jelly beans! That's why food loses its "taste" when you have a cold. It is probably fair to say that subjective flavor is half smell.

Interestingly, MSG's reputation as a "flavor enhancer" likely arises when the savory odors of, say, chicken soup, combine with the taste of glutamate (which does not taste very pleasant by itself) (McCabe & Rolls, 2007). At the very least, we may finally know why chicken soup is such a "comfort food." But remember to smell it first!

FIGURE 4.22 Receptors for taste: *(a)* The tongue is covered with small protrusions called *papillae.* *(b)* Most taste buds are found around the top edges of the tongue (shaded area). However, some are located elsewhere, including under the tongue. Stimulation of the central part of the tongue causes no taste sensations. All four primary taste sensations occur anywhere that taste buds exist. *(c)* An enlarged drawing shows that taste buds are located near the base of papillae. *(d)* Detail of a taste bud. These receptors also occur in other parts of the digestive system, such as the lining of the mouth.

Taste buds (taste-receptor cells) are located mainly on the top side of the tongue, especially around the edges. However, a few are found elsewhere inside the mouth (▸▸ Figure 4.22). As food is chewed, it dissolves and enters the taste buds, where it sets off nerve impulses to the brain (Northcutt, 2004). Much like smell, sweet and bitter tastes appear to be based on a lock-and-key match between molecules and intricately shaped receptors. Saltiness and sourness, however, are triggered by a direct flow of charged atoms into the tips of taste cells (Lindemann, 2001).

Taste bud The receptor organ for taste.

---

study break
Hearing, Smell, and Taste

RECITE

1. The frequency of a sound wave corresponds to how loud it is. T or F?
2. Which of the following is not a part of the cochlea?
   a. ossicles   b. pinna
   c. tympanic membrane   d. all of the above
3. According to the place theory of hearing, higher tones register most strongly near the base of the cochlea. T or F?
4. Sensorineural hearing loss occurs when the auditory ossicles are damaged. T or F?
5. Daily exposure to sounds with a loudness of _____ decibels may cause permanent hearing loss.
6. Cochlear implants have been used primarily to overcome
   a. conductive hearing loss   b. hunter's notch
   c. sensorineural hearing loss   d. tinnitus
7. Olfaction appears to be at least partially explained by the
   _____ _____ _____ theory of molecule shapes and receptor sites.
8. *Umami* is a type of "smell blindness" for a particular odor. T or F?

REFLECT
Critical Thinking

9. Why do you think your voice sounds so different when you hear a tape recording of your speech?
10. Smell and hearing differ from vision in a way that may aid survival. What is it?

Relate

Close your eyes and listen to the sounds around you. As you do, try to mentally trace the events necessary to convert vibrations in the air into the sounds you are hearing. Review the discussion of hearing if you leave out any steps.

What is your favorite food odor? What is your favorite taste? Can you explain how you are able to sense the aroma and taste of foods?

ANSWERS

10. Both smell and hearing can detect stimuli (including signals of approaching danger) around corners, behind objects, and behind the head. Other people hear your voice only as it is carried through the air. You hear not only that sound, but also vibrations conducted by the bones of your skull. 9. The answer lies in another question: How else might vibrations from the voice reach the cochlea? 1. F 2. d 3. T 4. F 5. 85 6. c 7. lock and key 8. F

The Somesthetic Senses—
Flying by the Seat of Your Pants

What are the somesthetic senses?

A gymnast "flying" through a routine on the uneven bars may rely as much on the **somesthetic senses** as on vision (*soma* means "body," *esthetic* means "feel"). Even the most routine activities, such as walking, running, or passing a sobriety test, would be impossible without the **skin senses** (touch), the **kinesthetic senses** (receptors in muscles and joints that detect body position and movement), and the **vestibular senses** (receptors in the inner ear for balance, gravity, and acceleration). Because of their importance, let's begin with the skin senses.

The Skin Senses

It's difficult to imagine what life would be like without the sense of touch, but the plight of Ian Waterman gives a hint. After an illness, Waterman permanently lost all feeling below his neck. Now, in order to know what position his body is in, he has to be able to see it. If he moves with his eyes closed, he has no idea where he is moving. If the lights go out in a room, he's in big trouble (Gallagher, 2004).

Skin receptors produce at least five different sensations: *light touch, pressure, pain, cold,* and *warmth.* Receptors with particular shapes appear to specialize somewhat in various sensations (▶▶ Figure 4.23). However, free nerve endings alone can produce all five sensations (Carlson, 2007). Altogether, the skin has about 200,000 nerve endings for temperature, 500,000 for touch and pressure, and 3 million for pain.

Does the number of receptors in an area of skin relate to its sensitivity? Yes. Your skin could be "mapped" by applying heat, cold, touch, pressure, or pain to points all over your body. Such testing would show that the number of skin receptors varies, and that sensitivity generally matches the number of receptors in a given area. Generally speaking, important areas such as the lips, tongue, face, hands, and genitals have a higher density of receptors. Of course, the sensation you ultimately feel will depend on brain activity.

Pain

The number of pain receptors also varies, right? Yes, like the other skin senses, pain receptors vary in their distribution. About 230 pain points per square centimeter (about a half inch) are found behind the knee, 180 per centimeter on the buttocks, 60 on the pad of the thumb,

▶▶ **FIGURE 4.23** The skin senses include touch, pressure, pain, cold, and warmth. This drawing shows different forms the skin receptors can take. The only clearly specialized receptor is the Pacinian corpuscle, which is highly sensitive to pressure. Free nerve endings are receptors for pain and any of the other sensations. For reasons that are not clear, cold is sensed near the surface of the skin, and warmth is sensed deeper (Carlson, 2007).

Outer layer of skin
Merkel's disks
Free nerve endings
Meissner corpuscle's
Krause's end-bulb
Nerve endings around hair follicle
Pacinian corpuscle

Somesthetic senses Sensations produced by the skin, muscles, joints, viscera, and organs of balance.

Skin senses The senses of touch, pressure, pain, heat, and cold.

Kinesthetic senses The senses of body movement and positioning.

Vestibular senses The senses of balance, position in space, and acceleration.

Receptors for touch

and 40 on the tip of the nose. (Is it better, then, to be pinched on the nose or behind the knee? It depends on what you like!)

Pain carried by *large nerve fibers* is sharp, bright, and fast and seems to come from specific body areas (McMahon & Koltzenburg, 2005). This is the body's **warning system.** Give yourself a small jab with a pin and you will feel this type of pain. As you do this, notice that warning pain quickly disappears. Much as we may dislike warning pain, it is usually a signal that the body has been, or is about to be, damaged. Without warning pain, we would be unable to detect or prevent injury. Children who are born with a rare inherited insensitivity to pain repeatedly burn themselves, break bones, bite off parts of their tongues, and become ill without knowing it (Cox et al., 2006). As you might imagine, it's also hard for people with *congenital pain insensitivity* to have empathy for the pain of others (Danziger, Prkachin, & Willer, 2006).

A second type of somatic pain is carried by *small nerve fibers.* This type of pain is slower, nagging, aching, widespread, and very unpleasant (McMahon & Koltzenburg, 2005). It gets worse if the pain stimulus is repeated. This is the body's **reminding system.** It reminds the brain that the body has been injured. For instance, lower back pain often has this quality. Sadly, the reminding system can cause agony long after an injury has healed or, in terminal illnesses, when the reminder is useless.

Pain Control

In some cultures, people endure tattooing, stretching, cutting, and burning with little apparent pain. How do they do it? Very likely the answer lies in a reliance on psychological factors that anyone can use to reduce pain, such as anxiety reduction, control, and attention (Mailis-Gagnon & Israelson, 2005).

In general, unpleasant emotions such as fear and anxiety increase pain; pleasant emotions decrease it (Rainville, 2004). Anytime you can anticipate pain (such as a trip to the doctor, dentist, or tattoo parlor), you can lower anxiety by making sure you are *fully informed.* Be sure everything that will happen is explained. In general, the more control you *feel* over a painful stimulus, the less pain is experienced (Vallerand, Saunders, & Anthony, 2007). To apply this principle, you might arrange a signal so your doctor, dentist, or body piercer will know when to start and stop a painful procedure. Finally, distraction also reduces pain. Instead of listening to the whirr of a dentist's drill, for example, you might imagine that you are lying in the sun at a beach, listening to the roar of the surf. Or take an iPod along and crank up your favorite MP3s (Bushnell, Villemure, & Duncan, 2004). At home, music can also be a good distractor from chronic pain (Mitchell et al., 2007).

The Vestibular System

Although space flight might look like fun, you are about 70 percent likely to throw up during your first experience in orbit. ("Weightless Wonder" is NASA's official nickname for the high-flying airplane that provides short periods of weightlessness to train astronauts. Unofficially it is called the "Vomit Comet.")

But why? Weightlessness and space flight affect the vestibular system, often causing severe motion sickness. Within the vestibular system, fluid-filled sacs called *otolith* (OH-toe-lith) *organs* are sensitive to movement, acceleration, and gravity (▶▶ Figure 4.24). The otolith organs contain tiny crystals in a soft, gelatin-like mass. The tug of gravity or rapid head movements can cause the mass to shift. This, in turn, stimulates hair-like receptor cells, allowing us to sense gravity, acceleration, and movement through space (Lackner & DiZio, 2005).

Three fluid-filled tubes called the *semicircular canals* are the sensory organs for balance. If you could climb inside these tubes, you would find that head movements cause the fluid to swirl about. As the fluid moves, it bends a small "flap," or "float," called the

Weightlessness presents astronauts with a real challenge in sensory adaptation.

Warning system Pain based on large nerve fibers; warns that bodily damage may be occurring.

Reminding system Pain based on small nerve fibers; reminds the brain that the body has been injured.

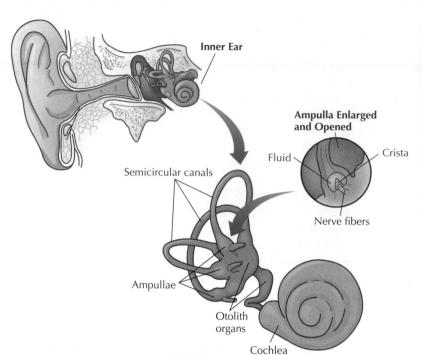

Inner Ear

Semicircular canals

Ampullae

Otolith organs

Cochlea

Ampulla Enlarged and Opened

Fluid

Crista

Nerve fibers

Many people become nauseated the first time they experience virtual reality. Why? Because virtual reality also creates a sensory conflict: Computer-generated visual images change as if the viewer's body is in motion, but the vestibular system tells viewers that they are standing still (Merhi et al., 2007). The result? The scenery may not be real but the nausea is.

▲ FIGURE 4.24 The vestibular system. (See text for explanation.)

crista, that detects movement in the semicircular canals. The bending of each crista again stimulates hair cells and signals head rotation.

What causes motion sickness? According to **sensory conflict theory,** dizziness and nausea occur when sensations from the vestibular system don't match sensations from the eyes and body (Flanagan, May, & Dobie, 2004). On solid ground, information from the vestibular system, vision, and kinesthesis usually matches. However, in a heaving, pitching boat, car, or airplane, a serious mismatch can occur—causing disorientation and heaving of another kind.

Why would sensory conflict cause nausea? You can probably blame (or thank) evolution. Many poisons disturb the vestibular system, vision, and the body. Therefore, we may have evolved so that we react to sensory conflict by vomiting to expel poison. The value of this reaction, however, may be of little comfort to anyone who has ever been "green" and miserable with motion sickness. To minimize such conflicts, try to keep your head still, fix your vision on a distant immobile object, and lie down if you can (Harm, 2002).

Adaptation, Attention, and Gating— Tuning In and Tuning Out

Why are we more aware of some sensations than others?

You are bombarded by sights, sounds, odors, tastes, and touch sensations. Which are you aware of? Each of the senses we have described is continuously active. Even so, many sensory events never reach awareness because of *sensory adaptation, selective attention,* and *sensory gating.* Let's see how information is filtered by these processes.

Sensory Adaptation

Sensory conflict theory Explains motion sickness as the result of a mismatch between information from vision, the vestibular system, and kinesthesis.

Think about walking into a house where fried squid, sauerkraut, and head cheese were prepared for dinner. (Some dinner!) You would probably pass out at the door, yet people who had been in the house for some time wouldn't be aware of the food odors. Similarly, smokers often don't get how much nonsmokers are bothered by the smell of tobacco smoke. Why? Because sensory receptors respond less to unchanging stimuli, a process called **sensory adaptation.**

Fortunately, the olfactory (smell) receptors adapt quickly. When exposed to a constant odor, they send fewer and fewer nerve impulses to the brain, until the odor is no longer noticed. Adaptation to pressure from a wristwatch, waistband, ring, or glasses is based on the same principle. Sensory receptors generally respond best to *changes* in stimulation. No one wants or needs to be reminded 16 hours a day that his or her shoes are on.

Selective Attention

As you sit reading this page, receptors for touch and pressure in the seat of your pants are sending nerve impulses to your brain. Although these sensations have been present all along, you were probably not aware of them until just now. This "seat-of-the-pants phenomenon" is an example of **selective attention** (voluntarily focusing on a specific sensory input). Selective attention appears to be based on the ability of brain structures to select and divert incoming sensory messages (Mather, 2008). We are able to "tune in on" a single sensory message while excluding others.

Another familiar example of this is the "cocktail party effect." When you are in a group of people, surrounded by voices, you can still select and attend to the voice of the person you are facing. Or if that person gets dull, you can eavesdrop on conversations all over the room. (Be sure to smile and nod your head occasionally!) Actually, no matter how interesting your companion may be, your attention will probably shift away if you hear your own name spoken somewhere in the room (Conway, Cowan, & Bunting, 2001). We do find what others say about us to be very interesting, don't we?

At times, we can even suffer from *inattentional blindness* (blindness caused by not attending to a stimulus) (Most et al., 2005). Not seeing something that is plainly before your eyes is most likely to occur when your attention is narrowly focused (Mack, 2002). Inattentional blindness is vividly illustrated by a study in which participants were shown a film of two basketball teams, one wearing black shirts and the other wearing white. Observers were asked to watch the film closely and count how many times a basketball passed between members of one of the teams, while ignoring the other team. As observers watched and counted, a person wearing a gorilla suit walked into the middle of the basketball game, faced the camera, thumped its chest, and walked out of view. Half the observers failed to notice this rather striking event (Simons & Chabris, 1999).

This effect probably explains why fans of opposing sports teams often act as if they had seen two completely different games. In a similar way, using a cell phone while driving can cause inattentional blindness. Instead of ignoring a gorilla, you might miss seeing another car, a motorcyclist, or a pedestrian while your attention is focused on the phone (Bressan & Pizzighello, 2008).

You might find it helpful to think of selective attention as a *bottleneck,* or narrowing in the information channel linking the senses to perception. When one message enters the bottleneck, it seems to prevent others from passing through (see ▸▸ Figure 4.25). Imagine, for instance, that you are driving a car and approaching an intersection. You need to be sure the traffic light is still green. Just as you are about to check it, your passenger points to a friend at the side of the road. If you then fail to notice the light just changed to red, an accident may be just seconds away.

Sensory Gating

What makes selective attention possible? Selective attention appears to be based on the ability of brain structures to select and divert incoming sensory messages (Mather, 2008). But what about messages that haven't reached the brain? Is it possible that some are blocked while others are allowed to pass? Evidence suggests there are *sensory gates* that control the flow of incoming nerve impulses in just this way. In particular, **sensory gating** refers to facilitating or blocking sensory messages in the spinal cord (Melzack & Katz, 2004; Melzack & Wall, 1996).

▲ **FIGURE 4.25** The attentional "bottleneck," or "spotlight," can be widened or narrowed. If you focus on local details in this drawing, you will see the letter *A* repeated 13 times. If you broaden your field of attention to encompass the overall pattern, you will see the letter *H*. (After Lamb & Yund, 1996.)

Sensory adaptation A decrease in sensory response to an unchanging stimulus.

Selective attention Giving priority to a particular incoming sensory message.

Sensory gating Alteration of sensory messages in the spinal cord.

The Matrix: Do Phantoms Live Here?

In the popular *Matrix* films, Neo, as played by Keanu Reeves, discovers that machines have imprisoned humans in a phantom world called the Matrix, in order to steal human energy for their own use. Actually, the idea of a "matrix" is not totally farfetched. Your own brain may create a *neuromatrix* that allows you to perceive your own body.

A person who suffers an amputation doesn't need to believe in the Matrix to encounter phantoms. Most amputees have *phantom limb* sensations, including pain, for months or years after losing a limb (Fraser, 2002; Halbert, Crotty, & Cameron, 2002). Because the phantom limb feels so "real," a patient with a recently amputated leg may inadvertently try to walk on it, risking further injury. Sometimes, phantom limbs feel like they

are stuck in awkward positions. For instance, one man can't sleep on his back because his missing arm feels like it is twisted behind him.

What causes phantom limbs? Gate control theory cannot explain phantom limb pain (Hunter, Katz, & Davis, 2003). Since pain can't be coming from the missing limb (after all, it's missing!), it cannot pass through pain gates to the brain. Instead, according to Ronald Melzack (1999; Melzack & Katz, 2006), over time the brain creates a body image called the *neuromatrix*. This internal model of the body generates our sense of bodily self. Although amputation may remove a limb, as far as the neuromatrix in the brain is concerned, the limb still exists. Functional magnetic resonance imaging (fMRI) confirms that sensory and motor areas of the brain

are more active when a person feels a phantom limb (Rosen et al., 2001). Even though pain signals no longer come from the amputated limb, the neuromatrix evidently interprets other sensory experiences as pain from the missing limb (Giummarra et al., 2007).

Sometimes the brain gradually reorganizes to adjust for the sensory loss (Wu & Kaas, 2002). For example, a person who loses an arm may at first have a phantom arm and hand. After many years, the phantom may shrink, until only a hand is felt at the shoulder. Perhaps more vividly than others, people with phantom limbs are reminded that the sensory world we experience is constructed, moment-by-moment, not by some futuristic machines, but by our own brain activity.

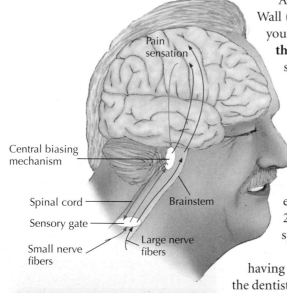

FIGURE 4.26 Diagram of a sensory gate for pain. A series of pain impulses going through the gate may prevent other pain messages from passing through. Or pain messages may relay through a "central biasing mechanism" that exerts control over the gate, closing it to other impulses.

Labels on figure:
- Pain sensation
- Central biasing mechanism
- Spinal cord
- Sensory gate
- Small nerve fibers
- Brainstem
- Large nerve fibers

Gate control theory Proposes that pain messages pass through neural "gates" in the spinal cord.

A fascinating example of sensory gating is provided by Ronald Melzack and Patrick Wall (1996), who studied "pain gates" in the spinal cord. Melzack and Wall noticed, as you may have, that one type of pain will sometimes cancel another. Their **gate control theory** suggests that pain messages from different nerve fibers pass through the same neural "gate" in the spinal cord. If the gate is "closed" by one pain message, other messages may not be able to pass through (Melzack & Katz, 2004; Melzack & Wall, 1996).

How is the gate closed? Messages carried by large, fast nerve fibers seem to close the spinal pain gate directly. Doing so can prevent slower, "reminding system" pain from reaching the brain. As a pain control technique, this is called *counterirritation*. Pain clinics use it by applying a mild electrical current to the skin. This sends *mild* pain messages to the spinal cord and brain, which may effectively close the neurological gates to reduce more agonizing pain (Köke et al., 2004). For more extreme pain, the electrical current can be applied directly to the spinal cord (Linderoth & Foreman, 2006).

You can use counterirritation to control your own pain. For instance, if you are having a tooth filled, try pinching yourself or digging a fingernail into a knuckle while the dentist is working. Focus your attention on the pain you are creating, and increase it any time the dentist's work becomes more painful. This strategy may seem strange, but it works. Generations of children have used it to take the edge off a spanking.

Messages from small, slow fibers seem to take a different route. After going through the pain gate, they pass on to a "central biasing system" in the brain. Under some circumstances, the brain then sends a message back down the spinal cord, closing the pain gates (▶▶ Figure 4.26). Melzack and Wall believe that gate control theory explains the painkilling effects of acupuncture (but see "The Matrix: Do Phantoms Live Here?").

Acupuncture is the Chinese medical art of relieving pain and illness by inserting thin needles into the body. As the acupuncturist's needles are twirled, heated, or electrified, they activate small pain fibers. These relay through the biasing system to close the gates to intense or chronic pain (Melzack & Wall, 1996). Studies have shown that acupuncture produces short-term pain relief for 40 to 80 percent of patients tested (Ernst, 1994; Weidenhammer et al., 2007).

(*Left*) An acupuncturist's chart. (*Right*) Thin stainless steel needles are inserted into areas defined by the chart. Modern research has begun to explain the pain-killing effects of acupuncture (see text). Acupuncture's claimed ability to cure diseases is more debatable.

Herve Donnezan/Photo Researchers, Inc.

Conclusion and a Look Ahead

The senses supply raw data to the brain, but the information remains mostly meaningless until it is interpreted. It's as if the senses provide only the jumbled pieces of a complex puzzle. Melzack's (1999) concept of a neuromatrix is one theory of how the brain tries to make sense of sensory input. In the remainder of this chapter we will further explore some perceptual processes that help us put the puzzle together. But first, here's a chance to rehearse what you've learned.

study break ✋

Somesthetic Senses, Adaptation, Attention, and Gating

Relate

Stand on one foot with your eyes closed. Now touch the tip of your nose with your index finger. Which of the somesthetic senses did you use to perform this feat?

Imagine you are on a boat ride with a friend who starts to feel queasy. Can you explain to your friend what causes motion sickness and what she or he can do to prevent it?

As you sit reading this book, which sensory inputs have undergone adaptation? What new inputs can you become aware of by shifting your focus of attention?

Think about a strategy you have used for reducing pain at the doctor or dentist or in some other painful situation. Did you alter anxiety, control, or attention? Can you think of any ways in which you have used counterirritation to lessen pain?

Visual perception involves finding meaningful patterns in complex stimuli. If you look closely at this painting by the artist Yvaral, you will see that it is entirely made up of small, featureless squares. An infant or newly sighted person would see only a jumble of meaningless colors. But because the squares form a familiar pattern, you should easily see Marilyn Monroe's face. (Or is that Madonna?) ("Marilyn Numerisée," 1990, courtesy Circle Gallery.)

Perception—That Second Step

In general, how do we construct our perceptions?

Imagine what it would be like to have your vision restored after a lifetime of blindness. Actually, a first look at the world can be disappointing because the newfound ability to *sense* the world does not guarantee that it can be *perceived*. Newly sighted persons must *learn* to identify objects, to read clocks, numbers, and letters, and to judge sizes and distances (Gregory, 2003). For instance, Mr. S. B. was a cataract patient who had been blind since birth. After an operation restored his sight at age 52, Mr. S. B. struggled to use his vision.

Mr. S. B. soon learned to tell time from a large clock and to read block letters he had known only from touch. At a zoo, he recognized an elephant from descriptions he had heard. However, handwriting meant nothing to him for more than a year after he regained sight, and many objects were meaningless until he touched them. Thus, Mr. S. B. slowly learned to organize his *sensations* into meaningful *perceptions*. Cases like those of Mr. S. B. show that your experiences are **perceptual constructions,** or mental models of external events, that *are actively created by your brain.*

Of course, perceptions can be misconstructed as they are filtered through our needs, expectations, attitudes, values, and beliefs (▶▶ Figure 4.27). At the beginning of this chapter we described how one of your authors "experienced" an apparent murder that turned out to be something quite different. The girl's description completely shaped his own initial perceptions. This perhaps is understandable. But he'll never forget the added shock he felt when he met the "murderer." The man he had seen a few moments before as vicious and horrible-looking was not even a stranger. He was a neighbor whom your author had seen dozens of times before. Clearly, we don't just believe what we see. We also see what we believe.

▶▶ **FIGURE 4.27** It is difficult to look at this simple drawing without perceiving depth. Yet the drawing is nothing more than a collection of flat shapes. Turn this page counterclockwise 90 degrees and you will see 3 Cs, one within another. When the drawing is turned sideways, it seems nearly flat. However, if you turn the page upright again, a sense of depth will reappear. Clearly, you have used your knowledge and expectations to *construct* an illusion of depth. The drawing itself would be only a flat design if you didn't invest it with meaning.

Illusions

Perceptual misconstruction is responsible for many *illusions*. In an **illusion,** length, position, motion, curvature, or direction is consistently misjudged. For example, because we have seen thousands of rooms shaped roughly like a box, we habitually construct perceptions based on this assumption. This need not be true, however. An *Ames room* (named for the man who designed it) is a lopsided space that appears square when viewed from a certain location (▶▶ Figure 4.28). This illusion is achieved by carefully distorting the proportions of the walls, floor, ceiling, and windows. Because the left corner of the Ames room is farther from a viewer than the right, a person standing in that corner looks very small; one standing in the nearer, shorter right corner looks very large. A person who walks from the left to the right corner will seem to "magically" grow larger.

Note that illusions are distorted perceptions of stimuli that actually exist. In a **hallucination,** people perceive objects or events that have no external reality (Lepore, 2002). For example, they hear voices that are not there (see "Staying in Touch with Reality"). If you think you are experiencing an illusion or a hallucination, try engaging in some reality testing.

What do you mean by reality testing? In any situation having an element of doubt or uncertainty, **reality testing** involves obtaining additional information to check your per-

Perceptual construction A mental model of external events.

Illusion A misleading or distorted perception.

Hallucination An imaginary sensation—such as seeing, hearing, or smelling something that does not exist in the external world.

Reality testing Obtaining additional information to check on the accuracy of perceptions.

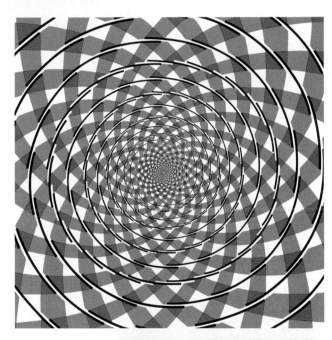

Mark McKenna

⬆ **FIGURE 4.28** The Ames room. From the front, the room looks normal; actually, the right-hand corner is very short, and the left-hand corner is very tall. In addition, the left side of the room slants away from viewers. The diagram shows the shape of the room and reveals why people appear to get bigger as they cross the room toward the nearer, shorter right corner.

ceptions. If you think you see a 3-foot-tall butterfly, you can confirm you are hallucinating by trying to touch its wings. To detect an illusion, you may have to measure a drawing or apply a straight-edge to it. ▶▶Figure 4.29 shows a powerful illusion called Fraser's spiral. What appears to be a spiral is actually made up of a series of closed circles. Most people cannot spontaneously see this reality. Instead, they must carefully trace one of the circles to confirm what is "real" in the design.

Let's explore the process of perceptual construction and some factors that shape or even distort it.

Bottom-up and Top-down Processing

Moment by moment, our perceptions are typically constructed in both *bottom-up* and *top-down* fashion. Think about the process of building a house: Raw materials, such as lumber, doors, tiles, carpets, screws, and nails, must be painstakingly fit together. At the same time, a building plan guides how the raw materials are assembled.

Our brain builds perceptions in similar ways. In **bottom-up processing,** we start constructing at the "bottom," with raw materials. That is, we begin with small sensory units (features), and build upward to a complete perception. The reverse also occurs. In **top-down processing,** preexisting knowledge is used to rapidly organize features into a meaningful whole (Goldstein, 2010). If you put together a picture puzzle you've never seen before, you are relying mainly on bottom-up processing: You must assemble small pieces until a recognizable pattern begins to emerge. Top-down processing is like putting together a puzzle you have solved many times: After only a few pieces are in place, your past experience gives you the plan to rapidly fill in the final picture.

Both types of processing are illustrated by ▶▶Figure 4.30. Also, look ahead to ▶▶Figure 4.33. The first time you see this photo, you will probably process it bottom-up, picking out features until it becomes recognizable. The next time you see it, because of top-down processing, you should recognize it instantly.

An excellent example of perceptual construction is found in the Gestalt organizing principles.

⬆ **FIGURE 4.29** The limits of pure perception. Even simple designs are easily misperceived. Fraser's spiral is actually a series of concentric circles. The illusion is so powerful that people who try to trace one of the circles sometimes follow the illusory spiral and jump from one circle to the next. (After Seckel, 2000.)

Bottom-up processing Organizing perceptions by beginning with low-level features.

Top-down processing Applying higher level knowledge to rapidly organize sensory information into a meaningful perception.

Staying in Touch with Reality

Just imagine that often, and without warning, you hear a voice shouting, "Buckets of blood!" or see blood spattering across the walls of your bedroom. Chances are people would think you are mentally disturbed. Hallucinations are a major symptom of psychosis, dementia, epilepsy, migraine headaches, alcohol withdrawal, and drug intoxication (Spence & David, 2004). They are also one of the clearest signs that a person has "lost touch with reality."

Yet consider the case of mathematician John Nash (the subject of *A Beautiful Mind,* the winner of the 2002 Oscar for best film). Even though Nash suffered from schizophrenia, he eventually learned to use his *reality testing* to sort out which of his experiences were perceptions and which were hallucinations. Unlike John Nash, most people who experience full-blown hallucinations have a limited ability to engage in reality testing (Hohwy & Rosenberg, 2005).

Curiously, "sane hallucinations" also occur. *Charles Bonnet syndrome* is a rare condition that afflicts mainly older people who are partially blind, but not mentally disturbed. Animals, buildings, plants, people, and other objects may seem to appear and disappear in front of their eyes. One older man suffering from partial blindness and leukemia complained of seeing animals in his house, including cattle and bears (Jacob et al., 2004). However, people experiencing "sane hallucinations" can more easily tell that their hallucinations aren't real because their capacity for reality testing is not impaired.

Such unusual experiences show how powerfully the brain seeks meaningful patterns in sensory input and the role that reality testing plays in our normal perceptual experience.

▲ **FIGURE 4.30** Check out this abstract design. If you process it "bottom-up," you will likely see only three small dark geometric shapes near the edges. Would you like to try some top-down processing? Knowing the title of the design will allow you to apply your knowledge and see it in an entirely different way. The title? It's *Special K.* Can you see it now?

Figure-ground organization Part of a stimulus appears to stand out as an object (figure) against a less prominent background (ground).

Gestalt Organizing Principles

How are sensations organized into perceptions? The Gestalt psychologists (see Chapter 1) proposed that the simplest organization involves grouping some sensations into an object, or figure, that stands out on a plainer background. **Figure-ground organization** is probably inborn, because it is the first perceptual ability to appear after cataract patients like Mr. S. B. regain sight. In normal figure-ground perception, only one figure is seen. In *reversible figures,* however, figure and ground can be switched. In ▶▶ Figure 4.31 it is equally possible to see either a wineglass on a dark background or two facial profiles on a light background. As you shift from one pattern to the other, you should get a clear sense of what figure-ground organization means.

Are there other Gestalt organizing principles? The Gestalt psychologists identified several other principles that bring some order to your perceptions (▶▶ Figure 4.32).

1. **Nearness.** All other things being equal, stimuli that are near each other tend to be grouped together (Quinn, Bhatt, & Hayden, 2008). Thus, if three people stand near each other and a fourth person stands 10 feet away, the adjacent three will be seen as a group and the distant person as an outsider (see Figure 4.32*a*).

2. **Similarity.** "Birds of a feather flock together," and stimuli that are similar in size, shape, color, or form tend to be grouped together (see Figure 4.32*b*). Picture two bands marching side by side. If their uniforms are different colors, the bands will be seen as two separate groups, not as one large group.

3. **Continuation, or continuity.** Perceptions tend toward simplicity and continuity. In Figure 4.32*c* it is easier to visualize a wavy line on a squared-off line than it is to see a complex row of shapes.

4. **Closure.** Closure refers to the tendency to *complete* a figure so that it has a consistent overall form. Each of the drawings in Figure 4.32*d* has one or more gaps, yet each is perceived as a recognizable figure. The "shapes" that appear in the two right drawings in Figure 4.32*d* are *illusory figures* (implied shapes that are not actually bounded by an edge or an outline). Even young children see these shapes, despite knowing that they are "not really there." Illusory figures reveal that our tendency to form shapes—even with minimal cues—is powerful.

5. **Contiguity.** A principle that can't be shown in Figure 4.32 is contiguity, or nearness in time *and* space. Contiguity is often responsible for the perception that one thing has *caused* another (Buehner & May, 2003). A psychologist friend of ours demonstrates this principle in class by knocking on his head with one hand while knocking on a wooden table (out of sight) with the other. The knocking sound is perfectly timed with the movements of his visible hand. This leads to the irresistible perception that his head is made of wood.

6. **Common region.** As you can see in Figure 4.32e, stimuli that are found within a common area tend to be seen as a group (Palmer & Beck, 2007). On the basis of similarity and nearness, the stars in Figure 4.32e should be one group and the dots another. However, the colored backgrounds define regions that create three groups of objects (four stars, two stars plus two dots, and four dots). Perhaps the principle of common region explains why we tend to mentally group together people from a particular country, state, province, or geographic region.

Clearly, the Gestalt principles offer us some basic "plans" for organizing parts of our day-to-day perceptions in top-down fashion. Take a moment and look for the camouflaged animal pictured in Figure 4.33. (Camouflage patterns break up figure-ground organization). Have you already seen this photo? If you had never seen similar animals before, could you have located this one? Mr. S. B. would have been at a total loss to find meaning in such a picture.

In a way, we are all detectives, seeking patterns in what we see. In this sense, a meaningful pattern represents a **perceptual hypothesis,** or initial plan or guess about how to organize sensations. Have you ever seen a "friend" in the distance, only to have the person turn into a stranger as you drew closer? Preexisting ideas and expectations *actively* guide our interpretation of sensations (Most et al., 2005).

⬆ FIGURE 4.31 A reversible figure-ground design. Do you see two faces in profile, or a wineglass?

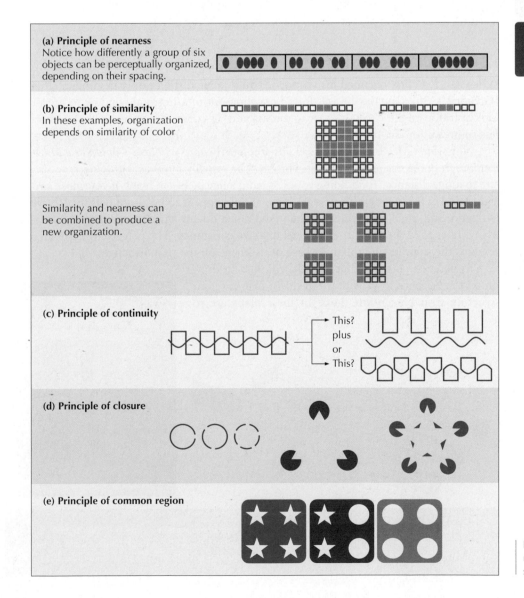

◀◀ FIGURE 4.32 How we organize perceptions.

(a) Principle of nearness
Notice how differently a group of six objects can be perceptually organized, depending on their spacing.

(b) Principle of similarity
In these examples, organization depends on similarity of color

Similarity and nearness can be combined to produce a new organization.

(c) Principle of continuity

This? plus or This?

(d) Principle of closure

(e) Principle of common region

Perceptual hypothesis An initial guess regarding how to organize (perceive) a stimulus pattern.

E. R. Degginger/Animals Animals

The active, constructive nature of perception is perhaps most apparent for *ambiguous stimuli* (patterns allowing more than one interpretation). If you look at a cloud, you may discover dozens of ways to organize its contours into fanciful shapes and scenes. Even clearly defined stimuli may permit more than one interpretation. Look at Necker's cube in ▶▶ Figure 4.34 if you doubt that perception is an active process. Visualize the top cube as a wire box. If you stare at the cube, its organization will change. Sometimes it will seem to project upward, like the lower left cube; other times it will project downward. The difference lies in how your brain interprets the same information. In short, we actively *construct* meaningful perceptions; we do not passively record the events and stimuli around us (Rolls, 2008).

In some instances, a stimulus may offer such conflicting information that perceptual organization becomes impossible. For example, the tendency to make a three-dimensional object out of a drawing is frustrated by the "three-pronged widget" (▶▶ Figure 4.35), an *impossible figure*. Such patterns cannot be organized into stable, consistent, or meaningful perceptions. If you cover either end of the drawing in Figure 4.35, it makes sense perceptually. However, a problem arises when you try to organize the entire drawing. Then, the conflicting information it contains prevents you from forming a stable perception.

Learning to organize his visual sensations was only one of the hurdles Mr. S. B. faced in learning to see. In the next section, we will consider some others.

▲ **FIGURE 4.33** A challenging example of perceptual organization. Once the camouflaged insect (known as a giant walkingstick) becomes visible, it is almost impossible to view the picture again without seeing the insect.

Perceptual Constancies

When Mr. S. B. first regained his vision, he could judge distance only in familiar situations (Gregory, 1990). One day he was found crawling out of a hospital window to get a closer look at traffic on the street. It's easy to understand his curiosity, but he had to be restrained. His room was on the fourth floor!

Why would Mr. S. B. try to crawl out of a fourth-story window? Couldn't he at least tell distance from the size of the cars? No, you must be visually familiar with objects to use their size to judge distance. Try holding your left hand a few inches in front of your nose and your right hand at arm's length. Your right hand should appear to be about half the size of your left hand. Still, you know your right hand did not suddenly shrink, because you have seen it many times at various distances. We call this **size constancy:** The perceived size of an object remains the same, even though the size of its image on the retina changes.

To perceive your hand accurately, you had to draw on past experience to provide a top-down plan for constructing your perception. Some of these plans are so

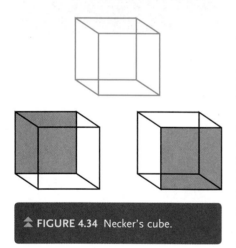

▲ **FIGURE 4.34** Necker's cube.

▲ **FIGURE 4.35** *(Left)* An impossible figure—the "three-pronged widget." *(Right)* It might seem that including more information in a drawing would make perceptual conflicts impossible. However, Japanese artist Shigeo Fukuda has shown otherwise. ("Disappearing Column" © Shigeo Fukuda, 1985.)

Size constancy The perceived size of an object remains constant, despite changes in its retinal image.

basic they seem to be *native* (inborn). An example is the ability to see a line on a piece of paper. Likewise, even newborn babies show some evidence of size constancy (Granrud, 2006; Slater, Mattock, & Brown, 1990). However, many of our perceptions are *empirical*, or based on prior experience. For instance, cars, houses, and people look like toys when seen from a great distance or from an unfamiliar perspective, such as from the top of a skyscraper. This suggests that although some size constancy is innate, it is also affected by learning (Granrud, 2004).

In **shape constancy** the shape of an object remains stable, even though the shape of its retinal image changes. You can demonstrate shape constancy by looking at this page from directly overhead and then from an angle. Obviously, the page is rectangular, but most of the images that reach your eyes are distorted. Yet, though the book's image changes, your perception of its shape remains constant. (For additional examples, see ▸▸ Figure 4.36.) On the highway, alcohol intoxication impairs size and shape constancy, adding to the accident rate among drunk drivers (Farrimond, 1990).

Let's say that you are outside in bright sunlight. Beside you, a friend is wearing a gray skirt and a white blouse. Suddenly a cloud shades the sun. It might seem that the blouse would grow dimmer, but it still appears to be bright white. This happens because the blouse continues to reflect a larger *proportion* of light than nearby objects. **Brightness constancy** refers to the fact that the brightness of objects appears to stay the same as lighting conditions change. However, this holds true only if the blouse and other objects are all illuminated by the same amount of light. You could make an area on your friend's gray skirt look whiter than the shaded blouse by shining a bright spotlight on the skirt.

To summarize, the energy patterns reaching our senses are constantly changing, even when they come from the same object. Size, shape, and brightness constancy rescue us from a confusing world in which objects would seem to shrink and grow, change shape as if made of rubber, and light up or fade like neon lamps.

One of the most amazing perceptual feats is our capacity to create three-dimensional space from flat retinal images. We'll explore that topic in a moment, but first here's a chance to rehearse what you've learned.

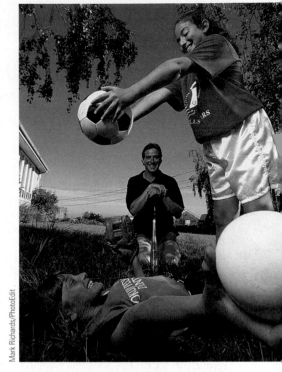

Mark Richards/PhotoEdit

Almost everyone's family album has at least one photo like this. Extreme viewing angles can make maintaining size constancy difficult, even for familiar objects.

(a)   (b)

▲ **FIGURE 4.36** Shape constancy. *(a)* When a door is open, its image actually forms a trapezoid. Shape constancy is indicated by the fact that it is still perceived as a rectangle. *(b)* With great effort you may be able to see this design as a collection of flat shapes. However, if you maintain shape constancy, the distorted pentagrams strongly suggest the surface of a sphere. (Paz-Ket [oil on canvas], Vasarely, Victor [1908–97]/Museo de Bellas Artes, Bilbao, Spain/ © DACS/The Bridgeman Art Library International.)

Shape constancy The perceived shape of an object is unaffected by changes in its retinal image.

Brightness constancy The apparent (or relative) brightness of objects remains the same as long as they are illuminated by the same amount of light.

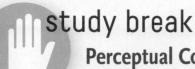

study break

Perceptual Construction, Gestalt Organizing Principles, and Perceptual Constancies

RECITE

1. The Ames room is used to test infants for depth perception. T or F?
2. In top-down processing of information, individual features are analyzed and assembled into a meaningful whole. T or F?
3. The first and most basic perceptual organization to emerge when sight is restored to a blind person is
   a. continuity
   b. nearness constancy
   c. recognition of numbers and letters
   d. figure-ground
4. At times, meaningful perceptual organization represents a _____, or "guess," held until the evidence contradicts it.
5. The design known as Necker's cube is a good example of an impossible figure. T or F?

6. Which among the following are subject to basic perceptual constancy?
   a. figure-ground organization
   b. size
   c. ambiguity
   d. brightness
   e. continuity
   f. closure
   g. shape
   h. nearness

REFLECT
Critical Thinking

7. People who have taken psychedelic drugs, such as LSD or mescaline, often report that the objects and people they see appear to be changing in size, shape, and brightness. This suggests that such drugs disrupt what perceptual process?

Relate

As you look around the area in which you are now, how are the Gestalt organizing principles helping to organize your perceptions? Try to find a specific example for each principle.

If you needed to explain the perceptual constancies to a friend, what would you say? Why are the constancies important for maintaining a stable perceptual world?

ANSWERS

1. F 2. F 3. d 4. hypothesis 5. F 6. b, d, g 7. Perceptual constancies (size, shape, and brightness).

Depth Perception—What If the World Were Flat?

How is it possible to see depth and judge distance?

Close one of your eyes, hold your head very still, and stare at a single point across the room. If you don't move your head or eyes, your surroundings will appear to be almost flat, like a painting or photograph. But even under these conditions you will still have some sense of depth. Now, open both eyes and move your head and eyes as usual. Suddenly, the "3-D" perceptual world returns. How are we able to perceive depth and space?

Depth perception is the ability to see three-dimensional space and to accurately judge distances. Without depth perception, another form of perceptual construction, you would be unable to drive a car or ride a bicycle, play catch, shoot baskets, thread a needle, or simply navigate around a room (Howard & Rogers, 2001a). The world would look like a flat surface.

Mr. S. B. had trouble with depth perception after his sight was restored. Is depth perception learned? Studies done with a visual cliff suggest that depth perception is partly learned and partly innate (Witherington et al., 2005). Basically, a visual cliff is a glass-topped table (▶▶ Figure 4.37). On one side a checkered surface lies directly beneath the glass. On the other side, the checkered surface is 4 feet below. This makes the glass look like a tabletop on one side and a cliff, or drop-off, on the other.

To test for depth perception, 6- to 14-month-old infants were placed in the middle of the visual cliff. This gave them a choice of crawling to the shallow side or the deep side. (The glass prevented them from doing any "skydiving" if they chose the deep side.) Most infants chose the shallow side. In fact, most refused the deep side even when their mothers tried to call them toward it (Gibson & Walk, 1960).

Depth perception The ability to see three-dimensional space and to accurately judge distances.

Glass only

Glass over patterned surface

Deep side

Shallow side

Floor pattern seen through glass

◀◀ **FIGURE 4.37** Human infants and newborn animals refuse to go over the edge of the visual cliff.

If the infants were at least 6 months old when they were tested, isn't it possible that they learned to perceive depth? Yes. More recent research has shown that depth perception begins to develop as early as 2 weeks of age (Yonas, Elieff, & Arterberry, 2002). It is very likely that at least a basic level of depth perception is innate. Yet, the development of depth perception is not complete until about 6 months, suggesting that it depends on both brain maturation and individual experience.

But don't some older babies crawl off tables or beds? As soon as infants become active crawlers, they refuse to cross the deep side of the visual cliff. However, older infants who have just learned to walk must again learn to avoid the "deep" side of the visual cliff (Witherington et al., 2005). Besides, even babies who perceive depth may not be able to catch themselves if they slip. A lack of coordination—not an inability to see depth—probably explains most "crash landings" after about 4 months of age.

Stereoscopic: optic nerve transmissions from each eye are relayed to both sides of brain

Binocular: both eyes have overlapping fields of vision

Allows depth perception with accurate distance estimation

(a)

We learn to construct our perception of three-dimensional space by using a variety of *depth cues.* **Depth cues** are features of the environment and messages from the body that supply information about distance and space. Some cues require two eyes (*binocular cues*), whereas others will work with just one eye (*monocular cues*).

Binocular Depth Cues

The most basic source of depth perception is *retinal disparity* (a discrepancy in the images that reach the right and left eyes). Retinal disparity, which is a binocular cue, is based on the fact that the eyes are about 2.5 inches apart. Because of this, each eye receives a slightly different view of the world. When the two images are fused into one overall image, **stereoscopic vision** (three-dimensional sight) occurs (Howard & Rogers, 2001b). The result is a powerful sensation of depth (▶▶ Figure 4.38 and ▶▶ Figure 4.39).

Convergence is a second binocular depth cue. When you look at a distant object, the lines of vision from your eyes are parallel. You are normally not aware of it, but whenever you estimate a distance under 50 feet (as when you play catch or shoot trash can hoops with the first draft of your essay), you are using convergence. How? Muscles attached to the

(b)

◀◀ **FIGURE 4.38** *(a)* Stereoscopic vision. *(b)* The photographs show what the right and left eyes would see when viewing a plant. Hold the page about 6 to 8 inches from your eyes. Allow your eyes to cross and focus on the overlapping image between the two photos. Then try to fuse the leaves into one image. If you are successful, the third dimension will appear like magic.

Depth cues Perceptual features that impart information about distance and three-dimensional space.

Stereoscopic vision Perception of space and depth caused chiefly by the fact that the eyes receive different images.

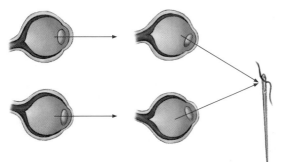

FIGURE 4.40 The eyes must converge, or turn in toward the nose, to focus close objects. The eyes shown are viewed from above the head.

eyeball feed information on eye position to the brain to help it judge distance (▶▶ Figure 4.40).

You can feel convergence by exaggerating it: Focus on your fingertip and bring it toward your eyes until they almost cross. You can actually feel the muscles that control eye movement working harder and harder as your fingertip gets closer.

Can a person with one eye perceive depth? Yes, but not as well as a person with two eyes. Overall, stereoscopic vision is 10 times better for judging depth than perception based on just one eye (Rosenberg, 1994). Try driving a car or riding a bicycle with one eye closed. You will find yourself braking too soon or too late, and you will have difficulty estimating your speed. ("But, officer, my psychology text said to. . . .") Despite this, you will be able to drive, although it will be more difficult than usual. This is possible because your single eye can still make use of monocular depth cues.

Monocular Depth Cues

As their name implies, monocular depth cues can be perceived with just one eye. One such cue is *accommodation,* the bending of the lens to focus on nearby objects. Sensations from muscles attached to each lens flow back to the brain. Changes in these sensations help us judge distances within about 4 feet of the eyes. This information is available even if you are just using one eye, so accommodation is a monocular cue. Beyond 4 feet, accommodation has limited value. Obviously, it is more important to a watchmaker or a person trying to thread a needle than it is to a basketball player or someone driving an automobile.

Other monocular depth cues are referred to as pictorial depth cues, because a good movie, painting, or photograph can create a convincing sense of depth where none exists.

How is the illusion of depth created on a two-dimensional surface? **Pictorial depth cues** are features found in paintings, drawings, and photographs that impart information about space, depth, and distance. To understand how these cues work, imagine that you are look-

Pictorial depth cues Features found in paintings, drawings, and photographs that impart information about space, depth, and distance.

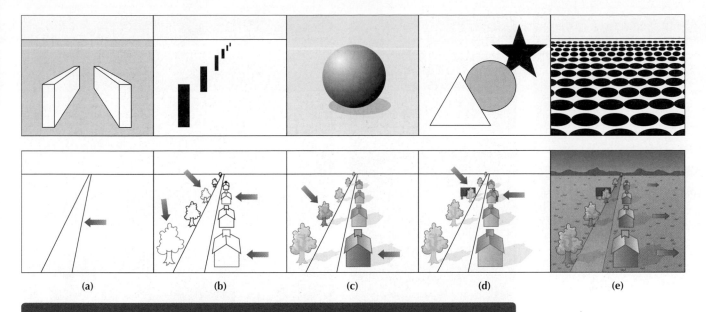

FIGURE 4.41 *(a)* Linear perspective. *(b)* Relative size. *(c)* Light and shadow. *(d)* Overlap. *(e)* Texture gradients. Drawings in the top row show fairly "pure" examples of each of the pictorial depth cues. In the bottom row, the pictorial depth cues are used to assemble a more realistic scene.

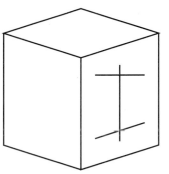

ing outdoors through a window. If you trace everything you see onto the glass, you will have an excellent drawing, with convincing depth. If you then analyze what is on the glass, you will find the following features:

Linear perspective is a very powerful cue for depth. Because of the depth cues implied in this drawing *(left)*, the upper cross on the vertical line appears to be diagonal. It is actually a right angle. The lower cross, which appears to be a right angle, is actually diagonal to the vertical line. (After Enns & Coren, 1995.)

1. **Linear perspective.** This cue is based on the apparent convergence of parallel lines in the environment. If you stand between two railroad tracks, they appear to meet near the horizon, even though they actually remain parallel. Because you know they are parallel, their convergence implies great distance (▶▶ Figure 4.41*a*).

2. **Relative size.** If an artist wishes to depict two objects of the same size at different distances, the artist makes the more distant object smaller (▶▶ Figure 4.41*b*). Special effects in films create sensational illusions of depth by rapidly changing the image size of planets, airplanes, monsters, or what have you. (Also see ▶▶ Figure 4.42.)

3. **Height in the picture plane.** Objects that are placed higher (closer to the horizon line) in a drawing tend to be perceived as more distant. In the upper frame of Figure 4.41*b* the black columns look like they are receding into the distance partly because they become smaller, but also because they move higher in the drawing.

4. **Light and shadow.** Most objects are lighted in ways that create clear patterns of light and shadow. Copying such patterns of light and shadow can give a two-dimensional design a three-dimensional appearance (▶▶ Figure 4.41*c*). (Also, look ahead to ▶▶ Figure 4.43 for more information on light and shadow.)

5. **Overlap.** Overlap (or *interposition*) occurs when one object partially blocks another object. Hold your hands up and ask a friend across the room which is nearer. Relative size will give the answer if one hand is much nearer to your friend than the other. But if one hand is only slightly closer than the other, your friend may not be able to tell—until you slide one hand in front of the other. Overlap then removes any doubt (▶▶ Figure 4.41*d*).

Dennis Coon

▲ **FIGURE 4.42** On a dry lake bed, relative size is just about the only depth cue available for judging the camera's distance from this vintage aircraft. What do you estimate the distance to be? For the answer, look ahead to ▶▶ Figure 4.46.

▶▶ **FIGURE 4.43** *(Above)* When judging depth, we usually assume that light comes mainly from one direction, usually from above. Squint a little to blur the image you see here. You should perceive a collection of globes projecting outward. If you turn this page upside down, the globes should become cavities. (After Ramachandran, 1995.) *(Below)* The famed Dutch artist M. C. Escher violated our assumptions about light to create the dramatic illusions of depth found in his 1955 lithograph *Convex and Concave*. In this print, light appears to come from all sides of the scene. (M. C. Escher's "Convex and Concave" © 2009 The M. C. Escher Company-Holland. All rights reserved. www.mcescher.com.)

● Table 4.1 Summary of Visual Depth Cues

Binocular Cues
- Retinal disparity
- Convergence

Monocular Cues
- Accommodation
- Pictorial depth cues
  Linear perspective
  Relative size
  Height in the picture plane
  Light and shadow
  Overlap
  Texture gradients
  Aerial perspective
  Relative motion (motion parallax)

6. **Texture gradients.** Changes in texture also contribute to depth perception. If you stand in the middle of a cobblestone street, the street will look coarse near your feet. However, its texture will get smaller and finer if you look into the distance (▶▶ Figure 4.41*e*).

7. **Aerial perspective.** Smog, fog, dust, and haze add to the apparent distance of an object. Because of aerial perspective, distant objects tend to be hazy, washed out in color, and lacking in detail. Aerial haze is often most noticeable when it is missing. If you have ever seen a distant mountain range on a crystal-clear day, it might have looked like it was only a few miles away.

8. **Relative motion.** Relative motion, also known as *motion parallax* (PAIR-ah-lax), can be seen by looking out a window and moving your head from side to side. Notice that nearby objects appear to move a sizable distance as your head moves. Trees, houses, and telephone poles that are farther away appear to move slightly in relation to the background. Distant objects like hills, mountains, or clouds don't seem to move at all.

When combined, pictorial cues can create a powerful illusion of depth. (See ● Table 4.1 for a summary of all the depth cues we have discussed.)

Is motion parallax really a pictorial cue? Strictly speaking it is not, except in the two-dimensional world of movies, television, or animated cartoons. However, when parallax is present, we almost always perceive depth. Much of the apparent depth of a good movie comes from relative motion captured by the camera. ▶▶ Figure 4.44 illustrates the defining feature of motion parallax. Imagine that you are in a bus and watching the passing scenery (with your gaze at a right angle to the road). Under these conditions, nearby objects will appear to rush *backward*. Those farther away, such as distant mountains, will seem to move

← Direction of travel

◄◄ FIGURE 4.44 The apparent motion of objects viewed during travel depends on their distance from the observer. Apparent motion can also be influenced by an observer's point of fixation. At middle distances, objects closer than the point of fixation appear to move backward; those beyond the point of fixation appear to move forward. Objects at great distances, such as the sun or moon, always appear to move forward.

very little or not at all. Objects that are more remote, such as the sun or moon, will appear to move in the *same* direction you are traveling. (That's why the moon appears to "follow" you when you take a stroll at night.)

The Moon Illusion

How do the depth perception cues relate to daily experience? We constantly use both pictorial cues and bodily cues to sense depth and judge distances. Consider an intriguing effect called the *moon illusion* (perceiving the moon as larger when it is low in the sky). When the moon is on the horizon, it tends to look like a silver dollar. When it is directly overhead, it looks more like a dime. Contrary to what some people believe, the moon is not magnified by the atmosphere. But the moon *looks* nearly twice as large when it's low in the sky (Ross & Plug, 2002). This occurs, in part, because the moon's *apparent distance* is greater when it is near the horizon than when it is overhead (Kaufman & Kaufman, 2000).

But if it seems farther away, shouldn't it look smaller? No. When the moon is overhead, few depth cues surround it. In contrast, when you see the moon on the horizon, it is behind houses, trees, telephone poles, and mountains. These objects add numerous depth cues, which cause the horizon to seem more distant than the sky overhead. Picture two balloons, one 10 feet away and the second 20 feet away. Suppose the more distant balloon is inflated until its image matches the image of the nearer balloon. How do we know the more distant balloon is larger? Because its image is the same size as a balloon that is closer. Similarly, the moon makes the same-size image on the horizon as it does overhead. However, the horizon seems more distant because more depth cues are present. As a result, the horizon moon must be perceived as larger (Kaufman & Kaufman, 2000). (See ▶▶ Figure 4.45.)

This explanation is known as the **apparent-distance hypothesis** (the horizon seems more distant than the night sky). You can test it by removing depth cues while looking at a horizon moon. Try looking at the moon through a rolled-up paper tube, or make your hands into a "telescope" and look at the next large moon you see. It will immediately appear to shrink when viewed without depth cues (Ross & Plug, 2002).

Can all illusions be explained? Not in all cases, or to everyone's satisfaction. In general, size and shape constancy, habitual eye movements, continuity, and perceptual habits combine in various ways to produce the illusions in ▶▶ Figure 4.47. Rather than attempt to explain all of them, let's focus on one deceptively simple example.

◄◄ FIGURE 4.45 The Ponzo illusion may help you understand the moon illusion. Picture the two white bars as resting on the railroad tracks. In the drawing, the upper bar is the same length as the lower bar. However, because the upper bar appears to be farther away than the lower bar, we perceive it as longer. The same logic applies to the moon illusion.

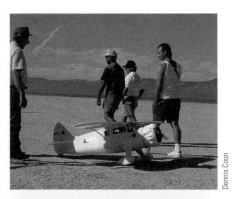

Dennis Coon

▲ FIGURE 4.46 Before you can use familiar size to judge distance, objects must actually be the size you assume they are. Either these men are giants, or the model airplane was closer than you may have thought when you looked at Figure 4.42.

Apparent-distance hypothesis An explanation of the moon illusion stating that the horizon seems more distant than the night sky.

(a) Which of the horizontal lines is longer?

(b) Is the diagonal a single straight line? Check it with a ruler.

(c) Is this a drawing of a staircase descending from upper left to lower right . . . or is it the view of the underneath of a staircase from lower right to upper left?

(d) Are these lines parallel? Cover some of the slash marks to see.

(e) Which line is longer, horizontal or vertical?

(f) Notice how the background distorts the square.

(g) Which quadrilateral is larger?

(h) Which column is shortest? Which is longest?

⬆ FIGURE 4.47 Some interesting perceptual illusions. Such illusions reveal that perceptual misconstructions are a normal part of visual perception.

Consider the drawing in Figure 4.47*a*. This is the familiar **Müller-Lyer** (MEOO-ler-LIE-er) **illusion** in which the horizontal line with arrowheads appears shorter than the line with V's. A quick measurement will show that they are the same length. How can we explain this illusion? Evidence suggests it is based on a lifetime of experience with the edges and corners of rooms and buildings. Richard Gregory (2000) believes you see the horizontal line with the V's as if it were the corner of a room viewed from inside (▶▶ Figure 4.48). The line with arrowheads, on the other hand, suggests the corner of a room or building seen from outside. In other words, cues that suggest a three-dimensional space alter our perception of a two-dimensional design (Enns & Coren, 1995).

Earlier, to explain the moon illusion, we said that if two objects make images of the same size, the more distant object must be larger. This is known formally as *size-distance invariance* (the size of an object's image is precisely related to its distance from the eyes). Gregory believes the same concept explains the Müller-Lyer illusion. If the V-tipped line looks farther away than the arrowhead-tipped line, you must compensate by seeing the V-tipped line as longer. This explanation presumes that you have had years of experience with straight lines, sharp edges, and corners—a pretty safe assumption in our culture.

Is there any way to show that past experience causes the illusion? If we could test someone who saw only curves and wavy lines as a child, we would know if experience with a "square" culture is important. Fortunately, the Zulus, a group of people in South Africa, live in a "round" culture. In their daily lives, traditional Zulus rarely encounter a straight line: Their houses are shaped like rounded mounds and arranged in a circle, tools and toys are curved, and there are few straight roads or square buildings.

What happens if a Zulu looks at the Müller-Lyer design? The typical Zulu villager does not experience the illusion. At most, she or he sees the V-shaped line as *slightly* longer than the other (Gregory, 1990). This seems to confirm the importance of perceptual habits in determining our view of the world.

Müller-Lyer illusion Two equal-length lines tipped with inward or outward pointing V's appear to be of different lengths.

FIGURE 4.48 Why does line *(b)* in the Müller-Lyer illusion look longer than line *(a)*? Probably because it looks more like a distant corner than a nearer one. Because the vertical lines form images of the same length, the more "distant" line must be perceived as larger. As you can see in the drawing on the right, additional depth cues accentuate the Müller-Lyer illusion. (After Enns & Coren, 1995.)

RECITE

1. The visual cliff is used to test for infant sensitivity to linear perspective. T or F?
2. Write an *M* or a *B* after each of the following to indicate if it is a monocular or binocular depth cue.
   accommodation _____ convergence _____ retinal disparity _____ linear perspective _____ motion parallax _____ overlap _____ relative size _____
3. Which of the depth cues listed in Question 2 are based on muscular feedback? _____.
4. Interpretation of pictorial depth cues requires no prior experience. T or F?
5. The moon's image is greatly magnified by the atmosphere near the horizon. T or F?
6. Size-distance relationships appear to underlie which two illusions? _____ and _____

REFLECT

Critical Thinking

7. What hearing ability would you say is most closely related to stereoscopic vision?
8. What size object do you think you would have to hold at arm's length to cover up a full moon?

Relate

Part of the rush of excitement produced by action movies and video games is based on the sense of depth they create. Return to the list of pictorial depth cues. What cues have you seen used to portray depth? Try to think of specific examples in a movie or game you have seen recently.

If you spent a year hiking the Amazon River Basin, what effect might it have on your perception of the Müller-Lyer illusion?

ANSWERS

1. F 2. accommodation (M); convergence (M); retinal disparity (B); linear perspective (B); motion parallax (M), overlap (M), relative size (M) 3. accommodation or convergence 4. F 5. F 6. moon illusion, Müller-Lyer illusion 7. If you close your eyes, you can usually tell the direction and perhaps the location of a sound source, such as a hand-clap. Locating sounds in space is heavily dependent on having two ears, just as stereoscopic vision depends on having two eyes. 8. The most popular answers range from a quarter to a softball. Actually, a pea held in the outstretched hand will cover a full moon (Kunkel, 1993). If you listed an object larger than a pea, be aware that perceptions, no matter how accurate they seem, may distort reality.

Perceptual Learning—Perception from the Top Down

How is perception altered by expectations, motives, emotions, and learning?

We use Gestalt organizing principles, perceptual constancies, and depth cues to construct our visual perceptions. All of these processes, and others, make up the common, partly inborn, core of our perceptual abilities. In addition, we each have specific life experiences that can, in top-down fashion, affect our perceptions. For instance, what you perceive can be altered by *perceptual expectancies,* motives, emotions, and *perceptual habits.*

Perceptual Expectancies

What is a perceptual expectancy? If you are a runner in the starting blocks at a track meet, you are *set* to respond in a certain way. If a car backfires, runners at a track meet may jump the gun. Likewise, past experience, motives, context, or suggestions may create a **perceptual expectancy** (or **set**) that prepares you to perceive in a certain way. As a matter of fact, we all frequently jump the gun when perceiving. In essence, an expectancy is a perceptual hypothesis we are *very likely* to apply to a stimulus—even if applying it is inappropriate.

Perceptual sets often lead us to see what we *expect* to see. For example, let's say you are driving across the desert. You are very low on gas. Finally, you see a sign approaching. On it are the words FUEL AHEAD. You relax, knowing you will not be stranded. But as you draw nearer, the words on the sign become FOOD AHEAD. Most people have had similar experiences in which expectations altered their perceptions. To observe perceptual expectancies firsthand, perform the demonstration described in ▶▶ Figure 4.49.

Perceptual expectancies are frequently created by *suggestion.* In one study (wine snobs take note), participants given a taste of a $90 wine reported that it tasted better than a $10 wine. Functional MRI images confirmed that brain areas related to pleasure were indeed more active when participants tasted the more expensive wine (Plassmann et al., 2008). The twist is that exactly the same wine was served in both cases. Suggesting that the wine was expensive created a perceptual expectancy that it would taste better. And so it did (advertisers also take note). In the same way, labeling people as "gang members," "mental patients," "queers," "illegal immigrants," "bitches," and so on, is very likely to distort perceptions.

View I

View II

View III

▲ **FIGURE 4.49** "Young woman/old woman" illustrations. As an interesting demonstration of perceptual expectancy, show some of your friends view I and some view II (cover all other views). Next show your friends view III and ask them what they see. Those who saw view I should see the old woman in view III; those who saw view II should see the young woman in view III. Can you see both? (After Leeper, 1935.)

Perceptual expectancy (or set) A readiness to perceive in a particular manner, induced by strong expectations.

Do They See What We See?

According to psychologist Richard Nisbett and his colleagues, people from different cultures do, in fact, perceive the world differently. European Americans are individualistic people who tend to focus on themselves and their sense of personal control. In contrast, East Asians are collectivist people who tend to focus on their personal relationships and social responsibilities. As a consequence, European Americans tend to explain actions in terms of internal factors ("she did it because she chose to do it"). In comparison, East Asians tend to explain actions in terms of their social context ("he did it because it was his responsibility to his family") (Norenzayan & Nisbett, 2000).

Do such cultural differences affect our everyday perception of objects and events? Apparently they do. In one study, American and Japanese participants were shown drawings of everyday scenes, such as a farm. Later, they saw a slightly changed version of the scene. Some of the changes were made to the focal point, or figure, of the scene. Other changes altered the surrounding context, or ground, of the scene. Americans, it turns out, were better at detecting changes in the figure of a scene. Japanese participants were better at finding alterations in the background (Nisbett & Miyamoto, 2005).

To explain this difference, Chua, Boland, and Nisbett (2005) presented American and Chinese participants with pictures of a figure (such as a tiger) placed on a ground (such as a jungle) and monitored their eye-movement patterns. The Americans focused their eye movements on the figure; Chinese participants made more eye movements around the ground. In other words, Westerners have a relatively narrow focus of attention, whereas Easterners have a broader focus of attention. Apparently, the society we live in can, indeed, influence even our most basic perceptual habits. This difference in perceptual style even influences the artistic and aesthetic preferences expressed in Eastern and Western art (Masuda et al., 2008).

Motives, Emotions, and Perception

Our motives and emotions also play a role in shaping our perceptions. For example, if you are hungry, food-related words are more likely to gain your attention than non-food-related words (Mogg et al., 1998). Advertisers take advantage of two motives that are widespread in our society: anxiety and sex. Everything from mouthwash to automobile tires is merchandised by using sex to gain attention (LaTour & Henthorne, 2003). Other ads combine sex with anxiety. Deodorant, soaps, toothpaste, and countless other articles are pushed in ads that play on desires to be attractive, to have "sex appeal," or to avoid embarrassment.

Our emotions can also shape our perceptions. According to psychologist Barbara Frederickson, negative emotions generally narrow our perceptual focus, or "spotlight," increasing the likelihood of inattentional blindness. In contrast, positive emotions can actually broaden the scope of attention (Fredrickson & Branigan, 2005). For example, positive emotions can affect how well people recognize people from other races. In recognizing faces, a consistent *other-race effect* occurs. This is a sort of "They all look alike to me" bias in perceiving persons from other racial and ethnic groups. In tests of facial recognition, people are much better at recognizing faces of their own race than others. But when people are in positive moods, their ability to recognize people from other races improves (Johnson & Fredrickson, 2005).

The main reason for the other-race effect is that we typically have more experience with people from our own race. As a result, we become very familiar with the features that help us recognize different persons. For other groups, we lack the perceptual expertise needed to accurately separate one face from another (Sporer, 2001). Such differences indicate the importance of perceptual learning, a topic we turn to next.

Okay, so maybe members of different races or ethnic groups have developed perceptual sets that lead them to see in-group faces differently, but we all see everything else the same, right? For an answer, see "Do They See What We See?"

Perceptual Learning

England is one of the few countries in the world where people drive on the left side of the road. Because of this reversal, it is not unusual for visitors to step off curbs in front of cars—after carefully looking for traffic in the *wrong* direction. As this example suggests, learning has a powerful impact on top-down processing in perception.

How does learning affect perception? The term **perceptual learning** refers to changes in the brain that alter how we construct sensory information into percepts (Fahle & Poggio, 2002).

Perceptual learning Changes in perception that can be attributed to prior experience; a result of changes in how the brain processes sensory information.

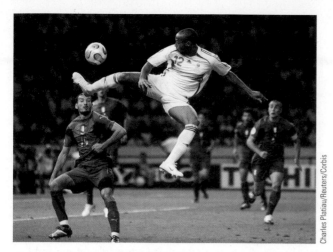

In many sports, expert players are much better than beginners at paying attention to key information. Compared with novices, experts scan actions and events more quickly, and they focus on only the most meaningful information. This helps experts to make decisions and react more quickly (Bard, Fleury, & Goulet, 1994).

For example, to use a computer, you must learn to pay attention to specific stimuli, such as icons and cursors. We also learn to tell the difference between stimuli that seemed identical at first. An example is the novice chef who discovers how to tell the difference between dried basil, oregano, and tarragon. In other situations, we learn to focus on just one part of a group of stimuli. This saves us from having to process all the stimuli in the group. For instance, a linebacker in football may be able to tell if the next play will be a run or a pass by watching one or two key players, rather than the entire opposing team (Seitz & Watanabe, 2005).

In general, learning creates *perceptual habits* (ingrained patterns of organization and attention) that affect our daily experience. Stop for a moment and look at ▶▶ Figure 4.50. The left face looks somewhat unusual, to be sure. But the distortion seems mild—until you turn the page upside down. Viewed normally, the face looks quite grotesque. Why is there a difference? Apparently, most people have little experience with upside-down faces. Perceptual learning, therefore, has less impact on our perceptions of an upside-down face. With a face in the normal position, you know what to expect and where to look. Also, you tend to see the entire face as a recognizable pattern. When a face is inverted, we are forced to perceive its individual features separately (Caharel et al., 2006).

In the next section, we will go beyond normal perception to ask, Is extrasensory perception possible? Before we do that, here's a chance to answer the question, Is remembering the preceding discussion possible?

⬆ **FIGURE 4.50** The effects of prior experience on perception. The doctored face looks far worse when viewed right side up because it can be related to past experience.

RECITE

1. When a person is prepared to perceive events in a particular way, it is said that a perceptual expectancy or _____ exists.
2. People around the world perceive in the same way regardless of culture. T or F?
3. Perceptual habits may become so ingrained that they lead us to misperceive a stimulus. T or F?
4. Perceptual learning seems to program the brain for sensitivity to important _____ of the environment.

REFLECT

Critical Thinking

5. Cigarette advertisements in the United States are required to carry a warning label about the health risks of smoking. How have tobacco companies made these labels less visible?

Perceptual Expectancies, Motives, Emotions, and Perceptual Learning

Relate

You have almost certainly misperceived a situation at some time because of a perceptual expectancy or the influence of your motives and emotions. How were your perceptions influenced?

How has perceptual learning affected your ability to safely drive a car? For example, what do you pay attention to at intersections? Where do you habitually look as you are driving?

ANSWERS

1. set 2. F 3. T 4. features 5. Advertisers place health warnings in the corners of ads, where they attract the least possible attention. Also, the labels are often placed on "busy" backgrounds so that they are partially camouflaged. Finally, the main images in ads are designed to strongly attract attention. This further distracts readers from seeing the warnings. Over time, perceptual learning renders these warnings practically invisible.

Extrasensory Perception— Do You Believe in Magic?

Is extrasensory perception possible?

Once, during the middle of the night, a woman away for a weekend visit suddenly had a strong impulse to return home. When she arrived, she found the house on fire with her husband asleep inside (Rhine, 1953). How could she have known? Could she have used **extrasensory perception (ESP)**—the purported ability to perceive events in ways that cannot be explained by known sensory capacities?

About half of the general public believes in the existence of ESP (Wiseman & Watt, 2006). ESP and other paranormal events are treated as accepted facts in many movies and television programs. Stage entertainers routinely "astound" their audiences. There is even a discipline, *parapsychology,* that studies ESP and other **psi phenomena** (events that seem to defy accepted scientific laws). (Psi is pronounced like "sigh.") Parapsychologists seek answers to the questions raised by three basic forms that ESP could take. These are:

1. **Telepathy.** The purported ability to communicate directly with another person's mind. When the other person is dead, the communications are called *mediumship.*
2. **Clairvoyance.** The purported ability to perceive events or gain information in ways that appear unaffected by distance or normal physical barriers.
3. **Precognition.** The purported ability to perceive or accurately predict future events. Precognition may take the form of prophetic dreams that foretell the future.
   While we are at it, we might as well toss in another purported psi ability:
4. **Psychokinesis.** The purported ability to exert influence over inanimate objects (such as bending spoons) by willpower ("mind over matter"). (Psychokinesis cannot be classed as a type of ESP, but it is frequently studied by parapsychologists.)

Extrasensory perception (ESP) The purported ability to perceive events in ways that cannot be explained by known capacities of the sensory organs.

Psi phenomena Events that seem to lie outside the realm of accepted scientific laws.

An Appraisal of ESP

Do psychologists also believe in ESP? Regardless of all of this enthusiasm, psychologists as a group are highly skeptical about psi abilities. Let's have a look at the evidence for and against extrasensory perception. The formal investigation of psi events owes much to the late J. B. Rhine, who tried to study ESP objectively. Many of Rhine's experiments made use of *Zener cards* (a deck of 25 cards, each bearing one of five symbols) (▶▶ Figure 4.51). In a typical clairvoyance test, people try to guess the symbols on the cards as they are turned up from a shuffled deck. In a typical telepathy test, a *receiver* tries to guess the correct symbol by reading the mind of a *sender* looking at a card. Pure guessing in these tests will produce an average score of 5 "hits" out of 25 cards. Rhine and others since have reported results much greater than might be expected by chance alone.

Doesn't evidence like that settle the issue? No it doesn't, for a number of reasons, including fraud, poorly designed experiments, and chance.

Fraud

Fraud continues to plague parapsychology. The need for skepticism is especially great anytime there's money to be made from purported psychic abilities. Stage demonstrations of ESP are based on deception and tricks, as are other "for profit" enterprises. For example, the

"I see a girl, I see a marriage, I see her not understanding you, I see a beer belly. Do you want me to go on?"

owners of the "Miss Cleo" TV-psychic operation were convicted of felony fraud in 2002. "Miss Cleo," supposedly a Jamaican-accented psychic, was really just an actress from Los Angeles. People who paid $4.99 a minute for a "reading" from "Miss Cleo" actually reached one of several hundred operators. These people were hired to do "cold readings" through ads that read, "No experience necessary." Despite being entirely faked, the "Miss Cleo" scam brought in more than $1 billion before it was shut down.

Anyone can learn to do "cold readings" well enough to produce satisfied customers (Wood et al., 2003). *Cold reading* is a set of techniques that are used to lead people to believe in the truth of what a psychic or medium is saying about them. These include a reliance on many of the same techniques used by astrologers, such as uncritical acceptance, positive instances, and the Barnum effect. (Remember Chapter 1?)

The "psychic" begins a "reading" by making general statements about a person. The psychic then plays "hot and cold" by attending to the person's facial expressions, body language, or tone of voice. When the psychic is "hot" (on the right track), he or she continues to make similar statements about the person. If the person's reactions signal that the psychic is "cold," the psychic drops that topic or line of thought and tries another (Hyman, 2007).

Poorly Designed Experiments

Unfortunately, some of Rhine's most dramatic early experiments used badly printed Zener cards that allowed the symbols to show faintly on the back. It is also very easy to cheat, by marking cards with a fingernail or by noting marks on the cards caused by normal use. Even if this were not the case, there is evidence that early experimenters sometimes unconsciously gave people cues about cards with their eyes, facial gestures, or lip movements. In short, none of the early studies in parapsychology were done in a way that eliminated the possibility of deliberate fraud or the accidental "leakage" of helpful information (Alcock, Burns, & Freeman, 2003).

Modern parapsychologists are now well aware of the need for double-blind experiments, security and accuracy in record keeping, meticulous control, and repeatability of experiments (Milton & Wiseman, 1997; O'Keeffe & Wiseman, 2005). In the last 10 years, hundreds of experiments have been reported in parapsychological journals. Many of them seem to support the existence of psi abilities.

Chance

Then why do most psychologists still remain skeptical about psi abilities? The most important reason has to do with chance. Remember the woman who had a premonition that something bad was about to happen to her husband? She returned home early to find her house on fire with him sleeping inside. An apparent clairvoyant or telepathic experience like this is certainly striking, but it does not confirm the existence of ESP. You may not realize it, but such *coincidences* occur quite often. On any given night, many, many people might act on a "premonition." If, by coincidence, one person's hunch turns out to be correct, it may be *reinterpreted* as precognition or clairvoyance (Marks, 2000; Wiseman & Watt, 2006). Then you read about it in the news the next day. No one reports the vast majority of false premonitions, which will simply be forgotten.

Inconsistency in psi research is a related problem. For every published study with positive results, there are many others that fail and are never reported (Alcock, 2003). Even experimental "successes" are weak. Many of the most spectacular findings in parapsychology simply cannot be *replicated* (reproduced or repeated) (Hyman, 1996a). Furthermore, improved research methods usually result in fewer positive results (Hyman, 1996b; O'Keeffe & Wiseman, 2005).

Even when a person does seems to show evidence of psi ability, it is rare—in fact, almost unheard of—for him or her to maintain that ability over any sustained period of time (Alcock, Burns, & Freeman, 2003). This is likely because a person who only temporarily scores above chance has just received credit for a **run of luck** (a statistically unusual outcome that could occur by chance alone).

Run of luck A statistically unusual outcome (as in getting 5 heads in a row when flipping a coin) that could still occur by chance alone.

To understand the run-of-luck criticism, imagine that you flip a coin 100 times and record the results. You then flip another coin 100 times, again recording the results. The two lists are compared. For any 10 pairs of flips, we would expect heads or tails to match 5 times. Let's say that you go through the list and find a set of 10 pairs where 9 out of 10 matched. This is far above chance expectation. But does it mean that the first coin "knew" what was going to come up on the second coin? The idea is obviously silly. Now, what if a person guesses 100 times what will come up on a coin. Again, we might find a set of 10 guesses that matches the results of flipping the coin. Does this mean that the person, for a time, had precognition—then lost it?

You may be surprised to learn that some ESP researchers believe this "decline effect" shows that parapsychological skills are very fragile, like a weak cell phone connection, fading in and out over time. If a person has a good short run of guessing, it is assumed that the person, for a time, had precognition. A subsequent run of poor guesses is interpreted to mean the person's precognition has temporarily faded out. In fact, creative interpretation is a common problem when it comes to psi. For example, ex-astronaut Edgar Mitchell claimed he did a successful telepathy experiment from space. Yet news accounts never mentioned that on some trials Mitchell's "receivers" scored above chance, whereas on others they scored *below* chance. Although you might assume that below-chance trials were failures to find telepathy, Mitchell reinterpreted them as "successes," claiming that they represented intentional "psi missing." But, as skeptics have noted, if both high scores and low scores count as successes, how can you lose?

Implications

After close to 130 years of investigation, it is still impossible to say conclusively whether psi events occur. As we have seen, a close look at psi experiments often reveals serious problems of evidence, procedure, and scientific rigor (Alcock, Burns, & Freeman, 2003; Hyman, 2007; Stokes, 2001). The more closely psi experiments are examined, the more likely it is that claimed successes will evaporate (Alcock, 2003; Stokes, 2001). As one critic put it, positive ESP results usually mean "Error Some Place" (Marks, 2000).

What would it take to scientifically demonstrate the existence of ESP? Quite simply, a set of instructions that would allow any competent, unbiased observer to produce a psi event under standardized conditions that rule out any possibility of fraud or chance (Schick & Vaughn, 2001). In fact, professional magician and skeptic James Randi even offers a $1,000,000 prize to anyone who can demonstrate evidence of psi events under standardized conditions. No one has yet claimed the prize. (You can read all about it if you Google the James Randi Educational Foundation.)

Undoubtedly, some intrepid researchers will continue their attempts to supply irrefutable evidence. Others remain skeptics and consider 130 years of inconclusive efforts reason enough to abandon the concept of ESP (Marks, 2000). Yet, being a skeptic does not mean a person is against something. It means that you are unconvinced. The purpose of this discussion, then, has been to counter the *uncritical* acceptance of psi events that is reported in the popular press or by researchers who are uncritical "true believers." (But then, you already knew we were going to say that, didn't you!)

Of course, in many ESP tests, the outcome is beyond debate. A good example is provided by ESP experiments done through newspapers, radio, and television. In these mass media studies, people attempted to identify ESP targets from a distance. The results of more than 1.5 million ESP trials done through the mass media are easy to summarize: There was no significant ESP effect (Milton & Wiseman, 1999). Zero. Zip. Nada. Clearly, state lottery organizers have nothing to fear!

A Look Ahead

In this chapter we have moved from basic sensations to the complexities of perceiving people and events. We have also probed some of the controversies concerning ESP. In the Psychology in Action section, we will return to "everyday" perception, for a look at perceptual awareness.

RECITE

1. Four purported psi events investigated by parapsychologists are clairvoyance, telepathy, precognition, and _____.
2. The _____ cards were used by J. B. Rhine in early tests of ESP.
3. Natural, or "real life," occurrences are regarded as the best evidence for the existence of ESP. T or F?
4. Skeptics attribute positive results in psi experiments to statistical runs of luck. T or F?
5. Replication rates are very high for ESP experiments. T or F?

REFLECT

Critical Thinking

6. What would you estimate is the chance that two people will have the same birthday (day and month, but not year) in a group of 30 people?

7. A "psychic" on television offers to fix broken watches for viewers. Moments later, dozens of viewers call the station to say that their watches miraculously started running again. What have they overlooked?

Relate

Let's say that a friend of yours is an avid fan of TV shows that feature paranormal themes. See if you can summarize for her or him what is known about ESP. Be sure to include evidence for and against the existence of ESP and some of the thinking errors associated with nonskeptical belief in the paranormal.

ANSWERS

1. psychokinesis 2. Zener 3. F 4. T 5. F 6. Most people assume that this would be a relatively rare event. Actually there is a 71 percent chance that two people will share a birthday in a group of 30. Most people probably underestimate the natural rate of occurrence of many seemingly mysterious coincidences (Alcock, Burns, & Freeman, 2003). 7. When psychologists handled watches awaiting repair at a store, 57 percent began running again, with no help from a "psychic." Believing the psychic's claim also overlooks the impact of big numbers: If the show reached a large audience, at least a few "broken" watches would start working merely by chance.

psychology in action

Becoming a Better Eyewitness to Life

AP Images

How can I learn to perceive events more accurately?

In the courtroom, eyewitness testimony can be a key to proving guilt or innocence. The claim "I saw it with my own eyes" still carries a lot of weight with a jury. Too many jurors (unless they have taken a psychology course) tend to assume that eyewitness testimony is nearly infallible (Durham & Dane, 1999). Even U.S. judges are vulnerable to overoptimism about eyewitness testimony (Wise & Safer, 2004). But, to put it bluntly, eyewitness testimony is frequently wrong (Wells & Olson, 2003). Recall, for instance, that one of your authors would have sworn in court that he had seen a murder taking place at the supermarket—*if* he hadn't received more information to correct his misperceptions.

What about witnesses who are certain that their perceptions were accurate? Should juries believe them? Actually, having confidence in your testimony has almost no bearing on its accuracy (Brewer & Wells, 2006)! Psychologists are gradually convincing lawyers, judges, and police that eyewitness errors are common (Yarmey, 2003). Even so, thousands of people have been wrongfully convicted (Scheck, Neufeld, & Dwyer, 2000).

Unfortunately, perception rarely provides an "instant replay" of events. Impressions formed when a person is surprised, threatened, or under stress are especially prone to distortion (Yuille & Daylen, 1998). One study of eyewitness cases found that the *wrong person* was chosen from police lineups 25 percent of the time (Levi, 1998).

Wouldn't the victim of a crime remember more than a mere witness? Not necessarily. A revealing study found that eyewitness accuracy is virtually the same for witnessing a crime (seeing a pocket calculator stolen) as it is for being a victim (seeing one's own watch stolen) (Hosch & Cooper, 1982). Placing more weight on the testimony of victims may be a serious mistake. In many crimes, victims fall prey to *weapon focus*. Understandably, they

Even in broad daylight, eyewitness testimony is untrustworthy. In 2001 an airliner crashed near Kennedy International Airport in New York. Hundreds of people saw the plane go down. Half of them said the plane was on fire. Flight recorders showed there was no fire. One witness in five saw the plane make a right turn. An equal number saw it make a left turn! As one investigator noted, the best witness may be a "kid under 12 years old who doesn't have his parents around." Adults, it seems, are easily swayed by their expectations.

fix their entire attention on the knife, gun, or other weapon used by an attacker. In doing so, they fail to notice details of appearance, dress, or other clues to identity (Pickel, French, & Betts, 2003). Additional factors that consistently lower eyewitness accuracy are summarized in ●Table 4.2 (Kassin et al., 2001; Wells & Olson, 2003).

Implications Now that DNA testing is available, more than 200 people who were convicted of murder, rape, and other crimes in the United States have been exonerated. Most of these innocent people were convicted mainly on the basis of eyewitness testimony. Each also spent *years* in prison before being cleared (Foxhall, 2000). How often are everyday perceptions as inaccurate or distorted as those of an emotional eyewitness? The answer we have been moving toward is very frequently. Bearing this in mind may help you be more tolerant of the views of others and more cautious about your own objectivity. It may also encourage more frequent *reality testing* on your part.

If you have ever concluded that someone was angry, upset, or unfriendly without checking the accuracy of your perceptions, you have fallen into a subtle trap. Personal objectivity is an elusive quality, requiring frequent reality testing to maintain. At the very least, it pays to ask a person what she or he is feeling when you are in doubt. Clearly, most of us could learn to be better "eyewitnesses" to daily events.

Positive Psychology: Perceptual Awareness

Do some people perceive things more accurately than others? Humanistic psychologist Abraham Maslow (1969) believed that some people perceive themselves and others with unusual accuracy. Maslow characterized these people as especially alive, open, aware, and mentally healthy. He found that their perceptual styles were marked by immersion in the present; a lack of self-consciousness; freedom from selecting, criticizing, or evaluating; and a general "surrender" to experience. The kind of perception Maslow described is

---

●Table 4.2 Factors Affecting the Accuracy of Eyewitness Perceptions

SOURCES OF ERROR	SUMMARY OF FINDINGS
1. Wording of questions	An eyewitness's testimony about an event can be affected by how the questions put to that witness are worded.
2. Postevent information	Eyewitness testimony about an event often reflects not only what was actually seen but also information obtained later on.
3. Attitudes, expectations	An eyewitness's perception and memory for an event may be affected by his or her attitudes and expectations.
4. Alcohol intoxication	Alcohol intoxication impairs later ability to recall events.
5. Cross-racial perceptions	Eyewitnesses are better at identifying members of their own race than they are at identifying people of other races.
6. Weapon focus	The presence of a weapon impairs an eyewitness's ability to accurately identify the culprit's face.
7. Accuracy-confidence	An eyewitness's confidence is not a good predictor of his or her accuracy.
8. Exposure time	The less time an eyewitness has to observe an event, the less well she or he will perceive and remember it.
9. Unconscious transference	Eyewitnesses sometimes identify as a culprit someone they have seen in another situation or context.
10. Color perception	Judgments of color made under monochromatic light (such as an orange street light) are highly unreliable.
11. Stress	Very high levels of stress impair the accuracy of eyewitness perceptions.

Source: Adapted from Kassin et al., 2001.

like that of a mother with her newborn infant, a child at Christmas, or two people in love.

In daily life, we quickly habituate (respond less) to predictable and unchanging stimuli. **Habituation** is a type of learning—basically, we learn to cease paying attention to familiar stimuli. For instance, when you download a new MP3, the music initially holds your attention all the way through. But when the MP3 becomes "old," the song may play without your really attending to it. When a stimulus is repeated *without change,* our response to it habituates, or decreases. Interestingly, creative people habituate *more slowly* than average. We might expect that they would rapidly become bored with a repeated stimulus. Instead, it seems that creative people actively attend to stimuli, even those that are repeated (Colin, Moore, & West, 1996).

The Value of Paying Attention Whereas the average person has not reached perceptual restriction of the "if you've seen one tree, you've seen them all" variety, the fact remains that most of us tend to look at a tree and classify it into the perceptual category of "trees in general" without really appreciating the miracle standing before us. How, then, can we bring about **dishabituation** (a reversal of habituation) on a day-to-day basis? Does perceptual clarity require years of effort? Fortunately, a more immediate avenue is available. The deceptively simple key to dishabituation is this: Pay attention. The following story summarizes the importance of attention:

> One day a man of the people said to Zen Master Ikkyu: "Master, will you please write for me some maxims of the highest wisdom?"
> Ikkyu immediately took his brush and wrote the word "Attention."
> "Is that all?" asked the man. "Will you not add something more?"
> Ikkyu then wrote twice running: "Attention. Attention."
> "Well," remarked the man rather irritably, "I really don't see much depth or subtlety in what you have just written."
> Then Ikkyu wrote the same word three times running: "Attention. Attention. Attention." Half angered, the man demanded, "What does that word 'Attention' mean anyway?"
> And Ikkyu answered gently: "Attention means attention." (Kapleau, 1966)

To this we can add only one thought, provided by the words of poet William Blake: "If the doors of perception were cleansed, man would see everything as it is, infinite."

How to Become a Better "Eyewitness" to Life

Here's a summary of ideas from this chapter to help you maintain and enhance perceptual awareness and accuracy:

1. *Remember that perceptions are constructions of reality.* Learn to regularly question your own perceptions. Are they accurate? Could another interpretation fit the facts? What assumptions are you making? Could they be false? How might your assumptions be distorting your perceptions?

2. *Break perceptual habits and interrupt habituation.* Each day, try to get away from habitual, top-down processing and do some activities in new ways. For example, take different routes when you travel to work or school. Do routines, such as brushing your teeth or combing your hair, with your nonpreferred hand. Try to look at friends and family members as if they are persons you just met for the first time.

3. *Seek out-of-the-ordinary experiences.* The possibilities here range from trying foods you don't normally eat to reading opinions very different from your own. Experiences ranging from a quiet walk in the woods to a trip to an amusement park may be perceptually refreshing.

4. *Beware of perceptual sets.* Anytime you pigeonhole people, objects, or events, there is a danger that your perceptions will be distorted by expectations or preexisting categories. Be especially wary of labels and stereotypes. Try to see people as individuals, and events as unique, one-time occurrences.

Habituation A decrease in perceptual response to a repeated stimulus.

Dishabituation A reversal of habituation.

5. *Be aware of the ways in which motives and emotions influence perceptions.* It is difficult to avoid being swayed by your own interests, needs, desires, and emotions. But be aware of this trap and actively try to see the world through the eyes of others. Taking the other person's perspective is especially valuable in disputes or arguments. Ask yourself, "How does this look to her or him?"

6. *Make a habit of engaging in reality testing.* Actively look for additional evidence to check the accuracy of your perceptions. Ask questions, seek clarifications, and find alternate channels of information. Remember that perception is not automatically accurate. You could be wrong—we all are frequently.

7. *Pay attention.* Make a conscious effort to pay attention to other people and your surroundings. Don't drift through life in a haze. Listen to others with full concentration. Watch their facial expressions. Make eye contact. Try to get in the habit of approaching perception as if you are going to have to testify later about what you saw and heard.

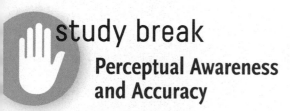

study break

Perceptual Awareness and Accuracy

RECITE

1. Most perceptions can be described as active constructions of external reality. T or F?
2. Inaccuracies in eyewitness perceptions obviously occur in "real life," but they cannot be reproduced in psychology experiments. T or F?
3. Accuracy scores for facts provided by witnesses to staged crimes may be as low as 25 percent correct. T or F?
4. Victims of crimes are more accurate eyewitnesses than are impartial observers. T or F?
5. *Reality testing* is another term for dishabituation. T or F?

REFLECT
Critical Thinking

6. Return for a moment to the incident described at the beginning of this chapter. What perceptual factors were involved in the first version of the "murder"? How did the girl affect what was seen?

Relate

Because perceptions are constructions or models of external events, we should all engage in more frequent reality testing. Can you think of a recent event when a little reality testing would have saved you from misjudging a situation?

In order to improve your own perceptual awareness and accuracy, which strategies would you emphasize first?

ANSWERS

1. T 2. F 3. T 4. F 5. F 6. The girl's misperception, communicated so forcefully to one of your authors, created a powerful expectancy that influenced what he perceived. Also, the event happened quickly (the exposure time was brief) and the stressful or emotional nature of the incident encouraged his own misperception.

chapter in review

Major Points

- Sensory systems select, analyze, and transduce information from the surrounding world.

- All of the senses rely on a complex series of mechanical, chemical, and neural events to generate messages understood by the brain.

- Sensory adaptation, selective attention, and sensory gating significantly modify our experiences.

- Perception is an active process of assembling sensations into meaningful patterns.

- We unconsciously use Gestalt organizing principles and perceptual constancies to construct perceptions.

- Our wondrous ability to perceive three-dimensional space is based on binocular and monocular depth cues.

- Perception is greatly affected by expectations, motives, emotions, and learning.

- Perceptual accuracy can be improved by conscious effort and an awareness of factors that contribute to erroneous perceptions.

Summary

In general, how do sensory systems function?

- Because of transduction, selectivity, limited sensitivity, feature detection, and coding patterns, the senses act as data reduction systems.
- Sensation can be partially understood in terms of sensory localization in the brain.

How does the visual system function?

- The eye is a visual system, not a photographic one. The entire visual system is structured to analyze visual information.
- Four common visual defects are myopia, hyperopia, astigmatism, and presbyopia.
- The rods and cones are photoreceptors in the retina of the eye.
- The rods specialize in peripheral vision, night vision, seeing black and white, and motion detection. The cones specialize in color vision, acuity, and daylight vision.
- Color vision is explained by the trichromatic theory in the retina and by the opponent-process theory in the visual system beyond the eyes.
- Total color blindness is rare, but 8 percent of males and 1 percent of females are red-green color-blind or color-weak.
- Dark adaptation is caused mainly by an increase in the amount of visual pigments in the rods.

What are the mechanisms of hearing?

- Sound waves are the stimulus for hearing. They are transduced by the eardrum, auditory ossicles, oval window, cochlea, and ultimately, the hair cells.
- The frequency theory and place theory of hearing together explain how pitch is sensed.
- Two basic types of hearing loss are conductive hearing loss and sensorineural hearing loss. Noise-induced hearing loss is a common form of sensorineural hearing loss caused by exposure to loud noise.

How do the chemical senses operate?

- Olfaction (smell) and gustation (taste) are chemical senses responsive to airborne or liquefied molecules.
- The lock and key theory of olfaction partially explains smell. In addition, the location of the olfactory receptors in the nose helps identify various scents.
- Sweet and bitter tastes are based on a lock-and-key coding of molecule shapes. Salty and sour tastes are triggered by a direct flow of ions into taste receptors.

What are the somesthetic senses?

- The somesthetic senses include the skin senses, vestibular senses, and kinesthetic senses (receptors that detect muscle and joint positioning).
- The skin senses are touch, pressure, pain, cold, and warmth. Sensitivity to each is related to the number of receptors found in an area of skin.
- Distinctions can be made between warning pain and reminding pain.
- Pain is greatly affected by anxiety, attention, and control over a stimulus. Pain can be reduced by controlling these factors.
- According to sensory conflict theory, motion sickness is caused by a mismatch of visual, kinesthetic, and vestibular sensations. Motion sickness can be avoided by minimizing sensory conflict.

Why are we more aware of some sensations than others?

- Incoming sensations are affected by sensory adaptation (a reduction in the number of nerve impulses sent), by selective attention (selection and diversion of messages in the brain), and by sensory gating (blocking or alteration of messages flowing toward the brain).
- Selective gating of pain messages takes place in the spinal cord, as explained by gate control theory. Gate control theory cannot explain phantom limb pain.

In general, how do we construct our perceptions?

- Perception is an active process of constructing sensations into a meaningful mental representation of the world.
- Perceptions are based on simultaneous bottom-up and top-down processing. Complete percepts are assembled out of small sensory features in "bottom-up" fashion guided by preexisting knowledge applied "top-down" to help organize features into a meaningful whole.
- Separating figure and ground is the most basic perceptual organization.
- The following Gestalt principles also help organize sensations: nearness, similarity, continuity, closure, contiguity, and common region.

- A perceptual organization may be thought of as a hypothesis held until evidence contradicts it.
- In vision, the image projected on the retina is constantly changing, but the external world appears stable and undistorted because of size, shape, and brightness constancy.

How is it possible to see depth and judge distance?

- A basic, innate capacity for depth perception is present soon after birth.
- Depth perception depends on binocular cues of retinal disparity and convergence.
- Depth perception also depends on the monocular cue of accommodation. • Monocular "pictorial" depth cues also underlie depth perception. They are linear perspective, relative size, height in the picture plane, light and shadow, overlap, texture gradients, aerial haze, and motion parallax.
- The moon illusion can be explained by the apparent-distance hypothesis, which emphasizes that many depth cues are present when the moon is near the horizon, and few are present when it is overhead.

How is perception altered by expectations, motives, emotions, and learning?

- Suggestion, motives, emotions, attention, and prior experience combine in various ways to create perceptual sets, or expectancies.
- Personal motives and values often alter perceptions by changing the evaluation of what is seen or by altering attention to specific details.

- Perceptual learning influences the top-down organization and interpretation of sensations.
- One of the most familiar of all illusions, the Müller-Lyer illusion, seems to be related to perceptual learning, linear perspective, and size–distance invariance relationships.

Is extrasensory perception possible?

- Parapsychology is the study of purported psi phenomena, including telepathy (including mediumship), clairvoyance, precognition, and psychokinesis.
- Research in parapsychology remains controversial because of a variety of problems and shortcomings. The bulk of the evidence to date is against the existence of ESP.

How can I learn to perceive events more accurately?

- Eyewitness testimony is surprisingly unreliable. Eyewitness accuracy is further damaged by weapon focus, and a number of similar factors.
- When a stimulus is repeated without change, our response to it undergoes habituation.
- Perceptual accuracy is enhanced by reality testing, dishabituation, and conscious efforts to pay attention.
- It is also valuable to break perceptual habits, to broaden frames of reference, to beware of perceptual sets, and to be aware of the ways in which motives and emotions influence perceptions.

Web Resources

For an up-to-date list of direct links to interesting sites, including those listed here, visit the student companion site for this book at www.cengage.com/psychology/coon

The Joy of Visual Perception An online book about visual perception, including information on the eye.

Virtual Tour of the Ear This site provides educational information about the ear and hearing and provides quick access to ear and hearing web resources.

Taste and Smell Disorders Read about various disorders of taste and smell and what can be done about them.

American Pain Foundation Find out more about pain and its treatment.

Gallery of Illusions An interesting and fun website that presents illusory stimuli that are fun to view and that provides a basis to learn about sensation and perception.

3-D Stereograms Find the 3-D images hidden in these pictures.

Perceptual Learning Explore an example of perceptual learning through wine tasting.

James Randi Education Foundation Win $1,000,000 for proving, under scientifically controlled conditions, that you have ESP.

The Innocence Project Read about real cases of people convicted through eyewitness testimony but later exonerated by DNA evidence.

Interactive Learning

PSYCHOLOGY: A JOURNEY BOOK COMPANION WEBSITE
WWW.CENGAGE.COM/PSYCHOLOGY/COON
Visit your book companion website, where you will find flash cards, practice quizzes, web links, and more to help you study.

JUST WHAT YOU NEED TO KNOW NOW! CENGAGE**NOW**
Spend time on what you need to master rather than on information you already have learned. Take a pretest for this chapter, and CengageNOW will generate a personalized study plan based on your results. The study plan will identify the topics you need to review and direct you to online resources to help you master those topics. You can then take a posttest to help you determine the concepts you have mastered and what you will need to work on. Try it out! Go to www.cengage.com/login to sign in with an access code or to purchase access to this product.

test your knowledge

Sensation and Perception

For additional review, get more practice with *CengageNOW, WebTutor*, the *Practice Quizzes*, and/or the printed *Study Guide* available with this book.

1. The senses divide the world into basic perceptual features and sensory patterns, a process known as
   a. sensory localization   b. sensory analysis
   c. accommodation   d. phosphenation

2. If you press on your closed eyelids you will experience phosphenes. This illustrates the concept of
   a. visual saturation   b. sensory coding
   c. accommodation   d. hyperopia

3. People who become farsighted as they get older have the condition known as
   a. hyperopia   b. myopia
   c. astigmatism   d. presbyopia

4. The greatest visual acuity is associated with the _____ and the _____.
   a. trichromat, rods   b. vitreous humor, cones
   c. fovea, cones   d. nanometer, cones

5. Black and white vision and a high degree of sensitivity to movement are characteristic of
   a. rod vision   b. cone vision
   c. the blind spot   d. the fovea

6. Colored afterimages are best explained by
   a. trichromatic theory   b. the effects of astigmatism
   c. sensory localization   d. opponent-process theory

7. Dark adaptation is directly related to an increase in
   a. visual pigments in   b. astigmatism
      the rods
   c. accommodation   d. saturation

8. The loudness of a sound is determined by the _____ of sound waves.
   a. frequency   b. amplitude
   c. rarefaction   d. ossicle

9. Sounds are ultimately transduced by movements of the
   a. pinna   b. malleus
   c. cochlea   d. hair cells

10. The term *umami* refers to
    a. smell blindness   b. temporary damage to the hair cells
    c. secondary olfaction   d. a taste quality

11. The lock and key theory appears to partly explain
    a. motion sickness   b. olfaction and gustation
    c. dark adaptation   d. color blindness

12. Which of the following is NOT a somesthetic sense?
    a. taste   b. touch
    c. balance   d. kinesthesis

13. As time passes, nerve endings in the skin under your wristwatch send fewer signals to the brain and you become able to feel the watch. This process is called
    a. sensory gating   b. the sensory bottleneck
    c. reverse attention   d. sensory adaptation

14. The fact that a mild surface pain can greatly reduce more agonizing pain is consistent with
    a. gate control theory   b. the concept of sensory adaptation
    c. sensory conflict theory d. perceptual constancy theory

15. Which of the following is LEAST likely to contribute to the formation of a perceptual figure?
    a. continuity   b. closure
    c. similarity   d. separation

16. The clearest example of a binocular depth cue is
    a. linear perspective   b. retinal disparity
    c. aerial perspective   d. motion parallax

17. The apparent distance hypothesis provides a good explanation of the
    a. moon illusion   b. horizontal-vertical illusion
    c. Zulu illusion   d. effects of inattentional blindness

18. Top-down perceptual processing is closely related to
    a. perceptual expectancies b. the Müller-Lyer illusion
    c. size-distance invariances d. precognition

19. The Zener cards were used in early studies of
    a. psi phenomena   b. inattentional blindness
    c. the Müller-Lyer illusion d. top-down processing

20. A good antidote to perceptual habituation can be found in conscious efforts to
    a. reverse sensory gating   b. pay attention
    c. achieve visual   d. counteract shape constancy
       accommodation

Answers   1. b 2. b 3. d 4. c 5. a 6. d 7. a 8. b 9. d 10. d 11. b 12. a 13. d 14. a 15. d 16. b 17. a 18. a 19. a 20. b

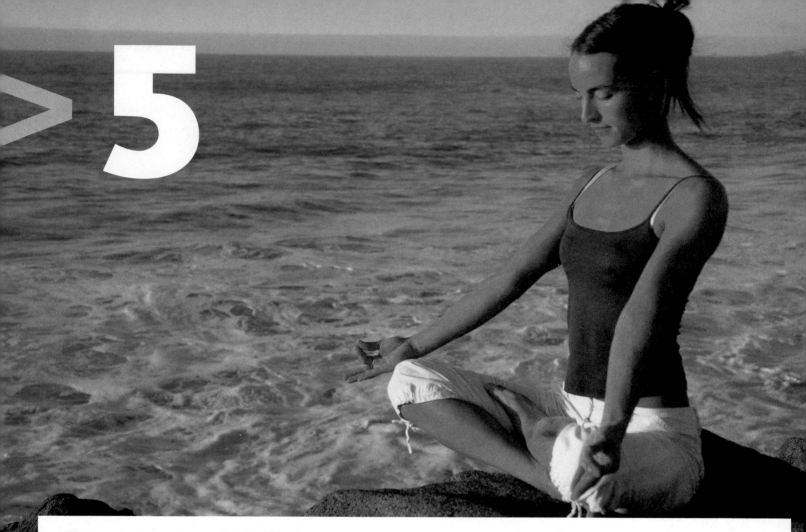

States of Consciousness

Journey into Psychology: Bending Your Mind

In Los Angeles, California, an aspiring actor consults a hypnotist for help in reducing her stage fright.

In the American Southwest, a Navajo elder gives his congregation peyote tea, a sacrament in the Native American Church, as a drumbeat resounds in the darkness.

In Toronto, Canada, three businesswomen head for a popular tavern after a particularly stressful day.

In Big Bend National Park in southern Texas, a college student spends a day walking through the wilderness, in a quiet state of mindfulness meditation.

In New Zealand, a Maori tohunga (priest) performs a nightlong ritual to talk to the spirits who created the world in the mythical period the Aborigines call Dreamtime.

In Northern Ireland, a nun living in a convent spends an entire week in silent prayer and contemplation.

In New York City, an artist spends 2 hours in a flotation chamber to clear her head before resuming work on a large painting.

At a park in Amsterdam, a group of street musicians smoke a joint and sing for spare change.

In Tucson, Arizona, one of your authors brews himself another cup of cappuccino.

Each of these people seeks to bend his or her mind—to alter consciousness—in different ways, to different degrees, and for different reasons. As these examples suggest, consciousness can take many forms. In the discussion that follows, we will begin with the familiar realms of sleep and dreaming and then move to some more exotic states of consciousness.

States of Consciousness— The Many Faces of Awareness

What is consciousness?

To be conscious means to be aware. **Consciousness** consists of all the sensations, perceptions, memories, and feelings you are aware of at any instant (Robinson, 2008). While this definition may seem obvious, it is based on your own subjective, *first-person* experience. You are the expert on what it feels like to be you. But what about other people? What does it feel like to be President Obama? Or your mother? And what about a dog (Bo, the first dog)? What runs through Bo's mind when he sniffs other dogs? Does he feel joy?

You simply can't answer these questions about *other minds* through your own first-person perspective. The difficulty of knowing other minds is one reason why the early behaviorists distrusted introspection. (Remember Chapter 1?) Instead you need to adopt an objective, *third-person* point of view. A key challenge for psychology is to use objective studies of the brain and behavior to help us understand the mind and consciousness, which are basically private phenomena (Koch, 2004; Robinson, 2008). This chapter summarizes some of what we have learned about different states of consciousness.

Altered States of Consciousness

We spend most of our lives in *waking consciousness,* a state of clear, organized alertness. In waking consciousness, we perceive times, places, and events as real, meaningful, and familiar. But states of consciousness related to fatigue, delirium, hypnosis, drugs, and euphoria may differ markedly from "normal" awareness. Everyone experiences at least some altered states, such as sleep, dreaming, and daydreaming (Blackmore, 2004). Some people experience dramatically altered states, such as the lower levels of awareness associated with strokes and other forms of brain damage (Morin, 2006). In everyday life, changes in consciousness may even accompany long-distance running, listening to music, making love, or other circumstances.

How are altered states distinguished from normal awareness? During an **altered state of consciousness (ASC),** changes occur in the *quality* and *pattern* of mental activity. Typically there are distinct shifts in our perceptions, emotions, memories, time sense, thoughts, feelings of self-control, and suggestibility (Siegel, 2005). Definitions aside, most people know when they have experienced an ASC.

Are there other causes of ASCs? In addition to the ones mentioned, we could add: sensory overload (a rave, Mardi Gras crowd, or mosh pit), monotonous stimulation (such as "highway hypnotism" on long drives), unusual physical conditions (high fever, hyperventilation, dehydration, sleep loss, near-death experiences), restricted sensory input, and many other possibilities. In some instances, altered states have important cultural meanings. (See "Consciousness and Culture" for more information.)

An unconscious person will die without constant care. Yet as crucial as consciousness is, we can't really explain how it occurs (Robinson, 2008). Nevertheless, it is possible to identify various states of consciousness and to explore the role they play in our lives. Let's begin with a look at the most common altered state, sleep and dreaming.

Sleep—Catching a Few ZZZ's

What are the effects of sleep loss or changes in sleep patterns?

Each of us will spend some 25 years of life asleep. Because sleep is familiar, many people think they know all about it. But many common-sense beliefs about sleep are false. For example, you are not totally unresponsive during sleep. A sleeping mother may ignore a jet

Survey Questions

- What is consciousness?
- What are the effects of sleep loss or changes in sleep patterns?
- Why do we sleep?
- What are some sleep disorders and unusual sleep events?
- Do dreams have meaning?
- What is hypnosis?
- Do meditation and sensory deprivation have any benefits?
- What are the effects of the more commonly used psychoactive drugs?
- How can dreams be used to promote personal understanding?

Consciousness Mental awareness of sensations, perceptions, memories, and feelings.

Altered state of consciousness (ASC) A condition of awareness distinctly different in quality or pattern from waking consciousness.

human diversity

Consciousness and Culture

Throughout history, people have found ways to alter consciousness (Siegel, 2005). A dramatic example is the sweat lodge ceremony of the Sioux Indians. During the ritual, several men sit in total darkness inside a small chamber heated by coals. Cedar smoke, bursts of steam, and sage fill the air. The men chant rhythmically. The heat builds. At last they can stand it no more. The door is thrown open. Cooling night breezes rush in. And then? The cycle begins again—often to be repeated four or five times more.

Like the yoga practices of Hindu mystics or the dances of the Whirling Dervishes of Turkey, the ritual "sweats" of the Sioux are meant to cleanse the mind and body. When they are espe-cially intense, they bring altered awareness and personal revelation.

People seek some altered states for pleasure, as is often true of drug intoxication. Yet, as the Sioux illustrate, many cultures regard altered consciousness as a pathway to personal enlight-enment. Indeed, all cultures and most religions recognize and accept some alterations of con-sciousness. However, the meaning given to these states varies greatly—from signs of "madness" and "possession" by spirits to life-enhancing breakthroughs. Thus, cultural conditioning greatly affects what altered states we recognize, seek, consider normal, and attain (de Rios & Grob, 2005).

Expuesto-Nicolas Randall/Alamy

In many cultures, rituals of healing, prayer, purification, or personal transformation are accompanied by altered states of consciousness.

---

thundering overhead but wake at the slightest whimper of her child. Likewise, you are more likely to awaken if you hear your own name spoken instead of another. It's even possible to do simple tasks while asleep. In one experiment, people learned to avoid an electric shock by touching a switch each time a tone sounded. Eventually, they could do it without waking. (This is much like the basic survival skill of turning off your alarm clock without waking.)

Of course, sleep does impose limitations. Don't expect to learn math, a foreign language, or other complex skills while asleep—especially if the snooze takes place in class (Froufe & Schwartz, 2001). But do expect that a good sleep will help you remember what you learned the day before (Fenn, Nusbaum, & Margoliash, 2003; Saxvig et al., 2008).

The Need for Sleep

How strong is the need for sleep? Sleep is an innate **biological rhythm** that can never be entirely ignored (Lavie, 2001; Mistlberger, 2005). Of course, sleep will give way temporarily, especially at times of great danger. As comedian and filmmaker Woody Allen once put it, "The lion and the lamb shall lie down together, but the lamb will not be very sleepy." However, there are limits to how long humans can go without sleep. A rare disease that prevents sleep always ends with stupor, coma, and death (Dauvilliers et al., 2004). (See ▶▶ Figure 5.1.)

How long could a person go without sleep? With few exceptions, 4 days or more without sleep becomes hell for everyone. The world record is held by Randy Gardner, who at age 17 went 264 hours (11 days) without sleep. Surprisingly, Randy needed only 14 hours of sleep to recover. As Randy found, most symptoms of **sleep deprivation** (sleep loss) are reversed by a single night's rest. (In 2007, a man named Tony Wright went 266 hours without sleep. However, *The Guinness Book of Records* no longer recognizes sleep deprivation competitions because of possible health risks, so Randy still holds the "official" record.)

What are the costs of sleep loss? At various times, Randy's speech was slurred, and he couldn't concentrate, remember clearly, or name common objects (Coren, 1996). Sleep loss also typically causes trembling hands, drooping eyelids, inattention, irritability, staring, increased pain sensitivity, and general discomfort (Doran, Van Dongen, & Dinges, 2001).

Most people experience *hypersomnia* (hi-per-SOM-nee-ah: excessive daytime sleepi-ness) after even a few hours of sleep loss. Hypersomnia is a common problem during ado-lescence (Carskadon, Acebo, & Jenni, 2004). Rapid physical changes during puberty increase

Timothy Ross/The Image Works

▲ FIGURE 5.1 Not all animals sleep, but like humans, those that do have powerful sleep needs. For example, dolphins must voluntarily breathe air, which means they face the choice of staying awake or drowning. The dolphin solves this problem by sleeping on just one side of its brain at a time! The other half of the brain, which remains awake, controls breathing (Jouvet, 1999).

Biological rhythm Any repeating cycle of biological activity, such as sleep and waking cycles or changes in body temperature.

Sleep deprivation Being prevented from getting desired or needed amounts of sleep.

the need for sleep. However, the quality and quantity of sleep time tends to decrease during the teen years (Fukuda & Ishihara, 2001).

Most people who have not slept for a day or two can still do interesting or complex mental tasks. But they have trouble paying attention, staying alert, and doing simple or boring routines (Belenky et al., 2003). They are also susceptible to **microsleeps,** which are brief shifts in brain activity to the pattern normally recorded during sleep. Imagine placing an animal on a moving treadmill, over a pool of water. Even under these conditions, animals soon drift into repeated microsleeps. For a pilot or machine operator, this can spell disaster (Hardaway & Gregory, 2005). If a task is monotonous (such as factory work or air traffic control), no amount of sleep loss is safe. In fact, if you lose just 1 hour of sleep a night, it can affect your mood, memory, ability to pay attention, and even your health (Maas, 1999). Sleep helps keep the brain healthy by regulating its temperature, conserving energy, and aiding brain development and repair. Biologically, sleep is a necessity, not a luxury.

When you drive, remember that microsleeps can lead to macro-accidents. Even if your eyes are open, you can fall asleep for a few seconds. A hundred thousand crashes every year are caused by sleepiness (Rau, 2005). Although coffee helps (Kamimori et al., 2005), if you are struggling to stay awake while driving, you should stop, quit fighting it, and take a short nap.

Severe sleep loss can even cause a temporary **sleep-deprivation psychosis** (loss of contact with reality). Confusion, disorientation, delusions, and hallucinations are typical of this reaction. Fortunately, such "crazy" behavior is uncommon. Hallucinations and delusions rarely appear before 60 hours of wakefulness (Naitoh, Kelly, & Englund, 1989).

How can I tell how much sleep I really need? Pick a day when you feel well rested. Then sleep that night until you wake without an alarm clock. If you feel rested when you wake up, that's your natural sleep need. If you're sleeping fewer hours than you need, you're building up a sleep debt (Maas, 1999).

Sleep Patterns

Sleep was described as an innate biological rhythm. What does that mean? Daily sleep and waking periods create a variety of sleep patterns. Rhythms of sleep and waking are so steady that they continue for many days, even when clocks and light–dark cycles are removed. However, under such conditions, humans eventually shift to a sleep–waking cycle that averages slightly more than 24 hours (Czeisler et al., 1999). (See ▶▶ Figure 5.2.) This suggests that external time markers, especially light and dark, help tie our sleep rhythms to days that are exactly 24 hours long. Otherwise, many of us would drift into our own unusual sleep cycles (Duffy & Wright, 2005).

What is the normal range of sleep? A few rare individuals can get by on an hour or two of sleep a night—and feel perfectly fine. Only a small percentage of the population are *short sleepers,* averaging 5 hours of sleep or less per night. On the other end of the scale we find *long sleepers,* who doze 9 hours or more (Grandner & Kripke, 2004). The majority of us sleep on a familiar 7- to 8-hour-per-night schedule. Urging everyone to sleep 8 hours would be like advising everyone to wear medium-size shoes.

We need less sleep as we get older, right? Yes, total sleep time declines throughout life. Those older than 50 average only 6 hours of sleep a night. In contrast, infants spend up to 20 hours a day sleeping, usually in 2- to 4-hour cycles. As they mature, most children go through a "nap" stage and eventually settle into a steady cycle of sleeping once a day. Perhaps we should all continue to take an afternoon "siesta." Midafternoon sleepiness is a natural part of the sleep cycle. Brief, well-timed naps can help maintain alertness in people like truck drivers and hospital interns, who often must fight to stay alert (Garbarino et al., 2004).

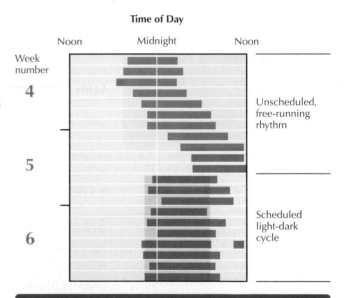

▲ **FIGURE 5.2** Sleep rhythms. Bars show periods of sleep during the fourth, fifth, and sixth weeks of an experiment with a human subject. During unscheduled periods, the subject was allowed to select times of sleep and lighting. The result was a sleep rhythm of about 25 hours. Notice how this free-running rhythm began to advance around the clock as the subject fell asleep later each day. When periods of darkness (shaded area) were imposed during the fifth week, the rhythm quickly resynchronized with 24-hour days. (Adapted from Czeisler, C. A., Richardson, G. S., Zimmerman, J. C., Moore-Ede, M. C., et al. [1981]. Entrainment of human circadian rhythms by light-dark cycles: A reassessment. Photochemistry, Photobiology, 34, 239–247. Fig 2. Copyright © 1981. Reprinted by permission of Blackwell Publishing Ltd.)

Microsleep A brief shift in brain-wave patterns to those of sleep.

Sleep-deprivation psychosis A major disruption of mental and emotional functioning brought about by sleep loss.

Busy people may be tempted to sleep less. However, people on *shortened* cycles—for example, 3 hours of sleep to 6 hours awake—often can't get to sleep when the cycle calls for it. That's why astronauts continue to sleep on their normal earth schedule while in space. Adapting to *longer* than normal days is more promising. Such days can be tailored to match natural sleep patterns, which have a ratio of 2 to 1 between time awake and time asleep (16 hours awake and 8 hours asleep). For instance, one study showed that 28-hour "days" work for some people. Overall, sleep patterns may be bent and stretched, but they rarely yield entirely to human whims (Åkerstedt, 2007).

▲ **FIGURE 5.3** These conjoined twins share the same blood supply, yet one sleeps while the other is awake. (Photo by Yale Joel, *Life Magazine.* © 1954 Time, Inc.)

Stages of Sleep—The Nightly Roller-Coaster

Why do we sleep?

What causes sleep? Early sleep experts thought that something in the blood-stream must cause sleep. But conjoined twins, whose bodies are joined at birth, show that this is false (▶▶ Figure 5.3). During waking hours, a **sleep hormone** (sleep-promoting chemical) collects in the brain and spinal cord, *not* in the blood. If this substance is extracted from one animal and injected into another, the second animal will sleep deeply for many hours (Cravatt et al., 1995). Notice, however, that this explanation is incomplete. For example, why would a well-rested person have to fight to stay awake during a boring midday meeting?

Whether you are awake or asleep right now depends on the *balance* between separate sleep and waking systems. Brain circuits and chemicals in one of the systems promote sleep (Steiger, 2007). A network of brain cells in the other system responds to chemicals that inhibit sleep. The two systems seesaw back and forth, switching the brain between sleep and wakefulness (Lavie, 2001). Note that the brain does not "shut down" during sleep. Rather, the *pattern* of activity changes.

Sleep Stages

How does brain activity change when you fall asleep? Changes in tiny electrical signals (brain waves) generated by the brain can be amplified and recorded with an **electroencephalograph** (eh-LEK-tro-en-SEF-uh-lo-graf), or **EEG.** When you are awake and alert, the EEG reveals a pattern of small, fast waves called **beta waves** (▶▶ Figure 5.4). Immediately before sleep, the pattern shifts to larger and slower waves called **alpha waves.** (Alpha waves also occur when you are relaxed and allow your thoughts to drift.) As the eyes close, breathing becomes slow and regular, the pulse rate slows, and body temperature drops. Soon after, we descend into *slow-wave sleep* through four distinct **sleep stages.**

Stage 1

As you enter **light sleep** (stage 1 sleep), your heart rate slows even more. Breathing becomes more irregular. The muscles of your body relax. This may trigger a reflex muscle twitch called a *hypnic* (HIP-nik: sleep) *jerk.* (This is quite normal, so have no fear about admitting to your friends that you fell asleep with a hypnic jerk.) In stage 1 sleep the EEG is made up mainly of small, irregular waves with some alpha. Persons awakened at this time may or may not say they were asleep.

Stage 2

As sleep deepens, body temperature drops further. Also, the EEG begins to include **sleep spindles,** which are short bursts of distinctive brain-wave activity (Fogel et al., 2007). Spindles seem to mark the true boundary of sleep. Within 4 minutes after spindles appear, most people will say they were asleep.

Sleep hormone A sleep-promoting substance found in the brain and spinal cord.

Electroencephalograph (EEG) A device designed to detect, amplify, and record electrical activity in the brain.

Beta waves Small fast brain waves associated with being awake and alert.

Alpha waves Large, slow brain waves associated with relaxation and falling asleep.

Sleep stages Levels of sleep identified by brain-wave patterns and behavioral changes.

Light sleep Stage 1 sleep, marked by small, irregular brain waves and some alpha waves.

Sleep spindles Distinctive bursts of brain-wave activity that indicate a person is asleep.

(a)   (b)

⬆ **FIGURE 5.4** *(a)* An EEG recording session. The boy in the background is asleep. *(b)* Changes in brain-wave patterns associated with various stages of sleep. Actually, most wave types are present at all times, but they occur more or less frequently in various sleep stages.

Stage 3

In stage 3, a new brain wave called delta begins to appear. **Delta waves** are very large and slow. They signal a move to deeper slow-wave sleep and a further loss of consciousness.

Stage 4

Most people reach **deep sleep** (the deepest level of normal sleep) in about 1 hour. Stage 4 brain waves are almost pure slow-wave delta, and the sleeper is in a state of oblivion. If you make a loud noise during stage 4, the sleeper will wake up in a state of confusion and may not remember the noise.

The Dual Process Hypothesis of Sleep

There is much more to a night's sleep than a simple descent into stage 4. Fluctuations in other sleep hormones cause recurring cycles of deeper and lighter sleep throughout the night (Steiger, 2007). During these repeated periods of lighter sleep, a curious thing happens: The sleeper's eyes occasionally move under the eyelids. (If you ever get a chance to watch a sleeping child, roommate, or spouse, you may see these eye movements.) **Rapid eye movements,** or **REMs,** are associated with dreaming (▶▶ Figure 5.5). In addition, **REM sleep** is marked by a return of fast, irregular EEG patterns similar to stage 1 sleep. In fact, the brain is so active during REM sleep that it looks as if the person is awake (Rock, 2004).

The two most basic states of sleep, then, are **non-REM (NREM) sleep,** which occurs during stages 1, 2, 3, and 4, and REM sleep, with its associated dreaming (Rock, 2004). Earlier, we noted some of the biological benefits of sleep. According to the *dual process hypothesis of sleep,* REM and NREM sleep have two added purposes: They help "refresh" the brain and store memories (Ficca & Salzarulo, 2004).

The Function of NREM Sleep

What is the function of NREM sleep? NREM sleep is dream free about 90 percent of the time and is deepest early in the night during the first few stage 4 periods. Your first period of stage 1 sleep usually lacks REMs and dreams. Later stage 1 periods typically include a shift into

Delta waves Large, slow brain waves that occur in deeper sleep (stages 3 and 4).

Deep sleep Stage 4 sleep; the deepest form of normal sleep.

Rapid eye movements (REMs) Swift eye movements during sleep.

REM sleep Sleep marked by rapid eye movements and a return to stage 1 EEG patterns.

NREM sleep Non-rapid eye movement sleep characteristic of stages 2, 3, and 4.

24 Hours

(a)

(b)

▲ **FIGURE 5.5** *(a)* Average proportion of time adults spend daily in REM sleep and NREM sleep. REM periods add up to about 20 percent of total sleep time. *(b)* Typical changes in stages of sleep during the night. Notice that dreams coincide mostly with REM periods.

REM sleep. Dreamless slow-wave NREM sleep increases after physical exertion and may help us recover from bodily fatigue. It also appears to "calm" the brain during the earlier part of a night's sleep (Tononi & Cirelli, 2003).

According to the dual process hypothesis, we are bombarded by information throughout the day, which causes our neural networks to become more and more active. As a result, your brain requires more and more energy to continue functioning. Slow-wave sleep early in the night brings overall brain activation levels back down, allowing a "fresh" approach to the next day.

Consider for a moment the amazing jumble of events that make up a day. Some experiences are worth remembering (like what you are reading right now, of course) and others are not so important (like what you were thinking when you put on your socks). As slow-wave sleep reduces overall activation in the brain, less important experiences may fade away and be forgotten. If you wake up feeling clearer about what you studied the previous night, it might be because your brain doesn't "sweat the small stuff"!

The Function of REM Sleep

What then, is the purpose of REM sleep? According to the dual process hypothesis, while NREM sleep "calms" the brain, REM sleep appears to "sharpen" our memories of the previous day's more important experiences (Saxvig et al., 2008). Daytime stress tends to increase REM sleep, which may rise dramatically when there is a death in the family, trouble at work, a marital conflict, or other emotionally charged events. The value of more REM sleep is that it helps us sort and retain memories, especially memories about strategies for solving problems (Walker & Stickgold, 2006). This is why, after studying for a long period, you may remember more if you go to sleep, rather than pulling an all-nighter. (REMember to get some REM!)

Early in life, REM sleep may stimulate the developing brain. Newborn babies have lots of new experiences to process, so they spend a hearty 8 or 9 hours a day in REM sleep. That's about 50 percent of their total sleep time.

REM Sleep and Dreaming

Roughly 85 percent of the time, people awakened during REMs report vivid dreams. Some eye movements correspond to dream activities. Dream that you are watching a tennis match, and you will probably move your eyes from side to side. However, people who were born blind still have REMs, so eye movements are not just a result of "watching" dream

They Came from Outer Space?

Imagine opening your eyes shortly before dawn, attempting to roll over in your bed, and suddenly realizing that you are entirely paralyzed. While lying helplessly on your back and unable to cry out for help, you become aware of sinister figures lurking in your bedroom. As they move closer to your bed, your heart begins to pound violently and you feel as if you are suffocating. You hear buzzing sounds and feel electrical sensations shooting throughout your body. Within moments, the visions vanish and you can move once again. Terrified, you wonder what just happened. (McNally & Clancy, 2005, p. 114)

Sleep paralysis, which normally prevents us from moving during REM sleep, can also occur just as you begin to wake up. During such episodes, people sometimes have *hypnopompic* (hip-neh-POM-pik: "upon awakening") hallucinations. According to psychologist Al Cheyne, these

hallucinations may include bizarre experiences, such as sensing that an alien being is in your bedroom; feeling something pressing on your chest, suffocating you; or feeling like you are floating out of your body (Cheyne, 2005; Cheyne, Rueffer, & Newby-Clark, 1999).

Although most of us shrug off these weird experiences, some people try to make sense of them. Earlier in history, people interpreted these hallucinated intruders as angels, demons, or witches and believed that their out-of-body experiences were real (Cheyne, Rueffer, & Newby-Clark, 1999). However, as our culture changes, so do our interpretations of sleep experiences. Today, for example, some people who have sleep-related hallucinations believe they have been abducted by space aliens or sexually abused (McNally & Clancy, 2005).

Swiss artist Henry Fuseli drew on hypnopompic imagery as an inspiration for his famous painting *The Nightmare*.

Detroit Institute of the Arts/SuperStock

---

images (Shafton, 1995). REM sleep is easy to observe in pets, such as dogs and cats. Watch for eye and face movements and irregular breathing. (You can forget about your pet iguana, though. Reptiles show no signs of REM sleep.)

Dreams during REM sleep tend to be longer, clearer, more detailed, more bizarre, and more "dream-like" than thoughts and images that occur in NREM sleep (Hobson, Pace-Schott, & Stickgold, 2000). Also, brain areas associated with imagery and emotion become more active during REM sleep. This may explain why REM dreams tend to be more vivid than NREM dreams (Braun, Balkin, & Herscovitch, 1998; Rock, 2004).

Speaking very loosely, it's as if the dreaming brain were reviewing messages left on a telephone answering machine, to decide which are worth keeping. During the day, when information is streaming in, the brain may be too busy to efficiently select useful memories. When the conscious brain is "offline," we are better able to build new memories.

What happens to the body when a person dreams? REM sleep is a time of high emotion. The heart beats irregularly. Blood pressure and breathing waver. Both males and females appear to be sexually aroused: Men usually have an erection, and genital blood flow increases in women. This occurs for all REM sleep, so it is not strictly related to erotic dreams (Jouvet, 1999).

During REM sleep, your body becomes quite still, as if you were paralyzed. Imagine for a moment the results of acting out some of your recent dreams. Very likely, REM-sleep paralysis prevents some hilarious—and dangerous—nighttime escapades. When it fails, some people thrash violently, leap out of bed, and may attack their bed partners. A lack of muscle paralysis during REM sleep is called *REM behavior disorder* (Ochoa & Pulido, 2005). One patient suffering from the disorder tied himself to his bed every night. That way, he couldn't jump up and crash into furniture or walls (Shafton, 1995). Sometimes sleep paralysis can go a little too far. See "They Came from Outer Space?" to find out why.

In a moment, we will survey some additional sleep problems—if you are still awake. First, here are a few questions to check your memory of our discussion so far.

RECITE

1. Changes in the quality and pattern of mental activity define
   a. an EEG
   b. REM
   c. SIDS
   d. an ASC
2. Delusions and hallucinations typically continue for several days after a sleep-deprived individual returns to normal sleep. T or F?
3. Alyssa experiences a microsleep while driving. Most likely, this indicates that she
   a. was producing mostly beta waves
   b. had high levels of sleep hormones in her bloodstream
   c. switched from delta waves to alpha waves
   d. was sleep deprived
4. Older adults, and particularly the elderly, sleep more than children do because the elderly are more easily fatigued. T or F?
5. Alpha waves are to presleep drowsiness as _____ _____ are to stage 4 sleep.

6. Rapid eye movements indicate that a person is in deep sleep. T or F?
7. Which of the following would normally be most incompatible with moving your arms and legs while asleep?
   a. REM sleep
   b. sleep spindles
   c. delta waves
   d. NREM sleep

REFLECT
Critical Thinking

8. Why might it be better for the unscheduled human sleep–waking cycle to average more than 24 hours, instead of less?
9. In addition to helping store memories, what biological advantages might sleeping provide?

Relate

Make a quick list of some altered states of consciousness you have experienced. What do they have in common? How are they different? What conditions caused them?

Imagine that you are a counselor at a sleep clinic. You must explain the basics of sleep and dreaming to a new client who knows little about these topics. Can you do it?

ANSWERS

1. d 2. F 3. d 4. F 5. delta waves 6. F 7. a 8. Sleep experts theorize that the 25-hour average leaves a little "slack" in the cycle. External time markers can then retard the body cycle slightly to synchronize it with light–dark cycles. If the body cycle were shorter than 24 hours, we all might have to "stretch" every day to adjust. 9. Lowering body activity and metabolism during sleep may help conserve energy and lengthen life. Also, natural selection may have favored sleep because animals that remained active at night probably had a higher chance of being killed. (We'll bet they had more fun, though.)

Sleep Disturbances—Showing Nightly: Sleep Wars!

What are some sleep disorders and unusual sleep events?

Sleep quality has taken a beating in North America. Artificial lighting, frenetic schedules, exciting pastimes, smoking, drinking, overstimulation, and many other factors have contributed to a near epidemic of sleep problems. Sleep disturbances are a serious risk to health and happiness (Shneerson, 2005). Sleep clinics treat thousands of people each year who suffer from sleep disorders or complaints. These disturbances range from daytime sleep attacks to sleepwalking and terrifying nightmares. (See ● Table 5.1.) Let's explore some of the more interesting problems these people face.

Insomnia

Staring at the ceiling at 2 AM is pretty low on most people's list of favorite pastimes. Yet about 60 million Americans have frequent or chronic insomnia (National Institute of Neurological Disorders and Stroke, 2007). **Insomnia** includes difficulty in going to sleep, frequent nighttime awakenings, waking too early, or a combination of these problems. Insomnia can harm people's work, health, and relationships (Sateia & Nowell, 2004).

Types and Causes of Insomnia

Worry, stress, and excitement can cause *temporary insomnia* and a self-defeating cycle. First, excess mental activity ("I can't stop turning things over in my mind") and heightened arousal block sleep. Then, frustration and anger over not being able to sleep cause more worry and

Insomnia Difficulty in getting to sleep or staying asleep.

● Table 5.1 Sleep Disturbances—Things That Go Wrong in the Night

Hypersomnia	Excessive daytime sleepiness. This can result from depression, insomnia, narcolepsy, sleep apnea, sleep drunkenness, periodic limb movements, drug abuse, and other problems.
Insomnia	Difficulty in getting to sleep or staying asleep; also, not feeling rested after sleeping.
Narcolepsy	Sudden, irresistible, daytime sleep attacks that may last anywhere from a few minutes to a half hour. Victims may fall asleep while standing, talking, or even driving.
Nightmare disorder	Vivid, recurrent nightmares that significantly disturb sleep.
Periodic limb movement syndrome	Muscle twitches (primarily affecting the legs) that occur every 20 to 40 seconds and severely disturb sleep.
REM behavior disorder	A failure of normal muscle paralysis, leading to violent actions during REM sleep.
Restless legs syndrome	An irresistible urge to move the legs to relieve sensations of creeping, tingling, prickling, aching, or tension.
Sleep apnea	During sleep, breathing stops for 20 seconds or more until the person wakes a little, gulps in air, and settles back to sleep; this cycle may be repeated hundreds of times per night.
Sleep drunkenness	A slow transition to clear consciousness after awakening; sometimes associated with irritable or aggressive behavior.
Sleep terror disorder	The repeated occurrence of night terrors that significantly disturb sleep.
Sleep–wake schedule disorder	A mismatch between the sleep–wake schedule demanded by a person's bodily rhythm and that demanded by the environment.
Sleepwalking disorder	Repeated incidents of leaving bed and walking about while asleep.

Sources: Carney, Geyer, & Berry, 2005; Shneerson, 2005

arousal. This further delays sleep, which causes more frustration, and so on (Espie, 2002). A good way to beat this cycle is to avoid fighting it. Get up and do something useful or satisfying when you can't sleep. (Reading a textbook might be a good choice of useful activities.) Return to bed only when you begin to feel that you are struggling to stay awake. If sleeping problems last for more than 3 weeks, then a diagnosis of *chronic insomnia* can be made.

Drug-dependency insomnia (sleep loss caused by withdrawal from sleeping pills) can also occur. There is real irony in the billion dollars a year North Americans spend on sleeping pills. Nonprescription sleeping pills such as Sominex, Nytol, and Sleep-Eze have little sleep-inducing effect. Barbiturates are even worse. These prescription sedatives decrease both stage 4 sleep and REM sleep, drastically lowering sleep quality. In addition, many users become "sleeping-pill junkies" who need an ever-greater number of pills to get to sleep. Victims must be painstakingly weaned from their sleep medicines. Otherwise, terrible nightmares and "rebound insomnia" may drive them back to drug use. It's worth remembering that although alcohol and other depressant drugs may help a person get to sleep, they greatly reduce sleep quality (Nau & Lichstein, 2005). Even newer drugs, such as Ambien and Lunesta, which induce sleep, have drawbacks. Possible side effects include amnesia, impaired judgment, increased appetite, decreased sex drive, depression, and sleepwalking. Rebound insomnia is also a risk, making these drugs at best a temporary remedy for insomnia.

"It's only insomnia if there's nothing good on."

Behavioral Remedies for Insomnia

If sleeping pills are a poor way to treat insomnia, what can be done? Sleep specialists prefer to treat insomnia with lifestyle changes and behavioral techniques (Montgomery & Dennis, 2004). Treatment for chronic insomnia usually begins with a careful analysis of a patient's sleep habits, lifestyle, stress levels, and medical problems. All the approaches discussed in the following list are helpful for treating insomnia (Nau & Lichstein, 2005):

1. **Stimulus control.** Insisting on a regular schedule helps establish a firm body rhythm, greatly improving sleep. This is best achieved by exercising **stimulus control,** which refers to linking a response with specific stimuli. It is important to get up and go to sleep at the same time each day, including weekends (Bootzin & Epstein, 2000). In addition, insomniacs are told to avoid doing anything but sleeping when they are in bed. They are not to study, eat, watch TV, read, pay the bills, worry, or even think in bed. (Lovemaking is okay, however.) In this way, only sleeping and relaxation become associated with going to bed at specific times (Bootzin & Epstein, 2000).
2. **Sleep restriction.** Even if an entire night's sleep is missed, it is important not to sleep late in the morning, nap more than an hour, sleep during the evening, or go to bed early the following night. Instead, restricting sleep to normal bedtime hours avoids fragmenting sleep rhythms (Shneerson, 2005).
3. **Paradoxical intention.** Another helpful approach is to remove the pressures of trying to go to sleep. Instead, the goal becomes trying to keep the eyes open (in the dark) and stay awake as long as possible (Nau & Lichstein, 2005). This allows sleep to come unexpectedly and lowers performance anxiety (Espie, 2002).
4. **Relaxation.** Some insomniacs lower their arousal before sleep by using a physical or mental strategy for relaxing, such as progressive muscle relaxation (see Chapter 13 for more information), meditation, or blotting out worries with calming images. It is also helpful to schedule time in the early evening to write down worries or concerns and plan what to do about them the next day, in order to set them aside before going to bed.
5. **Exercise.** Strenuous exercise during the day promotes sleep. It is best if done about 6 hours before bedtime (Maas, 1999). However, exercise in the evening is helpful only if it is very light.
6. **Food intake.** What you eat can affect how easily you get to sleep. Eating starchy foods increases the amount of *tryptophan* (TRIP-tuh-fan: an amino acid) reaching the brain. More tryptophan, in turn, increases the amount of serotonin in the brain, which is associated with relaxation, a positive mood, and sleepiness. Thus, to promote sleep, try eating a starchy snack, such as cookies, bread, pasta, oatmeal, pretzels, or dry cereal. If you really want to drop the bomb on insomnia, try eating a baked potato (which may be the world's largest sleeping pill!) (Sahelian, 1998).
7. **Stimulants.** Stimulants, such as coffee and cigarettes, should be avoided. It is also worth remembering that alcohol, although not a stimulant, impairs sleep quality.

Sleepwalking, Sleeptalking, and Sleepsex

Sleepsex? As strange as it may seem, many waking behaviors can be engaged in while asleep, such as driving a car, cooking, playing a musical instrument, and eating (Plazzi et al., 2005). The most famous, sleepwalking, is eerie and fascinating in its own right. **Somnambulists** (som-NAM-bue-lists: those who sleepwalk) avoid obstacles, descend stairways, and on rare occasions may step out of windows or in front of automobiles. Sleepwalkers have been observed jumping into lakes, urinating in garbage pails or closets (phew!), shuffling furniture around, and even brandishing weapons (Schenck & Mahowald, 2005).

The sleepwalker's eyes are usually open, but a blank face and shuffling feet reveal that the person is still asleep. If you find someone sleepwalking, you should gently guide the person back to bed. Awakening a sleepwalker does no harm, but it is not necessary.

Does sleepwalking occur during dreaming? No. Remember that people are normally immobilized during REM sleep. EEG studies have shown that somnambulism occurs dur-

Stimulus control Linking a particular response with specific stimuli.

Somnambulism Sleepwalking; occurs during NREM sleep.

ing NREM stages 3 and 4 (Stein & Ferber, 2001). *Sleeptalking* also occurs mostly during NREM sleep. The link with deep sleep explains why sleeptalking makes little sense and why sleepwalkers are confused and remember little when awakened (American Psychiatric Association, 2000).

Oh, yes, you're curious about sleepsex. There is, of course, an official name for it: *sexsomnia* (Shapiro, Trajanovic, & Fedoroff, 2003). Sexsomnia is not as exciting as it might sound: Just imagine being startled wide awake by your bed partner, who is asleep, but attempting to have sex with you (Mangan, 2004).

Nightmares and Night Terrors

Stage 4 sleep is also the realm of night terrors. These frightening episodes are quite different from ordinary nightmares. A **nightmare** is simply a bad dream that takes place during REM sleep. Frequently occurring nightmares (one a week or more) are associated with higher levels of psychological distress (Levin & Fireman, 2002). During stage 4 **night terrors,** a person suffers total panic and may hallucinate frightening dream images into the bedroom. An attack may last 15 or 20 minutes. When it is over, the person awakens drenched in sweat but only vaguely remembers the terror. Because night terrors occur during NREM sleep (when the body is not immobilized), victims may sit up, scream, get out of bed, or run around the room. Victims remember little afterward. (Other family members, however, may have a story to tell.) Night terrors are most common in childhood, but they continue to plague about 2 out of every 100 adults (Kataria, 2004; Ohayon, Guilleminault, & Priest, 1999).

How to Eliminate a Nightmare

Is there any way to stop a recurring nightmare? A bad nightmare can be worse than any horror movie. It's easy to leave a theater, but we often remain trapped in terrifying dreams. Nevertheless, most nightmares can be banished by following three simple steps. First, write down your nightmare, describing it in detail. Next, change the dream any way you wish, being sure to spell out the details of the new dream. The third step is *imagery rehearsal,* in which you mentally rehearse the changed dream before you fall asleep again (Krakow & Zadra, 2006). Imagery rehearsal may work because it makes upsetting dreams familiar while a person is awake and feeling safe. Or perhaps it mentally "re-programs" future dream content. In any case, the technique has helped many people.

Sleep Apnea

Some sage once said, "Laugh and the whole world laughs with you; snore and you sleep alone." Nightly "wood sawing" is often harmless, but it can signal a serious problem. A person who snores loudly, with short silences and loud gasps or snorts, may suffer from apnea (AP-nee-ah: interrupted breathing). In **sleep apnea,** breathing stops for periods of 20 seconds to 2 minutes. As the need for oxygen becomes intense, the person wakes a little and gulps in air. She or he then settles back to sleep. But soon, breathing stops again. This cycle is repeated hundreds of times a night. As you might guess, apnea victims are extremely sleepy during the day (Collop, 2005).

What causes sleep apnea? Some cases occur because the brain stops sending signals to the diaphragm to maintain breathing. Another cause is blockage of the upper air passages. One of the most effective treatments is the use of a continuous positive airway pressure (CPAP) mask to aid breathing during sleep. Other treatments include weight loss and surgery for breathing obstructions (Collop, 2005).

SIDS

Sleep apnea is suspected as one cause of **sudden infant death syndrome (SIDS),** or "crib death." Each year 2,500 babies are victims of SIDS (National Institute of Child Health and Human Development, 2008). In the "typical" crib death, a slightly premature or small baby with some signs of a cold or cough is bundled up and put to bed. A short time later, parents find the child has died. A baby deprived of air will normally struggle to begin

Nightmare A bad dream that occurs during REM sleep.

Night terror A state of panic during NREM sleep.

Sleep apnea Repeated interruption of breathing during sleep.

Sudden infant death syndrome (SIDS) The sudden, unexplained death of an apparently healthy infant.

breathing again. However, SIDS babies seem to have a weak arousal reflex. This prevents them from changing positions and resuming breathing after an episode of apnea (Horne et al., 2001).

Babies at risk for SIDS must be carefully watched for the first 6 months of life. To aid parents in this task, a special monitor may be used that sounds an alarm when breathing or pulse becomes weak (▶▶ Figure 5.6). Babies at risk for SIDS are often premature, have a shrill, high-pitched cry, engage in "snoring," breath-holding, or frequent awakening at night, breathe mainly through an open mouth, or remain passive when their face rolls into a pillow or blanket.

"Back to Sleep"

Sleeping position is another major risk factor for SIDS. Healthy infants are better off sleeping on their backs or sides (Shapiro-Mendoza et al., 2009). (Premature babies, those with respiratory problems, and those who often vomit may need to sleep facedown. Ask a pediatrician for guidance.) Remember, "*back* to sleep" is the safest position for most infants (Hauck et al., 2002). It is also worth eliminating soft objects such as pillows, quilts, comforters, or sheepskins from the baby's bed. Finally, parents sharing their beds with infants (co-sleeping) also take a risk. *Overlaying*, which occurs when a sleeping adult rolls over on top of an infant, is responsible for a considerable proportion of infant suffocation deaths (Shapiro-Mendoza et al., 2009).

> **FIGURE 5.6** Infants at risk for SIDS are often attached to devices that monitor breathing and heart rate during sleep. An alarm sounds to alert parents if either pulse or respiration falters. SIDS rarely occurs after an infant is 1 year old. Babies at risk for SIDS should be placed on their sides or on their backs. (Photo courtesy of Healthdyne, Inc.)

Dreams—A Separate Reality?

Do dreams have meaning?

When REM sleep was discovered in 1952, it ushered in a "golden era" of dream inquiry. To conclude our discussion of sleep, let's consider some age-old questions about dreaming.

Does everyone dream? Do dreams occur in an instant? Most people dream four or five times a night, but not all people remember their dreams. "Non-dreamers" are often surprised by their dreams when first awakened during REM sleep. Dreams are usually spaced about 90 minutes apart. The first dream lasts only about 10 minutes; the last averages 30 minutes and may run as long as 50. Dreams, therefore, occur in real time, not as "flashes" (Shafton, 1995).

REM Sleep Revisited

How important is REM sleep? To answer this question, sleep expert William Dement awakened volunteers each time they entered REM sleep. Soon, their need for "dream time" grew more urgent. By the fifth night, many had to be awakened 20 or 30 times to prevent REM sleep. When the volunteers were finally allowed to sleep undisturbed, they dreamed extra amounts. This effect, called a **REM rebound,** explains why alcoholics have horrible nightmares after they quit drinking. Alcohol reduces sleep quality by suppressing REM sleep, thus setting up a powerful rebound when it is withdrawn (Stein & Friedmann, 2005).

Dement's volunteers complained of memory lapses, poor concentration, and anxiety. For a while, it was thought that people deprived of REM sleep might go crazy. But later experiments showed that missing *any* sleep stage can cause a rebound for that stage. In general, daytime disturbances are related to the *total amount* of sleep lost, not to the *type* of sleep lost (Devoto et al., 1999).

Dream Theories

How meaningful are dreams? Some theorists believe that dreams have deeply hidden meanings. Others regard dreams as nearly meaningless. Yet others hold that dreams reflect our waking thoughts, fantasies, and emotions (Beck, 2004). Let's examine all three views.

REM rebound The occurrence of extra rapid eye movement sleep following REM sleep deprivation.

Psychodynamic Dream Theory

Psychodynamic theories of dreaming emphasize internal conflicts and unconscious forces. Sigmund Freud's (1900) landmark book, *The Interpretation of Dreams*, first advanced the idea that many dreams are based on *wish fulfillment* (an expression of unconscious desires). One of Freud's key proposals was that dreams express unconscious desires and conflicts as disguised **dream symbols** (images that have deeper symbolic meaning). Understanding a dream, then, requires analyzing the dream's obvious, visible meaning (*manifest content*) to uncover its hidden, symbolic meaning (*latent content*).

For instance, a woman who dreams of stealing her best friend's wedding ring and placing it on her own hand may be unwilling to consciously admit that she is sexually attracted to her best friend's husband. Similarly, a journey might symbolize death, and horseback riding or dancing, sexual intercourse.

Do all dreams have hidden meanings? Probably not. Freud realized that some dreams are trivial "day residues" or carryovers from ordinary waking events. On the other hand, dreams do tend to reflect a person's current concerns, so Freud wasn't entirely wrong.

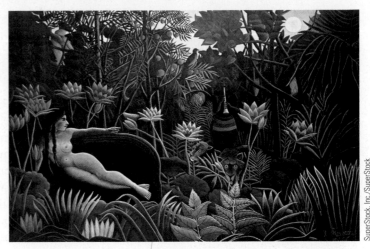

According to psychodynamic theory, dream imagery often has symbolic meaning. How would you interpret French artist Henri Rousseau's dream-like image, titled *The Dream*? The fact that dreams don't have a single unambiguous meaning is one of the shortcomings of Freudian dream theory.

The Activation-Synthesis Hypothesis

Psychiatrists Allan Hobson and Robert McCarley have a radically different view of dreaming, called the **activation-synthesis hypothesis.** They believe that during REM sleep several lower brain centers are "turned on" (*activated*) in more or less random fashion. However, messages from the cells are blocked from reaching the body, so no movement occurs. Nevertheless, the cells continue to tell higher brain areas of their activities. Struggling to interpret this random information, the brain searches through stored memories and manufactures (*synthesizes*) a dream (Hobson, 2000, 2005). However, frontal areas of the cortex, which control higher mental abilities, are mostly shut down during REM sleep. This explains why dreams are more primitive and more bizarre than daytime thoughts (Hobson, 2000).

How does that help explain dream content? According to the activation-synthesis hypothesis, dreams are basically meaningless. Let's use the classic chase dream as an example. In such dreams we feel we are running but not going anywhere. This occurs because the brain is told the body is running, but it gets no feedback from the motionless legs. To try to make sense of this information, the brain creates a chase drama. A similar process probably explains dreams of floating or flying.

So dreams have no meaning? The activation-synthesis hypothesis doesn't rule out the idea that dreams have some meaning. Because dreams are created from memories and past experiences, parts of dreams can sometimes reflect each person's mental life, emotions, and concerns (Hobson, 2000).

Neurocognitive Dream Theory

Can't dreams just be about normal day-to-day stuff? Yes they can. William Domhoff offers a third view of dreaming. According to his **neurocognitive dream theory,** dreams actually have much in common with waking thoughts and emotions. Most dreams reflect ordinary waking concerns. Domhoff believes this is true because many brain areas that are active when we are awake remain active during dreaming (Domhoff, 2001, 2003). From this perspective, our dreams are a conscious expression of REM sleep processes that are sorting and storing daily experiences. Thus, we shouldn't be surprised if a student who is angry at a teacher dreams of embarrassing the teacher in class, a lonely person dreams of romance, or a hungry child dreams of food. It is not necessary to seek deep symbolic meanings to understand these dreams.

Psychodynamic theory Any theory of behavior that emphasizes internal conflicts, motives, and unconscious forces.

Dream symbols Images in dreams that serve as visible signs of hidden ideas, desires, impulses, emotions, relationships, and so forth.

Activation-synthesis hypothesis An attempt to explain how dream content is affected by motor commands in the brain that occur during sleep, but are not carried out.

Neurocognitive dream theory Proposal that dreams reflect everyday waking thoughts and emotions.

Dream Worlds

Which dream theory is the most widely accepted? Each theory has strengths and weaknesses. However, studies of dream content do support neurocognitive theory's focus on the continuity between dreams and waking thought. Rather than being exotic or bizarre, most dreams reflect everyday events (Hall, 1966; Pesant & Zadra, 2006). For example, athletes tend to dream about the previous day's athletic activities (Erlacher & Schredl, 2004). In general, the favorite dream setting is a familiar room in a house. Action usually takes place between the dreamer and two or three other emotionally important people—friends, enemies, loved ones, or employers. Dream actions are also mostly familiar: running, jumping, riding, sitting, talking, and watching. About half of all dreams have sexual elements. Dreams of flying, floating, and falling occur less frequently. However, note that such dreams lend some support to the activation-synthesis hypothesis, because they are not everyday events. (Unless you are a trapeze artist.)

Are most dreams happy or sad? If you ask people in the morning what they dreamed about, they mention more unpleasant emotions than pleasant emotions (Merritt et al., 1994). However, it may be that dreams of fear, anger, or sadness are easier to remember. When people are awakened during REM sleep, they report equal numbers of positive and negative emotions (Fosse, Stickgold, & Hobson, 2001).

Even if many dreams can be viewed as just a different form of thought, many psychologists continue to believe that some dreams have deeper meaning (White & Taytroe, 2003; Wilkinson, 2006). There seems to be little doubt that dreams can make a difference in our lives: Veteran sleep researcher William Dement once dreamed that he had lung cancer. In the dream a doctor told Dement he would die soon. At the time, Dement was smoking two packs of cigarettes a day. He says, "I will never forget the surprise, joy, and exquisite relief of waking up. I felt reborn." Dement quit smoking the following day. (For more information about dreaming, see the Psychology in Action section later in this chapter.)

study break

Sleep Disturbances and Dreaming

RECITE

1. Which of the following is *not* a behavioral remedy for insomnia?
   a. daily hypersomnia   b. stimulus control
   c. progressive relaxation   d. paradoxical intention
2. Eating a snack that is nearly all starch can promote sleep because it increases _____ in the brain.
   a. beta waves   b. tryptophan
   c. EEG activity   d. hypnic cycling
3. Night terrors, sleepwalking, and sleeptalking all occur during stage 1, NREM sleep. T or F?
4. Sleep _____ is suspected as one cause of SIDS.
5. People who suffer from sudden daytime sleep attacks have which sleep disorder?
   a. narcolepsy   b. REM behavior disorder
   c. somnambulism   d. sleep spindling
6. According to the activation-synthesis hypothesis of dreaming, dreams are constructed from _____ to explain messages received from nerve cells controlling eye movement, balance, and bodily activity.

7. Sharpening memories and facilitating their storage is one function of
   a. activation-synthesis   b. REM sleep
      cycles
   c. deep sleep   d. NREM sleep

REFLECT

Critical Thinking

8. Even without being told that somnambulism is an NREM event, you could have predicted that sleepwalking doesn't occur during dreaming. Why?

Relate

Almost everyone suffers from insomnia at least occasionally. Are any of the techniques for combating insomnia similar to strategies you have discovered on your own?

How many sleep disturbances can you name (including those listed in Table 5.1)? Are there any that you have experienced? Which do you think would be most disruptive?

Do you think the activation-synthesis hypothesis provides an adequate explanation of your own dreams? Have you had dreams that seem to reflect Freudian wish fulfillment? Do you think your dreams have symbolic meaning or reflect everyday concerns?

ANSWERS

1. a 2. b 3. F 4. apnea 5. a 6. memories 7. b 8. Because people are immobilized during REM sleep and REM sleep is strongly associated with dreaming. This makes it unlikely that sleepwalkers are acting out dreams.

Hypnosis—Look into My Eyes

"Your body is becoming heavy. You can barely keep your eyes open. You are so tired you can't move. Relax. Let go. Relax. Close your eyes and relax." These are the last words a textbook should ever say to you, and the first a hypnotist might say.

Interest in hypnosis began in the 1700s with Austrian doctor Franz Mesmer, whose name gave us the term *mesmerize* (to hypnotize). Mesmer believed he could cure disease with magnets. Mesmer's strange "treatments" are related to hypnosis because they actually relied on the power of suggestion, not magnetism (Waterfield, 2002). For a time, Mesmer enjoyed quite a following. In the end, however, his theories of "animal magnetism" were rejected and he was branded a fraud.

The term *hypnosis* was later coined by English surgeon James Braid. The Greek word *hypnos* means "sleep," and Braid used it to describe the hypnotic state. Today we know that hypnosis is *not* sleep. Confusion about this point remains because some hypnotists give the suggestion, "Sleep, sleep." However, EEG patterns recorded during hypnosis are different from those observed when a person is asleep or pretending to be hypnotized (Barabasz, 2000).

Theories of Hypnosis

If hypnosis isn't sleep, then what is it? That's a good question. **Hypnosis** is often defined as an altered state of consciousness, characterized by narrowed attention and an increased openness to suggestion (Kallio & Revonsuo, 2003; Kosslyn et al., 2000). Notice that this definition assumes that hypnosis is a distinct state of consciousness.

The best-known *state theory* of hypnosis was proposed by Ernest Hilgard (1904–2001), who argued that hypnosis causes a *dissociative state,* or "split" in awareness. To illustrate, he asked hypnotized subjects to plunge one hand into a painful bath of ice water. Subjects told to feel no pain said they felt none. The same subjects were then asked if there was any part of their mind that did feel pain. With their free hand, many wrote, "It hurts," or "Stop it, you're hurting me," while they continued to act pain free (Hilgard, 1977, 1994). Thus, one part of the hypnotized person says there is no pain and acts as if there is none. Another part, which Hilgard calls the *hidden observer,* is aware of the pain but remains in the background. The **hidden observer** is a detached part of the hypnotized person's awareness that silently observes events.

In contrast, *nonstate theorists* argue that hypnosis is not a distinct state at all. Instead it is merely a blend of conformity, relaxation, imagination, obedience, and role-playing (Kirsch, 2005). For example, many theorists believe that all hypnosis is really self-hypnosis (autosuggestion). From this perspective, a hypnotist merely helps another person to follow a series of suggestions. These suggestions, in turn, alter sensations, perceptions, thoughts, feelings, and behaviors (Lynn & Kirsch, 2006). (See "Swinging Suggestions.")

Regardless of which theoretical approach finally prevails, both views suggest that hypnosis can be explained by normal principles. It is not mysterious or "magical," despite what stage hypnotists might have you think.

The Reality of Hypnosis

How is hypnosis done? Could I be hypnotized against my will? Hypnotists use many different methods. Still, all techniques encourage a person (1) to focus attention on what is being said, (2) to relax and feel tired, (3) to "let go" and accept suggestions easily, and (4) to use vivid imagination (Druckman & Bjork, 1994). Basically, you must cooperate to become hypnotized.

What does it feel like to be hypnotized? You might be surprised at some of your actions during hypnosis. You also might have mild feelings of floating, sinking, anesthesia, or sepa-

Hypnosis An altered state of consciousness characterized by narrowed attention and increased suggestibility.

Hidden observer A detached part of the hypnotized person's awareness that silently observes events.

Swinging Suggestions

Here's a demonstration you can use to gain insight into hypnosis. Tie a short length of string (about 6 inches) to a small, heavy object, such as a ring or a small metal nut. Hold the ring at eye level, about a foot from your face. Concentrate on the ring and notice that it will begin to move, ever so slightly. As it does, focus all your attention on the ring. Narrow your attention to a beam of energy and mentally push the ring away from you. Each time the ring swings away, push on it, using only mental force. Then release it and let it swing back toward you. Continue to mentally push and release the ring until it is swinging freely. For the best results, try this now, before reading more.

Did the ring move? If it did, you used *auto-suggestion* to influence your own behavior in a subtle way. Suggestions that the ring would swing caused your hand to make tiny micromuscular movements. These, in turn, caused the ring to move—no special mental powers or supernatural forces are involved.

As is true of hypnotic suggestion, the ring's movement probably seemed to be automatic. Obviously, you could just intentionally swing the ring. However, if you responded to suggestion, the movement seemed to happen without any effort on your part. In the same way, when people are hypnotized, their actions seem to occur without any voluntary intent. Incidentally, autosuggestion likely underlies other phenomena, such as how Ouija boards answer questions without any conscious movements by the person using the pointer.

Dennis Coon

---

ration from your body. Personal experiences vary widely. A key element in hypnosis is the **basic suggestion effect** (a tendency of hypnotized persons to carry out suggested actions as if they were involuntary). Hypnotized persons feel like their actions and experiences are *automatic*—they seem to happen without effort. Here is how one person described his hypnotic session:

> I felt lethargic, my eyes going out of focus and wanting to close. My hands felt real light. . . . I felt I was sinking deeper into the chair. . . . I felt like I wanted to relax more and more. . . . My responses were more automatic. I didn't have to *wish* to do things so much or *want* to do them. . . . I just did them. . . . I felt floating. . . . very close to sleep. (Hilgard, 1968)

Contrary to the way hypnosis is portrayed in movies, hypnotized people generally remain in control of their behavior and aware of what is going on. For instance, most people will not act out hypnotic suggestions that they consider immoral or repulsive (such as disrobing in public or harming someone) (Kirsch & Lynn, 1995).

Hypnotic Susceptibility

Can everyone be hypnotized? About 8 people out of 10 can be hypnotized, but only 4 out of 10 will be good hypnotic subjects. People who are imaginative and prone to fantasy are often highly responsive to hypnosis (Kallio & Revonsuo, 2003). But people who lack these traits may also be hypnotized. If you are willing to be hypnotized, chances are good that you could be. Hypnosis depends more on the efforts and abilities of the hypnotized person than the skills of the hypnotist. But make no mistake, people who are hypnotized are not merely faking their responses.

Hypnotic susceptibility refers to how easily a person can become hypnotized. It is measured by giving a series of suggestions and counting the number of times a person responds. A typical hypnotic test is the *Stanford Hypnotic Susceptibility Scale,* shown in ● Table 5.2. In the test, various suggestions are made, and the person's response is noted. For instance, you might be told that your left arm is becoming more and more rigid and that it will not bend. If you can't bend your arm during the next 10 seconds, you have shown susceptibility to hypnotic suggestions. (Also see ▶▶ Figure 5.7.)

Effects of Hypnosis

What can (and cannot) be achieved with hypnosis? Many abilities have been tested during hypnosis, leading to the following conclusions (Burgess & Kirsch, 1999; Chaves, 2000):

Basic suggestion effect The tendency of hypnotized persons to carry out suggested actions as if they were involuntary.

Hypnotic susceptibility One's capacity for becoming hypnotized.

● Table 5.2 Stanford Hypnotic Susceptibility Scale

SUGGESTED BEHAVIOR	CRITERION OF PASSING
1. Postural sway	Falls without forcing
2. Eye closure	Closes eyes without forcing
3. Hand lowering (left)	Lowers at least 6 inches by end of 10 seconds
4. Immobilization (right arm)	Arm rises less than 1 inch in 10 seconds
5. Finger lock	Incomplete separation of fingers at end of 10 seconds
6. Arm rigidity (left arm)	Less than 2 inches of arm bending in 10 seconds
7. Hands moving together	Hands at least as close as 6 inches after 10 seconds
8. Verbal inhibition (name)	Name unspoken in 10 seconds
9. Hallucination (fly)	Any movement, grimacing, acknowledgment of effect
10. Eye catalepsy	Eyes remain closed at end of 10 seconds
11. Posthypnotic (changes chairs)	Any partial movement response
12. Amnesia test	Three or fewer items recalled

Adapted from Weitzenhoffer & Hilgard, 1959.

1. **Superhuman acts of strength.** Hypnosis has no more effect on physical strength than instructions that encourage a person to make his or her best effort.

2. **Memory.** There is some evidence that hypnosis can enhance memory (Wagstaff et al., 2004). However, it frequently increases the number of false memories as well. For this reason, many states now bar persons from testifying in court if they were hypnotized to improve their memory of a crime they witnessed.

3. **Amnesia.** A person told not to remember something heard during hypnosis may claim not to remember. In some instances this may be nothing more than a deliberate attempt to avoid thinking about specific ideas. However, brief memory loss of this type actually does seem to occur (Barnier, McConkey, & Wright, 2004).

4. **Pain relief.** Hypnosis can relieve pain (Keefe, Abernethy, & Campbell, 2005). It can be especially useful when chemical painkillers are ineffective. For instance, hypnosis can reduce phantom limb pain (Oakley, Whitman, & Halligan, 2002). (As discussed in Chapter 4, amputees sometimes feel phantom pain that seems to come from a missing limb.)

5. **Age regression.** Given the proper suggestions, some hypnotized people appear to "regress" to childhood. However, most theorists now believe that "age-regressed" subjects are only acting out a suggested role.

6. **Sensory changes.** Hypnotic suggestions concerning sensations are among the most effective. Given the proper instructions, a person can be made to smell a small bottle of ammonia and respond as if it were a wonderful perfume. It is also possible to alter color vision, hearing sensitivity, time sense, perception of illusions, and many other sensory responses.

Hypnosis is a valuable tool. It can help people relax, feel less pain, and make better progress in therapy (Chapman, 2006). Generally, hypnosis is more successful at changing subjective experience than it is at modifying behaviors such as smoking or overeating.

Dennis Coon

▲ FIGURE 5.7 In one test of hypnotizability, subjects attempt to pull their hands apart after hearing suggestions that their fingers are "locked" together.

Stage Hypnosis

On stage the hypnotist intones, "When I count to three, you will imagine that you are on a train to Disneyland and growing younger and younger as the train approaches." Responding to these suggestions, grown men and women begin to giggle and squirm like children on their way to a circus.

How do stage entertainers use hypnosis to get people to do strange things? They don't. Little or no hypnosis is needed to do a good hypnosis act. **Stage hypnosis** is often merely a simu-

Stage hypnosis Use of hypnosis to entertain; often, merely a simulation of hypnosis for that purpose.

Dennis Coon

△ **FIGURE 5.8** Arrange three chairs as shown. Have someone recline as shown. Ask him to lift slightly while you remove the middle chair. Accept the applause gracefully! (Concerning hypnosis and similar phenomena, the moral, of course, is "Suspend judgment until you have something solid to stand on.")

lation of hypnotic effects. Stage hypnotists make use of several features of the stage setting to perform their act (Barber, 2000):

1. **Waking suggestibility.** We are all more or less open to suggestion, but on stage people are unusually cooperative because they don't want to "spoil the act." As a result, they will readily follow almost any instruction given by the entertainer.

2. **Selection of responsive subjects.** Participants in stage hypnotism (all *volunteers*) are first "hypnotized" as a group. Then, anyone who doesn't yield to instructions is eliminated.

3. **The hypnosis label disinhibits.** Once a person has been labeled "hypnotized," she or he can sing, dance, act silly, or whatever, without fear or embarrassment. On stage, being "hypnotized" takes away personal responsibility for one's actions.

4. **The hypnotist as a "director."** After volunteers loosen up and respond to a few suggestions, they find that they are suddenly the stars of the show. Audience response to the antics on stage brings out the "ham" in many people. All the "hypnotist" needs to do is direct the action.

5. **The stage hypnotist uses tricks.** Stage hypnosis is about 50 percent taking advantage of the situation and 50 percent deception. One of the more impressive stage tricks is to rigidly suspend a person between two chairs. This is astounding only because the audience does not question it. Anyone can do it, as is shown in the photographs and instructions in ▶▶ Figure 5.8. Try it!

To summarize, hypnosis is real, and it can significantly alter private experience. Hypnosis is a useful tool in a variety of settings. Nightclubs, however, are not one of these settings. Stage "hypnotists" entertain; they rarely hypnotize.

Meditation and Sensory Deprivation— Chilling, the Healthy Way

Do meditation and sensory deprivation have any benefits?

Throughout history, meditation and sensory deprivation have been widely used as a means of altering consciousness through deep relaxation. Let's see what they have in common and how they differ.

Meditation

Meditation is a mental exercise used to alter consciousness. In general, meditation focuses attention and interrupts the typical flow of thoughts, worries, and analysis. People who use meditation to reduce stress often report less daily physical tension and anxiety (Andresen, 2000). Brain scans (PET and fMRI) reveal changes in the activity of the frontal lobes during meditation, which suggests that it may be a distinct state of consciousness (Cahn & Polich, 2006; Farb et al., 2007).

Meditation takes two major forms. In **concentrative meditation,** you attend to a single focal point, such as an object, a thought, or your own breathing. In contrast, **mindfulness meditation** is "open," or expansive. In this case, you widen your attention to embrace a total, nonjudgmental awareness of the world (Lazar, 2005). An example is losing all self-consciousness while walking in the wilderness with a quiet and receptive mind. Although it may not seem so, mindfulness meditation is more difficult to attain than concentrative meditation. For this reason, we will discuss concentrative meditation as a practical self-control method.

Performing Concentrative Meditation

How is concentrative meditation done? The basic idea is to sit still and quietly focus on some external object or on a repetitive internal stimulus, such as your own breathing or humming (Blackmore, 2004). As an alternative, you can silently repeat a *mantra* (a word used as the focus of attention in concentrative meditation). Typical mantras are smooth, flowing sounds that are easily repeated. A widely used mantra is the word "om." A mantra could also be any pleasant word or a phrase from a familiar song, poem, or prayer. If other thoughts arise as you repeat a mantra, just return attention to it as often as necessary to maintain meditation.

The Relaxation Response

The benefits of meditation include lowered heart rate, blood pressure, muscle tension, and other signs of stress (Lazar et al., 2000). Medical researcher Herbert Benson believes that the core of meditation is the **relaxation response**—an innate physiological pattern that opposes your body's fight-or-flight mechanisms. Benson feels, quite simply, that most of us have forgotten how to relax deeply. People in his experiments learned to produce the relaxation response by following these instructions:

> Sit quietly and comfortably. Close your eyes. Relax your muscles, beginning at your feet and progressing up to your head. Relax them deeply. Become aware of breathing through your nose. As you breathe out, say a word like "peace" silently to yourself. Don't worry about how successful you are in relaxing deeply. Just let relaxation happen at its own pace. Don't be surprised by distracting thoughts. When they occur, ignore them and continue repeating "peace." (Adapted from Benson, 1977; Lazar et al., 2000)

As a stress-control technique, meditation may be a good choice for people who find it difficult to "turn off" upsetting thoughts when they need to relax. In one study, a group of college students who received just 90 minutes of training in the relaxation response experienced greatly reduced stress levels (Deckro et al., 2002). The physical benefits of meditation include lowered heart rate, blood pressure, muscle tension, and other signs of stress (Lazar et al., 2000), as well as improved immune system activity (Davidson et al., 2003).

According to Shauna Shapiro and Roger Walsh (2006), meditation has benefits beyond relaxation. Practiced regularly, meditation may foster mental well-being and positive mental skills such as clarity, concentration, and calm. In this sense, meditation may share much in common with psychotherapy. Indeed, research has shown that mindfulness meditation relieves a variety of psychological disorders, from insomnia to excessive anxiety. It can also reduce aggression and the illegal use of psychoactive drugs (Shapiro & Walsh, 2006). Regular meditation may even help people develop self-awareness and maturity (Travis, Arenander, & DuBois, 2004).

Meditation A mental exercise for producing relaxation or heightened awareness.

Concentrative meditation Mental exercise based on attending to a single object or thought.

Mindfulness meditation Mental exercise based on widening attention to become aware of everything experienced at any given moment.

Relaxation response The pattern of internal bodily changes that occurs at times of relaxation.

Sensory Deprivation

The relaxation response can also be produced by brief sensory deprivation. **Sensory deprivation (SD)** refers to any major reduction in the amount or variety of sensory stimulation.

What happens when stimulation is greatly reduced? A hint comes from reports by prisoners in solitary confinement, arctic explorers, high-altitude pilots, long-distance truck drivers, and radar operators. When faced with limited or monotonous stimulation, people sometimes have bizarre sensations, dangerous lapses in attention, and wildly distorted perceptions. Intense or prolonged SD is stressful and disorienting. Yet, oddly enough, brief periods of sensory restriction can be very relaxing.

Psychologists have explored the possible benefits of sensory restriction using small isolation tanks like the one pictured in ▶▶ Figure 5.9. An hour or two spent in a flotation tank, for instance, causes a large drop in blood pressure, muscle tension, and other signs of stress (van Dierendonck & Te Nijenhuis, 2005). Of course, it could be argued that a warm bath has the same effect. Nevertheless, brief SD appears to be one of the surest ways to induce deep relaxation (Suedfeld & Borrie, 1999).

Like meditation, sensory restriction may also help with more than relaxation. Mild SD can help people quit smoking, lose weight, and reduce their use of alcohol and drugs (van Dierendonck & Te Nijenhuis, 2005). Psychologist Peter Suedfeld calls such benefits **Restricted Environmental Stimulation Therapy (REST).** Deep relaxation makes people more open to suggestion, and sensory restriction interrupts habitual behavior patterns. As a result, REST can "loosen" belief systems and make it easier to change bad habits (Suedfeld & Borrie, 1999).

REST also shows promise as a way to stimulate creative thinking (Norlander, Bergman, & Archer, 1998). Other researchers have reported that REST sessions can enhance performance in skilled sports, such as gymnastics, tennis, basketball, darts, and marksmanship (Druckman & Bjork, 1994; Norlander, Bergman, & Archer, 1999). There is also evidence that REST can relieve chronic pain and reduce stress (Bood et al., 2006). Clearly, there is much yet to be learned from studying "nothingness."

Summary

To summarize, research suggests that meditation and mild sensory deprivation are ways to elicit the relaxation response. For many people, sitting quietly and "resting" can be as effective. Similar stress reduction occurs when people set aside time daily to engage in other restful activities, such as muscle relaxation, positive daydreaming, and even leisure reading. However, if you are the type of person who finds it difficult to ignore upsetting thoughts, then concentrative meditation might be a good way to promote relaxation. Practiced regularly, meditation and REST may even help improve overall mental health—something almost everyone could use in our fast-paced society.

Positive Psychology: Mindfulness and Well-Being

Did you "space out" anytime today? Most of us have occasional moments of reduced awareness. **Mindfulness** is the opposite of such mindless moments: It involves an open, nonjudgmental awareness of current experience. In other words, mindfulness is similar to the state that people who practice mindfulness meditation are trying to achieve. A person who is mindful is fully present, moment by moment. She or he is acutely aware of every thought, emotion, or sensation, but does not judge it or react to it. The person is fully "awake" and attuned to immediate reality.

Psychologists interested in positive mental states have begun to study the effects of mindfulness. For example, cancer patients who are taught mindfulness meditation have lower levels of distress and a greater sense of well-being. Such benefits apply to healthy people, too. In general, mindfulness is associated with self-knowledge and well-being (Brown & Ryan, 2003). Anyone who has a tendency to sleepwalk through life—and that's most of us at times—would be wise to be mindful of the value of mindfulness.

Pixtal/SuperStock

▲ FIGURE 5.9 A sensory isolation chamber. Small flotation tanks like the one pictured have been used by psychologists to study the effects of mild sensory deprivation. Subjects float in darkness and silence. The shallow body-temperature water contains hundreds of pounds of Epsom salts, so that subjects float near the surface. Mild sensory deprivation produces deep relaxation.

Sensory deprivation (SD) Any major reduction in the amount or variety of sensory stimulation.

Restricted Environmental Stimulation Therapy (REST) A form of sensory deprivation that results in a variety of psychological benefits.

Mindfulness A state of open, nonjudgmental awareness of current experience.

RECITE

1. In Ernest Hilgard's dissociative state theory of hypnosis, awareness is split between normal consciousness and
   a. disinhibition
   b. autosuggestion
   c. memory
   d. the hidden observer
2. Tests of hypnotic susceptibility measure a person's tendency to respond to
   a. suggestion
   b. imagery rehearsal
   c. stimulus control techniques
   d. the activation-synthesis effect
3. Which of the following can most definitely be achieved with hypnosis?
   a. unusual strength
   b. pain relief
   c. improved memory
   d. sleep-like brain waves
4. The focus of attention in concentrative meditation is "open," or expansive. T or F?
5. Mantras are words said silently to oneself to end a session of meditation. T or F?
6. The most immediate benefit of meditation appears to be its capacity for producing the relaxation response. T or F?
7. Prolonged periods of extreme sensory deprivation lower anxiety and induce deep relaxation. T or F?

REFLECT

Critical Thinking

8. What kind of control group would you need in order to identify the true effects of hypnosis?
9. Regular meditators report lower levels of stress and a greater sense of well-being. What other explanations must we eliminate before this effect can be regarded as genuine?

Relate

How have your beliefs about hypnosis changed after reading the preceding section? Can you think of specific examples in which hypnosis was misrepresented? For example, in high school assemblies, stage acts, movies, or TV dramas?

Various activities can produce the relaxation response. When do you experience states of deep relaxation, coupled with a sense of serene awareness? What similarities do these occurrences have to meditation or sensory deprivation?

ANSWERS

1. d 2. a 3. b 4. F 5. F 6. T 7. F 8. Most experiments on hypnosis include a control group in which people are asked to simulate being hypnotized. Without such controls, the tendency of subjects to cooperate with experimenters makes it difficult to identify true hypnotic effects. 9. Studies on the effects of meditation must control for the placebo effect and the fact that those who choose to learn meditation may not be a representative sample of the general population.

Drug-Altered Consciousness— The High and Low of It

What are the effects of the more commonly used psychoactive drugs?

The most common way to alter human consciousness is to administer a **psychoactive drug** (a substance capable of altering attention, judgment, memory, time sense, self-control, emotion, or perception). In fact, most Americans regularly use consciousness-altering drugs (don't forget that caffeine, alcohol, and nicotine are mildly psychoactive). Psychoactive drugs alter consciousness by directly influencing brain activity (Julien, 2005). (See "How Psychoactive Drugs Affect the Brain.") Many psychoactive drugs can be placed on a scale ranging from stimulation to depression (▶▶ Figure 5.10). A **stimulant** (upper) is a substance that increases activity in the body and nervous system. A **depressant** (downer) does the reverse.

Because drugs that can ease pain, induce sleep, or end depression have a high potential for abuse, the more powerful psychoactive drugs are controlled substances (Goldberg, 2006). Nevertheless, more than 20 million Americans are currently illicit drug users (Substance Abuse and Mental Health Services Administration [SAMHSA], 2005). Drug abuse has been one of the most persistent of all social problems in Western nations.

Why is drug abuse so common? People seek drug experiences for many reasons, ranging from curiosity and a desire to belong to a group, to a search for meaning or an escape from feelings of inadequacy. Many abusers turn to drugs in a self-defeating attempt to cope with life. All the frequently abused drugs produce immediate feelings of pleasure. The negative

Psychoactive drug A substance capable of altering attention, memory, judgment, time sense, self-control, mood, or perception.

Stimulant A substance that increases activity in the body and nervous system.

Depressant A substance that decreases activity in the body and nervous system.

brain waves

How Psychoactive Drugs Affect the Brain

Psychoactive drugs influence the activity of brain cells (Kalat, 2009). Typically, drugs imitate or alter the effects of neurotransmitters, the chemicals that carry messages between brain cells. Some drugs, such as Ecstasy, amphetamines, and some antidepressants, cause more neurotransmitters to be released, increasing the activity of brain cells. Other drugs, such as cocaine, slow the removal of neurotransmitters after they are released. This prolongs the action of transmitter chemicals and typically has a stimulating effect. Other drugs, such as nicotine and opiates, directly stimulate brain cells by mimicking neurotransmitters. Another possibility is illustrated by alcohol and tranquilizers. These drugs affect certain types of brain cells that cause relaxation and relieve anxiety. Some drugs fill receptor sites on brain cells and block incoming messages. Other possibilities also exist, which is why drugs can have such a wide variety of effects on the brain (Julien, 2005).

Dopamine projections to prefrontal cortex

Nucleus accumbens

Medial forebrain bundle (a path of axons that release dopamine)

Area in midbrain

△ FIGURE 5.11 Addictive drugs increase dopamine activity in the medial forebrain bundle and the nucleus accumbens, stimulating the frontal cortex and giving rise to intensified feelings of pleasure.

Nearly all addictive drugs stimulate the brain's reward circuitry, producing feelings of pleasure (Kalat, 2009). In particular, addictive drugs stimulate a brain region called the *nucleus accumbens* to release the neurotransmitter dopamine, which results in intensified feelings of pleasure (▶▶ Figure 5.11). As one expert put it, addictive drugs fool brain-reward pathways. "As a result, the reward pathway signals, 'That felt good. Let's do it again. Let's remember exactly how we did it.'" This creates a compulsion to repeat the drug experience. It's the hook that eventually snares the addict (Restak, 2001). In the end, the addictive drug physically changes the brain's reward circuitry, making it even harder for the addict to overcome his or her addiction (Robinson & Berridge, 2003). Adolescents are especially susceptible to addiction because brain systems that restrain their risk-taking are not as mature as those that reward pleasure seeking (Chambers, Taylor, & Potenza, 2003).

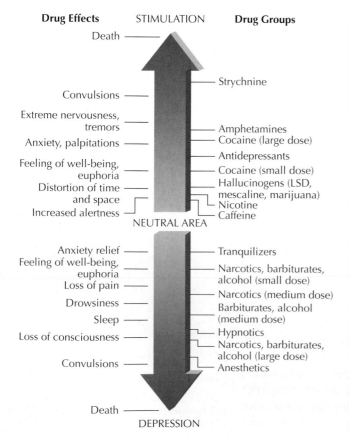

△ FIGURE 5.10 Spectrum and continuum of drug action. Many drugs can be rated on a stimulation–depression scale according to their effects on the central nervous system. Although LSD, mescaline, and marijuana are listed here, the stimulation–depression scale is less relevant to these drugs. The principal characteristic of such hallucinogens is their mind-altering quality.

consequences follow much later. This combination of immediate pleasure and delayed punishment allows abusers to feel good on demand.

In time, of course, most of the pleasure goes out of drug abuse and the abuser's problems get worse. But if an abuser merely feels better (however briefly) after taking a drug, drug taking can become compulsive (Higgins et al., 2004). In contrast, people who stop using drugs often say that they quit because the drawbacks had come to exceed the benefits (Toneatto et al., 1999).

The best predictors of adolescent drug use and abuse are drug use by peers, parental drug use, delinquency, parental maladjustment, poor self-esteem, social nonconformity, and stressful life changes. One study found that adolescents who abuse drugs tend to be maladjusted, alienated, impulsive, and emotionally distressed (Masse & Tremblay, 1997). Antisocial behavior, school failure, and risky sexual behavior are also commonly associated with drug abuse (Ary et al., 1999). Such patterns make it clear that taking drugs is a symptom, rather than a cause, of personal and social maladjustment (Ksir, Hart, & Ray, 2006).

Drug Dependence

Another reason why drug abuse is so common is that taking most psychoactive drugs tends to create dependencies. Once you get started, it can be hard to stop. Drug dependence falls into two broad categories. When a person compulsively uses a drug to maintain bodily comfort, a **physical dependence** (addiction) exists (Julien, 2005). Addiction occurs most often with drugs that cause **withdrawal symptoms** (physical illness that follows removal of a drug). Withdrawal from drugs such as alcohol, barbiturates, and opiates can cause violent flu-like symptoms of nausea, vomiting, diarrhea, chills, sweating, and cramps. Addiction is often accompanied by a **drug tolerance** (reduced response to a drug). This leads users to take larger and larger doses to get the desired effect.

Persons who develop a **psychological dependence** feel that a drug is necessary to maintain their comfort or well-being. Usually, they intensely crave the drug and its rewarding qualities (Winger et al., 2005). Psychological dependence can be just as powerful as physical addiction. That's why some psychologists define addiction as any compulsive habit pattern. By this definition, a person who has lost control over drug use, for whatever reason, is addicted. In fact, most people who answer yes to both of the following questions have an alcohol or drug problem and should seek professional help (Brown et al., 1997):

• In the last year, did you ever drink or use drugs more than you meant to?
• Have you felt you wanted or needed to cut down on your drinking or drug use in the last year?

Patterns of Abuse

Some drugs, of course, have a higher potential for abuse than others. Heroin is certainly more dangerous than caffeine. However, this is only one side of the picture. It can be as useful to classify drug-taking *behavior* as it is to rate drugs. For example, some people remain social drinkers for life, whereas others become alcoholics within weeks of taking their first drink (Robinson & Berridge, 2003). In this sense, drug use can be classified as *experimental* (short-term use based on curiosity), *social-recreational* (occasional social use for pleasure or relaxation), *situational* (use to cope with a specific problem, such as needing to stay awake), *intensive* (daily use with elements of dependence), or *compulsive* (intense use and extreme dependence). The last three categories of drug taking tend to be damaging no matter what drug is used.

Heath Ledger's Oscar-winning performance as the Joker in one of the Batman films was his last. His career was only the most recent one to be cut short by polydrug abuse.

Polydrug Abuse

There is one more pattern of drug abuse that bears mentioning: the abuse of more than one drug at the same time. According to the Florida Medical Examiners Commission (2008), polydrug abuse accounts for the "vast majority" of deaths due to drug overdose. When mixed, the effects of different drugs are multiplied by **drug interactions** (one drug enhances the effect of another) that are responsible for thousands of fatal drug overdoses every year (Goldberg, 2006). This is true whether the mixed drugs were legally or illegally obtained.

Drugs of Abuse

Note in ● Table 5.3 that the drugs most likely to lead to physical dependence are alcohol, amphetamines, barbiturates, cocaine, codeine, heroin, methadone, morphine, and tobacco (nicotine). Using *any* of the drugs listed in Table 5.3 can result in psychological dependence. Note too that people who take drugs intravenously are at high risk for developing hepatitis and AIDS (see Chapter 11). The discussion that follows focuses on the drugs most often abused by students.

Physical dependence Physical addiction, as indicated by the presence of drug tolerance and withdrawal symptoms.

Withdrawal symptoms Physical illness and discomfort following the withdrawal of a drug.

Drug tolerance A reduction in the body's response to a drug.

Psychological dependence Drug dependence that is based primarily on emotional or psychological needs.

Drug interaction A combined effect of two drugs that exceeds the addition of one drug's effects to the other.

● Table 5.3 Comparison of Psychoactive Drugs

NAME	CLASSIFICATION	MEDICAL USE	USUAL DOSE	DURATION OF EFFECT
Alcohol	Sedative-hypnotic	Solvent, antiseptic	Varies	1–4 hours
Amphetamines	Stimulant	Relief of mild depression, control of narcolepsy and hyperactivity	2.5–5 milligrams	4 hours
Barbiturates	Sedative-hypnotic	Sedation, relief of high blood pressure, anticonvulsant	50–100 milligrams	4 hours
Benzodiazepines	Anxiolytic (antianxiety drug)	Tranquilizer	2–100 milligrams	10 minutes–8 hours
Caffeine	Stimulant	Counteract depressant drugs, treatment of migraine headaches	Varies	Varies
Cocaine	Stimulant, local anesthetic	Local anesthesia	Varies	Varied, brief periods
Codeine	Narcotic	Ease pain and coughing	30 milligrams	4 hours
GHB	Sedative-hypnotic	Experimental treatment of narcolepsy, alcoholism	1–3 grams (powder)	1–3 hours
Heroin	Narcotic	Pain relief	Varies	4 hours
LSD	Narcotic	Experimental study of mental function, alcoholism	100–500 milligrams	10 hours
Marijuana (THC)	Relaxant, euphoriant; in high doses, hallucinogen	Treatment of glaucoma and side effects of chemotherapy	1–2 cigarettes	4 hours
MDMA	Stimulant/hallucinogen	None	125 milligrams	4–6 hours
Mescaline	Hallucinogen	None	350 micrograms	12 hours
Methadone	Narcotic	Pain relief	10 milligrams	4–6 hours
Morphine	Narcotic	Pain relief	15 milligrams	6 hours
PCP	Anesthetic	None	2–10 milligrams	4–6 hours, plus 12-hour recovery
Psilocybin	Hallucinogen	None	25 milligrams	6–8 hours
Tobacco (nicotine)	Stimulant	Emetic (nicotine)	Varies	Varies

Question marks indicate conflict of opinion. It should be noted that illicit drugs are frequently adulterated and thus pose unknown hazards to the user.

Uppers—Amphetamines, Cocaine, MDMA, Caffeine, Nicotine

Amphetamines are synthetic stimulants. Common street names for amphetamine are "speed," "bennies," "dexies," "go," and "uppers." These drugs were once widely prescribed for weight loss or depression. Today, the main legitimate medical use of amphetamines is to treat childhood hyperactivity and overdoses of depressant drugs. Illicit use of

EFFECTS SOUGHT	LONG-TERM SYMPTOMS	PHYSICAL DEPENDENCE POTENTIAL	PSYCHOLOGICAL DEPENDENCE POTENTIAL	ORGANIC DAMAGE POTENTIAL
Sense alteration, anxiety reduction, sociability	Cirrhosis, toxic psychosis, neurologic damage, addiction	Yes	Yes	Yes
Alertness, activeness	Loss of appetite, delusions, hallucinations, toxic psychosis	Yes	Yes	Yes
Anxiety reduction, euphoria	Addiction with severe withdrawal symptoms, possible convulsions, toxic psychosis	Yes	Yes	Yes
Anxiety relief	Irritability, confusion, depression, sleep disorders	Yes	Yes	No, But can affect fetus
Wakefulness, alertness	Insomnia, heart arrhythmias, high blood pressure	No?	Yes	Yes
Excitation, talkativeness	Depression, convulsions	Yes	Yes	Yes
Euphoria, prevent withdrawal discomfort	Addiction, constipation, loss of appetite	Yes	Yes	No
Intoxication, euphoria, relaxation	Anxiety, confusion, insomnia, hallucinations, seizures	Yes	Yes	No?
Euphoria, prevent withdrawal discomfort	Addiction, constipation, loss of appetite	Yes	Yes	No*
Insightful experiences, exhilaration, distortion of senses	May intensify existing psychosis, panic reactions	No	No?	No?
Relaxation; increased euphoria, perceptions, sociability	Possible lung cancer, other health risks	Yes	Yes	Yes?
Excitation, euphoria	Personality change, hyperthermia, liver damage	No	Yes	Yes
Insightful experiences, exhilaration, distortion of senses	May intensify existing psychosis, panic reactions	No	No?	No?
Prevent withdrawal discomfort	Addiction, constipation, loss of appetite	Yes	Yes	No
Euphoria, prevent withdrawal discomfort	Addiction, constipation, loss of appetite	Yes	Yes	No*
Euphoria	Unpredictable behavior, suspicion, hostility, psychosis	Debated	Yes	Yes
Insightful experiences, exhilaration, distortion of senses	May intensify existing psychosis, panic reactions	No	No?	No?
Alertness, calmness, sociability	Emphysema, lung cancer, mouth and throat cancer, cardiovascular damage, loss of appetite	Yes	Yes	Yes

*Persons who inject drugs under nonsterile conditions run a high risk of contracting AIDS, hepatitis, abscesses, or circulatory disorders.

amphetamines is widespread, however, especially by people seeking to stay awake and by those who think drugs can improve mental or physical performance (Iversen, 2006).

Methamphetamine is a more potent variation of amphetamine. It can be snorted, injected, or eaten. Of the various types of amphetamine, methamphetamine has created the largest drug problem. "Bergs," "glass," "meth," or "crystal," as it is known on the street, can be made cheaply in backyard labs and sold for massive profits. In addition to ruining lives through addiction, it has fueled a violent criminal subculture.

Amphetamines rapidly produce a drug tolerance. Most abusers end up taking ever-larger doses to get the desired effect. Eventually, some users switch to injecting methamphetamine directly into the bloodstream. True speed freaks typically go on binges lasting several days, after which they "crash" from lack of sleep and food.

Abuse

How dangerous are amphetamines? Amphetamines pose many dangers. Large doses can cause nausea, vomiting, extremely high blood pressure, fatal heart attacks, and disabling strokes. It is important to realize that amphetamines speed up the use of the body's resources; they do not magically supply energy. After an amphetamine binge, people suffer from crippling fatigue, depression, confusion, uncontrolled irritability, and aggression. Repeated amphetamine use damages the brain. Amphetamines can also cause *amphetamine psychosis,* a loss of contact with reality. Affected users have paranoid delusions that someone is out to get them. Acting on these delusions, they may become violent, resulting in suicide, self-injury, or injury to others (Iversen, 2006).

A potent smokable form of crystal methamphetamine has added to the risks of stimulant abuse. This drug, known as "ice" on the street, is highly addictive. Like "crack," the smokable form of cocaine, it produces an intense high. But also like crack (discussed in a moment), crystal methamphetamine leads very rapidly to compulsive abuse and severe drug dependence.

Cocaine was the main ingredient in many nonprescription elixirs before the turn of the twentieth century. Today cocaine is recognized as a powerful and dangerous drug. Its high potential for abuse has damaged the lives of countless users.

Cocaine

Cocaine ("coke," "snow," "blow," "snuff") is a powerful central nervous system stimulant extracted from the leaves of the coca plant. Cocaine produces feelings of alertness, euphoria, well-being, power, boundless energy, and pleasure (Julien, 2005). At the turn of the twentieth century, dozens of nonprescription potions and cure-alls contained cocaine. It was during this time that Coca-Cola was indeed the "real thing." From 1886 until 1906, when the U.S. Pure Food and Drug Act was passed, Coca-Cola contained cocaine (which has since been replaced with caffeine).

How does cocaine differ from amphetamines? The two are very much alike in their effects on the central nervous system. The main difference is that amphetamine lasts several hours; cocaine is snorted and quickly metabolized, so its effects last only about 15 to 30 minutes.

Abuse

How dangerous is cocaine? Cocaine's capacity for abuse and social damage rivals that of heroin. When rats and monkeys are given free access to cocaine, they find it irresistible. Many, in fact, end up dying of convulsions from self-administered overdoses of the drug. Even casual or first-time users risk having convulsions, a heart attack, or a stroke (Lacayo, 1995). Cocaine increases the chemical messengers dopamine (DOPE-ah-meen) and noradrenaline (nor-ah-DREN-ah-lin). Noradrenaline arouses the brain, and dopamine produces a "rush" of pleasure. This combination is so powerfully rewarding that cocaine users run a high risk of becoming compulsive abusers (Ridenour et al., 2005).

A person who stops using cocaine does not experience heroin-like withdrawal symptoms. Instead, the brain adapts to cocaine abuse in ways that upset its chemical balance, causing depression when cocaine is withdrawn. First, there is a jarring "crash" of mood and energy. Within a few days, the person enters a long period of fatigue, anxiety, paranoia, boredom, and **anhedonia** (an-he-DAWN-ee-ah: an inability to feel pleasure). Before long, the urge to use cocaine becomes intense. So, although cocaine does not fit the classic pattern of addiction, it is ripe for compulsive abuse. Even a person who gets through withdrawal may crave cocaine months or years later (Withers et al., 1995). If cocaine were cheaper, 9 out of 10 users would progress to compulsive abuse. In fact, rock cocaine ("crack," "rock," or "*roca*"), which is cheaper, produces very high abuse rates. Here are some signs of cocaine abuse:

Anhedonia An inability to feel pleasure.

- *Compulsive use.* If cocaine is available—say, at a party—you can't say no to it.
- *Loss of control.* Once you have had some cocaine, you will keep using it until you are exhausted or the cocaine is gone.
- *Disregarding consequences.* You don't care if the rent gets paid, your job is endangered, your lover disapproves, or your health is affected, you'll use cocaine anyway.

Anyone who thinks she or he has a cocaine problem should seek advice at a drug clinic or a Cocaine Anonymous meeting. Although quitting cocaine is extremely difficult, three out of four abusers who remain in treatment do succeed in breaking their coke dependence (Simpson et al., 1999; Sinha et al., 2006). There is also hope on the horizon in the form of a vaccine currently undergoing clinical trials that prevents cocaine from stimulating the nervous system (Kampman, 2005).

MDMA ("Ecstasy")

The drug MDMA (methylenedioxymethamphetamine, or "Ecstasy") is also chemically similar to amphetamine. In addition to producing a rush of energy, users say it makes them feel closer to others and heightens sensory experiences. Ecstasy causes brain cells to release extra amounts of serotonin. The physical effects of MDMA include dilated pupils, elevated blood pressure, jaw clenching, loss of appetite, and elevated body temperature (Braun, 2001). Although some users believe that Ecstasy increases sexual pleasure, it *diminishes* sexual performance, impairing erection in 40 percent of men and retarding orgasm in both men and women (Zemishlany, Aizenberg, & Weizman, 2001).

Abuse

Ecstasy use in North America has declined slightly from a peak around 2002, perhaps because of widespread negative publicity. Regardless, every year more than half a million Americans try Ecstasy for the first time (SAMHSA, 2005). Every year, emergency room doctors see many MDMA cases, including MDMA-related deaths. Some of these incidents are caused by elevated body temperature (hyperthermia) or heart arrhythmias, which can lead to collapse. Ecstasy users at "rave" parties try to prevent overheating by drinking water to cool themselves. This may help to a small degree, but the risk of fatal heat exhaustion is real. MDMA can also cause severe liver damage, which can be fatal (Braun, 2001). In addition, Ecstasy users are more likely to abuse alcohol and other drugs, to neglect studying, to party excessively, and to engage in risky sex (Strote, Lee, & Wechsler, 2002). Ironically, Ecstasy use at "rave" parties actually does intensify the impact of the music. We say ironically because the end result is often overstimulation of the brain, which can result in a "rebound" depression (Michelangelo et al., 2006).

Enough time has passed to assess the long-term effects of Ecstasy use. Feelings of anxiety or depression can persist for months after a person stops taking Ecstasy. In addition, heavy users typically do not perform well in tests of learning and memory and show some signs of underlying brain damage (Quednow et al., 2006). Fortunately, however, the long-term consequences are not as severe as once feared (Advisory Council on the Misuse of Drugs, 2009).

Caffeine

Caffeine is the most frequently used psychoactive drug in North America. (And that's not counting Seattle!) Caffeine stimulates the brain by blocking chemicals that normally inhibit or slow nerve activity (Julien, 2005). Its effects become apparent with doses as small as 50 milligrams, the amount found in about one-half cup of brewed coffee. Physically, caffeine causes sweating, talkativeness, tinnitus (ringing in the ears), and hand tremors (Nehlig, 2004). Psychologically, caffeine suppresses fatigue or drowsiness and increases feelings of alertness (Wesensten et al., 2002). Some people have a hard time starting a day (or writing another paragraph) without it.

How much caffeine did you consume today? It is common to think of coffee as the major source of caffeine, but there are many others. Caffeine is found in tea, many soft drinks (especially colas), chocolate, and cocoa. More than 2,000 nonprescription drugs also contain caffeine, including stay-awake pills, cold remedies, and many name-brand aspirin products.

Abuse

Are there any serious drawbacks to using caffeine? Overuse of caffeine may result in an unhealthy dependence known as **caffeinism.** Insomnia, irritability, loss of appetite, chills, racing heart, and elevated body temperature are all signs of caffeinism. Many people with these symptoms drink 15 or 20 cups of coffee a day. However, even at lower dosages, caffeine can intensify anxiety and other psychological problems (Hogan, Hornick, & Bouchoux, 2002).

Caffeine poses a variety of health risks. Caffeine encourages the growth of breast cysts in women, and it may contribute to bladder cancer, heart problems, and high blood pressure. Pregnant women should consider giving up caffeine entirely because of a suspected link between caffeine and birth defects. Pregnant women who consume as little as 2 cups of coffee a day increase the risk of having a miscarriage (Cnattingius et al., 2000).

It is customary to think that caffeine is not a drug. But as few as 2.5 cups of coffee a day (or the equivalent) can be a problem. People who consume even such modest amounts may experience anxiety, depression, fatigue, headaches, and flu-like symptoms during withdrawal (Juliano & Griffiths, 2004). About half of all caffeine users show some signs of dependence (Hughes et al., 1998). It is wise to remember that caffeine *is* a drug and use it in moderation.

Nicotine

Nicotine is a natural stimulant found mainly in tobacco. Next to caffeine and alcohol, it is the most widely used psychoactive drug (Julien, 2005).

How does nicotine compare with other stimulants? Nicotine is a potent drug. It is so toxic that it is sometimes used to kill insects! In large doses it causes stomach pain, vomiting and diarrhea, cold sweats, dizziness, confusion, and muscle tremors. In very large doses, nicotine may cause convulsions, respiratory failure, and death. For a nonsmoker, 50 to 75 milligrams of nicotine taken in a single dose could be lethal. (Chain-smoking about 17 to 25 cigarettes will produce this dosage.) Most first-time smokers get sick on one or two cigarettes. In contrast, regular smokers build a tolerance for nicotine. A heavy smoker may inhale 40 cigarettes a day without feeling ill.

Abuse

How addictive is nicotine? A vast array of evidence confirms that nicotine is very addictive (Spinella, 2005). The average age of first use is 15, and it takes about a year before dependence sets in (Baker, Brandon, & Chassin, 2004). Among regular smokers who are 15 to 24 years old, 60 percent are addicted (Breslau et al., 2001). For many smokers, withdrawal from nicotine causes headaches, sweating, cramps, insomnia, digestive upset, irritability, and a sharp craving for cigarettes (National Institute on Drug Abuse, 2006). These symptoms may last from 2 to 6 weeks and may be worse than heroin withdrawal. Indeed, relapse patterns are nearly identical for alcoholics, heroin addicts, cocaine abusers, and smokers who try to quit (Stolerman & Jarvis, 1995). Up to 90 percent of people who quit smoking relapse within a year, and 20 percent relapse even after 2 years of abstinence (Krall, Garvey, & Garcia, 2002).

Impact on Health

How serious are the health risks of smoking? If you think smoking is harmless or that there's no connection between smoking and cancer, you're kidding yourself. A burning cigarette releases a large variety of potent *carcinogens* (car-SIN-oh-jins: cancer-causing substances). According to the U.S. Surgeon General (U.S. Department of Health and Human Services, 2004), "smoking harms nearly every organ of the body," leading to an increased risk of many cancers (such as lung cancer), cardiovascular diseases (such as stroke), respiratory diseases (such as chronic bronchitis), and reproductive disorders (such as decreased fertility). Together, these health risks combine to reduce the life expectancy of the average smoker by 10 to 15 years. (Skeptics

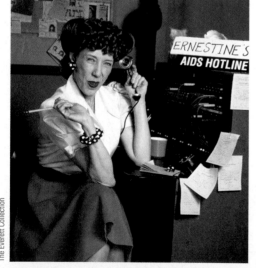

The Everett Collection

Actress and comedienne Lily Tomlin, here shown portraying one of her comedic characters, Ernestine, once took up smoking for a role in a movie (*Shadows and Fog*) and developed a 4-pack-a-day habit. As Tomlin's experience shows, the best way to avoid developing a nicotine addiction is to not begin smoking in the first place.

Caffeinism Excessive consumption of caffeine, leading to dependence and a variety of physical and psychological complaints.

please note: Wayne McLaren, who portrayed the rugged "Marlboro Man" in cigarette ads, died of lung cancer at age 51.) Every year almost 450,000 people die from tobacco use (National Center for Chronic Disease Prevention and Health Promotion, 2009).

By the way, urban cowboys and Skol bandits, the same applies to chewing tobacco and snuff. A 30-minute exposure to one pinch of smokeless tobacco is equivalent to smoking three or four cigarettes. Along with all the health risks of smoking, users of smokeless tobacco also run a higher risk of developing oral cancer (American Lung Association, 2006).

Smokers don't just risk their own health; they also endanger those who live and work nearby. Secondary smoke causes about 3,000 lung cancer deaths and as many as 62,000 heart disease deaths each year in the United States alone. It is particularly irresponsible of smokers to expose young children, who are especially vulnerable, to secondhand smoke (American Lung Association, 2009).

Quitting Smoking

Is it better for a person to quit smoking abruptly or taper down gradually? Most people try to quit by themselves. Some try to quit cold turkey, whereas others try to taper down gradually. Although going cold turkey has its advocates, gradually quitting works better for more people.

Going cold turkey makes quitting an all-or-nothing proposition. Smokers who smoke even one cigarette after "quitting forever" tend to feel they've failed. Many figure they might just as well resume smoking. Those who quit gradually accept that success may take many attempts, spread over several months. If you are going to quit by going cold turkey, you will have a better chance of success if you decide to quit *now* rather than at some time in the future (West & Sohal, 2006).

"Not for me thanks, mate - I'm only a passive smoker."

The best way to taper off is *scheduled gradual reduction* (Riley et al., 2002). There are many ways in which smoking can be gradually reduced. For example, the smoker can (1) delay having a first cigarette in the morning and then try to delay a little longer each day, (2) gradually reduce the total number of cigarettes smoked each day, or (3) quit completely, but for just 1 week, then quit again, a week at a time, for as many times as necessary to make it stick. Deliberately scheduling and then gradually stretching the length of time periods between cigarettes is a key part of this program. Scheduled smoking apparently helps people learn to cope with the urge to smoke. As a result, people using this method are more likely to remain permanent nonsmokers than people using other approaches (Cinciripini, Wetter, & McClure, 1997).

Whatever approach is taken, quitting smoking is not easy (Abrams et al., 2003). Many people find that using nicotine patches or gum helps them get through the withdrawal period (Shiffman et al., 2006). Also, as we have noted, anyone trying to quit should be prepared to make several attempts before succeeding. But the good news is that tens of millions of people have quit. (Behavioral self-management techniques can be very useful for breaking habits such as smoking. See Chapter 6 and Chapter 13.)

Downers—Sedatives, Tranquilizers, and Alcohol

The most widely used downers, or depressant drugs, are alcohol, barbiturates, GHB, and benzodiazepine (ben-zoe-die-AZ-eh-peen) tranquilizers. These drugs are much alike in their effects. In fact, barbiturates and tranquilizers are sometimes referred to as "solid alcohol." Let's examine the properties of each.

Barbiturates

Barbiturates are sedative drugs that depress brain activity. Common barbiturates include amobarbital, pentobarbital, secobarbital, and tuinal. On the street they are known as "downers," "blue heavens," "yellow jackets," "lows," "goof balls," "reds," "pink ladies," "rainbows," or "tooies." Medically, barbiturates are used to calm patients or to induce sleep. At mild dosages, barbiturates have an effect similar to alcohol intoxication. Higher dosages can cause severe mental confusion or even hallucinations. Barbiturates are often taken in excess amounts because a first dose may be followed by others, as the user becomes uninhibited or forgetful. Overdoses first cause a loss of consciousness. Then they severely depress brain centers that control heartbeat and breathing. The result is death (McKim, 2007).

GHB

Would you swallow a mixture of degreasing solvent and drain cleaner to get high? Apparently, a lot of people would. A mini-epidemic of GHB (gamma-hydroxybutyrate) use has taken place in recent years, especially at nightclubs and raves. GHB ("goop," "scoop," "max," "Georgia Home Boy") is a central nervous system depressant that relaxes and sedates the body. Users describe its effects as being similar to alcohol. Mild GHB intoxication tends to produce euphoria, a desire to socialize, and a mild loss of inhibitions. GHB's intoxicating effects typically last 3 to 4 hours, depending on the dosage.

Abuse

At lower dosages, GHB can relieve anxiety and produce relaxation. However, as the dose increases, its sedative effects may result in nausea, a loss of muscle control, and either sleep or a loss of consciousness. Potentially fatal doses of GHB are only three times the amount typically taken by users. This narrow margin of safety has led to numerous overdoses, especially when GHB was combined with alcohol. An overdose causes coma, breathing failure, and death. Also, GHB inhibits the gag reflex, so some users choke to death on their own vomit.

In 2000, the U.S. government classified GHB as a controlled substance, making its possession a felony. Clinical evidence increasingly suggests that GHB is addictive and a serious danger to users. Two out of three frequent users have lost consciousness after taking GHB. Heavy users who stop taking GHB have withdrawal symptoms that include anxiety, agitation, tremor, delirium, and hallucinations (Miotto et al., 2001).

As if the preceding weren't enough reason to be leery of GHB, here's one more to consider: GHB is often manufactured in homes with recipes and ingredients purchased on the Internet. As mentioned earlier, it can be produced by combining degreasing solvent with drain cleaner (Falkowski, 2000). If you want to degrease your brain, GHB will do the trick.

Tranquilizers

A **tranquilizer** is a drug that lowers anxiety and reduces tension. Doctors prescribe benzodiazepine tranquilizers to alleviate nervousness and stress. Valium is the best-known drug in this family; others are Xanax, Halcion, and Librium. Even at normal dosages these drugs can cause drowsiness, shakiness, and confusion. When used at too high a dosage or for too long, benzodiazepines are addictive (McKim, 2007).

A drug sold under the trade name Rohypnol (ro-HIP-nol) has added to the problem of tranquilizer abuse. This drug, which is related to Valium, is cheap and 10 times more potent. It lowers inhibitions and produces relaxation or intoxication. Large doses induce short-term amnesia and sleep. "Roofies," as they are known on the street, are odorless and tasteless. They have been used to spike drinks, which are given to the unwary. Victims of this "date rape" drug are then sexually assaulted or raped while they are unconscious. (Be aware, however, that drinking too much alcohol is by far the most common prelude to rape.)

Tranquilizer A drug that lowers anxiety and reduces tension.

Abuse

Repeated use of barbiturates can cause physical dependence. Some abusers suffer severe emotional depression that may end in suicide. Similarly, when tranquilizers are used at too high a dosage or for too long, addiction can occur. Many people have learned the hard way that their legally prescribed tranquilizers are as dangerous as many illicit drugs (McKim, 2007).

Combining barbiturates or tranquilizers with alcohol is especially risky. All too often, depressants are gulped down with alcohol or added to a spiked punch bowl. This is the lethal brew that left a young woman named Karen Ann Quinlan in a coma that lasted 10 years, ending with her death. It is no exaggeration to restate that mixing depressants with alcohol can be deadly.

Alcohol

Alcohol is the common name for ethyl alcohol, the intoxicating element in fermented and distilled liquors. Contrary to popular belief, alcohol is not a stimulant. The noisy animation at drinking parties is due to alcohol's effect as a *depressant*. As ▶▶ Figure 5.12 shows, small amounts of alcohol reduce inhibitions and produce feelings of relaxation and euphoria.

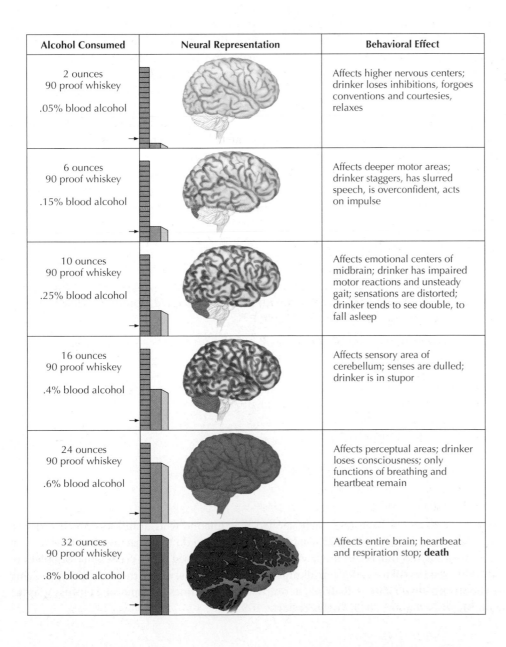

Alcohol Consumed	Neural Representation	Behavioral Effect
2 ounces 90 proof whiskey .05% blood alcohol		Affects higher nervous centers; drinker loses inhibitions, forgoes conventions and courtesies, relaxes
6 ounces 90 proof whiskey .15% blood alcohol		Affects deeper motor areas; drinker staggers, has slurred speech, is overconfident, acts on impulse
10 ounces 90 proof whiskey .25% blood alcohol		Affects emotional centers of midbrain; drinker has impaired motor reactions and unsteady gait; sensations are distorted; drinker tends to see double, to fall asleep
16 ounces 90 proof whiskey .4% blood alcohol		Affects sensory area of cerebellum; senses are dulled; drinker is in stupor
24 ounces 90 proof whiskey .6% blood alcohol		Affects perceptual areas; drinker loses consciousness; only functions of breathing and heartbeat remain
32 ounces 90 proof whiskey .8% blood alcohol		Affects entire brain; heartbeat and respiration stop; **death**

◀◀ **FIGURE 5.12** The behavioral effects of alcohol are related to blood alcohol content and the resulting suppression of higher mental function. Arrows indicate the typical threshold for legal intoxication in the United States. (From Jozef Cohen, Eyewitness Series in Psychology, p. 44. Copyright © Jozef Cohen. Reprinted by permission of Huguette Cohen.)

Dougie Wallace/Alamy

Binge drinking and alcohol abuse have become serious problems among college students (Tewksbury, Higgins, & Mustaine, 2008).

Larger amounts cause ever-greater impairment of the brain until the drinker loses consciousness. Alcohol is also not an aphrodisiac. Rather than enhancing sexual arousal, it usually impairs performance, especially in males. As William Shakespeare observed long ago, drink "provokes the desire, but it takes away the performance."

Abuse

Alcohol, the world's favorite depressant, breeds our biggest drug problem. More than 20 million people in the United States and Canada have serious drinking problems. One American dies every 20 minutes in an alcohol-related car crash. The level of alcohol abuse among adolescents and young adults is alarming. Of 18-year-olds, 15 percent are heavy drinkers and 40 percent have engaged in binge drinking (SAMHSA, 2005). **Binge drinking** is defined as downing five or more drinks in a short time (four drinks for women). Apparently, many students think it's entertaining to get completely wasted and throw up on their friends. However, binge drinking is a serious sign of alcohol abuse. It is responsible for 1,400 college student deaths each year and thousands of trips to the ER (Wechsler et al., 2002).

Binge drinking is of special concern because the brain continues to develop into the early twenties. Research has shown that teenagers and young adults who drink too much may lose as much as 10 percent of their brain power—especially their memory capacity (Brown et al., 2000). Such losses can have a long-term impact on a person's chances for success in life. In short, getting drunk is a slow but sure way to get stupid (Wechsler & Wuethrich, 2002).

Positive reinforcement—drinking for pleasure—motivates most people who consume alcohol. What sets alcohol abusers apart is that they also drink to cope with negative emotions, such as anxiety and depression. That's why alcohol abuse increases with the level of stress in people's lives. People who drink to relieve bad feelings are at great risk of becoming alcoholics (Kenneth, Carpenter, & Hasin, 1998).

Recognizing Problem Drinking

What are the signs of alcohol abuse? Because alcohol abuse is such a common problem, it is important to recognize the danger signals. If you can answer yes to even one of the following questions, you may have a problem with drinking (adapted from the College Alcohol Problems Scale, revised; Maddock et al., 2001):

As a result of drinking alcoholic beverages I....
1. engaged in unplanned sexual activity.
2. drove under the influence.
3. did not use protection when engaging in sex.
4. engaged in illegal activities associated with drug use.
5. felt sad, blue, or depressed.
6. was nervous or irritable.
7. felt bad about myself.
8. had problems with appetite or sleeping.

Moderated Drinking

Almost everyone has been to a party spoiled by someone who drank too much too fast. Those who avoid overdrinking have a better time, and so do their friends. But how do you avoid drinking too much? After all, as one wit once observed, "The conscience dissolves in alcohol." It takes skill to regulate drinking in social situations, where the temptation to drink can be strong. If you choose to drink, here are some guidelines that may be helpful (adapted from Miller & Munoz, 2005; Vogler & Bartz, 1992):

Binge drinking Consuming five or more drinks in a short time.

Paced Drinking

1. Think about your drinking beforehand and plan how you will manage it.
2. Drink slowly, eat while drinking or drink on a full stomach, and make every other drink (or more) a nonalcoholic beverage.
3. Limit drinking primarily to the first hour of a social event or party.
4. Practice how you will politely but firmly refuse drinks.
5. Learn how to relax, meet people, and socialize without relying on alcohol.

And remember, research has shown that you are likely to overestimate how much your fellow students are drinking (Maddock & Glanz, 2005). So don't let yourself be lured into overdrinking just because you have the (probably false) impression that other students are drinking more than you. Limiting your own drinking may help others as well. When people are tempted to drink too much, their main reason for stopping is that "other people were quitting and deciding they'd had enough" (Johnson, 2002).

Treatment

Treatment for alcohol dependence begins with sobering up the person and cutting off the supply. This phase is referred to as **detoxification** (literally, "to remove poison"). It frequently produces all the symptoms of drug withdrawal and can be extremely unpleasant. The next step is to try to restore the person's health. Heavy abuse of alcohol usually causes severe damage to body organs and the nervous system. After alcoholics have "dried out" and some degree of health has been restored, they may be treated with tranquilizers, antidepressants, or psychotherapy. Unfortunately, the success of these procedures has been limited.

One mutual-help approach that has been fairly successful is Alcoholics Anonymous (AA). AA takes a spiritual approach while acting on the premise that it takes a former alcoholic to understand and help a current alcoholic. Participants at AA meetings admit that they have a problem, share feelings, and resolve to stay "dry" one day at a time. Other group members provide support for those struggling to end dependency. (Other "12-step" programs, such as Cocaine Anonymous and Narcotics Anonymous, use the same approach.)

Eighty percent of those who remain in AA for more than 1 year get through the following year without a drink. However, AA's success rate may simply reflect the fact that members join voluntarily, meaning they have admitted they have a serious problem (Morgenstern et al., 1997). Sadly, it seems that alcohol abusers will often not face their problems until they have "hit rock bottom." If they are willing, though, AA presents a practical approach to the problem (Vaillant, 2005).

Other groups offer a rational, nonspiritual approach to alcohol abuse that better fits the needs of some people. Examples include Rational Recovery and Secular Organizations for Sobriety (SOS). Other alternatives to AA include medical treatment, group therapy, and individual psychotherapy (Buddie, 2004). There is a strong tendency for abusive drinkers to deny they have a problem. The sooner they seek help, the better.

Hallucinogens—Tripping the Light Fantastic

Marijuana is the most popular illicit drug in America (SAMHSA, 2005). The main active chemical in marijuana is tetrahydrocannabinol (tet-rah-hydro-cah-NAB-ih-nol), or THC, for short. THC is a mild **hallucinogen** (hal-LU-sin-oh-jin: a substance that alters sensory impressions). Other hallucinogenic drugs include LSD and PCP.

LSD and PCP

The drug LSD (lysergic acid diethylamide, or "acid") is perhaps the best-known hallucinogen. Even when taken in tiny amounts, LSD can produce hallucinations and psychotic-like disturbances in thinking and perception. Two other common hallucinogens are mescaline (peyote) and psilocybin ("magic mushrooms," or "shrooms"). Incidentally, the drug PCP

Detoxification In the treatment of alcoholism, the withdrawal of the patient from alcohol.

Hallucinogen A substance that alters or distorts sensory impressions.

Artists have tried at times to capture the effects of hallucinogens. Here, the artist depicts visual experiences he had while under the influence of LSD.

(phencyclidine, or "angel dust") can have hallucinogenic effects. However, PCP, which is an anesthetic, also has stimulant and depressant effects. This potent combination can cause extreme agitation, disorientation, violence—and too often, tragedy. All of the hallucinogens, including marijuana, typically affect neurotransmitter systems that carry messages between brain cells (Julien, 2005).

Marijuana

Marijuana and hashish are derived from the hemp plant *Cannabis sativa.* Marijuana ("pot," "grass," "Ganja," "MJ") consists of the dried leaves and flowers of the hemp plant. Hashish is a resinous material scraped from cannabis leaves. Marijuana's psychological effects include a sense of euphoria or well-being, relaxation, altered time sense, and perceptual distortions. At high dosages, however, paranoia, hallucinations, and delusions can occur (Ksir, Hart, & Ray, 2006). All considered, marijuana intoxication is relatively subtle by comparison to drugs such as LSD or alcohol. Despite this, driving a car while high on marijuana can be extremely hazardous. As a matter of fact, driving under the influence of any intoxicating drug is dangerous.

No overdose deaths from marijuana have been reported. However, marijuana cannot be considered harmless. Particularly worrisome is the fact that THC accumulates in the body's fatty tissues, especially in the brain and reproductive organs. Even if a person smokes marijuana just once a week, the body is never entirely free of THC. Scientists have located a specific receptor site on the surface of brain cells where THC binds to produce its effects (▶▶Figure 5.13). These receptor sites are found in large numbers in the cerebral cortex, which is the seat of human consciousness (Julien, 2005). In addition, THC receptors are found in areas involved in the control of skilled movement. Naturally occurring chemicals similar to THC may help the brain cope with pain and stress. However, when THC is used as a drug, high dosages can cause paranoia, hallucinations, and dizziness.

▶▶ **FIGURE 5.13** This thin slice of a rat's brain has been washed with a radioactive THC-like drug. Yellowish areas show where the brain is rich in THC receptors. In addition to the cortex, or outer layer of the brain, THC receptors are found in abundance in areas involved in the control of coordinated movement. Naturally occurring chemicals similar to THC may help the brain cope with pain and stress. However, when THC is used as a drug, high doses can cause paranoia, hallucinations, and dizziness (Julien, 2005).

Dangers of Marijuana Use

Does marijuana produce physical dependence? Yes, according to recent studies (Lichtman & Martin, 2006). Frequent users of marijuana find it very difficult to quit, so dependence is a risk (Budney & Hughes, 2006). But marijuana's potential for abuse lies primarily in the realm of psychological dependence, not physical addiction.

For about a day after a person smokes marijuana, his or her attention, coordination, and short-term memory are impaired (Pope, Gruber, & Yurgelun-Todd, 1995). Frequent marijuana users show small declines in learning, memory, attention, and thinking abilities (Solowij et al., 2002). When surveyed at age 29, nonusers are healthier, earn more, and are more satisfied with their lives than people who smoke marijuana regularly (Ellickson, Martino, & Collins, 2004).

People who smoke five or more "joints" a week score 4 points lower on IQ tests. This is enough to dull their learning capacity. In fact, many people who have stopped using marijuana say they quit because they were bothered by short-term memory loss and concentration problems. Fortunately, IQ scores and other cognitive measures rebound in about a month after a person quits using marijuana (Grant et al., 2001). In other words, people who smoke dope may act like dopes, but if they quit, there's a good chance they will regain their mental abilities.

Long-Term Health Risks

Marijuana's long-term effects include the following health risks:

1. Marijuana smoke contains 50 percent more cancer-causing hydrocarbons and 16 times more tar than tobacco smoke does. Thus, smoking several "joints" a week may be the equivalent of smoking a dozen cigarettes a day. In regular users, marijuana increases the risk of a variety of cancers, including prostate and cervical cancer (Hashibe et al., 2005).
2. Marijuana temporarily lowers sperm production in males, and users produce more abnormal sperm. This could be a problem for a man who is marginally fertile and wants to have a family (Schuel et al., 1999).
3. In experiments with female monkeys, THC causes abnormal menstrual cycles and disrupts ovulation. Other animal studies show that THC causes a higher rate of miscarriages and that it can reach the developing fetus. As is true for so many other drugs, it appears that marijuana should be avoided during pregnancy.
4. THC can suppress the body's immune system, increasing the risk of disease.
5. In animals, marijuana causes genetic damage within cells of the body. It is not known to what extent this happens in humans, but it does suggest that marijuana can be detrimental to health.
6. Activity levels in the cerebellum are lower than normal in marijuana abusers. This may explain why chronic marijuana users tend to show some loss of coordination (Volkow et al., 1996).
7. There is some evidence that THC damages parts of the brain important for memory (Chan et al., 1998).
8. Children whose mothers smoked marijuana during pregnancy show lowered ability to succeed in challenging, goal-oriented activities (Fried & Smith, 2001; Noland et al., 2005).

Although much is still unknown, marijuana appears to pose a wide range of health risks. Only future research will tell for sure "what's in the pot."

A Look Ahead

Of the many states of consciousness we have discussed, dreaming remains one of the most familiar—and the most surprising. Are there lessons to be learned from dreams? What personal insights lie hidden in the ebb and flow of your dream images? Let's find out in the upcoming Psychology in Action section.

study break

Psychoactive Drugs

RECITE

1. Addictive drugs stimulate the brain's reward circuitry by affecting
   - a. neurotransmitters
   - b. alpha waves
   - c. tryptophan levels
   - d. delta spindles
2. Which of the drugs listed below are known to cause a physical dependence?
   - a. heroin
   - b. morphine
   - c. codeine
   - d. methadone
   - e. barbiturates
   - f. alcohol
   - g. marijuana
   - h. amphetamines
   - i. nicotine
   - j. cocaine
   - k. GHB
3. Amphetamine psychosis is similar to extreme _____, in which the individual feels threatened and suffers from delusions.

4. Cocaine is very similar to which of the following in its effects on the central nervous system?
   - a. Seconal
   - b. codeine
   - c. cannabis
   - d. amphetamine
5. MDMA and GHB are classified as depressants. T or F?
6. The combination of _____ or _____ and alcohol can be fatal.
7. College students may overdrink as they try to keep up with how much they falsely imagine that their peers drink. T or F?

REFLECT

Critical Thinking

8. The U.S. government, which helps fund antismoking campaigns and smoking-related health research, also continues to subsidize tobacco growers. Can you explain this contradiction?
9. Why do you think there is such a contrast between the laws regulating marijuana and those regulating alcohol and tobacco?

Relate

What legal drugs did you use in the last year? Did any have psychoactive properties? How do psychoactive drugs differ from other substances in their potential for abuse?

ANSWERS

1. a 2. All of them do 3. paranoia 4. d 5. F 6. barbiturates, tranquilizers 7. T 8. Neither can we. 9. Drug laws in Western societies reflect cultural values and historical patterns of use. Inconsistencies in the law often cannot be justified on the basis of pharmacology, health risks, or abuse potential.

---

psychology in action

Exploring and Using Dreams

How can dreams be used to promote personal understanding?

No matter what theory of dreaming we favor, dreams can be thought of as a message *from* yourself *to* yourself. Thus, the way to understand dreams is to remember them, write them down, look for the messages they contain, and become deeply acquainted with *your own* symbol system. Here's how:

How to Catch a Dream

1. Before going to sleep, plan to remember your dreams. Keep a pen and paper or a tape recorder beside your bed.

2. If possible, arrange to awaken gradually without an alarm. Natural awakening almost always follows soon after a REM period.

3. If you rarely remember your dreams, you may want to set an alarm clock to go off an hour before you usually awaken. Although less desirable than awakening naturally, this may let you catch a dream.

4. Upon awakening, lie still and review the dream images with your eyes closed. Try to recall as many details as possible.

5. If you can, make your first dream record (whether by writing or by recording) with your eyes closed. Opening your eyes will disrupt dream recall.

6. Review the dream again and record as many additional details as you can remember. Dream memories disappear quickly. Be sure to describe feelings as well as the plot, characters, and actions of the dream.

7. Put your dreams into a permanent dream diary. Keep dreams in chronological order and review them periodically. This procedure will reveal recurrent themes, conflicts, and emotions. It almost always produces valuable insights.

8. Remember, a number of drugs suppress dreaming by interfering with REM sleep (see ● Table 5.4).

Dream Work

At one time or another almost everyone has had a dream that seemed to have deep meaning (Rock, 2004). Exploring everyday dream life can be a source of personal enrichment and personal growth (Cartwright & Lamberg, 1992). What strategies do psychologists use to interpret dreams? Let's start with Sigmund Freud's pioneering approach.

To unlock dreams, Freud identified four **dream processes,** or mental filters, that disguise the meanings of dreams. The first is **condensation,** in which several people, objects, or events are combined into a single dream image. A dream character that looks like a teacher, acts like your father, talks like your mother, and is dressed like your employer might be a condensation of authority figures in your life.

Displacement is a second way of disguising dream content. Displacement may cause important emotions or actions of a dream to be redirected toward safe or seemingly unimportant images. Thus, a student angry at his parents might dream of accidentally wrecking their car instead of directly attacking them.

A third dream process is **symbolization.** As mentioned earlier, Freud believed that dreams are often expressed in images that are symbolic rather than literal. That's why it helps to ask what feelings or ideas a dream image might symbolize. Let's say, for example, that a student dreams of coming to class naked. A literal interpretation would be that the student is an exhibitionist. A more likely symbolic meaning is that the student feels vulnerable or unprepared in the class.

Secondary elaboration is the fourth method by which dream meanings are disguised. **Secondary elaboration** is the tendency to make a dream more logical and to add details when remembering it. The fresher a dream memory is, the more useful it is likely to be.

Looking for condensation, displacement, symbolization, and secondary elaboration may help you unlock your dreams. But there are other techniques that may be more effective. Dream theorist Calvin Hall (1974) preferred to think of dreams as plays and the dreamer as a playwright. Although Hall points out that dream images and ideas tend to be more primitive than waking thoughts, much can be learned by simply considering the *setting, cast of characters, plot,* and *emotions* portrayed in a dream.

Another dream theorist, Rosalind Cartwright, suggests that dreams are primarily "feeling statements." According to her, the overall *emotional tone* (underlying mood) of a dream is a major clue to its meaning (Cartwright & Lamberg, 1992). Is the dream comical, threatening, joyous, or depressing? Were you lonely, jealous, frightened, in love, or angry?

Because each dream has several possible meanings or levels of meaning, there is no fixed way to work with it. Telling the dream to others and discussing its meaning can be a good start. Describing it may help you relive some of the feelings in the dream. Also, family members or friends may be able to offer interpretations to which you would be blind. Watch for verbal or visual puns and other playful elements in dreams. For example, if you dream that you are in a wrestling match and your arm is pinned behind your back, it may mean that you feel someone is "twisting your arm" in real life.

The meaning of most dreams will yield to a little detective work. Try asking a series of questions about dreams you would like to understand:

Probing Dreams

1. Who was in the dream? Were there humans, animals, or mythical characters? Do you recognize any of the characters?

2. What social interactions were taking place? Were those interactions friendly? Aggressive? Sexual?

● **Table 5.4 Effects of Selected Drugs on Dreaming**

DRUG	EFFECT ON REM SLEEP
Alcohol	Decrease
Amphetamines	Decrease
Barbiturates	Decrease
Caffeine	None
Cocaine	Decrease
LSD	Slight increase
Marijuana	Slight decrease or no effect
Opiates	Decrease
Valium	Decrease

Michael Schmitt/Jupiterimages

How would you try to find the meaning of a dream? A traditional approach is to look for symbolic messages, as well as literal meanings. If you find yourself wearing a mask in a dream, for instance, it could relate to important roles that you play at school, work, or home. It could also mean that you want to hide or that you are looking forward to a costume party. However, to accurately interpret a dream, it is important to learn your own "vocabulary" of dream images and meanings. Keeping a dream diary is the first step toward gaining valuable insights.

Dream processes Mental filters that hide the true meanings of dreams.

Condensation Combining several people, objects, or events into a single dream image.

Displacement Directing emotions or actions toward safe or unimportant dream images.

Symbolization The nonliteral expression of dream content.

Secondary elaboration Making a dream more logical and complete while remembering it.

3. What activities were taking place? Were they physical activities or not?

4. Was there striving? Was the striving successful or not?

5. Was the dream about good fortune or misfortune?

6. What emotions were present in the dream? Was there anger, apprehension, confusion, happiness, or sadness?

7. What were the physical surroundings like? What was the setting? Were there any physical objects present? (Adapted from the Hall–Van de Castle system of dream content analysis; Domhoff, 2003.)

If you still have trouble seeing the meaning of a dream, you may find it helpful to use a technique developed by Fritz Perls. Perls, the originator of Gestalt therapy, considered most dreams a special message about what's missing in our lives, what we avoid doing, or feelings that need to be "re-owned." Perls believed that dreams are a way of filling in gaps in personal experience (Perls, 1969).

An approach that Perls found helpful is to "take the part of" or "speak for" each of the characters and objects in the dream. In other words, if you dream about a strange man standing behind a doorway, you would speak aloud to the man, then answer for him. To use Perls's method, you would even speak for the door, perhaps saying something like, "I am a barrier. I keep you safe, but I also keep you locked inside. The stranger has something to tell you. You must risk opening me to learn it."

A particularly interesting dream exercise is to continue a dream as waking fantasy so that it may be concluded or carried on to a more meaningful ending. As the world of dreams and your personal dream language become more familiar, you will doubtless find many answers, paradoxes, intuitions, and insights into your own behavior.

Using Your Dreams

It is possible to learn to use dreams for our own purposes. For example, as mentioned previously, nightmare sufferers can use imagery rehearsal to modify their own nightmares (Germain et al., 2004; Krakow & Zadra, 2006). Similarly, it is possible to use your dreams to enhance creativity (Stickgold & Walker, 2004).

Dreams and Creativity History is full of cases where dreams have been a pathway to creativity and discovery. A striking example is provided by Dr. Otto Loewi, a pharmacologist and winner of a Nobel Prize. Loewi had spent years studying the chemical transmission of nerve impulses. A tremendous breakthrough in his research came when he dreamed of an experiment 3 nights in a row. The first 2 nights he woke up and scribbled the experiment on a pad. But the next morning, he couldn't tell what the notes meant. On the third night, he got up after having the dream. This time, instead of making notes, he went straight to his laboratory and performed the crucial experiment. Loewi later said that if the experiment had occurred to him while awake, he would have rejected it.

Loewi's experience gives some insight into using dreams to produce creative solutions. Inhibitions are reduced during dreaming, which may be especially useful in solving problems that require a fresh point of view. Even unimaginative people may create amazing worlds each night in their dreams. For many of us, this rich ability to create is lost in the daily rush of sensory input.

Being able to take advantage of dreams for problem solving is improved if you "set" yourself before retiring. Before you go to bed, try to visualize or think intently about a problem you wish to solve. Steep yourself in the problem by stating it clearly and reviewing all relevant information. Then use the suggestions listed previously to catch your dreams. Although this method is not guaranteed to produce a novel solution or a new insight, it is certain to be an adventure. About half of a group of college students using the method for 1 week recalled a dream that helped them solve a personal problem (Barrett, 1993).

Lucid Dreaming If you would like to press further into the territory of dreams, you may want to learn lucid dreaming, a relatively rare, but fascinating, experience. During a **lucid dream**

Lucid dream A dream in which the dreamer feels awake and capable of normal thought and action.

a person feels as if she or he is fully awake within the dream world and capable of normal thought and action. If you ask yourself, "Could this be a dream?" and answer "Yes," you are having a lucid dream (Holzinger, LaBerge, & Levitan, 2006; LaBerge, 2000).

Stephen LaBerge and his colleagues at the Stanford University Sleep Research Center have used a unique approach to show that lucid dreams are real and that they occur during REM sleep. In the sleep lab, lucid dreamers agree to make prearranged signals when they become aware they are dreaming. One such signal is to look up abruptly in a dream, causing a distinct upward eye movement. Another signal is to clench the right and left fists (in the dream) in a prearranged pattern. In other words, lucid dreamers can partially overcome REM sleep paralysis. Such signals show very clearly that lucid dreaming and voluntary action in dreams is possible (LaBerge, 2000).

How can a person learn to have lucid dreams? Try following this simple routine: When you awaken spontaneously from a dream, take a few minutes to try to memorize it. Next, engage in 10 to 15 minutes of reading or any other activity requiring full wakefulness. Then while lying in bed and returning to sleep, say to yourself, "Next time I'm dreaming, I want to remember I'm dreaming." Finally, visualize yourself lying in bed asleep while in the dream you just rehearsed. At the same time, picture yourself realizing that you are dreaming. Follow this routine each time you awaken (substitute a dream memory from another occasion if you don't awaken from a dream). Researchers have also found that stimulation from the vestibular system tends to increase lucidity. Thus, sleeping in a hammock, a boat, or on a waterbed might increase the number of lucid dreams you have (Leslie & Ogilvie, 1996).

Why would anyone want to have more lucid dreams? Researchers are interested in lucid dreams because they provide a tool for understanding dreaming (Paulsson & Parker, 2006). Using subjects who can signal while they are dreaming makes it possible to explore dreams with firsthand data from the dreamer's world itself.

On a more personal level, lucid dreaming can convert dreams into a nightly "workshop" for emotional growth. Consider, for example, a recently divorced woman who kept dreaming that she was being swallowed by a giant wave. Rosalind Cartwright asked the woman to try swimming the next time the wave engulfed her. She did, with great determination, and the nightmare lost its terror. More important, her revised dream made her feel that she could cope with life again. For reasons such as this, people who have lucid dreams tend to feel a sense of emotional well-being (Wolpin et al., 1992). Dream expert Allan Hobson believes that learning to voluntarily enter altered states of consciousness (through lucid dreaming or self-hypnosis, for example) has allowed him to have enlightening experiences without the risks of taking mind-altering drugs (Hobson, 2001). So, day or night, don't be afraid to dream a little.

RECITE

1. Which is NOT one of the four dream processes identified by Freud?
   a. condensation   b. lucidity
   c. displacement   d. symbolization
2. In secondary elaboration, one dream character stands for several others. T or F?
3. Calvin Hall's approach to dream interpretation emphasizes the setting, cast, plot, and emotions portrayed in a dream. T or F?
4. Rosalind Cartwright stresses that dreaming is a relatively mechanical process having little personal meaning. T or F?
5. Both alcohol and LSD cause a slight increase in dreaming. T or F?
6. "Taking the part of" or "speaking for" dream elements is a dream interpretation technique originated by Fritz Perls. T or F?
7. Recent research shows that lucid dreaming occurs primarily during NREM sleep or microawakenings. T or F?

REFLECT

Critical Thinking

8. The possibility of having a lucid dream raises an interesting question: If you were dreaming right now, how could you prove it?

Relate

Some people are very interested in remembering and interpreting their dreams. Others pay little attention to dreaming. What importance do you place on dreams? Do you think dreams and dream interpretation can increase self-awareness?

ANSWERS

1. b 2. F 3. T 4. F 5. F 6. T 7. F 8. In waking consciousness, our actions have consequences that produce immediate sensory feedback. Dreams lack such external feedback. Thus, trying to walk through a wall or doing similar tests would reveal if you were dreaming.

chapter in review

Major Points

- Consciousness and altered states of awareness are core features of mental life.

- Sleep is necessary for survival; dreaming appears to contribute to memory consolidation and perhaps to general mental and emotional health.

- Sleep loss and sleep disorders are serious health problems that should be corrected when they persist.

- Dreams can be meaningful. Whether they have deeper, symbolic meaning is still debated.

- Hypnosis is useful but not "magical." Hypnosis can change private experiences more readily than behaviors or habits.

- Meditation can be used to alter consciousness, as well as to reliably produce deep relaxation.

- Psychoactive drugs, which alter consciousness, are highly prone to abuse.

- Collecting and interpreting your dreams can promote self-awareness.

Summary

What is consciousness?

- States of awareness that differ from normal, alert, waking consciousness are called altered states of consciousness (ASCs). Altered states are especially associated with sleep and dreaming, hypnosis, sensory deprivation, and psychoactive drugs.
- Cultural conditioning greatly affects what altered states a person recognizes, seeks, considers normal, and attains.

What are the effects of sleep loss or changes in sleep patterns?

- Sleep is an innate biological rhythm essential for survival.
- Moderate sleep loss affects mainly vigilance and performance on routine or boring tasks.
- Higher animals and people deprived of sleep experience involuntary microsleep.
- Extended sleep loss can (somewhat rarely) produce a temporary sleep-deprivation psychosis.
- Sleep patterns show some flexibility, but 7 to 8 hours remains average. The amount of daily sleep decreases steadily from birth to old age.

Why do we sleep?

- Sleep occurs in four stages. Stage 1 is light sleep, and stage 4 is deep sleep. The sleeper alternates between stages 1 and 4 (passing through stages 2 and 3) several times each night.
- According to the dual process hypothesis, sleep "refreshes" the body and brain and helps form lasting memories.
- The two most basic sleep states are rapid eye movement (REM) sleep and non-REM (NREM) sleep. REM sleep is strongly associated with dreaming.
- NREM sleep brings overall brain activation levels down, "calming" the brain.
- REM sleep and dreaming help us store important memories.

What are some sleep disorders and unusual sleep events?

- Insomnia may be temporary or chronic. Behavioral approaches to managing insomnia, such as sleep restriction and stimulus control, are quite effective.
- Sleepwalking, sleeptalking, and sleepsex occur during NREM sleep.
- Night terrors occur in NREM sleep, whereas nightmares occur in REM sleep.

- Sleep apnea (interrupted breathing) is one source of insomnia and daytime hypersomnia (sleepiness).
- Apnea is suspected as one cause of sudden infant death syndrome (SIDS). With only a few exceptions, healthy infants should sleep face up or on their sides.

Do dreams have meaning?

- The Freudian, or psychodynamic, view is that dreams express unconscious wishes, frequently hidden by dream symbols.
- Many theorists have questioned Freud's view of dreams. For example, the activation-synthesis model portrays dreaming as a physiological process.
- The neurocognitive view of dreams holds that dreams are continuous with waking thoughts and emotions.
- Most dream content is about familiar settings, people, and actions. Positive and negative emotions occur about equally in dreams.

What is hypnosis?

- Hypnosis is an altered state characterized by narrowed attention and increased suggestibility. (Not all psychologists agree that hypnotic effects require an alteration of consciousness.)
- Hypnosis appears capable of producing relaxation, controlling pain, and altering perceptions.
- Hypnosis alters perceptions and behavior, but it is more capable of changing subjective experiences than habits, such as smoking.
- Stage hypnotism takes advantage of typical stage behavior and uses deception to simulate hypnosis.

Do meditation and sensory deprivation have any benefits?

- Meditation and sensory deprivation are beneficial ways to alter consciousness through relaxation.
- Concentrative meditation can be used to focus attention, alter consciousness, and reduce stress. Major benefits of meditation are its ability to interrupt anxious thoughts and to elicit the relaxation response.
- Brief exposure to sensory deprivation can also elicit the relaxation response. Under proper conditions, sensory deprivation may help break long-standing habits.

What are the effects of the more commonly used psychoactive drugs?

- Psychoactive drugs affect the brain in ways that alter consciousness. Most psychoactive drugs can be placed on a scale ranging from stimulation to depression.
- Drugs may cause a physical dependence (addiction) or a psychological dependence, or both. The physically addicting drugs are alcohol, amphetamines, barbiturates, cocaine, codeine, GHB, heroin, methadone, morphine, nicotine, and tranquilizers.
- Drug use can be classified as experimental, recreational, situational, intensive, and compulsive. Drug abuse is most often associated with the last three. Polydrug abuse is also a problem.
- Stimulant drugs are readily abused because of the period of depression that often follows stimulation. The greatest risks are associated with amphetamines (especially methamphetamine), cocaine, MDMA, and nicotine, but even caffeine can be a problem. Nicotine includes the added risk of lung cancer, heart disease, and other health problems.
- Barbiturates and tranquilizers are depressant drugs whose action is similar to that of alcohol. The overdose level for barbiturates and GHB is close to the intoxication

dosage, making them dangerous drugs. Mixing barbiturates, tranquilizers, or GHB and alcohol may result in a fatal drug interaction.
- Alcohol is the most heavily abused drug in common use today. Binge drinking is a problem among college students. It is possible to pace the consumption of alcohol.
- Marijuana is subject to an abuse pattern similar to alcohol. Studies have linked chronic marijuana use with lung cancer, various mental impairments, and other health problems.

How can dreams be used to promote personal understanding?

- Collecting and interpreting your dreams can promote self-awareness.
- Freud held that the meaning of dreams is hidden by condensation, displacement, symbolization, and secondary elaboration. Hall emphasizes the setting, cast, plot, and emotions of a dream. Cartwright's view of dreams as feeling statements and Perls's technique of speaking for dream elements are also helpful.
- Dreams may be used for creative problem solving, especially when dream awareness is achieved through lucid dreaming.

States of Consciousness

For additional review, get more practice with *CengageNOW, WebTutor,* the *Practice Quizzes,* and/or the printed *Study Guide* available with this book.

1. We can only know the consciousness of other minds through a(n) _____ point of view.
   a. introspective b. third-person
   c. psychodynamic d. first-person

2. If you are sleep deprived as you read this question, you may well be experiencing
   a. mostly alpha waves b. pain insensitivity
   c. stimulus control d. microsleeps

3. A person in deep sleep produces mostly
   a. beta waves b. alpha waves
   c. delta waves d. REMs

4. Which of the following would normally be most incompatible with moving your arms and legs while asleep?
   a. REM sleep b. sleep spindles
   c. delta waves d. NREM sleep

5. Which of the following is NOT a form of insomnia?
   a. NREM insomnia b. temporary insomnia
   c. drug-dependency insomnia d. chronic insomnia

6. Nightmares differ from night terrors because they occur during _____ sleep.
   a. NREM b. REM
   c. stage 1 d. stage 4

7. Sleep restriction and stimulus control are techniques used to treat
   a. sleep apnea b. sleeptalking
   c. night terrors d. insomnia

8. If REM sleep is interrupted, a person will experience REM
   a. nightmares b. rebound
   c. disturbance d. forgetfulness

9. Wish fulfillment and dream symbols are important concepts in which explanation of dream content?
   a. activation-synthesis b. the REST hypothesis
   c. imagery rehearsal d. psychodynamic

10. Suggestible people are more likely to be
    a. more hypnotizable b. unimaginative
    c. hidden observers d. less hypnotizable

11. Research has shown that hypnosis cannot produce
    a. unusual strength b. improved memory
    c. pain relief d. sensory changes

12. Which terms DO NOT belong together?
    a. concentrative meditation—relaxation response
    b. sensory deprivation—relaxation response
    c. mindfulness meditation—mantra
    d. sensory deprivation—REST

13. Addictive drugs trigger
    a. physical dependence b. drug tolerance
    c. psychological dependence d. all of the above

14. Drug tolerance is most closely associated with
    a. psychological dependence b. marijuana
    c. withdrawal symptoms d. anhedonia

15. When rats and monkeys are given free access to cocaine, they
    a. avoid it b. prefer it
    c. excrete it d. find it irresistible

16. Hyperthermia, heart arrhythmias, and severe liver damage are major risks in the use of
    a. marijuana b. benzodiazepine
    c. MDMA d. GHB

17. Drug interaction is a special danger when a person combines
    a. marijuana and amphetamine b. barbiturates and alcohol
    c. alcohol and cocaine d. marijuana and THC

18. Treatment for alcohol dependence begins with sobering up the person and cutting off the supply. This is referred to as
    a. "hitting bottom" b. the crucial phase
    c. detoxification d. clinical anhedonia

19. Drug abuse is partly explained by the fact that psychoactive drugs produce immediate pleasure and
    a. somnambulism b. enhanced self-esteem
    c. delayed punishment d. brain carcinogens

20. Freud's four dream processes _____ dreams.
    a. elaborate b. disguise
    c. disrupt d. clarify

Answers 1.b 2.d 3.c 4.a 5.a 6.b 7.d 8.b 9.d 10.a 11.a 12.c 13.d 14.c 15.d 16.d 17.b 18.c 19.c 20.b

Conditioning and Learning

Journey into Psychology: Rats!

Larry vividly remembers his mother describing how a rat had terrified her. She gestured excitedly as she relived the horror of seeing the creature scamper out of a camp stove. Although everyone else laughed, 6-year-old Larry shivered as he imagined the attacking rodent. That's the day he learned to fear rats.

Years later, while studying gorillas in Africa, he encountered his first live rat. Larry was shocked by his own reaction. Despite being a respected scientist, he ran away shrieking like a little child. After failing to control his fear a few

more times (and being good-naturedly ribbed about it by others), he resolved to conquer it.

Back home, Larry read about irrational fears and realized that a form of learning called *vicarious classical conditioning* explained how he had come to dread rats. After reading several more books, he returned to the jungle, certain that he could cope with his next close encounter. However, he was shocked to discover that his newfound knowledge was no help at all.

Larry had bumped into a strange truth: All his abstract "book learning," a form of *cogni-*

tive learning, was powerless to protect him in the presence of a rat. Chastened, he went to a therapist who used classical conditioning to help him overcome his fear. Larry eventually came to like rats and now has a pet rat named Einstein. Larry also went on to study how baby gorillas learn by observing others—much as he did when he observed his mother's story about the rat.

Different forms of learning reach into every corner of our lives. Are you ready to learn more? If so, let's begin!

Survey Questions

- What is learning?
- How does classical conditioning occur?
- Does conditioning affect emotions?
- How does operant conditioning occur?
- Are there different kinds of operant reinforcement?
- How are we influenced by patterns of reward?
- What does punishment do to behavior?
- What is cognitive learning?
- Does learning occur by imitation?
- How does conditioning apply to everyday problems?

What Is Learning—Does Practice Make Perfect?

What is learning?

Almost all human behavior is learned. Imagine if you suddenly lost all you had ever learned. What could you do? You would be unable to read, write, or speak. You couldn't feed yourself, find your way home, drive a car, play the bassoon, or "party." Needless to say, you would be totally incapacitated. (Dull, too!)

Learning is a relatively permanent change in behavior due to experience (Powell, Symbaluk, & Honey, 2009). Notice that this definition excludes both temporary changes and more permanent changes caused by motivation, fatigue, maturation, disease, injury, or drugs. Each of these can alter behavior, but none qualifies as learning.

Types of Learning

As Larry's rat experience illustrates, there are different types of learning. **Associative learning** occurs whenever a person or an animal forms a simple association among various stimuli and/or responses. Humans share the capacity for associative learning with many other species. In a moment, we will explore two types of associative learning called classical conditioning and operant conditioning.

Humans also engage in **cognitive learning,** which refers to understanding, knowing, anticipating, or otherwise making use of information-rich higher mental processes. More complex forms of cognitive learning, such as learning from written language, are unique to humans and are why our species is called *Homo sapiens* (from the Latin for *man* and *wise*). However, some animals do engage in simpler forms of cognitive learning, which we will describe later in this chapter.

Associative Learning

Isn't learning the result of practice? It depends on what you mean by practice. Merely repeating a response will not necessarily produce learning. You could close your eyes and swing a tennis racket hundreds of times without improving your swing. Reinforcement is the key to associative learning. **Reinforcement** refers to any event that increases the probability that a response will occur again. A response is any identifiable behavior. Responses may be observable actions, such as blinking, eating a piece of candy, or turning a doorknob. They can also be internal, such as having a faster heartbeat.

To teach a dog a trick, we could reinforce correct responses by giving the dog some food each time it sits up. Similarly, you could teach a child to be neat by praising him for picking up his toys. Learning can also occur in other ways. For instance, if a girl gets stung by a bee, she may learn to associate pain with bees and to fear them. In this case, the girl's fear is reinforced by the discomfort she feels immediately after seeing the bee.

Unlocking the secrets of associative learning begins with noting what happens before and after a response. Events that precede a response are **antecedents.** For example, Ashleigh, who is 3, has learned that when she hears a truck pull into the driveway, it means that Daddy is home. Ashleigh runs to the front door. Effects that follow a response are **consequences.** The hug she gets from her father is what reinforces Ashleigh's tendency to run to the door. As this suggests, paying careful attention to the "before and after" of associative learning is a key to understanding it.

Classical conditioning is based on what happens before we respond. It begins with a stimulus that reliably triggers a response. Imagine, for example, that a puff of air (the stimulus) is aimed at your eye. The air puff will make you blink (a response) every time. The eyeblink is a **reflex** (automatic, nonlearned response). Now, assume that we sound a horn (another stimulus) just before each puff of air hits your eye. If the horn and the air puff occur together many times, what happens? Soon, the horn alone will make

---

Learning Any relatively permanent change in behavior that can be attributed to experience.

Associative learning The formation of simple associations between various stimuli and responses.

Cognitive learning Higher-level learning involving thinking, knowing, understanding, and anticipation.

Reinforcement Any event that increases the probability that a particular response will occur.

Antecedents Events that precede a response.

Consequences Effects that follow a response.

Reflex An innate, automatic response to a stimulus; for example, an eyeblink.

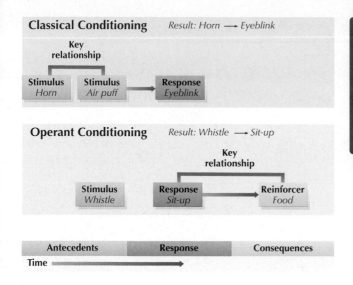

Classical Conditioning — Result: Horn → Eyeblink

Key relationship

Stimulus *Horn* — Stimulus *Air puff* → Response *Eyeblink*

Operant Conditioning — Result: Whistle → Sit-up

Key relationship

Stimulus *Whistle* — Response *Sit-up* → Reinforcer *Food*

| Antecedents | Response | Consequences |

Time

◀◀ **FIGURE 6.1** In classical conditioning, a stimulus that does not produce a response is paired with a stimulus that does elicit a response. After many such pairings, the stimulus that previously had no effect begins to produce a response. In the example shown, a horn precedes a puff of air to the eye. Eventually the horn alone will produce an eyeblink. In operant conditioning, a response that is followed by a reinforcing consequence becomes more likely to occur on future occasions. In the example shown, a dog learns to sit up when it hears a whistle.

you blink. Clearly, you've learned something. Before, the horn didn't make you blink. Now it does.

In **classical conditioning,** an antecedent stimulus that doesn't produce a response is linked with one that does (a horn is associated with a puff of air to the eye, for example). We can say that learning has occurred when the new stimulus will also elicit (bring forth) responses (▶▶ Figure 6.1).

In **operant conditioning,** learning is based on the consequences of responding. A response may be followed by a reinforcer (such as food). Or by punishment. Or by nothing. These results determine whether a response is likely to be made again (Figure 6.1). For example, if you wear a particular hat and get lots of compliments (reinforcement), you are likely to wear it more often. If people snicker, insult you, call the police, or scream (punishment), you will probably wear it less often.

Now that you have an idea of what happens in the two basic kinds of associative learning, let's look at classical conditioning in more detail.

Classical Conditioning—Does the Name Pavlov Ring a Bell?

How does classical conditioning occur?

At the beginning of the twentieth century, something happened in the lab of Russian physiologist Ivan Pavlov that brought him the Nobel Prize: Pavlov's subjects drooled at him. Actually, Pavlov was studying digestion. To observe salivation, he placed meat powder or some tidbit on a dog's tongue and measured the resulting flow of saliva. However, after repeating his procedure many times, Pavlov noticed that his dogs were salivating *before* the food reached their mouths. Later, the dogs even began to salivate when they saw Pavlov enter the room (Hergenhahn, 2009).

Pavlov believed that salivation is an automatic, inherited reflex. It really shouldn't change from one day to the next. His dogs were *supposed* to salivate when he put food in their mouths, but they were *not supposed* to salivate when they merely saw him. This was a change in behavior due to experience. Pavlov realized that some type of learning had occurred and soon began investigating "conditioning," as he called it (▶▶ Figure 6.2). Because of its place in history, this form of learning is now called *classical conditioning* (also known as *Pavlovian conditioning* or *respondent conditioning*) (Mackintosh, 2003).

▲ **FIGURE 6.2** An apparatus for Pavlovian conditioning. A tube carries saliva from the dog's mouth to a lever that activates a recording device *(far left)*. During conditioning, various stimuli can be paired with a dish of food placed in front of the dog. The device pictured here is more elaborate than the one Pavlov used in his early experiments.

Classical conditioning A form of learning in which reflex responses are associated with new stimuli.

Operant conditioning Learning based on the consequences of responding.

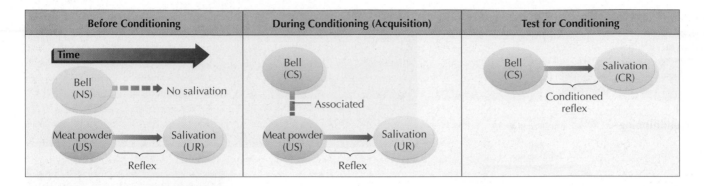

Before Conditioning	During Conditioning (Acquisition)	Test for Conditioning

Time

Bell (NS) ---> No salivation

Meat powder (US) ---> Salivation (UR)
Reflex

Bell (CS)
Associated
Meat powder (US) ---> Salivation (UR)
Reflex

Bell (CS) ---> Salivation (CR)
Conditioned reflex

▲ **FIGURE 6.3** The classical conditioning procedure.

Pavlov's Experiment

How did Pavlov study conditioning? To begin, he rang a bell. At first, the bell was a neutral stimulus (the dogs did not respond to it by salivating). Immediately after, he placed meat powder on the dogs' tongues, which caused reflex salivation. This sequence was repeated a number of times: bell, meat powder, salivation; bell, meat powder, salivation. Eventually (as conditioning took place), the dogs began to salivate when they heard the bell (▶▶ Figure 6.3). By association, the bell, which before had no effect, began to evoke the same response that food did. This was shown by sometimes ringing the bell alone. Then the dog salivated, even though no food had been placed in its mouth.

Psychologists use several terms to describe these events. The meat powder is an **unconditioned stimulus (US)** (a stimulus innately capable of producing a response; salivation in this case). Notice that the dog did not have to learn to respond to the US. Such stimuli naturally trigger reflexes or emotional reactions. Because a reflex is innate, or "built in," it is called an **unconditioned** (nonlearned) **response (UR).** Reflex salivation was the UR in Pavlov's experiment.

The bell starts out as a **neutral stimulus (NS).** In time, the bell becomes a **conditioned stimulus (CS)** (a stimulus that, because of learning, will elicit a response). When Pavlov's bell also produced salivation, the dog was making a new response. Thus, salivation had also become a **conditioned** (learned) **response (CR)** (Figure 6.3). ● Table 6.1 summarizes the important elements of classical conditioning.

Are all these terms really necessary? Yes, because they help us recognize similarities in various instances of learning. Let's summarize the terms using an earlier example:

Unconditioned stimulus (US) A stimulus innately capable of eliciting a response.

Unconditioned response (UR) An innate reflex response elicited by an unconditioned stimulus.

Neutral stimulus (NS) A stimulus that does not evoke a response.

Conditioned stimulus (CS) A stimulus that evokes a response because it has been repeatedly paired with an unconditioned stimulus.

Conditioned response (CR) A learned response elicited by a conditioned stimulus.

● Table 6.1 Elements of Classical Conditioning

ELEMENT	SYMBOL	DESCRIPTION	EXAMPLE
Unconditioned stimulus	US	A stimulus innately capable of eliciting a response	Meat powder
Unconditioned response	UR	An innate reflex response elicited by an unconditioned stimulus	Reflex salivation *to the US*
Neutral stimulus	NS	A stimulus that does not evoke the unconditioned response	Bell *before conditioning*
Conditioned stimulus	CS	A stimulus that evokes a response because it has been repeatedly paired with an unconditioned stimulus	Bell *after conditioning*
Conditioned response	CR	A learned response elicited by a conditioned stimulus	Salivation *to the CS*

Coping with Chemo

Our hearts go out to children with cancer. Even the treatment, chemotherapy, makes them miserable because it causes nausea and vomiting. In a cruel twist, after a few treatments, nausea can occur even when no chemotherapy is scheduled. Typically, it is triggered by certain sights or tastes, like the sight of the treatment center or the taste of a food the child ate before an earlier chemotherapy session.

In classical conditioning terms, chemotherapy is a US that leads to nausea, which is a UR. The sight of the treatment center or the taste of food eaten before treatment is initially a neutral stimu-

lus. However, because it is associated with nausea and vomiting, it becomes a CS. These sights or tastes can now elicit anticipatory nausea (a CR) even at times when the child doesn't receive chemotherapy (Chance, 2009).

In nature, many species are *biologically prepared* to associate specific locations and tastes with nausea. If animals eat contaminated food and then get sick and vomit, later the same locations or tastes may trigger anticipatory nausea and vomiting. These reactions discourage animals from eating potentially dangerous food. Unfortunately, conditioned nausea only compli-

cates treatment for young cancer patients. If Gita eats pepperoni pizza, her favorite meal, before she has a chemotherapy session, the taste of pepperoni may come to make her feel sick.

Is there any way to prevent conditioned nausea? No, but classical conditioning can provide some relief (Taylor, 2002). Meals eaten before chemotherapy can be flavored with an unusual taste, such as peppermint. The unique flavor overshadows other tastes, which don't become linked with nausea (Bovbjerg et al., 1992). In this way, Gita can continue to enjoy her pepperoni pizza.

Before Conditioning	Example
US → UR	Puff of air → eyeblink
NS → no effect	Horn → no effect

After Conditioning	Example
CS → CR	Horn → eyeblink

See "Coping with Chemo" for an example of how classical conditioning is used to solve a clinical problem.

Principles of Classical Conditioning— Here's Johnny

Imagine a boy named Johnny. To observe conditioning, you could ring a bell and squirt lemon juice into Johnny's mouth. By repeating this procedure several times, you could condition Johnny to salivate to the bell. Johnny might then be used to explore other aspects of classical conditioning.

▲ FIGURE 6.4 Acquisition and extinction of a conditioned response. (After Pavlov, 1927.)

Acquisition

During **acquisition,** or training, a conditioned response must be reinforced (strengthened) (▶▶ Figure 6.4). Classical conditioning is *reinforced* when the CS is followed by, or paired with, an unconditioned stimulus. This process is called **respondent reinforcement** because the US brings forth a *response,* which becomes associated with the CS. For Johnny, the bell is the CS, salivating is the UR, and the sour lemon juice is a US. To reinforce salivating to the bell, we must link the bell with the lemon juice. Conditioning will be most rapid if the US (lemon juice) follows *immediately* after the CS (the bell). With most reflexes, the optimal delay between CS and US is from ½ second to about 5 seconds (Chance, 2009).

Higher Order Conditioning

Once a response is learned, it can bring about **higher order conditioning.** In this case, a well-learned CS is used to reinforce further learning (Lefrançois, 2006). That is, the CS has become strong enough to be used like an unconditioned stimulus. Let's illustrate again with our salivating child.

Acquisition The period in conditioning during which a response is reinforced.

Respondent reinforcement Reinforcement that occurs when an unconditioned stimulus closely follows a conditioned stimulus.

Higher order conditioning Classical conditioning in which a conditioned stimulus is used to reinforce further learning; that is, a CS is used as if it were a US.

Before Conditioning		
	US *Lemon juice*	→ **UR** *Salivation*

During Conditioning		
CS *Bell*	— **US** *Lemon juice*	→ **UR** *Salivation*

Test for Conditioning		
	CR *Bell*	→ **CR** *Salivation*

Higher Order Conditioning		
CS₂ *Clap*	— **CS₁** *Bell*	→ **CR** *Salivation*

Test for Conditioning		
	CS₂ *Clap*	→ **CR** *Salivation*

FIGURE 6.5 Higher order conditioning takes place when a well-learned conditioned stimulus is used as if it were an unconditioned stimulus. In this example, a child is first conditioned to salivate to the sound of a bell. In time, the bell will elicit salivation. At that point, you could clap your hands and then ring the bell. Soon, after repeating the procedure, the child would learn to salivate when you clapped your hands.

As a result of earlier learning, the bell now makes Johnny salivate. (No lemon juice is needed.) To go a step further, you could clap your hands and then ring the bell. (Again, no lemon juice would be used.) Through higher order conditioning, Johnny would soon learn to salivate when you clapped your hands (▶▶ Figure 6.5). (This little trick could be a real hit with friends and neighbors.)

Higher order conditioning extends learning one or more steps beyond the original conditioned stimulus. Many advertisers use this effect by pairing images that evoke good feelings (such as people smiling and having fun) with pictures of their products. They hope that you will learn, by association, to feel good when you see their products (Priluck & Till, 2004).

Expectancies

Pavlov believed that classical conditioning does not involve any higher mental processes. Today, many psychologists think that classical conditioning does have cognitive origins because it is related to information that might aid survival. According to this **informational view,** we look for associations among events. Doing so creates new mental **expectancies,** or thoughts about how events are interconnected.

How does classical conditioning alter expectancies? Notice that the conditioned stimulus reliably precedes the unconditioned stimulus. Because it does, the CS *predicts* the US (Rescorla, 1987). During conditioning, the brain learns to *expect* that the US will follow the CS. As a result, the brain prepares the body to respond to the US. Here's an example: When you are about to get a shot with a hypodermic needle, your muscles tighten and there is a catch in your breathing. Why? Because your body is preparing for pain. You have learned to expect that getting poked with a needle will hurt. This expectancy, which was acquired during classical conditioning, changes your behavior.

Extinction and Spontaneous Recovery

Once an association has been classically conditioned, will it ever go away? If the US stops following the CS, conditioning will fade away, or extinguish. Let's return to Johnny. If you ring the bell many times and do not follow it with lemon juice, Johnny's expectancy that "bell precedes lemon juice" will weaken. As it does, he will lose his tendency to salivate when he hears the bell. Thus, we see that classical conditioning can be weakened by removing the connection between the conditioned and the unconditioned stimulus (see Figure 6.4). This process is called **extinction.**

If conditioning takes a while to build up, shouldn't it take time to reverse? Yes. In fact, it may take several extinction sessions to completely reverse conditioning. Let's say that we ring the bell until Johnny quits responding. It might seem that extinction is complete. However, Johnny will probably respond to the bell again on the following day, at least at first (Rescorla, 2004). The return of a learned response after apparent extinction is called **spontaneous recovery.** It explains why people who have had a car accident may need many slow, calm rides before their fear of driving extinguishes.

Generalization

After conditioning, other stimuli similar to the CS may also trigger a response. This is called **stimulus generalization.** For example, we might find that Johnny salivates to the sound of a ringing telephone or doorbell, even though they were never used as conditioning stimuli.

It is easy to see the value of stimulus generalization. Consider the child who burns her finger while playing with matches. Most likely, lighted matches will become conditioned fear stimuli for her. Because of stimulus generalization, she may also have a healthy fear of flames from lighters, fireplaces, stoves, and so forth. It's fortunate that generalization extends learning to related situations. Otherwise, we would all be far less adaptable.

As you may have guessed, stimulus generalization has limits. As stimuli become less like the original CS, responding decreases. If you condition a person to blink each time you play

Informational view Perspective that explains learning in terms of information imparted by events in the environment.

Expectancy An anticipation concerning future events or relationships.

Extinction The weakening of a conditioned response through removal of reinforcement.

Spontaneous recovery The reappearance of a learned response after its apparent extinction.

Stimulus generalization The tendency to respond to stimuli similar to, but not identical to, a conditioned stimulus.

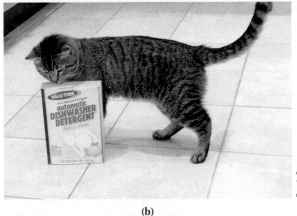

Lower tones   CS   Higher tones

Test stimuli   CS   Test stimuli

(a)

(b)

▲ FIGURE 6.6 *(a)* Stimulus generalization. Stimuli similar to the CS also elicit a response. *(b)* This cat has learned to salivate when it sees a cat food box. Because of stimulus generalization, it also salivates when shown a similar-looking detergent box.

a particular note on a piano, blinking will decline as you play higher or lower notes. If the notes are *much* higher or lower, the person will not respond at all (▶▶ Figure 6.6). Stimulus generalization explains why many stores carry imitations of nationally known products. For many customers, positive attitudes conditioned to the original products tend to generalize to the cheaper knockoffs (Till & Priluck, 2000).

Discrimination

Let's consider one more idea with Johnny (who by now must be ready to hide in the closet). Suppose we again condition Johnny, with a bell as the CS. As an experiment, we also occasionally sound a buzzer instead of ringing the bell. However, the buzzer is never followed by the US (lemon juice). At first, Johnny salivates when he hears the buzzer (because of generalization). But after we sound the buzzer several times more, Johnny will stop responding to it. Why? In essence, Johnny's generalized response to the buzzer has extinguished. As a result, he has learned to *discriminate,* or respond differently, to the bell and the buzzer.

Stimulus discrimination is the ability to respond differently to various stimuli. As an example, you might remember the feelings of anxiety or fear you had as a child when your mother's or father's voice changed to the dreaded put-away-that-PlayStation-controller tone. Most children quickly learn to discriminate voice tones associated with punishment from those associated with praise or affection.

Classical Conditioning in Humans— An Emotional Topic

Does conditioning affect emotions?

Is much human learning based on classical conditioning? At its simplest, classical conditioning depends on unconditioned reflex responses. As mentioned earlier, a reflex is a dependable, inborn stimulus-and-response connection. For example, your hand reflexively draws back

Stimulus discrimination The learned ability to respond differently to similar stimuli.

from pain. Bright light causes the pupil of the eye to narrow. A puff of air directed at your eye will make you blink. Various foods elicit salivation. Any of these reflexes, and others as well, can be associated with a new stimulus. At the very least, you have probably noticed how your mouth waters when you see or smell a bakery. Even pictures of food may make you salivate (a photo of a sliced lemon is great for this).

Conditioned Emotional Responses

More complex *emotional,* or "gut," responses may also be associated with new stimuli. For instance, if your face reddened when you were punished as a child, you may blush now when you are embarrassed or ashamed. Or think about the effects of associating pain with a dentist's office during your first visit. On later visits, did your heart pound and your palms sweat *before* the dentist began?

Many *involuntary,* autonomic nervous system, responses ("fight-or-flight" reflexes) are linked with new stimuli and situations by classical conditioning. For example, learned reactions worsen many cases of hypertension (high blood pressure). Traffic jams, arguments with a spouse, and similar situations can become conditioned stimuli that trigger a dangerous rise in blood pressure (Reiff, Katkin, & Friedman, 1999).

Of course, emotional conditioning also applies to animals. One of the most common mistakes people make with pets (especially dogs) is hitting them if they do not come when called. Calling the animal then becomes a conditioned stimulus for fear and withdrawal. No wonder the pet disobeys when called on future occasions. Parents who belittle, scream at, or physically abuse their children make the same mistake.

(a)   (b)

(c)   (d)

⬥ FIGURE 6.7 Hypothetical example of a CER becoming a phobia. Child approaches dog *(a)* and is frightened by it *(b)*. Fear generalizes to other household pets *(c)* and later to virtually all furry animals *(d)*.

Learned Fears

Some phobias (FOE-bee-ahs) are also based on emotional conditioning. A *phobia* is a fear that persists even when no realistic danger exists. Fears of animals, water, heights, thunder, fire, bugs, elevators, and the like are common. Psychologists believe that many phobias begin as **conditioned emotional responses (CERs),** or learned emotional reactions to a previously neutral stimulus. People who have phobias can often trace their fears to a time when they were frightened, injured, or upset by a particular stimulus, especially in childhood (King, Muris, & Ollendick, 2005). Just one bad experience in which you were frightened or disgusted by a spider may condition fears that last for years (de Jong & Muris, 2002). Stimulus generalization and higher order conditioning can spread CERs to other stimuli (Gewirtz & Davis, 1998). As a result, what began as a limited fear may become a disabling phobia (▶▶ Figure 6.7).

During a CER, an area of your brain called the amygdala becomes more active, producing feelings of fear. The amygdala is part of the limbic system, which is responsible for other emotions as well (see Chapter 2). Cognitive learning has little effect on these lower brain areas (Olsson, Nearing, & Phelps, 2007). Perhaps that's why fears and phobias cannot be readily eased by merely reading about how to control fears—as our friend Larry found with his rat phobia. However, conditioned fears do respond to a therapy called *desensitization.* This is done by gradually exposing the phobic person to feared stimuli while she or he remains calm and relaxed. For example, people who fear heights can be slowly taken to ever-higher elevations until their fears extinguish (Wiederhold & Wiederhold, 2005). (See Chapter 13 for more information about therapies based on learning principles.)

Undoubtedly, we acquire many of our likes, dislikes, and fears as conditioned emotional responses. As noted before, advertisers try to achieve the same effect by pairing products with pleasant images and music. So do many students on a first date.

 Conditioned emotional response (CER) An emotional response that has been linked to a previously nonemotional stimulus by classical conditioning.

Vicarious, or Secondhand, Conditioning

Conditioning can also occur indirectly. Let's say, for example, that you watch another person get an electric shock. Each time, a signal light comes on before the shock is delivered. Even if you don't receive a shock yourself, you will soon develop a CER to the light. Children who learn to fear thunder by watching their parents react to it have undergone similar conditioning. Many Americans were traumatized as a consequence of watching media coverage of the September 11, 2001, terrorist attacks in New York and Washington (Blanchard et al., 2004). Similarly, people who counsel traumatized victims of sexual abuse can themselves develop vicarious trauma (Rothschild & Rand, 2006; Way et al., 2004).

Vicarious classical conditioning occurs when we learn to respond emotionally to a stimulus by observing another person's emotional reactions (Olsson, Nearing, & Phelps, 2007). Such "secondhand" learning affects feelings in many situations. Being told that "snakes are dangerous" may not explain the child's *emotional* response. More likely, the child has observed others reacting fearfully to the word *snake* or to snake images on television (King, Muris, & Ollendick, 2005). That is exactly how Larry, the researcher we met at the beginning of this chapter, developed his fear of rats. As children grow up, the emotions of parents, friends, and relatives undoubtedly add to fears of snakes, caves, spiders, heights, and other terrors. Even "horror" movies filled with screaming actors can have a similar effect.

The emotional attitudes we develop toward foods, political parties, ethnic groups, escalators—whatever—are probably conditioned not only by direct experiences but vicariously as well. No one is born prejudiced—all attitudes are learned. Parents may do well to look in a mirror if they wonder how or where a child "picked up" a particular fear or emotional attitude.

Vicarious classical conditioning Classical conditioning brought about by observing another person react to a particular stimulus.

RECITE

1. The concept of reinforcement applies to both
   a. antecedents and consequences
   b. neutral stimuli and rewards
   c. classical and operant conditioning
   d. acquisition and spontaneous recovery
2. Classical conditioning, studied by the Russian physiologist _____, is also referred to as _____ conditioning.
3. You smell the odor of cookies being baked and your mouth waters. Apparently, the odor of cookies is a _____ and your salivation is a _____.
   a. CR, CS
   b. CS, CR
   c. consequence, neutral stimulus
   d. reflex, CS
4. The informational view says that classical conditioning is based on changes in mental _____ about the CS and US.
5. After you have acquired a conditioned response, it may be weakened by
   a. spontaneous recovery
   b. stimulus generalization
   c. removing reinforcement
   d. following the CS with a US
6. When a conditioned stimulus is used to reinforce the learning of a second conditioned stimulus, higher order conditioning has occurred. T or F?
7. Psychologists theorize that many phobias begin when a CER generalizes to other, similar situations. T or F?
8. Three-year-old Josh sees his 5-year-old sister get chased by a neighbor's dog. Now Josh is as afraid of the dog as his sister is. Josh's fear is a result of
   a. stimulus discrimination
   b. vicarious conditioning
   c. spontaneous recovery
   d. higher order conditioning

REFLECT

Critical Thinking

9. Lately you have been getting a shock of static electricity every time you touch a door handle. Now there is a hesitation in your door-opening movements. Can you analyze this situation in terms of classical conditioning?

Relate

US, CS, UR, CR—How will you remember these terms? First, you should note that we are interested in either a stimulus (S) or a response (R). What else do we need to know? Each S or R can be either conditioned (C) or unconditioned (U).

Can a stimulus provoke a response before any learning has occurred? If it can, then it's a US. Do you have to learn to respond to the stimulus? Then it's a CS.

Does a response occur without being learned? Then it's a UR. If it has to be learned, then it's a CR.

ANSWERS

1. c 2. Pavlov, Pavlovian or respondent 3. b 4. expectancies 5. c 6. T 7. T 8. b 9. Door handles have become conditioned stimuli that elicit the reflex withdrawal and muscle tensing that normally follows getting a shock.

Operant Conditioning— Can Pigeons Play Ping-Pong?

How does operant conditioning occur?

The principles of operant conditioning, another form of associative learning, are among the most powerful tools in psychology. You won't regret learning how to use them. Operant conditioning explains much day-to-day behavior and can be used to alter the behavior of pets, children, other adults, and your own behavior, too.

As stated earlier, in **operant conditioning** (also known as *instrumental learning*), we associate responses with their consequences. The basic principle is simple: Acts that are reinforced tend to be repeated (Mazur, 2006). Pioneer learning theorist Edward L. Thorndike called this the **law of effect,** the probability of a response is altered by the effect it has (Schultz & Schultz, 2008). Learning is strengthened each time a response is followed by a satisfying state of affairs. You are much more likely to keep telling a joke if people laugh at it. If the first three people frown when they hear the joke, you may not tell it again.

In operant conditioning, the learner actively "operates on" the environment. Thus, operant conditioning refers mainly to learning *voluntary* responses. For example, pushing buttons on a TV remote control is a learned operant response. Pushing a particular button is reinforced by gaining the consequence you desire, such as changing channels or muting an obnoxious commercial. In contrast, classical conditioning is passive. It simply "happens to" the learner when a US follows a CS. (See ● Table 6.2 for a further comparison of classical and operant conditioning.)

● Table 6.2 Comparison of Classical and Operant Conditioning

	CLASSICAL CONDITIONING	OPERANT CONDITIONING
Nature of response	Involuntary, reflex	Spontaneous, voluntary
Reinforcement	Occurs *before* response (CS paired with US)	Occurs *after* response (response is followed by reinforcing stimulus or event)
Role of learner	Passive (response is *elicited* by US)	Active (response is emitted)
Nature of learning	Neutral stimulus becomes a CS through association with a US	Probability of making a response is altered by consequences that follow it
Learned expectancy	US will follow CS	Response will have a specific effect

Positive Reinforcement

Isn't reinforcement another term for reward? Not exactly. To be correct, it is better to say *reinforcer.* Why? Because rewards do not always increase responding. If you give chocolate to a child as a "reward" for good behavior, it will work only if the child likes chocolate. What is reinforcing for one person may not be for another. As a practical rule of thumb, psychologists define an **operant reinforcer** as any event that follows a response and increases its probability of occurring again (►► Figure 6.8).

Acquiring an Operant Response

Many studies of operant conditioning in animals make use of an *operant conditioning chamber* (Skinner, 1938). This device is also called a Skinner box, after B. F. Skinner, who invented it (see ►► Figure 6.9). A look into a typical Skinner box will clarify the process of operant conditioning:

Einstein Snags a Snack

A smart and hungry rat (yes, it's Larry's rat) is placed in an operant conditioning chamber. For a while our subject walks around, grooms, sniffs at the corners, or stands on his hind legs—all typical rat behaviors. Then it happens. He places his paw on the lever to get a better view of the top of the cage. *Click!* The lever depresses, and a food pellet drops into the tray. The rat scurries to the tray, eats the pellet, and then grooms himself. Up and exploring the cage again, he leans on the lever. *Click!* After a trip to the food tray, he returns to the bar and sniffs it, then puts his foot on it. *Click!* Soon Einstein settles into a smooth pattern of frequent bar pressing.

Operant conditioning Learning based on the consequences of responding.

Law of effect Responses that lead to desirable effects are repeated; those that produce undesirable results are not.

Operant reinforcer Any event that reliably increases the probability or frequency of responses it follows.

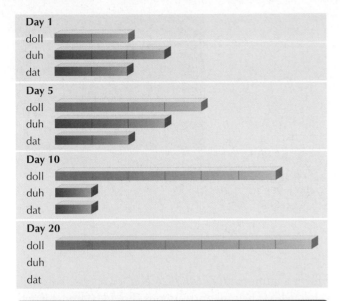

Day 1
doll
duh
dat

Day 5
doll
duh
dat

Day 10
doll
duh
dat

Day 20
doll
duh
dat

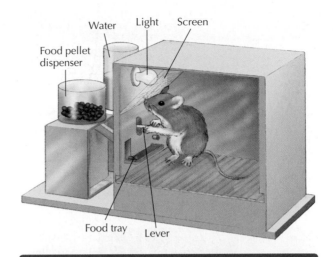

Water   Light   Screen

Food pellet
dispenser

Food tray   Lever

▲ FIGURE 6.8 Assume that a child who is learning to talk points to her favorite doll and says either "doll," "duh," or "dat" when she wants it. Day 1 shows the number of times the child uses each word to ask for the doll (each block represents one request). At first, she uses all three words interchangeably. To hasten learning, her parents decide to give her the doll only when she names it correctly. Notice how the child's behavior shifts as operant reinforcement is applied. By day 20, saying "doll" has become the most probable response.

▲ FIGURE 6.9 The Skinner box. This simple device, invented by B. F. Skinner, allows careful study of operant conditioning. When the rat presses the bar, a pellet of food or a drop of water is automatically released.

Notice that the rat did not acquire a new skill in this situation. He was already able to press the bar. Reinforcement alters only how *frequently* he presses the bar. In operant conditioning, new behavior patterns are molded by changing the probability that various responses will be made.

Information and Contingency

Like classical conditioning, we can think of operant learning as being based on information and expectancies (Pierce & Cheney, 2004). In operant conditioning, *we learn to expect that a certain response will have a certain effect at certain times.* That is, we learn that a particular response is associated with reinforcement (Hergenhahn & Olson, 2005). Further, operant reinforcement works best when it is *response contingent* (kon-TIN-jent). That is, it must be given only after a desired response has occurred. From this point of view, a reinforcer tells a person or an animal that a response was "right" and worth repeating.

For example, one severely disturbed 9-year-old child was taught to say "Please." Before, he typically just grabbed objects and became angry if he couldn't have them. When the child said "Please," he was reinforced in three ways: He received the object he asked for (a crayon, for example); he was given a small food treat, such as a piece of candy, popcorn, or a grape; and he was praised for his good behavior (Matson et al., 1990). When he was consistently reinforced for saying "Please," he soon learned to use the word nearly every time he wanted something.

In similar ways, operant principles greatly affect behavior in homes, schools, and businesses. It is always worthwhile to arrange reinforcers so that they encourage productive and responsible behavior.

The Timing of Reinforcement

Operant reinforcement is most effective when it rapidly follows a correct response (Mazur, 2006). For rats in a Skinner box, little or no learning occurs if the delay between bar pressing and receiving food exceeds 50 seconds (▶▶ Figure 6.10). In general, you will be most

◀◀ **FIGURE 6.10** The effect of delay of reinforcement. Notice how rapidly the learning score drops when reward is delayed. Animals learning to press a bar in a Skinner box showed no signs of learning if food reward followed a bar press by more than 100 seconds (Perin, 1943).

successful if you present a reinforcer *immediately* after a response you wish to change. Thus, a child who is helpful or courteous should be immediately praised for her good behavior.

Let's say I work hard all semester in a class to get an A grade. Wouldn't the delay in reinforcement keep me from learning anything? No, for several reasons. First, as a mature human you can anticipate future reward. Second, you get reinforced by quiz and test grades all through the semester. Third, a single reinforcer can often maintain a long response chain (a linked series of actions that lead to reinforcement).

An example of **response chaining** is provided by the sport of dog agility training. Dogs are taught to navigate a variety of obstacles. These include jumping over hurdles, walking over seesaws, climbing up and jumping off inclined walls, and running through tunnels made out of cloth (Helton, 2007). During competitions, a trainer can reinforce a dog with a snack or a hug only after the dog completes the entire response chain. The winning dog is the one who finishes the course with the fewest mistakes and the fastest time. (Good dog!)

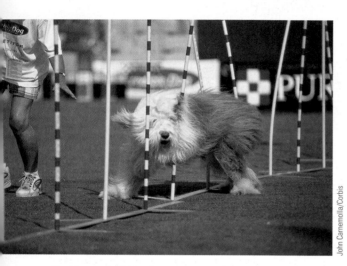

Dogs must build up long response chains to compete in agility training competitions.

John Carnemolla/Corbis

Many of the things we do every day involve similar response chains. The long series of events necessary to prepare a meal is rewarded by the final eating. A violinmaker may carry out thousands of steps for the final reward of hearing a first musical note. And as a student, you have built up long response chains for the final reward of getting good grades (right?).

Are You Superstitious?

If a golfer taps her club on the ground three times and then hits a great shot, what happens? The successful shot reinforces not only the correct swing but also the three taps. Reinforcers affect not only the specific response they follow but also other responses that occur shortly before. This helps explain many human superstitions. (During operant training, animals often develop similar unnecessary responses.) If this happens a few times more, the golfer may superstitiously tap her club three times before every shot. Some examples of actual superstitious behaviors of professional baseball players include drawing four lines in the dirt before getting in the batter's box, eating chicken before each game, and always playing in the same athletic supporter—for 4 years (phew!) (Burger & Lynn, 2005).

Superstitious behaviors are repeated because they appear to produce reinforcement, even though they are actually unnecessary. If you walk under a ladder and then break a leg, you may avoid ladders in the future. Each time you avoid a ladder and nothing bad happens, your superstitious action is reinforced. Belief in magic can also be explained along such lines. Rituals to bring rain, ward off illness, or produce abundant crops very likely earn the faith of participants because they occasionally appear to succeed.

Response chaining The assembly of separate responses into a series of actions that lead to reinforcement.

Superstitious behavior A behavior repeated because it seems to produce reinforcement, even though it is actually unnecessary.

Shaping

How is it possible to reinforce responses that rarely occur? Even in a barren Skinner box, it could take a long time for a rat (even one as smart as Einstein) to accidentally press the bar and get a food pellet. We might wait forever for more complicated responses to occur. For example, you would have to wait a long time for a duck to accidentally walk out of its cage, turn on a light, play a toy piano, turn off the light, and walk back to its cage. If this is what you wanted to reward, you would never get the chance.

Then how are the animals on TV and at amusement parks taught to perform complicated tricks? The answer lies in **shaping,** which is the gradual molding of responses to a desired pattern. Let's look again at our favorite rat, Einstein.

Einstein Shapes Up

Instead of waiting for Einstein's first accidental bar press, which might have taken a long time, we could have shaped his behavior. Assume that Einstein has not yet learned to press the bar. At first, we settle for just getting him to face the bar. Any time he turns toward the bar, he is reinforced with a bit of food. Soon Einstein spends much of his time facing the bar. Next, we reinforce him every time he takes a step toward the bar. If he turns toward the bar and walks away, nothing happens. But when he faces the bar and takes a step forward, *click!* His responses are being shaped.

By changing the rules about what makes a successful response, we can gradually train the rat to approach the bar and press it. In other words, *successive approximations* (ever-closer matches) to a desired response are reinforced during shaping. B. F. Skinner once taught two pigeons to play Ping-Pong in this way (►► Figure 6.11). Shaping applies to humans, too. Let's say you want to study more, clean the house more often, or exercise more. In each case, it would be best to set a series of gradual, daily goals. Then you can reward yourself for small steps in the right direction (Watson & Tharp, 2007).

FIGURE 6.11 Operant conditioning principles were used to train these pigeons to play Ping-Pong.

Operant Extinction

Would a rat stop bar pressing if no more food arrived? Yes, but not immediately. Through **operant extinction,** learned responses that are not reinforced gradually fade away. Just as acquiring an operant response takes time, so does extinction. For example, if a TV program repeatedly bores you, watching the program will likely extinguish over time.

Even after extinction seems complete, the previously reinforced response may return. If a rat is removed from a Skinner box after extinction and given a short rest, the rat will press the bar again when returned to the box. Similarly, a few weeks after they give up on buying state lottery tickets, many people are tempted to try again.

Does extinction take as long the second time? If reinforcement is still withheld, a rat's bar pressing will extinguish again, usually more quickly. The brief return of an operant response after extinction is another example of spontaneous recovery (mentioned earlier regarding classical conditioning). Spontaneous recovery is very adaptive. After a rest period, the rat responds again in a situation that produced food in the past: "Just checking to see if the rules have changed!"

Marked changes in behavior occur when reinforcement and extinction are combined. For example, parents often unknowingly reinforce children for *negative attention seeking* (using misbehavior to gain attention). Children are generally ignored when they are playing quietly. They get attention when they become louder and louder, yell "Hey, Mom!" at the top of their lungs, throw tantrums, show off, or break something. Granted, the attention they get is often a scolding, but attention is a powerful reinforcer, nevertheless. Parents report dramatic improvements when they *ignore* their children's disruptive behavior and praise or attend to a child who is quiet or playing constructively.

Shaping Gradually molding responses to a final desired pattern.

Operant extinction The weakening or disappearance of a nonreinforced operant response.

Time & Life Pictures/Getty Images

Negative Reinforcement

Until now, we have stressed **positive reinforcement,** which occurs when a pleasant or desirable event follows a response. How else could operant learning be reinforced? The time has come to consider **negative reinforcement,** which occurs when making a response removes an unpleasant event. Don't be fooled by the word *negative.* Negative reinforcement also increases responding. However, it does so by ending (negating) discomfort.

Let's say that you have a headache and take an aspirin. Your aspirin taking will be negatively reinforced if the headache stops. Likewise, a rat could be taught to press a bar to get food (positive reinforcement), or the rat could be given a continuous mild shock (through the floor of its cage) that is turned off by a bar press (negative reinforcement). Either way, the rat will learn to press the bar more often. Why? Because it leads to a desired state of affairs (food or an end to pain). Here's another example of negative reinforcement: A politician who irritates you is being interviewed on the evening news. You change channels so you won't have to listen to him. (Channel changing is negatively reinforced.)

Punishment

Many people mistake negative reinforcement for punishment. However, **punishment** refers to following a response with an *aversive* (unpleasant) consequence. Punishment *decreases* the likelihood that the response will occur again. As noted, negative reinforcement *increases* responding. The difference can be seen in a hypothetical example. Let's say you live in an apartment and your neighbor's stereo is blasting so loudly that you can't concentrate on reading this book. If you pound on the wall and the volume suddenly drops (negative reinforcement), future wall pounding will be more likely. But if you pound on the wall and the volume increases (punishment) or if the neighbor comes over and pounds on you (more punishment), wall pounding becomes less likely. Here's another example of punishment, in which an unpleasant result follows a response: Every time you give advice to a friend, she suddenly turns cold and distant. Lately, you've stopped offering her advice. (Giving advice was punished by rejection.)

Isn't it also punishing to have privileges, money, or other positive things taken away for making a particular response? Yes. Punishment also occurs when a reinforcer or positive state of affairs is removed, such as losing privileges. This second type of punishment is called **response cost.** The best-known form of response cost is *time out,* in which children are removed from situations that normally allow them to gain reinforcement. When your parents put you on time out by sending you to your room, they denied you the reinforcement of being with the rest of your family or hanging out with your friends. Parking tickets and other fines are also based on response cost. For your convenience, ● Table 6.3 summarizes four basic consequences of making a response.

Positive reinforcement Occurs when a response is followed by a reward or other positive event.

Negative reinforcement Occurs when a response is followed by an end to discomfort or by the removal of an unpleasant event.

Punishment Any event that follows a response and *decreases* its likelihood of occurring again.

Response cost Removal of a positive reinforcer after a response is made.

● Table 6.3 Behavioral Effects of Various Consequences

	CONSEQUENCE OF MAKING A RESPONSE	EXAMPLE	EFFECT ON RESPONSE PROBABILITY
Positive reinforcement	Positive event begins	Food given	Increase
Negative reinforcement	Negative event ends	Pain stops	Increase
Punishment	Negative event begins	Pain begins	Decrease
Punishment (response cost)	Positive event ends	Food removed	Decrease
Nonreinforcement	Nothing	—	Decrease

oose you could have an electrode implanted ur brain and connected to an iPod-style con- er. Twirl the controller and electrical impulses ulate one of your brain's "pleasure centers." very few humans who have ever had a nce to try direct brain stimulation report feel- ntense pleasure that is better than food, er, sex, drugs, or any other primary reinforcer ath, 1963). (See ▶▶ Figure 6.12.) Most of what we know about intracranial self- ulation comes from studying rats with similar ants (Olds & Fobes, 1981). A rat "wired for sure" can be trained to press the bar in a ner box to deliver electrical stimulation to its limbic system (refer back to Figure 2.26 in oter 2). Some rats will press the bar thousands mes per hour to obtain brain stimulation. After

15 or 20 hours of constant pressing, animals sometimes collapse from exhaustion. When they revive, they begin pressing again. If the reward cir- cuit is not turned off, an animal will ignore food, water, and sex in favor of bar pressing.

Many natural primary reinforcers activate the same pleasure pathways in the brain that make intracranial self-stimulation so powerful (McBride, Murphy, & Ikemoto, 1999). So do psychoactive drugs, such as alcohol and cocaine (Eisler, Justice, & Neill, 2004; Rodd et al., 2005). One shudders to think what might happen if brain implants were easy and practical to do. (They are not.) Every company from Playboy to Microsoft would have a device on the market, and we would have to keep a closer watch on politicians than usual!

▲ FIGURE 6.12 Humans have been "wired" for brain stimulation, as shown in *(a)*. Occasionally done as an experimental way to restrain uncontrollable outbursts of violence, temporary implants have rarely been done merely to produce pleasure. Most research has been carried out with rats. Using the apparatus shown in *(b)*, the rat can press a bar to deliver mild electric stimulation to a "pleasure center" in the brain.

Operant Reinforcers—What's Your Pleasure?

Are there different kinds of operant reinforcement?

For humans, learning may be reinforced by anything from a candy bar to a word of praise. In categorizing reinforcers, a useful distinction can be made between *primary reinforcers* and *secondary reinforcers.* It is also important to distinguish *reinforcement,* which exerts its effect through associative learning, from *feedback,* a key component of cognitive learning. Let's examine reinforcement and feedback in more detail.

Primary Reinforcers

Primary reinforcers produce comfort, end discomfort, or fill an immediate physical need: They are natural, nonlearned, and rooted in biology. Food, water, and sex are obvious examples. Every time you open the refrigerator, walk to a drinking fountain, turn up the heat, or order a double latte, your actions reflect primary reinforcement.

In addition to obvious examples, there are other, less obvious, primary reinforcers, such as psychoactive drugs. One of the most powerful reinforcers is *intracranial self-stimulation,* which involves the direct activation of "pleasure centers" in the brain. (See "Tickling Your Own Fancy.")

Secondary Reinforcers

Although human learning is still strongly tied to food, water, and other primary reinforcers, humans also respond to a much broader range of rewards and reinforcers. Money, praise, attention, approval, success, affection, grades, and the like, all serve as learned or **secondary reinforcers.**

How does a secondary reinforcer gain its ability to promote learning? Some secondary rein- forcers are simply associated with a primary reinforcer. For example, if you would like to train

Primary reinforcers Nonlearned reinforcers; usually those that satisfy physiological needs.

Secondary reinforcer A learned reinforcer; often one that gains reinforcing properties by association with a primary reinforcer.

FIGURE 6.13 Poker chips normally have little or no value for chimpanzees, but this chimp will work hard to earn them once he learns that the "Chimp-O-Mat" will dispense food in exchange for them.

Chimp-O-Mat, Yerkes Regional Primate Research Center, Emory University

a dog to follow you ("heel") when you take a walk, you could reward the dog with small food treats for staying near you. If you praise the dog each time you give it a treat, praise will become a secondary reinforcer. In time, you will be able to skip giving treats and simply praise your pup for doing the right thing. The same principle applies to children. One reason that parents' praise becomes a secondary reinforcer is because it is frequently associated with food, candy, hugs, and other primary reinforcers.

Tokens

Secondary reinforcers that can be *exchanged* for primary reinforcers gain their value more directly (Mazur, 2006). Printed money obviously has little or no value of its own. You can't eat it, drink it, or sleep with it. However, it can be exchanged for food, water, lodging, and other necessities.

A **token reinforcer** is a tangible secondary reinforcer, such as money, gold stars, poker chips, and the like. In a series of classic experiments, chimpanzees were taught to work for tokens. The chimps were first trained to put poker chips into a "Chimp-O-Mat" vending machine. Each chip dispensed a few grapes or raisins. Once the animals had learned to exchange tokens for food, they would learn new tasks to earn the chips. To maintain the value of the tokens, the chimps were occasionally allowed to use the "Chimp-O-Mat" (Wolfe, 1936) (▸▸ Figure 6.13).

A major advantage of tokens is that they don't lose reinforcing value as quickly as primary reinforcers do. For instance, if you use candy to reinforce a developmentally disabled child for correctly naming things, the child might lose interest once he is satiated (fully satisfied) or no longer hungry. It would be better to use tokens as immediate rewards for learning. Later, the child can exchange his tokens for candy, toys, or other treats.

Token economies, systems for managing and altering behavior through reinforcement of selected responses, have also been used with troubled children and adults in special programs, and even in ordinary elementary school classrooms (Alberto & Troutman, 2009; Spiegler & Guevremont, 2003) (▸▸ Figure 6.14). In each case the goal is to provide an immediate reward for learning. Typically, tokens may be exchanged for food, special privileges, or trips to movies, amusement parks, and so forth. Many parents find that tokens greatly reduce discipline problems with younger children. For example, children can earn points or gold stars during the week for good behavior. If they earn enough tokens, they are allowed on Sunday to choose one item out of a "grab bag" of small prizes.

FIGURE 6.14 Reinforcement in a token economy. This graph shows the effects of using tokens to reward socially desirable behavior in a mental hospital ward. Desirable behavior was defined as cleaning, making the bed, attending therapy sessions, and so forth. Tokens earned could be exchanged for basic amenities such as meals, snacks, coffee, game-room privileges, or weekend passes. The graph shows more than 24 hours per day because it represents the total number of hours of desirable behavior performed by all patients in the ward. (Adapted from Ayllon, T., & Azrin, N. H. [1965]. The measurement and reinforcement of behavior of psychotics. Journal of the Experimental Analysis of Behavior, 8, 357–383. Fig 4, p. 373. Reprinted by permission of the authors.)

In graph: Performance, total number of hours/day; Days; Reinforcement contingent upon performance; Reinforcement NOT contingent upon performance; Reinforcement contingent upon performance; N = 44

Social Reinforcers

As we have noted, learned desires for attention and approval, which are called **social reinforcers,** often influence human behavior. This fact can be used in a classic, if somewhat mischievous, demonstration.

Shaping a Teacher

For this activity, about one half (or more) of the students in a classroom must participate. First, select a target behavior. This should be something like "lecturing from the right side of the room." (Keep it simple, in case your teacher is a slow learner.) Begin training in this way: Each time the instructor turns toward the right or takes a step in that direction, participating students

Token reinforcer A tangible secondary reinforcer such as money, gold stars, poker chips, and the like.

Social reinforcer Reinforcement based on receiving attention, approval, or affection from another person.

Learning and Conservation

Psychologists enjoy helping to solve practical problems. One area of behavior very much in need of attention is our "throw-away" society. We burn fossil fuels; destroy forests; use chemical products; and strip, clear, and farm the land. In doing so, we alter the very face of the Earth. What can be done?

One approach involves changing the *consequences* of wasteful energy use, polluting, and the like. For example, energy taxes can be used to increase the cost of using fossil fuels (response cost). On the reinforcement side of the equation,

rebates can be offered for installing insulation or buying energy-efficient appliances or cars, and tax breaks can be given to companies that take steps to preserve the environment. Recycling is also more effective when entire families participate, with some family members (usually Mom, of course) reinforcing the recycling behavior of other family members (Meneses & Beerlipalacio, 2005).

Feedback is also important. Environmental psychologists have long known that a lack of prompt feedback is a major barrier to conservation (Abrahamse et al., 2005). When families,

work groups, factories, and dorms receive feedback, on a weekly basis, about how much they recycled, they typically recycle more. New tools, such as *ecological footprint calculators*, make it a lot easier for individuals to get feedback about their individual resource consumption (Global Footprint Network, 2009). With growing public concern over global warming, many people are now calculating their individual *carbon footprint*, the volume of greenhouse gases individual consumption adds to the atmosphere (The Nature Conservancy, 2009).

---

should look *really* interested. Also, smile, ask questions, lean forward, and make eye contact. If the teacher turns to the left or takes a step in that direction, participating students should lean back, yawn, check out their split ends, close their eyes, or generally look bored. Soon, without being aware of why, the instructor should be spending most of his or her time each class period lecturing from the right side of the classroom.

This trick has been a favorite of psychology graduate students for decades. For a time, one of your author's professors delivered all her lectures from the right side of the room while toying with the cords on the window shades. (We added the cords the second week!) The point to remember from this example is that attention and approval can change the behavior of children, family members, friends, roommates, and coworkers. Be aware of what you are reinforcing. And be aware that you may be unaware of some of the reinforcers that are changing your own behavior!

Feedback

His eyes, driven and blazing, dart from side to side. His body contorts while his hands furiously spin in circular motions. Does this describe some strange neurological disorder? Actually, it depicts 10-year-old Vikram as he plays his favorite Wii game, an animated snowboarding adventure!

How did Vikram learn the complex movements needed to excel at virtual snowboarding? After all, he was not rewarded with food or money. The answer lies in the fact that Vikram's favorite video game provides *feedback,* a key element that underlies learning. **Feedback** (information about the effect a response had) is particularly important in human cognitive learning (Lefrançois, 2006). Humans readily learn responses that merely have a desired effect or that bring a goal closer.

Every time a player does something, a video game responds instantly with sounds, animated actions, and a higher or lower score. The machine's responsiveness and the information flow it provides can be very motivating if you want to win. The same principle applies to many other learning situations: If you are trying to learn to use a computer, to play a musical instrument, to cook, to play a sport, or to solve math problems, feedback that you achieved a desired result can be reinforcing in its own right. Whenever you are trying to learn a complex skill, it pays to get more feedback (Jaehnig & Miller, 2007; Wulf et al., 2002). (Also see "Learning and Conservation.")

Learning Aids

How can feedback be applied? Since increased feedback almost always improves learning and performance, it makes sense to design learning aids to supply effective feedback (Horn et al., 2005). Feedback is most effective when it is *frequent, immediate,* and *detailed.*

> **Feedback** Information returned to a person about the effects a response has had.

Hypotenuse $= \sqrt{A^2 + B^2}$

3   H

4

Problem 4   H = ?

Set distance
SCORE: 2

3 miles

4 miles

⚓ **FIGURE 6.15** Computer-assisted instruction. The left-hand screen shows a simplified drill-and-practice math problem, in which students must find the hypotenuse of a triangle. The right-hand screen presents the same problem as a serious game to increase interest and motivation. In the game, a child is asked to set the proper distance on a ray gun in the hovering space ship to "vaporize" an attacker.

Programmed instruction teaches students in a format that presents information in small amounts, gives immediate practice, and provides continuous feedback to learners. Frequent feedback keeps learners from practicing errors. It also lets students work at their own pace.

To get a sense of the programmed instruction format, finish reading the next few paragraphs and complete the *Study Break* when you encounter it (just like you do with *all* of the Study Breaks you come across, right?). Work through the *Recite* questions one at a time, checking your answer before moving on. (You can find the correct answers upside down at the end of the Study Break.) In this way, your correct (or incorrect) responses will be followed by immediate feedback.

Today programmed instruction is often presented via computer (Emurian, 2005; McDonald, Yanchar, & Osguthorpe, 2005). You may know it as CAI (*computer-assisted instruction*) or drill-and-practice (or, affectionately, drill-and-kill). In addition to giving learners immediate feedback, the computer can give hints about why an answer was wrong and what is needed to correct it (Timmerman & Kruepke, 2006). Increasingly, CAI programs called *serious games* are making use of game formats such as stories, competition with a partner, sound effects, and rich computer graphics to increase interest and motivation (Michael & Chen, 2006) (▶▶ Figure 6.15).

Educational *simulations,* the most complex serious games, allow students to explore an imaginary situation or "microworld" to learn to solve real-world problems (▶▶ Figure 6.16). By seeing the effects of their choices, students discover basic principles of physics, biology, psychology, or other subjects (Grabe, 2006).

CAI software can save teachers and learners much time and effort, although the final level of skill or knowledge gained is not necessarily higher. In addition, people often do better with feedback from a computer because they can freely make mistakes and learn from them (Luyben, Hipworth, & Pappas, 2003; Norton, 2003). Let's pause now for some learning exercises (remember?) so that you can get some feedback about your mastery of the preceding ideas.

NASA

⚓ **FIGURE 6.16** Boeing 747 Airline Training Simulator. Student pilots can learn all the ins and outs of flying a jumbo jet in this flight simulator. Aren't you glad they don't have to do that with real planes (and passengers)? Your authors sure are!

Programmed instruction Any learning format that presents information in small amounts, gives immediate practice, and provides continuous feedback to learners.

RECITE

1. Responses in operant conditioning are _____ or _____, whereas those in classical conditioning are passive, _____, or _____ responses.
2. Changing the rules in small steps so that an animal (or person) is gradually trained to respond as desired is called _____.
3. Extinction in operant conditioning is also subject to _____ of a response.
   a. successive approximations
   b. shaping
   c. automation
   d. spontaneous recovery
4. Positive reinforcers increase the rate of responding and negative reinforcers decrease it. T or F?
5. Primary reinforcers are those learned through classical conditioning. T or F?
6. Which is a correct match?
   a. social reinforcer–primary reinforcement
   b. token reinforcer–secondary reinforcement
   c. intracranial stimulation–secondary reinforcement
   d. negative reinforcer–punishment
7. Superstitious responses are those that are
   a. shaped by secondary reinforcement
   b. extinguished
   c. prepotent
   d. unnecessary to obtain reinforcement
8. CAI is based on the same principles as
   a. negative reinforcement
   b. programmed instruction
   c. higher order conditioning
   d. stimulus generalization

REFLECT
Critical Thinking

9. Can you imagine different forms of feedback?

Relate

Can you explain the difference between positive reinforcement, negative reinforcement, and punishment? Can you give an example of each concept from your own experience?

A friend of yours punishes his dog all the time. What advice would you give him about how to use reinforcement, extinction, and shaping, instead of punishment?

ANSWERS

1. voluntary or emitted, involuntary or elicited   2. shaping   3. d   4. F   5. F   6. b   7. d   8. b   9. Knowledge of results means you find out if your response was right or wrong. Knowledge of correct response should have been. Elaboration feedback adds additional information, such as an explanation of the correct answer. Adding knowledge of correct response and/or some elaboration is more effective than knowledge of results alone (Jaehnig & Miller, 2007).

Partial Reinforcement— Las Vegas, a Human Skinner Box?

How are we influenced by patterns of reward?

If you would like to influence operant learning, you will need to know how patterns of reinforcement affect behavior. Imagine, for example, that a mother wants to reward her child for turning off the lights when he leaves a room. Contrary to what you might think, it is better to reinforce only some of her son's correct responses. Why should this be so? You'll find the answer in the following discussion.

Until now, we have treated operant reinforcement as if it were continuous. *Continuous reinforcement* means that a reinforcer follows every correct response. At the start, continuous reinforcement is useful for learning new responses (Lefrançois, 2006). To teach your dog to come to you, it is best to reinforce your dog every time it comes when called. Curiously, once your dog has learned to come when called, it is best to shift to **partial reinforcement,** in which reinforcers do not follow every response. Responses acquired by partial reinforcement are highly resistant to extinction (Svartdal, 2003). For some obscure reason, lost in the lore of psychology, this is called the **partial reinforcement effect.**

How does getting reinforced part of the time make a habit stronger? If you have ever visited a casino, you have probably seen row after row of people playing slot machines. To gain insight into the distinction between continuous and partial reinforcement, imagine that you put a dollar in a slot machine and pull the handle. Ten dollars spills into the tray. Let's say this continues for several minutes. Every pull is followed by a payoff. Because you are being

Partial reinforcement A pattern in which only a portion of all responses are reinforced.

Partial reinforcement effect Responses acquired with partial reinforcement are more resistant to extinction.

The one-armed bandit (slot machine) is a dispenser of partial reinforcement.

reinforced on a continuous schedule, you quickly "get hooked" (and begin to plan your retirement).

But, alas, suddenly each pull is followed by nothing. Obviously, you would respond several times more before giving up. However, when continuous reinforcement is followed by extinction, the message quickly becomes clear: No more payoffs (or early retirement).

Contrast this with partial reinforcement. This time, imagine that you put a dollar in a slot machine five times without a payoff. You are just about to quit, but decide to play once more. Bingo! The machine returns $20. After this, payoffs continue on a partial schedule; some are large, and some are small. All are unpredictable. Sometimes you hit two in a row, and sometimes 20 or 30 pulls go unrewarded.

Now let's say the payoff mechanism is turned off again. How many times do you think you would respond this time before your handle-pulling behavior extinguished? Because you have developed the expectation that any play may be "the one," it will be hard to resist just one more play.... and one more.... and one more. Also, because partial reinforcement includes long periods of nonreward, it will be harder to distinguish between periods of reinforcement and extinction. It is no exaggeration to say that the partial reinforcement effect has left many people penniless. Even psychologists visiting a casino may get "cleaned out" (not your authors, of course!).

To return to our examples, after using continuous reinforcement to teach a child to turn off the lights or a dog to come when called, it is best to shift to partial reinforcement. That way, the new behavior will become more resistant to extinction.

Schedules of Partial Reinforcement

Partial reinforcement can be given in several patterns, or partial *schedules of reinforcement* (plans for determining which responses will be reinforced) (Domjan, 2010). Let's consider the four most basic, which have some interesting effects on us. Typical responses to each pattern are shown in ▶▶ Figure 6.17. Results such as these are obtained when a *cumulative recorder* is connected to a Skinner box. The device consists of a moving strip of paper and a mechanical pen that jumps upward each time a response is made. Rapid responding causes the pen to draw a steep line; a horizontal line indicates no response. Small tick marks on the lines show when a reinforcer was given.

Fixed Ratio (FR)

What would happen if a reinforcer followed only every other response? Or what if we followed every third, fourth, fifth, or other number of responses with reinforcement? Each of these patterns is a **fixed ratio (FR) schedule** (a set number of correct responses must be made to obtain a reinforcer). Notice that in an FR schedule the ratio of reinforcers to responses is fixed: FR-2 means that every other response is rewarded; FR-3 means that every third response is reinforced; in an FR-10 schedule, exactly 10 responses must be made to obtain a reinforcer.

Fixed ratio schedules produce *very high response rates* (Figure 6.17). A hungry rat on an FR-10 schedule will quickly run off 10 responses, pause to eat, and then run off 10 more. A similar situation occurs when factory or farm workers are paid on a piecework basis. When a fixed number of items must be produced for a set amount of pay, work output is high.

Variable Ratio (VR)

In a **variable ratio (VR) schedule** a varied number of correct responses must be made to get a reinforcer. Instead of reinforcing every fourth response (FR-4), for example, a person or animal on a VR-4 schedule gets rewarded *on the average* every fourth response. Sometimes 2 responses must be made to obtain a reinforcer; sometimes it's 5; sometimes 4; and so on. The actual number varies, but it averages out to 4 (in this example). Variable ratio schedules also produce high response rates.

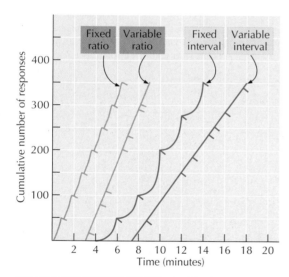

▲ **FIGURE 6.17** Typical response patterns for reinforcement schedules.

Fixed ratio (FR) schedule A set number of correct responses must be made to get a reinforcer. For example, a reinforcer is given for every four correct responses.

Variable ratio (VR) schedule A varied number of correct responses must be made to get a reinforcer. For example, a reinforcer is given after three to seven correct responses; the actual number changes randomly.

Are Animals Stuck in Time?

We humans are *cognitive time travelers,* regularly zooming back and forth through time in our minds. You can, for example, think about past events, such as what you had for breakfast this morning. We can also imagine events in the future. Brides-to-be are famous for planning their weddings down to the last detail. But what about animals? Are they cognitive time travelers or are they less cognitive and hence "stuck in time" (Roberts, 2002; Zentall, 2005)? Does the first dog Bo ever think about how hot it was yesterday or what he plans to do tomorrow? To answer such questions, psychologists have used operant conditioning as a research tool.

Conditioning studies have repeatedly shown that animals are sensitive to the passage of time (Zentall, 2005). For example, pigeons and rats reinforced on fixed interval schedules stop responding immediately after they receive a reinforcer and do not start again until just before the next scheduled reinforcement (Roberts, 2002). In one study, pigeons were put in a Skinner box with a pecking

key on each wall. They quickly learned to peck only at Key 1 if it was 9:30 in the morning and at Key 3 if it was 4:00 in the afternoon (Saksida & Wilkie, 1994).

Another study focused on scrub jays. These birds are hoarders; they store excess food at different locations and then go back later to eat it. Scrub jays were allowed to hoard some nuts in one location and some worms in another. If they were released 4 hours later, they went directly to the worms. However, if they were released 5 days later, they went straight for the nuts. Worms are a scrub jay's favorite food, which explains their choice after 4 hours. But worms decay after a day or so, while nuts stay edible. It seems that the jays knew exactly where they stored each type of food and how much time had passed (Clayton, Yu, & Dickinson, 2001).

While these studies are suggestive, they are part of an ongoing debate about animal cognition, including whether or not animals are stuck in time (Roberts & Roberts, 2002). Nevertheless, be care-

George McCarthy/NPL/Minden Pictures

Florida scrub jays are food hoarders. Does their food hoarding behavior prove they are not "trapped in time"?

ful if you forget to feed your beloved dog, Rover, at his usual mealtime. If he has been conditioned to think it's time to eat, he may settle for your favorite flip-flops instead of dog food!

VR schedules seem less predictable than FR. Does that have any effect on extinction? Yes. Because reinforcement is less predictable, VR schedules tend to produce greater resistance to extinction than fixed ratio schedules. Playing a slot machine is an example of behavior maintained by a variable ratio schedule. Another would be our plan to only occasionally reward a child for turning off the lights, once he has learned to do so. Golf, tennis, baseball, and many other sports are also reinforced on a variable ratio basis: Even the best batters in baseball rarely get a hit more than an average of 3 out of every 10 times they are at bat.

Fixed Interval (FI)

In another pattern, reinforcement is given only when a correct response is made after a fixed amount of time has passed. This time interval is measured from the last reinforced response. Responses made during the time interval are not reinforced. In a **fixed interval (FI) schedule** the first correct response made after the time period has passed is reinforced. Thus, a rat on an FI-30-second schedule has to wait 30 seconds after the last reinforced response before a bar press will pay off again. The rat can press the bar as often as it wants during the interval, but it will not be rewarded.

Fixed interval schedules produce *moderate response rates.* Animals working on an FI schedule seem to develop a keen sense of the passage of time (Eckerman, 1999). Few responses occur just after a reinforcement is delivered and a spurt of activity occurs just before the next reinforcement is due. (See "Are Animals Stuck in Time?")

Is getting paid weekly an FI schedule? Pure examples of fixed interval schedules are rare, but getting paid each week at work does come close. Notice, however, that most people do not work faster just before payday, as an FI schedule predicts. A closer parallel would be having a report due every 2 weeks for a class. Right after turning in a paper, your work would probably drop to zero for a week or more (Chance, 2009).

Variable Interval (VI)   (PAY OF SCHEDULES)

Variable interval (VI) schedules are a variation on fixed intervals. Here, reinforcement is given for the first correct response made after a varied amount of time. On a VI-30-second schedule, reinforcement is available after an interval that *averages* 30 seconds.

Fixed interval (FI) schedule A reinforcer is given only when a correct response is made after a set amount of time has passed since the last reinforced response. Responses made during the time interval are not reinforced.

Variable interval (VI) schedule A reinforcer is given for the first correct response made after a varied amount of time has passed since the last reinforced response. Responses made during the time interval are not reinforced.

VI schedules produce *slow, steady response rates* and tremendous resistance to extinction (Lattal, Reilly, & Kohn, 1998). When you dial a phone number and get a busy signal, reward (getting through) is on a VI schedule. You may have to wait 30 seconds or 30 minutes. If you are like most people, you will doggedly dial over and over again until you get a connection. Success in fishing is also on a VI schedule—which may explain the bulldog tenacity of many anglers (Chance, 2009).

Stimulus Control—Red Light, Green Light

When you are driving, your behavior at intersections is controlled by the red or green light. In similar fashion, many of the stimuli we encounter each day act like stop or go signals that guide our behavior. To state the idea more formally, stimuli that consistently precede a rewarded response tend to influence when and where the response will occur. This effect is called **stimulus control.** Notice how it works with our friend Einstein:

Lights Out for Einstein

While learning the bar-pressing response, Einstein has been in a Skinner box illuminated by a bright light. During several training sessions, the light is alternately turned on and off. When the light is on, a bar press will produce food. When the light is off, bar pressing goes unrewarded. We soon observe that the rat presses vigorously when the light is on and ignores the bar when the light is off.

In this example, the light signals what consequences will follow if a response is made. Evidence for stimulus control could be shown by turning the food delivery *on* when the light is *off.* A well-trained animal might never discover that the rules had changed (Powell, Symbaluk, & Honey, 2009). A similar example of stimulus control would be a child learning to ask for candy when her mother is in a good mood, but not asking at other times. Likewise, we pick up phones that are ringing, but rarely answer phones that are silent.

Generalization

Two important aspects of stimulus control are generalization and discrimination. Let's return to dogs to illustrate these concepts. First, generalization.

Is generalization the same in operant conditioning as it is in classical conditioning? Basically, yes. **Operant stimulus generalization** is the tendency to respond to stimuli similar to those that preceded operant reinforcement. That is, a reinforced response tends to be made again when similar antecedents are present.

Assume, for instance, that your dog has begun to jump up at you whenever you are eating dinner at the kitchen table (bad dog!). Mind you, that's because you have been rewarding its behavior with table scraps (bad master!). Now your dog begins to jump any time you sit at the kitchen table. The dog has learned that reinforcement tends to occur when you are at the kitchen table. The dog's behavior has come under stimulus control. Now let's say that there are some other tables in your house. Because they are similar, your dog will likely jump up if you sit at any of them because the jumping response *generalized* to other tables. Similar generalization explains why children may temporarily call all men *Daddy*—much to the embarrassment of their parents.

Discrimination

Meanwhile, back at the table. . . . As stated earlier, to discriminate means to respond differently to varied stimuli. Because one table signaled the availability of reinforcement to your dog, it began jumping up while you sat at other tables as well (generalization). If you do not feed your dog while sitting at any other table, the jumping response that originally generalized to them will extinguish because of nonreinforcement. Thus, your dog's jumping response is consistently rewarded in the presence of a specific table. The same response to different tables is extinguished. Through **operant stimulus discrimination,** your dog has learned to differentiate

Stimulus control Stimuli present when an operant response is acquired tend to control when and where the response is made.

Operant stimulus generalization The tendency to respond to stimuli similar to those that preceded operant reinforcement.

Operant stimulus discrimination The tendency to make an operant response when stimuli previously associated with reward are present and to withhold the response when stimuli associated with nonreward are present.

between antecedent stimuli that signal reward and nonreward. As a result, the dog's response pattern will shift to match these **discriminative stimuli** (stimuli that precede reinforced and nonreinforced responses).

Stimulus discrimination is aptly illustrated by the "sniffer" dogs that locate drugs and explosives at airports and border crossings. Operant discrimination is used to teach these dogs to recognize contraband. During training, they are reinforced only for approaching containers baited with drugs or explosives.

Stimulus discrimination also has a tremendous impact on human behavior. Learning to recognize different automobile brands, birds, animals, wines, types of music, and even the answers on psychology tests all depends, in part, on operant discrimination learning.

A discriminative stimulus that most drivers are familiar with is a police car on the freeway. This stimulus is a clear signal that a specific set of reinforcement contingencies applies. As you have probably observed, the presence of a police car brings about rapid reductions in driving speed, lane changes, and tailgating.

Would using different ringtones on my cellphone be an example of using discriminative stimuli? Excellent! Suppose you use one ringtone for people you want to speak to, one for people you don't, and yet another for calls from strangers. In no time at all you will be showing different telephone answering behavior in response to different ringtones.

Carleton Ray/Photo Researchers, Inc.

Stimulus control. Operant shaping was used to teach this whale to "bow" to an audience. Fish were used as reinforcers. Notice the trainer's hand signal, which serves as a discriminative stimulus to control the performance.

Discriminative stimuli Stimuli that precede rewarded and nonrewarded responses in operant conditioning.

RECITE

1. Two aspects of stimulus control are _____ and _____.
2. Responding tends to occur in the presence of discriminative stimuli associated with reinforcement and tends not to occur in the presence of discriminative stimuli associated with nonreinforcement. T or F?
3. Stimulus generalization refers to making an operant response in the presence of stimuli similar to those that preceded reinforcement. T or F?
4. Moderate response rates that are marked by spurts of activity and periods of inactivity are characteristic of
   a. FR schedules   b. VR schedules
   c. FI schedules   d. VI schedules
5. Partial reinforcement tends to produce slower responding and reduced resistance to extinction. T or F?
6. The schedule of reinforcement associated with playing slot machines and other types of gambling is
   a. fixed ratio   b. variable ratio
   c. fixed interval   d. variable interval

REFLECT

Critical Thinking

7. A business owner who pays employees an hourly wage wants to increase productivity. How could the owner make more effective use of reinforcement?

8. How could you use conditioning principles to teach a dog or a cat to come when called?

Relate

Think of something you do that is reinforced only part of the time. Do you pursue this activity persistently? How have you been affected by partial reinforcement?

See if you can think of at least one everyday example of the five basic schedules of reinforcement (continuous reinforcement and four types of partial reinforcement).

Doors that are meant to be pushed outward have metal plates on them. Those that are meant to be pulled inward have handles. Do these discriminative stimuli affect your behavior? (If they don't, how's your nose doing?)

ANSWERS

1. generalization, discrimination 2. T 3. T 4. c 5. F 6. b 7. Continuing to use fixed interval rewards (hourly wage or salary) would guarantee a basic level of income for employees. To reward extra effort, the owner could add some fixed ratio reinforcement (such as incentives, bonuses, commissions, or profit sharing) to employees' pay. 8. An excellent way to train a pet to come when you call is to give a distinctive call or whistle each time you feed the animal. This makes the signal a secondary reinforcer and a discriminative stimulus for reward (food). Of course, it also helps to directly reinforce an animal with praise, petting, or food for coming when called.

Punishment—Putting the Brakes on Behavior

What does punishment do to behavior?

Spankings, reprimands, fines, jail sentences, firings, failing grades, and the like are commonly used to control behavior. Clearly, the story of instrumental learning is unfinished without a return to the topic of punishment. Recall that **punishment** lowers the probability that a response will occur again. To be most effective, punishment must be given contingently (only after an undesired response occurs).

Punishers are consequences that lower the probability that a response will be made again. Receiving a traffic citation is directly punishing because the driver is delayed and reprimanded. Paying a fine and higher insurance rates add to the punishment in the form of response cost.

Punishers, like reinforcers, are defined by observing their effects on behavior. A **punisher** is any consequence that reduces the frequency of a target behavior. It is not always possible to know ahead of time what will act as a punisher for a particular person. For example, when Jason's mother reprimanded him for throwing toys, he stopped doing it. In this instance, the reprimand was a punisher. However, Chris is starved for attention of any kind from his parents, who both work full-time. For Chris, a reprimand, or even a spanking, might actually reinforce toy throwing. Remember, too, that a punisher can be either the onset of an unpleasant event or the removal of a positive state of affairs (response cost).

Variables Affecting Punishment

How effective is punishment? The effectiveness of punishers depends greatly on their *timing, consistency,* and *intensity.* Punishment works best when it occurs as the response is being made, or *immediately* afterward (timing), and when it is given *each time* a response occurs (consistency). Thus, if simply refusing to feed your dog table scraps is not enough to stop it from jumping at you when you sit at a table, you could effectively (and humanely) punish it by spraying water on its nose each time it jumps up. About 10 to 15 such treatments are usually enough. This would not be the case if you applied punishment haphazardly or long after the jumping stopped. If you discover that your dog dug up a tree and ate it while you were gone, punishing the dog hours later will do little good. Likewise, the commonly heard childhood threat "Wait 'til your father comes home, then you'll be sorry" just makes the father a feared brute; it doesn't effectively punish an undesirable response.

Severe punishment (following a response with an intensely aversive or unpleasant stimulus) can be extremely effective in stopping behavior. If 3-year-old Beavis sticks his finger in a light socket and gets a shock, that may be the last time he *ever* tries it. However, mild punishment only temporarily *suppresses* a response. If the response is still reinforced, punishment may be particularly ineffective.

This fact was demonstrated by slapping rats on the paw as they were bar pressing in a Skinner box. Two groups of well-trained rats were placed on extinction. One group was punished with a slap for each bar press, and the other group was not. It might seem that the slap would cause bar pressing to extinguish more quickly. Yet, this was not the case, as you can see in ▶▶ Figure 6.18. Punishment temporarily slowed responding, but it did not cause more rapid extinction. Slapping the paws of rats or children has little permanent effect on a reinforced response.

Similarly, if 7-year-old Alissa sneaks a snack from the refrigerator before dinner and is punished for it, she may pass up snacks for a short time. But because snack sneaking was

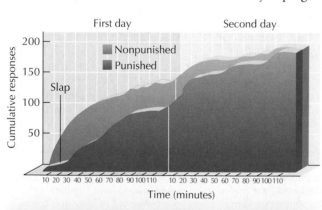

▲ **FIGURE 6.18** The effect of punishment on extinction. Immediately after punishment, the rate of bar pressing is suppressed, but by the end of the second day, the effects of punishment have disappeared. (After B. F. Skinner, *The Behavior of Organisms.*© 1938. D. Appleton-Century Co., Inc. Reprinted by permission of Prentice-Hall, Inc.)

Punishment The process of suppressing a response.

Punisher Any event that decreases the probability or frequency of responses it follows.

also rewarded by the sneaked snack, she will probably try sneaky snacking again, sometime later. But seriously, to reiterate, intense punishment may permanently suppress responding, even for actions as basic as eating. Animals severely punished while eating may never eat again (Bertsch, 1976).

The Downside of Punishment

Are there drawbacks to using punishment? There are several, all of which become more of a problem as punishment increases in severity. Basically, punishment is *aversive* (painful or uncomfortable). As a result, people and situations associated with punishment tend, through classical conditioning, to become feared, resented, or disliked. The aversive nature of punishment makes it especially poor to use when teaching children to eat politely or in toilet training.

Escape and Avoidance

A second major problem is that aversive stimuli encourage escape and avoidance learning. In **escape learning** we learn to make a response in order to end an aversive stimulus. For example, if you work with a loud and obnoxious person, you may at first escape from conversations with him to obtain relief. (Notice that escape learning is based on negative reinforcement.) Later you may dodge him altogether. This is an example of **avoidance learning** (making a response in order to postpone or prevent discomfort). Each time you sidestep him, your avoidance is again reinforced by a sense of relief. In many situations involving frequent punishment, similar desires to escape and avoid are activated. For example, children who run away from punishing parents (escape) may soon learn to lie about their behavior (avoidance) or to spend as much time away from home as possible (also an avoidance response).

Aggression

A third problem with punishment is that it can greatly increase *aggression*. Animals react to pain by attacking whomever or whatever else is around. A common example is the faithful dog that nips its owner during a painful procedure at the veterinarian's office. Likewise, humans who are in pain have a tendency to lash out at others.

We also know that one of the most common responses to frustration is aggression. Generally speaking, punishment is painful, frustrating, or both. Punishment, therefore, sets up a powerful environment for learning aggression. When spanked, a child may feel angry, frustrated, and hostile. What if that child then goes outside and hits a brother, a sister, or a neighbor? The danger is that aggressive acts may feel good because they release anger and frustration. If so, aggression has been rewarded and will tend to occur again in other frustrating situations.

One study found that children who are physically punished are more likely to engage in aggressive, impulsive, antisocial behavior (Thomas, 2004). Similarly, a classic study of angry adolescent boys found that they were severely punished at home. This suppressed their misbehavior at home but made them more aggressive elsewhere. Parents were often surprised to learn that their "good boys" were in trouble for fighting at school (Bandura & Walters, 1959). Fortunately, at least for younger children, if parents change to less punitive parenting, their children's levels of aggression will decline (Thomas, 2004).

In the classroom, physical punishment, yelling, and humiliation are also generally ineffective. Positive reinforcement, in the form of praise, approval, and reward, is much more likely to quell classroom disruptions, defiance, and inattention (Alberto & Troutman, 2009).

Using Punishment Wisely

In light of its limitations and drawbacks, should punishment be used to control behavior? Parents, teachers, animal trainers, and the like have three basic tools to control simple learning: (1) Reinforcement strengthens responses; (2) nonreinforcement causes responses to

Escape learning Learning to make a response in order to end an aversive stimulus.

Avoidance learning Learning to make a response in order to postpone or prevent discomfort.

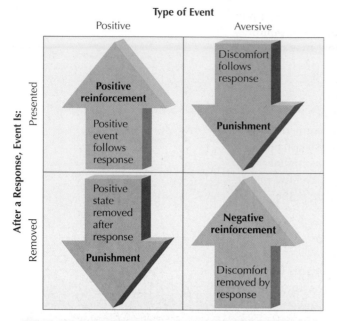

Type of Event

	Positive	Aversive
Presented	**Positive reinforcement** — Positive event follows response	Discomfort follows response — **Punishment**
Removed	Positive state removed after response — **Punishment**	**Negative reinforcement** — Discomfort removed by response

After a Response, Event Is:

FIGURE 6.19 Types of reinforcement and punishment. The impact of an event depends on whether it is presented or removed after a response is made. Each square defines one possibility: Arrows pointing upward indicate that responding is increased; downward-pointing arrows indicate that responding is decreased.

extinguish; (3) punishment suppresses responses. (Consult ▶ Figure 6.19 to refresh your memory about the different types of reinforcement and punishment.) These tools work best in combination. It is usually best to begin by making liberal use of positive reinforcement, especially praise, to encourage good behavior. Also, try extinction first: See what happens if you ignore a problem behavior, or shift attention to a desirable activity and then reinforce it with praise. Remember, it is much more effective to strengthen and encourage desirable behaviors than it is to punish unwanted behaviors (Gershoff, 2002). When all else fails, it may be necessary to use punishment to help manage the behavior of an animal, child, or even another adult. For those times, here are some tips to keep in mind:

1. *Avoid harsh punishment.* Harsh or excessive punishment has serious negative drawbacks (never slap a child's face, for instance). "Sparing the rod" will not spoil a child. In fact, the reverse is true. As we just discussed, harsh punishment can lead to negative emotional reactions, avoidance and escape behaviors, and increased aggression (Aucoin, Frick, & Bodin, 2006). It can even lead to long-term mental health problems (Afifi et al., 2006).

    What about spanking? Parents should minimize spanking or avoid it entirely (Gershoff, 2002). Although most children show no signs of long-term damage from spanking if it is backed up by supportive parenting, emotional damage does occur if spankings are severe, frequent, or coupled with harsh parenting (Baumrind, Larzelere, & Cowan, 2002). Like all harsh punishment, frequent spanking tends to increase aggression and leads to more problem behaviors, not fewer (McLoyd & Smith, 2002; Saadeh, Rizzo, & Roberts, 2002). In fact, antispanking laws have been passed in a number of countries around the world.

2. *Use the minimum punishment necessary to suppress misbehavior.* If punishment is used at all, it should be mild. In a situation that poses immediate danger, such as when a child reaches for something hot or a dog runs into the street, mild punishment may prevent disaster. Punishment in such cases works best when it produces actions *incompatible* with the response you want to suppress. Let's say a child reaches toward a stove burner. Would a swat on the bottom serve as an effective punisher? Probably so. It would be better, however, to slap the child's outstretched hand so that it will be *withdrawn* from the source of danger. Taking away privileges or other positive reinforcers (response cost) is usually best for older children and adults. Often, a verbal rebuke or a scolding is enough.

3. *Apply punishment during, or immediately after, misbehavior.* Of course, immediate punishment is not always possible. With older children and adults, you can bridge the delay by clearly stating what act you are punishing. If you cannot punish an animal or young child immediately, wait for the next instance of misbehavior.

4. *Be consistent.* Be very clear about what you regard as misbehavior. Punish every time the misbehavior occurs. Don't punish for something one time and ignore it the next. If you are usually willing to give a child three chances, don't change the rule and explode without warning after a first offense. Both parents should try to punish their children for the same things and in the same way.

5. *Use counter-conditioning.* Mild punishment tends to be ineffective if reinforcers are still available in the situation. That's why it is best to also reward an alternate, desired response. For example, a child who has a habit of taking toys from her sister should not just be reprimanded for it. She should be *counter-conditioned,* or rewarded for displaying any behavior that is counter to the unacceptable behavior, such as cooperative play or sharing her toys. As desired behaviors become more frequent, undesired behaviors become less frequent. The girl can't very well share her toys and take them from her sister at the same time.

    Remember, punishment tells a person or an animal only that a response was "wrong." Punishment does not say what the "right" response is, so it *does not teach new behaviors.* If reinforcement is missing, punishment becomes less effective (Gershoff, 2002).

6. *Expect anger from a punished person.* Briefly acknowledge this anger, but be careful not to reinforce it. Be willing to admit your mistake if you wrongfully punish someone or if you punished too severely.

7. *Punish with kindness and respect.* Avoid punishing when you are angry. It is easy to get carried away and become abusive (Gershoff, 2002). Two thirds of child abuse cases start out as attempts at physical punishment (Trocmé et al., 2001). One way to guard against doing harm is to punish with kindness and respect. Doing so also allows the punished person to retain self-respect. For instance, do not punish a person in front of others, if possible. A strong, trusting relationship tends to minimize behavior problems. Ideally, others should want to behave well to get your praise, not because they fear punishment.

To summarize, a common error is to rely too much on punishment for training or discipline. Frequent punishment makes a person or an animal unhappy, confused, anxious, aggressive, and fearful (Gershoff, 2002). The overall emotional adjustment of a child or pet disciplined mainly by reward is usually superior to one disciplined mainly by punishment.

Parents and teachers should also be aware that using punishment can be "habit forming." When children are being noisy, messy, disrespectful, or otherwise misbehaving, the temptation to punish them can be strong. The danger is that punishment often works. When it does, a sudden end to the adult's irritation acts as a negative reinforcer. This encourages the adult to use punishment more often in the future (Alberto & Troutman, 2009). Immediate silence may be "golden," but its cost can be very high in terms of a child's emotional health.

study break
Punishment

RECITE

1. Negative reinforcement increases responding; punishment suppresses responding. T or F?
2. Three factors that greatly influence the effects of punishment are timing, consistency, and _____ .
3. Mild punishment tends to only temporarily _____ a response that is also reinforced.
   a. enhance   b. aggravate
   c. replace   d. suppress
4. Three undesired side effects of punishment are (1) conditioning of fear and resentment, (2) encouragement of aggression, and (3) the learning of escape or _____ responses.
5. Using punishment can be "habit forming" because putting a stop to someone else's irritating behavior can _____ _____ the person who applies the punishment.

REFLECT
Critical Thinking

6. Using the concept of partial reinforcement, can you explain why inconsistent punishment is especially ineffective?
7. Escape and avoidance learning have been applied to encourage automobile seat belt use. Can you explain how?

Relate

Think of how you were punished as a child. Was the punishment immediate? Was it consistent? What effect did these factors have on your behavior? Was the punishment effective? Which of the side effects of punishment have you witnessed or experienced?

ANSWERS

1. T 2. intensity 3. d 4. avoidance 5. negatively reinforce 6. An inconsistently punished response will continue to be reinforced on a partial schedule, which can make it even more resistant to extinction. 7. Many automobiles have an unpleasant buzzer that sounds if the ignition key is turned before the driver's seat belt is fastened. Most drivers quickly learn to fasten the belt to stop the annoying sound. This is an example of escape conditioning. Avoidance conditioning is evident when a driver learns to buckle up before the buzzer sounds.

Cognitive Learning—Beyond Conditioning

What is cognitive learning?

Is all learning just an association between stimuli and responses? Much learning can be explained by classical and operant conditioning. But, as we have seen, even basic conditioning has "mental" elements. As a human, you can anticipate future reward or punishment and react accordingly. (You may wonder why this doesn't seem to work when a doctor or dentist says, "This won't hurt a bit." Here's why: They lie!) There is no doubt that human learning includes a large *cognitive,* or mental, dimension (Lefrançois, 2006). As humans, we are greatly affected by information, expectations, perceptions, mental images, and the like.

As we mentioned at the beginning of this chapter, loosely speaking, *cognitive learning* refers to understanding, knowing, anticipating, or otherwise making use of information-rich higher mental processes. Cognitive learning extends beyond basic conditioning into the realms of memory, thinking, problem solving, and language. Because these topics are covered in later chapters, our discussion here is limited to a first look at learning beyond conditioning.

Cognitive Maps

How do you navigate around the town you live in? Have you simply learned to make a series of right and left turns to get from one point to another? More likely, you have an overall mental picture of how the town is laid out. This *cognitive map* acts as a guide even when you must detour or take a new route (Foo et al., 2005). A **cognitive map** is an internal representation of an area, such as a maze, city, or campus. Even the lowly rat—not exactly a mental giant (well, except for Einstein)—learns *where* food is found in a maze, not just which turns to make to reach the food (Tolman, Ritchie, & Kalish, 1946). If you have ever learned your way through some of the levels found in many video games, you will have a good idea of what a cognitive map is. In a sense, cognitive maps also apply to other kinds of knowledge. For instance, it could be said that you have been developing a "map" of psychology while reading this book. That's why students sometimes find it helpful to draw pictures or diagrams of how they envision concepts fitting together.

Latent Learning

Cognitive learning is also revealed by latent (hidden) learning. **Latent learning** occurs without obvious reinforcement and remains hidden until reinforcement is provided (Davidson, 2000). Here's an example from a classic animal study: Two groups of rats were allowed to explore a maze. The animals in one group found food at the far end of the maze. Soon, they learned to rapidly make their way through the maze when released. Rats in the second group were unrewarded and showed no signs of learning. But later, when the "uneducated" rats were given food, they ran the maze as quickly as the rewarded group (Tolman & Honzik, 1930). Although there was no outward sign of it, the unrewarded animals had learned their way around the maze. Their learning, therefore, remained latent at first (▶▶ Figure 6.20).

How did they learn if there was no reinforcement? Just satisfying curiosity can be enough to reward learning (Harlow & Harlow, 1962). In humans, latent learning is related to higher-level abilities, such as anticipating future reward. For example, if you give an attractive classmate a ride home, you may make mental notes about how to get to his or her house, even if a date is only a remote future possibility.

Discovery Learning

Much of what is meant by cognitive learning is summarized by the word *understanding.* Each of us has, at times, learned ideas by **rote** (mechanical repetition and memorization). Although rote learning can be efficient, many psychologists believe that learning is more lasting and flexible when people *discover* facts and principles on their own. In **discovery learning,** skills

It's easy to get lost when visiting a new city if you don't have a cognitive map of the area. Printed maps help, but they may still leave you puzzled until you begin to form a mental representation of major landmarks and directions.

Cognitive map Internal images or other mental representations of an area (maze, city, campus, and so forth) that underlie an ability to choose alternative paths to the same goal.

Latent learning Learning that occurs without obvious reinforcement and that remains unexpressed until reinforcement is provided.

Rote learning Learning that takes place mechanically, through repetition and memorization, or by learning rules.

Discovery learning Learning based on insight and understanding.

(a)

(b)

Reinforced starting on eleventh day
Always reinforced

FIGURE 6.20 Latent learning. *(a)* The maze used by Tolman and Honzik to demonstrate latent learning by rats. *(b)* Results of the experiment. Notice the rapid improvement in performance that occurred when food was made available to the previously unreinforced animals. This indicates that learning had occurred but that it remained hidden or unexpressed. (Adapted from Tolman & Honzik, 1930.)

are gained by insight and understanding instead of by rote (Swaak, de Jong, & van Joolingen, 2004).

As long as learning occurs, what difference does it make if it is by discovery or by rote? ▶▶ Figure 6.21 illustrates the difference. Two groups of students were taught to calculate the area of a parallelogram by multiplying the height by the length of the base. Some were encouraged to see that a "piece" of a parallelogram could be "moved" to create a rectangle. Later, they were

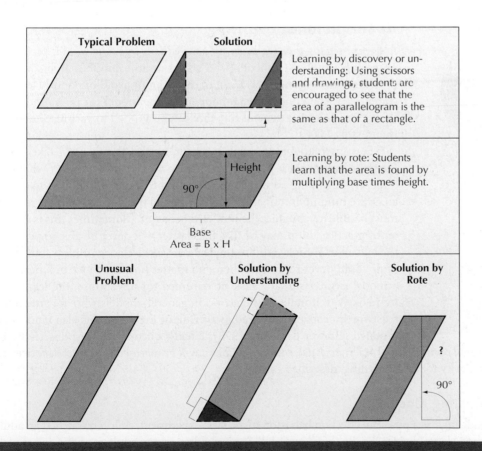

FIGURE 6.21 Learning by understanding and by rote. For some types of learning, understanding may be superior, although both types of learning are useful. (After Wertheimer, 1959.)

better able to solve unusual problems in which the height times base formula didn't seem to work. Students who simply memorized a rule were confused by similar problems (Wertheimer, 1959). As this implies, discovery can lead to a better understanding of new or unusual problems. When possible, people should try new strategies and discover new solutions during learning. However, this doesn't mean that students are supposed to stumble around and rediscover the principles of math, physics, or chemistry. The best teaching strategies are based on *guided discovery,* in which students are given enough freedom to actively think about problems and enough guidance so that they gain useful knowledge (Mayer, 2004).

Modeling—Do as I Do, Not as I Say

Does learning occur by imitation?

Many skills are learned by what Albert Bandura (1971) calls *observational learning,* or *modeling.* Watching and imitating the actions of another person or noting the consequences of the person's actions can lead to **observational learning** (Lefrançois, 2006). We humans share the capacity for observational learning with many mammals, like Larry's beloved gorillas (Meunier, Monfardini, & Boussaoud, 2007).

The value of learning by observation is obvious: Imagine trying to *tell* someone how to tie a shoe, do a dance step, or play a guitar. Bandura believes that anything that can be learned from direct experience can be learned by observation. Often, this allows a person to skip the tedious trial-and-error stage of learning.

Observational Learning

It seems obvious that we learn by observation, but how does it occur? By observing a **model** (someone who serves as an example), a person may (1) learn new responses, (2) learn to carry out or avoid previously learned responses (depending on what happens to the model for doing the same thing), or (3) learn a general rule that can be applied to various situations (Lefrançois, 2006).

For observational learning to occur, several things must take place. First, the learner must pay *attention* to the model and *remember* what was done. (A beginning auto mechanic might be interested enough to watch an entire tune-up but unable to remember all the steps.) Next, the learner must be able to *reproduce* the modeled behavior. (Sometimes this is a matter of practice, but it may be that the learner will never be able to perform the behavior. We may admire the feats of world-class gymnasts, but most of us could never reproduce them, no matter how much we practiced.) If a model is *successful* at a task or *rewarded* for a response, the learner is more likely to imitate the behavior. In general, models who are attractive, trustworthy, capable, admired, powerful, or high in status also tend to be imitated (Brewer & Wann, 1998). Finally, once a new response is tried, *normal reinforcement or feedback determines whether it will be repeated thereafter.* (Notice the similarity to latent learning, described earlier.)

Observational learning often imparts large amounts of information that would be difficult to obtain by reading instructions or memorizing rules.

Bambu Productions/Getty Images

Observational learning Learning achieved by watching and imitating the actions of another or noting the consequences of those actions.

Model A person who serves as an example in observational learning.

Imitating Models

Modeling has a powerful effect on behavior. In a classic experiment, children watched an adult attack a large blowup "Bo-Bo the Clown" doll. Some children saw an adult sit on the doll, punch it, hit it with a hammer, and kick it around the room. Others saw a movie of these actions. A third group saw a cartoon version of the aggression. Later, the children were frustrated by having some attractive toys taken away from them. Then, they were allowed to play with the Bo-Bo

FIGURE 6.22 A nursery school child imitates the aggressive behavior of an adult model he has just seen in a movie. (Courtesy of Albert Bandura/Stanford University.)

doll. Most imitated the adult's attack (▶▶ Figure 6.22). Some even added new aggressive acts of their own! Interestingly, the cartoon was only slightly less effective in encouraging aggression than the live adult model and the filmed model (Bandura, Ross, & Ross, 1963).

Then do children blindly imitate adults? No. Remember that observational learning only prepares a person to duplicate a response. Whether it is actually imitated depends on whether the model was rewarded or punished for what was done. Nevertheless, when parents tell a child to do one thing but model a completely different response, children tend to imitate what the parents *do,* and *not* what they *say.* Thus, through modeling, children learn not only attitudes, gestures, emotions, and personality traits, but fears, anxieties, and bad habits as well. A good example is the adolescent smoker, who is much more likely to begin smoking if her parents, siblings, and friends smoke (Wilkinson & Abraham, 2004). Tragically, children who witness domestic violence are more likely to commit it themselves (Murrell, Christoff, & Henning, 2007).

Now, consider a typical situation: Little Raymond has just been interrupted at play by his older brother, Robert. Angry and frustrated, he swats Robert. This behavior interrupts his father Frank's TV watching. Father promptly spanks little Raymond, saying, "This will teach you to hit your big brother." And it will. Because of modeling effects, it is unrealistic to expect a child to "Do as I say, not as I do." The message Frank has given the child is clear: "You have frustrated me; therefore, I will hit you." The next time little Raymond is frustrated, it won't be surprising if he imitates his father and hits his brother (so why does everybody love Raymond, anyway?).

Modeling and the Media

Does television promote observational learning? Today's 8- to 18-year-olds spend an average of 44.5 hours a week engaged with various media, including television, video games, movies, the Internet, music, and print media (Roberts, Foehr, & Rideout, 2005). Although overall use is falling, television still consumes the lion's share of media attention, averaging 21 hours every week.

By the time the average person has graduated from high school, she or he will have viewed some 15,000 hours of TV, compared with only 11,000 hours spent in the classroom. In that time, viewers will have seen some 18,000 murders and countless acts of robbery, arson, bombing, torture, and beatings. Even G-rated cartoons average 10 minutes of violence per hour (Yokota & Thompson, 2000). In short, typical TV viewers are exposed to a massive dose of media violence, which tends to promote observational learning of aggression (Bushman & Anderson, 2001).

Televised Aggression

The last finding should come as no surprise. Studies show conclusively that if children watch a great deal of televised violence, they will be more prone to behave aggressively (Anderson et al., 2003; Bushman & Anderson, 2001). In other words, not all children will

critical thinking

You Mean Video Games Might Be Bad for Me?

Today's kids can experience more gore in a day than most people used to experience in a lifetime, even during military combat. For example, in one video game you can kill an entire marching band with a flame-thrower. Some of your victims won't die right away. They will just writhe in pain, begging you to finish them off.

What effects do such experiences have on people who play violent video games? Reviews have concluded that violent video games increase aggressive behavior in children and young adults (Anderson & Bushman, 2001; Anderson, 2004). As with TV, young children are especially suscep-

tible to fantasy violence in video games (Anderson et al., 2003; Bensley & Van Eenwyk, 2001).

One study illustrates the impact of video game violence. First, college students played a violent (*Mortal Kombat*) or nonviolent (*PGA Tournament Golf*) video game. Next, they competed with another student (actually an actor) in a task that allowed aggression and retaliation to take place. Students who played *Mortal Kombat* were much more likely to aggress, by punishing their competitor (Bartholow & Anderson, 2002). (Don't mess with someone who just played *Mortal Kombat!*)

How does video game violence increase aggressive behavior? One possibility is that repeated exposure to violence desensitizes players, making them less likely to react negatively to violence and, hence, more prone to engage in it (Bartholow, Sestir, & Davis, 2005; Funk, 2005). Another possibility is that by practicing violence against other people, players may learn to be aggressive in real life (Unsworth & Ward, 2001). (Before you write off video games altogether, read "You Mean Video Games Might Be Good For Me?" in Chapter 8.)

▶▶ **FIGURE 6.23** This graph shows that preschoolers who watched low levels of television violence were less aggressive than average as young adults when contacted 15 years later. In contrast, preschoolers who watched high levels of television violence were more aggressive than average as young adults. The composite aggression score includes measures of indirect aggression (e.g., verbal abusiveness) and direct aggression (physical aggression). (Data adapted from Huesmann et al., 2003.)

become more aggressive, but many will. More ominously, the effect can last into early adulthood. A group of primary school students with known television viewing habits were later contacted in early adulthood (Huesmann et al., 2003). Those who watched more violence on television as elementary schoolers were more aggressive as adults 15 years later (see ▶▶ Figure 6.23).

Does the same conclusion apply to video games? Oh, yes. Children tend to imitate what they observe in all media. From professional wrestling (Bernthal, 2003) to rap music (Wingood et al., 2003) to video games (Carnagey & Anderson, 2004), children have plenty of opportunity to observe and imitate both the good and the bad. (See "You Mean Video Games Might Be Bad for Me?" for some recent evidence.)

Is it fair to say, then, that media violence causes aggression in consumers, especially children? Media violence can make aggression more *likely,* but it does not invariably "cause" it to occur for any given child (Kirsh, 2005). Many other factors affect the chances that hostile thoughts will be turned into actions. Youngsters who believe that aggression is an acceptable way to solve problems, who believe that TV violence is realistic, and who identify with TV characters are most likely to copy televised aggression (Huesmann et al., 2003). It is particularly troubling to find media *heroes* behaving aggressively, as well as villains. Younger children, in particular, are more likely to be influenced because they don't fully recognize that media characters and stories are fantasies (McKenna & Ossoff, 1998).

In view of such findings, it is understandable that countries like Canada, Norway, and Switzerland have restricted the amount of permissible violence on television. Should all countries do the same?

A Look Ahead

Conditioning principles are often derived from animal experiments. However, it should be apparent that the same principles apply to human behavior. Perhaps the best way to appreciate this fact is to observe how reinforcement affects your own behavior. With this in mind, the upcoming Psychology in Action section proposes a personal experiment in operant conditioning. Don't miss this coming attraction!

Erik S. Lesser/AP Images

TV heroes can act as powerful models for observational learning of aggression.

RECITE

1. An internal representation of relationships is referred to as a
   _____ .
2. Learning that suddenly appears when a reward or incentive for performance is given is called
   a. discovery learning   b. latent learning
   c. rote learning   d. reminiscence
3. Psychologists use the term _____ to describe observational learning.
4. If a model is successful, rewarded, attractive, or high in status, his or her behavior is
   a. difficult to reproduce   b. less likely to be attended to
   c. more likely to be imitated d. subject to positive transfer
5. Children who observed a live adult behave aggressively became more aggressive; those who observed movie and cartoon aggression did not. T or F?
6. Children are most likely to imitate TV characters with whom they identify. T or F?
7. Children who watch a great deal of media violence are more prone to be aggressive, an effect that is best explained by
   a. negative reinforcement   b. shaping and successive approximations
   c. observational learning   d. vicarious classical conditioning

ANSWERS

1. cognitive map 2. b 3. modeling 4. c 5. F 6. T 7. c 8. Your cognitive map of the campus has undoubtedly become more accurate and intricate over time as you have added details to it. Your drawings should reflect this change. 9. Because the observation is based on a correlation. Children who are already aggressive may choose to watch more aggressive programs, rather than being made aggressive by them. It took experimental studies to verify that televised aggression promotes aggression by viewers.

psychology in action
Behavioral Self-Management—A Rewarding Project

Would you like to exercise more, attend more classes, cut down on smoking, concentrate longer, or read more books? This is an invitation to carry out a self-management project of your own. As such, this could be the start of one of the most personal applications of psychology in this book.

Self-Managed Behavior

The principles of operant conditioning can be adapted to manage your own behavior (Martin & Pear, 2007; Watson & Tharp, 2007). Here's how:

1. **Choose a target behavior.** Identify the activity you want to change.

2. **Record a baseline.** Record how much time you currently spend performing the target activity or count the number of desired or undesired responses you make each day.

3. **Establish goals.** Remember the principle of shaping, and set realistic goals for gradual improvement on each successive week. Also, set daily goals that add up to the weekly goal.

4. **Choose reinforcers.** If you meet your daily goal, what reward will you allow yourself? Daily rewards might be watching television, eating a candy bar, socializing with friends, listening to your iPod, or whatever you enjoy. Also establish a weekly reward. If you reach your weekly goal, what reward will you allow yourself? A movie? A dinner out? Some time playing a game like *Guitar Hero?* A weekend hike?

5. **Record your progress.** Keep accurate records of the amount of time spent each day on the desired activity or the number of times you make the desired response.

6. **Reward successes.** If you meet your daily goal, collect your reward. If you fall short, be honest with yourself and skip the reward. Do the same for your weekly goal.

7. **Adjust your plan as you learn more about your behavior.** Overall progress will reinforce your attempts at self-management.

If you have trouble thinking of rewards, remember that anything done often can serve as reinforcement. This is known as the **Premack principle.** It is named after David Premack,

"RUNNING AWAY FROM YOUR PROBLEMS DOES NOT COUNT AS EXERCISE."

Premack principle Any high-frequency response can be used to reinforce a low-frequency response.

a psychologist who popularized its use. For example, if you like to watch television every night and want to study more, make it a rule not to turn on the set until you have studied for an hour (or whatever length of time you choose). Then lengthen the requirement each week. Here is a sample of one student's plan:

1. *Target behavior:* number of hours spent studying for school.

2. *Recorded baseline:* an average of 25 minutes per day for a weekly total of 3 hours.

3. *Goal for the first week:* an increase in study time to 40 minutes per day; weekly goal of 5 hours total study time. *Goal for second week:* 50 minutes per day and 6 hours per week. *Goal for third week:* 1 hour per day and 7 hours per week. *Ultimate goal:* to reach and maintain 14 hours per week study time.

4. *Daily reward for reaching goal:* 1/2 hour of guitar playing in the evening; no playing if the goal is not met. *Weekly reward for reaching goal:* going to a movie or buying a DVD.

Self-Recording Even if you find it difficult to give and withhold rewards, **self-recording** (keeping records of response frequencies, a form of feedback) can make a difference all by itself. This is because we tend to react to being observed, even when we are the ones watching our own behavior. In general, when you systematically (and honestly) observe yourself, you are more likely to engage in desired behaviors and less likely to perform undesired behaviors (Fireman, Kose, & Solomon, 2003; Watson & Tharp, 2007).

Keep track of the number of times that you exercise, arrive late to class, eat vegetables, smoke a cigarette, study, watch TV, drink a cappuccino, swear, or whatever you are interested in changing. A simple tally on a piece of paper will do, or you can get a small mechanical counter like those used to keep golf scores or count calories. Record keeping helps break patterns, and the feedback can be motivating as you begin to make progress.

Good Ways to Break Bad Habits

Are there any extra tips for breaking bad habits? By using the methods we have discussed, you can *decrease* unwanted behaviors, such as swearing, biting your nails, criticizing others, smoking, drinking coffee, watching TV too much, or engaging in any other behavior you choose to target. However, breaking bad habits may require some additional techniques. Here are four strategies to help you change bad habits.

Alternate Responses A good strategy for change is to try to get the same reinforcement with a new response.

Example: Marta often tells jokes at the expense of others. Her friends sometimes feel hurt by her sharp-edged humor. Marta senses this and wants to change. What can she do? Usually, Marta's joke telling is reinforced by attention and approval. She could just as easily get the same reinforcement by giving other people praise or compliments. Making a change in her behavior should be easy because she will continue to receive the reinforcement she seeks.

Extinction Try to discover what is reinforcing an unwanted response and remove, avoid, or delay the reinforcement.

Example: Fatima has developed a habit of taking longer and longer "breaks" to watch TV when she should be studying. Obviously, TV watching is reinforcing her break taking. To improve her study habits, Fatima could delay reinforcement by studying at the library or some other location a good distance from her TV.

Response Chains Break up response chains that precede an undesired behavior; this will help break the bad habit. The key idea is to scramble the chain of events that leads to an undesired response (Watson & Tharp, 2007).

Example: Most nights Ignacio comes home from work, turns on the TV, and eats a whole bag of cookies or chips. He then takes a shower and changes clothes. By dinnertime he has lost his appetite. Ignacio realizes he is substituting junk food for dinner. Ignacio could solve the problem by breaking the response chain that precedes dinner. For instance, he could shower immediately when he gets home or avoid turning on the television until after dinner.

Self-recording Self-management based on keeping records of response frequencies.

Cues and Antecedents Try to avoid, narrow down, or remove stimuli that elicit the bad habit.

Example: Brent wants to cut down on smoking. He can take many smoking cues out of his surroundings by removing ashtrays, matches, and extra cigarettes from his house, car, and office. Drug cravings are strongly related to cues conditioned to the drug, such as the odor of cigarettes (Lazev, Herzog, & Brandon, 1999). Brent can narrow antecedent stimuli even more. He could begin by smoking only in the lounge at work, never in his office or in his car. He could then limit his smoking to home. Then to only one room at home. Then to one chair at home. If he succeeds in getting this far, he may want to limit his smoking to only one unpleasant place, such as a bathroom, basement, or garage (Riley et al., 2002).

Contracting If you try the techniques described here and have difficulty sticking with them, you may want to try behavioral contracting. In a **behavioral contract,** you state a specific problem behavior you want to control, or a goal you want to achieve. Also state the rewards you will receive, privileges you will forfeit, or punishments you must accept. The contract should be signed by you and a person you trust.

A behavioral contract can be quite motivating, especially when mild punishment is part of the agreement. Here's a classic example, reported by Nurnberger and Zimmerman (1970): A student working on his Ph.D. had completed all requirements but his dissertation, yet for 2 years had not written a single page. A contract was drawn up for him in which he agreed to meet weekly deadlines on the number of pages he would complete. To make sure he would meet the deadlines, he wrote postdated checks. These were to be forfeited if he failed to reach his goal for the week. The checks were made out to organizations he despised (the Ku Klux Klan and American Nazi Party). From the time he signed the contract until he finished his degree, the student's work output was greatly improved.

Getting Help

Attempting to manage or alter your own behavior may be more difficult than it sounds. If you feel you need more information, consult the book listed below. You will also find helpful advice in the Psychology in Action section of Chapter 13. If you do try a self-modification project but find it impossible to reach your goals, be aware that professional advice is available.

Behavioral contract A formal agreement stating behaviors to be changed and consequences that apply.

Where to Obtain More Information: Watson, D. L., & Tharp, R. G. (2007). *Self-directed behavior* (9th ed.). Belmont, CA: Wadsworth.

---

study break
Behavioral Self-Management

RECITE

1. After a target behavior has been selected for reinforcement, it's a good idea to record a baseline so that you can set realistic goals for change. T or F?
2. Self-recording, even without the use of extra rewards, can bring about desired changes in target behaviors. T or F?
3. The Premack principle states that behavioral contracting can be used to reinforce changes in behavior. T or F?
4. A self-management plan should make use of the principle of shaping by setting a graduated series of goals. T or F?

5. Eleni ends up playing solitaire on her computer each time she tries to work on a term paper. Eventually she does get to work, but only after a long delay. To break this bad habit Eleni removes the solitaire icon from her computer screen so that she won't see it when she begins work. Eleni has used which strategy for breaking bad habits?
   a. alternative responses b. extinction
   c. avoid cues   d. contracting

REFLECT
Critical Thinking

6. How does setting daily goals in a behavioral self-management program help maximize the effects of reinforcement?

Relate

Even if you don't expect to carry out a self-management project right now, outline a plan for changing your own behavior. Be sure to describe the behavior you want to change, set goals, and identify reinforcers.

ANSWERS

1. T 2. T 3. F 4. T 5. c 6. Daily performance goals and rewards reduce the delay of reinforcement, which maximizes its impact.

chapter in review

Major Points

- Learning is a relatively permanent change in behavior due to experience.

- In classical conditioning, a neutral stimulus is repeatedly paired with a stimulus that reliably provokes a response. By association, the neutral stimulus also begins to elicit a response.

- In operant conditioning, responses that are followed by reinforcement occur more frequently.

- To understand why people behave as they do, it is important to identify how their responses are being reinforced.

- Cognitive learning involves acquiring higher level information, rather than just linking stimuli and responses.

- We also learn by observing and imitating the actions of others.

- Behavioral principles can be used to manage one's own behavior.

Summary

What is learning?

- Associative learning is a simple type of learning that affects many aspects of daily life.

- Cognitive learning involves making use of information-rich higher mental processes.

- Learning resulting from conditioning depends on reinforcement. Reinforcement increases the probability that a particular response will occur.

- Classical, or respondent, conditioning and instrumental, or operant, conditioning are two basic types of associative learning.

- In classical conditioning, a neutral stimulus is followed by an unconditioned stimulus. With repeated pairings, the neutral stimulus begins to elicit a response.

- In operant conditioning, responses that are followed by reinforcement occur more frequently.

How does classical conditioning occur?

- Classical conditioning, studied by Pavlov, occurs when a neutral stimulus (NS) is associated with an unconditioned stimulus (US).

- The US causes a reflex called the unconditioned response (UR). If the NS is consistently paired with the US, it becomes a conditioned stimulus (CS) capable of producing a conditioned (learned) response (CR).

- When the conditioned stimulus is followed by the unconditioned stimulus, conditioning is reinforced (strengthened).

- From an informational view, conditioning creates expectancies, which alter response patterns. In classical conditioning, the CS creates an expectancy that the US will follow.

- Higher order conditioning occurs when a well-learned conditioned stimulus is used as if it were an unconditioned stimulus, bringing about further learning.

- When the CS is repeatedly presented alone, conditioning is extinguished (weakened or inhibited). After extinction seems to be complete, a rest period may lead to the temporary reappearance of a conditioned response. This is called spontaneous recovery.

- Through stimulus generalization, stimuli similar to the conditioned stimulus will also produce a response. Generalization gives way to stimulus discrimination when an organism learns to respond to one stimulus but not to similar stimuli.

Does conditioning affect emotions?

- Conditioning applies to visceral or emotional responses as well as simple reflexes. As a result, conditioned emotional responses (CERs) also occur.

- Irrational fears called phobias may be CERs. Conditioning of emotional responses can occur vicariously (secondhand) as well as directly.

How does operant conditioning occur?

- Operant conditioning occurs when a voluntary action is followed by a reinforcer (which increases the frequency of the response) or a punisher (which decreases the frequency of the response).

- Delaying reinforcement greatly reduces its effectiveness, but long chains of responses may be maintained by a single reinforcer.

- Superstitious behaviors often become part of response chains because they appear to be associated with reinforcement.

- By rewarding successive approximations to a particular response, behavior can be shaped into desired patterns.

- If an operant response is not reinforced, it may extinguish (disappear). But after extinction seems complete, it may temporarily reappear (spontaneous recovery).

- Both positive reinforcement and negative reinforcement increase the likelihood that a response will be repeated. Punishment decreases the likelihood that the response will occur again.

Are there different kinds of operant reinforcement?

- Operant learning may be based on primary reinforcers (which are rooted in biology), secondary reinforcers (such as tokens and social reinforcers), and feedback (knowledge of results).

- Primary reinforcers are "natural," physiologically based rewards. Intracranial stimulation of "pleasure centers" in the brain can also serve as a primary reinforcer.

- Secondary reinforcers are learned. They typically gain their reinforcing value by direct association with primary reinforcers or because they can be exchanged for primary reinforcers. Tokens and money gain their reinforcing value in this way.

- Feedback aids learning and improves performance. It is most effective when it is immediate, detailed, and frequent.

- Programmed instruction breaks learning into a series of small steps and provides immediate feedback. Computer-assisted instruction (CAI) does the same but has the added advantage of providing alternative exercises and information when needed.

How are we influenced by patterns of reward?

- Reward or reinforcement may be given continuously (after every response) or on a schedule of partial reinforcement. Partial reinforcement produces greater resistance to extinction.
- The four most basic partial schedules of reinforcement are fixed ratio, variable ratio, fixed interval, and variable interval. Each produces a distinct pattern of responding.
- Stimuli that precede a reinforced response tend to control the response on future occasions (stimulus control). Two aspects of stimulus control are generalization and discrimination.
- In generalization, an operant response tends to occur when stimuli similar to those preceding reinforcement are present.
- In discrimination, responses are given in the presence of discriminative stimuli associated with reinforcement and withheld in the presence of stimuli associated with nonreinforcement.

What does punishment do to behavior?

- Punishment decreases response frequency.
- Punishment occurs when a response is followed by the onset of an aversive event or by the removal of a positive event (response cost).
- Punishment is most effective when it is immediate, consistent, and intense.

- Although severe punishment can virtually eliminate a particular behavior, mild punishment usually only temporarily suppresses responding. Reinforcement must be used to make lasting changes in the behavior of a person or an animal.
- The undesirable side effects of punishment include the conditioning of fear to punishing agents and situations associated with punishment, the learning of escape and avoidance responses, and the encouragement of aggression.

What is cognitive learning?

- Cognitive learning involves higher mental processes, such as understanding, knowing, or anticipating.
- Even in relatively simple learning situations, animals and people seem to form cognitive maps (internal representations of relationships).
- In latent learning, learning remains hidden or unseen until a reward or incentive for performance is offered.
- Discovery learning emphasizes insight and understanding, in contrast to rote learning.

Does learning occur by imitation?

- Learning can occur by merely observing and imitating the actions of another person or by noting the consequences of the person's actions.
- Observational learning is influenced by the personal characteristics of the model and the success or failure of the model's behavior. Studies have shown that aggression is readily learned and released by modeling.
- Media characters can act as powerful models for observational learning. Media violence increases the likelihood of aggression by viewers.

How does conditioning apply to everyday problems?

- By applying operant conditioning principles, it is possible to change or manage your own behavior.
- When managing behavior, self-reinforcement, self-recording, feedback, and behavioral contracting are all helpful.
- Four strategies that can help change bad habits are reinforcing alternative responses, promoting extinction, breaking response chains, and avoiding antecedent cues.

Web Resources

For an up-to-date list of direct links to interesting sites, including those listed here, visit the student companion site for this book at www.cengage.com/psychology/coon

Classical Conditioning Experiment Try this demonstration of classical conditioning.

Clicker Training for Animals One approach to using operant conditioning to train animals.

Ten Reasons Not to Hit Your Kids Read more about the limitations of spanking.

Guidelines for Using Time Out with Children and Preteens Read about the use of response cost as an effective form of punishment.

Psychological Self-Tools An online self-help book.

Interactive Learning

PSYCHOLOGY: A JOURNEY BOOK COMPANION WEBSITE
WWW.CENGAGE.COM/PSYCHOLOGY/COON
Visit your book companion website, where you will find flash cards, practice quizzes, web links, and more to help you study.

JUST WHAT YOU NEED TO KNOW NOW!
Spend time on what you need to master rather than on information you already have learned. Take a pretest for this chapter, and CengageNOW will generate a personalized study plan based on your results. The study plan will identify the topics you need to review and direct you to online resources to help you master those topics. You can then take a posttest to help you determine the concepts you have mastered and what you will need to work on. Try it out! Go to www.cengage.com/login to sign in with an access code or to purchase access to this product.

test your knowledge

Conditioning and Learning

For additional review, get more practice with *CengageNOW, WebTutor,* the *Practice Quizzes,* and/or the printed *Study Guide* available with this book.

1. Classical and operant conditioning can be distinguished by paying attention to which aspects of a response?
   a. associative and cognitive
   b. neutral stimuli and rewards
   c. antecedents and consequences
   d. acquisition and spontaneous recovery

2. You once got sick on a roller coaster. Now the sight of a roller coaster makes you feel queasy. Apparently, the sight of a roller coaster is a _____ and your queasiness is a _____.
   a. CR, CS
   b. CS, CR
   c. consequence, neutral stimulus
   d. reflex, CS

3. According to the informational view, classical conditioning creates new
   a. expectancies
   b. unconditioned responses
   c. unconditioned stimuli
   d. generalizations

4. After you have extinguished a conditioned response, it may recur because of
   a. removing reinforcement
   b. stimulus generalization
   c. spontaneous recovery
   d. following the CS with a US

5. At least some phobias can be thought of as
   a. NS-CR connections
   b. desensitization gradients
   c. extinction responses
   d. CERs

6. Conditioned fears respond to a therapy called
   a. desensitization
   b. CER
   c. spontaneous recovery
   d. conditioning

7. Mary watched her brother fall off a bike and hurt himself. Now she is afraid to ride her bike. Mary's fear is a result of
   a. stimulus discrimination
   b. vicarious conditioning
   c. spontaneous recovery
   d. higher order conditioning

8. The law of effect defines the role of _____ in learning.
   a. antecedent stimuli
   b. stimulus generalization
   c. operant reinforcers
   d. stimulus approximations

9. Operant reinforcement works best when it is
   a. delayed
   b. an antecedent
   c. response contingent
   d. aversive

10. Negative reinforcement _____ responding.
   a. increases
   b. decreases
   c. reverses
   d. extinguishes

11. Response cost is one form of
   a. discrimination conditioning
   b. generalization
   c. higher order conditioning
   d. punishment

12. Tokens are
   a. primary reinforcers
   b. secondary reinforcers
   c. social reinforcers
   d. a form of feedback

13. Programmed instruction presents information in small amounts, gives immediate practice, and provides _____ feedback to learners.
   a. negative
   b. continuous
   c. positive
   d. delayed

14. Studies have shown that animals are _____ to the passage of time.
   a. insensitive
   b. oblivious
   c. sensitive
   d. somewhat responsive

15. The "sniffer" dogs that locate drugs and explosives at airports learn to identify contraband through _____ _____ training.
   a. classical extinction
   b. classical desensitization
   c. vicarious feedback
   d. operant discrimination

16. Punishment tends to encourage escape learning, avoidance learning, and
   a. rapid extinction
   b. aggression
   c. correct responses
   d. the partial reinforcement effect

17. Discovery learning is often superior to its opposite:
   a. rote learning
   b. negative reinforcement
   c. observational learning
   d. cognitive learning

18. For observational learning to occur, the learner must pay attention to a model, remember what was done, and _____ the modeled behavior.
   a. reinforce
   b. reinvent
   c. reproduce
   d. repress

19. As a behavioral management strategy, self-recording applies _____ to change personal habits.
   a. vicarious conditioning
   b. feedback
   c. behavioral contracting
   d. the Premack principle

20. Bad habits can be altered by finding ways to remove, avoid, or delay the reinforcement that follows unwanted responses. This strategy is best described as
   a. seek alternate responses
   b. use operant extinction
   c. break up response chains
   d. narrow cues and antecedents

Answers 1. c 2. b 3. a 4. c 5. d 6. a 7. b 8. c 9. c 10. a 11. d 12. b 13. b 14. c 15. d 16. b 17. a 18. c 19. b 20. b

Memory

Journey into Psychology: Fuhgeddaboudit

That advice, offered New York City style, may not seem helpful at exam time. After all, the less you forget, the better, right? Not always.

Consider what A. J. thinks about her "perfect" memory: "My memory has ruled my life. . . . Whenever I see a date flash on the television (or anywhere else for that matter) I automatically go back to that day and remember where I was, what I was doing, what day it fell on and on and on and on and on. It is nonstop, uncontrollable and totally exhausting. . . . Most have called it a gift but I call it a burden.

I run my entire life through my head every day and it drives me crazy!!!" (Parker, Cahill, & McGaugh, 2006, pp. 35–36).

Another person with an amazing memory, known as Mr. S., even made a living as a professional memorizer, or *mnemonist* (Luria, 1968). He regularly wowed audiences with his ability to memorize, with equal ease, long strings of digits, meaningless consonants, mathematical formulas, and poems in foreign languages. Don't be too quick to envy Mr. S.'s abilities either. He remembered so much that

he couldn't separate important facts from trivia or facts from fantasy. His memory was so powerful that he had to devise ways to *forget*—such as writing information on a piece of paper and then burning it.

In a very real sense, who we are is determined by what we remember *and* what we forget (Behrend, Beike, & Lampinen, 2004). As you read this chapter on memory and forgetting, you'll almost certainly discover ways to improve your memory.

Stages of Memory—Do You Have a Mind Like a Sieve?

How does memory work?

Why are we always forgetting stuff? To understand forgetting, we first need to understand remembering. Do you remember what you had for breakfast this morning? Or any of what happened last month? Of course you do. But how is it possible for us to so easily travel back in time? Let's begin with a look at some basic memory concepts.

Many people think of memory as "a dusty storehouse of facts." In reality, human **memory** is an active system that receives, stores, organizes, alters, and recovers information (Baddeley, Eysenck, & Anderson, 2009). To be stored for a long time, information must pass through sensory memory, short-term memory, and long-term memory. These stages are summarized by the *Atkinson-Schiffrin model* of memory shown in ▶▶ Figure 7.1 (Atkinson & Schiffrin, 1968; Goldstein, 2008).

In some general ways, each of these three memory systems acts like a computer (▶▶ Figure 7.2). Incoming information is first **encoded,** or changed into a usable form. This step is like typing data into a computer. Next, information is **stored,** or held, in the memory system. Finally, information must be **retrieved,** or taken out of storage, to be useful. If you're going to remember all of the 9,856 new terms on your next psychology exam, you must successfully move them through sensory memory, short-term memory, and long-term memory. Let's trace the interesting series of memory events that must occur before you can pass that exam.

Sensory Memory

Let's say you sit down to memorize a few terms from this textbook. How will you remember them? Information is first encoded in **sensory memory,** which can hold an exact copy of what you see or hear, for a few seconds or less. We are normally unaware of the functioning of our sensory memories. For instance, look at a flower and then quickly close your eyes. If you are lucky, a fleeting visual image of the flower will persist. **Iconic** (eye-KON-ick) **memories** (sensory images) typically last for about one-half second (Keysers et al., 2005). Simi-

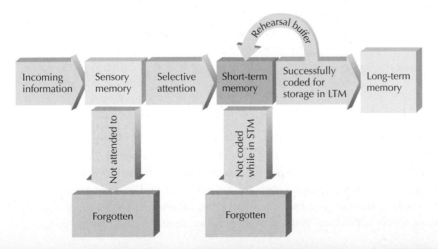

⬆ FIGURE 7.1 The Atkinson-Schiffrin model. Remembering is thought to involve at least three steps. Incoming information is first held for a second or two by sensory memory. Information selected by attention is then transferred to temporary storage in short-term memory (STM). If new information is not rapidly encoded, or rehearsed, it is forgotten. If it is transferred to long-term memory (LTM), it becomes relatively permanent, although retrieving it may be a problem. The preceding is a useful, but highly simplified, *model* of memory; it may not be literally true of what happens in the brain (Atkinson & Schiffrin, 1968; Goldstein, 2008).

Survey Questions

- How does memory work?
- What are the features of short-term memory?
- What are the features of long-term memory?
- How is memory measured?
- Why do we forget?
- How does the brain form and store memories?
- What are "photographic" memories?
- How can I improve my memory?
- Are there any tricks to help me with my memory?

Memory The mental system for receiving, encoding, storing, organizing, altering, and retrieving information.

Encoding Converting information into a form in which it will be retained in memory.

Storage Holding information in memory for later use.

Retrieval Recovering information from storage in memory.

Sensory memory The first stage of memory, which holds an exact record of incoming information for a few seconds or less.

▲ FIGURE 7.2 In some ways, a computer acts like a mechanical memory system. Both systems process information, and both allow encoding, storage, and retrieval of data.

larly, when you hear information, sensory memory stores it as an *echoic memory* for up to 2 seconds (Haenschel et al., 2005). (An **echoic memory** is a brief flurry of activity in the auditory system.) In general, sensory memory holds information just long enough to move it to the second memory system, short-term memory (Neath & Surprenant, 2003).

Short-Term Memory

Not everything we see or hear stays in memory. Imagine that a radio is playing in the background as you read this chapter. Will you remember what the announcer says, too? Probably not, because *selective attention* (focusing on a selected portion of sensory input) controls what information is retrieved from sensory memory and moved on to short-term memory. **Short-term memory (STM)** stores small amounts of information. We are consciously aware of short-term memories for a dozen seconds or so (Jonides et al., 2008). By paying attention to your textbook, you will place some psychological terms in short-term memory (while you ignore the voice on the radio saying, "Try Drizzle Diapers today").

How are short-term memories encoded? Short-term memories can be encoded as images. But more often they are encoded *phonetically* (by sound), especially in recalling words and letters (Page et al., 2007). If you are introduced to Tim at a party and you forget his name, you are more likely to call him by a name that sounds like Tim (Jim, Kim, or Slim, for instance), rather than a name that sounds different, such as Bob or Mike. On a psychology exam you may be lucky if you don't write "axon potential" instead of "action potential," or "depression" instead of "repression"!

Short-term memory briefly stores small amounts of information. When you dial a phone number or briefly remember a shopping list, you are using STM. Notice that unless you *rehearse* information (silently say it over and over to yourself), it is quickly "dumped" from STM and forever lost. Short-term memory prevents our minds from storing useless names, dates, telephone numbers, and other trivia.

As you may have noticed when dialing a telephone, STM is very sensitive to *interruption,* or *interference.* You've probably had something like this happen: Someone leaves a phone number on your answering machine. You repeat the number to yourself as you start to dial. Someone asks you a question. You answer, turn to the phone, and find that you have forgotten the number. Notice again that STM can handle only small amounts of information. It is very difficult to do more than one task at a time in STM (Miyake, 2001; Oberauer & Göthe, 2006).

Working Memory

Short-term memory is often used for more than just storing information. When STM is combined with other mental processes, it acts more like a sort of "mental scratchpad," or **working memory,** where we do much of our thinking. That is, working memory briefly holds the information we need when we are thinking and solving problems (Holmes & Adams, 2006). Whenever you read a book, do mental arithmetic, put together a puzzle, plan a meal, or follow directions, you are using working memory (Baddeley, 2003).

Long-Term Memory

If STM is so limited, how do we remember for longer periods? Information that is important or meaningful is transferred to **long-term memory (LTM),** which acts as a lasting storehouse for knowledge. LTM contains everything you know about the world—from aardvark to zebra, math to *Desperate Housewives,* facts to fantasy. Yet, there appears to be no danger of running out of room. LTM can store nearly limitless amounts of information. In fact, the more you know, the easier it becomes to add new information to memory. This is the

Iconic memory A mental image or visual representation.

Echoic memory A brief continuation of sensory activity in the auditory system after a sound is heard.

Short-term memory (STM) The memory system used to hold small amounts of information for relatively brief time periods.

Working memory Another name for short-term memory, especially when it is used for thinking and problem solving.

Long-term memory (LTM) The memory system used for relatively permanent storage of meaningful information.

reverse of what we would expect if LTM could be "filled up" (Goldstein, 2008). It is also one of many reasons for getting an education.

Are long-term memories also encoded as sounds? They can be. But typically, long-term memories are encoded on the basis of *meaning*, not sound. If you make an error in LTM, it will probably be related to meaning. For example, if you are trying to recall the phrase *test anxiety* for your psychology exam, you are more likely to mistakenly say *test nervousness* or *test worry* than *text anxiety* or *tent anxiety*.

If you can link information in STM to knowledge already stored in LTM, it gains meaning. This makes it easier to remember. If you can relate the definition of *test anxiety* to a memory of a time when you or a friend were nervous about taking a test, you are more likely to remember the definition. As another example, try to memorize this story:

> With hocked gems financing him, our hero bravely defied all scornful laughter. "Your eyes deceive," he had said. "An egg, not a table, correctly typifies this unexplored planet." Now three sturdy sisters sought proof. Forging along, days became weeks as many doubters spread fearful rumors about the edge. At last from nowhere welcome winged creatures appeared, signifying momentous success. (Adapted from Dooling & Lachman, 1971.)

This odd story emphasizes the impact that meaning has on memory. People given the title of the story were able to remember it far better than those not given a title. See if the title helps you as much as it did them: "Columbus Discovers America."

The Relationship Between STM and LTM

Although sensory memory is involved every time we store information, we are most likely to notice STM and LTM. To summarize their connection, picture short-term memory as a small desk at the front of a huge warehouse full of filing cabinets (LTM). As information enters the warehouse, it is first placed on the desk. Because the desk is small, it must be quickly cleared off to make room for new information. Unimportant items are simply tossed away. Meaningful or personally important information is placed in the files (LTM). When we want to use knowledge from LTM to answer a question, the information is returned to STM. Or, in our analogy, a folder is taken out of the files (LTM) and moved to the desk (STM), where it can be used.

Now that you have a general picture of memory, it is time to explore STM and LTM in more detail. But first, here's a chance to rehearse what you've learned.

study break
Memory Systems

RECITE

Match: **A.** Sensory memory   **B.** STM   **C.** LTM
1. _____ Information tends to be encoded phonetically
2. _____ Holds information for a few seconds or less
3. _____ Stores an iconic memory or echoic memory
4. _____ Permanent, unlimited capacity
5. _____ Temporarily holds small amounts of information
6. _____ Selective attention determines its contents
7. STM is improved by interruption, or interference, because attention is more focused at such times. T or F?

REFLECT
Critical Thinking
8. Why is sensory memory important to filmmakers?

Relate
Think of a time today when you used short-term memory (such as briefly remembering a phone number, a URL, or someone's name). How long did you retain the information? How did you encode it? How much do you remember now?

How is long-term memory helping you read this sentence? If the words weren't already stored in LTM, could you read at all? How else have you used LTM today?

ANSWERS

1. B 2. A 3. A 4. C 5. B 6. B 7. F 8. Without sensory memory, a movie would look like a series of still pictures. The split-second persistence of visual images helps blend one motion-picture frame into the next.

Short-Term Memory—Do You Know the Magic Number?

What are the features of short-term memory?

To make good use of your memory, it is valuable to know more about the quirks and characteristics of both STM and LTM. Let's start with a closer look at STM.

How much information can be held in short-term memory? For an answer, read the following numbers once. Then close the book and write as many as you can in the correct order.

> 8 5 1 7 4 9 3

This is called a digit-span test. It is a measure of attention and short-term memory. If you were able to correctly repeat seven digits, you have an average short-term memory. Now try to memorize the following list, again reading it only once.

> 7 1 8 3 5 4 2 9 1 6 3 4

This series was probably beyond your short-term memory capacity. Psychologist George Miller found that short-term memory is limited to the "magic number" seven (plus or minus two) **information bits** (Miller, 1956). A bit is a single meaningful "piece" of information, such as a digit. It is as if short-term memory has seven "slots" or "bins" into which separate items can be placed. Actually, a few people can remember up to nine bits, and for some types of information five bits is the limit. Thus, an *average* of seven information bits can be stored in short-term memory (Neath & Surprenant, 2003).

When all of the "slots" in STM are filled, there is no room for new information. Picture how this works at a party: Let's say your hostess begins introducing everyone who is there, "Chun, Dasia, Sandra, Roseanna, Cholik, Shawn, Kyrene. . . ." "Stop," you think to yourself. But she continues, "Nelia, Jay, Frank, Patty, Amit, Ricky." The hostess leaves, satisfied that you have met everyone. And you spend the evening talking with Chun, Dasia, and Ricky, the only people whose names you remember!

Chunking

Before we continue, try your short-term memory again, this time on letters. Read the following letters once, then look away and try to write them in the proper order.

> T V I B M U S N Y M C A

Notice that there are 12 letters, or "bits" of information. If you studied the letters one at a time, this should be beyond the 7-item limit of STM. However, you may have noticed that some of the letters can be grouped, or *chunked,* together. For example, you may have noticed that NY is the abbreviation for New York. If so, the two bits N and Y became one chunk. **Information chunks** are made up of bits of information grouped into larger units.

Does chunking make a difference? Yes. Chunking *recodes* (reorganizes) information into units that are already in LTM. In a classic experiment that used lists like this one, people remembered best when the letters were read as familiar meaningful chunks: TV, IBM, USN, YMCA (Bower & Springston, 1970). If you recoded the letters this way, you organized them into four *chunks* of information and probably remembered the entire list. If you didn't, go back and try it again; you'll notice a big difference.

Chunking suggests that STM holds about five to seven of whatever units we are using. A single chunk could be made up of numbers, letters, words, phrases, or familiar sentences. Picture STM as a small desk again. Through chunking, we combine several items into one "stack" of information. This allows us to place seven stacks on the desk, where before there was only room for seven separate items. While you are studying, try to find ways to link two,

Information bits Meaningful units of information, such as numbers, letters, words, or phrases.

Information chunks Information bits grouped into larger units.

three, or more separate facts or ideas into larger chunks, and your short-term memory will improve. In fact, some psychologists believe that STM may actually hold only four items, unless some chunking has occurred (Cowan, 2005; Jonides et al., 2008). The clear message is that creating information chunks is the key to making good use of your short-term memory (Gobet, 2005).

Rehearsing Information

How long are short-term memories stored? They disappear very rapidly. However, you can prolong a memory by silently repeating it, a process called **maintenance rehearsal.** In a sense, rehearsing information allows you to "hear" it many times, not just once (Nairne, 2002). You have probably used maintenance rehearsal to keep a phone number active in your mind while looking at your cell phone and dialing it.

Isn't saying stuff to yourself over and over also a way of studying? It *is* true that the more times a short-term memory is rehearsed, the greater its chances of being stored in LTM (Goldstein, 2008). This is *rote learning* (learning by simple repetition). But rote learning is not a very effective way to study.

Elaborative encoding, which makes information more meaningful, is a far better way to form lasting memories. Elaborative encoding links new information to memories that are already in LTM. When you are studying, you will remember more if you elaborate on the meaning of the information. As you read, try to reflect frequently. Ask yourself "why" questions, such as, "Why would that be true?" (Toyota & Kikuchi, 2005; Willoughby et al., 1997). Also, try to relate new ideas to your own experiences and knowledge (Hartlep & Forsyth, 2000). If you recognize this advice from *Psychology for Your Life—Self-Reflective Learning,* at the front of this book, good for you! (If not, do consider reading about *Self-Reflective Learning* if only to elaborate on your encoding of the idea of elaborative encoding.)

What if rehearsal is prevented, so a memory cannot be recycled or moved to LTM? Without maintenance rehearsal, STM storage is quite brief. In one experiment, subjects heard meaningless syllables like "xar," followed by a number like 67. As soon as subjects heard the number, they began counting backward by threes (to prevent them from repeating the syllable). After a delay of between 12 and 18 seconds, their memory for the syllables fell to zero (Peterson & Peterson, 1959). That's why if you are introduced to someone and that person's name slips out of STM, it is gone forever. To avoid embarrassment, pay careful attention to the name, repeat it to yourself several times, and try to use it in the next sentence or two—before you lose it (Neath & Surprenant, 2003).

▲ **FIGURE 7.3** Exposed cerebral cortex of a patient undergoing brain surgery. Numbers represent points that reportedly produced "memories" when electrically stimulated. A critical evaluation of such reports suggests that they are more like dreams than memories. This fact raises questions about claims that long-term memories are permanent. (From Penfield, 1958. Courtesy of the author and Charles C Thomas, Publisher, Springfield, Illinois.)

Maintenance rehearsal Silently repeating or mentally reviewing information to hold it in short-term memory.

Elaborative encoding Encoding that links new information with existing memories and knowledge.

Long-Term Memory—A Blast from the Past

What are the features of long-term memory?

An electrode touched the patient's brain. Immediately she said, "Yes, sir, I think I heard a mother calling her little boy somewhere. It seemed to be something happening years ago. It was somebody in the neighborhood where I live." A short time later the electrode was applied to the same spot. Again the patient said, "Yes, I hear the same familiar sounds, it seems to be a woman calling, the same lady" (Penfield, 1958). A woman made these statements while she was undergoing brain surgery. There are no pain receptors in the brain, so the patient was awake as her brain was electrically stimulated (▶▶ Figure 7.3). When activated, some brain areas seemed to produce vivid memories of long-forgotten events.

Permanence

Are all our experiences permanently recorded in memory? Results like those described led neurosurgeon Wilder Penfield to claim that the brain records the past like a "strip of movie film, complete with sound track" (Penfield, 1957). But as you already know, this is an exaggeration, since many events never get past sensory or short-term memory. Also, brain stimulation produces memory-like experiences in only about 3 percent of cases. Most reports resemble dreams more than memories, and many are clearly imaginary. Memory experts now believe that long-term memories are only *relatively* permanent (Goldstein, 2008).

Try It Yourself: How's Your Memory?
To better appreciate the next topic, pause for a moment and read the words you see here. Read through the list once. Then continue reading the next section of this chapter.

> bed dream blanket doze pillow nap snore mattress alarm
> clock rest slumber nod sheet bunk cot cradle groggy

Constructing Memories

There's another reason for doubting that all our experiences are permanently recorded. As new long-term memories are stored, older memories are often updated, changed, lost, or *revised* (Baddeley, Eysenck, & Anderson, 2009). To illustrate this point, Elizabeth Loftus and John Palmer (1974) showed people a filmed automobile accident. Afterward, some participants were asked to estimate how fast the cars were going when they "smashed" into each other. For others, the words "bumped," "contacted," or "hit" replaced "smashed." One week later, each person was asked, "Did you see any broken glass?" Those asked earlier about the cars that "smashed" into each other were more likely to say yes. (No broken glass was shown in the film.) The new information ("smashed") was included in memories and altered them.

Try It Yourself: Old or New?
Now, without looking back to the list of words you read a few minutes ago, see if you can tell which of the following are "old" words (items from the list you read) and which are "new" words (items that weren't on the list). Mark each of the following words as old or new:

> sofa sleep lamp kitchen

Updating memories is called **constructive processing.** Gaps in memory, which are common, may be filled in by logic, guessing, or new information (Schacter, Norman, & Koutstaal, 1998). Indeed, it is possible to have "memories" for things that never happened (such as remembering broken glass at an accident when there was none) (Loftus, 2003a, 2003b). In one study, people who had visited a Disney resort were shown several fake ads for Disney that featured Bugs Bunny. Later, about 16 percent of the people who saw these fake ads claimed that they had met Bugs at Disneyland. This is impossible, of course, because Bugs Bunny is a Warner Brothers character that would never be found at Disneyland (Braun, Ellis, & Loftus, 2002).

So constructive processing could be used to deliberately manipulate memory? Bingo. According to one theory, advertisers do it all the time (See "Do You Like Jam with Your Memory?").

Try It Yourself: And Now, the Results
Return now and look at the labels you wrote on the "old or new" word list. Contrary to what you may think you "remembered," all of the listed words are "new." None was on the original list!

If you thought you "remembered" that "sleep" was on the original list, you had a false memory. The word *sleep* is associated with most of the words on the original list, which creates a strong impression that you saw it before (Roediger & McDermott, 1995).

As the preceding examples show, thoughts, inferences, and mental associations may be mistaken for true memories (Loftus, 2003a, 2003b). People in Elizabeth Loftus's experi-

Constructive processing Reorganizing or updating memories on the basis of logic, reasoning, or the addition of new information.

Do You Like Jam with Your Memory?

Have you ever wondered why well-known companies, which already sell huge quantities of familiar products (such as soft drinks or beer), continue to advertise as heavily as they do? If you believe that the point of the advertising is to familiarize people with a product or to inform them about it, this *is* a mystery. But if you think about the constructive nature of memory, the mystery is solved. According to economist Jesse Shapiro (2006), the intent of much advertising is to "jam" your memory with positive impressions of a product.

How does "memory jamming" work? How many times have you had a bottle or can of your favorite beer or soft drink? And how many commercials for those beverages have you watched? Every extra commercial adds one more positive memory of the beverage to your long-term memory. Here's a typical commercial: Boy goes to cool party, sees a hot girl, flashes favorite beer, gets the girl. (Yes, beer commercials mainly target young men.) Because we cannot always easily tell which recollection is fact and which is fiction, storing enough of these commercials can eventually create "memories" that never happened. For example, you might remember that you enjoy drinking a particular beverage more than you actually do in reality.

According to Shapiro (2006), the more positive fictional commercials we see, the less likely we are to remember an actual negative experience with a product. In effect, the positive, fictional memories "jam," or block, our ability to remember actual negative memories when deciding whether to buy a product. Kathryn Braun-LaTour and Michael LaTour (2004) add that long-term advertising campaigns create a "brand" memory that can be remarkably strong. This appears to be especially true when the ads are first viewed in early childhood. So perhaps you have been having jam with your memories ever since you were a baby.

---

ments who had these *pseudo-memories* (false memories) were often quite upset to learn they had given false "testimony" (Loftus & Ketcham, 1994).

False long-term memories are a common problem in police work. For example, a witness may select a photo of a suspect from police files or see a photo in the news. Later, the witness identifies the suspect in a lineup or in court. Did the witness really remember the suspect from the scene of the crime? Or was it from the more recently seen photograph?

Does new information "overwrite" existing memories? No, the real problem is that we often can't remember the *source* of a memory (Simons et al., 2004). This can lead witnesses to "remember" a face that they actually saw somewhere other than the crime scene (Ruva, McEvoy, & Bryant, 2007). Many tragic cases of mistaken identity occur this way. One famous example involved memory expert Donald Thomson. After appearing live on Australian television, he was accused of rape. It turns out that the victim was watching him on TV when the actual rapist broke into her apartment (Schacter, 1996, 2001). She correctly remembered his face but attributed it to the wrong source.

Is there any way to avoid such problems? Forensic psychologists have tried a variety of techniques to help improve the memory of witnesses. "Telling Wrong from Right in Forensic Memory" examines research on this important question.

To summarize, forming and using long-term memories is an active, creative, highly personal process. Our memories are colored by emotions, judgments, and quirks of personality. If you and a friend were joined at the hip and you went through life side-by-side, you would still have different memories. What we remember depends on what we pay attention to, what we regard as meaningful or important, and what we feel strongly about (Schacter, 2000).

Eyewitness memories are notoriously inaccurate. By the time witnesses are asked to testify in court, information they learned after an incident may blend into their original memories.

Organizing Memories

Long-term memory stores huge amounts of information during a lifetime. How are we able to quickly find specific memories? The answer is that each person's "memory index" is highly organized.

Do you mean that information is arranged alphabetically, as in a dictionary? Not a chance! If we ask you to name a black and white animal that lives on ice, is related to a chicken, and cannot fly, you don't have to go from aardvark to zebra to find the answer. You will probably think of only black-and-white birds living in the Antarctic. *Voilá,* the answer is a penguin.

Imagine that you are a forensic psychologist, investigating a crime. Unfortunately, your witness can't remember much of what happened. As a "memory detective," what can you do to help?

Could hypnosis improve the witness's memory? It might seem so. In one California case, 26 children were abducted from a school bus and held captive for ransom. Under hypnosis, the bus driver recalled the license plate number of the kidnappers' van. This memory helped break the case. Such successes seem to imply that hypnosis can improve memory. But does it?

Research has shown that hypnosis increases false memories more than it does true ones. Eighty percent of the new memories produced by hypnotized subjects in one classic experiment were *incorrect* (Dywan & Bowers, 1983). This is in part because a hypnotized person is more likely than normal to use imagination to fill in gaps in memory. Also, if a questioner asks misleading or suggestive questions, hypnotized persons tend to weave the information into their memories (Scoboria et al., 2002). To make matters worse, even when a memory is completely false, the

hypnotized person's confidence in it can be unshakable (Burgess & Kirsch, 1999).

Thus, hypnosis sometimes uncovers more information, as it did with the bus driver (Schreiber & Schreiber, 1999). However, in the absence of corroborating evidence, there is no sure way to tell which of these memories are false and which are true (Newman & Thompson, 2001).

Is there a better way to improve eyewitness memory? To help police detectives, R. Edward Geiselman and Ron Fisher created the **cognitive interview,** a technique for jogging the memory of eyewitnesses (Fisher & Geiselman, 1987). The key to this approach is recreating the crime scene. Witnesses revisit the scene in their imaginations or in person. That way, aspects of the crime scene, such as sounds, smells, and objects, provide helpful retrieval cues (stimuli associated with a memory). Back in the context of the crime, the witness is encouraged to recall events in different orders and from different viewpoints. Every new memory, no matter how trivial it may seem, can serve as a cue to trigger the retrieval of yet more memories. (Later in this chapter, we will see why such cues are so effective for jogging memories.)

When used properly, the cognitive interview produces 35 percent more correct information than standard questioning (Davis, McMahon, &

Some police detectives, following the advice of psychologists, recreate crime scenes to help witnesses remember what they saw. Typically, people return to the scene at the time of day the crime occurred. They are also asked to wear the same clothing they wore and go through the same motions as they did before the crime. With so many memory cues available, witnesses sometimes remember key items of information they hadn't recalled before.

Greenwood, 2005; Geiselman et al., 1986). This improvement comes without adding to the number of false memories elicited, as occurs with hypnosis. The result is a procedure that is more effective in actual police work and in different cultures (Ginet & Py, 2001; Kebbell & Wagstaff, 1998; Stein & Memon, 2006).

Information in LTM may be arranged according to rules, images, categories, symbols, similarity, formal meaning, or personal meaning (Baddeley, Eysenck, & Anderson, 2009). In recent years, psychologists have begun to develop a picture of the *structure,* or organization, of memories. *Memory structure* refers to the pattern of associations among items of information. For example, assume that you are given two statements, to which you must answer yes or no: (1) *A canary is an animal.* (2) *A canary is a bird.* Which do you answer more quickly? Most people can say that *A canary is a bird* faster than they can recognize that *A canary is an animal* (Collins & Quillian, 1969).

Why should this be so? Psychologists believe that a **network model** of memory explains why. According to this view, LTM is organized as a network of linked ideas (▶▶ Figure 7.4). When ideas are "farther" apart, it takes a longer chain of associations to connect them. The more two items are separated, the longer it takes to answer. In terms of information links, *canary* is probably "close" to *bird* in your "memory files." *Animal* and *canary* are farther apart. Remember, though, this has nothing to do with alphabetical order. We are talking about a system of linked meanings.

Redintegration

Cognitive interview Use of various cues and strategies to improve the memory of eyewitnesses.

Network model A model of memory that views it as an organized system of linked information.

Networks of associated memories may also help explain a common experience: Imagine finding a picture taken on your sixth birthday or tenth Christmas. As you look at the photo, one memory leads to another, which leads to another, and another. Soon you have unleashed a flood of seemingly forgotten details. This process is called *redintegration* (ruh-DIN-tuh-GRAY-shun).

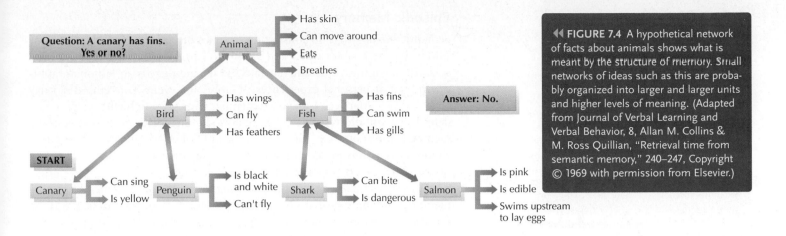

Question: A canary has fins. Yes or no?

Animal
- Has skin
- Can move around
- Eats
- Breathes

Answer: No.

Bird
- Has wings
- Can fly
- Has feathers

Fish
- Has fins
- Can swim
- Has gills

START

Canary
- Can sing
- Is yellow

Penguin
- Is black and white
- Can't fly

Shark
- Can bite
- Is dangerous

Salmon
- Is pink
- Is edible
- Swims upstream to lay eggs

FIGURE 7.4 A hypothetical network of facts about animals shows what is meant by the structure of memory. Small networks of ideas such as this are probably organized into larger and larger units and higher levels of meaning. (Adapted from Journal of Verbal Learning and Verbal Behavior, 8, Allan M. Collins & M. Ross Quillian, "Retrieval time from semantic memory," 240–247, Copyright © 1969 with permission from Elsevier.)

Redintegration seems to spread through the "branches" of memory networks. The key idea in redintegration is that one memory serves as a cue to trigger another. As a result, an entire past experience may be reconstructed from one small recollection. Many people find that redintegration can be touched off by distinctive odors from the past—from a farm visited in childhood, Grandma's kitchen, the seashore, the perfume or aftershave of a former lover, and so on (Willander & Larsson, 2006).

Skill Memory and Fact Memory

How many types of long-term memory are there? It is becoming clear that more than one type of long-term memory exists. For example, a curious thing happens to many people who develop amnesia. Amnesic patients may be unable to learn a telephone number, an address, or a person's name. Yet the same patients can learn to solve complex puzzles in a normal amount of time (Cavaco et al., 2004) (▶▶ Figure 7.5). These and other observations have led many psychologists to conclude that long-term memories fall into at least two categories. One is called *procedural memory* (or skill memory). The other is *declarative memory* (also sometimes called fact memory).

Skills — *Tieing shoes*

Procedural memory includes basic conditioned responses and learned actions, such as those involved in typing, driving, or swinging a golf club. Memories such as these can be fully expressed only as actions (or "know-how"). It is likely that skill memories register in "lower" brain areas, especially the cerebellum. They represent the more basic "automatic" elements of conditioning, learning, and memory (Hermann et al., 2004).

Facts

Declarative memory stores specific factual information, such as names, faces, words, dates, and ideas. Declarative memories are expressed as words or symbols. For example, knowing that *Peter* Jackson directed the *Lord of the Rings* trilogy, while *Randy* Jackson judges on *American Idol* is a declarative memory. This is the type of memory that a person with amnesia lacks and that most of us take for granted. Declarative memory can be further divided into *semantic memory* and *episodic memory* (Tulving, 2002).

Semantic Memory

Much of our basic factual knowledge about the world is almost totally immune to forgetting. The names of objects, the days of the week or months of the year, simple math skills, the seasons, words and language, and other general facts are all quite lasting. Such impersonal facts make up a part of LTM called **semantic memory,** which serves as a mental dictionary or encyclopedia of basic knowledge.

FIGURE 7.5 The tower puzzle. In this puzzle, all the colored disks must be moved to another post, without ever placing a larger disk on a smaller one. Only one disk may be moved at a time, and a disk must always be moved from one post to another (it cannot be held aside). An amnesic patient learned to solve the puzzle in 31 moves, the minimum possible. Even so, each time he began, he protested that he did not remember ever solving the puzzle before and that he did not know how to begin. Evidence like this suggests that memories for skills are distinct from memories for facts.

Redintegration Process by which memories are reconstructed or expanded by starting with one memory and then following chains of association to other, related memories.

Procedural memory Long-term memories of conditioned responses and learned skills.

Declarative memory That part of long-term memory containing specific factual information.

Semantic memory A subpart of declarative memory that records impersonal knowledge about the world.

FIGURE 7.6 In the model shown here, long-term memory is divided into procedural memory (learned actions and skills) and declarative memory (stored facts). Declarative memories can be either semantic (impersonal knowledge) or episodic (personal experiences associated with specific times and places).

Episodic memory A subpart of declarative memory that records personal experiences that are linked with specific times and places.

Episodic Memory

Semantic memory has no connection to times or places. It would be rare, for instance, to remember when and where you first learned the names of the seasons. In contrast, **episodic** (ep-ih-SOD-ik) **memory** is an "autobiographical" record of personal experiences. It stores life events (or "episodes") day after day, year after year. Can you remember your seventh birthday? Your first date? What you did yesterday? All are episodic memories. Note that episodic memories are about the "what," "where," and "when" of our lives. More than simply storing information, they allow us to mentally travel back in time and *re-experience* events (Tulving, 2002).

Are episodic memories as lasting as semantic memories? In general, episodic memories are more easily forgotten than semantic memories. In fact, it is the forgetting of episodic information that results in the formation of semantic memories. At first, you remembered when and where you were when you learned the names of the seasons (Mommy, Mommy, guess what I learned in kindergarten today!). Over time you forgot the episodic details but will likely remember the names for the rest of your life.

How Many Types of Memory?

In answer to the question posed at the beginning of this section, it is very likely that three kinds of long-term memories exist: procedural memory and two types of declarative memory, semantic and episodic (▶▶ Figure 7.6).

Measuring Memory—The Answer Is on the Tip of My Tongue

How is memory measured?

You either remember something or you don't, right? Wrong. Partial memories are common. For instance, have you ever tried to remember something only to find yourself stuck in a **tip-of-the-tongue (TOT) state?** This is the feeling that a memory is available but not quite retrievable (Schwartz, 2002). It is as if an answer or a memory is just out of reach—on the "tip of your tongue."

In a classic TOT study, university students read the definitions of words such as *sextant, sampan,* and *ambergris.* Students who "drew a blank" and couldn't name a defined word were asked to give any other information they could. Often, they could guess the first and last letter and the number of syllables of the word they were seeking. They also gave words that sounded like or meant the same thing as the defined word (Brown & McNeill, 1966).

Closely related to the TOT state is the fact that people can often tell beforehand if they are likely to remember something. This is called the *feeling of knowing* (Widner, Otani, & Winkelman, 2005). Feeling-of-knowing reactions are easy to observe on TV game shows, where they occur just before contestants are allowed to answer.

Déjà vu is the illusion that you have already experienced a new situation that you are actually seeing for the first time. Most likely, saying to yourself, "I feel like I've seen it before" is another example of partial retrieval. Déjà vu occurs when a new experience triggers vague memories of a past experience, without yielding any details (Brown, 2004). The new experience seems familiar even though the older memory is too weak to rise to the level of awareness.

Because memory is not an all-or-nothing event, there are several ways of measuring it. Three commonly used methods of measuring memory are *recall, recognition,* and *relearning.* Let's see how they differ.

Recalling Information

What is the name of the first song on your favorite CD? Who won the World Series last year? Who wrote *Hamlet?* If you can answer these questions, you are using **recall,** a direct retrieval of facts or information. Tests of recall often require *verbatim* (word-for-word) memory. If you study a poem until you can recite it without looking at it, you are recalling it. If you complete a fill-in-the-blank question, you are using recall. When you answer an essay question by providing facts and ideas, you are also using recall, even though you didn't learn your essay verbatim.

The order in which information is memorized has an interesting effect on recall. To experience it, try to memorize the following list, reading it only once:

> bread, apples, soda, ham, cookies, rice, lettuce, beets,
> mustard, cheese, oranges, ice cream, crackers, flour, eggs

If you are like most people, it will be hardest for you to recall items from the middle of the list. ▶▶ Figure 7.7 shows the results of a similar test. Notice that most errors occur with middle items of an ordered list. This is the **serial position effect.** You can remember the last items on a list because they are still in STM. The first items are also remembered well because they entered an "empty" short-term memory. This allows you to rehearse the items so they move into long-term memory (Addis & Kahana, 2004). The middle items are neither held in short-term memory nor moved to long-term memory, so they are often lost.

Recognizing Information

Try to write down everything you can remember learning from a class you took last year. If you actually did this, you might conclude that you had learned very little. However, a more sensitive test based on recognition could be used. In **recognition memory,** previ-

Tip-of-the-tongue (TOT) state The feeling that a memory is available but not quite retrievable.

Recall To supply or reproduce memorized information with a minimum of external cues.

Serial position effect The tendency to make the most errors in remembering the middle items of an ordered list.

Recognition memory An ability to correctly identify previously learned information.

FIGURE 7.7 The serial position effect. The graph shows the percentage of subjects correctly recalling each item in a 15-item list. Recall is best for the first and last items. (Data from Craik, 1970.)

ously learned material is correctly identified. For instance, you could take a multiple-choice test on facts and ideas from the course. Because you would have to recognize only correct answers, you would probably find that you had learned a lot.

Recognition memory can be amazingly accurate for pictures and photographs (Whitehouse, Maybery, & Durkin, 2006). In one classic study, people viewed 2,560 photographs at a rate of one every 10 seconds. Each person was then shown 280 pairs of photographs. Each pair included an "old" picture (from the first set of photos) and a similar "new" image. Subjects could tell 85 to 95 percent of the time which photograph they had seen before (Haber, 1970). This finding may explain why we rarely need to see our friends' vacation photos more than once.

Recognition is usually superior to recall. That's why people so often say, "I may forget a name, but I never forget a face." (You can't recall the name but recognize the face.) That's also why police departments use photographs or a lineup to identify criminal suspects. Witnesses who disagree when they try to recall a suspect's height, weight, age, or eye color often agree completely when they merely need to recognize the person.

Is recognition always superior? It depends greatly on the kind of *distractors* used (Flowe & Ebbese, 2007). These are false items included with an item to be recognized. If distractors are very similar to the correct item, memory may be poor. A reverse problem occurs when only one choice looks like it could be correct. This can produce a *false positive,* or false sense of recognition, like the false memory you had earlier when you thought you remembered seeing the word *sleep.*

Police lineups make use of the sensitivity of recognition memory. However, unless great care is taken, false identifications are still possible (Wells, 2001).

Many hundreds of people have been put in jail on the basis of mistaken eyewitness memories (Wells, Memon, & Penrod, 2006). There have been instances in which witnesses described a criminal as black, tall, or young. Then a lineup was held in which a suspect was the only African American among whites, the only tall suspect, or the only young person. In such cases a false identification is very likely. To avoid tragic mistakes, it's better to have *all* the distractors look like the person witnesses described. Also, to reduce false positives, witnesses should be warned that the culprit *may not be present.* It's also better to show witnesses one photo at a time (a sequential lineup). For each photo, the witness must decide whether the person is the culprit before another photo is shown (Wells, 2001; Wells & Olsen, 2003).

Relearning Information

In another classic experiment, a psychologist read a short passage in Greek to his son every day when the boy was between 15 months and 3 years of age. At age 8, the boy was asked if he remembered the Greek passage. He showed no evidence of recall. He was then shown selections from the passage he heard and selections from other Greek passages. Could he recognize the one he heard as an infant? "It's all Greek to me!" he said, indicating a lack of recognition (and drawing a frown from everyone in the room).

Had the psychologist stopped, he might have concluded that no memory of the Greek remained. However, the child was then asked to memorize the original quotation and others of equal difficulty. This time his earlier learning became evident. The boy memorized the passage he had heard in childhood 25 percent faster than the others (Burtt, 1941). As this experiment suggests, **relearning** is typically the most sensitive measure of memory.

When a person is tested by relearning, how do we know a memory still exists? As with the boy described, relearning is measured by a *savings score* (the amount of time saved when relearning information). Let's say it takes you 1 hour to memorize all the names in a tele-

Relearning Learning again something that was previously learned. Used to measure memory of prior learning.

phone book. (It's a small town.) Two years later you relearn them in 45 minutes. Because you "saved" 15 minutes, your savings score would be 25 percent (15 divided by 60 times 100). Savings of this type are a good reason for studying a wide range of subjects. It may seem that learning algebra, history, or a foreign language is wasted if you don't use the knowledge immediately. But when you do need such information, you will be able to relearn it quickly.

Explicit and Implicit Memories

Who were the last three presidents of the United States? What did you have for breakfast today? What is the title of Kanye West's latest album? Explicit memory is used in answering each of these questions. **Explicit memories** are past experiences that are consciously brought to mind. Recall, recognition, and the tests you take in school rely on explicit memories.

In contrast, **implicit memories** lie outside of awareness (Roediger & Amir, 2005). That is, we are not aware that a memory exists. For example, if you know how to type, it is apparent that you know where the letters are on the keyboard. But how many typists could correctly label blank keys in a drawing of a keyboard? Many people find that they cannot directly remember such information, even though they "know" it. Nevertheless, implicit memories—such as unconsciously knowing where the letters are on a keyboard—greatly influence our behavior (Neath & Surprenant, 2003).

Can you label the letter keys on this blank keyboard? If you can, you probably used implicit memory to do it.

Priming

How is it possible to show that a memory exists if it lies outside of awareness? Psychologists first noticed implicit memory while studying memory loss caused by brain injuries. Let's say, for example, that a patient is shown a list of common words, such as *chair, tree, lamp, table,* and so on. Later, the patient fails to recall any words from the list.

Now, instead of asking the patient to explicitly recall the list, we could "prime" his memory by giving him the first two letters of each word. "Just say whatever word comes to mind that begins with these letters," we tell him. Of course, many words could be made from each pair of letters. For example, the first item (from "chair") would be the letters CH. The patient could say "child," "chalk," "chain," "check," or many other words. Instead, he says "chair," a word from the original list. The patient is not aware that he is remembering the list, but as he gives a word for each letter pair, almost all are from the list. Apparently, the letters **primed** (activated) hidden memories, which then influenced his answers.

Similar effects have been found for people with normal memories. As the preceding example implies, implicit memories are often revealed by giving a person limited cues, such as the first letter of words or partial drawings of objects. Typically, the person believes that he or she is just saying whatever comes to mind. Nevertheless, information previously seen or heard affects his or her answers (Rueckl & Galantucci, 2005).

Explicit memory A memory that a person is aware of having; a memory that is consciously retrieved.

Implicit memory A memory that a person does not know exists; a memory that is retrieved unconsciously.

Priming Facilitating the retrieval of an implicit memory by using cues to activate hidden memories.

RECITE

1. Four techniques for measuring or demonstrating memory are
_____   _____

_____   _____

2. Essay tests require _____ of facts or ideas.
3. As a measure of memory, a savings score is associated with
   a. recognition   b. priming
   c. relearning   d. reconstruction
4. The two most sensitive tests of memory are
   a. recall and   b. recall and
      redintegration   relearning
   c. recognition   d. recognition
      and relearning   and digit-span
5. Priming is used to reveal which type of memories?
   a. explicit   b. sensory
   c. skill   d. implicit

REFLECT
Critical Thinking

6. When asked to explain why they may have failed to recall some information, people often claim it must be because the information is no longer in their memory. Why does the existence of implicit memories challenge this explanation?

Relate

Have you experienced a TOT state recently? Were you able to retrieve the word you were searching for? If not, what could you remember about it?

Do you prefer tests based primarily on recall or recognition? Have you observed a savings effect while relearning information you studied in the past (such as in high school)?

Can you think of things you do that are based on implicit memories? For instance, how do you know which way to turn various handles in your house, apartment, or dorm? Do you have to explicitly think, "Turn it to the right" before you act?

What kinds of information are you good at remembering? Why do you think your memory is better for those topics?

ANSWERS

1. recall, recognition, relearning, priming 2. recall 3. c 4. c 5. d 6. It is possible to have an implicit memory that cannot be consciously recalled. Memories like these (*available*) show that failing to recall something does not guarantee it is no longer in memory even though they are not consciously *accessible* (Allik, 2000).

Forgetting in LTM—Why We, Uh, Let's See; Why We, Uh. . . . Forget!

Why do we forget?

We don't expect sensory memories and short-term memories to remain with us for long. But when you deliberately encode and store information in long-term memory you want it to stay there (after all, it's supposed to be *long*-term). For example, when you study for an exam, you count on your long-term memory to retain the information at least until you take your exam.

Why do we forget long-term memories? The more you know about how we "lose" memories, the better you will be able to hang on to them. Most forgetting tends to occur immediately after memorization. Herman Ebbinghaus (1885) famously tested his own memory at various intervals after learning. To be sure he would not be swayed by prior learning, he memorized *nonsense syllables*. These are meaningless three-letter words such as "cef," "wol," and "gex." The importance of using meaningless words is shown by the fact that "Vel," "Fab," and "Duz" are no longer used on memory tests. People who recognize these words as detergent names find them very easy to remember. This is another reminder that relating new information to what you already know can improve memory.

By waiting various lengths of time before testing himself, Ebbinghaus plotted a **curve of forgetting.** This graph shows the amount of information remembered after varying lengths of time (▶▶ Figure 7.8). Notice that forgetting is rapid at first and is then followed by a slow decline (Hintzman, 2005). The same applies to meaningful information, but the forgetting curve is stretched over a longer time. As you might expect, recent events are recalled more accurately than those from the remote past (O'Connor et al., 2000). Thus, you are more likely to remember that *Slumdog Millionaire* won the "Best Picture" Academy Award for 2008 than you are to remember that *Million Dollar Baby* won it for 2004.

Curve of forgetting A graph that shows the amount of memorized information remembered after varying lengths of time.

As a student, you should note that a short delay between studying and taking a test minimizes forgetting. However, this is no reason for cramming. Most students make the error of *only* cramming. If you cram, you don't have to remember for very long, but you may not learn enough in the first place. If you use short, daily study sessions and review intensely before a test, you will get the benefit of good preparation and a minimum time lapse.

The Ebbinghaus curve shows less than 30 percent remembered after only 2 days have passed. Is forgetting really that rapid? No, not always. Meaningful information is not lost nearly as quickly as nonsense syllables. After 3 years, students who took a university psychology course had forgotten about 30 percent of the facts they learned. After that, little more forgetting occurred (Conway, Cohen, & Stanhope, 1992). Actually, as learning grows stronger, some knowledge may become nearly permanent (Berntsen & Thomsen, 2005).

While the Ebbinghaus curve gives a general picture of forgetting from long-term memory, it doesn't explain it. For explanations we must search further. (Before we do, look at "Card Magic!", where you will find an interesting demonstration.) Earlier in this chapter we pointed out that three processes are involved in successfully remembering: encoding, storage, and retrieval. Conversely, forgetting can be due to the failure of any one of these three processes.

When Encoding Fails

Can you accurately draw and label a U.S. penny? In an interesting experiment, Ray Nickerson and Marilyn Adams (1979) asked a large group of students to draw a penny. Few could. In fact, few could even recognize a drawing of a real penny among fakes. (Can you?) (See ▶▶ Figure 7.11.)

The most obvious reason for forgetting is also the most commonly overlooked. Obviously, few of us ever encode the details of a penny. Similarly, we may not encode the details of what we are reading in a book or studying for an exam. In such cases, we "forget" because of **encoding failure**. That is, a memory was never formed in the first place (the card trick you just saw is another example). If you are bothered by frequent forgetting or absent-mindedness, it is wise to ask yourself, "Have I been encoding the information in the first place?" (Schacter, 2001). By the way, if you like to study while watching television or instant messaging, beware. Dividing your attention between studying and other activities can also lead to encoding failure (Naveh-Benjamin, Guez, & Sorek, 2007).

Actively thinking about the information you are learning (elaborative encoding) is a good way to prevent encoding failure (Hall et al., 2007). You'll find more memory strategies in *Psychology for Your Life—Self-Reflective Learning* (at the beginning of this book). Check it out, if you haven't already.

College Students: They're All Alike!

Encoding failures also affect our memories of people. Imagine yourself in this situation: As you are walking on campus, a young man, who looks like a college student, approaches you and asks for directions. While you are talking, two workers carrying a door pass between you and the young man. While your view is blocked by the door, another man takes the place of the first. Now you are facing a different person than the one who was there just seconds earlier. If this happened to you, do you think you would notice the change? Remarkably, only half the people tested in this way noticed the switch (Simons & Levin, 1998)!

How could anyone fail to notice that one stranger had been replaced by another? The people who didn't remember the first man were all older adults. College students weren't fooled by the switch. Apparently, older adults encoded the first man in very general terms as a "college student." As a result, that's all they remembered about him. Because his replacement also looked like a college student, they thought he was the same person (Simons & Levin, 1998).

▲ **FIGURE 7.8** The curve of forgetting. This graph shows the amount remembered (measured by relearning) after varying lengths of time. Notice how rapidly forgetting occurs. The material learned was nonsense syllables. Forgetting curves for meaningful information also show early losses followed by a long gradual decline, but overall, forgetting occurs much more slowly. (After Ebbinghaus, 1885.)

Encoding failure Failure to store sufficient information to form a useful memory.

discovering psychology

Card Magic!

FIGURE 7.9

Naveh-Benjamin, Guez, & Sorek, 2007). The five cards you see below are all new (none is shown in Figure 7.9). Because you couldn't find it in the "remaining five," your card seemed to disappear. What looked like "card magic" is actually memory magic. Now return to "When Encoding Fails" and continue reading to learn more about forgetting.

Pick a card from the six shown in ▶▶ Figure 7.9, above. Look at it closely and be sure you can remember which card is yours. Now, snap your fingers and look at the cards in ▶▶ Figure 7.10, below. Poof! Only five cards remain, and the card you chose has disappeared. Obviously, you could have selected any one of the six cards in Figure 7.9. How did we know which one to remove?

This trick is based entirely on an illusion of memory. Recall that you were asked to concentrate on one card among the six cards in Figure 7.9. That prevented you from paying attention to the other cards, so they weren't stored in your memory (Mangels, Picton, & Craik, 2001;

FIGURE 7.10

Actually, we all tend to categorize strangers in general terms: Is the person young or old, male or female, a member of my ethnic group or another? This tendency is one reason why eyewitnesses are better at identifying members of their own ethnic group than persons from other groups (Burgess & Weaver, 2003; Michel, Caldara, & Rossion, 2006). It may seem harsh to say so, but during brief social contacts, people really do act as if members of other ethnic groups "all look alike." Of course, this bias disappears when people get acquainted and learn more about one another as individuals (McKone et al., 2007).

When Memory Storage Fails

One view of forgetting holds that **memory traces** (changes in nerve cells or brain activity) decay (fade or weaken) over time. **Memory decay** appears to be a factor in the loss of sensory memories. Such fading also applies to short-term memory. Information stored in STM

Memory traces Physical changes in nerve cells or brain activity that take place when memories are stored.

Memory decay The fading or weakening of memories assumed to occur when memory traces become weaker.

FIGURE 7.11 Some of the distractor items used in a study of recognition memory and encoding failure. Penny A is correct but was seldom recognized. Pennies G and J were popular wrong answers. (Adapted from Nickerson & Adams, 1979.)

seems to initiate a brief flurry of activity in the brain that quickly dies out. Short-term memory therefore operates like a "leaky bucket": New information constantly pours in, but it rapidly fades away and is replaced by still newer information. Let's say that you are trying to remember a short list of letters, numbers, or words after seeing or hearing them once. If it takes you more than 4 to 6 seconds to repeat the list, you will forget some of the items (Dosher & Ma, 1998).

Disuse

Does decay also occur in long-term memory? There is evidence that memories not retrieved and "used" or rehearsed become weaker over time (Schacter, 2001). That is, some long-term memory traces may fade from **disuse** (infrequent retrieval) and eventually become too weak to retrieve. However, disuse alone cannot fully explain forgetting.

Disuse doesn't seem to account for our ability to recover seemingly forgotten memories through redintegration, relearning, and priming. It also fails to explain why some unused memories fade, whereas others are carried for life. A third contradiction will be recognized by anyone who has spent time with the elderly. People growing senile may become so forgetful that they can't remember what happened a week ago. Yet at the same time that your Uncle Oscar's recent memories are fading, he may have vivid memories of trivial and long-forgotten events from the past. "Why, I remember it as clearly as if it were yesterday," he will say, forgetting that the story he is about to tell is one he told earlier the same day (twice). In short, disuse offers no more than a partial explanation of long-term forgetting.

When Retrieval Fails

If encoding failure and storage failure don't fully explain forgetting from long-term memory, what does? If you have encoded and stored information, that leaves retrieval failure as a likely cause of forgetting. Even if memories are **available** (stored in your memory), you still have to be able to **access** them (locate or retrieve them) in order to remember. For example, you've probably had the experience of knowing you know the answer to an exam question (you knew it was available), but being unable to retrieve it during the exam (it was inaccessible) (Landau & Leynes, 2006). You know what happens next, right? As you leave the exam, the answer "pops" into your head!

Cue-Dependent Forgetting

One reason retrieval may fail is because **memory cues** (stimuli associated with a memory) are missing when the time comes to retrieve information. For instance, if you were asked, "What were you doing on Monday afternoon of the third week in May, 2 years ago?", your reply might be, "Come on, how should I know?" However, if you were reminded, "That was the day the courthouse burned," or "That was the day Stacy had her automobile accident," you might remember immediately.

The presence of appropriate cues almost always enhances memory (Nairne, 2002). For example, memory will tend to be better if you study in the same room where you will be tested. Because this is often impossible, when you study, try to visualize the room where you will be tested. Doing so can enhance memory later (Jerabek & Standing, 1992). Similarly, people remember better if the same odor (such as lemon or lavender) is present when they study and are tested (Parker, Ngu, & Cassaday, 2001). If you wear a particular perfume or cologne while you prepare for a test, it might be wise to wear it when you take the test.

State-Dependent Learning

Have you heard the one about the drunk who misplaced his wallet and had to get drunk again to find it? Actually, this is not too farfetched. The bodily state that exists during learning can be a strong retrieval cue for later memory, an effect known as **state-dependent learning** (Neath & Surprenant, 2003). Being very thirsty, for instance, might prompt you to remember events that took place on another occasion when you were thirsty. Because of

Paul Conklin/PhotoEdit

External cues like those found in a photograph, in a scrapbook, or during a walk through an old neighborhood often aid recall of seemingly lost memories. For many veterans, finding a familiar name engraved in the Vietnam Veterans Memorial unleashes a flood of memories.

Disuse Theory that memory traces weaken when memories are not periodically used or retrieved.

Availability (in memory) Memories currently stored in memory are available.

Accessibility (in memory) Memories currently stored in memory which can be retrieved when necessary are both available and accessible.

Memory cue Any stimulus associated with a particular memory. Memory cues usually enhance retrieval.

State-dependent learning Memory influenced by one's bodily state at the time of learning and at the time of retrieval. Improved memory occurs when the bodily states match.

Sad mood during learning   Happy mood during learning

Mood while recalling words

FIGURE 7.12 The effect of mood on memory. Subjects best remembered a list of words when their mood during testing was the same as their mood was when they learned the list. (Adapted from Bower, 1981.)

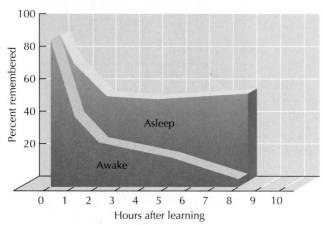

Hours after learning

FIGURE 7.13 The amount of forgetting after a period of sleep or of being awake. Notice that sleep causes less memory loss than activity that occurs while one is awake. (After Jenkins & Dallenbach, 1924.)

Interference The tendency for new memories to impair retrieval of older memories, and the reverse.

Retroactive interference The tendency for new memories to interfere with the retrieval of old memories.

such effects, information learned under the influence of a drug is best remembered when the drugged state occurs again (Slot & Colpaert, 1999). However, this is a laboratory finding. In school, it's far better to study with a clear mind in the first place.

A similar effect applies to emotional states (Wessel & Wright, 2004). For instance, Gordon Bower (1981) found that people who learned a list of words while in a happy mood recalled them better when they were again happy. People who learned while they felt sad remembered best when they were sad (▶▶ Figure 7.12). Similarly, if you are in a happy mood you are more likely to remember recent happy events. If you are in a bad mood you will tend to have unpleasant memories. Such links between emotional cues and memory could explain why couples who quarrel often end up remembering—and rehashing—old arguments.

Interference

Further insight into forgetting comes from a classic experiment in which college students learned lists of nonsense syllables. After studying, students in one group slept for 8 hours and were then tested for memory of the lists. A second group stayed awake for 8 hours and went about business as usual. When members of the second group were tested, they remembered *less* than the group that slept (▶▶ Figure 7.13.) This difference is based on the fact that new learning can interfere with the ability to retrieve previous learning. (Sleep can improve memory in another way: REM sleep and dreaming appear to help us form certain types of memories. See Chapter 5.) **Interference** refers to the tendency for new memories to impair retrieval of older memories (and the reverse). It seems to apply to both short-term and long-term memory (Lustig, May, & Hasher, 2001; Nairne, 2002).

It is not completely clear if new memories alter existing memory traces or if they make it harder to retrieve earlier memories. In any case, there is no doubt that interference is a major cause of forgetting (Neath & Surprenant, 2003). College students who memorized 20 lists of words (one list each day) were able to recall only 15 percent of the last list. Students who learned only one list remembered 80 percent (Underwood, 1957) (▶▶ Figure 7.14).

The sleeping college students remembered more because retroactive (RET-ro-AK-tiv) interference was held to a minimum. **Retroactive interference** refers to the tendency for new learning to inhibit retrieval of old learning. Avoiding new

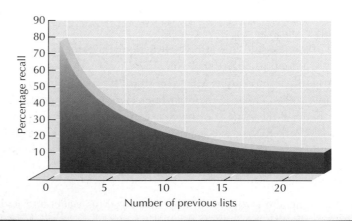

Number of previous lists

FIGURE 7.14 Effects of interference on memory. A graph of the approximate relationship between percentage recalled and number of different word lists memorized. (Adapted from Underwood, 1957.)

learning prevents retroactive interference. This doesn't exactly mean you should hide in a closet after you study for an exam. However, you should avoid studying other subjects until the exam. Sleeping after study can help you retain memories, and reading, writing, or even watching TV may cause interference.

Retroactive interference is easily demonstrated in the laboratory by this arrangement:

Experimental group:	**Learn A**	**Learn B**	**Test A**
Control group:	**Learn A**	**Rest**	**Test A**

Imagine yourself as a member of the experimental group. In task A, you learn a list of telephone numbers. In task B, you learn a list of Social Security numbers. How do you score on a test of task A (the telephone numbers)? If you do not remember as much as the control group that learns *only* task A, then retroactive interference has occurred. The second thing learned interfered with memory of the first thing learned; the interference went "backward," or was "retroactive" (▶▶ Figure 7.15).

Proactive (pro-AK-tiv) interference is the second type of interference. **Proactive interference** occurs when prior learning inhibits recall of later learning. A test for proactive interference would take this form:

Experimental group:	**Learn A**	**Learn B**	**Test B**
Control group:	**Rest**	**Learn B**	**Test B**

Let's assume that the experimental group remembers less than the control group on a test of task B. In that case, learning task A interfered with memory for task B.

Then proactive interference goes "forward"? Yes. For instance, if you cram for a psychology exam and then later the same night cram for a history exam, your memory for the second subject studied (history) will be less accurate than if you had studied only history. (Because of retroactive interference, your memory for psychology would probably also suffer.) The greater the similarity in the two subjects studied, the more interference takes place. The moral, of course, is don't procrastinate in preparing for exams. The more you can avoid competing information, the more likely you are to recall what you want to remember (Anderson & Bell, 2001; Wixted, 2004).

How could anyone lose something as large as a car? If you park your car in a different place every day, you may have experienced forgetting caused by interference. Today's memory about your car's location is easily confused with memories from yesterday, and the day before, and the day before that.

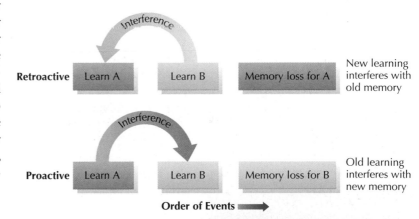

Repression and Suppression of Memories

Take a moment and scan over the events of the last few years of your life. What kinds of things most easily come to mind? Many people remember happy, positive events better than disappointments and irritations (Moore & Zoellner, 2007). This tendency is called **repression,** or motivated forgetting. Through repression, painful, threatening, or embarrassing memories are held out of consciousness (Anderson et al., 2004). An example is provided by soldiers who have repressed some of the horrors they saw during combat (Karon & Widener, 1997).

The forgetting of past failures, upsetting childhood events, the names of people you dislike, or appointments you don't want to keep may reveal repression. People prone to repression tend to be extremely sensitive to emotional events. As a result, they use repression to protect themselves from threatening thoughts (McNally, Clancy, & Barrett, 2004). See "The Recovered Memory/False Memory Debate" for further cautions.

FIGURE 7.15 Retroactive and proactive interference. The order of learning and testing shows whether interference is retroactive (backward) or proactive (forward).

Proactive interference The tendency for old memories to interfere with the retrieval of newer memories.

Repression Unconsciously pushing unwanted memories out of awareness.

The Recovered Memory/False Memory Debate

Many sexually abused children develop problems that persist into adulthood. In some instances, they repress all memory of the abuse. According to some psychologists, uncovering these hidden memories can be an important step toward regaining emotional health (Colangelo, 2007).

Although the preceding may be true, the search for repressed memories of sexual abuse has itself been a problem. Families have been torn apart by accusations of sexual abuse that later turned out to be completely false (Porter et al., 2003). For example, Gary Ramona lost his marriage and his $400,000-a-year job when his daughter Holly alleged that he molested her throughout her childhood. To prove to Holly that her memories were true, the therapists gave her the drug Amytal and told her that it was a "truth drug." (Amytal is a hypnotic drug that induces a twilight state of consciousness. People do not automatically tell the truth while under its influence.) Ramona sued Holly's therapists, claiming that they had been irresponsible. After reviewing the evidence, a jury awarded Gary Ramona $500,000 in damages. In a way, Gary Ramona was lucky. Most people who are falsely accused have no way to prove their innocence (Loftus & Ketcham, 1994).

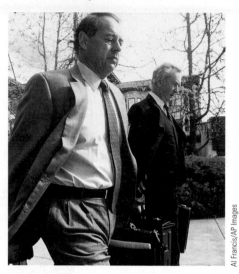

Al Francis/AP Images

Gary Ramona's life was shattered by "recovered" memories that turned out to be false.

Why would anyone have false memories about such disturbing events? Several popular books and a few misguided therapists have actively encouraged people to find repressed memories of abuse. Hypnosis, guided visualization, suggestion, age regression, and similar techniques can elicit fantasies that are mistaken for real memories. As we saw earlier, it is easy to create false

memories, especially by using hypnosis (Loftus, 2003b; Loftus & Bernstein, 2005).

In an effort to illustrate how easy it is to create false memories and to publicize *false memory syndrome,* memory expert Elizabeth Loftus once deliberately implanted a false memory in actor Alan Alda. As the host of the television series *Scientific American Frontiers,* he was scheduled to interview Loftus. Before the interview, Alda was asked to fill out a questionnaire about his tastes in food. When he arrived, Loftus told Alda that his answers revealed that he must once have gotten sick after eating hard-boiled eggs (which was false). Later that day, at a picnic, Alda would not eat hard-boiled eggs (Loftus, 2003a).

Certainly, some memories of abuse that return to awareness are genuine and must be dealt with. However, there is little doubt that some "recovered" memories are pure fantasy. No matter how real a recovered memory may seem, it could be false, unless it can be verified by others, or by court or medical records (Olio, 2004). The saddest thing about such claims is that they deaden public sensitivity to actual abuse. Childhood sexual abuse is widespread. Awareness of its existence must not be repressed.

If I try to forget a test I failed, am I repressing it? No. Repression can be distinguished from **suppression,** an active, conscious attempt to put something out of mind. By not thinking about the test, you have merely suppressed a memory. If you choose to, you can remember the test. Clinicians consider true repression an *unconscious* event and one of the major psychological defenses we use against emotional threats. (See Chapter 11 for details.) When a memory is repressed, we may be unaware that forgetting has even occurred.

Although some psychologists have questioned whether repression exists (Court & Court, 2001), evidence suggests that we can choose to actively suppress upsetting memories (Anderson, 2001). If you have experienced a painful emotional event, you will probably avoid all thoughts associated with it. This tends to keep cues out of mind that could trigger a painful memory. In time, your active suppression of the memory may become true repression (Anderson & Green, 2001).

Memory and the Brain—Some "Shocking" Findings

How does the brain form and store memories?

One possibility overlooked in our discussion of forgetting is that memories may be lost as they are being formed (Papanicolaou, 2006). For example, a head injury may cause a "gap" in memories preceding the accident. *Retrograde amnesia,* as this is called, involves forgetting events that occurred before an injury or trauma. In contrast, *anterograde amnesia* involves

Suppression A conscious effort to put something out of mind or to keep it from awareness.

forgetting events that follow an injury or trauma (Behrend, Beike, & Lampinen, 2004). (We will discuss an example of this type of amnesia in a moment.)

Consolidation

We can explain retrograde amnesia by assuming that it takes time to form a lasting memory, a process called **consolidation** (Vogel, Woodman, & Luck, 2006). You can think of consolidation as being somewhat like writing your name in wet concrete. Once the concrete is set, the information (your name) is fairly lasting. But while it is setting, it can be wiped out (amnesia) or scribbled over (interference).

Consider a classic experiment on consolidation, in which a rat is placed on a small platform. The rat steps down to the floor and receives a painful electric shock. After one shock, the rat can be returned to the platform repeatedly, but it will not step down. Obviously, the rat remembers the shock. Would it remember if consolidation were disturbed?

Curiously, one way to prevent consolidation is to give a different kind of shock called *electroconvulsive shock* (ECS). ECS is a mild electric shock to the brain. It does not harm the animal, but it does destroy any memory that is being formed. If each painful shock (the one the animal remembers) is followed by ECS (which wipes out memories during consolidation), the rat will step down over and over. Each time, ECS will erase the memory of the painful shock. (ECS is employed as a psychiatric treatment for severe depression in humans.)

What would happen if ECS were given several hours after the learning? Recent memories are more easily disrupted than older memories. If enough time is allowed to pass between learning and ECS, the memory will be unaffected because consolidation is already complete. That's why people with mild head injuries lose only memories from just before the accident, while older memories remain intact (Baddeley, Eysenck, & Anderson, 2009). Likewise, you would forget more if you studied, stayed awake 8 hours, and then slept 8 hours than you would if you studied, slept 8 hours, and were awake for 8 hours. Either way, 16 hours would pass. However, less forgetting would occur in the second instance, because more consolidation would occur before interference begins (Wixted, 2005).

Where does consolidation take place in the brain? Actually, many parts of the brain are responsible for memory, but the **hippocampus** is particularly important (Sutherland et al., 2006). The hippocampus acts as a sort of "switching station" between short-term and long-term memory (Squire, 2004). The hippocampus does this, in part, by growing new neurons (nerve cells) and by making new connections within the brain (Eichenbaum & Fortin, 2005).

If the hippocampus is damaged, patients usually develop anterograde amnesia and show a striking inability to consolidate new memories (Zola & Squire, 2001). A man described by Brenda Milner (1965) provides a dramatic example. Two years after an operation damaged his hippocampus, the 29-year-old H. M. continued to give his age as 27 and reported that the operation had just taken place. His memory of events before the operation remained clear, but he found forming new long-term memories almost impossible. When his parents moved to a new house a few blocks away on the same street, he could not remember the new address. Month after month, he read the same magazines over and over without finding them familiar. If you were to meet this man, he would seem fairly normal because he still has short-term memory. But if you were to leave the room and return 15 minutes later, he would act as if he had never seen you before. Lacking the ability to form new lasting memories, he lived eternally in the present until his death in 2008 at the age of 82 (Bohbot & Corkin, 2007; Corkin, 2002).

Memory and Emotion

Do you remember when you first learned about the terrorist attacks on New York City's World Trade Center in 2001? Can you recall lots of detail, including how you reacted? If so, you have a flashbulb memory for 9/11. A flashbulb memory is an especially vivid image that seems to be frozen in memory at times of emotionally significant personal or public events. Depending on your age, you may also have a "flashbulb" memory for the assassinations of John F. Kennedy or Martin Luther King, Jr., the *Challenger* or *Columbia* space shuttle disasters, or the death of Princess Diana (Curci & Luminet, 2006; Sharot et al., 2007).

Consolidation Process by which relatively permanent memories are formed in the brain.

Hippocampus A brain structure associated with emotion and the transfer of information from short-term memory to long-term memory.

Do you have a flashbulb memory for the November 4, 2008, election victory of President Obama? You do if someone alerted you about the news and you remember that person's call. You do if you saw the news on TV and you have clear memories of how you reacted.

Are flashbulb memories handled differently by the brain? Powerful experiences activate the limbic system, a part of the brain that processes emotions. Heightened activity in the limbic system, in turn, appears to intensify memory consolidation (LaBar, 2007; Kensinger, 2007). As a result, flashbulb memories tend to form at times of intense emotion.

Although flashbulb memories are often related to public tragedies, memories of both positive and negative events can have "flashbulb" clarity (Paradis et al., 2004; Rubin, 1985). Would you consider any of the following to be a flashbulb memory? Your first kiss, a special date, or your prom night? How about a time you had to speak in front of a large audience? A car accident you were in or witnessed?

The term **flashbulb memories** was first used to describe recollections that seemed to be unusually vivid and permanent (Brown & Kulik, 1977). It has become clear, however, that flashbulb memories are not always accurate (Greenberg, 2004; Kensinger, 2007). More than anything else, what sets flashbulb memories apart is that we tend to place great *confidence* in them—even when they are wrong (Niedzwienska, 2004). Perhaps that's because we review emotionally charged events over and over and tell others about them. Also, public events such as wars, earthquakes, and elections reappear many times in the news, which highlights them in memory. Over time, flashbulb memories tend to crystallize into consistent, if not entirely accurate, landmarks in our lives (Schmolck, Buffalo, & Squire, 2000).

Some memories go beyond flashbulb clarity and become so intense that they may haunt a person for years. Extremely traumatic experiences, such as military combat, can produce so much limbic system activation that the resulting memories and "flashbacks" leave a person emotionally handicapped (Nemeroff et al., 2006).

Long-Term Memory and the Brain

Somewhere within the 3-pound mass of the human brain lies all we know: ZIP codes, faces of loved ones, history, favorite melodies, the taste of an apple, and much, much more. Where is this information? According to neuroscientist Richard Thompson (2005), many parts of the brain become active when we form long-term memories, but some areas are more important for each type of memory.

For example, patterns of blood flow in the cerebral cortex (the wrinkled outer layer of the brain) can be used to map brain activity. ▶▶ Figure 7.16 shows the results of measuring

(a)   (b)   (c)

⬆ **FIGURE 7.16** Patterns of blood flow in the cerebral cortex (wrinkled outer layer of the brain) change as areas become more or less active. Thus, blood flow can be used to draw "maps" of brain activity. This drawing, which views the brain from the top, shows the results of measuring cerebral blood flow while people were thinking about a semantic memory (*a*) or an episodic memory (*b*). In the map, green indicates areas that are more active during semantic thinking. Reds show areas of greater activity during episodic thinking. The brain in view *c* shows the difference in activity between views *a* and *b*. The resulting pattern suggests that the front of the cortex is related to episodic memory. Areas toward the back and sides of the brain, especially the temporal lobes, are more associated with semantic memory (Gabrieli, 1998; Tulving, 1989, 2002).

 Flashbulb memories Memories created at times of high emotion that seem especially vivid.

blood flow while people were thinking about a semantic memory or an episodic memory. The resulting pattern indicates that we use the front of the cortex for episodic memory. Back areas are more associated with semantic memory (Tulving, 2002).

Let's summarize (and simplify greatly). Earlier we noted that the hippocampus handles memory consolidation (Zola & Squire, 2001). Once declarative long-term memories are formed, they appear to be stored in the cortex of the brain (episodic in the front, semantic in the back) (Squire, 2004). Long-term procedural (skill) memories are stored in the cerebellum, a part of the brain that is also responsible for muscular coordination (Hermann et al., 2004).

How are memories recorded in the brain? Scientists are beginning to identify the exact ways in which nerve cells record information. For example, Eric Kandel and his colleagues have studied learning in the marine snail *aplysia* (ah-PLEEZ-yah). Learning in *aplysia* occurs when certain nerve cells in a circuit alter the amount of transmitter chemicals they release (Bailey & Kandel, 2004). Learning also alters the activity, structure, and chemistry of brain cells. Such changes determine which connections get stronger and which become weaker. This "reprograms" the brain and records information (Abraham, 2006).

Scientists continue to study various chemicals, especially neurotransmitters that affect memory. Their research may eventually help the millions of persons who suffer from memory impairment (Elli & Nathan, 2001).

An *aplysia*. The relatively simple nervous system of this sea animal allows scientists to study memory as it occurs in single nerve cells.

[handwritten: CAN LEARN CLASSICAL CONDITIONING]

---

 study break
Forgetting

RECITE

1. According to the Ebbinghaus curve of forgetting, we forget slowly at first and then a rapid decline occurs. T or F?
2. Which explanation seems to account for the loss of short-term memories?
   a. decay b. disuse
   c. repression d. interference
3. When memories are available but not accessible, forgetting may be cue dependent. T or F?
4. When learning one thing makes it more difficult to recall another, forgetting may be caused by _____.
5. You are asked to memorize long lists of telephone numbers. You learn a new list each day for 10 days. When tested on list 3, you remember less than a person who learned only the first three lists. Your larger memory loss is probably caused by
   a. disuse b. retroactive interference
   c. regression d. proactive interference
6. If you consciously succeed at putting a painful memory out of mind, you have used
   a. redintegration b. suppression
   c. negative rehearsal d. repression
7. Retrograde amnesia results when consolidation is speeded up. T or F?

REFLECT
Critical Thinking

8. Based on state-dependent learning, why do you think that music often strongly evokes memories?
9. You must study French, Spanish, psychology, and biology in one evening (poor thing!). What do you think would be the best order in which to study these subjects so as to minimize interference?

Relate

Do you know someone whose name you have a hard time remembering? Do you like or dislike that person? Do you think your difficulty is an instance of repression? Suppression? Interference? Encoding failure?

Have you had a flashbulb memory? How vivid is the memory today? How accurate do you think it is?

ANSWERS

1. F 2. a and d 3. T 4. interference 5. b 6. b 7. F 8. Music tends to affect the mood a person is in, and moods tend to affect memory (Miranda & Kihlstrom, 2005). 9. Any order that separates French from Spanish and psychology from biology would be better (for instance: French, psychology, Spanish, biology).

Exceptional Memory—Wizards of Recall

What are "photographic" memories?

In this section we will explore exceptional memories. Is superior memory a biological gift, such as having a "photographic" memory? Or do excellent memorizers merely make better-than-average use of normal memory capacities?

▶▶ **FIGURE 7.17** *(a)* "Treasure map" similar to the one used by Kosslyn, Ball, and Reiser (1978) to study images in memory. *(b)* This graph shows how long it took subjects to move a visualized spot various distances on their mental images of the map. (See text for explanation.)

(a)

(b)

▲ **FIGURE 7.18** A test picture like that used to identify children with eidetic imagery. To test your eidetic imagery, look at the picture for 30 seconds. Then look at a blank surface and try to "project" the picture onto it. If you have good eidetic imagery, you will be able to see the picture in detail. Return now to the text and try to answer the questions there. (Redrawn from an illustration in Lewis Carroll's *Alice's Adventures in Wonderland*.)

Mental images Internal images or visual depictions used in memory and thinking.

Eidetic imagery The ability to retain a "projected" mental image long enough to use it as a source of information.

Can you remember how many doors there are in your house or apartment? To answer a question like this, many people form **mental images** (mental pictures) of each room and count the doorways they visualize. As this example implies, many memories are stored as mental images (Roeckelein, 2004).

Stephen Kosslyn, Thomas Ball, and Brian Reiser (1978) found an interesting way to show that memories do exist as images. Participants first memorized a sort of treasure map similar to the one shown in ▶▶ Figure 7.17*a*. They were then asked to picture a black dot moving from one object, such as one of the trees, to another, such as the hut at the top of the island. Did people really form an image to do this task? It seems they did. As shown in ▶▶ Figure 7.17*b*, the time it took to "move" the dot was directly related to actual distances on the map.

Is the "treasure map" task an example of photographic memory? In some ways, internal memory images do have "photographic" qualities. However, the term *photographic memory* is more often used to describe a memory ability called eidetic imagery.

Eidetic Imagery

Eidetic (eye-DET-ik) **imagery** occurs when a person has visual images clear enough to be "scanned" or retained for at least 30 seconds. Internal memory images can be "viewed" mentally with the eyes closed. In contrast, eidetic images are "projected" out in front of a person. That is, they are best "seen" on a plain surface, such as a blank piece of paper. In this respect, eidetic images are somewhat like the after-images you might have after looking at a flashbulb or a brightly lit neon sign (Haber & Haber, 2000).

In one series of tests, children were shown a picture from *Alice's Adventures in Wonderland* (▶▶ Figure 7.18). To test your eidetic imagery, look at the picture and read the instructions there.

Now, let's see how much you remember. Can you say (without looking again) which of Alice's apron strings is longer? Are the cat's front paws crossed? How many stripes are on the cat's tail? After the picture was removed from view, one 10-year-old boy was asked what he saw. He replied, "I see the tree, gray tree with three limbs. I see the cat with stripes around its tail." Asked to count the stripes, the boy replied, "There are about 16" (a correct count!). The boy then went on to describe the remainder of the picture in striking detail (Haber, 1969).

Don't be disappointed if you didn't do too well when you tried your eidetic skills. Eidetic memory is more common in childhood and becomes rare by adulthood (Haber & Haber, 2000).

A Case of Photographic Memory

Let's return now to the concept of mental images. In rare instances, such images may be so vivid that it is reasonable to say that a person has "photographic memory." For example, we met A. J. and Mr. S. at the beginning of this chapter. Besides having excellent memories, both attested to the importance of forgetting. If you didn't have selective memory, you would recall all the ingredients on your cereal box, every street number you've seen, and countless other scraps of information. Regardless, few people in history have possessed such amazing memory abilities. Instead most people with good memories have learned effective strategies for remembering. Let's investigate further.

Strategies for Remembering

At first, a student volunteer named Steve could remember 7 digits. Could he improve with practice? For 20 months Steve practiced memorizing ever-longer lists of digits. Ultimately, he was able to memorize approximately 80 digits, like this sample:

92842048050842268953990190252912807999706606574717310601080585269726026357332135

How did Steve do it? Basically, he worked by chunking digits into meaningful groups containing three or four digits each. Steve's avid interest in long-distance running helped greatly. For instance, to him the first three digits above represented 9 minutes and 28 seconds, a good time for a 2-mile run. When running times wouldn't work, Steve used other associations, such as ages or dates, to chunk digits (Ericsson & Chase, 1982). It seems apparent that Steve's success was based on learned strategies. By using similar memory systems, other people have trained themselves to equal Steve's feat (Bellezza, Six, & Phillips, 1992). In fact, the ability to organize information into chunks underlies expertise in many fields (Gobet, 2005).

Psychologist Anders Ericsson believes that exceptional memory is merely a learned extension of normal memory. As evidence, he notes that Steve's short-term memory did not improve during months of practice. For example, Steve could still memorize only seven consonants. Steve's phenomenal memory for numbers grew as he figured out new ways to chunk digits at encoding and store them in LTM. Steve began with a normal memory for digits. He extended his memory by diligent practice. Clearly, exceptional memory can be learned (Ericsson et al., 2004).

Memory Champions

Each year the World Memory Championship is held in England. Contestants must rapidly memorize daunting amounts of information, such as long lists of unrelated words and numbers. Psychologists John Wilding and Elizabeth Valentine saw this event as an opportunity to study exceptional memory and persuaded the contestants to take some additional memory tests. These ranged from ordinary (recall a story), to challenging (recall the telephone numbers of six different people), to diabolical (recall 48 numerals arranged in rows and columns) (Maguire et al., 2003; Wilding & Valentine, 1994).

Exceptional memorizers were found to:

- Use memory strategies and techniques
- Have specialized interests and knowledge that make certain types of information easier to encode and recall
- Have naturally superior memory abilities, often including vivid mental images
- Not have superior intellectual abilities or different brains

The first two points confirm what we learned from Steve's acquired memory ability. Many of the contestants, for example, actively used memory strategies, including special memory "tricks" called *mnemonics* (nee-MON-iks). Specialized interests and knowledge also helped for some tasks. For example, one contestant, a mathematician, was exceedingly good at memorizing numbers (Wilding & Valentine, 1994).

Several of the memory contestants were able to excel on tasks that prevented the use of learned strategies and techniques. This observation implies that superior memory ability can be a "gift" as well as a learned skill. Wilding and Valentine conclude that excep-

8	7	3	7	9	2	6	8
2	0	1	1	7	4	9	5
0	1	7	5	8	7	8	3
1	9	4	7	6	0	6	9
3	6	1	6	8	1	5	4
4	5	2	4	0	2	9	7

This number matrix is similar to the ones contestants in the World Memory Championship had to memorize. To be scored as correct, digits had to be recalled in their proper positions (Wilding & Valentine, 1994a).

tional memory may be based on either natural ability or learned strategies. Usually it requires both.

Improving Memory—Keys to the Memory Bank

How can I improve my memory?

Let's see how you can improve your memory. To begin, there is very little you can do to improve your brain's ability to store long-term memories. The jury is still out on the use of herbs (such as *Ginkgo biloba*) and vitamins (such as vitamin E) to improve human memory (McDaniel, Maier, & Einstein, 2002). However, until there's a memory pill, you can immediately use learned strategies to improve memory encoding and memory retrieval. Most super memorizers use these strategies to augment whatever natural talents they have. Some of their strategies are described in the remainder of this section. Later, mnemonics are explored in this chapter's Psychology in Action section. Please do remember to read it.

Encoding Strategies

One way to improve your memory is to be sure to fully encode information. That way you can avoid forgetting due to encoding failure. Here are some steps you can take to become a better encoder:

Elaborative Encoding

The more you *rehearse* (mentally review) information as you read, the better you will remember it. But remember that maintenance rehearsal alone is not very effective. Elaborative encoding, in which you rehearse by looking for connections to existing knowledge, is far better. Repeatedly thinking about facts helps link them together in memory. To learn college-level information, you must make active use of more reflective rehearsal strategies (Santrock & Halonen, 2007).

Selection

The Dutch scholar Erasmus said that a good memory should be like a fish net: It should keep all the big fish and let the little ones escape. If you boil down the paragraphs in most textbooks to one or two important terms or ideas, your memory chores will be more manageable. Practice very selective marking in your texts and use marginal notes to further summarize ideas. Most students mark their texts too much instead of too little. If everything is underlined, you haven't been selective. And, very likely, you didn't pay much attention in the first place (Peterson, 1992).

Organization

Assume that you must memorize the following list of words: north, man, red, spring, woman, east, autumn, yellow, summer, boy, blue, west, winter, girl, green, south. This rather difficult list could be reorganized into *chunks* as follows: north-east-south-west, spring-summer-autumn-winter, red-yellow-green-blue, man-woman-boy-girl. Organizing class notes and summarizing chapters can be quite helpful (Hettich, 2005). You may even want to summarize your summaries, so that the overall network of ideas becomes clearer and simpler. Summaries improve memory by encoding better encoding of information (Hadwin, Kirby, & Woodhouse, 1999).

Whole Versus Part Learning

If you have to memorize a speech, is it better to try to learn it from beginning to end? Or in smaller parts like paragraphs? Generally it is better to practice whole packages of information rather than smaller parts (*whole learning*). This is especially true for fairly short, organized information. An exception is that learning parts may be better for extremely long, complicated information. In *part learning,* subparts of a larger body of information are studied (such as sections of a textbook chapter). To decide which approach to use, remember to study the *largest meaningful amount of information* you can at one time.

For very long or complex material, try the *progressive-part method,* by breaking a learning task into a series of short sections. At first, you study part A until it is mastered. Next, you study parts A and B; then A, B, and C; and so forth. This is a good way to learn the lines of a play, a long piece of music, or a poem (Ash & Holding, 1990). After the material is learned, you should also practice by starting at points other than A (at C, D, or B, for example). This helps prevent getting "lost" or going blank in the middle of a performance.

Serial Position

Whenever you must learn something in order, be aware of the serial position effect. As you will recall, this is the tendency to make the most errors in remembering the middle of a list. If you are introduced to a long line of people, the names you are likely to forget will be those in the middle, so you should make an extra effort to attend to them. You should also give extra practice to the middle of a list, poem, or speech. Try to break long lists of information into short sub-lists, and make the middle sub-lists the shortest of all.

Cues

The best *memory cues* (stimuli that aid retrieval) are those that were present during encoding (Anderson, 2005). For example, students in one study had the daunting task of trying to recall a list of 600 words. As they read the list (which they did not know they would be tested on), the students gave three other words closely related in meaning to each listed word. In a test given later, the words each student supplied were used as cues to jog memory. The students recalled an astounding 90 percent of the original word list (Mantyla, 1986).

Now read the following sentence:

The fish bit the swimmer.

If you were tested a week from now, you would be more likely to recall the sentence if you were given a memory cue. And, surprisingly, the word *shark* would work better as a reminder than *fish* would. The reason for this is that most people think of a shark when they read the sentence. As a result, *shark* becomes a potent memory cue (Schacter, 2000).

The preceding example shows, once again, that it often helps to *elaborate* information as you learn. When you study, try to use new names, ideas, or terms in several sentences. Also, form images that include the new information and relate it to knowledge you already have. Your goal should be to knit meaningful cues into your memory code to help you retrieve information when you need it (▶▶ Figure 7.19).

Overlearning

Numerous studies have shown that memory is greatly improved when you *overlearn* or continue to study beyond bare mastery. After you have learned material well enough to remember it once without error, you should continue studying. Overlearning is your best insurance against going blank on a test because of being nervous.

Spaced Practice

To keep boredom and fatigue to a minimum, try alternating short study sessions with brief rest periods. This pattern, called **spaced practice,** is generally superior to **massed practice,** in which little or no rest is given between learning sessions. By improving attention and consolidation, three 20-minute study sessions can produce more learning than 1 hour of continuous study (Neath & Surprenant, 2003).

Gregg Segal/Getty Images

▲ FIGURE 7.19 Actors can remember large amounts of complex information for many months, even when learning new roles in between. During testing, they remember their lines best when they are allowed to move and gesture as they would when performing. Apparently their movements supply cues that aid recall (Noice & Noice, 1999).

Spaced practice A practice schedule that alternates study periods with brief rests.

Massed practice A practice schedule in which studying continues for long periods, without interruption.

Perhaps the best way to make use of spaced practice is to *schedule* your time. To make an effective schedule, designate times during the week before, after, and between classes when you will study particular subjects. Then treat these times just as if they are classes you have to attend.

Retrieval Strategies

Once you have successfully encoded information, you still have to retrieve it. Here are some strategies to help you avoid retrieval failure:

Retrieval Practice

Learning proceeds best when feedback allows you to check your progress. Feedback can help you identify ideas that need extra practice. In addition, knowing that you have remembered or answered correctly is rewarding. A prime way to provide feedback for yourself while studying is *recitation*. If you are going to remember something, eventually you will have to retrieve it. *Recitation* refers to summarizing aloud while you are learning. Recitation forces you to practice retrieving information. When you are reading a text, you should stop frequently and try to remember what you have just read by restating it in your own words. In one classic experiment, the best memory score was earned by a group of students who spent 80 percent of their time reciting and only 20 percent reading (Gates, 1958). Maybe students who talk to themselves aren't crazy after all.

If you have spaced your practice and overlearned, retrieval practice in the form of review will be like icing on your study cake. Reviewing shortly before an exam cuts down the time during which you must remember details that may be important for the test. When reviewing, hold the amount of new information you try to memorize to a minimum. It may be realistic to take what you have actually learned and add a little more to it at the last minute by cramming. But remember that more than a little new learning may interfere with what you already know.

Using a Strategy to Aid Recall

Successful retrieval is usually the result of a planned *search* of memory (Herrmann et al., 2006). For example, one study found that students were most likely to recall names that eluded them if they made use of partial information (Reed & Bruce, 1982). The students were trying to answer questions such as, "He is best remembered as the scarecrow in the Judy Garland movie *The Wizard of Oz*." (The answer is Ray Bolger.) Partial information that helped students remember included impressions about the length of the name, letter sounds within the name, similar names, and related information (such as the names of other characters in the movie). A similar helpful strategy is to go through the alphabet, trying each letter as the first sound of a name or word you are seeking.

The *cognitive interview* described earlier in this chapter (see "Telling Wrong from Right in Forensic Memory") offers some further hints for recapturing context and jogging memories:

1. Say or write down *everything* you can remember that relates to the information you are seeking. Don't worry about how trivial any of it seems; each bit of information you remember can serve as a cue to bring back others.
2. Try to recall events or information in different orders. Let your memories flow out backward or out of order, or start with whatever impressed you the most.
3. Recall from different viewpoints. Review events by mentally standing in a different place. Or try to view information as another person would remember it. When taking a test, for instance, ask yourself what other students or your professor would remember about the topic.
4. Mentally put yourself back in the situation where you learned the information. Try to mentally recreate the learning environment or relive the event. As you do, include sounds, smells, details of weather, nearby objects, other people present, what you said or thought, and how you felt as you learned the information (Fisher & Geiselman, 1987; Milne & Bull, 2002).

Extend How Long You Remember

When you are learning new information, practice retrieval repeatedly. As you do, gradually lengthen the amount of time that passes before you test yourself again. For example, if you are studying German words on flash cards, look at the first card and then move it a few cards back in the stack. Do the same with the next few cards. When you get to the first "old" card, test yourself on it and check the answer. Then, move it farther back in the stack. Do the same with other "old" cards as they come up. When "old" cards come up for the third time, put them clear to the back of the stack (Cull, Shaughnessy, & Zechmeister, 1996).

Sleep and Memory

Remember that sleeping after study reduces interference. However, unless you are a "night person," late evening may not be a very efficient time for you to study. Also, you obviously can't sleep after every study session or study everything just before you sleep. That's why your study schedule should include ample breaks between subjects as described earlier. (See "Spaced Practice.") The breaks and free time in your schedule are as important as your study periods.

Hunger and Memory

People who are hungry almost always score lower on memory tests. So Mother was right, it's a good idea to make sure you've had a good breakfast or lunch before you take tests at school (Smith, Clark, & Gallagher, 1999). And a cup of coffee won't hurt your test performance, either (Smith, 2005).

A Look Ahead

Psychologists still have much to learn about the nature of memory and how to improve it. For now, one thing stands out clearly: People who have good memories excel at organizing information and making it meaningful. Sometimes, however, you are faced with the need to memorize information without much inherent meaning. For example, a shopping list is just a list of more or less unrelated items. There isn't much of a meaningful relationship between carrots, rolls of toilet paper, TV dinners, and Twinkies except that you need more of them. With this in mind, the Psychology in Action discussion for this chapter tells how you can use mnemonics to better memorize when meaning-based memory strategies, like those described in this section, are not helpful.

RECITE

1. Children with eidetic imagery typically have no better than average long-term memory. T or F?
2. For most people, having an especially good memory is based on
   a. maintenance rehearsal   b. constructive processing
   c. phonetic imagery   d. learned strategies
3. As new information is encoded, it is helpful to elaborate on its meaning and connect it to other information. T or F?
4. Organizing information while studying has little effect on memory because long-term memory is already highly organized. T or F?
5. To improve memory, it is reasonable to spend as much or more time reciting as reading. T or F?

6. The cognitive interview helps people remember more by providing
   a. memory cues   b. a serial position effect
   c. phonetic priming   d. massed practice

REFLECT
Critical Thinking

7. Mr. S. had great difficulty remembering faces. Can you guess why?
8. What advantages would there be to taking notes as you read a textbook, as opposed to underlining words in the text?

Relate

What kinds of information are you good at remembering? Why do you think your memory is better for those topics?

Return to the topic headings in the preceding pages that list techniques for improving memory. Place a check mark next to those that you have used recently. Review any you didn't mark and think of a specific example of how you could use each technique at school, at home, or at work.

ANSWERS

1. T 2. d 3. T 4. F 5. T 6. a 7. Mr. S.'s memory was so specific that faces seemed different and unfamiliar if he saw them from a new angle or if a face had a different expression on it than Mr. S. last saw it. 8. Note-taking is a form of elaborative encoding and recitation; it facilitates the organization and selection of important ideas, and your notes can be used for review.

psychology in action
Mnemonics—Memory Magic

Are there any tricks to help me with my memory?

Just imagine the poor biology or psychology student who is required to learn the names of the 12 cranial nerves (in order, of course). Although the spinal nerves connect the brain to the body through the spinal cord, the cranial nerves do so directly. Just in case you wanted to know, their names of are: olfactory, optic, oculomotor, trochlear, trigeminal, abducens, facial, vestibulocochlear, glossopharyngeal, vagus, spinal accessory, and hypoglossal.

As you might imagine, most of us find it difficult to successfully encode this list. In the absence of any obvious meaningful relationship among these terms, it is difficult to apply the memory strategies we discussed earlier in the chapter and tempting to resort to *rote* learning (learning by simple repetition). Fortunately, there *is* an alternative: mnemonics (nee-MON-iks) (Baddeley, Eysenck, & Anderson, 2009; Neath & Surprenant, 2003). A **mnemonic** is any kind of memory system or aid. The superiority of mnemonic learning as opposed to rote learning has been demonstrated many times (Carney & Levin, 2003; Manalo, 2002).

Some mnemonic systems are so common that almost everyone knows them. If you are trying to remember how many days there are in a month, you may find the answer by reciting, "Thirty days hath September. . . ." Physics teachers often help students remember the colors of the spectrum by giving them the mnemonic "Roy G. Biv": **R**ed, **O**range, **Y**ellow, **G**reen, **B**lue, **I**ndigo, **V**iolet. The budding sailor who has trouble telling port from starboard may remember that "port" and "left" both have four letters or may remind herself, "I *left* port." And what beginning musician hasn't remembered the notes represented by the lines and spaces of the musical staff by learning "F-A-C-E" and "**E**very **G**ood **B**oy **D**oes **F**ine"?

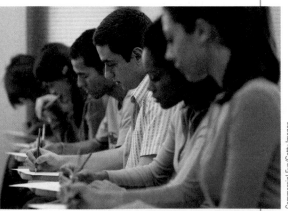

Mnemonics can be an aid in preparing for tests. However, because mnemonics help most in the initial stages of storing information, it is important to follow through with other elaborative learning strategies.

Mnemonic Any kind of memory system or aid.

Generations of students have learned the names of the spinal nerves by memorizing the sentence "**On Old O**lympus' **T**owering **T**op **A** **F**amous **V**ocal **G**erman **V**iewed **S**ome **H**ops. This mnemonic, which uses the first letter of each of the cranial nerves to generate a nonsense sentence, indeed produces better recall of the cranial nerves. Such *acrostics* are even more effective if you make up your own (Bloom & Lamkin, 2006). By practicing mnemonics you should be able to greatly improve your memory with little effort.

Here, then, are some basic principles of mnemonics:

1. **Make things meaningful.** In general, transferring information from short-term memory to long-term memory is aided by making it meaningful. If you encounter technical terms that have little or no immediate meaning for you, *give* them meaning, even if you have to stretch the term to do so. (This point is clarified by the examples following this list.)

2. **Make information familiar.** Another way to get information into long-term memory is to connect it to information already stored there. If some facts or ideas in a chapter seem to stay in your memory easily, associate other more difficult facts with them.

3. **Use mental pictures.** Visual pictures, or images, are generally easier to remember than words. Turning information into mental pictures is therefore very helpful. Make these images as vivid as possible (Neath & Surprenant, 2003).

4. **Form bizarre, unusual, or exaggerated mental associations.** Forming images that make sense is better in most situations. However, when associating two ideas, terms, or especially mental images, you may find that the more outrageous and exaggerated the association, the more likely you are to remember. Bizarre images make stored information more *distinctive* and therefore easier to retrieve (Worthen & Marshall, 1996). Imagine, for example, that you have just been introduced to Mr. Rehkop. To remember his name, you could picture him wearing a police uniform. Then replace his nose with a ray gun. This bizarre image will provide two hints when you want to remember Mr. Rehkop's name: *ray* and *cop*. This technique works for other kinds of information, too. College students who used exaggerated mental associations to remember the names of unfamiliar animals outperformed students who just used rote memory (Carney & Levin, 2001). Bizarre images help improve mainly immediate memory, and they work best for fairly simple information (Fritz et al., 2007; Robinson-Riegler & McDaniel, 1994). Nevertheless, they can be a first step toward learning.

A sampling of typical applications of mnemonics should make these four points clearer to you:

Example 1 Let's say you have some new vocabulary words to memorize in Spanish. You can learn them with little effort by using the **keyword method,** in which a familiar word or image is used to link two other words or items (Fritz et al., 2007; Pressley, 1987). To remember that the word *pajaro* (pronounced PAH-hah-ro) means bird, you can link it to a "key" word in English: *Pajaro* sounds a bit like "parked car-o." Therefore, to remember that *pajaro* means bird, you might visualize a parked car jam-packed full of birds. You should try to make this image as vivid and exaggerated as possible, with birds flapping and chirping and feathers flying everywhere. Similarly, for the word *carta* (which means "letter"), you might imagine a shopping *cart* filled with postal letters.

If you link similar keywords and images for the rest of the list, you may not remember them all, but you will get most without much more practice. As a matter of fact, if you have formed the *pajaro* and *carta* images just now, it is going to be almost impossible for you to ever see these words again without remembering what they mean.

What about a year from now? How long do keyword memories last? Mnemonic memories work best in the short run. Later, they may be more fragile than conventional memories. That's why it's usually best to use mnemonics during the initial stages of learning (Carney & Levin, 2003). To create more lasting memories, you'll need to use the techniques discussed earlier in this chapter.

Exaggerated mental images can link two words or ideas in ways that aid memory. Here, the keyword method is used to link the English word *letter* with the Spanish word *carta*.

Keyword method As an aid to memory, using a familiar word or image to link two items.

Example 2 Suppose you have to learn the names of all the bones and muscles in the human body for biology. To remember that the jawbone is the *mandible*, you can associate it to a *man nibbling*, or maybe you can picture a *man dribbling* a basketball with his jaw (make this image as ridiculous as possible). If the muscle name *latissimus dorsi* gives you trouble, familiarize it by turning it into "*the ladder misses the door, sigh.*" Then picture a ladder glued to your back where the muscle is found. Picture the ladder leading up to a small door at your shoulder. Picture the ladder missing the door. Picture the ladder sighing like an animated character in a cartoon.

This seems like more to remember, not less; and it seems like it would cause you to misspell things. Mnemonics are an aid, not a complete substitute for normal memory. Mnemonics are not likely to be helpful unless you make extensive use of *images* (Willoughby et al., 1997). Your mental pictures will come back to you easily. As for misspellings, mnemonics can be thought of as a built-in hint in your memory. Often, when taking a test, you will find that the slightest hint is all you need to remember correctly. A mnemonic image is like having someone leaning over your shoulder who says, "Psst, the name of that muscle sounds like 'ladder misses the door, sigh.'" If misspelling continues to be a problem, try to create memory aids for spelling, too.

Here are two more examples to help you appreciate the flexibility of a mnemonic approach to studying.

Example 3 Your art history teacher expects you to be able to name the artist when you are shown slides as part of exams. You have seen many of the slides only once before in class. How will you remember them? As the slides are shown in class, make each artist's name into an object or image. Then picture the object *in* the paintings done by the artist. For example, you can picture Van Gogh as a *van* (automobile) *going* through the middle of each Van Gogh painting. Picture the van running over things and knocking things over. Or, if you remember that Van Gogh cut off his ear, picture a giant bloody ear in each of his paintings.

Example 4 If you have trouble remembering history, try to avoid thinking of it as something from the dim past. Picture each historical personality as a person you know right now (a friend, teacher, parent, and so on). Then picture these people doing whatever the historical figures did. Also, try visualizing battles or other events as if they were happening in your town, or make parks and schools into countries. Use your imagination.

How can mnemonics be used to remember things in order? Here are three techniques that are helpful:

1. **Form a story or a chain.** To remember lists of ideas, objects, or words in order, try forming an exaggerated association (mental image) connecting the first item to the second, then the second to the third, and so on. To remember the following short list in order—elephant, doorknob, string, watch, rifle, oranges—picture a full-size *elephant* balanced on a *doorknob* playing with a *string* tied to him. Picture a *watch* tied to the string, and a *rifle* shooting *oranges* at the watch. This technique can be used quite successfully for lists of 20 or more items. In one test, people who used a linking mnemonic did much better at remembering lists of 15 and 22 errands (Higbee et al., 1990). Try it next time you go shopping and leave your list at home. Another helpful strategy is to make up a short story that links all the items on a list you want to remember (McNamara & Scott, 2001).

2. **Take a mental walk.** Ancient Greek orators had an interesting way to remember ideas in order when giving a speech. Their method was to take a mental walk along a familiar path. As they did, they associated topics with the images of statues found along the walk. You can do the same thing by "placing" objects or ideas along the way as you mentally take a familiar walk (Neath & Surprenant, 2003).

3. **Use a system.** As we have already seen, many times, the first letters or syllables of words or ideas can be formed into another word that will serve as a reminder of order. "Roy G. Biv" is an example. As an alternative, learn the following: 1 is a bun, 2 is a shoe, 3 is

a tree, 4 is a door, 5 is a hive, 6 is sticks, 7 is heaven, 8 is a gate, 9 is a line, 10 is a hen. To remember a list in order, form an image associating bun with the first item on your list. For example, if the first item is *frog,* picture a "frog-burger" on a bun to remember it. Then, associate shoe with the second item, and so on.

If you have never used mnemonics, you may still be skeptical, but give this approach a fair trial. Most people find they can greatly extend their memory through the use of mnemonics. But remember, like most things worthwhile, remembering takes effort.

study break
Mnemonics

RECITE

1. Memory systems and aids are referred to as
   _____.
2. Which of the following is least likely to improve memory?
   a. using exaggerated mental images
   b. forming a chain of associations
   c. turning visual information into verbal information
   d. associating new information with information that is already known or familiar
3. Bizarre images make stored information more distinctive and therefore easier to retrieve. T or F?
4. In general, mnemonics improve memory for only related words or ideas. T or F?

REFLECT
Critical Thinking

5. How are elaborative encoding and mnemonics alike?

Relate

The best mnemonics are your own. As an exercise, see if you can create a better acrostic for the 12 cranial nerves. One student generated **O**ld **O**tto **O**ctavius **T**ried **T**rigonometry **A**fter **F**acing **V**ery **G**rim **V**irgin's **S**ad **H**usbands (Bloom & Larrikin, 2006).

Go through the glossary items in this chapter and make up mnemonics for any terms you have difficulty remembering. Here is an example to help you get started. An iconic memory is a visual image: Picture an *eye* in a *can* to remember that iconic memories store visual information.

ANSWERS
1. mnemonics   2. c   3. T   4. F   5. Both attempt to relate new information to information stored in LTM that is familiar or already easy to retrieve.

chapter in review

Major Points

- Remembering is an active process. Our memories are frequently lost, altered, revised, or distorted.

- The best way to remember depends, to an extent, on which memory system you are using.

- Remembering is not an all-or-nothing process. Even when you think you can't recall anything, some information may continue to exist in memory.

- Understanding how and why forgetting occurs will allow you to make better use of your memory.

- Some people have naturally superior memories, but everyone can learn to improve his or her memory.

- Memory systems (mnemonics) greatly improve immediate memory. However, conventional learning tends to create the most lasting memories.

Summary

How does memory work?

- Memory is an active, computer-like system that encodes, stores, and retrieves information.
- The three stages of memory (sensory memory, short-term memory, and long-term memory) hold information for increasingly longer periods.
- Sensory memories are encoded as iconic memories or echoic memories. Short-term memories tend to be encoded by sound, and long-term memories by meaning.

What are the features of short-term memory?

- Selective attention determines what information moves from sensory memory, which is exact but very brief, on to STM.
- STM has a capacity of about five to seven bits of information, but this can be extended by chunking, or recoding. Short-term memories are brief and very sensitive to interruption, or interference; however, they can be prolonged by maintenance rehearsal.

What are the features of long-term memory?

- LTM serves as a general storehouse for meaningful information. Elaborative encoding helps us form lasting, long-term memories.
- Long-term memories are relatively permanent. LTM seems to have an almost unlimited storage capacity.
- Constructive processing tends to alter memories. Remembering is an active process. Our memories are frequently lost, altered, revised, or distorted.
- LTM is highly organized. The structure of memory networks is the subject of current research.
- In redintegration, memories are reconstructed, as one bit of information leads to others, which then serve as cues for further recall.
- LTM contains procedural (skill) and declarative (fact) memories. Declarative memories can be semantic or episodic.

How is memory measured?

- The tip-of-the-tongue state shows that memory is not an all-or-nothing event. Memories may therefore be revealed by recall, recognition, relearning, or priming.
- In recall, memories are retrieved without explicit cues, as in an essay exam. Recall of listed information often reveals a serial position effect.

- A common test of recognition is the multiple-choice question.
- In relearning, material that seems to be forgotten is learned again, and memory is revealed by a savings score.
- Recall, recognition, and relearning measure mainly explicit memories. Other techniques, such as priming, are necessary to reveal implicit memories.

Why do we forget?

- Forgetting can occur because of failures of encoding, of storage, or of retrieval.
- Herman Ebbinghaus found that forgetting is most rapid immediately after learning, as shown by the curve of forgetting.
- Failure to encode information is a common cause of "forgetting."
- Forgetting in sensory memory and STM is due to a failure of storage through a weakening (decay) of memory traces. Decay of memory traces may also explain some LTM losses.
- Failures of retrieval occur when information that resides in memory is nevertheless not retrieved.
- A lack of memory cues can produce retrieval failure. State-dependent learning is related to the effects of memory cues.
- Much forgetting in STM and LTM is caused by interference. In retroactive interference, new learning interferes with the ability to retrieve earlier learning. Proactive interference occurs when old learning interferes with the retrieval of new learning.
- Memories can be consciously suppressed and they may be unconsciously repressed.
- Extreme caution is warranted when "recovered" memories are the only basis for believing that a person was sexually abused during childhood.

How does the brain form and store memories?

- Lasting memories are recorded by changes in the activity, structure, and chemistry of brain cells.
- It takes time to consolidate memories. In the brain, memory consolidation takes place in the hippocampus. Until they are consolidated, long-term memories are easily destroyed.
- Intensely emotional experiences can result in flashbulb memories.
- After memories have been consolidated, they appear to be stored in the cortex of the brain.
- Memories are recorded in the brain through nerve cells and how they interconnect.

What are "photographic" memories?

- Eidetic imagery (photographic memory) occurs when a person is able to project an image onto a blank surface.
- Eidetic imagery is rarely found in adults. However, many adults have internal memory images, which can be very vivid.
- Although it's true that some people have naturally superior memories, everyone can learn to improve his or her memory.
- Exceptional memory may be based on natural ability or learned strategies. Usually it involves both.

How can I improve my memory?

- Excellent memory abilities are based on using strategies and techniques that make learning efficient and that compensate for natural weaknesses in human memory.
- Memory can be improved through better encoding strategies, such as elaborating, selecting and organizing information as well as whole learning, the progressive part method, encoding memory cues, overlearning, and spaced practice.
- Memory can also be improved through better retrieval strategies, such as using feedback, recitation, rehearsal, and active search strategies.
- When you are studying or memorizing, you should also keep in mind the effects of serial position, sleep, and hunger.

Are there any tricks to help me with my memory?

- Mnemonic systems use mental images and unusual associations to link new information with familiar memories already stored in LTM.
- Effective mnemonics tend to rely on mental images and bizarre or exaggerated mental associations.

Web Resources

For an up-to-date list of direct links to interesting sites, including those listed here, visit the student companion site for this book at www.cengage.com/psychology/coon

Playing Games with Memory Try some activities to test your memory.

The Atkinson-Schiffrin Model Further explore the three-store model of memory.

The Magical Number Seven, Plus or Minus Two Read George Miller's original paper on capacity limits in short-term memory.

Questions and Answers About Memories of Childhood Abuse Read a summary of the repressed memory issue from the American Psychological Association.

Free Recall Test Test your free recall ability.

Memory Strategies Read about a useful list of memory strategies for studying.

Memory Techniques and Mnemonics Follow links to information on mnemonics.

Interactive Learning

PSYCHOLOGY: A JOURNEY BOOK COMPANION WEBSITE
WWW.CENGAGE.COM/PSYCHOLOGY/COON

Visit your book companion website, where you will find flash cards, practice quizzes, web links, and more to help you study.

JUST WHAT YOU NEED TO KNOW NOW! CENGAGENOW

Spend time on what you need to master rather than on information you already have learned. Take a pretest for this chapter, and CengageNOW will generate a personalized study plan based on your results. The study plan will identify the topics you need to review and direct you to online resources to help you master those topics. You can then take a posttest to help you determine the concepts you have mastered and what you will need to work on. Try it out! Go to www.cengage.com/login to sign in with an access code or to purchase access to this product.

test your knowledge

Memory

For additional review, get more practice with *CengageNOW, WebTutor,* the *Practice Quizzes,* and/or the printed *Study Guide* available with this book.

1. The first step in forming a memory is
   a. retrieval
   b. storage
   c. rehearsal
   d. encoding

2. Storing information as an icon or an echo is most characteristic of
   a. sensory memory
   b. short-term memory
   c. long-term memory
   d. procedural memory

3. Selective attention controls which information moves from sensory memory to
   a. phonetic memory
   b. iconic memory
   c. STM
   d. LTM

4. Information in LTM is stored mainly on the basis of
   a. meaning
   b. sounds and phonetics
   c. icons and echos
   d. how it will be retrieved

5. The digit-span test is primarily a measure of
   a. LTM
   b. elaborative encoding
   c. recoding
   d. STM

6. Elaborative encoding is especially useful for forming
   a. memory icons
   b. long-term memories
   c. skill memories
   d. retroactive memories

7. Redintegration can be said to occur when one memory
   a. leads to another
   b. blocks retrieval
   c. is transferred to LTM
   d. is forgotten

8. Which of the following is a type of declarative memory?
   a. long-term memory
   b. redintegrative memory
   c. procedural memory
   d. episodic memory

9. The least sensitive test of memory is
   a. redintegration
   b. relearning
   c. recall
   d. recognition

10. Which type of memory test would be most likely to reveal a serial position effect?
    a. recall
    b. recognition
    c. relearning
    d. implicit

11. Implicit memories are which type of memories?
    a. explicit
    b. conscious
    c. skill
    d. unconscious

12. The fact that most people cannot correctly draw a U.S. penny is best explained by
    a. storage failure
    b. retrieval failure
    c. financial failure
    d. encoding failure

13. Decay of memory traces appears to apply most to the forgetting of
    a. sensory and short-term memories
    b. procedural memories
    c. semantic memories
    d. state-dependent memories

14. A saxophone player learns three new pieces of music, one after the other, in a single afternoon. The next day he is least able to remember the third piece because of
    a. state-dependent learning
    b. the time decay of memory traces
    c. proactive interference
    d. disuse of memory cues

15. If you can't remember putting a painful memory out of mind, you have used
    a. redintegration
    b. suppression
    c. negative rehearsal
    d. repression

16. Repressed memories could be thought of as the reverse of
    a. Flashbulb memories
    b. proactive memories
    c. retroactive memories
    d. episodic memories

17. Memory consolidation would most likely be disrupted by
    a. rehearsal
    b. ECS
    c. massed practice
    d. sleep

18. Which of the following is BAD advice for improving memory?
    a. Select and organize information.
    b. Use spaced practice.
    c. Take tests when you are hungry.
    d. Sleep after you study.

19. The cognitive interview is superior to hypnosis for helping people remember because it
    a. does not lead to more false memories
    b. leads to more false memories
    c. leads to less correct information
    d. uses fewer retrieval cues

20. The keyword method is a commonly used
    a. cognitive interviewing technique
    b. massed practice strategy
    c. mnemonic technique
    d. first step in the progressive-part method

Answers   1. d 2. a 3. c 4. a 5. d 6. b 7. a 8. d 9. c 10. a 11. d 12. d 13. a 14. c 15. d 16. a 17. b 18. c 19. a 20. c

Intelligence, Cognition, Language, and Creativity

Journey into Psychology: Homo sapiens

Unlike other species, humans owe their success more to intelligence and thinking abilities than to physical strength or speed (Goldstein, 2008). That's why our species is called *Homo sapiens* (from the Latin for *man* and *wise*). Our intelligence makes us highly adaptable creatures. We live in deserts, jungles, mountains, frenzied cities, placid retreats, and space stations.

Consider Steven Hawking. He can't walk or talk. When he was 13, Lou Gehrig's disease began to slowly destroy nerve cells in his spinal cord, short-circuiting messages between his brain and muscles. Today, he is confined to a wheelchair and "speaks" by manually controlling a speech synthesizer. Yet despite his severe disabilities, his brain is unaffected by the disease and remains fiercely active. He can still *think*. Steven is a theoretical physicist and one of the best-known scientific minds of modern times. With courage and determination, he has used his intellect to advance our understanding of the universe.

But what exactly is wisdom? What is intelligence? How do we think? How are we able to solve problems? How do people like Steven Hawking create works of science, art, and literature? For some preliminary answers, we will investigate intelligence, thinking, problem solving, language, and creativity, in the following pages.

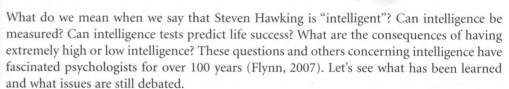

Survey Questions

- How is human intelligence defined and measured?
- How much does intelligence vary from person to person?
- What are some controversies in the study of intelligence?
- What is the nature of thought?
- In what ways are images related to thinking?
- What are concepts?
- What is the role of language in thinking?
- What do we know about problem solving?
- What is creative thinking?
- How accurate is intuition?
- What can be done to improve thinking and promote creativity?

Human Intelligence—The IQ and You

How is human intelligence defined and measured?

What do we mean when we say that Steven Hawking is "intelligent"? Can intelligence be measured? Can intelligence tests predict life success? What are the consequences of having extremely high or low intelligence? These questions and others concerning intelligence have fascinated psychologists for over 100 years (Flynn, 2007). Let's see what has been learned and what issues are still debated.

Like many important concepts in psychology, intelligence cannot be observed directly. Nevertheless, we feel certain it exists. Let's compare two children:

> When she was 14 months old, Anne wrote her own name. She taught herself to read at age 2. At age 5, she astounded her kindergarten teacher by bringing a notebook computer to class—on which she was reading an encyclopedia. At 10 she breezed through an entire high school algebra course in 12 hours.

> Billy, who is 10 years old, can write his name and can count, but he has trouble with simple addition and subtraction problems and finds multiplication impossible. He has been held back in school twice and is still incapable of doing the work his 8-year-old classmates find easy.

Anne is considered a genius; Billy, a slow learner. There seems little doubt that they differ in intelligence.

Wait! Anne's ability is obvious, but how do we know that Billy isn't just lazy? That's the same question that Alfred Binet faced in 1904 (Jarvin & Sternberg, 2003). The French minister of education in Paris wanted to find a way to distinguish slower students from the more capable (or the capable but lazy). In a flash of brilliance, Binet and an associate created a test made up of "intellectual" questions and problems. Next, they learned which questions an average child could answer at each age. By giving children the test, they could tell if a child was performing up to his or her potential (Kaufman, 2000).

Binet's approach gave rise to modern intelligence tests. At the same time, it launched an ongoing debate. Part of the debate is related to the basic difficulty of defining intelligence (Sternberg, Grigorenko, & Kidd, 2005).

Defining Intelligence

Isn't there an accepted definition of intelligence? Broadly speaking, yes. **Intelligence** is the global capacity to act purposefully, to think rationally, and to deal effectively with the environment. The core of intelligence is usually thought to consist of a small set of *general mental abilities* (called the **g-factor**) in the areas of reasoning, problem solving, knowledge, memory, and successful adaptation to one's surroundings (Sternberg, 2004). Beyond this, however, there is much disagreement. In fact, many psychologists simply accept an *operational definition* of intelligence by spelling out the procedures they use to measure it. Thus, by selecting items for an intelligence test, a psychologist is saying in a very direct way, "This is what I mean by intelligence." A test that measures memory, reasoning, and verbal fluency offers a very different definition of intelligence than one that measures strength of grip, shoe size, length of the nose, or the person's best *Mario Cart* video game score.

Measuring Intelligence

American psychologists quickly saw the value of Alfred Binet's test. In 1916, Lewis Terman and others at Stanford University revised it for use in North America. After more revisions, the *Stanford-Binet Intelligence Scales, Fifth Edition* (SB5) continues to be widely used. The SB5 is made up primarily of age-ranked questions. Naturally, these questions get a little harder at each age level. The SB5 is appropriate for people from age 2 to 85+ years (Roid, 2003).

The SB5 measures five cognitive factors (types of mental abilities) that make up general intelligence. These are *fluid reasoning, knowledge, quantitative reasoning, visual-spatial pro-*

Modern intelligence tests are widely used to measure intellectual abilities. When properly administered, such tests provide an operational definition of intelligence.

Intelligence An overall capacity to think rationally, act purposefully, and deal effectively with the environment.

g-factor A general ability factor or core of general intellectual ability that involves reasoning, problem-solving ability, knowledge, memory, and successful adaptation to one's surroundings.

cessing, and *working memory*. Each factor is measured with verbal questions (those involving words and numbers) and nonverbal questions (items that use pictures and objects). Let's see what each factor looks like.

Fluid Reasoning

Fluid reasoning is tested with questions like the following:

How are an apple, a plum, and a banana different from a beet?
An apprentice is to a master as a novice is to an _____.
"I knew my bag was going to be in the last place I looked, so I looked there first." What is silly or impossible about that?

Other items ask people to fill in the missing shape in a group of shapes and to tell a story that explains what's going on in a series of pictures.

Knowledge

The Knowledge factor assesses what a person knows about a wide range of topics.

Why is yeast added to bread dough?
What does "cryptic" mean?
What is silly or impossible about this picture? (For example, a bicycle has square wheels.)

Quantitative Reasoning

Test items for Quantitative Reasoning measure a person's ability to solve problems involving numbers. Here are some samples:

If I have six marbles and you give me another one, how many marbles will I have?
Given the numbers 3, 6, 9, 12, what number would come next?
If a shirt is being sold for 50 percent of the normal price, and the price tag is $60, what is the cost of the shirt?

Visual-Spatial Processing

People who have visual-spatial skills are good at putting picture puzzles together and copying geometric shapes (such as triangles, rectangles, and circles). Visual-Spatial Processing questions ask test takers to reproduce patterns of blocks and choose pictures that show how a piece of paper would look if it were folded or cut. Verbal questions can also require visual-spatial abilities:

Suppose that you are going east, then turn right, then turn right again, then turn left. In what direction are you facing now?

Working Memory

The Working Memory part of the SB5 measures the ability to use short-term memory. Some typical memory tasks include the following:

Correctly remember the order of colored beads on a stick.
After hearing several sentences, name the last word from each sentence.
Repeat a series of digits (forward or backward) after hearing them once.

If you were to take the SB5, it would yield a score for your general intelligence, verbal intelligence, nonverbal intelligence, and each of the five cognitive factors (Bain & Allin, 2005).

The Wechsler Tests

Is the Stanford-Binet the only intelligence test? A widely used alternative is the *Wechsler Adult Intelligence Scale—Third Edition* (WAIS-III). A version for children is called the *Wechsler Intelligence Scale for Children—Fourth Edition* (WISC-IV) (Baron, 2005).

Table 8.1 Sample Items Similar to Those Used on the WAIS-III

VERBAL SUBTESTS	SAMPLE ITEMS
Information	How many wings does a bird have?
	Who wrote *Paradise Lost*?
Digit span	Repeat from memory a series of digits, such as 3 1 0 6 7 4 2 5, after hearing it once.
General	What is the advantage of keeping money in the bank?
Comprehension	Why is copper often used in electrical wires?
Arithmetic	Three men divided 18 golf balls equally among themselves. How many golf balls did each man receive?
	If 2 apples cost 15¢, what will be the cost of a dozen apples?
Similarities	In what way are a lion and a tiger alike?
	In what way are a saw and a hammer alike?
Vocabulary	The test consists simply of asking, "What is a _____?" or "What does _____ mean?"
	The words cover a wide range of difficulty or familiarity.

PERFORMANCE SUBTESTS	DESCRIPTION OF ITEM
Picture arrangement	Arrange a series of cartoon panels to make a meaningful story.
Picture completion	What is missing from these pictures?
Block design	Copy designs with blocks (as shown at right).
Object assembly	Put together a jigsaw puzzle.
Digit symbol	Fill in the symbols:

1	2	3	4
X	III	I	0

3	4	1	3	4	2	1	2

Although the Wechsler tests are similar to the Stanford-Binet, there are some differences as well. For one thing, the WAIS-III was specifically designed to test adult intelligence. The original Stanford-Binet was better suited for children and adolescents. The latest Stanford-Binet (the SB5) can now be used for all ages, but the WAIS was the first "adult" intelligence test. Like the Stanford-Binet, the Wechsler tests yield a single overall intelligence score. In addition, the WAIS and WISC give separate scores for **performance** (nonverbal) **intelligence** and **verbal** (language- or symbol-oriented) **intelligence.** (Note that this feature was also recently added to the SB5.) The abilities measured by the Wechsler tests and some sample test items are listed in ● Table 8.1.

Intelligence Quotients

What is an IQ score? Imagine that a child named Yuan can answer questions an average 7-year-old can answer. How smart is she? Actually, we can't say yet, because we don't know how old Yuan is. If she is 10, she's not very smart. If she's 5, she is very bright. Thus, to estimate a child's intelligence we need to compare her **mental age** (average intellectual performance) and her **chronological age** (age in years). This yields an **intelligence quotient,** or **IQ.** When the Stanford-Binet was first used, IQ was defined as mental age (MA) divided by chronological age (CA) and multiplied by 100. (Multiplying by 100 changes the IQ into a whole number, rather than a decimal.)

$$\frac{MA}{CA} \times 100 = IQ$$

Calculating IQ scores allows a comparison between children with different chronological and mental ages. For instance, 10-year-old Justin has a mental age of 12. Thus, his IQ is 120. Justin's friend Suke also has a mental age of 12. However, Suke's chronological age is 12,

Performance intelligence Intelligence measured by solving puzzles, assembling objects, completing pictures, and other nonverbal tasks.

Verbal intelligence Intelligence measured by answering questions involving vocabulary, general information, arithmetic, and other language- or symbol-oriented tasks.

Mental age The average mental ability people display at a given age.

Chronological age A person's age in years.

Intelligence quotient (IQ) An index of intelligence defined as a person's mental age divided by his or her chronological age and multiplied by 100.

so his IQ is 100. The IQ shows that 10-year-old Justin is brighter than his 12-year-old friend Suke, even though their intellectual skills are about the same. Notice that a person's IQ will be 100 when mental age equals chronological age. An IQ score of 100 is therefore defined as average intelligence.

Then does a person with an IQ score below 100 have below average intelligence? Not unless the IQ is well below 100, since average intelligence is usually defined as any score from 90 to 109. The important point is that IQ scores will be over 100 when mental age is higher than age in years. IQ scores below 100 occur when a person's age in years exceeds his or her mental age.

Deviation IQs

Although the preceding examples may give you insight into IQ scores, it's no longer necessary to directly calculate IQs. Instead, modern tests use **deviation IQs.** Tables supplied with the test are used to convert a person's relative standing in the group to an IQ score. That is, they tell how far above or below average the person's score falls. For example, if you score at the 50th percentile, half the people your age who take the test score higher than you and half score lower. In this case, your IQ score is 100. If you score at the 84th percentile, your IQ score is 115. If you score at the 97th percentile, your IQ score is 130. (For more information, see the Statistics appendix near the end of this book.)

Group Tests

The SB5 and the Wechsler tests are individual intelligence tests, which must be given to a single person by a trained specialist. In contrast, group intelligence tests can be given to a large group of people with minimal supervision. Group tests usually require people to read, to follow instructions, and to solve problems of logic, reasoning, mathematics, or spatial skills. If you're wondering if you have ever taken an intelligence test, the answer is probably yes. The well-known *SAT Reasoning Test* (SAT) measures aptitudes for language, math, and reasoning. The SAT is designed to predict your chances for success in college. Because it measures a number of different mental aptitudes, it can also be used to estimate general intelligence (Frey & Detterman, 2004).

Artificial Intelligence

While most efforts have focused on measuring intelligence in humans, a small group of psychologists and computer scientists have taken an entirely different approach. Their basic idea is to build machines that display **artificial intelligence (AI).** This usually refers to creating computer programs capable of doing things that require intelligence when done by people (Russell & Norvig, 2003). As computer scientist Aaron Sloman explains it, "Human brains don't work by magic, so whatever it is they do should be doable by machine" (Brooks, 2009). The resulting programs can then help us understand how people do those same things.

Consider, for example, Aaron Sloman's robot, the "Cubinator," which does a spiffy job of solving Rubik's Cube puzzles. Sloman hopes the Cubinator's expertise will help him better understand how humans do mathematics (Sloman, 2008).

How smart are computers and robots? Don't worry, they are not very smart yet. Let's say you are exchanging instant messages over the Internet with someone you don't know. You are allowed to make any comments and ask any questions you like, for as long as you like. In reality, the "person" you are communicating with is a computer. Do you think a computer could fool you into believing it was human? If it did, wouldn't that qualify it as "intelligent"? You may be surprised to learn that, to date, no machine has come close to passing this test (Moor, 2003).

The problem computers face is that we humans can mentally "shift gears" from one topic to another with incredible flexibility. In contrast, machine "intelligence" is currently "blind" outside its underlying set of rules. As a tiny example, u cann understnd wrds thet ar mizpeld. Computers are very literal and easily stymied by such errors.

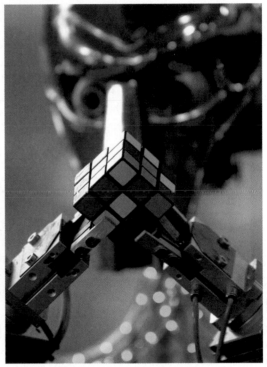

Bela Szandelszky/AP Images

The "Cubinator" solving a Rubik's Cube at the 2007 Rubik's Cube World Championships. The winner, in 10 seconds, was a person. The Cubinator took 26 seconds. To what extent is the way the Cubinator comes up with solutions helpful for understanding how humans do it?

Deviation IQ An IQ obtained statistically from a person's relative standing in his or her age group; that is, how far above or below average the person's score was relative to other scores.

Artificial intelligence (AI) Any artificial system (often a computer program) that is capable of human-like problem solving or intelligent responding.

Regardless, AI has been successful at very specific tasks (such as playing chess or solving Rubik's Cubes). Much of current AI is based on the fact that many tasks—from harmonizing music to diagnosing disease—can be reduced to a set of rules applied to a collection of information. AI is valuable in situations where speed, vast memory, and persistence are required. In fact, AI programs are better at some tasks than humans are. An example is world chess champion Garry Kasparov's loss, in 1997, to a computer called Deep Blue.

Artificial Intelligence and Cognition

Although AI is a long way from duplicating general human intelligence, AI systems like the Cubinator offer a way to probe some of our specific cognitive skills, or intelligences. For instance, computer simulations and expert systems provide good examples of how AI is being used as a research tool.

Computer simulations are programs that attempt to duplicate specific human behaviors, especially thinking, decision making, and problem solving. Here, the computer acts as a "laboratory" for testing models of cognition. If a computer program behaves as humans do (including making the same errors), then the program may be a good model of how we think.

Expert systems are computer programs that respond as a human expert would (Giarratano & Riley, 2005). They have demystified some human abilities by converting complex skills into clearly stated rules a computer can follow. Expert systems can predict the weather, analyze geological formations, diagnose disease, play chess, read, tell when to buy or sell stocks, and perform many other tasks.

Eventually, AI will almost certainly lead to robots that recognize voices and that speak and act "intelligently" in specific areas of ability. To achieve this, should intelligence be directly programmed into computers? Or should computers be designed to learn from experience, like the human brain does? (McClelland & Rogers, 2003). Only time will tell. For now, let's turn to a look at how much measured intelligence varies from person to person.

Variations in Intelligence—Curved Like a Bell

How much does intelligence vary from person to person?

IQ scores are classified as shown in ▶▶ Figure 8.1. The distribution (or scattering) of IQ scores approximates a **normal** (bell-shaped) **curve.** That is, most scores fall close to the average and very few are found at the extremes.

The Mentally Gifted

How high is the IQ of a genius? Only 2 people out of 100 score above 130 on IQ tests. These bright individuals are usually described as "gifted." Less than one half of 1 percent of the population scores above 140. These people are certainly gifted or perhaps even "geniuses."

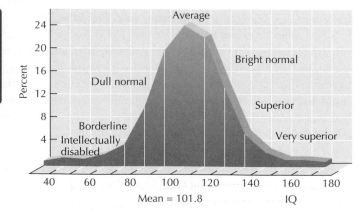

▶▶ **FIGURE 8.1** Distribution of Stanford-Binet Intelligence Test scores for 3,184 children. (After Terman & Merrill, 1937/1960.)

Normal curve A bell-shaped curve characterized by a large number of scores in a middle area, tapering to very few extremely high and low scores.

However, some psychologists reserve the term *genius* for people with even higher IQs or those who are exceptionally creative (Hallahan & Kauffman, 2006).

Gifted Children

Do high IQ scores in childhood predict later ability? To directly answer this question, Lewis Terman selected 1,500 children with IQs of 140 or more. Terman followed this gifted group (the "Termites" as he called them) into adulthood and found that most were quite successful. A majority finished college, earned advanced degrees, or held professional positions, and many had written books or scientific articles (Terman & Oden, 1959).

In general, the correlation between IQ scores and school grades is .50, a sizable association. The link would be even stronger, but motivation, special talents, off-campus learning, and many other factors also affect grades. The same is true of "real world" success beyond school. IQ is not at all good at predicting success in art, music, writing, dramatics, science, and leadership. Creativity is much more strongly related to doing well in these areas (Preckel, Holling, & Wiese, 2006; Runco, 2004). Regardless, when people score in the gifted range, their chances for high achievement do seem to rise (Shurkin, 1992).

Were all the Termites superior as adults? No. Although most were mentally healthy and successful, some had committed crimes, were unemployable, or were emotionally troubled. Remember that a high IQ reveals *potential.* It does not guarantee success. Nor does a lower IQ guarantee failure. Nobel prize–winning physicist Richard Feynman, whom many regarded as a genius, had an IQ of 122 (Michalko, 1998).

How did Terman's more successful Termites differ from the less successful? Most of them had educated parents who taught them to value learning. They also had *intellectual determination,* which is a desire to know, to excel, and to persevere (Winner, 2003). Thus, successful gifted persons tend to be persistent and motivated to learn. No one is paid to sit around being capable of achievement. What you do is always more important than what you should be able to do. That's why children's talents are most likely to blossom when they are nurtured with support, encouragement, education, and effort (Callahan, 2006).

Identifying Gifted Children

How might a parent spot an unusually bright child? Early signs of giftedness are not always purely "intellectual." **Giftedness** can be the possession of either a high IQ or of special talents or aptitudes, such as creativity.

The following signs may reveal that a child is gifted: A tendency to seek out older children and adults; an early fascination with explanations and problem solving; talking in complete sentences as early as 2 or 3 years of age; an unusually good memory; precocious talent in art, music, or number skills; an early interest in books, along with early reading (often by age 3); showing of kindness, understanding, and cooperation toward others (Alvino & Editors, 1996; Distin, 2006).

It is wise to remember that there are many ways in which a child may be gifted. Many schools now offer Gifted and Talented Education programs for students with a variety of special abilities—not just for those who score well on IQ tests.

Notice that this list goes beyond straight g-factor, or general "academic" intelligence. In fact, if artistic talent, mechanical aptitude, musical aptitude, athletic potential, and so on are considered, many children have a special "gift" of one kind or another. Limiting giftedness

Giftedness Either the possession of a high IQ or special talents or aptitudes.

Meet the Rain Man

Meet Kim Peek, the model for Dustin Hoffman's character in the Academy Award–winning movie *Rain Man*. Kim began memorizing books at 18 months of age. Today, he can recite from memory more than 9,000 books. He knows all the ZIP codes and area codes in the United States and can give accurate travel directions between any two major U.S. cities. He can also discuss hundreds of pieces of classical music in detail and is even learning to play all that music. Amazingly, though, for someone with such skills, Kim has difficulty with abstract thinking and tests of general intelligence. He is poorly coordinated and cannot button his own clothes (Treffert & Christensen, 2005).

Kim Peek has *savant syndrome,* in which a person of limited intelligence shows exceptional mental ability in one or more narrow areas, such as mental arithmetic, calendar calculations, art, or music (Young, 2005).

Richard Green

Once, four months after reading a Tom Clancy novel, *The Hunt for Red October,* Kim was asked about a character, a Russian radio operator. He immediately named the character, gave the page number on which a description appeared, and accurately recited several paragraphs about the character (Treffert & Christensen, 2005).

Do savants have special mental powers not shared by most people? According to one theory, many savants have suffered some form of damage to their left hemispheres, freeing them from the "distractions" of language, concepts, and higher-level thought. This allows them to focus with crystal clarity on music, drawing, prime numbers, license plates, TV commercials, and other specific information (Young, 2005). Another theory holds that the performances of many savants result from intense practice (Miller, 1999). Perhaps each of us harbors embers of mental brilliance that intense practice could fan into full flame (Snyder et al., 2006).

Although savant syndrome hasn't been fully explained, it does show that extraordinary abilities can exist apart from general intelligence.

to high IQ can shortchange children with special talents. This is especially true of ethnic minority children, who may be the victims of subtle biases in standardized intelligence tests. These children, as well as children with physical disabilities, are less likely to be recognized as gifted (Ford & Moore, 2006; Robinson & Clinkenbeard, 1998).

In the next section, we will discuss intellectual disability. Before you begin, take a few moments to read "Meet the Rain Man," where you will find information about a remarkable mixture of brilliance and mental disability.

Intellectual Disability

A person with mental abilities far below average is termed **intellectually disabled** (the former term, **mentally retarded,** is now regarded by many as offensive). Intellectual disability begins at an IQ of approximately 70 or below. However, a person's ability to perform *adaptive behaviors* (basic skills such as dressing, eating, communicating, shopping, and working) also figures into evaluating this disability (American Psychiatric Association, 2000; Hallahan & Kauffman, 2006). (See ● Table 8.2.)

Intellectual disability (formerly mental retardation) The presence of a developmental disability, a formal IQ score below 70, or a significant impairment of adaptive behavior.

● Table 8.2 Levels of Intellectual Disability

IQ RANGE	DEGREE OF INTELLECTUAL DISABILITY	EDUCATIONAL CLASSIFICATION	REQUIRED LEVEL OF SUPPORT
50–55 to 70	Mild	Educable	Intermittent
35–40 to 50–55	Moderate	Trainable	Limited
20–25 to 35–40	Severe	Dependent	Extensive
Below 20–25	Profound	Life support	Pervasive

(American Psychiatric Association, 2000; Hodapp, 1994.)

It's important to realize that intellectually disabled persons have no handicap where feelings are concerned. They are easily hurt by rejection, teasing, or ridicule. Likewise, they respond warmly to love and acceptance. They have a right to self-respect and a place in the community (Montreal Declaration on Intellectual Disabilities, 2004). This is especially important during childhood, when support from others adds greatly to the person's chances of becoming a well-adjusted member of society.

Causes of Intellectual Disability

What causes intellectual disability? About half of all cases of intellectual disability are *organic,* or related to physical disorders (Das, 2000). These include *genetic abnormalities,* such as missing genes, extra genes, or defective genes; *fetal damage* (prenatal damage from teratogens such as disease, infection, or drugs); and *birth injuries* (such as lack of oxygen during delivery). *Metabolic disorders,* which affect energy production and use in the body, also cause intellectual disability. Malnutrition and exposure to lead, PCBs, and other toxins early in childhood can also cause organic intellectual disability (Beirne-Smith, Patton, & Shannon, 2006).

These youngsters are participants in the Special Olympics—an athletic event for the intellectually disabled. It is often said of the Special Olympics that "everyone is a winner—participants, coaches, and spectators."

In 30 to 40 percent of cases, no known biological problem can be identified. In many such instances, the degree of intellectual disability is mild, in the 50 to 70 IQ range. Often, other family members are also mildly intellectually disabled. *Familial intellectual disability,* as this is called, occurs mostly in very poor households where nutrition, intellectual stimulation, medical care, and emotional support may be inadequate. This suggests that familial intellectual disability is based largely on an impoverished environment. Thus, better nutrition, education, and early childhood enrichment programs could prevent many cases of intellectual disability (Beirne-Smith, Patton, & Shannon, 2006).

Questioning Intelligence—How Intelligent Is the Idea of Intelligence?

What are some controversies in the study of intelligence?

The idea that intelligence can be defined in terms of a small set of general mental abilities and measured with IQ tests like the SB5 or the Wechsler scales has been controversial for several reasons. To begin, not every culture values the intellectual skills assessed by these tests. (For a glimpse at how some other cultures define "intelligence," see "Intelligence— How Would a Fool Do It?"). In view of such differences, psychologists have tried to create "culture fair" intelligence tests. Some have questioned the value of defining intelligence in terms of any general intelligence factor. Others have wondered whether intelligence is mainly inherited from our parents or shaped through life experiences.

Culture and Intelligence

Imagine giving the SB5 to a young Pulawat islander. If navigating from island to island is what he values and is good at, then what would it mean if he got a low IQ score? Psychologist Jerome Kagan once remarked, "If the Wechsler and Binet scales were translated into Spanish, Swahili, and Chinese and given to every 10-year-old in Latin America, East Africa, and China, the majority would obtain IQ scores in the mentally retarded range."

Certainly we cannot believe that children of other cultures are all intellectually disabled. The fault must lie with the test (White, 2006). As noted earlier, cultural values, knowledge, language patterns, and traditions can greatly affect performance on tests designed for

human diversity

Intelligence—How Would a Fool Do It?

You have been asked to sort some objects into categories. Wouldn't it be smart to put the clothes, containers, implements, and foods in separate piles? Not necessarily. When members of the Kpelle culture in Liberia were asked to sort objects, they grouped them together by function. For example, a potato (food) would be placed together with a knife (implement). When the Kpelle were asked why they grouped the objects this way, they often said that that was how a wise man would do it. The researchers finally asked the Kpelle, "How would a fool do it?" Only then did the Kpelle sort the objects into the nice, neat categories we Westerners prefer.

This anecdote, related by cultural psychologist Patricia Greenfield (1997), raises serious questions about general definitions of intelligence. For example, among the Cree of northern Canada, "smart" people are the ones who have visual skills needed to find food on the frozen tundra (Darou, 1992). For the Puluwat people in the South Pacific, being smart means having ocean-going navigation skills necessary to get from island to island (Sternberg, 2004). And so it goes, as each culture teaches its children the kinds of "intelligence" valued in that culture—how the wise man would do it, not the fool (Correa-Chávez, Rogoff, & Arauz, 2005).

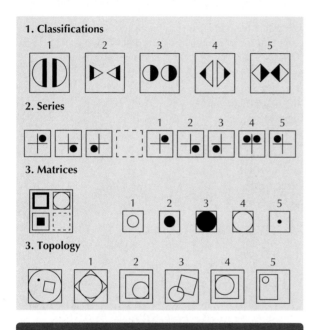

Culture-fair test A test (such as an intelligence test) designed to minimize the importance of skills and knowledge that may be more common in some cultures than in others.

Western cultures (Neisser et al., 1996; Sternberg & Grigorenko, 2005). To avoid this problem, some psychologists have tried to develop culture-fair tests that do not disadvantage certain groups. A **culture-fair test** is designed to minimize the importance of skills and knowledge that may be more common in some cultures than in others. (For a sample of culture-fair test items, see ▶▶ Figure 8.2.)

Culture-fair tests attempt to measure intelligence without, as much as possible, being influenced by a person's verbal skills, cultural background, and educational level. Their value lies not just in testing people from other cultures. They are also useful for testing children in the United States who come from poor communities, rural areas, or ethnic minority families (Stephens et al., 1999). However, no intelligence test can be entirely free of cultural influences. For instance, our culture is very "visual," because children are constantly exposed to television, movies, video games, and the like. Thus, compared with children in developing countries, a child who grows up in the United States may be better prepared to take *both* nonverbal tests and traditional IQ tests.

Because the concept of intelligence exhibits such diversity across cultures, many psychologists have begun to stress the need to rethink the concept of intelligence itself (Greenfield, 1997; Sternberg & Grigorenko, 2005). If we are to find a truly culture-fair way to measure intelligence, we first need to better identify those core cognitive skills, or multiple intelligences, that lie at the heart of human intelligence the world around (Sternberg & Grigorenko, 2006).

Multiple Intelligences

Defining intelligence as a g-factor (general ability) has been controversial. As we noted earlier in our discussion of "intelligent" behavior in other cultures, there are many ways to be smart. For example, consider William, a grade-school student two years behind in reading, who shows his teacher how to solve a difficult computer-programming problem. Or what about his classmate, Malika, who is poor in math but plays intricate pieces of piano music? Both of these children show clear signs of intelligence. And yet, each might score below average on a traditional IQ test. And, as we have seen, autistic savants like Kim Peek have even more extreme intellectual strengths and weaknesses. Such observations have convinced many psychologists that it is time to forge new, broader definitions of intelligence. Their basic goal is to better predict "real world" success—not just the likelihood of success in school (Sternberg & Grigorenko, 2006).

One such psychologist is Howard Gardner of Harvard University. Gardner (2003, 2004) theorizes that there are actually eight distinctly different kinds of intelligence. These are different mental "languages" that people use for thinking. Each is listed below, with examples of pursuits that make use of them:

1. *Language* (linguistic abilities)—writer, lawyer, comedian
2. *Logic and math* (numeric abilities)—scientist, accountant, programmer
3. *Visual and spatial* (pictorial abilities)—engineer, inventor, artist
4. *Music* (musical abilities)—composer, musician, music critic
5. *Bodily-kinesthetic* (physical abilities)—dancer, athlete, surgeon
6. *Intrapersonal* (self-knowledge)—poet, actor, minister
7. *Interpersonal* (social abilities)—psychologist, teacher, politician
8. *Naturalist* (an ability to understand the natural environment)—biologist, medicine man, organic farmer

To simplify a great deal, people can be "word smart," "number smart," "picture smart," "music smart," "body smart," "self smart," "people smart," and/or "nature smart."

Most of us are probably strong in only a few types of intelligence. In contrast, geniuses like Albert Einstein seem to be able to use nearly all of the intelligences, as needed, to solve problems.

If Gardner's theory of **multiple intelligences** is correct, traditional IQ tests measure only a part of real-world intelligence—namely, linguistic, logical-mathematical, and spatial abilities. A further implication is that our schools may be wasting a lot of human potential (Campbell, Campbell, & Dickinson, 2003). For example, some children might find it easier to learn math or reading if these topics were tied into art, music, dance, drama, and so on. Already, many schools are using Gardner's theory to cultivate a wider range of skills and talents (Campbell, Campbell, & Dickinson, 2003; Kornhaber & Gardner, 2006).

Let's end this section with a look at the controversial question of how much intelligence is inherited from our parents.

According to Howard Gardner's theory, bodily-kinesthetic skills reflect one of eight distinct types of intelligence.

IQ and Heredity

Is intelligence inherited? Most people are aware that there is a moderate similarity in the intelligence of parents and their children, or between brothers and sisters. As ▶▶ Figure 8.3 shows, the similarity in IQ scores among relatives grows in proportion to how close they are on the family tree.

Does this indicate that intelligence is hereditary? Not necessarily. Brothers, sisters, and parents share similar environments as well as similar heredity. To separate nature and nurture, **twin studies** may be done. Such studies compare the IQs of twins who were raised together or separated at birth. This allows us to estimate how much heredity and environment affect intelligence.

Twin Studies

Notice in Figure 8.3 that the IQs of fraternal twins are more alike than the IQs of ordinary siblings. *Fraternal twins* come from two separate eggs fertilized at the same time. Genetically, they are no more alike than ordinary siblings. Why, then, should the twins' IQs be more similar? The reason may be environmental: Parents treat twins more alike than ordinary siblings, resulting in a closer match in IQs.

More striking similarities are observed with *identical twins,* who develop from a single egg and have identical genes. At the top of Figure 8.3 you can see that identical twins who grow up in the same family have highly correlated IQs. This is what we would expect with identical heredity and very similar environments. Now, let's consider what happens when identical twins are reared apart. As you can see, the correlation drops, but only from 0.86 to 0.72. Psychologists who emphasize genetics believe these figures show that adult intelligence is roughly 50 percent hereditary (Grigorenko & Sternberg, 2003).

⬆ FIGURE 8.3 Approximate correlations between IQ scores for persons with varying degrees of genetic and environmental similarity. Notice that the correlations grow smaller as the degree of genetic similarity declines. Also note that a shared environment increases the correlation in all cases. (Estimates from Bouchard, 1983; Henderson, 1982.)

Multiple intelligences Howard Gardner's theory that there are several specialized types of intellectual ability.

Twin study A comparison of the characteristics of twins who were raised together or separated at birth; used to identify the relative impact of heredity and environment.

How do environmentalists interpret the figures? They point out that the IQs of some separated twins differ by as much as 20 points. Such IQ gaps occur when the twins grow up with big educational and environmental differences. It is more common for separated twins to be placed in homes socially and educationally similar to those of their biological parents. This fact would tend to inflate apparent genetic effects by making the separated twins' IQs more alike. Another frequently overlooked fact is that twins grow up in the same environment *before birth* (in the womb). If we take such environmental similarities into account, intelligence would seem to be less than 50 percent hereditary (Devlin, Daniels, & Roeder, 1997; Turkheimer et al., 2003).

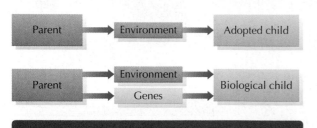

FIGURE 8.4 Comparison of an adopted child and a biological child reared in the same family. (After Kamin, 1981.)

IQ and Environment

How much can environment alter intelligence? Intriguing evidence for an environmental view of intelligence comes from adoption studies. Consider families having one adopted child and one biological child. As ▶▶ Figure 8.4 shows, parents contribute genes *and* environment to their biological child. With an adopted child they contribute only environment. If intelligence is highly genetic, the IQs of biological children should be more like their parents' IQs than are the IQs of adopted children. However, one study found that children reared by the same mother tend to resemble her IQ to the same degree. It does not matter whether or not they share her genes (Kamin, 1981; Weinberg, 1989).

In another study, striking increases in IQ occurred in 25 children who were moved from an orphanage and were eventually adopted by parents who gave them love, a family, and a stimulating home environment. Once considered intellectually disabled and unadoptable, the children gained an average of 29 IQ points. A second group of initially less "intellectually disabled" children, who stayed in the orphanage, *lost* an average of 26 IQ points! (Skeels, 1966).

A particularly dramatic environmental effect is the gain in Westernized nations of an average of 15 IQ points during the last 30 years (Dickens & Flynn, 2001; Flynn, 2007). These IQ boosts occurred in far too short a time for genetics to explain them. It is more likely that the gains reflect environmental forces, such as improved education and nutrition and living in a technologically complex society (Johnson, 2005). If you've ever tried to play a computer game or set up a wireless network in your home, you'll understand why people may be getting better at answering IQ test questions. (See "You Mean Video Games Might Be Good for Me?")

IQ and Race

Historically, African-American children in the United States scored an average of about 15 points lower on standardized IQ tests than European-American children. As a group, Japanese-American children scored above average in IQ. Could such differences be genetic? One persistent claim is that African Americans score below average in IQ because of their "genetic heritage" and because they are genetically incapable of climbing out of poverty (Hernstein & Murray, 1994; Rushton & Jensen, 2005). Psychologists have responded to such claims with a number of counterarguments.

To begin, it is no secret that as a group African Americans are more likely than European Americans to live in environments that are physically, educationally, and intellectually impoverished. When unequal education is part of the equation, IQs may tell us little about how heredity affects intelligence (Sternberg, Grigorenko, & Kidd, 2005; Suzuki & Aronson, 2005). Indeed, one study found that placing poor African-American children into European-American adoptive families increased the children's IQs by an average of 13 points, bringing them into line with those of European-American children (Nisbett, 2005). That is, providing African-American children with the same environmental experiences available to European-American children erased IQ differences.

One tantalizing hint that lower African-American IQ scores are not genetic is provided by the "Obama effect." Ray Friedman and his colleagues at Vanderbilt University administered a

You Mean Video Games Might Be Good for Me?

Although rapidly rising Western IQ scores suggest that environmental factors influence intelligence (Flynn, 2007; Schooler, 1998), we are left with the question, Which factors? Writer Steven Johnson (2005) believes that popular culture is responsible. Although he agrees that much popular media content is too violent or sexual in nature, he points out that video games, the Internet, and even television are becoming more complex. As a result, they demand ever-greater cognitive effort from us. In other words, it is as important to understand *how* we experience the environment as it is to understand *what* we experience.

For example, early video games, such as *Pong* or *Pac Man*, offered simple, repetitive visual experiences. In contrast, today's popular games, such as *The World of Warcraft* or *Second Life*, offer rich, complicated experiences that can take many hours of intense problem solving to complete. Furthermore, players must usually figure out the rules by themselves. Instructions that fans have written for popular games are typically much longer than chapters in this book. Only a complex and engaging game would prompt players to use such instructions, much less write them for others to use (Johnson, 2005).

According to Johnson, other forms of popular culture have also become more complex, including the Internet, computer software, and even popular television. For example, compared with television dramas of the past, modern dramas weave plot lines and characters through an entire season of programs. In the end, popular culture may well be inviting us to read, reflect, and problem-solve more than ever before (Jaeggi et al., 2008). (Before you uncritically embrace video games, read "You Mean Video Games Might Be Bad for Me?" in Chapter 6.)

20-item test to African-American and European-American students. Before the election of Barack Obama, African-American students performed more poorly than European-American students. During the election, African-American students performed just as well as their European-American counterparts. Apparently President Obama is providing a role model, inspiring better academic performance in African-American students (Wolf, 2009).

Further, although IQ predicts school performance, it does not predict later career success (McClelland, 1994). In this regard, "street smarts," or what psychologist Robert Sternberg calls *practical intelligence* (Stemler & Sternberg, 2006), may be seen by minority cultures as more important than "book learning," or what Sternberg calls *analytic intelligence* (Sankofa et al., 2005).

Most psychologists have concluded that there is no scientific evidence that group differences in average IQ are based on genetics. In fact, studies that used actual blood group testing found no significant correlations between ethnic ancestry and IQ scores. This is because it does not even make genetic sense to talk about "races" at all—obvious external markers, like skin color, have little to do with underlying genetic differences (Bonham et al., 2005; Sternberg, 2007). Group differences in IQ scores are based on cultural and environmental diversity, as much as on heredity (Neisser et al., 1996; Nisbett, 2005). To conclude otherwise reflects political beliefs and biases, not scientific facts.

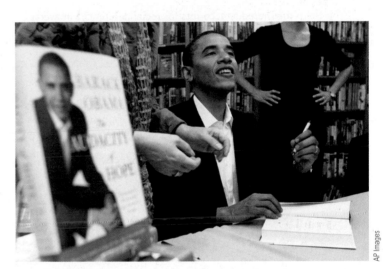

"Yes We Can." President Obama's intelligence is inspiring millions of Americans and others around the world to aspire to greater academic success. His example is particularly important to African Americans.

Summary

In the final analysis, intelligence reflects development as well as potential, nurture as well as nature (Grigorenko, 2005). Moreover, the fact that intelligence is partly determined by heredity tells us little of any real value. Genes are fixed at birth. Improving the environments in which children learn and grow is the main way in which we can ensure that they reach their full potential (Grigorenko & Sternberg, 2003; White, 2006).

What Is Thinking?—Brains over Brawn

What is the nature of thought?

We have seen that intelligence consists of various mental abilities. Let's explore some of them in more detail. How do concepts, language, and mental images make abstract, intelligent thinking possible?

Cognition refers to mentally processing information. Our thoughts take many forms, including daydreaming, problem solving, and reasoning (to name but a few). Although thinking is not limited to humans, imagine trying to teach an animal to match the feats of Shakuntala Devi, who once set a "world's record" for mental calculation by multiplying two randomly chosen 13-digit numbers (7,686,369,774,870 times 2,465,099,745,779) in her head, giving the answer in 28 seconds. (That's 18,947,668,104,042,434,089,403,730 if you haven't already figured it out.)

Some Basic Units of Thought

At its most basic, thinking is an *internal representation* (mental expression) of a problem or situation. Picture a chess player who mentally tries out several moves before actually touching a chess piece. By *planning* her moves, she can avoid many mistakes. Imagine planning what to study for an exam, what to say at a job interview, or how to get to your spring break hotel. Better yet, in each of these cases imagine what might happen if you couldn't, or didn't, plan at all.

The power of being able to mentally represent problems is dramatically illustrated by chess grand master Miguel Najdorf, who once simultaneously played 45 chess games while

Cognition The process of thinking or mentally processing information (images, concepts, words, rules, and symbols).

blindfolded. How did Najdorf do it? Like most people, he used the basic units of thought: images, concepts, and language (or symbols). **Images** are picture-like mental representations. **Concepts** are ideas that represent categories of objects or events. **Language** consists of words or symbols, and rules for combining them. Thinking often involves all three units. For example, blindfolded chess players rely on visual images, concepts ("Game 2 begins with a strategy called an English opening"), and the notational system, or "language," of chess.

In a moment we will delve further into imagery, concepts, and language. Be aware, however, that thinking involves attention, pattern recognition, memory, decision making, intuition, knowledge, and more. The rest of this chapter is just a sample of what cognitive psychology is about.

Mental Imagery—Does a Frog Have Lips?

In what ways are images related to thinking?

Almost everyone has visual and auditory images. More than half of us have imagery for movement, touch, taste, smell, and pain. Thus, mental images are sometimes more than just "pictures." For example, your image of a bakery may also include its delicious odor. Some people even have a rare form of imagery called *synaesthesia* (sin-es-THEE-zyah). For these individuals, images cross normal sensory barriers (Kadosh & Henik, 2007). For one such person, spiced chicken tastes "pointy," for another, pain is the color orange and, for a third, human voices unleash a flood of colors and tastes (Dixon, Smilek, & Merikle, 2004; Robertson & Sagiv, 2005). Despite such variations, most of us use images to think, remember, and solve problems. For instance, we may use mental images to:

(a)   **(b)**   **(c)**

(d)   **(e)**   **(f)**

- Make a decision or solve a problem (choosing what clothes to wear; figuring out how to arrange furniture in a room).
- Change feelings (thinking of pleasant images to get out of a bad mood; imagining yourself as thin to stay on a diet).
- Improve a skill or prepare for some action (using images to improve a tennis stroke; mentally rehearsing how you will ask for a raise).
- Aid memory (picturing Mr. Cook wearing a chef's hat, so you can remember his name).

The Nature of Mental Images

Mental images are not flat, like photographs. Researcher Stephen Kosslyn showed this by asking people, Does a frog have lips and a stubby tail? Unless you often kiss frogs, you will probably tackle this question by using mental images. Most people picture a frog, "look" at its mouth, and then mentally "rotate" the frog in mental space to check its tail (Kosslyn, 1983). Mental rotation is partly based on imagined movements (▶▶ Figure 8.5). That is, we mentally "pick up" an object and turn it around (Wraga et al., 2005).

▲ FIGURE 8.5 Imagery in thinking. *(Top)* Subjects were shown a drawing similar to *(a)* and drawings of how *(a)* would look in other positions, such as *(b)* and *(c)*. Subjects could recognize *(a)* after it had been "rotated" from its original position. However, the more *(a)* was rotated in space, the longer it took to recognize it. This result suggests that people actually formed a three-dimensional image of *(a)* and rotated the image to see if it matched (Shepard, 1975). *(Bottom)* Try your ability to manipulate mental images: Picture each of these shapes as a piece of paper that can be folded to make a cube. After they have been folded, on which cubes do the arrow tips meet? (Kosslyn, 1985).

"Reverse Vision"

What happens in the brain when a person has visual images? Seeing something in your "mind's eye" is similar to seeing real objects. Information from the eyes normally activates the brain's primary visual area, creating an image (▶▶ Figure 8.6). Other brain areas then help us recognize the image by relating it to stored knowledge. When you form a mental image, the system works in reverse. Brain areas where memories are stored send signals back

Image Most often, a mental representation that has picture-like qualities; an icon.

Concept An idea representing a category of related objects or events.

Language Words or symbols, and rules for combining them, that are used for thinking and communication.

Vision

Frontal lobe

Parietal lobe

Occipital lobe

Temporal lobe

Cerebellum

Visual Image

Frontal lobe

Parietal lobe

Occipital lobe

Temporal lobe

Cerebellum

> ▲ **FIGURE 8.6** When you see a flower, its image is represented by activity in the primary visual area of the cortex, at the back of the brain. Information about the flower is also relayed to other brain areas. If you form a mental image of a flower, information follows a reverse path. The result, once again, is activation of the primary visual area.

The Guggenheim Museum in Bilbao, Spain, was designed by architect Frank Gehry. Could a person lacking mental imagery design such a masterpiece? Three people out of 100 find it impossible to produce mental images, and 3 out of 100 have very strong imagery. Most artists, architects, designers, sculptors, and filmmakers have excellent visual imagery.

to the visual cortex, where once again an image is created (Ganis, Thompson, & Kosslyn, 2004; Kosslyn, 2005). For example, if you visualize a friend's face right now, the area of your brain that specializes in perceiving faces will become more active (O'Craven & Kanwisher, 2000).

Using Mental Images

How are images used to solve problems? We use *stored images* (information from memory) to apply past experiences to problem solving. Let's say you are asked, "How many ways can you use an empty egg carton?" You might begin by picturing uses you have already seen, such as sorting buttons into a carton. To give more original answers, you will probably need to use *created* images, which are assembled or invented, rather than simply remembered. Thus, an artist may completely picture a proposed sculpture before beginning work. People with good imaging abilities tend to score higher on tests of creativity (Morrison & Wallace, 2001). In fact, Albert Einstein, Thomas Edison, Lewis Carroll, and many other of history's most original intellects relied heavily on imagery (West, 1991).

Does the "size" of a mental image affect thinking? To find out, first picture a cat sitting beside a housefly. Now try to "zoom in" on the cat's ears so you see them clearly. Next, picture a rabbit sitting beside an elephant. How quickly can you "see" the rabbit's front feet? Did it take longer than picturing the cat's ears?

When a rabbit is pictured with an elephant, the rabbit's image must be small because the elephant is large. Using such tasks, Stephen Kosslyn (1985) found that the smaller an image is, the harder it is to "see" its details. To put this finding to use, try forming oversize images of things you want to think about. For example, to understand electricity, picture the wires as large pipes with electrons the size of golf balls moving through them; to understand the human ear, explore it (in your mind's eye) like a large cave; and so forth.

Kinesthetic Imagery

Do muscular responses relate to thinking? In a sense, we think with our bodies as well as our heads. *Kinesthetic images* are created from muscular sensations (Holmes & Collins, 2001). Such images help us think about movements and actions.

As you think and talk, kinesthetic sensations can guide the flow of ideas. For example, if a friend calls and asks you the combination of a lock you loaned her, you may move your hands as if twirling the dial on the lock. Or, try answering this question: Which direction do you turn the hot-water handle in your kitchen to shut off the water? Most people haven't simply memorized the words "Turn it clockwise" or "Turn it counterclockwise." Instead you will probably "turn" the faucet in your imagination before answering. You may even make a turning motion with your hand before answering.

Kinesthetic images are especially important in music, sports, dance, skateboarding, martial arts, and other movement-oriented skills. People with good kinesthetic imagery (or high *bodily-kinesthetic intelligence*) learn such skills faster than those with poor imagery (Glisky, Williams, & Kihlstrom, 1996).

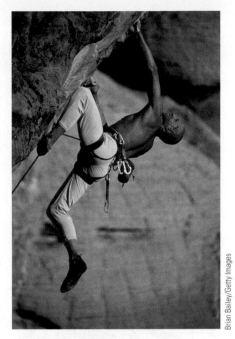

A study found that rock climbers use kinesthetic imagery to learn climbing routes and to plan their next few moves (Smyth & Waller, 1998).

Concepts—I'm Positive, It's a Whatchamacallit

What are concepts?

A concept is an idea that represents a category of objects or events. Concepts help us identify important features of the world. That's why experts in various areas of knowledge are good at classifying objects. Bird watchers, tropical fish fanciers, 5-year-old dinosaur enthusiasts, and other experts all learn to look for identifying details that beginners tend to miss. If you are knowledgeable about a topic, such as horses, flowers, or football, you literally see things differently than less well informed people do (Johnson & Mervis, 1997; Ross, 2006).

Forming Concepts

How are concepts learned? **Concept formation** is the process of classifying information into meaningful categories (Ashby & Maddox, 2005). At its most basic, concept formation is based on experience with *positive* and *negative instances* (examples that belong, or do not belong, to the concept class). Concept formation is not as simple as it might seem. Imagine a child learning the concept of *dog*:

> **Dog Daze**
> A child and her father go for a walk. At a neighbor's house, they see a medium-sized dog. The father says, "See the dog." As they pass the next yard, the child sees a cat and says, "Dog!" Her father corrects her, "No, that's a *cat.*" The child now thinks, "Aha, dogs are large and cats are small." In the next yard, she sees a Pekingese and says, "Cat!" "No, that's a dog," replies her father.

The child's confusion is understandable. At first she might even mistake a Pekingese for a dust mop. However, with more positive and negative instances, the child will eventually recognize everything from Great Danes to Chihuahuas as members of the same category—dogs.

As adults, we often acquire concepts by learning or forming rules. A **conceptual rule** is a guideline for deciding whether objects or events belong to a concept class. For example, a triangle must be a closed shape with three sides made of straight lines. Rules are an efficient way to learn concepts, but examples remain important. It's unlikely that memorizing rules would allow a new listener to accurately categorize punk, hip-hop, fusion, salsa, metal, country, and rap music.

Types of Concepts

Are there different kinds of concepts? Yes, **conjunctive concepts,** or "and concepts," are defined by the presence of two or more features (Reed, 2010). In other words, an item must have "this feature *and* this feature *and* this feature." For example, a *motorcycle* must have two wheels *and* an engine *and* handlebars.

Concept formation The process of classifying information into meaningful categories.

Conceptual rule A formal rule for deciding if an object or event is an example of a particular concept.

Conjunctive concept A class of objects that have two or more features in common. (For example, to qualify as an example of the concept an object must be both red *and* triangular.)

▲ **FIGURE 8.7** When does a cup become a bowl or a vase? Deciding if an object belongs to a conceptual class is aided by relating it to a prototype, or ideal example. Subjects in one experiment chose Number 5 as the "best" cup. (After Labov, 1973.)

▲ **FIGURE 8.8** Use of prototypes in concept identification. Even though its shape is unusual, item *(a)* can be related to a model (an ordinary set of pliers) and thus recognized. But what are items *(b)* and *(c)*? If you don't recognize them, look ahead to ▶▶ Figure 8.10. (Adapted from Bransford, J. D., McCarrell, N. S., A sketch of cognitive approach to comprehension: some thoughts about understanding what it means, Figures b & d on p. 381, in Johnson-Laird, P. N., and Watson, P. C., Thinking: Readings in Cognitive Sciences. Copyright © 1977. Reprinted by permission of Cambridge University Press.)

Relational concept A concept defined by the relationship between features of an object or between an object and its surroundings (for example, "greater than," "lopsided").

Disjunctive concept A concept defined by the presence of at least one of several possible features. (For example, to qualify an object must be either blue *or* circular.)

Prototype An ideal model used as a prime example of a particular concept.

Denotative meaning The exact, dictionary definition of a word or concept; its objective meaning.

Connotative meaning The subjective, personal, or emotional meaning of a word or concept.

Relational concepts are based on how an object relates to something else, or how its features relate to one another. All of the following are relational concepts: *larger, above, left, north,* and *upside down.* Another example is *brother,* which is defined as "a male considered in his relation to another person having the same parents."

Disjunctive concepts have *at least one* of several possible features. These are "either/or" concepts. To belong to the category, an item must have "this feature *or* that feature *or* another feature." For example, in baseball, a *strike* is *either* a swing and a miss *or* a pitch over the plate *or* a foul ball. The either/or quality of disjunctive concepts makes them hard to learn.

Prototypes

When you think of the concept *bird,* do you mentally list the features that birds have? Probably not. In addition to rules and features, we use **prototypes,** or ideal models, to identify concepts (Burnett et al., 2005; Rosch, 1977). A robin, for example, is a prototypical bird; an ostrich is not. In other words, some items are better examples of a concept than others are. Which of the drawings in ▶▶ Figure 8.7 best represents a cup? At some point, as a cup grows taller or wider it becomes a vase or a bowl. How do we know when the line is crossed? Probably, we mentally compare objects to an "ideal" cup, like Number 5. That's why it's hard to identify concepts when we can't come up with relevant prototypes. What, for example, are the objects shown in ▶▶ Figure 8.8? As you can see, prototypes are especially helpful when we try to categorize complex stimuli (Minda & Smith, 2001).

Faulty Concepts

Using inaccurate concepts often leads to thinking errors. For example, *social stereotypes* are oversimplified concepts of groups of people. Stereotypes about men, African Americans, women, conservatives, liberals, police officers, or other groups often muddle thinking about members of the group. (See Chapter 14 for more information about stereotypes, prejudice, and discrimination.) A related problem is *all-or-nothing thinking* (one-dimensional thought). In this case, we classify things as absolutely right or wrong, good or bad, fair or unfair, black or white, honest or dishonest. Thinking this way prevents us from appreciating the subtleties of most life problems (Bastian & Haslam, 2006).

Connotative Meaning

Generally speaking, concepts have two types of meaning. The **denotative meaning** of a word or concept is its exact definition. The **connotative meaning** is its emotional or personal meaning. The denotative meaning of the word *naked* (having no clothes) is the same for a nudist as it is for a movie censor, but we could expect their connotations to differ. Connotative differences can influence how we think about important issues. For example, the term *enhanced radiation device* has a more positive connotation than *neutron bomb* does (Gruner & Tighe, 1995).

Rate this word: JAZZ

Rounded		Angular
Strong		Weak
Smooth		Rough
Passive		Active
Large		Small
Hot		Cold
Bad		Good
Relaxed		Tense
Dry		Wet
Stale		Fresh

◀◀ **FIGURE 8.9** This is an example of Osgood's (1952) semantic differential. The connotative meaning of the word *jazz* can be established by rating it on the scales. Mark your own rating by placing dots or X's in the spaces. Connect the marks with a line; then have a friend rate the word and compare your responses. It might be interesting to do the same for *rock and roll, classical,* and *rap.* You also might want to try the word *psychology.* (From *Psychological Bulletin,* Vol. 49, No. 3, May 1952.)

Can you clarify what a connotative meaning is? Yes, connotative meaning can be measured with a technique called the *semantic differential,* as shown in ▶▶ Figure 8.9. When we rate words or concepts, most of their connotative meaning boils down to the dimensions *good/bad, strong/weak,* and *active/passive.* These dimensions give words very different connotations, even when their denotative meanings are similar. For example, I am *conscientious;* you are *careful;* he is *nitpicky!* Because we are conscientious (not nitpicky, right?), let's further explore language.

▲ **FIGURE 8.10** Context can substitute for a lack of appropriate prototypes in concept identification.

Language—Don't Leave Home Without It

What is the role of language in thinking?

As we have seen, thinking may occur without language. Everyone has searched for a word to express an idea that exists as a vague image or feeling. Nevertheless, most thinking relies heavily on language, because words *encode* (translate) the world into symbols that are easy to manipulate (▶▶ Figure 8.11).

The study of meaning in words and language is known as **semantics.** It is here that the link between words and thinking becomes most evident. Suppose, on an intelligence test, you were asked to circle the word that does not belong in this series:

SKYSCRAPER   CATHEDRAL   TEMPLE   PRAYER

If you circled *prayer,* you answered as most people do. Now try another problem, again circling the odd item:

CATHEDRAL   PRAYER   TEMPLE   SKYSCRAPER

Did you circle *skyscraper* this time? The new order subtly alters the meaning of the last word (Mayer, 1995). This occurs because words get much of their meaning from *context.* For example, the word *shot* means different things when we are thinking of marksmanship, bartending, medicine, photography, or golf (Carroll, 2008; Miller, 1999).

Likewise, the words we use can greatly affect our thinking: Has one country's army "invaded" another country or "liberated" it? Is the martini glass "half full" or "half empty"? Would you rather eat "rare prime beef" or "bloody slab of dead cow"? More subtle effects

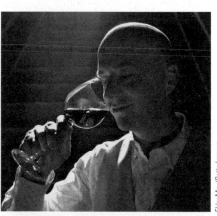

▲ **FIGURE 8.11** Wine tasting illustrates the encoding function of language. To communicate their experiences to others, wine connoisseurs must put taste sensations into words. The wine you see here is "marked by deeply concentrated nuances of plum, blackberry, and currant, with a nice balance of tannins and acid, building to a spicy oak finish." (Don't try this with a Pop-tart!)

Semantics The study of meanings in words and language.

Bilingualism—*Si o No, Oui ou Non,* Yes or No?

Are there advantages to being able to speak more than one language? Definitely. **Bilingualism** is the ability to speak two languages. Studies have found that students who learn to speak two languages well have better mental flexibility, general language skills, control of attention, and problem-solving abilities (Bialystok & DePape, 2009; Craik & Bialystok, 2005).

Unfortunately, millions of minority American children who do not speak English at home experience *subtractive bilingualism*. Immersed in English-only classrooms, where they are expected to "sink or swim," they usually end up losing some of their native language skills. Such children risk becoming less than fully competent in *both* their first and second languages. In addition, they tend to fall behind educationally. As they struggle with English, their grasp of arithmetic, social studies, science, and other subjects may

also suffer. In short, English-only instruction can leave them poorly prepared to succeed in the majority culture (Genesee, Paradis, & Crago, 2004; Matthews & Matthews, 2004).

For the majority of children who speak English at home, the picture can be quite different, because learning a second language is almost always beneficial. It poses no threat to the child's home language and improves a variety of cognitive skills. This has been called *additive bilingualism* because learning a second language adds to a child's overall competence (Hinkel, 2005).

An approach called **two-way bilingual education** can help children benefit from bilingualism and avoid its drawbacks (Lessow-Hurley, 2005). In such programs, majority group children and children with limited English skills are taught part of the day in English and part in a second language. Both majority and minority language

speakers become fluent in two languages, and they perform as well or better than single-language students in English and general academic abilities.

Then why isn't two-way bilingual education more widely used? Bilingual education tends to be politically unpopular among majority language speakers (Garcia, 2008). Language is an important sign of group membership. Even where the majority culture is highly dominant, some of its members may feel that recent immigrants and "foreign languages" are eroding their culture. Regardless, an ability to think and communicate in a second language is a wonderful gift. Given the cognitive benefits, fostering bilingualism may also turn out to be one of the best ways to improve competitiveness in our rapidly globalizing information economy.

| PURPLE | BLUE | GREEN | GREEN |
| RED | PURPLE | RED | GREEN |

⬆ **FIGURE 8.12** The Stroop interference task. Test yourself by naming the colors in the top two rows as quickly as you can. Then name the colors of the *ink* used to print the words in the bottom two rows (do not read the words themselves). Was it harder to name the ink colors in the bottom rows? (Adapted from MacLeod, 2005.)

Bilingualism An ability to speak two languages.

Two-way bilingual education A program in which English-speaking children and children with limited English proficiency are taught half the day in English and half in a second language.

 Phonemes The basic speech sounds of a language.

 Morphemes The smallest meaningful units in a language, such as syllables or words.

Grammar A set of rules for combining language units into meaningful speech or writing.

Syntax Rules for ordering words when forming sentences.

Transformation rules Rules by which a simple declarative sentence may be changed to other voices or forms (past tense, passive voice, and so forth).

also occur. For example, most people have difficulty quickly naming the color of the ink used to print the words in the bottom two rows of ▶▶ Figure 8.12. The word meanings are just too strong to ignore.

Language also plays a major role in defining ethnic communities and other social groups. Thus, language can be a bridge or a barrier between cultures. Translating languages can cause a rash of semantic problems. Perhaps the San Jose, California, public library can be excused for once displaying a large banner that was supposed to say "You are welcome" in a native Philippine language. The banner actually said "You are circumcised." However, in more important situations, such as in international business and diplomacy, avoiding semantic confusion may be vital. (See "Bilingualism—*Si o No, Oui ou Non,* Yes or No?")

The Structure of Language

What does it take to make a language? First, a language must provide *symbols* that stand for objects and ideas (Jay, 2003). The symbols we call words are built out of **phonemes** (FOE-neems: basic speech sounds) and **morphemes** (MOR-feems: speech sounds collected into meaningful units, such as syllables or words). For instance, in English the sounds *m, b, w,* and *a* cannot form a syllable *mbwa*. In Swahili, they can. (Also see ▶▶ Figure 8.13.)

Next, a language must have a **grammar,** or set of rules for making sounds into words and words into sentences (Reed, 2010). One part of grammar, known as **syntax,** concerns rules for word order. Syntax is important because rearranging words almost always changes the meaning of a sentence: "Dog bites man" versus "Man bites dog."

Traditional grammar is concerned with "surface" language—the sentences we actually speak. Linguist Noam Chomsky has focused instead on the unspoken rules we use to change core ideas into various sentences. Chomsky (1986) believes that we do not learn all the sentences we might ever say. Rather, we actively *create* them by applying **transformation rules** to universal, core patterns. We use these rules to change a simple declarative sentence to other voices or forms (past tense, passive voice, and so forth). For example, the core sentence "Dog bites man" can be transformed to these patterns (and others as well):

Past: The dog bit the man.
Passive: The man was bitten by the dog.
Negative: The dog did not bite the man.
Question: Did the dog bite the man?

Children seem to be using transformation rules when they say things such as "I runned home." That is, the child applied the normal past tense rule to the irregular verb *to run.*

A true language is also *productive*—it can generate new thoughts or ideas. In fact, words can be rearranged to produce a nearly infinite number of sentences. Some are silly: "Please don't feed me to the goldfish." Some are profound: "We hold these truths to be self-evident, that all men are created equal." In either case, the productive quality of language makes it a powerful tool for thinking.

Albanian	mak, mak
Chinese	gua, gua
Dutch	rap, rap
English	quack, quack
French	coin, coin
Italian	qua, qua
Spanish	cuá, cuá
Swedish	kvack, kvack
Turkish	vak, vak

⬆ **FIGURE 8.13** Animals around the world make pretty much the same sounds. Notice, however, how various languages use slightly different phonemes to express the sound a duck makes.

Gestural Languages

Contrary to common belief, language is not limited to speech. Consider the case of Ildefonso, a young man who was born deaf. At age 24, Ildefonso had never communicated with another human, except by mime. Then at last, Ildefonso had a breakthrough: After much hard work with a sign language teacher, he understood the link between a cat and the gesture for it. At that magic moment, he grasped the idea that "cat" could be communicated to another person, just by signing the word.

American Sign Language (ASL), a gestural language, made Ildefonso's long-awaited breakthrough possible. ASL is not pantomime or a code. It is a true language, like German, Spanish, or Japanese (Liddell, 2003). In fact, those who use other gestural languages, such as French Sign, Mexican Sign, or Old Kentish Sign, may not easily understand ASL (Quinto-Pozos, 2008).

Although ASL has a *spatial* grammar, syntax, and semantics all its own (⏵⏵ Figure 8.14), both speech and signing follow similar universal language patterns. Signing children pass through the stages of language development at about the same age as speaking children do. Some psychologists now believe that speech evolved from gestures, far back in human history (Corballis, 2002). Gestures help us string words together as we speak

Look at

Stare

⬆ **FIGURE 8.14** ASL has only 3,000 root signs, compared with roughly 600,000 words in English. However, variations in signs make ASL a highly expressive language. For example, the sign LOOK AT can be varied in ways to make it mean look at me, look at her, look at each, stare at, gaze, watch, look for a long time, look at again and again, reminisce, sightsee, look forward to, predict, anticipate, browse, and many more variations.

Infants can express the idea "pick me up" in gestures before they can make the same request in words. Their progression from gestures to speech may mirror the evolution of human language abilities (Stokoe, 2001).

(Morsella & Krauss, 2004). Some people would have difficulty speaking with their hands tied to their sides. Do you ever make hand gestures when you are speaking on the phone? If so, you may be displaying a remnant of the gestural origins of language. Perhaps that's also why the same brain areas become more active when a person speaks or signs (Emmorey et al., 2003).

Sign languages naturally arise out of a need to communicate visually. But they also embody a personal identity and define a distinct community. Those who "speak" sign share not just a language but a rich culture as well (Singleton & Newport, 2004).

Animal Language

Do animals use language? Animals do communicate. The cries, gestures, and mating calls of animals have broad meanings immediately understood by other animals of the same species (Searcy & Nowicki, 2005). For the most part, however, natural animal communication is quite limited. Even apes and monkeys make only a few dozen distinct cries, which carry messages such as "attack," "flee," or "food here." More important, animal communication lacks the productive quality of human language. For example, when a monkey gives an "eagle distress call," it means something like, "I see an eagle." The monkey has no way of saying, "I don't see an eagle," or "Thank heavens that wasn't an eagle," or "That sucker I saw yesterday was some huge eagle" (Pinker & Jackendoff, 2005). Let's consider some of psychology's experiences in trying to teach chimpanzees to use language.

Chimp Language

In the late 1960s, Beatrix and Allen Gardner used operant conditioning and imitation to teach a female chimp named Washoe to use ASL. Washoe learned to put together primitive sentence strings like "Come-gimme sweet," "Gimme tickle," and "Open food drink." At her peak, Washoe could construct six-word sentences and use about 240 signs (Gardner & Gardner, 1989).

At around the same time, David Premack taught Sarah the chimpanzee to use 130 "words" consisting of plastic chips arranged on a magnetized board (▶▶ Figure 8.15). From the beginning of her training, Sarah was required to use proper word order. She learned to answer questions; to label things "same" or "different"; to classify objects by color, shape, and size; and to form compound sentences (Premack & Premack, 1983). Sarah has even learned to use conditional sentences. A *conditional statement* contains a qualification, often in the if/then form: "If Sarah take apple, then Mary give Sarah chocolate." "If Sarah take banana, then Mary no give Sarah chocolate" (▶▶ Figure 8.16).

Can it be said with certainty that the chimps understand such interchanges? Most researchers working with chimps believe that they have indeed communicated with them. Especially striking are the chimps' spontaneous responses. Washoe once "wet" on psychologist Roger Fouts' back while riding on his shoulders. When Fouts asked, with some annoyance, why she had done it, Washoe signed, "It's funny!"

Nouns		Verbs		Concepts Conditionals		Adjectives (Colors)	
Sarah	Chocolate	Is	Give	Same	Different	Red	Yellow

▲ **FIGURE 8.15** Here is a sample of some of the word-symbols that Sarah the chimpanzee used to communicate with humans. (After Premack & Premack, 1972.)

Criticisms

While such interchanges are impressive, communication and real language usage are different things. Even untrained chimps use simple gestures to communicate with humans. For example, a chimp will point at a banana that is out of reach, while glancing back and forth between the banana and a person standing nearby (Leavens & Hopkins, 1998). (The meaning of the gesture is clear. The meaning of the exasperated look on the chimp's face is less certain, but it probably means, "Give me the banana, you idiot.")

Also problems with syntax (word order) have plagued almost all animal language studies. For example, when a chimp named Nim Chimpsky (no relation to Noam Chomsky) wanted an orange, he would typically signal a grammarless string of words: "Give orange me give eat orange me eat orange give me eat orange give me you." This might be communication, but it is not language.

Kanzi's Lexigrams

In the 1980s, Duane Rumbaugh and Sue Savage-Rumbaugh taught Kanzi, a pygmy chimpanzee, to communicate by pushing buttons on a computer keyboard. Each of the 250 buttons is marked with a *lexigram,* or geometric word-symbol (▶▶ Figure 8.17). Using the lexigrams, Kanzi can create primitive sentences several words long. He can also understand about 650 spoken sentences.

Kanzi's sentences consistently follow correct word order. Like a child learning language, Kanzi picked up some rules from his caregivers (Segerdahl, Fields, & Savage-Rumbaugh, 2005). However, he has developed other patterns on his own. For example, Kanzi usually places action symbols in the order he wants to carry them out, such as "chase tickle" or "chase hide." In this respect, Kanzi's grammar is on a par with that of a 2-year-old child.

Kanzi's ability to invent a simple grammar may help us better understand the roots of human language. It is certainly the strongest answer yet to critics (Benson et al., 2002). On the other hand, Chomsky insists that if chimps were biologically capable of language, they would use it on their own. Although the issue is far from resolved, such research may unravel the mysteries of language learning.

▲ FIGURE 8.16 After reading the message "Sarah insert apple pail banana dish" on the magnetic board, Sarah performed the actions as directed. (From "Teaching Language to an Ape," by Ann J. Premack and David Premack. © 1972 Scientific American, Inc. Reprinted by permission of Eric Mose Jr.)

The Great Ape Trust of Iowa

▲ FIGURE 8.17 Kanzi's language learning has been impressive. He can comprehend spoken English words. He can identify lexigram symbols when he hears corresponding words. He can use lexigrams when the objects they refer to are absent, and he can, if asked, lead someone to the object. All these skills were acquired through observation, not conditioning (Savage-Rumbaugh et al., 1990).

study break

Imagery, Concepts, and Language

RECITE

1. List three primary units of thought:
   _____ _____
   _____
2. Our reliance on imagery in thinking means that problem solving is impaired by the use of language or symbols. T or F?
3. Humans appear capable of forming three-dimensional images that can be moved or rotated in mental space. T or F?
4. A *mup* is defined as anything that is small, blue, and hairy. *Mup* is a _____ concept.
5. The connotative meaning of the word *naked* is "having no clothes." T or F?
6. True languages are _____ because they can be used to generate new possibilities.
7. The basic speech sounds are called _____; the smallest meaningful units of speech are called _____.

REFLECT

Critical Thinking

8. A Democrat and a Republican are asked to rate the word *democratic* on the semantic differential. Under what conditions would their ratings be most alike?
9. Chimpanzees and other apes are intelligent and entertaining animals. If you were doing language research with a chimp, what major problem would you have to guard against?

Relate

Name some ways in which you have used imagery in the thinking you have done today.

Write a conceptual rule for the following idea: *unicycle*. Were you able to define the concept with a rule? Would positive and negative instances help make the concept clearer for others?

A true sports car has two seats, a powerful engine, good brakes, and excellent handling. What kind of a concept is the term *sports car*? What do you think of as a prototypical sports car?

You must learn to communicate with an alien life form whose language cannot be reproduced by the human voice. Do you think it would be better to use a gestural language or lexigrams? Why?

ANSWERS

1. images, concepts, language or symbols (others could be listed)   2. F   3. T   4. conjunctive   5. F   6. productive   7. phonemes, morphemes   8. If they both assume the word refers to a form of government, not a political party or a candidate.   9. The problem of anthropomorphizing (ascribing human characteristics to animals) is especially difficult to avoid when researchers spend many hours "conversing" with chimps.

Problem Solving—Getting an Answer in Sight

What do we know about problem solving?

We all solve many problems every day. Problem solving can be as commonplace as figuring out how to make a nonpoisonous meal out of leftovers or as significant as developing a cure for cancer. How do we solve such problems? A good way to start a discussion of problem solving is to solve a problem. Give this one a try:

> A famous ocean liner (the *Queen Latifah*) is steaming toward port at 20 miles per hour. The ocean liner is 50 miles from shore when a seagull takes off from its deck and flies toward port. At the same instant, a speedboat leaves port at 30 miles per hour. The bird flies back and forth between the speedboat and the *Queen Latifah* at a speed of 40 miles per hour. How far will the bird have flown when the two boats pass?

If you don't immediately see the answer to this problem, read it again. (The answer is revealed in the "Insightful Solutions" section.)

Mechanical Solutions

For routine problems, a **mechanical solution** may be adequate. Mechanical solutions are achieved by trial and error or by rote. If you forget the combination to your bike lock, you may be able to discover it by trial and error. In an era of high-speed computers, many trial-and-error solutions are best left to machines. A computer could generate all possible combinations of the five numbers on the lock in a split second. (Of course, it would take a long time to try them all.) When a problem is solved by *rote*, thinking is guided by an **algorithm,** or learned set of rules that always leads to a correct solution. A simple example of an algorithm are the steps needed to divide one number into another (by doing arithmetic, not by using a calculator).

Mechanical solution A problem solution achieved by trial and error or by a fixed procedure based on learned rules.

Algorithm A learned set of rules that always leads to the correct solution of a problem.

If you have a good background in math, you may have solved the problem of the bird and the boats by rote. (Your authors hope you didn't. There is an easier solution.)

Solutions by Understanding

Many problems cannot be solved mechanically. In that case, **understanding** (deeper comprehension of a problem) is necessary. Try this problem:

> A person has an inoperable stomach tumor. A device is available that produces rays that at high intensity will destroy tissue (both healthy and diseased). How can the tumor be destroyed without damaging surrounding tissue? (Also see the sketch in ▶▶ Figure 8.18.)

What does this problem show about problem solving? German psychologist Karl Duncker gave college students this problem in a classic series of studies. Duncker asked them to think aloud as they worked. He found that successful students first had to discover the *general properties* of a correct solution. A **general solution** defines the requirements for success, but not in enough detail to guide further action. This phase was complete when students realized that the intensity of the rays had to be lowered on their way to the tumor. Then, in the second phase, they proposed a number of **functional** (workable) **solutions** and selected the best one (Duncker, 1945). (One solution is to focus weak rays on the tumor from several angles. Another is to rotate the person's body, to minimize exposure of healthy tissue.)

It might help to summarize with a more familiar example. Almost everyone who has tried to play a poker game like Texas Hold'em begins at the mechanical, trial-and-error level. If you want to take the easy (i.e., rote) route, printed odds tables are available for every stage of play. In time, those who persist begin to understand the general properties of the game. After that, they can play fast enough to keep up with other players.

Heuristics

"You can't get there from here," or so it often seems when facing a problem. Solving problems often requires a strategy. If the number of alternatives is small, a **random search strategy** may work. This is another example of trial-and-error thinking in which all possibilities are tried, more or less randomly. Imagine that you are traveling and you decide to look up an old friend, Janet Smith, in a city you are visiting. You open the phone book and find 47 J. Smiths listed. Of course, you could dial each number until you find the right one. "Forget it," you say to yourself. "Is there any way I can narrow the search?" "Oh, yeah! I remember hearing that Janet lives by the beach." Then you take out a map and call only the numbers with addresses near the waterfront (Hunt & Ellis, 2004).

The approach used in this example is a **heuristic** (hew-RIS-tik: a strategy for identifying and evaluating problem solutions). Typically, a heuristic is a "rule of thumb" that *reduces the number of alternatives* thinkers must consider (Solso, MacLin, & MacLin, 2008). Although this raises the odds of success, it does not guarantee a solution. Here are some heuristic strategies that often work:

- Try to identify how the current state of affairs differs from the desired goal. Then find steps that will reduce the difference.
- Try working backward from the desired goal to the starting point or current state.
- If you can't reach the goal directly, try to identify an intermediate goal or subproblem that at least gets you closer.
- Represent the problem in other ways—with graphs, diagrams, or analogies, for instance.
- Generate a possible solution and test it. Doing so may eliminate many alternatives, or it may clarify what is needed for a solution.

Experts and Novices

Research has shown that expert skills are based on *acquired strategies* (learned heuristics) and specific *organized knowledge* (systematic information). Experts are better able to see the true nature of problems and to define them in terms of general principles (Anderson, 2005).

▲ FIGURE 8.18 A schematic representation of Duncker's tumor problem. The dark spot represents a tumor surrounded by healthy tissue. How can the tumor be destroyed without injuring surrounding tissue? (Adapted from Duncker, 1945.)

Understanding In problem solving, a deeper comprehension of the nature of the problem.

General solution A solution that correctly states the requirements for success but not in enough detail for further action.

Functional solution A detailed, practical, and workable solution.

Random search strategy Trying possible solutions to a problem in a more or less random order.

Heuristic Any strategy or technique that aids problem solving, especially by limiting the number of possible solutions to be tried.

Real Game

Black

White

Random Placement

▲ FIGURE 8.19 The left chessboard shows a realistic game. The right chessboard is a random arrangement of pieces. Expert chess players can memorize the left board at a glance, yet they are no better than beginners at memorizing the random board (Ross, 2006). Expert performance at most thinking tasks is based on acquired strategies and knowledge. If you would like to excel at a profession or a mental skill, plan on adding to your knowledge every day (Goldstein, 2008).

For example, chess experts are much more likely than novices to have heuristics available for solving problems. However, what really sets master players apart is their ability to intuitively recognize *patterns* that suggest what lines of play should be explored next. This helps eliminate a large number of possible moves. The chess master, therefore, does not waste time exploring unproductive pathways (Ross, 2006).

In other words, becoming a star performer does not come from some general strengthening of the mind. Master chess players don't necessarily have better memories than beginners (except for realistic chess positions) (Gobet & Simon, 1996; Solso, MacLin, & MacLin, 2008). (See ▶▶ Figure 8.19.) And, typically, they don't explore more moves ahead than lesser players.

Insightful Solutions

A thinker who suddenly solves a problem has experienced **insight.** Insight is so rapid and clear that we may wonder why we didn't see the solution sooner (Schilling, 2005). Insights are usually based on reorganizing a problem. This allows us to see problems in new ways and makes their solutions seem obvious (Robertson, 2001).

Let's return now to the problem of the boats and the bird. The best way to solve it is by insight. Because the boats will cover the 50-mile distance in exactly 1 hour, and the bird flies 40 miles per hour, the bird will have flown 40 miles when the boats meet. Very little math is necessary if you have insight into this problem. ▶▶ Figure 8.20 lists some additional insight problems you may want to try. (The answers can be found in ● Table 8.3.)

Water lilies

Problem: Water lilies growing in a pond double in area every 24 hours. On the first day of spring, only one lily pad is on the surface of the pond. Sixty days later, the pond is entirely covered. On what day is the pond half-covered?

Twenty dollars

Problem: Jessica and Blair both have the same amount of money. How much must Jessica give Blair so that Blair has $20 more than Jessica?

How many pets?

Problem: How many pets do you have if all of them are birds except two, all of them are cats except two, and all of them are dogs except two?

Between 2 and 3

Problem: What one mathematical symbol can you place between 2 and 3 that results in a number greater than 2 and less than 3?

One word

Problem: Rearrange the letters NEWDOOR to make one word.

▲ FIGURE 8.20

Insight A sudden mental reorganization of a problem that makes the solution obvious.

▲ **FIGURE 8.21** Solution to the hat rack problem.

The Nature of Insight

Psychologists Robert Sternberg and Janet Davidson (1982) believe that insight involves three abilities. The first is *selective encoding,* which refers to selecting information that is relevant to a problem while ignoring distractions. For example, consider the following problem:

> If you have white socks and black socks in your drawer, mixed in the ratio of 4 to 5, how many socks will you have to take out to ensure you have a pair of the same color?

A person who recognizes that "mixed in a ratio of 4 to 5" is irrelevant will be more likely to come up with the correct answer of 3 socks.

Insight also relies on *selective combination,* or bringing together seemingly unrelated bits of useful information. Try this sample problem:

> With a 7-minute hourglass and an 11-minute hourglass, what is the simplest way to time the boiling of an egg for 15 minutes?

The answer requires using both hourglasses in combination. First, the 7-minute and the 11-minute hourglasses are started. When the 7-minute hourglass runs out, it's time to begin boiling the egg. At this point, 4 minutes remain on the 11-minute hourglass. Thus, when it runs out, it is simply turned over. When it runs out again, 15 minutes will have passed.

A third source of insights is *selective comparison.* This is the ability to compare new problems with old information or with problems already solved. A good example is the hat rack problem, in which subjects must build a structure that can support an overcoat in the middle of a room. Each person is given only two long sticks and a C-clamp to work with. The solution, shown in ▶▶ Figure 8.21, is to clamp the two sticks together so that they are wedged between the floor and ceiling. If you were given this problem, you would be more likely to solve it if you first thought of how pole lamps are wedged between floor and ceiling.

Fixations

One of the most important barriers to problem solving is **fixation,** the tendency to get "hung up" on wrong solutions or to become blind to alternatives. Usually this occurs when we place unnecessary restrictions on our thinking (German & Barrett, 2005). How, for example, could you plant four small trees so that each is an equal distance from all the others? (The answer is shown in ▶▶ Figure 8.22.)

A prime example of restricted thinking is **functional fixedness.** This is an inability to see new uses (functions) for familiar objects or for things that were used in a particular way (German & Barrett, 2005). If you have ever used a dime as a screwdriver, you've overcome functional fixedness.

How does functional fixedness affect problem solving? Karl Duncker illustrated the effects of functional fixedness by asking students to mount a candle on a vertical board so the candle could burn normally. Duncker gave each student three candles, some matches, some cardboard boxes, some thumbtacks, and other items. Half of Duncker's subjects received

▲ **FIGURE 8.22** Four trees can be placed equidistant from one another by piling dirt into a mound. Three of the trees are planted equal distances apart around the base of the mound. The fourth tree is planted on the top of the mound. If you were fixated on arrangements that involve level ground, you may have been blind to this three-dimensional solution.

Fixation The tendency to repeat wrong solutions or faulty responses, especially as a result of becoming blind to alternatives.

Functional fixedness A rigidity in problem solving caused by an inability to see new uses for familiar objects.

(a)   (b)   (c)

FIGURE 8.23 Materials for solving the candle problem were given to subjects in boxes *(a)* or separately *(b)*. Functional fixedness caused by condition *(a)* interfered with solving the problem. The solution to the problem is shown in *(c)*.

these items *inside* the cardboard boxes. The others were given all the items, including the boxes, spread out on a tabletop.

Duncker found that when the items were in the boxes, solving the problem was very difficult. Why? If students saw the boxes as *containers,* they didn't realize the boxes might be part of the solution. (If you haven't guessed the solution, check ▶▶ Figure 8.23.) Undoubtedly, we could avoid many fixations by being more flexible in categorizing the world (Langer, 2000). For instance, creative thinking could be facilitated in the container problem by saying "This *could be* a box," instead of "This *is* a box." When tested with the candle problem, 5-year-old children show no signs of functional fixedness. Apparently, this is because they have had less experience with the use of various objects. It is sometimes said that to be more creative, you should try to see the world without preconceptions, as if through the eyes of a child. In the case of functional fixedness, that may actually be true (German & Defeyter, 2000).

Common Barriers to Problem Solving

Functional fixedness is just one of the mental blocks that prevent insight. Here's an example of another: A $5 bill is placed on a table and a stack of objects is balanced precariously on top of the bill. How can the bill be removed without touching or moving the objects? A good answer is to split the bill on one of its edges. Gently pulling from opposite ends will tear the bill in half and remove it without toppling the objects. Many people fail to see this solution because they have learned not to destroy money (Adams, 2001). Notice again the impact of placing something in a category, in this case, "things of value" (which should not be destroyed). Other common mental blocks can hinder problem solving, too, as listed here:

1. **Emotional barriers:** inhibition and fear of making a fool of oneself, fear of making a mistake, inability to tolerate ambiguity, excessive self-criticism
   Example: An architect is afraid to try an unconventional design because she fears that other architects will think it is frivolous.
2. **Cultural barriers:** values that hold that fantasy is a waste of time; that playfulness is for children only; that reason, logic, and numbers
   are good; that feelings, intuitions, pleasure, and humor are bad or have no value in the serious business of problem solving
   Example: A corporate manager wants to solve a business problem but becomes stern and angry when members of his marketing team joke playfully about possible solutions.
3. **Learned barriers:** conventions about uses (functional fixedness), meanings, possibilities, taboos
   Example: A cook doesn't have any clean mixing bowls and fails to see that he could use a frying pan as a bowl.
4. **Perceptual barriers:** habits leading to a failure to identify important elements of a problem
   Example: A beginning artist concentrates on drawing a vase of flowers without seeing that the "empty" spaces around the vase are part of the composition, too.

RECITE

1. Insight refers to rote, or trial-and-error, problem solving. T or F?
2. The first phase in problem solving by understanding is to discover the general properties of a correct solution. T or F?
3. Problem-solving strategies that guide the search for solutions are called _____ .
4. A common element underlying insight is that information is encoded, combined, and compared _____ .
   a. mechanically   b. by rote
   c. functionally   d. selectively
5. The term *fixation* refers to the point at which a helpful insight becomes fixed in one's thinking. T or F?
6. Organized knowledge, acquired strategies, and the ability to recognize patterns are all characteristics of human expertise. T or F?

REFLECT

Critical Thinking

7. Do you think that it is true that "a problem clearly defined is a problem half solved"?

8. Sea otters select suitably sized rocks and use them to hammer shellfish loose for eating. They then use the rock to open the shell. Does this qualify as thinking?

Relate

Identify at least one problem you have solved mechanically or by rote. Now identify a problem you solved by understanding. Did the second problem involve finding a general solution or a functional solution? Or both? What heuristics did you use to solve the problem?

What is the best insightful solution you've ever come up with? Did it involve selective encoding, combination, or comparison?

Can you think of a time when you overcame functional fixedness to solve a problem?

ANSWERS

1. F   2. T   3. heuristics   4. d   5. F   6. T   7. Although this might be an overstatement, it is true that clearly defining a starting point and the desired goal can serve as a heuristic in problem solving.   8. Psychologist Donald Griffin (1992) believes it does because thinking is implied by actions that appear to be planned with an awareness of likely results.

Creative Thinking—Down Roads Less Traveled

What is creative thinking?

Original ideas have changed the course of human history. Much of what we now take for granted in art, medicine, music, technology, and science was once regarded as radical or impossible. How do creative thinkers like Steven Hawking achieve the breakthroughs that advance us into new realms? Psychologists have learned a great deal about how creativity occurs and how to promote it, as you will soon learn.

We have seen that problem solving may be mechanical, insightful, or based on understanding. To this we can add that thinking may be **inductive** (going from specific facts or observations to general principles) or **deductive** (going from general principles to specific situations). Thinking may also be **logical** (proceeding from given information to new conclusions on the basis of explicit rules) or **illogical** (intuitive, associative, or personal).

What distinguishes creative thinking from more routine problem solving? Creative thinking involves all these thinking styles, plus *fluency, flexibility,* and *originality.* Let's say that you would like to find creative uses for the billions of plastic containers discarded each year. The creativity of your suggestions could be rated in this way: **Fluency** is defined as the total number of suggestions you are able to make. **Flexibility** is the number of times you shift from one class of possible uses to another. **Originality** refers to how novel or unusual your ideas are. By counting the number of times you showed fluency, flexibility, and originality, we could rate your creativity, or capacity for *divergent thinking* (Baer, 1993; Runco, 2004).

In routine problem solving or thinking, there is one correct answer, and the problem is to find it. This leads to **convergent thinking** (lines of thought converge on the answer). **Divergent thinking** is the reverse, in which many possibilities are developed from one starting point (Cropley, 2006). (See ● Table 8.4 for some examples.) Rather than repeating learned solutions, creative thinking produces new answers, ideas, or patterns (Davidovitch & Milgram, 2006).

Inductive thought Thinking in which a general rule or principle is gathered from a series of specific examples; for instance, inferring the laws of gravity by observing many falling objects.

Deductive thought Thought that applies a general set of rules to specific situations; for example, using the laws of gravity to predict the behavior of a single falling object.

Logical thought Drawing conclusions on the basis of formal principles of reasoning.

Illogical thought Thought that is intuitive, haphazard, or irrational.

Fluency In tests of creativity, fluency refers to the total number of solutions produced.

Flexibility In tests of creativity, flexibility is indicated by the number of different types of solutions produced.

Originality In tests of creativity, originality refers to how novel or unusual solutions are.

Convergent thinking Thinking directed toward discovery of a single established correct answer; conventional thinking.

Divergent thinking Thinking that produces many ideas or alternatives; a major element in original or creative thought.

Fluency is an important part of creative thinking. Mozart produced more than 600 pieces of music. Shakespeare wrote 154 sonnets. Salvador Dalí (shown here) created more than 1,500 paintings as well as sculptures, drawings, illustrations, books, and even an animated cartoon. Not all of these works were masterpieces. However, a fluent outpouring of ideas fed the creative efforts of each of these geniuses.

John Bryson/Sygma/Corbis

> ● Table 8.4 Convergent and Divergent Problems
>
> **CONVERGENT PROBLEMS**
>
> - What is the area of a triangle that is 3 feet wide at the base and 2 feet tall?
> - Erica is shorter than Zoey but taller than Carlo, and Carlo is taller than Jared. Who is the second tallest?
> - If you simultaneously drop a baseball and a bowling ball from a tall building, which will hit the ground first?
>
> **DIVERGENT PROBLEMS**
>
> - What objects can you think of that begin with the letters BR?
> - How could discarded aluminum cans be put to use?
> - Write a poem about fire and ice.

Tests of Creativity

Divergent thinking can be measured in several ways. In the *Unusual Uses Test,* you would be asked to think of as many uses as possible for some object, such as the plastic containers mentioned earlier. In the *Consequences Test,* you would list the consequences that would follow a basic change in the world. For example, you might be asked, "What would happen if everyone suddenly lost their sense of balance and could no longer stay upright?" People try to list as many reactions as possible. If you were to take the *Anagrams Test,* you would be given a word such as *creativity* and asked to make as many new words as possible by rearranging the letters. Each of these tests can be scored for fluency, flexibility, and originality. (For an example of other tests of divergent thinking, see ▶▶ Figure 8.24.) Tests of divergent thinking seem to tap something quite different from intelligence. Generally, there is little correlation between creativity tests and IQ test scores (Preckel, Holling, & Wiese, 2006).

Isn't creativity more than divergent thought? What if a person comes up with a large number of useless answers to a problem? A good question. Divergent thinking is an important part of creativity, but there is more to it. To be creative, the solution to a problem must be more than novel, unusual, or original. It must also be *practical* if it is an invention and *sensible* if it is an idea. This is the dividing line between a "harebrained scheme" and a "stroke of genius." In other words, the creative person brings reasoning and critical thinking to bear on new ideas once they are produced (Runco, 2003).

Stages of Creative Thought

Is there any pattern to creative thinking? Typically, five stages occur during creative problem solving:

1. **Orientation.** As a first step, the person defines the problem and identifies its most important dimensions.
2. **Preparation.** In the second stage, creative thinkers saturate themselves with as much information about the problem as possible.

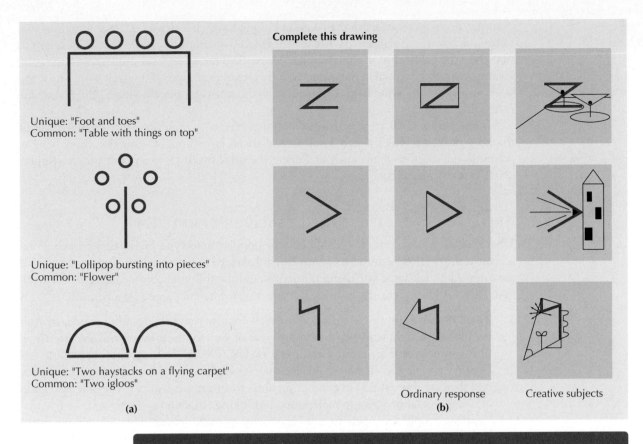

Complete this drawing

Unique: "Foot and toes"
Common: "Table with things on top"

Unique: "Lollipop bursting into pieces"
Common: "Flower"

Unique: "Two haystacks on a flying carpet"
Common: "Two igloos"

(a)

Ordinary response   Creative subjects

(b)

▲ **FIGURE 8.24** Some tests of divergent thinking. Creative responses are more original and more complex. [(a) Adapted from Wallach & Kogan, 1965; (b) adapted from Barron, 1958.]

3. **Incubation.** Most major problems produce a period during which all attempted solutions will be futile. At this point, problem solving may proceed on a subconscious level: Although the problem seems to have been set aside, it is still "cooking" in the background.

4. **Illumination.** The stage of incubation is often ended by a rapid insight or series of insights. These produce the "Aha!" experience, often depicted in cartoons as a lightbulb appearing over the thinker's head.

5. **Verification.** The final step is to test and critically evaluate the solution obtained during the stage of illumination. If the solution proves faulty, the thinker reverts to the stage of incubation.

Of course, creative thought is not always so neat. Nevertheless, the stages listed are a good summary of the most typical sequence of events.

You may find it helpful to relate the stages to the following true (more or less) story. Legend has it that the king of Syracuse (a city in ancient Greece) once suspected that his goldsmith had substituted cheaper metals for some of the gold in a crown and kept the extra gold. Archimedes, a famous mathematician and thinker, was given the problem of discovering whether the king had been cheated.

Archimedes began by defining the problem *(orientation):* "How can I tell what metals have been used in the crown without damaging it?" He then checked all known methods of analyzing metals *(preparation).* All involved cutting or melting the crown, so he was forced to temporarily set the problem aside *(incubation).* Then one day as he stepped into his bath, Archimedes suddenly knew he had the solution *(illumination).* He was so excited he is said to have run naked through the streets shouting, "Eureka, eureka!" (I have found it, I have found it!).

On observing his own body floating in the bath, Archimedes realized that different metals of equal weight would displace different amounts of water. A pound of brass, for

Hat-tipping device. According to the patent, it is for "automatically effecting polite salutations by the elevation and rotation of the hat on the head of the saluting party when said person bows to the person or persons saluted." In addition to being original or novel, a creative solution must fit the demands of the problem. Is this a creative solution to the "problem" of hat tipping? (U.S. Patent No. 556,248. From *Absolutely Mad Inventions,* by A. E. Brown and H. A. Jeffcott [1970].)

example, occupies more space than a pound of gold, which is denser. All that remained was to test the solution *(verification)*. Archimedes placed an amount of gold (equal in weight to that given the goldsmith) in a tub of water. He marked the water level and removed the gold. He then placed the crown in the water. Was the crown pure gold? If it was, it would raise the water to exactly the same level. Unfortunately, the purity of the crown and the fate of the goldsmith are to this day unknown!

Some authors believe that truly exceptional creativity requires a rare combination of thinking skills, personality, and a supportive social environment. This mix, they believe, accounts for creative giants such as Edison, Freud, Mozart, Picasso, and others (Runco, 2004; Tardif & Sternberg, 1988).

Positive Psychology: The Creative Personality

What makes a person creative? According to the popular stereotype, highly creative people are eccentric, introverted, neurotic, socially inept, unbalanced in their interests, and on the edge of madness. Although some artists and musicians cultivate this public image, there is little truth in it. Direct studies of creative individuals paint a very different picture (Winner, 2003):

1. There is a small positive correlation between creativity and IQ. In other words, smarter people have a slight tendency to be more creative. But, for the most part, at any given level of IQ, some people are creative and some are not (Preckel, Holling, & Wiese, 2006).
2. Creative people usually have a greater-than-average range of knowledge and interests, and they are more fluent in combining ideas from various sources. They are also good at using mental images and metaphors in thinking (Riquelme, 2002).
3. Creative people are open to a wide variety of experiences. They accept irrational thoughts and are uninhibited about their feelings and fantasies. They tend to use broad categories, to question assumptions, to break mental sets, and they find order in chaos. They also experience more unusual states of consciousness, such as vivid dreams and mystical experiences (Ayers, Beaton, & Hunt, 1999).
4. Creative people enjoy symbolic thought, ideas, concepts, and possibilities. They tend to be interested in truth, form, and beauty, rather than in fame or success. Their creative work is an end in itself (Sternberg & Lubart, 1995).
5. Creative people value their independence and prefer complexity. However, they are unconventional and nonconforming primarily in their work; otherwise, they do not have unusual, outlandish, or bizarre personalities.

Can creativity be learned? It is beginning to look as if some creative thinking skills can be learned. In particular, you can become more creative by practicing divergent thinking and by taking risks, analyzing ideas, and seeking unusual connections between ideas (Baer, 1993; Sternberg, 2001). Don't forget to read this chapter's Psychology in Action section for more on creativity.

Intuitive Thought—Mental Shortcut? Or Dangerous Detour?

How accurate is intuition?

At the same time that irrational, intuitive thought may contribute to creative problem solving, it can also lead to thinking errors. To see how this can happen, try the following problems:

> *Problem 1* An epidemic breaks out, and 600 people are about to die. Doctors have two choices. If they give drug A, 200 lives will be saved. If they give drug B, there is a one-third chance that 600 people will be saved, and a two-thirds chance that none will be saved. Which drug should they choose?

Have You Ever Thin-Sliced Your Teacher?

Think back to your least favorite teacher (not your current one, of course!). How long did it take you to figure out that he or she wasn't going to make your list of star teachers?

In an intriguing study, psychologist Nalini Ambady asked people to watch video clips of teachers they did not know. After watching three 10-second segments, participants were asked to rate the teachers. Amazingly, their ratings correlated highly with year-end course evaluations made by actual students (Ambady & Rosenthal, 1993). Ambady obtained the same result when she presented an even thinner "slice" of teaching

behavior, just three 2-second clips. A mere 6 seconds is all that participants needed to form intuitive judgments of the instructors' teaching!

In his book *Blink*, Malcolm Gladwell (2005) argues that this was not a case of hurried irrationality. Instead, it was "thin-slicing," or quickly making sense of thin slivers of experience. According to Gladwell, these immediate, intuitive reactions can sometimes form the basis of more carefully reasoned judgments. They are a testament to the power of the cognitive unconscious, which is a part of the brain that does automatic,

unconscious processing (Wilson, 2002). Far from being irrational, intuition may be an important part of how we think.

The trick, of course, is figuring out when thin-slicing can be trusted and when it can't. After all, first impressions aren't always right. For example, have you ever had a teacher you came to appreciate only after classes were well under way or only after the course was over? In many circumstances, quick impressions are most valuable when you take the time to verify them through further observation.

Problem 2 Again, 600 people are about to die, and doctors must make a choice. If they give drug A, 400 people will die. If they give drug B, there is a one-third chance that no one will die, and a two-thirds chance that 600 will die. Which drug should they choose?

Most people choose drug A for the first problem and drug B for the second. This is fascinating because the two problems are identical. The only difference is that the first is stated in terms of lives saved, the second in terms of lives lost. Yet, even people who realize that their answers are contradictory find it difficult to change them (Kahneman & Tversky, 1972, 1973).

Intuition

As the example shows, we often make decisions intuitively, rather than logically or rationally. **Intuition** is quick, impulsive thought. It may provide fast answers, but it can also be misleading and sometimes disastrous. (But see "Have You Ever Thin-Sliced Your Teacher?")

Two noted psychologists, Daniel Kahneman (KON-eh-man) and Amos Tversky (tuh-VER-ski) (1937–1996), studied how we make decisions in the face of uncertainty. They found that human judgment is often seriously flawed (Kahneman, 2003; Kahneman, Slovic, & Tversky, 1982). Let's explore some common intuitive thinking errors, so you will be better prepared to avoid them.

Representativeness

One very common pitfall in judgment is illustrated by the question, Which is more probable?

A. Tiger Woods will not be in the lead after the first round of golf of a tournament but win the tournament.

B. Tiger Woods will not be in the lead after the first round of golf of a tournament.

Tversky and Kahneman (1982) found that most people regard statements like A as more probable than B. However, this intuitive answer overlooks an important fact: The likelihood of two events occurring together is lower than the probability of either one alone. (For example, the probability of getting one head when flipping a coin is one half, or .5. The probability of getting two heads when flipping two coins is one fourth, or .25.) Therefore, A is less likely to be true than B.

According to Tversky and Kahneman, such faulty conclusions are based on the **representativeness heuristic.** That is, we tend to give a choice greater weight if it seems to be representative of what we already know. Thus, you probably compared the information

Intuition Quick, impulsive thought that does not make use of formal logic or clear reasoning.

Representativeness heuristic A tendency to select wrong answers because they seem to match pre-existing mental categories.

about Tiger Woods with your mental model of what a golf pro's behavior should be like. Answer A seems to better represent the model. Therefore, it seems more likely than answer B, even though it isn't. In courtrooms, jurors are more likely to think a defendant is guilty if the person appears to fit the profile of a person likely to commit a crime (Davis & Follette, 2002). For example, a young single male from a poor neighborhood would be more likely to be judged guilty of theft than a middle-aged married father from an affluent suburb.

Hot Cognition

Feelings also tend to affect good judgment. When we must make a choice, our emotional reactions to various alternatives can determine what intuitively seems to be the right answer. Emotions such as fear, hope, anxiety, liking, or disgust can eliminate possibilities from consideration or promote them to the top of the list (Kahneman, 2003). For many people, choosing which political candidate to vote for is a good example of how emotions can cloud clear thinking. Rather than comparing candidates' records and policies, it is tempting to vote for the person we like, rather than the person who is most qualified for the job.

Underlying Odds

A second common error in judgment involves ignoring the **base rate,** or underlying probability, of an event. People in one experiment were told that they would be given descriptions of 100 people—70 lawyers and 30 engineers. Subjects were then asked to guess, without knowing anything about a person, whether she or he was an engineer or a lawyer. All correctly stated the probabilities as 70 percent for lawyer and 30 percent for engineer. Participants were then given this description:

> Eric is a 30-year-old man. He is married with no children. A man of high ability and high motivation, he promises to be quite successful in his field. He is well liked by his colleagues.

Notice that the description gives no new information about Eric's occupation. He could still be either an engineer or a lawyer. Therefore, the odds should again be estimated as 70-30. However, most people changed the odds to 50-50. Intuitively it seems that Eric has an equal chance of being either an engineer or a lawyer. But this guess completely ignores the underlying odds.

Perhaps it is fortunate that we do at times ignore underlying odds. Were this not the case, how many people would get married in the face of a 50 percent divorce rate? Or how many would start high-risk businesses? On the other hand, people who smoke, drink and then drive, or skip wearing auto seat belts ignore rather high odds of injury or illness. In many high-risk situations, ignoring base rates is the same as thinking you are an exception to the rule.

Framing

The most general conclusion about intuition is that the way a problem is stated, or **framed,** affects decisions (Tversky & Kahneman, 1981). As the first example in this discussion revealed, people often give different answers to the same problem if it is stated in slightly different ways. To gain some added insight into framing, try another thinking problem:

> A couple are divorcing. Both parents seek custody of their only child, but custody can be granted to just one parent. If you had to make a decision based on the following information, to which parent would you award custody of the child?
>
> **Parent A:** average income, average health, average working hours, reasonable rapport with the child, relatively stable social life.
>
> **Parent B:** above-average income, minor health problems, lots of work-related travel, very close relationship with the child, extremely active social life.

Most people choose to award custody to Parent B, the parent who has some drawbacks but also several advantages (such as above-average income). That's because people tend to look for *positive qualities* that can be *awarded* to the child. However, how would you choose

Base rate The basic rate at which an event occurs over time; the basic probability of an event.

Framing In thought, the terms in which a problem is stated or the way that it is structured.

if you were asked this question: Which parent should be denied custody? In this case, most people choose to deny custody to Parent B. Why is Parent B a good choice one moment and a poor choice the next? It's because the second question asked who should be *denied* custody. To answer this question, people tend to look for *negative qualities* that would *disqualify* a parent. As you can see, the way a question is framed can channel us down a narrow path so we attend to only part of the information provided, rather than weighing all the pros and cons (Shafir, 1993).

Usually, the *broadest* way of framing or stating a problem produces the best decisions. However, people often state problems in increasingly narrow terms until a single, seemingly "obvious" answer emerges. For example, to select a career, it would be wise to consider pay, working conditions, job satisfaction, needed skills, future employment outlook, and many other factors. Instead, such decisions are often narrowed to thoughts such as, "I like to write, so I'll be a journalist," "I want to make good money, and law pays well," or "I can be creative in photography." Framing decisions so narrowly greatly increases the risk of making a poor choice. If you would like to think more critically and analytically, it is important to pay attention to how you are defining problems before you try to solve them. Remember, shortcuts to answers often short-circuit clear thinking.

Wisdom

People can be intelligent without being wise. For example, a person who does well in school and on IQ tests may make a total mess of her life. Likewise, people can be intelligent without being creative; and clear, rational thinking can lead to correct, but uninspired, answers (Solomon, Marshall, & Gardner, 2005). In many areas of human life, wisdom represents a mixture of convergent thinking, intelligence, and reason, spiced with creativity and originality. People who are wise approach life with openness and tolerance (Helson & Srivastava, 2002).

RECITE

1. Fluency, flexibility, and originality are characteristics of
   a. convergent thought   b. deductive thinking
   c. creative thought   d. trial-and-error solutions
2. List the typical stages of creative thinking in the correct order.
   _____ _____
   _____ _____
   _____
3. Reasoning and critical thinking tend to block creativity; these are noncreative qualities. T or F?
4. To be creative, an original idea must also be practical or feasible. T or F?
5. Intelligence and creativity are highly correlated; the higher a person's IQ, the more likely he or she is to be creative. T or F?
6. Kate is single, outspoken, and very bright. As a college student, she was deeply concerned with discrimination and other social issues and participated in several protests. Which statement is more likely to be true?
   a. Kate is a bank teller.   b. Kate is a bank teller and a feminist.

REFLECT

Critical Thinking

7. A coin is flipped four times with one of the following results: (a) H T T H, (b) T T T T, (c) H H H H, (d) H H T H. Which sequence would most likely precede getting a head on the fifth coin flip?

Relate

Make up a question that would require convergent thinking to answer. Now do the same for divergent thinking.

Which of the tests of creativity described in the text do you think you would do best on? (Look back if you can't remember them all.)

To better remember the stages of creative thinking, make up a short story that includes these words: *orient, prepare, in Cuba, illuminate, verify*.

Explain in your own words how representativeness and base rates contribute to thinking errors.

ANSWERS

1. c   2. orientation, preparation, incubation, illumination, verification   3. F   4. T   5. F   6. a   7. The chance of getting a head on the fifth flip is the same in each case. Each time you flip a coin, the chance of getting heads is 50 percent, no matter what happened before. However, many people intuitively think that b is the answer because heads is "overdue," or that c is correct because the coin is "on a roll" for heads.

psychology in action
Enhancing Creativity—Brainstorms

What can be done to improve thinking and promote creativity?

Thomas Edison explained his creativity by saying, "Genius is 1 percent inspiration and 99 percent perspiration." Many studies of creativity show that "genius" and "eminence" owe as much to persistence and dedication as they do to inspiration (Glueck, Ernst, & Unger, 2002; Winner, 2003). Once it is recognized that creativity can be hard work, then something can be done to enhance it. Here are some suggestions:

1. Break mental sets and challenge assumptions.

A *mental set* is the tendency to perceive a problem in a way that blinds us to possible solutions. Mental sets are a major barrier to creative thinking. Usually, they lead us to see a problem in preconceived terms that impede our problem-solving attempts. (Fixations and functional fixedness, which were described earlier, are specific types of mental sets.)

Try the problems pictured in ▶▶ Figure 8.25. If you have difficulty, try asking yourself what assumptions you are making. The problems are designed to demonstrate the limiting effects of a mental set. (The answers to these problems, along with an explanation of the sets that prevent their solution, are found in ▶▶ Figure 8.26.)

Now that you have been forewarned about the danger of faulty assumptions, see if you can correctly answer the following questions. If you get caught on any of them, consider it an additional reminder of the value of actively challenging the assumptions you are making in any instance of problem solving.

1. A farmer had 19 sheep. All but 9 died. How many sheep did the farmer have left?

2. It is not unlawful for a man living in Winston-Salem, North Carolina, to be buried west of the Mississippi River. T or F?

3. I have two coins that together total 30 cents. One of the coins is not a nickel. What are the two coins?

These questions are designed to cause thinking errors. Here are the answers:

1. Nineteen—9 alive and 10 dead.   2. F. It is against the law to bury a living person anywhere.   3. A quarter and a nickel. One of the coins is not a nickel, but the other one is!

(a)   (b)

▲ **FIGURE 8.25** Nine dots are arranged in a square. Can you connect them by drawing four continuous straight lines without lifting your pencil from the paper? (b) Six matches must be arranged to make four triangles. The triangles must be the same size, with each side equal to the length of one match. (The solutions to these problems appear in Figure 8.26.)

2. Define problems broadly.

An effective way to break mental sets is to enlarge the definition of a problem. For instance, assume that your problem is to design a better doorway. This is likely to lead to ordinary solutions. Why not change the problem to design a better way to get through a wall? Now your solutions will be more original. Best of all might be to state the problem as follows: Find a better way to define separate areas for living and working. This could lead to truly creative solutions (Adams, 2001).

Let's say you are leading a group that's designing a new can opener. Wisely, you ask the group to think about *opening* in general, rather than about can openers. This was just the approach that led to the pop-top can. As the design group discussed the concept of opening, one member suggested that nature has its own openers, like the soft seam on a pea pod. Instead of a new can-opening tool, the group invented the self-opening can (Stein, 1974).

3. Restate the problem in different ways.

Stating problems in novel ways also tends to produce more creative solutions. See if you can cross out six letters to make a single word out of the following:

C S R I E X L E A T T T E R E S

If you're having difficulty, it may be that you need to restate the problem. Were you trying to cross out six letters? The real solution is to cross out the letters in the words "six letters," which yields the word CREATE.

One way to restate a problem is to imagine how another person would view it. What would a child, engineer, professor, mechanic, artist, psychologist, judge, or minister ask about the problem? Also, don't be afraid to ask "silly" or playful questions such as: If the problem were alive, what would it look like? If the problem were edible, how would it taste?

At the very least, you should almost always ask the following questions: What information do I have? What don't I know? Have I used all of the information? What additional information do I need? What are the parts of the problem? How are the parts related? How could the parts be related? Remember, to think more creatively you must find ways to jog yourself out of mental sets and habitual modes of thought (Michalko, 1998).

4. Allow time for incubation.

If you are feeling hurried by a sense of time pressure, you are almost always less likely to think creatively (Amabile, Hadley, & Kramer, 2002). You need to be able to revise or embellish initial solutions, even those based on rapid insight. Incubation is especially fruitful when you are exposed to external cues that relate to the problem (remember Archimedes' bath?). For example, Johannes Gutenberg, creator of the printing press, realized while at a wine harvest that the mechanical pressure used to crush grapes could also be used to imprint letters on paper (Dorfman, Shames, & Kihlstrom, 1996).

5. Seek varied input.

Remember, creativity requires divergent thinking. Rather than digging deeper with logic, you are attempting to shift your mental "prospecting" to new areas. As an example of this strategy, Edward de Bono (1992) recommends that you randomly look up words in the dictionary and relate them to the problem. Often the words will trigger a fresh perspective or open a new avenue. For instance, let's say you are asked to come up with new ways to clean oil off a beach. Following de Bono's suggestion, you would read the following randomly selected words, relate each to the problem, and see what thoughts are triggered: *weed, rust, poor, magnify, foam, gold, frame, hole, diagonal, vacuum, tribe, puppet, nose, link, drift, portrait, cheese, coal.* You may get similar benefits from relating various objects to a problem. Or, take a walk, skim through a newspaper, or look through a stack of photographs to see what thoughts they trigger (Michalko, 1998). Exposing yourself to a wide variety of information is a good way to encourage divergent thinking (Clapham, 2001).

6. Look for analogies.

Many "new" problems are really old problems in new clothing (Siegler, 1989). Representing a problem in a variety of ways is often the key to solution. Most problems become easier to solve when they are effectively represented. For example, consider this problem:

> Two backpackers start up a steep trail at 6 a.m. They hike all day, resting occasionally, and arrive at the top at 6 p.m. The next day they start back down the trail at 6 a.m. On the way down, they stop several times and vary their pace. They arrive back at 6 p.m. On the way down, one of the hikers, who is a mathematician, tells the other that she has realized that they will pass a point on the trail at exactly the same time as they did the day before. Her non-mathematical friend finds this hard to believe, since on both days they have stopped and started many times and changed their pace. The problem: Is the mathematician right?

Perhaps you will see the answer to this problem immediately. If not, think of it this way: What if there were two pairs of backpackers, one going up the trail, the second coming down, and both hiking *on the same day*? As one pair of hikers goes up the trail and the other goes down, they *must* pass each other at some point on the trail, right? Therefore, at that point they will be at the same place at the same time. Now, would your conclusion change

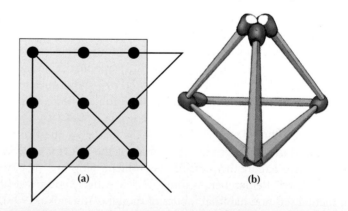

(a) (b)

⬆ FIGURE 8.26 Problem solutions. *(a)* The dot problem can be solved by extending the lines beyond the square formed by the dots. Most people assume incorrectly that they may not do this. *(b)* The match problem can be solved by building a three-dimensional pyramid. Most people assume that the matches must be arranged on a flat surface. If you remembered the four-tree problem from earlier in the chapter, the match problem may have been easy to solve.

if one of the pairs was going up the trail one day and the other was coming down the trail the next? If you mentally draw their path up the mountain and then visualize them coming back down it the next day, do you see that at some point the two paths will meet at the same point at the same time on both days? Well, what if the same pair of hikers were going up one day and coming back down the next? As you can now see, the mathematician was right.

7. Delay evaluation.

Various studies suggest that people are most likely to be creative when they are given the freedom to play with ideas and solutions without having to worry about whether they will be evaluated. In the first stages of creative thinking, it is important to avoid criticizing your efforts. Worrying about the correctness of solutions tends to inhibit creativity (Basadur, Runco, & Vega, 2000).

Living More Creatively

Many conventional thinkers live intelligent, successful, and fulfilling lives. Just the same, creative thinking can add spice to life and lead to exciting personal insights. Psychologist Mihalyi Csikszentmihalyi (sik-sent-me-HALE-yee) (1997) makes these recommendations about how to become more creative:

- Find something that surprises you every day.
- Try to surprise at least one person every day.
- If something sparks your interest, follow it.
- Make a commitment to doing things well.
- Seek challenges.
- Take time for thinking and relaxing.
- Start doing more of what you really enjoy, and less of what you dislike.
- Try to look at problems from as many viewpoints as you can.

Even if you don't become more creative by following these suggestions, they are still good advice. Life is not a standardized test with a single set of correct answers. It is much more like a blank canvas on which you can create designs that uniquely express your talents and interests. To live more creatively, you must be ready to seek new ways of doing things. Try to surprise at least one person today—yourself, if no one else.

---

study break
Enhancing Creativity

RECITE

1. Fixations and functional fixedness are specific types of mental sets. T or F?
2. The incubation period in creative problem solving usually lasts just a matter of minutes. T or F?
3. Exposure to creative models has been shown to enhance creativity. T or F?
4. One way to live more creatively is to surprise yourself every day. T or F?

REFLECT
Critical Thinking

5. Do you think there is any connection between your mood and your creativity?

Relate

Review the preceding pages and note which methods you could use more often to improve the quality of your thinking. Now mentally summarize the points you especially want to remember.

ANSWERS

1. T 2. F 3. T 4. T 5. In general, more intense moods are associated with higher creativity (Davis, 2009).

chapter in review

Major Points

- Intelligence is often defined as a single general human quality and operationally defined as performance on an IQ test.

- Simplistic definitions of intelligence have been questioned. IQ is influenced by nurture as well as nature.

- Thinking, problem solving, language, and creativity are the origins of intelligent behavior.

- Thinking is influenced by the form in which information is represented—as images, concepts, or symbols.

- Language is an especially powerful way to encode information and manipulate ideas.

- Understanding problem solving can make you more effective at finding solutions.

- Expert problem solving is based on acquired knowledge and strategies.

- Creative thinking is novel, divergent, and tempered with a dash of practicality.

- Some thinking errors can be avoided if you know the pitfalls of intuitive thought.

- Creativity can be enhanced by strategies that promote divergent thinking.

Summary

How is human intelligence defined and measured?

- Intelligence refers to the general capacity (or g-factor) to act purposefully, think rationally, and deal effectively with the environment.

- In practice, intelligence is operationally defined by intelligence tests, which provide a useful but narrow estimate of real-world intelligence.

- *Artificial intelligence* refers to any artificial system that can perform tasks that require intelligence when done by people. Two principal areas of artificial intelligence research on particular human skills are computer simulations and expert systems.

- The first intelligence test was assembled by Alfred Binet. A modern version of Binet's test is the *Stanford-Binet Intelligence Scale*.

- Another major intelligence test is the *Wechsler Adult Intelligence Scale* (WAIS). The WAIS measures both verbal and performance intelligence. Group intelligence tests are also available.

- Intelligence is expressed as an intelligence quotient (IQ), defined as mental age divided by chronological age and then multiplied by 100. The distribution of IQ scores approximates a normal curve.

How much does intelligence vary from person to person?

- Most people score in the mid-range on intelligence tests. Only a small percentage of people have exceptionally high and low IQ scores.

- People with IQs in the gifted or "genius" range of above 140 tend to be superior in many respects. However, by criteria other than IQ, many children can be considered gifted or talented in one way or another.

- The term *developmentally disabled* is applied to those whose IQ falls below 70 or who lack various adaptive behaviors. About 50 percent of the cases of developmental disability are organic. Many of the remaining cases are thought to reflect familial intellectual disability.

What are some controversies in the study of intelligence?

- Traditional IQ tests often suffer from a degree of cultural and racial bias. For this and other reasons, it is wise to remember that IQ is merely an index of intelligence and that intelligence is narrowly defined by most tests.

- Many psychologists have begun to forge new, broader definitions of intelligence. Howard Gardner's theory of multiple intelligences is a good example.

- Intelligence is partially determined by heredity. However, environment is also important, as revealed by IQ increases induced by education and stimulating environments.

What is the nature of thought?

- Thinking is an internal representation of external stimuli or situations.

- Three basic units of thought are images, concepts, and language (or symbols).

In what ways are images related to thinking?

- Images may be stored in memory or created to solve problems.

- Images can be three-dimensional, they can be rotated in space, and their size may change.

- Kinesthetic images are used to represent movements and actions. Kinesthetic sensations help structure the flow of thoughts for many people.

What are concepts?

- A concept is a generalized idea of a class of objects or events.

- Concept formation may be based on positive and negative instances or rule learning.

- In practice, concept identification frequently makes use of prototypes, or ideal models.

- Concepts may be conjunctive ("and" concepts), disjunctive ("either/or" concepts), or relational.

- The denotative meaning of a word or concept is its dictionary definition. Connotative meaning is personal or emotional.

What is the role of language in thinking?

- Language encodes events into symbols, for easy mental manipulation. The study of meaning in language is called *semantics*.

- Bilingualism is a valuable ability. Two-way bilingual education allows children to develop additive bilingualism while in school.

- Language carries meaning by combining a set of symbols according to a set of rules (grammar), which includes rules about word order (syntax).

- True languages are productive and can be used to generate new ideas or possibilities.

- Complex gestural systems, such as American Sign Language, are true languages.

- Chimpanzees and other primates have been taught American Sign Language and similar systems. This suggests to some that primates are capable of very basic language use. Others question this conclusion.

What do we know about problem solving?

- The solution to a problem may be arrived at mechanically (by trial and error or by rote application of rules), but mechanical solutions are often inefficient.
- Solutions by understanding usually begin with discovery of the general properties of an answer, followed by a functional solution.
- Problem solving is aided by heuristics, which narrow the search for solutions.
- When understanding leads to a rapid solution, insight has occurred. Three elements of insight are selective encoding, selective combination, and selective comparison.
- Insight can be blocked by fixations. Functional fixedness is a common fixation, but emotional blocks, cultural values, learned conventions, and perceptual habits are also problems.

What is creative thinking?

- To be creative, a solution must be practical and sensible as well as original. Creative thinking requires divergent thought, characterized by fluency, flexibility, and originality. Tests of creativity measure these qualities.

- Five stages often seen in creative problem solving are orientation, preparation, incubation, illumination, and verification. Not all creative thinking fits this pattern.
- Studies suggest that the creative personality has a number of characteristics, most of which contradict popular stereotypes. There is only a very small correlation between IQ and creativity.
- Some creative thinking skills can be learned.

How accurate is intuition?

- Intuitive thinking can be fast and accurate but also often leads to errors. Wrong conclusions may be drawn when an answer seems highly representative of what we already believe is true.
- Emotions also lead to intuitive thinking and poor choices.
- A second problem is ignoring the base rate (or underlying probability) of an event.
- Clear thinking is usually aided by stating or framing a problem in broad terms.

What can be done to improve thinking and promote creativity?

- Various strategies that promote divergent thinking tend to enhance creative problem solving.
- In group situations, brainstorming may lead to creative solutions. The principles of brainstorming can also be applied to individual problem solving.

Cognition, Intelligence, and Creativity

For additional review, get more practice with *CengageNOW, WebTutor,* the *Practice Quizzes,* and/or the printed *Study Guide* available with this book.

1. Which modern intelligence test originated as a test for adults?
   - a. SB5
   - b. WAIS
   - c. SAT
   - d. WISC

2. By definition, a person has above-average intelligence when
   - a. MA > CA
   - b. CA > 100
   - c. MA > 100
   - d. MA < CA

3. One thing that the mentally gifted and the developmentally disabled have in common is that both
   - a. have a tendency to suffer from metabolic disorders
   - b. have to be tested with the WAIS, rather than the SB5
   - c. have MAs that are higher than their CAs
   - d. have extreme IQ scores

4. Which is NOT one of the eight types of intelligence identified by Howard Gardner?
   - a. cyber skills
   - b. music skills
   - c. visual and spatial skills
   - d. naturalist skills

5. Computer simulations and expert systems are primary research tools in
   - a. psycholinguistics
   - b. the field of AI
   - c. studies of divergent thinking
   - d. studies of the semantic differential

6. When racial or cultural groups differ in access to education, IQs tell us little about how _____ affect(s) intelligence.
   - a. stimulating environments
   - b. teaching adaptive behaviors
   - c. genetics
   - d. applying deviation IQs

7. Concepts are
   - a. picture-like mental representations
   - b. generalized ideas about a class of objects or events
   - c. symbols and rules for combining symbols
   - d. symbolic notational systems

8. A person doing mental rotation would need to use which basic unit of thought?
   - a. concepts
   - b. language
   - c. images
   - d. symbols

9. Our ability to think about movements and actions is aided by
   - a. kinesthetic imagery
   - b. rotational concepts
   - c. mental calculation
   - d. relational concepts

10. A triangle must be a closed shape and have three sides and the sides must be straight lines. *Triangle* is a
    - a. conjunctive concept
    - b. relational concept
    - c. disjunctive concept
    - d. connotative concept

11. When you are trying to categorize complex stimuli, _____ are especially helpful.
    - a. kinesthetic images
    - b. connotative concepts
    - c. denotative concepts
    - d. prototypes

12. Which of the following is NOT an element of spoken language?
    - a. grammar
    - b. morphemes
    - c. phonemes
    - d. lexigrams

13. Noam Chomsky believes that we use _____ to change core declarative sentences into other voices and forms.
    - a. phonemes
    - b. transformation rules
    - c. conditional statements
    - d. conjunctive encoding

14. Which statement is the best summary of animal language research with chimpanzees?
    - a. Chimps can learn to use signs, but they can't make word sounds.
    - b. Chimps can learn to communicate with signs.
    - c. Chimps who learn signs use language on a par with 5-year-old children.
    - d. Because of serious problems with syntax, chimps have been unable to communicate with humans.

15. After you find a general solution to a problem, you must usually also find a
    - a. heuristic
    - b. search strategy
    - c. fixation
    - d. functional solution

16. Functional fixedness is a major barrier to
    - a. insightful problem solving
    - b. using random search strategies
    - c. mechanical problem solving
    - d. achieving fixations through problem solving

17. A test scored for fluency and flexibility is obviously designed to measure
    - a. intuitive thinking
    - b. convergent thinking
    - c. divergent thinking
    - d. algorithms

18. The stage of creative thinking that corresponds to insightful problem solving is
    - a. verification
    - b. incubation
    - c. induction
    - d. illumination

19. Our decisions are greatly affected by the way a problem is stated, a process called
    - a. framing
    - b. base rating
    - c. induction
    - d. selective encoding

20. Creativity also involves
    - a. hard work
    - b. operant conditioning IQs
    - c. a high IQ
    - d. defining problems more narrowly

Answers   1.b 2.a 3.d 4.a 5.b 6.c 7.b 8.c 9.a 10.a 11.d 12.d 13.b 14.b 15.d 16.a 17.c 18.d 19.a 20.a

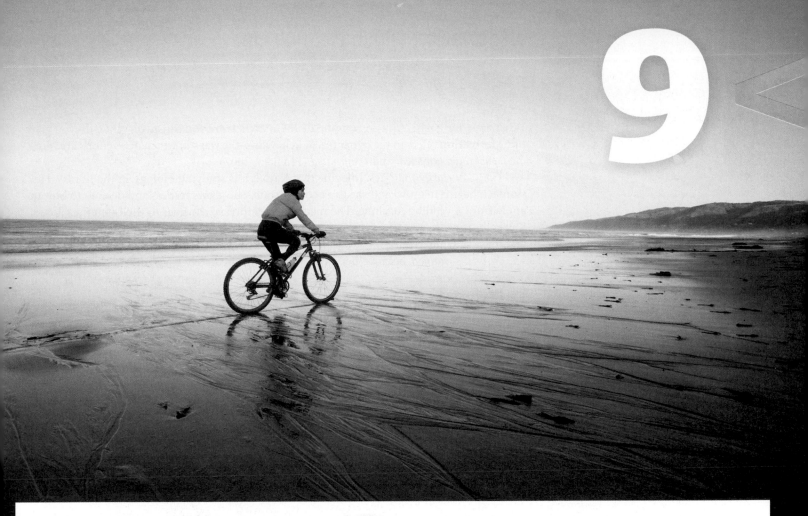

Motivation and Emotion

Journey into Psychology: Are You Moved by the Music of Life?

Robert was in his doctor's waiting room when he suffered a "strange attack." He recalls that the "atmosphere changed, the walls seemed to close in, and the voices of other patients became a buzz." However, months of therapy were no help because Robert simply couldn't talk about his feelings. When asked how he felt, Robert might reply, "Fine" or "I don't know." Or he might describe a bodily sensation instead of an emotion, by replying, "My stomach hurts" (Lumley, 2004). The scientific name for Robert's problem is *alexithymia* (a-LEX-ih-THIGH-me-ah), from the Latin for "can't name emotions."

In a sense, you could say that emotion is the "music" that enriches the rhythms of our lives. Sadly, Robert is not moved by this music as intensely as most of us are. Not only is Robert unable to name his emotions, he is only vaguely aware of them in the first place. As you might suspect, people like Robert find it hard to form close relationships because they cannot easily empathize with the feelings of others. This lack of inner awareness can also lead to health problems, such as depression or addictive behaviors (Lumley, 2004).

In this chapter you will learn how motives

provide the drumbeat of human behavior and emotions color its rhythms. The words *motivation* and *emotion* both derive from the Latin word *movere* (to move). As we will see, both play complex roles in our daily lives. Even "simple" motivated activities, such as eating, are not solely under the control of the body. In many instances, external cues, expectations, learning, cultural values, and other factors influence our motives and emotions (Franken, 2007). Let's begin with basic motives, such as hunger and thirst, and end by exploring how emotions affect us.

Survey Questions

- What is motivation? Are there different types of motives?

- What causes hunger? Overeating? Eating disorders?

- Is there more than one type of thirst? In what ways are pain avoidance and the sex drive unusual?

- What are the typical patterns of human sexual response?

- How does arousal relate to motivation?

- What are social motives? Why are they important?

- Are some motives more basic than others?

- What happens during emotion?

- What physiological changes underlie emotion? Can "lie detectors" really detect lies?

- How accurately are emotions expressed by the face and "body language"?

- How do psychologists explain emotions?

- What does it mean to have "emotional intelligence"?

Motivation—Push Me, Pull Me

What is motivation? Are there different types of motives?

What are your goals? Why do you pursue them? When are you satisfied? When do you give up? **Motivation** refers to the dynamics of behavior—the ways in which our actions are *initiated, sustained, directed,* and *terminated* (Franken, 2007).

Can you clarify that? Yes. Imagine that Kayleigh is studying biology in the library. Her stomach begins to growl and she can't concentrate. She grows restless and decides to buy an apple from a vending machine. The machine is empty, so she goes to the cafeteria. Closed. Kayleigh drives to a nearby fast food outlet, where she finally eats. Her hunger satisfied, she resumes studying. Notice how Kayleigh's food seeking was *initiated* by a bodily need. Her search was *sustained* because her need was not immediately met, and her actions were *directed* by possible sources of food. Finally, achieving her goal *terminated* her food seeking.

A Model of Motivation

Many motivated activities begin with a **need,** or internal deficiency. The need that initiated Kayleigh's search was a shortage of key substances in her body. Needs cause a **drive** (an energized motivational state) to develop. The drive was hunger, in Kayleigh's case. Drives activate a **response** (an action or series of actions) designed to push us toward a **goal** (the "target" of motivated behavior). Reaching a goal that satisfies the need will end the chain of events. Thus, a simple model of motivation can be shown in this way:

Aren't needs and drives the same thing? No, because the strength of needs and drives can differ (Beck, 2004). For example, it is not uncommon for older people to suffer from dehydration (a bodily need for water) despite experiencing a lack of thirst (the drive to drink) (Farrell et al., 2008).

Now let's observe Kayleigh again. It's a holiday weekend and she's home from school: For dinner, Kayleigh has soup, salad, a large steak, a baked potato, two pieces of cheesecake, and three cups of coffee. After dinner, she complains that she is "too full to move." Soon after, Kayleigh's aunt arrives with a strawberry pie. Kayleigh exclaims that strawberry pie is her favorite and eats three large pieces! Is this hunger? Certainly, Kayleigh's dinner already satisfied her biological needs for food.

How does that change the model of motivation? Kayleigh's "pie lust" illustrates that motivated behavior can be energized by the "pull" of external stimuli, as well as by the "push" of internal needs.

Incentives

The "pull" of a goal is called its **incentive value** (the goal's appeal beyond its ability to fill a need). Some goals are so desirable (strawberry pie, for example) that they can motivate behavior in the absence of an internal need. Other goals are so low in incentive value that they may be rejected even if they meet the internal need. Fresh silkworms, for instance, are highly nutritious. However, it is doubtful that you would eat one no matter how hungry you might be. Regardless, because they are also easy to grow and produce few waste products, silkworms may become the preferred food for astronauts on long space voyages (Yang et al., 2009). (Attention, aspiring astronauts: Are you ready for silkworms *and* motion sickness?)

Motivation Internal processes that initiate, sustain, direct, and terminate activities.

Need An internal deficiency that may energize behavior.

Drive The psychological expression of internal needs or valued goals. For example, hunger, thirst, or a drive for success.

Response Any action, glandular activity, or other identifiable behavior.

Goal The target or objective of motivated behavior.

Incentive value The value of a goal above and beyond its ability to fill a need.

Usually, our actions are energized by a mixture of internal needs *and* external incentives. That's why a strong need may change an unpleasant incentive into a desired goal. Perhaps you've never eaten a silkworm, but we'll bet you've eaten some pretty horrible leftovers when the refrigerator was bare. The incentive value of goals also helps explain motives that don't seem to come from internal needs, such as drives for success, status, or approval (▶▶ Figure 9.1).

Types of Motives

For our purposes, motives can be divided into three major categories:

1. **Biological motives** are based on biological needs that must be met for survival. The most important biological motives are hunger, thirst, pain avoidance, and needs for air, sleep, elimination of wastes, and regulation of body temperature. Biological motives are innate.
2. **Stimulus motives** express our needs for stimulation and information. Examples include activity, curiosity, exploration, manipulation, and physical contact. Although such motives also appear to be innate, they are not strictly necessary for survival.
3. **Learned motives** are based on learned needs, drives, and goals. Learned motives, which are often social in nature, help explain many human activities, such as standing for election or auditioning for *American Idol*. Many learned motives are related to learned needs for power, affiliation (the need to be with others), approval, status, security, and achievement.

(a) High-incentive value goal

(b) Low-incentive value goal

Anna Clopet/Corbis

Biological Motives and Homeostasis

How important is air in your life? Water? Sleep? Food? Temperature regulation? Finding a public rest room? For most of us, satisfying biological needs is so routine that we tend to overlook how much of our behavior they direct. But exaggerate any of these needs through famine, shipwreck, poverty, near drowning, bitter cold, or drinking ten cups of coffee, and their powerful grip on behavior becomes evident.

Biological drives are essential because they maintain *homeostasis* (HOE-me-oh-STAY-sis), or bodily equilibrium (Cooper, 2008). The term **homeostasis** means "standing steady," or "steady state." Optimal levels exist for body temperature, for chemicals in the blood, for blood pressure, and so forth (Levin, 2006). When the body deviates from these "ideal" levels, automatic reactions begin to restore equilibrium (Deckers, 2005). Thus, it might help to think of homeostasis as being similar to a thermostat set at a particular temperature.

A (Very) Short Course on Thermostats

The thermostat in your house constantly compares the actual room temperature to a *set point*, or ideal temperature, which you can control. When room temperature falls below the set point, the heat is automatically turned on to warm the room. When the heat equals or slightly exceeds the set point, it is automatically turned off or the air conditioning is turned on. In this way room temperature is kept in a state of equilibrium hovering around the set point.

The first reactions to disequilibrium in the human body are also automatic. For example, if you become too hot, more blood will flow through your skin and you will begin to perspire, thus lowering body temperature. We are often unaware of such changes, unless continued disequilibrium drives us to seek shade, warmth, food, or water.

Circadian Rhythms

Our needs and drives can change from moment to moment. After eating, our motivation to eat more food tends to diminish, and a few minutes in the hot sun can leave us feeling thirsty. But our motivation can also vary over longer cycles. Scientists have long known

▲ **FIGURE 9.1** Needs and incentives interact to determine drive strength *(above)*. *(a)* Moderate need combined with a high-incentive goal produces a strong drive. *(b)* Even when a strong need exists, drive strength may be moderate if a goal's incentive value is low. It is important to remember, however, that incentive value lies "in the eye of the beholder" *(photo)*. No matter how hungry, few people would be able to eat the pictured silkworms.

Biological motives Innate motives based on biological needs.

Stimulus motives Innate needs for stimulation and information.

Learned motives Motives based on learned needs, drives, and goals.

Homeostasis A steady state of bodily equilibrium.

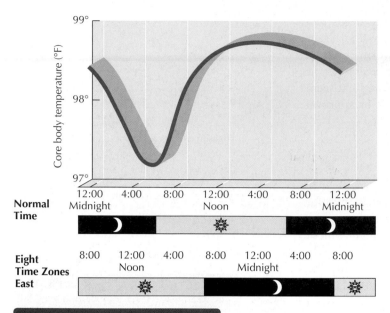

Normal Time

12:00 Midnight	4:00	8:00	12:00 Noon	4:00	8:00	12:00 Midnight

Eight Time Zones East

8:00	12:00 Noon	4:00	8:00	12:00 Midnight	4:00	8:00

▲ **FIGURE 9.2** Core body temperature is a good indicator of a person's circadian rhythm. Most people reach a low point 2 to 3 hours before their normal waking time. It's no wonder that both the Chernobyl and Three-Mile Island nuclear power plant accidents occurred around 4 A.M. Rapid travel to a different time zone, shift work, depression, and illness can throw sleep and waking patterns out of synchronization with the body's core rhythm. Mismatches of this kind are very disruptive (Reinberg & Ashkenazi, 2008).

Circadian rhythms Cyclical changes in bodily functions and arousal levels that vary on a schedule approximating a 24-hour day.

that body activity is guided by internal "biological clocks." Every 24 hours, your body undergoes a cycle of changes called **circadian** (SUR-kay-dee-AN) **rhythms** (*circa:* about; *diem:* a day) (Beersma & Gordijn, 2007). Throughout the day, activities in the liver, kidneys, and endocrine glands undergo large changes. Body temperature, blood pressure, and amino acid levels also shift from hour to hour. These activities, and many others, peak once a day (▶▶ Figure 9.2). People are usually more motivated and alert at the high point of their circadian rhythms (Antle & Mistlberger, 2005).

Jet Lag and Shift Work

Circadian rhythms are most noticeable after a major change in time schedules. Businesspersons, athletes, and other time zone travelers tend to perform poorly when their body rhythms are disturbed. If you travel great distances east or west, the peaks and valleys of your circadian rhythms will be out of phase with the sun and clocks. For example, you might be wide-awake at midnight and feel like you're sleepwalking during the day. (Return to Figure 9.2.) Shift work has the same effect, causing fatigue, irritability, upset stomach, and depression (Garbarino, 2002; Shen et al., 2006).

How fast do people adapt to rhythm changes? For major time zone shifts (5 hours or more) it can take up to 2 weeks to resynchronize. The *direction* of travel also affects adaptation (Herxheimer & Waterhouse, 2003). If you fly west, adapting is relatively easy; if you fly east, adapting takes much longer. When you fly east, the sun comes up *earlier* relative to your "home" time. Let's say that you live in San Diego and fly to Philadelphia. If you get up at 7 A.M. in Philadelphia, it's 4 A.M. back in San Diego—and your body knows it. If you fly west, the sun comes up later. In this case, it is easier for people to "advance" (stay up later and sleep in) than it is to shift backward.

Adjusting to jet lag is slowest when you stay indoors, where you can sleep and eat on "home time." Getting outdoors speeds adaptation. A few intermittent 5-minute periods of exposure to bright light early in the morning are also helpful for resetting your circadian rhythm (Duffy & Wright, 2005). Bright light affects the timing of body rhythms by reducing the amount of melatonin produced by the pineal gland. When melatonin levels rise late in the evening, it's bedtime as far as the brain is concerned.

How does this affect those of us who are not world travelers? There are few college students who have not at one time or another "burned the midnight oil," especially for final exams. At such times it is wise to remember that departing from your regular schedule usually costs more than it's worth. You may be motivated to do as much during 1 hour in the morning as you could have done in 3 hours of work after midnight. You might just as well go to sleep 2 hours earlier.

In general, if you can anticipate an upcoming body rhythm change, it is best to preadapt to your new schedule. *Preadaptation* refers to gradually matching your sleep–waking cycle to a new time schedule. Before traveling, for instance, you should go to sleep 1 hour later (or earlier) each day until your sleep cycle matches the time at your destination.

RECITE

1. Motives _____, sustain, _____, and terminate activities.
2. Needs provide the _____ of motivation, whereas incentives provide the _____.

Classify the following needs or motives by placing the correct letter in the blank.

A. Biological motive **B.** Stimulus motive **C.** Learned motive

3. _____ curiosity
4. _____ status
5. _____ sleep
6. _____ thirst
7. _____ achievement
8. _____ physical contact
9. The maintenance of bodily equilibrium is called thermostasis. T or F?
10. A goal high in incentive value may create a drive in the absence of any internal need. T or F?

REFLECT

Critical Thinking

11. Many people mistakenly believe that they suffer from "hypoglycemia" (low blood sugar), which is often blamed for fatigue, difficulty concentrating, irritability, and other symptoms. Why is it unlikely that many people actually have hypoglycemia?

Relate

Motives help explain why we do what we do. See if you can think of something you do that illustrates the concepts of need, drive, response, and goal. Does the goal in your example vary in incentive value? What effects do high- and low-incentive-value goals have on your behavior? Mentally list some biological motives you have satisfied today.

ANSWERS

1. initiate, direct 2. push, pull 3. B 4. C 5. A 6. A 7. C 8. B 9. F 10. T 11. Because of homeostasis: Blood sugar is normally maintained within narrow bounds. While blood sugar levels fluctuate enough to affect hunger, true hypoglycemia is an infrequent medical problem.

Hunger—Pardon Me, My Hypothalamus Is Growling

What causes hunger? Overeating? Eating disorders?

You get hungry, you find food, and you eat: Hunger might seem like a "simple" motive, but we have only recently begun to understand it. Hunger provides a good model of how both internal and external factors direct our behavior.

Internal Factors in Hunger

Don't feelings of hunger originate in the stomach? To find out, Walter Cannon and A. L. Washburn (1912) decided to see if stomach contractions cause hunger. In an early study, Washburn trained himself to swallow a balloon, which could be inflated through an attached tube. (You, too, will do anything for science, right?) This allowed Cannon to record the movements of Washburn's stomach (▶▶ Figure 9.3). When Washburn's stomach contracted, he reported that he felt "hunger pangs." In view of this, the two scientists concluded that hunger is nothing more than the contractions of an empty stomach. (This, however, proved to be an inflated conclusion.)

For many people, hunger produces an overall feeling of weakness or shakiness, rather than a "growling" stomach. Of course, eating *does* slow when the stomach is stretched or distended (full). (Remember last Thanksgiving?) However, we now know that the stomach is not essential for feeling hunger. Even people who have had

Record of stomach contractions

Time record in minutes

Record of hunger pangs

Record of breathing

Gastric balloon

▲ FIGURE 9.3 In Walter Cannon's early study of hunger, a simple apparatus was used to simultaneously record hunger pangs and stomach contractions. (After Cannon, 1934.)

their stomachs removed for medical reasons continue to feel hungry and eat regularly (Woods et al., 2000).

Then what does cause hunger? Many different factors combine to promote and suppress hunger. The brain receives many signals from parts of the digestive system, ranging from the tongue and stomach to the intestines and the liver.

Brain Mechanisms

What part of the brain controls hunger? Although no single "hunger thermostat" exists, a small area called the **hypothalamus** (HI-po-THAL-ah-mus) is especially important because it regulates many motives, including hunger, thirst, and the sex drive (▶▶ Figure 9.4).

The hypothalamus is sensitive to levels of sugar in the blood (and other substances described in a moment). It also receives neural messages from the liver and stomach. When combined, these signals determine if you are hungry or not (Woods et al., 2000).

One part of the hypothalamus acts as a feeding system that initiates eating. If the *lateral hypothalamus* is "turned on" with an electrified probe, even a well-fed animal will immediately begin eating. (The term *lateral* simply refers to the *sides* of the hypothalamus. See ▶▶ Figure 9.5.) If the same area is destroyed, the animal may never eat again.

The lateral hypothalamus is normally activated in a variety of ways. For example, when you are hungry your stomach lining produces *ghrelin* (GREL-in), a hormone that activates your lateral hypothalamus (Olszewski et al., 2003). (If your stomach is growlin' it's probably releasing ghrelin.) Ghrelin also activates parts of your brain involved in learning. This means you should consider studying before you eat, not immediately afterward (Diano et al., 2006).

How do we know when to stop eating? A second area in the hypothalamus is part of a satiety system, or "stop mechanism" for eating. If the *ventromedial* (VENT-ro-MEE-dee-al) *hypothalamus* is destroyed, dramatic overeating results. (*Ventromedial* refers to the bottom middle of the hypothalamus.) Rats with such damage will eat until they balloon up to weights of 1,000 grams or more (▶▶ Figure 9.6). A normal rat weighs about 180 grams. To put this weight gain in human terms, picture someone you know who weighs 180 pounds growing to a weight of 1,000 pounds.

The *paraventricular* (PAIR-uh-ven-TRICK-you-ler) *nucleus* of the hypothalamus also affects hunger. This area helps keep blood sugar levels steady by both starting and stopping eating. The paraventricular nucleus is sensitive to a substance called neuropeptide Y (NPY). If NPY is present in large amounts, an animal will eat until it cannot hold another bite (Williams et al., 2004). Incidentally, the hypothalamus also responds to a chemical in marijuana, which can produce intense hunger (the "munchies") (Di Marzo et al., 2001).

A chemical called glucagon-like peptide 1 (GLP-1) is also involved in causing eating to cease. After you eat a meal, GLP-1 is released by the intestines. From there, it travels in the bloodstream to the brain. When enough GLP-1 arrives, your desire to eat ends (Nori, 1998). As you might imagine, GLP-1 pills show promise in the treatment of obesity (Raun et al., 2007). By the way, it takes at least 10 minutes for the hypothalamus to respond after you begin eating. That's why you are less likely to overeat if you eat slowly, which gives your brain time to get the message that you've had enough (Liu et al., 2000).

▲ **FIGURE 9.4** Location of the hypothalamus in the human brain.

▶▶ **FIGURE 9.5** This is a cross section through the middle of the brain (viewed from the front of the brain). Indicated areas of the hypothalamus are associated with hunger and the regulation of body weight.

Corpus callosum

Lateral hypothalamus

Ventromedial hypothalamus

Paraventricular nucleus

Hypothalamus A small area at the base of the brain that regulates many aspects of motivation and emotion, especially hunger, thirst, and sexual behavior.

brain waves

Your Brain's "Fat Point"

Like a thermostat, your brain maintains a **set point** in order to control your weight over the long term. It does this by monitoring the amount of fat stored in your body in specialized *fat cells* (Ahima & Osei, 2004).

Your set point is the weight you maintain when you are making no effort to gain or lose weight. When your body weight goes below its set point, you will feel hungry most of the time. On the other hand, fat cells release a substance called *leptin* when your "spare tire" is well inflated. Leptin is carried in the bloodstream to the hypothalamus, where it tells us to eat less (Williams et al., 2004).

Can you change your fat set point? Good question. Your leptin levels are partly under genetic control. In rare cases mice (and we humans)

The mouse on the left has a genetic defect that prevents its fat cells from producing normal amounts of leptin. Without this chemical signal, the mouse's body acts as if its set point for fat storage is, shall we say, rather high.

inherit a genetic defect that reduces leptin levels in the body, leading to obesity. In such cases, taking leptin can help (Williamson et al., 2005).

For the rest of us, the news is not so encouraging because there is currently no known way to lower your set point for fat, since the number of fat cells remains unchanged throughout adult life (Spalding et al., 2008). To make matters worse, radical diets do not help (but you knew that already, didn't you?). They may even raise the set point for fat, resulting in *diet-induced obesity* (Ahima & Osei, 2004). You may not be able to lose weight by resetting your hypothalamus, but psychologists have studied more effective approaches to weight loss. We will examine some later in this chapter.

In addition to knowing when to start eating, and when meals are over, your brain also controls your weight over long periods of time. (See "Your Brain's 'Fat Point.'")

The substances we have reviewed are only some of the chemical signals that start and stop eating (Geary, 2004). Others continue to be discovered. In time, they may make it possible to artificially control hunger. If so, better treatments for extreme obesity and self-starvation could follow (Batterham et al., 2003).

External Factors in Hunger and Obesity

As we have seen, "hunger" is affected by more than just our biological needs for food. In fact, if internal needs alone controlled eating, many fewer people would overeat (Stroebe, Papies, & Aarts, 2008). Nevertheless, roughly 65 percent of adults in the United States are overweight (▶▶ Figure 9.7). In 2006, more than one third were obese (Ogden et al., 2007). As a

▲ **FIGURE 9.6** Damage to the hunger satiety system in the hypothalamus can produce a very fat rat, a condition called hypothalamic *hyperphagia* (Hi-per-FAGE-yah: overeating). This rat weighs 1,080 grams. (The pointer has gone completely around the dial and beyond.) (Courtesy of Neal E. Miller. Rockefeller University.)

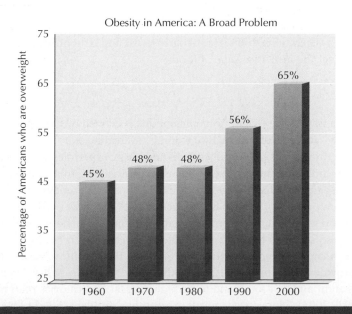

Obesity in America: A Broad Problem

(Bar graph: Percentage of Americans who are overweight)

- 1960: 45%
- 1970: 48%
- 1980: 48%
- 1990: 56%
- 2000: 65%

▲ **FIGURE 9.7** A near epidemic of obesity has occurred in the United States during the last 20 years, with 65 percent of all Americans now classified as overweight (Ogden et al., 2007).

Set point (for fat) The proportion of body fat that tends to be maintained by changes in hunger and eating.

result, obesity is overtaking smoking as a cause of needless deaths (Murray, 2001). Let's consider some external influences on hunger and their role in obesity, a major health risk and, for many, a source of social stigma and low self-esteem.

External Eating Cues

Most of us are sensitive to *external eating cues*, signs and signals linked with food. For example, do you tend to eat more when food is highly visible and easy to get? In cultures like ours, where food is plentiful, eating cues add greatly to the risk of overeating (Woods et al., 2000). Many college freshmen gain weight rapidly during their first 3 months on campus (the famous "Frosh 15"). All-you-can-eat dining halls in the dorms and nighttime snacking appear to be the culprits (Levitsky et al., 2003). The presence of others can also affect whether people overeat (or undereat), depending on how much everyone else is eating and how important it is to impress them (Pliner & Mann, 2004).

Taste

The availability of a variety of tasty foods can also lead to overeating and obesity in societies where such foods are plentiful. Normally, tastes for foods vary considerably. For example, if you are well fed, leptin dulls the tongue's sensitivity to sweet tastes (Kawai et al., 2000). If you have noticed that you lose your "sweet tooth" when you are full, you may have observed this effect. Actually, if you eat too much of any particular food, it will become less appealing. This probably helps us maintain variety in our diets. However, it also encourages obesity. If you overdose on hamburgers or French fries, moving on to some cookies or chocolate cheesecake certainly won't do your body much good (Pinel, Assanand, & Lehman, 2000).

Emotional Eating

Is it true that people also overeat when they are emotionally upset? Yes. People with weight problems are prone to overeat when they are anxious, angry, or sad (Geliebter & Aversa, 2003). Furthermore, obese individuals are often unhappy in our fat-conscious culture. The result is overeating that leads to emotional distress and still more overeating (Rutledge & Linden, 1998).

Cultural Factors

Learning to think of some foods as desirable and others as revolting has a large impact on what we eat. In North America we would never consider eating the eyes out of the steamed head of a monkey, but in some parts of the world they are considered a delicacy. By the same token, vegans and vegetarians think it is barbaric to eat any kind of meat. In short, cultural values greatly affect the *incentive value* of foods.

Dieting

A diet is not just a way to lose weight. Your current diet is defined by the types and amounts of food you regularly eat. Some diets actually encourage overeating. For instance, placing animals on a "supermarket" diet leads to gross obesity. In one classic experiment, rats were given meals of chocolate chip cookies, salami, cheese, bananas, marshmallows, milk chocolate, peanut butter, and fat. These pampered rodents overate, gaining almost three times as much weight as rats that ate only laboratory chow (Sclafani & Springer, 1976). (Rat chow is a dry mixture of several bland grains. If you were a rat, you'd probably eat more cookies than rat chow, too.)

People are also sensitive to dietary content. In general, *sweetness*, high *fat content*, and *variety* tend to encourage overeating (Lucas & Sclafani, 1990). Unfortunately, North American culture provides the worst kinds of foods for people who suffer from obesity. For example, restaurant and fast food tend to be higher in fat and calories than meals made at home (Brownell, 2003). "Supersized" meals are another problem. Food portions at restaurants in the United States are 25 percent larger, or more, than they are in France. Far fewer people are obese in France, most likely because they simply eat less. The French also take longer to eat a meal, which discourages overeating (Rozin et al., 2003).

discovering psychology

Behavioral Dieting

As we have noted, dieting is usually followed by rapid weight gains. If you really want to lose weight, you must overhaul your eating and exercise habits, an approach called **behavioral dieting**. Here are some helpful behavioral techniques:

1. **Get yourself committed to weight loss.** Involve other people in your efforts. Programs such as Overeaters Anonymous or Take Off Pounds Sensibly can be a good source of social support.

2. **Exercise.** No diet can succeed for long without an increase in exercise. To lose weight, you must use more calories than you take in. Burning just 200 extra calories a day can help prevent rebound weight gains. Add activity to your routine in every way you can think of. Stop saving steps and riding elevators. Buy a *step counter* to track the number of steps you take every day. Walking 10,000 steps per day will burn between 2,000 and 3,500 calories a week (depending on your weight). The more frequently and vigorously you exercise, the more weight you will lose (Jeffery & Wing, 2001).

3. **Learn your eating habits by observing yourself and keeping a "diet diary."** Begin by making a complete, 2-week record of when and where you eat, what you eat, and the feelings and events that occur just before and after eating. Is a roommate, relative, or spouse encouraging you to overeat? What are your most "dangerous" times and places for overeating?

4. **Learn to weaken your personal eating cues.** When you have learned when and where you do most of your eating, avoid these situations. Try to restrict your eating to one room, and do not read, watch TV, study, or talk on the phone while eating. Require yourself to interrupt what you are doing in order to eat.

5. **Count calories, but don't starve yourself.** To lose weight, you must eat less, and calories allow you to keep a record of your food intake. If you have trouble eating less every day, try dieting 4 days a week. People who diet intensely every other day lose as much as those who diet moderately every day (Viegener et al., 1990).

6. **Develop techniques to control the act of eating.** Whenever you can, check for nutritional information and buy groceries and meals lower in calories and fats. Begin to take smaller portions. Carry to the table only what you plan to eat. Put all other food away before leaving the kitchen. Eat slowly, sip water between bites of food, leave food on your plate, and stop eating before you are completely full. Be especially wary of the extra large servings at fast-food restaurants (Murray, 2001).

7. **Avoid snacks.** It is generally better to eat more small meals a day than fewer large ones because more calories are burned (Assanand, Pinel, & Lehman, 1998). (No, we don't mean high-calorie snacks *in addition to* meals.) If you have an impulse to snack, set a timer for 20 minutes and see if you are still hungry then. Delay the impulse to snack several times if possible. Dull your appetite by filling up on raw carrots, bouillon, water, coffee, or tea.

8. **Chart your daily progress.** Record your weight, the number of calories eaten, and whether you met your daily goal. Set realistic goals by cutting down calories gradually. Losing about a pound per week is realistic, but remember, you are changing habits, not just dieting. "Diets" don't work!

9. **Set a "threshold" for weight control.** Maintaining weight loss can be even more challenging than losing weight. It is easier to maintain weight losses if you set a regain limit of 3 pounds or less. In other words, if you gain more than 2 or 3 pounds, you immediately begin to make corrections in your eating habits and amount of exercise (Brownell, 2003).

Be patient. It takes years to develop eating habits. You can expect it to take at least several months to change them. If you are unsuccessful at losing weight with these techniques, you might find it helpful to seek the aid of a psychologist familiar with behavioral weight-loss techniques.

An added problem faced by people who want to control their weight concerns "yo-yo" dieting.

The Paradox of Yo-Yo Dieting

If dieting works, why are hundreds of "new" diets published each year? The answer is that although dieters do lose weight, most regain it soon after they stop dieting. In fact, many people end up weighing even more than before. Why should this be so? Dieting (starving) slows the body's rate of metabolism (the rate at which energy is used up). In effect, a dieter's body becomes highly efficient at *conserving* calories and storing them as fat (Pinel, Assanand, & Lehman, 2000).

Apparently, evolution prepared us to save energy when food is scarce and to stock up on fat when food is plentiful. Briefly starving yourself, therefore, may have little lasting effect on weight. "Yo-yo dieting," or repeatedly losing and gaining weight, is especially dangerous.

Behavioral dieting Weight reduction based on changing exercise and eating habits, rather than temporary self-starvation.

Actress Valerie Bertinelli has been a lifelong yo-yo dieter who tried many different diets. As a spokeswoman for a national weight-loss program, Valerie lost about 40 pounds. Will she maintain her weight loss after she reaches her target weight?

Anorexia nervosa is far more dangerous than many people realize. This haunting Italian anti-anorexia poster shows 68-pound model Isabelle Caro, who has struggled with anorexia for 15 years. Many celebrities have struggled with eating disorders, including Karen Carpenter (who died of starvation-induced heart failure), Paula Abdul, Kirstie Alley, Fiona Apple, Victoria Beckham (Posh Spice), Princess Diana, Tracey Gold, Janet Jackson, and Mary-Kate Olsen.

 Anorexia nervosa Active self-starvation or a sustained loss of appetite that has psychological origins.

Frequent changes in weight can dramatically slow the body's metabolic rate. As noted earlier, this may raise the body's set point for fat and makes it harder to lose weight each time a person diets and easier to regain weight when the diet ends. Frequent weight changes also increase the risk for heart disease and premature death (Wang & Brownell, 2005). To avoid bouncing between feast and famine requires a permanent change in eating habits and exercise.

To summarize, eating and overeating are related to internal and external influences, diet, emotions, genetics, exercise, and many other factors. People become obese in different ways and for different reasons. We live in a culture that provides inexpensive, good-tasting food everywhere and have a brain that evolved to say "Eat whenever food is available." Nevertheless, many people have learned to take control of eating by applying psychological principles (see "Behavioral Dieting").

Eating Disorders

Under the sheets of her hospital bed Krystal looks like a skeleton. Victims of anorexia, who are mostly adolescent females, suffer devastating weight losses from severe, self-inflicted dieting (Cooper, 2005). If she cannot overcome her **anorexia nervosa** (AN-uh-REK-see-yah ner-VOH-sah: self-starvation), Krystal may die of malnutrition.

Do anorexics lose their appetite? Although a compulsive attempt to lose weight causes them to not seek or desire food, they usually still feel physical hunger. Often, anorexia starts with "normal" dieting that slowly begins to dominate the person's life. In time, anorexics suffer debilitating health problems. From 5 to 8 percent (more than 1 in 20) die of malnutrition (Polivy & Herman, 2002). ● Table 9.1 lists the symptoms of anorexia nervosa.

● Table 9.1 Recognizing Eating Disorders

ANOREXIA NERVOSA

- Body weight below 85 percent of normal for one's height and age
- Refusal to maintain body weight in normal range
- Intense fear of becoming fat or gaining weight, even though underweight
- Disturbance in one's body image or perceived weight
- Self-evaluation unduly influenced by body weight
- Denial of seriousness of abnormally low body weight
- Absence of menstrual periods
- Purging behavior (vomiting or misuse of laxatives or diuretics)

BULIMIA NERVOSA

- Normal or above-normal weight
- Recurring binge eating
- Eating within an hour or two an amount of food that is much larger than most people would consume
- Feeling a lack of control over eating
- Purging behavior (vomiting or misuse of laxatives or diuretics)
- Excessive exercise to prevent weight gain
- Fasting to prevent weight gain
- Self-evaluation unduly influenced by body weight

Source: American Psychiatric Association, 2000.

Bulimia nervosa (bue-LIHM-ee-yah) is a second major eating disorder. Bulimic persons gorge on food, then vomit or take laxatives to avoid gaining weight (see Table 9.1). As with anorexia, most victims of bulimia are girls or women. Approximately 5 percent of college women are bulimic, and as many as 60 percent have milder eating problems. Bingeing and purging can seriously damage health. Typical risks include sore throat, hair loss, muscle spasms, kidney damage, dehydration, tooth erosion, swollen salivary glands, menstrual irregularities, loss of sex drive, and even heart attack.

Men and Eating Disorders

Eating disorders are on the rise among men. Currently, one third of men say they want less body fat and another third want more muscles (McCabe & Ricciardelli, 2004). As a result, many men are altering what they eat and exercising excessively. Some are going too far: About 10 percent of anorexics and 25 percent of bulimics are now males (Weltzin et al., 2005).

Causes

What causes anorexia and bulimia? People who suffer from eating disorders are extremely dissatisfied with their bodies (Crisp et al., 2006). Usually, they have distorted views of themselves, exaggerated fears of becoming fat, and low self-esteem. Many overestimate their body size by 25 percent or more. As a result, they think they are disgustingly "fat" when they are actually wasting away (▶▶ Figure 9.8) (Polivy & Herman, 2002).

Many of these problems are related to the idealized body images presented in the media (Levine & Harrison, 2004). Some websites even go so far as to celebrate anorexia and bulimia (referred to by "fans" as "Ana" and "Mia") (Tierney, 2008). Girls who spend a lot of time reading fashion magazines or visiting these websites are more likely to have distorted body images and unrealistic ideas about how they compare with others (Martinez-Gonzalez et al., 2003).

The popularity of fitness, exercise, and sports has also contributed to eating disorders. Today, more people are changing their diets in search of a lean, muscular look. People engaged in sports that require low body fat or extreme weight loss (such as wrestling, gymnastics, pole vaulting, high jumping, and even cycling) are particularly likely to develop eating disorders (Weltzin et al., 2005).

People with eating disorders appear to be trying to gain some measure of control. Anorexic teen girls are usually described as "perfect" daughters—helpful, considerate, conforming, and obedient. They seem to be seeking perfect control in their lives by being perfectly slim (Castro et al., 2004). People suffering from bulimia are also concerned with control. Typically they are obsessed with thoughts of weight, food, eating, and ridding themselves of food. As a result, they feel guilt, shame, self-contempt, and anxiety. Vomiting reduces their anxiety, which makes purging highly reinforcing (Powell & Thelen, 1996).

Treatment

Most people suffering from eating disorders will not seek help on their own. This is especially true for men, because eating disorders are still widely perceived to be a female problem (Weltzin et al., 2005). Typically, it takes strong urging by family or friends to get victims into treatment.

■ **Perceived ideal weight**   ■ **Actually most attractive to men**
■ **Perceived as most attractive to men**   ■ **Perceived current weight**

▲ **FIGURE 9.8** Women with abnormal eating habits were asked to rate their body shape on a scale similar to the one you see here. As a group, they chose ideal figures much thinner than what they thought their current weights were. (Most women say they want to be thinner than they currently are, but to a lesser degree than women with eating problems.) Notice that the women with eating problems chose an ideal weight that was even thinner than what they thought men prefer. This is not typical of most women. In this study, only women with eating problems wanted to be thinner than what they thought men find attractive (Zellner, Harner, & Adler, 1989).

Bulimia nervosa Excessive eating (gorging) usually followed by self-induced vomiting and/or taking laxatives.

Treatment for anorexia usually begins with giving drugs to relieve obsessive fears of gaining weight. Then a medical diet is used to restore weight and health. Next, a counselor may help patients work on the emotional conflicts that led to weight loss. For bulimia, behavioral counseling may include self-monitoring of food intake. A related cognitive-behavioral approach focuses on changing the thinking patterns and beliefs about weight and body shape that perpetuate eating disorders (Byrne & McLean, 2002; Cooper, 2005).

Biological Motives Revisited— Thirst, Pain, and Sex

Is there more than one type of thirst? In what ways are pain avoidance and the sex drive unusual?

Most biological motives work in ways that are similar to hunger. For example, thirst is only partially controlled by dryness of the mouth. If you were to take a drug that made your mouth constantly wet, or dry, your water intake would remain normal. Like hunger, thirst is regulated by separate *thirst* and *thirst satiety* systems in the hypothalamus. Also like hunger, thirst is strongly affected by learning and cultural values.

Thirst

You may not have noticed, but there are actually two kinds of thirst. **Extracellular thirst** occurs when water is lost from the fluids surrounding the cells of your body. Bleeding, vomiting, diarrhea, sweating, and drinking alcohol cause this type of thirst (Franken, 2007). When a person loses both water and minerals in any of these ways—especially by perspiration—a slightly salty liquid may be more satisfying than plain water.

Why would a thirsty person want to drink salty water? The reason is that before the body can retain water, minerals lost through perspiration (mainly salt) must be replaced. In lab tests, animals greatly prefer saltwater after salt levels in their bodies are lowered (Strickler & Verbalis, 1988). Similarly, some nomadic peoples of the Sahara Desert prize blood as a beverage, probably because of its saltiness. (Maybe they should try Gatorade?)

A second type of thirst occurs when you eat a salty meal. In this instance your body does not lose fluid. Instead, excess salt causes fluid to be drawn out of cells. As the cells "shrink," **intracellular thirst** is triggered. Thirst of this type is best quenched by plain water.

The drives for food, water, air, sleep, and elimination are all similar in that they are generated by a combination of activities in the body and the brain, and they are influenced by various external factors. However, the drive to avoid pain and the sex drive are more unusual.

Pain

How is the drive to avoid pain different? Hunger, thirst, and sleepiness come and go in a fairly regular cycle each day. Pain avoidance, by contrast, is an **episodic drive** (ep-ih-SOD-ik). That is, it occurs in distinct episodes when bodily damage takes place or is about to occur. Most drives prompt us to actively seek a desired goal (food, drink, warmth, and so forth). Pain prompts us to *avoid* or *eliminate* sources of discomfort.

Some people feel they must be "tough" and not show any distress. Others complain loudly at the smallest ache or pain. The first attitude raises pain tolerance, and the second lowers it. As this suggests, the drive to avoid pain is partly learned. That's why members of some societies endure cutting, burning, whipping, tattooing, and piercing of the skin that would agonize most people (but apparently not devotees of piercing and "body art"). In general, we learn how to react to pain by observing family members, friends, and other role models (McMahon & Koltzenburg, 2005).

Extracellular thirst Thirst caused by a reduction in the volume of fluids found between body cells.

Intracellular thirst Thirst triggered when fluid is drawn out of cells due to an increased concentration of salts and minerals outside the cell.

Episodic drive A drive that occurs in distinct episodes.

The Sex Drive

Sex is unlike other biological motives because sex (contrary to anything your personal experience might suggest) is not necessary for *individual* survival. It is necessary, of course, for *group* survival.

The term **sex drive** refers to the strength of one's motivation to engage in sexual behavior. In lower animals the sex drive is directly related to hormones. Female mammals (other than humans) are interested in mating only when their fertility cycles are in the stage of **estrus,** or "heat." Estrus is caused by a release of **estrogen** (a female sex hormone) into the bloodstream. Hormones are important in males as well. In most animals, castration will abolish the sex drive. But in contrast to females, the normal male animal is almost always ready to mate. His sex drive is aroused primarily by the behavior and scent of a receptive female. Therefore, in many species, mating is closely tied to female fertility cycles.

How much do hormones affect human sex drives? Hormones affect the human sex drive, but not as directly as in animals (Crooks & Baur, 2008). The sex drive in men is related to the amount of **androgens** (male hormones such as testosterone) provided by the testes. When the supply of androgens dramatically increases at puberty, so does the male sex drive. Likewise, the sex drive in women is related to their estrogen levels (Hyde & DeLamater, 2006). However, "male" hormones also affect the female sex drive. In addition to estrogen, a woman's body produces small amounts of androgens. When their androgen levels increase, many women experience a corresponding increase in sex drive (Van Goozen et al., 1995). Testosterone levels decline with age, and various medical problems can lower sexual desire. In some instances, taking testosterone supplements can restore the sex drive in both men and women (Crooks & Baur, 2008).

Does alcohol increase the sex drive? In general, no. Alcohol is a *depressant*. As such, it may, in small doses, stimulate erotic desire by lowering inhibitions. This effect no doubt accounts for alcohol's reputation as an aid to seduction. (Humorist Ogden Nash once summarized this bit of folklore by saying, "Candy is dandy, but liquor is quicker.") However, in larger doses alcohol suppresses orgasm in women and erection in men. Getting drunk *decreases* sexual desire, arousal, pleasure, and performance (McKay, 2005).

Numerous other drugs are reputed to be *aphrodisiacs* (af ruh DEEZ ee aks: substances that increase sexual desire or pleasure). However, like alcohol, many other drugs actually impair sexual response, rather than enhance it (McKay, 2005). Some examples are amphetamines, amyl nitrite, barbiturates, cocaine, Ecstasy, LSD, and marijuana. In the end, love is the best aphrodisiac (Crooks & Baur, 2008).

Perhaps the most interesting fact about the sex drive is that it is largely *non-homeostatic* (relatively independent of bodily need states). In humans, the sex drive can be aroused at virtually any time by almost anything. It therefore shows no clear relationship to deprivation (the amount of time since the drive was last satisfied). Certainly, an increase in desire may occur as time passes. But recent sexual activity does not prevent sexual desire from occurring again. Notice, too, that people may seek to arouse the sex drive as well as to reduce it. This unusual quality makes the sex drive capable of motivating a wide range of behaviors. It also explains why sex is used to sell almost everything imaginable.

Let's explore human sexuality in a little more detail.

Tolerance for pain and the strength of a person's motivation to avoid discomfort are greatly affected by cultural practices and beliefs.

Sexual Behavior—Mapping the Erogenous Zones

What are the typical patterns of human sexual response?

Human sexual arousal is complex. It may, of course, be produced by direct stimulation of the body's **erogenous zones** (eh-ROJ-eh-nus: productive of pleasure or erotic desire). Human erogenous zones include the genitals, mouth, breasts, ears, anus, and to a lesser degree, the entire surface of the body. It is clear, however, that more than physical contact is involved: A urological

Sex drive The strength of one's motivation to engage in sexual behavior.

Estrus Changes in the sexual drives of animals that create a desire for mating; particularly used to refer to females in heat.

Estrogen Any of a number of female sex hormones.

Androgen Any of a number of male sex hormones, especially testosterone.

Erogenous zones Areas of the body that produce pleasure and/or provoke erotic desire.

(a)

(b)

or gynecological exam rarely results in any sexual arousal. Likewise, an unwanted sexual advance may produce only revulsion. Human sexual arousal obviously includes a large mental element.

Sexual Arousal

Are men more easily sexually aroused than women? Overall, women and men have equal potential for sexual arousal, and women are no less *physically* responsive than men. However, women tend to place more emphasis on emotional closeness with a lover than men do (Basson et al., 2005; Peplau, 2003).

Based on the frequency of orgasm (from masturbation or intercourse), the peak of male sexual activity is at age 18. The peak rate of female sexual activity appears to occur a little later (Janus & Janus, 1993). However, male and female sexual patterns are rapidly becoming more alike. ▶▶ Figure 9.9 presents some of the data on sexual behavior from a major national health survey of American men and women ages 25 to 44. As you can see, in any given year men and women do not differ in their average number of opposite-sex partners or in their overall pattern of sexual activity (Mosher, Chandra, & Jones, 2005). Exaggerating the differences between male and female sexuality is not only inaccurate, it can also create artificial barriers to sexual satisfaction (Wiederman, 2001). For example, assuming that men should always initiate sex denies the fact that women have comparable sexual interests and needs.

Human Sexual Response

The pioneering work of gynecologist William Masters and psychologist Virginia Johnson greatly expanded our understanding of sexual response (Masters & Johnson, 1966, 1970). In a series of experiments, interviews, and controlled observations, Masters and Johnson directly studied sexual intercourse and masturbation in nearly 700 males and females. According to Masters and Johnson, sexual response can be divided into four phases: (1) *excitement,* (2) *plateau,* (3) *orgasm,* and (4) *resolution* (▶▶ Figures 9.10 and 9.11). These four

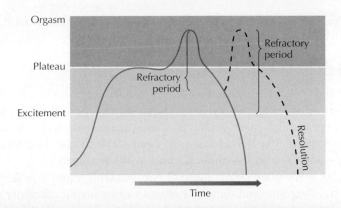

FIGURE 9.11 Male sexual response cycle. The green line shows that sexual arousal rises through the excitement phase and levels off for a time during the plateau phase. Arousal peaks during orgasm and then returns to pre-excitement levels. During the refractory period, immediately after orgasm, a second sexual climax is typically impossible. However, after the refractory period has passed, there may be a return to the plateau phase, followed by a second orgasm (dotted line). (From Frank A. Beach, ed., *Sex and Behavior*. New York: John Wiley & Sons, Inc., 1965. Reproduced by permission of the author's Estate.)

phases, which are the same for people of all sexual orientations (Garnets & Kimmel, 1991), can be described as follows:

Excitement phase The first level of sexual response, indicated by initial signs of sexual arousal.

Plateau phase The second level of sexual response, during which physical arousal intensifies.

Orgasm A climax and release of sexual excitement.

Resolution The final phase of sexual response, involving a return to lower levels of sexual tension and arousal.

Female Response

In women, the excitement phase is marked by a complex pattern of changes in the body. The vagina is prepared for intercourse, the nipples become erect, pulse rate rises, and the skin may become flushed or reddened. If sexual stimulation ends, the excitement phase will gradually subside. If a woman moves into the plateau phase, physical changes and subjective feelings of arousal become more intense. Sexual arousal that ends during this phase tends to ebb more slowly, which may produce considerable frustration. Occasionally, women skip the plateau phase (see Figure 9.10). For some women, this is almost always the case. Orgasm is usually followed by resolution, a return to lower levels of sexual tension and arousal. After orgasm, about 15 percent of all women return to the plateau phase and may have one or more additional orgasms (Mah & Binik, 2001).

Male Response

Sexual arousal in the male is signaled by erection of the penis during the excitement phase. A rise in heart rate, increased blood flow to the genitals, enlargement of the testicles, erection of the nipples, and numerous other body changes also occur. As is true of female sexual response, continued stimulation moves the male into the plateau phase. Again, physical changes and subjective feelings of arousal become more intense. Further stimulation during the plateau phase brings about a reflex release of sexual tension, resulting in orgasm.

In the mature male, orgasm is usually accompanied by *ejaculation* (release of sperm and seminal fluid). Afterward, it is followed by a short *refractory period* during which a second orgasm is impossible. Only rarely is the male refractory period immediately followed

Excitement phase The first phase of sexual response, indicated by initial signs of sexual arousal.

Plateau phase The second phase of sexual response during which physical arousal is further heightened.

Orgasm A climax and release of sexual excitement.

Resolution The fourth phase of sexual response, involving a return to lower levels of sexual tension and arousal.

by a second orgasm. Both orgasm and resolution in the male usually do not last as long as they do for females.

Comparing Male and Female Responses

Although male and female sexual responses are generally quite similar, the differences that do exist can affect sexual compatibility. For example, women typically go through the sexual phases more slowly than do men. However, during masturbation, 70 percent of females reach orgasm in 4 minutes or less. This is quite comparable to male response times. It suggests again that women are no less physically responsive than men.

In one regard, women are clearly more responsive. Only about 5 percent of males are capable of multiple orgasm (and then only after an unavoidable refractory period). Most men are limited to a second orgasm at best. In contrast, Masters and Johnson's findings suggest that most women who regularly experience orgasm are capable of multiple orgasm. According to one survey, 48 percent of all women have had multiple orgasms (Darling, Davidson, & Passarello, 1992). Remember though, that only about 15 percent regularly have multiple orgasms. A woman should not automatically assume that something is wrong if she isn't orgasmic or multiorgasmic. Many women have satisfying sexual experiences even when orgasm is not involved. (For information about common sexual complaints, see "Sexual Problems.")

Sexual Scripts

In a restaurant we commonly expect certain things to occur. It could even be said that each of us has a restaurant "script" that defines a plot, dialogue, and actions that should take place. We also learn a variety of **sexual scripts,** or unspoken mental plans that guide our sexual behavior. Such scripts determine when and where we are likely to express sexual feelings, and with whom (Lenton & Bryan, 2005). They provide a "plot" for the order of events in lovemaking and they outline "approved" actions, motives, and outcomes.

When two people follow markedly different scripts, misunderstandings are almost sure to occur. Consider, for instance, what happens when a woman acting out a "romantic first date" script is paired with a man following a "friends with benefits" script: The result is often anger, hurt feelings, or worse (Schleicher & Gilbert, 2005). Even newlyweds may find that their sexual "agendas" differ. In such cases, considerable "rewriting" of scripts is often needed for sexual compatibility. For humans the mind (or brain) is the ultimate erogenous zone. (To read more about contemporary sexual scripts, see "What's Love Got to Do with It?")

Sexual Orientation—Who Do You Love?

Another aspect of sexuality is **sexual orientation,** your degree of emotional and erotic attraction to members of the same sex, opposite sex, or both sexes. *Heterosexuals* are romantically and erotically attracted to members of the opposite sex. *Homosexuals* are attracted to people whose sex matches their own. *Bisexuals* are attracted to both men and women. In short, sexual orientation answers these questions: Who are you attracted to? Who do you have erotic fantasies about? Do you love men, or women, or both? (Garnets, 2002).

Sexual orientation is a deep part of personal identity. Starting with their earliest erotic feelings, most people remember being attracted to either the opposite sex or the same sex. The chances are practically nil of an exclusively heterosexual or homosexual person being "converted" from one orientation to the other. If you are heterosexual, you are probably certain that nothing could ever make you have homoerotic feelings. If so, then you know how homosexual persons feel about the prospects for changing *their* sexual orientation (Seligman, 1994).

What determines a person's sexual orientation? Available evidence suggests that sexual orientation is mainly genetic and biological, although social, cultural, and psychological influences are also involved (LeVay & Valente, 2006).

Sexual script An unspoken mental plan that defines a "plot," dialogue, and actions expected to take place in a sexual encounter.

Sexual orientation One's degree of emotional and erotic attraction to members of the same sex, opposite sex, or both sexes.

What's Love Got to Do with It?

Younger Americans are shifting toward scripts favoring casual sex (Hughes, Morrison, & Asada, 2005). One such script includes sex in a friendship, without traditional romance. According to one survey, more than half of all college students have been *friends with benefits* (friends who have sex but aren't romantically involved) (Puentes, Knox, & Zusman, 2008). Even more casual is the *hook-up* script, in which two people having sex are more or less strangers (seek pleasure first, ask questions later?). In contrast, traditional sexual scripts stress courtship, romance, and marriage. Sex in such relationships might be premarital, but it is still romantic (Roese et al., 2006).

As casual sexual scripts become more common, the traditional focus on intercourse is fading in favor of oral sex, which tends to be seen as less risky, more acceptable, and "not a big deal." Casual sexual scripts are also spreading to younger children. One study found that 20 percent of American ninth graders have already had oral sex and more than 30 percent intend to try it soon (Halpern-Felsher et al., 2005).

Casual sex is often viewed as easier than facing the challenges of romantic attachment and finding a lifelong partner. However, it is not without its own risks. Casual sex is usually associated with alcohol use and unsafe sexual behaviors, such as unprotected sex (Grello, Welsh, & Harper, 2006). Although oral sex is safer than intercourse, a significant chance of getting a sexually transmitted disease remains (Boskey, 2008).

Another downside of casual sex is the letdown that can occur when one person follows a romantic script and the other follows a casual script ("He[or she] is just not that into you"). For example, young women who are having casual sex are more likely to be depressed (Grello, Welsh, & Harper, 2006).

Adolescents and young adults have always engaged in experimentation and exploration. Most young people emerge unscathed from their explorations if they clearly understand that their encounters are casual and practice safe sex. Most eventually also "graduate" to a more traditional search for love.

How could genes and biology affect sexual orientation? Possibly, heredity shapes areas of the brain that orchestrate sexual behavior. Support for this idea comes from the work of neuroscientists who have shown that various brain structures and brain chemicals differ in heterosexuals and homosexuals (Kinnunen et al., 2004; LeVay, 1993). Some researchers now estimate that sexual orientation is from 30 to 70 percent genetic (Mustanski, Chivers, & Bailey, 2002).

One popular theory holds that prenatal hormone levels influence the developing fetus (LeVay & Valente, 2006). According to the *prenatal hormonal theory of homosexuality,* some male fetuses are exposed to too little testosterone. Similarly, some female fetuses are exposed to too much testosterone. These differences, in turn, can impact sexual orientation (Mustanski, Chivers, & Bailey, 2002). Regardless, homosexuality is not caused by hormone imbalances in adulthood; the hormone levels of most gay men and lesbians are within the normal range (Banks & Gartrell, 1995).

Consistent with the genetic and biological view of sexual orientation, it is unlikely that parenting makes children homosexual. There is little difference in the development of children with gay or lesbian parents and those who have heterosexual parents (Patterson, 2002; Wainwright, Russell, & Patterson, 2004).

It appears that nature strongly prepares people to be either homosexual or heterosexual. In view of this, discriminating against homosexuals is much like rejecting a person for being blue-eyed or left-handed (Rathus, Nevid, & Fichner-Rathus, 2005). Homosexual people are found in all walks of life, at all social and economic levels, and in all cultural groups (Garnets, 2002). Perhaps as more people come to see gay and lesbian people in terms of their humanity, rather than their sexuality, the prejudices they have faced will wane.

Healthy Sexual Relationships

Regardless of sexual responsiveness or sexual orientation, as a shared pleasure, a form of intimacy, a means of communication, and a haven from everyday tensions, a positive sexual relationship can do much to enhance a couple's mutual understanding and caring. People are most likely to value their sexuality when they develop a respectful, trusting, and intimate relationship with their partner. A sense of closeness helps maintain sexual interest and mutually satisfying lovemaking, especially in long-term relationships (McCarthy, 1995; McCarthy & Fucito, 2005).

Sexual Problems—When Pleasure Fades

Sexual dysfunctions are far more common than many people realize. Most people who seek sexual counseling have one or more of the following types of problems (Crooks & Baur, 2008; American Psychiatric Association, 2000):

Desire Disorders: The person has little or no sexual motivation or desire.

Arousal Disorders: The person desires sexual activity but does not become sexually aroused.

Orgasm Disorders: The person does not have orgasms or experiences orgasm too soon or too late.

Sexual Pain Disorders: The person experiences pain that makes lovemaking uncomfortable or impossible.

There was a time when people suffered such problems in silence. However, in recent years effective treatments have been found for many complaints. Medical treatments or drugs (such as Viagra and Cialis for men) may be helpful for sexual problems that clearly have physical causes. In other cases, counseling or psychotherapy may be the best approach.

For example, many patients benefit from a technique called *sensate focus*. In sensate focus, distressed couples begin by taking turns caressing each other in nonsexual ways. They are told to concentrate on giving pleasure and on signaling what feels good to them. This relieves the pressure to perform and it builds communication skills. Slowly, the couple moves on to mutually satisfying lovemaking, as natural arousal begins to replace fear and anger. Similar solutions exist for many sexual problems. In most communities, professional help can be obtained from appropriately trained psychologists, physicians, or counselors.

study break

Hunger, Thirst, Pain, and Sex

RECITE

1. The hunger satiety system in the hypothalamus signals the body to start eating when it receives signals from the liver or detects changes in blood sugar. T or F?
2. People who diet frequently tend to benefit from practice: They lose weight more quickly each time they diet. T or F?
3. Bulimia nervosa is also known as the binge–purge syndrome. T or F?
4. In addition to burning calories, physical exercise can lower the body's set point. T or F?
5. Thirst may be either intracellular or _____.
6. Pain avoidance is a(n) _____ drive.
7. Sexual behavior in animals is largely controlled by estrogen levels in the female and the occurrence of estrus in the male. T or F?

8. List the four phases of sexual response identified by Masters and Johnson:

   _____, _____, _____, _____.

REFLECT

Critical Thinking

9. Kim, who is overweight, is highly sensitive to external eating cues. How might her wristwatch contribute to her overeating?

Relate

Think of the last meal you ate. What caused you to feel hungry? What internal signals told your body to stop eating? How sensitive are you to external eating cues? How were you influenced by portion size?

A friend of yours seems to be engaging in yo-yo dieting. Can you tell your friend why such dieting is ineffective and summarize how behavioral dieting is done?

In what ways are sexual responses of members of the opposite sex similar to your own? In what ways are they different?

ANSWERS

1. F 2. F 3. T 4. F 5. extracellular 6. episodic 7. F 8. excitement, plateau, orgasm, resolution 9. The time of day can influence eating, especially for externally cued eaters, who tend to get hungry at mealtimes, irrespective of their internal needs for food.

Stimulus Motives—Monkey Business

How does arousal relate to motivation?

Are you full of energy right now? Or are you tired? Clearly, the level of arousal you are experiencing is closely linked with your motivation. Are there ideal levels of arousal for different people and different activities? Let's find out.

Most people enjoy a steady "diet" of new movies, novels, tunes, fashions, games, news, websites, and adventures. Yet *stimulus motives,* which reflect needs for information, exploration, manipulation, and sensory input, go beyond mere entertainment. Stimulus drives also help us survive. As we scan our surroundings, we constantly identify sources of food, danger, shelter, and other key details. The drive for stimulation is already present during infancy. By the time a child can walk, there are few things in the home that have not been tasted, touched, viewed, handled, or, in the case of toys, destroyed!

Stimulus drives are readily apparent in animals as well as humans. For example, monkeys will quickly learn to solve a mechanical puzzle made up of interlocking metal pins, hooks, and latches (Butler, 1954) (▶▶ Figure 9.12). No food treats or other external rewards are needed to get them to explore and manipulate their surroundings. The monkeys seem to work for the sheer fun of it.

▲ **FIGURE 9.12** Monkeys happily open locks that are placed in their cage. Because no reward is given for this activity, it provides evidence for the existence of stimulus needs. (Photo courtesy of Harry F. Harlow.)

Arousal Theory

Are stimulus drives homeostatic? Yes. According to **arousal theory** we try to keep arousal at an optimal level (Franken, 2007; Hancock & Ganey, 2003). In other words, when your level of arousal is too low or too high, you will seek ways to raise or lower it.

What do you mean by arousal? Arousal refers to activation of the body and nervous system. Arousal is zero at death, low during sleep, moderate during normal daily activities, and high at times of excitement, emotion, or panic. Arousal theory assumes that we become uncomfortable when arousal is too low ("I'm bored") or when it is too high, as in fear, anxiety, or panic ("The dentist will see you now"). Most adults vary music, parties, sports, conversation, sleep, surfing the Web, and the like, to keep arousal at moderate levels. The right mix of activities prevents boredom *and* overstimulation (Csikszentmihalyi, Abuhamdeh, & Nakamura, 2005).

Sensation Seekers

Do people vary in their needs for stimulation? Arousal theory also suggests that people learn to seek particular levels of arousal. Where would you prefer to go on your next summer vacation? Your back yard? How about a week with your best friends at a cottage on a nearby lake? Or a shopping and museum trip to New York City? Better yet, how about cage diving with great white sharks in South Africa? If the shark adventure attracts you, you are probably high in sensation seeking and would be interested in a vacation that includes activities like bungee-jumping, scuba diving, skiing, skydiving, and white-water rafting (Pizam et al., 2004).

Sensation seeking is a trait of people who prefer high levels of stimulation (Gray & Wilson, 2007). Whether you are high or low in sensation seeking is probably based on how your body responds to new, unusual, or intense stimulation (Zuckerman, 2002). People high in sensation seeking tend to be bold and independent, and value change. They also report more sexual partners, are more likely to smoke, and prefer spicy, sour, and crunchy foods over bland foods. Low sensation seekers are orderly, nurturant, and giving, and enjoy the company of others.

Jeffrey L. Rotman/Corbis

Thrill seeking is an element of the sensation-seeking personality.

Arousal theory Assumes that people prefer to maintain ideal, or comfortable, levels of arousal.

(a) Inverted U function

(b) Simple task

(c) Complex task

▲ **FIGURE 9.13** *(a)* The general relationship between arousal and efficiency can be described by an inverted U curve. The optimal level of arousal or motivation is higher for a simple task *(b)* than for a complex task *(c)*.

Exciting lives aside, there is a dark side to sensation seeking. High sensation seekers are more likely to engage in high-risk behaviors such as substance abuse (Horvath et al., 2004) and casual unprotected sex (Gullette & Lyons, 2005).

Levels of Arousal

Is there an ideal level of arousal for peak performance? If we set aside individual differences, most people perform best when their arousal level is *moderate*. Let's say that you have to take an essay exam. If you are feeling sleepy or lazy (arousal level too low), your performance will suffer. If you are in a state of anxiety or panic about the test (arousal level too high), you will also perform below par. Thus, the relationship between arousal and performance forms an *inverted U function* (a curve in the shape of an upside-down U) (▶▶ Figure 9.13) (Hancock & Ganey, 2003).

The inverted U tells us that at very low levels of arousal, you're not sufficiently energized to perform well. Performance will improve as your arousal level increases, up to the middle of the curve. Then it begins to drop off as you become emotional, frenzied, or disorganized. For example, imagine trying to start a car stalled on a railroad track, with a speeding train bearing down on you. That's what the high-arousal end of the curve feels like.

Is performance always best at moderate levels of arousal? No, the ideal level of arousal depends on the complexity of a task. If a task is relatively simple, it is best for arousal to be high. When a task is more complex, your best performance will occur at lower levels of arousal. This relationship is called the **Yerkes-Dodson law** (see Figure 9.13). It applies to a wide variety of tasks and to measures of motivation other than arousal.

For example, at a track meet, it is almost impossible for sprinters to get too aroused for a race. The task is direct and simple: Run as fast as you can for a short distance. On the other hand, a golfer making a tournament-deciding putt faces a more sensitive and complex task. Excessive arousal is almost certain to hurt his or her performance. In school, most students have had experience with "test anxiety," a familiar example of how too much arousal can lower performance.

Coping with Test Anxiety

Then is it true that by learning to calm down, a person would do better on tests? Usually, but not always. To begin with, some arousal is healthy; it focuses us on the task at hand. It is only when arousal interferes with performance that we refer to anxiety. **Test anxiety** is a mixture of *heightened physiological arousal* (nervousness, sweating, pounding heart) and *excessive worry*. This combination—arousal plus worry—tends to distract students with a rush of

Yerkes-Dodson law A summary of the relationships among arousal, task complexity, and performance.

Test anxiety High levels of arousal and worry that seriously impair test performance.

upsetting thoughts and feelings (Stipek, 2001). Here are some suggestions for coping with test anxiety:

Preparation

Hard work is the most direct antidote for test anxiety. Many test-anxious students simply study too little, too late. That's why improving your study skills is a good way to reduce test anxiety (Cassady, 2004). If test anxiety is a problem for you, it would be wise to return to the Introduction in this book and review the learning and test-taking skills described there. The best solution is to *overprepare* by studying long before the "big day." Well-prepared students score higher, worry less, and are less likely to panic (Zohar, 1998).

Relaxation

Learning to relax is another way to lower test anxiety (Powell, 2004). You can learn self-relaxation skills by looking at Chapter 11, where a relaxation technique is described. Emotional support also helps (Stöber, 2004). If you are test anxious, discuss the problem with your professors or study for tests with a supportive classmate.

Rehearsal

To reduce nervousness, rehearse how you will cope with upsetting events. Before taking a test, imagine yourself going blank, running out of time, or feeling panicked. Then calmly plan how you will handle each situation—by keeping your attention on the task, by focusing on one question at a time, and so forth (Watson & Tharp, 2007).

Restructuring Thoughts

Another helpful strategy involves listing the upsetting thoughts you have during exams. Then you can learn to combat these worries with calming, rational replies (Jones & Petruzzi, 1995). (These are called *coping statements;* see Chapter 11 for more information.) Let's say you think, "I'm going to fail this test and everybody will think I'm stupid." A good reply to this upsetting thought would be to say, "If I prepare well and control my worries, I will probably pass the test. Even if I don't, it won't be the end of the world. My friends will still like me, and I can try to improve on the next test."

Students who cope well with exams usually try to do the best they can, even under difficult circumstances. Becoming a more confident test taker can actually increase your scores, because it helps you remain calm. With practice, most people can learn to be less testy at test-taking time (Smith, 2002).

Learned Motives—The Pursuit of Excellence

What are social motives? Why are they important?

Some of your friends are more interested than others in success, achievement, competition, money, possessions, status, love, approval, grades, dominance, power, or belonging to groups—all of which are *social motives* or goals. We acquire **social motives** in complex ways, through socialization and cultural conditioning (Franken, 2007). The behavior of outstanding artists, scientists, athletes, educators, and leaders is best understood in terms of such learned needs, particularly the need for achievement.

The Need for Achievement

To many people, being "motivated" means being interested in achievement (Wigfield & Eccles, 2002). In a later chapter we will investigate aggression, helping, affiliation, seeking approval, and other social motives. For now, let us focus on the **need for achievement (nAch)**, which is

Social motives Learned motives acquired as part of growing up in a particular society or culture.

Need for achievement (nAch) The desire to excel or meet some internalized standard of excellence.

a desire to meet an internal standard of excellence (McClelland, 1961). People with a high need for achievement strive to do well any time they are evaluated.

Is that like the aggressive businessperson who strives for success? Not necessarily. Needs for achievement may lead to wealth and prestige, but people who are high achievers in art, music, science, or amateur sports may excel without seeking riches. Such people typically enjoy challenges and relish a chance to test their abilities (Puca & Schmalt, 1999).

Power

The need for achievement differs from the **need for power,** which is a desire to have impact upon or control over others (McClelland, 1975). People with strong needs for power want their importance to be visible: They buy expensive possessions, wear prestigious clothes, and exploit relationships. In some ways, the pursuit of power and financial success is the dark side of the American dream. People whose main goal in life is to make lots of money tend to be poorly adjusted and unhappy (Kasser & Ryan, 1993).

Characteristics of Achievers

Using a simple measure, David McClelland (1965) found that he could predict the behavior of high and low achievers. Here's a test: In front of you are five targets. Each is placed at an increasing distance from where you are standing. You are given a bean-bag to toss at the target of your choice. Target A, anyone can hit; target B, most people can hit; target C, some people can hit; target D, very few people can hit; target E is rarely if ever hit. If you hit A, you will receive $2; B, $4; C, $8; D, $16; and E, $32. You get only one toss. Which one would you choose? McClelland's research suggests that if you have a high need for achievement, you will select C or perhaps D. Those high in nAch are *moderate* risk takers. When faced with a problem or a challenge, persons high in nAch avoid goals that are too easy.

Why do they pass up sure success? They do it because easy goals offer no sense of satisfaction. They also avoid long shots because there is either no hope of success, or "winning" will be due to luck rather than skill. Persons low in nAch select sure things or impossible goals. Either way, they don't have to take any responsibility for failure.

Desires for achievement and calculated risk taking lead to success in many situations. People high in nAch complete difficult tasks, they earn better grades, and they tend to excel in their occupations. College students high in nAch attribute success to their own ability, and failure to insufficient effort. Thus, high nAch students are more likely to renew their efforts when they perform poorly. When the going gets tough, high achievers get going.

Kevin Lamarque/Reuters/Corbis

The person with high needs for achievement strives to do well in any situation in which evaluation takes place.

The Key to Success

What does it take to achieve extraordinary success? Psychologist Benjamin Bloom (1985) studied America's top concert pianists, Olympic swimmers, sculptors, tennis players, mathematicians, and research neurologists. He found that drive and determination, not great natural talent, led to exceptional success.

The first steps toward high achievement began when parents exposed their children to music, swimming, scientific ideas, and so forth, "just for fun." At first, many of the children had very ordinary skills. One Olympic swimmer, for instance, remembers repeatedly losing races as a 10-year-old. At some point, however, the children began to actively cultivate their abilities. Before long, parents noticed the child's rapid progress and found an expert instructor or coach. After more successes, the youngsters began "living" for their talent and practiced many hours daily. This continued for many years before they reached truly outstanding heights of achievement.

The upshot of Bloom's work is that talent is nurtured by dedication and hard work (R. C. Beck, 2004). It is most likely to blossom when parents actively support a child's special interest and emphasize doing one's best at all times. Studies of child prodigies and eminent adults also show that intensive practice and expert coaching are common ingredients of high achievement. Elite performance in music, sports, chess, the arts, and many other pur-

Need for power The desire to have social impact and control over others.

suits requires at least 10 years of dedicated practice (Ericsson & Charness, 1994; Ross, 2006). The old belief that "talent will surface" on its own is largely a myth.

Self-Confidence

Achieving elite performance may be reserved for the dedicated few. Nevertheless, like elite athletes, you may be able to improve your motivation by increasing your self-confidence (Hanton, Mellalieu, & Hall, 2004). People with self-confidence believe they can successfully carry out an activity or reach a goal. To enhance self-confidence, it is wise to do the following (Druckman & Bjork, 1994):

- Set goals that are specific and challenging, but attainable.
- Visualize the steps you need to take to reach your goal.
- Advance in small steps.
- When you first acquire a skill, your goal should be to make progress in learning. Later, you can concentrate on improving your performance, compared with other people.
- Get expert instruction that helps you master the skill.
- Find a skilled model (someone good at the skill) to emulate.
- Get support and encouragement from an observer.
- If you fail, regard it as a sign that you need to try harder, not that you lack ability.

Self-confidence affects motivation by influencing the challenges you will undertake, the effort you will make, and how long you will persist when things don't go well. You can be confident that self-confidence is worth cultivating.

Motives in Perspective—The View from the Pyramid

Are some motives more basic than others?

Are all these motives equally important? Abraham Maslow proposed a **hierarchy of human needs,** in which some needs are more basic or powerful than others. (As you may recall from Chapter 1, Maslow called the full use of personal potential *self-actualization.*) Think about the needs that influence your own behavior. Which seem strongest? Which do you spend the most time and energy satisfying? Now look at Maslow's hierarchy (▶▶ Figure 9.14).

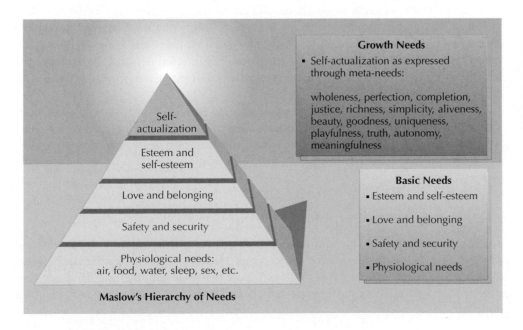

Maslow's Hierarchy of Needs

Growth Needs
- Self-actualization as expressed through meta-needs:

  wholeness, perfection, completion, justice, richness, simplicity, aliveness, beauty, goodness, uniqueness, playfulness, truth, autonomy, meaningfulness

Basic Needs
- Esteem and self-esteem
- Love and belonging
- Safety and security
- Physiological needs

(Pyramid levels, top to bottom: Self-actualization; Esteem and self-esteem; Love and belonging; Safety and security; Physiological needs: air, food, water, sleep, sex, etc.)

◀◀ **FIGURE 9.14** Maslow believed that lower needs in the hierarchy are dominant. Basic needs must be satisfied before growth motives are fully expressed. Desires for self-actualization are reflected in various meta-needs (see text).

Hierarchy of human needs Abraham Maslow's ordering of needs, based on their presumed strength or potency.

Note that biological needs are at the base of the pyramid. Because these needs must be met if we are to survive, they tend to be *prepotent,* or dominant over the higher needs. That's why, when you are really hungry, you can think of little else but food. Maslow believed that higher, more fragile needs are expressed only after we satisfy our biological needs. This is also true of needs for safety and security. Until they are met, we may have little interest in higher pursuits. For instance, a person who is feeling threatened might have little interest in writing poetry or even talking with friends. For this reason, Maslow described the first four levels of the hierarchy as **basic needs.** Other basic needs are for love and belonging (family, friendship, caring) and esteem and self-esteem (recognition and self-respect).

All the basic needs are *deficiency* motives. That is, they are activated by a *lack* of food, water, security, love, esteem, or other basic needs. At the top of the hierarchy we find **growth needs,** which are expressed as a need for self-actualization. The need for self-actualization is not based on deficiencies. Rather, it is a positive, life-enhancing force for personal growth (Reiss & Havercamp, 2005). Like other humanistic psychologists, Maslow believed that people are basically good. If our basic needs are met, he said, we will tend to move on to actualizing our potentials.

How are needs for self-actualization expressed? Maslow also called the less powerful but humanly important actualization motives **meta-needs** (Maslow, 1970). Meta-needs are an expression of tendencies to fully develop your personal potentials. The meta-needs are:

Francois-Xavier Marit/Getty Images

Wheelchair athletes engage in vigorous competition. Maslow considered such behavior an expression of the need for self-actualization.

1. Wholeness (unity)
2. Perfection (balance and harmony)
3. Completion (ending)
4. Justice (fairness)
5. Richness (complexity)
6. Simplicity (essence)
7. Aliveness (spontaneity)
8. Beauty (rightness of form)
9. Goodness (benevolence)
10. Uniqueness (individuality)
11. Playfulness (ease)
12. Truth (reality)
13. Autonomy (self-sufficiency)
14. Meaningfulness (values)

According to Maslow, we tend to move up through the hierarchy of needs, toward the meta-needs. When the meta-needs are unfulfilled, people fall into a "syndrome of decay" marked by despair, apathy, and alienation. Maslow's point is that mere survival or comfort is usually not enough to make a full and satisfying life. It's interesting to note, in this regard, that college students who are concerned primarily with money, personal appearance, and social recognition score lower than average in vitality, self-actualization, and general well-being (Kasser & Ryan, 1996).

Are many people motivated by meta-needs? Maslow estimated that few people are motivated primarily by needs for self-actualization. Most of us are more concerned with esteem, love, or security. Perhaps this is because rewards in our society tend to encourage conformity, uniformity, and security in schools, jobs, and relationships. When was the last time you met a meta-need?

Intrinsic and Extrinsic Motivation

Some people cook for a living and consider it hard work. Others cook for pleasure and dream of opening a restaurant. For some people, mountain biking, gardening, writing, photography, or jewelry making is fun. For others the same activities are drudgery they must be paid to do. How can the same activity be "work" for one person and "play" for another?

Basic needs The first four levels of needs in Maslow's hierarchy; lower needs tend to be more potent than higher needs.

Growth needs In Maslow's hierarchy, the higher level needs associated with self-actualization.

Meta-needs In Maslow's hierarchy, needs associated with impulses for self-actualization.

People who are intrinsically motivated feel free to explore creative solutions to problems. *(left)* Dean Kaman, inventor of the Segway personal transportation device. *(right)* "Extreme Makeover," an entrant in The Great Arcata to Ferndale World Championship Cross Country Kinetic Sculpture Race.

When you do something for enjoyment or to improve your abilities, your motivation is usually *intrinsic*. **Intrinsic motivation** occurs when we act without any obvious external rewards. We simply enjoy an activity or see it as an opportunity to explore, learn, and actualize our potentials. In contrast, **extrinsic motivation** stems from external factors, such as pay, grades, rewards, obligations, and approval. Most of the activities we think of as "work" are extrinsically rewarded (Baard, Deci, & Ryan, 2004; Ryan & Deci, 2000).

Turning Play into Work

Don't extrinsic incentives strengthen motivation? Yes they can, but not always. In fact, *excessive* rewards can decrease intrinsic motivation and spontaneous interest. For instance, in one classic study, children who were lavishly rewarded for drawing with felt-tip pens later showed little interest in playing with the pens again (Greene & Lepper, 1974). Apparently, "play" can be turned into "work" by *requiring* people to do something they would otherwise enjoy. When we are coerced or "bribed" to act, we tend to feel as if we are "faking it." Employees who lack initiative and teenagers who reject school and learning are good examples of those who have such a reaction (Ryan & Deci, 2000).

Creativity

People are more likely to be creative when they are intrinsically motivated. On the job, for instance, salaries and bonuses may increase the amount of work done. However, work *quality* is affected more by intrinsic factors, such as personal interest and freedom of choice (Nakamura & Csikszentmihalyi, 2003). When a person is intrinsically motivated, a certain amount of challenge, surprise, and complexity makes a task rewarding. When extrinsic motivation is stressed, people are less likely to solve tricky problems and come up with innovative ideas (Amabile, Hadley, & Kramer, 2002).

Should extrinsic motivation always be avoided? No, but extrinsic motivation shouldn't be overused, especially with children. In general, (1) if there's no intrinsic interest in an activity to begin with, you have nothing to lose by using extrinsic rewards; (2) if basic skills are lacking, extrinsic rewards may be necessary at first; (3) extrinsic rewards can focus attention on an activity so that real interest will develop; and (4) if extrinsic rewards are used, they should be small and phased out as soon as possible (Buckworth et al., 2007; Cameron & Pierce, 2002).

motivation

Intrinsic motivation Motivation that comes from within, rather than from external rewards; motivation based on personal enjoyment of a task or activity.

Extrinsic motivation Motivation based on obvious external rewards, obligations, or similar factors.

At work, it is valuable for managers to find out what each employee's interests and career goals are. People are not motivated solely by money. A chance to do challenging, interesting, and intrinsically rewarding work is often just as important. In many situations it is important to encourage intrinsic motivation, especially when children are learning new skills.

study break

Stimulus Motives, Learned Motives, Maslow, and Intrinsic Motivation

RECITE

1. Exploration, manipulation, and curiosity provide evidence for the existence of _____ drives.
2. Sensation seekers tend to be extroverted, independent, and individuals who value change. T or F?
3. Two key elements of test anxiety that must be controlled are _____ and excessive _____.
4. People high in nAch are attracted to "long shots" and "sure things." T or F?
5. According to Maslow, meta-needs are the most basic and prepotent sources of human motivation. T or F?
6. Intrinsic motivation is often undermined in situations in which obvious external rewards are applied to a naturally enjoyable activity. T or F?

REFLECT
Critical Thinking

7. Many U.S. college freshmen say that "being well-off financially" is an essential life goal and that "making more money" was a very important factor in their decision to attend college. Which meta-needs are fulfilled by "making more money"?

Relate

Does arousal theory seem to explain any of your own behavior? Think of at least one time when your performance was impaired by arousal that was too low or too high. Now think of some personal examples that illustrate the Yerkes-Dodson law.

Are you high or low in your need for stimulation?

In situations involving risk and skill, do you like to "go for broke"? Or do you prefer sure things? Do you think you are high, medium, or low in nAch?

Which levels of Maslow's hierarchy of needs occupy most of your time and energy?

Name an activity you do that is intrinsically motivated and one that is extrinsically motivated. How do they differ?

ANSWERS

1. stimulus 2. T 3. arousal, worry 4. F 5. F 6. T 7. None of them.

Inside an Emotion—How Do You Feel?

What happens during emotion?

Picture the faces of terrified people fleeing a tornado and it's easy to see that motivation and emotion are closely related. Emotions shape our relationships and color our daily activities. **Emotion** is characterized by physiological arousal and changes in facial expressions, gestures, posture, and subjective feelings. As mentioned earlier, the word emotion derives from the Latin word meaning "to move."

What "moves" during an emotion? First of all, your body is physically aroused during emotion. Such bodily stirrings are what cause us to say we were "moved" by a play, a funeral, or an act of kindness. Second, we are often motivated, or moved to take action, by emotions such as fear, anger, or joy. Many of the goals we seek make us feel good. Many of the activities we avoid make us feel bad. We feel happy when we succeed and sad when we fail (Kalat & Shiota, 2007).

Emotions are linked to many basic **adaptive behaviors,** such as attacking, fleeing, seeking comfort, helping others, and reproducing. Such behaviors help us survive and adjust to changing conditions (Plutchik, 2003). However, it is also apparent that emotions can have negative effects. Stage fright or "choking" in sports can spoil performances. Hate, anger, contempt, disgust, and fear disrupt behavior and relationships. But more often, emotions

Emotion A state characterized by physiological arousal, changes in facial expression, gestures, posture, and subjective feelings.

Adaptive behaviors Actions that aid attempts to survive and adapt to changing conditions.

aid survival. As social animals, it would be impossible for humans to live in groups, cooperate in raising children, and defend one another without positive emotional bonds of love, caring, and friendship (Buss, 2000).

A pounding heart, sweating palms, "butterflies" in the stomach, and other bodily reactions are major elements of fear, anger, joy, and other emotions. Typical **physiological changes** take place in heart rate, blood pressure, perspiration, and other bodily stirrings. Most are caused by activity in the sympathetic nervous system and by the hormones *adrenaline* and *noradrenaline*, which the adrenal glands release into the bloodstream.

Emotional expressions, or outward signs of what a person is feeling, are another ingredient of emotion. For example, when you are intensely afraid, your hands tremble, your face contorts, your posture becomes tense and defensive, and your voice changes. In general, these expressions serve to tell others what emotions we are experiencing (Hortman, 2003). **Emotional feelings** (a person's private emotional experience) are a final major element of emotion. This is the part of emotion with which we are usually most familiar.

Primary Emotions

Are some emotions more basic than others? Yes, Robert Plutchik (2003) has identified eight **primary emotions.** These are fear, surprise, sadness, disgust, anger, anticipation, joy, and trust (acceptance). If the list seems too short, it's because each emotion can vary in *intensity.* When you're angry, for instance, you may feel anything from rage to simple annoyance (see ▶▶ Figure 9.15).

As shown in Figure 9.15, each pair of adjacent primary emotions can be mixed to yield a third, more complex emotion. Other mixtures are also possible. For example, 5-year-old Tupac feels both joy and fear as he eats a cookie he stole from Mom's cookie jar. The result? Guilt—as you may recall from your own childhood. Likewise, jealousy could be a mixture of love, anger, and fear.

A **mood** is the mildest form of emotion (▶▶ Figure 9.16). Moods are low-intensity emotional states that can last for many hours, or even days. Moods often affect day-to-day behavior by preparing us to act in certain ways. For example, when your neighbor Roseanne is in an irritable mood, she may react angrily to almost anything you say. When she is in a happy mood, she can easily laugh off an insult. Happy, positive moods tend to make us more adaptable in several ways. For example, when you are in a good mood, you are likely to make better decisions and you will be more helpful, efficient, creative, and peaceful (Compton, 2005).

Like our motives, our moods are closely tied to circadian rhythms. When your body temperature is at its daily low point, you are more likely to feel "down" emotionally. When body temperature is at its peak, your mood is likely to be positive—even if you missed a night of sleep (Boivin, Czeisler, & Waterhouse, 1997).

Emotion and the Brain

Emotions can be either positive or negative. Ordinarily, we might think that positive and negative emotions are mutually exclusive. But this is not the case. As Tupac's "cookie guilt" implies, you can have positive and negative emotions at the same time. How is that possible? In the brain, positive emotions are processed mainly in the left hemisphere. In contrast, negative emotions are processed in the right hemisphere (Simon-Thomas, Role, & Knight, 2005). The fact that positive and negative emotions are based in different brain areas helps

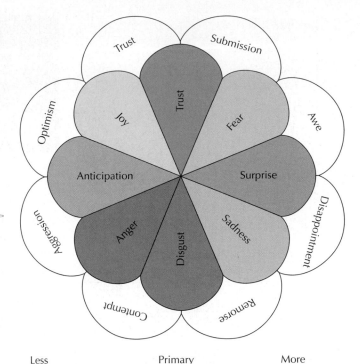

Less intense	Primary emotion	More intense
Interest	Anticipation	Vigilance
Serenity	Joy	Ecstasy
Acceptance	Trust	Admiration
Apprehension	Fear	Terror
Distraction	Surprise	Amazement
Pensiveness	Sadness	Grief
Boredom	Disgust	Loathing
Annoyance	Anger	Rage

▲ **FIGURE 9.15** Primary and mixed emotions. In Robert Plutchik's model, there are eight primary emotions, as listed in the inner areas. Adjacent emotions may combine to give the emotions listed around the perimeter. Mixtures involving more widely separated emotions are also possible. For example, fear plus anticipation produces anxiety. (Adapted from Plutchik, 2003.)

Physiological changes (in emotion) Alterations in heart rate, blood pressure, perspiration, and other involuntary responses.

Emotional expression Outward signs that an emotion is occurring.

Emotional feelings The private, subjective experience of having an emotion.

Primary emotions According to Robert Plutchik's theory, the most basic emotions are fear, surprise, sadness, disgust, anger, anticipation, joy, and acceptance.

Mood A low-intensity, long-lasting emotional state.

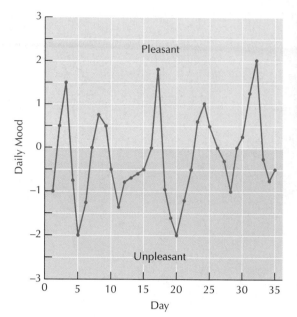

◀◀ **FIGURE 9.16** Folklore holds that people who work or attend school on a weekly schedule experience their lowest moods on "Blue Monday." Actually, moods tend to be generally lower for *most* weekdays than they are on weekends. The graph shown here plots the average daily moods of a group of college students over a 5-week period. As you can see, many people find that their moods rise and fall on a 7-day cycle. For most students, a low point tends to occur around Monday or Tuesday and a peak on Friday or Saturday. In other words, moods are shaped by weekly schedules. (Adapted from Larsen & Kasimatis, 1990.)

explain why we can feel happy and sad at the same time (Canli et al., 1998). It also explains why your right foot is more ticklish than your left foot! The left hemisphere controls the right side of the body and processes positive emotions (Smith & Cahusac, 2001). Thus, most people are more ticklish on their right side. If you really want to tickle someone, be sure to "do it right."

Scientists used to think that all emotions are processed by the cerebral cortex. However, this is not always the case. Imagine this test of willpower: Go to a zoo and place your face close to the glass in front of a rattlesnake display. Suddenly, the rattlesnake strikes at your face. Do you flinch? Even though you know you are safe, Joseph LeDoux predicts that you will recoil from the snake's attack (LeDoux, 2000).

LeDoux and other researchers have found that an area of the brain called the **amygdala** (ah-MIG-duh-la) specializes in producing fear (▶▶ Figure 9.17). (See Chapter 2 for more information.) The amygdala receives sensory information very directly and quickly, bypassing the cortex (Walker & Davis, 2008). As a result, it allows us to respond to potential danger before we really know what's happening. This primitive fear response is not under the control of higher brain centers. The role of the amygdala in emotion may explain why people who suffer from phobias and disabling anxiety often feel afraid without knowing why (Fellous & Ledoux, 2005).

People who suffer damage to the amygdala become "blind" to emotion. An armed robber could hold a gun to a person's head and the person wouldn't feel fear. Such people are also unable to "read" or understand other people's emotional expressions, especially as conveyed by their eyes (Adolphs, 2008). Like Robert, whom you met at the beginning of this chapter, many lose their ability to relate normally to friends, family, and coworkers (Goleman, 1995).

Later we will attempt to put all the elements of emotion together into a single picture. But first, we need to look more closely at bodily arousal and emotional expressions.

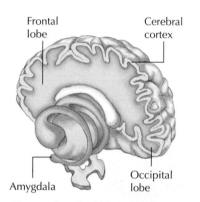

Frontal lobe
Cerebral cortex
Amygdala
Occipital lobe

▲ **FIGURE 9.17** An amygdala can be found buried within the temporal lobes on each side of the brain (see Chapter 2). The amygdala appears to provide "quick and dirty" processing of emotional stimuli that allows us to react involuntarily to danger.

Physiology and Emotion— Arousal, Sudden Death, and Lying

What physiological changes underlie emotion?
Can "lie detectors" really detect lies?

An African Bushman frightened by a lion and a city dweller frightened by a prowler will react in much the same way. Such encounters usually produce muscle tension, a pounding heart, irritability, dryness of the throat and mouth, sweating, butterflies in the stomach, frequent urination, trembling, restlessness, sensitivity to loud noises, and numerous other body changes. These reactions are nearly universal because they are innate. Specifically, they are caused by the **autonomic nervous system (ANS)** (the neural system that connects the brain with internal organs and glands). As you may recall from Chapter 2, activity of the ANS is *automatic*, rather than voluntary (Kalat & Shiota, 2007).

Amygdala A part of the limbic system (within the brain) that produces fear responses.

Autonomic nervous system (ANS) The system of nerves that connects the brain with the internal organs and glands.

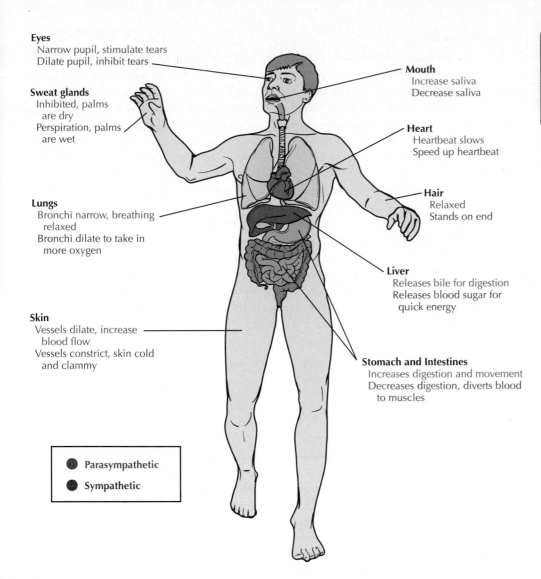

Eyes
Narrow pupil, stimulate tears
Dilate pupil, inhibit tears

Sweat glands
Inhibited, palms
are dry
Perspiration, palms
are wet

Lungs
Bronchi narrow, breathing
relaxed
Bronchi dilate to take in
more oxygen

Skin
Vessels dilate, increase
blood flow
Vessels constrict, skin cold
and clammy

Mouth
Increase saliva
Decrease saliva

Heart
Heartbeat slows
Speed up heartbeat

Hair
Relaxed
Stands on end

Liver
Releases bile for digestion
Releases blood sugar for
quick energy

Stomach and Intestines
Increases digestion and movement
Decreases digestion, diverts blood
to muscles

● **Parasympathetic**
● **Sympathetic**

◀◀ **FIGURE 9.18** The parasympathetic branch of the ANS calms and quiets the body. The sympathetic branch arouses the body and prepares it for emergency action.

Fight or Flight

The ANS has two divisions, the sympathetic branch and the parasympathetic branch. The two branches are active at all times. Whether you are relaxed or aroused at any moment depends on the relative activity of both branches.

What does the ANS do during emotion? In general, the **sympathetic branch** activates the body for emergency action—for "fighting or fleeing." It does this by arousing some body systems and inhibiting others (▶▶ Figure 9.18). Sugar is released into the bloodstream for quick energy, the heart beats faster to supply blood to the muscles, digestion is temporarily slowed, blood flow in the skin is restricted to reduce bleeding, and so forth. Such reactions improve the chances of surviving an emergency.

The **parasympathetic branch** reverses emotional arousal. This calms and relaxes the body. After a period of high emotion, the heart is slowed, the pupils return to normal size, blood pressure drops, and so forth. In addition to restoring balance, the parasympathetic system helps build up and conserve the body's energy.

The parasympathetic system responds much more slowly than the sympathetic system. That's why a pounding heart, muscle tension, and other signs of arousal don't fade for 20 or 30 minutes after you feel an intense emotion, such as fear. Moreover, after a strong emotional shock, the parasympathetic system may overreact and lower blood pressure too much. This can cause you to become dizzy or faint after seeing something shocking, such as a horrifying accident.

Sympathetic branch The part of the ANS that activates the body at times of stress.

Parasympathetic branch The part of the autonomic system that quiets the body and conserves energy.

Sudden Death

Strong emotions can kill you in two ways. The first can occur if the sympathetic system becomes too active, resulting in excessive stress. For older persons or those with heart problems, stress-related sympathetic effects may be enough to bring about heart attack and collapse. For example, five times more people than usual died of heart attacks on the day of a major 1994 earthquake in Los Angeles (Leor, Poole, & Kloner, 1996). Similarly, in Asia, the number 4 is considered unlucky, and more heart patients die on the fourth day of the month than any other day. Because of the extra stress due to the fear that they will die on an "unlucky day," their chance of dying actually increases (Phillips et al., 2001).

Second, the **parasympathetic rebound** to sympathetic arousal can also be severe enough to cause death. In times of war, for instance, combat can be so savage that some soldiers literally die of fear (Moritz & Zamchech, 1946). Apparently, such deaths occur because the parasympathetic nervous system slows the heart to a stop. Even in civilian life this is possible. In one case, a terrified young woman was admitted to a hospital because she felt she was going to die. A backwoods midwife had predicted that the woman's two sisters would die before their 16th and 21st birthdays. Both died as predicted. The midwife also predicted that this woman would die before her 23rd birthday. She was found dead in her hospital bed the day after she was admitted. It was 2 days before her 23rd birthday (Seligman, 1989). The woman was an apparent victim of her own terror.

Lie Detectors

You undoubtedly know that criminals are not always truthful. But what you may not know is that up to 25 percent of all wrongful convictions include false confessions as evidence (Kassin, 2005). If you can't count on someone's word, what can you trust? The most popular method for detecting falsehoods measures the bodily changes that accompany emotion. However, the accuracy of "lie detector" tests is doubtful, and they can be a serious invasion of privacy (Lykken, 2001; National Academy of Sciences, 2002).

What is a lie detector? Do lie detectors really detect lies? The lie detector is more accurately called a **polygraph**, a word that means "many writings" (▶▶ Figure 9.19). The polygraph was invented in 1915 by psychologist William Marston, who also created the comic book character Wonder Woman, a superhero whose "magic lasso" could force people to tell the truth (Grubin & Madsen, 2005). Although popularly known as a lie detector because the police use it for that purpose, in reality the polygraph is not a lie detector at all (Bunn, 2007). A suspect is questioned while "hooked up" to a polygraph, which typically records changes in heart rate, blood pressure, breathing, and the galvanic skin response (GSR). The GSR is

FIGURE 9.19 *(left)* A typical polygraph measures heart rate, blood pressure, respiration, and galvanic skin response. Pens mounted on the top of the machine record bodily responses on a moving strip of paper. *(right)* Changes in the area marked by the arrow indicate emotional arousal. If such responses appear when a person answers a question, he or she may be lying, but arousal may have other causes.

Parasympathetic rebound Excess activity in the parasympathetic nervous system following a period of intense emotion.

Polygraph A device for recording heart rate, blood pressure, respiration, and galvanic skin response; commonly called a "lie detector."

recorded from the hand by electrodes that measure skin conductance, or, more simply, sweating. Because the device records only general emotional arousal, it can't tell the difference between lying and fear, anxiety and excitement (Iacono, 2008).

Wouldn't a person be nervous just from being questioned? Yes, but to minimize this problem, skilled polygraph examiners use the *comparison questions test* (Honts & Alloway, 2007). A series of neutral questions is asked interspersed with relevant items. For example, the polygraph operator may ask some neutral (irrelevant, non-emotional) questions, such as, "Is your name (person's name)?" "Did you eat lunch today?" and so forth, along with relevant items like "Did you murder Hensley?" or "Was it $52,000 you took from that bank?" An innocent person may respond emotionally to the whole procedure, but only a guilty person is supposed to respond more to relevant questions when compared with neutral ones (Iacono, 2008).

Even when questioning is done properly, lie detection may be inaccurate (Grubin & Madsen, 2005). A woman named Donna was arrested for violating a restraining order against Marie. Even though she claimed she was having lunch instead of harassing Marie, she failed a polygraph test (Geddes, 2008).

If Donna was innocent, why did she fail the test? Put yourself in her place, and it's easy to see why. Imagine the examiner asking, "Did you drive up to Marie, curse at her, and then drive away?" Because you know Marie, and you already know what you have been charged with, it's no secret that this is a critical question. What would happen to *your* heart rate, blood pressure, breathing, and perspiration under such circumstances? Psychologist David Lykken (1998, 2001) has documented many cases in which innocent people were convicted on the basis of polygraph evidence.

Proponents of lie detection claim it is 95 percent accurate. But in one study, accuracy was dramatically lowered when people thought about past emotional experiences as they answered irrelevant questions (Ben-Shakhar & Dolev, 1996). Similarly, the polygraph may be thrown off by self-inflicted pain, by tranquilizing drugs, or by people who can lie without anxiety (Waid & Orne, 1982). Worst of all, the test is much more likely to label an innocent person guilty, rather than a guilty person innocent. In studies involving real crimes, an average of one innocent person in five was rated as guilty by the lie detector (Lykken, 2001). For such reasons, the National Academy of Sciences (2002) has concluded that polygraph tests should not be used to screen employees.

Despite the lie detector's flaws, you may be tested for employment or for other reasons. Should this occur, the best advice is to remain calm; then actively challenge the results if the machine wrongly questions your honesty.

Isn't there a better way to detect lies? Possibly. Harassment charges against Donna were dropped when a functional magnetic resonance imaging (fMRI) scan revealed she was indeed telling the truth. Brain scans like fMRI directly measure brain activity, thus bypassing the traditional approach of measuring indirect signs of emotional arousal (Lefebvre et al., 2007). For example, researchers have found that different brain areas are involved in telling a lie (Abe et al., 2007). Psychiatrist Daniel Langleben (2008) theorizes that a liar must inhibit telling the truth in order to lie. Thus, extra brain areas must be activated to tell a lie, which can be seen in brain images when people are lying (see Chapter 2).

Even if new methods are used, the key problem remains: How can we avoid falsely classifying liars as truth tellers and truth tellers as liars? Until that can be done with acceptable accuracy, any new technique may have no more value than the polygraph does.

study break

Emotion and Physiological Arousal

RECITE

1. Many of the physiological changes associated with emotion are caused by secretion of the hormone
   a. atropine
   b. adrenaline
   c. attributine
   d. amoduline
2. Emotional _____ often serve to communicate a person's emotional state to others.
3. Awe, remorse, and disappointment are among the primary emotions listed by Robert Plutchik. T or F?
4. Emotional arousal is closely related to activity of the _____ nervous system.
5. The sympathetic system prepares the body for "fight or flight" by activating the parasympathetic system. T or F?
6. The parasympathetic system inhibits digestion and raises blood pressure and heart rate. T or F?
7. What body changes are measured by a polygraph?

REFLECT

Critical Thinking

8. Can you explain why people "cursed" by shamans or "witch doctors" sometimes actually die?

Relate

How did your most emotional moment of the past week affect your behavior, expressions, feelings, and bodily state? Could you detect both sympathetic and parasympathetic effects?

Make a list of the emotions you consider to be most basic. To what extent do they agree with Plutchik's list?

What did you think about lie detectors before reading this chapter? What do you think now?

ANSWERS

1. b 2. expressions 3. F 4. autonomic 5. F 6. F 7. heart rate, blood pressure, breathing rate, galvanic skin response 8. In cultures where there is deep belief in magic or voodoo, a person who thinks that she or he has been cursed may become uncontrollably emotional. After several days of intense terror, a parasympathetic rebound is likely. If the rebound is severe enough, it can lead to physical collapse and death.

Expressing Emotions—Making Faces and Talking Bodies

How accurately are emotions expressed by the face and "body language"?

Next to our own feelings, the expressions of others are the most familiar part of emotion. Are emotional expressions a carryover from human evolution? Charles Darwin thought so. Darwin (1872) observed that angry tigers, monkeys, dogs, and humans all bare their teeth in the same way. Psychologists believe that emotional expressions evolved to communicate our feelings to others, which aids survival. Such messages give valuable hints about what other people are likely to do next (Kalat & Shiota, 2007). For instance, in one study, people were able to detect angry and scheming faces faster than happy, sad, or neutral faces (▶▶ Figure 9.20). Presumably, we are especially sensitive to threatening faces because they warn us of possible harm (Adolphs, 2008; Tipples, Atkinson, & Young, 2002).

Angry   Sad   Happy   Scheming   Neutral

⬆ FIGURE 9.20 When shown groups of simplified faces (without labels), the angry and scheming faces "jumped out" at people faster than sad, happy, or neutral faces. An ability to rapidly detect threatening expressions probably helped our ancestors survive (Adapted from Tipples, Atkinson, & Young, 2002.)

Facial Expressions

Are emotional expressions the same for all people? Basic expressions appear to be fairly universal (Figure 9.21). Facial expressions of fear, anger, disgust, sadness, surprise, and happiness (enjoyment) are recognized around the world (Smith et al., 2005). Expressions of contempt and interest may also be universal, but researchers are less certain of this (Ekman, 1993). Notice that this list covers most of the primary emotions described earlier. Children who are born blind have little opportunity to learn emotional expressions from others. Even so, they also display basic expressions in the same way sighted people do (Galati, Scherer, & Ricci-Bitti, 1997). It's also nice to note that a smile is the most universal and easily recognized facial expression of emotion.

There are more than a few facial expressions, aren't there? Yes. Your face can produce some 20,000 different expressions, which makes it the most expressive part of your body. Most of these are *facial blends* (a mixture of two or more basic expressions). Imagine, for example, that you just received an F on an unfair test. Quite likely, your eyes, eyebrows, and forehead would reveal anger, and your mouth would be turned downward in a sad frown.

Most of us believe we can fairly accurately tell what others are feeling by observing their facial expressions. If thousands of facial blends occur, how do we make such judgments? The answer is that facial expressions can be boiled down to three basic dimensions: *pleasantness–unpleasantness, attention–rejection,* and *activation* (or arousal) (Schlosberg, 1954). By smiling when you give a friend a hard time, you add an emotional message of acceptance to the verbal insult, which changes its meaning. As they say in movie Westerns, it makes a big difference to "smile when you say that, pardner."

Cultural Differences in Expressing Emotion

Some facial expressions are shaped by learning and may be found only in specific cultures. Among the Chinese, for example, sticking out the tongue is a gesture of surprise, not of disrespect or teasing. If a person comes from another culture, it is wise to remember that you may easily misunderstand his or her expressions. At such times, knowing the social *context* in which an expression occurs helps clarify its meaning (Carroll & Russell, 1996; Kalat & Shiota, 2007).

How many times have you been angry this week? If it was more than once, you're not unusual. Anger is a very common emotion in Western cultures. Very likely this is because our culture emphasizes personal independence and a free expression of individual rights and needs. In North America, anger is widely viewed as a "natural" reaction to feeling that you have been treated unfairly.

In contrast, many Asian cultures place a high value on group harmony. In Asia, expressing anger in public is less common, and anger is regarded as less "natural." The reason for this is that anger tends to separate people. Thus, being angry is at odds with a culture that values cooperation. Culture also influences positive emotions. In America, we tend to have positive feelings such as pride, happiness, and superiority, which emphasize our role as *individuals*. In Japan, positive feelings are more often linked with membership in groups (friendly feelings, closeness to others, and respect) (Kitayama, Markus, & Kurokawa, 2000; Markus et al., 2006).

It is common to think of emotion as an individual event. However, as you can see, emotion is shaped by cultural ideas, values, and practices (Mesquita & Markus, 2004).

Gender and Emotional Expression

Women have a reputation for being "more emotional" than men. Are they? Compared with women, men in Western cultures are more likely to have difficulty expressing their emotions. According to psychologist Ronald Levant and colleagues (2006), although male babies start out life more emotionally expressive than female babies, little boys soon learn to "toughen up," beginning in early childhood. As a result, men have learned to curtail the expression of most of their emotions, although not to the extent of Robert, the alexithymic man we met at the beginning of the chapter. While girls are encouraged to express sadness, fear, shame, and guilt,

Photodisc/Getty Images

▲ **FIGURE 9.21** Is anger expressed the same way in different cultures? Masks that are meant to be frightening or threatening are strikingly similar around the world. Most have an open, downward-curved mouth and diagonal or triangular eyes, eyebrows, nose, cheeks, and chin. (Keep this list in mind next Halloween.) Obviously, the pictured mask is not meant to be warm and cuddly. Your ability to "read" its emotional message suggests that basic emotional expressions have universal biological roots (Adolphs, 2008).

The expression of emotion is strongly influenced by learning. As you have no doubt observed, women cry more often, longer, and more intensely than men do. Men begin learning early in childhood to suppress crying—possibly to the detriment of their emotional health (Williams & Morris, 1996). Many men are especially unwilling to engage in public displays of emotion, in contrast to these women, who are grieving for the victims of a 2005 school siege in Breslan, Russia, which left hundreds of children dead.

Emotions are often unconsciously revealed by gestures and body positioning.

boys are more likely to be allowed to express only anger and hostility (Fischer et al., 2004).

But does this mean that men experience emotions less than women? Levant believes that men who fail to express emotions become less aware of their own emotions. For many men, an inability to express feelings or to even be aware of them is a major barrier to having close, satisfying relationships with others (Levant, 2003). Blunted emotions may even contribute to tragedies like the mass murder at Columbine High School in Littleton, Colorado. For many young males, anger is the only emotion they can freely feel and express.

Body Language

If a friend walked up to you and said, "Hey, ugly, what are you doing?" would you be offended? Probably not, because such remarks are usually delivered with a big grin. The facial and bodily gestures of emotion speak a language all their own and add to what a person says.

Kinesics (kih-NEEZ-iks) is the study of communication through body movement, posture, gestures, and facial expressions (Harrigan, 2006). Informally, we call it body language. To see a masterful use of body language, turn off the sound on a television and watch a popular entertainer or politician at work.

What kinds of messages are sent with body language? It is important to realize cultural learning also affects the meaning of gestures. What, for instance, does it mean if you touch your thumb and first finger together to form a circle? In North America it means "Everything is fine" or "A-okay." In France and Belgium it means "You're worth zero." In southern Italy it means "You're an ass!" When the layer of culturally defined meanings is removed, it is more realistic to say that body language reveals an overall emotional tone (underlying emotional state).

The body telegraphs other feelings. The most general "messages" involve *relaxation* or *tension,* and *liking* or *disliking.* Relaxation is expressed by casually positioning the arms and legs, leaning back (if sitting), and spreading the arms and legs. Liking is expressed mainly by leaning toward a person or object. Thus, body positioning can reveal feelings that would normally be concealed. Who do you "lean toward"?

Theories of Emotion—Several Ways to Fear a Bear

How do psychologists explain emotions?

Is it possible to explain what takes place during emotion? Theories of emotion offer different answers to these questions. Let's explore some prominent views. Each appears to have a part of the truth, so we will try to put them all together in the end.

The James-Lange Theory

Kinesics Study of the meaning of body movements, posture, hand gestures, and facial expressions; commonly called body language.

You're hiking in the woods when a bear steps onto the trail. What will happen next? Common sense tells us that we will then feel fear, become aroused, and run (and sweat and yell). But is this the true order of events? In the 1880s, William James and Carl Lange (LON-geh) proposed that common sense had it backward. According to the **James-Lange theory,** bodily arousal (such as increased heart rate) does not *follow* a feeling such as fear. Instead, they argued, *emotional feelings follow bodily arousal.* Thus, we see a bear, run, are aroused, and *then* feel fear as we become aware of our bodily reactions (▸▸ Figure 9.22).

To support his ideas, James pointed out that we often do not experience an emotion until after reacting. For example, imagine that you are driving. Suddenly a car pulls out in front of you. You swerve and skid to an abrupt halt. Only then do you notice your pounding heart, rapid breathing, and tense muscles—and recognize your fear.

The Cannon-Bard Theory

Walter Cannon (1932) and Phillip Bard disagreed with the James-Lange theory. According to the **Cannon-Bard theory,** emotional feelings and bodily arousal *occur at the same time.* Cannon and Bard believed that seeing a bear activates the thalamus in the brain. The thalamus, in turn, alerts the cortex and the hypothalamus for action. The cortex produces our emotional feelings and emotional behavior. The hypothalamus triggers a chain of events that arouses the body. Thus, if you see a dangerous-looking bear, brain activity will simultaneously produce bodily arousal, running, and a feeling of fear (Figure 9.22).

Schachter's Cognitive Theory of Emotion

The previous theories are concerned mostly with our physical responses. Stanley Schachter realized that cognitive (mental) factors also enter into emotion. According to **Schachter's cognitive theory,** emotion occurs when we apply a particular *label* to general physiological *arousal.* We likely choose the appropriate label through a process of **attribution,** by deciding which source is leading to the arousal (Valins, 1967).

Assume, for instance, that someone sneaks up behind you on a dark street and says, "Boo!" Your body is now aroused (pounding heart, sweating palms, and so on). If you attribute your arousal to a total stranger, you might label your arousal as fear; if you attribute your arousal to a close friend, you may experience surprise or delight. The label (such as anger, fear, or happiness) you apply to bodily arousal is influenced by your past experiences, the situation, and the reactions of others (Figure 9.22).

Support for the cognitive theory of emotion comes from an experiment in which people watched a slapstick movie (Schachter & Wheeler, 1962). Before viewing the movie, everyone got an injection but no one was told what he or she was injected with. One third

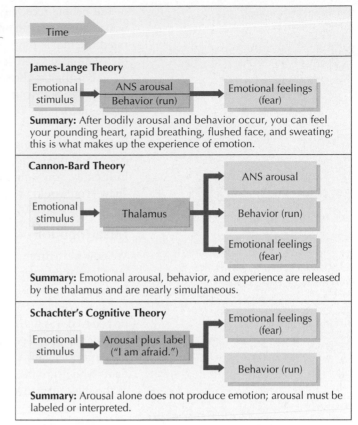

▲ **FIGURE 9.22** Theories of emotion.

Which theory of emotion best describes the reactions of these people? Given the complexity of emotion, each theory appears to possess an element of truth.

James-Lange theory States that emotional feelings follow bodily arousal and come from awareness of such arousal.

Cannon-Bard theory States that activity in the thalamus causes emotional feelings and bodily arousal to occur simultaneously.

Schachter's cognitive theory States that emotions occur when physical arousal is labeled or interpreted on the basis of experience and situational cues.

Attribution The mental process of assigning causes to events. In emotion, the process of attributing arousal to a particular source.

of the people received an arousing injection of adrenaline, one third got a placebo (salt water) injection, and one third was given a tranquilizer. People who received the adrenaline rated the movie funniest and laughed the most while watching it. In contrast, those given the tranquilizer were least amused. The placebo group fell in between.

According to the cognitive theory of emotion, individuals who received adrenaline had a stirred-up body, but no explanation for what they were feeling. By attributing their arousal to the movie, they became happy and amused. This and similar experiments make it clear that emotion is much more than just an agitated body. Perception, experience, attitudes, judgment, and many other mental factors also affect the emotions we feel. Schachter's theory would predict, then, that if you met a bear, you would be aroused. If the bear seemed unfriendly, you would interpret your arousal as fear, and if the bear offered to shake your "paw," you would be happy, amazed, and relieved!

Misattribution

We now move from slapstick movies and fear of bear bodies to an appreciation of bare bodies. There is no guarantee that we always make the correct attributions about our emotions. For example, Valins (1966) showed male college students a series of photographs of nude females. While watching the photographs, each student heard an amplified heartbeat that he believed was his own. In reality, students were listening to a recorded heartbeat carefully designed to beat *louder* and *stronger* when some (but not all) of the slides were shown.

After watching the slides, each student was asked to say which was most attractive. Students who heard the false heartbeat consistently rated slides paired with a "pounding heart" as the most attractive. In other words, when a student saw a slide and heard his heart beat louder, he attributed his "emotion" to the slide. His attribution seems to have been, "Now that one I like!" His next reaction, perhaps, was "But why?" Later research suggests that subjects persuaded themselves that the slide really was more attractive in order to explain their apparent arousal (Truax, 1983).

That seems somewhat artificial. Does it really make any difference what arousal is attributed to? Yes. Attribution theory predicts that you are most likely to "love" someone who gets you stirred up emotionally (Foster et al., 1998). This is true even when fear, anger, frustration, or rejection is part of the formula. Thus, if you want to successfully propose marriage, take your intended to the middle of a narrow, windswept suspension bridge over a deep chasm and look deeply into his or her eyes. As your beloved's heart pounds wildly (from being on the bridge, not from your irresistible charms), say, "I love you." Attribution theory predicts that your companion will conclude, "Oh wow, I must love you too."

The preceding is not as far-fetched as it may seem. In an ingenious study, a female psychologist interviewed men in a park. Some were on a swaying suspension bridge 230 feet above a river. The rest were on a solid wooden bridge just 10 feet above the ground. After the interview, the psychologist gave each man her telephone number, so he could "find out about the results" of the study. Men interviewed on the suspension bridge were much more likely to give the "lady from the park" a call (Dutton & Aron, 1974). Apparently, these men experienced heightened arousal, which they misinterpreted as attraction to the experimenter—a clear case of love at first fright!

Emotional Appraisal

According to Richard Lazarus (1991a, 1991b), the role of cognition in experiencing emotions is not restricted to making attributions about arousal *after* it has occurred. Rather, emotions you experience are greatly influenced by how you think about an event *in the first place*. **Emotional appraisal** refers to evaluating the personal meaning of a stimulus: Is it good/bad, threatening/supportive, relevant/irrelevant, and so on. Some examples of emotional appraisals and the emotions they give rise to can be found in ● Table 9.2.

● Table 9.2 Appraisals and Corresponding Emotions

APPRAISAL	EMOTION
You have been slighted or demeaned.	Anger
You feel threatened.	Anxiety
You have experienced a loss.	Sadness
You have broken a moral rule.	Guilt
You have not lived up to your ideals.	Shame
You desire something another has.	Envy
You are near something repulsive.	Disgust
You fear the worst but yearn for better.	Hope
You are moving toward a desired goal.	Happiness
You are linked with a valued object or accomplishment.	Pride
You have been treated well by another.	Gratitude
You desire affection from another person.	Love
You are moved by someone's suffering.	Compassion

Source: Paraphrased from Lazarus, 1991a.

Emotional appraisal Evaluating the personal meaning of a stimulus or situation.

The Facial Feedback Hypothesis

Schachter and Lazarus added thinking and interpretation (cognition) to our view of emotion, but the picture still seems incomplete. What about expressions? How do they influence emotion? As Charles Darwin observed, the face is very central to emotion—perhaps it is more than just an "emotional billboard."

Psychologist Carrol Izard (1977, 1990) was among the first to suggest that the face does, indeed, affect emotion. According to Izard, emotions cause innately programmed changes in facial expression. Sensations from the face then provide cues to the brain that help us determine what emotion we are feeling. This idea is known as the **facial feedback hypothesis** (Soussignan, 2002). Stated another way, it says that having facial expressions and becoming aware of them influences our private emotional experience. Exercise, for instance, arouses the body, but we don't experience this arousal as emotion because it does not trigger emotional expressions.

Psychologist Paul Ekman takes this idea one step further. He believes that "making faces" can actually cause emotion (Ekman, 1993). In one study, participants were guided as they arranged their faces, muscle by muscle, into expressions of surprise, disgust, sadness, anger, fear, and happiness (▶▶ Figure 9.23). At the same time, each person's bodily reactions were monitored.

Contrary to what you might expect, "making faces" can affect the autonomic nervous system, as shown by changes in heart rate and skin temperature. In addition, each facial expression produces a different pattern of activity. An angry face, for instance, raises heart rate and skin temperature, whereas disgust lowers both (Ekman, Levenson, & Friesen, 1983). Other studies have confirmed that posed expressions alter emotions and bodily activity (Duclos & Laird, 2001; Soussignan, 2002).

In a fascinating experiment on facial feedback, people rated how funny they thought cartoons were while holding a pen crosswise in their mouths. Those who held the pen in their teeth thought the cartoons were funnier than did people who held the pen in their lips. Can you guess why? The answer is that if you hold a pen with your teeth, you are forced to form a smile. Holding it with the lips makes a frown. As predicted by the facial feedback hypothesis, emotional experiences were influenced by the facial expressions that people made (Strack, Martin, & Stepper, 1988). Next time you're feeling sad, bite a pen!

It appears, then, that not only do emotions influence expressions, but expressions influence emotions, as shown here (Duclos & Laird, 2001):

Contracted Facial Muscles	Felt Emotion
Forehead	Surprise
Brow	Anger
Mouth (down)	Sadness
Mouth (smile)	Joy

Dennis Coon

▲ **FIGURE 9.23** Facial feedback and emotion. Participants in Ekman's study formed facial expressions like those normally observed during emotion. When they did this, emotion-like changes took place in their bodily activity. (After Ekman, Levenson, & Friesen, 1983.)

Facial feedback hypothesis States that sensations from facial expressions help define what emotion a person feels.

Suppressing Emotion—Don't Turn the Music Off

According to popular media, we are supposed to be happy all the time (Hecht, 2007). Yet real emotional life has its ups and downs. Often we try to appear less emotional than we really are, especially when we are feeling negative emotions. Have you ever been angry with a friend in public? Embarrassed by someone's behavior at a party? Disgusted by someone's table manners? In such circumstances, people are quite good at suppressing outward signs of emotion.

However, restraining emotion can actually increase activity in the sympathetic nervous sys-

tem. In other words, hiding emotion requires a lot of effort. Suppressing emotions can also impair thinking and memory, as you devote energy to self-control. Thus, while suppressing emotion allows us to appear calm and collected on the outside, this cool appearance comes at a high cost (Richards & Gross, 2000). People who constantly suppress their emotions cope poorly with life and are prone to depression and other problems (Lynch et al., 2001).

Conversely, people who express their emotions generally experience better emotional and

physical health (Lumley, 2004; Pennebaker, 2004). Paying attention to our negative emotions can also lead us to think more clearly about the positive *and* the negative. The end result is better decision making, which can increase our overall happiness in the long run (Norem, 2002). Usually, it's better to manage emotions than it is to suppress them. You will find some suggestions for managing emotions in the upcoming "Psychology in Action" section.

This could explain an interesting effect you have probably observed. When you are feeling "down," forcing yourself to smile will sometimes be followed by an actual improvement in your mood (Kleinke, Peterson, & Rutledge, 1998).

If smiling can improve a person's mood, is it a good idea to inhibit negative emotions? For an answer, see "Suppressing Emotion—Don't Turn the Music Off."

FIGURE 9.24 A contemporary model of emotion. Appraisal gives rise to arousal and cognitive labeling, behavior, facial/postural expressions, and emotional feelings. Arousal, attribution, behavior, and expressions add to emotional feelings. Emotional feelings influence appraisal, which further affects arousal, behavior, expressions, and feelings.

A Contemporary Model of Emotion

To summarize, James and Lange were right that feedback from arousal and behavior adds to our emotional experiences. Cannon and Bard were right about the timing of events. Schachter showed us that cognition is important. In fact, psychologists are increasingly aware that how you *appraise* a situation greatly affects your emotions (Strongman, 2003). Richard Lazarus stressed the importance of emotional appraisal. Carrol Izard focused on facial expressions. Let's put these ideas together in a single model of emotion (▶▶ Figure 9.24).

Imagine that a large snarling dog lunges at you with its teeth bared. A modern view of your emotional reactions goes something like this: An *emotional stimulus* (the dog) is *appraised* (judged) as a threat or other cause for emotion (You think to yourself, "Uh oh, big trouble!"). Your appraisal gives rise to *ANS arousal* (your heart pounds and your body becomes stirred up) and *cognitive labeling*. At the same time, your appraisal leads to *adaptive behavior* (you run from the dog). The appraisal also releases *innate emotional expressions* (your face twists into a mask of fear and your posture becomes tense). It also causes a change in consciousness that you recognize as the subjective experience of fear. (The intensity of this *emotional feeling* is directly related to the amount of ANS arousal taking place in your body.)

Each element of emotion—ANS arousal, labeling, adaptive behavior, subjective experience, and your emotional expressions—may further alter your emotional appraisal of the situation, as well as your thoughts, judgments, and perceptions. Thus, according to the facial feedback hypothesis, your facial expression may further influence your emotion. Such changes affect each of the other reactions, which again alters your appraisal and interpretation of events. Thus, emotion may blossom, change course, or diminish as it proceeds. Note too that the original emotional stimulus can be external, like the attacking dog, or internal, such as a memory of being chased by a dog, rejected by a lover, or praised by a friend. That's why mere thoughts and memories can make us fearful, sad, or happy (Strongman, 2003).

A Look Ahead

In the Psychology in Action section of this chapter we will look further at the impact of emotional appraisals through an examination of *emotional intelligence*. Before we continue, you might want to appraise your learning with the exercises that follow.

Emotional Expression and Theories of Emotion

RECITE

1. Charles Darwin held that emotional expressions aid survival for animals. T or F?
2. A formal term for "body language" is _____.
3. Which three dimensions of emotion are communicated by facial expressions?
   a. pleasantness–unpleasantness
   b. complexity
   c. attention–rejection
   d. anger
   e. curiosity–disinterest
   f. activation
4. According to the James-Lange theory, emotional experience precedes physical arousal and emotional behavior. (We see a bear, are frightened, and run.) T or F?
5. The Cannon-Bard theory of emotion says that bodily arousal and emotional experience occur _____.
6. According to Schachter's cognitive theory, bodily arousal must be labeled or interpreted for an emotional experience to occur. T or F?
7. As you try to wiggle your ears, you keep pulling the corners of your mouth back into a smile. Each time you do, you find yourself giggling. Which of the following provides the best explanation for this reaction?
   a. attribution
   b. the Cannon-Bard theory
   c. appraisal
   d. facial feedback

REFLECT

Critical Thinking

8. People with high spinal injuries may feel almost no signs of physiological arousal from their bodies. Nevertheless they still feel emotion, which can be intense at times. What theory of emotion does this observation contradict?

Relate

Write a list of emotions that you think you can accurately detect from facial expressions. Does your list match Paul Ekman's? Would you be more confident in rating pleasantness–unpleasantness, attention–rejection, and activation? Why?

Try frowning or smiling for 5 minutes. Did facial feedback have any effect on your mood?

Cover the left column of Table 9.2. Read each emotional label in the right column. What appraisal do you think would lead to the listed emotion?

ANSWERS

1. T 2. kinesics 3. a, c, f 4. F 5. simultaneously 6. T 7. d 8. The James-Lange theory and Schachter's cognitive theory. The facial feedback hypothesis also helps explain the observation.

---

psychology in action

Emotional Intelligence—The Fine Art of Self-Control

What does it mean to have "emotional intelligence"?

The Greek philosopher Aristotle had a recipe for handling relationships smoothly: "Be angry with the right person, to the right degree, at the right time, for the right purpose, and in the right way." Psychologists Peter Salovey and John Mayer call such self-control **emotional intelligence,** the ability to perceive, use, understand, and manage emotions (Salovey & Mayer, 1997). In general, being emotionally intelligent means accepting that emotions are an essential part of who we are and how we survive. Being emotionally skilled can make us more flexible, adaptable, and emotionally mature (Bonanno et al., 2004).

People who excel in life tend to be emotionally intelligent (Mehrabian, 2000). If our emotions are the music of life, then emotionally intelligent people are good musicians. They do not stifle their emotions or overindulge in them. Instead they compose them into sustaining life rhythms that mesh well with other people. They are more *agreeable* than people with low emotional skills (Haas et al., 2007).

Emotional intelligence Emotional competence, including empathy, self-control, self-awareness, and other skills.

Peter Beavis/Getty Images

Indeed, the costs of poor emotional skills can be high. They range from problems in marriage and parenting to poor physical health. A lack of emotional intelligence can ruin careers and sabotage achievement. Perhaps the greatest toll falls on children and teenagers. For them, having poor emotional skills can contribute to depression, eating disorders, unwanted pregnancy, aggression, violent crime, and poor academic performance (Parker, 2005). Thus, in many life circumstances, emotional intelligence is as important as IQ (Dulewicz & Higgs, 2000).

Are there specific skills that make up emotional intelligence? Many elements contribute to emotional intelligence (Larsen & Prizmic, 2004; Mayer et al., 2001). A description of some of the most important skills follows:

Perceiving Emotions The foundation of emotional intelligence is the ability to perceive emotions in yourself and others. Unlike alexithymic people such as Robert, emotionally intelligent people are tuned in to their own feelings (Taylor & Taylor-Allan, 2007). They are able to recognize quickly if they are angry, envious, feeling guilty, or depressed. This is valuable because many people have disruptive emotions without being able to pinpoint why they are uncomfortable. At the same time, emotionally intelligent people have *empathy*. They accurately perceive emotions in others and sense what others are feeling. They are good at "reading" facial expressions, tone of voice, and other signs of emotion.

Using Emotions People who are emotionally intelligent use their feelings to enhance thinking and decision making. For example, if you can remember how you reacted emotionally in the past, it can help you react better to new situations. You can also use emotions to promote personal growth and improve relationships with others. For instance, you may have noticed that helping someone else makes you feel better, too. Likewise, when good fortune comes their way, people who are emotionally smart share the news with others. Almost always, doing so strengthens relationships and increases emotional well-being (Gable et al., 2004).

Understanding Emotions Emotions contain useful information. For instance, anger is a cue that something is wrong; anxiety indicates uncertainty; embarrassment communicates shame; depression means we feel helpless; enthusiasm tells us we're excited. People who are emotionally intelligent know what causes various emotions, what they mean, and how they affect behavior.

Managing Emotions Emotional intelligence involves an ability to manage your own emotions and those of others. For example, you know how to calm down when you are angry and you also know how to calm others. As Aristotle noted so long ago, people who are emotionally intelligent have an ability to amplify or restrain emotions, depending on the situation (Bonanno et al., 2004).

Positive Psychology and Your Emotions

It's obvious that joy, interest, contentment, love, and similar emotions are pleasant and rewarding. There is a natural tendency to enjoy positive emotions while treating negative emotions as unwelcome misery. Make no mistake, though. Negative emotions can also be valuable and constructive. For example, persistent distress may motivate a person to seek help, mend a relationship, or find a new direction in life (Plutchik, 2003). Negative emotions are associated with actions that probably helped our ancestors save their skins: escaping, attacking, expelling poison, and the like. As useful as these reactions may be, they tend to narrow our focus of attention and limit our ideas about possible actions.

In contrast, positive emotions tend to broaden our focus (Fredrickson & Branigan, 2005). This opens up new possibilities and builds up our personal resources. For instance, emotions such as joy, interest, and contentment create an urge to play, to be creative, to explore, to savor life, to seek new experiences, to integrate, and to grow.

In short, positive emotions are not just a pleasant side effect of happy circumstances. They also encourage personal growth and social connection. Happiness can be cultivated by using the strengths we already possess—including kindness, originality, humor, optimism, and generosity. Such strengths are natural buffers against misfortune, and they can help people live more positive, genuinely happy lives (Seligman, 2002). A capacity for having positive emotions is a basic human strength, and cultivating good feelings is a part of emotional intelligence (Fredrickson, 2003).

Becoming Emotionally Smart

How would a person learn the skills that make up emotional intelligence? Emotional skills can be learned. Accepting that emotions are valuable is an important first step. There are many valuable lessons to learn from paying close attention to your emotions and the emotions of others. It's a good bet that many of the people you admire the most are not just smart, but also emotionally smart. They are people who know how to offer a toast at a wedding, tell a joke at a roast, comfort the bereaved at a funeral, add to the fun at a party, or calm a frightened child. These are skills worth cultivating.

study break
Emotional Intelligence

RECITE

1. People who rate high in emotional intelligence tend to be highly aware of their own feelings and unaware of emotions experienced by others. T or F?
2. Using the information imparted by emotional reactions can enhance thinking and decision making. T or F?
3. Positive emotions may be pleasant, but they tend to narrow our focus of attention and limit the range of possible actions we are likely to consider. T or F?
4. Which of the following is *not* an element of emotional intelligence?
   a. empathy
   b. self-control
   c. misattribution
   d. self-awareness

REFLECT

Critical Thinking

5. You are angry because a friend borrowed money from you and hasn't repaid it. What would be an emotionally intelligent response to this situation?

Relate

Think of a person you know who is smart, but low in emotional intelligence. Think of another person who is smart cognitively *and* emotionally. How does the second person differ from the first? Which person do you think would make a better parent, friend, supervisor, roommate, or teacher?

ANSWERS

1. F 2. T 3. F 4. c 5. There's no single right answer. Rather than being angry, it might be better to reflect on whether friendship or money is more important in life. If you appreciate your friend's virtues, accept that no one is perfect, and reappraise the loan as a gift, you could save a valued relationship and reduce your anger at the same time. Alternately, if you become aware that your friend persistently manipulates other people with emotional appeals for support, it may be worth reappraising your friendship.

chapter in review

Major Points

- Motives and goals greatly influence what we do and how we expend our energies.

- The brain monitors various internal signals to control basic motives, such as hunger and thirst.

- Motivated behavior is also influenced by learned habits, external cues, and cultural values.

- Many activities are related to needs for stimulation and our efforts to maintain desired levels of arousal.

- Emotions can be disruptive, but overall they help us to adapt and survive.

- Emotional intelligence involves managing emotions, not suppressing them.

Summary

What is motivation? Are there different types of motives?

- Motives initiate, sustain, direct, and terminate activities. Motivation typically involves the sequence: need, drive, goal, and goal attainment (need reduction).
- Behavior can be activated either by needs (push) or by goals (pull).
- The attractiveness of a goal and its ability to initiate action are related to its incentive value.
- Three principal types of motives are biological motives, stimulus motives, and learned motives.
- Most primary motives operate to maintain homeostasis.
- Circadian rhythms are closely tied to sleep, activity, and energy cycles. Time zone travel and shift work can seriously disrupt motivation, sleep, and bodily rhythms.

What causes hunger? Overeating? Eating disorders?

- Hunger is influenced by a complex interplay between fullness of the stomach, blood sugar levels, metabolism in the liver, and fat stores in the body.
- The most direct control of eating is effected by the hypothalamus, which has areas that act like feeding and satiety systems. The hypothalamus is sensitive to both neural and chemical messages, which affect eating.
- Other factors influencing hunger are the body's set point, external eating cues, the attractiveness and variety of diet, emotions, learned taste preferences and aversions, and cultural values.
- Obesity is the result of internal and external influences, diet, emotions, genetics, and exercise.
- The most effective way to lose weight is behavioral dieting, which is based on techniques that change eating patterns and exercise habits.
- Anorexia nervosa and bulimia nervosa are two prominent eating disorders. Both tend to involve conflicts about self-image, self-control, and anxiety.

Is there more than one type of thirst? In what ways are pain avoidance and the sex drive unusual?

- Like hunger, thirst and other basic motives are primarily under the central control of the hypothalamus.
- Thirst may be either intracellular or extracellular.

- Pain avoidance is unusual because it is episodic as opposed to cyclic. Pain avoidance and pain tolerance are partially learned.
- The sex drive is also unusual because it is nonhomeostatic.

What are the typical patterns of human sexual response?

- Sexual arousal is related to the body's erogenous zones, but mental and emotional reactions are the ultimate source of sexual responsiveness.
- Human sexual response can be divided into four phases: excitement, plateau, orgasm, and resolution.
- Overall, male and female sexual responses are similar. However, males experience a refractory period after orgasm, and only 5 percent of men are multiorgasmic. Fifteen percent of women are multiorgasmic.
- Sexual orientation refers to one's degree of emotional and erotic attraction to members of the same sex, opposite sex, or both sexes.
- A combination of hereditary, biological, social, and psychological influences combine to produce one's sexual orientation.

How does arousal relate to motivation?

- Drives for stimulation are partially explained by arousal theory, which states that an ideal level of bodily arousal will be maintained if possible.
- The desired level of arousal or stimulation varies from person to person.
- Optimal performance usually occurs at *moderate* levels of arousal, as described by an inverted U function. The Yerkes-Dodson law further states that for simple tasks, the ideal arousal level is higher, and for complex tasks it is lower.

What are social motives? Why are they important?

- Social motives are learned through socialization and cultural conditioning.
- Such motives account for much of the diversity of human motivation.
- A high need for achievement (nAch) is correlated with success in many situations, with career choice, and with *moderate* risk taking.
- Self-confidence greatly affects motivation in everyday life.

Are some motives more basic than others?

- Maslow's hierarchy of motives categorizes needs as either basic or growth oriented. Lower needs are assumed to be prepotent (dominant) over higher needs. Self-actualization, the highest and most fragile need, is reflected in meta-needs.
- Meta-needs are closely related to intrinsic motivation. In some situations, external rewards can undermine intrinsic motivation, enjoyment, and creativity.

What happens during emotion?

- An emotion consists of physiological changes, adaptive behavior, emotional expressions, and emotional feelings.
- The primary emotions of fear, surprise, sadness, disgust, anger, anticipation, joy, and acceptance can be mixed to produce more complex emotional experiences.
- The left hemisphere of the brain primarily processes positive emotions. Negative emotions are processed in the right hemisphere.
- The amygdala provides a "quick and dirty" pathway for the arousal of fear that bypasses the cerebral cortex.

What physiological changes underlie emotion? Can "lie detectors" really detect lies?

- Physical changes associated with emotion are caused by the hormone adrenaline and by activity in the autonomic nervous system (ANS).
- The sympathetic branch of the ANS is responsible primarily for arousing the body; the parasympathetic branch, for quieting it.
- The polygraph, or "lie detector," measures emotional arousal (rather than lying) by monitoring heart rate, blood pressure, breathing rate, and the galvanic skin response (GSR).
- The accuracy of the lie detector can be quite low.

How accurately are emotions expressed by the face and "body language"?

- Basic facial expressions of fear, anger, disgust, sadness, and happiness are universally recognized.
- Facial expressions reveal pleasantness versus unpleasantness, attention versus rejection, and a person's degree of emotional activation.
- The formal study of body language is known as kinesics. Body gestures and movements (body language) also express feelings, mainly by communicating emotional tone rather than specific universal messages.
- Body positioning expresses relaxation or tension and liking or disliking.

How do psychologists explain emotions?

- The James-Lange theory says that emotional experience follows bodily reactions. In contrast, the Cannon-Bard theory says that bodily reactions and emotional experiences occur at the same time.
- Schachter's cognitive theory emphasizes that labeling bodily arousal can determine what emotion you feel. Appropriate labels are chosen by attribution (ascribing arousal to a particular source).
- Contemporary views of emotion place greater emphasis on the effects of emotional appraisals.
- The facial feedback hypothesis holds that facial expressions help define the emotions we feel.
- Contemporary views of emotion emphasize that all of the elements of emotion are interrelated and interact with each other.

What does it mean to have "emotional intelligence"?

- Emotional intelligence is the ability to consciously make your emotions work for you in a wide variety of life circumstances.
- People who are "smart" emotionally are self-aware and empathetic; know how to use emotions to enhance thinking, decision making, and relationships; and have an ability to understand and manage emotions.
- Positive emotions are valuable because they tend to broaden our focus and they encourage personal growth and social connection.

Motivation and Emotion

For additional review, get more practice with *CengageNOW*, *WebTutor*, the *Practice Quizzes*, and/or the printed *Study Guide* available with this book.

1. Human needs for activity and exploration are an expression of
   a. learned motives
   b. biological motives
   c. incentive values
   d. stimulus motives

2. Desirable goals are motivating because they are high in
   a. secondary value
   b. stimulus value
   c. homeostatic value
   d. incentive value

3. The term *jet lag* is commonly used to refer to disruptions of
   a. the inverted U function
   b. circadian rhythms
   c. any of the episodic drives
   d. the body's set point

4. A feeding system exists in the _____ _____ of the brain.
   a. medial leptothalamus
   b. ventral paraventriculum
   c. lateral hypothalamus
   d. leptothalamic nucleus

5. Maintaining your body's set point for fat is closely linked with the amount of _____ in the bloodstream.
   a. hypothalamic factor-1
   b. ventromedial peptide-1
   c. NPY
   d. leptin

6. Chronic self-starvation is most characteristic of people who have
   a. taste aversions
   b. anorexia
   c. bulimia
   d. strong sensitivity to external eating cues

7. In addition to changing eating habits, a key element of behavioral dieting is
   a. exercise
   b. well-timed snacking
   c. better eating cues
   d. commitment to "starving" every day

8. One thing that men and women have in common is that their sex drive is
   a. affected by androgens
   b. extracellular
   c. controlled by estrogen
   d. homeostatic and episodic

9. The typical phases of human sexual arousal are
   a. estrus, refractory period, orgasm, resolution
   b. excitement, orgasm, resolution, refractory period
   c. estrus, orgasm, plateau, resolution
   d. excitement, plateau, orgasm, resolution

10. Sensate focus is a technique used to treat
    a. estrus disorders in men
    b. bulimia nervosa
    c. excessive weight cycling
    d. sexual disorders

11. Which of the following is NOT a characteristic of people who are sensation seekers?
    a. boredom susceptibility
    b. experience seeking
    c. inhibition
    d. thrill seeking

12. Complex tasks, such as taking a classroom test, tend to be disrupted by high levels of arousal, an effect predicted by
    a. the Sensation-Seeking Scale
    b. the Yerkes-Dodson law
    c. studies of circadian arousal patterns
    d. studies of the need for achievement

13. People high in nAch
    a. prefer long shots
    b. prefer sure things
    c. are moderate risk takers
    d. prefer change and high levels of stimulation

14. The highest level of Maslow's hierarchy of motives involves
    a. meta-needs
    b. needs for safety and security
    c. needs for love and belonging
    d. extrinsic needs

15. Polygraph operators try to use which component of emotion to detect deception?
    a. adaptive behaviors
    b. physiological changes
    c. emotional expressions
    d. the parasympathetic rebound

16. Preparing the body for "fighting or fleeing" is largely the job of the
    a. paraventricular nucleus
    b. sympathetic branch
    c. GSR
    d. androgens

17. The idea that labeling arousal helps define what emotions we experience is associated with
    a. the James-Lange theory
    b. Schachter's cognitive theory
    c. the Cannon-Bard theory
    d. Darwin's theory of innate emotional expressions

18. Holding a pen crosswise in your mouth is likely to improve your mood, a result predicted by
    a. the Cannon-Bard theory
    b. attribution theory
    c. the facial-feedback hypothesis
    d. Schachter's cognitive theory

19. Emotionally intelligent people have which of the following skills?
    a. empathy
    b. self-awareness
    c. understanding of emotions
    d. all three of the previously mentioned skills

20. One benefit of positive emotions is the capacity to
    a. broaden our focus
    b. limit our ideas about possible actions
    c. narrow our focus
    d. help our ancestors escape attack

Answers   1. d 2. d 3. b 4. c 5. d 6. b 7. a 8. a 9. d 10. d 11. c 12. b 13. c 14. a 15. b 16. b 17. b 18. c 19. d 20. a

Personality

Journey into Psychology: The Hidden Essence

Rural Colorado. The car banged over one last, brain-jarring rut and lurched toward the dilapidated farmhouse. Annette awaited one of your authors on the porch, hooting and whooping and obviously happy to see an old friend arrive.

If anyone was suited for a move to the "wilds" of Colorado, it was Annette, a strong and resourceful woman. Still, it was hard to imagine a more radical change. After separating from her husband, she had traded a comfortable life in the city for rough times in the high country. Annette was working as a ranch hand and a lumberjack (lumberjill?), trying to make it through some hard winters. She had

even recently decked a guy twice her size who was harassing her in a tavern. Nevertheless, the changes in Annette's life were radical and we worried that she might be entirely different. She was, on the contrary, more her "old self" than ever.

Perhaps you have had a similar experience. After several years of separation, it is always intriguing to see an old friend. At first you may be struck by how the person has changed ("Where did you get that haircut!?"). Soon, however, you will probably be delighted to discover that the semi-stranger before you is still the person you once knew. It is exactly this

core of consistency that psychologists have in mind when they use the term *personality*.

Without doubt, personality touches our daily lives. Falling in love, choosing friends, getting along with coworkers, voting for a president, or coping with your zaniest relatives all raise questions about personality.

What is personality? How does it differ from temperament, character, or attitudes? Is it possible to measure personality? Can we change our personality? We'll address these questions and more in this chapter.

Survey Questions

- How do psychologists use the term *personality*?
- Are some personality traits more basic or important than others?
- How do psychodynamic theories explain personality?
- What do behaviorists and social learning theorists emphasize in their approach to personality?
- How do humanistic theories differ from other perspectives?
- How do traits and situations affect personality?
- How do psychologists measure personality?
- What causes shyness? What can be done about it?

The Psychology of Personality— Do You Have Personality?

How do psychologists use the term personality?

"Annette has a very optimistic personality." "Ramiro's not handsome, but he has a great personality." "My father's business friends think he's a nice guy. They should see him at home where his real personality comes out." "It's hard to believe Tanya and Nikki are sisters. They have such opposite personalities."

It's obvious that we all frequently use the term *personality.* But if you think that personality means "charm," "charisma," or "style," you have misused the term. Many people also confuse personality with the term **character,** which implies that a person has been evaluated, not just described (Skipton, 1997). If, by saying someone has "personality," you mean the person is friendly, outgoing, and upstanding, you are describing what we regard as good character in our culture. But in some cultures it is deemed good for people to be fierce, warlike, and cruel.

Psychologists regard **personality** as a person's unique long-term pattern of thinking, emotions, and behavior (Burger, 2008; Mischel, 2004). In other words, personality refers to the consistency in who you are, have been, and will become. It also refers to the special blend of talents, values, hopes, loves, hates, and habits that makes each of us a unique person. So, everyone in a particular culture has personality, whereas not everyone has character—or at least not good character. (Do you know any good characters?)

Psychologists use a large number of models and concepts to explain personality. It might be wise, therefore, to start with a few key concepts. These ideas should help you keep your bearings as you read this chapter.

Traits

We use the idea of traits every day to talk about personality. For instance, Allan is *sociable, orderly,* and *intelligent.* His sister Kayla is *shy, sensitive,* and *creative.* As we observed in our reunion with Annette, personality traits like these can be quite stable (Gustavsson et al., 1997; Engler, 2009). Think about how little your best friends have changed in the last 5 years. It would be strange indeed to feel like you were talking with a different person every time you met a friend or an acquaintance. In general, then, **personality traits** like these are stable qualities that a person shows in most situations (Matthews, Deary, & Whiteman, 2003). As you will see when you read further into this chapter, there is considerable debate about just *why* traits are stable qualities. But more about that later.

Typically, traits are inferred from behavior. If you see Allan talking to strangers—first at a supermarket and later at a party—you might deduce that he is "sociable." Once person-

Does this man have personality? Do you?

Psychologists and employers are especially interested in the personality traits of individuals who hold high-risk, high-stress positions involving public safety, such as police, air-traffic controllers, and nuclear power plant employees.

Character Personal characteristics that have been judged or evaluated; a person's desirable or undesirable qualities.

Personality A person's unique and relatively stable behavior patterns.

Personality trait A stable, enduring quality that a person shows in most situations.

ality traits are identified, they can be used to predict future behavior. For example, noting that Allan is outgoing might lead you to predict that he will be sociable at school or at work. In fact, such consistencies can span many years. A study of women who appeared to be happy in their college yearbook photos (they had genuine smiles) found that most were still happy people 30 years later (Harker & Keltner, 2001).

Traits even influence our health as well as our marital and occupational success (Roberts et al., 2007). For example, who do you think will be more successful in her chosen career: Jane, who is conscientious, or Sally, who is not (Chamorro-Premuzic & Furnham, 2003)?

Types

Have you ever asked the question, "What type of person is she (or he)?" A **personality type** refers to people who have *several traits in common* (Larsen & Buss, 2005). Informally, your own thinking might include categories such as the executive type, the athletic type, the motherly type, the hip-hop type, the techno geek, and so forth. If you tried to define these informal types, you would probably list a different collection of traits for each one.

How valid is it to speak of personality "types"? Over the years, psychologists have proposed many ways to categorize personalities into types. For example, Swiss psychiatrist Carl Jung (yoong) proposed that people are either *introverts* or *extroverts*. An **introvert** is a shy, reserved person whose attention is usually focused inward. An **extrovert** is a bold, outgoing person whose attention is usually directed outward. These terms are so widely used that you may think of yourself and your friends as being one type or the other. However, knowing if someone is extroverted or introverted tells you little about how conscientious she is, or how kind or open to new ideas he is. In short, two categories (or even several) are often inadequate to fully capture differences in personality. That's why rating people on a list of traits tends to be more informative than classifying them into two or three types (Engler, 2009).

Even though types tend to oversimplify personality, they do have value. Most often, types are a shorthand way of labeling people who have several key traits in common. For example, in the next chapter we will discuss Type A and Type B personalities. Type A's are people who have personality traits that increase their chance of suffering a heart attack; Type B's take a more laid-back approach to life (see ▶▶ Figure 10.1). Similarly, you will read in Chapter 12 about unhealthy personality types such as the paranoid personality, the dependent personality, and the antisocial personality. Each problem type is defined by a specific collection of maladaptive traits.

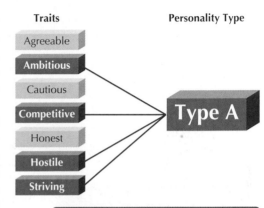

▲ **FIGURE 10.1** Personality types are defined by the presence of several specific traits. For example, several possible personality traits are shown in the left column. A person who has a Type A personality typically possesses all or most of the highlighted traits. Type A persons are especially prone to heart disease (see Chapter 11).

Self-Concept

Self-concepts provide another way of understanding personality. The rough outlines of your self-concept could be revealed by this request: "Please tell us about yourself." In other words, your **self-concept** consists of all your ideas, perceptions, stories, and feelings about who you are. It is the mental "picture" you have of your own personality (Swann, Chang-Schneider, & Larsen McClarty, 2007).

We creatively build our self-concepts out of daily experiences. Then we slowly revise them as we have new experiences.

Matt Cardy/Getty Images

Self-concepts can be remarkably consistent. In an interesting study, old people were asked how they had changed over the years. Almost all thought they were essentially the same person they were when they were young (Troll & Skaff, 1997). Mick Jagger, for example, has been the charismatic and passionate lead singer of the Rolling Stones for over 40 years.

Personality type A style of personality defined by a group of related traits.

Introvert A person whose attention is focused inward; a shy, reserved, self-centered person.

Extrovert A person whose attention is directed outward; a bold, outgoing person.

Self-concept A person's perception of his or her own personality traits.

Self-Esteem and Culture—Hotshot or Team Player?!

You and some friends are playing soccer. Your team wins, in part because you make some good plays. After the game, you bask in the glow of having performed well. You don't want to brag about being a hotshot, but your self-esteem gets a boost from your personal success.

In Japan, Shinobu and some of his friends are playing soccer. His team wins, in part because he makes some good plays. After the game Shinobu is happy because his team did well. However, Shinobu also dwells on the ways in which he let his team down. He thinks about how he could improve, and he resolves to be a better team player.

These sketches illustrate a basic difference in Eastern and Western psychology. In individualistic cultures such as the United States, self-esteem is based on personal success and outstanding performance (Lay & Verkuyten, 1999). For us, the path to higher self-esteem lies in self-enhancement. We are pumped up by our successes and tend to downplay our faults and failures (Ross et al., 2005).

Japanese and other Asian cultures place a greater emphasis on collectivism or interdependence among people. For them, self-esteem is based on a secure sense of belonging to social groups. As a result, people in Asian cultures are more apt to engage in self-criticism (Ross et al., 2005). By correcting personal faults, they add to the well-being of the group (Kitayama, Markus, & Kurokawa, 2000). And, when the *group* succeeds, individual members feel better about themselves, which raises their self-esteem.

Perhaps self-esteem is still based on success in both Eastern and Western cultures. However, it is fascinating that cultures define success in such different ways (Schmitt & Allik, 2005). The North American emphasis on winning is not the only way to feel good about yourself.

Once a stable self-concept exists, it tends to guide what we pay attention to, remember, and think about. Because of this, self-concepts can greatly affect our behavior and personal adjustment—especially when they are inaccurate (Ryckman, 2008). For instance, Alesha is a student who thinks she is stupid, worthless, and a failure, despite getting good grades. With such an inaccurate self-concept, she tends to be depressed regardless of how well she does.

Self-Esteem

Note that in addition to having a faulty self-concept, Alesha has low **self-esteem** (a negative self-evaluation). A person with high self-esteem is confident, proud, and self-respecting. One who has low self-esteem is insecure, lacking in confidence, and self-critical. Like Alesha, people with low self-esteem are usually anxious and unhappy. People who have low self-esteem typically also suffer from poor self-knowledge. Their self-concepts are inconsistent, inaccurate, and confused. Problems of this type are explored later in this chapter.

Self-esteem tends to rise when we experience success or praise. A person who is competent and effective and who is loved, admired, and respected by others will almost always have high self-esteem (Baumeister et al., 2003). (The reasons for having high self-esteem can vary in different cultures. See "Self-Esteem and Culture" for more information.)

What if you "think you're hot," but you're not? Genuine self-esteem is based on an accurate appraisal of your strengths and weaknesses. A positive self-evaluation that is bestowed too easily may not be healthy (Twenge & Campbell, 2001). People who think very highly of themselves (and let others know it) may at first seem confident, but their arrogance quickly turns off other people (Paulhus, 1998).

Personality Theories

As you can already see, it would be easy to get lost without a framework for understanding personality. How do our thoughts, actions, and feelings relate to one another? How does personality develop? Why do some people suffer from psychological problems? How can they be helped? To answer such questions, psychologists have created a dazzling array of theories. A **personality theory** is a system of concepts, assumptions, ideas, and principles proposed to explain personality (▶▶ Figure 10.2). In this chapter, we can explore only a few of the many personality theories. These are the four major perspectives we will consider:

1. **Trait theories** attempt to learn what traits make up personality and how they relate to actual behavior.
2. **Psychodynamic theories** focus on the inner workings of personality, especially internal conflicts and struggles.

Self-esteem Regarding oneself as a worthwhile person; a positive evaluation of oneself.

Personality theory A system of concepts, assumptions, ideas, and principles used to understand and explain personality.

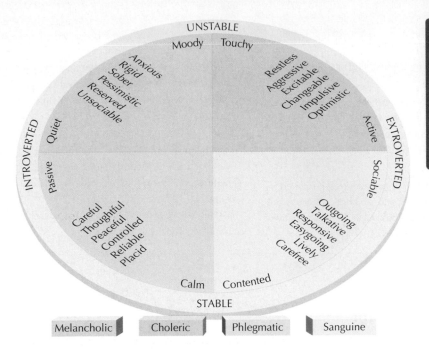

◀◀ **FIGURE 10.2** English psychologist Hans Eysenck (1916–1997) believed that many personality traits are related to whether you are mainly introverted or extroverted and whether you tend to be emotionally stable or unstable (highly emotional). These characteristics, in turn, are related to four basic types of temperament first recognized by the early Greeks. The types are: *melancholic* (sad, gloomy), *choleric* (hot-tempered, irritable), *phlegmatic* (sluggish, calm), and *sanguine* (cheerful, hopeful). (Adapted from Eysenck, 1981.)

3. **Behavioristic and social learning theories** place importance on the external environment and on the effects of conditioning and learning. Social learning theories attribute differences in personality to socialization, expectations, and mental processes.
4. **Humanistic theories** stress private, subjective experience and personal growth. With these broad perspectives in mind, let's take a deeper look at personality.

The Trait Approach—Describe Yourself in 18,000 Words or Less

Are some personality traits more basic or important than others?

The trait approach is currently the dominant method for studying personality. Psychologists seek to describe personality with a small number of key traits or factors. Take a moment to check the traits in ● Table 10.1 that describe your personality.

Don't worry if some of your key traits weren't in the table. More than 18,000 English words refer to personal characteristics. Are the traits you checked of equal importance? Are some stronger or more basic than others? Do any overlap? For example, if you checked "dominant," did you also check "confident" and "bold"?

Answers to these questions would interest a trait theorist. To better understand personality, **trait theorists** attempt to analyze, classify, and interrelate traits. In addition, trait theorists often think of traits as **biological predispositions,** a hereditary readiness of humans to behave in particular ways. (We have encountered this idea before, in Chapter 3, where we humans were described as having a biological predisposition to learn language.)

As we have noted, traits are stable dispositions that a person shows in most situations (Matthews, Deary, & Whiteman, 2003). For example, if you are usually friendly, optimistic, and cautious, these qualities are traits of your personality.

What if I am also sometimes shy, pessimistic, or uninhibited? The original three qualities are still traits as long as they are most *typical* of your behavior. Let's say our friend Annette approaches most situations with optimism but tends to expect the worst each time she applies for a job and worries that she won't get it. If her pessimism is limited to this situation or just a few others, it is still accurate and useful to describe her as an optimistic person.

● Table 10.1 **Adjective Checklist**

Check the traits you feel are characteristic of your personality. Are some more basic than others?

aggressive	ambitious
confident	generous
warm	cautious
sensitive	talented
sociable	funny
dominant	accurate
humble	visionary
thoughtful	helpful
orderly	conforming
liberal	optimistic
meek	passionate
organized	clever
loyal	calm
bold	reliable
mature	jealous
honest	religious
dull	nervous
uninhibited	cheerful
serious	emotional
anxious	good-natured
curious	kind
neighborly	compulsive

Trait theorist A psychologist interested in classifying, analyzing, and interrelating traits to understand personality.

Biological predisposition The presumed hereditary readiness of humans to learn certain skills, such as how to use language, or a readiness to behave in particular ways.

What's Your Musical Personality?

Even if you like all kinds of music, you probably prefer some styles to others. Of the styles listed here, which three do you enjoy the most? (Circle your choices.)

blues jazz classical folk rock alternative heavy metal country soundtrack religious pop rap/hip-hop soul/funk electronic/dance

In one study, Peter Rentfrow and Samuel Gosling found that the types of music people prefer tend to be associated with their personality characteristics (Rentfrow & Gosling, 2003). See if your musical tastes match their findings (Rentfrow & Gosling, 2007):

- People who value aesthetic experiences, have good verbal abilities, and are liberal and tolerant of others tend to like music that is reflective and complex (blues, jazz, classical, and folk music).

- People who are curious about new experiences, enjoy taking risks, and are physically active prefer intense, rebellious music (rock, alternative, and heavy metal music).

- People who are cheerful, conventional, extroverted, reliable, helpful, and conservative tend to enjoy upbeat conventional music (country, soundtrack, religious, and pop music).

- People who are talkative, full of energy, forgiving, and physically attractive and who reject conservative ideals tend to prefer energetic, rhythmic music (rap/hip-hop, soul/funk, and electronic/dance music).

Unmistakably, personality traits affect our everyday behavior.

Predicting Behavior

As we have noted, separating people into broad types, such as "introvert" or "extrovert," may oversimplify personality. However, introversion/extroversion can also be thought of as a trait. Knowing how you rate on this single dimension would allow us to predict how you will behave in a variety of settings. Where, for example, do you prefer to meet people—face-to-face or through the Internet? Researchers have found that students high in the trait of introversion are more likely to prefer the Internet because they find it easier to talk with people online (Koch & Pratarelli, 2004). (Other interesting links exist between traits and behavior. See "What's Your Musical Personality?")

Classifying Traits

Are there different types of traits? Yes, psychologist Gordon Allport (1961) identified several kinds. **Common traits** are characteristics shared by most members of a culture. Common traits tell us how people from a particular nation or culture are similar, or which traits a culture emphasizes. In America, for example, competitiveness is a fairly common trait. Among the Hopi of northern Arizona, however, it is relatively rare.

Of course, common traits don't tell us much about individuals. Although many people are competitive in American culture, various people you know may rate high, medium, or low in this trait. Usually we are also interested in **individual traits,** which describe a person's unique qualities.

Here's an analogy to help you separate common traits from individual traits: If you decide to buy a pet dog, you will want to know the general characteristics of the dog's breed (its common traits). In addition, you will want to know about the "personality" of a specific dog (its individual traits) before you decide to take it home.

Allport also made distinctions between *cardinal traits, central traits,* and *secondary traits.* **Cardinal traits** are so basic that all of a person's activities can be traced to the trait. For instance, compassion was an overriding trait of Mother Teresa's personality. Likewise, Abraham Lincoln's personality was dominated by the cardinal trait of honesty. According to Allport, few people have cardinal traits.

Central Traits

How do central and secondary traits differ from cardinal traits? **Central traits** are the basic building blocks of personality. A surprisingly small number of central traits can capture the essence of a person. For instance, just six traits would provide a good description of Annette's personality: dominant, sociable, honest, cheerful, intelligent, and optimistic. When college students were asked to describe someone they knew well, they mentioned an average of seven central traits (Allport, 1961).

Common traits Personality traits that are shared by most members of a particular culture.

Individual traits Personality traits that define a person's unique individual qualities.

Cardinal trait A personality trait so basic that all of a person's activities relate to it.

Central traits The core traits that characterize an individual personality.

Secondary traits are more superficial personal qualities, such as food preferences, attitudes, political opinions, musical tastes, and so forth. In Allport's terms, a personality description might therefore include the following items:

Name: Jane Doe
Age: 22
Cardinal traits: None
Central traits: Possessive, autonomous, artistic, dramatic, self-centered, trusting
Secondary traits: Prefers colorful clothes, likes to work alone, politically liberal, always late.

Source Traits

How can you tell if a personality trait is central or secondary? Raymond B. Cattell (1906–1998) tried to answer this question by directly studying the traits of a large number of people. Cattell began by measuring visible features of personality, which he called **surface traits.** Soon, Cattell noticed that these surface traits often appeared together in groups. In fact, some traits clustered together so often that they seemed to represent a single more basic trait. Cattell called these deeper characteristics, or dimensions, **source traits** (Cattell, 1965). They are the core of each individual's personality.

How do source traits differ from Allport's central traits? Allport classified traits subjectively, and it's possible that he was wrong at times. To look for connections among traits, Cattell used *factor analysis,* a statistical technique used to correlate multiple measurements and identify general underlying factors. For example, he found that imaginative people are almost always inventive, original, curious, creative, innovative, and ingenious. If you are an imaginative person, we automatically know that you have several other traits, too. Thus, *imaginative* is a source trait. (Source traits are also called factors.)

Cattell (1973) identified 16 source traits. According to him, all 16 are needed to fully describe a personality. Source traits are measured by a test called the *Sixteen Personality Factor Questionnaire* (often referred to as the 16 PF). Like many personality tests, the 16 PF can be used to produce a **trait profile,** or graph of a person's score on each trait. Trait profiles draw a "picture" of individual personalities, which makes it easier to compare them (▶▶ Figure 10.3).

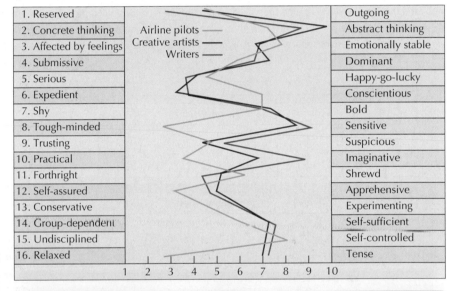

▲ **FIGURE 10.3** The 16 source traits measured by Cattell's 16 PF are listed beside the graph. Scores can be plotted as a profile for an individual or a group. The profiles shown here are group averages for airline pilots, creative artists, and writers. Notice the similarity between artists and writers and the difference between these two groups and pilots. (Data derived from Cattell, Eber and Tatsuoka: *Handbook for the Sixteen Personality Factor Questionnaire* [16PF®], Copyright © 1970, 1988, 1992 by the Institute for Personality and Ability Testing, [IPAT] Inc., Champaign, Illinois, USA. All rights reserved. 16PF is a registered trade mark of IPAT Inc.)

The Big Five

Noel is outgoing, friendly, conscientious, even-tempered, and curious. His brother Joel is reserved, hostile, irresponsible, temperamental, and disinterested in ideas. You will be spending a week in a space capsule with either Noel or Joel. Who would you choose? If the answer seems obvious, it's because Noel and Joel were described with the **five-factor model,** a system that identifies the five most basic dimensions of personality.

Five Key Dimensions

The "Big Five" factors listed in ▶▶ Figure 10.4 attempt to further reduce Cattell's 16 factors to just five universal dimensions, or source traits (Costa & McCrae, 2006). The Big Five may be the best answer of all to the question, What is the essence of human personality (McCrae & Terracciano, 2005)?

Secondary traits Traits that are inconsistent or relatively superficial.

Surface traits The visible or observable traits of one's personality.

Source traits Basic underlying traits, or dimensions, of personality; each source trait is reflected in a number of surface traits.

Trait profile A graph of the scores obtained on several personality traits.

Five-factor model Proposes that there are five universal dimensions of personality.

Which Personality Are You (and Which Is Best)?

According to the *five-factor model,* your rating on each of five basic personality dimensions, or factors, gives a good overall description of your personality. Try it (see Figure 10.4). How well do you think your ratings describe you?

When you were rating yourself, did you notice that some of the traits in Figure 10.4 don't seem very attractive? After all, who would want to score low in *extroversion*? What could be good about being a quiet, passive, and reserved loner? In other words, aren't some personality patterns better than others?

What is the best personality pattern? You might be surprised to learn that there is no one "best" personality pattern. For example, extroverts tend to earn more during their careers than introverts and they have more sexual partners. But they are also more likely to take risks than introverts (and to land in the hospital with an injury).

Extroverts are also more likely to divorce. Because of this, extroverted men are less likely to live with their children. In other words, extroversion tends to open the doors to some life experiences and close doors to others (Nettle, 2005).

The same is true for *agreeableness.* Agreeable people attract more friends and enjoy strong social support from others. But agreeable people often put the interests of friends and family ahead of their own. This leaves agreeable people at a disadvantage. To do creative, artistic work or to succeed in the business world often involves putting your own interests first (Nettle, 2008).

How about conscientiousness? Up to a point, being conscientious is associated with high achievement. However, having impossibly high standards, a trait called *perfectionism,* can be a problem. As you might expect, college students who are perfectionists tend to get good grades.

Yet some students cross the line into maladaptive perfectionism, which typically *lowers* performance at school and elsewhere (Accordino, Accordino, & Slaney, 2000). Authentic Navajo rugs always have a flaw in their intricate designs. Navajo weavers intentionally make a "mistake" in each rug as a reminder that humans are not perfect. There is a lesson in this: It is not always necessary, or even desirable, to be "perfect." To learn from your experiences you must feel free to make mistakes (Castro & Rice, 2003). Success, in the long run, is more often based on seeking "excellence" rather than "perfection" (Enns, Cox, & Clara, 2005).

Except for very extreme personality patterns, which are often maladaptive, most "personalities" involve a mixture of costs and benefits. We all face the task of pursuing life experiences that best suit our own unique personality patterns (Nettle, 2008).

Extroversion

	Low	1	2	3	4	5	6	7	High	
Loner Quiet Passive Reserved										Joiner Talkative Active Affectionate

Agreeableness

	Low	1	2	3	4	5	6	7	High	
Suspicious Critical Ruthless Irritable										Trusting Lenient Soft-hearted Good-natured

Conscientiousness

	Low	1	2	3	4	5	6	7	High	
Negligent Lazy Disorganized Late										Conscientious Hard-working Well-organized Punctual

Neuroticism

	Low	1	2	3	4	5	6	7	High	
Calm Even-tempered Comfortable Unemotional										Worried Temperamental Self-conscious Emotional

Openness to Experience

	Low	1	2	3	4	5	6	7	High	
Down-to-earth Uncreative Conventional Uncurious										Imaginative Creative Original Curious

◀◀ **FIGURE 10.4** The Big Five. According to the five-factor model, basic differences in personality can be "boiled down" to the dimensions shown here. Rate yourself on each factor. The five-factor model answers these essential questions about a person: Is she/he extroverted or introverted? Agreeable or difficult? Conscientious or irresponsible? Emotionally stable or unstable? Smart or unintelligent? These questions cover a large measure of what we might want to know about someone's personality. (Trait descriptions adapted from McCrae & Costa, 2001.)

If you would like to compare the personalities of two people, try rating them informally on the five dimensions shown in Figure 10.4. For factor 1, *extroversion,* rate how introverted or extroverted each person is. Factor 2, *agreeableness,* refers to how friendly, nurturant, and caring a person is, as opposed to cold, indifferent, self-centered, or spiteful. A person who is *conscientious* (factor 3) is self-disciplined, responsible, and achieving. People low on this factor are irresponsible, careless, and undependable. Factor 4, *neuroticism,* refers to negative, upsetting emotions. People who are high in neuroticism tend to be anxious, emotionally "sour," irritable, and unhappy. Finally, people who rate high on factor 5, *openness to experience,* are intelligent and open to new ideas (McCrae & Costa, 2001). The beauty of the Big Five model is that almost any trait you can name will be related to one of the five factors. If you were selecting a college roommate, hiring an employee, or answering a singles ad, you would probably like to know all the personal dimensions covered by the Big Five. Now, try rating yourself as you read "Which Personality Are You (and Which Is Best)?"

The Big Five traits have been related to different brain systems and chemicals (Ashton, 2007; Nettle, 2008). They also predict how people will act in various circumstances. For example, people who score high in conscientiousness tend to perform well at work, do well in school, and rarely have automobile accidents (Arthur & Doverspike, 2001; Barrick, Moun, & Judge, 2001; Chamorro-Premuzic & Furnham, 2003). They even live longer (Martin, Friedman, & Schwartz, 2007).

Knowing where a person stands on the "Big Five" personality factors helps predict his or her behavior. For example, people who score high on conscientiousness tend to be safe drivers who are unlikely to have automobile accidents (Arthur & Doverspike, 2001).

RECITE

1. The term _____ refers to the presence or absence of desirable personal qualities.
   a. personality   b. source trait
   c. character   d. temperament
2. A system that classifies all people as either introverts or extroverts is an example of a _____ approach to personality.
3. An individual's perception of his or her own personality constitutes that person's _____ .
4. Central traits are those shared by most members of a culture. T or F?
5. Cattell believes that clusters of _____ traits reveal the presence of underlying _____ traits.
6. Which of the following is *not* one of the Big Five personality factors?
   a. submissiveness   b. agreeableness
   c. extroversion   d. neuroticism

study break ✋

Personality and Trait Theories

REFLECT
Critical Thinking
7. In what way would memory contribute to the formation of an accurate or inaccurate self-image?

Relate
See if you can define or describe the following terms in your own words: personality, character, temperament, trait, type, self-concept, self-esteem.

List six or seven traits that best describe your personality. Which system of traits seems to best match your list, Allport's, Cattell's, or the Big Five?

Choose a prominent trait from your list. Does its expression seem to be influenced by specific situations? Do you think that heredity contributed to the trait?

ANSWERS

1. c   2. type   3. self-concept   4. F   5. surface, source   6. a   7. As discussed in Chapter 7, memory is highly selective, and long-term memories are often distorted by recent information. Such properties add to the moldability of self-concept.

Psychoanalytic Theory—Id Came to Me in a Dream

How do psychodynamic theories explain personality?

Psychodynamic theorists differ from trait theorists in that they are not content with studying traits. Instead, they prefer to probe under the surface of personality—to learn what drives, conflicts, and energies animate us. Psychodynamic theorists believe that many of our actions are based on hidden, or unconscious, thoughts, needs, and emotions. What psychodynamic theorists tend to share in common with trait theorists is the view that human personality is based on a set of biological dispositions.

Psychoanalytic theory, the best-known psychodynamic approach, grew out of the work of Sigmund Freud, a Viennese physician. As a doctor, Freud was fascinated by patients whose problems seemed to be more emotional than physical. From about 1890 until he died in 1939, Freud evolved a theory of personality that deeply influenced modern thought (Jacobs, 2003; Schultz & Schultz, 2005). Let's consider some of its main features.

The Structure of Personality

How did Freud view personality? Freud's model portrays personality as a dynamic system directed by three mental structures, the **id,** the **superego,** and the **ego.** According to Freud, most behavior involves activity of all three systems. (Freud's theory includes a large number of concepts. For your convenience, they are defined in ● Table 10.2 rather than in glossary boxes.)

 Psychoanalytic theory Freudian theory of personality that emphasizes unconscious forces and conflicts.

● Table 10.2 Key Freudian Concepts

Anal stage The psychosexual stage corresponding roughly to the period of toilet training (ages 1 to 3).

Anal-expulsive personality A disorderly, destructive, cruel, or messy person.

Anal-retentive personality A person who is obstinate, stingy, or compulsive and who generally has difficulty "letting go."

Conscience The part of the superego that causes guilt when its standards are not met.

Conscious Region of the mind that includes all mental contents a person is aware of at any given moment.

Ego The executive part of personality that directs rational behavior.

Ego ideal The part of the superego representing ideal behavior; a source of pride when its standards are met.

Electra conflict A girl's sexual attraction to her father and feelings of rivalry with her mother.

Erogenous zone Any body area that produces pleasurable sensations.

Eros Freud's name for the "life instincts."

Fixation A lasting conflict developed as a result of frustration or overindulgence.

Genital stage Period of full psychosexual development, marked by the attainment of mature adult sexuality.

Id The primitive part of personality that remains unconscious, supplies energy, and demands pleasure.

Latency According to Freud, a period in childhood when psychosexual development is more or less interrupted.

Libido In Freudian theory, the force, primarily pleasure oriented, that energizes the personality.

Moral anxiety Apprehension felt when thoughts, impulses, or actions conflict with the superego's standards.

Neurotic anxiety Apprehension felt when the ego struggles to control id impulses.

Oedipus conflict A boy's sexual attraction to his mother, and feelings of rivalry with his father.

Oral stage The period when infants are preoccupied with the mouth as a source of pleasure and means of expression.

Oral-aggressive personality A person who uses the mouth to express hostility by shouting, cursing, biting, and so forth. Also, one who actively exploits others.

Oral-dependent personality A person who wants to passively receive attention, gifts, love, and so forth.

Phallic personality A person who is vain, exhibitionistic, sensitive, and narcissistic.

Phallic stage The psychosexual stage (roughly ages 3 to 6) when a child is preoccupied with the genitals.

Pleasure principle A desire for immediate satisfaction of wishes, desires, or needs.

Preconscious An area of the mind containing information that can be voluntarily brought to awareness.

Psyche The mind, mental life, and personality as a whole.

Psychosexual stages The oral, anal, phallic, and genital stages, during which various personality traits are formed.

Reality principle Delaying action (or pleasure) until it is appropriate.

Superego A judge or censor for thoughts and actions.

Thanatos The death instinct.

Unconscious The region of the mind that is beyond awareness, especially impulses and desires not directly known to a person.

The Id

The id is made up of innate biological instincts and urges. The id operates on the **pleasure principle.** It is self-serving, irrational, impulsive, and totally unconscious. That is, it seeks to freely express pleasure-seeking urges of all kinds. If we were solely under control of the id, the world would be chaotic beyond belief.

The id acts as a well of energy for the entire **psyche** (sigh-KEY), or personality. This energy, called **libido** (lih-BEE-doe), flows from the **life instincts** (or **Eros**). According to Freud, libido underlies our efforts to survive, as well as our sexual desires and pleasure seeking. Freud also described a **death instinct. Thanatos,** as he called it, produces aggressive and destructive urges. Freud offered humanity's long history of wars and violence as evidence of such urges. Most id energies, then, are aimed at discharging tensions related to sex and aggression.

The Ego

2/3/12

The ego is sometimes described as the "executive," because it directs energies supplied by the id. The id is like a blind king or queen whose power is awesome but who must rely on others to carry out orders. The id can only form mental images of things it desires. The ego wins power to direct behavior by relating the desires of the id to external reality.

Are there other differences between the ego and the id? Yes. Recall that the id operates on the pleasure principle. The ego, in contrast, is guided by the **reality principle.** The ego is the system of thinking, planning, problem solving, and deciding. It is in conscious control of the personality and often delays action until it is practical or appropriate.

Freud considered personality an expression of two conflicting forces, life instincts and the death instinct. Both are symbolized in this drawing by Allan Gilbert. (If you don't immediately see the death symbolism, stand farther from the drawing.)

The Superego

What is the role of the superego? The superego acts as a judge or censor for the thoughts and actions of the ego. One part of the superego, called the **conscience,** reflects actions for which a person has been punished. When standards of the conscience are not met, you are punished internally by *guilt* feelings.

A second part of the superego is the **ego ideal.** The ego ideal reflects all behavior one's parents approved of or rewarded. The ego ideal is a source of goals and aspirations. When its standards are met, we feel *pride.*

The superego acts as an "internalized parent" to bring behavior under control. In Freudian terms, a person with a weak superego will be a delinquent, criminal, or antisocial personality. In contrast, an overly strict or harsh superego may cause inhibition, rigidity, or unbearable guilt.

The Dynamics of Personality

How do the id, ego, and superego interact? Freud didn't picture the id, ego, and superego as parts of the brain or as "little people" running the human psyche. Instead, they are conflicting mental processes. Freud theorized a delicate balance of power among the three. For example, the id's demands for immediate pleasure often clash with the superego's moral restrictions. Perhaps an example will help clarify the role of each part of the personality:

Freud in a Nutshell

Let's say you are sexually attracted to an acquaintance. The id clamors for immediate satisfaction of its sexual desires but is opposed by the superego (which finds the very thought of sex shocking). The id says, "Go for it!" The superego icily replies, "Never even think that again!" And what does the ego say? The ego says, "I have a plan!"

This is, of course, a drastic simplification, but it does capture the core of Freudian thinking. To reduce tension, the ego could begin actions leading to friendship, romance, courtship, and marriage. If the id is unusually powerful, the ego may give in and attempt a seduction. If the superego prevails, the ego may be forced to *displace* or *sublimate* sexual energies to other activities (sports, music, dancing, push-ups, cold showers). According to Freud, internal struggles and rechanneled energies typify most personality functioning.

Is the ego always caught in the middle? Basically yes, and the pressures on it can be intense. In addition to meeting the conflicting demands of the id and superego, the overworked ego must deal with external reality.

According to Freud, you feel anxiety when your ego is threatened or overwhelmed. Impulses from the id cause **neurotic anxiety** when the ego can barely keep them under control. Threats of punishment from the superego cause **moral anxiety.** Each person develops habitual ways of calming these anxieties, and many resort to using *ego-defense mechanisms* to lessen internal conflicts. Defense mechanisms are mental processes that deny, distort, or otherwise block out sources of threat and anxiety. (The ego defense mechanisms that Freud identified are used as a form of protection against stress, anxiety, and threatening events. See Chapter 11.)

Levels of Awareness

Like other psychodynamic theorists, Freud believed that our behavior often expresses unconscious (or hidden) forces. The **unconscious** holds repressed memories and emotions, plus the instinctual drives of the id. Interestingly, modern scientists have found that the brain's limbic system does, in fact, seem to trigger unconscious emotions and memories (LeDoux, 2000).

Even though they are beyond awareness, unconscious thoughts, feelings, or urges may slip into behavior in disguised or symbolic form. For example, if you meet someone you would like to know better, you may unconsciously leave a book or a jacket at that person's house to ensure another meeting.

Are the actions of the ego and superego also unconscious, like the id? At times, yes, but they also operate on two other levels of awareness (▶▶ Figure 10.5). The **conscious** level includes everything you are aware of at a given moment, including thoughts, perceptions, feelings, and memories. The **preconscious** contains material that can be easily brought to awareness. If you stop to think about a time when you felt angry or rejected, you will be moving this memory from the preconscious to the conscious level of awareness.

The superego's activities also reveal differing levels of awareness. At times we consciously try to live up to moral codes or standards. Yet, at other times a person may feel guilty without knowing why. Psychoanalytic theory credits such guilt to unconscious workings of the superego. Indeed, Freud believed that the unconscious origins of many feelings cannot be easily brought to awareness.

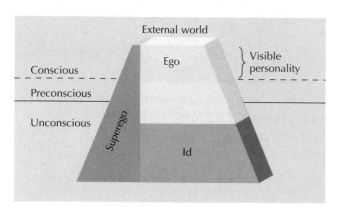

⬆ FIGURE 10.5 The approximate relationship between the id, ego, and superego, and the levels of awareness.

Personality Development

How does psychoanalytic theory explain personality development? Freud theorized that the core of personality is formed before age 6 in a series of **psychosexual stages.** Freud believed that erotic urges in childhood have lasting effects on development. As you might expect, this is a controversial idea. However, Freud used the terms *sex* and *erotic* very broadly to refer to many physical sources of pleasure.

A Freudian Fable?

Freud identified four psychosexual stages, the **oral, anal, phallic,** and **genital.** (He also described a period of "latency" between the phallic and genital stages. Latency is explained in a moment.) At each stage, a different part of the body becomes a child's primary **erogenous zone** (an area capable of producing pleasure). Each area then serves as the main source of pleasure, frustration, and self-expression. Freud believed that many adult personality traits can be traced to **fixations** in one or more of the stages.

What is a fixation? A fixation is an unresolved conflict or emotional hang-up caused by overindulgence or by frustration. As we describe the psychosexual stages, you'll see why Freud considered fixations important.

The Oral Stage

During the first year of life, most of an infant's pleasure comes from stimulation of the mouth. If a child is overfed or frustrated, oral traits may be created. Adult expressions of oral needs include gum chewing, nail biting, smoking, kissing, overeating, and alcoholism.

What if there is an oral fixation? Fixation early in the oral stage produces an **oral-dependent personality.** Oral-dependent persons are gullible (they swallow things easily!) and passive and need lots of attention (they want to be mothered and showered with gifts). Frustrations later in the oral stage may cause aggression, often in the form of biting. Fixations here create cynical, **oral-aggressive** adults who exploit others. They also like to argue ("Biting sarcasm" is their forte!).

The Anal Stage

Between the ages of 1 and 3, the child's attention shifts to the process of elimination. When parents attempt toilet training, the child can gain approval or express rebellion or aggression by "holding on" or by "letting go." Therefore, harsh or lenient toilet training can cause an anal fixation that may lock such responses into personality. Freud described the **anal-retentive** (holding-on) personality as obstinate, stingy, orderly, and compulsively clean. The **anal-expulsive** (letting-go) personality is disorderly, destructive, cruel, or messy.

The Phallic Stage

Adult traits of the **phallic personality** are vanity, exhibitionism, sensitive pride, and narcissism (self-love). Freud theorized that phallic fixations develop between the ages of 3 and 6. At this time, increased sexual interest causes the child to be physically attracted to the parent of the opposite sex. In males this attraction leads to an **Oedipus conflict.** In it, the boy feels a rivalry with his father for the affection of his mother. Freud believed that the male child feels threatened by the father (specifically, the boy fears castration). To ease his anxieties, the boy must identify with the father. Their rivalry ends when the boy seeks to become more like his father. As he does, he begins to accept the father's values and forms a conscience.

What about the female child? Girls experience an **Electra conflict.** In this case, the girl loves her father and competes with her mother. However, according to Freud, the girl identifies with the mother more gradually.

Freud believed that females already feel castrated. Because of this, they are less driven to identify with their mothers than boys are with their fathers. This, he said, is less effective in creating a conscience. This particular part of Freudian thought has been thoroughly (and rightfully) rejected by modern experts in the psychology of women. It is better understood as a reflection of the male-dominated times in which Freud lived.

Latency

According to Freud, there is a period of **latency** from age 6 to puberty. Latency is not so much a stage as it is a quiet time during which psychosexual development is dormant. Freud's belief that psychosexual development is "on hold" at this time is hard to accept. Nevertheless, Freud saw latency as a relatively quiet time compared with the stormy first 6 years of life.

The Genital Stage

At puberty an upswing in sexual energies activates all the unresolved conflicts of earlier years. This upsurge, according to Freud, is the reason why adolescence can be filled with emotion and turmoil. The genital stage begins at puberty. It is marked, during adolescence, by a growing capacity for responsible social-sexual relationships. The genital stage ends with a mature capacity for love and the realization of full adult sexuality.

Was Freud's ever-present cigar a sign of an oral fixation? Was it a phallic symbol? Was it both? Or was it neither? Once, when he was asked, Freud himself apparently replied, "Sometimes a cigar is just a cigar." An inability to say for sure is one of the shortcomings of psychoanalytic theory.

Critical Comments

As bizarre as Freud's theory might seem, it has been influential for several reasons. First, it pioneered the idea that the first years of life help shape adult personality. Second, it identified feeding, toilet training, and early sexual experiences as critical events in personality formation. Third, Freud was among the first to propose that development proceeds through a series of stages. (Erik Erikson's psycho*social* stages, which cover development from birth to old age, are a modern offshoot of Freudian thinking. See Chapter 3.)

Is the Freudian view of development widely accepted? Few psychologists wholeheartedly embrace Freud's theory today. In some cases Freud was clearly wrong. His portrayal of the elementary school years (latency) as free from sexuality and unimportant for personality development is hard to believe. His idea of the role of a stern or threatening father in the development of a strong conscience in males has also been challenged. Studies show that a son is more likely to develop a strong conscience if his father is affectionate and accepting, rather than stern and punishing. Freud also overemphasized sexuality in personality development. Other motives and cognitive factors are of equal importance.

Freud has been criticized for his views of patients who believed they were sexually molested as children. Freud assumed that such events were merely childhood fantasies. This view led to a long-standing tendency to disbelieve children who have been molested and women who have been raped (Brannon, 1996).

Another important criticism is that Freud's concepts are almost impossible to verify scientifically. The theory provides numerous ways to explain almost any thought, action, or feeling *after* it has occurred. However, it leads to few predictions, which makes its claims difficult to test. Although more criticisms of Freud could be listed, the fact remains that there is an element of truth to much of what he said (Jacob, 2003). Because of this, some clinical psychologists continue to regard Freudian theory as a useful way to think about human problems.

study break
Psychodynamic Theory

RECITE

1. List the three divisions of personality postulated by Freud.
   _____
2. Which division is totally unconscious? _____
3. Which division is responsible for moral anxiety? _____
4. Freud proposed the existence of a life instinct known as Thanatos. T or F?
5. Freud's view of personality development is based on the concept of _____ stages.
6. Arrange these stages in the proper order: phallic, anal, genital, oral.
   _____
7. Freud considered the anal-retentive personality to be obstinate and stingy. T or F?

REFLECT
Critical Thinking

8. Many adults would find it embarrassing or humiliating to drink from a baby bottle. Can you explain why?

Relate

Try to think of at least one time when your thoughts, feelings, or actions seemed to reflect the workings of each of the following: the id, the ego, and the superego.

Do you know anyone who seems to have oral, anal, or phallic personality traits? Do you think Freud's concept of fixation explains their characteristics?

Do any of your personal experiences support the existence of an Oedipus conflict or an Electra conflict? If not, is it possible that you have repressed feelings related to these conflicts?

ANSWERS

1. id, ego, superego 2. id 3. superego 4. F 5. psychosexual 6. oral, anal, phallic, genital 7. T 8. A psychoanalytic theorist would say that it is because the bottle rekindles oral conflicts and feelings of vulnerability and dependence.

Learning Theories of Personality— Habit I Seen You Before?

What do behaviorists and social learning theorists emphasize in their approach to personality?

After exploring Freud's psychodynamic theory, you might be relieved to know that behavioral theorists explain personality through straightforward concepts, such as learning, reinforcement, and imitation. Behavioral and social learning theories are based on scientific research, which makes them powerful ways of looking at personality.

How do behaviorists approach personality? According to some critics, as if people are robots. Actually, the behaviorist position is not nearly that mechanistic, and its value is well established. Behaviorists have shown repeatedly that children can *learn* things like kindness, hostility, generosity, or destructiveness. What does this have to do with personality? Everything, according to the behavioral viewpoint.

Behavioral personality theories emphasize that personality is no more (or less) than a collection of learned behavior patterns. Personality, like other learned behavior, is acquired through classical and operant conditioning, observational learning, reinforcement, extinction, generalization, and discrimination. When Mother says, "It's not nice to make mud pies with Mommy's blender. If we want to grow up to be a big girl, we won't do it again, will we?" she serves as a model and in other ways shapes her daughter's personality.

Strict learning theorists reject the idea that personality is made up of traits. They would assert, for instance, that there is no such thing as a trait of "honesty" (Mischel, 2004).

Certainly some people are honest and others are not. How can honesty not be a trait? Learning theorists recognize that some people are honest *more often* than others. According to learning theorists, this is not a biological disposition; rather, it is a learned response. If his parents consistently reward little Alexander for honesty, he is more likely to become an honest adult. If his parents are less scrupulous, Alexander might well grow up differently.

Learning theorists also stress the **situational determinants** (external causes) of actions. Knowing that someone is honest does not automatically allow us to predict whether that person will be honest in a specific situation. It would not be unusual, for example, to find that a person honored for returning a lost wallet had cheated on a test, bought a term paper, or broken the speed limit. If you were to ask a learning theorist, "Are you an honest person?" the reply might be, "In what situation?"

A good example of how situations can influence behavior is a study in which people were intentionally overpaid for doing an assigned task. Under normal circumstances, 80 percent kept the extra money without mentioning it. But as few as 17 percent were dishonest if the situation was altered. For instance, if people thought the money was coming out of the pocket of the person doing the study, far fewer were dishonest (Bersoff, 1999). Thus, situations always interact with our prior learning to activate behavior.

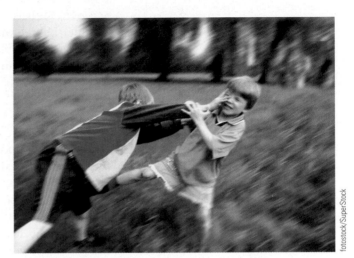

Freud believed that aggressive urges are "instinctual." In contrast, behavioral theories assume that personal characteristics such as aggressiveness are learned. Is this boy's aggression the result of observational learning, harsh punishment, or prior reinforcement?

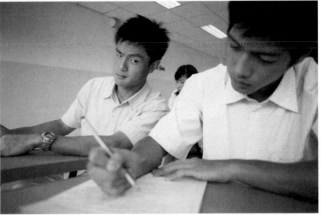

Seventy-five percent of American college students admit that they have been academically dishonest in one way or another. What can be done about these high rates of dishonesty? The behavioral perspective holds that honesty is determined as much by circumstances as it is by personality. In line with this, simple measures like announcing in classes that integrity codes will be enforced can significantly reduce cheating. Using multiple forms of exams and web-based plagiarism software and educating students about plagiarism also tend to deter dishonesty (Altschuler, 2001; McKeever, 2006.)

How Situations Affect Behavior

Situations vary greatly in their impact. Some are powerful. Others are trivial and have little effect on behavior. The more powerful the situation, the easier it is to see what is meant by *situational determinants*. For example, each of the following situations would undoubtedly

Behavioral personality theory Any model of personality that emphasizes learning and observable behavior.

Situational determinants External conditions that strongly influence behavior.

have a strong influence on your behavior: An armed person walks into your classroom; you accidentally sit on a lighted cigarette; you find your lover in bed with your best friend. Yet even these situations could provoke very different reactions from different personalities. That's why behavior is always a product of both prior learning and the situations in which we find ourselves (Mischel, Shoda, & Smith, 2004).

Ultimately, what is predictable about personality is that we respond in fairly consistent ways to certain types of situations. Consider, for example, two people who are easily angered: One person might get angry when she is delayed (for example, in traffic or a check-out line), but not when she misplaces something at home; the other person might get angry whenever she misplaces things, but not when she is delayed. Overall, the two women are equally prone to anger, but their anger tends to occur in different patterns and different types of situations (Mischel, 2004).

Personality = Behavior

How do learning theorists view the structure of personality? The behavioral view of personality can be illustrated with an early theory proposed by John Dollard and Neal Miller (1950). In their view, *habits* (learned behavior patterns) make up the structure of personality. As for the dynamics of personality, habits are governed by four elements of learning: *drive, cue, response,* and *reward.* A *drive* is any stimulus strong enough to goad a person to action (such as hunger, pain, lust, frustration, or fear). *Cues* are signals from the environment. These signals guide *responses* (actions) so that they are most likely to bring about *reward* (positive reinforcement).

How does that relate to personality? Let's say a child named Amina is frustrated by her older brother Kelvin, who takes a toy from her. Amina could respond in several ways: She could throw a temper tantrum, hit Kelvin, tell Mother, and so forth. The response she chooses is guided by available cues and the previous effects of each response. If telling Mother has paid off in the past, and the mother is present, telling again may be her immediate response. If a different set of cues exists (if Mother is absent or if Kelvin looks particularly menacing), Amina may select some other response. To an outside observer, Amina's actions seem to reflect her personality. To a learning theorist, they simply express the combined effects of drive, cue, response, and reward. Behavioral theories have contributed greatly to the creation of therapies for various psychological problems and disorders. See the discussion of behavior therapy in Chapter 13.

Doesn't this analysis leave out a lot? Yes. Learning theorists first set out to provide a simple, clear model of personality. But in recent years they have had to face a fact that they originally tended to overlook: People think. The new breed of behavioral psychologists—whose views include perception, thinking, expectations, and other mental events—are called social learning theorists. Learning principles, modeling, thought patterns, perceptions, expectations, beliefs, goals, emotions, and social relationships are combined in **social learning theory** to explain personality (Mischel, Shoda, & Smith, 2004).

Social Learning Theory

The "cognitive behaviorism" of social learning theory can be illustrated by three concepts proposed by Julian Rotter: the psychological situation, expectancy, and reinforcement value (Rotter & Hochreich, 1975). Let's examine each.

Someone trips you. How do you respond? Your reaction probably depends on whether you think it was planned or an accident. It is not enough to know the setting in which a person responds. We also need to know the person's **psychological situation** (how the person interprets or defines the situation). As another example, let's say you score low on an exam. Do you consider it a challenge to work harder, a sign that you should drop the class, or an excuse to get drunk? Again, your interpretation is important.

Our actions are affected by an **expectancy,** or anticipation, that making a response will lead to reinforcement. To continue the example, if working harder has paid off in the past, it is a likely reaction to a low test score. But to predict your response, we would also have to know

Social learning theory An explanation of personality that combines learning principles, cognition, and the effects of social relationships.

Psychological situation A situation as it is perceived and interpreted by an individual, not as it exists objectively.

Expectancy Anticipation about the effect a response will have, especially regarding reinforcement.

if you *expect* your efforts to pay off in the present situation. In fact, expected reinforcement may be more important than actual past reinforcement. And what about the *value* you attach to grades, school success, or personal ability? The third concept, **reinforcement value,** states that we attach different subjective values to various activities or rewards. You will likely choose to study harder if passing your courses and obtaining a degree is highly valued. This, too, must be taken into account to understand personality.

Self-Efficacy

An ability to control your own life is the essence of what it means to be human. Because of this, Albert Bandura believes that one of the most important expectancies we develop concerns **self-efficacy** (EF-uh-keh-see: a capacity for producing a desired result). You're attracted to someone in your anthropology class. Will you ask him or her out? You're beginning to consider a career in psychology. Will you take the courses you need to get into graduate school? You'd like to exercise more on the weekends. Will you join a hiking club? In these and countless other situations, efficacy beliefs play a key role in shaping our lives. Believing that our actions will produce desired results influences the activities and environments we choose (Bandura, 2001; Schultz & Schultz, 2005).

Self-Reinforcement

One more idea deserves mention. At times, we all evaluate our actions and may reward ourselves with special privileges or treats for "good behavior." With this in mind, social learning theory adds the concept of self-reinforcement to the behavioristic view. **Self-reinforcement** refers to praising or rewarding yourself for having made a particular response (such as completing a school assignment). Thus, habits of self-praise and self-blame become an important part of personality (Schultz & Schultz, 2005). In fact, self-reinforcement can be thought of as the social learning theorist's counterpart to the superego.

Self-reinforcement is closely related to high self-esteem. The reverse is also true: Mildly depressed college students tend to have low rates of self-reinforcement. It is not known if low self-reinforcement leads to depression, or the reverse. In either case, higher rates of self-reinforcement are associated with less depression and greater life satisfaction (Seybolt & Wagner, 1997). From a behavioral viewpoint, there is value in learning to be "good to yourself."

Iconica/Getty Images

Through self-reinforcement we reward ourselves for personal achievements and other "good" behavior.

© Vic Lee. Reprinted with special permission of King Features Syndicate.

I WISH YOU WOULD QUIT BEING SO HARD ON YOURSELF. IT LEAVES *ME* WITH NOTHING TO DO.

Behavioristic View of Development

How do learning theorists account for personality development? Many of Freud's ideas can be restated in terms of learning theory. John Dollard and Neal Miller (1950) agree with Freud that the first 6 years are crucial for personality development, but for different reasons. Rather than thinking in terms of psychosexual urges and fixations, they ask, "What makes early learning experiences so lasting in their effects?" Their answer is that childhood is a

Reinforcement value The subjective value a person attaches to a particular activity or reinforcer.

Self-efficacy Belief in your capacity to produce a desired result.

Self-reinforcement Praising or rewarding oneself for having made a particular response (such as completing a school assignment).

time of urgent drives, powerful rewards and punishments, and crushing frustrations. Also important is *social reinforcement*, which is based on praise, attention, or approval from others. These forces combine to shape the core of personality.

Critical Situations

Dollard and Miller believe that during childhood, four **critical situations** are capable of leaving a lasting imprint on personality. These are (1) feeding, (2) toilet or cleanliness training, (3) sex training, and (4) learning to express anger or aggression.

Why are these of special importance? Feeding serves as an illustration. If children are fed when they cry, it encourages them to actively manipulate their parents. The child allowed to cry without being fed learns to be passive. Thus, a basic active or passive orientation toward the world may be created by early feeding experiences. Feeding can also affect later social relationships because the child learns to associate people with pleasure or with frustration and discomfort.

Toilet and cleanliness training can be a particularly strong source of emotion for both parents and children. Rashad's parents were aghast the day they found him smearing feces about with joyful abandon. They reacted with sharp punishment, which frustrated and confused Rashad. Many attitudes toward cleanliness, conformity, and bodily functions are formed at such times. Studies have also long shown that severe, punishing, or frustrating toilet training can have undesirable effects on personality development (Christophersen & Mortweet, 2003). Because of this, toilet and cleanliness training demand patience and a sense of humor.

What about sex and anger? When, where, and how a child learns to express anger and sexual feelings can leave an imprint on personality. Specifically, permissiveness for sexual and aggressive behavior in childhood is linked to adult needs for power (McClelland & Pilon, 1983). This link probably occurs because permitting such behaviors allows children to get pleasure from asserting themselves. Sex training also involves learning socially defined "male" and "female" gender roles—which, in turn, affects personality (Pervin, Cervone, & John, 2005).

Personality and Gender

From birth onward, children are labeled as boys or girls and encouraged to learn sex-appropriate behavior (Denmark, Rabinowitz, & Sechzer, 2005).

What does it mean to have a "masculine" or "feminine" personality? According to social learning theory, identification and imitation contribute greatly to personality development and to sex training. **Identification** refers to the child's emotional attachment to admired adults, especially those who provide love and care. Identification typically encourages **imitation,** a desire to act like the admired person. Many "male" or "female" traits come from children's attempts to imitate a same-sex parent with whom they identify.

If children are around parents of both sexes, why don't they imitate behavior typical of the opposite sex as well as of the same sex? You may recall from Chapter 6 that learning takes place vicariously as well as directly. This means that we can learn without direct reward by observing and remembering the actions of others. But the actions we choose to imitate depend on their outcomes. For example, boys and girls have equal chances to observe adults and other children acting aggressively. However, girls are less likely than boys to imitate directly aggressive behavior (shouting at or hitting another person). Instead, girls are more likely to rely on indirectly aggressive behavior (excluding others from friendship, spreading rumors). This may well be because the expression of direct aggression is thought to be inappropriate for girls. As a consequence, girls rarely see direct female aggression rewarded or approved (Richardson & Green, 1999). In others words, "girlfighting" is likely a culturally reinforced pattern (Brown, 2005). Intriguingly, over the last

It begins

THIS DIAPER MAKES MY BUTT LOOK BIG...

P. BYRNES.

Critical situations Situations during childhood that are capable of leaving a lasting imprint on personality.

Identification Feeling emotionally connected to a person and seeing oneself as like him or her.

Imitation An attempt to match one's own behavior to another person's behavior.

few years, girls have become more willing to engage in direct aggression as popular culture presents more and more images of directly aggressive women (Artz, 2005).

We have considered only a few examples of the links between social learning and personality. Nevertheless, the connection is unmistakable. When parents accept their children and give them affection, the children become sociable, positive, and emotionally stable, and they have high self-esteem. When parents are rejecting, punishing, sarcastic, humiliating, or neglectful, their children become hostile, unresponsive, unstable, and dependent and have impaired self-esteem (Triandis & Suh, 2002).

Historically, parents and other adults in Western countries like the United States tended to encourage boys to engage in **instrumental** (goal-directed) **behaviors,** to be directly aggressive, to hide their emotions, and to prepare for the world of work. Girls, on the other hand, were encouraged in **expressive** (emotion-oriented) **behaviors** and, to a lesser degree, were socialized for indirect aggression and for motherhood. Thus, from an early age, males and females tended to grow up in different, gender-defined cultures (Martin & Fabes, 2001). But these differences are becoming less and less noticeable as traditional male and female gender roles have been called into question.

Androgyny

Are you aggressive, ambitious, analytical, assertive, athletic, competitive, decisive, dominant, forceful, independent, individualistic, self-reliant, and willing to take risks? If so, you are quite "masculine." Are you affectionate, cheerful, childlike, compassionate, flatterable, gentle, gullible, loyal, sensitive, shy, soft-spoken, sympathetic, tender, understanding, warm, and yielding? If so, then you are quite "feminine." What if you have traits from both lists? In that case, you may be *androgynous* (an-DROJ-ih-nus).

The two lists you just read are from the seminal work of psychologist Sandra Bem (1974). By combining 20 traditionally "masculine" traits (self-reliant, assertive, and so forth), 20 traditionally "feminine" traits (affectionate, gentle), and 20 neutral traits (truthful, friendly), Bem created the *Bem Sex Role Inventory* (BSRI). (Some psychologists prefer to use the term *sex role* instead of gender role.) Next, she and her associates gave the BSRI to thousands of people, asking them to say whether each trait applied to them. Of those surveyed, 50 percent fell into traditional feminine or masculine categories, 15 percent scored higher on traits of the opposite sex, and 35 percent were androgynous, getting high scores on both feminine and masculine items.

The word **androgyny** (an-DROJ-ih-nee) literally means "man-woman" and refers to having both masculine and feminine traits (Helgeson, 2005). Bem is convinced that our complex society requires flexibility with respect to gender roles. She believes that it is necessary for men to also be gentle, compassionate, sensitive, and yielding and for women to also be forceful, self-reliant, independent, and ambitious—*as the situation requires*. In short, Bem feels that more people should be androgynous and has shown that androgynous individuals are more adaptable. They seem especially to be less hindered by images of "feminine" or "masculine" behavior. In contrast, rigid gender stereotypes and gender roles can seriously restrict behavior.

For example, in one study people were given the choice of doing either a "masculine" activity (oil a hinge, nail boards together, and so forth) or a "feminine" activity (prepare a baby bottle, wind yarn into a ball, and so on). Masculine men and feminine women consistently chose to do gender-appropriate activities, even when the opposite choice paid more!

Bem has concluded that masculine males have great difficulty expressing warmth, playfulness, and concern—even when they are appropriate (Bem, 1975, 1981). Masculine men, it seems, tend to view such feelings as unacceptably "feminine." Masculine men (let's call them "manly men") also find it hard to accept emotional support from others, particularly from women (Levant, 2001, 2003).

Problems faced by highly feminine women are the reverse of those faced by masculine men. Such women have trouble being independent and assertive, even when these qualities are desirable. In contrast, more androgynous individuals are higher in emotional intelligence (remember Chapter 9?) (Guastello & Guastello, 2003).

Androgynous individuals adapt easily to both traditionally "feminine" and "masculine" situations.

Instrumental behaviors Behaviors directed toward the achievement of some goal; behaviors that are instrumental in producing some effect.

Expressive behaviors Behaviors that express or communicate emotion or personal feelings.

Androgyny The presence of both "masculine" and "feminine" traits in a single person (as masculinity and femininity are defined within one's culture).

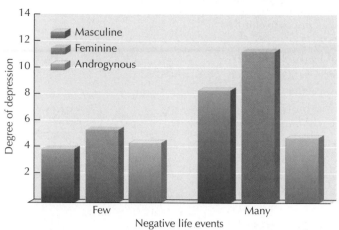

► FIGURE 10.6 Another indication of the possible benefits of androgyny is found in a study of reactions to stress. When confronted with an onslaught of negative events, strongly masculine or feminine persons become more depressed than androgynous individuals do (adapted from Roos & Cohen, 1987).

Gender in Perspective

Androgyny has been hotly debated over the years. Now, as the dust begins to settle, the picture looks like this:

• Having "masculine" traits means primarily that a person is independent and assertive. Scoring high in "masculinity," therefore, is related to high self-esteem and to success in many situations (Long, 1989).

• Having "feminine" traits means primarily that a person is nurturing and interpersonally oriented. People who score high in "femininity," therefore, are more likely to seek and receive social support. They tend to experience greater social closeness with others and more happiness in marriage (Reevy & Maslach, 2001).

In sum, there are advantages to possessing both "feminine" and "masculine" traits (Guastello & Guastello, 2003; Lefkowitz & Zeldow, 2006). In general, androgynous persons are more flexible when it comes to coping with difficult situations (Crooks & Baur, 2008; Woodhill & Samuels, 2004) (see ►► Figure 10.6). Androgynous persons also tend to be more satisfied with their lives. Apparently, they can use both instrumental and emotionally expressive capacities to enhance their lives and relationships (Lefkowitz & Zeldow, 2006).

It is worth saying again that many people remain comfortable with traditional views of gender. Nevertheless, "feminine" traits and "masculine" traits can exist in the same person, and androgyny can be a highly adaptive balance.

study break
Behavioral and Social Learning Theories

RECITE

1. Learning theorists believe that personality "traits" really are _____ acquired through prior learning. They also emphasize _____ determinants of behavior.
2. Dollard and Miller consider cues the basic structure of personality. T or F?
3. To explain behavior, social learning theorists include mental elements, such as _____ (the anticipation that a response will lead to reinforcement).
4. Self-reinforcement is to behavioristic theory as superego is to psychoanalytic theory. T or F?
5. Which of the following is *not* a "critical situation" in the behaviorist theory of personality development?
   a. feeding   b. sex training
   c. language training   d. anger training
6. In addition to basic rewards and punishments, a child's personality is also shaped by _____ reinforcement.

7. Social learning theories of development emphasize the impact of identification and _____ .
8. A person who is aggressive, ambitious, analytical, and assertive would be rated as androgynous on the BSRI. T or F?

REFLECT
Critical Thinking

9. The concept of *reinforcement value* is closely related to a motivational principle discussed in Chapter 9. Can you name it?

Relate

What is your favorite style of food? Can you relate Dollard and Miller's concepts of habit, drive, cue, response, and reward to explain your preference?

Some people love to shop. Others hate it. How have the psychological situation, expectancy, and reinforcement value affected your willingness to "shop 'til you drop"?

Who did you identify with as a child? What aspects of that person's behavior did you imitate?

Think of three people you know, one who is androgynous, one who is traditionally feminine, and one who is traditionally masculine. What advantages and disadvantages do you see in each collection of traits? How do you think you would be classified if you took the BSRI?

ANSWERS

1. habits, situational   2. F   3. expectancies   4. T   5. c   6. social   7. imitation   8. F   9. incentive value

Humanistic Theory—Peak Experiences and Personal Growth

How do humanistic theories differ from other perspectives?

At the beginning of this chapter, you met Annette. A few years ago, Annette and her husband spent a year riding mules across the country as a unique way to see America and get to know themselves better. Where do such desires for personal growth come from? Humanistic theories pay special attention to the fuller use of human potentials and they help bring balance to our overall views of personality.

Humanism focuses on human experience, problems, potentials, and ideals. It is a reaction to the rigidity of traits, the pessimism of psychoanalytic theory, and the mechanical nature of learning theory. At its core is a positive image of what it means to be human. Humanists reject the Freudian view of personality as a battleground for instincts and unconscious forces. Instead, they view human nature as inherently good. (*Human nature* consists of the traits, qualities, potentials, and behavior patterns most characteristic of the human species.) Humanists also oppose the machine-like overtones of behaviorism. We are not, they say, merely a bundle of moldable responses. Rather, we are creative beings capable of *free choice* (an ability to choose that is not determined by genetics, learning, or unconscious forces). In short, humanists seek ways to encourage our potentials to blossom.

To a humanist the person you are today is largely the product of all the choices you have made. Humanists also emphasize immediate *subjective experience* (private perceptions of reality), rather than prior learning. They believe that there are as many "real worlds" as there are people. To understand behavior, we must learn how a person subjectively views the world—what is "real" for her or him.

Who are the major humanistic theorists? Many psychologists have added to the humanistic tradition. Of these, the best known are Abraham Maslow (1908–1970) and Carl Rogers (1902–1987). Because Maslow's idea of self-actualization was introduced in Chapter 1, let's begin with a more detailed look at this facet of his thinking.

Maslow and Self-Actualization

Abraham Maslow became interested in people who were living unusually effective lives. How were they different? To find an answer, Maslow began by studying the lives of great men and women from history, such as Albert Einstein, William James, Jane Addams, Eleanor Roosevelt, Abraham Lincoln, John Muir, and Walt Whitman. From there he moved on to directly study living artists, writers, poets, and other creative individuals.

Along the way, Maslow's thinking changed radically. At first he studied only people of obvious creativity or high achievement. However, it eventually became clear that a housewife, clerk, student, or someone like our friend Annette could live a rich, creative, and satisfying life. Maslow referred to the process of fully developing personal potentials as **self-actualization** (Maslow, 1954). The heart of self-actualization is a continuous search for personal fulfillment (Ewen, 2003; Reiss & Havercamp, 2005).

Characteristics of Self-Actualizers

A *self-actualizer* is a person who is living creatively and fully using his or her potentials. In his studies, Maslow found that self-actualizers share many similarities. Whether famous or unknown, well schooled or uneducated, rich or poor, self-actualizers tend to fit the following profile:

1. **Efficient perceptions of reality.** Self-actualizers are able to judge situations correctly and honestly. They are very sensitive to the fake and dishonest.
2. **Comfortable acceptance of self, others, nature.** Self-actualizers accept their own human nature with all its flaws. The shortcomings of others and the contradictions of the human condition are accepted with humor and tolerance.

Humanism An approach that focuses on human experience, problems, potentials, and ideals.

Self-actualization The process of fully developing personal potentials.

3. **Spontaneity.** Maslow's subjects extended their creativity into everyday activities. Actualizers tend to be unusually alive, engaged, and spontaneous.

4. **Task centering.** Most of Maslow's subjects had a mission to fulfill in life or some task or problem outside of themselves to pursue. Humanitarians such as Albert Schweitzer and Mother Teresa represent this quality.

5. **Autonomy.** Self-actualizers are free from reliance on external authorities or other people. They tend to be resourceful and independent.

6. **Continued freshness of appreciation.** The self-actualizer seems to constantly renew appreciation of life's basic good. A sunset or a flower will be experienced as intensely time after time as it was at first. There is an "innocence of vision," like that of an artist or child.

7. **Fellowship with humanity.** Maslow's subjects felt a deep identification with others and the human situation in general.

8. **Profound interpersonal relationships.** The interpersonal relationships of self-actualizers are marked by deep, loving bonds (Hanley & Abell, 2002).

9. **Comfort with solitude.** Despite their satisfying relationships with others, self-actualizing persons value solitude and are comfortable being alone (Sumerlin & Bundrick, 1996).

10. **Nonhostile sense of humor.** This refers to the wonderful capacity to laugh at oneself. It also describes the kind of humor a man like Abraham Lincoln had. Lincoln probably never made a joke that hurt anybody. His wry comments were a gentle prodding of human shortcomings.

11. **Peak experiences.** All of Maslow's subjects reported the frequent occurrence of *peak experiences* (temporary moments of self-actualization). These occasions were marked by feelings of ecstasy, harmony, and deep meaning. Self-actualizers reported feeling at one with the universe, stronger and calmer than ever before, filled with light, beautiful and good, and so forth.

In summary, self-actualizers feel safe, nonanxious, accepted, loved, loving, and alive.

Maslow's choice of people for study seems pretty subjective. Do they really provide a fair representation of self-actualization? Although Maslow tried to investigate self-actualization empirically, his choice of people for study was subjective. Undoubtedly there are many ways to make full use of personal potential. Maslow's primary contribution was to draw our attention to the possibility of lifelong personal growth.

What steps can be taken to promote self-actualization? Maslow made few specific recommendations about how to proceed. There is no magic formula for leading a more creative life. Self-actualization is primarily a *process,* not a goal or an end point. As such, it requires hard work, patience, and commitment. Nevertheless, some helpful suggestions can be gleaned from his writings (Maslow, 1954, 1967, 1971). Here are some ways to begin:

1. **Be willing to change.** Begin by asking yourself, "Am I living in a way that is deeply satisfying to me and that truly expresses me?" If not, be prepared to make changes in your life. Indeed, ask yourself this question often and accept the need for continual change.

2. **Take responsibility.** You can become an architect of self by acting as if you are personally responsible for every aspect of your life. Shouldering responsibility in this way helps end the habit of blaming others for your own shortcomings.

3. **Examine your motives.** Self-discovery involves an element of risk. If your behavior is restricted by a desire for safety or security, it may be time to test some limits. Try to make each life decision a choice for growth, not a response to fear or anxiety.

4. **Experience honestly and directly.** Wishful thinking is another barrier to personal growth. Self-actualizers trust themselves enough to accept all kinds of information without distorting it to fit their fears and desires. Try to see yourself as others do. Be willing to admit, "I was wrong," or, "I failed because I was irresponsible."

5. **Make use of positive experiences.** Maslow considered peak experiences temporary moments of self-actualization. Therefore, you might actively repeat activities that have caused feelings of awe, amazement, exaltation, renewal, reverence, humility, fulfillment, or joy.

6. **Be prepared to be different.** Maslow felt that everyone has a potential for "greatness," but most fear becoming what they might. As part of personal growth, be prepared to trust your own impulses and feelings; don't automatically judge yourself by the standards of others. Accept your uniqueness.

7. **Get involved.** With few exceptions, self-actualizers tend to have a mission or "calling" in life. For these people, "work" is not done just to fill deficiency needs, but to satisfy higher yearnings for truth, beauty, community, and meaning. Get personally involved and committed. Turn your attention to problems outside yourself.

8. **Assess your progress.** There is no final point at which one becomes self-actualized. It's important to gauge your progress frequently and to renew your efforts. If you feel bored at school, at a job, or in a relationship, consider it a challenge. Have you been taking responsibility for your own personal growth? Almost any activity can be used as a chance for self-enhancement if it is approached creatively.

Carl Rogers' Self Theory

Carl Rogers, another well-known humanist, also emphasized the human capacity for inner peace and happiness. The *fully functioning person,* he said, lives in harmony with his or her deepest feelings and impulses. Such people are open to their experiences and they trust their inner urges and intuitions (Rogers, 1961). Rogers believed that this attitude is most likely to occur when a person receives ample amounts of love and acceptance from others.

Humanists consider self-image a central determinant of behavior and personal adjustment.

Personality Structure and Dynamics

Rogers' theory emphasizes the **self,** a flexible and changing perception of personal identity. Much behavior can be understood as an attempt to maintain consistency between our *self-image* and our actions. (Your **self-image** is a total subjective perception of your body and personality.) For example, people who think of themselves as kind tend to be considerate in most situations.

Let's say I know a person who thinks she is kind, but she really isn't. How does that fit Rogers' theory? According to Rogers, we allow experiences that match our self-image into awareness, where they gradually change the self. Information or feelings inconsistent with the self-image are said to be incongruent. Thus, a person who thinks she is kind but really isn't is in a state of **incongruence.** In other words, there is a discrepancy between her experiences and her self-image. As another example, it would be incongruent to believe that you are a person who "never gets angry" if you spend much of each day seething inside.

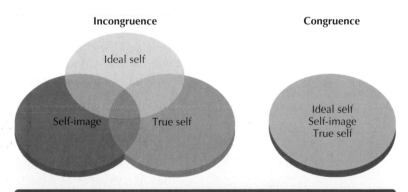

▲ FIGURE 10.7 Incongruence occurs when there is a mismatch between any of these three entities: the ideal self (the person you would like to be), your self-image (the person you think you are), and the true self (the person you actually are). Self-esteem suffers when there is a large difference between one's ideal self and self-image. Anxiety and defensiveness are common when the self-image does not match the true self.

Experiences seriously incongruent with the self-image can be threatening, and are often distorted or denied conscious recognition. Blocking, denying, or distorting experiences prevents the self from changing. This creates a gulf between the self-image and reality. As the self-image grows more unrealistic, the **incongruent person** becomes confused, vulnerable, dissatisfied, or seriously maladjusted (▶▶ Figure 10.7). In line with Rogers' observations, a study of college students confirmed that being *authentic* is vital for healthy functioning. That is, we need to feel that our behavior accurately expresses who we are (Sheldon et al., 1997). Please note, however, that being authentic doesn't mean you can do whatever you want. Being true to yourself is no excuse for acting irresponsibly or ignoring the feelings of others (Kernis & Goldman, 2005).

When your self-image is consistent with what you really think, feel, do, and experience, you are best able to actualize your potentials. Rogers also considered it essential to have

Self A continuously evolving conception of one's personal identity.

Self-image Total subjective perception of one's body and personality (another term for self-concept).

Incongruence State that exists when there is a discrepancy between one's experiences and self-image or between one's self-image and ideal self.

Incongruent person A person who has an inaccurate self-image or whose self-image differs greatly from the ideal self.

Telling Stories About Ourselves

You know these two student types: the carefree party animal and the conscientious bookworm. Perhaps you even think of yourself as one or the other. Is there any truth to these (stereo)types? Can you change your type?

College life often creates a conflict between opportunities for fun with friends and the need to study hard. In general, our personality traits are relatively stable characteristics (McAdams & Pals, 2006). As a result, a person high in the Big Five traits of extroversion and agreeableness will tend to embrace a carefree college lifestyle. In comparison, someone high in conscientiousness will find it easier to hit the books (McGregor, McAdams, & Little, 2006).

Does that mean a partyer can't become a bookworm (or vice versa)? It depends: Do you mean over a week? Or a lifetime? Personality traits do slowly change as we age. In particular,

we tend to become more agreeable, conscientious, and emotionally stable as we grow older (Roberts & Mroczek, 2008).

Oh, you need to change by the end of the semester? That's a taller order. In that case, you might want to try telling yourself stories about possible selves you could become. The *narrative approach* to personality asserts that our personalities are shaped by the stories we tell about ourselves (Lodi-Smith et al., 2009; Pals, 2006). In other words, alternate life stories are not just fantasies or daydreams. They actually influence who we are and who we become.

So, if you feel that you are being too careless and carefree at school, start imagining yourself studying more, getting to classes on time, and getting good grades. Listen to the stories of successful students and use them to revise your own story. Visit your campus counseling center to

learn more about how to succeed at school. In other words, imagine yourself as a bit more of a bookworm. (Don't worry, your carefree nature won't desert you!)

If you feel you are too conscientious and working too hard, imagine yourself going out with friends more often. Listen to the stories of your extroverted classmates. Imagine the benefits of balancing work and play in your life. If you are shy or perfectionistic, visit your campus counseling center to learn how to become more sociable or relaxed. And, again, don't worry: Having more fun won't make you irresponsible.

Whatever possible self you choose to pursue, you are more likely to become what you imagine if you elaborate your story, making it more detailed and "real" as you gradually adopt new patterns. You *can* create a new narrative identity for yourself (Bauer, McAdams, & Pals, 2008).

---

congruence between the self-image and the **ideal self.** The ideal self is similar to Freud's ego ideal. It is an image of the person you would most like to be.

Is it really incongruent not to live up to your ideal self? Rogers was aware that we never fully attain our ideals. Nevertheless, the greater the gap between the way you see yourself and the way you would like to be, the more tension and anxiety you will experience.

Rogers emphasized that to maximize our potentials, we must accept information about ourselves as honestly as possible. In accord with his thinking, researchers have found that people with a close match between their self-image and ideal self tend to be socially poised, confident, and resourceful. Those with a poor match tend to be depressed, anxious, and insecure (Boldero et al., 2005).

According to psychologists Hazel Markus and Paula Nurius (1986), our ideal self is only one of a number of *possible selves* (persons we could become or are afraid of becoming). Annette, who was described earlier, is an interesting personality, to say the least. Annette is one of those people who seems to have lived many lives in the time that most of us manage only one. Like Annette, you may have pondered many possible personal identities. (See "Telling Stories About Ourselves.")

Possible selves translate our hopes, fears, fantasies, and goals into specific images of who we *could* be. Thus, a beginning law student might picture herself as a successful attorney; an enterprising college student might imagine himself as an Internet entrepreneur; and a person on a diet might imagine both slim and grossly obese possible selves. Such images tend to direct our future behavior (Oyserman et al., 2004).

Of course, almost everyone over age 30 has probably felt the anguish of realizing that some cherished possible selves will never be realized. Nevertheless, there is value in asking yourself not just "Who am I?" but also "Who would I like to become?" As you do, remember Maslow's advice that everyone has a potential for "greatness," but most fear becoming what they might.

Humanistic View of Development

Why do mirrors, photographs, video cameras, and the reactions of others hold such fascination and threat for many people? Carl Rogers' theory suggests it is because they provide information about one's self. The development of a self-image depends greatly on informa-

Ideal self An idealized image of oneself (the person one would like to be).

tion from the environment. It begins with a sorting of perceptions and feelings: my body, my toes, my nose, I want, I like, I am, and so on. Soon, it expands to include self-evaluation: I am a good person, I did something bad just now, and so forth.

How does development of the self contribute to later personality functioning? Rogers believed that positive and negative evaluations by others cause children to develop internal standards of evaluation called **conditions of worth.** In other words, we learn that some actions win our parents' love and approval, whereas others are rejected. More important, parents may label some *feelings* as bad or wrong. For example, a child might be told that it is wrong to feel angry toward a brother or sister—even when anger is justified. Likewise, a little boy might be told that he must not cry or show fear, two very normal emotions.

Learning to evaluate some experiences or feelings as "good" and others as "bad" is directly related to a later capacity for self-esteem, positive self-evaluation, or **positive self-regard,** to use Rogers' term. To think of yourself as a good, lovable, worthwhile person, your behavior and experiences must match your internal conditions of worth. The problem is that this can cause incongruence by leading to the denial of many true feelings and experiences.

To put it simply, Rogers blamed many adult emotional problems on attempts to live by the standards of others. He believed that congruence and self-actualization are encouraged by replacing conditions of worth with **organismic valuing** (a natural, undistorted, full-body reaction to an experience). Organismic valuing is a direct, gut-level response to life that avoids the filtering and distortion of incongruence. It involves trusting one's own feelings and perceptions. Organismic valuing is most likely to develop, Rogers felt, when children (or adults) receive **unconditional positive regard** (unshakable love and approval) from others. That is, when they are "prized" as worthwhile human beings, just for being themselves, without any conditions or strings attached. Although this may be a luxury few people enjoy, we are more likely to move toward our ideal selves if we receive affirmation and support from a close partner (Drigotas et al., 1999).

Traits and Situations—The Great Debate

How do traits and situations affect personality?

Personality theorists have long grappled with the relative roles of nature and nurture in shaping personalities. Some theories, such as trait theory and psychoanalytic theory, stress the role of inherited biological predispositions, while others, including behavioral and humanist theories, stress the role of learning and life experiences. Before we conclude with an overview of the four major theories of personality, let's look at the roles that heredity, biological predispositions, and environmental situations play in forming personality.

Do We Inherit Personality?

Even newborn babies differ in temperament, which implies that it is hereditary. **Temperament,** the "raw material" from which personalities are formed, refers to the hereditary aspects of your personality, such as biological predispositions to be sensitive, irritable, and distractible and to display a typical mood (Rothbart, 2007). Temperament has a large impact on how infants interact with their parents (see Chapter 3). Judging from Annette's adult personality, you might guess that she was an active, happy baby.

At what age are personality traits firmly established? Personality starts to stabilize at around age 3 and continues to "harden" through age 50 (Caspi, Roberts, & Shiner, 2005). However, as mentioned earlier, personality slowly matures during old age as most people continue to become more conscientious, agreeable, and emotionally stable (Roberts & Mroczek, 2008). It appears that stereotypes of the "grumpy old man" and "cranky old woman" are largely unfounded.

Conditions of worth Internal standards used to judge the value of one's thoughts, actions, feelings, or experiences.

Positive self-regard Thinking of oneself as a good, lovable, worthwhile person.

Organismic valuing A natural, undistorted, full-body reaction to an experience.

Unconditional positive regard Unshakable love and approval given without qualification.

Temperament The hereditary aspects of personality, including sensitivity, activity levels, prevailing mood, irritability, and adaptability.

Amazing Twins

Many reunited twins in the Minnesota study (the Minnesota Twins?) have displayed similarities far beyond what would be expected on the basis of heredity. The "Jim twins," James Lewis and James Springer, are one famous example. Both Jims had married and divorced women named Linda. Both had undergone police training. One named his firstborn son James Allan, the other named *his* firstborn son James Alan. Both drove Chevrolets and vacationed at the same beach each summer. Both listed carpentry and mechanical drawing among their hobbies. Both had built benches around trees in their yards. And so forth (Holden, 1980).

Are all identical twins so, well, identical? No, they aren't. Consider identical twins Carolyn Spiro and Pamela Spiro Wagner, who, unlike the "Jim Twins," lived together throughout their childhood. While in sixth grade, they found out that President Kennedy had been assassinated. Carolyn wasn't sure why everyone was so upset. Pamela heard voices announcing that she was responsible for his death. After years of hiding her voices from everyone, Pamela tried to commit suicide while the twins were attending Brown University. She was diagnosed with schizophrenia. Never to be cured, she has gone on to write award-winning poetry. Carolyn eventually became a Harvard psychiatrist (Spiro Wagner & Spiro, 2005). Some twins reared apart appear very similar; some reared together appear rather different.

So why are some identical twins, like the Jim Twins, so much alike even if they were reared apart? Although genetics is important, it is preposterous to suggest that there are child-naming genes and bench-building genes. How, then, do we explain the eerie similarities in some separated twins' lives? Imagine that you were separated at birth from a twin brother or sister. If you were reunited with your twin today, what would you do? Quite likely, you would spend the next several days comparing every imaginable detail of your lives. Under such circumstances, it is virtually certain that you and your twin would notice and compile a long list of similarities ("Wow! I use the same brand of toothpaste you do!"). Yet, two unrelated persons of the same age, sex, and race could probably rival your list—*if* they were as motivated to find similarities.

In fact, one study compared twins with unrelated pairs of students. The unrelated pairs, who were the same age and sex, were almost as alike as the twins. They had highly similar political beliefs, musical interests, religious preferences, job histories, hobbies, favorite foods, and so on (Wyatt et al., 1984). Why were the unrelated students so similar? Basically, it's because people of the same age and sex live in the same historical times and select from similar societal options. As just one example, in nearly every elementary school classroom, you will find several children with the same first name.

It appears then that many of the seemingly "astounding" coincidences shared by reunited twins may be a special case of the fallacy of positive instances, described in Chapter 1. Reunited twins tend to notice the similarities and ignore the differences.

Identical twins Pam (*left*) and Carolyn (*right*) were raised together. Regardless, Carolyn became a psychiatrist while Pamela developed schizophrenia and went on to become an award-winning poet (Spiro Wagner & Spiro, 2005). Their story illustrates the complex interplay of forces that shape our adult personalities.

Does the stability of personality traits mean that they are affected by heredity? Some breeds of dogs have reputations for being friendly, aggressive, intelligent, calm, or emotional. Such differences fall in the realm of **behavioral genetics,** the study of inherited behavioral traits. We know that facial features, eye color, body type, and many other physical characteristics are inherited. So are many of our behavioral dispositions (Bouchard, 2004; Kalat, 2007). Genetic studies have shown that intelligence, language, some mental disorders, temperament, and other complex qualities are influenced by heredity. In view of such findings, it wouldn't be a surprise to find that genes affect personality as well (Nettle, 2006).

Wouldn't comparing the personalities of identical twins help answer the question? It would indeed—especially if the twins were separated at birth or soon after.

Twins and Traits

For several decades, psychologists at the University of Minnesota have been studying identical twins who grew up in different homes. Medical and psychological tests reveal that reunited twins are very much alike, even when they are reared apart (Bouchard, 2004; Bouchard et al., 1990). They may even be similar in appearance, voice quality, facial gestures, hand movements, and nervous tics, such as nail biting. Separated twins also tend to have similar talents. If one twin excels at art, music, dance, drama, or athletics, the other is likely to as well—despite wide differences in childhood environment. However, as "The Amazing Twins" explains, it's wise to be cautious about some reports of extraordinary similarities in reunited twins.

Behavioral genetics The study of inherited behavioral traits and tendencies.

Summary

Studies of twins make it clear that heredity has a sizable effect on each of us. All told, it seems reasonable to conclude that heredity is responsible for about 25 to 50 percent of the variation in many personality traits (Caspi, Roberts, & Shiner, 2005; Loehlin et al., 1998). Notice, however, that the same figures imply that personality is shaped as much, or more, by environment as it is by biological predispositions.

Each personality, then, is a unique blend of heredity and environment, biology and culture. We are not—thank goodness—genetically programmed robots whose behavior and personality traits are "wired in" for life. Where you go in life is the result of the choices you make. Although these choices are influenced by inherited tendencies, they are not merely a product of your genes (Funder, 2006).

Is Personality Affected by Situations?

Remember Annette? When we heard she actually decked a man who was harassing her, we were surprised. The Annette we had known was always quite calm and peaceful. Had she changed so much? Before we try to provide an answer, take a moment to answer the questions that follow. Doing so will add to your understanding of a long-running controversy in the psychology of personality.

Rate Yourself: How Do You View Personality?
1. My friends' actions are fairly consistent from day to day and in different situations. T or F?
2. Whether a person is honest or dishonest, kind or cruel, a hero or a coward depends mainly on circumstances. T or F?
3. Most people I have known for several years have pretty much the same personalities now as they did when I first met them. T or F?
4. The reason people in some professions (such as teachers, lawyers, or doctors) seem so much alike is because their work requires that they act in particular ways. T or F?
5. One of the first things I would want to know about a potential roommate is what the person's personality is like. T or F?
6. I believe that immediate circumstances usually determine how people act at any given time. T or F?
7. To be comfortable in a particular job, a person's personality must match the nature of the work. T or F?
8. Almost anyone would be polite at a wedding reception; it doesn't matter what kind of personality the person has. T or F?

Now count the number of times you marked true for the odd-numbered items. Do the same for the even-numbered items.

If you agreed with most of the odd-numbered items, you tend to view behavior as strongly influenced by personality traits or lasting personal dispositions, whether biological or learned.

If you agreed with most of the even-numbered items, you view behavior as strongly influenced by external situations and circumstances.

What if I answered true about equally for odd and even items? Then you place equal weight on traits and situations as ways to explain behavior. This is the view now held by many personality psychologists (Funder, 2006; Mischel & Shoda, 1998).

Traits, Consistency, and Situations

Does that mean that to predict how a person will act, it is better to focus on both personality traits and external circumstances? Yes, it's best to take both into account. Because personality traits are consistent, they can predict such things as job performance, dangerous driving, or a successful marriage (Funder, 2006). Yet, *situations* also greatly influence our behavior. Annette's normally calm demeanor became aggressive only because the situation was unusual and extreme: The man in the bar seriously harassed her, making her uncharacteristically angry and upset.

Can all unusual behaviors be "blamed" on unusual situations? Great question. Consider Fred Cowan, a model student in school and described by those who knew him as quiet, gentle, and a man who loved children. Despite his size (6 feet tall, 250 pounds), Fred was described by a coworker as "someone you could easily push around." Two weeks after he was suspended from his job, Fred returned to work determined to get even with his supervisor. Unable to find the man, he killed four coworkers and a policeman before taking his own life (Lee, Zimbardo, & Bertholf, 1977).

Sudden murderers like Fred Cowan tend to be quiet, overcontrolled individuals. They are likely to be especially violent if they ever lose control. While their attacks may be triggered by a minor irritation or frustration, the attack reflects years of unexpressed feelings of anger and belittlement. When sudden murderers finally release the strict controls they have maintained on their overcontrolled behavior, a furious and frenzied attack ensues (Cartwright, 2002b). Usually it is totally out of proportion to the offense against them, and many have amnesia for their violent actions. So, unlike Annette, who reacted in an unexpected way to an unusual situation, Fred Cowan's overreaction was typical of people who share his personality pattern.

Trait-Situation Interactions

It would be unusual for you to dance at a movie or read a book at a football game. Likewise, few people sleep in roller coasters or tell off-color jokes at funerals. However, your personality traits may predict whether you choose to read a book, go to a movie, or attend a football game in the first place. Typically, traits *interact* with situations to determine how we will act (Mischel, 2004).

In a **trait–situation interaction,** external circumstances influence the expression of a personality trait. For instance, imagine what would happen if you moved from a church to a classroom to a party to a football game. As the setting changed, you would probably become louder and more boisterous. This change would show situational effects on behavior. At the same time, your personality traits would also be apparent: If you were quieter than average in church and class, you would probably be quieter than average in the other settings, too.

Overview and Comparison of Personality Theories

Which of the personality theories is right? To date, each theory has added to our understanding by providing a sort of lens through which human behavior can be viewed. Nevertheless, theories can't be fully proved or disproved. We can only ask, Does the evidence tend to support this theory or disconfirm it? Yet, although theories are neither true nor false, their implications or predictions may be. The best way to judge a theory, then, is in terms of its *usefulness*. Does the theory adequately explain behavior? Does it stimulate new research? Does it suggest how to treat psychological disorders? Each theory has fared differently in these areas (Pervin, Cervone, & John, 2005). ● Table 10.3 provides an over-

Trait–situation interaction The influence that external settings or circumstances have on the expression of personality traits.

● Table 10.3 Comparison of Personality Theories

	TRAIT THEORIES	PSYCHOANALYTIC THEORY	BEHAVIORISTIC AND SOCIAL LEARNING THEORIES	HUMANISTIC THEORY
Role of inheritance (genetics)	Maximized	Stressed	Minimized	Minimized
Role of environment	Recognized	Recognized	Maximized	Maximized
View of human nature	Neutral	Negative	Neutral	Positive
Is behavior free or determined?	Determined	Determined	Determined	Free choice
Principal motives	Depends on one's traits	Sex and aggression	Drives of all kinds	Self-actualization
Personality structure	Traits	Id, ego, superego	Habits, expectancies	Self
Role of unconscious	Minimized	Maximized	Practically nonexistent	Minimized
Conception of conscience	Traits of honesty, etc.	Superego	Self-reinforcement, punishment history	Ideal self, valuing process
Developmental emphasis	Combined effects of heredity and environment	Psychosexual stages	Critical learning situations, identification, and imitation	Development of self-image
Barriers to personal growth	Unhealthy traits	Unconscious conflicts, fixations	Maladaptive habits, unhealthy environment	Conditions of worth, incongruence

Body text continues from previous page:

view of the four principal approaches to personality. The challenge now facing theorists is how to combine the four perspectives into a single, complete explanation of personality (Mayer, 2005).

study break

Humanistic Theory and Traits and Situations

RECITE

1. Humanists view human nature as basically good and they emphasize the effects of subjective learning and unconscious choice. T or F?
2. Maslow used the term _____ to describe the tendency of certain individuals to fully use their talents and potentials.
3. According to Rogers, a close match between the self-image and the ideal self creates a condition called incongruence. T or F?
4. Rogers' theory considers acceptance of conditions of _____ a troublesome aspect of development of the self.
5. According to Maslow, a preoccupation with one's own thoughts, feelings, and needs is characteristic of self-actualizing individuals. T or F?
6. Maslow regarded _____ experiences as times of temporary self-actualization.
7. _____ refers to the hereditary aspects of a person's emotional nature.
8. To understand personality, it is wise to remember that traits and situations _____ to determine our behavior.

REFLECT

Critical Thinking

9. What role have your possible selves played in your choice of a college major?
10. Are situations equally powerful in their impact on behavior?

Relate

Do you know anyone who seems to be making especially good use of his or her personal potential? Does that person fit Maslow's profile of a self-actualizer?

How much difference do you think there is between your self-image, your ideal self, and your true self? Do you think Rogers is right about the effects of applying conditions of worth to your perceptions and feelings?

Which of the four views of personality has most helped you reflect on your own personality? Have the others helped at all?

ANSWERS

1. F   2. self-actualization   3. F   4. worth   5. F   6. peak   7. Temperament   8. interact   9. Career decisions almost always involve, in part, picturing oneself occupying various occupational roles. Such "future selves" play a role in many of the major decisions we make (Masters & Holley, 2006).   10. No. Circumstances can have a strong or weak influence. In some situations, almost everyone will act the same, no matter what their personality traits may be. In other situations, traits may be of greater importance.

Personality Assessment— Psychological Yardsticks

How do psychologists measure personality?

Measuring personality can help predict how people will behave at work, at school, and in therapy. However, painting a detailed picture can be a challenge. In many instances, it requires several of the techniques described in the following discussion. To capture a personality as unique as Annette's, it might take all of them!

How is personality "measured"? Psychologists use interviews, observation, questionnaires, and projective tests to assess personality (Burger, 2008). Each method has strengths and limitations. For this reason, they are often used in combination.

Formal personality measures are refinements of more casual ways of judging a person. At one time or another, you have probably "sized up" a potential date, friend, or roommate by engaging in conversation (interview). Perhaps you have asked a friend, "When I am delayed I get angry. Do you?" (questionnaire). Maybe you watch your professors when they are angry or embarrassed to learn what they are "really" like when they're caught off-guard (observation). Or possibly you have noticed that when you say, "I think people feel...," you may be expressing your own feelings (projection). Let's see how psychologists apply each of these methods to probe personality.

The Interview

In an **interview,** direct questioning is used to learn about a person's life history, personality traits, or current mental state (Sommers-Flanagan & Sommers-Flanagan, 2002). In an *unstructured interview,* conversation is informal and topics are taken up freely as they arise. In a *structured interview,* information is gathered by asking a planned series of questions.

How are interviews used? Interviews are used to identify personality disturbances; to select people for jobs, college, or special programs; and to study the dynamics of personality. Interviews also provide information for counseling or therapy. For instance, a counselor might ask a depressed person, "Have you ever contemplated suicide? What were the circumstances?" The counselor might then follow by asking, "How did you feel about it?" or, "How is what you are now feeling different from what you felt then?"

In addition to providing information, interviews make it possible to observe a person's tone of voice, hand gestures, posture, and facial expressions. Such "body language" cues are important because they may radically alter the message sent, as when a person claims to be "completely calm" but trembles uncontrollably.

Limitations

Interviews give rapid insight into personality, but they have limitations. For one thing, interviewers can be swayed by preconceptions. A person identified as a "housewife," "college student," "high school athlete," "punk," "geek," or "ski bum" may be misjudged because of an interviewer's personal biases. Second, an interviewer's own personality, or even gender, may influence a client's behavior. When this occurs, it can accentuate or distort the person's apparent traits (Pollner, 1998). A third problem is that people sometimes try to deceive interviewers. For example, a person accused of a crime might try to avoid punishment by pretending to be mentally disabled.

A fourth problem is the **halo effect,** which is the tendency to generalize a favorable (or unfavorable) impression to an entire personality (Lance, LaPointe, & Stewart, 1994). Because of the halo effect, a person who is likable or physically attractive may be rated more mature, intelligent, or mentally healthy than she or he actually is. The halo effect is something to keep in mind at job interviews. First impressions do make a difference (Lance, LaPointe, & Stewart, 1994).

Even with their limitations, interviews are a respected method of assessment. In many cases, interviews are the first step in evaluating personality and an essential prelude to therapy. Nevertheless, interviews are usually not enough and must be supplemented by other measures and tests (Meyer et al., 2001).

Direct Observation and Rating Scales

Are you fascinated by airports, bus depots, parks, taverns, subway stations, or other public places? Many people relish a chance to observe the actions of others. When used for assessment, **direct observation** (looking at behavior) is a simple extension of this natural interest in "people watching." For instance, a psychologist might arrange to observe a disturbed child as she plays with other children. Is the child withdrawn? Does she become hostile or aggressive without warning? By careful observation, the psychologist can identify the girl's personality traits and clarify the nature of her problems.

Wouldn't observation be subject to the same problems of misperception as an interview? Yes. Misperceptions can be a difficulty, which is why rating scales are sometimes used (▶▶ Figure 10.8). A **rating scale** is a list of personality traits or aspects of behavior that can be used to evaluate a person. Rating scales limit the chance that some traits will be over-

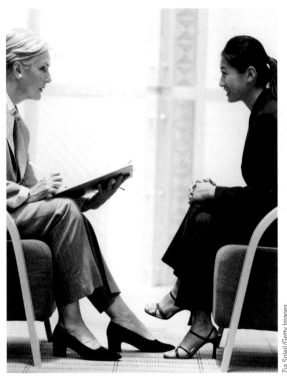

What is your impression of the person wearing the black suit? If you think that she looks friendly, attractive, or neat, your other perceptions of her might be altered by that impression. Interviewers are often influenced by the halo effect (see text).

Zia Soleil/Getty Images

Interview (personality) A face-to-face meeting held for the purpose of gaining information about an individual's personal history, personality traits, current psychological state, and so forth.

Halo effect The tendency to generalize a favorable or unfavorable impression to unrelated details of personality.

Direct observation Assessing behavior through direct surveillance.

Rating scale A list of personality traits or aspects of behavior on which a person is rated.

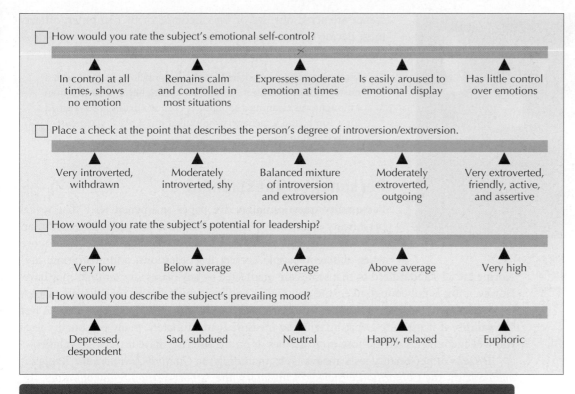

How would you rate the subject's emotional self-control?

| In control at all times, shows no emotion | Remains calm and controlled in most situations | Expresses moderate emotion at times | Is easily aroused to emotional display | Has little control over emotions |

Place a check at the point that describes the person's degree of introversion/extroversion.

| Very introverted, withdrawn | Moderately introverted, shy | Balanced mixture of introversion and extroversion | Moderately extroverted, outgoing | Very extroverted, friendly, active, and assertive |

How would you rate the subject's potential for leadership?

| Very low | Below average | Average | Above average | Very high |

How would you describe the subject's prevailing mood?

| Depressed, despondent | Sad, subdued | Neutral | Happy, relaxed | Euphoric |

FIGURE 10.8 Sample rating scale items. To understand how the scale works, imagine someone you know well. Where would you place check marks on each of the scales to rate that person's characteristics?

looked while others are exaggerated (Synhorst et al., 2005). Perhaps they should be a standard procedure for choosing a roommate, spouse, or lover!

An alternative approach is to do a **behavioral assessment** by counting the frequency of specific behaviors. In this case, observers record *actions,* not what traits they think a person has (Ramsay, Reynolds, & Kamphaus, 2002). For example, a psychologist working with hospitalized mental patients might note the frequency of a patient's aggression, self-care, speech, and unusual behaviors. Behavioral assessments can also be used to probe thought processes. In one study, for example, couples were assessed while talking with each other about their sexuality. Couples with sexual difficulties were less likely to be receptive to discussing their sexuality and more likely to blame each other than were couples with no sexual difficulties (Kelly, Strassberg, & Turner, 2006).

Situational Testing

In **situational testing,** real-life conditions are simulated so that a person's spontaneous reactions can be observed. Such tests assume that the best way to learn how people react is to put them in realistic situations and watch what happens. Situational tests expose people to frustration, temptation, pressure, boredom, or other conditions capable of revealing personality characteristics (Olson-Buchanan & Drasgow, 2006; Weekley & Jones, 1997). Some popular "reality TV" programs, such as *American Idol, Survivor,* and *The Amazing Race,* bear some similarity to situational tests—which may account for their ability to attract millions of viewers.

How are situational tests done? An interesting example of situational testing is the judgmental firearms training provided by many police departments. At times, police officers must make split-second decisions about using their weapons. A mistake could be fatal. In a typical shoot–don't shoot test, actors play the part of armed criminals. As various high-risk

Behavioral assessment Recording the frequency of various behaviors.

Situational test Simulating real-life conditions so that a person's reactions may be directly observed.

A police officer undergoes judgmental fire-arms training. Variations on this situational test are used by a growing number of police departments. All officers must score a passing grade.

scenes are acted out live or on videotape or by computer, officers must decide to shoot or hold fire. A newspaper reporter who once took the test (and failed it) gives this account (Gersh, 1982):

> I judged wrong. I was killed by a man in a closet, a man with a hostage, a woman interrupted when kissing her lover, and a man I thought was cleaning a shotgun. . . . I shot a drunk who reached for a comb, and a teenager who pulled out a black water pistol. Looked real to me.

Personality Questionnaires

Personality questionnaires are paper-and-pencil tests that reveal personality characteristics. Questionnaires are more objective than interviews or observation. (An objective test gives the same score when different people correct it.) Questions, administration, and scoring are all standardized so that scores are unaffected by any biases an examiner may have. However, this is not enough to ensure accuracy. A good test must also be reliable and valid. A test is **reliable** if it yields close to the same score each time it is given to the same person. A test has **validity** if it measures what it claims to measure. Unfortunately, many personality tests you will encounter, such as those in magazines or on the Internet, have little or no validity.

Dozens of personality tests are available, including the *Guilford-Zimmerman Temperament Survey,* the *California Psychological Inventory,* the *Allport-Vernon Study of Values,* the 16 PF, and many more. One of the best-known and most widely used objective tests is the **Minnesota Multiphasic Personality Inventory-2 (MMPI-2)** (Butcher, 2005). The MMPI-2 is composed of 567 items to which a test taker must respond "true" or "false." Items include statements such as the following:

Everything tastes the same. F
I am very normal, sexually. F
I like birds. T
I usually daydream in the afternoon. T
Mostly I stay away from other people. T
Someone has been trying to hurt me. F
Sometimes I think strange thoughts.* T

How can these items show anything about personality? For instance, what if a person has a cold so that "everything tastes the same"? For an answer (and a little bit of fun), read the following items. Answer "Yes," "No," or "Don't bother me, I can't cope!"

I would enjoy the work of a chicken flicker. N
My eyes are always cold. N
Frantic screaming makes me nervous. Y
I believe I smell as good as most people. N
I use shoe polish to excess. N
The sight of blood no longer excites me. N
As an infant I had very few hobbies. Y
Dirty stories make me think about sex. Y
I stay in the bathtub until I look like a raisin. Y
I salivate at the sight of mittens. N
I never finish what I† Y

These items were written by humorist Art Buchwald (1965) to satirize personality questionnaires. Such questions may seem ridiculous, but they are not very different from the real thing. How, then, do the items on tests such as the MMPI-2 reveal anything about personal-

Personality questionnaire A paper-and-pencil test consisting of questions that reveal aspects of personality.

Reliability The ability of a test to yield nearly the same score each time it is given to the same person.

Validity The ability of a test to measure what it purports to measure.

Minnesota Multiphasic Personality Inventory-2 (MMPI-2) One of the best-known and most widely used objective personality questionnaires.

---

*MMPI-2 statements themselves cannot be reproduced, to protect the validity of the test.

†Art Buchwald, "Psyching Out," Washington Post, June 1965. Reprinted courtesy of the Estate of Art Buchwald.

● Table 10.4 MMPI-2 Basic Clinical Subscales

1. **Hypochondriasis** (HI-po-kon-DRY-uh-sis). Exaggerated concern about one's physical health.
2. **Depression.** Feelings of worthlessness, hopelessness, and pessimism.
3. **Hysteria.** The presence of physical complaints for which no physical basis can be established.
4. **Psychopathic deviate.** Emotional shallowness in relationships and a disregard for social and moral standards.
5. **Masculinity/femininity.** One's degree of traditional "masculine" aggressiveness or "feminine" sensitivity.
6. **Paranoia.** Extreme suspiciousness and feelings of persecution.
7. **Psychasthenia** (sike-as-THEE-nee-ah). The presence of obsessive worries, irrational fears (phobias), and compulsive (ritualistic) actions.
8. **Schizophrenia.** Emotional withdrawal and unusual or bizarre thinking and actions.
9. **Mania.** Emotional excitability, manic moods or behavior, and excessive activity.
10. **Social introversion.** One's tendency to be socially withdrawn.

ity? The answer is that a single item tells little about personality. For example, a person who agrees that "Everything tastes the same" might simply have a cold. It is only through *patterns* of response that personality dimensions are revealed.

Items on the MMPI-2 were selected for their ability to correctly identify persons with particular psychological problems (Butcher, 2005). For instance, if depressed persons consistently answer a series of items in a particular way, it is assumed that others who answer the same way are also prone to depression. As silly as the gag items in the preceding list may seem, it is possible that some could actually work in a legitimate test. But before an item could be part of a test, it would have to be shown to correlate highly with some trait or dimension of personality.

The MMPI-2 measures 10 major aspects of personality (listed in ● Table 10.4). After the MMPI-2 is scored, results are charted graphically as an **MMPI-2 profile** (►► Figure 10.9). By comparing a person's profile with scores produced by typical, normal adults, a psychologist can identify various personality disorders. Additional scales can identify substance abuse, eating disorders, Type A (heart-attack prone) behavior, repression, anger, cynicism, low self-esteem, family problems, inability to function in a job, and other problems (Butcher, 2006).

How accurate is the MMPI-2? Personality questionnaires are accurate only if people tell the truth about themselves. Because of this, the MMPI-2 has additional **validity scales** that

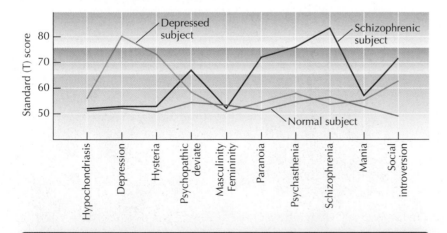

▲ **FIGURE 10.9** An MMPI-2 profile showing hypothetical scores indicating normality, depression, and psychosis. High scores begin at 66 and very high scores at 76. An unusually low score (40 and below) may also reveal personality characteristics or problems.

MMPI-2 profile A graphic representation of an individual's scores on each of the primary scales of the MMPI-2.

Validity scales Scales that tell whether test scores should be invalidated for lying, inconsistency, or "faking good."

reveal whether a person's scores should be discarded. The validity scales detect attempts by test takers to "fake good" (make themselves look good) or "fake bad" (make it look like they have problems). Other scales uncover defensiveness or tendencies to exaggerate shortcomings and troubles. When taking the MMPI-2, it is best to answer honestly, without trying to second-guess the test.

A clinical psychologist trying to decide if a person has emotional problems would be wise to take more than the MMPI-2 into account. Test scores are informative, but they can incorrectly label some people (Urbina, 2004). Fortunately, clinical judgments usually rely on information from interviews, tests, and other sources. Also, despite their limitations, it is reassuring to note that psychological assessments are at least as accurate as commonly used medical tests (Meyer et al., 2001).

Projective Tests of Personality

Projective tests take a different approach to personality. Interviews, observation, rating scales, and inventories try to directly identify overt, observable traits (Leichtman, 2004). By contrast, projective tests seek to uncover deeply hidden or *unconscious* wishes, thoughts, and needs.

As a child you may have delighted in finding faces and objects in cloud formations. Or perhaps you have learned something about your friends' personalities from their reactions to movies or paintings. If so, you will have some insight into the rationale for projective tests. In a **projective test,** a person is asked to describe ambiguous stimuli or make up stories about them. Describing an unambiguous stimulus (a picture of an automobile, for example) tells little about your personality. But when you are faced with an unstructured stimulus, you must organize what you see in terms of your own life experiences. Everyone sees something different in a projective test, and what is perceived can reveal the inner workings of personality.

Projective tests have no right or wrong answers, which makes them difficult to fake (Leichtman, 2004). Moreover, projective tests can be a rich source of information, because responses are not restricted to simple true/false or yes/no answers.

The Rorschach Inkblot Test

Is the inkblot test a projective technique? The inkblot test, or **Rorschach** (ROAR-shock) **Technique,** is one of the oldest and most widely used projective tests. Developed by Swiss psychologist Hermann Rorschach in the 1920s, it consists of 10 standardized inkblots. These vary in color, shading, form, and complexity.

How does the test work? First, a person is shown each blot and asked to describe what she or he sees in it (▶▶ Figure 10.10). Later the psychologist may return to a blot, asking the

Projective tests Psychological tests making use of ambiguous or unstructured stimuli.

Rorschach Technique A projective test comprised of ten standardized inkblots.

⬆ **FIGURE 10.10** Inkblots similar to those used on the Rorschach. What do you see?

person to identify specific sections of it, to expand previous descriptions, or to give new impressions about what it contains. Obvious differences in content—such as "blood dripping from a dagger" versus "flowers blooming in a basket"—are important for identifying personal conflicts and fantasies. But surprisingly, content is less important than what parts of the inkblot are used to organize images. These factors allow psychologists to detect emotional disturbances by observing how a person perceives the world (Hilsenroth, 2000).

The Thematic Apperception Test

Another popular projective test is the **Thematic Apperception Test (TAT)** developed by personality theorist Henry Murray (1893–1988).

How does the TAT differ from the Rorschach? The TAT consists of 20 sketches depicting various scenes and life situations (▶▶ Figure 10.11). During testing, a person is shown each sketch and asked to make up a story about the people in it. Later, the person looks at each sketch a second or a third time and elaborates on previous stories or creates new stories.

To score the TAT, a psychologist analyzes the content of the stories. Interpretations focus on how people feel, how they interact, what events led up to the incidents depicted in the sketch, and how the story will end. For example, TAT stories told by bereaved college students typically include themes of death, grief, and coping with loss (Balk et al., 1998).

A psychologist might also count the number of times the central figure in a TAT story is angry, overlooked, apathetic, jealous, or threatened. Here is a story written by a student to describe Figure 10.11:

> The girl has been seeing this guy her mother doesn't like. The mother is telling her that she better not see him again. The mother says, "He's just like your father." The mother and father are divorced. The mother is smiling because she thinks she is right. But she doesn't really know what the girl wants. The girl is going to see the guy again, anyway.

As this example implies, the TAT is especially good at revealing feelings about a person's social relationships (Alvarado, 1994; Aronow, Altman Weiss, & Reznikoff, 2001).

Limitations of Projective Testing

Although projective tests have been popular, their validity is considered lowest among tests of personality (Lilienfeld, 1999; Wood et al., 2003). Objectivity and reliability (consistency) are also low for different users of the TAT and Rorschach. Note that after a person interprets an ambiguous stimulus, the scorer must interpret the person's (sometimes) ambiguous responses. In a sense, the interpretation of a projective test may be a projective test for the scorer!

Despite their drawbacks, projective tests still have value (Hilsenroth, 2000). This is especially true when they are used as part of a *test battery* (collection of assessment devices and interviews). In the hands of a skilled clinician, projective tests can be a good way to detect major conflicts, to get clients to talk about upsetting topics, and to set goals for therapy (O'Roark, 2001).

A Look Ahead

The "Psychology in Action" section that follows should add balance to your view of personality. Don't be shy. Read on!

▲ **FIGURE 10.11** This is a picture like those used for the Thematic Apperception Test. If you wish to simulate the test, tell a story that explains what led up to the pictured situation, what is happening now, and how the action will end.

Thematic Apperception Test (TAT) A projective test consisting of 20 different scenes and life situations about which respondents make up stories.

study break
Personality Assessment

RECITE

1. The halo effect is the tendency of an interviewer to influence what is said by the interviewee. T or F?
2. Which of the following is considered the most objective measure of personality?
   a. rating scales   b. personality questionnaires
   c. projective tests   d. TAT
3. Situational testing allows direct _____ of personality characteristics.
4. A psychotic person would probably score highest on which MMPI-2 scale?
   a. depression   b. hysteria
   c. schizophrenia   d. mania
5. The use of ambiguous stimuli is most characteristic of
   a. interviews   b. projective tests
   c. personality inventories d. direct observation

6. The content of one's responses to the MMPI-2 is considered an indication of unconscious wishes, thoughts, and needs. T or F?
7. Doing a behavioral assessment requires direct observation of the person's actions or a direct report of the person's thoughts. T or F?
8. A test is considered valid if it consistently yields the same score when the same person takes it on different occasions. T or F?

REFLECT
Critical Thinking

9. Can you think of one more reason why personality traits may not be accurately revealed by interviews?
10. Projective testing would be of greatest interest to which type of personality theorist?

RELATE

How do *you* assess personality? Do you informally make use of any of the methods described in this chapter?

You are a candidate for a desirable job. Your personality is going to be assessed by a psychologist. What method (or methods) would you prefer that she or he use? Why?

ANSWERS

1. F   2. b   3. observation   4. c   5. b   6. F   7. T   8. F   9. Because of trait–situation interactions, a person may not behave in a normal fashion while being evaluated in an interview.   10. Psychodynamic: Because projective testing is designed to uncover unconscious thoughts, feelings, and conflicts.

---

psychology in action
Barriers and Bridges—Understanding Shyness

What causes shyness? What can be done about it?

Do you

- Find it hard to talk to strangers?
- Lack confidence with people?
- Feel uncomfortable in social situations?
- Feel nervous with people who are not close friends?

As a personality trait, **shyness** refers to a tendency to avoid others, as well as feelings of anxiety, preoccupation, and social inhibition (uneasiness and strain when socializing) (Bruch, 2001). Shy persons fail to make eye contact, retreat when spoken to, speak too quietly, and display little interest or animation in conversations. Mild shyness may be no more than a nuisance. However, extreme shyness (which may be diagnosed as *social anxiety disorder*) is often associated with depression, loneliness, fearfulness, social anxiety, inhibition, and low self-esteem (Derlega, Winstead, & Jones, 2005; Stein & Stein, 2008).

Elements of Shyness

What causes shyness? To begin with, shy persons often lack *social skills* (proficiency at interacting with others). Many simply

Digital Vision/Getty Images

Shyness A tendency to avoid others plus uneasiness and strain when socializing.

have not learned how to meet people or how to start a conversation and keep it going. **Social anxiety** (a feeling of apprehension in the presence of others) is also a factor in shyness. Almost everyone feels nervous in some social situations (such as meeting an attractive stranger). Typically, this is a reaction to evaluation fears (fears of being inadequate, embarrassed, ridiculed, or rejected). Although fears of rejection are common, they are much more frequent or intense for shy persons (Bradshaw, 2006; Jackson, Towson, & Narduzzi, 1997). A third problem for shy persons is a self-defeating bias (distortion) in their thinking. Specifically, shy persons almost always blame themselves when a social encounter doesn't go well. They are unnecessarily self-critical in social situations (Lundh et al., 2002).

Situational Causes of Shyness Shyness is most often triggered by *novel* or *unfamiliar* social situations. A person who does fine with family or close friends may become shy and awkward when meeting a stranger. Shyness is also magnified by formality, meeting someone of higher status, being noticeably different from others, or being the focus of attention (as in giving a speech) (Larsen & Buss, 2005).

Don't most people become cautious and inhibited in such circumstances? Yes. That's why we need to see how the personalities of shy and not-shy persons differ.

Dynamics of the Shy Personality

There is a tendency to think that shy persons are wrapped up in their own feelings and thoughts. But surprisingly, researchers Jonathan Cheek and Arnold Buss (1979) found no connection between shyness and **private self-consciousness** (attention to inner feelings, thoughts, and fantasies). Instead, they discovered that shyness is linked to **public self-consciousness** (acute awareness of oneself as a social object).

Persons who rate high in public self-consciousness are intensely concerned about what others think of them (Cowden, 2005). They worry about saying the wrong thing or appearing foolish. In public, they may feel "naked" or as if others can "see through them." Such feelings trigger anxiety or outright fear during social encounters, leading to awkwardness and inhibition (Cowden, 2005). The shy person's anxiety, in turn, often causes her or him to misperceive others in social situations (Schroeder, 1995).

As mentioned, almost everyone feels anxious in at least some social situations. But there is a key difference in the way shy and not-shy persons *label* this anxiety. Shy persons tend to consider their social anxiety a *lasting personality trait*. Shyness, in other words, becomes part of their self-concept. In contrast, not-shy persons believe that *external situations* cause their occasional feelings of shyness. When not-shy persons feel anxiety or "stage fright," they assume that almost anyone would feel as they do under the same circumstances (Zimbardo, Pilkonis, & Norwood, 1978).

Labeling is important because it affects *self-esteem*. In general, not-shy persons tend to have higher self-esteem than shy persons. This is because not-shy persons give themselves credit for their social successes and recognize that failures are often due to circumstances. In contrast, shy people blame themselves for social failures, never give themselves credit for successes, and expect to be rejected (Jackson et al., 2002).

Shy Beliefs

What can be done to reduce shyness? Shyness is often maintained by unrealistic or self-defeating beliefs (Antony, 2004; Butler, 2001). Here's a sample of such beliefs:

1. *If you wait around long enough at a social gathering, something will happen.*
    Comment: This is really a cover-up for fear of starting a conversation. For two people to meet, at least one has to make an effort, and it might as well be you.
2. *Other people who are popular are just lucky when it comes to being invited to social events or asked out.*
    Comment: Except for times when a person is formally introduced to someone new, this is false. People who are more active socially typically make an effort to meet and spend time with others. They join clubs, invite others to do things, strike up conversations, and generally leave little to luck.

Social anxiety A feeling of apprehension in the presence of others.

Private self-consciousness Preoccupation with inner feelings, thoughts, and fantasies.

Public self-consciousness Intense awareness of oneself as a social object.

3. *The odds of meeting someone interested in socializing are always the same, no matter where I am.*
   Comment: This is another excuse for inaction. It pays to seek out situations that have a higher probability of leading to social contact, such as clubs, teams, and school events.
4. *If someone doesn't seem to like you right away, they really don't like you and never will.*
   Comment: This belief leads to much needless shyness. Even when a person doesn't show immediate interest, it doesn't mean the person dislikes you. Liking takes time and opportunity to develop.

Unproductive beliefs like the preceding can be replaced with statements such as the following:

1. I've got to be active in social situations.
2. I can't wait until I'm completely relaxed or comfortable before taking a social risk.
3. I don't need to pretend to be someone I'm not; it just makes me more anxious.
4. I may think other people are harshly evaluating me, but actually I'm being too hard on myself.
5. I can set reasonable goals for expanding my social experience and skills.
6. Even people who are very socially skillful are never successful 100 percent of the time. I shouldn't get so upset when an encounter goes badly. (Adapted from Antony, 2004; Butler, 2001.)

Social Skills

Learning social skills takes practice (Carducci & Fields, 2007). There is nothing "innate" about knowing how to meet people or start a conversation. Social skills can be directly practiced in a variety of ways. It can be helpful, for instance, to get a tape recorder and listen to several of your conversations. You may be surprised by the way you pause, interrupt, miss cues, or seem disinterested. Similarly, it can be useful to look at yourself in a mirror and exaggerate facial expressions of surprise, interest, dislike, pleasure, and so forth. By such methods, most people can learn to put more animation and skill into their self-presentation. (For a discussion of related skills, see the section on self-assertion in Chapter 14.)

Conversation One of the simplest ways to make better conversation is by learning to ask questions. A good series of questions shifts attention to the other person and shows you are interested. Nothing fancy is needed. You can do fine with questions such as, "Where do you (work, study, live)? Do you like (dancing, travel, music)? How long have you (been at this school, worked here, lived here)?" After you've broken the ice, the best questions are often those that are *open ended* (they can't be answered yes or no):

"What parts of the country have you seen?" (as opposed to: "Have you ever been to Florida?")

"What's it like living on the West Side?" (as opposed to: "Do you like living on the West Side?")

"What kinds of food do you like?" (as opposed to: "Do you like Chinese cooking?")

It's easy to see why open-ended questions are helpful. In replying to open-ended questions, people often give "free information" about themselves. This extra information can be used to ask other questions or to lead into other topics of conversation.

This brief sampling of ideas is no substitute for actual practice. Overcoming shyness requires a real effort to learn new skills and test old beliefs and attitudes. It may even require the help of a counselor or therapist. At the very least, a shy person must be willing to take social risks. Breaking down the barriers of shyness will always include some awkward or unsuccessful encounters. Nevertheless, the rewards are powerful: human companionship and personal freedom.

RECITE

1. Social anxiety and evaluation fears are seen almost exclusively in shy individuals; the not-shy rarely have such experiences. T or F?
2. Unfamiliar people and situations most often trigger shyness. T or F?
3. Public self-consciousness plus a tendency to label oneself as shy are major characteristics of the shy personality. T or F?
4. Changing personal beliefs and practicing social skills can be helpful in overcoming shyness. T or F?

REFLECT

Critical Thinking

5. Shyness is a trait of Vonda's personality. Like most shy people, Vonda is most likely to feel shy in unfamiliar social settings. Vonda's shy behavior demonstrates that the expression of traits is governed by what concept?

Relate

If you are shy, see if you can summarize how social skills, social anxiety, evaluation fears, self-defeating thoughts, and public self-consciousness contribute to your social inhibition. If you're not shy, imagine how you would explain these concepts to a shy friend.

ANSWERS

1. F 2. T 3. T 4. T 5. trait-situation interactions (again)

chapter in review

Major Points

- Each of us displays consistent behavior patterns that define our own personalities and allow us to predict how other people will act.

- Personality can be understood by identifying traits, by probing mental conflicts and dynamics, by noting the effects of prior learning and situations, and by knowing how people perceive themselves.

- Psychologists use interviews, direct observation, questionnaires, and projective tests to measure and assess personality.

- Shyness is related to public self-consciousness and other psychological factors that can be altered, which makes it possible for some people to overcome shyness.

Summary

How do psychologists use the term personality?

- Personality is made up of one's unique and enduring behavior patterns.
- Character is personality evaluated, or the possession of desirable qualities.
- Personality traits are lasting personal qualities that are inferred from behavior.
- Personality types group people into categories on the basis of shared traits.
- Behavior is influenced by self-concept, which is a perception of one's own personality traits.
- A positive self-evaluation leads to high self-esteem. Low self-esteem is associated with stress, unhappiness, and depression.
- Personality theories combine interrelated assumptions, ideas, and principles to explain personality.

Are some personality traits more basic or important than others?

- Trait theories identify qualities that are most lasting or characteristic of a person.
- Allport made useful distinctions between common traits and individual traits and among cardinal, central, and secondary traits.

- Cattell's theory attributes visible surface traits to the existence of 16 underlying source traits.
- Source traits are measured by the *Sixteen Personality Factor Questionnaire* (16 PF).
- The five-factor model identifies five universal dimensions of personality: extroversion, agreeableness, conscientiousness, neuroticism, and openness to experience.

How do psychodynamic theories explain personality?

- Like other psychodynamic approaches, Sigmund Freud's psychoanalytic theory emphasizes unconscious forces and conflicts within the personality.
- In Freud's theory, personality is made up of the id, ego, and superego.
- Libido, derived from the life instincts, is the primary energy running the personality. Conflicts within the personality may cause neurotic anxiety or moral anxiety and motivate us to use ego-defense mechanisms.
- The personality operates on three levels, the conscious, preconscious, and unconscious.
- The Freudian view of personality development is based on a series of psychosexual stages: the oral, anal, phallic, and genital stages. Fixation at any stage can leave a lasting imprint on personality.

What do behaviorists and social learning theorists emphasize in their approach to personality?

- Behavioral theories of personality emphasize learning, conditioning, and immediate effects of the environment (situational determinants).
- Learning theorists Dollard and Miller consider habits the basic core of personality. Habits express the combined effects of drive, cue, response, and reward.
- Social learning theory adds cognitive elements, such as perception, thinking, and understanding to the behavioral view of personality.
- Social learning theory is exemplified by the concepts of psychological situation, expectancies, and reinforcement value.
- The behavioristic view of personality development holds that social reinforcement in four situations is critical. The situations are feeding, toilet or cleanliness training, sex training, and anger or aggression training.
- Identification and imitation are of particular importance in learning to be "male" or "female."
- Psychological androgyny is related to greater behavioral adaptability and flexibility.

How do humanistic theories differ from other perspectives?

- Humanistic theory emphasizes subjective experience and needs for self-actualization.
- Abraham Maslow found that self-actualizers share characteristics that range from efficient perceptions of reality to frequent peak experiences.
- Carl Rogers viewed the self as an entity that emerges from personal experience. We tend to become aware of experiences that match our self-image and exclude those that are incongruent with it.
- The incongruent person has a highly unrealistic self-image and/or a mismatch between the self-image and the ideal self. The congruent or fully functioning person is flexible and open to experiences and feelings.

- As parents apply conditions of worth to children's behavior, thoughts, and feelings, children begin to do the same. Internalized conditions of worth then contribute to incongruence that disrupts the organismic valuing process.

How do traits and situations affect personality?

- Temperament refers to the hereditary and physiological aspects of one's emotional nature.
- Behavioral genetics and studies of identical twins suggest that heredity contributes significantly to adult personality traits.
- Traits (biological predispositions) interact with situations to explain our behavior.
- Each of the four major theories of personality is useful for understanding some aspects of personality.

How do psychologists measure personality?

- Techniques typically used for personality assessment are interviews, observation, questionnaires, and projective tests.
- Structured and unstructured interviews provide much information, but they are subject to interviewer bias and misperceptions. The halo effect may also lower the accuracy of an interview.
- Direct observation, sometimes involving situational tests, behavioral assessment, or the use of rating scales, allows evaluation of a person's actual behavior.
- Personality questionnaires, such as the *Minnesota Multiphasic Personality Inventory-2* (MMPI-2), are objective and reliable, but their validity is open to question.
- Projective tests ask a person to project thoughts or feelings to an ambiguous stimulus or unstructured situation.
- The *Rorschach Technique,* or inkblot test, is a well-known projective technique. A second is the *Thematic Apperception Test* (TAT).
- Projective tests are low in validity and objectivity. Nevertheless, they are considered useful by many clinicians, particularly as part of a test battery.

What causes shyness? What can be done about it?

- Shyness is a mixture of social inhibition and social anxiety. It is marked by heightened public self-consciousness and a tendency to regard one's shyness as a lasting trait.
- Shyness can be lessened by changing self-defeating beliefs and by improving social skills.

Web Resources

For an up-to-date list of direct links to interesting sites, including those listed here, visit the student companion site for this book at www.cengage.com/psychology/coon

Personality Theories Explore an electronic textbook about personality theories.

Internet Personality Inventory Test yourself on the Big Five.

Psychodynamic and Neo-Freudian Theories Freud's followers did not always agree with his views. Read about their views on personality.

Information on Self-Efficacy Read about Albert Bandura and the idea of self-efficacy.

Maslow's Hierarchy of Needs Read more about Maslow's hierarchy of needs and self-actualization.

MMPI Explore a research project about the MMPI.

The Classical Rorschach Explore Hermann Rorschach and his famous inkblot test.

The Shyness Home Page Try several shyness surveys.

Interactive Learning

PSYCHOLOGY: A JOURNEY BOOK COMPANION WEBSITE
WWW.CENGAGE.COM/PSYCHOLOGY/COON
Visit your book companion website, where you will find flash cards, practice quizzes, web links, and more to help you study.

JUST WHAT YOU NEED TO KNOW NOW! CENGAGENOW™
Spend time on what you need to master rather than on information you already have learned. Take a pretest for this chapter, and CengageNOW will generate a personalized study plan based on your results. The study plan will identify the topics you need to review and direct you to online resources to help you master those topics. You can then take a posttest to help you determine the concepts you have mastered and what you will need to work on. Try it out! Go to www.cengage.com/login to sign in with an access code or to purchase access to this product.

test your knowledge

Personality

For additional review, get more practice with *CengageNOW, WebTutor,* the *Practice Quizzes,* and/or the printed *Study Guide* available with this book.

1. When someone's personality has been evaluated, we are making a judgment about his or her
   a. temperament
   b. character
   c. extroversion
   d. self-esteem

2. A personality type is usually defined by the presence of
   a. all five personality dimensions
   b. a stable self concept
   c. several specific traits
   d. a source trait

3. Personality theorist Raymond Cattell used factor analysis to identify 16
   a. common traits
   b. source traits
   c. cardinal traits
   d. trait-situation interactions

4. Which of the following is NOT one of the Big Five personality dimensions?
   a. extroversion
   b. agreeableness
   c. neuroticism
   d. androgyny

5. According to Freud, which division of personality is governed by the reality principle?
   a. ego
   b. id
   c. ego ideal
   d. superego

6. Freud stated that the mind functions on three levels: the conscious, the unconscious, and the
   a. psyche
   b. preconscious
   c. superego
   d. subconscious

7. Freudian theory states that a person who is passive and dependent and needs lots of attention has a fixation in the
   a. oral stage
   b. superego
   c. Oedipal stage
   d. genital stage

8. The situational determinants of our actions are of special interest and importance to
   a. psychodynamic theorists
   b. humanistic theorists
   c. learning theorists
   d. behavioral geneticists

9. Which of the following is NOT a concept of social learning theory?
   a. incongruence
   b. expectancy
   c. self-efficacy
   d. reinforcement value

10. Maslow thought of peak experiences as temporary moments of
    a. congruence
    b. positive self-regard
    c. self-actualization
    d. self-reinforcement

11. Carl Rogers believed that personal growth is encouraged when conditions of worth are replaced by
    a. self-efficacy
    b. instrumental worth
    c. latency
    d. organismic valuing

12. The research methods of _____ have been used to study the extent to which we inherit personality characteristics.
    a. behavioral genetics
    b. social learning theory
    c. factor analysis
    d. trait profiling

13. The halo effect can be a serious problem in accurate personality assessment that is based on
    a. projective testing
    b. behavioral recording
    c. interviewing
    d. the TAT

14. Situational testing is primarily an example of using _____ to assess personality.
    a. direct observation
    b. structured interviewing
    c. cardinal traits
    d. projective techniques

15. Which of the following items DOES NOT belong with the others?
    a. Rorschach technique
    b. TAT
    c. MMPI-2
    d. projective testing

16. By definition, a test that measures what it claims to measure is
    a. valid
    b. situational
    c. objective
    d. reliable

17. Which of the following is an objective personality questionnaire?
    a. the TAT
    b. the In-basket Test
    c. the NDE-16
    d. the MMPI-2

18. Which MMPI-2 scale is designed to detect phobias and compulsive actions?
    a. Hysteria
    b. Paranoia
    c. Psychasthenia
    d. Mania

19. Contrary to what many people think, shyness is NOT related to
    a. private self-consciousness
    b. social anxiety
    c. self-esteem
    d. blaming oneself for social failures

20. Shy persons tend to consider their social anxiety to be a
    a. situational reaction
    b. personality trait
    c. public efficacy
    d. habit

Answers 1.b 2.c 3.b 4.d 5.a 6.b 7.a 8.c 9.a 10.c 11.d 12.a 13.c 14.a 15.c 16.a 17.d 18.c 19.a 20.b

Health, Stress, and Coping

Journey into Psychology: Jennifer's Amazing Race

What a year! Jennifer had barely managed to survive the rush of make-or-break term papers, projects, and classroom presentations. Then it was on to the last leg of her race to the end of term: finals. Perfectly timed to inflict as much suffering as possible, her two hardest exams fell on the same day! Great.

On the last day of finals, Jennifer got caught in a traffic jam on her way to school. Two drivers cut her off, and another gave her a one-finger salute. When Jennifer finally got to campus the parking lot was swarming with frantic students. Most of them, like her, were within minutes of missing a final exam. At last,

Jennifer spied an empty space. As she started toward it, a Mini Cooper darted around the corner and into "her" place. The driver of the car behind her began to honk impatiently. For a moment, Jennifer was seized by a colossal desire to run over anything in sight.

Finally, after a week and a half of stress, pressure, and frustration, Jennifer had crossed the finish line. Sleep deprivation, gallons of coffee, junk food, and equal portions of cramming and complaining had carried her through finals. She was off for a summer of rock climbing. At last, she could kick back, relax, and have some fun. Or could she? Just 4 days after the end of

school, Jennifer got a bad cold, followed by bronchitis that lasted for nearly a month.

Jennifer's experience illustrates what happens when stress, emotion, personal habits, and health collide. Though the timing of her cold might have been a coincidence, odds are it wasn't. Periods of stress are frequently followed by illness.

In the first part of this chapter we will explore a variety of behavioral health risks. Then we will look more closely at what stress is and how it affects us. After that, we will emphasize ways of coping with stress, so you can do a better job of staying healthy than Jennifer did.

Health Psychology—Here's to Your Good Health

What is health psychology? How does behavior affect health?

Most of us agree that our health is priceless. Yet many diseases and half of all deaths in North America can be traced to our unhealthy behaviors (Mokdad et al., 2004). **Health psychology** aims to use behavioral principles to prevent illness and death and to promote health. Psychologists working in the allied field of **behavioral medicine** apply psychology to manage medical problems, such as diabetes or asthma. Their interests include pain control, helping people cope with chronic illness, stress-related diseases, self-screening for diseases (such as breast cancer), and similar topics (Brannon & Feist, 2010).

Behavioral Risk Factors

A century ago, people died primarily from infectious diseases and accidents. Today, people generally die from **lifestyle diseases,** which are related to health-damaging personal habits (Mokdad et al., 2004). Examples include heart disease, stroke, HIV/AIDS, and lung cancer (▶▶ Figure 11.1). Clearly, some lifestyles promote health, whereas others lead to illness and death. As one observer put it, "If you don't take care of yourself, the undertaker will take on that responsibility for you."

What are some unhealthy behaviors? Some causes of illness are beyond our control, but many behavioral risks can be reduced. **Behavioral risk factors** are actions that increase the chances of disease, injury, or early death. For example, approximately 440,000 people die every year from smoking-related diseases (CDC, 2005). Similarly, being overweight *doubles* the chance of dying from cancer or heart disease. Roughly 65 percent of all American adults are overweight (CDC, 2003). As a result, obesity may soon overtake smoking as the main cause of preventable deaths. Being fat is not just a matter of fashion—in the long run it could kill you. A person who is overweight at age 20 can expect to lose 5 to 20 years of life expectancy (Fontaine et al., 2003).

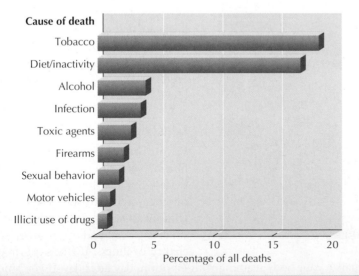

▲ FIGURE 11.1 The nine leading causes of death in the United States are shown in this graph. As you can see, eight of the top nine causes are directly related to behavioral risk factors (infection is the exception). At least 45 percent of all deaths can be traced to unhealthful behavior. The percentage of day-to-day health problems related to unhealthful behavior is even higher. (Data from Mokdad et al., 2004.)

Survey Questions

- What is health psychology? How does behavior affect health?
- How can sexually transmitted diseases be prevented?
- What is stress? What factors determine its severity?
- What causes frustration and what are typical reactions to it?
- Are there different types of conflict? How do people react to conflict?
- What are defense mechanisms?
- What do we know about coping with feelings of helplessness and depression?
- How is stress related to health and disease?
- What are the best strategies for managing stress?

Health psychology Study of the ways in which behavioral principles can be used to prevent illness and promote health.

Behavioral medicine The study of behavioral factors in medicine, physical illness, and medical treatment.

Lifestyle disease A disease related to health-damaging personal habits.

Behavioral risk factors Behaviors that increase the chances of disease, injury, or premature death.

● Table 11.1 **Percentage of U.S. High School Students Who Engaged in Health-Endangering Behaviors**

RISKY BEHAVIOR	PERCENTAGE
Rode with drinking driver	30
Was in a physical fight	33
Carried a weapon	17
Drank alcohol	45
Used marijuana	22
Engaged in sexual intercourse	47
Did not use condom during last sexual intercourse	37
Smoked cigarettes	22
Did not eat enough fruits and vegetables	78
Did not get enough physical exercise	33

Source: Grunbaum et al., 2004

Each of the following factors is a major behavioral risk (Baum & Posluszny, 1999): high levels of stress, untreated high blood pressure, cigarette smoking, abuse of alcohol or other drugs, overeating, inadequate exercise, unsafe sexual behavior, exposure to toxic substances, violence, excess sun exposure, reckless driving, and disregarding personal safety (avoidable accidents). Seventy percent of all medical costs are related to just six of the listed factors—smoking, alcohol abuse, drug abuse, poor diet, insufficient exercise, and risky sexual practices (Orleans, Gruman, & Hollendonner, 1999). (Unsafe sex is discussed in the next section.)

The personal habits you have by the time you are 18 or 19 greatly affect your health, happiness, and life expectancy years later (Gurung, 2010; Vaillant & Mukamal, 2001). ● Table 11.1 shows how many American high school students engage in various kinds of risky behaviors.

Specific risk factors are not the only concern. Some people have a general **disease-prone personality** that leaves them depressed, anxious, hostile, and. . . . frequently ill. In contrast, people who are intellectually resourceful, compassionate, optimistic, and non-hostile tend to enjoy good health (Taylor, 2006; Taylor et al., 2000). Depression, in particular, is likely to damage health (Allgower, Wardle, & Steptoe, 2001; Luppa et al., 2007). People who are depressed eat poorly, sleep poorly, rarely exercise, fail to use seat belts in cars, smoke more, and so on.

Lifestyle

In your mind's eye, fast-forward an imaginary film of your life all the way to old age. Do it twice—once with a lifestyle including a large number of behavioral risk factors, and again without them. It should be obvious that many small risks can add up, dramatically raising the chance of illness. If stress is a frequent part of your life, visualize your body seething with emotion, day after day. If you smoke, picture a lifetime's worth of cigarette smoke blown through your lungs in a week. If you drink, take a lifetime of alcohol's assaults on the brain, stomach, and liver and squeeze them into a month: Your body would be poisoned, ravaged, and soon dead. If you eat a high-fat, high-cholesterol diet, fast-forward a lifetime of heart-killing plaque clogging your arteries.

We don't mean to sermonize. We just want to remind you that risk factors make a difference. To make matters worse, unhealthy lifestyles almost always create multiple risks.

In the long run, behavioral risk factors and lifestyles do make a difference in health and life expectancy.

Disease-prone personality A personality type associated with poor health; marked by persistent negative emotions, including anxiety, depression, and hostility.

That is, people who smoke are also likely to drink excessively. Those who overeat usually do not get enough exercise, and so on (Straub, 2006). Even infectious diseases are often linked to behavioral risks. For example, pneumonia and other infections occur at higher rates in people who have cancer, heart disease, lung disease, or liver disease. Thus, many deaths attributed to infections can actually be traced back to smoking, poor diet, or alcohol abuse (Mokdad et al., 2004).

Health-Promoting Behaviors

To prevent disease, health psychologists first try to remove behavioral risk factors. All the medicine in the world may not be enough to restore health without changes in behavior. We all know someone who has had a heart attack or lung disease who couldn't change the habits that led to his or her illness.

In some cases, lifestyle diseases can be treated or prevented by making specific, minor changes in behavior. For example, hypertension (high blood pressure) can be deadly. Yet, consuming less sodium (salt) can help fend off this "silent killer." (Losing weight, using alcohol sparingly, and getting more exercise will also help [Georgiades et al., 2000].)

In addition to removing specific risk factors, psychologists are interested in getting people to increase behaviors that promote health. Health-promoting behaviors include such obvious practices as getting regular exercise, controlling smoking and alcohol use, maintaining a balanced diet, getting good medical care, and managing stress (Zarcadoolas, Pleasant, & Greer, 2006). In one study, the risk of dying was cut by 65 percent during a 10-year period for adults who were careful about diet, alcohol, exercise, and smoking (Knoops et al., 2004).

Health-promoting behaviors don't have to be restrictive or burdensome. For instance, maintaining a healthy diet doesn't mean surviving on tofu and wheatgrass. The healthiest people in the study just described ate a tasty "Mediterranean diet" higher in fruit, vegetables, and fish and lower in red meat and dairy products. Likewise, you don't need to exercise like an Olympic athlete to benefit from physical activity. All you need is 30 minutes of exercise (the equivalent of a brisk walk) three or four times a week. Almost everyone can fit such "lifestyle physical activity" into his or her schedule (Pescatello, 2001).

What about alcohol? Moderation in drinking doesn't mean that you must be a teetotaler. Consuming one or two alcoholic drinks per day is generally safe for most people, especially if you remain alcohol free 2 or 3 days a week. A glass of red wine daily may even be healthy (Anekonda, 2006). However, having three or more drinks a day greatly increases the risk for stroke, cirrhosis of the liver, cancer, high blood pressure, heart disorders, and other diseases (Knoops et al., 2004).

To summarize, a small number of behavioral patterns accounts for many common health problems (Grunbaum et al., 2004). ● Table 11.2 lists several major ways to promote good health. (To explore an interesting social factor underlying common health problems, see "Unhealthy Birds of a Feather.")

Early Prevention

Of the behavioral risks we have discussed, smoking is the largest preventable cause of death and the single most lethal factor (Mokdad et al., 2004). As such, it illustrates the prospect for preventing illness.

What have health psychologists done to lessen the risks of smoking? Attempts to "immunize" youths against pressures to start smoking are a good example. When humorist Mark Twain said, "Giving up smoking is the easiest thing in the world. I know because I've done it thousands of times," he stated a basic truth—only 1 smoker in 10 has long-term success at quitting. Thus, the best way to deal with smoking is to prevent it before it becomes a lifelong habit. For example, prevention programs in schools discourage smoking with quizzes about smoking, antismoking art contests, poster and T-shirt giveaways, antismoking pamphlets for parents,

RODNEY KICKED OFF HIS NEW FITNESS REGIME BY BUYING A HEAVIER REMOTE CONTROL ...THIS WAS NOT ENOUGH!

Unhealthy Birds of a Feather

Would you like to eat better, exercise more, or quit smoking? Researchers Nicholas Christakis and James Fowler believe they know why it can be difficult to alter unhealthy behaviors. Often, social factors are a barrier to change. If you are a smoker, do your friends also smoke? Are your family members fast-food junkies just like you? Unhealthy behaviors such as overeating or smoking seem to spread almost like a "mental virus."

One study of social contagion found that people were 57 percent more likely to become obese if they had a friend who became fat first (Christakis & Fowler, 2007). Another study noted that smokers tend to "hang out" with other smokers (Christakis & Fowler, 2008). Apparently, we tend to flock together with like-minded people and adopt many of their habits.

Does that mean I am doomed to be unhealthy if my family and friends have unhealthy habits? Not necessarily. Social networks can also spread healthful behaviors. If one smoker in a group of smokers quits, others are more likely to follow suit. If your spouse quits smoking, you are 67 percent more likely to quit. If a good friend quits smoking, your chances of abandoning tobacco go up by 36 percent (Christakis & Fowler, 2008). The growing social unpopularity of smoking may explain why American adults who still smoke (now only 19 percent) are becoming an endangered species (Schroeder, 2008).

The implication? Don't wait for your friends or family to adopt healthier habits. Take the lead and get them to join you. Failing that, start hanging out with a healthier crowd. You might catch something healthy.

---

and questions for students to ask their parents (Zarcadoolas, Pleasant, & Greer, 2006). Such efforts are designed to persuade kids that smoking is dangerous and "uncool." Apparently, many teens are getting the message, as attitudes toward smoking are now more negative than they were 20 years ago (Chassin et al., 2003).

Some antismoking programs include **refusal skills training.** In this case, youths learn to resist pressures to begin smoking (or using other drugs). For example, junior high students can role-play ways to resist smoking pressures from peers, adults, and cigarette ads. Similar methods can be applied to other health risks, such as sexually transmitted diseases and teen pregnancy (Wandersman & Florin, 2003).

Many health programs also teach students general life skills. The idea is to give kids skills that will help them cope with day-to-day stresses. That way, they will be less tempted to escape problems through drug use or other destructive behaviors. **Life skills training**

Refusal skills training Program that teaches youths how to resist pressures to begin smoking. (Can also be applied to other drugs and health risks.)

Life skills training A program that teaches stress reduction, self-protection, decision making, self-control, and social skills.

● Table 11.2 Major Health-Promoting Behaviors

	SOURCE	DESIRABLE BEHAVIORS
	Tobacco	Do not smoke; do not use smokeless tobacco
	Nutrition	Eating a balanced, low-fat diet; appropriate caloric intake; maintenance of healthy body weight
	Exercise	At least 30 minutes of aerobic exercise, 5 days per week
	Blood pressure	Lower blood pressure with diet and exercise, or medicine if necessary
	Alcohol and drugs	No more than two drinks per day; abstain from using drugs
	Sleep and relaxation	Avoid sleep deprivation; provide for periods of relaxation every day
	Sex	Practice safer sex; avoid unplanned pregnancy
	Injury	Curb dangerous driving habits, use seat belts; minimize sun exposure; forgo dangerous activities
	Stress	Learn stress management; lower hostility

includes practice in stress reduction, self-protection, decision making, goal setting, self-control, and social skills (Tobler et al., 2000).

Community Health

In addition to early prevention, health psychologists have had some success with **community health campaigns.** These are community-wide education projects designed to lessen major risk factors (Orleans, 2000). Health campaigns inform people of risks such as stress, alcohol abuse, high blood pressure, high cholesterol, smoking, sexually transmitted diseases, or excessive sun exposure. This is followed by efforts to motivate people to change their behavior. Campaigns sometimes provide *role models* (positive examples) who show people how to improve their own health. They also direct people to services for health screening, advice, and treatment. Health campaigns may reach people through the mass media, public schools, health fairs, workplaces, or self-help programs.

Positive Psychology: Wellness

Health is not just an absence of disease (Allen, Carlson, & Ham, 2007). People who are truly healthy enjoy a positive state of **wellness** or well-being. Maintaining wellness is a lifelong pursuit and, hopefully, a labor of love. People who attain optimal wellness are both physically and psychologically healthy. They are happy, optimistic, self-confident individuals who can bounce back emotionally from adversity (Tugade, Fredrickson, & Barrett, 2004).

People who enjoy a sense of well-being also have supportive relationships with others, do meaningful work, and live in a clean environment. Many of these aspects of wellness are addressed elsewhere in this book.

One major risk factor young people are likely to face is the danger of contracting a sexually transmitted disease. Yet this serious, and possibly fatal, health risk can be dramatically reduced by making small changes in behavior. Let's apply your new understanding of health psychology to this important topic (right after you pause for a healthy Study Break).

Centers for Disease Control

Celebrities can also help persuade young people to not start smoking in the first place.

Community health campaign A community-wide education program that provides information about how to lessen risk factors and promote health.

Wellness A positive state of good health; more than the absence of disease.

RECITE

1. Adjustment to chronic illness and the control of pain are topics that would more likely be of interest to a specialist in _____ _____ rather than a health psychologist.
2. With respect to health, which of the following is *not* a major behavioral risk factor?
   a. overexercise   b. cigarette smoking
   c. stress   d. high blood pressure
3. Lifestyle diseases related to just six behaviors account for 70 percent of all medical costs. The behaviors are smoking, alcohol abuse, drug abuse, poor diet, insufficient exercise, and
   a. driving too fast   b. excessive sun exposure
   c. unsafe sex   d. exposure to toxins
4. Health psychologists tend to prefer _____ rather than modifying habits (like smoking) that become difficult to break once they are established.
5. The disease-prone personality is marked by _____, anxiety, and hostility.

REFLECT

Critical Thinking

6. The general public is increasingly well informed about health risks and healthful behavior. Can you apply the concept of reinforcement to explain why so many people fail to act on this information?

Relate

Make a list of the major behavioral risk factors that apply to you. Are you laying the foundation for a lifestyle disease?

Which of the health-promoting behaviors listed in Table 11.2 would you like to increase?

If you were designing a community health campaign, who would you use as role models of healthful behavior?

ANSWERS

1. behavioral medicine 2. a 3. c 4. prevention 5. depression 6. Many of the health payoffs are delayed by months or years, greatly lessening the immediate rewards for healthful behavior.

STDs and Safer Sex—Choice, Risk, and Responsibility

How can sexually transmitted diseases be prevented?

In general, most adults favor greater freedom of choice for themselves, including choice about sexual behavior. Yet, as the upcoming discussion of AIDS suggests, there are new and compelling reasons for caution in sexual behavior. This is especially true for younger people who are exploring their identities, sexual or otherwise, in an era of more casual sex (Puentes, Knox, & Zusman, 2008).

Sexually Transmitted Diseases

A **sexually transmitted disease (STD)** is an infection passed from one person to another by intimate physical contact. Sexually active people run higher risks for chlamydia (klah-MID-ee-ah), gonorrhea, hepatitis B, herpes, syphilis, and other STDs. Many people who carry STDs remain *asymptomatic* (a-SIMP-teh-mat-ik: lacking obvious symptoms). It is easy to have an infection without knowing it. Likewise, it is often impossible to tell if a sexual partner is infectious. Thus, risky sex is a serious hazard. A study of sexually active teenage girls engaging in risky sex is a case in point. Nearly 90 percent of the girls thought that they had virtually no chance of getting an STD. In reality, over the next 18 months, 1 in 4 got chlamydia or gonorrhea (Ethier et al., 2003).

A major problem is that people who are sexually active may have indirect contact with many other people. One study of sexual relationships at a high school in a Midwestern city found long chains of sexual contact between students. Thus, a student at the end of the chain might have had sex with only one person, but in reality she or he had indirect contact with dozens or even hundreds of others (Bearman, Moody, & Stovel, 2004).

For many sexually active people, the human immunodeficiency virus (HIV) has added a new threat. HIV is a sexually transmitted disease that disables the immune system. Whereas most other STDs are treatable, HIV infections can be lethal. Check your knowledge about HIV against the following summary.

HIV/AIDS

Acquired immune deficiency syndrome (AIDS) is caused by an HIV infection. As the immune system weakens, other "opportunistic" diseases invade the body. Most AIDS victims eventually die of multiple infections (although newer multidrug therapies have greatly improved the odds of survival). The first symptoms of AIDS may show up as little as 2 months after infection, but they typically don't appear for 10 years. Because of this long incubation period, infected persons often pass the AIDS virus on to others without knowing it. Medical testing can detect an HIV infection. However, for at least the first 6 months after becoming infected, a person can test negative while carrying the virus. A negative test result, therefore, is no guarantee that a person is a "safe" sex partner.

HIV infections are spread by direct contact with body fluids—especially blood, semen, and vaginal secretions. The AIDS virus cannot be transmitted by casual contact. People do not get AIDS from shaking hands, touching or using objects touched by an AIDS patient, eating food prepared by an infected person, or from social kissing, sweat or tears, sharing drinking glasses, sharing towels, and so forth.

HIV can be spread by all forms of sexual intercourse, and it has affected persons of all sexual orientations. Recently, the AIDS epidemic has spread more quickly among heterosexuals, women, African Americans, Hispanics, and children (Taylor-Seehafer & Rew, 2000). Around the world, almost half of all HIV cases are female (UNAIDS, 2006). HIV infection

The AIDS Memorial Quilt was begun in 1985 to commemorate those who have died from AIDS. The photo is of the last public display of the complete quilt, in 1996. Today, the quilt has grown to immense size, symbolizing the extent of the AIDS epidemic. Originally the quilt memorialized only homosexual victims. It now includes heterosexual men, women, and children, signifying that AIDS respects no boundaries.

Leonard Lessin/Photo Researchers, Inc.

Sexually transmitted disease (STD) A disease that is typically passed from one person to the next by intimate physical contact; a venereal disease.

is the leading cause of death among women and men between the ages of 25 and 44 (Gayle, 2000). Worldwide, 2.9 million people die each year from HIV/AIDS, and 4.3 million new infections occur (UNAIDS, 2006).

Behavioral Risk Factors

Sexually active people can do much to protect their own health. The behaviors listed here are risky when performed with an infected person:

Risky Behaviors
- Sharing drug needles and syringes
- Anal sex, with or without a condom
- Vaginal or oral sex with someone who injects drugs or engages in anal sex
- Sex with someone you don't know well, or with someone you know has had several partners
- Unprotected sex (without a condom) with an infected partner
- Having two or more sex partners (additional partners further increase the risk)

In the United States, between 2 and 4 of every 100 adults put themselves at high risk by engaging in the behaviors just listed (Gayle, 2000). It's important to remember that you can't tell from appearance if a person is infected. Many people would be surprised to learn that their partners have engaged in behavior that places them both at risk.

The preceding high-risk behaviors can be contrasted with the following list of safer sexual practices. Note, however, that unless a person completely abstains, sex can be made safer but not risk free.

Safer Sex Practices
- Not having sex
- Sex with one mutually faithful, uninfected partner
- Not injecting drugs
- Discussing contraception with partner
- Being selective regarding sexual partners
- Reducing the number of sexual partners
- Discussing partner's sexual health prior to engaging in sex
- Not engaging in sex while intoxicated
- Using a condom

Sexually active persons should practice safer sex until their partner's sexual history and/or health has been clearly established. And remember, a condom offers little or no protection if it is misused. Sadly, one of three sexually active teens don't know how to use a condom correctly (and virgins of both sexes are even more clueless) (Crosby & Yarber, 2001).

HIV and AIDS initially had a strong impact on sexual behavior in some groups. Among gay men there was a sharp decrease in risky sex and an increase in monogamous relationships. Unfortunately, this trend has recently reversed. Once again, STD rates are rising dramatically among gay men. In part, this may be due to the fact that new medical treatments are helping people with HIV live longer. Many victims simply do not look or act sick. This gives a false impression about the dangers of HIV infection and encourages foolish risk taking (Handsfield, 2001).

Other groups are also not getting the message. The AIDS epidemic has thus far had little impact on the willingness of high school and college age students to engage in risky behavior (casual sex) or to use condoms (Bauman, Karasz, & Hamilton, 2007). A study of heterosexual adults found that the majority did not practice safer sex with their last partner. Most of these "gamblers" knew too little about their partners to be sure they were not taking a big risk. For many people, drinking alcohol greatly increases the likelihood of taking sexual risks (Corbin & Fromme, 2002).

Apparently, heterosexual people still don't feel that they are truly at risk. However, *75 percent* of people with HIV were infected through heterosexual sex. Over the next 20 to 30 years, heterosexual transmission is expected to become the primary means of spreading HIV. Over the next 15 years, 65 million more people will die of AIDS unless prevention efforts are greatly expanded (Altman, 2002).

Isn't it possible that practicing safer sex would be interpreted as a sign that you mistrust your lover? Actually, taking precautions could, instead, be defined as a way of showing that you really care about the welfare of your partner. As is the case with other behavioral risk factors, it's certainly a way of showing that you care about your own health.

We'll next turn our attention to the effect that stress has on health and sickness. Understanding stress and learning to control it can improve not only your health, but the quality of your life as well (Suinn, 2001). For these reasons, a discussion of stress and stress management follows.

Stress—Threat or Thrill?

What is stress? What factors determine its severity?

Stress can be a major behavioral risk factor if it is prolonged or severe, but it isn't always bad. As Canadian stress research pioneer Hans Selye (SEL-yay) (1976) observed, "To be totally without stress is to be dead." That's because **stress** is the mental and physical condition that occurs when we adjust or adapt to the environment. Unpleasant events such as work pressures, marital problems, or financial woes naturally produce stress. But so do travel, sports, a new job, rock climbing, dating, and other positive activities. Even if you aren't a thrill seeker, a healthy lifestyle may include a fair amount of *eustress* (good stress). Activities that provoke "good stress" are usually challenging, rewarding, and energizing.

It might seem that stressful events "happen to" people. Although this is sometimes the case, more often stress is a matter of how we perceive events and react to them. Because of this, stress can often be managed or controlled. Let's explore how stress occurs and typical reactions to it.

A **stress reaction** begins with the same autonomic nervous system (ANS) arousal that occurs during emotion. Imagine you are standing at the top of a wind-whipped ski jump for the first time. Internally, you would experience a rapid surge in your heart rate, blood pressure, respiration, muscle tension, and other ANS responses. *Short-term* stresses of this kind can be uncomfortable, but they rarely do any damage. (Your landing might, however.) *Long-term* stresses are another matter entirely (Sternberg, 2000).

Stress The mental and physical condition that occurs when a person must adjust or adapt to the environment.

Stress reaction The physical response to stress, consisting mainly of bodily changes related to autonomic nervous system arousal.

General Adaptation Syndrome

The impact of long-term stresses can be understood by examining the body's defenses against stress, a pattern known as the general adaptation syndrome.

The **general adaptation syndrome (GAS)** is a series of bodily reactions to prolonged stress. Selye (1976) noticed that the first symptoms of almost any disease or trauma (poisoning, infection, injury, or stress) are almost identical. The body responds in the same way to any stress, be it infection, failure, embarrassment, a new job, trouble at school, or a stormy romance.

How does the body respond to stress? The GAS consists of three stages: an alarm reaction, a stage of resistance, and a stage of exhaustion (▶▶ Figure 11.2) (Selye, 1976).

In the **alarm reaction,** your body mobilizes its resources to cope with added stress. The pituitary gland signals the adrenal glands to produce more adrenaline, noradrenaline, and cortisol. As these stress hormones are dumped into the bloodstream, some bodily processes are speeded up and others are slowed. This allows bodily resources to be applied where they are needed (Lyons & Chamberlain, 2006).

We should all be thankful that our bodies automatically respond to emergencies. But brilliant as this emergency system is, it can also cause problems. In the first phase of the alarm reaction, people have such symptoms as headache, fever, fatigue, sore muscles, shortness of breath, diarrhea, upset stomach, loss of appetite, and a lack of energy. Notice that these are also the symptoms of being sick, of stressful travel, of high-altitude sickness, of final exams week, and (possibly) of falling in love!

During the **stage of resistance,** bodily adjustments to stress stabilize. As the body's defenses come into balance, symptoms of the alarm reaction disappear. Outwardly, everything seems normal. However, this appearance of normality comes at a high cost. The body is better able to cope with the original stressor, but its resistance to other stresses is lowered. For example, animals placed in extreme cold become more resistant to the cold, but more susceptible to infection. It is during the stage of resistance that the first signs of psychosomatic disorders (physical disorders triggered by psychological factors) begin to appear.

Continued stress leads to the **stage of exhaustion,** in which the body's resources are drained and stress hormones are depleted. Some of the typical signs or symptoms of impending exhaustion include the following (Friedman, 2002):

Emotional signs: Anxiety, apathy, irritability, mental fatigue

Behavioral signs: Avoidance of responsibilities and relationships, extreme or self-destructive behavior, self-neglect, poor judgment

Physical signs: Excessive worry about illness, frequent illness, exhaustion, overuse of medicines, physical ailments and complaints

The GAS may sound melodramatic if you are young and healthy or if you've never endured prolonged stress. However, you should not take stress lightly. Unless a way of relieving stress is found, the result will be a psychosomatic disease, a serious loss of health, or complete collapse. When Selye examined animals in the later stages of the GAS, he found that their adrenal glands were enlarged and discolored. There was intense shrinkage of internal organs, such as the thymus, spleen, and lymph nodes, and many animals had stomach ulcers. In addition to such direct effects, stress can disrupt the body's immune system, as described next.

Stress, Illness, and Your Immune System

How can prolonged stress result in a physical illness? An answer can be found in your body's immune system, which mobilizes defenses (such as white blood cells) against invading microbes and other disease agents. The immune system is regulated, in part, by the brain. Because of this link, stress and upsetting emotions can affect the immune system in ways that increase susceptibility to disease (Miller, Cohen, & Ritchey, 2002). By the way, the study

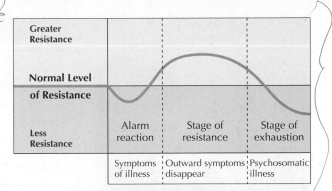

▲ FIGURE 11.2 The general adaptation syndrome. During the initial alarm reaction to stress, resistance falls below normal. It rises again as bodily resources are mobilized, and it remains high during the stage of resistance. Eventually, resistance falls again as the stage of exhaustion is reached. (From *The Stress of Life* by Hans Selye. Copyright © 1976 by Hans Selye. Used by permission of McGraw-Hill Book Company.)

General adaptation syndrome (GAS) A series of bodily reactions to prolonged stress; occurs in three stages: alarm, resistance, and exhaustion.

Alarm reaction First stage of the GAS, during which bodily resources are mobilized to cope with a stressor.

Stage of resistance Second stage of the GAS, during which bodily adjustments to stress stabilize, but at a high physical cost.

Stage of exhaustion Third stage of the GAS, at which time the body's resources are exhausted and serious health consequences occur.

Stress and negative emotions lower immune system activity and increase inflammation. This, in turn, raises our vulnerability to infection, worsens illness, and delays recovery.

of links among behavior, stress, disease, and the immune system is called **psychoneuroimmunology** (Daruna, 2004). (Try dropping that into a conversation sometime if you want to see a stress reaction!)

Studies show that the immune system is weakened in students during major exam times, as Jennifer found out during her mad dash to the end of term. Immunity is also lowered by divorce, bereavement, a troubled marriage, job loss, poor sleep, depression, and similar stresses (Deinzer et al., 2000; Motivala & Irwin, 2007; Segerstrom & Miller, 2004). Lowered immunity explains why the "double whammy" of getting sick when you are trying to cope with prolonged or severe stress is so common (Lyons & Chamberlain, 2006). Stress causes the body to release substances that increase inflammation. This is part of the body's self-protective response to threats, but it can prolong infections and delay healing (Kiecolt-Glaser et al., 2002; Wargo, 2007). It's also worth noting again the value of positive emotions. Happiness, laughter, and delight tend to strengthen immune system response. Doing things that make you happy can also protect your health (Rosenkranz et al., 2003).

Could reducing stress help prevent illness? Yes. Various psychological approaches, such as support groups, relaxation exercises, guided imagery, and stress management training can actually boost immune system functioning (Dougall & Baum, 2003). By doing so, they help promote and restore health. For example, stress management reduced the severity of cold and flu symptoms in a group of university students (Reid, Mackinnon, & Drummond, 2001).

There is even evidence that stress management can improve the chances of survival in people with life-threatening diseases, such as cancer, heart disease, and HIV/AIDS (Schneiderman et al., 2001). With some successes to encourage them, psychologists are now searching for the best combination of treatments to help people resist disease (Miller & Cohen, 2001).

When Is Stress a Strain?

It goes almost without saying that some events are more likely to cause stress than others. A **stressor** is a condition or event that challenges or threatens a person. Police officers, for instance, suffer from a high rate of stress-related diseases. The threat of injury or death, plus occasional confrontations with angry, drunk, or hostile citizens, takes a toll. A major factor is the *unpredictable* nature of police work. An officer who stops a car to issue a traffic ticket never knows if a cooperative citizen or an armed gang member is waiting inside.

Air traffic control is stressful work. Employees must pay intense attention for long periods of time and have little control over the pace of work, and the consequences of making a mistake can be dire.

A revealing study shows how unpredictability adds to stress. In a series of 1-minute trials, college students breathed air through a mask. In some trials, the air contained 20 percent more carbon dioxide (CO_2) than normal. If you were to inhale this air, you would feel anxious, stressed, and a little like you were suffocating. Students tested this way hated the "surprise" doses of CO_2. They found it much less stressful to be told in advance which trials would include a choking whiff of CO_2 (Lejuez et al., 2000).

Pressure is another element of stress, especially job stress. **Pressure** occurs when a person must meet *urgent* external demands or expectations (Weiten, 1998). For example, we feel pressured when activities must be speeded up, when deadlines must be met, when extra work is added, or when we must work near maximum capacity for long periods. Most students who have survived final exams are familiar with the effects of pressure.

What if I set deadlines for myself? Does it make a difference where the pressure comes from? Yes. People generally feel more stress in situations over which they have little or no control (Taris et al., 2005). In one study, nurses with a high sense of control (e.g., over the pacing of work and the physical arrangement of the working environment) were less likely to get sick,

Psychoneuroimmunology Study of the links among behavior, stress, disease, and the immune system.

Stressor A specific condition or event in the environment that challenges or threatens a person.

Pressure A stressful condition that occurs when a person must meet urgent external demands or expectations.

either physically or mentally, than nurses with a low sense of control (Ganster, Fox, & Dwyer, 2001).

To summarize, when emotional "shocks" are *intense* or *repeated, unpredictable, uncontrollable,* and linked to *pressure,* stress will be magnified and damage is likely to result. At work, people face many of these sources of stress every day. (See ● Table 11.3 for a list of the most common sources of stress at work.) In fact, chronic job stress can even result in *burnout.*

Burnout

Burnout occurs when workers are physically, mentally, and emotionally drained (Greenglass, Burke, & Moore, 2003). When people become burned out, they experience emotional exhaustion, cynicism or detachment, and feelings of reduced personal accomplishment (Maslach, Schaufeli, & Leiter, 2001).

Burnout may occur in any job, but it is a special problem in emotionally demanding helping professions, such as nursing, teaching, social work, childcare, counseling, or police work. By the way, college students can also experience burnout (Jacobs & Dodd, 2003).

Appraising Stressors

It might seem that stressful events "happen to" us. Sometimes this is true, but as noted in Chapter 9, our emotions are greatly affected by how we appraise situations. That's why some people are distressed by events that others view as a thrill or a challenge (eustress). Ultimately, stress depends on how you perceive a situation. Our friend Akihito would find it stressful to listen to five of his son's hip-hop CDs in a row. His son Takashi would find it stressful to listen to *one* of his father's opera CDs. To know if you are stressed, we must know what meaning you place on events. As we will see in a moment, whenever a stressor is appraised as a *threat* (potentially harmful), a powerful stress reaction follows (Folkman & Moskowitz, 2004; Lazarus, 1991a).

"Am I Okay or in Trouble?"

You have been selected to give a speech to 300 people. Or, a doctor tells you that you must undergo a dangerous and painful operation. Or, the one true love of your life walks out the door. What would your emotional response to these events be? How do you cope with a threat?

According to Richard Lazarus (1991a), there are two important steps in managing a threat. The first is a **primary appraisal,** in which you decide if a situation is relevant or irrelevant, positive or threatening. In essence, this step answers the question "Am I okay or in trouble?" Then you make a **secondary appraisal,** in which you assess your resources and choose a way to meet the threat or challenge ("What can I do about this situation?"). Thus, the way a situation is "sized up" greatly affects our ability to cope with it (▶▶ Figure 11.3). Public speaking, for instance, can be appraised as an intense threat or as a chance to perform. Emphasizing the threat—by imagining failure, rejection, or embarrassment—obviously invites disaster (Strongman, 2003).

The Nature of Threat

What does it mean to feel threatened by a stressor? Certainly in most day-to-day situations it doesn't mean you think your life is in danger. (Unless, of course, you owe money to "Eddie the Enforcer.") Threat has more to do with the idea of control. We are particularly prone to feel stressed when we can't—or think we can't—control our immediate environment. In short, a *perceived* lack of control is just as threatening as an actual lack of control. For example, college students who *feel* overloaded experience stress even though their workload may not actually be heavier than that of their classmates (Jacobs & Dodd, 2003).

A sense of control also comes from believing you can reach desired goals. It is threatening to feel that we lack *competence* to cope with life's demands (Bandura, 2001). Because of

Burnout A job-related condition of mental, physical, and emotional exhaustion.

Primary appraisal Deciding if a situation is relevant to oneself and if it is a threat.

Secondary appraisal Deciding how to cope with a threat or challenge.

Primary Appraisal ➔ **Secondary Appraisal**
relevant?   coping resources available?
threatening?   course of action?

Stressor
intense?
repeated?
unpredictable?
uncontrollable?
pressure?

Notice of Workforce Reduction

⏶ FIGURE 11.3 Stress is the product of an interchange between a person and the environment.

this, the intensity of your body's stress reaction often depends on what you think and tell yourself about a stressor. That's why it's valuable to learn to think in ways that ward off the body's stress response. (Some strategies for controlling upsetting thoughts are described in the Psychology in Action section on "Stress Management.")

Coping with Threat

You have appraised a situation as threatening. What will you do next? You have two major choices. In **emotion-focused coping,** we try to control our emotional reactions to the situation. For example, a distressed person may distract herself by listening to music, taking a walk to relax, or seeking emotional support from others. In contrast, **problem-focused coping** is aimed at managing or correcting the distressing situation itself. Some examples are making a plan of action or concentrating on your next step (Folkman & Moskowitz, 2004).

Couldn't both types of coping occur together? Yes. Sometimes the two types of coping aid one another. For instance, quieting your emotions may make it easier for you to find a way to solve a problem. Say, for example, that a woman feels anxious as she steps to the podium to give a speech. If she does some deep breathing to reduce her anxiety (emotion-focused coping) she will be better able to glance over her notes to improve her delivery (problem-focused coping).

It is also possible for coping efforts to clash. For instance, if you have to make a difficult decision, you may suffer intense emotional distress. In such circumstances there is a temptation to make a quick, ill-advised choice, just to end the suffering. Doing so may allow you to cope with your emotions, but it shortchanges problem-focused coping.

In general, problem-focused coping tends to be especially useful when you are facing a controllable stressor—that is, a situation you can actually do something about. Emotion-focused efforts are best suited to managing your reaction to stressors you cannot control (Folkman & Moskowitz, 2004). To improve your chances of coping effectively, the stress-fighting strategies described in this chapter include a mixture of both techniques.

So far, our discussion has focused on everyday stresses. How do people react to the extreme stresses imposed by war, violence, or disaster? "Coping with Traumatic Stress" discusses this important topic.

Frustration—Blind Alleys and Lead Balloons

What causes frustration and what are typical reactions to it?

Do you remember how frustrated Jennifer was when she couldn't find a parking place? **Frustration** is a negative emotional state that occurs when people are prevented from reaching desired goals. In Jennifer's case, the goal of finding a parking space was blocked by another car.

Obstacles of many kinds cause frustration. A useful distinction can be made between external and personal sources of frustration. *External frustration* is based on conditions outside a person that impede progress toward a goal. All the following are external frustrations: getting stuck with a flat tire; having a marriage proposal rejected; finding the cupboard bare when you go to get your poor dog a bone; being chased out of the house by your starving dog. In other words, external frustrations are based on *delays, failure, rejection, loss,* and other direct blocking of motivated behavior.

Notice that external obstacles can be either *social* (slow drivers, tall people in theaters, people who cut into lines) or *nonsocial* (stuck doors, a dead battery, rain on the day of the game). If you ask your friends what has frustrated them recently, most will probably men-

Emotion-focused coping Managing or controlling one's emotional reaction to a stressful or threatening situation.

Problem-focused coping Directly managing or remedying a stressful or threatening situation.

Frustration A negative emotional state that occurs when one is prevented from reaching a goal.

Coping with Traumatic Stress

Traumatic experiences produce psychological injury or intense emotional pain. Victims of **traumatic stresses,** such as war, torture, rape, assassination, plane crashes, natural disasters, and street violence, may suffer from nightmares, flashbacks, insomnia, irritability, nervousness, grief, emotional numbing, and depression. There is little doubt that the 2008 earthquake in Sichuan, China, caused these effects for those people living or working in the quake zone. Like most traumatic stresses, the impact was, and continues to be, overwhelming.

Lui Jin/AFP/Getty Images

With a death toll of over 60,000 victims, there can be little doubt that the 2008 earthquake in China was a traumatically stressful event. Even people who merely witnessed the aftermath of the disaster on television will suffer from stress symptoms.

People who personally witness or survive a disaster are most affected by traumatic stress. Twenty percent of the people who lived close to the World Trade Center in New York City suffered serious stress disorders after the 9/11 terrorist attack (Galea et al., 2002). Yet even those who experience horror at a distance may be traumatized (Galea & Resnick, 2005). Forty-four percent of U.S. adults who only saw the 9/11 attacks on television had at least some stress symptoms (Schuster et al., 2001). For example, Americans faced elevated risks of hypertension and heart problems for 3 years after 9/11 (Holman et al., 2008). Indirect exposure to such terrorist attacks, coupled with the ongoing risk of more attacks, has ensured that many people will suffer ongoing stress into the foreseeable future (Marshall et al., 2007).

Traumatic stress produces feelings of helplessness and vulnerability (Fields & Margolin, 2001). Victims realize that disaster could strike again without warning. In addition to feeling threatened, many victims sense that they are losing control of their lives (Scurfield, 2002).

What can people do about such reactions? Psychologists recommend the following:

- Identify what you are feeling and talk to others about your fears and concerns.

- Think about the skills that have helped you overcome adversity in the past and apply them to the present situation.

- Continue to do the things that you enjoy and that make life meaningful (LeDoux & Gorman, 2001).

- Get support from others. This is a major element in recovery from all traumatic events.

- Give yourself time to heal. Fortunately, most people are more resilient than they think.

When traumatic stresses are severe or repeated, some people have even more serious symptoms. They suffer from crippling anxiety or become emotionally numb. Typically, they can't stop thinking about the disturbing event; they anxiously avoid anything associated with the event; and they are constantly fearful or nervous. (These are the symptoms of *stress disorders,* which are discussed in Chapter 12.) Such reactions can leave victims emotionally handicapped for months or years after a disaster. The consequences can last a lifetime for children who are the victims of trauma (Gillespie & Nemeroff, 2007). If you feel that you are having trouble coping with a severe emotional shock, consider seeking help from a psychologist or other professional (Bisson et al., 2007).

---

tion someone's behavior ("My sister wore one of my dresses when I wanted to wear it," "My supervisor is unfair," "My history teacher grades too hard"). As social animals, we humans are highly sensitive to social sources of frustration (Taylor, 2006). That's probably why unfair treatment associated with racial or ethnic prejudice is a major source of frustration and stress in the lives of many African Americans and other minority group members (Clark et al., 1999; Gurung, 2010).

Frustration usually increases as the *strength, urgency,* or *importance* of a blocked motive increases. Jennifer was especially frustrated in the parking lot because she was late for an exam. Likewise, an escape artist submerged in a tank of water and bound with 200 pounds of chain would become *quite* frustrated if a trick lock jammed. Remember, too, that motivation becomes stronger as we near a goal. As a result, frustration is more intense when a person runs into an obstacle very close to a goal. If you've ever missed an A grade by five points, you were probably very frustrated. If you've missed an A by one point—well, frustration builds character, right?

A final factor affecting frustration is summarized by the old phrase "the straw that broke the camel's back." The effects of *repeated* frustrations can accumulate until a small irritation sets off an unexpectedly violent response. A case in point is the fact that people with long daily commutes are more likely to display "road rage" (angry, aggressive driving) (Harding et al., 1998).

Personal frustrations are based on personal characteristics. If you are 4 feet tall and aspire to be a professional basketball player, you very likely will be frustrated. If you want to go to medical school but can earn only D grades, you will likewise be frustrated. In both examples, frustration is actually based on personal limitations. Yet, failure may be

Traumatic stresses Extreme events that cause psychological injury or intense emotional pain.

FIGURE 11.4 Frustration and common reactions to it.

Person → *Goal* | *Barrier* | **Frustration**

Goal | **Persistence, vigorous effort**

Goal | **Variability, circumvention**

Goal | **Direct aggression**

Goal | **Displaced aggression**

Goal | **Withdrawal, escape**

Paintball seems to bring out aggressive impulses in many players. Wild shoot-outs are part of the fun, but are some players displacing aggressive urges related to frustration in other areas of their lives?

Steve Nagy/Photolibrary

Aggression Any response made with the intent of causing harm.

Displaced aggression Redirecting aggression to a target other than the actual source of one's frustration.

Scapegoating Blaming a person or a group of people for conditions not of their making.

Escape Reducing discomfort by leaving frustrating situations or by psychologically withdrawing from them.

perceived as externally caused. We will return to this point in a discussion of stress management. In the meantime, let's look at some typical reactions to frustration.

Reactions to Frustration

Aggression is any response made with the intent of harming a person or an object. It is one of the most persistent and frequent responses to frustration (Anderson & Bushman, 2002).

Does frustration always cause aggression? Aren't there other reactions? Although the connection is strong, frustration does not always incite aggression. More often, frustration is met first with *persistence,* often in the form of more vigorous efforts and varied responses (▶▶ Figure 11.4). For example, if you put your last quarter in a vending machine and pressing the button has no effect, you will probably press harder and faster (vigorous effort). Then you will press all the other buttons (varied response). Persistence may help you reach your goal by getting *around* a barrier. However, if the machine *still* refuses to deliver, or return your quarter, you may become aggressive and kick the machine (or at least tell it what you think of it).

Persistence can be very adaptive. Overcoming a barrier ends the frustration and allows the need or motive to be satisfied. The same is true of aggression that removes or destroys a barrier. Picture a small band of nomadic humans, parched by thirst but separated from a water hole by a menacing animal. It is easy to see that attacking the animal may ensure their survival. In modern society such direct aggression is seldom acceptable. If you find a long line at the drinking fountain, aggression is hardly appropriate. Because direct aggression is discouraged, it is frequently *displaced.*

How is aggression displaced? Directing aggression toward a source of frustration may be impossible, or it may be too dangerous. If you are frustrated by your boss at work or by a teacher at school, the cost of direct aggression may be too high (losing your job or failing a class). Instead, the aggression may be displaced, or redirected, toward whomever or whatever is available. Targets of **displaced aggression** tend to be safer, or less likely to retaliate, than the original source of frustration. At one time or another, you have probably lashed out at a friend or relative who was not the real cause of your annoyance. As this suggests, excessive anger over a minor irritation is a common form of displaced aggression (Miller et al., 2003).

Psychologists attribute much hostility to displaced aggression. A disturbing example is the finding that unemployment and divorce are associated with increased child abuse (Weissman, Jogerst, & Dawson, 2003). In a pattern known as **scapegoating,** a person or a group is blamed for conditions not of their making. A *scapegoat* is a person who has become a habitual target of displaced aggression. Despite recent progress, many minority groups continue to face hostility based on scapegoating. Think, for example, about the hostility expressed toward illegal immigrants during times of economic hardship. In many communities, layoffs and job losses are closely linked to increased violence (Catalano, Novaco, & McConnell, 1997). Or think about the hostility expressed toward anyone in the United States who looked even vaguely "foreign" right after the 9/11 terrorist attacks.

I have a friend who dropped out of school to hitchhike around the country. He seemed very frustrated before he quit. What type of response to frustration is that? Another major reaction to frustration is escape, or withdrawal. It is stressful and unpleasant to be frustrated. If other reactions do not reduce frustration, a person may try to escape. **Escape** may mean actually leaving a source of frustration (dropping out of school, quitting a job, leaving an unhappy marriage), or it may mean psychologically escaping. Two common forms of psychological escape are feigned apathy (pretending not to care) and the use of drugs such as cocaine, alcohol, marijuana, or narcotics. (Notice that these are examples of ineffective emotion-focused coping.) (See Figure 11.4 for a summary of common reactions to frustration.)

Coping with Frustration

In a classic experiment, a psychologist studying frustration placed rats on a small platform at the top of a tall pole. Then he forced them to jump off the platform toward two elevated doors, one locked and the other unlocked. If the rat chose the correct door, it swung open and the rat landed safely on another platform. Rats who chose the locked door bounced off it and fell into a net far below.

The problem of choosing the open door was made unsolvable and very frustrating by randomly alternating which door was locked. After a time, most rats adopted a stereotyped response. That is, they chose the same door every time. This door was then permanently locked. All the rat had to do was jump to the other door to avoid a fall, but time after time the rat bounced off the locked door (Maier, 1949).

Isn't that an example of persistence? No. Persistence that is *inflexible* can turn into "stupid," stereotyped behavior like that of a rat on a jumping platform. When dealing with frustration, you must know when to quit and establish a new direction. Here are some suggestions to help you avoid needless frustration:

1. Try to identify the source of your frustration. Is it external or personal?
2. Is the source of frustration something that can be changed? How hard would you have to work to change it? Is it under your control at all?
3. If the source of your frustration can be changed or removed, are the necessary efforts worth it?

The answers to these questions help determine if persistence will be futile. There is value in learning to accept gracefully those things that cannot be changed.

It is also important to distinguish between *real* barriers and *imagined* barriers. All too often we create our own imaginary barriers. For example, Corazon wants a part-time job to earn extra money. At the first place she applied, she was told that she didn't have enough "experience." Now she complains of being frustrated because she wants to work but cannot. She needs "experience" to work, but can't get experience without working. She has quit looking for a job.

Is Corazon's need for experience a real barrier? Unless she applies for *many* jobs, it is impossible to tell if she has overestimated its importance. For her the barrier is real enough to prevent further efforts, but with persistence she might locate an "unlocked door." If a reasonable amount of effort does show that experience is essential, it might be obtained in other ways—through temporary volunteer work, for instance.

Conflict—Yes, No, Yes, No, Yes, No, Well, Maybe

Are there different types of conflict? How do people react to conflict?

Conflict occurs whenever a person must choose between contradictory needs, desires, motives, or demands. Choosing between college and work, marriage and single life, or study and failure are common conflicts. There are four basic forms of conflict. As we will see, each has its own properties (▶▶ Figure 11.5 and ▶▶ Figure 11.6).

Approach-Approach Conflicts

A simple **approach-approach conflict** comes from having to choose between two positive, or desirable, alternatives. Choosing between tutti-frutti-coconut-mocha-champagne ice and orange-marmalade-peanut butter-coffee swirl at the ice cream parlor may throw you into a temporary conflict. However, if you really like both choices, your decision will be quickly made. Even when more important decisions are at stake, approach-approach con-

Choice

Conflict A stressful condition that occurs when a person must <u>choose</u> between incompatible or contradictory alternatives.

Approach-approach conflict Choosing between two positive, or desirable, alternatives.

▲ **FIGURE 11.5** Three basic forms of conflict. For this woman, choosing between pie and ice cream is a minor approach-approach conflict; deciding whether to take a job that will require weekend work is an approach-avoidance conflict; and choosing between paying higher rent and moving is an avoidance-avoidance conflict.

flicts tend to be the easiest to resolve. When both options are positive, the scales of decision are easily tipped one direction or the other.

Avoidance-Avoidance Conflicts

Being forced to choose between two negative, or undesirable, alternatives creates an **avoidance-avoidance conflict.** A person in an avoidance conflict is caught between "the devil and the deep blue sea," between "the frying pan and the fire," or "a rock and a hard place." In real life, double-avoidance conflicts involve dilemmas such as choosing between unwanted pregnancy and abortion, the dentist and tooth decay, a monotonous job and poverty, or dorm food and starvation.

Suppose that I consider any pregnancy sacred and not to be tampered with. Or suppose I don't object to abortion. Like many other stressful situations, these examples can be defined as conflicts only on the basis of personal needs and values. If a woman wants to end a pregnancy and does not object to abortion, she experiences no conflict. If she would not consider abortion under any circumstances, there is also no conflict.

Avoidance conflicts often have a "damned if you do, damned if you don't" quality. In other words, both choices are negative, but *not choosing* may be impossible or equally undesirable. To illustrate, imagine the plight of a person trapped in a hotel fire 20 stories from the ground. Should she jump from the window and almost surely die on the pavement? Or should she try to dash through the flames and almost surely die of smoke inhalation and burns? When faced with a choice such as this, it is easy to see why people often *freeze,* finding it impossible to decide or take action. In actual disasters of this sort, people are often found dead in their rooms, victims of an inability to take action.

Indecision, inaction, and freezing are not the only reactions to double-avoidance conflicts. Because avoidance conflicts are stressful and difficult to solve, people sometimes pull out of them entirely. This reaction, called *leaving the field,* is another form of escape. It may explain the behavior of a student who could not attend school unless he worked. However,

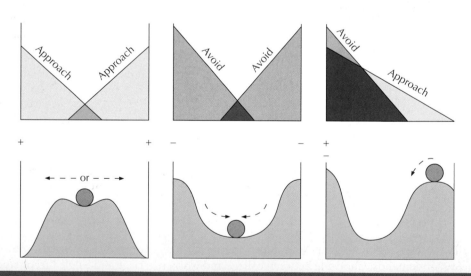

▲ **FIGURE 11.6** Conflict diagrams. As shown by the colored areas in the graphs, desires to approach and to avoid increase near a goal. The effects of these tendencies are depicted below each graph. The "behavior" of the ball in each example illustrates the nature of the conflict above it. An approach conflict (*left*) is easily decided. Moving toward one goal will increase its attraction (*graph*) and will lead to a rapid resolution. (If the ball moves in either direction, it will go all the way to one of the goals.) In an avoidance conflict (*center*), tendencies to avoid are deadlocked, resulting in inaction. In an approach-avoidance conflict (*right*), approach proceeds to the point where desires to approach and avoid cancel each other. Again, these tendencies are depicted (*below*) by the action of the ball. (Graphs after Miller, 1944.)

 Avoidance-avoidance conflict Choosing between two negative, undesirable alternatives.

if he worked, he could not earn passing grades. His solution after much conflict and indecision? He joined the navy.

Approach-Avoidance Conflicts

Approach-avoidance conflicts are also difficult to resolve. In some ways they are more troublesome than avoidance conflicts because people seldom escape them. A person in an **approach-avoidance conflict** is "caught" by being attracted to, and repelled by, the same goal or activity. Attraction keeps the person in the situation, but its negative aspects cause turmoil and distress. For example, a high school student arrives to pick up his date for the first time. He is met at the door by her father, who is a professional wrestler—7 feet tall, 300 pounds, and entirely covered with hair. The father gives the boy a crushing handshake and growls that he will break him in half if the girl is not home on time. The student considers the girl attractive and has a good time. But does he ask her out again? It depends on the relative strength of his attraction and his fear. Almost certainly he will feel *ambivalent* about asking her out again, knowing that another encounter with her father awaits him.

Ambivalence (mixed positive and negative feelings) is a central characteristic of approach-avoidance conflicts. Ambivalence is usually translated into *partial approach* (Miller, 1944). Because our student is still attracted to the girl, he may spend time with her at school and elsewhere. But he may not actually date her again. Some more realistic examples of approach-avoidance conflicts are planning to marry someone your parents strongly disapprove of, wanting to be in a play but suffering stage fright, wanting to buy a car but not wanting to make monthly payments, and wanting to eat when you're already overweight. Many of life's important decisions have approach-avoidance dimensions.

Multiple Conflicts

Aren't real-life conflicts more complex than the ones described here? Yes. Conflicts are rarely as clear-cut as those described. People in conflict are usually faced with several dilemmas at once, so several types of conflict may be intermingled. The fourth type of conflict moves us closer to reality. In a **double approach-avoidance conflict,** each alternative has both positive and negative qualities. For example, you are offered two jobs: One has good pay but poor hours and dull work; the second has interesting work and excellent hours, but low pay. Which do you select? This situation is more typical of the choices we must usually make. It offers neither completely positive nor completely negative options.

As with single approach-avoidance conflicts, people faced with double approach-avoidance conflicts feel ambivalent about each choice. This causes them to *vacillate,* or waver between the alternatives. Just as you are about to choose one such alternative, its undesirable aspects tend to loom large. So, what do you do? You swing back toward the other choice. If you have ever been romantically attracted to two people at once—each having qualities you like and dislike—then you have probably experienced vacillation. Another example that may be familiar is trying to decide between two college majors, each with advantages and disadvantages.

In real life it is common to face **multiple approach-avoidance conflicts** in which several alternatives each have positive and negative features. An example would be trying to choose which automobile to buy among several brands. When multiple approach-avoidance conflicts involve major life decisions, such as choosing a career, a school, a mate, or a job, they can add greatly to the amount of stress we experience.

Managing Conflicts

How can I handle conflicts more effectively? Most of the suggestions made earlier concerning frustration also apply to conflicts. However, here are some additional things to remember when you are in conflict or must make a difficult decision:

1. Don't be hasty when making important decisions. Hasty decisions are often regretted. Even if you do make a faulty decision, it will trouble you less if you know that you did everything possible to avoid a mistake.

Approach-avoidance conflict Being attracted to and repelled by the same goal or activity.

Double approach-avoidance conflict Being simultaneously attracted to and repelled by each of two alternatives.

Multiple approach-avoidance conflict Being simultaneously attracted to and repelled by each of several alternatives.

2. Try out important decisions *partially* when possible. If you are thinking about moving to a new town, try to spend a few days there first. If you are choosing between colleges, do the same. If classes are in progress, sit in on some. If you want to learn to scuba dive, rent equipment for a reasonable length of time before buying.

3. Look for workable compromises. Again it is important to get all available information. If you think that you have only one or two alternatives and they are undesirable or unbearable, seek the aid of a teacher, counselor, minister, or social service agency. You may be overlooking possible alternatives these people will know about.

4. When all else fails, make a decision and live with it. Indecision and conflict exact a high cost. Sometimes it is best to select a course of action and stick with it unless it is very obviously wrong after you have taken it.

Conflicts are a normal part of life. With practice you can learn to manage many of the conflicts you will face.

study break
Stress, Frustration, and Conflict

RECITE

1. The first stage of the GAS is called the _____ reaction.
2. Whereas stressful incidents suppress the immune system, stress management techniques have almost no effect on immune system functioning. T or F?
3. Emotional exhaustion, cynicism, and reduced accomplishment are characteristics of job _____.
4. Stress tends to be greatest when a situation is appraised as a _____ and a person does not feel _____ to cope with the situation.
5. According to Lazarus, coping with threatening situations can be both problem focused and _____ focused.
6. Which of the following is *not* a common reaction to frustration?
   a. ambivalence   b. aggression
   c. displaced aggression   d. persistence
7. Sampson Goliath is 7 feet tall and weighs 300 pounds. He has failed miserably in his aspirations to become a jockey. The source of his frustration is mainly _____.
8. Inaction and freezing are most characteristic of avoidance-avoidance conflicts. T or F?
9. Approach-avoidance conflicts produce mixed feelings called _____.

REFLECT
Critical Thinking

10. Which do you think would produce more stress: (a) appraising a situation as mildly threatening but feeling like you are totally incompetent to cope with it, or (b) appraising a situation as very threatening but feeling that you have the resources and skills to cope with it?
11. Being frustrated is unpleasant. If some action, including aggression, ends frustration, why might we expect the action to be repeated on other occasions?

Relate

What impact did pressure, control, predictability, repetition, and intensity have on your last stress reaction?

What type of coping do you tend to use when you face a stressor such as public speaking or taking an important exam?

Think of a time when you were frustrated. What was your goal? What prevented you from reaching it? Was your frustration external or personal?

Have you ever displaced aggression? Why did you choose another target for your hostility?

Review the major types of conflict and think of a conflict you have faced that illustrates each type. Did your reactions match those described in the text?

ANSWERS

1. alarm 2. F 3. burnout 4. threat, competent 5. emotion 6. a 7. personal 8. T 9. ambivalence 10. There is no correct answer here because individual stress reactions vary greatly. However, the secondary appraisal of a situation often determines just how stressful it is. Feeling incapable of coping is very threatening. 11. If a response ends discomfort, the response has been negatively reinforced. This makes it more likely to occur in the future (see Chapter 6).

Psychological Defense—Mental Karate?

What are defense mechanisms?

Threatening situations tend to produce **anxiety.** When you are anxious, you feel tense, uneasy, apprehensive, worried, and vulnerable. This unpleasant state can lead to emotion-focused coping that is defensive in nature (Lazarus, 1991b). Psychodynamic psychologists have identified various defense mechanisms that allow us to reduce anxiety caused by stressful situations or our own shortcomings.

What are psychological defense mechanisms and how do they reduce anxiety? A **defense mechanism** is any mental process used to avoid, deny, or distort sources of threat or anxiety, especially threats to one's self-image. Many of the defenses were first identified by Sigmund Freud, who assumed they operate *unconsciously.* Often, defense mechanisms create large blind spots in awareness. For instance, you might know an extremely stingy person who is completely unaware that he is a tightwad.

Everyone has at one time or another used defense mechanisms. Let's consider some of the most common. (A more complete listing is given in ● Table 11.4.)

Denial

One of the most basic defenses is **denial** (protecting oneself from an unpleasant reality by refusing to accept it or believe it). We are prone to deny death, illness, and similar painful and threatening events. For instance, if you were told that you had only 3 months to live, how would you react? Your first thoughts might be "Aw, come on, someone must have mixed up the X-rays" or "The doctor must be mistaken" or simply "It can't be true!" Similar denial and disbelief are common reactions to the unexpected death of a friend or relative: "It's just not real. I don't believe it!"

Repression

Freud noticed that his patients had tremendous difficulty recalling shocking or traumatic events from childhood. It seemed that powerful forces were holding these painful memories from awareness. Freud called this **repression,** and said we use it to protect ourselves by blocking out threatening thoughts and impulses. Feelings of hostility toward a family member, the

---

● Table 11.4 Psychological Defense Mechanisms

Compensation Counteracting a real or imagined weakness by emphasizing desirable traits or seeking to excel in the area of weakness or in other areas.

Denial Protecting oneself from an unpleasant reality by refusing to perceive it.

Fantasy Fulfilling unmet desires in imagined achievements or activities.

Identification Taking on some of the characteristics of an admired person, usually as a way of compensating for perceived personal weaknesses or faults.

Intellectualization Separating emotion from a threatening or anxiety-provoking situation by talking or thinking about it in impersonal "intellectual" terms.

Isolation Separating contradictory thoughts or feelings into "logic-tight" mental compartments so that they do not come into conflict.

Projection Attributing one's own feelings, shortcomings, or unacceptable impulses to others.

Rationalization Justifying your behavior by giving reasonable and "rational," but false, reasons for it.

Reaction formation Preventing dangerous impulses from being expressed in behavior by exaggerating opposite behavior.

Regression Retreating to an earlier level of development or to earlier, less demanding habits or situations.

Repression Unconsciously preventing painful or dangerous thoughts from entering awareness.

Sublimation Working off unmet desires, or unacceptable impulses, in activities that are constructive.

Anxiety Apprehension, dread, or uneasiness similar to fear but based on an unclear threat.

Defense mechanism A habitual and often unconscious psychological process used to reduce anxiety.

names of people we dislike, and past failures are common targets of repression. Research suggests that you are most likely to repress information that threatens your self-image (Mendolia, 2002).

Reaction Formation

In a **reaction formation,** impulses are not just repressed; they are also held in check by exaggerating opposite behavior. For example, a mother who unconsciously resents her children may, through reaction formation, become absurdly overprotective and overindulgent. Her real thoughts of "I hate them" and "I wish they were gone" are replaced by "I love them" and "I don't know what I would do without them." The mother's hostile impulses are traded for "smother" love, so that she won't have to admit she hates her children. Thus, the basic idea in a reaction formation is that the individual acts out an opposite behavior to block threatening impulses or feelings.

Regression

In its broadest meaning, **regression** refers to any return to earlier, less demanding situations or habits. Most parents who have a second child have to put up with at least some regression by the older child. Threatened by a new rival for affection, an older child may regress to childish speech, bed-wetting, or infantile play after the new baby arrives. If you've ever seen a child get homesick at summer camp or on a vacation, you've observed regression. The child wants to go home, where it's "safe." An adult who throws a temper tantrum or a married adult who "goes home to mother" is also regressing.

Projection

Projection is an unconscious process that protects us from the anxiety we would feel if we were to discern our faults. A person who is projecting tends to see his or her own feelings, shortcomings, or unacceptable impulses in others. **Projection** lowers anxiety by exaggerating negative traits in others. This justifies one's own actions and directs attention away from personal failings.

One of your authors once worked for a greedy shop owner who cheated many of his customers. This same man considered himself a pillar of the community and very moral and religious. How did he justify to himself his greed and dishonesty? He believed that everyone who entered his store was bent on cheating *him* any way they could. In reality, few, if any, of his customers shared his motives, but he projected his own greed and dishonesty onto them.

Rationalization

Every teacher is familiar with this strange phenomenon: On the day of an exam, an incredible wave of disasters sweeps through the city. Mothers, fathers, sisters, brothers, aunts, uncles, grandparents, friends, relatives, and pets of students become ill or die. Motors suddenly fall out of cars. Books are lost or stolen. Alarm clocks go belly-up and ring no more. All manner of computer equipment malfunctions.

The making of excuses comes from a natural tendency to explain our behavior. **Rationalization** refers to justifying personal actions by giving "rational" but false reasons for them. When the explanation you give for your behavior is reasonable and convincing— but not the real reason—you are *rationalizing*. For example, Jennifer failed to turn in an assignment made at the beginning of the semester in one of her classes. Here's the explanation she gave her professor:

> My car broke down 2 days ago, and I couldn't get to the library until yesterday. Then I couldn't get all the books I needed because some were checked out, but I wrote what I could. Then last night, as the last straw, the ink cartridge in my printer ran out, and since all the stores were closed, I couldn't finish the paper on time.

When asked why she left the assignment until the last minute (the real reason it was late), Jennifer offered another set of rationalizations. Like many people, Jennifer had difficulty seeing herself without the protection of her rationalizations.

All of the defense mechanisms described seem pretty undesirable. Do they have a positive side? People who overuse defense mechanisms become less adaptable, because they consume great amounts of emotional energy to control anxiety and maintain an unrealistic self-image. Defense mechanisms do have value, though. Often, they help keep us from being overwhelmed by immediate threats. This can provide time for a person to learn to cope in a more effective, problem-focused manner. If you recognize some of your own behavior in the descriptions here, it is hardly a sign that you are hopelessly defensive. As noted earlier, most people occasionally use defense mechanisms.

Two defense mechanisms that have a decidedly more positive quality are compensation and sublimation.

Compensation

Compensatory reactions are defenses against feelings of inferiority. A person who has a defect or weakness (real or imagined) may go to unusual lengths to overcome the weakness or to *compensate* for it by excelling in other areas. One of the pioneers of "pumping iron" is Jack LaLanne, who opened the first modern health club in America. LaLanne made a successful career out of bodybuilding in spite of the fact that he was thin and sickly as a young man. Or perhaps it would be more accurate to say *because* he was thin and sickly. You can find dozens of examples of **compensation** at work. A childhood stutterer may excel in debate at college. As a child, Helen Keller was unable to see or hear, but she became an outstanding thinker and writer. Perhaps Ray Charles, Stevie Wonder, Andrea Bocelli, and other blind entertainers were drawn to music because of their handicap.

Sublimation

The defense called **sublimation** (sub-lih-MAY-shun) is defined as working off frustrated desires (especially sexual desires) through socially acceptable activities. Freud believed that art, music, dance, poetry, scientific investigation, and other creative activities could serve to rechannel sexual energies into productive behavior. Freud also felt that almost any strong desire could be sublimated. For example, a very aggressive person may find social acceptance as a professional soldier, boxer, or football player. Greed may be refined into a successful business career. Lying may be sublimated into storytelling, creative writing, or politics.

Sexual motives appear to be the most easily and widely sublimated (Jacobs, 2003). Freud would have had a field day with such modern pastimes as surfing, motorcycle riding, drag racing, and dancing to or playing rock music, to name but a few. People enjoy each of these activities for a multitude of reasons, but it is hard to overlook the rich sexual symbolism apparent in each.

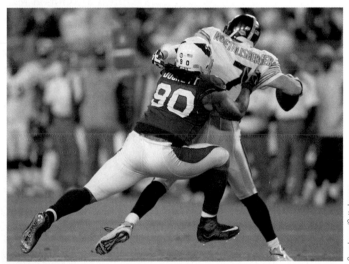

For some players—and fans—football probably allows sublimation of aggressive urges. *Grand Theft Auto* and similar computer games may serve the same purpose.

Learned Helplessness—Is There Hope?

What do we know about coping with feelings of helplessness and depression?

What would happen if a person's defenses failed or if the person appraised a threatening situation as hopeless? Martin Seligman studied the case of a young marine who seemed to have adapted to the stresses of being held prisoner during the Vietnam War. The marine's health was related to a promise made by his captors: If he cooperated, they said, he would be released on a certain date. As the date approached, his spirits soared. Then came a devastating blow. He had been deceived. His captors had no intention of ever releasing him. He immediately lapsed into a deep depression, refused to eat or drink, and died shortly thereafter.

That seems like an extreme example. Does anything similar occur outside of concentration camps? Apparently so. For example, researchers in San Antonio, Texas, asked older people if they were hopeful about the future. Those who answered "No" died at elevated rates (Stern, Dhanda, & Hazuda, 2001).

 To explain such patterns psychologists have focused on the concept of **learned helplessness,** an acquired inability to overcome obstacles and avoid aversive stimuli (Seligman, 1989). To observe learned helplessness, let's see what happens when animals are tested in a shuttle box (▶▶ Figure 11.7). If placed in one side of a divided box, dogs will quickly learn to leap to the other side to escape an electric shock. If they are given a warning before the shock occurs (for example, a light that dims), most dogs learn to avoid the shock by leaping the barrier before the shock arrives. This is true of most dogs, but not those who have learned to feel helpless (Overmier & LoLordo, 1998).

How is a dog made to feel helpless? Before being tested in the shuttle box, a dog can be placed in a harness (from which the dog cannot escape) and then given several painful shocks. The animal is helpless to prevent these shocks. When placed in the shuttle box, dogs prepared this way react to the first shock by crouching, howling, and whining. None of them try to escape. They helplessly resign themselves to their fate. After all, they have already learned that there is nothing they can do about shock.

As the shuttle box experiments suggest, helplessness is a psychological state that occurs when events *appear to be uncontrollable* (Seligman, 1989). Helplessness also afflicts humans. It is a common reaction to repeated failure and to unpredictable or unavoidable punishment. A prime example is college students who feel helpless about their schoolwork. Such students tend to procrastinate, give up easily, and drop out of school (Perry, 2003).

Where humans are concerned, attributions (discussed in Chapter 9) have a large effect on helplessness. Persons who are made to feel helpless in one situation are more likely to act helpless in other situations if they attribute their failure to *lasting, general* factors. An example would be concluding "I must be stupid" after doing poorly on a test in a biology class. In contrast, attributing a low score to specific factors in the situation ("I'm not too good at

FIGURE 11.7 In the normal course of escape and avoidance learning, a light dims shortly before the floor is electrified *(a)*. Because the light does not yet have meaning for the dog, the dog receives a shock (non-injurious, by the way) and leaps the barrier *(b)*. Dogs soon learn to watch for the dimming of the light *(c)* and to jump before receiving a shock *(d)*. Dogs made to feel "helpless" rarely even learn to escape shock, much less to avoid it.

Learned helplessness A learned inability to overcome obstacles or to avoid punishment; learned passivity and inaction to aversive stimuli.

the type of test my biology professor uses" or "I'm not very interested in biology") tends to prevent learned helplessness from spreading (Peterson & Vaidya, 2001).

Depression

Seligman and others have pointed out the similarities between learned helplessness and **depression.** Both are marked by feelings of despondency, powerlessness, and hopelessness. "Helpless" animals display decreased activity, lowered aggression, blunted appetite, and a loss of sex drive. Humans suffer from similar effects and also tend to see themselves as failing, even when they're not (LoLordo, 2001; Seligman, 1989).

Depression is one of the most widespread emotional problems, and it undoubtedly has many causes. However, learned helplessness seems to explain many cases of depression and hopelessness. For example, Seligman (1972) describes the fate of Archie, a 15-year-old boy. For Archie, school is an unending series of shocks and failures. Other students treat him as if he's stupid; in class he rarely answers questions because he doesn't know some of the words. He feels knocked down everywhere he turns. These may not be electric shocks, but they are certainly emotional "shocks," and Archie has learned to feel helpless to prevent them. When he leaves school his chances of success will be poor. He has learned to passively endure whatever shocks life has in store for him. Archie is not alone in this regard. Hopelessness is almost always a major element of depression (Ciarrochi, Dean, & Anderson, 2002).

Hope

Does Seligman's research give any clues about how to "unlearn" helplessness? With dogs, an effective technique is to forcibly drag them away from shock into the "safe" compartment. After this is done several times, the animals regain "hope" and feelings of control over the environment. Just how this can be done with humans is a question psychologists are exploring. It seems obvious, for instance, that someone like Archie would benefit from an educational program that would allow him to "succeed" repeatedly.

In **mastery training,** responses are reinforced that lead to mastery of a threat or control over one's environment. Animals who undergo such training become more resistant to learned helplessness (Volpicelli et al., 1983). For example, animals that first learn to escape shock become more persistent in trying to flee inescapable shock. In effect, they won't give up, even when the situation really is "hopeless."

Such findings suggest that we might be able to "immunize" people against helplessness and depression by allowing them to master difficult challenges. The Outward Bound schools, in which people pit themselves against the rigors of mountaineering, whitewater canoeing, and wilderness survival, might serve as a model for such a program.

The value of hope should not be overlooked. As fragile as this emotion seems to be, it is a powerful antidote to depression and helplessness. As an individual, you may find hope in religion, nature, human companionship, or even technology. Wherever you find it, remember its value: Hope is among the most important of all human emotions. Having positive beliefs, such as optimism, hope, and a sense of meaning and control is closely related to overall well-being (Taylor et al., 2000, 2003).

Mastery training can occur informally when people learn to cope with challenges. For example, 18- to 21-year-old trainees on a transatlantic sailing voyage showed marked improvements in their ability to cope with stress (Norris & Weinman, 1996).

Depression: Why Students Get the Blues

During the school year, many college students suffer some symptoms of depression, which can exert a toll on academic performance. In one study, students diagnosed with depression scored half a grade point below nondepressed students (Hysenbegasi, Hass, & Rowland, 2005). Why do students get "blue"? Various problems contribute to depressive feelings. Here are some of the most common:

Depression A state of despondency marked by feelings of powerlessness and hopelessness.

Mastery training Reinforcement of responses that lead to mastery of a threat or control over one's environment.

In a survey, college students reported that they were depressed from one to two times a month. These episodes lasted from a few hours to several days.

1. Stresses from college work and pressures to choose a career can leave students feeling that they are missing out on fun or that all their hard work is meaningless.
2. Isolation and loneliness are common when students leave their support groups behind. In the past, family, a circle of high school friends, and often a boyfriend or girlfriend could be counted on for support and encouragement.
3. Problems with studying and grades frequently trigger depression. Many students start college with high aspirations and little prior experience with failure. At the same time, many lack basic skills necessary for academic success and are afraid of failure (Martin & Marsh, 2003).
4. Depression can be triggered by the breakup of an intimate relationship, either with a former boyfriend or girlfriend or with a newly formed college romance.
5. Students who find it difficult to live up to their idealized images of themselves are especially prone to depression (Scott & O'Hara, 1993).
6. An added danger is that depressed students are more likely to abuse alcohol, which is a depressant (Weitzman, 2004).

Recognizing Depression

Most people know, obviously enough, when they are "down." Aaron Beck, an authority on depression, suggests that you assume that more than a minor fluctuation in mood is involved when five conditions exist (Beck & Greenberg, 1974):

1. You have a consistently negative opinion of yourself.
2. You engage in frequent self-criticism and self-blame.
3. You place negative interpretations on events that usually wouldn't bother you.
4. The future looks bleak and negative.
5. You feel that your responsibilities are overwhelming.

What can be done to combat depression? Bouts of the college blues are closely related to stressful events. Learning to manage college work and to challenge self-critical thinking can help alleviate mild school-related depression.

Attacks of the college blues are common and should be distinguished from more serious cases of depression. Severe depression is a serious problem that can lead to suicide or a major impairment of emotional functioning. In such cases it would be wise to seek professional help.

Coping with Depression

If you don't do well on a test or a class assignment, how do you react? If you see it as a small, isolated setback, you probably won't feel too bad. However, if you feel like you have "blown it" in a big way, depression may follow. Students who strongly link everyday events to long-term goals (such as a successful career or high income) tend to overreact to day-to-day disappointments (McIntosh, Harlow, & Martin, 1995).

What does the preceding tell us about the college blues? The implication is that it's important to take daily tasks one step at a time and chip away at them. That way, you are less likely to feel overwhelmed, helpless, or hopeless. One classic suggestion comes from Aaron Beck and Ruth Greenberg (1974): When you feel "blue," you should make a *daily schedule* for yourself. Try to schedule activities to fill up every hour during the day. It is best to start with easy activities and progress to more difficult tasks. Check off each item as it is completed. That way, you will begin to break the self-defeating cycle of feeling helpless and falling further behind. (Depressed students spend much of their time sleeping.) A series of small accomplishments, successes, or pleasures may be all that you need to get going again. However, if you are lacking skills needed for success in college, ask for help in getting them. Don't remain "helpless."

Feelings of worthlessness and hopelessness are usually supported by self-critical or negative thoughts. Beck and Greenberg recommend writing down such thoughts as they occur, especially those that immediately precede feelings of sadness. After you have collected these thoughts, write a rational answer to each. For example, the thought "No one loves me" should be answered with a list of those who do care. (See Chapter 13 for more information.) One more point to keep in mind is this: When events begin to improve, try to accept it as a sign that better times lie ahead. Positive events are most likely to end depression if you view them as stable and continuing, rather than temporary and fragile (Needles & Abramson, 1990).

study break
Defense Mechanisms, Helplessness, and Depression

RECITE

1. Fulfilling frustrated desires in imaginary achievements or activities defines the defense mechanism of
   a. compensation   b. isolation
   c. fantasy   d. sublimation
2. Of the defense mechanisms, two that are considered relatively constructive are
   a. compensation   b. denial
   c. isolation   d. projection
   e. regression   f. rationalization
   g. sublimation
3. Depression in humans is similar to _____ _____ observed in animal experiments.
4. College students suffering from depression have lower grades than nondepressed students. T or F?
5. Frequent self-criticism and self-blame are a natural consequence of doing college work. T or F?

REFLECT

Critical Thinking

6. Learned helplessness is MOST closely related to which of the factors that determine the severity of stress?

Relate

We tend to be blind to our own reliance on defense mechanisms. Return to the definitions in Table 11.4 and see if you can think of one example of each defense that you have observed someone else using.

Have you ever felt helpless in a particular situation? What caused you to feel that way? Does any part of Seligman's description of learned helplessness match your own experience?

Imagine that a friend of yours is suffering from the college blues. What advice would you give your friend?

ANSWERS

1. c 2. a, g 3. learned helplessness 4. T 5. F 6. Feelings of incompetence and lack of control.

Stress and Health—Unmasking a Hidden Killer

How is stress related to health and disease?

At the beginning of this chapter you read about Jennifer, our intrepid student who became ill after a stressful final exam period. Was Jennifer's illness a coincidence? Psychologists have now firmly established that stress affects our health. Let's see how this occurs. We will also explore some factors that limit the health risks we face. Because we live in a fast-paced and often stressful society, these are topics worth stressing.

Disaster, depression, and sorrow often precede illness (Brannon & Feist, 2010). As Jennifer learned after finals week, stressful events reduce the body's natural defenses against disease. More surprising is the finding that *life changes*—both good and bad—can increase susceptibility to accidents or illness. Major changes in our surroundings or routines require us to be vigilant, on guard, and ready to react. Over long periods, this can be quite stressful (Sternberg, 2000).

Life Events and Stress

How can I tell if I am subjecting myself to too much stress? Psychiatrist Thomas Holmes and graduate student Richard Rahe developed the first rating scale to estimate the health hazards we face when stresses add up (Holmes & Rahe, 1967). Still widely used today, a version of the **Social Readjustment Rating Scale (SRRS)** is reprinted in

Social Readjustment Rating Scale (SRRS) A scale that rates the impact of various life events on the likelihood of illness.

Table 11.5 Social Readjustment Rating Scale

RANK	LIFE EVENT	LIFE CHANGE UNITS	RANK	LIFE EVENT	LIFE CHANGE UNITS
1	Death of spouse or child	119	22	Child leaving home	44
2	Divorce	98	23	Mortgage or loan greater than $10,000	44
3	Death of close family member	92	24	Change in responsibilities at work	43
4	Marital separation	79	25	Change in living conditions	42
5	Fired from work	79	26	Change in residence	41
6	Major personal injury or illness	77	27	Begin or end school	38
7	Jail term	75	28	Trouble with in-laws	38
8	Death of close friend	70	29	Outstanding personal achievement	37
9	Pregnancy	66	30	Change in work hours or conditions	36
10	Major business readjustment	62	31	Change in schools	35
11	Foreclosure on a mortgage or loan	61	32	Christmas	30
12	Gain of new family member	57	33	Trouble with boss	29
13	Marital reconciliation	57	34	Change in recreation	29
14	Change in health or behavior of family member	56	35	Mortgage or loan less than $10,000	28
15	Change in financial state	56	36	Change in personal habits	27
16	Retirement	54	37	Change in eating habits	27
17	Change to different line of work	51	38	Change in social activities	27
18	Change in number of arguments with spouse	51	39	Change in number of family get-togethers	26
19	Marriage	50	40	Change in sleeping habits	26
20	Spouse begins or ends work	46	41	Vacation	25
21	Sexual difficulties	45	42	Change in church activities	22
			43	Minor violations of the law	22

Reprinted from M. A. Miller & R. H. Rahe, 'Life changes scaling for the 1990s' in "Journal of Psychosomatic Research": 43(3): pp. 279–292, Table II, copyright © 1997 Elsevier Ltd., with permission from Elsevier.

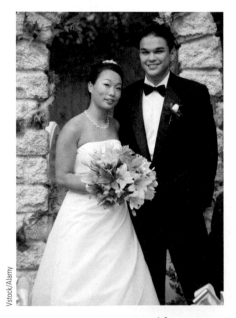

Marriage is usually a positive life event. Nevertheless, the many changes it brings can be stressful.

● Table 11.5 (Scully, Tosi, & Banning, 2000). Notice that the impact of life events is expressed in *life change units* (*LCUs*) (numerical values assigned to each life event).

As you read the scale, note again that positive life events may be as costly as disasters. Marriage rates 50 LCUs, even though it is usually a happy event. You'll also see many items that read, "Change in. . . ." This means that an improvement in life conditions can be as costly as a decline. A stressful adjustment may be required in either case.

To use the scale shown in Table 11.5, add up the LCUs for all life events you have experienced during the last year and compare the total to the following standards:

> 0–150: No significant problems
>
> 150–199: Mild life crisis (33 percent chance of illness)
>
> 200–299: Moderate life crisis (50 percent chance of illness)
>
> 300 or more: Major life crisis (80 percent chance of illness)

According to Holmes, there is a high chance of illness or accident when your LCU total exceeds 300 points. A more conservative rating of stress can be obtained by totaling LCU points for only the previous 6 months.

Many of the listed life changes don't seem relevant to young adults or college students. Does the SRRS apply to them? The SRRS tends to be more appropriate for older, more established adults. The health of college students is also affected by stressful events, such as entering college, changing majors, or breaking up in a steady relationship. (For a student-oriented rating of stress, see ● Table 11.8 in the "Psychology in Action" section.)

human diversity

Acculturative Stress—Stranger in a Strange Land

Around the world, an increasing number of emigrants and refugees must adapt to dramatic changes in language, dress, values, and social customs. For many, the result is a period of culture shock or **acculturative stress** (stress caused by adapting to a foreign culture). Typical reactions to acculturative stress are anxiety, hostility, depression, alienation, physical illness, or identity confusion (Rummens, Beiser, & Noh, 2003). For many young immigrants, acculturative stress is a major source of mental health problems (Yeh, 2003).

The severity of acculturative stress is related, in part, to how a person adapts to a new culture. Four main patterns are (Berry, 1990; Berry et al., 2005):

Integration—maintain your old cultural identity but participate in the new culture

Separation—maintain your old cultural identity and avoid contact with the new culture

Assimilation—adopt the new culture as your own and have contact with its members

Marginalization—reject your old culture but suffer rejection by members of the new culture

To illustrate each pattern, let's consider a family that has immigrated to the United States from the imaginary country of Farlandia.

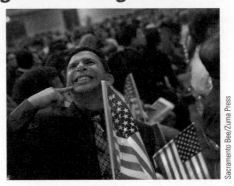

Sacramento Bee/Zuma Press

One of the best antidotes for acculturative stress is a society that tolerates or even celebrates ethnic diversity. Although some people find it hard to accept new immigrants, the fact is, nearly everyone's family tree includes people who were once strangers in a strange land.

The father favors integration. He is learning English and wants to get involved in American life. At the same time, he is a leader in the Farlandian-American community and spends much of his leisure time with other Farlandian-Americans. His level of acculturative stress is low.

The mother speaks only Farlandish and interacts with only other Farlandian-Americans. She remains almost completely separate from American society. Her stress level is high.

The teenage daughter is annoyed by hearing Farlandish spoken at home, by her mother's serving only Farlandian food, and by having to spend her leisure time with her extended Farlandian family. She would prefer to speak English and to be with her American friends. Her desire to assimilate creates moderate stress.

The son doesn't particularly value his Farlandian heritage, yet his schoolmates reject him because he speaks with a Farlandian accent. He feels trapped between two cultures. His position is marginal and his stress level is high.

To summarize, those who feel marginalized tend to be highly stressed; those who seek to remain separate are also highly stressed; those who pursue integration into their new culture are minimally stressed; and those who assimilate are moderately stressed.

As you can see, integration and assimilation are the best options. However, a big benefit of assimilating is that people who embrace their new culture experience fewer social difficulties. For many, this justifies the stress of adopting new customs and cultural values (Gurung, 2010; Ward & Rana-Deuba, 1999).

Evaluation

People differ greatly in their reactions to the same event. For this reason, the SRRS is at best a rough index of stress. Nevertheless, it's hard to ignore a classic study in which people were deliberately exposed to the virus that causes common colds. The results were nothing to sneeze at: If a person had a high stress score, she or he was much more likely to actually get a cold (Cohen, Waltzman, & Fisher, 1993). In view of such findings, a high LCU score should be taken seriously. If your score goes much over 300, an adjustment in your activities or lifestyle may be needed. Remember, "To be forewarned is to be forearmed."

The Hazards of Hassles

There must be more to stress than major life changes. Isn't there a link between ongoing stresses and health? In addition to having a direct impact, major life events spawn countless daily frustrations and irritations (Pillow, Zautra, & Sandler, 1996). Also, many of us face ongoing stresses at work or at home that do not involve major life changes (Pett & Johnson, 2005). Such minor but frequent stresses are called **hassles,** or **microstressors.** (See ● Table 11.6 for some examples of hassles faced by college students.)

In a yearlong study, 100 men and women recorded the hassles they endured. Participants also reported on their physical and mental health. Frequent and severe hassles turned out to be better predictors of day-to-day health than major life events were. However, major life events did predict changes in health 1 or 2 years after the events took place. It appears that daily hassles are closely linked to immediate health and psychological well-being (Crowther et al., 2001). Major life changes have more of a long-term impact.

One way to guarantee that you will experience a large number of life changes and hassles is to live in a foreign culture. "Acculturative Stress—Stranger in a Strange Land" offers a brief glimpse into some of the consequences of culture shock.

● Table 11.6 **Examples of Common Hassles Faced by College Students**

Too many things to do
Not enough money for housing
Feeling discriminated against
People making gender jokes
Communication problems with friends
Driving to school
People making fun of my religion
Fear of losing valuables
Work schedule
Getting into shape
Parents' expectations
Source: Pett & Johnson, 2005.

Acculturative stress Stress caused by the many changes and adaptations required when a person moves to a foreign culture.

Hassle (microstressor) Any distressing, day-to-day annoyance.

Have you ever had someone dismiss a health concern by saying, "Its all in your mind," as if your problem might be imaginary? For centuries the *medical model* has dominated Western thinking. From this perspective, health is an absence of illness and your body is a complex biological machine that can break down and become ill. Sometimes, you inflict the damage yourself through poor lifestyle choices, such as smoking or overeating. Sometimes, an external cause, such as a virus, is the culprit. In either event, the problem is physical and your mind has little to do with it. Moreover, physical problems call for physical treat-

ments ("Take your medicine"), so your mind has little to do with your recovery. In the medical model, *any* impact of the mind on health was dismissed as a mere placebo effect. (To remind yourself about placebo effects, see Chapter 1.)

Over the last 50 years, the medical model has slowly given way to the *biopsychosocial model*. This view states that diseases are caused by a combination of biological, psychological, and social factors. Most important, the biopsychosocial model defines health as a state of well-being that we can *actively* attain and maintain (Oakley, 2004). Instead of passively getting treatments from a doctor, this

model says that you play a role in fostering your own health. Thus, it may no longer be inaccurate to say, "It's all in your mind," *if* you mean that a person's beliefs—which affect behavior—can have a dramatic impact on health (Brooks, 2008). It is becoming clear that medicine works best when doctors help people *make sense* of their medical condition, to maximize healing (Moerman, 2002). So, as you take responsibility for your own well-being, remember that in some ways health *is* all in your mind!

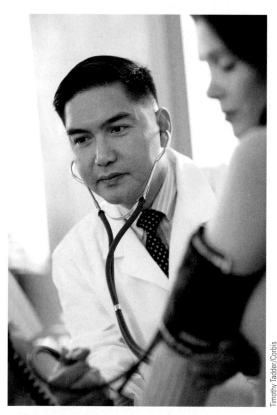

It is estimated that at least half of all patients who see a doctor have a psychosomatic disorder or an illness that is complicated by psychosomatic symptoms.

Timothy Tadder/Corbis

What can be done about a high LCU score or feeling excessively hassled? A good response is to use stress management skills. For serious problems, stress management should be learned directly from a therapist or a stress clinic. When ordinary stresses are involved, there is much you can do on your own. An upcoming discussion of stress management will give you a start. In the meantime, take it easy!

Psychosomatic Disorders

As we have seen, chronic or repeated stress can damage physical health, as well as upset emotional well-being. Prolonged stress reactions are closely related to a large number of psychosomatic (SIKE-oh-so-MAT-ik) illnesses. In **psychosomatic disorders** (*psyche:* mind; *soma:* body), psychological factors contribute to actual bodily damage or to damaging changes in bodily functioning (Asmundson & Taylor, 2005). Psychosomatic problems, therefore, are *not* the same as hypochondria. **Hypochondriacs** (HI-po-KON-dree-aks) imagine that they have diseases. There is nothing imaginary about asthma, a migraine headache, or high blood pressure. Severe psychosomatic disorders can be fatal. The person who says, "Oh it's *just* psychosomatic" doesn't understand how serious stress-related diseases really are. (See "It's All in Your Mind.")

The most common psychosomatic problems are gastrointestinal and respiratory (stomach pain and asthma, for example), but many others exist. Typical problems include eczema (skin rash), hives, migraine headaches, rheumatoid arthritis, hypertension (high blood pressure), colitis (ulceration of the colon), and heart disease. Actually, these are only the major problems. Many lesser health complaints are also stress related. Typical examples include sore muscles, headaches, neckaches, backaches, indigestion, constipation, chronic diarrhea, fatigue, insomnia, premenstrual problems, and sexual dysfunctions (Taylor, 2006). For some of these problems, biofeedback may be helpful. The next section explains how.

Biofeedback

Psychologists have discovered that people can learn to control bodily activities once thought to be involuntary. This is done by applying informational feedback to bodily control, a process called **biofeedback.** If I were to say to you, "Raise the temperature of your right hand," you probably couldn't, because you wouldn't know if you were succeeding. To make your task easier, we could attach a sensitive thermometer to your hand. The thermometer could

Psychosomatic disorders Illnesses in which psychological factors contribute to bodily damage or to damaging changes in bodily functioning.

Hypochondriac A person who complains about illnesses that appear to be imaginary.

Biofeedback Information given to a person about his or her ongoing bodily activities; aids voluntary regulation of bodily states.

be wired so that an increase in temperature would activate a signal light. Then, all you would have to do is try to keep the light on as much as possible. With practice and the help of biofeedback, you could learn to raise your hand temperature at will.

Biofeedback holds promise as a way to treat some psychosomatic problems (▶▶ Figure 11.8). For instance, people have been trained to prevent migraine headaches with biofeedback. Sensors are taped to patients' hands and foreheads. Patients then learn to redirect blood flow away from the head to their extremities. Because migraine headaches involve excessive blood flow to the head, biofeedback helps patients reduce the frequency of their headaches (Andrasik, 2003; Larsson et al., 2005).

Early successes led many to predict that biofeedback would offer a cure for psychosomatic illnesses, anxiety, phobias, drug abuse, and a long list of other problems. In reality, biofeedback has proved helpful, but not an instant cure (Schwartz & Andrasik, 2003). Biofeedback can help relieve muscle-tension headaches, migraine headaches, and chronic pain (Middaugh & Pawlick, 2002). It shows promise for lowering blood pressure and controlling heart rhythms (Rau, Bührer, & Weitkunat, 2003). The technique has been used with some success to control epileptic seizures and hyperactivity in children (Demos, 2005). Insomnia also responds to biofeedback therapy (Gathchel & Oordt, 2003).

How does biofeedback help? Some researchers believe that many of its benefits arise from *general relaxation.* Others stress that there is no magic in biofeedback itself. The method simply acts as a "mirror" to help a person perform tasks involving *self-regulation.* Just as a mirror does not comb your hair, biofeedback does not do anything by itself. It can, however, help people make desired changes in their behavior (Weems, 1998).

▲ **FIGURE 11.8** In biofeedback training, bodily processes are monitored and processed electronically. A signal is then routed back to the patient through headphones, signal lights, or other means. This information helps the patient alter bodily activities not normally under voluntary control.

The Cardiac Personality

It would be a mistake to assume that stress is the sole cause of psychosomatic diseases. Genetic differences, organ weaknesses, and learned reactions to stress combine to do damage. Personality also enters the picture. As mentioned earlier, a general disease-prone personality type exists. To a degree, there are also "headache personalities," "asthma personalities," and so on. The best documented of such patterns is the "cardiac personality"—a person at high risk for heart disease.

Two cardiologists, Meyer Friedman and Ray Rosenman, offer a glimpse at how some people create stress for themselves. In a landmark study of heart problems, Friedman and Rosenman (1983) classified people as either **Type A personalities** (those who run a high risk for heart attack) or **Type B personalities** (those who are unlikely to have a heart attack). In an 8-year follow-up, they found more than twice the rate of heart disease in Type A's than in Type B's (Rosenman et al., 1975).

Type A

What is the Type A personality like? Type A people are hard driving, ambitious, highly competitive, achievement oriented, and striving. Type A people believe that with enough effort they can overcome any obstacle, and they "push" themselves accordingly.

Perhaps the most telltale signs of a Type A personality are *time urgency* and chronic *anger* or *hostility.* Type A's seem to chafe at the normal pace of events. They hurry from one activity to another, racing the clock in self-imposed urgency. As they do, they feel a constant sense of frustration and anger. Feelings of anger and hostility, in particular, are strongly related to increased risk for heart attack (Boyle et al., 2004; Bunde & Suls, 2006). One study found that 15 percent of a group of 25-year-old doctors and lawyers who scored high on a hostility test were dead by age 50. The most damaging pattern may occur in hostile persons who keep their anger "bottled up." Such people seethe with anger but don't express it outwardly. This increases their pulse rate and blood pressure and puts a tremendous strain on the heart (Bongard, al'Absi, & Lovallo, 1998).

Individuals with Type A personalities feel a continuous sense of anger, irritation, and hostility.

Type A personality A personality type with an elevated risk for heart disease; characterized by time urgency, anger, and hostility.

Type B personality All personality types other than Type A; a low-cardiac-risk personality.

> ● Table 11.7 Characteristics of the Type A Person
>
> Check the items that apply to you. Do you:
>
> _____ Have a habit of explosively accentuating various key words in ordinary speech even when there is no need for such accentuation (I HATE it when you do THAT!)?
>
> _____ Finish other persons' sentences for them?
>
> ___X___ *Always* move, walk, and eat rapidly?
>
> _____ Quickly skim reading material and prefer summaries or condensations of books?
>
> _____ Become easily angered by slow-moving lines or traffic?
>
> _____ Feel an impatience with the rate at which most events take place?
>
> _____ Tend to be unaware of the details or beauty of your surroundings?
>
> _____ Frequently strive to think of or do two or more things simultaneously?
>
> _____ Almost always feel vaguely guilty when you relax, vacation, or do absolutely nothing for several days?
>
> _____ Tend to evaluate your worth in quantitative terms (number of A's earned, amount of income, number of games won, and so forth)?
>
> ___X___ Have nervous gestures or muscle twitches, such as grinding your teeth, clenching your fists, or drumming your fingers?
>
> _____ Attempt to schedule more and more activities into less time and in so doing make fewer allowances for unforeseen problems?
>
> _____ Frequently think about other things while talking to someone?
>
> _____ Repeatedly take on more responsibilities than you can comfortably handle?
>
> *Source:* Shortened and adapted from Friedman & Rosenman, 1983.

To summarize, there is growing evidence that anger or hostility may be the core lethal factor of Type A behavior (Krantz & McCeney, 2002; Niaura et al., 2002). To date, hundreds of studies have supported the validity of the Type A concept. In view of this, Type A's would be wise to take their increased health risks seriously.

How are Type A people identified? Characteristics of Type A people are summarized in the short self-identification test presented in ● Table 11.7. If most of the list applies to you, you might be a Type A. However, confirmation of your type would require more powerful testing methods. Also, remember that the original definition of Type A behavior was probably too broad. The key psychological factors that increase heart disease risk appear to be anger, hostility, and mistrust (Krantz & McCeney, 2002; Smith et al., 2004). Also, although Type A behavior appears to promote heart disease, depression or distress may be what finally triggers a heart attack (Denollet & Van Heck, 2001; Dinan, 2001).

Because our society places a premium on achievement, competition, and mastery, it is not surprising that many people develop Type A personalities. The best way to avoid the self-made stress this causes is to adopt behavior that is the opposite of that listed in Table 11.7 (Williams, Barefoot, & Schneiderman, 2003).

People who frequently feel angry and hostile toward others may benefit from the advice of Redford Williams (1989). According to Williams, reducing hostility involves three goals. First, you must stop mistrusting the motives of others. Second, you must find ways to reduce how often you feel anger, indignation, irritation, and rage. Third, you must learn to be kinder and more considerate. It is entirely possible to succeed in life without sacrificing your health or happiness in the process.

Hardy Personality

How do Type A people who do not develop heart disease differ from those who do? Psychologist Salvatore Maddi has studied people who have a **hardy personality.** Such people seem to be unusually resistant to stress. The first study of hardiness began with two groups of managers at a large utility company. All the managers held high-stress positions. Yet some tended to get sick after stressful events, whereas others were rarely ill. How did the people who were thriving differ from their "stressed-out" colleagues? Both groups seemed to have traits typical of the Type A personality, so that wasn't the explanation. They were also quite similar in most other respects. The main difference was that the hardy group seemed to hold a worldview that consisted of three traits (Maddi, 2006):

1. They had a sense of personal *commitment* to self, work, family, and other stabilizing values.
2. They felt that they had *control* over their lives and their work.
3. They had a tendency to see life as a series of *challenges,* rather than as a series of threats or problems.

How do such traits protect people from the effects of stress? Persons strong in *commitment* find ways of turning whatever they are doing into something that seems interesting and important. They tend to get involved rather than feeling alienated.

Persons strong in *control* believe that they can more often than not influence the course of events around them. This prevents them from passively seeing themselves as victims of circumstance.

Finally, people strong in *challenge* find fulfillment in continual growth. They seek to learn from their experiences, rather than accepting easy comfort, security, and routine (Maddi, 2006). Indeed, many "negative" experiences can actually enhance personal growth—if you have support from others and the skills needed to cope with challenge (Armeli, Gunthert, & Cohen, 2001).

Positive Psychology: Hardiness and Happiness

Good and bad events occur in all lives. What separates happy people from those who are unhappy is largely a matter of attitude. Happy people tend to see their lives in more positive terms, even when trouble comes their way. For example, happier people tend to find humor in disappointments. They look at setbacks as challenges. They are strengthened by losses (Lyubomirsky & Tucker, 1998). In short, happiness tends to be related to hardiness (Maddi, 2006). Why is there a connection? As psychologist Barbara Fredrickson has pointed out, positive emotions tend to broaden our mental focus. Emotions such as joy, interest, and contentment create an urge to play, to be creative, to explore, to savor life, to seek new experiences, to integrate, and to grow. When you are stressed, experiencing positive emotions can make it more likely that you will find creative solutions to your problems. Positive emotions also tend to reduce the bodily arousal that occurs when we are stressed, possibly limiting stress-related damage (Fredrickson, 2003).

The work we have reviewed here has drawn new attention to the fact that each of us has a personal responsibility for maintaining and promoting good health. In the discussion that follows, we will look at what you can do to better cope with stress. But first, the following questions may help you maintain a healthy grade on your next psychology test.

Hardy personality A personality style associated with superior stress resistance.

study break
Stress and Health

RECITE

1. Holmes's SRRS appears to predict long-range changes in health, whereas the frequency and severity of daily microstressors is closely related to immediate ratings of health. T or F?
2. Ulcers, migraine headaches, and hypochondria are all frequently psychosomatic disorders. T or F?
3. Which of the following is *not* classified as a psychosomatic disorder?
   a. hypertension   b. colitis
   c. eczema   d. thymus
4. Two major elements of biofeedback training appear to be relaxation and self-regulation. T or F?
5. Evidence suggests that the most important feature of the Type A personality is a sense of time urgency rather than feelings of anger and hostility. T or F?
6. A sense of commitment, challenge, and control characterizes the hardy personality. T or F?

REFLECT
Critical Thinking

7. People with a hardy personality type appear to be especially resistant to which of the problems discussed earlier in this chapter?

Relate

Use the SRRS to find your LCU score for the past year. Do you think there is a connection between your LCU score and your health? Or have you observed more of a connection between microstressors and your health?

Suppose you moved to a foreign country. How much acculturative stress do you think you would face? Which pattern of adaptation do you think you would adopt?

Mindy complains about her health all the time, but she actually seems to be just fine. An acquaintance of Mindy's dismisses her problems by saying, "Oh, she's not really sick. It's just psychosomatic." What's wrong with this use of the term *psychosomatic*?

Do you think you are basically a Type A or a Type B personality? To what extent do you possess traits of the hardy personality?

ANSWERS

1. T 2. F 3. d 4. T 5. F 6. T 7. Learned helplessness.

psychology in action
Stress Management—Winning the Stress Game

What are the best strategies for managing stress?

Stress management is the use of behavioral strategies to reduce stress and improve coping skills. As promised, this section describes strategies for managing stress. Before you continue reading, you may want to assess your level of stress again, this time using a scale developed for undergraduate students. (See Table 11.8.) Like the SRRS, high scores on the *College Life Stress Inventory* suggest that you have been exposed to health-threatening levels of stress (Renner & Mackin, 1998).

The *College Life Stress Inventory* is scored by adding the ratings for all of the items that have happened to you in the last year. The following scale is an approximate guide to the meaning of your score. But remember, stress is an internal state. If you are good at coping with stressors, a high score may not be a problem for you.

> 0–150: Very low
> 151–590: Low
> 591–1030: Below average
> 1031–1470: Average
> 1471–1910: High
> 1911–2350: Very high
> 2351 or more: Extremely high

Stress management The application of behavioral strategies to reduce stress and improve coping skills.

Table 11.8 College Life Stress Inventory

Circle the "stress rating" number for any item that has happened to you in the last year, then add them.

EVENT	STRESS RATING	EVENT	STRESS RATING
Being raped	100	Lack of sleep	69
Finding out that you are HIV-positive	100	Change in housing situation (hassles, moves)	69
Being accused of rape	98	Competing or performing in public	69
Death of a close friend	97	Getting in a physical fight	66
Death of a close family member	96	Difficulties with a roommate	66
Contracting a sexually transmitted disease (other than AIDS)	94	Job changes (applying, new job, work hassles)	65
Concerns about being pregnant	91	Declaring a major or concerns about future plans	65
Finals week	90	A class you hate	62
Concerns about your partner being pregnant	90	Drinking or use of drugs	61
Oversleeping for an exam	89	Confrontations with professors	60
Flunking a class	89	Starting a new semester	58
Having a boyfriend or girlfriend cheat on you	85	Going on a first date	57
Ending a steady dating relationship	85	Registration	55
Serious illness in a close friend or family member	85	Maintaining a steady dating relationship	55
Financial difficulties	84	Commuting to campus or work, or both	54
Writing a major term paper	83	Peer pressures	53
Being caught cheating on a test	83	Being away from home for the first time	53
Drunk driving	82	Getting sick	52
Sense of overload in school or work	82	Concerns about your appearance	52
Two exams in one day	80	Getting straight A's	51
Cheating on your boyfriend or girlfriend	77	A difficult class that you love	48
Getting married	76	Making new friends; getting along with friends	47
Negative consequences of drinking or drug use	75	Fraternity or sorority rush	47
Depression or crisis in your best friend	73	Falling asleep in class	40
Difficulties with parents	73	Attending an athletic event (e.g., football game)	20
Talking in front of a class	72		

Now that you have a picture of your current level of stress, what can you do about it? The simplest way of coping with stress is to modify or remove its source—by leaving a stressful job, for example. Obviously this is often impossible, which is why learning to manage stress is so important.

As shown in ▶▶ Figure 11.9, stress triggers *bodily effects, upsetting thoughts,* and *ineffective behavior.* Also shown is the fact that each element worsens the others in a vicious cycle. Indeed, the basic idea of the "Stress Game" is that once it begins, *you lose*—unless you take action to break the cycle. The information that follows tells how.

Managing Bodily Reactions

Much of the immediate discomfort of stress is caused by fight-or-flight emotional responses. The body is ready to act, with tight muscles and a pounding heart. If action is prevented, we merely remain "uptight." A sensible remedy is to learn a reliable, drug-free way of relaxing.

Exercise Stress-based arousal can be dissipated by using the body. Any full-body exercise can be effective. Our intrepid student, Jennifer, enjoys rock climbing. Swimming, dancing, jumping rope, yoga, most sports, and especially walking are valuable outlets. Regular exercise alters hormones, circulation, muscle tone, and a number of other aspects of physical functioning. Together, such changes can reduce anxiety and lower the risks for disease (Linden, 2005; Salmon, 2001).

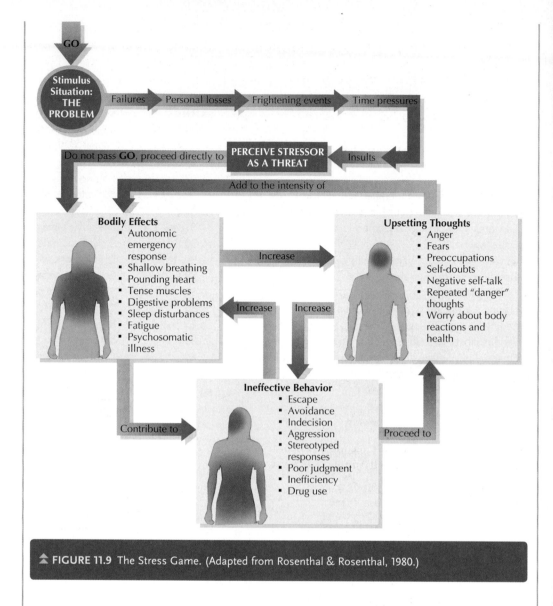

FIGURE 11.9 The Stress Game. (Adapted from Rosenthal & Rosenthal, 1980.)

Be sure to choose activities that are vigorous enough to relieve tension, yet enjoyable enough to be done repeatedly. Exercising for stress management is most effective when it is done daily. As little as 30 minutes of total exercise per day, even if it occurs in short 10- to 20-minute sessions, can improve mood and energy (Hansen, Stevens, & Coast, 2001).

Meditation Many stress counselors recommend *meditation* for quieting the body and promoting relaxation. Meditation and its effects were discussed in Chapter 5. For now, it is enough to state that meditation is easy to learn—taking an expensive commercial course is unnecessary.

Meditation is one of the most effective ways to relax (Deckro et al., 2002). But be aware that listening to or playing music, taking nature walks, enjoying hobbies, and the like can be meditations of sorts. Anything that reliably interrupts upsetting thoughts and promotes relaxation can be helpful.

Progressive Relaxation It is possible to relax systematically, completely, and by choice. To learn the details of how this is done, consult Chapter 13 of this book. The basic idea of **progressive relaxation** is to tighten all the muscles in a given area of your body (the arms, for instance) and then voluntarily relax them. By first tensing and relaxing each area of the body, you can learn what muscle tension feels like. Then when each area is relaxed, the change is more noticeable and more controllable. In this way it is possible, with practice, to greatly reduce tension.

Progressive relaxation A method for producing deep relaxation of all parts of the body.

Guided Imagery In a technique called **guided imagery,** people visualize images that are calming, relaxing, or beneficial in other ways. Relaxation, for instance, can be promoted by visualizing peaceful scenes. Pick several places where you feel safe, calm, and at ease. Typical locations might be a beach or lake, the woods, floating on an air mattress in a warm pool, or lying in the sun at a quiet park. To relax, vividly imagine yourself in one of these locations. In the visualized scene, you should be alone and in a comfortable position. It is important to visualize the scene as realistically as possible. Try to feel, taste, smell, hear, and see what you would actually experience in the calming scene. Practice forming such images several times a day for about 5 minutes each time. When your scenes become familiar and detailed, they can be used to reduce anxiety and encourage relaxation (Rosenthal, 1993). Remember, too, that imagining that a supportive friend or a loving pet is nearby can reduce tension and anxiety (Allen, Blascovich, & Mendes, 2002; Smith, Ruiz, & Uchino, 2004).

Modifying Ineffective Behavior

Stress is often made worse by our misguided responses to it. The following suggestions may help you deal with stress more effectively.

Slow Down Remember that stress can be self-generated. Try to deliberately do things at a slower pace—especially if your pace has speeded up over the years. Tell yourself, "What counts most is not if I get there first, but if I get there at all" or "My goal is distance, not speed."

Organize Disorganization creates stress. Try to take a fresh look at your situation and get organized. Setting priorities can be a real stress fighter. Ask yourself what's really important and concentrate on the things that count. Learn to let go of trivial but upsetting irritations. And above all, when you are feeling stressed, remember to K.I.S.: **K**eep **I**t **S**imple. (Some people prefer K.I.S.S.: Keep It Simple, Stupid.)

Strike a Balance Work, school, family, friends, interests, hobbies, recreation, community, church—there are many important elements in a satisfying life. Damaging stress often comes from letting one element—especially work or school—get blown out of proportion. Your goal should be quality in life, not quantity. Try to strike a balance between challenging "good stress" and relaxation. Remember, when you are "doing nothing" you are actually doing something very important: Set aside time for "me acts" such as loafing, browsing, puttering, playing, and napping.

Recognize and Accept Your Limits Many of us set unrealistic and perfectionist goals. Given that no one can ever be perfect, this attitude leaves many people feeling inadequate, no matter how well they have performed. Set gradual, achievable goals for yourself. Also, set realistic limits on what you try to do on any given day. Learn to say no to added demands or responsibilities.

Seek Social Support **Social support** (close, positive relationships with others) facilitates good health and morale (Manne, 2003). People with close, supportive relationships have better immune responses and better health (Kiecolt-Glaser et al., 2002). Apparently, support from family and friends serves as a buffer to cushion the impact of stressful events.

Women tend to make better use of social support than men do. Women who are stressed seek support, and they nurture others. Men are more likely to become aggressive or to withdraw emotionally (Taylor et al., 2000). This may be why "manly men" won't ask for help, whereas women in trouble call their friends! Where stress is concerned, many men could benefit from adopting women's tendency to tend and befriend others.

How else might social support help? Most people share positive events, such as marriages, births, graduations, and birthdays, with others. When things go well, we like to tell others. Sharing such events tends to amplify positive emotions and to further increase social support. In many ways, the sharing of good news is an important means by which positive events contribute to individual well-being (Gable et al., 2004).

Guided imagery Intentional visualization of images that are calming, relaxing, or beneficial in other ways.

Social support Close, positive relationships with other people.

Write about Your Feelings

If you don't have someone you can talk to about stressful events, you might try expressing your thoughts and feelings in writing. Several studies have found that students who write about their upsetting experiences, thoughts, and feelings are better able to cope with stress. They also experience fewer illnesses, and they get better grades (Esterling et al., 1999; Pennebaker, 2004). Writing about your feelings tends to leave your mind clearer. This makes it easier to pay attention to life's challenges and come up with effective coping strategies (Klein & Boals, 2001a, 2001b). Thus, after you write about your feelings, it helps to make specific plans for coping with upsetting experiences (Pennebaker & Chung, 2007).

As an alternative, you might want to try writing about positive experiences. In one study, college students who wrote about intensely positive experiences had fewer illnesses over the next 3 months. Writing just 20 minutes a day for 3 days improved the students' moods and had a surprisingly long-lasting effect on their health (Burton & King, 2004).

Avoiding Upsetting Thoughts

Assume you are taking a test. Suddenly you realize that you are running short of time. If you say to yourself, "Oh no, this is terrible, I've blown it now," your body's response will probably be sweating, tenseness, and a knot in your stomach. On the other hand, if you say, "I should have watched the time, but getting upset won't help, I'll just take one question at a time," your stress level will be much lower.

As stated earlier, stress is greatly affected by the views we take of events. Physical symptoms and a tendency to make poor decisions are increased by negative thoughts or "self-talk." In many cases what you say to yourself can be the difference between coping and collapsing (Matheny et al., 1996).

Coping Statements Psychologist Donald Meichenbaum has popularized a technique called **stress inoculation.** In it, clients learn to fight fear and anxiety with an internal monologue of positive coping statements. First, clients learn to identify and monitor **negative self-statements** (self-critical thoughts that increase anxiety). Negative thoughts are a problem because they tend to directly elevate physical arousal. To counter this effect, clients learn to replace negative statements with coping statements from a supplied list. Eventually they are encouraged to make their own lists (Saunders et al., 1996).

How are coping statements applied? **Coping statements** are reassuring and self-enhancing. They are used to block out, or counteract, negative self-talk in stressful situations. Before giving a short speech, for instance, you would replace "I'm scared," "I can't do this," "My mind will go blank and I'll panic," or "I'll sound stupid and boring" with "I'll give my speech on something I like," or "I'll breathe deeply before I start my speech," or "My pounding heart just means I'm psyched up to do my best." Additional examples of coping statements follow:

Preparing for Stressful Situation
- I'll just take things one step at a time.
- If I get nervous, I'll just pause a moment.
- Tomorrow I'll be through it.
- I've managed to do this before.
- What exactly do I have to do?

Confronting the Stressful Situation
- Relax now, this can't really hurt me.
- Stay organized, focus on the task.
- There's no hurry, take it step by step.
- Nobody's perfect, I'll just do my best.
- It will be over soon, just be calm.

Meichenbaum cautions that saying the "right" things to yourself may not be enough to improve stress tolerance. You must practice this approach in actual stress situations. Also, it is important to develop your own personal list of coping statements by finding what works for you. Ultimately, the value of learning this and other stress management skills ties back

Stress inoculation Use of positive coping statements to control fear and anxiety.

Negative self-statements Self-critical thoughts that increase anxiety and lower performance.

Coping statements Reassuring, self-enhancing statements that are used to stop self-critical thinking.

into the idea that much stress is self-generated. Knowing that you can manage a demanding situation is in itself a major antidote for stress. In a recent study, college students who learned stress inoculation not only had less anxiety and depression, but better self-esteem as well (Schiraldi & Brown, 2001).

Lighten Up Humor is worth cultivating as a way to reduce stress. A good sense of humor can lower your distress/stress reaction to difficult events (Lefcourt, 2003). In addition, an ability to laugh at life's ups and downs is associated with better immunity to disease (McClelland & Cheriff, 1997). Don't be afraid to laugh at yourself and at the many ways in which we humans make things difficult for ourselves. You've probably heard the following advice about everyday stresses: "Don't sweat the small stuff" and "It's all small stuff." Humor is one of the best antidotes for anxiety and emotional distress because it helps put things into perspective (Henman, 2001; Szabo, 2003). The vast majority of events are only as stressful as you allow them to be. Have some fun. It's perfectly healthy.

study break
Coping with Stress

RECITE

1. Exercise, meditation, and progressive relaxation are considered effective ways of countering negative self-statements. T or F?
2. Research shows that social support from family and friends has little effect on the health consequences of stress. T or F?
3. One element of stress inoculation is training in the use of positive coping statements. T or F?
4. People who write about their feelings tend to dwell on stressful events, which reduces their ability to meet life challenges. T or F?

REFLECT
Critical Thinking

5. Steve always feels extremely pressured when the due date arrives for his major term papers. How could he reduce stress in such instances?

Relate

If you were going to put together a "tool kit" for stress management, what items would you include?

ANSWERS

1. F 2. F 3. T 4. F 5. The stress associated with doing term papers can be almost completely eliminated by breaking up a long-term assignment into many small daily or weekly assignments (Ariely & Wertenbroch, 2002). Students who habitually procrastinate are often amazed at how pleasant college work can be once they renounce "brinkmanship" (pushing things off to the limits of tolerance).

Major Points

- A variety of personal habits and behavior patterns affect health.

- Maintaining good health is a personal responsibility, not a matter of luck. Wellness is based on minimizing risk factors and engaging in health-promoting behaviors.

- Stress is a normal part of life; however, it is also a major risk factor for illness and disease.

- Although some events are more stressful than others, stress always represents an interaction between people and the environments in which they live.

- Personality characteristics affect the amount of stress a person experiences and the subsequent risk for illness.

- The body's reactions to stress can directly damage internal organs, and stress impairs the body's immune system, increasing susceptibility to disease.

- The damaging effects of stress can be reduced with stress management techniques.

Summary

What is health psychology? How does behavior affect health?

- Health psychologists are interested in behavior that helps maintain and promote health.

- Studies of health and illness have identified a number of behavioral risk factors and health-promoting behaviors.

- Health psychologists have pioneered efforts to prevent the development of unhealthy habits and to improve well-being through community health campaigns.

How can sexually transmitted diseases be prevented?

- Many sexually active people continue to take unnecessary risks with their health by failing to follow safer sex practices.

- Safe-sex practices help protect your own health and they show that you care about the welfare of your partner.

What is stress? What factors determine its severity?

- Stress occurs when demands are placed on an organism to adjust or adapt.

- The body reacts to stress in a series of stages called the general adaptation syndrome (GAS).

- The stages of the GAS are alarm, resistance, and exhaustion. Bodily reactions in the GAS follow the pattern observed in the development of psychosomatic disorders.

- Studies of psychoneuroimmunology show that stress lowers the body's resistance to disease by weakening the immune system.

- Stress is more damaging in situations involving pressure, a lack of control, unpredictability of the stressor, and intense or repeated emotional shocks.

- Stress is intensified when a situation is perceived as a threat and when a person does not feel competent to cope with it.

- In work settings, prolonged stress can lead to burnout.

- Making a primary appraisal greatly affects our emotional responses to a situation.

- During a secondary appraisal, we select problem-focused coping or emotion-focused coping (or both) as a way of managing stress.

What causes frustration and what are typical reactions to it?

- Frustration is the negative emotional state that occurs when progress toward a goal is blocked.

- External frustrations are based on delay, failure, rejection, loss, and other direct blocking of motives. Personal frustration is related to personal characteristics over which one has little control.

- Frustrations of all types become more intense as the strength, urgency, or importance of the blocked motive increases.

- Major behavioral reactions to frustration include persistence, more vigorous responding, circumvention, direct aggression, displaced aggression (including scapegoating), and escape or withdrawal.

Are there different types of conflict? How do people react to conflict?

- Conflict occurs when one must choose between contradictory alternatives.

- Four major types of conflict are approach-approach, avoidance-avoidance, approach-avoidance, and multiple conflicts (double approach-avoidance and multiple approach-avoidance).

- Approach-approach conflicts are usually the easiest to resolve.

- Avoidance conflicts are difficult to resolve and are characterized by inaction, indecision, freezing, and a desire to escape (called leaving the field).

- People usually remain in approach-avoidance conflicts but fail to fully resolve them. Approach-avoidance conflicts are associated with ambivalence and partial approach.

- Vacillation is a common reaction to double and multiple approach-avoidance conflicts.

What are defense mechanisms?

- Defense mechanisms are mental processes used to avoid, deny, or distort sources of threat or anxiety, including threats to one's self-image.

- A large number of defense mechanisms have been identified, including compensation, denial, fantasy, intellectualization, isolation, projection, rationalization, reaction formation, regression, repression, and sublimation.

What do we know about coping with feelings of helplessness and depression?

- Learned helplessness can be used as a model for understanding depression. Mastery training, optimism, and hope all act as antidotes for learned helplessness.
- Depression is a major, and surprisingly common, emotional problem. Actions and thoughts that counter feelings of helplessness tend to reduce depression.
- The college blues are a relatively mild form of depression. Learning to manage college work and to challenge self-critical thinking can help alleviate the college blues.

How is stress related to health and disease?

- Work with the Social Readjustment Rating Scale indicates that multiple life changes tend to increase long-range susceptibility to accident or illness.
- Immediate psychological and mental health is more closely related to the intensity and severity of daily hassles (microstressors).

- Intense or prolonged stress may cause damage in the form of psychosomatic problems.
- During biofeedback training, bodily processes are monitored and converted to a signal that tells what the body is doing. Biofeedback allows people to alleviate some psychosomatic illnesses by altering bodily activities.
- People with Type A personalities are competitive, striving, hostile, impatient, and prone to having heart attacks.
- People who have traits of the hardy personality seem to be unusually resistant to stress.

What are the best strategies for managing stress?

- A sizable number of coping skills can be applied to manage stress. Most of these focus on one of three areas: bodily effects, ineffective behavior, and upsetting thoughts.

Web Resources

For an up-to-date list of direct links to interesting sites, including those listed here, visit the student companion site for this book at www.cengage.com/psychology/coon

The Longevity Game Find out how long you might live; explore your options.

Defense Mechanisms Try to role-play various defense mechanisms.

Depression and Control Explore the relationship between learned helplessness and depression.

SRRS Fill out an online version of the Social Readjustment Rating Scale.

Stress, Anxiety, Fears, and Psychosomatic Disorders A comprehensive source on stress, anxiety, and related disorders.

Type A Behavior Describes Type A behavior, with links to an online test and related sites.

Self-Growth.com Explore a self-improvement and personal growth website that provides many links to stress management resources, including online articles and information on related topics such as biofeedback and stress.

Stress Management Resources A site that helps you deal with job-related stress.

Interactive Learning

PSYCHOLOGY: A JOURNEY BOOK COMPANION WEBSITE
WWW.CENGAGE.COM/PSYCHOLOGY/COON
Visit your book companion website, where you will find flash cards, practice quizzes, web links, and more to help you study.

JUST WHAT YOU NEED TO KNOW NOW!
Spend time on what you need to master rather than on information you already have learned. Take a pretest for this chapter, and CengageNOW will generate a personalized study plan based on your results. The study plan will identify the topics you need to review and direct you to online resources to help you master those topics. You can then take a posttest to help you determine the concepts you have mastered and what you will need to work on. Try it out! Go to www.cengage.com/login to sign in with an access code or to purchase access to this product.

Conditioning and Learning

For additional review, get more practice with *CengageNOW, WebTutor,* the *Practice Quizzes,* and/or the printed *Study Guide* available with this book.

1. Actions that increase the chances of disease, injury, or early death are termed behavioral
   a. health factors
   b. personalities
   c. risk factors
   d. habits

2. People who have a disease-prone personality style are anxious and hostile. These traits can also be observed in the _____ personality.
   a. emotion-focused
   b. problem-focused
   c. SRRS-prone
   d. Type A

3. Health promoting behaviors that combat hypertension include the following: lose weight, consume less sodium, use alcohol sparingly, and get more
   a. sleep
   b. exercise
   c. LCUs
   d. cholesterol

4. Which of the following is NOT an STD?
   a. herpes
   b. eczema
   c. chlamydia
   d. hepatitis B

5. For the first _____ after infection, a negative test result for the HIV virus is no guarantee that a person is a "safe" sex partner.
   a. 3 weeks
   b. 6 weeks
   c. 6 months
   d. 3 years

6. The first signs of psychosomatic disorders begin to appear during the stage of
   a. alarm
   b. exhaustion
   c. resistance
   d. appraisal

7. Students taking stressful final exams are more susceptible to the cold virus, a pattern best explained by the concept of
   a. the disease-prone personality
   b. psychoneuroimmunology
   c. emotion-focused coping
   d. reaction formation

8. A good indication that stress is a normal part of life is provided by the existence of
   a. learned helplessness
   b. hypochondria
   c. sublimation
   d. eustress

9. According to Richard Lazarus, choosing a way to meet a threat or challenge takes place during the
   a. primary stress reaction
   b. secondary stress reaction
   c. primary appraisal
   d. secondary appraisal

10. Aggression is an especially common reaction to
   a. frustration
   b. scapegoating
   c. approach conflicts
   d. ambivalence

11. Displaced aggression is closely related to the pattern of behavior known as
   a. scapegoating
   b. leaving the field
   c. stereotyped responding
   d. burnout

12. You would be most likely to experience vacillation if you found yourself in
   a. an approach-approach conflict
   b. an avoidance-avoidance conflict
   c. a double approach-avoidance conflict
   d. the condition called emotion-focused coping

13. Justifying your actions by making excuses that appear to explain your behavior is called
   a. sublimation
   b. reaction formation
   c. compensation
   d. rationalization

14. Learned helplessness tends to occur when events appear to be
   a. frustrating
   b. in conflict
   c. uncontrollable
   d. problem-focused

15. Ratings on the SRRS are based on the total number of _____ a person has for the preceding year.
   a. hassles
   b. LCUs
   c. STDs
   d. psychosomatic illnesses

16. Anger, hostility, and mistrust appear to be the core lethal factors in
   a. hypochondria
   b. learned helplessness
   c. the GAS
   d. Type A behavior

17. In many ways, a person who has a hardy personality is the opposite of a person who has
   a. a high STD score
   b. a low LCU score
   c. Type A traits
   d. Type B traits

18. A person using progressive relaxation for stress management is most likely trying to control which component of stress?
   a. bodily reactions
   b. upsetting thoughts
   c. ineffective behavior
   d. the primary appraisal

19. Exercise, meditation, progressive relaxation, and guided imagery would be least likely to help a person who is in the GAS stage of
   a. alarm
   b. resistance
   c. exhaustion
   d. adaptation

20. While taking a stressful classroom test you say to yourself "Stay organized, focus on the task." It's obvious that you are using
   a. guided imagery
   b. a coping statement
   c. LCUs
   d. guided relaxation

Answers   1. c 2. d 3. b 4. b 5. c 6. c 7. b 8. d 9. d 10. a 11. a 12. c 13. d 14. c 15. b 16. d 17. c 18. a 19. c 20. b

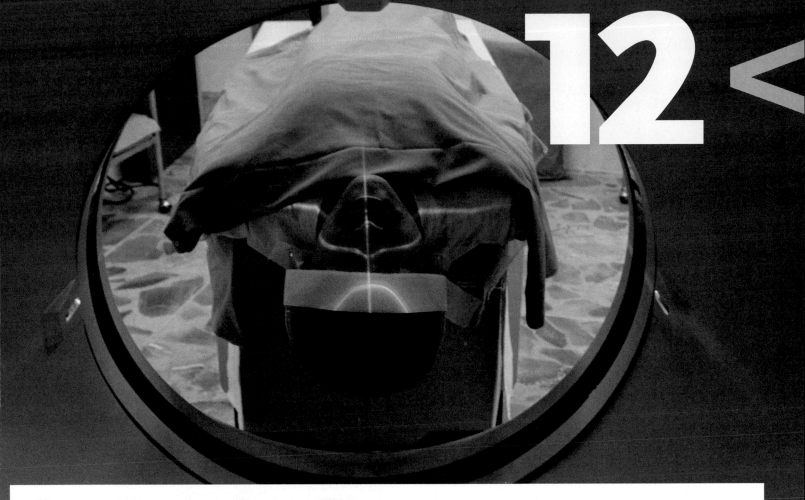

Psychological Disorders

Journey into Psychology: Beware the Helicopters

"The helicopters. Oh no, not the helicopters. Have come to tear the feathers out of my frontal lobes. Help me, nurse, help me, can't you hear them? Gotta get back into my body to save it . . . . The doctor is thinking I would make good glue."

These are the words of Carol North, a psychiatrist who survived schizophrenia. In addition to being plagued by hallucinated helicopters, Carol heard voices that said: "Be good," "Do bad," "Stand up," "Sit down," "Collide with the other world," "Do you want a cigar?" (North, 1987).

Carol North's painful journey into the shadows of madness left her incapacitated for nearly 20 years. Wonderfully, she has since forged her career as an eminent psychiatrist. Today, she is helping others escape the maze of mental illness that once imprisoned her (see, for example, North et al., 2008). Her case is but one hint of the magnitude of mental health problems. One quarter of American adults suffer from a diagnosable mental disorder in any given year. In 2002, almost 32,000 Americans committed suicide (National Institute of Mental Health, 2006b).

What does it mean to be "crazy"? A hundred years ago, doctors and nonprofessionals alike used terms such as "crazy," "insane," "cracked," and "lunatic" quite freely. The "insane" were thought of as bizarre and definitely different from the rest of us. Today, our understanding of psychological disorders is more sophisticated. To draw the line between normal and abnormal, we must weigh some complex issues. We'll explore some of them in this chapter, as well as an array of psychological problems.

Survey Questions

- How is abnormality defined?
- What are the major psychological disorders?
- What are the general characteristics of psychotic disorders?
- What is the nature of a delusional disorder?
- What forms does schizophrenia take? What causes it?
- What are mood disorders? What causes them?
- What problems result when a person suffers high levels of anxiety?
- How do psychologists explain anxiety-based disorders?
- What is a personality disorder?
- Why do people commit suicide? Can suicide be prevented?

Normality—What's Normal?

How is abnormality defined?

"That guy's not playing with a full deck." "Yeah, the butter's sliding off his waffle. He's ready to go postal." Informally, it's tempting to make such snap judgments about mental health. But deciding if a person's behavior is abnormal is harder than it might seem. To seriously classify people as psychologically unhealthy raises complex and age-old issues. The conservative, churchgoing housewife down the street might be flagrantly psychotic and a lethal danger to her children. The reclusive eccentric who hangs out at the park could be the sanest person in town. Let's begin our discussion with some basic factors that affect judgments of normality.

The scientific study of mental, emotional, and behavioral disorders is known as **psychopathology.** The term also refers to mental disorders themselves, such as schizophrenia or depression, and to behavior patterns that make people unhappy and impair their personal growth (Butcher, Mineka, & Hooley, 2007). Defining abnormality can be tricky. We might begin by saying that psychopathology is characterized by *subjective discomfort* (private feelings of pain, unhappiness, or emotional distress) like Carol North endured.

But couldn't a person be seriously disturbed without feeling discomfort? Yes. Psychopathology doesn't always cause personal anguish. A person suffering from mania might feel elated and "on top of the world." Also, a *lack* of discomfort may reveal a problem. For example, if you showed no signs of grief after the death of a close friend, we might suspect psychopathology. In practice, subjective discomfort explains most instances in which people voluntarily seek professional help.

Some psychologists use statistics to define normality more objectively. **Statistical abnormality** refers to scoring very high or low on some dimension, such as intelligence, anxiety, or depression. Anxiety, for example, is a feature of several psychological disorders. To measure it, we could create a test to learn how many people show low, medium, or high levels of anxiety. Usually, the results of such tests will form a *normal* (bell-shaped) *curve.* (*Normal* in this case refers only to the *shape* of the curve.) Notice that most people score near the middle of a normal curve; very few have extremely high or low scores (▶▶ Figure 12.1). A person who deviates from the average by being anxious all the time (high anxiety) might be abnormal. So, too, might a person who never feels anxiety.

Then statistical abnormality tells us nothing about the meaning of deviations from the norm? Right. It is as statistically "abnormal" (unusual) for a person to score above 145 on an IQ test as it is to score below 55. However, only the lower score is regarded as "abnormal" or undesirable. In the same sense, it is unusual for a person to speak four languages or to win an event at the Olympics, but these are desirable, if rare, accomplishments.

Statistical definitions also can't tell us *where to draw the line* between normality and abnormality. To take a new example, we could obtain the average frequency of sexual intercourse for persons of a particular age, sex, sexual orientation, and marital status. Clearly, a person who feels driven to have sex dozens of times a day has a problem. But as we move back toward the norm, we face the problem of drawing lines. How often does a normal behavior have to occur before it becomes abnormal? As you can see, statistical boundary lines tend to be somewhat arbitrary (Comer, 2005).

Atypical behavior or nonconformity may underlie some disorders. **Social nonconformity** refers to disobeying public standards for acceptable conduct. Extreme nonconformity can lead to destructive or self-destructive behavior. (Think, for instance, of a drug abuser or a prostitute.) However, we must be careful to separate unhealthy nonconformity from creative lifestyles. Many eccentric "characters" are charming and emotionally stable. Note, too, that strictly following social norms is no guarantee of mental health. In some cases, psychopathology involves rigid conformity. (See "Crazy for a Day.")

FIGURE 12.1 The number of people displaying a personal characteristic may help define what is statistically abnormal.

[Graph: Number of cases (y-axis) vs. Characteristic level of anxiety (x-axis: Extremely low, Low, Moderate, High, Extremely high), with "Abnormal?" labeled at both extreme ends of the bell curve]

Psychopathology The scientific study of mental, emotional, and behavioral disorders; also, abnormal or maladaptive behavior.

Statistical abnormality Abnormality defined on the basis of an extreme score on some dimension, such as IQ or anxiety.

Social nonconformity Failure to conform to societal norms or the usual minimum standards for social conduct.

Crazy for a Day

Performing a mildly abnormal behavior is a good way to get a sense of how social norms define "normality" in daily life. Here's your assignment: Do something strange in public and observe how people react to you. (Please don't do anything dangerous, harmful, or offensive—and don't get arrested!) Here are some deviant behaviors that other students have staged:

- Sit in the dining area of a fast-food restaurant and loudly carry on a conversation with an imaginary companion.

- Stand in a busy hallway on campus and adopt a kung fu stance. Remain in that position for 10 minutes.

- Walk around campus on a sunny day while wearing a raincoat and carrying an open umbrella. Keep the umbrella over your head when you are inside buildings.

- Stick one finger in your nose and another in your ear. Walk through a busy shopping mall.

- Cover your head with aluminum foil for a day.

Does the idea of performing any of these actions make you uncomfortable? If so, you may not need to do anything more to appreciate how powerfully social norms constrain our actions. As we have noted, social nonconformity is just one facet of abnormal behavior. Nevertheless, actions that are regarded as "strange" within a particular culture are often the first sign to others that a person has a problem.

A young woman ties a thick rubber cord around her ankles, screams hysterically, and jumps headfirst off a bridge. Thirty years ago, the woman's behavior might have seemed completely crazy. Today, it is a routine form of entertainment (called "bungee jumping"). Before any behavior can be defined as abnormal, we must consider the *situational context* (social situation, behavioral setting, or general circumstances) in which it occurs. Is it normal to stand outside and water a lawn with a hose? It depends on whether it is raining. Is it abnormal for a grown man to remove his pants and expose himself to another man or woman in a place of business? It depends on whether the other person is a bank clerk or a doctor.

Almost any imaginable behavior can be considered normal in some contexts. In 1972, an airplane carrying a rugby team crashed in the snow-capped Andes of South America. Incredibly, 16 of the 45 people onboard survived 73 days in deep snow and subfreezing temperatures. They were forced to use extremely grim measures to do so—they ate the bodies of those who died in the crash.

As implied by our earlier discussion of social norms, culture is one of the most influential contexts in which any behavior is judged (Fabrega, 2004). In some cultures it is considered normal to defecate or urinate in public or to appear naked in public. In our culture such behaviors would be considered unusual or abnormal. In Muslim cultures, women who remain completely housebound are considered normal or even virtuous. In Western cultures they might be diagnosed as suffering from a disorder called agoraphobia. (Agoraphobia is described later in this chapter.)

Thus, *cultural relativity* (the idea that judgments are made relative to the values of one's culture) can affect the diagnosis of psychological disorders. Still, *all* cultures classify people as abnormal if they fail to communicate with others or are consistently unpredictable in their actions.

Rick Friedman/Corbis

Social nonconformity does not automatically indicate psychopathology.

Core Features of Disordered Behavior

If abnormality is so hard to define, how are judgments of psychopathology made? Although the standards we have discussed are *relative*, abnormal behavior does have two core features. First, it is **maladaptive.** Rather than helping people cope successfully, abnormal behavior makes it more difficult for them to meet the demands of day-to-day life. Second, people suffering from psychological disorders *lose the ability to control* their thoughts, behaviors, or feelings adequately. For example, gambling is not a problem if people bet for entertainment and can maintain self-control. However, compulsive gambling is a sign of psychopathology. The voices that Carol North kept hearing are a prime example of what it means to lose control of one's thoughts. In the most extreme cases, people become a danger to themselves or others, which is clearly maladaptive (Hansell, 2007).

In practice, deciding that a person needs help usually occurs when the person *does something* (hits a person, hallucinates, stares into space, collects rolls of toilet paper, and so forth)

Maladaptive behavior Behavior that makes it difficult to adapt to the environment and meet the demands of day-to-day life.

that *annoys* or *gains the attention* of a person in a *position of power* in the person's life (an employer, teacher, parent, spouse, or the person himself or herself). That person then *does something* about it. (A police officer may be called, the person may be urged to see a psychologist, a relative may start commitment proceedings, or the person may voluntarily seek help.)

Insanity

Commitment proceedings may result in the finding of **insanity,** which is a legal term. It refers to an inability to manage one's affairs or foresee the consequences of one's actions. People who are declared insane are not legally responsible for their actions. If necessary, they can be involuntarily committed to a mental hospital.

Legally, insanity is established by testimony from *expert witnesses* (psychologists and psychiatrists) recognized by a court of law as being qualified to give opinions on a specific topic. Involuntary commitments happen most often when people are brought to emergency rooms. People who are involuntarily committed are usually judged to be a danger to themselves or to others, or they are severely mentally disabled (Luchins et al., 2004).

Classifying Mental Disorders— Problems by the Book

What are the major psychological disorders?

Psychological problems are classified by using the *Diagnostic and Statistical Manual of Mental Disorders* (DSM) (American Psychiatric Association, 2000). The DSM helps psychologists correctly identify mental disorders and select the best therapies to treat them (First & Pincus, 2002).

A **mental disorder** is a significant impairment in psychological functioning. If you were to glance through the DSM-IV-TR (the fourth edition, text revision), you would see many disorders described. It's impossible here to discuss all these problems. However, a simplified list of some major disorders can be found in ● Table 12.1. Those disorders are further described in the next section.

Insanity A legal term that refers to a mental inability to manage one's affairs or to be aware of the consequences of one's actions.

Mental disorder A significant impairment in psychological functioning.

● Table 12.1 Some Selected Categories of Psychopathology

PROBLEM	PRIMARY SYMPTOM	TYPICAL SIGNS OF TROUBLE
Psychotic disorders	Loss of contact with reality	You hear or see things that others don't; your mind has been playing tricks on you.
Mood disorders	Mania or depression	You feel sad and hopeless; or you talk too loud and too fast and have a rush of ideas and feelings that others think are unreasonable.
Anxiety disorders	High anxiety or anxiety-based distortions of behavior	You have anxiety attacks and feel like you are going to die; or you are afraid to do things that most people can do; or you spend unusual amounts of time doing things like washing your hands or counting your heartbeats.
Somatoform disorders	Bodily complaints without an organic (physical) basis	You feel physically sick, but your doctor says nothing is wrong with you; or you suffer from pain that has no physical basis; or you are preoccupied with thoughts about being sick.
Dissociative disorders	Amnesia, feelings of unreality, multiple identities	There are major gaps in your memory of events; you feel like you are a robot or a stranger to yourself; others tell you that you have done things that you don't remember doing.
Personality disorders	Unhealthy personality patterns	Your behavior patterns repeatedly cause problems at work, at school, and in your relationships with others.
Sexual and gender identity disorders	Disturbed gender identity, deviant sexual behavior, problems in sexual adjustment	You feel that you are a man trapped in a woman's body (or the reverse); or you can gain sexual satisfaction only by engaging in highly atypical sexual behavior; or you have problems with sexual desire, arousal, or performance.
Substance-related disorders	Disturbances related to drug abuse or dependence	You have been drinking too much, using illegal drugs, or taking prescription drugs more often than you should.

An Overview of Psychological Disorders

People suffering from **psychotic disorders** have "retreated from reality." That is, they suffer from hallucinations and delusions and are socially withdrawn. Psychotic disorders are severely disabling and often lead to hospitalization. Typically, psychotic patients cannot control their thoughts and actions. For example, David often heard the voice of his Uncle Bill: "He told me to turn off the TV. He said, 'It's too damn loud, turn it down, turn it down.' Other times he talks about fishing. 'Good day for fishing. Got to go fishing'" (Durand & Barlow, 2010). Psychotic symptoms occur in schizophrenia, delusional disorders, and some mood disorders. Also, psychosis may be related to medical problems, drug abuse, and other conditions.

Organic mental disorders are problems caused by brain pathology; that is, by drug damage, diseases of the brain, injuries, poisons, and so on (▶▶ Figure 12.2). A person with an organic disorder may have severe emotional disturbances, impaired thinking, memory loss, personality changes, delirium, or psychotic symptoms (Nolen-Hoeksema, 2007).

In reality, almost all mental disorders are partly biological (Hansell, 2007). That's why the DSM-IV-TR does not list "organic mental disorders" as a separate category. Nevertheless, all the following problems are closely associated with organic damage: delirium, dementia, amnesia, and other cognitive disorders; mental disorders due to a general medical condition; and substance-related disorders (drug abuse).

Mood disorders are defined primarily by the presence of extreme, intense, and long-lasting emotions. Afflicted persons may be *manic,* meaning agitated, elated, and hyperactive, or they may be *depressed.* Some people with mood disorders alternate between mania and depression and may have psychotic symptoms as well.

Anxiety disorders are marked by fear or anxiety and by distorted behavior. Some anxiety disorders involve feelings of panic. Others take the form of phobias (irrational fears) or just overwhelming anxiety and nervousness. Two additional anxiety disorders are acute stress disorder and posttraumatic stress disorder. Obsessive-compulsive behavior patterns are also associated with high anxiety. (These problems are described later in this chapter.)

Somatoform (so-MAT-oh-form) **disorders** occur when a person has physical symptoms that mimic disease or injury (e.g., paralysis, blindness, illness, chronic pain), for which there is no identifiable physical cause. In such cases, psychological factors appear to explain the symptoms.

> ◀◀ **FIGURE 12.2** This MRI scan of a human brain (viewed from the top) reveals a tumor (dark spot). Mental disorders sometimes have organic causes of this sort. However, in many instances no obvious organic damage can be found.

Scott Camazine/Photo Researchers, Inc.

Courtesy of Ulrike Kantor, Ulrike Kantor Gallery

The self-portraits shown here were painted by Andy Wilf during a 4-year period. At that time, Wilf is said to have increasingly abused drugs and alcohol. This dramatic series of images is a record of his self-destructive descent into a private hell. The third painting shows a shrouded skull—and foretells the artist's fate. Wilf died of a drug overdose. Drug abuse is but one of the many psychopathologies, or "problems in living," that psychologists seek to alleviate.

Psychotic disorder A severe mental disorder characterized by a retreat from reality, by hallucinations and delusions, and by social withdrawal.

Organic mental disorder A mental or emotional problem caused by brain diseases or injuries.

Mood disorder A major disturbance in mood or emotion, such as depression or mania.

Anxiety disorder Disruptive feelings of fear, apprehension, or anxiety, or distortions in behavior that are anxiety related.

Somatoform disorder Physical symptoms that mimic disease or injury for which there is no identifiable physical cause.

human diversity

Running Amok with Cultural Maladies

Every culture recognizes the existence of psychopathology, and most have at least a few folk names for afflictions you won't find in the DSM-IV-TR. Here are some examples of *culture-bound syndromes* from around the world (Durand & Barlow, 2010; López & Guarnaccia, 2000; Sumathipala, Siribaddana, & Bhugra, 2004):

- **Amok** Men in Malaysia, Laos, the Philippines, and Polynesia who believe they have been insulted are sometimes known to go *amok*. After a period of brooding, they erupt into an outburst of violent, aggressive, or homicidal behavior randomly directed at people and objects.

- **Susto** Among Latin Americans, the symptoms of *susto* include insomnia, irritability, phobias, and an increase in sweating and heart rate. Susto can result if someone is badly frightened by a black magic curse. In extreme cases, *voodoo death* can result, as the person is literally scared to death.

- **Ghost sickness** Among many American Indian tribes, people who become preoccupied with death and the deceased are said to suffer from *ghost sickness*. The symptoms of ghost sickness include bad dreams, weakness, loss of appetite, fainting, dizziness, fear, anxiety, hallucinations, loss of consciousness, confusion, feelings of futility, and a sense of suffocation.

- **Koro** In South and East Asia, a man may experience sudden and intense anxiety that his penis (or, in females, the vulva and nipples) will recede into the body. In addition to the terror this incites, victims also believe that advanced cases of *koro* can cause death. A similar fear of shrinking genitals has also been reported from West Africa (Dzokoto & Adams, 2005).

- **Zar** In North African and Middle Eastern societies, *zar* is said to occur when spirits possess an individual. Zar is marked by shouting, laughing, hitting the head against a wall, singing, or weeping. Victims may become apathetic or withdrawn and may refuse to eat or carry out daily tasks.

- **Dhat** In Indian society, *dhat* is the fear of the loss of semen during nocturnal emissions. A man suffering from *dhat* will feel anxious and perhaps also guilty. He may also experience fatigue, loss of appetite, weakness, anxiety, and sexual dysfunction.

It's clear that people have a need to label and categorize disturbed behavior. As you can see, however, folk terminology tends to be vague. The terms listed here provide little guidance about the true nature of a person's problems or the best ways to treat them. That's why the DSM is based on empirical data and clinical observations. Otherwise, psychologists and psychiatrists would be no better than folk healers when making diagnoses (Ancis, Chen, & Schultz, 2004).

By the way, culture-bound disorders occur in all societies. For example, American psychologists Pamela Keel and Kelly Klump believe that the eating disorder bulimia is primarily a syndrome of Western cultures like the United States (Keel & Klump, 2003).

A person with a **dissociative disorder** may have temporary amnesia or multiple personalities. Also included in this category are frightening episodes of depersonalization, in which people feel like they are outside of their bodies, are behaving like robots, or are lost in a dream world.

Personality disorders are deeply ingrained, unhealthy personality patterns. Such patterns usually appear in adolescence and continue through much of adult life. They include paranoid (overly suspicious), narcissistic (self-loving), dependent, borderline, and antisocial personality types, as well as others.

Sexual and gender identity disorders include any of a wide range of difficulties with sexual identity, deviant sexual behavior, or sexual adjustment. In gender identity disorders, sexual identity does not match a person's physical sex, and the person may seek a sex-change operation. Deviations in sexual behavior known as *paraphilias* include exhibitionism, fetishism, voyeurism, and so on. Also found in this category are a variety of *sexual dysfunctions* (problems in sexual desire, arousal, or response).

Substance-related disorders involve abuse of, or dependence on, psychoactive drugs. Typical culprits include alcohol, barbiturates, opiates, cocaine, amphetamines, hallucinogens, marijuana, and nicotine. A person with a substance-related disorder cannot stop using the drug and may also suffer from withdrawal symptoms, delirium, dementia, amnesia, psychosis, emotional outbursts, sexual problems, and sleep disturbances. (Problems related to drug abuse are discussed in Chapter 5.)

In addition to the formal mental disorders we have reviewed, many cultures have names for "unofficial" psychological "disorders." See "Running Amok with Cultural Maladies" for some examples.

DSM-V

Isn't neurosis a psychological disorder? You might be surprised to learn that definitions of mental disorders change over time. When the DSM was first published in 1952, *neurosis* was included. The term was dropped in later editions because it is too imprecise. "Neurotic"

Dissociative disorder Temporary amnesia, multiple personality, or depersonalization.

Personality disorder A maladaptive personality pattern.

Sexual and gender identity disorders Any of a wide range of difficulties with sexual identity, deviant sexual behavior, or sexual adjustment.

Substance-related disorder Abuse of or dependence on a mood- or behavior-altering drug.

behavior is now part of anxiety, somatoform, or dissociative disorders. Even though **neurosis** is an outdated term, you may still hear it used to loosely refer to problems involving excessive anxiety.

A new edition, the DSM-V, is due in 2012. Like previous manuals, it will reflect updated research and changing social attitudes (Thomas, 2009; Ronningstam, 2009). For example, *gender identity disorder,* which was mentioned earlier, may be omitted from the DSM-V (Gever, 2009; Zucker & Spitzer, 2005). Opponents of this term believe that many people whose physical sex does not match their sexual identity are well adjusted and should not be labeled as "disordered."

New mental disorders may also be added to the DSM-V. One possibility being considered is *posttraumatic embitterment disorder,* which occurs when a person is left so bitter after a perceived injustice that he or she cannot let it go (Linden et al., 2008). For example, Jack's wife left him 3 years ago. He is embittered, angry, and humiliated. He cannot forget or forgive her. Jack sits at home alone every night, is not seeing anyone else, is having troubles at work, and is estranged from his children.

If added, posttraumatic embitterment disorder would join an ever-growing list of recognized disorders. Other possibilities include *rage disorder, apathy disorder,* and *hostile personality disorder.* Such terms have led some to worry that more and more normal human behavior is being redefined as problematic (Lane, 2009). Yet, each of the problems listed here can seriously disrupt a person's life and perhaps should be part of the next DSM.

General Risk Factors

What causes psychological disorders like those listed in Table 12.1? We will soon explore the causes of some specific problems. For now, here are some general risk factors that contribute to psychopathology:

- **Biological/physical factors:** genetic defects or inherited vulnerabilities, poor prenatal care, very low birth weight, chronic physical illness or disability, exposure to toxic chemicals or drugs, head injuries
- **Psychological factors:** stress, low intelligence, learning disorders, lack of control or mastery
- **Family factors:** parents who are immature, mentally disturbed, criminal, or abusive; severe marital strife; extremely poor child discipline; disordered family communication patterns
- **Social conditions:** poverty, stressful living conditions, homelessness, social disorganization, overcrowding

An Important Note—You're Okay, Really!

In upcoming sections we will explore some disorders in more detail, beginning with psychotic disorders. (See ● Table 12.2 for a more detailed list of disorders, including those in Table 12.1. You don't need to memorize all of them.) As you read further, we hope that you will not fall prey to "medical student's disease." Medical students, it seems, have a predictable tendency to notice in themselves the symptoms of each dreaded disease they study. As a psychology student you may notice what seem to be abnormal tendencies in your own behavior. If so, don't panic. In most instances, this only shows that pathological behavior is an *exaggeration* of normal defenses and reactions, not that your behavior is abnormal. Before we go on, though, there's a Study Break on page 477 to help you diagnose your grasp of psychopathology.

Neurosis An outdated term once used to refer, as a group, to anxiety disorders, somatoform disorders, dissociative disorders, and some forms of depression.

● Table 12.2 Major DSM-IV-TR Categories

Disorders Usually First Diagnosed in Infancy, Childhood, or Adolescence

Mental retardation
  Example: Mild mental retardation
Learning disorders
  Example: Reading disorder
Motor skills disorder
  Example: Developmental coordination disorder
Communication disorders
  Example: Stuttering
Pervasive developmental disorders
  Example: Autistic disorder
Attention-deficit and disruptive behavior disorders
  Example: Attention-deficit/hyperactivity disorder
Feeding and eating disorders of infancy or early childhood
  Example: Pica (eating inedible substances)
Tic disorders
  Example: Tourette's disorder
Elimination disorders
  Example: Enuresis (bed-wetting)
Other disorders of infancy, childhood, or adolescence
  Example: Separation anxiety disorder

Delirium, Dementia, Amnestic, and Other Cognitive Disorders

Delirium
  Example: Delirium due to a general medical condition
Dementia
  Example: Dementia of the Alzheimer's type
Amnestic disorders (memory loss)
  Example: Amnestic disorder due to a general medical condition
Cognitive disorder not otherwise specified

Mental Disorders Due to a General Medical Condition Not Elsewhere Classified

Catatonic disorder due to a general medical condition
Personality change due to a general medical condition
Mental disorder not otherwise specified due to a general medical condition

Substance-Related Disorders
  Example: Cocaine use disorders

Schizophrenia and Other Psychotic Disorders

Schizophrenia
  Example: Schizophrenia, paranoid type
Schizophreniform disorder
Schizoaffective disorder
Delusional disorder
  Example: Delusional disorder, grandiose type
Brief psychotic disorder
Shared psychotic disorder (folie a deux)
Psychotic disorder due to a general medical condition
Substance-induced psychotic disorder
Psychotic disorder not otherwise specified

Mood Disorders

Depressive disorders
  Example: Major depressive disorder
Bipolar disorders
  Example: Bipolar I disorder
Mood disorder due to a general medical condition
Substance-induced mood disorder
Mood disorder not otherwise specified

Anxiety Disorders
  Example: Panic disorder

Somatoform Disorders
  Example: Conversion disorder

Factitious Disorders (Faked Disability or Illness)
  Example: Factitious disorder

Dissociative Disorders
  Example: Dissociative identity disorder

Sexual and Gender Identity Disorders

Sexual dysfunctions
  Example: Sexual arousal disorders
Paraphilias
  Example: Voyeurism
Sexual disorder not otherwise specified
Gender identity disorders
  Example: Gender identity disorder

Eating Disorders
  Example: Anorexia nervosa

Sleep Disorders

Primary sleep disorders
Dyssomnias
  Example: Primary insomnia
Parasomnias
  Example: Sleep terror disorder
Sleep disorders related to another mental disorder
  Example: Insomnia related to posttraumatic stress disorder
Other sleep disorders
  Example: Substance-induced sleep disorder

Impulse Control Disorders Not Elsewhere Classified
  Example: Kleptomania

Adjustment Disorders
  Example: Adjustment disorder

Personality Disorders
  Example: Antisocial personality disorder

Source: American Psychiatric Association, 2000.

study break
Normality and Psychopathology

7. Someone who engages in one of the paraphilias has what type of disorder?
   a. dissociative   b. somatoform
   c. substance   d. sexual

REFLECT
Critical Thinking

8. Brian, a fan of grunge rock, occasionally wears a skirt in public. Does Brian's cross-dressing indicate that he has a mental disorder?

Relate

Think of an instance of abnormal behavior you have witnessed. By what formal standards would the behavior be regarded as abnormal? In every society? Was the behavior maladaptive in any way?

ANSWERS

1. F 2. d 3. d 4. c 5. delusions, hallucinations 6. b 7. d 8. Probably not. Undoubtedly, Brian's cross-dressing is socially disapproved by many people. Nevertheless, to be classified as a mental disorder it must cause him to feel disabling shame, guilt, depression, or anxiety. The cultural relativity of behavior like Brian's is revealed by the fact that it is fashionable and acceptable for women to wear men's clothing.

Psychotic Disorders—The Dark Side of the Moon

What are the general characteristics of psychotic disorders?

Psychotic disorders are among the most dramatic and serious of all mental problems. Imagine that a member of your family (Floyd?) has been hearing voices, is talking strangely, has covered his head with aluminum foil, and believes that houseflies are speaking to him in code. If you observed such symptoms, would you be concerned? Of course you would, and rightly so.

A person who is psychotic undergoes a number of striking changes in thinking, behavior, and emotion. Basic to all these changes is the fact that **psychosis** reflects a loss of contact with shared views of reality (psycho*sis*, singular; psycho*ses*, plural). The following comments, made by a psychotic patient, illustrate what is meant by a "split" from reality (Durand & Barlow, 2010):

> When you do the 25 of the clock, it means that you leave the house 25 after 1 to mail letters so they can check on you. . . . and they know where you're at. That's the Eagle.

The Nature of Psychosis

What are the major features of psychotic disorders? Delusions and hallucinations are core features, but there are others as well.

People who suffer from **delusions** hold false beliefs that they insist are true, regardless of how much the facts contradict them. An example is a 43-year-old schizophrenic man who was convinced he was pregnant (Mansouri & Adityanjee, 1995).

Psychosis A withdrawal from reality marked by hallucinations and delusions, disturbed thought and emotions, and by personality disorganization.

Delusion A false belief held against all contrary evidence.

A scene in a state mental hospital.

Are there different types of delusions? Yes, some common types of delusions are: (1) *depressive* delusions, in which people feel that they have committed horrible crimes or sinful deeds; (2) *somatic* delusions, such as believing your body is "rotting away" or that it is emitting foul odors; (3) delusions of *grandeur,* in which people think they are extremely important; (4) delusions of *influence,* in which people feel they are being controlled or influenced by others or by unseen forces; (5) delusions of *persecution,* in which people believe that others are "out to get them"; and (6) delusions of *reference,* in which people give great personal meaning to unrelated events. For instance, delusional people sometimes think that television programs are giving them a special personal message (American Psychiatric Association, 2000).

Hallucinations are imaginary sensations, such as seeing, hearing, or smelling things that don't exist in the real world. The most common psychotic hallucination is hearing voices, like the voice that told Carol North to "collide with the other world." Sometimes these voices command patients to hurt themselves. Unfortunately, sometimes people obey (Barrowcliff & Haddock, 2006). More rarely, psychotic people may feel "insects crawling under their skin," taste "poisons" in their food, or smell "gas" their "enemies" are using to "get" them. Sensory changes, such as anesthesia (numbness, or a loss of sensation) or extreme sensitivity to heat, cold, pain, or touch, can also occur.

During a psychotic episode, emotions are often severely disturbed. For instance, the psychotic person may be wildly elated, depressed, hyperemotional, or apathetic. Sometimes psychotic patients display flat affect, a condition in which the face is frozen in a blank expression. Brain images from psychotic patients with "frozen faces" reveal that their brains process emotions abnormally (Fahim et al., 2005).

Some psychotic symptoms can be thought of as a primitive type of communication. That is, many patients can use their actions to say "I need help" or "I can't handle it anymore." Disturbed verbal communication is a nearly universal symptom of psychosis. In fact, psychotic speech tends to be so garbled and chaotic that it sometimes sounds like a "word salad."

Major disturbances such as those just described—as well as added problems with thinking, memory, and attention—bring about personality disintegration and a break with reality. *Personality disintegration* occurs when a person's thoughts, actions, and emotions are no longer coordinated. When psychotic disturbances and a fragmented personality are evident for weeks or months, the person has suffered a psychosis (American Psychiatric Association, 2000). (See ● Table 12.3.)

● **Table 12.3 Warning Signs of Psychotic Disorders and Major Mood Disorders**

- You express bizarre thoughts or beliefs that defy reality.
- You have withdrawn from family members and other relationships.
- You hear unreal voices or see things others don't.
- You are extremely sad, persistently despondent, or suicidal.
- You are excessively energetic and have little need for sleep.
- You lose your appetite, sleep excessively, and have no energy.
- You exhibit extreme mood swings.
- You believe someone is trying to get you.
- You have engaged in antisocial, destructive, or self-destructive behavior.

Sources: Harvey et al., 1996; Durand & Barlow, 2010.

Organic Psychosis

In a sense, all psychoses are partly organic, involving physical changes in the brain. However, the general term *organic psychosis* is usually reserved for problems involving clear-cut brain injuries or diseases.

For example, poisoning by lead or mercury can damage the brain, causing hallucinations, delusions, and a loss of emotional control (▶▶ Figure 12.3). Children who eat leaded paint flakes or breathe leaded paint powder can become psychotic or intellectually disabled (Mielke, 1999). Children with higher levels of lead in their blood are more likely to be arrested as adults for criminal offenses (Wright et al., 2008). On a much larger scale, "poisoning" of another type, in the form of drug abuse, can also produce deviant behavior and psychotic symptoms (American Psychiatric Association, 2000).

The most common organic problem is **dementia** (duh-MEN-sha), a serious mental impairment in old age caused by deterioration of the brain (Gatz, 2007). In dementia, we see major disturbances in memory, reasoning, judgment, impulse control, and personality. This combination usually leaves people confused, suspicious, apathetic, or withdrawn. Some common causes of dementia are circulatory problems, repeated strokes, or general

Hallucination An imaginary sensation, such as seeing, hearing, or smelling things that don't exist in the real world.

Dementia A serious mental impairment in old age caused by physical deterioration of the brain.

FIGURE 12.3 The Mad Hatter, from Lewis Carroll's *Alice's Adventures in Wonderland*. History provides numerous examples of psychosis caused by toxic chemicals. Carroll's Mad Hatter character is modeled after an occupational disease of the eighteenth and nineteenth centuries. In that era, hat makers were heavily exposed to mercury used in the preparation of felt. Consequently, many suffered brain damage and became psychotic, or "mad" (Kety, 1979).

The soil and dust in cities and near busy streets is often heavily contaminated with lead. This lead came from automobile exhaust before leaded gasoline was banned. Young children frequently put objects and their hands in their mouths. This is a major source of lead poisoning for many children. Paving play areas or covering them with clean soil can greatly reduce lead exposure (Mielke, 1999).

shrinkage and atrophy of the brain. The most common form of dementia is **Alzheimer's** (ALLS-hi-merz) **disease.** Alzheimer's victims slowly lose the ability to work, cook, drive, read, write, or do arithmetic. Eventually they are mute and bedridden. Alzheimer's disease appears to be caused by unusual webs and tangles in the brain that damage areas important for memory and learning (Ingram, 2003). Genetic factors can increase the risk of developing this devastating disease (Gatz, 2007).

Are there specific kinds of psychotic disorders? Two major types of psychosis are *delusional disorders* and *schizophrenia*. You'll find information on each of these problems in upcoming discussions.

Former U.S. President Ronald Reagan was diagnosed with Alzheimer's disease in 1995. Like many Alzheimer's victims, Reagan slipped into a slow mental decline. He died in 2004.

Delusional Disorders—An Enemy Behind Every Tree

What is the nature of a delusional disorder?

People with delusional disorders usually do not suffer from hallucinations, emotional excesses, or personality disintegration. Even so, their break with reality is unmistakable. The main feature of **delusional disorders** is the presence of deeply held false beliefs, which may take the following forms (American Psychiatric Association, 2000):

- **Erotomanic type:** In this disorder, people have erotic delusions that they are loved by another person, especially by someone famous or of higher status. As you might imagine, some celebrity stalkers suffer from erotomania.
- **Grandiose type:** In this case, people suffer from the delusion that they have some great, unrecognized talent, knowledge, or insight. They may also believe that they have a special relationship with an important person or with God or that they are a famous person. (If the famous person is alive, the deluded person regards her or him as an imposter.)

Alzheimer's disease An age-related disease characterized by memory loss, mental confusion, and, in its later stages, a nearly total loss of mental abilities.

Delusional disorder A psychosis marked by severe delusions of grandeur, jealousy, persecution, or similar preoccupations.

- **Jealous type:** An example of this type of delusion would be having an all-consuming, but unfounded, belief that your spouse or lover is unfaithful.
- **Persecutory type:** Delusions of persecution involve belief that you are being conspired against, cheated, spied on, followed, poisoned, maligned, or harassed.
- **Somatic type:** People suffering from somatic delusions typically believe that their bodies are diseased or rotting, or infested with insects or parasites, or that parts of their bodies are defective.

Although they are false, and sometimes far-fetched, all these delusions are about experiences that could occur in real life (Manschreck, 1996). In other types of psychosis, delusions tend to be more bizarre. For example, a person with schizophrenia might believe that space aliens have replaced all his internal organs with electronic monitoring devices. In contrast, people with ordinary delusions merely believe that someone is trying to steal their money, that they are being deceived by a lover, that the FBI is watching them, and the like (American Psychiatric Association, 2000).

Paranoid Psychosis

The most common delusional disorder, often called **paranoid psychosis,** centers on delusions of persecution. Many self-styled reformers, crank letter writers, conspiracy theorists, "UFO abductees," and the like suffer paranoid delusions. Paranoid individuals often believe that they are being cheated, spied on, followed, poisoned, harassed, or plotted against. Usually they are intensely suspicious, believing they must be on guard at all times.

The evidence such people find to support their beliefs usually fails to persuade others. Every detail of the paranoid person's existence is woven into a private version of "what's really going on." Buzzing during a telephone conversation may be interpreted as "someone listening"; a stranger who comes to the door asking for directions may be seen as "really trying to get information"; and so forth.

It is difficult to treat people suffering from paranoid delusions because it is almost impossible for them to accept that they need help. Anyone who suggests that they have a problem simply becomes part of the "conspiracy" to "persecute" them. Consequently, paranoid people frequently lead lonely, isolated, and humorless lives dominated by constant suspicion and hostility.

Delusional disorders are rare. By far, the most common form of psychosis is schizophrenia. Let's explore schizophrenia in more detail and see how it differs from a delusional disorder.

Schizophrenia—Shattered Reality

What forms does schizophrenia take? What causes it?

Schizophrenia (SKIT-soh-FREN-ee-uh) is marked by delusions, hallucinations, apathy, thinking abnormalities, and a "split" between thought and emotion. In schizophrenia, emotions may become blunted or very inappropriate. For example, if a person with schizophrenia is told his mother just died, he might smile, or giggle, or show no emotion at all. Schizophrenic delusions may include the idea that the person's thoughts and actions are being controlled, that thoughts are being broadcast (so others can hear them), that thoughts have been "inserted" into the person's mind, or that thoughts have been removed. In addition, schizophrenia involves withdrawal from contact with others, a loss of interest in external activities, a breakdown of personal habits, and an inability to deal with daily events (Neufeld et al., 2003). One person in 100 has schizophrenia in any given year (National Institute of Mental Health, 2006b).

Many schizophrenic symptoms appear to be related to problems with *selective attention*. In other words, it is hard for people with schizophrenia to focus on one item of information at a time. Having an impaired "sensory filter" in their brains may be why they are overwhelmed by a jumble of thoughts, sensations, images, and feelings (Heinrichs, 2001).

Paranoid psychosis A delusional disorder centered especially on delusions of persecution.

Schizophrenia A psychosis characterized by delusions, hallucinations, apathy, and a "split" between thought and emotion.

Is there more than one type of schizophrenia? Schizophrenia appears to be a group of related disturbances. It has four major subtypes:

- **Disorganized type:** Schizophrenia marked by incoherence, grossly disorganized behavior, bizarre thinking, and flat or grossly inappropriate emotions
- **Catatonic type:** Schizophrenia marked by stupor, rigidity, unresponsiveness, posturing, mutism, and, sometimes, agitated, purposeless behavior
- **Paranoid type:** Schizophrenia marked by a preoccupation with delusions or by frequent auditory hallucinations related to a single theme, especially grandeur or persecution
- **Undifferentiated type:** Schizophrenia in which there are prominent psychotic symptoms, but none of the specific features of catatonic, disorganized, or paranoid types

Disorganized Schizophrenia

The disorder known as **disorganized schizophrenia** (sometimes called *hebephrenic* schizophrenia) comes close to matching the stereotyped images of "madness" seen in movies. In disorganized schizophrenia, personality disintegration is almost complete: Emotions, speech, and behavior are all highly disorganized. The result is silliness, laughter, and bizarre or obscene behavior, as shown by this intake interview of a patient named Edna:

Dr. Tell me, how do you feel?

Patient London's bell is a long, long dock. Hee! Hee! (Giggles uncontrollably.)

Dr. Do you know where you are now?

Patient D_____n! S_____t on you all who rip into my internals! The grudgerometer will take care of you all! (Shouting) I am the Queen, see my magic, I shall turn you all into smidgelings forever!

I. . . . I. . . . I. . . . I! (Makes grotesque faces.)

Edna was placed in the women's ward where she proceeded to masturbate. Occasionally, she would scream or shout obscenities. At other times she giggled to herself. She was known to attack other patients. She began to complain that her uterus was attached to a "pipeline to the Kremlin" and that she was being "infernally invaded" by Communism. (Suinn, 1975*)

Disorganized schizophrenia typically develops in adolescence or young adulthood. Chances of improvement are limited, and social impairment is usually extreme (American Psychiatric Association, 2000).

In disorganized schizophrenia, behavior is marked by silliness, laughter, and bizarre or obscene behavior.

Peter Granser/Laif/Aurora Photos

Catatonic Schizophrenia

The catatonic person seems to be in a state of total panic (Fink & Taylor, 2003). **Catatonic schizophrenia** brings about a stuporous condition in which odd positions may be held for hours or even days. These periods of rigidity may be similar to the tendency to "freeze" at times of great emergency or panic. Catatonic individuals appear to be struggling desperately to control their inner turmoil. One sign of this is the fact that stupor may occasionally give way to agitated outbursts or violent behavior. The following excerpt describes a catatonic episode:

Manuel appeared to be physically healthy upon examination. Yet he did not regain his awareness of his surroundings. He remained motionless, speechless, and seemingly unconscious. One evening an aide turned him on his side to straighten out the sheet, was called away to tend to another patient, and forgot to return. Manuel was found the next morning, still on his side, his arm tucked under his body, as he had been left the night before. His arm was turning blue from lack of circulation, but he seemed to be experiencing no discomfort. (Suinn, 1975)

most severe

Disorganized schizophrenia Schizophrenia marked by incoherence, grossly disorganized behavior, bizarre thinking, and flat or grossly inappropriate emotions.

Catatonic schizophrenia Schizophrenia marked by stupor, rigidity, unresponsiveness, posturing, mutism, and, sometimes, agitated, purposeless behavior.

*Suinn Excerpts: From *Fundamentals of Behavior Pathology* by R. M. Suinn. Copyright © 1975. Reprinted by permission of John Wiley & Sons, Inc. Additional Suinn quotes in this chapter are from the same source.

Can the rigid postures and stupor of a person with catatonic schizophrenia be understood in terms of abnormal body chemistry? Environment? Heredity?

Notice that Manuel did not speak. *Mutism,* along with a marked decrease in responsiveness to the environment, makes patients with catatonic schizophrenia difficult to "reach." Fortunately, this bizarre disorder has become rare in Europe and North America (American Psychiatric Association, 2000).

Paranoid Schizophrenia

Paranoid schizophrenia is the most common schizophrenic disorder. As in paranoid delusional disorders, **paranoid schizophrenia** centers on delusions of grandeur and persecution. However, paranoid schizophrenics also hallucinate, and their delusions are more bizarre and unconvincing than those in a delusional disorder (Freeman & Garety, 2004).

Thinking that God, the government, or "cosmic rays from space" are controlling their minds or that someone is trying to poison them, people suffering from paranoid schizophrenia may feel forced into violence to "protect" themselves (▶▶ Figure 12.4). An example is James Huberty, who brutally murdered 21 people at a McDonald's restaurant in San Ysidro, California. Huberty, who had paranoid schizophrenia, felt persecuted and cheated by life. Shortly before he announced to his wife that he was "going hunting humans," Huberty had been hearing hallucinated voices.

How dangerous are the mentally ill? Horrific crimes, like the San Ysidro murders, lead many people to believe that the mentally ill are dangerous. While sensationalized media reports tend to exaggerate the connection between mental illness and violence, the reality is just the opposite (Corrigan et al., 2005). According to the largest study ever conducted on this question, mentally ill individuals who are not also substance abusers are no more prone to violence than are normal individuals (Monahan et al., 2001). In general, only persons who are *actively psychotic* and *currently* experiencing psychotic symptoms are at increased risk for violence. In fact, the risk of violence from mental patients is actually many times lower than that from persons who have the following attributes: young, male, poor, and intoxicated (Corrigan & Watson, 2005).

▶▶ **FIGURE 12.4** Over a period of years, Theodore Kaczynski mailed bombs to unsuspecting victims, many of whom were maimed or killed. As a young adult, Kaczynski was a brilliant mathematician. At the time of his arrest, he had become the Unabomber—a reclusive "loner" who deeply mistrusted other people and modern technology. After his arrest, Kaczynski was judged to be suffering from paranoid schizophrenia.

The Causes of Schizophrenia

What causes schizophrenia? Former British Prime Minister Winston Churchill once described a question that perplexed him as "a riddle wrapped in a mystery inside an enigma." The same words might describe the causes of schizophrenia.

Environment

An increased risk of developing schizophrenia may begin at birth or even before. Women who are exposed to the influenza (flu) virus or to rubella (German measles) during the middle of pregnancy have children who are more likely to become schizophrenic (Brown et al., 2001). Malnutrition during pregnancy and complications at the time of birth can have a similar impact. Possibly, such events disturb brain development, leaving people more vulnerable to a psychotic break with reality (Walker et al., 2004).

Early **psychological trauma** (a psychological injury or shock) may also add to the risk. Often, the victims of schizophrenia were exposed to violence, sexual abuse, death, divorce,

Paranoid schizophrenia Schizophrenia marked by a preoccupation with delusions or by frequent auditory hallucinations related to a single theme, especially grandeur or persecution.

Psychological trauma A psychological injury or shock, such as that caused by violence, abuse, neglect, separation, and so forth.

separation, or other stresses in childhood (Walker et al., 2004). Living in a troubled family is a related risk factor. In a disturbed family environment, stressful relationships, communication patterns, and negative emotions prevail. Deviant communication patterns cause anxiety, confusion, anger, conflict, and turmoil. Typically, disturbed families interact in ways that are laden with guilt, prying, criticism, negativity, and emotional attacks (Bressi, Albonetti, & Razzoli, 1998; Davison & Neale, 2006).

Although they are attractive, environmental explanations alone are not enough to account for schizophrenia. For example, when the children of schizophrenic parents are raised away from their chaotic home environment, they are still more likely to become psychotic (Walker et al., 2004).

Heredity

Does that mean that heredity affects the risk of developing schizophrenia? There is now little doubt that heredity is a factor in schizophrenia. It appears that some individuals inherit a *potential* for developing schizophrenia. They are, in other words, more *vulnerable* to the disorder (Harrison & Weinberger, 2005; Walker et al., 2004).

How has that been shown? If one identical twin becomes schizophrenic (remember, identical twins have identical genes), then the other twin has a *48 percent* chance of also becoming schizophrenic (Lenzenweger & Gottesman, 1994). The figure for twins can be compared with the risk of schizophrenia for the population in general, which is 1 percent. (See ▶▶ Figure 12.5 for other relationships.) In general, schizophrenia is clearly more common among close relatives and tends to run in families. There's even a case on record of *four* identical quadruplets *all* developing schizophrenia (Mirsky et al., 2000). In light of such evidence, researchers are now beginning to search for specific genes related to schizophrenia.

One possibility is suggested by the fact that the older a man is (even if he doesn't suffer from schizophrenia) when he fathers a child, the more likely it is that the child will develop schizophrenia. Apparently, genetic mutations occur in aging male reproductive cells and increase the risk of schizophrenia (as well as other medical problems) (Malaspina et al., 2005; Sipos et al., 2004).

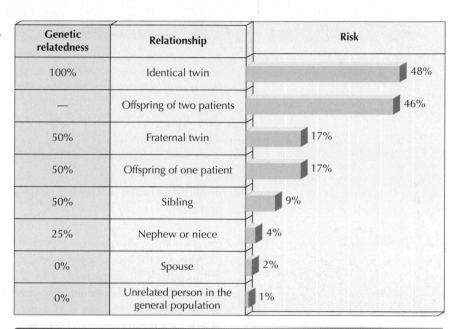

Genetic relatedness	Relationship	Risk
100%	Identical twin	48%
—	Offspring of two patients	46%
50%	Fraternal twin	17%
50%	Offspring of one patient	17%
50%	Sibling	9%
25%	Nephew or niece	4%
0%	Spouse	2%
0%	Unrelated person in the general population	1%

▲ **FIGURE 12.5** Lifetime risk of developing schizophrenia is associated with how closely a person is genetically related to a schizophrenic person. A shared environment also increases the risk. (Estimates from Lenzenweger & Gottesman, 1994.)

Brain Chemistry

Amphetamine, LSD, PCP ("angel dust"), and similar drugs produce effects that partially mimic the symptoms of schizophrenia. Also, the same drugs (phenothiazines) used to treat LSD overdoses tend to alleviate psychotic symptoms. Facts such as these suggest that biochemical abnormalities (disturbances in brain chemicals or neurotransmitters) may occur in schizophrenic people. It is possible that the schizophrenic brain produces some substance similar to a *psychedelic* (mind-altering) drug. At present, one likely candidate is dopamine (DOPE-ah-meen), an important chemical messenger found in the brain.

Many researchers believe that schizophrenia is related to overactivity in brain dopamine systems (Durand & Barlow, 2010; Kapur & Lecrubier, 2003). Another possibility is that dopamine receptors become super-responsive to normal amounts of dopamine. Dopamine appears to trigger a flood of unrelated thoughts, feelings, and perceptions, which may account for the voices, hallucinations, and delusions of schizophrenia. The

This series of paintings by Louis Wain reflects a troubled personality. Wain was a British illustrator who became schizophrenic in middle age. As Wain's psychosis progressed, his cat paintings became highly abstract and fragmented. In many ways, Wain's paintings resemble the perceptual changes caused by psychedelic drugs such as mescaline and LSD. Recent research suggests that psychosis may, in fact, be the result of mind-altering changes in brain chemistry.

implication is that schizophrenic people may be on a sort of drug trip caused by their own bodies (▶▶ Figure 12.6).

Dopamine is not the only brain chemical that has caught scientists' attention. The neurotransmitter glutamate also appears to be related to schizophrenia (van Elst et al., 2005). People who take the hallucinogenic drug PCP, which affects glutamate, have symptoms that closely mimic schizophrenia (Murray, 2002). This occurs because glutamate influences brain activity in areas that control emotions and sensory information (Tsai & Coyle, 2002). Another tantalizing connection is the fact that stress alters glutamate levels, which in turn alter dopamine systems (Moghaddam, 2002). The story is far from complete, but it appears that dopamine,

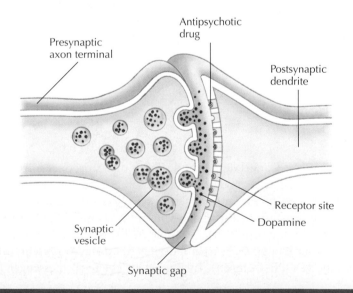

▲ FIGURE 12.6 Dopamine normally crosses the synapse between two neurons, activating the second cell. Antipsychotic drugs bind to the same receptor sites as dopamine does, blocking its action. In people suffering from schizophrenia, a reduction in dopamine activity can quiet a person's agitation and psychotic symptoms.

The Schizophrenic Brain

Several brain imaging methods (remember Chapter 2?) have made it possible to directly observe the living schizophrenic brain. Computed tomography (CT) scans and magnetic resonance imaging (MRI) scans, which can reveal brain structure, suggest that the brains of schizophrenics have shrunk (atrophied). For example, ▶▶ Figure 12.7 shows a CT scan (a computer-enhanced X-ray image) of the brain of John Hinkley, Jr., who shot former U.S. President Ronald Reagan and three other men in 1981. In the ensuing trial, Hinkley was declared insane. As you can see, his brain had wider than normal surface fissuring.

Similarly, MRI scans indicate that schizophrenic people tend to have enlarged ventricles (fluid-filled spaces

within the brain), again suggesting that surrounding brain tissue has withered (Barkataki et al., 2006). One possible explanation is that the schizophrenic brain may be unable to continually create new neurons to replace old ones that have died. In contrast, normal brains continue to produce new neurons (a process referred to as neurogenesis) throughout life (Toro & Deakin, 2007). It is telling that the affected areas are crucial for regulating

motivation, emotion, perception, actions, and attention (Gur et al., 1998; Walker et al., 2004).

Other methods provide images of brain activity, including positron emission tomography (PET) scans. To make a PET scan, a radioactive sugar solution is injected into a vein. When the sugar reaches the brain, an electronic device measures how much is used in each area. These data are then translated into a color map, or scan, of brain activity (▶▶ Figure 12.8). Researchers are finding patterns in such scans that are consistently linked with schizophrenia, affective disorders, and other problems. For instance, activity tends to be abnormally low in the frontal lobes of the schizophrenic brain (Durand & Barlow, 2010; Velakoulis & Pantelis, 1996).

Dennis Brack/stockphoto.com

▲ FIGURE 12.7 *(left)* CT scan of would-be presidential assassin John Hinkley, Jr., taken when he was 25. The X-ray image shows widened fissures in the wrinkled surface of Hinkley's brain. *(right)* CT scan of a normal 25-year-old's brain. In most young adults the surface folds of the brain are pressed together too tightly to be seen. As a person ages, surface folds of the brain normally become more visible. Pronounced brain fissuring in young adults may be a sign of schizophrenia, chronic alcoholism, or other problems.

NORMAL

SCHIZOPHRENIC

MANIC-DEPRESSIVE

The Brookhaven National Laboratory

▲ FIGURE 12.8 Positron emission tomography produces PET scans of the human brain. In the scans shown here, red, pink, and orange indicate lower levels of brain activity; white and blue indicate higher activity levels. Notice that activity in the schizophrenic brain is quite low in the frontal lobes (top area of each scan) (Velakoulis & Pantelis, 1996). Activity in the manic-depressive brain is low in the left brain hemisphere and high in the right brain hemisphere. The reverse is more often true of the schizophrenic brain. Researchers are trying to identify consistent patterns like these to aid diagnosis of mental disorders.

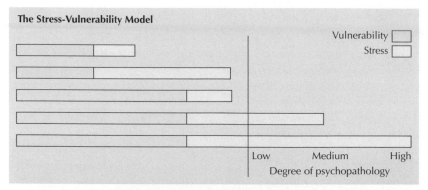

The Stress-Vulnerability Model

Vulnerability □
Stress □

Low   Medium   High
Degree of psychopathology

▲ **FIGURE 12.9** Various combinations of vulnerability and stress may produce psychological problems. The top bar shows low vulnerability and low stress. The result? No problem. The same is true of the next bar down, where low vulnerability is combined with moderate stress. Even high vulnerability (third bar) may not lead to problems if stress levels remain low. However, when high vulnerability combines with moderate or high stress (bottom two bars), the person "crosses the line" and suffers from psychopathology.

Stress-vulnerability model Attributes mental disorder like psychosis to a combination of environmental stress and inherited susceptibility.

glutamate, and other brain chemicals partly explain the devastating symptoms of schizophrenia (Walker et al., 2004). (See "The Schizophrenic Brain.")

Implications

In summary, the emerging picture of psychotic disorders such as schizophrenia takes this form: Anyone subjected to enough stress may be pushed to a psychotic break. (Battlefield psychosis is an example.) However, some people inherit a difference in brain chemistry or brain structure that makes them more susceptible—even to normal life stresses.

Thus, the right mix of inherited potential and environmental stress brings about mind-altering changes in brain chemicals and brain structure. This explanation is called a **stress-vulnerability model.** It attributes psychotic disorders to a blend of environmental stress and inherited susceptibility (Walker et al., 2004). The model seems to apply to other forms of psychopathology as well, such as depression (▶▶ Figure 12.9).

Despite advances in our understanding, psychosis remains "a riddle wrapped in a mystery inside an enigma." Let us hope that recent progress toward a cure for schizophrenia will continue.

study break

Psychosis, Delusional Disorders, and Schizophrenia

RECITE

1. Carol wrongly believes that her body is "rotting away." She is suffering from
   a. depressive hallucinations
   b. a delusion
   c. flat affect
   d. Alzheimer's disease
2. Colin, who has suffered a psychotic break, is hearing voices. This symptom is referred to as
   a. flat affect
   b. hallucination
   c. a word salad
   d. organic delusions
3. A psychosis caused by lead poisoning would be regarded as an organic disorder. T or F?
4. Hallucinations and personality disintegration are the principal features of paranoid psychosis. T or F?
5. Environmental explanations of schizophrenia emphasize emotional trauma and
   a. manic parents
   b. schizoaffective interactions
   c. psychedelic interactions
   d. disturbed family relationships

6. The _____ _____ of a schizophrenic person runs a 48 percent chance of also becoming psychotic.
7. Enlarged surface fissures and ventricles, as revealed by CT scans, are found only in the brains of chronic schizophrenics. T or F?

REFLECT

Critical Thinking

8. Researchers have found nearly double the normal number of dopamine receptor sites in the brains of schizophrenics. Why might that be important?
9. Enlarged surface fissures and ventricles are frequently found in the brains of chronic schizophrenics. Why is it a mistake to conclude that such features cause schizophrenia?

Relate

If you were writing a "recipe" for psychosis, what would the main "ingredients" be?

If you were asked to play the role of a paranoid person for a theater production, what symptoms would you emphasize?

You have been asked to explain the causes of schizophrenia to the parents of a schizophrenic teenager. What would you tell them?

ANSWERS

1. b 2. b 3. T 4. F 5. d 6. identical twin 7. F 8. Because of the extra receptors, schizophrenics may get psychedelic effects from normal levels of dopamine in the brain. 9. Because correlation does not confirm causation. Structural brain abnormalities are merely *correlated* with schizophrenia. They could be additional symptoms, rather than causes, of the disorder.

Mood Disorders—Peaks and Valleys

What are mood disorders? What causes them?

For some people, minor bouts of depression are as common as colds. But extreme swings of mood can be as disabling as a serious physical illness. In fact, depression can be deadly, because depressed persons may be suicidal. It is difficult to imagine how bleak and hopeless the world looks to a person who is deeply depressed, or how "crazy" it can be to ride a wave of mania. Let's explore mood disorders and their causes.

Psychologists have come to realize that **mood disorders** (major disturbances in emotion) are among the most serious of all psychological conditions. In any given year, roughly 9.5 percent of the U.S. population suffers from a mood disorder (National Institute of Mental Health, 2006b).

Two general types of mood disorder are depressive disorders and bipolar disorders (Nevid & Greene, 2005). (See ● Table 12.4.) In **depressive disorders,** sadness and despondency are exaggerated, prolonged, or unreasonable. Signs of a depressive disorder are dejection, hopelessness, and an inability to feel pleasure or to take interest in anything. Other common symptoms are fatigue, disturbed sleep and eating patterns, feelings of worthlessness, a very negative self-image, and thoughts of suicide. In **bipolar disorders,** people go both "up" and "down" emotionally (American Psychiatric Association, 2000).

Some mood disorders are long lasting but relatively moderate. If a person is mildly depressed for at least 2 years, the problem is called a **dysthymic disorder** (dis-THY-mik). If depression alternates with periods when the person's mood is cheerful, expansive, or irritable, the problem is a **cyclothymic disorder** (SIKE-lo-THY-mik). Even at this level, mood disorders can be debilitating. However, major mood disorders are much more damaging.

● Table 12.4 Mood Disorders

Depressive Disorders
  Major depressive disorder
  Dysthymic disorder
Bipolar Disorders
  Bipolar I disorder
  Bipolar II disorder
  Cyclothymic disorder

Source: American Psychiatric Association, 2000.

Major Mood Disorders

Major mood disorders are characterized by emotional extremes. The person who only goes "down" emotionally suffers from a **major depressive disorder.** During major depressive episodes, everything looks bleak and hopeless. The person has feelings of failure, worthlessness, and total despair. Suffering is intense and the person may become extremely subdued, withdrawn, or intensely suicidal. Suicide attempted during a major depression is rarely a "plea for help." Usually, the person intends to succeed and may give no prior warning.

In a **bipolar I disorder,** people experience both extreme mania and deep depression. During manic episodes, the person is loud, elated, hyperactive, grandiose, and energetic. Manic patients may go bankrupt in a matter of days, get arrested, or go on a binge of promiscuous sex. During periods of depression, the person is deeply despondent and possibly suicidal.

In a **bipolar II disorder** the person is mostly sad and guilt ridden, but has had one or more mildly manic episodes (called *hypomania*). That is, in a bipolar II disorder both elation and depression occur, but the person's mania is not as extreme as in a bipolar I disorder. Bipolar II patients who are hypomanic usually just manage to irritate everyone around them. They are excessively cheerful, aggressive, or irritable, and they may brag, talk too fast, interrupt conversations, or spend too much money (Nolen-Hoeksema, 2007).

In major depressive disorders, suicidal impulses can be intense and despair total.

Mood disorder Major disturbances in mood or emotion, such as depression or mania

Depressive disorders Emotional disorders primarily involving sadness, despondency, and depression.

Bipolar disorders Emotional disorders involving both depression and mania or hypomania.

Dysthymic disorder Moderate depression that persists for 2 years or more.

Cyclothymic disorder Moderate manic and depressive behavior that persists for 2 years or more.

Major mood disorders Disorders marked by lasting extremes of mood or emotion and sometimes accompanied by psychotic symptoms.

Major depressive disorder A mood disorder in which the person has suffered one or more intense episodes of depression.

Bipolar I disorder A mood disorder in which a person has episodes of mania (excited, hyperactive, energetic, grandiose behavior) and also periods of deep depression.

Bipolar II disorder A mood disorder in which a person is mostly depressed (sad, despondent, guilt ridden) but has also had one or more episodes of mild mania (hypomania).

In serious cases of depression it is impossible for a person to function at work or at school. Sometimes, depressed individuals cannot even feed or dress themselves. In cases of depression and/or mania that are even more severe, the person may also lose touch with reality and display psychotic symptoms.

How do major mood disorders differ from dysthymic and cyclothymic disorders? As mentioned, the major mood disorders involve more severe emotional changes. Also, major mood disorders more often appear to be **endogenous** (en-DODGE-eh-nus: produced from within) rather than a reaction to external events.

What Causes Mood Disorders?

Depression and other mood disorders have resisted adequate explanation and treatment. Some scientists are focusing on the biology of mood changes. They are interested in brain chemicals and transmitter substances, especially serotonin, noradrenaline, and dopamine levels. Their findings are incomplete, but progress has been made. For example, the chemical lithium carbonate can be effective for treating some cases of bipolar depression.

Other researchers seek psychological explanations. Psychoanalytic theory, for instance, holds that depression is caused by repressed anger. This rage is displaced and turned inward as self-blame and self-hate. As discussed in Chapter 11, behavioral theories of depression emphasize learned helplessness (LoLordo, 2001; Seligman, 1989). Cognitive psychologists believe that self-criticism and negative, distorted, or self-defeating thoughts underlie many cases of depression. (This view is discussed in Chapter 13.) Clearly, life stresses trigger many mood disorders (Maier, 2001). This is especially true for people who have personality traits and thinking patterns that make them vulnerable to depression (Dozois & Dobson, 2002).

Gender and Depression

Overall, women are twice as likely as men to experience depression (Kuehner, 2003). Researchers believe that social and environmental conditions are the main reason for this difference (Winstead & Sanchez, 2005). Factors that contribute to women's greater risk for depression include conflicts about birth control and pregnancy, work and parenting, and the strain of providing emotional support for others. Marital strife, sexual and physical abuse, and poverty are also factors. Nationwide, women and children are most likely to live in poverty. As a result, poor women frequently suffer the stresses associated with single parenthood, loss of control over their lives, poor housing, and dangerous neighborhoods (Stoppard & McMullen, 2003). One study found that women in the United States were most likely to be depressed if they lacked education, were unmarried, were Latina, had high stress levels, and experienced feelings of hopelessness (Myers et al., 2002).

Biology and Depression

Is heredity involved in the major mood disorders? Yes, especially in bipolar disorders (McGuffin et al., 2003). As a case in point, if one identical twin is depressed, the other has a 67 percent chance of suffering depression, too. For fraternal twins the probability is 19 percent. This difference may be related to the finding that people who have a particular version of a gene are more likely to become depressed when they are stressed (Caspi et al., 2003). As we have noted, psychological causes are important in many cases of depression. But for major mood disorders, biological factors seem to play a larger role. Surprisingly, one additional source of depression is related to the seasons.

Seasonal Affective Disorder

Unless you have experienced a winter of "cabin fever" in the far north, you may be surprised to learn that the rhythms of the seasons underlie **seasonal affective disorder (SAD),** or depression that occurs during only the fall and winter months. Almost anyone can get a little depressed when days are short, dark, and cold. But when a person's symptoms are lasting and disabling, the problem may be SAD. Here are some of the major symptoms of SAD,

Endogenous depression Depression that appears to be produced from within (perhaps by chemical imbalances in the brain), rather than as a reaction to life events.

Seasonal affective disorder (SAD) Depression that occurs only during fall and winter; presumably related to decreased exposure to sunlight.

according to Swedish psychiatrist Åsa Westrin and Canadian neuroscientist Raymond Lam (Westrin & Lam, 2007a):

- **Fatigue:** You feel too tired to maintain a normal routine.
- **Oversleeping and difficulty staying awake:** Your sleep patterns may be disturbed, and waking very early in the morning is common.
- **Craving:** You hunger for carbohydrates and sweets, leading to overeating and weight gain.
- **Inability to cope:** You feel irritable and stressed.
- **Social withdrawal:** You become unsocial in the winter but are socially active during other seasons.

Starting in the fall, people with SAD sleep longer but more poorly. During the day they feel tired and drowsy, and they tend to overeat. With each passing day, they become more sad, anxious, irritable, and socially withdrawn.

Although their depressions are usually not severe, many victims of SAD face each winter with a sense of foreboding. SAD is especially prevalent in northern latitudes (think of countries like Sweden and Canada), where days are very short during the winter (Michalak & Lam, 2002) (▶▶ Figure 12.10). For instance, one study found that 13 percent of college students living in northern New England showed signs of suffering from SAD (Low & Feissner, 1998). The students most likely to be affected were those who had moved from the South to attend college!

Seasonal depressions are related to the release of more melatonin during the winter. This hormone, which is secreted by the pineal gland in the brain, regulates the body's response to changing light conditions (Wehr et al., 2001). That's why 80 percent of SAD patients can be helped by extra doses of bright light, a remedy called phototherapy (▶▶ Figure 12.11). **Phototherapy** involves exposing SAD patients to one or more hours of very bright fluorescent light each day (Neumeister, 2004; Westrin & Lam, 2007b). This is best done early in the morning, where it simulates dawn in the summer (Avery et al., 2001). For many SAD sufferers, a hearty dose of morning "sunshine" appears to be the next best thing to vacationing in the tropics.

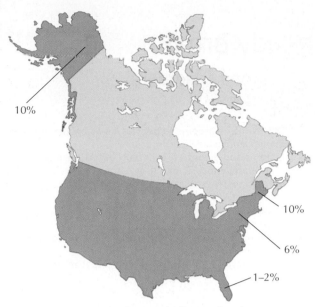

Rates of seasonal affective disorder, by latitude

▲ **FIGURE 12.10** Seasonal affective disorder appears to be related to reduced exposure to daylight during the winter. SAD affects 1 to 2 percent of Florida's population, about 6 percent of the people living in Maryland and New York City, and nearly 10 percent of the residents of New Hampshire and Alaska (Booker & Hellekson, 1992).

Angela Hampton/Alamy

▲ **FIGURE 12.11** An hour or more of bright light a day can dramatically reduce the symptoms of seasonal affective disorder. Treatment is usually necessary from fall through spring. Light therapy typically works best when it is used early in the morning (Avery et al., 2001).

Phototherapy A treatment for seasonal affective disorder that involves exposure to bright, full-spectrum light.

study break
Mood Disorders

RECITE

1. Dysthymic disorder is to depression as cyclothymic disorder is to manic depression. T or F?
2. Major mood disorders, especially bipolar disorders, often appear to be endogenous. T or F?
3. Learned helplessness is emphasized by _____ theories of depression.
   a. humanistic   b. biological
   c. behaviorist   d. psychoanalytic
4. The drug lithium carbonate has been shown to be an effective treatment for anxiety disorders. T or F?
5. The acronym SAD stands for schizotypal affective disorder. T or F?

REFLECT
Critical Thinking

6. How might relationships contribute to the higher rates of depression experienced by women?

Relate

How are the mentally ill stigmatized in movies and television dramas? Can you think of any positive portrayals (such as the film *A Beautiful Mind*)? How do you think such portrayals affect attitudes about mental disorders?

ANSWERS

1. T 2. T 3. c 4. F 5. F 6. Women tend to be more focused on relationships than men are. When listing the stresses in their lives, depressed women consistently report higher rates of relationship problems, such as loss of a friend, spouse, or lover, problems getting along with others, and illnesses suffered by people they care about. Depressed men tend to mention issues such as job loss, legal problems, and work problems (Kendler, Thornton, & Prescott, 2001).

Anxiety-Based Disorders—When Anxiety Rules

What problems result when a person suffers high levels of anxiety?

Anxiety refers to feelings of apprehension, dread, or uneasiness. We all feel anxiety, but anxiety that is out of proportion to a situation may reveal a problem. An example is a college student named Jian, who became unbearably anxious when he took exams. By the time Jian went to see a counselor, he had skipped several tests and was in danger of dropping out of school. In general, people with anxiety-related problems like Jian's display the following characteristics:

- High levels of anxiety and/or restrictive, self-defeating behavior patterns
- A tendency to use elaborate defense mechanisms or avoidance responses to get through the day
- Pervasive feelings of stress, insecurity, inferiority, and dissatisfaction with life

People with anxiety-related problems feel threatened and often can't do anything constructive about it. They struggle to control themselves but remain ineffective and unhappy (Rachman, 2004). In any given year, roughly 18 percent of the adult population suffers from an anxiety disorder (National Institute of Mental Health, 2006b).

If anxiety is a normal emotion, when does it signify a problem? A problem exists when intense anxiety prevents people from doing what they want or need to do. Also, their anxieties are out of control—they simply cannot stop worrying.

Adjustment Disorders

Do such problems cause a "nervous breakdown"? People suffering from anxiety-based problems may be miserable, but they rarely experience a "breakdown." Actually, the term *nervous breakdown* has no formal meaning. Nevertheless, a problem known as an *adjustment disorder* does come close to being something of a "breakdown."

Adjustment disorders occur when ordinary stresses push people beyond their ability to cope with life. Examples of such stresses are job loss, intense marital strife, and chronic physical illness. People suffering from an adjustment disorder may be extremely irritable, anxious, apathetic, or depressed. They also have trouble sleeping, lose their appetite, and suffer from various physical complaints. Often, their problems can be relieved by rest, sedation, supportive counseling, and a chance to "talk through" their fears and anxieties (American Psychiatric Association, 2000).

How is an adjustment disorder different from an anxiety disorder? The outward symptoms are similar. However, adjustment disorders disappear when a person's life circumstances improve (Jones, Yates, & Zhou, 2002). People suffering from anxiety disorders seem to generate their own misery, regardless of what's happening around them. They feel that they must be on guard against *future* threats that *could happen* at any time (Barlow, 2000).

Anxiety Disorders

In most anxiety disorders, distress seems greatly out of proportion to a person's circumstances. For example, consider the following description of Adrian H:

> She becomes very anxious that her children "might have been hurt or killed if they were out of the neighborhood playing and she hadn't heard from them in a couple of hours." She also worries all the time about her job performance and her relationships with men. Adrian believes that men rarely call back after a date or two because "they can sense I'm not a fun person." She never really relaxes, has difficulty focusing at work, has frequent headaches, and suffers from insomnia. (Adapted from Brown & Barlow, 2007)

Distress like Adrian H's is a key ingredient in anxiety disorders. It also may underlie dissociative and somatoform disorders, where maladaptive behavior serves to reduce anxiety and discomfort. To deepen your understanding, let's first examine the anxiety disorders themselves (● Table 12.5). Then we will see how anxiety contributes to other problems.

Generalized Anxiety Disorder

A person with a **generalized anxiety disorder** has been extremely anxious and worried for at least 6 months. Sufferers typically complain of sweating, a racing heart, clammy hands, dizziness, upset stomach, rapid breathing, irritability, and poor concentration. Overall, more women than men have these symptoms (Brown & Barlow, 2007).

Was Adrian H's problem a generalized anxiety disorder? Yes. However, if she also experienced *anxiety attacks,* then she would likely be diagnosed with panic disorder.

Panic Disorder (Without Agoraphobia)

In a **panic disorder (without agoraphobia),** people are highly anxious and also feel sudden, intense, unexpected panic. During a panic attack, victims experience chest pain, a racing heart, dizziness, choking, feelings of unreality, trembling, or fears of losing control. Many believe that they are having a heart attack, are going insane, or are about to die. Needless to say, this pattern leaves victims unhappy and uncomfortable much of the time. Again, the majority of people who suffer from panic disorder are women (Foot & Koszycki, 2004).

To get an idea of how a panic attack feels, imagine that you are trapped in your stateroom on a sinking ocean liner (the Titanic?). The room fills with water. When only a small air space remains near the ceiling and you are gasping for air, you'll know what a panic attack feels like.

Panic Disorder (with Agoraphobia)

In a **panic disorder (with agoraphobia),** people suffer from chronic anxiety and sudden panic. In addition, they have agoraphobia (ah-go-rah-FOBE-ee-ah), which is an intense *fear that a panic attack will occur* in a public place or unfamiliar situation. That is, agoraphobics intensely fear leaving their home and familiar surroundings. Typically, they find ways of avoiding places that frighten them—such as crowds, open roads, supermarkets, automo-

> ● Table 12.5 Anxiety Disorders
>
> **Generalized anxiety disorder**
> **Panic disorder**
> Without agoraphobia
> With agoraphobia
> **Agoraphobia (without a history of panic disorder)**
> **Specific phobia**
> **Social phobia**
> **Obsessive-compulsive disorder**
> **Acute stress disorder**
> **Posttraumatic stress disorder**
>
> *Source:* American Psychiatric Association, 2000.

Adjustment disorder An emotional disturbance caused by on-going stressors within the range of common experience.

Generalized anxiety disorder A chronic state of tension and worries about work, relationships, ability, or impending disaster.

Panic disorder (without agoraphobia) A chronic state of anxiety and also brief moments of sudden, intense, unexpected panic.

Panic disorder (with agoraphobia) A chronic state of anxiety and brief moments of sudden panic. The person fears that these panic attacks will occur in public places or unfamiliar situations.

biles, and so on. As a result, some agoraphobics are prisoners in their own homes (American Psychiatric Association, 2000).

Agoraphobia

The problem known as **agoraphobia** can also occur without panic. In this case, people *fear that something extremely embarrassing will happen* if they leave home or enter an unfamiliar situation. For example, an agoraphobic person may refuse to go outside because he or she fears having a sudden attack of dizziness, or diarrhea, or shortness of breath. Going outside the home alone, being in a crowd, standing in line, crossing a bridge, or riding in a car can be impossible for an agoraphobic person (American Psychiatric Association, 2000). About 4.2 percent of all adults suffer from agoraphobia (with or without panic) during their lifetime (Grant et al., 2006).

Specific Phobia

As we noted earlier, phobias are intense, irrational fears that a person cannot shake off, even when there is no real danger. In a **specific phobia,** the person's fear, anxiety, and avoidance are focused on particular objects, activities, or situations. People affected by phobias recognize that their fears are unreasonable, but they cannot control them. For example, a person with a spider phobia would find it impossible to ignore a picture of a spider, even though a photograph can't bite anyone (Miltner et al., 2004). Specific phobias can be linked to nearly any object or situation. In descending order of prevalence (Stinson et al., 2007), the most common specific phobias among Americans are:

Fear of insects, birds, snakes, or other animals (including, of course, arachnophobia, the fear of spiders, and zoophobia, fear of animals)

Acrophobia—fear of heights

Astraphobia—fear of storms, thunder, lightning

Aquaphobia—fear of being on or in water

Aviophobia—fear of airplanes

Claustrophobia—fear of closed spaces

Agoraphobia—fear of crowds

By combining the appropriate root word with the word "phobia," any number of fears can be named. Some are: triskaidekaphobia, fear of the number 13; xenophobia, fear of strangers; and hematophobia, fear of blood. One of your authors' favorites is coulrophobia, fear of clowns. Another is arachibutyrophobia, fear of peanut butter sticking to the roof of the mouth.

Almost everyone has a few mild phobias, such as fear of heights, closed spaces, or bugs and crawly things. A phobic disorder differs from such garden-variety fears in that it produces overwhelming fear. True phobias may lead to vomiting, wild climbing and running, or fainting. For a phobic disorder to exist, the person's fear must disrupt his or her daily life. Phobic persons are so threatened that they will go to almost any length to avoid the feared object or situation, such as driving 50 miles out of the way to avoid crossing a bridge. About 8 percent of all adults have phobic disorders during their lifetime (National Institute of Mental Health, 2006a).

Social Phobia

In **social phobia,** people fear situations in which they can be observed, evaluated, embarrassed, or humiliated by others. This leads them to avoid certain social situations, such as eating, writing, using the rest room, or speaking in public. When such situations cannot be avoided, people endure them with intense anxiety or distress. It is common for them to have uncomfortable physical symptoms, such as a pounding heart, shaking hands, sweating, diarrhea, mental confusion, and blushing. Social phobias greatly impair a person's ability to

For a person with a strong fear of snakes (ophidiophobia), merely looking at this picture may be unsettling.

Brent Stirton/The Image Bank/Getty Images

Agoraphobia (without panic) The fear that something extremely embarrassing will happen to if one leaves the house or enter unfamiliar situations.

Specific phobia An intense, irrational fear of specific objects, activities, or situations.

Social phobia An intense, irrational fear of being observed, evaluated, embarrassed, or humiliated by others in social situations.

work, attend school, and form personal relationships (American Psychiatric Association, 2000). About 7 percent of all adults are affected by social phobias in a given year (National Institute of Mental Health, 2006b).

Obsessive-Compulsive Disorder

People who suffer from **obsessive-compulsive disorder** are preoccupied with certain distressing thoughts and feel compelled to perform certain behaviors. You have probably experienced a mild obsessional thought, such as a song or stupid commercial jingle that repeats over and over in your mind. This may be irritating, but it's usually not terribly disturbing. True obsessions are images or thoughts that force their way into awareness against a person's will. They are so disturbing that they cause intense anxiety. The most common obsessions are about violence or harm (such as one's spouse being poisoned or hit by a car), about being "dirty" or "unclean," about whether one has performed some action (such as locking the door), and about committing immoral acts (Grabill et al., 2008).

Obsessions usually give rise to compulsions. These are irrational acts that a person feels driven to repeat. Often, compulsive acts help control or block out anxiety caused by an obsession. For example, a minister who finds profanities popping into her mind might start compulsively counting her heartbeat. Doing this would prevent her from thinking "dirty" words.

Many compulsive people are *checkers* or *cleaners*. For instance, a young mother who repeatedly pictures a knife plunging into her baby might check once an hour to make sure all the knives in her house are locked away. Doing so may reduce her anxieties, but it will probably also take over her life. Likewise, a person who feels "contaminated" from touching ordinary objects because "germs are everywhere" may be driven to wash his hands hundreds of times a day.

Of course, not all obsessive-compulsive disorders are so dramatic. Many simply involve extreme orderliness and rigid routine. Compulsive attention to detail and rigid following of rules help keep activities totally under control and make the highly anxious person feel more secure. (If such patterns are long-standing but less intense, they are classified as personality disorders, which we will discuss later in more detail.)

Bettmann/Corbis

Dennis Coon

The severe obsessions and compulsions of billionaire Howard Hughes led him to live as a recluse for more than 20 years. Hughes had an intense fear of contamination. To avoid infection, he constructed sterile, isolated environments in which his contact with people and objects was strictly limited by complicated rituals. Before handling a spoon, for instance, Hughes had his attendants wrap the handle in tissue paper and seal it with tape. A second piece of tissue was then wrapped around the first before he would touch it (Hodgson & Miller, 1982). A spoon prepared as Hughes required is shown at right.

Stress Disorders

Stress disorders occur when people experience stresses outside the range of normal human experience, such as floods, tornadoes, earthquakes, or horrible accidents. They affect many political hostages; combat veterans; prisoners of war; victims of terrorism, torture, violent crime, child molestation, rape, or domestic violence; and people who have witnessed a death or serious injury (Brown & Barlow, 2007).

Symptoms of stress disorders include repeated reliving of the traumatic event, avoidance of reminders of the event, and blunted emotions. Also common are insomnia, nightmares, wariness, poor concentration, irritability, and explosive anger or aggression. If such reactions last *less* than a month after a traumatic event, the problem is called an **acute stress disorder.** If they last *more* than a month, the person is suffering from **posttraumatic stress disorder (PTSD)** (Nemeroff et al., 2006).

If a situation causes distress, anxiety, or fear, we tend to avoid it in the future. This is a normal survival instinct. However, victims of PTSD fail to recover from these reactions. Military combat accounts for more than a quarter of the cases of PTSD among American men (Prigerson, Maciejewski, & Rosenheck, 2002). The constant threat of death and the gruesome sights and sounds of war take a terrible toll. Psychologists are already seeing high rates of PTSD among soldiers involved in combat in Iraq (Hoge et al., 2004). Sadly, 8 percent of

Obsessive-compulsive disorder An extreme preoccupation with certain thoughts and compulsive performance of certain behaviors.

Stress disorder A significant emotional disturbance caused by stresses outside the range of normal human experience.

Acute stress disorder A psychological disturbance lasting up to 1 month following stresses that would produce anxiety in anyone who experienced them.

Posttraumatic stress disorder (PTSD) A psychological disturbance lasting more than 1 month following stresses that would produce anxiety in anyone who experienced them.

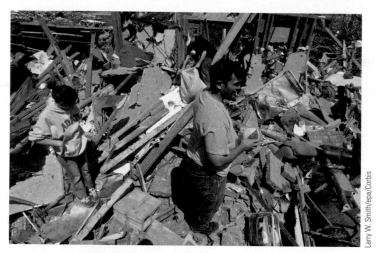
The 2008 U.S. tornado season killed many people and upset the lives of many more. In the aftermath of such disasters, many survivors suffer from acute stress reactions. For some, the flare-up of anxiety and distress occurs months or years after the stressful event, an example of a posttraumatic stress reaction.

military veterans still suffer from PTSD decades after they were in combat (Dirkzwager, Bramsen, & Van Der Ploeg, 2001). About 3.5 percent of adults suffer from posttraumatic stress in any given year (National Institute of Mental Health, 2006b).

Dissociative Disorders

In dissociative reactions we see striking episodes of *amnesia, fugue,* or *multiple identity*. **Dissociative amnesia** is an inability to recall one's name, address, or past. **Dissociative fugue** (fewg) involves sudden, unplanned travel away from home and confusion about personal identity. Dissociations are often triggered by highly traumatic events (McLewin & Muller, 2006). In such cases, forgetting personal identity and fleeing unpleasant situations appear to be defenses against intolerable anxiety.

A person suffering from a **dissociative identity disorder** has two or more separate identities or personality states. (Note that identity disorders are not the same as schizophrenia. Schizophrenia, which is a psychotic disorder, was discussed earlier in this chapter.) One famous and dramatic example of multiple identities is described in the book *Sybil* (Schreiber, 1973). Sybil reportedly had 16 different personality states. Each identity had a distinct voice, vocabulary, and posture. One personality could play the piano (not Sybil), but the others could not.

When an identity other than Sybil was in control, Sybil experienced a "time lapse," or memory blackout. Sybil's amnesia and alternate identities first appeared during childhood. As a girl she was beaten, locked in closets, perversely tortured, sexually abused, and almost killed. Sybil's first dissociations allowed her to escape by creating another person who would suffer torture in her place. Identity disorders often begin with unbearable childhood experiences, like those that Sybil endured. A history of childhood trauma, especially sexual abuse, is found in a high percentage of persons whose personalities split into multiple identities (McLewin & Muller, 2006; Simeon et al., 2002).

Flamboyant cases like Sybil's have led some experts to question the existence of multiple personalities (Casey, 2001). However, a majority of psychologists continue to believe that multiple identity is a real, if rare, problem (Cormier & Thelen, 1998).

Therapy for dissociative identity disorders may make use of hypnosis, which allows contact with the various personality states. The goal of therapy is *integration* and *fusion* of the identities into a single, balanced personality. Fortunately, multiple identity disorders are far rarer in real life than they are in TV dramas!

Somatoform Disorders

Have you ever known someone who appeared to be healthy but seemed to constantly worry about disease? These people are preoccupied with bodily functions, such as their heartbeat or breathing or digestion. Minor physical problems—even a small sore or an occasional cough—may convince them that they have cancer or some other dreaded disease. Typically, they can't give up their fears of illness, even if doctors can find no medical basis for their complaints (Korol, Craig, & Firestone, 2003).

Are you describing hypochondria? Yes. In **hypochondriasis** (HI-po-kon-DRY-uh-sis), people interpret normal bodily sensations as proof that they have a terrible disease. (See "Sick of Being Sick" for a related disorder with a curious twist.) In a problem called **somatization disorder** (som-ah-tuh-ZAY-shun), people express their anxieties through various bodily complaints. That is, they suffer from problems such as vomiting or nausea, shortness of breath, difficulty swallowing, or painful menstrual periods. Typically, the person feels ill much of the time and visits doctors repeatedly. Most sufferers take medicines or other treatments, but no physical cause can be found for their distress. Similarly, a person with **pain disorder** is disabled by pain that has no identifiable physical basis.

A rarer somatoform disorder ("body-form" disorder) is called a *conversion reaction*. In a **conversion disorder,** severe emotional conflicts are "converted" into symptoms that actu-

Dissociative amnesia Loss of memory (partial or complete) for important information related to personal identity.

Dissociative fugue Sudden travel away from home, plus confusion about one's personal identity.

Dissociative identity disorder The presence of two or more distinct personalities (multiple personality).

Hypochondriasis A preoccupation with fears of having a serious disease. Ordinary physical signs are interpreted as proof that the person has a disease, but no physical disorder can be found.

Somatization disorder Afflicted persons have numerous physical complaints. Typically, they have consulted many doctors, but no organic cause for their distress can be identified.

Pain disorder Pain that has no identifiable physical cause and appears to be of psychological origin.

Conversion disorder A bodily symptom that mimics a physical disability but is actually caused by anxiety or emotional distress.

Sick of Being Sick

At 14, Ben was in the hospital again for his sinus problem. He had already undergone 40 surgeries since the age of 8. In addition, he had been diagnosed at various times with bipolar disorder, oppositional defiant disorder, and attention deficit disorder. Ben was taking 19 different medications, and his mother said she desperately wanted him to be "healed." She sought numerous tests and never missed an appointment. But at long last, it became clear that there was nothing wrong with Ben. Left alone with doctors, Ben revealed that he was "sick of being sick."

In reality, it was Ben's mother who was sick. She was eventually diagnosed as suffering from **Munchausen syndrome by proxy** (Awadallah et al., 2005). This is a pattern in which a person fakes the medical problems of someone in his or her care. (In **Munchausen syndrome,** the person fakes his or her own medical problems.) As in Ben's case, most people with the syndrome are mothers who fabricate their children's illnesses. Sometimes they even deliberately harm their children. For example, one mother injected her son with 7-Up (Reisner, 2006).

But why? People who suffer from Munchausen syndrome and Munchausen syndrome by proxy appear to have a pathological need to seek attention and sympathy from medical profes-sionals. They may also win praise for being health conscious or a good parent (American Psychiatric Association, 2000).

This case illustrates another point about psychological disorders: Ben's mother was eventually diagnosed with several disorders, including Munchausen by proxy, schizoaffective disorder, and borderline personality disorder. As this suggests, many disturbed people are *comorbid.* That is, they suffer from more than one disorder at a time. Not only does comorbidity increase their misery, it makes it more difficult for health care providers to diagnose and treat them.

---

ally disturb physical functioning or closely resemble a physical disability. For instance, a soldier might become deaf or lame or develop "glove anesthesia" just before a battle.

What is "glove anesthesia"? "Glove anesthesia" is a loss of sensitivity in the areas of the skin that would normally be covered by a glove. Glove anesthesia shows that conversion symptoms often contradict known medical facts. The system of nerves in the hands does not form a glove-like pattern and could not cause such symptoms (▸▸ Figure 12.12).

Uncontrollable sneezing, which is often a conversion disorder, may continue for days or weeks. In such cases, sneezing is abnormal in rate and rhythm. In addition, the person's eyes do not close during a sneeze and sneezing does not occur during sleep. (A normal sneeze is shown here.) All of these signs suggest that the cause of the sneezing is psychological, not physical (Fochtmann, 1995).

Adam Barnes/Getty Images

Response in Conversion Reaction

Arm extension is followed by involuntary flexion of the stretched muscle, indicating reserve strength

Response in Organic Paralysis

Arm is easily extended by examiner's force

(a)

(b)

⏶ **FIGURE 12.12** *(left)* "Glove" anesthesia is a conversion reaction involving loss of feeling in areas of the hand that would be covered by a glove *(a)*. If the anesthesia were physically caused, it would follow the pattern shown in *(b)*. *(right)* To test for organic paralysis of the arm, an examiner can suddenly extend the arm, stretching the muscles. A conversion reaction is indicated if the arm pulls back involuntarily. (Adapted from Weintraub, 1983.)

Munchausen syndrome by proxy An affected person fakes the medical problems of someone in his or her care in order to gain attention.

Munchausen syndrome An affected person fakes his or her own medical problems in order to gain attention.

If symptoms disappear when a victim is asleep, hypnotized, or anesthetized, a conversion reaction must be suspected (Russo et al., 1998). Another sign to watch for is that victims of conversion reactions are strangely unconcerned about suddenly being disabled.

Anxiety and Disorder—Four Pathways to Trouble

How do psychologists explain anxiety-based disorders?

What causes anxiety disorders? Susceptibility to anxiety-based disorders appears to be partly inherited (Rachman, 2004). Studies show that being high strung, nervous, or emotional runs in families. For example, 60 percent of children born to parents suffering from panic disorder have a fearful, inhibited temperament. Such children are irritable and wary as infants, shy and fearful as toddlers, and quiet and cautious introverts in elementary school. By the time they reach adulthood, they are at high risk for anxiety problems, such as panic attacks (Barlow, 2000; Durand & Barlow, 2010).

There are at least four major psychological perspectives on the causes of dissociative, anxiety-based, and somatoform disorders. These are (1) the *psychodynamic* approach, (2) the *humanistic-existential* approach, (3) the *behavioral* approach, and (4) the *cognitive* approach.

Psychodynamic Approach

The term *psychodynamic* refers to internal motives, conflicts, unconscious forces, and other dynamics of mental life. Freud was the first to propose a psychodynamic explanation for what he called "neurosis." According to Freud, disturbances like those we have described represent a raging conflict among subparts of the personality—the id, ego, and superego.

Freud emphasized that intense anxiety can be caused by forbidden id impulses for sex or aggression that threaten to break through into behavior. The person constantly fears doing something "crazy" or forbidden. She or he may also be tortured by guilt, which the superego uses to suppress forbidden impulses. Caught in the middle, the ego is eventually overwhelmed. This forces the person to use rigid defense mechanisms and misguided, inflexible behavior to prevent a disastrous loss of control (see Chapter 10).

Humanistic-Existential Approaches

Humanistic theories emphasize subjective experience, human problems, and personal potentials. Humanistic psychologist Carl Rogers regarded emotional disorders as the end product of a faulty self-image or self-concept (Rogers, 1959). Rogers believed that anxious individuals have built up unrealistic mental images of themselves. This leaves them vulnerable to contradictory information. Let's say, for example, that an essential part of Cheyenne's self-image is the idea that she is highly intelligent. If Cheyenne does poorly in school, she may deny or distort her perceptions of herself and the situation. Should Cheyenne's anxiety become severe, she may resort to using defense mechanisms. A conversion reaction, anxiety attacks, or similar symptoms could also result from threats to her self-image. These symptoms, in turn, would become new threats that provoke further distortions. Soon, she would fall into a vicious cycle of maladjustment and anxiety that feeds on itself once started.

Existentialism focuses on the elemental problems of existence, such as death, meaning, choice, and responsibility. Psychologists who take a more existential view stress that unhealthy anxiety reflects a loss of *meaning* in one's life. According to them, we must show *courage* and *responsibility* in our choices if life is to have meaning. Too often, they say, we give in to "existential anxiety" and back away from life-enhancing choices. Existential anxiety is the unavoidable anguish that comes from knowing we are personally responsible for our lives. Hence, we have a crushing need to choose wisely and courageously as we face life's empty and impersonal void. Adolescents may experience considerable existential anxiety as they develop their identity (Berman, Weems, & Stickle, 2006).

From the existential view, people who are anxious are living in "bad faith." That is, they have collapsed in the face of the awesome responsibility to choose a meaningful existence. In short, they have lost their way in life. From this point of view, making choices that don't truly reflect what you value, feel, and believe can make you sick.

Behavioral Approach

Behaviorist approaches emphasize overt, observable behavior and the effects of learning and conditioning. Behaviorists assume that the "symptoms" we have discussed are learned, just as other behaviors are. You might recall from Chapter 6, for instance, that phobias can be acquired through classical conditioning. Similarly, anxiety attacks may reflect conditioned emotional responses that generalize to new situations, and the hypochondriac's "sickness behavior" may be reinforced by the sympathy and attention he or she gets. One point that all theorists agree on is that disordered behavior is ultimately self-defeating because it makes the person more miserable in the long run, even though it temporarily lowers anxiety.

But if the person becomes more miserable in the long run, how does the pattern get started? The behavioral explanation is that self-defeating behavior begins with avoidance learning (described in Chapter 6). Avoidance learning occurs when making a response delays or prevents the onset of a painful or unpleasant stimulus. Here's a quick review to refresh your memory:

> An animal is placed in a special cage. After a few minutes a light comes on, followed a moment later by a painful shock. Quickly, the animal escapes into a second chamber. After a few minutes, a light comes on in this chamber, and the shock is repeated. Soon the animal learns to avoid pain by moving before the shock occurs. Once an animal learns to avoid the shock, it can be turned off altogether. A well trained animal may avoid the nonexistent shock indefinitely.

The same analysis can be applied to human behavior. A behaviorist would say that the powerful reward of immediate relief from anxiety keeps self-defeating avoidance behaviors alive. This view, known as the **anxiety reduction hypothesis,** seems to explain why the behavior patterns we have discussed often look very "stupid" to outside observers.

Cognitive Approach

The cognitive view is that distorted thinking causes people to magnify ordinary threats and failures, which leads to distress (Provencher, Dugas, & Ladouceur, 2004). For example, Bonnie, who is socially phobic, constantly has upsetting thoughts about being evaluated at school. One reason for this is that people with social phobias tend to be perfectionists. Like other social phobics, Bonnie is excessively concerned about making mistakes. She also perceives criticism where none exists. If Bonnie expects that a social situation will focus too much attention on her, she avoids it (Brown & Barlow, 2007). Even when socially phobic persons are successful, distorted thoughts lead them to believe they have failed (Barlow, 2002). In short, changing the thinking patterns of anxious individuals like Bonnie can greatly lessen their fears (Hall, 2006).

Implications

All four psychological explanations probably contain a core of truth. For this reason, understanding anxiety-based disorders may be aided by combining parts of each perspective. Each viewpoint also suggests a different approach to treatment. Because many possibilities exist, therapy is discussed later, in Chapter 13.

Anxiety reduction hypothesis Explains the self-defeating nature of avoidance responses as a result of the reinforcing effects of relief from anxiety.

Personality Disorders—Blueprints for Maladjustment

What is a personality disorder?

"Get out of here and leave me alone so I can die in peace," Judy screamed at her nurses in the seclusion room of the psychiatric hospital. On one of her arms, long dark red marks mingled with the scars of previous suicide attempts. Judy once bragged that her record was 67 stitches. Today, the nurses had to strap her into restraints to keep her from gouging her own eyes. She was given a sedative and slept for 12 hours. She woke calmly and asked for her therapist—even though her latest outburst began when he canceled a morning appointment and changed it to afternoon.

Judy has a condition called *borderline personality disorder*. Although she is capable of working, Judy has repeatedly lost jobs because of her turbulent relationships with other people. At times she can be friendly and a real charmer. At other times she is extremely unpredictable, moody, and even suicidal. Being a friend to Judy can be a fearsome challenge. Canceling an appointment, forgetting a special date, making a wrong turn of phrase—these and similar small incidents may trigger Judy's rage or a suicide attempt. Like other people with borderline personality disorder, Judy is extremely sensitive to ordinary criticism, which leaves her feeling rejected and abandoned. Typically, she reacts with anger, self-hatred, and impulsive behavior. These "emotional storms" damage her personal relationships and leave her confused about who she is (Siever & Koenigsberg, 2000).

Maladaptive Personality Patterns

As stated earlier, a person with a personality disorder has maladaptive personality traits. For example, people with a paranoid personality disorder are suspicious, hypersensitive, and wary of others. Narcissistic persons need constant admiration, and they are lost in fantasies of power, wealth, brilliance, beauty, or love. Celebrities appear more likely to be narcissistic than noncelebrities, perhaps because they receive so much attention (Young & Pinsky, 2006). The dependent personality suffers from extremely low self-confidence. Dependent persons allow others to run their lives, and they place everyone else's needs ahead of their own. People with a histrionic personality disorder constantly seek attention by dramatizing their emotions and actions.

Typically, patterns such as the ones just described begin during adolescence or even childhood. Thus, personality disorders are deeply rooted and usually span many years. The list of personality disorders is long (● Table 12.6), so let us focus on a single frequently misunderstood problem, the antisocial personality.

Antisocial Personality

What are the characteristics of an antisocial personality? A person with an **antisocial personality** lacks a conscience. Such people are impulsive, selfish, dishonest, emotionally shallow, and manipulative. Antisocial persons, who are sometimes called *sociopaths* or *psychopaths,* are poorly socialized and seem to be incapable of feeling guilt, shame, fear, loyalty, or love (American Psychiatric Association, 2000).

● **Table 12.6 Personality Disorders and Typical Degree of Impairment**

MODERATE IMPAIRMENT

Dependent	You lack confidence and you are extremely submissive and dependent on others (clinging).
Histrionic	You are dramatic and flamboyant; you exaggerate your emotions to get attention from others.
Narcissistic	You think you are wonderful, brilliant, important, and worthy of constant admiration.
Antisocial	You are irresponsible, lack guilt or remorse, and engage in antisocial behavior, such as aggression, deceit, or recklessness.

HIGH IMPAIRMENT

Obsessive-compulsive	You demand order, perfection, control, and rigid routine at all times.
Schizoid	You feel very little emotion and can't form close personal relationships with others.
Avoidant	You are timid, uncomfortable in social situations, and fear evaluation.

SEVERE IMPAIRMENT

Borderline	Your self-image, moods, and impulses are erratic, and you are extremely sensitive to any hint of criticism, rejection, or abandonment by others.
Paranoid	You deeply distrust others and are suspicious of their motives, which you perceive as insulting or threatening.
Schizotypal	You are a loner, you engage in extremely odd behavior, and your thought patterns are bizarre, but you are not actively psychotic.

Source: American Psychiatric Association, 2000.

Antisocial personality A person who lacks a conscience, is emotionally shallow, impulsive, selfish, and tends to manipulate others.

Are sociopaths dangerous? Sociopaths tend to have a long history of conflict with society. Many are delinquents or criminals who may be a threat to the general public (Ogloff, 2006). However, sociopaths are rarely the crazed murderers you may have seen portrayed on TV and in movies. In fact, many sociopaths are "charming" at first. Their "friends" only gradually become aware of the sociopath's lying and self-serving manipulation. One study found that psychopaths are "blind" to signs of disgust in others. This may add to their capacity for cruelty and their ability to use others (Kosson et al., 2002). Many successful businesspersons, entertainers, politicians, and other seemingly normal people have sociopathic leanings. Basically, antisocial persons coldly use others and cheat their way through life (Ogloff, 2006).

More than 65 percent of all persons with antisocial personalities have been arrested, usually for crimes such as robbery, vandalism, and rape.

Causes

What causes sociopathy? Typically, people with antisocial personalities showed similar problems in childhood (Burt et al., 2007). Many were emotionally deprived and physically abused as children (Pollock et al., 1990). Adult sociopaths also display subtle neurological problems (▶▶ Figure 12.13). For example, they have unusual brain-wave patterns that suggest underarousal of the brain. This may explain why sociopaths tend to be thrill seekers. Quite likely, they are searching for stimulation strong enough to overcome their chronic underarousal and feelings of "boredom" (Hare, 2006).

In a revealing study, sociopaths were shown extremely grisly and unpleasant photographs of mutilations. The photos were so upsetting that they visibly startled normal people. The sociopaths, however, showed no startle response to the photos (Levenston et al., 2000). (They didn't "bat an eyelash.") Those with antisocial personalities might therefore be described as *emotionally cold*. They simply do not feel normal pangs of conscience, guilt, or anxiety (Blair et al., 2006). Again, this coldness seems to account for an unusual ability to calmly lie, cheat, steal, or take advantage of others.

Can sociopathy be treated? Antisocial personality disorders are rarely treated with success (Hare, 2006). All too often, sociopaths manipulate therapy, just like any other situation. If it is to their advantage to act "cured," they will do so. However, they return to their former behavior patterns as soon as possible. On a more positive note, antisocial behavior does tend to decline somewhat after age 40, even without treatment, because people tend to become more "mellow" as they age (Laub & Sampson, 2003).

▲ **FIGURE 12.13** Using PET scans, Canadian psychologist Robert Hare found that the normally functioning brain *(left)* lights up with activity when a person sees emotion-laden words such as "maggot" or "cancer." But the brain of a psychopath *(right)* remains inactive, especially in areas associated with feelings and self-control. When Dr. Hare showed the right image to several neurologists, one asked, "Is this person from Mars?"

Disorders in Perspective—Psychiatric Labeling

As we conclude our survey of psychological disorders, a caution is in order. The terms we have reviewed in this chapter are meant to aid communication about human problems. But if used maliciously or carelessly, they can hurt people. (See "A Disease Called Freedom.") Everyone has felt or acted "crazy" during brief periods of stress or high emotion. People with psychological disorders have problems that are more severe or long lasting than most of us experience. Otherwise, they may not be that different from the rest of us.

A fascinating classic study carried out by psychologist David Rosenhan illustrates the impact of psychiatric labeling. Rosenhan and several colleagues had themselves committed to mental hospitals with a diagnosis of "schizophrenia" (Rosenhan, 1973). After being admitted, each of these "pseudo-patients" dropped all pretense of mental illness. Yet, even

human diversity

A Disease Called Freedom

The year is 1840. You are a slave who has tried repeatedly to escape from a cruel and abusive master. You want to be free. An expert is consulted about your "abnormal" behavior. His conclusion? You are suffering from "drapetomania," a mental "disorder" that causes slaves to run away (Wakefield, 1992). Your "cure"? The expert will cut off your toes.

As this example suggests, psychiatric terms are easily abused. Historically, some have been applied to culturally disapproved behaviors that are not really disorders. Another of our personal favorites is the long-outdated diagnosis of "anarchia," a form of insanity that leads one to seek a more democratic society (Brown, 1990).

All of the following were also once considered disorders: childhood masturbation, lack of vaginal orgasm, self-defeating personality (applied mainly to women), homosexuality, and nymphomania (a woman with a healthy sexual appetite) (Wakefield, 1992). Even today, race, gender, and social class continue to affect the diagnosis of various disorders (Durand & Barlow, 2010; Poland & Caplan, 2004).

Gender is probably the most common source of bias in judging normality because standards tend to be based on males (Nolen-Hoeksema, 2007; Widiger, 2005). According to psychologist Paula Caplan (1995) and others, women are penalized both for conforming to female stereotypes and for ignoring them. If a woman is independent, aggressive, and unemotional, she may be considered "unhealthy." Yet at the same time, a woman who is vain, emotional, irrational, and dependent on others (all "feminine" traits in our culture) may be classified as having a personality disorder (Bornstein, 1996). Indeed, a majority of persons classified as having dependent personality disorder are women. In view of this, Paula Caplan asks, why isn't there a category called "delusional dominating personality disorder" for obnoxious men (Caplan, 1995)?

Because biases can influence perceptions of disorder and normality, it is worth being cautious before you leap to conclusions about the mental health of others (American Psychiatric Association, 2000). (They might be doing an assignment for their psychology class!)

---

though they acted completely normal, none of the researchers was ever recognized by hospital *staff* as a phony patient. Real patients were not so easily fooled. It was not unusual for a patient to say to one of the researchers, "You're not crazy, you're checking up on the hospital!" or "You're a journalist."

To record his observations, Rosenhan took notes by carefully jotting things on a small piece of paper hidden in his hand. However, he soon learned that stealth was totally unnecessary. Rosenhan simply walked around with a clipboard, recording observations. No one questioned this behavior. Rosenhan's note taking was just regarded as a symptom of his "illness." This observation clarifies why staff members failed to detect the fake patients. Because they were in a mental ward, and because they had been *labeled* schizophrenic, anything the pseudo-patients did was seen as a symptom of psychopathology.

As Rosenhan's study shows, it is far better to label *problems* than to label people. Think of the difference in impact between saying, "You are experiencing a serious psychological disorder" and, "You're a schizophrenic." Which statement would you prefer to have said about yourself?

Social Stigma

An added problem with psychiatric labeling is that it frequently leads to prejudice and discrimination. That is, the mentally ill in our culture are often *stigmatized* (rejected and disgraced). People who have been labeled mentally ill (at any time in their lives) are less likely to be hired. They also tend to be denied housing and they are more likely to be falsely accused of crimes. Thus, people who are grappling with mental illness may be harmed as much by social stigma as they are by their immediate psychological problems (Corrigan & Penn, 1999).

A Look Ahead

Treatments for psychological problems range from counseling and psychotherapy to mental hospitalization and drug therapy. Because they vary greatly, a complete discussion of therapies is found in the next chapter. For now, it's worth noting that many milder mental disorders can be treated successfully. Even major disorders may respond well to drugs and other techniques. It is wrong to fear "former mental patients" or to exclude them from work, friendships, and other social situations. A struggle with major depression or a psychotic episode does not inevitably lead to lifelong dysfunction. Too often, however, it does lead to unnecessary rejection based on groundless fears (Sarason & Sarason, 2005).

Let's conclude with a look at a widely misunderstood problem: By the time you finish reading this page, someone in the United States will have attempted suicide. What can be done about suicide? The upcoming Psychology in Action section provides some answers.

RECITE

1. Excessive anxiety over ordinary life stresses is characteristic of which of the following disorders?
   a. PTSD   b. agoraphobia
   c. hypochondriasis   d. adjustment disorder
2. Panic disorder can occur with or without agoraphobia, but agoraphobia cannot occur alone, without the presence of a panic disorder. T or F?
3. Alice has a phobic fear of closed spaces. What is the formal term for her fear?
   a. nyctophobia   b. claustrophobia
   c. pathophobia   d. pyrophobia
4. A person who intensely fears eating, writing, or speaking in public suffers from _____ _____.
5. "Checkers" and "cleaners" suffer from which disorder?
   a. acarophobia   b. panic disorder with agoraphobia
   c. generalized anxiety disorder   d. obsessive-compulsive disorder
6. Which of the following is NOT a dissociative disorder?
   a. fugue   b. amnesia
   c. conversion reaction   d. multiple identity
7. Which of the following personality disorders is associated with an inflated sense of self-importance and a constant need for attention and admiration?
   a. narcissistic   b. antisocial
   c. paranoid   d. manipulative
8. Antisocial personality disorders are difficult to treat, but there is typically a decline in antisocial behavior a year or two after adolescence. T or F?

REFLECT

Critical Thinking

9. Many of the physical complaints associated with anxiety disorders are closely related to activity of what part of the nervous system?

Relate

Many of the qualities that define personality disorders exist to a minor degree in normal personalities. Try to think of a person you know who has some of the characteristics described for each type of personality disorder.

Which of the anxiety disorders would you *least* want to suffer from? Why?

What is the key difference between a stress disorder and an adjustment disorder? (Review both discussions if you don't immediately know the answer.)

ANSWERS

1. d   2. F   3. b   4. social phobia   5. d   6. c   7. a   8. F   9. The autonomic nervous system (ANS), especially the sympathetic branch of the ANS.

psychology in action
Suicide—Lives on the Brink

Why do people commit suicide? Can suicide be prevented?

Talk show host Phil Donahue once commented that "suicide is a permanent solution to a temporary problem." If this is so obvious, then why is suicide so distressingly common? In North America, for every three people who die by homicide, five will kill themselves. And there may be as many as 25 attempts for every "successful" suicide (National Institute of Mental Health [NIMH], 2003). Sooner or later you are likely to be affected by the suicide attempt of someone you know.

What factors affect suicide rates? Suicide rates vary greatly, but some general patterns do emerge.

Sex Men are "better" at suicide than women. Four times as many men *complete* suicide, but women make more attempts (NIMH, 2006b). Male suicide attempts are more lethal because men typically use a gun or an equally fatal method (Garland & Zigler, 1993). Women most often attempt a drug overdose, so there's a better chance of help arriving before death occurs. Sadly, women are beginning to use more deadly methods and may soon equal men in their likelihood of death by suicide.

Ethnicity Suicide rates vary dramatically from country to country. The rate in the United States is almost ten times higher than the rate in Azerbaijan, and in turn the rate in Hungary is more than three times the U.S. rate (Lester & Yang, 2005). Within the United States, Caucasians generally have higher suicide rates than non-Caucasians (▶▶ Figure 12.14), although rates have increased among African Americans in recent years (Griffin-Fennell & Williams, 2006). Sadly, the suicide rate among Native Americans is by far the highest in the country (suicide rates are equally high among the aboriginal peoples of Australia and New Zealand) (Goldston et al., 2008; McKenzie, Serfaty, & Crawford, 2003).

Age Suicide rates increase with advancing age. More than half of all suicide victims are over 45 years old (see Figure 12.14). White males 65 years and older are particularly at risk. Of special concern is the rate of suicide among younger people. Between 1950 and 1990, suicide rates for adolescents and young adults doubled (Durand & Barlow, 2006). Among college students, suicide is the third leading cause of death (Jamison, 2001). School is a factor in some suicides, but only in the sense that suicidal students were not living up to their own extremely high standards. Many were good students. Other important factors in student suicide are cocaine or alcohol use (Garlow, Purselle, & Heninger, 2007), chronic health problems (real or imagined), and interpersonal difficulties (some who commit suicide are rejected lovers, but others are simply withdrawn and friendless people).

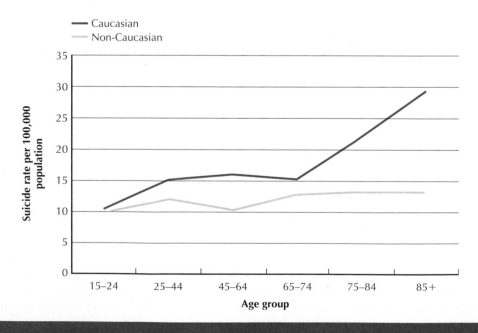

FIGURE 12.14 In the United States, suicide rates for Caucasians are higher than those for non-Caucasians. Also, older people have higher suicide rates than younger people (CDC, 2003).

Marital Status Marriage (when successful) may be the best natural guard against suicidal impulses. Married individuals have lower rates than the divorced, the widowed, and single persons (Yip & Thorburn, 2004).

Immediate Causes of Suicide

Why do people try to kill themselves? The best explanation for suicide may simply come from a look at the conditions that precede it. A diagnosable mental disorder (usually depression or substance abuse disorder) is a factor in 90 percent of all suicides (NIMH, 2006). Suicidal people usually have a history of trouble with family, a lover, or a spouse. Often they have drinking or drug abuse problems, sexual adjustment problems, or job difficulties.

The following are all major risk factors for suicide (NIMH, 2003; Rudd, Joiner, & Rajab, 2001): drug or alcohol abuse; a prior suicide attempt; depression or other mood disorder; feelings of hopelessness or worthlessness; antisocial, impulsive, or aggressive behavior; severe anxiety; panic attacks; a family history of suicidal behavior; shame, humiliation, failure, or rejection; and the availability of a firearm. Among ethnic adolescents, loss of face, acculturative stress, racism, and discrimination have been identified as additional risk factors (Goldston et al., 2008).

Typically, suicidal people isolate themselves from others, feel worthless, helpless, and misunderstood, and want to die. An extremely negative self-image and severe feelings of hopelessness are warnings that the risk for suicide is very high (Heisel, Flett, & Hewitt, 2003). However, a long history of such conditions is not always necessary to produce a desire for suicide. Anyone may temporarily reach a state of depression severe enough to attempt suicide. Most dangerous for the average person are times of divorce, separation, rejection, failure, and bereavement. Such situations can seem intolerable and motivate an intense desire to escape, to obtain relief, or to die (Boergers, Spirito, & Donaldson, 1998). For young people, feelings of anger and hostility add to the danger. When the impulse to harm others is turned inward, the risk for suicide increases dramatically (Jamison, 2001).

Preventing Suicide

Is it true that people who talk about or threaten suicide are rarely the ones who try it? No, this is a major fallacy. Of every ten potential suicides, eight give warning beforehand. A person who threatens suicide should be taken seriously. (See ▶▶ Figure 12.15.) A suicidal person may say nothing more than "I feel sometimes like I'd be better off dead." Warnings may also come indirectly. If a friend gives you a favorite ring and says, "Here, I won't be needing this anymore," or comments, "I guess I won't get my watch fixed—it doesn't matter anyway," it may be a plea for help.

| Suicidal thoughts | → | Suicidal threats | → | Suicide attempts | → | Completed suicide |

▲ FIGURE 12.15 Suicidal behavior usually progresses from suicidal thoughts, to threats, to attempts. A person is unlikely to make an attempt without first making threats. Thus, suicide threats should be taken seriously (Garland & Zigler, 1993).

The warning signs in the list that follows, especially if they are observed in combination, can signal an impending suicide attempt (Leenaars, Lester, & Wenckstern, 2005; Slaby, Garfinkel, & Garfinkel, 1994):

- Withdrawal from contact with others
- Sudden swings in mood
- Recent occurrence of life crisis or emotional shock
- Personality change
- Gift giving of prized possessions
- Depression/hopelessness
- Aggression and/or risk taking
- Single-car accident
- Preoccupation with death
- Drug use
- Death imagery in art
- Direct threats to commit suicide

Is it true that suicide can't be prevented, that the person will find a way to do it anyway? No. Suicide attempts usually come when a person is alone, depressed, and unable to view matters objectively. You *should* intervene if someone seems to be threatening suicide.

It is estimated that about two thirds of all suicide attempts are made by people who do not really want to die. Almost a third more are *ambivalent* or undecided about dying. Only 3 to 5 percent of suicide cases involve people who really want to die. Most people, therefore, are relieved when someone comes to their aid. Remember that suicide is almost always a cry for help and that you *can* help.

How to Help

What is the best thing to do if someone hints at thinking about suicide? It helps to know some of the common characteristics of suicidal thoughts and feelings (Leenaars, Lester, & Wenckstern, 2005):

1. **Escape.** At times, everyone feels like running away from an upsetting situation. Running away from home, quitting school, abandoning a marriage—these are all departures. Suicide, of course, is the ultimate escape. It helps when suicidal persons see that the natural wish for escape doesn't have to be expressed by ending it all.

2. **Unbearable psychological pain.** Emotional pain is what the suicidal person is seeking to escape. A goal of anyone hoping to prevent suicide should be to reduce the pain in any way possible. Ask the person, "Where does it hurt?" Suicide occurs when pain exceeds a person's resources for coping with pain.

3. **Frustrated psychological needs.** Often, suicide can be prevented if a distressed person's frustrated needs can be identified and eased. Is the person deeply frustrated in his or her search for love, achievement, trust, security, or friendship?

4. **Constriction of options.** The suicidal person feels helpless and decides that death is the *only* solution. The person has narrowed all his or her options solely to death. The rescuer's goal, then, is to help broaden the person's perspective. Even when all the choices are unpleasant, suicidal persons can usually be made to see that their *least unpleasant option* is better than death.

Knowing these patterns will give some guidance in talking to a suicidal person. In addition, your most important task may be to establish *rapport* (a harmonious connection) with the person. You should offer support, acceptance, and legitimate caring.

Remember that a suicidal person feels misunderstood. Try to accept and understand the feelings the person is expressing. Acceptance should also extend to the idea of suicide itself. It is completely acceptable to ask, "Are you thinking of suicide?"

Establishing communication with suicidal persons may be enough to carry them through a difficult time. You may also find it helpful to get day-by-day commitments from them to meet for lunch, share a ride, and the like. Let the person know you *expect* her or him to be there. Such commitments, even though small, can be enough to tip the scales when a person is alone and thinking about suicide.

Don't end your efforts too soon. A dangerous time for suicide is when a person suddenly seems to get better after a severe depression. This often means the person has finally decided to end it all. The improvement in mood is deceptive because it comes from an anticipation that suffering is about to end.

Crisis Intervention Most cities have mental health crisis intervention teams or centers for suicide prevention trained to talk with suicidal persons over the phone. Give a person who seems to be suicidal the number of one of these services. Urge the person to call you or the other number if she or he becomes frightened or impulsive. Or better yet, help the person make an appointment to get psychological treatment (Weishaar, 2006).

The preceding applies mainly to persons who are having mild suicidal thoughts. If a person actually threatens suicide, or if a suicide attempt seems to be imminent, don't worry about overreacting. Immediately seek professional assistance by calling the police, crisis intervention, or a rescue unit. If that is infeasible, ask how the person plans to carry out the suicide. A person who has a *specific, workable plan,* and the means to carry it out, should be asked to accompany you to the emergency ward of a hospital.

Needless to say, you should call immediately if a person is in the act of attempting suicide or if a drug has already been taken. The majority of suicide attempts come at temporary low points in a person's life and may never be repeated. Get involved—you may save a life!

RECITE

1. More women than men use guns in their suicide attempts. T or F?
2. While the overall suicide rate has remained about the same, there has been a decrease in adolescent suicides. T or F?
3. The highest suicide rates are found among the divorced. T or F?
4. The majority (two thirds) of suicide attempts are made by people who do not want to die. T or F?

REFLECT

Critical Thinking

5. If you follow the history of popular music, see if you can answer this question: What two major risk factors contributed to the 1994 suicide of Kurt Cobain, lead singer for the rock group Nirvana?

study break
Suicide and Suicide Prevention

Relate

You're working a suicide hotline and you take a call from a very distressed young man. What risk factors will you look for as he tells you about his anguish?

What are the common characteristics of suicidal thoughts and feelings? If a friend of yours were to express any of these thoughts or feelings, how would you respond?

ANSWERS

1. F 2. F 3. T 4. T 5. Drug or alcohol abuse and availability of a firearm.

chapter in review

Major Points

- Judgments of normality are relative, but psychological disorders clearly exist and need to be classified, explained, and treated.

- Two key elements of mental disorder are that abnormal behavior is maladaptive and involves a loss of self-control.

- The most severe forms of psychopathology involve emotional extremes and/or a break with reality.

- Psychological disorders are complex and have multiple causes.

- Suicide is a relatively frequent cause of death that can, in many cases, be prevented.

Summary

How is abnormality defined?

- Psychopathology refers to maladaptive behavior and to the scientific study of mental disorders.

- Factors that typically affect judgments of abnormality include subjective discomfort, statistical abnormality, nonconformity, context, and culture.

- Two key elements in judgments of disorder are that a person's behavior must be maladaptive and it must involve a loss of control.

- "Insanity" is a legal term defining whether a person may be held responsible for his or her actions. Sanity is determined in court on the basis of testimony by expert witnesses.

What are the major psychological disorders?

- Major mental problems include psychotic disorders, organic disorders, mood disorders, anxiety disorders, somatoform disorders, dissociative disorders, personality disorders, sexual or gender identity disorders, and substance-related disorders.

- Psychological problems are classified by using the *Diagnostic and Statistical Manual of Mental Disorders.*

What are the general characteristics of psychotic disorders?

- Psychosis is a break in contact with reality that is marked by delusions, hallucinations, sensory changes, disturbed emotions, disturbed communication, and personality disintegration.

- An organic psychosis is based on known injuries or diseases of the brain. Some common causes of organic psychosis are poisoning, drug abuse, and dementia (especially Alzheimer's disease).

What is the nature of a delusional disorder?

- Delusional disorders are almost totally based on the presence of delusions of grandeur, persecution, infidelity, romantic attraction, or physical disease.

- The most common delusional disorder is paranoid psychosis.

What forms does schizophrenia take? What causes it?

- The varieties of schizophrenia all involve delusions, hallucinations, communication difficulties, and a split between thought and emotion.

- Disorganized schizophrenia is marked by extreme personality disintegration and silly, bizarre, or obscene behavior.

- Catatonic schizophrenia is associated with stupor, mutism, and odd postures. Sometimes violent and agitated behavior also occurs.

- In paranoid schizophrenia (the most common type), outlandish delusions of grandeur and persecution are coupled with psychotic symptoms and personality breakdown.

- Current explanations of schizophrenia emphasize a combination of prenatal injuries, early trauma, environmental stress, inherited susceptibility, and abnormalities in the brain.

- Environmental factors that increase the risk for schizophrenia include viral infection or malnutrition during the mother's pregnancy, birth complications, early psychological trauma, and a disturbed family environment.

- Heredity is a major factor in schizophrenia.

- Recent biochemical studies have focused on the brain transmitter dopamine and its receptor sites.

- The dominant explanation of schizophrenia, and other problems as well, is the stress-vulnerability model.

What are mood disorders? What causes them?

- Mood disorders involve primarily disturbances of mood or emotion, producing manic or depressive states. Severe mood disorders may include psychotic features.

- In a dysthymic disorder, depression is long lasting, though moderate. In a cyclothymic disorder, people suffer from long-lasting, though moderate, swings between depression and elation.

- Bipolar disorders combine mania and depression. In a bipolar I disorder the person swings between severe mania and severe depression. In a bipolar II disorder the person is mostly depressed but has had periods of mild mania.

- A major depressive disorder involves extreme sadness and despondency but no signs of mania.

- Seasonal affective disorder (SAD), which occurs during the winter months, is another common form of depression. SAD is typically treated with phototherapy.

- Major mood disorders are partially explained by genetic vulnerability and changes in brain chemistry. Other important factors are loss, anger, learned helplessness, stress, and self-defeating thinking patterns.

What problems result when a person suffers high levels of anxiety?

- Anxiety disorders, dissociative disorders, and somatoform disorders are characterized by high levels of anxiety, rigid defense mechanisms, and self-defeating behavior patterns.
- Anxiety disorders include generalized anxiety disorder, panic disorder with or without agoraphobia, agoraphobia (without panic), specific phobias, social phobia, obsessive-compulsive disorders, acute stress disorder, and posttraumatic stress disorder.
- Dissociative disorders may take the form of amnesia, fugue, or multiple identities.
- Somatoform disorders center on physical complaints that mimic disease or disability. Four examples of somatoform disorders are hypochondriasis, somatization disorder, somatoform pain disorder, and conversion disorders.

How do psychologists explain anxiety-based disorders?

- The psychodynamic approach emphasizes unconscious conflicts as the cause of disabling anxiety.
- The humanistic approach emphasizes the effects of a faulty self-image.
- The behaviorists emphasize the effects of previous learning, particularly avoidance learning.
- Cognitive theories of anxiety focus on distorted thinking, judgment, and attention.

What is a personality disorder?

- Personality disorders are persistent, maladaptive personality patterns.
- Sociopathy is a common personality disorder. Antisocial persons seem to lack a conscience. They are emotionally unresponsive, manipulative, shallow, and dishonest.

Why do people commit suicide? Can suicide be prevented?

- Suicide is statistically related to such factors as age, sex, and marital status.
- In individual cases, the potential for suicide is best identified by a desire to escape, unbearable psychological pain, and frustrated psychological needs.
- People contemplating suicide narrow their options until death seems like the only way out.
- The impulse to attempt suicide is usually temporary. Efforts to prevent suicide are worthwhile.

Web Resources

For an up-to-date list of direct links to interesting sites, including those listed here, visit the student companion site for this book at www.cengage.com/psychology/coon

Against All Odds Read an article about Carol North, the psychiatrist who overcame schizophrenia.

Psychiatric Disorders Explore a complete listing of the DSM-IV-TR diagnostic categories.

Psychotic Disorders Read more about the psychotic disorders.

William Utermohlen's Self-Portraits View these remarkable paintings by a man descending into Alzheimer's disease.

Schizophrenia Explore this extensive website, which includes brain images and videos about schizophrenia.

Depression Take a depression test and find out more about depression.

Famous People with Phobias Find out more about famous phobias and how to live with them.

Are You Worried About a Friend or Loved One? Visit this website if you are worried about someone near to you committing suicide.

Interactive Learning

PSYCHOLOGY: A JOURNEY BOOK COMPANION WEBSITE
WWW.CENGAGE.COM/PSYCHOLOGY/COON

Visit your book companion website, where you will find flash cards, practice quizzes, web links, and more to help you study.

JUST WHAT YOU NEED TO KNOW NOW! CENGAGENOW

Spend time on what you need to master rather than on information you already have learned. Take a pretest for this chapter, and CengageNOW will generate a personalized study plan based on your results. The study plan will identify the topics you need to review and direct you to online resources to help you master those topics. You can then take a posttest to help you determine the concepts you have mastered and what you will need to work on. Try it out! Go to www.cengage.com/login to sign in with an access code or to purchase access to this product.

Psychological Disorders

For additional review, get more practice with *CengageNOW, WebTutor,* the *Practice Quizzes,* and/or the printed *Study Guide* available with this book.

1. The core feature of abnormal behavior is that it is
a. statistically unusual
b. maladaptive
c. socially nonconforming
d. a source of subjective discomfort

2. In North America, the most widely used standard for classifying mental disorders is the
a. PTSD
b. *Schedule of Personality Dysfunctions*
c. DSM
d. *Psychiatrist's Desk Reference*

3. People are said to have "retreated from reality" when they suffer from
a. psychotic disorders
b. mood disorders
c. somatoform disorders
d. personality disorders

4. A person who has periods of extreme mania suffers from
a. a somatoform disorder
b. a mood disorder
c. an anxiety disorder
d. a neurosis

5. *Koro* and *dhat* are
a. somatoform disorders
b. forms of psychosis
c. folk terminology
d. organic mental disorders

6. Which of the following is a *legal* concept?
a. neurosis
b. psychosis
c. drapetomania
d. insanity

7. Delusions and hallucinations are most characteristic of
a. neurosis
b. psychosis
c. Alzheimer's disease
d. dysthymic disorder

8. Paranoid psychosis is the most common type of
a. catatonic schizophrenia
b. delusional disorder
c. personality disorder
d. dementia

9. Which of the following is NOT one of the subtypes of schizophrenia?
a. erotomanic type
b. catatonic type
c. paranoid type
d. disorganized type

10. Biochemical explanations of schizophrenia have focused on excessive amounts of _____ in the brain.
a. radioactive sugar
b. webs and tangles
c. PCP
d. dopamine and glutamate

11. The stress-vulnerability model of psychosis explains mental disorders as a product of environmental stresses and
a. psychological trauma
b. deviant communication
c. exposure to the flu virus during pregnancy
d. heredity

12. Bipolar disorders that are not too severe are called
a. endogenous disorders
b. cyclothymic disorders
c. seasonal affective disorders
d. dysthymic disorders

13. The fact that lithium carbonate is effective in treating some cases of bipolar depression suggests that the causes of bipolar disorders are at least partly _____.
a. biological
b. existential
c. environmental
d. neurotic

14. Depression that occurs only in the winter is likely to be classified as
a. SAD
b. PTSD
c. bipolar
d. endogenous

15. When prolonged unemployment, a bad marriage, or physical illness pushes a person beyond his or her ability to cope, it is most likely that which of the following problems will occur?
a. a dissociative disorder
b. agoraphobia
c. an adjustment disorder
d. a conversion disorder

16. Agoraphobia is most often a feature of
a. adjustment disorder
b. panic disorder
c. DSM
d. obsessive-compulsive disorder

17. According to the _____ view, anxiety disorders are the end result of a faulty self-image.
a. psychodynamic
b. humanistic
c. behaviorist
d. cognitive

18. Which of the following is NOT a type of personality disorder?
a. schizoid
b. borderline
c. neurotic
d. dependent

19. A person who is impulsive, dishonest, emotionally cold, and manipulative may suffer from
a. antisocial personality disorder
b. histrionic personality disorder
c. dependent personality disorder
d. obsessive-compulsive personality disorder

20. The risk that a person may attempt suicide is greatest if the person has
a. a concrete, workable plan
b. had a recent life crisis
c. withdrawn from contact with others
d. frustrated psychological needs

Answers 1.b 2.c 3.a 4.b 5.c 6.d 7.b 8.b 9.a 10.d 11.d 12.b 13.a 14.a 15.c 16.b 17.b 18.c 19.a 20.a

Therapies

Journey into Psychology: The Duck Syndrome

Outside, some ducks quacked as they explored the campus pond. Susan's psychology professor could hear them between Susan's frightened sobs. As psychologists, we meet many students with personal problems. Still, Susan's teacher was surprised to see her at his office door. Her excellent work in class and her healthy, casual appearance left him unprepared for her first words. "I feel like I'm losing my mind," she said. "Can I talk to you?"

In the next hour, Susan described her own personal hell. In a sense, she was like the ducks outside, appearing peaceful on the surface, but madly paddling underneath. She was working hard to hide a world of crippling fear, anxiety, and depression. At work, she was deathly afraid of talking to co-workers and cus-

tomers. Her social phobia led to frequent absenteeism and embarrassing behavior. At each job she held, it was only a matter of time until she got fired.

At school Susan felt "different" and was sure that other students could tell she was "weird." Several disastrous romances had left her terrified of men. Lately she had been so depressed that she thought of suicide. Often, she became terrified for no apparent reason. Each time, her heart pounded wildly and she felt that she was about to completely lose control.

Susan's request for help was an important turning point. Emotional conflicts had made her existence a nightmare. At a time when she was becoming her own worst enemy, Susan

realized she needed help from another person. In Susan's case, that person was a talented psychologist to whom her teacher referred her. With psychotherapy, the psychologist was able to help Susan come to grips with her emotions and regain her balance.

This chapter discusses methods used to alleviate problems like Susan's. First, we will describe therapies that emphasize the value of gaining *insight* into personal problems. Then, we will focus on *behavior therapies* and *cognitive therapies,* which directly change troublesome actions and thoughts. Later, we will conclude with *medical therapies,* which are based on psychiatric drugs and other physical treatments.

Survey Questions

- • How do psychotherapies differ?
- • How did psychotherapy originate?
- Is Freudian psychoanalysis still used?
- What are the major humanistic therapies?
- Can therapy be conducted at a distance?
- What is behavior therapy?
- What role do operant principles play in behavior therapy?
- Can therapy change thoughts and emotions?
- Can psychotherapy be done with groups of people?
- What do various therapies have in common?
- How do psychiatrists treat psychological disorders?
- How are behavioral principles applied to everyday problems? How could a person find professional help?

Psychotherapy—The Talking Cure

How do psychotherapies differ?

Psychotherapy refers to any psychological technique that can bring about positive changes in personality, behavior, or personal adjustment. Psychotherapy is usually based on a dialogue between therapists and their clients, although some therapists also use learning principles to directly alter troublesome behaviors.

Therapists have many approaches to choose from: psychoanalysis, client-centered therapy, Gestalt therapy, behavior therapy, and cognitive therapy—to name but a few. As we will see, each therapy emphasizes different concepts and methods. For this reason, the best approach for a particular person or problem may vary (Prochaska & Norcross, 2010).

Dimensions of Therapy

The terms in the list that follows describe some basic aspects of various therapies (Sharf, 2008). Notice that more than one term may apply to a particular therapy. For example, it is possible to have a directive, action-oriented, open-ended group therapy or a nondirective, individual, insight-oriented, time-limited therapy:

- **Insight vs. action therapy:** Does the therapy aim to bring clients to a deeper understanding of their thoughts, emotions, and behavior? Or is it designed to bring about direct changes in troublesome thoughts, habits, feelings, or behavior, without seeking insight into their origins or meanings?
- **Directive vs. nondirective therapy:** Does the therapist provide strong guidance and advice? Or does the therapist assist clients, who are responsible for solving their own problems?
- **Individual vs. group therapy:** Does the therapy involve one therapist with one client? Or do several clients participate at the same time?
- **Open-ended vs. time-limited therapy:** Is the therapy open-ended? Or is it begun with the expectation that it will last only a limited number of sessions?

Myths

Psychotherapy has been depicted as a complete personal transformation—a sort of "major overhaul" of the psyche. But therapy is *not* equally effective for all problems. Chances of improvement are fairly good for phobias, low self-esteem, some sexual problems, and marital conflicts. More complex problems can be difficult to solve. For many people, the major benefit of therapy is that it provides comfort, support, and a way to make constructive changes (Bloch, 2006; Hellerstein et al., 1998).

In short, it is often unrealistic to expect psychotherapy to undo a person's entire past. Yet even when problems are severe, therapy may help a person gain a new perspective or learn behaviors to better cope with life. Psychotherapy can be hard work for both clients and therapists, but when it succeeds, few activities are more worthwhile.

It's also a mistake to think that psychotherapy is used only to solve problems or end a crisis. Even if a person is already doing well, therapy can be a way to promote personal growth (Bloch, 2006). Therapists in the positive psychology movement are developing ways to help people make use of their personal strengths. Rather than trying to fix what is "wrong" with a person, they seek to nurture positive traits and actively solve problems (Compton, 2005). ● Table 13.1 lists some of the elements of positive mental health that therapists seek to restore or promote.

● Table 13.1 Elements of Positive Mental Health

- · Personal autonomy and independence
- · A sense of identity
- · Feelings of personal worth
- · Skilled interpersonal communication
- · Sensitivity, nurturance, and trust
- · Genuineness and honesty with self and others
- · Self-control and personal responsibility
- · Committed and loving personal relationships
- · Capacity to forgive others and oneself
- · Personal values and a purpose in life
- · Self-awareness and motivation for personal growth
- · Adaptive coping strategies for managing stresses and crises
- · Fulfillment and satisfaction in work
- · Good habits of physical health

Source: Adapted from Bergin, 1991; Bloch, 2006.

Psychotherapy Any psychological technique used to facilitate positive changes in a person's personality, behavior, or adjustment.

Origins of Therapy—Bored Out of Your Skull

How did psychotherapy originate?

Early treatments for mental problems give good reasons to appreciate modern therapies (Sharf, 2008). Archaeological findings dating to the Stone Age suggest that most primitive approaches were marked by fear and superstitious belief in demons, witchcraft, and magic. One of the more dramatic "cures" practiced by primitive "therapists" was a process called *trepanning* (treh-PAN-ing), also sometimes spelled *trephining* (Terry, 2006). In modern usage, trepanning is any surgical procedure in which a hole is bored in the skull. In the hands of primitive therapists, it meant boring, chipping, or bashing holes in a patient's head. Presumably this was done to relieve pressure or release evil spirits. Surprisingly, some "patients" actually survived the "treatment" (▶▶ Figure 13.1).

During the Middle Ages, treatments for mental illness in Europe focused on **demonology,** the study of demons and persons plagued by spirits. Medieval "therapists" commonly blamed abnormal behavior on supernatural forces, such as possession by the devil, or on curses from witches and wizards. As a cure, they used exorcism to "cast out evil spirits." For the fortunate, exorcism was a religious ritual. More often, physical torture was used to make the body an inhospitable place for the devil to reside. Modern analyses of "demonic possession" suggest that many victims were suffering from epilepsy, schizophrenia (Mirsky & Duncan, 2005), dissociative disorders (van der Hart, Lierens, & Goodwin, 1996), and depression (Thase, 2006).

One reason for the rise of demonology may lie in *ergotism* (AIR-got-ism), a psychotic-like condition caused by ergot poisoning. In the Middle Ages, rye (grain) fields were often infested with ergot fungus. Ergot, we now know, is a natural source of LSD and other mind-altering chemicals. Eating tainted bread could have caused symptoms that were easily mistaken for bewitchment or madness. Pinching sensations, muscle twitches, facial spasms, delirium, and hallucinations are all signs of ergot poisoning (Matossian, 1982). Thus, many people "treated" by demonologists may have been doubly victimized.

In 1793, a French doctor named Philippe Pinel changed the Bicêtre Asylum in Paris from a squalid "madhouse" into a mental hospital by unchaining the inmates (Harris, 2003). Finally, the emotionally disturbed were regarded as "mentally ill" and given compassionate treatment. Although it has been more than 200 years since Pinel began humane treatment, the process of improving care continues today.

When was psychotherapy developed? The first true psychotherapy was created by Sigmund Freud little more than 100 years ago (Jacobs, 2003). As a physician in Vienna, Freud was intrigued by cases of *hysteria*. People suffering from hysteria have physical symptoms (such as paralysis or numbness) for which no physical causes can be found. (Such problems are now called somatoform disorders, as discussed in Chapter 12.) Slowly, Freud became convinced that hysteria was related to deeply hidden unconscious conflicts and developed an individual, directive therapy called psychoanalysis in order to help patients gain insight into those conflicts. Because it is the "granddaddy" of more modern therapies, let us examine psychoanalysis in some detail.

▲ **FIGURE 13.1** Primitive "treatment" for mental disorders sometimes took the form of boring a hole in the skull. This example shows signs of healing, which means the patient survived the treatment. Many didn't.

(left) Many early asylums were no more than prisons, with inmates held in chains. *(right)* One late-nineteenth-century "treatment" was based on swinging the patient in a harness—presumably to calm the patient's nerves.

Demonology In medieval Europe, the study of demons and the treatment of persons "possessed" by demons.

Psychoanalysis—Expedition into the Unconscious

Is Freudian psychoanalysis still used?

Isn't psychoanalysis the therapy where the patient lies on a couch? Freud's patients usually reclined on a couch during therapy, while Freud sat out of sight taking notes and offering interpretations. This procedure was supposed to encourage a free flow of thoughts and images from the unconscious. However, it is the least important element of psychoanalysis, and many modern analysts have abandoned it.

How did Freud treat emotional problems? Freud's theory stressed that "neurosis" and "hysteria" are caused by repressed memories, motives, and conflicts—particularly those stemming from instinctual drives for sex and aggression. Although they are hidden, these forces remain active in the personality and cause some people to develop rigid ego defenses and compulsive, self-defeating behavior. Thus, the main goal of **psychoanalysis** is to reduce internal conflicts that lead to emotional suffering (Marcus, 2002).

Freud developed four basic techniques to uncover the unconscious roots of neurosis (Freud, 1949). These are *free association, dream analysis, analysis of resistance,* and *analysis of transference.*

Pioneering psychotherapist Sigmund Freud's famous couch.

Peter Aprahamian/Corbis

Freudian

Free Association

The basis for **free association** is saying whatever comes to mind without worrying whether ideas are painful, embarrassing, or illogical. Thoughts are simply allowed to move freely from one idea to the next, without self-censorship. The purpose of free association is to lower defenses so that unconscious thoughts and feelings can emerge (Hoffer & Youngren, 2004).

Dream Analysis

Freud believed that dreams provide a "royal road to the unconscious," which disguises consciously unacceptable feelings and forbidden desires in dream form (Rock, 2004). The job of the psychoanalyst is to help the patient work past the obvious, visible meaning of the dream (**manifest content**) to uncover the hidden, symbolic meaning (**latent content).** This is achieved by analyzing **dream symbols** (images that have personal or emotional meanings).

Suppose a young man dreams of pulling a pistol from his waistband and aiming at a target while his wife watches. The pistol repeatedly fails to discharge, and the man's wife laughs at him. Freud might have seen this as an indication of repressed feelings of sexual impotence, with the gun serving as a disguised image of the penis.

Analysis of Resistance

When free associating or describing dreams, patients may *resist* talking about or thinking about certain topics. Such **resistances** (blockages in the flow of ideas) reveal particularly important unconscious conflicts. As analysts become aware of resistances, they bring them to the patient's awareness so the patient can deal with them realistically. Rather than being roadblocks in therapy, resistances can be challenges and guides (Engle & Arkowitz, 2006).

Analysis of Transference

Transference is the tendency to "transfer" feelings to a therapist similar to those the patient had for important persons in his or her past. At times, the patient may act as if the analyst is a rejecting father, an unloving or overprotective mother, or

Psychoanalysis A Freudian therapy that emphasizes the use of free association, dream interpretation, resistances, and transference to uncover unconscious conflicts.

Free association In psychoanalysis, the technique of having a client say anything that comes to mind, regardless of how embarrassing or unimportant it may seem.

Manifest dream content The surface, "visible" content of a dream; dream images as they are remembered by the dreamer.

Latent dream content The hidden or symbolic meaning of a dream, as revealed by dream interpretation and analysis.

Dream symbols Images in dreams whose personal or emotional meanings differ from their literal meanings.

Resistance A blockage in the flow of free association; topics the client resists thinking or talking about.

Transference The tendency of patients to transfer feelings to a therapist that correspond to those the patient had for important persons in his or her past.

a former lover, for example. As the patient re-experiences repressed emotions, the therapist can help the patient recognize and understand them. Troubled persons often provoke anger, rejection, boredom, criticism, and other negative reactions from others. Effective therapists learn to avoid reacting as others do and playing the patient's habitual resistance and transference "games." This, too, contributes to therapeutic change (Marcus, 2002).

Psychoanalysis Today

What is the status of psychoanalysis today? Traditional psychoanalysis was open-ended, calling for three to five therapy sessions a week, often for many years. Today, most patients are seen only once or twice per week, but treatment may still go on for years (Friedman et al., 1998). Because of the huge amounts of time and money this requires, psychoanalysts have become relatively rare. Nevertheless, psychoanalysis made a major contribution to modern therapies by highlighting the importance of unconscious conflicts (Friedman, 2006).

Many therapists have switched to doing time-limited **brief psychodynamic therapy,** which uses direct questioning to reveal unconscious conflicts (Binder, 2004). Modern therapists also actively provoke emotional reactions that will lower defenses and provide insights. Interestingly, brief therapy appears to accelerate recovery. Patients seem to realize that they need to get to the heart of their problems quickly (Messer & Kaplan, 2004).

Interpersonal Psychotherapy

One example of a brief dynamic therapy is **interpersonal psychotherapy (IPT),** which was first developed to help depressed people improve their relationships with others (Prochaska & Norcross, 2010). Research has confirmed that IPT is effective for depressive disorders, as well as eating disorders, substance abuse, social phobias, and personality disorders (Fiore et al., 2008; Hoffart, 2005; Prochaska, & Norcross, 2010; Talbot & Gamble, 2008).

Liona's therapy is a good example of IPT (Brown & Barlow, 2007). Liona was suffering from depression that a therapist helped her trace to a conflict with her parents. When her father was absent, Liona adopted the role of her mother's protector and friend. However, when her father was home, she was expected to resume her role as a daughter. She was angry at her father for frequently abandoning her mother and upset about having to switch roles so often. Liona's IPT sessions (which sometimes included her mother) focused on clarifying Liona's family roles. Her mood improved a lot after her mother urged her to "stick to being herself."

Is Traditional Psychoanalysis Effective?

The development of newer, more streamlined dynamic therapies is in part due to questions about whether traditional psychoanalysis "works." In a classic criticism, Hans Eysenck (1994) suggested that psychoanalysis simply takes so long that patients experience a *spontaneous remission* of symptoms (improvement due to the mere passage of time).

How seriously should the possibility of spontaneous remission be taken? It's true that problems ranging from hyperactivity to anxiety do improve with the passage of time. Regardless, researchers have confirmed that psychoanalysis does, in fact, produce improvement in a majority of patients (Doidge, 1997).

The real value of Eysenck's critique is that it encouraged psychologists to try new ideas and techniques. Researchers began to ask, "When psychoanalysis works, why does it work? Which parts of it are essential and which are unnecessary?" Modern therapists have given surprisingly varied answers to these questions. Upcoming sections will acquaint you with some of the therapies currently in use.

Brief psychodynamic therapy A modern therapy based on psychoanalytic theory but designed to produce insights more quickly.

Interpersonal psychotherapy (IPT) A brief dynamic psychotherapy designed to help people by improving their relationships with other people.

study break

Psychotherapy and Psychoanalysis

Humanistic Therapies—Restoring Human Potential

What are the major humanistic therapies?

When most people picture clinical psychologists at work, they probably imagine them doing insight therapy. As stated earlier, insight therapists help clients gain a deeper understanding of their thoughts, emotions, and behavior. Let's sample a variety of insight-oriented approaches, including therapies done at a distance (by telephone or over the Internet).

Better self-knowledge was the goal of traditional psychoanalysis. However, Freud claimed that his patients could expect only to change their "hysterical misery into common unhappiness"! Humanistic therapists are more optimistic, believing that humans have a natural urge to seek health and self-growth. Most assume that it is possible for people to use their potentials fully and live rich, rewarding lives.

Client-Centered Therapy

What is client-centered therapy? How is it different from psychoanalysis? Psychoanalysts delve into the unconscious. Psychologist Carl Rogers (1902–1987) found it more beneficial to explore *conscious* thoughts and feelings. The psychoanalyst tends to take a position of authority, stating what dreams, thoughts, or memories "mean." In contrast, Rogers believed that what is right or valuable for the therapist may be wrong for the client. (Rogers preferred the term "client" to "patient" because "patient" implies that a person is "sick" and needs to be "cured.") Consequently, the client determines what will be discussed during each session. Thus, **client-centered therapy** (also called **person-centered therapy**) is individual, nondirective, and based on insights from conscious thoughts and feelings (Brodley, 2006; Schneider, 2002).

If the client runs things, what does the therapist do? The therapist cannot "fix" the client. Instead, the client must actively seek to solve his or her problems (Whitton, 2003). The therapist's job is to create a safe "atmosphere of growth" by providing opportunities for change.

Client-centered (or person-centered) therapy A nondirective therapy based on insights gained from conscious thoughts and feelings; emphasizes accepting one's true self.

Health-Promoting Conditions

Rogers believed that effective therapists maintain four basic conditions. First, the therapist offers the client **unconditional positive regard** (unshakable personal acceptance). The therapist refuses to react with shock, dismay, or disapproval to anything the client says or feels. Total acceptance by the therapist is the first step to self-acceptance by the client.

Second, the therapist attempts to achieve genuine **empathy** by trying to see the world through the client's eyes and feeling some part of what the client is feeling.

As a third essential condition, the therapist strives to be **authentic** (genuine and honest). The therapist must not hide behind a professional role. Rogers believed that phony fronts destroy the growth atmosphere sought in client-centered therapy.

Fourth, the therapist does not make interpretations, propose solutions, or offer advice. Instead, the therapist **reflects** (rephrases, summarizes, or repeats) the client's thoughts and feelings. This enables the therapist to act as a psychological "mirror" so clients can see themselves more clearly. Rogers theorized that a person armed with a realistic self-image and greater self-acceptance will gradually discover solutions to life's problems.

Courtesy of UC Santa Barbara Archives

Psychotherapist Carl Rogers, who originated client-centered therapy.

Existential Therapy

According to the existentialists, "being in the world" (existence) creates deep anxiety. Each of us must deal with the realities of death. We must face the fact that we create our private world by making choices. We must overcome isolation on a vast and indifferent planet. Most of all, we must confront feelings of meaninglessness.

What do these concerns have to do with psychotherapy? **Existential therapy** focuses on the problems of existence, such as meaning, choice, and responsibility. Like client-centered therapy, it promotes self-knowledge. However, there are important differences. Client-centered therapy seeks to uncover a "true self" hidden behind a screen of defenses. In contrast, existential therapy emphasizes free will, the human ability to make choices. Accordingly, existential therapists believe you can *choose to become* the person you want to be.

Existential therapists try to give clients the *courage* to make rewarding and socially constructive choices. Typically, therapy focuses on death, freedom, isolation, and meaninglessness, the "ultimate concerns" of existence (van Deurzen & Kenward, 2005). These universal human challenges include: an awareness of one's mortality, the responsibility that comes with freedom to choose, being alone in your own private world, and the need to create meaning in your life.

What does the existential therapist do? The therapist helps clients discover self-imposed limitations in personal identity. To be successful, the client must fully accept the challenge of changing his or her life (Bretherton & Orner, 2004). Interestingly, Buddhists seek a similar state that they call "radical acceptance" (Brach, 2003).

A key aspect of existential therapy is *confrontation,* in which clients are challenged to examine their values and choices and to take responsibility for the quality of their existence (Gerwood, 1998). An important part of confrontation is the unique, intense, here-and-now *encounter* between two human beings. When existential therapy is successful, it brings about a renewed sense of purpose and a reappraisal of what's important in life. Some clients even experience an emotional rebirth, as if they had survived a close brush with death. As Marcel Proust wrote, "The real voyage of discovery consists not in seeing new landscapes but in having new eyes."

Gestalt Therapy

Gestalt therapy is based on the idea that perception, or *awareness,* is disjointed and incomplete in maladjusted persons. The German word *Gestalt* means "whole," or "complete." **Gestalt therapy** helps people rebuild thinking, feeling, and acting into connected wholes. This is achieved by expanding personal awareness; by accepting responsibility for one's thoughts, feelings, and actions; and by filling in gaps in experience (Joyce & Sills, 2001).

What are "gaps in experience"? Gestalt therapists believe that we often shy away from expressing or "owning" upsetting feelings. This creates a gap in self-awareness that may

Unconditional positive regard An unqualified, unshakable acceptance of another person.

Empathy A capacity for taking another's point of view; the ability to feel what another is feeling.

Authenticity In Carl Rogers' terms, the ability of a therapist to be genuine and honest about his or her own feelings.

Reflection In client-centered therapy, the process of rephrasing or repeating thoughts and feelings expressed by clients so they can become aware of what they are saying.

Existential therapy An insight therapy that focuses on the elemental problems of existence, such as death, meaning, choice, and responsibility; emphasizes making courageous life choices.

Gestalt therapy An approach that focuses on immediate experience and awareness to help clients rebuild thinking, feeling, and acting into connected wholes; emphasizes the integration of fragmented experiences.

become a barrier to personal growth. For example, a person who feels anger after the death of a parent might go for years without fully expressing it. This and similar threatening gaps may impair emotional health.

The Gestalt approach is more directive than client-centered or existential therapy and it is less insight-oriented and instead emphasizes immediate experience. Working either one-to-one or in a group setting, the Gestalt therapist encourages clients to become more aware of their moment-to-moment thoughts, perceptions, and emotions (Staemmler, 2004). Rather than discussing *why* clients feel guilt, anger, fear, or boredom, the therapist encourages them to have these feelings in the "here and now" and become fully aware of them. The therapist promotes awareness by drawing attention to a client's posture, voice, eye movements, and hand gestures. Clients may also be asked to exaggerate vague feelings until they become clear. Gestalt therapists believe that expressing such feelings allows people to "take care of unfinished business" and break through emotional impasses (O'Leary, 2006).

Gestalt therapy is often associated with the work of Fritz Perls (1969). According to Perls, emotional health comes from knowing what you *want* to do, not dwelling on what you *should* do, *ought* to do, or *should want* to do (Rosenberg & Lynch, 2002). In other words, emotional health comes from taking full responsibility for one's feelings and actions. For example, it means changing "I can't" to "I won't," or "I must" to "I choose to."

How does Gestalt therapy help people discover their real wants? Above all else, Gestalt therapy emphasizes *present* experience. Clients are urged to stop intellectualizing and talking *about* feelings. Instead, they learn to live now; live here; stop imagining; experience the real; stop unnecessary thinking; taste and see; express rather than explain, justify, or judge; give in to unpleasantness and pain just as to pleasure; and surrender to being as you are. Gestalt therapists believe that, paradoxically, the best way to change is to become who you really are (Joyce & Sills, 2001).

Because of their emphasis on verbal interaction, insight therapies may be conducted at a distance, by telephone, e-mail, or videoconferencing. Let's investigate this possibility.

Therapy at a Distance—Psych Jockeys and Cybertherapy

Can therapy be conducted at a distance?

How valid are psychological services offered at a distance? For better or worse, high-tech psychotherapy and counseling are rapidly becoming commonplace (Ormay, 2006). Today, psychological services are available through radio, telephone, e-mail, Internet chat rooms, and videoconferencing (Maheu et al., 2004). What are the advantages and disadvantages of getting help at a distance?

Media Psychologists

By now you have probably heard a phone-in radio psychologist or watched one on television. On a typical program, participants describe problems arising from child abuse, loneliness, love affairs, phobias, sexual adjustment, or depression. The media psychologist then offers reassurance, advice, or suggestions for getting help. Such talk-radio and television programs may seem harmless, but they raise some important questions. For instance, is it reasonable to give advice without knowing anything about a person's background? Could the advice do harm? What good can a psychologist do in 3 minutes or even an hour?

In their own defense, media psychologists point out that listeners and viewers may learn solutions to their problems by hearing others talk. Many also stress that their work is educational, not therapeutic. The well-known media psychologist Dr. Phil McGraw has even been awarded a President's Citation from the American Psychological Association for his work in publicizing mental health issues (Meyers, 2006).

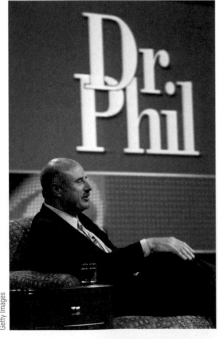

Getty Images

Media psychologists have been urged to educate without actually doing therapy on the air. Some overstep this boundary, however. Do you think popular TV psychologist Dr. Phil sometimes goes too far?

Nevertheless, the question arises: When does advice become therapy? The American Psychological Association urges media psychologists to discuss problems only of a general nature, instead of actually counseling anyone. For example, if a caller complains about insomnia, the radio psychologist should talk about insomnia in general, not probe the caller's personal life. A good guide for anyone tempted to call a radio psychologist or accept advice from a TV psychologist might be "let the consumer beware."

Telephone and Internet Therapists

The same caution applies to commercial telephone and Internet therapists. A key feature of successful face-to-face therapy is the establishment of a continuing *relationship* between two people. In this regard, distance therapies are more or less limited by a lack of interpersonal cues, such as facial expressions and body language. For example, brief e-mail messages are no way to make a diagnosis. And forget about facial expressions or body language—not even tone of voice reaches the e-mail therapist. Typing emotional icons (called *emoticons*) like little smiley faces (☺) or frowns (☹) is a poor substitute for real human interaction.

Of special concern is the fact that distance therapists may or may not be trained professionals (Bloom, 1998). And even if they are, questions exist about whether a psychologist licensed in one state can legally do therapy in another state via the telephone or the Internet.

Regardless, distance counseling and therapy services do have some advantages. For one thing, clients can more easily remain anonymous. (But beware that e-mail counseling may not be completely confidential and could be intercepted and misused.) Thus, a person who might hesitate to see a psychologist can seek help privately, on the phone or online. Likewise, people who live in rural areas can more easily work with psychologists living in large cities. And, compared with traditional office visits, distance therapies are less expensive.

Under the right circumstances, distance therapies can be successful (Day & Schneider, 2002). For example, in one study, telephone counseling helped improve success rates for smokers who wanted to quit (Rabius et al., 2004). Other studies have shown that depressed people benefit from telephone therapy (Mohr et al., 2005; Simon et al., 2004). Psychologists have also demonstrated success providing therapy over the Internet, at least for certain types of problems (Carlbring et al., 2007; Chester & Glass, 2006; Klein, Richards, & Austin, 2006).

The Ever-Evolving Internet

The Internet continues to provide new communication tools that blend voice, text, graphics, and video. Widely available and inexpensive technologies, such as Skype, make it easy to create two-way audio-video links that allow a client and therapist to see one another on computer monitors and to talk via speakerphones. Doing therapy this way still lacks the close personal contact of face-to-face interaction. However, it does remove many of the objections to doing therapy at a distance. It's very likely that distance services will continue to evolve (Riva & Wiederhold, 2006) and become a major source of mental health care in coming years (Schopp, Demiris, & Glueckauf, 2006).

RECITE

Match:

_____ 1. Client-centered therapy   A. Electronic advice
_____ 2. Gestalt therapy   B. Unconditional positive regard
_____ 3. Existential therapy   C. Gaps in awareness
_____ 4. Internet therapy   D. Choice and becoming

5. The Gestalt therapist tries to reflect a client's thoughts and feelings. T or F?
6. Client-centered therapy is directive. T or F?
7. Confrontation and encounter are concepts of existential therapy. T or F?

REFLECT
Critical Thinking

8. How might using the term "patient" affect the relationship between an individual and a therapist?

Relate

Here's a mnemonic for the elements of client-centered therapy: Picture a therapist saying "I ear u" to a client. The E stands for empathy, A for authenticity, R for reflection, and U for unconditional positive regard.

What would an existential therapist say about the choices you have made so far in your life? Should you be choosing more "courageously"?

You are going to play the role of a therapist for a classroom demonstration. How would you act if you were a client-centered therapist? An existential therapist? A Gestalt therapist?

A neighbor of yours is thinking about getting counseling on the Internet. What would you tell her about the pros and cons of distance therapy?

ANSWERS

1. B 2. C 3. D 4. A 5. F 6. F 7. T 8. The terms "doctor" and "patient" imply a large gap in status and authority between the individual and his or her therapist. Client-centered therapy attempts to narrow this gap by making the person the final authority concerning solutions to his or her problems. Also, the word "patient" implies that a person is "sick" and needs to be "cured." Many regard this as an inappropriate way to think about human problems.

Behavior Therapy—Healing by Learning

What is behavior therapy?

Jay repeatedly and vividly imagined himself going into a store to steal something. He then pictured himself being caught and turned over to the police, who handcuffed him and hauled him off to jail. Once there, he imagined calling his wife to tell her he had been arrested for shoplifting. He became very distressed as he faced her anger and his son's disappointment (Kohn & Antonuccio, 2002).

Why would anyone imagine such a thing? Jay's behavior is not as strange as it may seem. His goal was self-control: Jay is a *kleptomaniac* (a compulsive thief). The method he chose (called *covert sensitization*) is a form of behavior therapy (Corsini, 2001). **Behavior therapy** is an action therapy that uses learning principles to make constructive changes in behavior.

In general, how does behavior therapy work? Behavior therapists believe that deep insight into one's problems is often unnecessary for improvement. Instead, they try to directly alter troublesome thoughts and actions. Jay didn't need to probe into his past or his emotions and conflicts; he simply wanted to break his shoplifting habit.

Behavior therapists assume that people have *learned* to be the way they are. If they have learned responses that cause problems, then they can change them by *relearning* more appropriate behaviors. Broadly speaking, **behavior modification** refers to any use of classical or operant conditioning to directly alter human behavior (Miltenberger, 2008; Spiegler & Guevremont, 2003). (Some therapists prefer to call this approach *applied behavior analysis*.) Behavioral approaches include aversion therapy, desensitization, token economies, and other techniques (Forsyth & Savsevitz, 2002).

Behavior therapy Any therapy designed to actively change behavior.

Behavior modification The application of learning principles to change human behavior, especially maladaptive behavior.

How does classical conditioning work? I'm not sure I remember. Classical conditioning is a form of learning in which simple responses (especially reflexes) are associated with new stimuli. Perhaps a brief review would be helpful. In classical conditioning, a neutral stimulus is followed by an *unconditioned stimulus* (US) that consistently produces an unlearned reaction, called the *unconditioned response* (UR). Eventually, the previously neutral stimulus begins to produce this response directly. The response is then called a *conditioned response* (CR), and the stimulus becomes a *conditioned stimulus* (CS). Thus, for a child the sight of a hypodermic needle (CS) is followed by an injection (US), which causes anxiety or fear (UR). Eventually the sight of a hypodermic (the conditioned stimulus) may produce anxiety or fear (a conditioned response) *before* the child gets an injection. (For a more thorough review of classical conditioning, return to Chapter 6.)

What does classical conditioning have to do with behavior modification? Classical conditioning can be used to associate discomfort with a bad habit, as Jay did. More powerful versions of this approach are called aversion therapy.

Aversion Therapy

Imagine that you are eating an apple. Suddenly you discover that you just bit a large green worm in half. You vomit. Months later you cannot eat an apple again without feeling ill. It's apparent that you have developed a conditioned aversion to apples. (A *conditioned aversion* is a learned dislike or negative emotional response to some stimulus.)

How are conditioned aversions used in therapy? In **aversion therapy,** an individual learns to associate a strong aversion to an undesirable habit such as smoking, drinking, or gambling. Aversion therapy has been used to cure hiccups, sneezing, stuttering, vomiting, nail-biting, bed-wetting, compulsive hair-pulling, alcoholism, and the smoking of tobacco, marijuana, or crack cocaine. Actually, aversive conditioning happens every day. For example, not many physicians who treat lung cancer patients are smokers, nor do many emergency room doctors drive without using their seat belts (Eifert & Lejuez, 2000).

Puffing Up an Aversion

The fact that nicotine is toxic makes it easy to create an aversion that helps people give up smoking. Behavior therapists have found that electric shock, nauseating drugs, and similar aversive stimuli are not required to make smokers uncomfortable. All that is needed is for the smoker to smoke—rapidly, for a long time, at a forced pace. During rapid smoking, clients are told to smoke continuously, taking a puff every 6 to 8 seconds. Rapid smoking continues until the smoker is miserable and can stand it no more. By then, most people are thinking, "I never want to see another cigarette for the rest of my life."

Rapid smoking has long been known as an effective behavior therapy for smoking (McRobbie & Hajek, 2007). Nevertheless, anyone tempted to try rapid smoking should realize that it is very unpleasant. Without the help of a therapist, most people quit too soon for the procedure to succeed. In addition, rapid smoking can be dangerous. It should be done only with professional supervision. (An alternative method that is more practical is described in the Psychology in Action section of this chapter.)

Aversive Therapy for Drinking

Another excellent example of aversion therapy was pioneered by Roger Vogler and his associates (1977). Vogler worked with alcoholics who were unable to stop drinking and for whom aversion therapy was a last chance. While drinking an alcoholic beverage, clients receive a painful (although not injurious) electric shock to the hand. Most of the time, these shocks occur as the client is beginning to take a drink of alcohol.

These *response-contingent shocks* (shocks that are linked to a response) obviously take the pleasure out of drinking. Shocks also cause the alcohol abuser to develop a conditioned aversion to drinking. Normally, the misery caused by alcohol abuse comes long after the act of drinking—too late to have much effect. But if alcohol can be linked with *immediate* discomfort, then drinking will begin to make the individual very uncomfortable.

Aversion therapy Suppressing an undesirable response by associating it with aversive (painful or uncomfortable) stimuli.

Is it really acceptable to treat clients this way? People are often disturbed (shocked?) by such methods. However, clients usually *volunteer* for aversion therapy because it helps them overcome a destructive habit. Indeed, commercial aversion programs for overeating, smoking, and alcohol abuse have attracted many willing customers. More important, aversion therapy can be justified by its long-term benefits. As behaviorist Donald Baer put it, "A small number of brief, painful experiences is a reasonable exchange for the interminable pain of a lifelong maladjustment."

Desensitization

How is behavior therapy used to treat phobias, fears, and anxieties? Suppose you want to help a child, named Janice, overcome fear of the high diving board. How might you proceed? Directly forcing Janice off the high board could be a psychological disaster. A better approach would be to begin by teaching her to dive off the edge of the pool. Then she could be taught to dive off the low board, followed by a platform 6 feet above the water and then an 8-foot platform. As a last step, Janice could try the high board.

Who's Afraid of a Hierarchy?

This rank-ordered series of steps (called a **hierarchy**) allows Janice to undergo *adaptation*. Gradually, she adapts to the high dive and overcomes her fear. When Janice has conquered her fear, we can say that *desensitization* (dee-SEN-sih-tih-ZAY-shun) has occurred (Spiegler & Guevremont, 2003).

Desensitization is also based on **reciprocal inhibition** (using one emotional state to block another) (Heriot & Pritchard, 2004). For instance, it is impossible to be anxious and relaxed at the same time. If we can get Janice onto the high board in a relaxed state, her anxiety and fear will be inhibited. Repeated visits to the high board should cause fear to disappear in this situation. Again we would say that Janice has been desensitized. Typically, **systematic desensitization** (a guided reduction in fear, anxiety, or aversion) is attained by gradually approaching a feared stimulus while maintaining relaxation.

What is desensitization used for? Desensitization is used primarily to help people unlearn phobias (intense, unrealistic fears) or strong anxieties. For example, each of these people might be a candidate for desensitization: a teacher with stage fright, a student with test anxiety, a salesperson who fears people, or a newlywed with an aversion to sexual intimacy.

Performing Desensitization

How is desensitization done? First, the client and the therapist *construct a hierarchy*. This is a list of fear-provoking situations, arranged from least disturbing to most frightening. Second, the client is taught *exercises that produce deep relaxation*. (See "Feeling a Little Tense? Relax!") Third, once the client is relaxed, she or he tries to *perform the least disturbing item* on the list. For a fear of heights (acrophobia), this might be: "(1) Stand on a chair." The first item is repeated until no anxiety is felt. Any change from complete relaxation is a signal that clients must relax again before continuing. Slowly, clients move up the hierarchy: "(2) Climb to the top of a small stepladder"; "(3) Look down a flight of stairs"; and so on, until the last item is performed without fear: "(20) Fly in an airplane."

For many phobias, desensitization works best when people are directly exposed to the stimuli and situations they fear (Bourne, 2005). For something like a simple spider phobia, this exposure can even be done in groups. Also, for some fears (such as fear of riding an elevator) desensitization may be completed in a single session (Sturges & Sturges, 1998).

Programs for treating fears of flying combine relaxation, systematic desensitization, group support, and lots of direct exposure to airliners. Many such programs conclude with a brief flight, so that participants can "test their wings."

Rubberball/Getty Images

Hierarchy A rank-ordered series of higher and lower amounts, levels, degrees, or steps.

Reciprocal inhibition The presence of one emotional state can inhibit the occurrence of another, such as joy preventing fear or anxiety inhibiting pleasure.

Systematic desensitization A reduction in fear, anxiety, or aversion brought about by planned exposure to aversive stimuli.

Feeling a Little Tense? Relax!

The key to desensitization is relaxation. To inhibit fear, you must *learn* to relax. One way to voluntarily relax is by using the **tension-release method.** To achieve deep-muscle relaxation, try the following exercise:

Tense the muscles in your right arm until they tremble. Hold them tight as you slowly count to ten and then let go. Allow your hand and arm to go limp and to relax completely. Repeat the procedure. Releasing tension two or three times will allow you to feel whether or not your arm muscles have relaxed. Repeat the tension-release procedure with your left arm. Compare it with your right arm. Repeat until the left arm is equally relaxed. Apply the tension-release technique to your right leg; to your left leg; to your abdomen; to your chest and shoulders. Clench and release your chin, neck, and throat. Wrinkle and release your forehead and scalp. Tighten and release your mouth and face muscles. As a last step, curl your toes and tense your feet. Then release.

If you carried out these instructions, you should be noticeably more relaxed than you were before you began. Practice the tension-release method until you can achieve complete relaxation quickly (5 to 10 minutes). After you have practiced relaxation once a day for a week or two, you will begin to be able to tell when your body (or a group of muscles) is tense. Also, you will begin to be able to relax on command. This is a valuable skill that you can apply in any situation that makes you feel tense or anxious.

Vicarious Desensitization

What if it's not practical to directly act out the steps of a hierarchy? For a fear of heights, the steps of the hierarchy might be acted out. However, if this is impractical, as it might be in the case of a fear of flying, the problem can be handled by having clients observe *models* who are performing the feared behavior (Eifert & Lejuez, 2000) (▶▶ Figure 13.2). A model is a person (either live or filmed) who serves as an example for observational learning. If such **vicarious desensitization** (secondhand learning) can't be used, there is yet another option. Fortunately, desensitization works almost as well when a person *vividly imagines* each step in the hierarchy (Yahnke, Sheikh, & Beckman, 2003). If the steps can be visualized without anxiety, fear in the actual situation is reduced. Because imagining feared stimuli can be done at a therapist's office, it is the most common way of doing desensitization.

Virtual Reality Exposure

In an important new development, psychologists are now also using virtual reality to treat phobias. Virtual reality is a computer-generated, three-dimensional "world" that viewers enter by wearing a head-mounted video display. **Virtual reality exposure** presents computerized fear stimuli to clients in a realistic, yet carefully controlled fashion (Wiederhold & Wiederhold, 2005). It has already been used to treat fears of flying, driving, and public speaking as well as acrophobia (fear of heights), claustrophobia, and spider phobias (Arbona

Tension-release method A procedure for systematically achieving deep relaxation of the body.

Vicarious desensitization A reduction in fear or anxiety that takes place vicariously ("secondhand") when a client watches models perform the feared behavior.

Virtual reality exposure Use of computer-generated images to present fear stimuli. The virtual environment responds to a viewer's head movements and other inputs.

◀◀ **FIGURE 13.2** Treatment of a snake phobia by vicarious desensitization. These classic photographs show models interacting with snakes. To overcome their own fears, phobic subjects observed the models. (Bandura, Blanchard, & Ritter, 1969. Photos courtesy of Albert Bandura.)

FIGURE 13.3 *(top)* Dr. Larry Hodges (in the head-mounted display) and Dr. Page Anderson show how a virtual reality system is used to expose people to feared stimuli. *(bottom)* A computer image from a virtual Iraq. Iraq veterans suffering from posttraumatic stress disorder (PTSD) can re-experience their traumas. For example, someone whose Humvee was destroyed by an improvised explosive device can relive that moment complete with sights, sounds, vibrations, and even smells. Successive exposures result in a reduction of PTSD symptoms (Gerardi et al., 2008).

et al., 2004; Giuseppe, 2005; Hoffman et al., 2003; Lee et al., 2002; Wald and Taylor, 2000). (See ▶▶ Figure 13.3.)

Desensitization has been one of the most successful behavior therapies. A relatively new technique may provide yet another way to lower fears, anxieties, and psychological pain.

Eye Movement Desensitization

Traumatic events produce painful memories. Disturbing flashbacks often haunt victims of accidents, disasters, molestations, muggings, rapes, or emotional abuse. To help ease traumatic memories and posttraumatic stress, Dr. Francine Shapiro developed **eye movement desensitization and reprocessing (EMDR).**

In a typical EMDR session, the client is asked to visualize the images that most upset her or him. At the same time, a pencil (or other object) is moved rapidly from side to side in front of the person's eyes. Watching the moving object causes the person's eyes to dart swiftly back and forth. After about 30 seconds, clients describe any memories, feelings, and thoughts that emerged and discuss them with the therapist. These steps are repeated until troubling thoughts and emotions no longer surface (Shapiro, 2001; Shapiro & Forrest, 2004).

A number of studies suggest that EMDR lowers anxieties and takes the pain out of traumatic memories (Seidler & Wagner, 2006; Silver et al., 2005). However, EMDR is highly controversial. Some studies, for example, have found that eye movements add nothing to the treatment. The apparent success of EMDR may simply be based on gradual exposure to upsetting stimuli, as in other forms of desensitization (Cahill, Carrigan, & Frueh, 1999; Davidson & Parker, 2001). On the other hand, some researchers continue to find that EMDR is superior to traditional therapies (Greenwald, 2006; Rogers & Silver, 2002).

Is EMDR a breakthrough? Given the frequency of traumas in modern society, it shouldn't be long before we find out.

Eye movement desensitization and reprocessing (EMDR) A technique for reducing fear or anxiety; based on holding upsetting thoughts in mind while rapidly moving the eyes from side to side.

RECITE

1. What two types of conditioning are used in behavior modification? _____ and _____
2. Shock, pain, and discomfort play what role in conditioning an aversion?
   a. conditioned stimulus b. unconditioned response
   c. unconditioned stimulus d. conditioned response
3. If shock is used to control drinking, it must be _____ contingent.
4. What two principles underlie systematic desensitization? _____ and _____
5. When desensitization is carried out through the use of live or filmed models, it is called
   a. cognitive therapy b. flooding
   c. covert desensitization d. vicarious desensitization
6. The three basic steps in systematic desensitization are: constructing a hierarchy, flooding the person with anxiety, and imagining relaxation. T or F?
7. In EMDR therapy, computer-generated virtual reality images are used to expose clients to fear-provoking stimuli. T or F?

REFLECT

Critical Thinking

8. Alcoholics who take a drug called Antabuse become ill after drinking alcohol. Why, then, don't they develop an aversion to drinking?
9. A natural form of desensitization often takes place in hospitals. Can you guess what it is?

Relate

Can you describe three problems for which you think behavior therapy would be an appropriate treatment?

A friend of yours has a dog that goes berserk during thunderstorms. You own a CD of a thunderstorm. How could you use the CD to desensitize the dog? (Hint: The CD player has a volume control.)

Have you ever become naturally desensitized to a stimulus or situation that at first made you anxious (for instance, heights, public speaking, or driving on freeways)? How would you explain your reduced fear?

Operant Therapies—All the World Is a Skinner Box?

What role do operant principles play in behavior therapy?

Aversion therapy and desensitization are based on classical conditioning. Where does operant conditioning fit in? As you may recall, operant conditioning refers to learning based on the consequences of making a response. The operant principles most often used by behavior therapists to deal with human behavior are:

1. **Positive reinforcement.** Responses that are followed by reward tend to occur more frequently. If children whine and get attention, they will whine more frequently. If you get A's in your psychology class, you may become a psychology major.
2. **Nonreinforcement.** A response that is not followed by reward will occur less frequently.
3. **Extinction.** If a response is not followed by reward after it has been repeated many times, it will go away. After winning 3 times, you pull the handle on a slot machine 30 times more without a payoff. What do you do? You go away. So does the response of handle pulling (for that particular machine, at any rate).
4. **Punishment.** If a response is followed by discomfort or an undesirable effect, the response will be suppressed (but not necessarily extinguished).
5. **Shaping.** Shaping means rewarding actions that are closer and closer approximations to a desired response. For example, to reward an intellectually disabled child for saying "ball," you might begin by rewarding the child for saying anything that starts with a *b* sound.

6. **Stimulus control.** Responses tend to come under the control of the situation in which they occur. If you set your clock 10 minutes fast, it may be easier to leave the house on time in the morning. Your departure is under the stimulus control of the clock, even though you know it is fast.

7. **Time out.** A time-out procedure usually involves removing the individual from a situation in which reinforcement occurs. Time out is a variation of response cost: It prevents reward from following an undesirable response. For example, children who fight with each other can be sent to separate rooms and allowed out only when they are able to behave more calmly. (For a more thorough review of operant learning, return to Chapter 6.)

As simple as these principles may seem, they have been used very effectively to overcome difficulties in work, home, school, and industrial settings. Let's see how.

Nonreinforcement and Extinction

An extremely overweight mental patient had a persistent and disturbing habit: She stole food from other patients. No one could persuade her to stop stealing or to diet. For the sake of her health, a behavior therapist assigned her a special table in the ward dining room. If she approached any other table, she was immediately removed from the dining room. Any attempt to steal from others caused the patient to miss her own meal (Ayllon, 1963). Because her attempts to steal food went unrewarded, they rapidly disappeared.

What operant principles did the therapist in this example use? The therapist used *nonreward* to produce *extinction.* The most frequently occurring human behaviors lead to some form of reward. An undesirable response can be eliminated by *identifying* and *removing* the rewards that maintain it. But people don't always do things for food, money, or other obvious rewards. Most of the rewards maintaining human behavior are subtler. *Attention, approval,* and *concern* are common yet powerful reinforcers for humans (▶▶ Figure 13.4).

Nonreward and extinction can eliminate many problem behaviors, especially in schools, hospitals, and institutions. Often, difficulties center around a limited number of particularly disturbing responses. *Time out* is a good way to remove such responses, usually by refusing to pay attention to a person who is misbehaving. For example, 14-year-old Terrel periodically appeared in the nude in the activity room of a training center for disturbed adolescents. This behavior always generated a great deal of attention from staff and other patients. As an experiment, the next time he appeared nude, counselors and other staff members greeted him normally and then ignored him. Attention from other patients rapidly subsided. Sheepishly he returned to his room and dressed.

Behavioristic

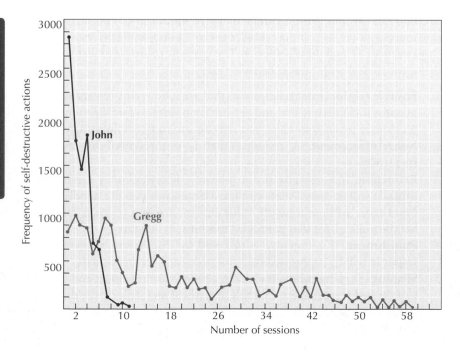

▶▶ **FIGURE 13.4** This graph shows extinction of self-destructive behavior in two autistic boys. Before extinction began, the boys received attention and concern from adults for injuring themselves. During extinction, the adults were taught to ignore the boys' self-damaging behavior. As you can see, the number of times that the boys tried to injure themselves declined rapidly. (Adapted from Lovaas & Simons, "Manipulation of self-destruction in three retarded children." From Journal of Applied Behavior Analysis, 1969 [2], 3. p. 147, Fig 1. Reprinted by permission of the authors.)

Reinforcement and Token Economies

A distressing problem therapists sometimes face is how to break through to severely disturbed patients who won't talk. Conventional psychotherapy offers little hope of improvement for such patients.

What can be done for them? One widely used approach is based on *tokens* (symbolic rewards that can be exchanged for real rewards). Tokens may be printed slips of paper, check marks, points, or gold stars. Whatever form they take, tokens serve as rewards because they may be exchanged for candy, food, cigarettes, recreation, or privileges, such as private time with a therapist, outings, or watching TV. Tokens are used in mental hospitals, half-way houses, schools for the intellectually disabled, programs for delinquents, and ordinary classrooms. They usually produce improvements in behavior (Dickerson, Tenhula, & Green-Paden, 2005; Reitman et al., 2004).

By using tokens, a therapist can *immediately reward* positive responses. For maximum impact, therapists select specific *target behaviors* (actions or other behaviors the therapist seeks to modify). Target behaviors are then reinforced with tokens. For example, a mute mental patient might first be given a token each time he or she says a word. Next, tokens may be given for speaking a complete sentence. Later, the patient could gradually be required to speak more often, then to answer questions, and eventually to carry on a short conversation in order to receive tokens. In this way, deeply withdrawn patients have been returned to the world of normal communication.

Full-scale use of tokens in an institutional setting produces a *token economy*. In a **token economy,** patients are rewarded with tokens for a wide range of socially desirable or productive activities (Spiegler & Guevremont, 2003). They must *pay* tokens for privileges and for engaging in problem behaviors (▶▶ Figure 13.5). For example, tokens are given to patients who get out of bed, dress themselves, take required medication, arrive for meals on time, and so on. Constructive activities, such as gardening, cooking, or cleaning, may also earn tokens. Patients must *exchange* tokens for meals and private rooms, movies, passes,

Credit Card

OXNARD DAY TREATMENT CENTER CREDIT INCENTIVE SYSTEM

EARN CREDITS BY		SPEND CREDITS FOR	
MONITOR DAILY	15	COFFEE	5
MENU PLANNING CHAIRMAN	50	LUNCH	10
PARTICIPATE	5	EXCEPT THURSDAY	15
BUY FOOD AT STORE	10	BUS TRIP	5
COOK FOR/PREPARE LUNCH	5	BOWLING	8
WIPE OFF KITCHEN TABLE	3	GROUP THERAPY	5
WASH DISHES	5-10	PRIVATE STAFF TIME	5
DRY AND PUT AWAY DISHES	5	DAY OFF	5-20
MAKE COFFEE AND CLEAN URN	15	WINDOW SHOPPING	5
CLEAN REFRIGERATOR	20	REVIEW WITH DR.	10
ATTEND PLANNING CONFERENCE	1	DOING OWN THING	1
OT PREPARATION	1-5	LATE 1 PER EVERY 10 MIN	
COMPLETE OT PROJECT	5	PRESCRIPTION FROM DR.	10
RETURN OT PROJECT	2		
DUST AND POLISH TABLES	5		
PUT AWAY GROCERIES	3		
CLEAN TABLE	5		
CLEAN 6 ASH TRAYS	2		
CLEAN SINK	5		
CARRY OUT CUPS & BOTTLES	5		
CLEAN CHAIRS	5		
CLEAN KITCHEN CUPBOARDS	5		
ASSIST STAFF	5		
ARRANGE MAGAZINES NEATLY	3		
BEING ON TIME	5		
MONITOR-ANN			

▲ **FIGURE 13.5** Shown here is a token used in one token economy system. In this instance the token is a card that records the number of credits earned by a patient. Also pictured is a list of credit values for various activities. Tokens may be exchanged for items or for privileges listed on the board. (After photographs by Robert P. Liberman.)

Token economy A therapeutic program in which desirable behaviors are reinforced with tokens that can be exchanged for goods, services, activities, and privileges.

off-ward activities, and other privileges. They are *charged* tokens for staying in bed, disrobing in public, talking to themselves, fighting, crying, and similar target behaviors (Morisse et al., 1996).

Token economies can radically change a patient's overall adjustment and morale. Patients are given an incentive to change, and they are held responsible for their actions. The use of tokens may seem manipulative, but it actually empowers patients. Many "hopelessly" intellectually disabled, mentally ill, and delinquent people have been returned to productive lives by means of token economies (Field et al., 2004).

By the time they are ready to leave, patients may be earning tokens on a weekly basis for maintaining sane, responsible, and productive behavior (Miltenberger, 2008). Typically, the most effective token economies are those that gradually switch from tokens to *social rewards* such as praise, recognition, and approval. Such rewards are what patients will receive when they return to family, friends, and community.

Cognitive Therapy—Think Positive!

Can therapy change thoughts and emotions?

How would a behavior therapist treat a problem like depression? None of the techniques described seem to apply. As we have discussed, behavior therapists usually try to change troublesome actions. However, in recent years cognitive therapists have become interested in what people think, believe, and feel, as well as how they act. In general, **cognitive therapy** helps clients change thinking patterns that lead to troublesome emotions or behaviors (Hall, 2006). For example, compulsive hand-washing can be greatly reduced by changing a client's thoughts and beliefs about dirt and contamination (Jones & Menzies, 1998). Cognitive therapy has been used as a remedy for many problems, but it has been especially successful in treating depression (Chambless & Ollendick, 2001; Hollon, Stewart, & Strunk, 2006).

Cognitive Therapy for Depression

As you may recall from Chapter 12, cognitive psychologists believe that negative, self-defeating thoughts underlie depression. According to Aaron Beck (1991), depressed persons see themselves, the world, and the future in negative terms because of some major distortions in thinking. The first is **selective perception,** which refers to perceiving only certain stimuli in a larger array. If five good things and three bad things happen during the day, depressed people focus only on the bad. A second thinking error in depression is **overgeneralization,** the tendency to think that an upsetting event applies to other, unrelated situations. An example would be considering yourself a total failure or completely worthless if you were to lose a part-time job or fail a test. To complete the picture, depressed persons tend to magnify the importance of undesirable events by engaging in **all-or-nothing thinking.** That is, they see events as completely good or bad, right or wrong, and themselves as either successful or failing miserably (J. S. Beck, 2002; Gilbert, 2001).

How do cognitive therapists alter such patterns? Cognitive therapists make a step-by-step effort to correct negative thoughts that lead to depression or similar problems. At first, clients are taught to recognize and keep track of their own thoughts. The client and therapist then look for ideas and beliefs that cause depression, anger, and avoidance. For example, here's how a therapist might challenge all-or-nothing thinking (Burns & Persons, 1982):

Client: I'm feeling even more depressed. No one wants to hire me, and I can't even clean up my apartment. I feel completely incompetent!

Therapist: I see. The fact that you are unemployed and have a messy apartment proves that you are completely incompetent?

Client: Well. . . . I can see that doesn't add up.

Cognitive therapy A therapy directed at changing the maladaptive thoughts, beliefs, and feelings that underlie emotional and behavioral problems.

Selective perception Perceiving only certain stimuli among a larger array of possibilities.

Overgeneralization Blowing a single event out of proportion by extending it to a large number of unrelated situations.

All-or-nothing thinking Classifying objects or events as absolutely right or wrong, good or bad, acceptable or unacceptable, and so forth.

Ten Irrational Beliefs—Which Do You Hold?

Rational-emotive behavior therapists have identified numerous beliefs that commonly lead to emotional upsets and conflicts. See if you recognize any of the following irrational beliefs:

1. I must be loved and approved by almost every significant person in my life or it's awful and I'm worthless.
   Example: "One of my roommates doesn't seem to like me. I must be a total zero."

2. I should be completely competent and achieving in all ways to be a worthwhile person.
   Example: "I don't understand my chemistry class. I guess I really am a stupid person."

3. Certain people I must deal with are thoroughly bad and should be severely blamed and punished for it.
   Example: "The old man next door is such a pain. I'm going to play my stereo even louder the next time he complains."

4. It is awful and upsetting when things are not the way I would very much like them to be.
   Example: "I should have gotten a B in that class. The teacher is unfair."

5. My unhappiness is always caused by external events; I cannot control my emotional reactions.
   Example: "You make me feel awful. I would be happy if it weren't for you."

6. If something unpleasant might happen, I should keep dwelling on it.
   Example: "I'll never forget the time my boss insulted me. I think about it every day at work."

7. It is easier to avoid difficulties and responsibilities than to face them.
   Example: "I don't know why my wife seems angry. Maybe it will just pass by if I ignore it."

8. I should depend on others who are stronger than I am.
   Example: "I couldn't survive if he left me."

9. Because something once strongly affected my life, it will do so indefinitely.
   Example: "My girlfriend dumped me during my junior year in college. I don't know if I can ever trust a woman again."

10. There is always a perfect solution to human problems and it is awful if this solution is not found.
    Example: "I'm so depressed about politics in this country. It all seems hopeless."

(Adapted from J. S. Beck, 2002; Ellis, 2004; Rohsenow & Smith, 1982.)

If any of the listed beliefs sound familiar, you may be creating unnecessary emotional distress for yourself by holding on to unrealistic expectations.

Next, clients are asked to gather information to test their beliefs. For instance, a depressed person might list his or her activities for a week. The list is then used to challenge all-or-nothing thoughts, such as "I had a terrible week" or "I'm a complete failure." With more coaching, clients learn to alter their thoughts in ways that improve their moods, actions, and relationships.

Cognitive therapy is as effective as drugs for treating many cases of depression. More important, people who have adopted new thinking patterns are less likely to become depressed again—a benefit that drugs can't impart (Dozois & Dobson, 2004; Hollon, Stewart, & Strunk, 2006).

In an alternate approach, cognitive therapists look for an *absence* of effective coping skills and thinking patterns, not for the *presence* of self-defeating thoughts (Dobson, Backs-Dermott, & Dozois, 2000). The aim is to teach clients how to cope with anger, depression, shyness, stress, and similar problems. Stress inoculation, which was described in Chapter 11, is a good example of this approach.

Cognitive therapy is a rapidly expanding specialty. Before we leave the topic, let's explore another widely used cognitive therapy.

Rational-Emotive Behavior Therapy

Rational-emotive behavior therapy (REBT) attempts to change irrational beliefs that cause emotional problems. According to Albert Ellis (1913–2007), the basic idea of REBT is as easy as A-B-C (Ellis, 1995, 2004). Ellis assumes that people become unhappy and develop self-defeating habits because they have unrealistic or faulty *beliefs.*

How are beliefs important? Ellis analyzes problems in this way: The letter A stands for an *activating experience,* which the person assumes to be the cause of C, an *emotional consequence.* For instance, a person who is rejected (the activating experience) feels depressed, threatened, or hurt (the consequence). Rational-emotive behavior therapy shows the client that the real problem is what comes between A and C: In between is B, the client's irrational and unrealistic *beliefs.* In this example, an unrealistic belief leading to unnecessary suffering is: "I must be loved and approved by everyone at all times." REBT holds that events do not *cause* us to have feelings. We feel as we do because of our beliefs (Kottler, 2004). (For some examples, see "Ten Irrational Beliefs—Which Do You Hold?")

Rational-emotive behavior therapy (REBT)
An approach that states that irrational beliefs cause many emotional problems and that such beliefs must be changed or abandoned.

Overcoming the Gambler's Fallacy

Seventeen-year-old Jonathan just lost his shirt again. This time he did it playing online blackjack. Jonathan started out making $5 bets and then doubled his bet over and over. Surely, he thought, his luck would eventually change. However, he ran out of money after just eight hands, having lost more than $1,000. Last week he lost a lot of money playing Texas Hold 'Em. Now Jonathan is in tears—he has lost most of his summer earnings, and he is worried about having to drop out of school and tell his parents about his losses. Jonathan has had to admit that he is part of the growing ranks of underage gambling addicts (LaBrie & Shaffer, 2007; Wilber & Potenza, 2006).

Like many problem gamblers, Jonathan suffers from several cognitive distortions related to gambling. Here are some of his mistaken beliefs (adapted from Toneatto, 2002):

Magnified gambling skill: Your self-confidence is exaggerated, despite the fact that you lose persistently.

Attribution errors: You ascribe your wins to skill but blame losses on bad luck.

Gambler's fallacy: You believe that a string of losses soon must be followed by wins.

Selective memory: You remember your wins but forget your losses.

Overinterpretation of cues: You put too much faith in irrelevant cues such as bodily sensations or a feeling that your next bet will be a winner.

Luck as a trait: You believe that you are a "lucky" person in general.

Probability biases: You have incorrect beliefs about randomness and chance events.

Do you have any of these mistaken beliefs? Taken together, Jonathan's cognitive distortions created an illusion of control. That is, he believed that if he worked hard enough, he could figure out how to win. Fortunately, a cognitive therapist helped Jonathan *cognitively restructure* his beliefs. He now no longer believes he can control chance events. Jonathan still gambles a bit, but he does so only recreationally, keeping his losses within his budget and enjoying himself in the process.

Ellis (1979, 2004) says that most irrational beliefs come from three core ideas, each of which is unrealistic:

1. I *must* perform well and be approved of by significant others. If I don't, then it is awful, I cannot stand it, and I am a rotten person.
2. You *must* treat me fairly. When you don't, it is horrible, and I cannot bear it.
3. Conditions *must* be the way I want them to be. It is terrible when they are not, and I cannot stand living in such an awful world.

It's easy to see that such beliefs can lead to much grief and needless suffering in a less than perfect world. Rational-emotive behavior therapists are very directive in their attempts to change a client's irrational beliefs and "self-talk." The therapist may directly attack clients' logic, challenge their thinking, confront them with evidence contrary to their beliefs, and even assign "homework." Here, for instance, are some examples of statements that dispute irrational beliefs (after Kottler, 2004):

*   "Where is the evidence that you are a loser just because you didn't do well this one time?"
*   "Who said the world should be fair? That's your rule."
*   "What are you telling yourself to make yourself feel so upset?"
*   "Is it really terrible that things aren't working out as you would like? Or is it just inconvenient?"

Many of us would probably do well to give up our irrational beliefs. Improved self-acceptance and a better tolerance of daily annoyances are the benefits of doing so. (See "Overcoming the Gambler's Fallacy.")

The value of cognitive approaches is further illustrated by three techniques (*covert sensitization, thought stopping,* and *covert reinforcement*) described in this chapter's Psychology in Action section. A little later you can see what you think of them.

RECITE

1. Behavior modification programs aimed at extinction of an undesirable behavior typically make use of what operant principles?
   a. punishment and stimulus control
   b. punishment and shaping
   c. nonreinforcement and time out
   d. stimulus control and time out
2. Attention can be a powerful _____ for humans.
3. Token economies depend on the time-out procedure. T or F?
4. Tokens basically allow the operant shaping of desired responses or "target behaviors." T or F?
5. According to Beck, selective perception, overgeneralization, and _____ thinking are cognitive habits that underlie depression.
6. REBT teaches people to change the antecedents of irrational behavior. T or F?

REFLECT

Critical Thinking

7. In Aaron Beck's terms, a belief such as "I must perform well or I am a rotten person" involves two thinking errors. These are:
   1. _____
   2. _____

Relate

See if you can give a personal example of how the following principles have affected your behavior: positive reinforcement, extinction, punishment, shaping, stimulus control, and time out.

You are setting up a token economy for troubled elementary school children. What target behaviors will you attempt to reinforce? For what behaviors will you charge tokens?

We all occasionally engage in negative thinking. Can you remember a time recently when you engaged in selective perception? Overgeneralization? All-or-nothing thinking?

Which of REBT's irrational beliefs have affected your feelings? Which beliefs would you like to change?

ANSWERS

1. c 2. reinforcer 3. F 4. T 5. all-or-nothing 6. F 7. Overgeneralization and all-or-nothing thinking.

Group Therapy—People Who Need People

Can psychotherapy be done with groups of people?

To complete our discussion of psychotherapies, we will begin with a brief look at group therapy. After that, we will try to identify the core features and helping skills that make psychotherapy "work."

Group therapy is psychotherapy done with more than one person. Many of the therapies we have discussed can be adapted for use in groups (Corey, 2008). Psychologists first tried working with groups because there was a shortage of therapists. Surprisingly, group therapy has turned out to be just as effective as individual therapy and has some special advantages (Burlingame, Fuhriman, & Mosier, 2003).

What are the advantages? In group therapy, a person can *act out* or directly experience problems. Doing so often produces insights that might not occur from merely talking about an issue. In addition, other group members with similar problems can offer support and useful input. Group therapy is especially good for helping people understand their personal relationships (McCluskey, 2002). For reasons such as these, a number of specialized groups have emerged. Because they range from Alcoholics Anonymous to Marriage Encounter, we will sample only a few examples.

A group therapy session. Group members offer mutual support while sharing problems and insights.

Group therapy Psychotherapy conducted in a group setting to make therapeutic use of group dynamics.

Psychodrama

One of the first group therapies was developed by Jacob Moreno (1953), who called his technique *psychodrama*. In **psychodrama,** clients act out personal conflicts with others who play supporting roles (Blatner, 2006). Through role-playing, the client re-enacts incidents that cause problems in real life. Moreno believed that insights gained in this way transfer to real-life situations. For example, Don, a disturbed teenager, might act out a typical family fight, with the therapist playing his father and with other clients playing his mother, brothers, and sisters.

Therapists using psychodrama often find that role reversals are helpful. A **role reversal** involves taking the part of another person to learn how he or she feels. For instance, Don might role-play his father or mother, to better understand their feelings. A related method is the **mirror technique,** in which clients observe another person re-enact their behavior. Thus, Don might briefly join the audience and watch as another group member plays his role. This would allow him to see himself as others do. Later, the group may summarize what happened and reflect on its meaning (Turner, 1997).

Family and Couples Therapy

Family relationships are the source of great pleasure and, all too often, of great pain. In **family therapy,** husband, wife, and children work as a group to resolve the problems of each family member. This is also called *couples therapy* when children are not involved (Scheinkman, 2008). Family and couples therapy tends to be time limited and focused on specific problems, such as frequent fights or a depressed teenager. For some types of problems, family therapy may be superior to other approaches (Capuzzi, 2003; Eisler et al., 2007).

Family therapists believe that a problem experienced by one family member is really the whole family's problem. If the entire pattern of behavior in a family doesn't change, improvements in any single family member may not last. Thus family therapists treat the family as a unit, although they may not meet with the entire family at each session (Eisler et al., 2007). Family members work together to improve communication, to change destructive patterns, and to see themselves and each other in new ways (Goldenberg & Goldenberg, 2004; Griffin, 2002).

Group Awareness Training

During the 1960s and 1970s, the human potential movement led many people to seek personal growth experiences. Often, their interest was expressed by participation in sensitivity training or encounter groups.

What is the difference between sensitivity groups and encounter groups? Sensitivity groups tend to be less confrontational than encounter groups. Participants in **sensitivity groups** take part in exercises that gently enlarge self-awareness and sensitivity to others. For example, in a *trust walk,* participants expand their confidence in others by allowing themselves to be led around while blindfolded.

Encounter groups are based on an honest expression of feelings, and intensely personal communication may take place. Typically, the emphasis is on tearing down defenses and false fronts. Because there is a danger of hostile confrontation, participation is safest when members are carefully screened and a trained leader guides the group. Encounter group "casualties" are rare, but they do occur (Shaffer & Galinsky, 1989).

There has also been much public interest in various forms of large-group awareness training. **Large-group awareness training** refers to programs that claim to increase self-awareness and facilitate constructive personal change. The Garden Company, Lifespring, the Forum, the Hoffman Quadrinity Process, and similar commercial programs are examples. Like the smaller groups that preceded them, large-group training combines psychological exercises, confrontation, new viewpoints, and group dynamics to promote personal change.

Are sensitivity, encounter, and awareness groups really psychotherapies? These experiences tend to be positive, but they produce only moderate benefits (Faith, Wong, &

Psychodrama A therapy in which clients act out personal conflicts and feelings in the presence of others who play supporting roles.

Role reversal Taking the role of another person to learn how one's own behavior appears from the other person's perspective.

Mirror technique Observing another person re-enact one's own behavior, like a character in a play; designed to help persons see themselves more clearly.

Family therapy Technique in which all family members participate, both individually and as a group, to change destructive relationships and communication patterns.

Sensitivity group A group experience consisting of exercises designed to increase self-awareness and sensitivity to others.

Encounter group A group experience that emphasizes intensely honest interchanges among participants regarding feelings and reactions to one another.

Large-group awareness training Any of a number of programs (many of them commercialized) that claim to increase self-awareness and facilitate constructive personal change.

Why is it risky to believe people who say their therapy was effective? An old joke among doctors is that a cold lasts a week without treatment and seven days with it. Perhaps the same is true of therapy. Someone who feels better after 6 months of therapy may have experienced a spontaneous remission—they just feel better because so much time has passed. Or perhaps the crisis that triggered the therapy is now nearly forgotten. Or maybe some sort of therapy placebo effect has occurred. Also, it's possible that the person has received help from other people, such as family, friends, or clergy.

To find out if therapy works, we could randomly place clients in an experimental group that receives therapy and a control group that does not. When this is done, the control group may show some improvement, even without receiving therapy (Lambert & Ogles, 2002). Thus, we can conclude that the therapy is effective only if people in the experimental group improve more than those in the control group.

But isn't it unethical to withhold treatment from someone who really needs therapy? That's right. One way to deal with this is to use a *waiting-list control group*. In this case, people who are waiting to see a therapist are compared with those who receive therapy. Later, those on the waiting list will eventually also receive therapy.

If we combine the results of many experiments, it becomes clear that therapy *is* effective (Lipsey & Wilson, 1993). In addition, studies have revealed that some therapies work best for specific problems (Bradley et al., 2005; Eddy et al., 2004). For example, behavioral, cognitive-behavioral, and drug therapies are most helpful in treating obsessive-compulsive disorder.

Carpenter, 1995). Moreover, many of the claimed benefits may result simply from a kind of **therapy placebo effect,** in which improvement is based on a client's belief that therapy will help. Positive expectations, a break in daily routine, and an excuse to act differently can have quite an impact. Also, less ambitious goals may be easier to attain. For example, one program succeeded in teaching stress-management techniques in a large group setting (Timmerman, Emmelkamp, & Sanderman, 1998). Because of their versatility, groups undoubtedly will continue to be a major tool for solving problems and improving lives (Corey, 2008).

Psychotherapy—An Overview

What do various therapies have in common?

How effective is psychotherapy? Judging the outcome of therapy is tricky. In a national survey, nearly 9 out of 10 people who have sought mental health care say their lives improved as a result of the treatment (Kotkin, Daviet, & Gurin, 1996). Unfortunately, you can't just take people's word for it. (See "How Do We Know Therapy Actually Works?") Fortunately, there is direct evidence that therapy is beneficial. Hundreds of studies show a strong pattern of positive effects for psychotherapy, counseling, and other psychological treatments (Barlow, 2004; Lambert & Cattani-Thompson, 1996; Moras, 2002).

Of course, results vary in individual cases. For some people therapy is immensely helpful; for others it is unsuccessful; overall it is effective for more people than not. Speaking more subjectively, a real success, in which a person's life is changed for the better, can be worth the frustration of several cases in which little progress is made.

Although it is common to think of therapy as a long, slow process, this is not normally the case (Shapiro et al., 2003). Research shows that about 50 percent of all clients feel better after between 13 and 18 weekly 1-hour therapy sessions (Howard et al., 1986). This means that the majority of clients improve after 6 months of therapy. Such rapid improvement is impressive in view of the fact that people often suffer for several years before seeking help. Unfortunately, because of high costs and limited insurance coverage, the average client receives only 5 therapy sessions, after which only 20 percent of all patients feel better (Hansen, Lambert, & Forman, 2002).

Therapy placebo effect Improvement caused not by the actual process of therapy but by a client's expectation that therapy will help.

● Table 13.2 Comparison of Psychotherapies

	INSIGHT OR ACTION?	DIRECTIVE OR NONDIRECTIVE?	INDIVIDUAL OR GROUP?	THERAPY'S STRENGTH[*]
Psychoanalysis	Insight	Directive	Individual	Searching honesty
Brief psychodynamic therapy	Insight	Directive	Individual	Productive use of conflict
Client-centered therapy	Insight	Nondirective	Both	Acceptance, empathy
Existential therapy	Insight	Both	Individual	Personal empowerment
Gestalt therapy	Insight	Directive	Both	Focus on immediate awareness
Behavior therapy	Action	Directive	Both	Observable changes in behavior
Cognitive therapy	Action	Directive	Individual	Constructive guidance
Rational-emotive behavior therapy	Action	Directive	Individual	Clarity of thinking and goals
Psychodrama	Insight	Directive	Group	Constructive re-enactments
Family therapy	Both	Directive	Group	Shared responsibility for problems

[*]This column based in part on Andrews (1989).

Core Features of Psychotherapy

What do psychotherapies have in common? We have sampled only a few of the many therapies in use today. For a summary of major differences among psychotherapies, see ● Table 13.2. To add to your understanding, let us briefly summarize what all techniques have in common.

Psychotherapies of various types share all or most of these goals: restoring hope, courage, and optimism; gaining insight; resolving conflicts; improving one's sense of self; changing unacceptable patterns of behavior; finding purpose; mending interpersonal relations; and learning to approach problems rationally (Frank & Frank, 2004; Seligman, 1998). To accomplish these goals, psychotherapies offer the following:

1. Therapy provides a **therapeutic alliance,** a *caring relationship* that unites the client and therapist as they work together to solve the client's problems. The strength of this alliance has a major impact on whether therapy succeeds (Kozart, 2002; Meier et al., 2006). The basis for this relationship is emotional rapport, warmth, friendship, understanding, acceptance, and empathy.

2. Therapy offers a *protected setting* in which emotional *catharsis* (release) can take place. Therapy is a sanctuary in which the client is free to express fears, anxieties, and personal secrets without fearing rejection or loss of confidentiality.

3. All therapies to some extent offer an *explanation* or *rationale* for the client's suffering. Additionally, they propose a line of action that will end this suffering.

4. Therapy provides clients with a *new perspective* about themselves and their situations and a chance to practice *new behaviors* (Crencavage & Norcross, 1990; Prochaska & Norcross, 2010). Insights gained during therapy can bring about lasting changes in clients' lives (Grande et al., 2003).

The Future of Psychotherapy

Psychotherapy has come a long way since the days of trepanning and demonology. Still, the search for ways to improve psychotherapy remains an urgent challenge for those who devote their lives to helping others.

What will psychotherapy look like in the future? A group of experts predicted the following (Norcross, Hedges, & Prochaska, 2002):

- There will be an increase in the use of short-term therapy and solution-focused, problem solving approaches.
- More therapy will be provided by master's-level practitioners (counselors, social workers, and psychiatric nurses).

Therapeutic alliance A caring relationship that unites a therapist and a client in working to solve the client's problems.

- The use of lower-cost Internet services, telephone counseling, paraprofessionals, and self-help groups will grow.
- The use of psychiatrists and psychoanalysis will decrease.

As you might guess, many of these predicted changes are based on pressures to reduce the cost of mental health services. Another interesting cost-saving measure is the idea that computer software may be able to treat some relatively minor problems (Craske et al., 2009). In one study, clients worked through ten computer-guided sessions that helped them identify a problem, form a plan of action, and work through carrying out the plan. Most were satisfied with the help they received (Jacobs et al., 2001).

In another major development, psychologists are making progress in identifying "empirically supported" (or "evidence-based") therapies (Westen & Bradley, 2005). Rather than just relying on intuition, clinicians are seeking guidance from research experiments and guidelines developed through clinical practice (Carroll & Rounsaville, 2007; Miller & Binder, 2002). The end result is a better understanding of which therapies "work" best for specific types of problems. This trend is also helping to weed out fringe "therapies" that have little or no value.

Basic Counseling Skills

A number of general helping skills can be distilled from the various approaches to therapy. These are points to keep in mind if you would like to comfort a person in distress, such as a troubled friend or relative (● Table 13.3).

Active Listening

People frequently talk "at" each other without really listening. A person with problems needs to be heard. Make a sincere effort to listen to and understand the person. Try to accept the person's message without judging it or leaping to conclusions. Let the person know you are listening, through eye contact, posture, your tone of voice, and your replies (Kottler, 2004).

Reflect Thoughts and Feelings

One of the best things you can do when offering support to another person is to give feedback by simply restating what is said. This is also a good way to encourage a person to talk. If your friend seems to be at a loss for words, *restate* or *paraphrase* his or her last sentence. Here's an example:

Friend: I'm really down about school. I can't get interested in any of my classes. I flunked my Spanish test, and somebody stole my notebook for psychology.

You: You're really upset about school, aren't you?

Friend: Yeah, and my parents are hassling me about my grades again.

You: You're feeling pressured by your parents?

Friend: Yeah, damn.

You: It must make you angry to be pressured by them.

As simple as this sounds, it is very helpful to someone trying to sort out feelings. Try it. If nothing else, you'll develop a reputation as a fantastic conversationalist!

Silence

Counselors tend to wait longer before responding than do people in everyday conversations. Pauses of 5 seconds or more are not unusual, and interrupting is rare. Listening patiently lets the person feel unhurried and encourages her or him to speak freely.

● **Table 13.3 Helping Behaviors**

To help another person gain insight into a personal problem, it is valuable to keep the following comparison in mind.

BEHAVIORS THAT HELP	BEHAVIORS THAT HINDER
Active listening	Probing painful topics
Acceptance	Judging/moralizing
Reflecting feelings	Criticism
Open-ended questioning	Threats
Supportive statements	Rejection
Respect	Ridicule/sarcasm
Patience	Impatience
Genuineness	Placing blame
Paraphrasing	Opinionated statements

Source: Adapted from Kottler, 2004.

Therapy and Culture—A Bad Case of "Ifufunyane"

At the age of 23, the patient was clearly suffering from "ifufunyane," a form of bewitchment common in the Xhosa culture of South Africa. However, he was treated at a local hospital by psychiatrists, who said he had schizophrenia and gave him antipsychotic drugs. The drugs helped, but his family shunned his fancy medical treatment and took him to a traditional healer who gave him herbs for his ifufunyane. Unfortunately, he got worse and was readmitted to the hospital. This time, the psychiatrists included the patient's family in his treatment. Together, they agreed to treat him with a combination of antipsychotic drugs *and* traditional herbs. This time, the patient got much better and his ifufunyane was alleviated (Niehaus et al., 2005).

As this example illustrates, **culturally skilled therapists** are trained to work with clients from various cultural backgrounds. To be culturally skilled, a counselor must be able to do all of the following (American Psychological Association, 2003; Draguns, Gielen, & Fish, 2004; Fowers & Davidov, 2006):

- Adapt traditional theories and techniques to meet the needs of clients from non-European ethnic or racial groups.
- Be aware of his or her own cultural values and biases.
- Establish rapport with a person from a different cultural background.
- Be open to cultural differences without resorting to stereotypes.

- Treat members of racial or ethnic communities as individuals.
- Be aware of a client's ethnic identity and degree of acculturation to the majority society.
- Use existing helping resources within a cultural group to support efforts to resolve problems.

Cultural awareness has helped broaden our ideas about mental health and optimal development (Draguns, Gielen, & Fish, 2004). It is also worth remembering that cultural barriers apply to communication in all areas of life, not just therapy. Although such differences can be challenging, they are also frequently enriching (Gielen, Draguns, & Fish, 2008).

Questions

Because your goal is to encourage free expression, *open-ended questions* tend to be the most helpful. A *closed question* is one that can be answered yes or no. Open-ended questions call for an open-ended reply. Say, for example, that a friend tells you, "I feel like my boss has it in for me at work." A closed question would be, "Oh yeah? So, are you going to quit?" Open-ended questions such as "Do you want to talk about it?" or "How do you feel about it?" are more likely to be helpful.

Clarify the Problem

People who have a clear idea of what is wrong in their lives are more likely to discover solutions. Try to understand the problem from the person's point of view. As you do, check your understanding often. For example, you might ask, "Are you saying that you feel depressed just at school? Or in general?" Remember, a problem well defined is often half solved.

Teams of psychologists and counselors are often assembled to provide support to victims of major accidents and natural disasters. Because their work is stressful and often heart wrenching, relief workers also benefit from on-site counseling. Expressing emotions and talking about feelings are major elements of disaster counseling.

AFP/Getty Images

Focus on Feelings

Feelings are neither right nor wrong. By focusing on feelings you can encourage the outpouring of emotion that is the basis for catharsis. Passing judgment on what is said just makes people defensive. For example, if a friend confides that he has failed a test and you say, "Just study more and you will do better," he will probably become defensive or hostile. Much more can be accomplished by saying, "You must feel very frustrated" or simply, "How do you feel about it?"

Avoid Giving Advice

Many people mistakenly think that they must solve problems for others. Remember that your goal is to provide understanding and support, not solutions. Of course, it is reasonable to give advice when you are asked for it, but make sure your advice is appropriate. For example, the student described earlier knows he needs to study. His problem is to understand why he doesn't *want* to study.

Accept the Person's Frame of Reference

W. I. Thomas said, "Things perceived as real are real in their effects." Because we all live in different psychological worlds, there is no "correct" view of a life situation. Try to resist imposing your views on the problems of others. A person who feels that his or her view-

Culturally skilled therapist A therapist who has the awareness, knowledge, and skills necessary to treat clients from diverse cultural backgrounds.

point has been understood feels freer to examine it objectively and to question it. Understanding another person's perspective is especially important when cultural differences may create a barrier between a client and a therapist (Draguns, Gielen, & Fish, 2004). (See "Therapy and Culture—A Bad Case of 'Ifufunyane.'")

Maintain Confidentiality

Your efforts to help will be wasted if you fail to respect the privacy of someone who has confided in you. Put yourself in the person's place. Don't gossip.

These guidelines are not an invitation to play "junior therapist." Professional therapists are trained to approach serious problems with skills far exceeding those described here. However, the points made help define the qualities of a therapeutic relationship. They also emphasize that each of us can supply two of the greatest mental health resources available at any cost: friendship and honest communication.

Medical Therapies—Psychiatric Care

How do psychiatrists treat psychological disorders?

Psychotherapy may be applied to anything from a brief crisis to a full-scale psychosis. However, most psychotherapists *do not* treat patients with major depressive disorders, schizophrenia, or other severe conditions. Major mental disorders are more often treated medically (Julien, 2005).

Three main types of **somatic** (bodily) **therapy** are *pharmacotherapy, electrical stimulation therapy,* and *psychosurgery*. Somatic therapy is often done in the context of psychiatric hospitalization. All the somatic approaches have a strong medical slant and are typically administered by psychiatrists.

Drug Therapies

The atmosphere in psychiatric wards and mental hospitals changed radically in the mid-1950s with the widespread adoption of **pharmacotherapy** (FAR-meh-koe-THER-eh-pea), the use of drugs to treat psychopathology. Drugs may relieve the anxiety attacks and other discomforts of milder psychological disorders. More often, however, they are used to combat schizophrenia and major mood disorders.

What sort of drugs are used in pharmacotherapy? Three major types of drugs are used. All achieve their effects by influencing the activity of different brain neurotransmitters. **Anxiolytics** (ANG-zee-eh LIT-iks) such as Valium produce relaxation or reduce anxiety. **Antidepressants** are mood-elevating drugs that combat depression. **Antipsychotics** (also called **major tranquilizers**) have tranquilizing effects and reduce hallucinations and delusions. (See ● Table 13.4 for examples of each class of drugs.)

● Table 13.4 Commonly Prescribed Psychiatric Drugs

CLASS	EXAMPLES (TRADE NAMES)	EFFECTS
Anxiolytics (minor tranquilizers)	Ativan, Halcion, Librium, Restoril, Valium, Xanax	Reduce anxiety, tension, fear
Antidepressants	Anafranil, Elavil, Nardil, Norpramin, Parnate, Paxil, Prozac, Tofranil, Zoloft	Counteract depression
Antipsychotics (major tranquilizers)	Clozaril, Haldol, Mellaril, Navane, Risperdal, Thorazine	Reduce agitation, delusions, hallucinations, thought disorders

Somatic therapy Any bodily therapy, such as drug therapy, electroconvulsive therapy, or psychosurgery.

Pharmacotherapy The use of drugs to treat psychopathology.

Anxiolytics Drugs (such as Valium) that produce relaxation or reduce anxiety.

Antidepressants Mood-elevating drugs.

Antipsychotics Drugs that, in addition to having tranquilizing effects, also tend to reduce hallucinations and delusional thinking. (Also called **major tranquilizers.**)

The work of artist Rodger Casier illustrates the value of psychiatric care. Despite having a form of schizophrenia, Casier produces artwork that has received public acclaim and has been featured in professional journals.

Courtesy of Rodger Casier

Are drugs a valid approach to treatment? Drugs have shortened hospital stays and greatly improved the chances that people will recover from major psychological disorders. Drug therapy has also made it possible for many people to return to the community, where they can be treated on an outpatient basis.

Limitations of Drug Therapy

Regardless of their benefits, all drugs involve risks as well. For example, 15 percent of patients taking major tranquilizers for long periods develop a neurological disorder that causes rhythmic facial and mouth movements (Chakos et al., 1996). Similarly, while the drug *clozapine* (Clozaril) can relieve the symptoms of schizophrenia, 2 out of 100 patients taking the drug suffer from a potentially fatal blood disease (Ginsberg, 2006).

Is the risk worth it? Many experts think it is, because chronic schizophrenia robs people of almost everything that makes life worth living. It's possible, of course, that newer drugs will improve the risk/benefit ratio in the treatment of severe problems like schizophrenia. For example, the drug risperidone (Risperdal) appears to be as effective as Clozaril, without the same degree of lethal risk. But even the best new drugs are not cure-alls. They help some people and relieve some problems, but not all. It is noteworthy that for serious mental disorders, a combination of medication and psychotherapy almost always works better than drugs alone (Manber et al., 2008). Nevertheless, where schizophrenia and major mood disorders are concerned, drugs will undoubtedly remain the primary mode of treatment (Vasa, Carlino, & Pine, 2006; Walker et al., 2004).

Electrical Stimulation Therapy

In contrast to drug therapies, electrical stimulation therapies achieve their effects by altering the electrical activity of the brain. Electroconvulsive therapy is the first, and most dramatic, of these therapies. Widely used since the 1940s, it remains controversial to this day (Hirshbein & Sarvananda, 2008).

Electroshock

In **electroconvulsive therapy (ECT)** a 150-volt electrical current is passed through the brain for slightly less than a second. This rather drastic medical treatment for depression triggers a convulsion and causes the patient to lose consciousness for a short time. Muscle relaxants and sedative drugs are given before ECT to soften its impact. Treatments are given in a series of six to eight sessions spread over 3 to 4 weeks.

How does shock help? Actually, it is the seizure activity that is believed to be helpful. Proponents of ECT claim that shock-induced seizures alter or "reset" the biochemical and hormonal balance in the brain and body, bringing an end to severe depression and suicidal behavior (Fink, 2000) as well as improving long-term quality of life (McCall et al., 2006). Others have charged that ECT works only by confusing patients so they can't remember why they were depressed.

Not all professionals support the use of ECT. However, most experts seem to agree on the following: (1) At best, ECT produces only temporary improvement—it gets the patient out of a bad spot, but it must be combined with other treatments; (2) ECT can cause memory losses in some patients; (3) ECT should be used only after other treatments have failed; and (4) to lower the chance of a relapse, ECT should be followed by antidepressant drugs (Sackeim et al., 2001). All told, ECT is considered by many to be a valid treatment for selected cases of depression—especially when it rapidly ends wildly self-destructive or suicidal behavior (Pagnin et al., 2004). It's interesting to note that most ECT patients feel that the treatment helped them. Most, in fact, would have it done again (Bernstein et al., 1998).

Implanted Electrodes

Unlike ECT, implanting electrodes requires surgery but allows for electrical stimulation of precisely targeted brain regions. (See Chapter 2 for more information about electrical stimulation of the brain.) In one study, depressed patients who hadn't benefited from drug therapy

In electroconvulsive therapy, electrodes are attached to the head, and a brief electrical current is passed through the brain. ECT is used in the treatment of severe depression.

Will & Deni McIntyre/Photo Researchers, Inc.

Electroconvulsive therapy (ECT) A treatment for severe depression, consisting of an electric shock passed directly through the brain, which induces a convulsion.

and ECT improved when a specific brain region was stimulated (Mayberg et al., 2005). Stimulating pleasure centers in the brains of another group of patients also relieved depression (Schlaepfer et al., 2008). Also unlike ECT, implanted electrodes can be used to treat disorders other than depression, such as obsessive-compulsive disorder (Nuttin et al., 1999).

Psychosurgery

Psychosurgery (any surgical alteration of the brain) is the most extreme medical treatment. The oldest and most radical psychosurgery is the lobotomy. In *prefrontal lobotomy* the frontal lobes are surgically disconnected from other brain areas. This procedure was supposed to calm persons who didn't respond to any other type of treatment.

When the lobotomy was first introduced in the 1940s, there were enthusiastic claims for its success. But later studies suggested that some patients were calmed, some showed no change, and some became mental "vegetables." Lobotomies also produced a high rate of undesirable side effects, such as seizures, blunted emotions, major personality changes, and stupor. At about the same time that such problems became apparent, the first antipsychotic drugs became available. Soon after, the lobotomy was abandoned (Mashour, Walker, & Martuza, 2005).

To what extent is psychosurgery used now? Psychosurgery is still considered valid by many neurosurgeons. However, most now use *deep lesioning*, in which small target areas are destroyed in the brain's interior. The appeal of deep lesioning is that it can have value as a remedy for some very specific disorders (Mashour, Walker, & Martuza, 2005). For instance, patients suffering from a severe type of obsessive-compulsive disorder may be helped by psychosurgery (Dougherty et al., 2002).

It is worth remembering that psychosurgery cannot be reversed. Whereas a drug can be given or taken away and electrical stimulation can be turned off, you can't take back psychosurgery. Critics argue that psychosurgery should be banned altogether; others continue to report success with brain surgery. Nevertheless, it may have value as a remedy for some very specific disorders (Fenton, 1998; Mashour, Walker, & Martuza, 2005).

Hospitalization

Mental hospitalization for major mental disorders involves placing a person in a protected setting where medical therapy is provided. Hospitalization, by itself, can be a form of treatment. Staying in a hospital takes patients out of situations that may be sustaining their problems. For example, people with drug addictions may find it nearly impossible to resist the temptations for drug abuse in their daily lives. Hospitalization can help them make a clean break from their self-destructive behavior patterns (André et al., 2003).

At their best, hospitals are sanctuaries that provide diagnosis, support, refuge, and therapy. This is frequently true of psychiatric units in general hospitals and private psychiatric hospitals. At worst, confinement to an institution can be a brutal experience that leaves people less prepared to face the world than when they arrived. This is more often the case in large state mental hospitals (Gorman, 1996).

In most instances, hospitals are best used as a last resort, after other forms of treatment within the community have been exhausted. Actually, most psychiatric patients do as well with short-term hospitalization as they do with longer periods. For this reason, the average stay in psychiatric hospitals is now just 20 days, rather than 3 to 4 months, as it was 20 years ago.

Another trend in treatment is **partial hospitalization.** In this approach, some patients spend their days in the hospital but go home at night. Others attend therapy sessions during the evening. A major advantage of partial hospitalization is that patients can go home and practice what they've been learning. Overall, partial hospitalization can be just as effective as full hospitalization (Kiser, Heston, & Paavola, 2006).

Peter Southwick/Stock, Boston

Depending on the quality of the institution, hospitalization may be a refuge or a brutalizing experience. Many state "asylums" or mental hospitals are antiquated and in need of drastic improvement.

Psychosurgery Any surgical alteration of the brain designed to bring about desirable behavioral or emotional changes.

Mental hospitalization Placing a person in a protected, therapeutic environment staffed by mental health professionals.

Partial hospitalization An approach in which patients receive treatment at a hospital during the day but return home at night.

Deinstitutionalization

In the last 50 years the population in large mental hospitals has dropped by two thirds. This is largely a result of **deinstitutionalization,** or reduced use of full-time commitment to mental institutions. Long-term "institutionalization" can lead to dependency, isolation, and continued emotional disturbance (Chamberlin & Rogers, 1990). Deinstitutionalization was meant to remedy this problem.

How successful has deinstitutionalization been? In truth, its success has been limited (Talbott, 2004). Many states reduced mental hospital populations primarily as a way to save money. The upsetting result is that many chronic patients have been discharged to hostile communities without adequate care. Many former patients have joined the ranks of the homeless. Others are repeatedly jailed for minor crimes. Sadly, patients who trade hospitalization for unemployment, homelessness, and social isolation all too often end up rehospitalized (Goldman, 1998). Even worse, one in five of the 2 million Americans who are in jail or prison are mentally ill—three times the number who are in mental hospitals (Human Rights Watch, 2003). These figures suggest that jails are replacing mental hospitals as our society's "solution" for mental illness.

Halfway houses may be a better way to ease a patient's return to the community (Soyez & Broekaert, 2003). **Halfway houses** are short-term group living facilities for people making the transition from an institution (mental hospital, prison, and so forth) to independent living. Typically, they offer supervision and support, without being as restricted and medically oriented as hospitals. They also keep people near their families. Most important, halfway houses can reduce a person's chances of being readmitted to a hospital (Coursey, Ward-Alexander, & Katz, 1990).

A well-run halfway house can be a humane and cost-effective way to ease former mental patients back into the community (Coursey, Ward-Alexander, & Katz, 1990).

Ed Kashi/Corbis

Community Mental Health Programs

Community mental health centers, which offer a wide range of mental health services and psychiatric care, are a bright spot in the area of mental health care. Such centers try to help people avoid hospitalization and find answers to mental health problems (Burns, 2004). Typically, they do this by providing short-term treatment, counseling, outpatient care, emergency services, and suicide prevention.

Mental health centers are also concerned with *prevention.* Consultation, education, and **crisis intervention** (skilled management of a psychological emergency) are used to prevent problems before they become serious. Also, some centers attempt to raise the general level of mental health in a community by combating unemployment, delinquency, and drug abuse (Tausig, Michello, & Subedi, 2004).

Have community mental health centers succeeded in meeting their goals? In practice, they have concentrated much more on providing clinical services than they have on preventing problems. This appears to be primarily the result of wavering government support (translation: money). Overall, community mental health centers have succeeded in making psychological services more accessible than ever before. Many of their programs rely on **paraprofessionals** (individuals who work in a near-professional capacity under the supervision of more highly trained staff). Some paraprofessionals are ex-addicts, ex-alcoholics, or ex-patients who have "been there." Many more are persons (paid or volunteer) who have skills in tutoring, crafts, or counseling or who are simply warm, understanding, and skilled at communication. Often, paraprofessionals are more approachable than "doctors." This encourages people to seek mental health services that they might otherwise be reluctant to use (Everly, 2002).

A Look Ahead

In the Psychology in Action section that follows, we will return briefly to behavioral approaches. There you will find a number of useful techniques that you may be able to apply to your own behavior. You'll also find a discussion of when to seek professional help and how to find it. Here's your authors' professional advice: This is information you won't want to skip.

Deinstitutionalization Reduced use of full-time commitment to mental institutions to treat mental disorders.

Halfway house A community-based facility for individuals making the transition from an institution (mental hospital, prison, and so forth) to independent living.

Community mental health center A facility offering a wide range of mental health services, such as prevention, counseling, consultation, and crisis intervention.

Crisis intervention Skilled management of a psychological emergency.

Paraprofessional An individual who works in a near-professional capacity under the supervision of a more highly trained person.

RECITE

1. In psychodrama, people attempt to form meaningful wholes out of disjointed thoughts, feelings, and actions. T or F?
2. Most large-group awareness trainings make use of Gestalt therapy. T or F?
3. Which therapy places great emphasis on role-playing?
   a. psychodrama   b. awareness training
   c. family therapy   d. encounter
4. Emotional _____ (release) in a protected setting is an element of most psychotherapies.
5. To aid a troubled friend, you should focus on facts rather than feelings, and you should critically evaluate what the person is saying to help him or her grasp reality. T or F?
6. ECT is a modern form of pharmacotherapy. T or F?
7. Currently, the frontal lobotomy is the most widely used form of psychosurgery. T or F?

REFLECT

Critical Thinking

8. In your opinion, do psychologists have a duty to protect others who may be harmed by their clients? For example, if a patient has homicidal fantasies about his ex-wife, should she be informed?

ANSWERS

psychology in action

Self-Management and Seeking Professional Help

How are behavioral principles applied to everyday problems? How could a person find professional help?

As mentioned elsewhere in this book, you should seek professional help when a significant problem exists. For lesser difficulties, you may want to try applying behavioral principles yourself (Watson & Tharp, 2007).

Covert Reward and Punishment— Boosting Your "Willpower"

Behavior therapy is not a cure-all. Its use is often quite complicated and requires a great deal of expertise. Still, behavior therapy offers a straightforward solution to many problems.

Let us see how this might be done:

Client: I have decided several times to quit smoking.

Therapist: When have you decided?

Client: Usually after I am reminded of how dangerous smoking is—like when I heard that my uncle had died of lung cancer. He smoked constantly.

Sheila Terry/Photo Researchers, Inc.

Therapist: If you have decided to quit "several times," I assume you haven't succeeded.

Client: No, the usual pattern is for me to become upset about smoking and then to cut down for a day or two.

Therapist: You forget the disturbing image of your uncle's death, or whatever, and start smoking again.

Client: Yes, I suppose if I had an uncle die every day or so, I might actually quit!

The use of intensive behavioral principles, such as electric shock, to condition an aversion seems remote from everyday problems. Even naturally aversive actions are difficult to apply to personal behavior. As mentioned earlier, for instance, rapid smoking is difficult for most smokers to carry out on their own. And what about a problem like overeating? It would be difficult indeed to eat enough to create a lasting aversion to overeating. (Although it's sometimes tempting to try.)

In view of such limitations, psychologists have developed an alternative procedure that can be used to curb smoking, overeating, and other habits (Cautela & Kearney, 1986; Watson & Tharp, 2007).

Covert Sensitization

In **covert sensitization,** aversive imagery is used to reduce the occurrence of an undesired response. Here's how it's done: Obtain six 3 by 5 cards and on each write a brief description of a scene related to the habit you wish to control. The scene should be so *disturbing* or *disgusting* that thinking about it would temporarily make you very uncomfortable about indulging in the habit. For smoking, the cards might read:

- "I am in a doctor's office. The doctor looks at some reports and tells me I have lung cancer. She says a lung will have to be removed and schedules the operation for next week."
- "I am in bed under an oxygen tent. My chest feels caved in. There is a tube in my throat. I can barely breathe."
- "I wake up in the morning and smoke a cigarette. I begin coughing up blood."
- "My lover won't even kiss me because my breath smells bad."

Other cards would continue along the same line.

The trick is to get yourself to imagine or picture vividly each of these disturbing scenes *several times* a day. Imagining the scenes can be accomplished by placing them under *stimulus control.* Simply choose something you do *frequently* each day (such as getting a cup of coffee or getting up from your chair). Next make a rule: Before you can get a cup of coffee or get up from your chair, or whatever you have selected as a cue, you must take out your cards and *vividly picture* yourself engaging in the action you wish to curb (eating or smoking, for example). Then *vividly picture* the scene described on the top card. Imagine the scene for 30 seconds.

After visualizing the top card, move it to the bottom so the cards are rotated. Make up new cards each week. The scenes can be made much more upsetting than the samples given here, which are toned down to keep you from being "grossed out."

Covert sensitization can also be used directly in situations that test your self-control. If you are trying to lose weight, for instance, you might be able to turn down a tempting dessert in this way: As you look at the dessert, visualize maggots crawling all over it. If you make this image as vivid and nauseating as possible, losing your appetite is almost a certainty. If you want to apply this technique to other situations, be aware that vomiting scenes are especially effective. Covert sensitization may sound as if you are "playing games with yourself," but it can be a great help if you want to cut down on a bad habit (Cautela & Kearney, 1986). Try it!

Thought Stopping

As discussed earlier, behavior therapists accept that thoughts, like visible responses, can also cause trouble. Think of times when you have repeatedly "put yourself down" mentally or when you have been preoccupied by needless worries, fears, or other negative and upsetting

Covert sensitization Use of aversive imagery to reduce the occurrence of an undesired response.

thoughts. If you would like to gain control over such thoughts, thought stopping may help you do it.

In **thought stopping,** aversive stimuli are used to interrupt or prevent upsetting thoughts. The simplest thought-stopping technique makes use of mild punishment to suppress upsetting mental images and internal "talk." Simply place a large, flat rubber band around your wrist. As you go through the day, apply this rule: Each time you catch yourself thinking the upsetting image or thought, pull the rubber band away from your wrist and snap it. You need not make this terribly painful. Its value lies in drawing your attention to how often you form negative thoughts and in interrupting the flow of thoughts.

A second thought-stopping procedure requires only that you interrupt upsetting thoughts each time they occur. Begin by setting aside time each day during which you will deliberately think the unwanted thought. As you begin to form the thought, shout "Stop!" aloud, with conviction. (Obviously, you should choose a private spot for this part of the procedure!)

Repeat the thought-stopping procedure 10 to 20 times for the first 2 or 3 days. Then switch to shouting "Stop!" covertly (to yourself) rather than aloud. Thereafter, thought stopping can be carried out throughout the day, whenever upsetting thoughts occur (Williams & Long, 1991). After several days of practice, you should be able to stop unwanted thoughts whenever they occur.

Covert Reinforcement

Earlier we discussed how punishing images can be used to decrease undesirable responses, such as smoking or overeating. Many people also find it helpful to covertly *reinforce* desired actions. **Covert reinforcement** is the use of positive imagery to reinforce desired behavior. For example, suppose your target behavior is, once again, not eating dessert. If this were the case, you could do the following (Cautela & Kearney, 1986; Watson & Tharp, 2007):

> Imagine that you are standing at the dessert table with your friends. As dessert is passed, you politely refuse and feel good about staying on your diet.

These images would then be followed by imagining a pleasant, reinforcing scene:

> Imagine that you are your ideal weight. You look really slim in your favorite color and style. Someone you really like says to you, "Gee, you've lost weight. I've never seen you look so good."

For many people, of course, actual direct reinforcement (as described in the Psychology in Action section of Chapter 6) is the best way to alter behavior. Nevertheless, covert or "visualized" reinforcement can have similar effects. To make use of covert reinforcement, choose one or more target behaviors and rehearse them mentally. Then follow each rehearsal with a vivid, rewarding image.

Self-Directed Desensitization—Overcoming Common Fears

You have prepared for 2 weeks to give a speech in a large class. As your turn approaches, your hands begin to tremble. Your heart pounds and you find it difficult to breathe. You say to your body, "Relax!" What happens? Nothing! That's why the first step in desensitization is learning to relax voluntarily, by using the tension-release method described earlier in this chapter. As an alternative, you might want to try imagining a very safe, pleasant, and relaxing scene. Some people find such images as relaxing as the tension-release method (Rosenthal, 1993). Another helpful technique is to do some deep breathing. Typically, a person who is breathing deeply is relaxed. Shallow breathing involves little movement of the diaphragm. If you place your hand on your abdomen, it will move up and down if you are breathing deeply.

Once you have learned to relax, the next step is to identify the fear you would like to control and construct a hierarchy.

Procedure for Constructing a Hierarchy

Make a list of situations (related to the fear) that make you anxious. Try to list at least 10 situations. Some should be very frightening and others only mildly frightening. Write a short description of each situation on a separate 3 by 5 card. Place the cards in order from

Thought stopping Use of aversive stimuli to interrupt or prevent upsetting thoughts.

Covert reinforcement Using positive imagery to reinforce desired behavior.

the least disturbing situation to the most disturbing. Here is a sample hierarchy for a student afraid of public speaking:

1. Being given an assignment to speak in class
2. Thinking about the topic and the date the speech must be given
3. Writing the speech; thinking about delivering the speech
4. Watching other students speak in class the week before the speech date
5. Rehearsing the speech alone; pretending to give it to the class
6. Delivering the speech to my roommate; pretending my roommate is the teacher
7. Reviewing the speech on the day it is to be presented
8. Entering the classroom; waiting and thinking about the speech
9. Being called; standing up; facing the audience
10. Delivering the speech

Using the Hierarchy

When you have mastered the relaxation exercises and have the hierarchy constructed, set aside time each day to work on reducing your fear. Begin by performing the relaxation exercises. When you are completely relaxed, visualize the scene on the first card (the least frightening scene). If you can *vividly* picture and imagine yourself in the first situation twice *without a noticeable increase in muscle tension*, proceed to the next card. Also, as you progress, relax yourself between cards.

Each day, stop when you reach a card that you cannot visualize without becoming tense in three attempts. Each day, begin one or two cards before the one on which you stopped the previous day. Continue to work with the cards until you can visualize the last situation without experiencing tension (techniques are based on Wolpe, 1974).

By using this approach you should be able to reduce the fear or anxiety associated with things such as public speaking, entering darkened rooms, asking questions in large classes, heights, talking to members of the opposite sex, and taking tests (Watson & Tharp, 2007). Even if you are not always able to reduce a fear, you will have learned to place relaxation under voluntary control. This alone is valuable because controlling unnecessary tension can increase energy and efficiency.

Seeking Professional Help—When, Where, and How?

Chances are good that at some point you or someone in your family will benefit from mental health services of one kind or another. In one survey, half of all American households included someone who received mental health treatment during the preceding year (Chamberlin, 2004).

How would I know if I should seek professional help at some point in my life? Although there is no simple answer to this question, the following guidelines may be helpful:

1. If your level of psychological discomfort (unhappiness, anxiety, or depression, for example) is comparable to a level of physical discomfort that would cause you to see a doctor or dentist, you should consider seeing a psychologist or a psychiatrist.

2. Another signal to watch for is significant changes in behavior, such as the quality of your work (or schoolwork), your rate of absenteeism, your use of drugs (including alcohol), or your relationships with others.

3. Perhaps you have urged a friend or relative to seek professional help and were dismayed because he or she refused to do so. If *you* find friends or relatives making a similar suggestion, recognize that they may be seeing things more clearly than you are.

4. If you have persistent or disturbing suicidal thoughts or impulses, you should seek help immediately.

Locating a Therapist

If I wanted to talk to a therapist, how would I find one? Here are some suggestions that could help you get started:

1. **Colleges and universities.** If you are a student, don't overlook counseling services offered by a student health center or special student counseling facilities.

2. **Workplaces.** If you have a job, check with your employer. Some employers have employee assistance programs that offer confidential free or low-cost therapy for employees.

3. **The Yellow Pages.** Psychologists are listed in the telephone book or on the Internet under "Psychologists," or in some cases under "Counseling Services." Psychiatrists are generally listed as a subheading under "Physicians." Counselors are usually found under the heading "Marriage and Family Counselors." These listings will usually put you in touch with individuals in private practice.

4. **Community or county mental health centers.** Most counties and many cities offer public mental health services. (These are listed in the phone book.) Public mental health centers usually provide counseling and therapy services directly, and they can refer you to private therapists.

5. **Mental health associations.** Many cities have mental health associations organized by concerned citizens. Groups such as these usually keep listings of qualified therapists and other services and programs in the community.

6. **Crisis hotlines.** The typical crisis hotline is a telephone service staffed by community volunteers. These people are trained to provide information concerning a wide range of mental health problems. They also have lists of organizations, services, and other resources in the community where you can go for help.

● Table 13.5 summarizes all the sources for psychotherapy, counseling, and referrals we have discussed, as well as some additional possibilities.

Options *How would I know what kind of a therapist to see? How would I pick one?* The choice between a psychiatrist and a psychologist is somewhat arbitrary. Both are trained to do psychotherapy and can be equally effective as therapists (Seligman, 1995). Although a psychiatrist can administer somatic therapy and prescribe drugs, so can psychologists in New Mexico and Louisiana (Munsey, 2006). Besides, a psychologist can work in conjunction with a physician if such services are needed.

Fees for psychiatrists are usually higher, averaging about $160 to $200 an hour. Psychologists average about $100 an hour. Counselors and social workers typically charge about $80 per hour. Group therapy averages only about $40 an hour because the therapist's fee is divided among several people.

Be aware that most health insurance plans will pay for psychological services. If fees are a problem, keep in mind that many therapists charge on a sliding scale, or ability-to-pay basis, and that community mental health centers almost always charge on a sliding scale. In one way or another, help is almost always available for anyone who needs it.

Some communities and college campuses have counseling services staffed by sympathetic paraprofessionals or peer counselors. These services are free or very low cost. As mentioned earlier, paraprofessionals are people who work in a near-professional capacity

---

● **Table 13.5 Mental Health Resources**

- Family doctors (for referrals to mental health professionals)
- Mental health specialists, such as psychiatrists, psychologists, social workers, and mental health counselors
- Health maintenance organizations (HMOs)
- Community mental health centers
- Hospital psychiatry departments and outpatient clinics
- University- or medical school–affiliated programs
- State hospital outpatient clinics
- Family service/social agencies
- Private clinics and facilities
- Employee assistance programs
- Local medical, psychiatric, or psychological societies

Source: National Institute of Mental Health (2005).

under professional supervision. **Peer counselors** are nonprofessional persons who have learned basic counseling skills. There is a natural tendency, perhaps, to doubt the abilities of paraprofessionals. However, many studies have shown that paraprofessional counselors are often as effective as professionals (Christensen & Jacobson, 1994).

Also, don't overlook self-help groups, which can add valuable support to professional treatment. Members of a self-help group typically share a particular type of problem, such as eating disorders or coping with an alcoholic parent. **Self-help groups** offer members mutual support and a chance to discuss problems. In many instances helping others also serves as therapy for those who give help (Burlingame & Davies, 2002). For some problems, self-help groups may be the best choice of all (Fobair, 1997; Galanter et al., 2005).

Qualifications You can usually find out about a therapist's qualifications simply by asking. A reputable therapist will be glad to reveal his or her background. If you have any doubts, credentials may be checked and other helpful information can be obtained from local branches of any of the following organizations. You can also browse the websites listed here:

American Association for Marriage and Family Therapy (www.aamft.org)

American Family Therapy Association (www.afta.org)

American Psychiatric Association (www.psych.org)

American Psychological Association (www.apa.org)

Association of Humanistic Psychology (www.ahpweb.org)

Canadian Psychiatric Association (www.cpa-apc.org)

Canadian Psychological Association (www.cpa.ca)

National Mental Health Association (www.nmha.org)

The question of how to pick a particular therapist remains. The best way is to start with a short consultation with a respected psychiatrist, psychologist, or counselor. This will allow the person you consult to evaluate your difficulty and recommend a type of therapy or a therapist who is likely to be helpful. As an alternative you might ask the person teaching this course for a referral.

Evaluating a Therapist *How would I know whether or not to quit or ignore a therapist?* A balanced look at psychotherapies suggests that all techniques can be successful (Wampold et al., 1997). However, all *therapists* are not equally successful. Far more important than the approach used are the therapist's personal qualities (Okiishi et al., 2003; Prochaska & Norcross, 2010). The most consistently successful therapists are those who are willing to use whatever method seems most helpful for a client. They are also marked by personal characteristics of warmth, integrity, sincerity, and empathy. Former clients consistently rate the person doing the therapy as more important than the type of therapy used (Elliott & Williams, 2003).

It is perhaps most accurate to say that at this stage of development, psychotherapy is an art, not a science. The *relationship* between a client and therapist is the therapist's most basic tool (Hubble, Duncan, & Miller, 1999; Prochaska & Norcross, 2010). This is why you must trust and easily relate to a therapist for therapy to be effective. Here are some danger signals to watch for in psychotherapy:

- Sexual advances by therapist
- Therapist makes repeated verbal threats or is physically aggressive
- Therapist is excessively blaming, belittling, hostile, or controlling
- Therapist makes excessive small talk; talks repeatedly about his/her own problems
- Therapist encourages prolonged dependence on him/her
- Therapist demands absolute trust or tells client not to discuss therapy with anyone else

Peer counselor A nonprofessional person who has learned basic counseling skills.

Self-help group A group of people who share a particular type of problem and provide mutual support to one another.

Clients who like their therapist are generally more successful in therapy (Talley, Strupp, & Morey, 1990). An especially important part of the therapeutic alliance is agreement about the goals of therapy (Meier et al., 2006). It is therefore a good idea to think about what you would like to accomplish by entering therapy. Write down your goals and discuss them with your therapist during the first session. Your first meeting with a therapist should also answer all of the following questions (Somberg, Stone, & Claiborn, 1993):

- Will the information I reveal in therapy remain completely confidential?
- What risks do I face if I begin therapy?
- How long do you expect treatment to last?
- What form of treatment do you expect to use?
- Are there alternatives to therapy that might help me as much or more?

It's always tempting to avoid facing up to personal problems. With this in mind, you should give a therapist a fair chance and not give up too easily. But don't hesitate to change therapists or to terminate therapy if you lose confidence in the therapist or if you don't relate well to the therapist as a person.

RECITE

1. Covert sensitization and thought stopping combine aversion therapy and cognitive therapy. T or F?
2. Like covert aversion conditioning, covert reinforcement of desired responses is also possible. T or F?
3. Exercises that bring about deep-muscle relaxation are an essential element in covert sensitization. T or F?
4. Items in a desensitization hierarchy should be placed in order from the least disturbing to the most disturbing. T or F?
5. The first step in desensitization is to place the visualization of disturbing images under stimulus control. T or F?
6. Persistent emotional discomfort is a clear sign that professional psychological counseling should be sought. T or F?
7. Community mental health centers rarely offer counseling or therapy themselves; they do only referrals. T or F?
8. In many instances, a therapist's personal qualities have more of an effect on the outcome of therapy than does the type of therapy used. T or F?

REFLECT

Critical Thinking

9. Would it be acceptable for a therapist to urge a client to break all ties with a troublesome family member?

study break ✋

Self-Management and Seeking Professional Help

Relate

How could you use covert sensitization, thought stopping, and covert reinforcement to change your behavior? Try to apply each technique to a specific example.

Just for practice, make a fear hierarchy for a situation you find frightening. Does vividly picturing items in the hierarchy make you tense or anxious? If so, can you intentionally relax using the tension-release method?

Assume that you want to seek help from a psychologist or other mental health professional. How would you proceed? Take some time to actually find out what mental health services are available to you.

ANSWERS

1. T 2. T 3. F 4. T 5. F 6. T 7. F 8. T 9. Such decisions must be made by clients themselves. Therapists can help clients evaluate important decisions and feelings about significant persons in their lives. However, actively urging a client to sever a relationship borders on unethical behavior.

chapter in review

Major Points

- Psychotherapy facilitates positive changes in personality, behavior, or adjustment.

- Before the development of modern therapies, superstition dominated attempts to treat psychological problems.

- Five major categories of psychotherapy are psychodynamic, insight, behavioral, cognitive, and group therapies.

- Psychotherapy is generally effective, although no single form of therapy is superior to others.

- All medical treatments for psychological disorders have pros and cons. Overall, however, their effectiveness is improving.

- Some personal problems can be successfully treated using self-management techniques.

- Everyone should know how to obtain high-quality mental health care in his or her community.

Summary

How do psychotherapies differ?

- Psychotherapies may be classified as insight, action, directive, nondirective, or supportive therapies, and combinations of these.

- Therapies may be conducted either individually or in groups, and they may be time limited.

How did psychotherapy originate?

- Early approaches to mental illness were dominated by superstition and moral condemnation.

- Demonology attributed mental disturbance to demonic possession and prescribed exorcism as the cure.

- In some instances, the actual cause of bizarre behavior may have been ergot poisoning.

- More humane treatment began in 1793 with the work of Philippe Pinel in Paris.

Is Freudian psychoanalysis still used?

- Psychoanalysts have become relatively rare because psychoanalysis is expensive and time intensive. However, as the first true psychotherapy, Freud's psychoanalysis gave rise to modern psychodynamic therapies.

- The psychoanalyst uses free association, dream analysis, and analysis of resistance and transference to reveal health-producing insights.

- Some critics argue that traditional psychoanalysis receives credit for spontaneous remissions of symptoms. However, psychoanalysis is successful for many patients.

- Brief psychodynamic therapy (which relies on psychoanalytic theory but is brief and focused) is as effective as other major therapies. One example is interpersonal psychotherapy.

What are the major humanistic therapies?

- Client-centered (or person-centered) therapy is nondirective, based on insights gained from conscious thoughts and feelings, and dedicated to creating an atmosphere of growth.

- Unconditional positive regard, empathy, authenticity, and reflection are combined to give the client a chance to solve his or her own problems.

- Existential therapies focus on the end result of the choices one makes in life. Clients are encouraged through confrontation and encounter to exercise free will and to take responsibility for their choices.

- Gestalt therapy emphasizes immediate awareness of thoughts and feelings. Its goal is to rebuild thinking, feeling, and acting into connected wholes and to help clients break through emotional blockages.

Can therapy be conducted at a distance?

- Media psychologists, telephone counselors, and cybertherapists may, on occasion, do some good. However, each has serious drawbacks, and the effectiveness of telephone counseling and cybertherapy has not been established.

- Therapy by videoconferencing shows more promise as a way to provide mental health services at a distance.

What is behavior therapy?

- Behavior therapists use the learning principles of classical or operant conditioning to directly change human behavior.

- In aversion therapy, classical conditioning is used to associate maladaptive behavior (such as smoking or drinking) with pain or other aversive events in order to inhibit undesirable responses.

- In desensitization, gradual adaptation and reciprocal inhibition break the link between fear and particular situations.

- Typical steps in desensitization are: Construct a fear hierarchy; learn to produce total relaxation; and perform items on the hierarchy (from least to most disturbing).

- Desensitization may be carried out with real settings or it may be done by vividly imagining the fear hierarchy or by watching models perform the feared responses.

- In some cases, virtual reality exposure can be used to present fear stimuli in a controlled manner.

- A new technique called eye movement desensitization and reprocessing (EMDR) shows promise as a treatment for traumatic memories and stress disorders. At present, however, EMDR is highly controversial.

What role do operant principles play in behavior therapy?

- Operant principles, such as positive reinforcement, nonreinforcement, extinction, punishment, shaping, stimulus control, and time out, are used to extinguish undesirable responses and to promote constructive behavior.

- Nonreward can extinguish troublesome behaviors. Often this is done by simply identifying and eliminating reinforcers, particularly attention and social approval.

- To apply positive reinforcement and operant shaping, tokens are often used to reinforce selected target behaviors.
- Full-scale use of tokens in an institutional setting produces a token economy. Toward the end of a token economy program, patients are shifted to social rewards such as recognition and approval.

Can therapy change thoughts and emotions?

- Cognitive therapy emphasizes changing thought patterns that underlie emotional or behavioral problems. Its goals are to correct distorted thinking and/or teach improved coping skills.
- Irrational beliefs are the core of many maladaptive thinking patterns. Changing such beliefs can have a positive impact on emotions and behavior.
- In a variation of cognitive therapy called rational-emotive behavior therapy (REBT), clients learn to recognize and challenge their own irrational beliefs.

Can psychotherapy be done with groups of people?

- Therapy can be done with groups of people based on a simple extension of individual methods or based on techniques developed specifically for groups.
- In psychodrama, individuals enact roles and incidents resembling their real-life problems. In family therapy, the family group is treated as a unit.
- Sensitivity and encounter groups encourage positive personality change. Large-group awareness training attempts to do the same, but the benefits of such programs are questionable.

What do various therapies have in common?

- Effective psychotherapies are based on the therapeutic alliance, a protected setting, catharsis, insights, new perspectives, and a chance to practice new behaviors.

- Psychotherapy is generally effective, although no single form of therapy is superior to others.
- All of the following are helping skills that can be learned: active listening, acceptance, reflection, open-ended questioning, support, respect, patience, genuineness, and paraphrasing.
- The culturally skilled counselor must be able to establish rapport with a person from a different cultural background and adapt traditional theories and techniques to meet the needs of clients from non-European ethnic groups.

How do psychiatrists treat psychological disorders?

- Three medical, or somatic, approaches to treatment are pharmacotherapy, electrical stimulation therapy (including electroconvulsive therapy [ECT]), and psychosurgery.
- Community mental health centers seek to avoid or minimize mental hospitalization. They also seek to prevent mental health problems through education, consultation, and crisis intervention.

How are behavioral principles applied to everyday problems? How could a person find professional help?

- Cognitive techniques can be an aid to managing personal behavior.
- In covert sensitization, aversive images are used to discourage unwanted behavior.
- Thought stopping uses mild punishment to prevent upsetting thoughts.
- Covert reinforcement is a way to encourage desired responses by mental rehearsal.
- Desensitization pairs relaxation with a hierarchy of upsetting images in order to lessen fears.

- In most communities, a competent and reputable therapist can be located with public sources of information or through a referral.
- Practical considerations such as cost and qualifications enter into choosing a therapist. However, the therapist's personal characteristics are of equal importance.

Web Resources

For an up-to-date list of direct links to interesting sites, including those listed here, visit the student companion site for this book at www.cengage.com/psychology/coon

Pre-Columbian Trephination Read about the first psychosurgery as a treatment for mental illness.

Dr. Phil See for yourself how Dr. Phil publicizes mental health issues.

Aversion Therapy Read more about aversion therapy.

Systematic Desensitization Explore this self-administered procedure.

American Self-Help Group Clearinghouse Explore this database of more than 1,000 self-help groups.

Lobotomy Read a case study of lobotomy and the history of the transorbital lobotomy procedure.

Finding a Therapist in Your Hometown Use the Internet to locate a local therapist.

Interactive Learning

PSYCHOLOGY: A JOURNEY BOOK COMPANION WEBSITE
WWW.CENGAGE.COM/PSYCHOLOGY/COON
Visit your book companion website, where you will find flash cards, practice quizzes, web links, and more to help you study.

JUST WHAT YOU NEED TO KNOW NOW! CENGAGENOW™
Spend time on what you need to master rather than on information you already have learned. Take a pretest for this chapter, and CengageNOW will generate a personalized study plan based on your results. The study plan will identify the topics you need to review and direct you to online resources to help you master those topics. You can then take a posttest to help you determine the concepts you have mastered and what you will need to work on. Try it out! Go to www.cengage.com/login to sign in with an access code or to purchase access to this product.

test your knowledge

Therapies

For additional review, get more practice with *CengageNOW*, *WebTutor*, the *Practice Quizzes*, and/or the printed *Study Guide* available with this book.

1. An approach that is incompatible with insight therapy is
   a. individual therapy   b. action therapy
   c. nondirective therapy   d. group therapy

2. Which type of therapy is LEAST likely to bring about personal change?
   a. nondirective therapy   b. supportive therapy
   c. time-limited therapy   d. group therapy

3. A scientific explanation of medieval "possessions" by "demons" is related to the effects of
   a. ergot poisoning   b. trepanning
   c. exorcism   d. unconscious transference

4. Which of the following is NOT a psychoanalytic concept?
   a. free association   b. resistance
   c. transference   d. storytelling

5. Carl Rogers did not believe in using _____ in therapy.
   a. empathy   b. authenticity
   c. reflection   d. confrontation

6. Filling in gaps in immediate self-awareness is one of the principal goals of
   a. REBT   b. existential therapy
   c. person-centered therapy d. Gestalt therapy

7. To date, the most acceptable type of "distance therapy" is
   a. media psychology   b. commercial telephone counseling
   c. Internet therapy   d. telehealth

8. Classical conditioning principles are the basis for
   a. aversion therapy   b. time out
   c. token economies   d. EMDR

9. Reciprocal inhibition is an important principle in
   a. EMDR   b. REBT
   c. desensitization   d. the design of a token economy

10. A psychologist who is interested in overgeneralization and irrational beliefs is obviously a proponent of
    a. exposure therapy   b. token economies
    c. systematic desensitization d. cognitive therapy

11. The B in the A-B-C of REBT stands for
    a. behavior   b. belief
    c. being   d. backward

12. The mirror technique is frequently used in
    a. exposure therapy   b. psychodrama
    c. family therapy   d. EMDR

13. Research shows that about _____ percent of people who have sought mental health treatment feel that the treatment helped.
    a. 90   b. 50
    c. 80   d. 100

14. When evaluating a therapy, one way to avoid being misled by a spontaneous remission of symptoms is to use a _____ control group.
    a. nondirective   b. latent
    c. psychodynamic   d. waiting-list

15. Emotional rapport, warmth, understanding, acceptance, and empathy are the core of
    a. the therapeutic alliance b. large-group awareness training
    c. role reversals   d. action therapies

16. Culturally skilled therapists do all but one of the following; which does NOT apply?
    a. Be aware of the client's degree of acculturation.
    b. Use helping resources within the client's cultural group.
    c. Adapt standard techniques to match cultural stereotypes
    d. Be aware of their own cultural values.

17. Major tranquilizers are also known as
    a. anxiolytics   b. antipsychotics
    c. antidepressants   d. prefrontal sedatives

18. ECT is classified as a type of
    a. somatic therapy   b. pharmacotherapy
    c. psychosurgery   d. deep lesioning

19. Mild punishment is used in which self-management technique?
    a. thought stopping   b. desensitization
    c. REBT   d. time out

20. The tension-release method is an important part of
    a. covert reinforcement   b. thought stopping
    c. desensitization   d. peer counseling

Answers 1. b 2. b 3. a 4. d 5. d 6. d 7. d 8. a 9. c 10. d 11. b 12. b 13. c 14. d 15. a 16. c 17. b 18. a 19. a 20. c

Social Behavior

Journey into Psychology: Love and Hate

Jasmine and Osama are tearing themselves away from home and moving to Europe. As Jasmine wryly comments, "We were naïve and thought we could win this fight, but we can't. So we have to go abroad and start a new life." The fight they lost was a struggle between love and hate. You see, Jasmine is a Jewish Israeli and Osama is a Palestinian Muslim. They met, fell in love, and were married. Since then they have been endlessly harassed. Because of deep hatred built up during the Palestinian–Israeli conflict, both sides were hostile to the love Jasmine and Osama share. They were repeatedly insulted, threatened, shunned, and reviled.

The Middle East is no place for them to live anymore (Price, 2007).

Jasmine and Osama are not alone. Prejudice and hatred exists between groups around the world. Examples include clashes between Catholics and Protestants in Northern Ireland, Hutus and Tutsis in Rwanda, and African Americans and European Americans here at home. Each conflict has produced tragic "Romeo and Juliet" stories like Jasmine and Osama's. These two lovers can be thankful they escaped with their lives.

From intimate couples to nations, classes to mobs, families to ethnic groups—each of us

is part of a rich tapestry of social relationships. Social life strongly influences our behavior, which is probably why we spend so much time thinking about other people. Love, hate, and related topics have been the target of an immense amount of study—too much, in fact, for us to cover in detail. Therefore, this chapter is a social psychology "sampler." We will look at how we think about social situations and various ways in which we influence others. We hope that you will find the topics interesting and thought provoking.

Survey Questions

- Why do people affiliate? What factors influence interpersonal attraction?

- How does group membership affect our behavior?

- What have social psychologists learned about social influence?

- How does self-assertion differ from aggression?

- How are attitudes acquired and changed?

- What causes prejudice and intergroup conflict?

- How do psychologists explain human aggression?

- Why are bystanders so often unwilling to help in an emergency?

- How can we promote multiculturalism and social harmony?

Affiliation and Attraction—Come Together

Why do people affiliate? What factors influence interpersonal attraction?

Each of us is immersed in a complex social world of communities, families, clans, crowds, tribes, companies, parties, troops, bands, sects, gangs, crews, teams, and nations. **Social psychology** is the scientific study of how individuals behave, think, and feel in social situations (that is, in the presence, actual or implied, of others) (Baron, Byrne, & Branscombe, 2009).

But what brings us together in the first place? We are social beings with a *need to affiliate* (a desire to associate with other people) based on basic human desires for approval, support, security, friendship, and information (Baumeister & Bushman, 2008).

Information? Yes. Other people provide information that helps us evaluate our own reactions. Whenever we are in doubt, we tend to rely on *social comparisons* to guide our behavior (Kulik, Mahler, & Moore, 2003).

Social Comparison Theory

If you want to know how heavy you are, you simply get on a scale. But how do you know if you are a good athlete, worker, parent, or friend? How do you know if your views on politics, religion, or music are unusual or widely shared? When there are no objective standards, the only available yardstick is provided by comparing yourself with others (Miller, 2006).

Social psychologist Leon Festinger (1919–1989) theorized that group membership fills needs for **social comparison** (comparing your own actions, feelings, opinions, or abilities to those of others). Have you ever "compared notes" with other students after taking an exam? ("How did you do?" "Wasn't that last question hard?") If you have, you were satisfying needs for social comparison (Festinger, 1957).

Typically, we don't make social comparisons randomly or on some absolute scale. Meaningful evaluations are based on comparing yourself with people of similar backgrounds, abilities, and circumstances (Stapel & Marx, 2007). To illustrate, let's ask a student named Wendy if she is a good tennis player. If Wendy compares herself with a professional, the answer will be no. But within her tennis group, Wendy is regarded as an excellent player. On a fair scale of comparison, Wendy knows she is good and she takes pride in her tennis skills. In the same way, thinking of yourself as successful, talented, responsible, or fairly paid depends entirely on whom you choose for comparison. Thus, a desire for social comparison provides a motive for associating with others and influences which groups we join (Franzoi & Klaiber, 2007).

Don't people also affiliate out of attraction for one another? Of course they do. That's what brought Jasmine and Osama together. Let's see why.

High school class reunions are notorious for the rampant social comparison they often encourage. Apparently it's hard to resist comparing yourself with former classmates to see how you are doing in life.

Interpersonal Attraction

"Birds of a feather flock together." "Familiarity breeds contempt." "Opposites attract." "Absence makes the heart grow fonder." Are these statements true? Actually, the folklore about friendship is, at best, a mixture of fact and fiction.

What does attract people to each other? **Interpersonal attraction** (affinity to another person) is the basis for most voluntary social relationships (Berscheid & Regan, 2005). As you might expect, we look for friends and lovers who are kind and understanding, who have attractive personalities, and who like us in return (Sprecher, 1998). Deciding whether you would like to know another person can happen very quickly, sometimes within just minutes

Social psychology The scientific study of how individuals behave, think, and feel in social situations.

Social comparison Making judgments about ourselves through comparison with others.

Interpersonal attraction Social attraction to another person.

of meeting (Sunnafrank, Ramirez, & Metts, 2004). In addition, several less obvious factors influence attraction.

Physical Proximity

Our choice of friends (and even lovers) is based more on *physical proximity* (nearness) than we might care to believe. For example, the closer people live to each other, the more likely they are to become friends. Likewise, lovers like to think they have found the "one and only" person in the universe for them. In reality, they have probably found the best match in a 5-mile radius! (Buss, 1985). Marriages are not made in heaven—they are made in local schools, businesses, churches, bars, clubs, and neighborhoods. It's not surprising that Jasmine and Osama worked together in the same business in Jerusalem.

Proximity promotes attraction by increasing the *frequency of contact* between people. In general, we are attracted to people we see often. (That's one reason why actors costarring in movies together often become romantically involved.) In short, there does seem to be a "boy-next-door" or "girl-next-door" effect in romantic attraction, and a "folks-next-door" effect in friendship. Notice, however, that the Internet is making it increasingly easier to stay in constant "virtual contact," which is leading to more and more long-distance friendships and romances (Lawson & Leck, 2006; Ridings & Gefen, 2004).

What attracts people to each other? Proximity and frequency of contact have a surprisingly large impact.

Physical Attractiveness

People who are *physically attractive* are regarded as good-looking by others. Beautiful people are generally rated as more appealing than average. This is due, in part, to the *halo effect*, a tendency to generalize a favorable impression to unrelated personal characteristics. Because of it, we assume that beautiful people are also likable, intelligent, warm, witty, mentally healthy, and socially skilled. In reality, physical attractiveness has almost *no* connection to intelligence, talents, or abilities. Perhaps that's why beauty affects mainly our initial interest in getting to know others (Keller & Young, 1996). Later, more meaningful qualities gain in importance (Berscheid, 2000; Miller, Perlman, & Brehm, 2007). As you discover that someone has a good personality, he or she will even start looking more attractive to you (Lewandowski, Aron, & Gee, 2007). It takes more than appearance to make a lasting relationship.

Physical beauty can be socially advantageous because of the widespread belief that "what is beautiful is good." However, physical beauty is generally unrelated to actual personal traits and talents.

Competence

People who are *competent* have knowledge, ability, or proficiency. All other things being equal, we are more attracted to people who are talented or competent. However, there's an interesting twist to this. In a revealing classic study, college students listened to audio-tapes of candidates for a "college quiz bowl." Two of the candidates seemed to be highly intelligent. The other two were of average ability. In addition, one "intelligent" candidate and one "average" candidate could be heard to clumsily spill coffee on themselves. Later, students rated the intelligent candidate who blundered as *most* attractive. In contrast, the average person who blundered was rated *least* attractive (Aronson, 1969). Thus, the superior but clumsy person was more attractive than the person who was only superior. Apparently, we like people who are competent but imperfect—which makes them more "human."

Similarity

Take a moment to make a list of your closest friends. What do they have in common (other than the joy of knowing you)? It is likely that their ages are similar to yours and you are of the same sex and ethnicity. There will be exceptions, of course. But similarity on these three dimensions is the general rule for friendships.

Similarity refers to how alike you are to another person in background, age, interests, attitudes, beliefs, and so forth. In everything from casual acquaintance to marriage, similar people are attracted to each other (Figueredo, Sefcek, & Jones, 2006; Miller, Perlman, & Brehm, 2007). And why not? It's reinforcing to see our beliefs and attitudes shared by others. It shows we are "right" and reveals that they are clever people as well!

So similarity also influences mate selection? Yes, in choosing a mate we tend to marry someone who is like us in almost every way, a pattern called *homogamy* (huh-MOG-ah-me) (Blackwell & Lichter, 2004). Studies show that married couples are highly similar in age, education, ethnicity, and religion. (You go, Jasmine and Osama!) To a lesser degree, they are also similar in attitudes and opinions, mental abilities, status, height, weight, and eye color. In case you're wondering, homogamy also applies to unmarried couples who are living together (Blackwell & Lichter, 2004). Homogamy is probably a good thing. The risk of divorce is highest among couples with sizable differences in age and education (Tzeng, 1992).

Excessive self-disclosure is a staple of many television talk shows. Guests frequently reveal intimate details about their personal lives, including private family matters, sex and dating, physical or sexual abuse, major embarrassments, and criminal activities. Viewers probably find such intimate disclosures entertaining, rather than threatening, because they don't have to reciprocate.

Everett Collection

Self-Disclosure

How do people who are not yet friends learn whether they are similar? To get acquainted, you must be willing to talk about more than just the weather, sports, or nuclear physics. At some point you must begin to share private thoughts and feelings and reveal yourself to others. This process, which is called **self-disclosure,** is essential for developing close relationships. In general, as friends talk, they gradually deepen the level of liking, trust, and self-disclosure (Levesque, Steciuk, & Ledley, 2002).

Self-disclosure is governed by unspoken rules about what's acceptable. Moderate self-disclosure leads to *reciprocity* (a return in kind). In contrast, *overdisclosure* exceeds what is appropriate for a relationship or social situation, giving rise to suspicion and reducing attraction. For example, imagine standing in line at a store and having the stranger in front of you say, "Lately I've been thinking about how I really feel about myself. I think I'm pretty well adjusted, but I occasionally have some questions about my sexual adequacy." It's interesting to note that on the Internet (and especially on social networking websites like Facebook and MySpace), people often feel freer to express their true feelings, which can lead to genuine, face-to-face friendships (Bargh, McKenna, & Fitzsimons, 2002). However, it can also lead to some very dramatic overdisclosure (George, 2006).

Self-disclosure The process of revealing private thoughts, feelings, and one's personal history to others.

Romantic love Love that is associated with high levels of interpersonal attraction, heightened arousal, mutual absorption, and sexual desire.

Intimacy Feelings of connectedness and affection for another person.

Passion Deep emotional and/or sexual feelings for another person.

Commitment The determination to stay in a long-term relationship with another person.

Liking and Loving—Dating, Rating, Mating

How does love differ from interpersonal attraction? It depends on what you mean by the word "love." **Romantic love,** for example, is based on interpersonal attraction, but it also involves high levels of passion: emotional arousal and/or sexual desire (Berscheid & Regan, 2005; Miller, Perlman, & Brehm, 2007).

To get another (tri?)angle on love, psychologist Robert Sternberg (1988) created his influential *triangular theory of love*. According to Sternberg, different forms of love arise from different combinations of three basic components (▶▶ Figure 14.1). **Intimacy** refers to feelings of connectedness and affection. **Passion** refers to deep emotional and/or sexual feelings. **Commitment** involves the determination to stay in a long-term relationship with another person.

Liking
Intimacy

Romantic love
Passion + intimacy

Companionate love
Intimacy + commitment

Consummate love
Intimacy + passion + commitment

Infatuation
Passion

Fatuous love
Passion + commitment

Empty love
Decision/commitment

FIGURE 14.1 The Triangle of Love. Each of the three basic components of love (intimacy, passion, and commitment) appears at one corner of the triangle and is associated with a form of love. Pairs of components and their associated form of love appear on lines of the triangle. Consummate love, which involves all three components, is pictured at the center of the triangle. (Adapted from Sternberg, 1988).

● Table 14.1 Sternberg's Triangular Theory of Love

Combinations of intimacy, passion, and commitment

TYPE OF LOVE	INTIMACY	PASSION	COMMITMENT
Nonlove			
Liking	Yes		
Infatuated love		Yes	
Empty love			Yes
Romantic love	Yes	Yes	
Companionate love	Yes		Yes
Fatuous love		Yes	Yes
Consummate love	Yes	Yes	Yes

Source: Sternberg, 1988.

How does the system work? Try it for yourself. Think of a person you love. Now read
● Table 14.1 as you ask yourself three yes/no questions: Do I feel intimate with this person? Do I feel passion for this person? Am I committed to this person? Find the kind of love that fits your answers. For example, if you answered *yes* to intimacy but *no* to passion and commitment, you **like** that person; you are friends. Alternately, if you answered *yes* to intimacy and commitment but *no* to passion, then you are feeling **companionate love.** This form of love is more common among couples who have been together for a long time.

Does that mean that the most complete form of love is consummate love? You've got it! We experience **consummate love** when we feel intimacy and passion for another person, *and* we are strongly committed to him or her.

Romantic love differs from friendship in another interesting way. In contrast to simple liking, romantic love usually involves deep *mutual absorption.* In other words, lovers (unlike friends) attend almost exclusively to one another.

What do lovers see when they gaze into each other's eyes? A final interesting characteristic of romantic love is lovers' ability to see their partners in idealized ways. Nobody's perfect, of course. That's why it's no surprise that relationships are most likely to persist when lovers idealize one another. Doing so doesn't just blind them to their partner's faults, it actually helps them create the relationship they wish for (Murray, Holmes, & Griffin, 1996, 2003).

Evolution and Mate Selection

Evolutionary psychology is the study of the evolutionary origins of human behavior patterns. Many psychologists believe that evolution left an imprint on men and women that influences everything from sexual attraction and infidelity to jealousy and divorce. According to David Buss, the key to understanding human mating patterns is to understand how evolved behavior patterns guide our choices (Buss, 2004, 2007).

In a study of 37 cultures on six continents, Buss found the following patterns: Compared with women, men are more interested in casual sex; they prefer younger, more physi-

Liking A relationship based on intimacy but lacking passion and commitment.

Companionate love Form of love characterized by intimacy and commitment but not passion.

Consummate love Form of love characterized by intimacy, passion, *and* commitment.

Evolutionary psychology Study of the evolutionary origins of human behavior patterns.

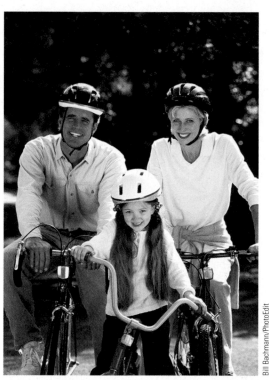

| | Number of responses to personal ad |
(chart labels: Beautiful waitress, Average-looking female lawyer, Average-looking male lawyer, Handsome cabdriver; axis 100 200 300 400 500 600)

▲ FIGURE 14.2 What do people look for when considering potential dating partners? Here are the results of a study in which personal ads were placed in newspapers. As you can see, men were more influenced by looks, and women by success (Goode, 1996).

According to evolutionary psychologists, women tend to be concerned with whether mates will devote time and resources to a relationship. Men place more emphasis on physical attractiveness and sexual fidelity.

cally attractive partners; and they get more jealous over real or imagined sexual infidelities than they do over a loss of emotional commitment. Compared with men, women prefer slightly older partners who appear to be industrious, higher in status, or economically successful; women are more upset by a partner who becomes emotionally involved with someone else, rather than one who is sexually unfaithful (Buss, 2000; Regan et al., 2000) (▶▶ Figure 14.2).

Why do such differences exist? Buss and others believe that mating preferences evolved in response to the differing reproductive challenges faced by men and women. As a rule, women must invest more time and energy in reproduction and nurturing the young than men do. Consequently, women evolved an interest in whether their partners will stay with them and whether their mates have the resources to provide for their children (Buss, 2004, 2007; Regan et al., 2000).

In contrast, the reproductive success of men depends on their mates' fertility. Men, therefore, tend to look for health, youth, and beauty in a prospective mate, as signs of suitability for reproduction (Buss, 2007). This preference, perhaps, is why some older men abandon their first wives in favor of young, beautiful "trophy wives." Evolutionary theory further proposes that the male emphasis on mates' sexual fidelity is based on concerns about the paternity of offspring. From a biological perspective, men do not benefit from investing resources in children they did not sire (Buller, 2005).

Although some evidence supports the evolutionary view of mating, it is important to remember that evolved mating tendencies are subtle at best and easily overruled by other factors. Some mating patterns may simply reflect the fact that men still tend to control the power and resources in most societies (Feingold, 1992). Also, early research may be misleading because women tend to give "polite" answers to questions about jealousy. Privately, they may be just as furious about a mate's sexual infidelity as any man would be (Harris, 2004).

Whatever the outcome of the debate about evolution and mate selection, it is important to remember this: Potential mates are rated as most attractive if they are kind, secure, intelligent, and supportive (Klohnen & Luo, 2003; Regan et al., 2000). These qualities are love's greatest allies.

Needs for affiliation and interpersonal attraction inevitably bring people together in groups. In the next section we will explore several interesting aspects of group membership. But first, here's a chance to review what you have learned.

RECITE

1. Interpersonal attraction is increased by all but one of the following. (Which does NOT fit?)
   a. physical proximity   b. competence
   c. similarity   d. overdisclosure
2. High levels of self-disclosure are reciprocated in most social encounters. T or F?
3. In Sternberg's triangular theory, infatuated love involves passion but not commitment or intimacy. T or F?
4. The most striking finding about marriage patterns is that most people choose mates whose personalities are quite unlike their own. T or F?
5. Compared with men, women tend to be more upset by sexual infidelity than by a loss of emotional commitment on the part of their mates. T or F?

study break
Affiliation, Friendship, and Love

REFLECT
Critical Thinking

6. How has the Internet altered the effects of proximity on interpersonal attraction?

Relate

How has social comparison affected your behavior? Has it influenced who you associate with?

Think of three close friends. Which of the attraction factors described earlier apply to your friendships?

To what extent does Sternberg's triangular theory of love apply to your own loving relationships with others?

ANSWERS

1. d 2. F 3. T 4. F 5. F 6. As mentioned earlier, it is now possible to interact with another person through the Internet. This makes actual physical proximity less crucial in interpersonal attraction, because frequent contact is possible even at great distances. Internet romances are a good example of this possibility.

Humans in a Social Context—People, People, Everywhere

How does group membership affect our behavior?

We all belong to many overlapping social groups, and in each, we occupy a *position* in the *structure* of the group. **Social roles** are patterns of behavior expected of persons in various social positions (Breckler, Olson, & Wiggins, 2006). For instance, playing the role of mother, boss, or student involves different sets of behaviors and expectations. Some roles are *ascribed* (they are assigned to a person or are not under personal control): male or female, son, adolescent, inmate. *Achieved roles* are voluntarily attained by special effort: spouse, teacher, scientist, bandleader, criminal.

What effect does role-playing have on behavior? Roles streamline daily interactions by allowing us to anticipate what others will do. When a person is acting as a doctor, mother, clerk, or police officer, we expect certain behaviors. However, roles have a negative side too. Many people experience **role conflicts,** in which two or more roles make conflicting demands on them. Consider, for example, a teacher who must flunk a close friend's daughter; a mother who has a full-time job; or a soccer coach whose son is on the team but isn't a very good athlete. Likewise, the clashing demands of work, family, and school create role conflicts for many students (Hammer, Grigsby, & Woods, 1998; Senécal, Julien, & Guay, 2003). Role conflicts at work (such as being a good team player vs. being a strong manager) lead to job burnout (Jawahar, Stone, & Kisamore, 2007) and negative health outcomes (Pomaki, Supeli, & Verhoeven, 2007). The brave couple Jasmine and Osama experience tremendous conflict. Their roles as husband and wife often clash with roles they play in their families and in their different religious and cultural groups.

Roles have a powerful impact on social behavior. What kinds of behavior do you expect from your teachers? What behaviors do they expect from you? What happens if either of you fails to match the other's expectations?

Social role Expected behavior patterns associated with particular social positions (such as daughter, worker, student).

Role conflict Trying to occupy two or more roles that make conflicting demands on behavior.

Group Structure, Cohesion, and Norms

Are there other dimensions of group membership? Two important dimensions of any group are its structure and its cohesiveness. **Group structure** consists of the network of roles, communication pathways, and power in a group. Organized groups such as an army or an athletic team have a high degree of structure. Informal friendship groups may or may not be very structured.

Group cohesiveness refers to the degree of attraction among group members or the strength of their desire to remain in the group. Members of cohesive groups literally stick together: They tend to stand or sit close together, they pay more attention to one another, and they show more signs of mutual affection. Also, their behavior tends to be closely coordinated (Chansler, Swamidass, & Cammann, 2003). Cohesiveness is the basis for much of the power that groups exert over us. Therapy groups, businesses, sports teams, and the like seek to increase cohesion because it helps people work together better (Craig & Kelly, 1999; Marmarosh, Holtz, & Schottenbauer, 2005).

In-groups

Cohesiveness is particularly strong for **in-groups** (groups with which a person mainly identifies). Very likely, your own in-groups are defined by a combination of prominent social dimensions, such as nationality, ethnicity, age, education, religion, income, political values, gender, sexual orientation, and so forth. In-group membership helps define who we are socially. Predictably, we tend to attribute positive characteristics to our in-group and negative qualities to **out-groups** (groups with which we do not identify). We also tend to exaggerate differences between members of out-groups and our own groups. This sort of "us-and-them" thinking seems to be a basic fact of social life. It also sets the stage for conflict between groups and for racial and ethnic prejudice—topics we will explore later in this chapter.

Status

In addition to defining roles, a person's social position within groups determines his or her **status,** or level of social power and importance. Higher status bestows special privileges and respect. For example, in one experiment, a man walked into a number of bakeries and asked for a pastry while claiming he did not have enough money to pay for it. Half the time he was well dressed and half the time he was poorly dressed. If the man was polite when he asked, he was equally likely to be given a free pastry no matter how he was dressed (95 vs. 90 percent). But if he was impolite when he asked, he was much less likely to get a pastry if he was poorly dressed than if he was well dressed (75 vs. 20 percent) (Guéguen & Pascual, 2003).

You don't have to be in a bakery for this to work. In most situations, we are more likely to comply with a request made by a high-status (well-dressed) person (Guéguen, 2002). Perhaps the better treatment given "higher status" persons, even when they are impolite, explains some of our society's preoccupation with expensive clothes, cars, and other status symbols.

Norms

We are also greatly affected by group norms. A **norm** is a widely accepted (but often unspoken) standard for appropriate behavior. If you have the slightest doubt about the power of norms, try this test: Walk into a crowded supermarket, get in a checkout line, and begin singing loudly in your fullest voice. Are you the 1 person in 100 who could actually carry out these instructions?

The impact of norms is shown by an interesting study of littering. The question was, Does the amount of trash in an area affect littering? To find out, people were given flyers as they walked into a public parking garage. As you can see in ▸▸ Figure 14.3, the more litter there was on the floor, the more likely people were to add to it by dropping their

Group structure The network of roles, communication pathways, and power in a group.

Group cohesiveness The degree of attraction among group members or their commitment to remaining in the group.

In-group A group with which a person identifies.

Out-group A group with which a person does not identify.

Status An individual's position in a social structure, especially with respect to power, privilege, or importance.

Norm A widely accepted (but often unspoken) standard of conduct for appropriate behavior.

flyer. Apparently, seeing that others had already littered implied a lax norm about whether littering is acceptable. The moral? The cleaner a public area is kept, the less likely people are to "trash" it (Cialdini, Reno, & Kallgren, 1990).

Making Attributions

Vonda just insulted Sutchai. But why? Every day we must guess how people will act, and why, often from small shreds of evidence. We do this through a process called **attribution.** As we observe others, we make inferences about them. Why did Nick change his college major? Why does Kirti talk so fast when she's around men? In answering such questions, we *attribute* people's behavior to various causes. It doesn't matter whether we are right or wrong about the causes of their behavior, our conclusions still affect how *we* act. To learn how we fill in the "person behind the mask," let's explore the making of attributions.

Two people enter a restaurant and order different meals. Nell tastes her food, then salts it. Bert salts his food before he tastes it. How would you explain their behavior? In Nell's case, you might assume that the *food* needed salt. If so, you have attributed her actions to an *external cause* (one that lies outside a person). With Bert, you might be more inclined to conclude that he must really *like* salt. If so, the cause of his behavior is internal. *Internal causes,* such as needs, personality traits, and Bert's taste for salt, lie within the person.

What effects do such interpretations have? It is difficult to fully understand social behavior without considering the attributions that we make. For instance, let's say that at the last five parties you've been to, you've seen a woman named Macy. Based on this, you assume that Macy likes to socialize. You see Macy at yet another gathering and mention that she seems to like parties. She says, "Actually, I hate these parties, but I get invited to play my tuba at them. My music teacher says I need to practice in front of an audience, so I keep attending these dumb events. Want to hear a Sousa march?"

We seldom know the real reasons for others' actions. That's why we tend to infer causes from *circumstances.* However, in doing so, we often make mistakes like the one with Macy. The most common error is to attribute the actions of others to internal causes (Follett & Hess, 2002; Jones & Nisbett, 1971). This mistake is called the **fundamental attribution error.** We tend to think the actions of others have internal causes even if they are actually caused by external forces or circumstances. One amusing example of this error is the tendency of people to attribute the actions of actors in television programs to the personality of the actor rather than the obvious external cause (that they are playing a character) (Tal-Or & Papirman, 2007).

Where our own behavior is concerned, we are more likely to think that external causes explain our actions. In other words, there is an **actor–observer bias** in how we explain behavior. As *observers,* we attribute the behavior of others to their wants, motives, and personality traits (this is the fundamental attribution error). As *actors,* we tend to find external explanations for our own behavior (Gordon & Kaplar, 2002). No doubt you chose your major in school because of what it has to offer. Other students choose *their* majors because of the kind of people they are. Other people who don't leave tips in restaurants are cheapskates. If you don't leave a tip, it's because the service was bad. And, of course, other people are always late because they are irresponsible. You are late because you were held up by events beyond your control.

FIGURE 14.3 Results of an experiment on norms concerning littering. The prior existence of litter in a public setting implies that littering is acceptable. This encourages others to "trash" the area. (From Cialdini, Reno, & Kallgren, 1990.)

Y-axis: Percentage of persons who littered
X-axis: Number of pieces of litter in environment

AFP/Getty Images

As of 2009, Madonna has adopted two children from Malawi. Do you attribute her actions to selfless concern for the suffering of children in Malawi? Or was she motivated by a selfish desire to hog the limelight? Such attributions greatly affect how we perceive and respond to the social behavior of others.

Attribution The process of making inferences about the causes of one's own behavior and that of others.

Fundamental attribution error The tendency to attribute the behavior of others to internal causes (personality, likes, and so forth).

Actor–observer bias The tendency to attribute the behavior of others to internal causes while attributing one's own behavior to external causes (situations and circumstances).

Social Influence—Follow the Leader

What have social psychologists learned about social influence?

No topic lies nearer the heart of social psychology than **social influence** (changes in behavior induced by the actions of others). When people interact, they almost always affect one another's behavior (Crano, 2000; Kassin, Fein, & Markus, 2008). For example, in a sidewalk experiment, various numbers of people stood on a busy New York City street. On cue they all looked at a sixth-floor window across the street. A camera recorded how many passersby also stopped to stare. The larger the influencing group, the more people were swayed to join in staring at the window (Milgram, Bickman, & Berkowitz, 1969).

Are there different kinds of social influence? Social influence ranges from mild to strong. The gentlest form of social influence is *mere presence* (changing behavior just because other people are nearby). We *conform* when we spontaneously change our behavior to bring it into agreement with others. Compliance is a more directed form of social influence. We *comply* when we change our behavior in response to another person who has little or no social power, or authority. Obedience is an even stronger form of social influence. We *obey* when we change our behavior in direct response to the demands of an authority. The strongest form of social influence is *coercion* (changing behavior because you are forced to).

Mere Presence

Suppose you just happened to be alone in a room, picking your nose (we know, none of us would do that, right?). Would you continue if a stranger entered the room? **Mere presence** refers to the tendency for people to change their behavior just because of the presence of other people. Let's explore some of the ways mere presence can induce us to modify our behavior.

Imagine you are out riding your mountain bike when another rider pulls up beside you. Will you pick up your pace? Slow down? Completely ignore the other rider? Psychologist Norman Triplett's 1898 investigation of just such a social situation was the first published social psychology experiment (Strube, 2005). According to Triplett, you are more likely to speed up. This is **social facilitation,** the tendency to perform better when in the presence of others.

Does mere presence always improve performance? No. If you are confident in your abilities, your behavior will most likely be facilitated in the presence of others. If you are not, then your performance is more likely to be impaired (Uziel, 2007). Another classic study focused on college students shooting pool at a student union. Good players who were confident (sharks?) normally made 71 percent of their shots. Their accuracy improved to 80 percent when they were being watched by others. Less confident, average players (marks?) who normally made 36 percent of their shots dropped to 25 percent accuracy when someone was watching them (Michaels et al., 1982).

Social loafing is another consequence of having other people nearby. People tend to work less hard (loaf) when they are part of a group than they do when they are solely responsible for their work. In one study, people playing tug-of-war while blindfolded pulled harder if they thought they were competing alone. When they thought others were on their team, they made less of an effort (Ingham et al., 1974).

Conformity

When Harry met Sally, they fell in love and were not shy about expressing themselves around campus. Some students in Harry's classes advised him to be a bit more discreet. Increasingly, Sally noticed other students staring at her and Harry when they were, well, expressing their love. Although they never made a conscious decision to conform, in another week their publicly intimate moments were a thing of the past. Perhaps the most basic of all group norms is, as Harry and Sally discovered, "Thou shalt conform." Like it or not, life is filled with instances of conformity.

Social influence Changes in a person's behavior induced by the presence or actions of others.

Mere presence The tendency for people to change their behavior just because of the presence of other people.

Social facilitation The tendency to perform better when in the presence of others.

Social loafing The tendency for people to work less hard when part of a group than when they are solely responsible for their work.

Groupthink—Agreement at Any Cost

Yale psychologist Irving Janis (1918–1990) first proposed the concept of groupthink in an attempt to understand a series of disastrous decisions made by government officials (Janis, 1989). The core of **groupthink** is misguided loyalty—an urge by decision makers to maintain each other's approval, even at the cost of critical thinking (Singer, 2005). Group members are hesitant to "rock the boat," question sloppy thinking, or tolerate alternative views. This self-censorship leads people to believe they agree more than they actually do (Henningsen et al., 2006; Whyte, 2000).

Groupthink has been blamed for contributing to many crises, such as the invasion and occupation of Iraq (Houghton, 2008; Singer, 2005), the *Columbia* space shuttle disaster in 2003, and the loss, in 1999, of the $165 million *Mars Climate Orbiter*. An analysis of 19 international crises found that groupthink contributed to most (Schafer & Crichlow, 1996).

To prevent groupthink, group leaders should take the following steps:

- Define each group member's role as a "critical evaluator."

- Avoid revealing any personal preferences in the beginning.

- State the problem factually, without bias.

- Invite a group member or outside person to play devil's advocate.

- Make it clear that group members will be held accountable for decisions.

- Encourage open inquiry and a search for alternate solutions (Baron, 2005; Chen et al., 1996).

In addition, Janis suggested that there should be a "second-chance" meeting to re-evaluate important decisions. That is, each decision should be reached twice.

In fairness to our decision makers, it is worth noting that the presence of too many alternatives can lead to *deadlock,* which can delay taking necessary action (Kowert, 2002). Regardless, in an age clouded by the threat of war, global warming, and terrorism, even stronger solutions to the problem of groupthink would be welcome. Perhaps we should form a group to think about it!

Daily behavior is probably most influenced by group pressures for conformity (Baron, Byrne, & Branscombe, 2007). We all **conform** to a degree. In fact, some uniformity is a necessity. Imagine being totally unable to anticipate the actions of others. In stores, schools, and homes this would be frustrating and disturbing. On the highways it would be lethal.

The Asch Experiment

How strong are group pressures for conformity? One of the first experiments on conformity was staged by Solomon Asch (1907–1996). To fully appreciate it, imagine yourself as a subject. Assume that you are seated at a table with six other students. Your task is actually quite simple. On each trial, you are shown three lines. Your job is to select the line that matches a "standard" line (▶▶ Figure 14.4).

As the testing begins, each person announces an answer for the first card. When your turn comes, you agree with the others. "This isn't hard at all," you say to yourself. For several more trials your answers agree with those of the group. Then comes a shock. All six people announce that line 1 matches the standard, and you were about to say line 2 matches. Suddenly you feel alone and upset. You nervously look at the lines again. The room falls silent. Everyone seems to be staring at you. The experimenter awaits your answer. Do you yield to the group?

In this study the other "students" were all actors who gave the wrong answer on about a third of the trials to create group pressure (Asch, 1956). Real students conformed to the group on about one third of the critical trials. Of those tested, 75 percent yielded at least once. People who were tested alone erred in less than 1 percent of their judgments. Clearly, those who yielded to group pressures were denying what their eyes told them.

Are some people more susceptible to group pressures than others? People with high needs for structure or certainty are more likely to conform. So are people who are anxious, low in self-confidence, or concerned with the approval of others. People who live in cultures that emphasize group cooperation (such as many Asian cultures) are also more likely to conform (Bond & Smith, 1996).

In addition to personal characteristics, certain situations tend to encourage conformity—sometimes with disastrous results. The feature titled "Groupthink—Agreement at Any Cost" offers a prime example.

Conformity is a subtle dimension of daily life. Notice the similarities in clothing and hairstyles among these couples.

(a)	(1) (2) (3)
Standard Line	**Comparison Lines**

▲ **FIGURE 14.4** Stimuli used in Solomon Asch's conformity experiments.

Groupthink A compulsion by members of decision-making groups to maintain agreement, even at the cost of critical thinking.

Conformity Bringing one's behavior into agreement or harmony with norms or with the behavior of others in a group in the absence of any direct pressure.

Group Factors in Conformity

How do groups enforce norms? In most groups, we have been rewarded with acceptance and approval for conformity and threatened with rejection or ridicule for nonconformity. These reactions are called *group sanctions.* Negative sanctions range from laughter, staring, or social disapproval to complete rejection or formal exclusion. If you've ever felt the sudden chill of disapproval by others, you will understand the power of group sanctions—just as Harry and Sally did.

Wouldn't the effectiveness of group sanctions depend on the importance of the group? Yes. The more important group membership is to a person, the more he or she will be influenced by other group members. The risk of being rejected can be a threat to our sense of personal identity (Crano, 2000). That's why the Asch experiments are impressive. Because these were only temporary groups, sanctions were informal and rejection had no lasting importance. Just the same, the power of the group was evident.

What other factors, besides importance of the group, affect the degree of conformity? In the sidewalk experiment described earlier, we noted that large groups had more influence. In Asch's face-to-face groups the size of the majority also made a difference, but a surprisingly small one. In other studies, the number of people who conformed increased dramatically as the majority grew from two to three people. However, a majority of three produced about as much yielding as a majority of eight. The next time you want to talk someone into (or out of) something, take two friends along and see what a difference it makes! (Sometimes it helps if the two are large and mean looking.)

Even more important than the size of the majority is its *unanimity* (total agreement). Having at least one person in your corner can greatly reduce pressures to conform. When Asch gave subjects an ally (who also opposed the majority by giving the correct answer), conformity was lessened. In terms of numbers, a unanimous majority of three is more powerful than a majority of eight with one dissenting. Perhaps this accounts for the rich diversity of human attitudes, beliefs, opinions, and lifestyles. If you can find at least one other person who sees things as you do (no matter how weird), you can be relatively secure in your opposition to other viewpoints. Incidentally, the Internet now makes it much easier to find that other like-minded person.

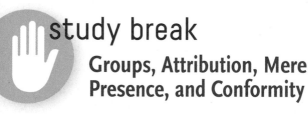

study break

Groups, Attribution, Mere Presence, and Conformity

RECITE

1. Status refers to a set of expected behaviors associated with a social position. T or F?
2. The fundamental attribution error is to attribute the actions of others to internal causes. T or F?
3. The effect one person's behavior has on another is called _____ _____.
4. The mere presence of others always improves performance. T or F?
5. Subjects in Solomon Asch's conformity study yielded on about 75 percent of the critical trials. T or F?
6. Nonconformity is punished by negative group _____.

7. Janis used the term _____ to describe a compulsion among decision-making groups to maintain an illusion of unanimity.

REFLECT

Critical Thinking

8. Would it be possible to be completely nonconforming (that is, to not conform to some group norm)?

Relate

How do you feel about participating in group projects at college? Have you ever encountered a social loafer? (*You* were never one, right?) How did you react?

Do you commit the fundamental attribution error? Try to think of a specific example that illustrates the concept.

Identify a recent time when you conformed in some way. How did norms, group pressure, sanctions, and unanimity contribute to your tendency to conform?

ANSWERS

1. F 2. T 3. social influence 4. F 5. F 6. sanctions 7. groupthink 8. A person who did not follow at least some norms concerning normal social behavior would very likely be perceived as extremely bizarre, disturbed, or psychotic.

Compliance—A Foot in the Door

Pressures to "fit in" and conform are usually indirect. In contrast, the term **compliance** refers to situations in which one person bends to the requests of another person who has little or no authority. These more direct pressures to comply are quite common. For example, a stranger might ask to borrow your cell phone so he can make a call; a saleswoman might suggest that you buy a more expensive watch than you had planned on; or a co-worker might ask you for the money to buy a cappuccino.

What determines whether a person will comply with a request? Many factors could be listed, but three stand out as especially interesting.

The Foot-in-the-Door Effect

People who sell door-to-door have long recognized that once they get a foot in the door, a sale is almost a sure thing. To state the **foot-in-the-door effect** more formally, a person who first agrees to a small request is later more likely to comply with a larger demand (Pascual & Guéguen, 2005). For instance, if someone asked you to put a large, ugly sign in your front yard to promote safe driving, you would probably refuse. If, however, you had first agreed to put a small sign in your window, you would later be much more likely to allow the big sign in your yard.

Apparently, the foot-in-the-door effect is based on observing one's own behavior. Seeing yourself agree to a small request helps convince you that you didn't mind doing what was asked. After that, you are more likely to comply with a larger request (Pascual & Guéguen, 2005).

The Door-in-the-Face Effect

Let's say that a neighbor comes to your door and asks you to feed his dogs, water his plants, and mow his yard while he is out of town for a month. This is quite a major request—one that most people would probably turn down. Feeling only slightly guilty, you tell your neighbor that you're sorry but you can't help him. Now, what if the same neighbor returns the next day and asks if you would at least pick up his mail while he is gone. Chances are very good that you would honor this request, even if you might have originally turned it down, too.

Psychologist Robert Cialdini coined the term **door-in-the-face effect** to describe the tendency for a person who has refused a major request to agree to a smaller request. In other words, after a person has turned down a major request ("slammed the door in your face"), he or she may be more willing to comply with a lesser demand. This strategy works because a person who abandons a large request appears to have given up something. In response, many people feel that they must repay her or him by giving in to the smaller request (Cialdini & Goldstein, 2004). In fact, a good way to get another person to comply with a request is to first do a small favor for the person.

Compliance Bending to the requests of a person who has little or no authority or other form of social power.

Foot-in-the-door effect The tendency for a person who has first complied with a small request to be more likely later to fulfill a larger request.

Door-in-the-face effect The tendency for a person who has refused a major request to subsequently be more likely to comply with a minor request.

The Low-Ball Technique

Anyone who has purchased an automobile will recognize a third way of inducing compliance. Automobile dealers are notorious for convincing customers to buy cars by offering "low-ball" prices that undercut the competition. The dealer first gets the customer to agree to buy at an attractively low price. Then, once the customer is committed, various techniques are used to bump the price up before the sale is concluded.

The **low-ball technique** consists of getting a person committed to act and then making the terms of acting less desirable (Guéguen, Pascual, & Dagot, 2002). Here's another example: A fellow student asks to borrow $25 for a day. This seems reasonable and you agree. However, once you have given your classmate the money, he explains that it would be easier to repay you after payday, in 2 weeks. If you agree, you've succumbed to the low-ball technique. Here's another example: Let's say you ask someone to give you a ride to school in the morning. Only after the person has agreed do you tell her that you have to be there at 6 A.M.

Obedience—Would You Electrocute a Stranger?

A person who has social power in one situation may have very little in another. In those situations where a person has power, she or he is described as an *authority*. When an authority commands **obedience,** the pressure to conform is greater than when someone with little or no authority requests compliance. Let's investigate obedience, a special type of conformity to the demands of an authority.

The question is this: If ordered to do so, would you shock a man with a heart condition who is screaming and asking to be released? Certainly, few people would obey. Or would they? In Nazi Germany, obedient soldiers (once average citizens) helped slaughter more than 6 million people in concentration camps. Do such inhumane acts reflect deep character flaws? Are they the acts of heartless psychopaths or crazed killers? Or are they simply the result of obedience to authority? These are questions that puzzled social psychologist Stanley Milgram (1965) when he began a provocative series of studies on obedience.

How did Milgram study obedience? As was true of the Asch experiments, Milgram's research is best appreciated by imagining yourself as a subject. Place yourself in the following situation.

Milgram's Obedience Studies

Imagine answering a newspaper ad to take part in a "learning" experiment at Yale University. When you arrive, a coin is flipped and a second person, a pleasant-looking man in his 50s, is designated the "learner." By chance you have become the "teacher."

Your task is to read a list of word pairs. The learner's task is to memorize them. You are to punish him with an electric shock each time he makes a mistake. The learner is taken to an adjacent room and you watch as he is seated in an "electric chair" apparatus. Electrodes are attached to his wrists. You are then escorted to your position in front of a "shock generator." On this device is a row of 30 switches marked from 15 to 450 volts. Corresponding labels range from "Slight Shock" to "Extreme Intensity Shock" and finally "Danger Severe Shock." Your instructions are to shock the learner each time he makes a mistake. You must begin with 15 volts and then move one switch (15 volts) higher for each additional mistake (▶▶ Figure 14.5).

The experiment begins, and the learner soon makes his first error. You flip a switch. More mistakes. Rapidly you reach the 75-volt level. The learner moans after each shock. At 100 volts he complains that he has a heart condition. At 150 volts he says he no longer wants to continue and demands to be released. At 300 volts he screams and says he can no longer give answers.

Low-ball technique A strategy in which commitment is gained first to reasonable or desirable terms, which are then made less reasonable or desirable.

Obedience Conformity to the demands of an authority.

discovering psychology

Quack Like a Duck

Imagine your response to the following events. On the first day of class, your psychology professor begins to establish the basic rules of behavior for the course. Draw a line under the first instruction you think you would refuse to carry out.

1. Seats are assigned and you are told to move to a new location.

2. You are told not to talk during class.

3. Your professor tells you that you must have permission to leave early.

4. You are told to bring your textbook to class at all times.

5. Your professor tells you to use only a pencil for taking notes.

6. You are directed to take off your watch.

7. The professor tells you to keep both hands on your desktop at all times.

8. You are instructed to keep both of your feet flat on the floor.

9. You are told to stand up and clap your hands three times.

10. Your professor says, "Stick two fingers up your nose and quack like a duck."

At what point would you stop obeying such orders? In reality, you might find yourself obeying a legitimate authority long after that person's demands had become unreasonable (Aronson, Wilson, & Akert, 2007).

From the film "Obedience" © 1968 by Stanley Milgram, © renewed by Alexandra Milgram, and distributed by The Pennsylvania State University Media Sales. Permission granted by Alexandra Milgram.

▲ FIGURE 14.5 Scenes from Stanley Milgram's classic study of obedience: the "shock generator," strapping a "learner" into his chair, and a "teacher" being told to administer a severe shock to the learner.

At some point, you begin to protest to the experimenter. "That man has a heart condition," you say. "I'm not going to kill that man." The experimenter says, "Please continue." Another shock and another scream from the learner and you say, "You mean I've got to keep going up the scale? No, sir. I'm not going to give him 450 volts!" The experimenter says, "The experiment requires that you continue." For a time the learner refuses to answer any more questions and screams with each shock (Milgram, 1965). Then he falls chillingly silent for the rest of the experiment.

It's hard to believe many people would do this. What happened? Milgram also doubted that many people would obey his orders. When he polled a group of psychiatrists before the experiment, they predicted that less than 1 percent of those tested would obey. The astounding fact is that 65 percent obeyed completely by going all the way to the 450-volt level. Virtually no one stopped short of 300 volts ("Severe Shock") (▶▶ Figure 14.6).

Was the learner injured? No. The "learner" was actually an actor who turned a tape recorder on and off in the shock room. No shocks were ever administered, but the dilemma for the "teacher" was quite real. Subjects protested, sweated, trembled, stuttered, bit their lips, and laughed nervously. Clearly they were disturbed by what they were doing. Nevertheless, most obeyed the experimenter's orders. You may doubt that Milgram's study of obedience applies to you. If so, take a moment to read "Quack Like a Duck."

Shock level

Slight	15 Volts	
Moderate		
Strong		
Very strong		
Intense	Victim screams
Extreme intensity	Victim pounds on wall
Danger: severe shock	Victim silent
XXX	450 Volts	Victim silent

10 20 30 40 50 60 70 80 90 100
Percentage of subjects obeying command at each shock level

▲ FIGURE 14.6 Results of Milgram's obedience experiment. Only a minority of subjects refused to provide shocks, even at the most extreme intensities. The first substantial drop in obedience occurred at the 300-volt level (Milgram, 1963).

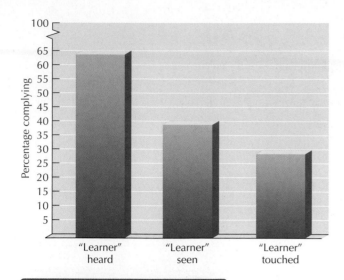

Milgram's Follow-Up

Why did so many people obey? Some have suggested that the prestige of Yale University added to subjects' willingness to obey. Could it be that they assumed that the professor running the experiment would not really allow anyone to be hurt? To test this possibility, the study was rerun in a shabby office building in nearby Bridgeport, Connecticut. Under these conditions, fewer people obeyed (48 percent), but the reduction was minor.

Milgram was disturbed by the willingness of people to knuckle under to authority and senselessly shock someone. In later experiments, he tried to reduce obedience. He found that the distance between the teacher and the learner was important. When subjects were in the *same room* as the learner, only 40 percent obeyed fully. When they were *face-to-face* with the learner and were required to force his hand down on a simulated "shock plate," only 30 percent obeyed (▶▶ Figure 14.7). Distance from the authority also had an effect. When the experimenter gave his orders over the phone, only 22 percent obeyed.

Implications

Milgram's research raises nagging questions about our willingness to commit antisocial or inhumane acts commanded by a "legitimate authority." The excuse so often given by war criminals—"I was only following orders"—takes on new meaning in this light. Milgram suggested that when directions come from an authority, people rationalize that they are not personally responsible for their actions. In locales as diverse as Cambodia, Rwanda, Bosnia, Vietnam, Darfur, Sri Lanka, and Iraq, the tragic result has been "sanctioned massacres" of chilling proportions. Even in everyday life, crimes of obedience are common (Zimbardo, 2007). In order to keep their jobs, many people obey orders to do things that they know are dishonest, unethical, or harmful (Hamilton & Sanders, 1995).

Let us end on a more positive note. In one of his experiments, Milgram found that group support can greatly reduce destructive obedience. When real subjects saw two other "teachers" (both actors) resist orders and walk out of the experiment, only 10 percent continued to obey. Thus, a personal assertion of courage or moral fortitude by one or two members of a group may free others to disobey misguided or unjust authority.

Coercion—Brainwashing and Cults

We close this section on social influence by examining some forms of *coercion,* the most extreme type of social influence. You are being **coerced** if you are forced to change your beliefs or your behavior against your will.

If you're a history enthusiast, you may associate *brainwashing* with techniques used by the Communist Chinese on prisoners during the Korean War. Through various types of "thought reform," the Chinese were able to coerce some of these prisoners to sign false confessions. More recently, the mass murder/suicide at Jonestown, the Branch Davidian tragedy at Waco, the Heaven's Gate group suicide in San Diego, and Osama bin Laden's al-Qaeda movement have heightened public interest in forced attitude change.

How does coercion differ from other forms of social influence? Brainwashing requires a captive audience. If you are offended by a television commercial, you can tune it out. Prisoners in POW camps are completely at the mercy of their captors. Complete control over the environment allows a degree of psychological manipulation that would be impossible in a normal setting.

Coercion Being forced to change your beliefs or your behavior against your will.

Brainwashing

How does captivity facilitate coercion? Brainwashing typically begins by making the target person feel completely helpless. Physical and psychological abuse, lack of sleep, humiliation, and isolation serve to *unfreeze,* or loosen, former values and beliefs. When exhaustion, pressure, and fear become unbearable, *change* occurs as the person begins to abandon former beliefs. Prisoners who reach the breaking point may sign a false confession or cooperate to gain relief. When they do, they are suddenly rewarded with praise, privileges, food, or rest. From that point on, a mixture of hope and fear, plus pressures to conform, serves to *refreeze* (solidify) new attitudes (Taylor, 2004).

How permanent are changes caused by brainwashing? In most cases, the dramatic shift in attitudes brought about by brainwashing is temporary. Most "converted" prisoners who returned to the United States after the Korean War eventually reverted to their original beliefs. Nevertheless, brainwashing can be powerful, as shown by the success of cults in recruiting new members.

Cults

Exhorted by their leader, some 900 members of the Reverend Jim Jones's People's Temple picked up paper cups and drank purple Kool-Aid laced with the deadly poison cyanide. Psychologically the mass suicide at Jonestown in 1978 is not so incredible as it might seem (Dein & Littlewood, 2005). The inhabitants of Jonestown were isolated in the jungles of Guyana, intimidated by guards, and lulled with sedatives. They were also cut off from friends and relatives and totally accustomed to obeying rigid rules of conduct, which primed them for Jones's final "loyalty test." Of greater psychological interest is the question of how people reach such a state of commitment and dependency.

Why do people join groups such as the People's Temple? The People's Temple was a classic example of a **cult,** an authoritarian group in which the leader's personality is more important than the beliefs she or he preaches. Cult members give their allegiance to this person, who is regarded as infallible, and they follow his or her dictates without question. Almost always, cult members are victimized by their leaders in one way or another.

For example, in April 1993, David Koresh and members of his Branch Davidian group perished in a fire at their Waco, Texas, compound. Like Jim Jones had done years before in Jonestown, Koresh took nearly total control of his followers' lives. He told them what to eat, dictated sexual mores, and had errant followers paddled. Followers were persuaded to surrender money, property, and even their children and wives. Like Jones, Koresh also took mistresses and had children out of wedlock. And like other cult leaders, Jones and Koresh demanded absolute loyalty and obedience to themselves and to their cult, with tragic results (Dein & Littlewood, 2005; Reiterman, 1993).

Psychologist and pioneering brainwashing expert Margaret Singer (1921–2003) studied and aided hundreds of former cult members. Her interviews reveal that in recruiting new members, cults use a powerful blend of guilt, manipulation, isolation, deception, fear, and escalating commitment. In this respect, cults employ high-pressure indoctrination techniques not unlike those used in brainwashing (Singer, 2003; Singer & Addis, 1992). In the United States alone, an estimated 2 to 5 million people have succumbed to the lure of cults (Robinson, Frye, & Bradley, 1997).

In the tragic fire at the Branch Davidian compound near Waco, Texas, some members paid with their lives for giving total allegiance to cult leader David Koresh.

Recruitment

Some people studied by Singer were seriously distressed when they joined a cult. Most, however, were simply undergoing a period of mild depression, indecision, or alienation from family and friends (Hunter, 1998). Cult members try to catch potential converts at

Cult A group that professes great devotion to some person and follows that person almost without question; cult members are typically victimized by their leaders in various ways.

a time of need—especially when a sense of belonging will be attractive to converts. For instance, many people were approached just after a romance had broken up, or when they were struggling with exams, or were trying to become independent from their families (Sirkin, 1990). At such times, people are easily persuaded that joining the group is all they need to do to be happy again (Hunter, 1998). Adolescents are especially vulnerable to recruitment into cults as they may be seeking a cause to conform to as a replacement for the parental authority they are rebelling against (Richmond, 2004).

Conversion

How is conversion achieved? Often it begins with intense displays of affection and understanding ("love bombing"). Next comes isolation from people who are not cult members, and drills, discipline, and rituals (all-night meditation or continuous chanting, for instance). These rituals wear down physical and emotional resistance, discourage critical thinking, and generate feelings of commitment (Langone, 2002).

Many cults make clever use of the foot-in-the-door technique, described earlier. At first, recruits make small commitments (to stay after a meeting, for example). Then, larger commitments are encouraged (to stay an extra day, to call in sick at work, and so forth). Making a major commitment is usually the final step. The new devotee signs over a bank account or property to the group, moves in with the group, and so forth. Making such major public commitments creates a powerful cognitive dissonance effect. Before long, it becomes virtually impossible for converts to admit they have made a mistake.

Once in the group, members are cut off from family and friends (former reference groups), and the cult can control the flow and interpretation of information to them. Members are isolated from their former value systems and social structures. Conversion is complete when they come to think of themselves more as group members than as individuals. At this point obedience is nearly total (Wexler, 1995).

Implications

Behind the "throne" from which Jim Jones ruled Jonestown was a sign bearing these words: "Those who do not remember the past are condemned to repeat it." Sadly, another cult-related tragedy occurred in 2001. The terrorist attacks on the United States were carried out by followers of cult leader Osama bin Laden (Olsson, 2007). At his direction, they learned hatred and contempt for everyone outside their band of true believers. If there is a lesson to be learned from such destructive cults, it is this: All true spiritual leaders have taught love and compassion. They also encourage followers to question their beliefs and to reach their own conclusions about how to live. In contrast, destructive cults show that it is dangerous to trade personal independence and critical thinking for security (Goldberg, 2001).

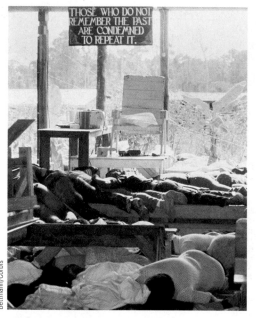

Aftermath of the mass suicide at Jonestown. How do cult-like groups recruit new devotees?

Assertiveness Training—Standing Up for Your Rights

How does self-assertion differ from aggression?

Most of us have been rewarded, first as children and later as adults, for compliant, obedient, or "good" behavior. Perhaps this is why so many people find it difficult to assert themselves. Or perhaps not asserting yourself is related to anxiety about "making a scene" or feeling disliked by others. Whatever the causes, some people suffer tremendous anguish in any situation requiring poise, self-confidence, or self-assertion. Have you ever done any of the following?

- Hesitated to question an error on a restaurant bill because you were afraid of making a scene?
- Backed out of asking for a raise or a change in working conditions?
- Said yes when you wanted to say no?
- Been afraid to question a grade that seemed unfair?

If you've ever had trouble with similar situations, *assertiveness training* (instruction in how to be self-assertive) may offer a solution. The first step in assertiveness training is to convince yourself of three basic rights: You have the right to refuse, to request, and to right a wrong. **Self-assertion** involves standing up for these rights by speaking out in your own behalf.

Is self-assertion just getting things your own way? Not at all. A basic distinction can be made between *self-assertion* and *aggressive* behavior. Self-assertion is a direct, honest expression of feelings and desires. It is not exclusively self-serving. People who are nonassertive are usually patient to a fault. Sometimes their pent-up anger explodes with unexpected fury, which can damage relationships. In contrast to assertive behavior, **aggression** involves hurting another person or achieving one's goals at the expense of another. Aggression does not take into account the feelings or rights of others. It is an attempt to get one's own way no matter what. Assertion techniques emphasize firmness, not attack (● Table 14.2).

The basic idea in assertiveness training is that each assertive action is practiced until it can be repeated even under stress. For example, let's say it really angers you when a store clerk waits on several people who arrived after you did. To improve your assertiveness in this situation, you would begin by *rehearsing* the dialogue, posture, and gestures you would use to confront the clerk or the other customer. Working in front of a mirror can be very helpful. If possible, you should *role-play* the scene with a friend. Be sure to have your friend take the part of a really aggressive or irresponsible clerk, as well as a cooperative one. Rehearsal and role-playing should also be used when you expect a possible confrontation with someone— for example, if you are going to ask for a raise, challenge a grade, or confront a landlord.

Self-assertion does not supply instant poise, confidence, or self-assurance. However, it is a way of combating anxieties associated with life in an impersonal and sometimes intimidating society. If you are interested in more information, you can consult a book entitled *Your Perfect Right* by Robert Alberti and Michael Emmons (2008).

Associated Press photographer Jeff Widener snapped this timeless photo of a lone protester literally standing up on his own behalf while he halted a column of tanks during the 1989 pro-democracy rallies in Tiananmen Square in Beijing, China. How many of us would find the courage to assert ourselves against such direct expressions of authority?

● Table 14.2 Comparison of Assertive, Aggressive, and Nonassertive Behavior

	ACTOR	RECEIVER OF BEHAVIOR
Nonassertive behavior	Self-denying, inhibited, hurt, and anxious; lets others make choices; goals not achieved	Feels sympathy, guilt, or contempt for actor; achieves goals at actor's expense
Aggressive behavior	Achieves goals at others' expense; expresses feelings, but hurts others; chooses for others or puts them down	Feels hurt, defensive, humiliated, or taken advantage of; does not meet own needs
Assertive behavior	Self-enhancing; acts in own best interests; expresses feelings; respects rights of others; goals usually achieved; self-respect maintained	Needs respected and feelings expressed; may achieve goal; self-worth maintained

Self-assertion A direct, honest expression of feelings and desires.

Aggression Hurting another person or achieving one's goals at the expense of another person.

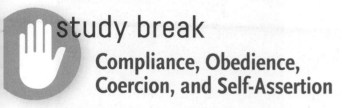
RECITE

1. The term *compliance* refers to situations in which a person complies with commands made by a person who has authority. T or F?
2. Obedience in Milgram's experiments was related to
   a. distance between learner and teacher
   b. distance between experimenter and teacher
   c. obedience of other teachers
   d. all of these
3. By repeating his obedience experiment in a downtown office building, Milgram demonstrated that the prestige of Yale University was the main reason for subjects' willingness to obey in the original experiment. T or F?
4. Brainwashing differs from other persuasive attempts in that brainwashing requires a _____ _____.

5. In assertiveness training, people learn techniques for getting their way in social situations and angry interchanges. T or F?
6. Nonassertive behavior causes hurt, anxiety, and self-denial in the actor and sympathy, guilt, or contempt in the receiver. T or F?

REFLECT

Critical Thinking

7. Modern warfare allows killing to take place impersonally and at a distance. How does this relate to Milgram's experiments?

Relate

Return to the description of various types of social power. Can you think of a setting in which you have (to a greater or lesser degree) each type of power?

You would like to persuade people to donate to a deserving charity. How, specifically, could you use compliance techniques to get people to donate?

Are you surprised that so many people obeyed orders in Milgram's experiments? Do you think you would have obeyed? How actively do you question authority?

To what extent are governments entitled to use coercion to modify the attitudes or behavior of their citizens?

ANSWERS

1. F 2. d 3. F 4. captive audience 5. F 6. T 7. There is a big difference between killing someone in hand-to-hand combat and killing someone by lining up images on a video screen. Milgram's research suggests that it is easier for a person to follow orders to kill another human when the victim is at a distance and removed from personal contact.

Attitudes—Belief + Emotion + Action

How are attitudes acquired and changed?

What is your attitude toward affirmative action, euthanasia, environmental groups, the situation in the Middle East, the death penalty, legalized abortion, junk food, psychology? Your answers, which are often influenced by social situations, can have far-reaching effects on your behavior. Attitudes are intimately woven into our actions and views of the world. Our tastes, friendships, votes, preferences, goals, and behavior in many other situations are all touched by attitudes (Baumeister & Bushman, 2008).

What specifically is an attitude? An **attitude** is a mixture of belief and emotion that predisposes a person to respond to other people, objects, or groups in a positive or negative way. Attitudes summarize your *evaluation* of objects (Oskamp & Schultz, 2005). As a result, they predict or direct future actions.

"Your attitude is showing," is sometimes said. Actually, attitudes are expressed through beliefs, emotions, and actions. The *belief component* of an attitude is what you believe about a particular object or issue. The *emotional component* consists of your feelings toward the attitudinal object. The *action component* refers to your actions toward various people, objects, or institutions. Consider, for example, your attitude toward gun control. You will have beliefs about whether gun control would affect rates of crime or violence. You will respond emotionally to guns, finding them either attractive and desirable or threatening and destructive. And you will have a tendency to seek out or avoid gun ownership. The action component of your attitude may well include support of organizations that urge or oppose gun control. As you can see, attitudes orient us to the social world. In doing so, they prepare us to act in certain ways (Albarracín, Johnson, & Zanna, 2005). (For another example, see ▶▶ Figure 14.8.)

Attitude A learned tendency to respond to people, objects, or institutions in a positive or negative way.

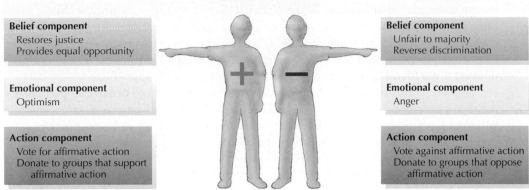

Issue: Affirmative Action

Belief component
Restores justice
Provides equal opportunity

Emotional component
Optimism

Action component
Vote for affirmative action
Donate to groups that support affirmative action

Belief component
Unfair to majority
Reverse discrimination

Emotional component
Anger

Action component
Vote against affirmative action
Donate to groups that oppose affirmative action

◄◄ **FIGURE 14.8** Elements of positive and negative attitudes toward affirmative action.

Forming Attitudes

How do people acquire attitudes? Attitudes are acquired in several basic ways. Sometimes, attitudes come from *direct contact* (personal experience) with the object of the attitude—such as opposing pollution when a nearby factory ruins your favorite river (Ajzen, 2005). Some attitudes are simply formed through *chance conditioning* (learning that takes place by chance or coincidence) (Olson & Zanna, 1993). Let's say, for instance, that you have had three encounters in your lifetime with psychologists. If all three were negative, you might take an unduly dim view of psychology. In the same way, people often develop strong attitudes toward cities, foods, or parts of the country on the basis of one or two unusually good or bad experiences.

Attitudes are also learned through *interaction with others;* that is, through discussion with people holding a particular attitude. For instance, if three of your good friends are volunteers at a local recycling center and you talk with them about their beliefs, you may well come to favor recycling, too. More generally, there is little doubt that many of our attitudes are influenced by *group membership.* In most groups, pressures to conform shape our attitudes, just as they do our behavior. *Child rearing* (the effects of parental values, beliefs, and practices) also affects attitudes (Bartram, 2006). For example, if both parents belong to the same political party, chances are that their children will belong to that party as adults. That's what makes Jasmine and Osama unusual; they have found love in opposition to their group membership and their childhood experiences.

Finally, there can be no doubt that attitudes are influenced by the media, such as newspapers, television, and the Internet. Every day we are coaxed, persuaded, and skillfully manipulated by messages in mass media. Consider, for example, the impact of television. Ninety-nine percent of North American homes have a television set, which is on an average of more than 7 hours a day (Steuer & Hustedt, 2002). The information thus channeled into homes has a powerful impact. For instance, frequent viewers mistrust others and overestimate their own chances of being harmed. This suggests that a steady diet of TV violence leads some people to develop a *mean worldview,* in which they regard the world as a dangerous and threatening place (Eschholz, Chiricos, & Gertz, 2003).

Attitudes and Behavior

Why are some attitudes acted on, while others are not? To answer this question, let's consider an example. Assume that a woman named Lorraine knows that automobiles are expensive to operate and add to air pollution, and she hates smog. Why would Lorraine continue to drive to work every day? Probably it is because the *immediate consequences* of our actions weigh heavily on the choices we make. No matter what Lorraine's attitude may be, it is difficult for her to resist the immediate convenience of driving. Our expectations of how *others will evaluate* our actions are also important. Lorraine may resist taking public transit to work for fear that her co-workers will be critical of her environmental stand. By taking this factor into account, researchers have been able to predict family planning choices, alcohol use by teenagers, re-enlistment in the National Guard, voting on a nuclear power plant initiative, and so forth (Cialdini, 2001). Finally, we must not overlook the effects of long-standing *habits* (Oskamp & Schultz, 2005). Let's say that after years of driving to work Lorraine finally vows to shift to public transit. Despite her good intentions, it would not be unusual if she found herself driving again two months later because of habit.

In short, there are often large differences between attitudes and behavior—particularly between privately held attitudes and public behavior. However, barriers to action typically fall when a person holds an attitude with *conviction*. If you have *conviction* about an issue, it evokes strong feelings, you think about it and discuss it often, and you are knowledgeable about it. Attitudes held with passionate conviction often lead to major changes in personal behavior (Oskamp & Schultz, 2005).

Attitude Change—Meet the "Seekers"

Although attitudes are fairly stable, they do change. Some attitude change can be understood in terms of **reference groups** (any group an individual uses as a standard for social comparison). It is not necessary to have face-to-face contact with other people for them to be a reference group. It depends instead on whom you identify with or whose attitudes and values you care about (Ajzen, 2005).

In the 1930s, Theodore Newcomb studied real-life attitude change among students at Bennington College, Vermont (Alwin, Cohen, & Newcomb, 1991). Most students came from conservative homes, but Bennington was a very liberal school. Newcomb found that most students shifted significantly toward more liberal attitudes during their 4 years at Bennington. Those who didn't change kept their parents and hometown friends as primary reference groups. This is typified by a student who said, "I decided I'd rather stick to my father's ideas." Those who did change identified primarily with the campus community. Notice that all students could count the college and their families as *membership* groups. However, one group or the other tended to become their point of reference.

Do you exercise regularly? Like students in the Bennington study, your intentions to exercise are probably influenced by the exercise habits of your reference groups (Terry & Hogg, 1996).

Persuasion

What about advertising and other direct attempts to change attitudes? Are they effective? **Persuasion** is any deliberate attempt to change attitudes or beliefs through information and arguments (Brock & Green, 2005). Businesses, politicians, and others who seek to persuade us obviously believe that attitudes can be changed. Billions of dollars are spent yearly on television advertising in the United States and Canada alone. Persuasion can range from the daily blitz of media commercials to personal discussion among friends. In most cases, the success or failure of persuasion can be understood if we consider the *communicator*, the *message*, and the *audience*.

At a community meeting, let's say you have a chance to promote an issue important to you (for or against building a new mall nearby, for instance). Whom should you choose to make the presentation, and how should that person present it? Research suggests that attitude change is encouraged when the following conditions are met. You should have little trouble seeing how these principles are applied to sell everything from underarm deodorants to presidents:

1. The communicator is likable, expressive, trustworthy, an expert on the topic, and similar to the audience in some respect.
2. The communicator appears to have nothing to gain if the audience accepts the message.
3. The message appeals to emotions, particularly to fear or anxiety.
4. The message also provides a clear course of action that will, if followed, reduce fear or produce personally desirable results.

Reference group Any group that an individual uses as a standard for social comparison.

Persuasion A deliberate attempt to change attitudes or beliefs with information and arguments.

5. The message states clear-cut conclusions.
6. The message is backed up by facts and statistics.
7. The message is repeated as frequently as possible.
8. Both sides of the argument are presented in the case of a well-informed audience.
9. Only one side of the argument is presented in the case of a poorly informed audience (Aronson, 1992; Oskamp & Schultz, 2005).

As we have just seen, we sometimes change our attitudes in response to external persuasion (Gass & Seiter, 2007). Sometimes, however, the internal process of *cognitive dissonance* can also lead to attitude change.

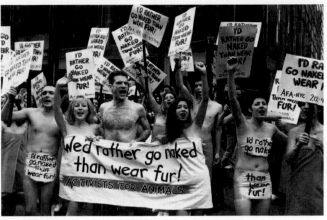

Persuasion. Would you be likely to be swayed by this group's message? Successful persuasion is related to characteristics of the communicator, the message, and the audience.

Cognitive Dissonance Theory

Cognitions are thoughts. Dissonance means clashing. The influential theory of **cognitive dissonance** states that contradicting or clashing thoughts cause discomfort. That is, we have a need for *consistency* in our thoughts, perceptions, and images of ourselves (Cooper, Mirabile, & Scher, 2005; Festinger, 1957). Inconsistency, then, can motivate people to make their thoughts or attitudes agree with their actions (Oskamp & Schultz, 2005).

For example, smokers are told on every pack of cigarettes that smoking endangers their lives. They light up and smoke anyway. How do they resolve the tension between this information and their actions? They could quit smoking, but it may be easier to convince themselves that smoking is not really so dangerous. To do this, a smoker might seek examples of heavy smokers who have lived long lives, spend time with other smokers, and avoid information about the link between smoking and cancer. According to cognitive dissonance theory, we also tend to reject new information that contradicts ideas we already hold. We're all guilty of this "don't bother me with the facts, my mind is made up" strategy at times.

A famous example of cognitive dissonance in action involves a woman named Mrs. Keech, who claimed she was in communication with beings on a planet called Clarion (Festinger, 1957). The messages foretold the destruction of North America. Mrs. Keech and her followers, the Seekers, were to be rescued by a flying saucer. The news media became involved and reported on the proceedings. When nothing happened, the Seekers suffered a bitter and embarrassing disappointment.

Did the group break up then? Amazingly, instead of breaking up, the Seekers became *more* convinced than ever before that they were right. Mrs. Keech announced that she had received a new message explaining that the Seekers had saved the world. Before, the Seekers were uninterested in persuading other people that the world was coming to an end. Now they called newspapers and radio stations to convince others of their accomplishment.

Why did their belief in Mrs. Keech's messages *increase* after the world failed to end? Why did the group suddenly become interested in convincing others that they were right? Cognitive dissonance theory explains that after publicly committing themselves to their beliefs, they had a strong need to maintain consistency (Tavris & Aronson, 2007). In effect, convincing others was a way of adding proof that they were correct (see ● Table 14.3).

Acting contrary to one's attitudes doesn't always bring about change. How does cognitive dissonance explain that? The amount of justification for acting contrary to your attitudes and beliefs affects how much dissonance you feel. (*Justification* is the degree to which a person's actions are explained by rewards or other circumstances.) In a classic study, college students did an extremely boring task (turning wooden pegs on a board) for a *long* time. Afterward, they were asked to help lure others into the experiment by pretending that the task was interesting and enjoyable. Students paid $20 for lying to others did not change their own negative opinion of the task: "That was *really* boring!" Those who were paid only $1 later rated the task as "pleasant" and "interesting." How can we explain these results? Apparently, students paid $20 experienced no dissonance. These students could reassure themselves that anybody would tell a little white lie for $20. Those paid $1 were faced with the conflicting thoughts: "I lied" and " I had no good reason to do it." Rather than admit to themselves that they had lied, these students changed their attitude toward what they had done (Festinger & Carlsmith, 1959) (▶▶ Figure 14.9).

Cognitive dissonance An uncomfortable clash between self-image, thoughts, beliefs, attitudes, or perceptions and one's behavior.

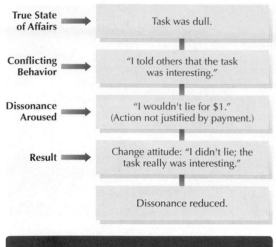

True State of Affairs →	Task was dull.
Conflicting Behavior →	"I told others that the task was interesting."
Dissonance Aroused →	"I wouldn't lie for $1." (Action not justified by payment.)
Result →	Change attitude: "I didn't lie; the task really was interesting."
	Dissonance reduced.

▲ **FIGURE 14.9** Summary of the Festinger and Carlsmith (1959) study from the viewpoint of a person experiencing cognitive dissonance.

● **Table 14.3 Strategies for Reducing Cognitive Dissonance**

LeShawn, who is a college student, has always thought of himself as an environmental activist. Recently, LeShawn "inherited" a car from his parents, who were replacing the family "clunker." In the past, LeShawn biked or used public transportation to get around. His parents' old car is an antiquated gas guzzler, but he has begun to drive it every day. How might LeShawn reduce the cognitive dissonance created by the clash between his environmentalism and his use of an inefficient automobile?

STRATEGY	EXAMPLE
Change your attitude	"Cars are not really a major environmental problem."
Add consonant thoughts	"This is an old car, so keeping it on the road makes good use of the resources consumed when it was manufactured."
Change the importance of the dissonant thoughts	"It's more important for me to support the environmental movement politically than it is to worry about how I get to school and work."
Reduce the amount of perceived choice	"My schedule has become too hectic, I really can't afford to bike or take the bus anymore."
Change your behavior	"I'm only going to use the car when it's impossible to bike or take the bus."

Source: After Franzoi, 2002.

study break
Attitudes and Attitude Change

RECITE

1. Attitudes have three parts: a _____ component, an _____ component, and an _____ component.
2. Which of the following is associated with attitude formation?
   a. group membership   b. mass media
   c. chance conditioning   d. child rearing
   e. all of the preceding   f. a and d only
3. In presenting a persuasive message, it is best to give both sides of the argument if the audience is already well informed on the topic. T or F?
4. Much attitude change is related to a desire to avoid clashing or contradictory thoughts, an idea summarized by _____ _____ theory.

REFLECT
Critical Thinking

5. Students entering a college gym are asked to sign a banner promoting water conservation. Later, the students shower at the gym. What effect would you expect signing the banner to have on how long students stay in the showers?
6. Cognitive dissonance theory predicts that false confessions obtained during brainwashing are not likely to bring about lasting changes in attitudes. Why?

Relate

Describe an attitude that is important to you. What are its three components?

Which of the various sources of attitudes best explain your own attitudes?

Who belongs to your most important reference group?

Imagine that you would like to persuade voters to support an initiative to preserve a small wilderness area by converting it to a park. Using research on persuasion as a guide, what could you do to be more effective?

How would you explain cognitive dissonance theory to a person who knows nothing about it?

ANSWERS

1. belief, emotional, action   2. e   3. T   4. cognitive dissonance   5. Cognitive dissonance theory predicts that students who sign the banner will take shorter showers, to be consistent with their publicly expressed support of water conservation. This is exactly the result observed in a study done by social psychologist Elliot Aronson.   6. Because there is strong justification for such actions. As a result, little cognitive dissonance is created when a prisoner makes statements that contradict his or her beliefs.

Prejudice—Attitudes that Injure

—#32

Love and friendship bring people together. Prejudice, which is marked by suspicion, fear, or hatred, has the opposite effect. After their marriage, Jasmine and Osama faced overwhelming **prejudice,** a negative emotional attitude held toward members of specific social groups. Prejudices may be reflected in the policies of police departments, schools, or government institutions (Dovidio, Glick, & Rudman, 2005). In such cases, prejudice is referred to as *racism, sexism, ageism,* or *heterosexism,* depending on the group affected. Because it is so prevalent and damaging, let's focus on racism.

Both racial prejudice and racism lead to **discrimination,** or unequal treatment of people who should have the same rights as others. Discrimination prevents people from doing things they should be able to do, such as buying a house, getting a job, or attending a high-quality school. For example, in many cities, African Americans have been the target of "racial profiling" in which they are stopped by police without reason. Sometimes, they are merely questioned, but many are cited for minor infractions, such as a cracked taillight or an illegal lane change. For many law-abiding citizens, being detained in this manner is a rude awakening (Plous, 2003). It's also one reason why many African Americans and other minority persons in America distrust police and the legal system (Dovidio et al., 2002). As distinguished African-American psychologist Kenneth Clark said, "Racial prejudice. . . . debases all human beings—those who are its victims, those who victimize, and in quite subtle ways, those who are merely accessories."

Becoming Prejudiced

How do prejudices develop? One major theory suggests that prejudice is a form of *scapegoating* (blaming a person or a group for the actions of others or for conditions not of their making). Scapegoating is a type of *displaced aggression* in which hostilities triggered by frustration are redirected at "safer" targets (Nelson, 2006). One interesting classic test of this hypothesis was conducted at a summer camp for young men. The men were given a difficult test they were sure to fail. Additionally, completing the test caused them to miss a trip to the movies, which was normally the high point of their weekly entertainment. Attitudes toward Mexicans and Japanese were measured before the test and after the men had failed the test and missed the movie. Subjects in this study, all European Americans, consistently rated members of the two ethnic groups lower after being frustrated (Miller & Bugelski, 1970). This effect was easy to observe after the September 11, 2001, terrorist attacks in the United States, when people who looked "foreign" became targets for displaced anger and hostility.

At times, the development of prejudice (like other attitudes) can be traced to direct experiences with members of the rejected group. A child who is repeatedly bullied by members of a particular ethnic group might develop a lifelong dislike for all members of the group. Yet even subtle influences, such as parents' attitudes, the depiction of people in books and on TV, and exposure to children of other races can have an impact. By the time they are 3 years old, many children show signs of race bias (Katz, 2003). Sadly, once prejudices are established, they prevent us from accepting more positive experiences that could reverse the damage (Wilder, Simon, & Faith, 1996).

Distinguished psychologist Gordon Allport (1958) concluded that there are two important sources of prejudice. *Personal prejudice* occurs when members of another ethnic group are perceived as a threat to one's own interests. For example, members of another group may be viewed as competitors for jobs. *Group prejudice* occurs when a person conforms to group norms. Let's say, for instance, that you have no personal reason for disliking out-group members. Nevertheless, your friends, acquaintances, or co-workers expect it of you.

Prejudice A negative emotional attitude held against members of a particular group of people.

Discrimination Treating members of various social groups differently in circumstances where their rights or treatment should be identical.

The Prejudiced Personality

Other research suggests that prejudice can be a general personality characteristic. Theodore Adorno and his associates (1950) carefully probed what they called the *authoritarian* (ah-thor-ih-TARE-ee-un) *personality*. These researchers started out by studying anti-Semitism. In the process, they found that people who are prejudiced against one group tend to be prejudiced against *all* out-groups (Perreault & Bourhis, 1999).

What are the characteristics of the prejudice-prone personality? The **authoritarian personality** is marked by rigidity, inhibition, prejudice, and oversimplification. Authoritarians also tend to be very *ethnocentric*. **Ethnocentrism** refers to placing one's own group "at the center," usually by rejecting all other groups. Put more simply, authoritarians consider their own ethnic group superior to others. In fact, authoritarians think they are superior to everyone who is different, not just other ethnic groups (Altemeyer, 2004; Whitley, 1999).

In addition to rejecting out-groups, authoritarians are overwhelmingly concerned with power, authority, and obedience. To measure these qualities, the *F scale* was created (the *F* stands for "fascism"). This scale is made up of statements such as the ones that follow—to which authoritarians readily agree (Adorno et al., 1950):

Authoritarian Beliefs
- Obedience and respect for authority are the most important virtues children should learn.
- People can be divided into two distinct classes: the weak and the strong.
- If people would talk less and work more, everybody would be better off.
- What this country needs most, more than laws and political programs, is a few courageous, tireless, devoted leaders, in whom the people can put their faith.
- Nobody ever learns anything really important except through suffering.
- Every person should have complete faith in some supernatural power whose decisions are obeyed without question.
- Certain religious sects that refuse to salute the flag should be forced to conform to such patriotic action or else be abolished.

As you can see, authoritarians are rather closed minded (Butler, 2000). As children, authoritarians were usually severely punished. Most learned to fear authority (and to covet it) at an early age. Authoritarians are not happy people.

Even if we discount the obvious bigotry of the authoritarian personality, racial prejudice runs deep in many nations. Let's probe deeper into the roots of such prejudiced behavior.

Intergroup Conflict—The Roots of Prejudice

An unfortunate by-product of group membership is that it often limits contact with people in other groups. Additionally, groups themselves may come into conflict. Both events tend to foster hatred and prejudice toward the out-group. The bloody clash of opposing forces in the Middle East, Africa, Ireland, and Hometown, U.S.A. are reminders that intergroup conflict is widespread. Daily, we read of jarring strife between political, religious, or ethnic groups.

Shared beliefs concerning *superiority, injustice, vulnerability,* and *distrust* are common triggers for hostility between groups. Pick almost any group in conflict with others and you will find people thinking along these lines: "We are special people who are superior to other groups, but we have been unjustly exploited, wronged, or humiliated [superiority and injustice]. Other groups are a threat to us [vulnerability]. They are dishonest and have repeatedly betrayed us [distrust]. Naturally, we are hostile toward them. They don't deserve our respect or cooperation" (Eidelson & Eidelson, 2003).

In addition to hostile beliefs about other groups, conflicts are almost always amplified by stereotyped images of out-group members (Bar-Tal & Labin, 2001).

What exactly is a stereotype? **Social stereotypes** are oversimplified images of people in various groups. There is a good chance that you have stereotyped images of some of the

Authoritarian personality A personality pattern characterized by rigidity, inhibition, prejudice, and an excessive concern with power, authority, and obedience.

Ethnocentrism Placing one's own group or race at the center—that is, tending to reject all other groups but one's own.

Social stereotypes Oversimplified images of the traits of individuals who belong to a particular social group.

Choking on Stereotypes

Bill, a retired aircraft mechanic, has agreed to talk to a group of high school students about the early days of commercial aviation. During his talk, Bill is concerned that any slip in his memory will confirm stereotypes about older people being forgetful. Because he is anxious and preoccupied about possible memory lapses, Bill actually "chokes" as he suffers problems with his memory (Chasteen et al. 2005).

As Bill's example suggests, negative stereotypes can have a self-fulfilling quality. This is especially true in situations in which a person's abilities are evaluated. For example, African Americans must often cope with negative stereotypes about their academic abilities (Steele & Aronson, 1995). Could such stereotypes actually impair school performance?

Psychologist Claude Steele has amassed evidence that victims of stereotyping tend to feel *stereotype threat*. They can feel threatened when they think they are being judged in terms of a stereotype. The anxiety that this causes can then lower performance, seemingly confirming the stereotype. An experiment Steele did demonstrates this effect. In the study, African-American and European-American college students took a very difficult verbal test. Some students were told the test measured *academic ability*. Others were told that the test was a laboratory *problem-solving task* unrelated to ability. In the ability condition, African-American students performed worse than European Americans. In the problem-solving condition, they performed the same as European Americans (Steele, 1997; Steele & Aronson, 1995). A similar effect occurred with women, who scored lower on a math test after being reminded of the stereotype that "women aren't good at math" (Cadinu et al., 2005; Keller, 2002).

In light of such findings, Steele and others are currently working on ways to remove stereotype threat, so that all students can use their potentials more fully (Steele, 1997).

---

following: African Americans, European Americans, Hispanics, Jews, women, Christians, old people, men, Asian Americans, blue-collar workers, rednecks, politicians, business executives, teenagers, and billionaires (▶▶ Figure 14.10). In general, the top three categories on which most stereotypes are based are sex, age, and race (Fiske et al., 2002).

Stereotypes tend to simplify people into "us" and "them" categories. Actually, aside from the fact that they always oversimplify, stereotypes often include a mixture of *positive* or *negative* qualities (Fiske et al., 2002). Even though stereotypes sometimes include positive traits, they are often used to maintain control over other people. When a person is stereotyped, the easiest thing for her or him to do is to abide by others' expectations—even if they are demeaning. That's why no one likes to be stereotyped. Being forced into a small, distorted social "box" is limiting and insulting. Stereotypes rob people of their individuality (Maddox, 2004). (See "Choking on Stereotypes.") Without stereotypes, there would be far less hate, prejudice, exclusion, and conflict.

When a prejudiced person meets a pleasant or likable member of a rejected group, the out-group member tends to be perceived as "an exception to the rule," not as evidence against the stereotype. This prevents prejudiced persons from changing their stereotyped beliefs (Wilder, Simon, & Faith, 1996). In addition, some elements of prejudice are unconscious, which makes them difficult to change (Dovidio et al., 2002).

Today's racism is often disguised by **symbolic prejudice.** That is, many people realize that crude and obvious racism is socially unacceptable. However, this may not stop them from expressing prejudice in thinly veiled forms when they state their opinions about affirmative action, busing, immigration, crime, and so on. In effect, modern racists find ways to rationalize their prejudice so that it seems to be based on issues other than raw racism. For instance, an African-American candidate and a European-American candidate apply for a job. Both are only moderately qualified for the position. If the person making the hiring decision is European American, who gets the job? As you might guess, the European-American candidate is much more likely to be hired. In other words, the European-American candidate will be given "the benefit of the doubt" about his or her abilities, whereas the African-American candidate won't. People making such decisions often believe that they aren't being prejudiced, but they unconsciously discriminate against minorities (Dovidio et al., 2002).

NBAE/Getty Images

▲ **FIGURE 14.10** Racial stereotypes are common in sports. For example, a study confirmed that many people actually do believe that "white men can't jump." This stereotype implies that African-American basketball players are naturally superior in athletic ability. European-American players, in contrast, are falsely perceived as smarter and harder working than African Americans. Such stereotypes set up expectations that distort the perceptions of fans, coaches, and sportswriters. The resulting misperceptions, in turn, help perpetuate the stereotypes (Stone, Perry, & Darley, 1997).

Symbolic prejudice Prejudice that is expressed in disguised fashion.

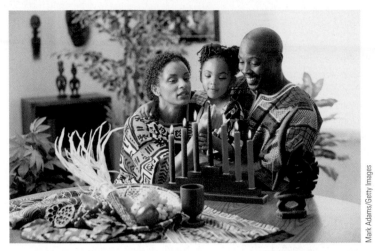

Ethnic pride is slowly replacing stereotypes and discrimination. For example, the African-American festival of Kwanzaa, a holiday celebrated late in December, emphasizes commitment to family, community, and African culture. However, despite affirmations of ethnic heritage, the problem of prejudice is far from solved.

Two experiments, both in unlikely settings and both using children, offer some additional insights into how stereotypes and intergroup tensions develop.

Experiments in Prejudice

What is it like to be discriminated against? In a unique experiment, elementary school teacher Jane Elliot sought to give her pupils direct experience with prejudice. On the first day of the experiment, Elliot announced that brown-eyed children were to sit in the back of the room and that they could not use the drinking fountain. Blue-eyed children were given extra recess time and got to leave first for lunch. At lunch, brown-eyed children were prevented from taking second helpings because they would "just waste it." Brown-eyed and blue-eyed children were kept from mingling, and the blue-eyed children were told they were "cleaner" and "smarter" (Peters, 1971).

Eye color might seem like a trivial basis for creating prejudices. However, people primarily use skin color to make decisions about the race of another person (Brown, Dane, & Durham, 1998). Surely, this is just as superficial a way of judging people as eye color is, especially given recent biological evidence that it does not even make genetic sense to talk about "races" (Bonham, Warshauer-Baker, & Collins, 2005). (See "Understand That Race Is a Social Construction" later in this chapter.)

At first, Elliot made an effort to constantly criticize and belittle the brown-eyed children. To her surprise, the blue-eyed children rapidly joined in and were soon outdoing her in the viciousness of their attacks. The blue-eyed children began to feel superior, and the brown-eyed children felt just plain awful. Fights broke out. Test scores of the brown-eyed children fell.

How lasting were the effects of this experiment? The effects were short lived, because two days later the children's roles were reversed. Before long, the same destructive effects occurred again, but this time in reverse. The implications of this experiment are unmistakable. In less than one day it was possible to get children to hate each other because of eye color and *status inequalities* (differences in power, prestige, or privileges). Certainly the effects of a lifetime of real racial or ethnic prejudice are infinitely more powerful and destructive (Clark et al., 1999). (See "Is America Purple?")

Equal-Status Contact

What can be done to combat prejudice? Several lines of thought (including cognitive dissonance theory) suggest that more frequent *equal-status contact* between groups in conflict should reduce prejudice and stereotyping (Olson & Zanna, 1993; Wernet et al., 2003). Equal-status contact refers to interacting on an equal footing, without obvious differences in power or status. In various studies, mixed-race groups have been formed at work, in the laboratory, and at schools. The conclusion from such research is that personal contact with a disliked group tends to induce friendly behavior, respect, and liking. However, these benefits occur only when personal contact is cooperative and on an equal footing (Grack & Richman, 1996).

Many school districts in the United States have begun requiring students to wear uniforms. Appearance (including gang colors) is one of the major reasons kids treat each other differently. Uniforms help minimize status inequalities and in-group/out-group distinctions. In Long Beach, California, a switch to uniforms was followed by a 91 percent drop in student assaults, thefts, vandalism, and weapons and drug violations (Ritter, 1998).

Superordinate Goals

Let us now consider a revealing study done with 11-year-old boys. When the boys arrived at a summer camp, they were split into two groups and housed in separate cabins. At first the groups were kept apart to build up separate group identities and friendships. Soon each group had a flag and a name (the "Rattlers" and the "Eagles") and each had staked out its territory. At this point the two groups were placed in competition with each other. After a number of clashes, disliking between the groups bordered on hatred: The boys baited each other, started fights, and raided each other's cabins (Sherif et al., 1961).

critical thinking

Is America Purple?

As research shows, it is easy to create prejudice. Pick any simplistic way to divide a group of people into "us" and "them" and popularize it. That's what teacher Jane Elliott did when she divided her class into the brown-eyed kids and the blue-eyed kids. In no time at all, the groups were prejudiced against each other.

But that was just an experiment. It couldn't happen in the real world, right? According to psychologists Conor Seyle and Matthew Newman (2006), we have witnessed just such a real-world example in America today. In order to graphically convey the outcome of the presidential vote in the 2000 election, *USA Today* created a state-by-state map, color coded red and blue to denote states that had voted for the Republican candidate or the Democratic candidate.

Within a few years, "Red" and "Blue" became a national shorthand for dividing Americans into opposing camps. The "Reds" are supposed to be Republican, conservative, middle-class, rural, religious, and live in the American heartland. The "Blues" are supposed to be Democrat, liberal, upper class, urban, nonreligious, and live on the coasts. The end result is that the complex American social world is reduced to two oversimplified stereotypes, leading to an increase in between-group prejudice (Mundy, 2004).

This oversimplification ignores the fact that, in many states, the presidential votes are very

FIGURE 14.11 Purple America Map. Counties within states voting more than 70 percent Republican appear in red; areas voting more than 70 percent Democratic appear in blue. Shades of purple represent intermediate percentages of voters. (Source: http://www.personal.umich.edu/~mejn/election/2008/. © 2008 M. E. J. Newman. Some rights reserved.)

close. Thus, a state that is "Red" by 51 percent is nevertheless 49 percent "Blue." Besides, many different combinations exist. President Clinton is originally from Arkansas (a "Red" state), but identifies himself as a Southern Baptist and worships in a Methodist church. Is he "Blue"? How do you categorize someone from California (a "Blue" state) who is an economic conservative, attends church occasionally, lives in San Francisco, supports gay marriage, and yet votes Republican?

According to Seyle & Newman (2006), a better approach is to recognize that America is made up of a full spectrum of political, social, religious, and economic views and that most Americans are "Purple." Thinking this way also highlights the fact that Americans of all political persuasions share more similarities than they do differences when compared with the citizens of other countries.

This more tolerant, less polarizing view of America is reflected in the "Purple America" map (▶▶ Figure 14.11) (Gastner, Shalizi, & Newman, 2005). Thinking purple just might result in a more productive national discussion about the important issues facing America today.

Were they allowed to go home hating each other? As an experiment in reducing intergroup conflict, and to prevent the boys from remaining enemies, various strategies to reduce tensions were tried. Holding meetings between group leaders did nothing. When the groups were invited to eat together, the event turned into a free-for-all. Finally, emergencies that required *cooperation* among members of both groups were staged at the camp. For example, the water supply was damaged so that all the boys had to work together to repair it. Creating this and other *superordinate goals* helped restore peace between the two groups. (A **superordinate goal** exceeds or overrides other, lesser goals.)

Cooperation and shared goals seem to help reduce conflict by encouraging people in opposing groups to see themselves as members of a single, larger group (Gaertner et al., 2000). Superordinate goals, in other words, have a "we're all in the same boat" effect on perceptions of group membership (Olson & Zanna, 1993). The power of superordinate goals can be seen in the unity that prevailed in the United States (and throughout much of the rest of the world) for months after the September 11 terrorist attacks. Superordinate goals are also an important factor in helping peacekeepers constructively engage with people from other nationalities (Boniecki & Britt, 2003).

Can such goals exist on a global scale? One example might be a desire to avoid nuclear holocaust. Another that comes to mind is the need to preserve the natural environment on a global scale. Still another is the continuing threat posed by terrorism and religious extremism. Politically, such goals may be far from universal. But their superordinate quality is clearly evident.

Superordinate goal A goal that exceeds or overrides all others; a goal that renders other goals relatively less important.

"Jigsaw" Classrooms

Contrary to the hopes of many, integrating public schools often has little positive effect on racial prejudice. In fact, prejudice may be made worse, and the self-esteem of minority students frequently decreases (Aronson, 2008).

If integrated schools provide equal-status contact, shouldn't prejudice be reduced? Theoretically, yes. But in practice, minority group children often enter schools unprepared to compete on an equal footing. The competitive nature of schools almost guarantees that children will *not* learn to like and understand each other.

With the preceding in mind, social psychologist Elliot Aronson pioneered a way to apply superordinate goals to ordinary classrooms. According to Aronson, such goals are effective because they create **mutual interdependence.** That is, people must depend on one another to meet each person's goals. When individual needs are linked, cooperation is encouraged (Deutsch, 1993).

How has that idea been applied? Aronson has successfully created "jigsaw" classrooms that emphasize cooperation rather than competition. The term *jigsaw* refers to the pieces of a jigsaw puzzle. In a **jigsaw classroom,** each child is given a "piece" of the information needed to complete a project or prepare for a test.

In a typical session, children are divided into groups of five or six and given a topic to study for a later exam. Each child is given his or her "piece" of information and asked to learn it. For example, one child might have information on Thomas Edison's invention of the light bulb; another, facts about his invention of the long-playing phonograph record; and a third, information about Edison's childhood. After the children have learned their parts, they teach them to others in the group. Even the most competitive children quickly realize that they cannot do well without the aid of everyone in the group. Each child makes a unique and essential contribution, so the children learn to listen to and respect each other.

Does the jigsaw method work? Compared with children in traditional classrooms, children in jigsaw groups are less prejudiced, like their classmates more, and have more positive attitudes toward school, their grades improve, and their self-esteem increases (Aronson, 2008; Walker & Crogan, 1998). Such results are quite encouraging.

To summarize, prejudice will be reduced when:

- Members of different groups have equal status *within the situation* that brings them together.
- Members of all groups seek a common goal.
- Group members must cooperate to reach the goal.
- Group members spend enough time together for cross-group friendships to develop.

Sports teams are an excellent example of a situation in which all of these conditions apply. The close contact and interdependent effort required in team sports often creates lifelong friendships and breaks down the walls of prejudice.

Jonathan Nourok/PhotoEdit

In a "jigsaw" classroom, children help each other prepare for tests. As they teach each other what they know, the children learn to cooperate and to respect the unique strengths of each individual.

Mutual interdependence A condition in which people must depend on one another to meet each person's goals.

Jigsaw classroom A method of reducing prejudice; each student receives only part of the information needed to complete a project or prepare for a test.

RECITE

1. As a basis for prejudice, _____ is frequently related to frustration and displaced _____.
2. The authoritarian personality tends to be prejudiced against all out-groups, a quality referred to as _____.
3. The stereotypes underlying racial and ethnic prejudice tend to evolve from the superordinate goals that often separate groups. T or F?
4. The term *symbolic prejudice* refers to racism or prejudice that is expressed in disguised or hidden form. T or F?
5. Jane Elliot's classroom experiment in prejudice showed that children could be made to dislike one another by imposing status inequalities. T or F?
6. Research suggests that prejudice and intergroup conflict may be reduced by _____ interaction and _____ goals.

study break
Prejudice and Intergroup Conflict

REFLECT
Critical Thinking

7. In court trials, defense lawyers sometimes try to identify and eliminate prospective jurors who have authoritarian personality traits. Can you guess why?

Relate

Mentally scan over the events of the last week. How would they have changed if prejudices of all types ceased to exist?

Think of the most rigid person you know. Does he or she match the profile of the authoritarian personality?

Stereotypes exist for many social categories, even ordinary ones such as "college student" and "unmarried young adult." What stereotypes do you think you face in daily life?

ANSWERS

1. scapegoating, aggression 2. ethnocentrism 3. F 4. T 5. T 6. equal-status, superordinate 7. Because authoritarians tend to believe that punishment is effective, they are more likely to vote for conviction.

Aggression—The World's Most Dangerous Animal

How do psychologists explain human aggression?

"I know not with what weapons World War III will be fought, but World War IV will be fought with sticks and stones."—Albert Einstein

For a time, the City Zoo of Los Angeles, California, had on display two examples of the world's most dangerous animal—the only animal capable of destroying the Earth and all other animal species. Perhaps you have already guessed which animal it was. In the cage were two college students, representing the species *Homo sapiens!*

The human capacity for aggression is staggering. About 58 million humans were killed by other humans (an average of nearly one person per minute) during the 125-year period ending with World War II. War, homicide, riots, family violence, assassination, rape, assault, forcible robbery, and other violent acts offer sad testimony to the realities of human aggression.

What causes aggression? **Aggression** refers to any action carried out with the intention of harming another person. Aggression has many potential causes. Brief descriptions of some of the major possibilities follow.

Instincts

Some ethologists argue that we are naturally aggressive creatures, having inherited a "killer instinct" from our animal ancestors (Blanchard & Blanchard, 2003). (An *ethologist* is a person who studies the natural behavior patterns of animals.) Noted ethologist Konrad Lorenz (1966, 1974) also believed that humans lack certain innate patterns that inhibit aggression in animals. For example, in a dispute over territory, two wolves may growl, lunge, bare their

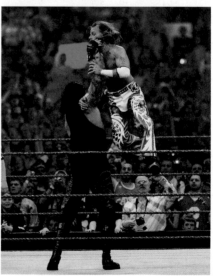

WireImage/Getty Images

Ritualized human aggression. Violent and aggressive behavior is so commonplace it may be viewed as entertainment. How "natural" is aggressive behavior?

Aggression Any action carried out with the intention of harming another person.

SOCIAL BEHAVIOR **579**

teeth, and fiercely threaten each other. In most instances, though, neither is killed or even wounded. One wolf, recognizing the dominance of the other, will typically bare its throat in a gesture of submission. The dominant wolf could kill in an instant, but it is inhibited by the other wolf's submissive gesture. In contrast, human confrontations of equal intensity almost always end in injury or death.

The idea that humans are "naturally" aggressive has an intuitive appeal, but many psychologists question it. Many of Lorenz's "explanations" of aggression are little more than loose comparisons between human and animal behavior. Just labeling a behavior "instinctive" does little to explain it. More important, we are left with the question of why some individuals or human groups (the Arapesh, the Senoi, the Navajo, the Eskimo, and others) show little hostility or aggression. And, thankfully, the vast majority of humans *do not* kill or harm others.

Biology

Despite problems with the instinctive view, aggression does have biological roots. Physiological studies have shown that some brain areas are capable of triggering or ending aggressive behavior. Also, researchers have found a relationship between aggression and such physical factors as hypoglycemia (low blood sugar), allergy, and specific brain injuries and diseases. For both men and women, higher levels of the hormone testosterone may be associated with more aggressive behavior (Harris et al., 1996; McDermott et al., 2007). Perhaps because of their higher testosterone levels, men are more likely to engage in physical aggression than women (Anderson & Bushman, 2002). However, none of these biological factors can be considered a direct *cause* of aggression (Moore, 2001; Popma et al., 2007). Instead, they probably lower the threshold for aggression, making hostile behavior more likely to occur.

The effects of alcohol and other drugs provide another indication of the role of the brain and biology in violence and aggression. A variety of studies show that alcohol is involved in large percentages of murders and violent crimes. Intoxicating drugs also seem to lower inhibitions to act aggressively—often with tragic results (Anderson & Bushman, 2002; Quigley & Leonard, 2000).

To summarize, the fact that we are biologically *capable* of aggression does not mean that aggression is inevitable or "part of human nature." Twenty eminent scientists who studied the question concluded: "Biology does not condemn humanity to war. . . . Violence is neither in our evolutionary legacy nor in our genes. The same species that invented war is capable of inventing peace" (Scott & Ginsburg, 1994; UNESCO, 1990). Humans are fully capable of learning to inhibit aggression. For example, American Quakers and Amish, who live in this country's increasingly violent culture, adopt nonviolence as a way of life (Bandura, 2001).

Frustration

Step on a dog's tail and you may get nipped. Frustrate a human and you may get insulted. The **frustration-aggression hypothesis** states that frustration tends to lead to aggression.

Does frustration always produce aggression? Although the connection is strong, a moment's thought will show that frustration does not *always* lead to aggression. Frustration, for instance, may lead to stereotyped responding or perhaps to a state of "learned helplessness" (see Chapter 11). Also, aggression can occur in the absence of frustration. This possibility is illustrated by sports spectators who start fights, throw bottles, tear down goal posts, and so forth, after their team has *won*.

Aversive Stimuli

Frustration probably encourages aggression because it is uncomfortable. Various *aversive stimuli*, which produce discomfort or displeasure, can heighten hostility and aggression (Anderson, Anderson, & Deuser, 1996; Morgan, 2005) (▶▶ Figure 14.12). Examples include insults, high temperatures, pain, and even disgusting scenes or odors. Such stimuli probably raise overall

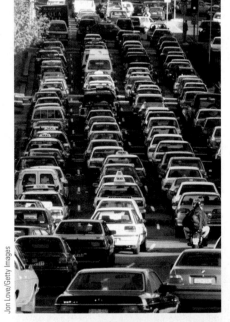

Road rage and some freeway shootings may be a reaction to the frustration of traffic congestion. The fact that automobiles provide anonymity, or a loss of personal identity, may also encourage aggressive actions that would not otherwise occur.

Frustration-aggression hypothesis States that frustration tends to lead to aggression.

arousal levels so that we become more sensitive to *aggression cues* (signals that are associated with aggression) (Carlson, Marcus-Newhall, & Miller, 1990). Aversive stimuli also tend to activate ideas, memories, and expressions associated with anger and aggression (Morgan, 2005).

Some cues for aggression are internal (angry thoughts, for instance). Many are external: Certain words, actions, and gestures made by others are strongly associated with aggressive responses. A raised middle finger, for instance, is an almost universal invitation to aggression in North America. Weapons serve as particularly strong cues for aggressive behavior (Morgan, 2005). The implication of this *weapons effect* seems to be that the symbols and trappings of aggression encourage aggression. A prime example is the fact that murders are almost three times more likely to occur in homes where guns are kept. Nearly 80 percent of the victims in such homes are killed by a family member or acquaintance (Kellermann et al., 1993).

Social Learning

One of the most widely accepted explanations of aggression is also the simplest. Social learning theory holds that we learn to be aggressive by observing aggression in others (Bandura, 2001). **Social learning theory** combines learning principles with cognitive processes, socialization, and modeling to explain behavior. According to this view, there is no instinctive human programming for fistfighting, pipe bombing, knife wielding, gun loading, 95-mile-an-hour "bean balls," or other violent or aggressive behaviors. Hence, aggression must be learned (▶▶ Figure 14.13). Is it any wonder that people who were the victims of violence during childhood are likely to become violent themselves? (Murrell, Christoff, & Henning, 2007)

Social learning theorists predict that people growing up in nonaggressive cultures will themselves be nonaggressive. Those raised in a culture with aggressive models and heroes will learn aggressive responses (Bandura, 2001). Considered in such terms, it is no wonder that America has become one of the most violent of all countries. A violent crime occurred every 23 seconds in the United States during 2005 (Federal Bureau of Investigation, 2005). Approximately 40 percent of the population owns firearms. Nationally, 70 percent agree that when a boy is growing up, it is "very important" for him to have a few fistfights. Children and adults are treated to an almost nonstop parade of aggressive models, in the media as well as in actual behavior. We are, without a doubt, an aggressive culture.

Media Violence

Every day, mainstream media provide an endless stream of bad models, especially concerning violence. TV, movies, computer games, and even music lyrics all contain violence. According to the organization Adults and Children Together (ACT) Against Violence, young children spend about 35 hours a week in front of TV or computer screens. By the end of elementary school, children will have seen about 8,000 murders and 100,000 other violent acts depicted on TV. Eighty percent of popular video games contain violent content. Many popular toys are also linked to violent media (ACT Against Violence, 2005a). And, of course, teenagers and young people are also chronically exposed to violence in the media.

How much does media violence affect children? There is now little doubt that widespread exposure to media violence contributes to aggression (Anderson et al., 2003; DeGaetano, 2005). As Albert Bandura showed in his studies of imitation (see Chapter 6), children may learn new aggressive actions by watching violent or aggressive behavior, or they may learn that violence is "okay." Either way, they are more likely to act aggressively. Heroes on TV are as violent as the villains, and they usually receive praise for their violence. Boys and girls who watch

▲ **FIGURE 14.12** Personal discomfort caused by aversive (unpleasant) stimuli can make aggressive behavior more likely. For example, studies of crime rates show that the incidence of highly aggressive behavior, such as murder, rape, and assault, rises as the air temperature goes from warm to hot to sweltering (Anderson, 1989). The results you see here further confirm the heat–aggression link. The graph shows that there is a strong association between the temperatures at major league baseball games and the number of batters hit by a pitch during those games. When the temperature goes over 90 degrees, watch out for that fastball! (Reifman, Larrick, & Fein, 1991)

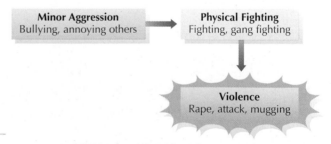

▲ **FIGURE 14.13** Violent behavior among delinquent boys doesn't appear overnight. Usually, their capacity for violence develops slowly, as they move from minor aggression to increasingly brutal acts. Overall aggression increases dramatically in early adolescence as boys gain physical strength and more access to weapons (Loeber & Hay, 1997).

Social learning theory Combines learning principles with cognitive processes, socialization, and modeling to explain behavior.

a lot of violence on TV are much more likely to be aggressive as adults (Huesmann et al., 2003). Violent video games are at least as problematic (Bartholow, Bushman, & Sestir, 2006), and even violent song lyrics increase aggressive tendencies (Anderson, Carnagey, & Eubanks, 2003).

In addition to teaching new antisocial actions, media such as TV and video games may disinhibit dangerous impulses that viewers already have. *Disinhibition* (the removal of inhibition) results in acting out behavior that normally would be restrained. For example, many TV programs give the message that violence is acceptable behavior that leads to success and popularity. For some people, this message can lower inhibitions against acting out hostile feelings (Anderson et al., 2003).

Another effect of media violence is that it tends to lower sensitivity to violent acts (Funk, 2005). As anyone who has seen a street fight or a mugging can tell you, TV violence is sanitized and unrealistic. The real thing is gross, ugly, and gut wrenching. Even when media violence is graphic, as it is in many video games, it is experienced in the relaxed and familiar setting of the home. For at least some viewers, this combination diminishes emotional reactions to violent scenes. Media, it seems, can cause a *desensitization* (reduced emotional sensitivity) to violence (Huesmann et al., 2003).

Preventing Aggression

What can be done about aggression? Social learning theory implies that "aggression begets aggression." For example, children who are physically abused at home, those who suffer severe physical punishment, and those who merely witness violence in the community are more likely to be involved in fighting, aggressive play, and antisocial behavior at school (Bartholow, Sestir, & Davis, 2005; Margolin & Gordis, 2000).

According to social learning theorists, watching a mixed martial arts fight or violent TV program may increase aggression, rather than drain off aggressive urges. A case in point is provided by psychologist Leonard Eron, who spent 22 years following more than 600 children into adulthood. Eron (1987) observes, "Among the most influential models for children were those observed on television. One of the best predictors of how aggressive a young man would be at age 19 was the violence of the television programs he preferred when he was 8 years old" (▶▶ Figure 14.14). According to Eron, children learn aggressive strategies and actions from TV violence. Because of this, they are more prone to aggress when they face frustrating situations or cues. Others have found that viewers who experience violent media have more aggressive thoughts. As we have noted, violent thoughts often precede violent actions (Anderson, Carnagey, & Eubanks, 2003). Thus, the spiral of aggression might be broken if we did not so often portray it, reward it, and glorify it (Hughes & Hasbrouck, 1996).

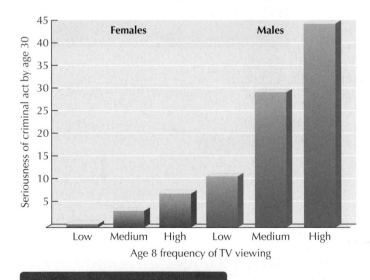

▲ **FIGURE 14.14** Although TV violence does not cause aggression, it can encourage it. The likelihood of committing criminal acts by age 30 is related to the amount of TV watching a person did when she or he was a child (Eron, 1987). (Graph copyright 1987 by the American Psychological Association, Inc. Reprinted by permission of the author.)

Parents as Media Guides

As the preceding studies show, reducing exposure to violent media is one way to lower aggression. However, other than pulling the plug, what can parents do about media's negative effects on children? Actually, quite a lot. Parents can make a big difference if they do the following (ACT Against Violence, 2005b; Frydman, 1999):

1. Start by creating a safe, warm environment at home and school and by modeling positive ways of getting along in the world. Children typically model parents' behavior, including their media viewing habits, and they are guided by parents' reactions to media.
2. Limit total media time so that TV and computer games do not dominate your child's view of the world. If necessary, set schedules for when watching TV or playing video games is allowed. Don't use media as a babysitter.

3. Closely monitor what your child does experience. Change channels or turn off the TV if you object to a program. Be prepared to offer games and activities that stimulate your child's imagination and creativity as well as model positive behavior and social attitudes.

4. Explore media with your child so that you can counter what is shown. Help your child distinguish between reality and fantasy in media. Reply to distortions, stereotypes, and violence as they appear on screen. Encourage the child to propose more mature, realistic, and positive responses to situations.

5. Show by your own disapproval that violent TV and computer game heroes are not the ones to emulate. Remember, children who identify with media characters are more likely to be influenced by media aggression.

By following these guidelines you can help children learn to enjoy media without being overly influenced by programs and advertisers. One study found that elementary school children become less aggressive when they decrease the amount of time they spend watching TV and playing video games (Robinson et al., 2001).

Beyond this, the question remains, How shall we tame the world's most dangerous animal? There is no easy answer, only a challenge of pressing importance (Lench, 2004). For the immediate future, it is clear that we need more people who are willing to engage in helpful, altruistic, **prosocial behavior** (actions that are constructive, altruistic, or helpful to others). In the next section we will examine some of the forces that prevent people from helping others and how to encourage prosocial behavior.

Prosocial Behavior—Helping Others

Why are bystanders so often unwilling to help in an emergency?

Let's begin our exploration of helping behavior by first asking why people sometimes do not help. That will make it clearer just how remarkable it is when people do help others.

Late one night in 1964, tenants of a Queens, New York, apartment building watched and listened in horror as a young woman named Kitty Genovese was murdered on the sidewalk outside. From the safety of their rooms, no fewer than 38 people heard the agonized screams as her assailant stabbed her, was frightened off, and returned to stab her again.

Kitty Genovese's murder took more than 30 minutes, but none of her neighbors tried to help. None even called the police until after the attack had ended. Perhaps it is understandable that no one wanted to get involved. After all, it could have been a violent lovers' quarrel. Or helping might have meant risking personal injury. But what prevented these people from at least calling the police? Although many details of the Kitty Genovese murder have been called into question, the episode was instrumental in launching research into *bystander apathy* (Manning, Levine, & Collins, 2007).

Isn't this an example of the alienation of city life? News reports treated this incident as evidence of a breakdown in social ties caused by the impersonality of the city. Although it is true that urban living can be dehumanizing, this does not fully explain such *bystander apathy* (the unwillingness of bystanders to offer help during emergencies is also referred to as the *bystander effect*). According to landmark work by psychologists John Darley and Bibb Latané (1968), failure to help is related to the number of people present. Over the years many studies have shown that the *more* potential helpers present, the *less* likely people are to help (Latané, Nida, & Wilson, 1981; Miller, 2006).

Does the person lying on the ground need help? What factors determine whether a person in trouble will receive help in an emergency? Surprisingly, more potential helpers tend to lower the chances that help will be given.

Prosocial behavior Behavior toward others that is helpful, constructive, or altruistic.

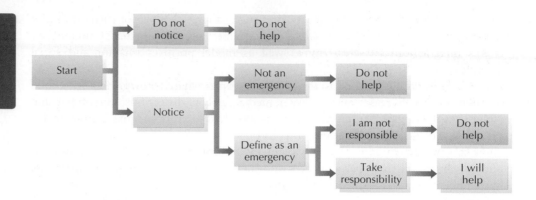

Why would people be less willing to help when others are present? In Kitty Genovese's case, the answer is that everyone thought *someone else* would help. The dynamics of this effect are easily illustrated: Suppose that two motorists have stalled at roadside, one on a sparsely traveled country road and the other on a busy freeway. Who gets help first?

On the freeway, where hundreds of cars pass every minute, each driver can assume that someone else will help. Personal responsibility for helping is spread so thin that no one takes action. On the country road, one of the first few people to arrive will probably stop, since the responsibility is clearly theirs. In general, Darley and Latané assume that bystanders are not apathetic or uncaring; they are inhibited by the presence of others.

Bystander Intervention

People must pass through four decision points before giving help. First they must notice that something is happening. Next they must define the event as an emergency. Then they must take responsibility. Finally, they must select a course of action (Figure 14.15). Laboratory experiments have shown that each step can be influenced by the presence of other people.

Noticing

What would happen if you fainted and collapsed on the sidewalk? Would someone stop to help? Would people think you were drunk? Would they even notice you? Darley and Latané suggest that if the sidewalk is crowded, few people will even see you. This has nothing to do with people blocking each other's vision. Instead, it is related to widely accepted norms against staring at others in public. People in crowds typically "keep their eyes to themselves."

Is there any way to show that this is a factor in bystander apathy? To test this idea, students were asked to fill out a questionnaire either alone or in a room full of people. While the students worked, a thick cloud of smoke was blown into the room through a vent.

Most students left alone in the room noticed the smoke immediately. Few of the people in groups noticed the smoke until it actually became difficult to see through it. Subjects working in groups politely kept their eyes on their papers and avoided looking at others (or the smoke). In contrast, those who were alone scanned the room from time to time.

Defining an Emergency

The smoke-filled room also shows the influence others have on defining a situation as an emergency. When subjects in groups finally noticed the smoke, they cast sidelong glances at others in the room. (Remember *social comparison?*) Apparently, they were searching for clues to help interpret what was happening. No one wanted to overreact or act like a fool if there was no emergency. However, as subjects coolly surveyed the reactions of others, they were themselves being watched. In real emergencies, people sometimes "fake each other out" and underestimate the need for action because each person attempts to appear calm. In short, until someone acts, no one acts.

Taking Responsibility

Perhaps the most crucial step in helping is assuming responsibility. In this case, groups limit helping by causing a *diffusion of responsibility* (spreading responsibility among several people).

Is that like the unwillingness of drivers to offer help on a crowded freeway? Exactly. It is the feeling that no one is personally responsible for helping. This problem was demonstrated in an experiment in which students took part in a group discussion over an intercom system. Actually, there was only one real subject in each group; the others were tape-recorded actors. Each subject was placed in a separate room (supposedly to maintain confidentiality), and discussions of college life were begun. During the discussion, one of the "students" simulated an epileptic-like seizure and called out for help. In some cases, subjects thought they were alone with the seizure victim. Others believed they were members of three- or six-person groups.

People who thought they were alone with the "victim" of this staged emergency reported it immediately or tried to help. Some subjects in the three-person groups failed to respond, and those who did were slower. In the six-person groups, over a third of the subjects took no action at all. People in this experiment were obviously faced with a conflict like that in many real emergencies: Should they be helpful and responsible, or should they mind their own business? Many were influenced toward inaction by the presence of others.

People do help in some emergencies. How are these different? It is not always clear what makes the difference. Helping behavior is complex and influenced by many variables. One naturalistic experiment staged in a New York City subway gives a hint of the kinds of things that may be important. When a "victim" (actor) "passed out" in a subway car, he received more help when carrying a cane than when carrying a liquor bottle (Piliavin, Rodin, & Piliavin, 1969).

To better answer the question, we need to consider some factors not included in Darley and Latané's account of helping.

Who Will Help Whom?

Many studies suggest that when we see a person in trouble, it tends to cause *heightened arousal* (Dovidio & Penner, 2001). This aroused, keyed-up feeling can motivate us to give aid, but only if the rewards of helping outweigh the costs. Higher costs (such as great effort, personal risk, or possible embarrassment) almost always decrease helping. In addition to general arousal, potential helpers may also feel **empathic arousal.** This means they empathize with the person in need or feel some of the person's pain, fear, or anguish. Helping is much more likely when we are able to take the perspective of others and feel sympathy for their plight (Batson & Powell, 2003).

Empathic arousal is especially likely to motivate helping when the person in need seems to be similar to ourselves (Batson & Powell, 2003). In fact, a feeling of connection to the victim may be one of the most important factors in helping. This, perhaps, is why being in a good mood also increases helping. When we are feeling successful, happy, or fortunate, we may also feel more connected to others (Dovidio & Penner, 2001). In summary, there is a strong **empathy-helping relationship:** We are most likely to help someone in need when we "feel for" that person and experience emotions such as empathy, sympathy, and compassion (Batson, 2006).

Is there anything that can be done to encourage prosocial behavior? People who see others helping are more likely to offer help themselves. Also, persons who give help in one situation tend to perceive themselves as helpful people. This change in self-image encourages them to help in other situations. One more point is that norms of fairness encourage us to help others who have helped us (Dovidio & Penner, 2001). For all these reasons, helping others not only assists them directly, it encourages others to help too.

"De-victimize" Yourself

If you should find yourself in need of help during an emergency, what can you do to avoid being a victim of bystander apathy? The work we have reviewed here suggests that you should make sure that you are noticed, that people realize there's an emergency, and that

Empathic arousal Emotional arousal that occurs when you feel some of another person's pain, fear, or anguish.

Empathy-helping relationship Observation that we are most likely to help someone else when we feel emotions such as empathy and compassion.

they need to take action. Being noticed can be promoted in some situations by shouting "Fire!" Bystanders who might run away from a robbery or an assault may rush to see where the fire is. At the very least, remember to not just scream. Instead, you should call out, "Help," or, "I need help right now." Whenever possible, define your situation for bystanders. Say, for instance, "I'm being attacked, call the police." Or, "Stop that man, he has my purse." You can also directly assign responsibility to a bystander by pointing to someone and saying, "You, call the police," or, "I'm injured, I need you to call an ambulance" (Cummins, 1995).

A Look Ahead

The Psychology in Action section of this chapter returns to the topic of prejudice for some further thoughts about how to promote tolerance. Don't miss this interesting conclusion to our discussion of social psychology.

study break

Aggression and Prosocial Behavior

RECITE

1. The position of ethologists is that there is no biological basis for aggression. T or F?
2. Higher levels of testosterone are associated with more aggressive behavior. T or F?
3. Frustration and aversive stimuli are more likely to produce aggression when cues for aggressive behavior are present. T or F?
4. Social learning theory holds that exposure to aggressive models helps drain off aggressive energies. T or F?
5. Heavy exposure to media results in lowered emotional sensitivity to violence. T or F?
6. _____ behavior refers to actions that are constructive, altruistic, or helpful to others.

7. Seeing that a person in need is similar to ourselves tends to increase empathic arousal and the likelihood that help will be given. T or F?

REFLECT
Critical Thinking

8. If media violence contributes to aggressive behavior in our society, do you think it is possible that the media could also promote prosocial behavior?

Relate

Most people have been angry enough at some time to behave aggressively. Which concepts or theories do you think best explain your own aggressive actions?

An elderly woman is at the side of the road, trying to change a flat tire. She obviously needs help. You are approaching her in your car. What must happen before you are likely to stop and help her?

ANSWERS

1. F 2. T 3. T 4. F 5. T 6. Prosocial 7. T 8. Yes. The media could be used to promote helping, cooperation, charity, and brotherhood in the same way that it has encouraged aggression. Numerous studies show that portraying prosocial behavior in the media increases prosocial behavior (Greitemeyer, 2009).

psychology in action

Multiculturalism—Living with Diversity

How can we promote multiculturalism and social harmony?

Today's society is more like a "tossed salad" than a cultural "melting pot." Rather than expecting everyone to be alike, psychologists believe that we must learn to respect and appreciate our differences. **Multiculturalism,** as this is called, is a recognition and acceptance of human diversity. It gives equal status to different ethnic, racial, and cultural groups (Moghaddam, 2007).

Breaking the Prejudice Habit

Most people publicly support policies of equality and fairness. Yet, many still have lingering biases and negative images of African Americans, Latinos, Muslim Americans, and other ethnic minorities. How can we make sense of such conflicting attitudes? A decision to for-

Multiculturalism Giving equal status, recognition, and acceptance to different ethnic and cultural groups.

sake prejudice does not immediately eliminate prejudiced thoughts and feelings. People who are not consciously prejudiced may continue to respond emotionally to members of other ethnic groups (Nosek, Greenwald, & Banaji, 2005). Quite likely this reflects lingering stereotypes and prejudices learned in childhood (Dion, 2003).

For many people, becoming less prejudiced begins by accepting the value of *openness to the other,* the ability to genuinely appreciate those who differ from us culturally (Fowers & Davidov, 2006). It is important to remember that being open to someone else does not mean that you have to agree with that person or turn your back on your own culture. Openness, in turn, leads to the acceptance of the values of tolerance and equality. People who value tolerance resist intolerant thoughts or feelings, which motivates them to try to alter their own biased reactions (Dovidio & Gaertner, 1999; Zuwerink et al., 1996). But doing so is not easy. Typically, it requires repeated efforts to learn to think, feel, and act differently. Nevertheless, many people have succeeded in overcoming the "prejudice habit" and becoming more open to life experiences in general (Fowers & Davidov, 2006). If you would like to be more open and tolerant, the following points may be helpful to you.

Beware of Stereotyping Stereotypes make the social world more manageable. But placing people in categories almost always causes them to appear more similar than they really are. As a result, we tend to see out-group members as very much alike, even when they are as varied as our friends and family. People who are not prejudiced work hard to actively inhibit stereotyped thoughts and to emphasize fairness and equality.

Seek Individuating Information A good way to tear down stereotypes is to get to know individuals from various ethnic and cultural groups (Giliovich, Keltner, & Nisbett, 2005). Typically, we are most tempted to apply stereotypes when we have only minimal information about a person. Stereotypes help us guess what a person is like and how she or he will act. Unfortunately, these inferences are usually wrong.

One of the best antidotes for stereotypes is **individuating information** (information that helps us see a person as an individual, rather than as a member of a group) (Cameron & Trope, 2004). Anything that keeps us from placing a person in a particular social category tends to negate stereotyped thinking. When you meet individuals from various backgrounds, focus on the *person,* not the *label* attached to her or him.

A good example of the effects of individuating information comes from a Canadian study of English-speaking students in a French language program. Students who were "immersed" (spent most of their waking hours with French Canadians) became more positive toward them. Immersed students were more likely to say they had come to appreciate and like French Canadians, they were more willing to meet and interact with them, and they saw themselves as less different from French Canadians (Lambert, 1987). In fact, with more subtle kinds of symbolic prejudice, such contact may be the best way to reduce intergroup conflict (Dovidio & Gaertner, 1999).

Don't Fall Prey to Just-World Beliefs Do you believe that the world is basically fair? Even if you don't, you may believe that the world is sufficiently just so that people generally get what they deserve. It may not be obvious, but such beliefs can directly increase prejudiced thinking (Hafer & Bègue, 2005).

As a result of discrimination, social conditions, and circumstances (such as recent immigration), minorities may occupy lower socioeconomic positions. **Just-world beliefs** (beliefs that people generally get what they deserve) can lead us to assume that minority group members wouldn't be in such positions if they weren't inferior in some way. This bit of faulty thinking amounts to blaming people who are *victims* of prejudice and discrimination for their plight. For example, assuming that a poor person is lazy may overlook the fact that discrimination in hiring has made it very difficult for him or her to find a good job.

Be Aware of Self-Fulfilling Prophecies You may recall from Chapter 1 that people tend to act in accordance with the behavior expected by others. If you hold strong stereotypes about members of various groups, a vicious cycle can occur. When you meet someone who is dif-

Individuating information Information that helps define a person as an individual, rather than as a member of a group or social category.

Just-world beliefs Beliefs that people generally get what they deserve.

ferent from yourself, you may treat her or him in a way that is consistent with your stereotypes. If the other person is influenced by your behavior, she or he may act in ways that seem to match your stereotype. For example, a person who believes that members of another ethnic group are hostile and unfriendly will probably treat people in that group in ways that provoke hostile and unfriendly response. This creates a self-fulfilling prophecy and reinforces belief in the stereotype. (A **self-fulfilling prophecy** is an expectation that prompts people to act in ways that make the expectation come true.)

Remember, Different Does Not Mean Inferior Some conflicts between groups cannot be avoided. What *can* be avoided is unnecessary **social competition** (rivalry among groups, each of which regards itself as superior to others). The concept of social competition refers to the fact that some individuals seek to enhance their self-esteem by identifying with a group. However, this works only if the group can be seen as superior to others. Because of social competition, groups tend to view themselves as better than their rivals (Baron, Byrne, & Branscombe, 2009). In one survey, *every* major ethnic group in the United States rated itself as better than any other group (Njeri, 1991).

A person who has high self-esteem does not need to treat others as inferior in order to feel good about himself or herself. Similarly, it is not necessary to degrade other groups in order to feel positive about one's own group identity (Fowers & Davidov, 2006). In fact, each ethnic group has strengths that members of other groups could benefit from emulating. For instance, African Americans, Asian Americans, and Latinos emphasize family networks that help buffer them from some of the stresses of daily life (Suinn, 1999).

Understand That Race Is a Social Construction From the viewpoint of modern genetics, the concept of race has absolutely no meaning (Bonham, Warshauer-Baker, & Collins, 2005; Sternberg, Grigorenko, & Kidd, 2005). Members of various groups are so varied genetically and human groups have intermixed for so many centuries that it is impossible to tell, biologically, to what "race" any given individual belongs. Thus, race is an illusion based on superficial physical differences and learned ethnic identities. Certainly people *act as if* different races exist. But this is a matter of social labeling, not biological reality. To assume that any human group is biologically superior or inferior is simply wrong. In fact, the best available evidence suggests that all people are descended from the same ancient ancestors. The origins of our species lie in Africa, about 100,000 years ago. Among early human populations, darker skin was a protective adaptation to sun exposure near the equator (Jablonski & Chaplin, 2000). Biologically, we are all brothers and sisters under the skin (Graves, 2001; Smedley & Smedley, 2005).

Look for Commonalities We live in a society that puts a premium on competition and individual effort. One problem with this is that competing with others fosters desires to demean, defeat, and vanquish them. When we cooperate with others we tend to share their joys and to suffer when they are in distress (Aronson, 2008). If we don't find ways to cooperate and live in greater harmony, everyone will suffer. That, if nothing else, is one thing that we all have in common. Everyone knows what it feels like to be different. Greater tolerance comes from remembering those times.

Tolerance and Cultural Awareness

Living comfortably in a multicultural society means being open to other groups. Getting acquainted with a person whose cultural background is different from your own can be a wonderful learning experience (Matsumoto & Juang, 2008). No one culture has all the answers or the best ways of doing things. Multicultural populations enrich a community's food, music, arts, and philosophy. Likewise, openness toward different racial, cultural, and ethnic groups can be personally rewarding (Fowers & Davidov, 2006).

The importance of cultural awareness often lies in subtleties and details. For example, in large American cities, many small stores are owned by Korean immigrants. Some of these Korean-American merchants have been criticized for being cold and hostile to their customers. Refusing to place change directly in customers' hands, for instance, helped trigger

Self-fulfilling prophecy An expectation that prompts people to act in ways that make the expectation come true.

Social competition Rivalry among groups, each of which regards itself as superior to others.

an African-American boycott of Korean grocers in New York City. The core of the problem was a lack of cultural awareness on both sides.

In America, if you walk into a store, you expect the clerk to be courteous to you. One way of showing politeness is by smiling. But in the Confucian-steeped Korean culture, a smile is reserved for family members and close friends. If a Korean or Korean American has no reason to smile, he or she just doesn't smile. There's a Korean saying: "If you smile a lot, you're silly." Expressions such as "thank you" and "excuse me" are also used sparingly and strangers rarely touch each other—not even to return change.

Here's another example of how ignorance of cultural practices can lead to needless friction and misunderstanding: An African-American woman who wanted to ease racial tensions took a freshly baked pie to her neighbors across the way, who were Orthodox Jews. At the front door the woman extended her hand, not knowing that Orthodox Jews don't shake women's hands, unless the woman is a close family member. Once she was inside, she picked up a kitchen knife to cut the pie, not knowing the couple kept a kosher household and used different knives for different foods. The woman's well-intentioned attempt at neighborliness ended in an argument! Knowing a little more about each other's cultures could have prevented both of the conflicts just described.

The Journey Continues—Psychology and You

The technological advances of the last 50 years have dramatically changed what is humanly possible. Yet, as a species we still have much in common with people who lived many hundreds and thousands of years ago. Although we might like to think otherwise, we cannot count on technology to solve all of our problems. The threat of war, social conflict, crime, prejudice, infectious disease, overpopulation, environmental damage, famine, homicide, economic disaster—these and most other major dilemmas facing us are *behavioral*. Will the human family endure? It's a psychological question.

At the beginning of this book we described psychology as a journey of self-discovery. It is our sincere hope that you have found enough relevance and value here to spark a lifelong interest in psychology. As your personal journey continues, one thing is certain: Many of your greatest challenges and most treasured moments will involve other people. You would be wise to continue adding to your understanding of human behavior. Psychology's future looks exciting. What role will it play in your life?

---

study break
Multiculturalism

RECITE

1. Multiculturalism refers to the belief that various subcultures and ethnic groups should be blended into a single emergent culture. T or F?
2. Many people who don't have prejudiced beliefs still have prejudiced thoughts and feelings in the presence of minority group individuals. T or F?
3. Individuating information tends to be a good antidote for stereotypes. T or F?
4. Just-world beliefs are the primary cause of social competition. T or F?

REFLECT
Critical Thinking

5. Why is it valuable to learn the terms by which members of various groups prefer to be addressed (for example, Mexican-American, Latino [or Latina], Hispanic, or Chicano [Chicana])?

Relate

Which strategies for breaking the prejudice habit do you already use? How could you apply the remaining strategies to become more tolerant?

ANSWERS

1. F   2. T   3. T   4. F   5. Because labels might have negative meanings that are not apparent to persons outside the group. People who are culturally aware allow others to define their own identities, rather than imposing labels on them.

chapter in review

Major Points

- Social psychology studies humans as social animals enmeshed in complex networks of social relationships.

- We are attracted to other people for reasons that are fairly universal.

- To understand social behavior, we must know what roles people play, their status, the norms they follow, and the attributions they make.

- Everyone is affected by social influence, ranging from mild (mere influence, conformity, and compliance) to strong (obedience and coercion). There are times when it is valuable to resist such pressures.

- Attitudes subtly affect nearly all aspects of social behavior.

- To persuade others, you must be aware of your role as a communicator, the nature of the audience, and messages that will appeal to them.

- Prejudice is reduced by equal-status contact and mutual interdependence.

- Aggression is a fact of life, but humans are not inevitably aggressive.

- We can encourage helping and altruism by removing barriers to prosocial behavior.

- Multicultural harmony can be attained through conscious efforts to be more tolerant of others.

Summary

Why do people affiliate? What factors influence interpersonal attraction?

- Affiliation is tied to needs for approval, support, friendship, and information.
- Social comparison theory holds that we affiliate to evaluate our actions, feelings, and abilities.
- Interpersonal attraction is increased by proximity, frequent contact, beauty, competence, and similarity.
- Mate selection is characterized by a large degree of similarity on many dimensions.
- Self-disclosure follows a reciprocity norm: Low levels of self-disclosure are met with low levels in return; moderate self-disclosure elicits more personal replies. However, over-disclosure tends to inhibit self-disclosure by others.
- In comparison with liking, romantic love involves higher levels of emotional arousal and is accompanied by mutual absorption between lovers. Consummate love, involving intimacy, passion, *and* commitment, is the most complete form of love.
- Evolutionary psychology attributes human mating patterns to the differing reproductive challenges faced by men and women during the course of evolution.

How does group membership affect our behavior?

- Social roles, which may be achieved or ascribed, are particular behavior patterns associated with social positions. When two or more contradictory roles are held, role conflict may occur.
- Higher status within groups is associated with special privileges and respect.
- Group structure refers to the organization of roles, communication pathways, and power within a group. Group cohesiveness is basically the degree of attraction among group members.
- Norms are standards of conduct enforced (formally or informally) by groups.
- Attribution theory is concerned with how we make inferences about behavior.
- The fundamental attribution error is to ascribe the actions of others to internal causes. Because of actor–observer differences, we tend to attribute our own behavior to external causes.

What have social psychologists learned about social influence?

- Social influence refers to alterations in behavior brought about by the behavior of others. Social influence ranges from mild (mere influence, conformity, and compliance) to strong (obedience and coercion).
- The presence of others may facilitate (or inhibit) performance. People may also engage in social loafing, working less hard when they are part of a group.
- The famous Asch experiments demonstrated that various group sanctions encourage conformity. Victims of groupthink seek to maintain each other's approval, even at the cost of critical thinking.
- Three strategies for gaining compliance are the foot-in-the-door technique, the door-in-the-face approach, and the low-ball technique.
- Obedience in Milgram's studies decreased when the victim was in the same room, when the victim and subject were face to face, when the authority figure was absent, and when others refused to obey.
- Coercion involves forcing people to change their beliefs or behavior against their will. Forced attitude change (brainwashing) is sometimes used by cults and other coercive groups.

How does self-assertion differ from aggression?

- Self-assertion involves standing up for yourself, while aggression involves achieving your goals at the expense of another.

How are attitudes acquired and changed?

- Attitudes are learned dispositions made up of a belief component, an emotional component, and an action component.
- Attitudes may be formed by direct contact, interaction with others, child-rearing practices, and group pressures. Peer group influences, reference group membership, the media, and chance conditioning also appear to be important in attitude formation.
- Effective persuasion occurs when characteristics of the communicator, the message, and the audience are well matched.
- In general, a likable and believable communicator who repeats a credible message that arouses emotion in the audience and states clear-cut conclusions will be persuasive.

- Maintaining and changing attitudes is closely related to cognitive dissonance and our needs to be consistent in our thoughts and actions.

What causes prejudice and intergroup conflict?

- Prejudice is a negative attitude held toward members of various out-groups. One theory attributes prejudice to scapegoating. A second account says that prejudices may be held for personal reasons (personal prejudice) or simply through adherence to group norms (group prejudice).
- Prejudiced individuals tend to have an authoritarian or dogmatic personality, characterized by rigidity, inhibition, intolerance, oversimplification, and ethnocentrism.
- Intergroup conflict gives rise to hostility and the formation of social stereotypes. Status inequalities tend to build prejudice. Equal-status contact tends to reduce it.
- Superordinate goals are a key to reducing intergroup conflict.
- On a smaller scale, jigsaw classrooms (which encourage cooperation through mutual interdependence) have been shown to be an effective way of combating prejudice.

How do psychologists explain human aggression?

- Ethological explanations of aggression attribute it to inherited instincts. Biological explanations emphasize brain mechanisms and physical factors related to thresholds for aggression.
- According to the frustration-aggression hypothesis, frustration and aggression are closely linked.

- Frustration is only one of many aversive stimuli that can arouse a person and make aggression more likely. Aggression is especially likely to occur when aggression cues are present.
- Social learning theory has focused attention on the role of aggressive models in the development of aggressive behavior.

Why are bystanders so often unwilling to help in an emergency?

- Four decision points that must be passed before a person gives help are: noticing, defining an emergency, taking responsibility, and selecting a course of action. Helping is less likely at each point when other potential helpers are present.
- Helping is encouraged by general arousal, empathic arousal, being in a good mood, low effort or risk, and perceived similarity between the victim and the helper. For several reasons, giving help tends to encourage others to help too.

How can we promote multiculturalism and social harmony?

- Multicultural harmony is attainable through conscious efforts to be more tolerant.
- Greater tolerance can be encouraged by neutralizing stereotypes with individuating information; by looking for commonalities with others; and by avoiding the effects of just world beliefs, self fulfilling prophecies, and social competition.
- Cultural awareness is a key element in promoting greater social harmony.

Web Resources

For an up-to-date list of direct links to interesting sites, including those listed here, visit the student companion site for this book at www.cengage.com/psychology/coon

Social Psychology Network Explore this massive website devoted to social psychology.

Assertiveness Access a collection of virtual pamphlets on assertiveness.

Information About Cults and Psychological Manipulation The home page of the International Cultic Studies Association offers a wealth of information about cults.

Project Implicit Test yourself to see if you are unconsciously prejudiced.

Multiculturalism Guidelines Read these guidelines from the American Psychological Association.

Diversity in College Read some relevant research about diversity in college.

Interactive Learning

PSYCHOLOGY: A JOURNEY BOOK COMPANION WEBSITE
WWW.CENGAGE.COM/PSYCHOLOGY/COON
Visit your book companion website, where you will find flash cards, practice quizzes, web links, and more to help you study.

JUST WHAT YOU NEED TO KNOW NOW!
Spend time on what you need to master rather than on information you already have learned. Take a pretest for this chapter, and CengageNOW will generate a personalized study plan based on your results. The study plan will identify the topics you need to review and direct you to online resources to help you master those topics. You can then take a posttest to help you determine the concepts you have mastered and what you will need to work on. Try it out! Go to www.cengage.com/login to sign in with an access code or to purchase access to this product.

Conditioning and Learning

For additional review, get more practice with *CengageNOW*, *WebTutor*, the *Practice Quizzes*, and/or the printed *Study Guide* available with this book.

1. The pattern known as homogamy shows the powerful effect that _____ has on interpersonal attraction.
   a. physical beauty
   b. similarity
   c. competence
   d. physical proximity

2. The fact that men tend to prefer younger, more physically attractive partners is predicted by
   a. evolutionary psychology
   b. the overdisclosure hypothesis
   c. social comparison theory
   d. studies of mutual absorption

3. Away from the office, Jan has become friends with Fran, a woman she supervises at work. Jan must do an evaluation of Fran, who hasn't been very efficient lately. It is most likely that Jan will experience
   a. groupthink
   b. role conflict
   c. group sanctions
   d. overdisclosure

4. A common error we all make is to attribute the actions of others to internal causes. This is known as the fundamental
   a. reciprocity norm
   b. role conflict
   c. social comparison
   d. attribution error

5. In Solomon Asch's conformity experiment, subjects yielded to group pressure on about _____ of the critical trials.
   a. 1 percent
   b. 10 percent
   c. one third
   d. two thirds

6. Groupthink is an example of the danger that lies in powerful pressures for group
   a. cohesion
   b. conformity
   c. attribution
   d. reciprocity

7. Which compliance technique involves getting a person committed to act and then making the terms of acting less desirable?
   a. foot-in-the-door
   b. low-ball
   c. door-in-the-face
   d. groupthink

8. In Milgram's experiments, the lowest level of obedience occurred when subjects
   a. saw another person refuse to obey
   b. were in the same room with the "learner"
   c. were face-to-face with the "learner"
   d. received orders over the phone

9. "Achieving one's goals without taking into account the rights of others." This statement describes
   a. self-assertion
   b. overdisclosure
   c. cognitive dissonance
   d. aggression

10. The three parts of an attitude are
    a. internal, external, group
    b. conviction, attribution, absorption
    c. status, norm, cohesion
    d. belief, emotion, action

11. Which of the following is NOT one of the factors that typically determines whether our attitudes are expressed as actions?
    a. empathic arousal
    b. existing habits
    c. immediate consequences
    d. anticipated evaluations by others

12. If you are trying to persuade a poorly informed audience, it is usually best to present
    a. one side of the argument
    b. both sides of the argument
    c. the unfreezing, change, refreezing cycle
    d. negative sanctions

13. The amount of cognitive dissonance a person feels is related to how much _____ exists for his or her actions.
    a. reciprocity
    b. justification
    c. chance conditioning
    d. reference

14. Some expressions of prejudice can be thought of as scapegoating or
    a. displaced aggression
    b. empathic arousal
    c. reference group reversal
    d. external attribution

15. One of the reasons that superordinate goals tend to reduce prejudice is that they require cooperation and
    a. social stereotyping
    b. ethnocentrism
    c. unfreezing
    d. equal-status contact

16. Jigsaw classrooms use _____ to create mutual interdependence.
    a. social competition
    b. just-world beliefs
    c. self-fulfilling prophecies
    d. superordinate goals

17. The *weapons effect* refers to the impact that _____ have on behavior.
    a. just-world beliefs
    b. aggression cues
    c. self-fulfilling prophecies
    d. televised models

18. The point of view most at odds with the idea that humans are instinctively aggressive is
    a. social learning theory
    b. the frustration-aggression hypothesis
    c. ethology
    d. the aversive stimuli effect

19. People are more likely to help another who is in trouble if
    a. many other helpers are present
    b. a diffusion of responsibility occurs
    c. they experience empathic arousal
    d. desensitization has taken place

20. One of the best antidotes for stereotypes is
    a. accepting just-world beliefs
    b. individuating information
    c. accepting self-fulfilling prophecies
    d. honest social competition

Answers   1. b 2. a 3. b 4. d 5. c 6. a 7. b 8. a 9. d 10. d 11. a 12. a 13. b 14. a 15. d 16. d 17. b 18. a 19. c 20. b

Behavioral Statistics

Journey into Psychology: Statistics from "Heads" to "Tails"

Let's say a friend of yours invites you to try your hand at a "game of chance." He offers to flip a coin and pay you a dollar if the coin comes up heads. If the coin shows tails, you must pay him a dollar. He flips the coin: tails—you pay him a dollar. He flips it again: tails. Again: tails. And again: tails. And again: tails. For good luck, one more time: rats! tails!

At this point you are faced with a choice. Should you continue the game in an attempt to recoup your losses? Or should you assume that the coin is biased and quit before you really get "skinned"? Taking out your trusty pocket calculator (and, of course, the statistics book you carry with you at all times), you com-

pute the odds of obtaining 6 tails in a row from an unbiased coin. The probability is 0.016 (less than 2 times out of 100).

If the coin really is honest, 6 consecutive tails is a rare event. Wisely, you decide that the coin is probably biased and refuse to play again. (Unless, of course, your "friend" is willing to take "tails" for the next 6 tosses!)

Perhaps a decision could have been made in this hypothetical example without using statistics. But notice how much clearer the situation becomes when it is expressed statistically.

The results of psychological studies are often expressed as numbers, which psychologists

must summarize and interpret before these numbers have any meaning. To do so, they use two major types of statistics. **Descriptive statistics** summarize or "boil down" numbers so they become more meaningful and easier to communicate to others. In comparison, **inferential statistics** are used for decision making, for generalizing from small samples, and for drawing conclusions. As was the case in the coin-flipping example, psychologists must often base decisions on limited data. Such decisions are much easier to make with the help of inferential statistics. Let's see how statistics are used in psychology.

Survey Questions

- What are descriptive statistics?
- How are correlations used in psychology?
- What are inferential statistics?

Descriptive Statistics—Psychology by the Numbers

What are descriptive statistics?

Let's say you have completed a study on human behavior. The results seem interesting, but can you really tell what your data reveal just by looking at a jumble of numbers? To get a clear picture of how people behaved, you will probably turn to descriptive statistics. Statistics bring greater clarity and precision to psychological thought and research (Gravetter & Wallnau, 2010). By summarizing the results of your study, statistics will help you draw valid conclusions about what you observed.

To see how, let's begin by considering three basic types of descriptive statistics: *graphical statistics,* measures of *central tendency,* and measures of *variability.* Let's start with **graphical statistics,** which present numbers pictorially, so they are easier to visualize.

Graphical Statistics

● Table A.1 shows simulated scores on a test of hypnotic susceptibility given to 100 college students. With such disorganized data, it is hard to form an overall "picture" of the differences in hypnotic susceptibility. But by using a *frequency distribution,* large amounts of information can be neatly organized and summarized. A **frequency distribution** is made by breaking down the entire range of possible scores into classes of equal size. Next, the number of scores falling into each class is recorded. In ● Table A.2, the raw data from Table A.1 have been condensed into a frequency distribution. Notice how much clearer the pattern of scores for the entire group becomes.

Frequency distributions are often shown *graphically* to make them more "visual." A **histogram,** or graph of a frequency distribution, is made by labeling class intervals on the *abscissa* (*x*-axis, or horizontal line) and frequencies (the number of scores in each class) on the *ordinate* (*y*-axis, or vertical line). Next, bars are drawn for each class interval; the height of each bar is determined by the number of scores in each class (▶▶ Figure A.1). An alternate way of graphing scores is the more familiar **frequency polygon** (▶▶ Figure A.2). Here, points are placed at the center of each class interval to indicate the number of scores. Then the dots are connected by straight lines.

Measures of Central Tendency

Notice in Table A.2 that more scores fall in the range 40–59 than elsewhere. How can we show this fact? A measure of **central tendency** is simply a number describing a "typical score" around which other scores fall. A familiar measure of central tendency is the mean,

Descriptive statistics Mathematical tools used to describe and summarize numeric data.

Inferential statistics Mathematical tools used for decision making, for generalizing from small samples, and for drawing conclusions.

Graphical statistics Techniques for presenting numbers pictorially, often by plotting them on a graph.

Frequency distribution A table that divides an entire range of scores into a series of classes and then records the number of scores that fall into each class.

Histogram A graph of a frequency distribution in which the number of scores falling in each class is represented by vertical bars.

Frequency polygon A graph of a frequency distribution in which the number of scores falling in each class is represented by points on a line.

Central tendency The tendency for a majority of scores to fall in the mid-range of possible values.

● Table A.1 Raw Scores of Hypnotic Susceptibility

55	86	52	17	61	57	84	51	16	64
22	56	25	38	35	24	54	26	37	38
52	42	59	26	21	55	40	59	25	57
91	27	38	53	19	93	25	39	52	56
66	14	18	63	59	68	12	19	62	45
47	98	88	72	50	49	96	89	71	66
50	44	71	57	90	53	41	72	56	93
57	38	55	49	87	59	36	56	48	70
33	69	50	50	60	35	67	51	50	52
11	73	46	16	67	13	71	47	25	77

● Table A.2 Frequency Distribution of Hypnotic Susceptibility Scores

CLASS INTERVAL	NUMBER OF PERSONS IN CLASS
0–19	10
20–39	20
40–59	40
60–79	20
80–99	10

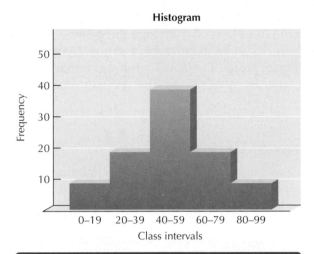

Figure A.1 Frequency histogram of hypnotic suscepti-bility scores contained in Table A.2.

Figure A.2 Frequency polygon of hypnotic suscepti-bility scores contained in Table A.2.

or "average." But as we shall see in a moment, other types of "averages" can be used. To illustrate each, we need an example: ● Table A.3 shows the raw data for an imaginary experiment in which two groups of subjects were given a test of memory. Assume that one group was given a drug that might improve memory (let's call the drug Rememberine). The second group received a placebo. Is there a difference in memory scores between the two groups? It's difficult to tell without computing an average.

The Mean

As one type of "average," the **mean** is calculated by adding all the scores for each group and then dividing by the total number of scores. Notice in Table A.3 that the means reveal a difference between the two groups.

The mean is sensitive to extremely high or low scores in a distribution. For this reason it is not always the best measure of central tendency. (Imagine how distorted it would be to calculate average yearly incomes from a small sample of people that happened to include a multimillionaire, such as actor Johnny Depp.) In such cases the middle score in a group of scores—called the *median*—is used instead.

The Median

The **median** is found by arranging scores from the highest to the lowest and selecting the score that falls in the middle. In other words, half the values in a group of scores fall below the median and half fall above. Consider, for example, the following weights obtained from

Mean A measure of central tendency calculated by adding a group of scores and then dividing by the total number of scores.

Median A measure of central tendency found by arranging scores from the highest to the lowest and selecting the score that falls in the middle. That is, half the values in a group of scores fall above the median and half fall below.

Table A.3 Raw Scores on a Memory Test for Subjects Taking Rememberine or a Placebo

SUBJECT	GROUP 1 REMEMBERINE	GROUP 2 PLACEBO
1	65	54
2	67	60
3	73	63
4	65	33
5	58	56
6	55	60
7	70	60
8	69	31
9	60	62
10	68	61
Sum	650	540
Mean	65	54
Median	66	60

Mean $= \dfrac{\Sigma X}{N}$ or $\dfrac{\text{Sum of all scores, X}}{\text{number of scores}}$

Mean Group 1 $= \dfrac{65 + 67 + 73 + 65 + 58 + 55 + 70 + 69 + 60 + 68}{10}$

$= \dfrac{650}{10} = 65$

Mean Group 2 $= \dfrac{54 + 60 + 63 + 33 + 56 + 60 + 60 + 31 + 62 + 61}{10}$

$= \dfrac{540}{10} = 54$

Median $=$ the middle score or the mean of the two middle scores*

Median Group 1 $=$ 55 58 60 65 $\boxed{65 \quad 67}$ 68 69 70 73

$= \dfrac{65 + 67}{2} = 66$

Median Group 2 $=$ 31 33 54 56 60 $\boxed{60 \quad 60}$ 61 62 63

$= \dfrac{60 + 60}{2} = 60$

* $\boxed{}$ indicates middle score(s).

Mode A measure of central tendency found by identifying the most frequently occurring score in a group of scores.

Variability The tendency for a group of scores to differ in value. Measures of variability indicate the degree to which a group of scores differ from one another.

Range The difference between the highest and lowest scores in a group of scores.

Standard deviation An index of how much a typical score differs from the mean of a group of scores.

a small class of college students: 105, 111, 123, 126, 148, 151, 154, 162, 182. The median for the group is 148, the middle score. Of course, if there is an even number of scores, there will be no "middle score." This problem is handled by averaging the two scores that "share" the middle spot. This procedure yields a single number to serve as the median (See bottom panel of Table A.3).

The Mode

A final measure of central tendency is the *mode*. The **mode** is simply the most frequently occurring score in a group of scores. If you were to take the time to count the scores in Table A.3, you would find that the mode of Group l is 65, and the mode of Group 2 is 60. Although the mode is usually easy to obtain, it can be an unreliable measure, especially in a small group of scores. The mode's advantage is that it gives the score actually obtained by the greatest number of people.

Measures of Variability

Let's say a researcher discovers two drugs that lower anxiety in agitated patients. However, let's also assume that one drug consistently lowers anxiety by moderate amounts, whereas the second sometimes lowers it by large amounts, sometimes has no effect, or may even increase anxiety in some patients. Overall, there is no difference in the *average* (mean) amount of anxiety reduction. Even so, an important difference exists between the two drugs. As this example shows, it is not enough to simply know the average score in a distribution. Usually, we would also like to know if scores are grouped closely together or scattered widely.

Measures of **variability** provide a single number that tells how "spread out" scores are. When the scores are widely spread, this number gets larger. When they are close together it gets smaller. If you look again at the example in Table A.3, you will notice that the scores within each group vary widely. How can we show this fact?

The Range

The simplest way would be to use the **range,** which is the difference between the highest and lowest scores. In Group 1 of our experiment, the highest score is 73, and the lowest is 55; thus, the range is 18 (73 − 55 = 18). In Group 2, the highest score is 63, and the lowest is 31; this makes the range 32. Scores in Group 2 are more spread out (are more variable) than those in Group 1.

The Standard Deviation

A better measure of variability is the **standard deviation** (an index of how much a typical score differs from the mean of a group of scores). To obtain the standard deviation, we find the deviation (or difference) of each score from the mean and then square it (multiply it by itself). These squared deviations are then added and averaged (the total is divided by the number of deviations). Taking the square root of this average yields the standard deviation

(● Table A.4). Notice again that the variability for Group 1 (5.4) is smaller than that for Group 2 (where the standard deviation is 11.3).

Standard Scores

A particular advantage of the standard deviation is that it can be used to "standardize" scores in a way that gives them greater meaning. For example, John and Heather both took psychology midterms, but in different classes. John earned a score of 118, and Heather scored 110. Who did better? It is impossible to tell without knowing what the average score was on each test, and whether John and Heather scored at the top, middle, or bottom of their classes. We would like to have one number that gives all this information. A number that does this is the *z*-score.

To convert an original score to a **z-score,** we subtract the mean from the score. The resulting number is then divided by the standard deviation for that group of scores. To illustrate, Heather had a score of 110 in a class with a mean of 100 and a standard deviation of 10. Therefore, her *z*-score is +1.0 (● Table A.5). John's score of 118 came from a class having a mean of 100 and a standard deviation of 18; thus his *z*-score is also +1.0 (see Table A.5). Originally it looked as if John did better on his midterm than Heather did. But we now see that relatively speaking, their scores were equivalent. Compared with other students, each was an equal distance above average.

The Normal Curve

When chance events are recorded, we find that some outcomes have a high probability and occur very often, others have a lower probability and occur infrequently, still others have little probability and occur rarely. As a result, the distribution (or tally) of chance events typically resembles a *normal curve* (▶▶ Figure A.3). A **normal curve** is bell shaped, with a large number of scores in the middle, tapering to very few extremely high and low scores. Most psychological traits or events are determined by the action of a large number of factors. Therefore, like chance events, measures of psychological variables tend to roughly match a normal curve. For example, direct measurement has shown such characteristics as height, memory span, and intelligence to be distributed approximately along a normal curve. In other words, many people have average height, memory ability, and intelligence. However, as we move above or below average, fewer and fewer people are found.

It is very fortunate that so many psychological variables tend to form a normal curve, because much is known about the curve. One valuable property concerns the relationship between the standard deviation and the normal curve. Specifically, the standard deviation measures off set proportions of the curve above and below the mean. For example, in ▶▶ Figure A.4, notice that roughly 68 percent of all cases (IQ scores, memory scores, heights, or whatever) fall between one standard deviation (SD) above and below the mean (±1 SD); 95 percent of all cases fall between ±2 SD; and 99 percent of the cases can be found between ±3 SD from the mean.

● Table A.6 gives a more complete account of the relationship between *z*-scores and the percentage of cases found in a particular area of the normal curve. Notice, for example, that 93.3 percent of all cases fall below a *z*-score of +1.5. A *z*-score of 1.5 on a test (no matter what the original, or "raw," score was) would be a good performance, because roughly 93 percent of all scores fall below this mark. Relationships between the standard deviation (or *z*-scores) and the normal curve do not change. This makes it possible to compare various tests or groups of scores if they come from distributions that are approximately normal.

● Table A.4 Computation of the Standard Deviation

GROUP 1 MEAN = 65		
SCORE − MEAN	DEVIATION (d)	DEVIATION SQUARED (d²)
65 − 65 =	0	0
67 − 65 =	2	4
73 − 65 =	8	64
65 − 65 =	0	0
58 − 65 =	−7	49
55 − 65 =	−10	100
70 − 65 =	5	25
69 − 65 =	4	16
60 − 65 =	−5	25
68 − 65 =	3	9
		292

$$SD = \sqrt{\frac{\text{sum of } d^2}{n}} = \sqrt{\frac{292}{10}} = \sqrt{29.2} = 5.4$$

GROUP 2 MEAN = 54		
SCORE − MEAN	DEVIATION (d)	DEVIATION SQUARED (d²)
54 − 54 =	0	0
60 − 54 =	6	36
63 − 54 =	9	81
33 − 54 =	−21	441
56 − 54 =	2	4
60 − 54 =	6	36
60 − 54 =	6	36
31 − 54 =	−23	529
62 − 54 =	8	64
61 − 54 =	7	49
		1276

$$SD = \sqrt{\frac{\text{sum of } d^2}{n}} = \sqrt{\frac{1276}{10}} = \sqrt{127.6} = 11.3$$

● Table A.5 Computation of a z-Score

$$z = \frac{X - \bar{X}}{SD} = \text{or} \frac{\text{score} - \text{mean}}{\text{standard deviation}}$$

$$\text{Heather: } z = \frac{110 - 100}{10} = \frac{+10}{10} = +1.0$$

$$\text{John: } z = \frac{118 - 100}{18} = \frac{+18}{18} = +1.0$$

z-Score A number that tells how many standard deviations above or below the mean a score is.

Normal curve A bell-shaped distribution, with a large number of scores in the middle, tapering to very few extremely high and low scores.

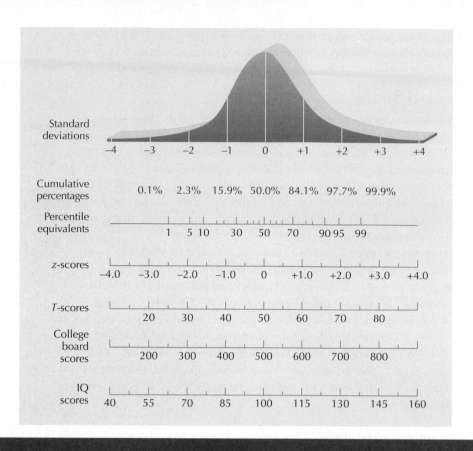

Figure A.3 The normal curve. The normal curve is an idealized mathematical model. However, many measurements in psychology closely approximate a normal curve. The scales you see here show the relationship of standard deviations, z-scores, and other measures to the curve.

Figure A.4 Relationship between the standard deviation and the normal curve.

Table A.6 Computation of a z-Score

Z-SCORE	PERCENTAGE OF AREA TO THE LEFT OF THIS VALUE	PERCENTAGE OF AREA TO THE RIGHT OF THIS VALUE
−3.0 SD	00.1	99.9
−2.5 SD	00.6	99.4
−2.0 SD	02.3	97.7
−1.5 SD	06.7	93.3
−1.0 SD	15.9	84.1
−0.5 SD	30.9	69.1
0.0 SD	50.0	50.0
+0.5 SD	69.1	30.9
+1.0 SD	84.1	15.9
+1.5 SD	93.3	06.7
+2.0 SD	97.7	02.3
+2.5 SD	99.4	00.6
+3.0 SD	99.9	00.1

RECITE

1. _____ statistics summarize numbers so they become more meaningful or easier to communicate; _____ statistics are used for decision making, generalizing, or drawing conclusions.
2. Histograms and frequency polygons are graphs of frequency distributions. T or F?
3. Three measures of central tendency are the mean, the median, and the _____.
4. If scores are placed in order, from the smallest to the largest, the median is defined as the middle score. T or F?
5. As a measure of variability, the standard deviation is defined as the difference between the highest and lowest scores. T or F?
6. A z-score of −1 tells us that a score fell one standard deviation below the mean in a group of scores. T or F?
7. In a normal curve, 99 percent of all scores can be found between +1 and −1 standard deviations from the mean. T or F?

REFLECT

Critical Thinking

8. You are asked to calculate the mean income of the following annual salaries: $2,000,000, $33,000, $27,000, $22,000, $21,000. Why might you refuse? What statistic might you propose to calculate instead?

Relate

Let's say you ask 100 people how long they sleep each night and record their answers. How could you show these scores graphically?

To find the average amount of sleep for your subjects, would you prefer to know the most frequent score (the mode), the middle score (the median), or the arithmetic average (the mean)?

How could you determine how much sleep times vary? That is, would you prefer to know the highest and lowest scores (the range), or the average amount of variation (the standard deviation)?

How would you feel about receiving your scores on classroom tests in the form of z-scores?

Do you think the distribution of scores in your study of sleep would form a normal curve? Why or why not?

ANSWERS

1. Descriptive, inferential 2. T 3. mode 4. T 5. F 6. T 7. F 8. The single large salary in this small group will distort the mean. In cases like this, the median is a better measure of central tendency.

Correlation—Rating Relationships

How are correlations used in psychology?

As we noted in Chapter 1, many of the statements that psychologists make about behavior do not result from the use of experimental methods. Rather, they come from keen observations and measures of existing phenomena. A psychologist might note, for example, that the higher a couple's socioeconomic and educational status, the smaller the number of children they are likely to have. Or that grades in high school are related to how well a person is likely to do in college. Or even that as rainfall levels increase within a given metropolitan area, crime rates decline. In these instances, we are dealing with the fact that two variables are **correlating** (varying together in some orderly fashion).

Relationships

Psychologists are very interested in describing relationships between events: Are children from single-parent families more likely to misbehave at school? Is wealth related to happiness? Is there a relationship between childhood exposure to the Internet and IQ at age 20? Is the chance of having a heart attack related to having a hostile personality? All these are questions about correlation (Howell, 2008).

The simplest way of visualizing a correlation is to construct a **scatter diagram.** In a scatter diagram, two measures (grades in high school and grades in college, for instance) are obtained. One measure is indicated by the *x*-axis and the second by the *y*-axis. The scatter diagram plots the intersection (crossing) of each pair of measurements as a single point. Many such measurement pairs give pictures like those shown in Figure A.5.

Correlation The existence of a consistent, systematic relationship between two events, measures, or variables.

Scatter diagram A graph that plots the intersection of paired measures; that is, the points at which paired X and Y measures cross.

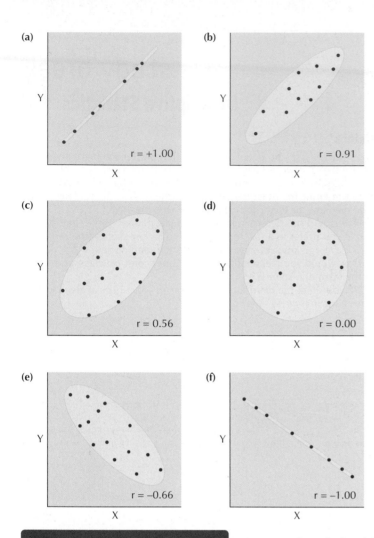

Figure A.5 Scatter diagrams showing various degrees of relationship for a positive, zero, and negative correlation.

Positive relationship A mathematical relationship in which increases in one measure are matched by increases in the other (or decreases correspond with decreases).

Zero correlation The absence of a (linear) mathematical relationship between two measures.

Negative relationship A mathematical relationship in which increases in one measure are matched by decreases in the other.

Coefficient of correlation A statistical index ranging from −1.00 to +1.00 that indicates the direction and degree of correlation.

Perfect positive relationship A mathematical relationship in which the correlation between two measures is +1.00.

Perfect negative relationship A mathematical relationship in which the correlation between two measures is −1.00.

Percent of variance A portion of the total amount of variation in a group of scores.

Figure A.5 also shows scatter diagrams of three basic kinds of relationships between variables (or measures). Graphs a, b, and c show *positive relationships* of varying strength. As you can see, in a **positive relationship,** increases in the X measure (or score) are matched by increases on the Y measure (or score). An example would be finding that higher IQ scores (X) are associated with higher college grades (Y). A **zero correlation** suggests that no relationship exists between two measures (see graph d). This might be the result of comparing subjects' hat sizes (X) to their college grades (Y). Graphs e and f both show a **negative relationship** (or correlation). Notice that as values of one measure increase, those of the second become smaller. An example might be the relationship between amount of alcohol consumed and scores on a test of coordination: Higher alcohol levels are correlated with lower coordination scores.

The Correlation Coefficient

The strength of a correlation can also be expressed as a **coefficient of correlation.** This coefficient is simply a number falling somewhere between +1.00 and −1.00. If the number is zero or close to zero, it indicates a weak or nonexistent relationship. If the correlation is +1.00, a **perfect positive relationship** exists; if the correlation is −1.00, a **perfect negative relationship** has been discovered. The most commonly used correlation coefficient is called the Pearson *r*. Calculation of the Pearson *r* is relatively simple, as shown in ● Table A.7. (The numbers shown are hypothetical.)

As stated in Chapter 1, correlations in psychology are rarely perfect. Most fall somewhere between zero and plus or minus 1. The closer the correlation coefficient is to +1.00 or −1.00, the stronger the relationship. An interesting example of some typical correlations is provided by a study that compared the IQs of adopted children with the IQs of their biological mothers. At age 4, the children's IQs correlated .28 with their biological mothers' IQs. By age 7 the correlation was .35. And by age 13 it had grown to .38. Over time, the IQs of adopted children become more similar to the IQs of their biological mothers.

Prediction

Correlations often provide highly useful information. For instance, it is valuable to know that there is a correlation between cigarette smoking and lung cancer rates. Another example is the fact that higher consumption of alcohol during pregnancy is correlated with lower birth weight and a higher rate of birth defects. There is a correlation between the number of recent life stresses experienced and the likelihood of emotional disturbance. Many more examples could be cited, but the point is, correlations help us to identify relationships that are worth knowing.

Correlations are particularly valuable for making *predictions.* If we know that two measures are correlated, and we know a person's score on one measure, we can predict his or her score on the other. For example, most colleges have formulas that use multiple correlations to decide which applicants have the best chances for success. Usually the formula includes such predictors as high school grade point average (GPA), teacher ratings, extracurricular activities, and scores on the SAT Reasoning Test (SAT) or some similar test. Although no single predictor is perfectly correlated with success in college, together the various predictors correlate highly and provide a useful technique for screening applicants.

There is an interesting "trick" you can do with correlations that you may find useful. It works like this: If you *square* the correlation coefficient (multiply *r* by itself), you will get a number telling the **percent of variance** (amount of variation in scores) accounted for by the

Table A.7 IQ and Grade Point Average for Computing Pearson *r*

STUDENT NO.	IQ (X)	GRADE POINT AVERAGE (Y)	X SCORE SQUARED (X²)	Y SCORE SQUARED (Y²)	X TIMES Y (XY)
1	110	1.0	12,100	1.00	110.0
2	112	1.6	12,544	2.56	179.2
3	118	1.2	13,924	1.44	141.6
4	119	2.1	14,161	4.41	249.9
5	122	2.6	14,884	6.76	317.2
6	125	1.8	15,625	3.24	225.0
7	127	2.6	16,124	6.76	330.2
8	130	2.0	16,900	4.00	260.0
9	132	3.2	17,424	10.24	422.4
10	134	2.6	17,956	6.76	348.4
11	136	3.0	18,496	9.00	408.0
12	138	3.6	19,044	12.96	496.8
Total	1503	27.3	189,187	69.13	3488.7

$$r = \frac{\Sigma XY - \dfrac{(\Sigma X)(\Sigma Y)}{N}}{\sqrt{\left[\Sigma X^2 - \dfrac{(\Sigma X)^2}{N}\right]\left[\Sigma Y^2 - \dfrac{(\Sigma Y)^2}{N}\right]}}$$

$$= \frac{3488.7 - \dfrac{1503(27.3)}{12}}{\sqrt{\left[189,187 - \dfrac{(1503)^2}{2}\right]\left[69.13\ 2\dfrac{(27.3)^2}{12}\right]}}$$

$$\frac{69.375}{81.088} = 0.856 = 0.86$$

correlation. For example, the correlation between IQ scores and college grade point average is .5. Multiplying .5 times .5 gives .25, or 25 percent. This means that 25 percent of the variation in college grades is accounted for by knowing IQ scores. In other words, with a correlation of .5, college grades are "squeezed" into an oval like the one shown in graph c, Figure A.5. IQ scores take away some of the possible variation in corresponding grade point averages. If there were no correlation between IQ and grades, grades would be completely free to vary, as shown in graph d, Figure A.5.

Along the same line, a correlation of +1.00 or −1.00 means that 100 percent of the variation in the Y measure is accounted for by knowing the X measure: If you know a person's X score, you can tell exactly what the Y score is. An example that comes close to this state of affairs is the high correlation (.86) between the IQs of identical twins. In any group of identical twins, 74 percent of the variation in the Y twins' IQs is accounted for by knowing the IQs of their siblings (the X twins).

Squaring correlations to obtain the *percent variance* accounted for is a useful tool for interpreting the correlations encountered in the media and the psychological literature. For example, sweeping pronouncements about relationships are occasionally made on the basis of correlations in the .25 to .30 range, even though the values mean that only 6 to 9 percent of the variance is accounted for by the observed correlation. Such correlations may document relationships worth noting, but they are rarely something to get excited about.

Correlation and Causation

It is very important to reiterate that finding a correlation between two measures does not automatically mean that one **causes** the other: Correlation does not demonstrate causation. When a correlation exists, the best we can say is that two variables are related. Of course, this does not mean that it is impossible for two correlated variables to have a cause-and-effect relationship. Rather, it means that we cannot *conclude,* solely on the basis of correlation, that a causal link exists. To gain greater confidence that a cause-and-effect relationship exists, an experiment must be performed (see Chapter 1).

Often, two correlated measures are related as a result of the influence of a third variable. For example, we might observe that the more hours students devote to studying, the better their grades. Although it is tempting to conclude that more studying produces (causes) better grades, it is possible (indeed, it is probable) that grades and the amount of study time are both related to the amount of motivation or interest a student has.

The difference between cause-and-effect data and data that reveal a relationship of unknown origin is one that should not be forgotten. Because we rarely run experiments in daily life, the information on which we act is largely correlational. This should make us more humble and more tentative in the confidence with which we make pronouncements about human behavior.

Inferential Statistics—Significant Numbers

What are inferential statistics?

You would like to know if boys are more aggressive than girls. You observe a group of 5-year-old boys and girls on a playground. After collecting data for a week, you find that the boys committed more aggressive acts than the girls. Could this difference just be a meaningless fluctuation in aggression? Or does it show conclusively that boys are more aggressive than girls? Inferential statistics were created to answer just such questions (Sprinthall, 2007).

Let's say that a researcher studies the effects of a new therapy on a small group of depressed individuals. Is she or he interested only in these particular individuals? Usually not, because except in rare instances, psychologists seek to discover general laws of behavior that apply widely to humans and animals. Undoubtedly the researcher would like to know if the therapy holds any promise for all depressed people. As stated earlier, *inferential statistics* are techniques that allow us to make inferences. That is, they allow us to generalize from the behavior of small groups of subjects to that of the larger groups they represent.

Samples and Populations

In any scientific study, we would like to observe the entire set, or **population,** of subjects, objects, or events of interest. However, this is usually impossible or impractical. Observing all terrorists, all cancer patients, or all mothers-in-law could be both impractical (because all are large populations) and impossible (because people change political views, may be unaware of having cancer, and change their status as relatives). In such cases, **samples** (smaller cross sections of a population) are selected, and observations of the sample are used to draw conclusions about the entire population.

For any sample to be meaningful, it must be **representative.** That is, the sample group must truly reflect the membership and characteristics of the larger population. In our earlier hypothetical study of a memory drug, it would be essential for the sample of 20 people to be representative of the general population. A very important aspect of representative samples is that their members are chosen at **random.** In other words, each member of the population must have an equal chance of being included in the sample.

Causation The act of causing some effect.

Population An entire group of animals, people, or objects belonging to a particular category (for example, all college students or all married women).

Sample A smaller subpart of a population.

Representative sample A small, randomly selected part of a larger population that accurately reflects characteristics of the whole population.

Random selection Choosing a sample so that each member of the population has an equal chance of being included in the sample.

Significant Differences

In our imaginary drug experiment, we found that the average memory score was higher for the group given the drug than it was for persons who didn't take the drug (the placebo group). Certainly this result is interesting, but could it have occurred by chance? If two groups were repeatedly tested (with neither receiving any drug), their average memory scores would sometimes differ. How much must two means differ before we can consider the difference "real" (not due to chance)?

Notice that the question is similar to one discussed earlier: How many tails in a row must we obtain when flipping a coin before we can conclude that the coin is biased? In the case of the coin, we noted that obtaining 6 tails in a row is a rare event. Thus, it became reasonable to assume that the coin was biased. Of course, it is possible to get 6 tails in a row when flipping an honest coin. But because this outcome is unlikely, we have good reason to suspect that something other than chance (a loaded coin, for instance) caused the results. Similar reasoning is used in tests of statistical significance.

Tests of **statistical significance** provide an estimate of how often experimental results could have occurred by chance alone. The results of a significance test are stated as a probability. This probability gives the odds that the observed difference was due to chance. In psychology, any experimental result that could have occurred by chance 5 times (or less) out of 100 (in other words, a probability of .05 or less) is considered *significant*. In our memory experiment, the probability is .025 ($p = .025$) that the group means would differ as much as they do by chance alone. This allows us to conclude with reasonable certainty that the drug actually did improve memory scores.

> **Statistical significance** The degree to which an event (such as the results of an experiment) is unlikely to have occurred by chance alone.

RECITE

1. A scatter diagram can be used to plot and visualize a _____ between two groups of scores.
2. In a negative relationship, increases in X scores correspond to decreases in Y scores. T or F?
3. A perfect positive correlation exists when the correlation coefficient is 0.00. T or F?
4. It is important to remember that correlation does not demonstrate _____.
5. In inferential statistics, observations of a _____ are used to make inferences and draw conclusions about an entire _____.
6. A representative sample can be obtained by selecting members of the sample at _____.
7. If the results of an experiment could have occurred by chance alone less than 25 times out of 100, the result is considered statistically significant. T or F?

REFLECT

Critical Thinking

8. Suppose it was found that sleeping with your clothes on is correlated with waking up with a headache. Could you conclude that sleeping with your clothes on causes headaches?

ANSWERS

1. correlation 2. T 3. F 4. causation 5. sample, population 6. random 7. F 8. No. To reiterate, correlation does not prove causality. It is more likely here that a third factor is causing *both* the sleeping with the clothes on at night *and* the headaches (too much alcohol, anyone?).

appendix in review

Major Points

- The results of psychological studies are often expressed as numbers, which must be summarized and interpreted before they have any meaning.

- Summarizing numbers visually, by using various types of graphs, makes it easier to see trends and patterns in the results of psychological investigations.

- It is helpful to know the "average" of a group of scores as well as how much they vary.

- Many psychological measures produce scores that form a normal curve. This is useful because the characteristics of normal curves are well known.

- When there is a correlation, or consistent relationship, between scores on two measures, knowing a person's score on one measure allows us to predict his or her score on the second measure.

- Some statistical techniques can be used to generalize results from samples to populations, to draw conclusions, and to tell if the results of a study could have occurred by chance.

Summary

What are descriptive statistics?

- Descriptive statistics organize and summarize numbers.

- Summarizing numbers visually, by using various types of graphs such as histograms and frequency polygons, makes it easier to see trends and patterns in the results of psychological investigations.

- Measures of central tendency define the "typical score" in a group of scores.

- The mean is found by adding all the scores in a group and then dividing by the total number of scores.

- The median is found by arranging a group of scores from the highest to the lowest and selecting the middle score.

- The mode is the score that occurs most frequently in a group of scores.

- Measures of variability provide a number that shows how much scores vary.

- The range is the difference between the highest score and the lowest score in a group of scores.

- The standard deviation shows how much, on average, all the scores in a group differ from the mean.

- To change an original score into a standard score (or z-score), you must subtract the mean from the score and then divide the result by the standard deviation.

- Standard scores (z-scores) tell, in standard deviation units, how far above or below the mean a score is. This allows meaningful comparisons between scores from different groups.

- Scores that form a normal curve are easy to interpret because the properties of the normal curve are well known.

How are correlations used in psychology?

- When there is a correlation, or consistent relationship, between scores on two measures, knowing a person's score on one measure allows us to predict his or her score on the second measure.

- The relationship between two variables or measures can be positive or negative.

- Correlation coefficients tell how strongly two groups of scores are related.

- Correlation alone does not demonstrate cause-and-effect links between variables or measures.

What are inferential statistics?

- Inferential statistics can be used to generalize results from samples to populations, to draw conclusions, and to tell if the results of a study could have occurred by chance.

- Most studies in psychology are based on samples. Findings from representative samples are assumed to also apply to entire populations.

- In psychology experiments, differences in the average performance of groups could occur purely by chance. Tests of statistical significance tell us if the observed differences between groups are common or rare. If a difference is large enough to be improbable, it suggests that the results did not occur by chance alone.

Web Resources

For an up-to-date list of direct links to interesting sites, including those listed here, visit the student companion site for this book at www.cengage.com/psychology/coon

Frequency Distribution of Tossing Coins and Dice Automatically calculate frequency distributions for tossing coins or dice and plot the results as a frequency polygon.

Descriptive Statistics Further explore descriptive statistics.

Concepts and Applications of Inferential Statistics Browse this full online statistics textbook.

Correlations Vary the correlations and view the corresponding scatter diagram.

Interactive Learning

PSYCHOLOGY: A JOURNEY BOOK COMPANION WEBSITE
WWW.CENGAGE.COM/PSYCHOLOGY/COON
Visit your book companion website, where you will find flash cards, practice quizzes, web links, and more to help you study.

JUST WHAT YOU NEED TO KNOW NOW! CENGAGENOW™
Spend time on what you need to master rather than on information you already have learned. Take a pretest for this chapter, and CengageNOW will generate a personalized study plan based on your results. The study plan will identify the topics you need to review and direct you to online resources to help you master those topics. You can then take a posttest to help you determine the concepts you have mastered and what you will need to work on. Try it out! Go to www.cengage.com/login to sign in with an access code or to purchase access to this product.

Ablation (ab-LAY-shun) Surgical removal of tissue.

Absolute threshold The minimum amount of physical energy necessary to produce a sensation.

Abstract Research reports begin with a very brief summary of the study and its findings. The abstract allows you to get an overview without reading the entire article.

Accessibility (in memory) Memories currently stored in memory which can be retrieved when necessary are both available and accessible.

Accommodation (perceptual) Changes in the shape of the lens of the eye.

Accommodation (Piaget) In Piaget's theory, the modification of existing mental patterns to fit new demands (that is, mental schemes are changed to accommodate new information or experiences).

Acculturative stress Stress caused by the many changes and adaptations required when a person moves to a foreign culture.

Acetylcholine (ah-SEET ul KOH-leen) The neurotransmitter released by neurons to activate muscles.

Acquaintance (date) rape Forced intercourse that occurs in the context of a date or other voluntary encounter.

Action component How one tends to act toward the object of an attitude.

Acquisition The period in conditioning during which a response is reinforced.

Action potential The nerve impulse.

Activation-synthesis hypothesis An attempt to explain how dream content is affected by motor commands in the brain that occur during sleep, but are not carried out.

Active listener A person who knows how to maintain attention, avoid distractions, and actively gather information from lectures.

Actor–observer bias The tendency to attribute the behavior of others to internal causes while attributing one's own behavior to external causes (situations and circumstances).

Acute stress disorder A psychological disturbance lasting up to 1 month following stresses that would produce anxiety in anyone who experienced them.

Adaptive behaviors Actions that aid attempts to survive and adapt to changing conditions.

Adjustment disorder An emotional disturbance caused by on-going stressors within the range of common experience.

Adolescence The culturally defined period between childhood and adulthood.

Adrenal glands Endocrine glands that arouse the body, regulate salt balance, adjust the body to stress, and affect sexual functioning.

Adrenaline A hormone produced by the adrenal glands that tends to arouse the body.

Affectional needs Emotional needs for love and affection.

Ageism Discrimination or prejudice based on a person's age.

Aggression Any action carried out with the intention of causing harm; hurting another person or achieving one's goals at the expense of another person.

Aggression cues Stimuli or signals that are associated with aggression and that tend to elicit it.

Aggressive pornography Media depictions of sexual violence or of forced participation in sexual activity.

Agnosia An inability to grasp the meaning of stimuli, such as words, objects, or pictures.

Agoraphobia (ah-go-rah-FOBE-ee-ah) **(without panic)** The fear that something extremely embarrassing will happen to if one leaves the house or enter unfamiliar situations.

Alarm reaction First stage of the GAS, during which bodily resources are mobilized to cope with a stressor.

Alcohol myopia (my-OH-pea-ah) Shortsighted thinking and perception that occurs during alcohol intoxication.

Algorithm A learned set of rules that always leads to the correct solution of a problem.

All-or-nothing thinking Classifying objects or events as absolutely right or wrong, good or bad, acceptable or unacceptable, and so forth.

Alpha waves Large, slow brain waves associated with relaxation and falling asleep.

Altered state of consciousness (ASC) A condition of awareness distinctly different in quality or pattern from waking consciousness.

Alzheimer's (ALLS-hi-merz) **disease** An age-related disease characterized by memory loss, mental confusion, and, in its later stages, a nearly total loss of mental abilities.

Ambivalence Mixed positive and negative feelings or simultaneous attraction and repulsion.

Ambivalent attachment An emotional bond marked by conflicting feelings of affection, anger, and emotional turmoil.

Amygdala (ah-MIG-dah-luh) A part of the limbic system (within the brain) associated with fear responses.

Anal stage The psychosexual stage corresponding roughly to the period of toilet training (ages 1 to 3).

Anal-expulsive personality A disorderly, destructive, cruel, or messy person.

Anal-retentive personality A person who is obstinate, stingy, or compulsive and who generally has difficulty "letting go."

Androgen (an-dro-JEN) Any of a number of male sex hormones, especially testosterone.

Androgyny (an-DROJ-ih-nee) The presence of both "masculine" and "feminine" traits in a single person (as masculinity and femininity are defined within one's culture).

Anger control Personal strategies for reducing or curbing anger.

Anhedonia (an-he-DAWN-ee-ah) An inability to feel pleasure.

Anima An archetype representing the female principle.

Animal model In research, an animal whose behavior is used to derive principles that may apply to human behavior.

Animus An archetype representing the male principle.

Anorexia nervosa (AN-uh-REK-see-yah ner-VOH-sah) Active self-starvation or a sustained loss of appetite that has psychological origins.

Antecedents Events that precede a response.

Anthropomorphic (AN-thro-po-MORE-fik) **error** The error of attributing human thoughts, feelings, or motives to animals, especially as a way of explaining their behavior.

Antidepressants Mood-elevating drugs.

Antipsychotics Drugs that, in addition to having tranquilizing effects, also tend to reduce hallucinations and delusional thinking. (Also called **major tranquilizers.**)

Antisocial behavior Any behavior that has a negative impact on other people.

Antisocial personality A person who lacks a conscience, is emotionally shallow, impulsive, selfish, and tends to manipulate others.

Anxiety Apprehension, dread, or uneasiness similar to fear but based on an unclear threat.

Anxiety disorder Disruptive feelings of fear, apprehension, or anxiety, or distortions in behavior that are anxiety related.

Anxiety reduction hypothesis Explains the self-defeating nature of avoidance responses as a result of the reinforcing effects of relief from anxiety.

Anxiolytics Drugs (such as Valium) that produce relaxation or reduce anxiety.

Aphasia (ah-FAZE-yah) A speech disturbance resulting from brain damage.

Apparent-distance hypothesis An explanation of the moon illusion stating that the horizon seems more distant than the night sky.

Applied psychology The use of psychological principles and research methods to solve practical problems.

Approach-approach conflict Choosing between two positive, or desirable, alternatives.

Approach-avoidance conflict Being attracted to and repelled by the same goal or activity.

Aptitude test A test that rates a person's potential to learn skills required by various occupations.

Archetype A universal idea, image, or pattern, found in the collective unconscious.

Architectural psychology Study of the effects buildings have on behavior and the design of buildings using behavioral principles.

Arousal theory Assumes that people prefer to maintain ideal, or comfortable, levels of arousal.

Artificial intelligence (AI) Any artificial system (often a computer program) that is capable of human-like problem solving or intelligent responding.

Assertiveness training Instruction in how to be self-assertive.

Assessment center A program set up within an organization to conduct in-depth evaluations of job candidates.

Assimilation In Piaget's theory, the application of existing mental patterns to new situations (that is, the new situation is assimilated to existing mental schemes).

Association area (association cortex) All areas of the cerebral cortex that are not primarily sensory or motor in function.

Associative learning The formation of simple associations between various stimuli and responses.

Astigmatism (ah-STIG-mah-tiz-em) Defects in the cornea, lens, or eye that cause some areas of vision to be out of focus.

Attention Voluntarily focusing on a specific sensory input.

Attention deficit/hyperactivity disorder (ADHD) A behavioral problem characterized by short attention span, restless movement, and impaired learning capacity.

Attentional overload A stressful condition caused when sensory stimulation, information, and social contacts make excessive demands on attention.

Attitude A learned tendency to respond to people, objects, or institutions in a positive or negative way.

Attitude scale A collection of attitudinal statements with which respondents indicate agreement or disagreement.

Attribution The mental process of assigning causes to events, including making inferences about the causes of one's own behavior, and that of others. In emotion, the process of attributing arousal to a particular source.

Authenticity In Carl Rogers' terms, the ability of a therapist to be genuine and honest about his or her own feelings.

Authoritarian parents Parents who enforce rigid rules and demand strict obedience to authority.

Authoritarian (ah-thor-ih-TARE-ee-un) **personality** A personality pattern characterized by rigidity, inhibition, prejudice, and an excessive concern with power, authority, and obedience.

Authoritative parents Parents who supply firm and consistent guidance combined with love and affection.

Autism Spectrum Disorders A range of disorders, from less to more severe, involving mutism, sensory spin-outs, sensory blocking, tantrums, unresponsiveness to others, and other difficulties.

Autokinetic effect The apparent movement of a stationary pinpoint of light displayed in a darkened room.

Autonomic nervous system (ANS) The system of nerves carrying information to and from the internal organs and glands.

Autonomy versus shame and doubt A conflict created when growing self-control (autonomy) is pitted against feelings of shame and doubt.

Availability (in memory) Memories currently stored in memory are available.

Aversion therapy Suppressing an undesirable response by associating it with aversive (painful or uncomfortable) stimuli.

Aversive stimulus A stimulus that is painful or uncomfortable.

Avoidance learning Learning to make a response in order to postpone or prevent discomfort.

Avoidance-avoidance conflict Choosing between two negative, undesirable alternatives.

Avoidant attachment An emotional bond marked by a tendency to resist commitment to others.

Axon (AK-sahn) Fiber that carries information away from the cell body of a neuron.

Axon terminals Bulb-shaped structures at the ends of axons that form synapses with the dendrites and somas of other neurons.

Bait shyness An unwillingness or hesitation on the part of animals to eat a particular food.

Barnum effect The tendency to consider a personal description accurate if it is stated in very general terms.

Base rate The basic rate at which an event occurs over time; the basic probability of an event.

Basic anxiety A primary form of anxiety that arises from living in a hostile world.

Basic needs The first four levels of needs in Maslow's hierarchy; lower needs tend to be more potent than higher needs.

Basic suggestion effect The tendency of hypnotized persons to carry out suggested actions as if they were involuntary.

Behavior modification The application of learning principles to change human behavior, especially maladaptive behavior.

Behavior therapy Any therapy designed to actively change behavior.

Behavioral assessment Recording the frequency of various behaviors.

Behavioral contract A formal agreement stating behaviors to be changed and consequences that apply.

Behavioral dieting Weight reduction based on changing exercise and eating habits, rather than temporary self-starvation.

Behavioral genetics The study of inherited behavioral traits and tendencies.

Behavioral medicine The study of behavioral factors in medicine, physical illness, and medical treatment.

Behavioral personality theory Any model of personality that emphasizes learning and observable behavior.

Behavioral risk factors Behaviors that increase the chances of disease, injury, or premature death.

Behavioral setting A smaller area within an environment whose use is well defined, such as a bus depot, waiting room, or lounge.

Behaviorism The school of psychology that emphasizes the study of overt, observable behavior.

Belief component What a person thinks or believes about the object of an attitude.

Beta waves Small fast brain waves associated with being awake and alert.

Beta-endorphin (BAY-tah-en-DOR-fin) A natural, painkilling brain chemical similar to morphine.

Biased sample A subpart of a larger population that does not accurately reflect characteristics of the whole population.

Bilingualism An ability to speak two languages.

Binge drinking Consuming five or more drinks in a short time (four drinks for women).

Binocular depth cues Perceptual features that impart information about distance and three-dimensional space which require two eyes.

Biodata Detailed biographical information about a job applicant.

Biofeedback Information given to a person about his or her ongoing bodily activities; aids voluntary regulation of bodily states.

Biological biasing effect Hypothesized effect that prenatal exposure to sex hormones has on development of the body, nervous system, and later behavior patterns.

Biological motives Innate motives based on biological needs.

Biological perspective The attempt to explain behavior in terms of underlying biological principles.

Biological predisposition The presumed hereditary readiness of humans to learn certain skills, such as how to use language, or a readiness to behave in particular ways.

Biological rhythm Any repeating cycle of biological activity, such as sleep and waking cycles or changes in body temperature.

Bipolar disorders Emotional disorders involving both depression and mania or hypomania.

Bipolar I disorder A mood disorder in which a person has episodes of mania (excited, hyperactive, energetic, grandiose behavior) and also periods of deep depression.

Bipolar II disorder A mood disorder in which a person is mostly depressed (sad, despondent, guilt ridden) but has also had one or more episodes of mild mania (hypomania).

Bisexual A person romantically and erotically attracted to both men and women.

Blind spot An area of the retina lacking visual receptors.

Bottom-up processing Organizing perceptions by beginning with low-level features.

Brainstem The lowest portions of the brain, including the cerebellum, medulla, pons, and reticular formation.

Brainwashing Engineered or forced attitude change involving a captive audience.

Brief psychodynamic therapy A modern therapy based on psychoanalytic theory but designed to produce insights more quickly.

Brightness constancy The apparent (or relative) brightness of objects remains the same as long as they are illuminated by the same amount of light.

Broca's (BRO-cahs) **area** A language area related to grammar and pronunciation.

Broken record A self-assertion technique involving repeating a request until it is acknowledged.

Browser Software that facilitates access to text, images, sounds, video, and other information stored in formats used on the Internet.

Bulimia (bue-LIHM-ee-yah) **nervosa** Excessive eating (gorging) usually followed by self-induced vomiting and/or taking laxatives.

Burnout A job-related condition of mental, physical, and emotional exhaustion.

Bystander apathy Unwillingness of bystanders to offer help during emergencies or to become involved in others' problems.

Caffeinism Excessive consumption of caffeine, leading to dependence and a variety of physical and psychological complaints.

Cannon-Bard theory States that activity in the thalamus causes emotional feelings and bodily arousal to occur simultaneously.

Carbon footprint The volume of greenhouse gases individual consumption adds to the atmosphere.

Cardinal trait A personality trait so basic that all of a person's activities relate to it.

Case study An in-depth focus on all aspects of a single person.

Castration Surgical removal of the testicles or ovaries.

Cataplexy (CAT-uh-plex-see) A sudden temporary paralysis of the muscles.

Catatonic schizophrenia Schizophrenia marked by stupor, rigidity, unresponsiveness, posturing, mutism, and, sometimes, agitated, purposeless behavior.

Causation The act of causing some effect.

Central nervous system (CNS) The brain and spinal cord.

Central tendency The tendency for a majority of scores to fall in the mid-range of possible values.

Central traits The core traits that characterize an individual personality.

Cerebellum (ser-ah-BEL-uhm) A brain structure that controls posture and coordination.

Cerebral (seh-REE-brel or ser-EH-brel) **cortex** The outer layer of the brain.

Cervix (SER-vix) The lower end of the uterus that projects into the vagina.

Character Personal characteristics that have been judged or evaluated; a person's desirable or undesirable qualities.

Chromosomes Thread-like "colored bodies" in the nucleus of each cell that are made up of DNA.

Chronological age A person's age in years.

Circadian (SUR-kay-dee-AN) **rhythms** Cyclical changes in bodily functions and arousal levels that vary on a schedule approximating a 24-hour day.

Clairvoyance The purported ability to perceive events at a distance or through physical barriers.

Classical conditioning A form of learning in which reflex responses are associated with new stimuli.

Client-centered (or person-centered) therapy A nondirective therapy based on insights gained from conscious thoughts and feelings; emphasizes accepting one's true self.

Clinical case study A detailed investigation of a single person, especially one suffering from some injury or disease.

Clinical method Studying psychological problems and therapies in clinical settings.

Clinical psychologist A psychologist who specializes in the treatment of psychological and behavioral disturbances or who does research on such disturbances.

Clitoris (KLIT-er-iss) Small, sensitive organ made up of erectile tissue; located above the vaginal opening.

Coefficient of correlation A statistical index ranging from −1.00 to +1.00 that indicates the direction and degree of correlation.

Coercion Being forced to change your beliefs or your behavior against your will.

Coercive power Social power based on the ability to punish others.

Cognition The process of thinking or mentally processing information (images, concepts, words, rules, and symbols).

Cognitive behaviorism An approach that combines behavioral principles with cognition (perception, thinking, anticipation) to explain behavior.

Cognitive dissonance An uncomfortable clash between self-image, thoughts, beliefs, attitudes, or perceptions and one's behavior.

Cognitive interview Use of various cues and strategies to improve the memory of eyewitnesses.

Cognitive learning Higher-level learning involving thinking, knowing, understanding, and anticipation.

Cognitive map Internal images or other mental representations of an area (maze, city, campus, and so forth) that underlie an ability to choose alternative paths to the same goal.

Cognitive therapy A therapy directed at changing the maladaptive thoughts, beliefs, and feelings that underlie emotional and behavioral problems.

Collective unconscious A mental storehouse for unconscious ideas and images shared by all humans.

Color blindness A total inability to perceive colors.

Color weakness An inability to distinguish some colors.

Commitment The determination to stay in a long-term relationship with another person.

Common traits Personality traits that are shared by most members of a particular culture.

Community health campaign A community-wide education program that provides information about how to lessen risk factors and promote health.

Community mental health center A facility offering a wide range of mental health services, such as prevention, counseling, consultation, and crisis intervention.

Companionate love Form of love characterized by intimacy and commitment but not passion.

Comparison level A personal standard used to evaluate rewards and costs in a social exchange.

Compensation Counteracting a real or imagined weakness by emphasizing desirable traits or seeking to excel in the area of weakness or in other areas.

Compressed workweek A work schedule that allows an employee to work fewer days per week by putting in more hours per day.

Compliance Bending to the requests of a person who has little or no authority or other form of social power.

Computed tomographic scan (CT scan) A computer-enhanced X-ray image of the brain or body.

Computerized test A test that uses a computer to present life-like situations; test takers react to problems posed by the situations.

Concentrative meditation Mental exercise based on attending to a single object or thought.

Concept An idea representing a category of related objects or events.

Concept formation The process of classifying information into meaningful categories.

Conceptual rule A formal rule for deciding if an object or event is an example of a particular concept.

Concrete operational stage Period of intellectual development during which children become able to use the concepts of time, space, volume, and number, but in ways that remain simplified and concrete, rather than abstract.

Condensation Combining several people, objects, or events into a single dream image.

Conditioned emotional response (CER) An emotional response that has been linked to a previously nonemotional stimulus by classical conditioning.

Conditioned response (CR) A learned response elicited by a conditioned stimulus.

Conditioned stimulus (CS) A stimulus that evokes a response because it has been repeatedly paired with an unconditioned stimulus.

Conditions of worth Internal standards used to judge the value of one's thoughts, actions, feelings, or experiences.

Conductive hearing loss Poor transfer of sounds from the eardrum to the inner ear.

Cones Visual receptors for colors and daylight visual acuity.

Conflict A stressful condition that occurs when a person must choose between incompatible or contradictory alternatives.

Conformity Bringing one's behavior into agreement or harmony with norms or with the behavior of others in a group in the absence of any direct pressure.

Congenital problems Problems or defects that originate during prenatal development in the womb.

Conjunctive concept A class of objects that have two or more features in common. (For example, to qualify as an example of the concept an object must be both red *and* triangular.)

Connotative meaning The subjective, personal, or emotional meaning of a word or concept.

Conscience The part of the superego that causes guilt when its standards are not met.

Conscious The region of the mind that includes all mental contents a person is aware of at any given moment.

Consciousness Mental awareness of sensations, perceptions, memories, and feelings.

Consequences Effects that follow a response.

Conservation In Piaget's theory, mastery of the concept that the weight, mass, and volume of matter remains unchanged (is conserved) even when the shape or appearance of objects changes.

Consistency With respect to child discipline, the maintenance of stable rules of conduct.

Consolidation Process by which relatively permanent memories are formed in the brain.

Constructive processing Reorganizing or updating memories on the basis of logic, reasoning, or the addition of new information.

Consummate love Form of love characterized by intimacy, passion, *and* commitment.

Contact comfort A pleasant and reassuring feeling human and animal infants get from touching or clinging to something soft and warm, usually their mother.

Context Information surrounding a stimulus.

Continuous reinforcement A schedule in which every correct response is followed by a reinforcer.

Control Altering conditions that influence behavior.

Control group In a controlled experiment, the group of subjects exposed to all experimental conditions or variables *except* the independent variable.

Control questions In a polygraph exam, questions that almost always provoke anxiety.

Conventional moral reasoning Moral thinking based on a desire to please others or to follow accepted rules and values.

Convergent thinking Thinking directed toward discovery of a single established correct answer; conventional thinking.

Conversion disorder A bodily symptom that mimics a physical disability but is actually caused by anxiety or emotional distress.

Conviction Beliefs that are important to a person and that evoke strong emotion.

Coping statements Reassuring, self-enhancing statements that are used to stop self-critical thinking.

Correlation The existence of a consistent, systematic relationship between two events, measures, or variables.

Correlational method Making measurements to discover relationships between events.

Correlational study A nonexperimental study designed to measure the degree of relationship (if any) between two or more events, measures, or variables.

Corticalization (KORE-tih-kal-ih-ZAY-shun) An increase in the relative size of the cerebral cortex.

Counseling psychologist A psychologist who specializes in the treatment of milder emotional and behavioral disturbances.

Counselor A mental health professional who specializes in helping people with problems not involving serious mental disorder; for example, marriage counselors, career counselors, or school counselors.

Counterirritation Using mild pain to block more intense or long-lasting pain.

Covert reinforcement Using positive imagery to reinforce desired behavior.

Covert sensitization Use of aversive imagery to reduce the occurrence of an undesired response.

Cowper's glands Two small glands that secrete a clear fluid into the urethra during sexual excitement.

Cranial nerves Major nerves that leave the brain without passing through the spinal cord.

Creative self The "artist" in each of us that creates a unique identity and style of life.

Crisis intervention Skilled management of a psychological emergency.

Critical situations Situations during childhood that are capable of leaving a lasting imprint on personality.

Critical thinking An ability to reflect on, evaluate, compare, analyze, critique, and synthesize information.

Crowding A subjective feeling of being overstimulated by a loss of privacy or by the nearness of others (especially when social contact with them is unavoidable).

Cue External stimuli that guide responses, especially by signaling the presence or absence of reinforcement.

Cult A group that professes great devotion to some person and follows that person almost without question; cult members are typically victimized by their leaders in various ways.

Cultural relativity The idea that behavior must be judged relative to the values of the culture in which it occurs.

Culturally skilled therapist A therapist who has the awareness, knowledge, and skills necessary to treat clients from diverse cultural backgrounds.

Culture An ongoing pattern of life, characterizing a society at a given point in history.

Culture-fair test A test (such as an intelligence test) designed to minimize the importance of skills and knowledge that may be more common in some cultures than in others.

Curve of forgetting A graph that shows the amount of memorized information remembered after varying lengths of time.

Cyclothymic (SIKE-lo-THY-mik) **disorder** Moderate manic and depressive behavior that persists for 2 years or more.

Dark adaptation Increased retinal sensitivity to light.

Death-qualified jury A jury composed of people who favor the death penalty or at least are indifferent to it.

Declarative memory That part of long-term memory containing specific factual information.

Deductive thought Thought that applies a general set of rules to specific situations; for example, using the laws of gravity to predict the behavior of a single falling object.

Deep lesioning (LEE-zhun-ing) Removal of tissue within the brain by use of an electrode.

Deep sleep Stage 4 sleep; the deepest form of normal sleep.

Defense mechanism A habitual and often unconscious psychological process used to reduce anxiety.

Deinstitutionalization Reduced use of full-time commitment to mental institutions to treat mental disorders.

Delta waves Large, slow brain waves that occur in deeper sleep (stages 3 and 4).

Delusion A false belief held against all contrary evidence.

Delusional disorder A psychosis marked by severe delusions of grandeur, jealousy, persecution, or similar preoccupations.

Dementia (duh-MEN-sha) A serious mental impairment in old age caused by physical deterioration of the brain.

Demonology In medieval Europe, the study of demons and the treatment of persons "possessed" by demons.

Dendrites (DEN-drytes) Neuron fibers that receive incoming messages.

Denial Protecting oneself from an unpleasant reality by refusing to perceive it.

Denotative meaning The exact, dictionary definition of a word or concept; its objective meaning.

Density The number of people in a given space or, inversely, the amount of space available to each person.

Dependent variable In an experiment, the condition (usually a behavior) that is affected by the independent variable.

Depressant (downer) A substance that decreases activity in the body and nervous system.

Depression A state of despondency marked by feelings of powerlessness and hopelessness.

Depressive disorders Emotional disorders primarily involving sadness, despondency, and depression.

Deprivation In development, the loss or withholding of normal stimulation, nutrition, comfort, love, and so forth; a condition of lacking.

Depth cues Perceptual features that impart information about distance and three-dimensional space.

Depth perception The ability to see three-dimensional space and to accurately judge distances.

Description In scientific research, the process of naming and classifying.

Descriptive statistics Mathematical tools used to describe and summarize numeric data.

Desensitization Reducing fear or anxiety by repeatedly exposing a person to emotional stimuli while the person is deeply relaxed.

Determinism The idea that all behavior has prior causes that would completely explain one's choices and actions if all such causes were known.

Detoxification In the treatment of alcoholism, the withdrawal of the patient from alcohol.

Developmental level An individual's current state of physical, emotional, and intellectual development.

Developmental psychology The study of progressive changes in behavior and abilities from conception to death.

Developmental task Any skill that must be mastered, or personal change that must take place, for optimal development.

Deviation IQ An IQ obtained statistically from a person's relative standing in his or her age group; that is, how far above or below average the person's score was relative to other scores.

Difference threshold A change in stimulus intensity that is detectable to an observer.

Diffusion of responsibility Spreading the responsibility to act among several people; reduces the likelihood that help will be given to a person in need.

Direct instruction Presentation of factual information by lecture, demonstration, and rote practice.

Direct observation Assessing behavior through direct surveillance.

Discovery learning Learning based on insight and understanding.

Discrimination Treating members of various social groups differently in circumstances where their rights or treatment should be identical.

Discriminative stimuli Stimuli that precede rewarded and nonrewarded responses in operant conditioning.

Discussion The results of the study are discussed in relation to the original question. Implications of the study are explored and further studies may be proposed.

Disease-prone personality A personality type associated with poor health; marked by persistent negative emotions, including anxiety, depression, and hostility.

Dishabituation A reversal of habituation.

Disinhibition The removal of inhibition; results in acting out behavior that normally would be restrained.

Disjunctive concept A concept defined by the presence of at least one of several possible features. (For example, to qualify an object must be either blue *or* circular.)

Disorganized schizophrenia Schizophrenia marked by incoherence, grossly disorganized behavior, bizarre thinking, and flat or grossly inappropriate emotions.

Displaced aggression Redirecting aggression to a target other than the actual source of one's frustration.

Displacement Directing emotions or actions toward safe or unimportant dream images.

Dissociative amnesia Loss of memory (partial or complete) for important information related to personal identity.

Dissociative disorder Temporary amnesia, multiple personality, or depersonalization.

Dissociative fugue Sudden travel away from home, plus confusion about one's personal identity.

Dissociative identity disorder The presence of two or more distinct personalities (multiple personality).

Disuse Theory that memory traces weaken when memories are not periodically used or retrieved.

Divergent thinking Thinking that produces many ideas or alternatives; a major element in original or creative thought.

Divided attention Allotting mental space or effort to various tasks or parts of a task.

DNA Deoxyribonucleic acid, a molecular structure that contains coded genetic information.

Dogmatism An unwarranted positiveness or certainty in matters of belief or opinion.

Dominant gene A gene whose influence will be expressed each time the gene is present.

Dominant hemisphere A term usually applied to the side of a person's brain that produces language.

Door-in-the-face effect The tendency for a person who has refused a major request to subsequently be more likely to comply with a minor request.

Double approach-avoidance conflict Being simultaneously attracted to and repelled by each of two alternatives.

Double standard Applying different standards for judging the appropriateness of male and female sexual behavior.

Double-blind experiment An arrangement in which both participants and experimenters are unaware of whether participants are in the experimental group or the control group, including who might have been administered a drug or a placebo.

Downward comparison Comparing yourself with a person who ranks lower than you on some dimension.

Dream processes Mental filters that hide the true meanings of dreams.

Dream symbols Images in dreams that serve as visible signs of hidden ideas, desires, impulses, emotions, relationships, and so forth.

Drive The psychological expression of internal needs or valued goals. For example, hunger, thirst, or a drive for success.

Drug interaction A combined effect of two drugs that exceeds the addition of one drug's effects to the other.

Drug tolerance A reduction in the body's response to a drug.

Dynamic touch Touch experienced when the body is in motion; a combination of sensations from skin receptors, muscles, and joints.

Dysosmia (dis-OZE-me-ah) Loss or impairment of the sense of smell.

Dyspareunia (DIS-pah-ROO-nee-ah) Genital pain before, during, or after sexual intercourse.

Dysthymic (dis-THY-mik) **disorder** Moderate depression that persists for 2 years or more.

Echoic memory A brief continuation of sensory activity in the auditory system after a sound is heard.

Ecological footprint The amount of land and water area required to replenish the resources that a human population consumes.

Educational psychology The field that seeks to understand how people learn and how teachers instruct.

Ego The executive part of personality that directs rational behavior.

Ego ideal The part of the superego representing ideal behavior; a source of pride when its standards are met.

Egocentric thought Thought that is self-centered and fails to consider the viewpoints of others.

Eidetic (eye-DET-ik) **imagery** The ability to retain a "projected" mental image long enough to use it as a source of information.

Elaborative encoding Encoding that links new information with existing memories and knowledge.

Electra conflict A girl's sexual attraction to her father and feelings of rivalry with her mother.

Electrical stimulation of the brain (ESB) Direct electrical stimulation and activation of brain tissue.

Electroconvulsive shock (ECS) An electric current passed directly through the brain, producing a convulsion.

Electroconvulsive therapy (ECT) A treatment for severe depression, consisting of an electric shock passed directly through the brain, which induces a convulsion.

Electrode Any device (such as a wire, needle, or metal plate) used to electrically stimulate or destroy nerve tissue or to record its activity.

Electroencephalograph (eh-LEK-tro-en-SEF-uh-lo-graf) **(EEG)** A device designed to detect, amplify, and record electrical activity in the brain.

Emblems Gestures that have widely understood meanings within a particular culture.

Emotion A state characterized by physiological arousal, changes in facial expression, gestures, posture, and subjective feelings.

Emotional appraisal Evaluating the personal meaning of a stimulus or situation.

Emotional attachment An especially close emotional bond that infants form with their parents, caregivers, or others.

Emotional component One's feelings toward the object of an attitude.

Emotional expression Outward signs that an emotion is occurring.

Emotional feelings The private, subjective experience of having an emotion.

Emotional intelligence Emotional competence, including empathy, self-control, self-awareness, and other skills.

Emotion-focused coping Managing or controlling one's emotional reaction to a stressful or threatening situation.

Empathic arousal Emotional arousal that occurs when you feel some of another person's pain, fear, or anguish.

Empathy A capacity for taking another's point of view; the ability to feel what another is feeling.

Empathy-helping relationship Observation that we are most likely to help someone else when we feel emotions such as empathy and compassion.

Encoding Converting information into a form in which it will be retained in memory.

Encoding failure Failure to store sufficient information to form a useful memory.

Encounter group A group experience that emphasizes intensely honest interchanges among participants regarding feelings and reactions to one another.

Endocrine system Glands whose secretions pass directly into the bloodstream or lymph system.

Endogenous (en-DODGE-eh-nus) **depression** Depression that appears to be produced from within (perhaps by chemical imbalances in the brain), rather than as a reaction to life events.

Enrichment In development, deliberately making an environment more stimulating, nutritional, comforting, loving, and so forth.

Environment ("nurture") The sum of all external conditions affecting development, including especially the effects of learning.

Environmental assessment Measurement and analysis of the effects an environment has on the behavior and perceptions of people within that environment.

Environmental psychology The formal study of how environments affect behavior.

Epididymis (ep-ih-DID-ih-mus) A coiled structure at the top of the testes in which sperm are stored.

Epinephrine (ep-eh-NEF-rin) An adrenal hormone that tends to arouse the body; epinephrine is associated with fear. (Also known as adrenaline.)

Episodic (ep-ih-SOD-ik) **drive** A drive that occurs in distinct episodes.

Episodic (ep-ih-SOD-ik) **memory** A subpart of declarative memory that records personal experiences that are linked with specific times and places.

Equal-status contact Social interaction that occurs on an equal footing, without obvious differences in power or status.

Erectile disorder An inability to maintain an erection for lovemaking.

Erogenous (eh-ROJ-eh-nus) **zones** Areas of the body that produce pleasure and/or provoke erotic desire.

Eros Freud's name for the "life instincts."

Escape Reducing discomfort by leaving frustrating situations or by psychologically withdrawing from them.

Escape learning Learning to make a response in order to end an aversive stimulus.

Estrogen Any of a number of female sex hormones.

Estrus Changes in the sexual drives of animals that create a desire for mating; particularly used to refer to females in heat.

Ethnocentrism Placing one's own group or race at the center—that is, tending to reject all other groups but one's own.

Ethologist A person who studies the natural behavior patterns of animals.

Evolutionary psychology Study of the evolutionary origins of human behavior patterns.

Excitement phase The first phase of sexual response, indicated by initial signs of sexual arousal.

Exhibitionism "Flashing," or displaying the genitals to unwilling viewers

Existential therapy An insight therapy that focuses on the elemental problems of existence, such as death, meaning, choice, and responsibility; emphasizes making courageous life choices.

Expectancy An anticipation concerning future events, relationships or about the effect a response will have, especially regarding reinforcement.

Experiential cognition Style of thinking arising during passive experience.

Experiment A formal trial undertaken to confirm or disconfirm a hypothesis about cause and effect.

Experimental group In a controlled experiment, the group of subjects exposed to the independent variable or experimental condition.

Experimental method Investigating causes of behavior through controlled experimentation.

Experimental subjects Humans (also referred to as **participants**) or animals whose behavior is investigated in an experiment.

Expert power Social power derived from possession of knowledge or expertise.

Explicit memory A memory that a person is aware of having; a memory that is consciously retrieved.

Expressive behaviors Behaviors that express or communicate emotion or personal feelings.

External cause A cause of behavior that is assumed to lie outside a person.

External urethral orifice (yoo-REE-thral OR-ih-fis) The opening at the tip of the penis through which urine and semen pass.

Extinction The weakening of a conditioned response through removal of reinforcement.

Extracellular thirst Thirst caused by a reduction in the volume of fluids found between body cells.

Extraneous variables Conditions or factors excluded from influencing the outcome of an experiment.

Extrasensory perception (ESP) The purported ability to perceive events in ways that cannot be explained by known capacities of the sensory organs.

Extrinsic motivation Motivation based on obvious external rewards, obligations, or similar factors.

Extroversion Ego attitude in which energy is mainly directed outward.

Extrovert A person whose attention is directed outward; a bold, outgoing person.

Eye movement desensitization and reprocessing (EMDR) A technique for reducing fear or anxiety; based on holding upsetting thoughts in mind while rapidly moving the eyes from side to side.

Facial agnosia An inability to perceive familiar faces.

Facial feedback hypothesis States that sensations from facial expressions help define what emotion a person feels.

Factor analysis A statistical technique used to correlate multiple measurements and identify general underlying factors.

Fallacy of positive instances The tendency to remember or notice information that fits one's expectations, while forgetting discrepancies.

Fallopian (feh-LOPE-ee-en) **tube** One of two tubes that carry eggs from the ovaries to the uterus.

Family therapy Technique in which all family members participate, both individually and as a group, to change destructive relationships and communication patterns.

Fantasy Fulfilling unmet desires in imagined achievements or activities.

Feedback Information returned to a person about the effects a response has had.

Feeling of knowing A feeling that allows people to predict beforehand whether they will be able to remember something.

Female orgasmic disorder A persistent inability to reach orgasm during lovemaking.

Female sexual arousal disorder A lack of physical arousal to sexual stimulation.

Fetishism Sexual arousal associated with inanimate objects

Figure-ground organization Part of a stimulus appears to stand out as an object (figure) against a less prominent background (ground).

Five-factor model Proposes that there are five universal dimensions of personality.

Fixation A lasting conflict developed as a result of frustration or overindulgence; the tendency to repeat wrong solutions or faulty responses, especially as a result of becoming blind to alternatives.

Fixed interval (FI) schedule A reinforcer is given only when a correct response is made after a set amount of time has passed since the last reinforced response. Responses made during the time interval are not reinforced.

Fixed ratio (FR) schedule A set number of correct responses must be made to get a reinforcer. For example, a reinforcer is given for every four correct responses.

Flashbulb memories Memories created at times of high emotion that seem especially vivid.

Flexibility In tests of creativity, flexibility is indicated by the number of different types of solutions produced.

Flextime A work schedule that allows flexible starting and quitting times.

Fluency In tests of creativity, fluency refers to the total number of solutions produced.

Foot-in-the-door effect The tendency for a person who has first complied with a small request to be more likely later to fulfill a larger request.

Forcible rape Sexual intercourse carried out against the victim's will, under the threat of violence or bodily injury.

Formal operations stage Period of intellectual development characterized by thinking that includes abstract, theoretical, and hypothetical ideas.

Fovea (FOE-vee-ah) An area at the center of the retina containing only cones.

Framing In thought, the terms in which a problem is stated or the way that it is structured.

Free association In psychoanalysis, the technique of having a client say anything that comes to mind, regardless of how embarrassing or unimportant it may seem.

Free will The idea that human beings are capable of freely making choices or decisions.

Frequency distribution A table that divides an entire range of scores into a series of classes and then records the number of scores that fall into each class.

Frequency polygon A graph of a frequency distribution in which the number of scores falling in each class is represented by points on a line.

Frequency theory Holds that tones up to 4,000 hertz are converted to nerve impulses that match the frequency of each tone.

Frontal lobes A brain area associated with movement, the sense of self, and higher mental functions.

Frotteurism Sexually touching or rubbing against a nonconsenting person, usually in a public place such as a subway.

Frustration A negative emotional state that occurs when one is prevented from reaching a goal.

Frustration-aggression hypothesis States that frustration tends to lead to aggression.

Fully functioning person A person living in harmony with her or his deepest feelings, impulses, and intuitions.

Functional fixedness A rigidity in problem solving caused by an inability to see new uses for familiar objects.

Functional MRI (fMRI) Functional magnetic resonance imaging that records brain activity.

Functional solution A detailed, practical, and workable solution.

Functionalism The school of psychology concerned with how behavior and mental abilities help people adapt to their environments.

Fundamental attribution error The tendency to attribute the behavior of others to internal causes (personality, likes, and so forth).

Galvanic skin response (GSR) A change in the electrical resistance (or inversely, the conductance) of the skin, due to sweating.

Gate control theory Proposes that pain messages pass through neural "gates" in the spinal cord.

Gender Psychological and social characteristics associated with being male or female; defined especially by one's gender identity and learned gender roles.

Gender bias (in research) A tendency for females and female issues to be underrepresented in research, psychological or otherwise.

Gender identity One's personal, private sense of maleness or femaleness as expressed in appearance, behavior, and attitudes.

Gender role The pattern of behaviors that are regarded as "male" or "female" by one's culture; sometimes also referred to as a sex role.

Gender role socialization The process of learning gender behaviors considered appropriate for one's sex in a given culture.

Gender role stereotypes Oversimplified and widely held beliefs about the basic characteristics of men and women.

General adaptation syndrome (GAS) A series of bodily reactions to prolonged stress; occurs in three stages: alarm, resistance, and exhaustion.

General solution A solution that correctly states the requirements for success but not in enough detail for further action.

Generalized anxiety disorder A chronic state of tension and worries about work, relationships, ability, or impending disaster.

Generativity versus stagnation A conflict of middle adulthood in which self-interest is countered by an interest in guiding the next generation.

Genes Specific areas on a strand of DNA that carry hereditary information.

Genetic disorders Problems caused by defects in the genes or by inherited characteristics.

Genetic sex Sex as indicated by the presence of *XX* (female) or *XY* (male) chromosomes.

Genital stage Period of full psychosexual development, marked by the attainment of mature adult sexuality.

Genital sex Sex as indicated by the presence of male or female genitals.

Gestalt psychology A school of psychology emphasizing the study of thinking, learning, and perception in whole units, not by analysis into parts.

Gestalt therapy An approach that focuses on immediate experience and awareness to help clients rebuild thinking, feeling, and acting into connected wholes; emphasizes the integration of fragmented experiences.

g-factor A general ability factor or core of general intellectual ability that involves reasoning, problem-solving ability, knowledge, memory, and successful adaptation to one's surroundings.

Giftedness Either the possession of a high IQ or special talents or aptitudes.

Glans penis (glanz PEA-nis) The tip of the penis.

Goal The target or objective of motivated behavior.

Gonadal sex Sex as indicated by the presence of ovaries (female) or testes (male).

Gonads The primary sex glands—the testes in males and ovaries in females.

Grammar A set of rules for combining language units into meaningful speech or writing.

Graphical statistics Techniques for presenting numbers pictorially, often by plotting them on a graph.

Group cohesiveness The degree of attraction among group members or their commitment to remaining in the group.

Group intelligence test Any intelligence test that can be administered to a group of people with minimal supervision.

Group prejudice Prejudice held out of conformity to group views.

Group sanctions Rewards and punishments (such as approval or disapproval) administered by groups to enforce conformity among members.

Group structure The network of roles, communication pathways, and power in a group.

Group therapy Psychotherapy conducted in a group setting to make therapeutic use of group dynamics.

Groupthink A compulsion by members of decision-making groups to maintain agreement, even at the cost of critical thinking.

Growth hormone A hormone, secreted by the pituitary gland, that promotes body growth.

Growth needs In Maslow's hierarchy, the higher level needs associated with self-actualization.

Guided imagery Intentional visualization of images that are calming, relaxing, or beneficial in other ways.

Gustation The sense of taste.

Habit A deeply ingrained, learned pattern of behavior.

Habituation A decrease in perceptual response to a repeated stimulus.

Hair cells Receptor cells within the cochlea that transduce vibrations into nerve impulses.

Halfway house A community-based facility for individuals making the transition from an institution (mental hospital, prison, and so forth) to independent living.

Hallucination An imaginary sensation—such as seeing, hearing, or smelling something that does not exist in the external world.

Hallucinogen (hal-LU-sin-oh-jin) A substance that alters or distorts sensory impressions.

Halo effect The tendency to generalize a favorable or unfavorable impression to unrelated details of personality.

Handedness A preference for the right or left hand in most activities.

Hardy personality A personality style associated with superior stress resistance.

Hassle (microstressor) Any distressing, day-to-day annoyance.

Health psychology Study of the ways in which behavioral principles can be used to prevent illness and promote health.

Heredity ("nature") The transmission of physical and psychological characteristics from parents to offspring through genes.

Heterosexism The belief that heterosexuality is better or more natural than homosexuality.

Heterosexual A person romantically and erotically attracted to members of the opposite sex.

Heuristic (hew-RIS-tik) Any strategy or technique that aids problem solving, especially by limiting the number of possible solutions to be tried.

Hidden observer A detached part of the hypnotized person's awareness that silently observes events.

Hierarchy A rank-ordered series of higher and lower amounts, levels, degrees, or steps.

Hierarchy of human needs Abraham Maslow's ordering of needs, based on their presumed strength or potency.

Higher order conditioning Classical conditioning in which a conditioned stimulus is used to reinforce further learning; that is, a CS is used as if it were a US.

Hippocampus (HIP-oh-CAMP-us) A part of the limbic system in the brain associated with emotion, storing memories, and the transfer of information from short-term memory to long-term memory.

Histogram A graph of a frequency distribution in which the number of scores falling in each class is represented by vertical bars.

Homeostasis (HOE-me-oh-STAY-sis) A steady state of bodily equilibrium.

Homogamy (huh-MOG-ah-me) Marriage of two people who are similar to one another.

Homosexual A person romantically and erotically attracted to same-sex persons.

Hormonal sex Sex as indicated by a preponderance of estrogens (female) or androgens (male) in the body.

Hormone A glandular secretion that affects bodily functions or behavior.

Human factors psychology (ergonomics) A specialty concerned with making machines and work environments compatible with human perceptual and physical capacities.

Human nature Those traits, qualities, potentials, and behavior patterns most characteristic of the human species.

Human–computer interaction (HCI) The application of human factors to the design of computers and computer software.

Humanism An approach to psychology that focuses on human experience, problems, potentials, and ideals.

Hyperopia (HI-per-OPE-ee-ah) Difficulty focusing nearby objects (farsightedness).

Hypersomnia (hi-per-SOM-nee-ah) Excessive daytime sleepiness. This can result from depression, insomnia, narcolepsy, sleep apnea, sleep drunkenness, periodic limb movements, drug abuse, and other problems.

Hypnosis An altered state of consciousness characterized by narrowed attention and increased suggestibility.

Hypnotic susceptibility One's capacity for becoming hypnotized.

Hypoactive sexual desire A persistent, upsetting loss of sexual desire.

Hypochondriac (HI-po-KON-dree-ak) A person who complains about illnesses that appear to be imaginary.

Hypochondriasis (HI-po-kon-DRY-uh-sis) A preoccupation with fears of having a serious disease. Ordinary physical signs are interpreted as proof that the person has a disease, but no physical disorder can be found.

Hypothalamus (HI-po-THAL-ah-mus) A small area at the base of the brain that regulates many aspects of motivation and emotion, especially hunger, thirst, and sexual behavior.

Hypothesis The predicted outcome of an experiment or an educated guess about the relationship between variables.

Iconic (eye-KON-ick) **memory** A mental image or visual representation.

Id The primitive part of personality that remains unconscious, supplies energy, and demands pleasure.

Ideal self An idealized image of oneself (the person one would like to be).

Identification Feeling emotionally connected to a person and seeing oneself as like him or her.

Identity versus role confusion A conflict of adolescence, involving the need to establish a personal identity.

Illogical thought Thought that is intuitive, haphazard, or irrational.

Illusion A misleading or distorted perception.

Illustrators Gestures people use to illustrate what they are saying.

Image Most often, a mental representation that has picture-like qualities; an icon.

I-message A message that states the effect someone else's behavior has on you.

Imitation An attempt to match one's own behavior to another person's behavior.

Implicit memory A memory that a person does not know exists; a memory that is retrieved unconsciously.

Inattentional blindness Failure to perceive a stimulus that is in plain view, but not the focus of attention.

In-basket test A testing procedure that simulates the individual decision-making challenges that executives face.

Incentive value The value of a goal above and beyond its ability to fill a need.

Incongruence State that exists when there is a discrepancy between one's experiences and self-image or between one's self-image and ideal self.

Incongruent person A person who has an inaccurate self-image or whose self-image differs greatly from the ideal self.

Independent variable In an experiment, the condition being investigated as a possible cause of some change in behavior. The values that this variable takes are chosen by the experimenter.

Individual intelligence test A test of intelligence designed to be given to a single individual by a trained specialist.

Individual traits Personality traits that define a person's unique individual qualities.

Individuating information Information that helps define a person as an individual, rather than as a member of a group or social category.

Inductive thought Thinking in which a general rule or principle is gathered from a series of specific examples; for instance, inferring the laws of gravity by observing many falling objects.

Industrial/organizational psychology A field that focuses on the psychology of work and on behavior within organizations.

Industry versus inferiority A conflict in middle childhood centered around lack of support for industrious behavior, which can result in feelings of inferiority.

Inferential statistics Mathematical tools used for decision making, for generalizing from small samples, and for drawing conclusions.

Information bits Meaningful units of information, such as numbers, letters, words, or phrases.

Information chunks Information bits grouped into larger units.

Informational view Perspective that explains learning in terms of information imparted by events in the environment.

In-group A group with which a person identifies.

Initiative versus guilt A conflict between learning to take initiative and overcoming feelings of guilt about doing so.

Insanity A legal term that refers to a mental inability to manage one's affairs or to be aware of the consequences of one's actions.

Insecure-ambivalent attachment An anxious emotional bond marked by both a desire to be with a parent or caregiver and some resistance to being reunited.

Insecure-avoidant attachment An anxious emotional bond marked by a tendency to avoid reunion with a parent or caregiver.

Insight A sudden mental reorganization of a problem that makes the solution obvious.

Insomnia Difficulty in getting to sleep or staying asleep.

Instrumental behaviors Behaviors directed toward the achievement of some goal; behaviors that are instrumental in producing some effect.

Integrity versus despair A conflict in old age between feelings of integrity and the despair of viewing previous life events with regret.

Intellectual disability (formerly **mental retardation**) The presence of a developmental disability, a formal IQ score below 70, or a significant impairment of adaptive behavior.

Intellectualization Separating emotion from a threatening or anxiety-provoking situation by talking or thinking about it in impersonal "intellectual" terms.

Intelligence An overall capacity to think rationally, act purposefully, and deal effectively with the environment.

Intelligence quotient (IQ) An index of intelligence defined as a person's mental age divided by his or her chronological age and multiplied by 100.

Interference The tendency for new memories to impair retrieval of older memories, and the reverse.

Internal cause A cause of behavior assumed to lie within a person—for instance, a need, preference, or personality trait.

Internet An electronic network of interlinked computers.

Interpersonal attraction Social attraction to another person.

Interpersonal psychotherapy (IPT) A brief dynamic psychotherapy designed to help people by improving their relationships with other people.

Interpretation Where pain is concerned, the meaning given to a stimulus.

Intersexual person A person who has genitals suggestive of both sexes.

Interview (personality) A face-to-face meeting held for the purpose of gaining information about an individual's personal history, personality traits, current psychological state, and so forth.

Intimacy Feelings of connectedness and affection for another person.

Intimacy versus isolation The challenge of overcoming a sense of isolation by establishing intimacy with others.

Intimate distance The most private space immediately surrounding the body (up to about 18 inches from the skin).

Intracellular thirst Thirst triggered when fluid is drawn out of cells due to an increased concentration of salts and minerals outside the cell.

Intrinsic motivation Motivation that comes from within, rather than from external rewards; motivation based on personal enjoyment of a task or activity.

Introduction The introduction describes the question to be investigated. It also provides background information by reviewing prior studies on the same or related topics.

Introspection To look within; to examine one's own thoughts, feelings, or sensations.

Introversion Ego attitude in which energy is mainly directed inward.

Introvert A person whose attention is focused inward; a shy, reserved, self-centered person.

Intuition Quick, impulsive thought that does not make use of formal logic or clear reasoning.

Intuitive thought Thinking that makes little or no use of reasoning and logic.

Ion (EYE-on) **channels** Tiny openings through the axon membrane.

Iris Circular muscle that controls the amount of light entering the eye.

Isolation Separating contradictory thoughts or feelings into "logic-tight" mental compartments so that they do not come into conflict.

James-Lange theory States that emotional feelings follow bodily arousal and come from awareness of such arousal.

Jigsaw classroom A method of reducing prejudice; each student receives only part of the information needed to complete a project or prepare for a test.

Job analysis A detailed description of the skills, knowledge, and activities required by a particular job.

Job enrichment Making a job more personally rewarding, interesting, or intrinsically motivating; typically involves increasing worker knowledge.

Job satisfaction The degree to which a person is comfortable with or satisfied with his or her work.

Just noticeable difference (JND) Any noticeable difference in a stimulus.

Just-world beliefs Beliefs that people generally get what they deserve.

Keyword method As an aid to memory, using a familiar word or image to link two items.

Kinesics (kih-NEEZ-iks) Study of the meaning of body movements, posture, hand gestures, and facial expressions; commonly called body language.

Kinesthetic senses The senses of body movement and positioning.

Knowledge of results (KR) Informational feedback.

Knowledge workers Workers who add value to their company by creating and manipulating information.

Labia majora (LAY-bee-ah mah-JOR-ah) The larger outer lips of the vulva.

Labia minora (LAY-bee-ah mih-NOR-ah) Inner lips of the vulva, surrounding the vaginal opening.

Language Words or symbols, and rules for combining them, that are used for thinking and communication.

Large-group awareness training Any of a number of programs (many of them commercialized) that claim to increase self-awareness and facilitate constructive personal change.

Latency According to Freud, a period in childhood when psychosexual development is more or less interrupted.

Latent dream content The hidden or symbolic meaning of a dream, as revealed by dream interpretation and analysis.

Latent learning Learning that occurs without obvious reinforcement and that remains unexpressed until reinforcement is provided.

Lateralization Differences between the two sides of the body; especially, differences in the abilities of the brain hemispheres.

Law of effect Responses that lead to desirable effects are repeated; those that produce undesirable results are not.

Leaderless group discussion A test of leadership that simulates group decision making and problem solving.

Legitimate power Social power based on a person's position as an agent of an accepted social order.

Learned helplessness A learned inability to overcome obstacles or to avoid punishment; learned passivity and inaction to aversive stimuli.

Learned motives Motives based on learned needs, drives, and goals.

Learning Any relatively permanent change in behavior that can be attributed to experience.

Libido (lih-BEE-doe) In Freudian theory, the force, primarily pleasure oriented, that energizes the personality.

Life skills training A program that teaches stress reduction, self-protection, decision making, self-control, and social skills.

Lifestyle disease A disease related to health-damaging personal habits.

Light sleep Stage 1 sleep, marked by small, irregular brain waves and some alpha waves.

Liking A relationship based on intimacy but lacking passion and commitment.

Limbic system A system in the forebrain that is closely linked with emotional response.

Links Connections built into websites that let you "jump" from one site to the next.

Lobes of the cerebral cortex Areas on the cortex bordered by major fissures or defined by their functions.

Localization of function The research strategy of linking specific structures in the brain with specific psychological or behavioral functions.

Lock and key theory of olfaction Holds that odors are related to the shapes of chemical molecules.

Logical consequences Reasonable consequences that are defined by parents.

Logical thought Drawing conclusions on the basis of formal principles of reasoning.

Long-term memory (LTM) The memory system used for relatively permanent storage of meaningful information.

Low-ball technique A strategy in which commitment is gained first to reasonable or desirable terms, which are then made less reasonable or desirable.

Lucid dream A dream in which the dreamer feels awake and capable of normal thought and action.

Magnetic resonance imaging (MRI) An imaging technique that results in a three-dimensional image of the brain or body, based on its response to a magnetic field.

Maintenance rehearsal Silently repeating or mentally reviewing information to hold it in short-term memory.

Major depressive disorder A mood disorder in which the person has suffered one or more intense episodes of depression.

Major mood disorders Disorders marked by lasting extremes of mood or emotion and sometimes accompanied by psychotic symptoms.

Maladaptive behavior Behavior that makes it difficult to adapt to the environment and meet the demands of day-to-day life.

Male orgasmic disorder A persistent inability to reach orgasm during lovemaking.

Management by objectives A management technique in which employees are given specific goals to meet in their work.

Management techniques Combining praise, recognition, approval, rules, and reasoning to enforce child discipline.

Mandala A circular design representing balance, unity, and completion.

Manifest dream content The surface, "visible" content of a dream; dream images as they are remembered by the dreamer.

Massed practice Practice done in a long, uninterrupted study session.

Mastery training Reinforcement of responses that lead to mastery of a threat or control over one's environment.

Masturbation Self-stimulation that causes sexual pleasure or orgasm.

Maternal influences The aggregate of all psychological effects mothers have on their children.

Maturation The physical growth and development of the body and nervous system.

Mean A measure of central tendency calculated by adding a group of scores and then dividing by the total number of scores.

Mechanical solution A problem solution achieved by trial and error or by a fixed procedure based on learned rules.

Median A measure of central tendency found by arranging scores from the highest to the lowest and selecting the score that falls in the middle. That is, half the values in a group of scores fall above the median and half fall below.

Meditation A mental exercise for producing relaxation or heightened awareness.

Medulla (meh-DUL-ah) The structure that connects the brain with the spinal cord and controls vital life functions.

Melatonin (mel-ah-TONE-in) Hormone released by the pineal gland in response to daily cycles of light and dark.

Memory The mental system for receiving, encoding, storing, organizing, altering, and retrieving information.

Memory cue Any stimulus associated with a particular memory. Memory cues usually enhance retrieval.

Memory decay The fading or weakening of memories assumed to occur when memory traces become weaker.

Memory task Any task designed to test or assess memory.

Memory traces Physical changes in nerve cells or brain activity that take place when memories are stored.

Mental age The average mental ability people display at a given age.

Mental disorder A significant impairment in psychological functioning.

Mental hospitalization Placing a person in a protected, therapeutic environment staffed by mental health professionals.

Mental images Internal images or visual depictions used in memory and thinking.

Mental practice Imagining a skilled performance to aid learning.

Mere presence The tendency for people to change their behavior just because of the presence of other people.

Meta-analysis A statistical technique for combining the results of many studies on the same subject.

Meta-needs In Maslow's hierarchy, needs associated with impulses for self-actualization.

Method This section of a research report tells how and why observations were made. It also describes the specific procedures used to gather data. That way, other researchers can repeat the study to see if they get the same results.

Microsleep A brief shift in brain-wave patterns to those of sleep.

Mindfulness A state of open, non-judgmental awareness of current experience.

Mindfulness meditation Mental exercise based on widening attention to become aware of everything experienced at any given moment.

Minnesota Multiphasic Personality Inventory-2 (MMPI-2) One of the best-known and most widely used objective personality questionnaires.

Mirror neuron A neuron that becomes active when a motor action is carried out and when another organism is observed carrying out the same action.

Mirror technique Observing another person re-enact one's own behavior, like a character in a play; designed to help persons see themselves more clearly.

MMPI-2 profile A graphic representation of an individual's scores on each of the primary scales of the MMPI-2.

Mnemonic (nee-MON-ik) Any kind of memory system or aid.

Mode A measure of central tendency found by identifying the most frequently occurring score in a group of scores.

Model A person who serves as an example in observational learning.

Monocular depth cues Perceptual features that impart information about distance and three-dimensional space which require just one eye.

Mood A low-intensity, long-lasting emotional state.

Mood disorder A major disturbance in mood or emotion, such as depression or mania.

Moon illusion The apparent change in size that occurs as the moon moves from the horizon (large moon) to overhead (small moon).

Moral anxiety Apprehension felt when thoughts, impulses, or actions conflict with the superego's standards.

Moral development The development of values, beliefs, and thinking abilities that act as a guide regarding what is acceptable behavior.

Morphemes (MOR-feems) The smallest meaningful units in a language, such as syllables or words.

Motherese (or parentese) A pattern of speech used when talking to infants, marked by a higher-pitched voice; short, simple sentences; repetition, slower speech; and exaggerated voice inflections.

Motivation Internal processes that initiate, sustain, direct, and terminate activities.

Motor program A mental plan or model that guides skilled movement.

Motor skill A series of actions molded into a smooth and efficient performance.

Müller-Lyer (MEOO-ler-LIE-er) **illusion** Two equal-length lines tipped with inward or outward pointing V's appear to be of different lengths.

Multiculturalism Giving equal status, recognition, and acceptance to different ethnic and cultural groups.

Multiple approach-avoidance conflict Being simultaneously attracted to and repelled by each of several alternatives.

Multiple intelligences Howard Gardner's theory that there are several specialized types of intellectual ability.

Munchausen syndrome An affected person fakes his or her own medical problems in order to gain attention.

Munchausen syndrome by proxy An affected person fakes the medical problems of someone in his or her care in order to gain attention.

Mutual absorption With regard to romantic love, the nearly exclusive attention lovers give to one another.

Mutual interdependence A condition in which people must depend on one another to meet each person's goals.

Myelin (MY-eh-lin) A fatty layer coating some axons.

Myopia (my-OPE-ee-ah) Difficulty focusing distant objects (nearsightedness).

Narcolepsy (NAR-koe-lep-see) Sudden, irresistible, daytime sleep attacks that may last anywhere from a few minutes to a half hour. Victims may fall asleep while standing, talking, or even driving.

Natural consequences The effects that naturally tend to follow a particular behavior.

Natural design Human factors engineering that makes use of naturally understood perceptual signals.

Natural selection Darwin's theory that evolution favors those plants and animals best suited to their living conditions.

Naturalistic observation Observing behavior as it unfolds in natural settings.

Need An internal deficiency that may energize behavior.

Need for achievement (nAch) The desire to excel or meet some internalized standard of excellence.

Need for power The desire to have social impact and control over others.

Need to affiliate The desire to associate with other people.

Negative after-potential A drop in electrical charge below the resting potential.

Negative correlation A statistical relationship in which increases in one measure are matched by decreases in the other.

Negative reinforcement Occurs when a response is followed by an end to discomfort or by the removal of an unpleasant event.

Negative relationship A mathematical relationship in which increases in one measure are matched by decreases in the other.

Negative self-statements Self-critical thoughts that increase anxiety and lower performance.

Negative transfer Mastery of one task conflicts with learning or performing another.

Neo-Freudian A psychologist who accepts the broad features of Freud's theory but has revised the theory to fit his or her own concepts.

Nerve A bundle of neuron axons.

Network model A model of memory that views it as an organized system of linked information.

Neural networks Interlinked collections of neurons that process information in the brain.

Neurilemma (NOOR-rih-LEM-ah) A layer of cells that encases many axons.

Neurocognitive dream theory Proposal that dreams reflect everyday waking thoughts and emotions.

Neurogenesis (noor-oh-JEN-uh-sis) The production of new brain cells.

Neurological soft signs Subtle behavioral signs of brain dysfunction, including clumsiness, an awkward gait, poor hand–eye coordination, and other perceptual and motor problems.

Neuron (NOOR-on) An individual nerve cell.

Neuropeptides (NOOR-oh-PEP-tides) Brain chemicals, such as enkephalins and endorphins, that regulate the activity of neurons.

Neuroplasticity The capacity of the brain to change in response to experience.

Neurosis An outdated term once used to refer, as a group, to anxiety disorders, somatoform disorders, dissociative disorders, and some forms of depression.

Neurotic anxiety Apprehension felt when the ego struggles to control id impulses.

Neurotransmitter (NOOR-oh-TRANS-mit-er) Any chemical released by a neuron that alters activity in other neurons.

Neutral stimulus (NS) A stimulus that does not evoke a response.

Night blindness Blindness under conditions of low illumination.

Night terror A state of panic during NREM sleep.

Nightmare A bad dream that occurs during REM sleep.

Nightmare disorder Vivid, recurrent nightmares that significantly disturb sleep.

Noise pollution Stressful and intrusive noise; usually artificially generated by machinery, but also including noises made by animals and humans.

Noise-induced hearing loss Damage caused by exposing the hair cells to excessively loud sounds.

Non-homeostatic drive A drive that is relatively independent of physical deprivation cycles or bodily need states.

Norepinephrine An adrenal hormone that tends to arouse the body; norepinephrine is associated with anger. (Also known as noradrenaline.)

Norm A widely accepted (but often unspoken) standard of conduct for appropriate behavior.

Normal curve A bell-shaped curve characterized by a large number of scores in a middle area, tapering to very few extremely high and low scores.

NREM (Non-REM) sleep Non-rapid eye movement sleep characteristic of stages 2, 3, and 4.

Obedience Conformity to the demands of an authority.

Object permanence Concept, gained in infancy, that objects continue to exist even when they are hidden from view.

Objective test A test that gives the same score when different people correct it.

Observational learning Learning achieved by watching and imitating the actions of another or noting the consequences of those actions.

Observational record A detailed summary of observed events or a videotape of observed behavior.

Observer bias The tendency of an observer to distort observations or perceptions to match his or her expectations.

Observer effect Changes in an organism's behavior brought about by an awareness of being observed.

Obsessive-compulsive disorder An extreme preoccupation with certain thoughts and compulsive performance of certain behaviors.

Occipital (awk-SIP-ih-tal) **lobes** Portion of the cerebral cortex where vision registers in the brain.

Oedipus conflict A boy's sexual attraction to his mother, and feelings of rivalry with his father.

Olfaction The sense of smell.

Open-ended interview An interview in which persons are allowed to freely state their views.

Operant conditioning Learning based on the consequences of responding.

Operant conditioning chamber (Skinner box) An apparatus designed to study operant conditioning in animals; a Skinner box.

Operant extinction The weakening or disappearance of a nonreinforced operant response.

Operant reinforcer Any event that reliably increases the probability or frequency of responses it follows.

Operant stimulus discrimination The tendency to make an operant response when stimuli previously associated with reward are present and to withhold the response when stimuli associated with nonreward are present.

Operant stimulus generalization The tendency to respond to stimuli similar to those that preceded operant reinforcement.

Operational definition Defining a scientific concept by stating the specific actions or procedures used to measure it. For example, "hunger" might be defined as "the number of hours of food deprivation."

Opponent-process theory (of color vision) Theory of color vision based on three coding systems (red or green, yellow or blue, black or white).

Opponent-process theory (of emotions) States that strong emotions tend to be followed by an opposite emotional state; also the strength of both emotional states changes over time.

Oral stage The period when infants are preoccupied with the mouth as a source of pleasure and means of expression.

Oral-aggressive personality A person who uses the mouth to express hostility by shouting, cursing, biting, and so forth. Also, one who actively exploits others.

Oral-dependent personality A person who wants to passively receive attention, gifts, love, and so forth.

Organ of Corti (KOR-tee) Center part of the cochlea, containing hair cells, canals, and membranes.

Organic mental disorder A mental or emotional problem caused by brain diseases or injuries.

Organismic valuing A natural, undistorted, full-body reaction to an experience.

Organizational citizenship Making positive contributions to the success of an organization in ways that go beyond one's job description.

Organizational culture The social climate within an organization.

Orgasm A climax and release of sexual excitement.

Originality In tests of creativity, originality refers to how novel or unusual solutions are.

Out-group A group with which a person does not identify.

Overgeneralization Blowing a single event out of proportion by extending it to a large number of unrelated situations.

Orientation response Bodily changes that prepare an organism to receive information from a particular stimulus.

Ovary (OH-vah-ree) One of the two female reproductive glands; ovaries are the source of hormones and eggs.

Overlearning Continuing to study and learn after you first think you've mastered a topic.

Overly permissive parents Parents who give little guidance, allow too much freedom, or do not require the child to take responsibility.

Pain disorder Pain that has no identifiable physical cause and appears to be of psychological origin.

Panic disorder (with agoraphobia) A chronic state of anxiety and brief moments of sudden panic. The person fears that these panic attacks will occur in public places or unfamiliar situations.

Panic disorder (without agoraphobia) A chronic state of anxiety and also brief moments of sudden, intense, unexpected panic.

Paranoid psychosis A delusional disorder centered especially on delusions of persecution.

Paranoid schizophrenia Schizophrenia marked by a preoccupation with delusions or by frequent auditory hallucinations related to a single theme, especially grandeur or persecution.

Paraphilias (PAIR-eh-FIL-ih-ahs) Compulsive or destructive deviations in sexual preferences or behavior.

Paraprofessional An individual who works in a near-professional capacity under the supervision of a more highly trained person.

Parapsychology The study of extra-normal psychological events, such as extrasensory perception.

Parasympathetic branch The part of the autonomic system that quiets the body and conserves energy.

Parasympathetic rebound Excess activity in the parasympathetic nervous system following a period of intense emotion.

Parental styles Identifiable patterns of parental caretaking and interaction with children.

Parietal (puh-RYE-ih-tal) **lobes** Area of the brain where bodily sensations register.

Partial hospitalization An approach in which patients receive treatment at a hospital during the day but return home at night.

Partial reinforcement A pattern in which only a portion of all responses are reinforced.

Partial reinforcement effect Responses acquired with partial reinforcement are more resistant to extinction.

Passion Deep emotional and/or sexual feelings for another person.

Passive compliance Passively bending to unreasonable demands or circumstances.

Paternal influences The aggregate of all psychological effects fathers have on their children.

Peak performance A performance during which physical, mental, and emotional states are harmonious and optimal.

Pedophilia Sex with children, or child molesting.

Peer counselor A nonprofessional person who has learned basic counseling skills.

Pelvic bone One of the bones at the front of the pelvis (the pelvis connects the spine with the legs).

Percent of variance A portion of the total amount of variation in a group of scores.

Perception The mental process of organizing sensations into meaningful patterns.

Perceptual construction A mental model of external events.

Perceptual expectancy (or set) A readiness to perceive in a particular manner, induced by strong expectations.

Perceptual features Basic elements of a stimulus, such as lines, shapes, edges, or colors.

Perceptual habits Well-established patterns of perceptual organization and attention.

Perceptual hypothesis An initial guess regarding how to organize (perceive) a stimulus pattern.

Perceptual learning Changes in perception that can be attributed to prior experience; a result of changes in how the brain processes sensory information.

Perfect negative relationship A mathematical relationship in which the correlation between two measures is −1.00.

Perfect positive relationship A mathematical relationship in which the correlation between two measures is +1.00.

Performance intelligence Intelligence measured by solving puzzles, assembling objects, completing pictures, and other nonverbal tasks.

Periodic limb movement syndrome Muscle twitches (primarily affecting the legs) that occur every 20 to 40 seconds and severely disturb sleep.

Peripheral nervous system (PNS) All parts of the nervous system outside the brain and spinal cord.

Peripheral vision Vision at the edges of the visual field.

Persona The "mask" or public self presented to others.

Personal distance The distance maintained when interacting with close friends (about 18 inches to 4 feet from the body).

Personal interview Formal or informal questioning of job applicants to learn their qualifications and to gain an impression of their personalities.

Personal prejudice Prejudicial attitudes held toward persons who are perceived as a direct threat to one's own interests.

Personal space An area surrounding the body that is regarded as private and subject to personal control.

Personal unconscious A mental storehouse for a single individual's unconscious thoughts.

Personality A person's unique and relatively stable behavior patterns.

Personality disorder A maladaptive personality pattern.

Personality questionnaire A paper-and-pencil test consisting of questions that reveal aspects of personality.

Personality theory A system of concepts, assumptions, ideas, and principles used to understand and explain personality.

Personality trait A stable, enduring quality that a person shows in most situations.

Personality type A style of personality defined by a group of related traits.

Personnel psychology Branch of industrial/organizational psychology concerned with testing, selection, placement, and promotion of employees.

Persuasion A deliberate attempt to change attitudes or beliefs with information and arguments.

PET scan Positron emission tomography; a computer-generated image of brain activity based on glucose consumption in the brain.

Phallic personality A person who is vain, exhibitionistic, sensitive, and narcissistic.

Phallic stage The psychosexual stage (roughly ages 3 to 6) when a child is preoccupied with the genitals.

Phantom limb The illusory sensation that a limb still exists after it is lost through accident or amputation.

Pharmacotherapy (FAR-meh-koe-THER-eh-pea) The use of drugs to treat psychopathology.

Pheromone An airborne chemical signal.

Phonemes (FOE-neems) The basic speech sounds of a language.

Phototherapy A treatment for seasonal affective disorder that involves exposure to bright, full-spectrum light.

Physical dependence (addiction) Physical addiction, as indicated by the presence of drug tolerance and withdrawal symptoms.

Physical environments Natural settings, such as forests and beaches, as well as environments built by humans, such as buildings, ships, and cities.

Physiological changes (in emotion) Alterations in heart rate, blood pressure, perspiration, and other involuntary responses.

Pictorial depth cues Features found in paintings, drawings, and photographs that impart information about space, depth, and distance.

Pineal gland Gland in the brain that helps regulate body rhythms and sleep cycles.

Pituitary gland The "master gland" whose hormones influence other endocrine glands.

Place theory Theory that higher and lower tones excite specific areas of the cochlea.

Placebo (plah-SEE-bo) An inactive substance given in the place of a drug in psychological research or by physicians who wish to treat a complaint by suggestion.

Placebo (plah-SEE-bo) **effect** Changes in behavior due to a participant's expectations that a drug (or other treatment) will have some effect.

Plateau phase The second phase of sexual response during which physical arousal is further heightened.

Pleasure principle A desire for immediate satisfaction of wishes, desires, or needs.

Polygenic (pol-ih-JEN-ik) **characteristics** Personal traits or physical properties that are influenced by many genes working in combination.

Polygraph A device for recording heart rate, blood pressure, respiration, and galvanic skin response; commonly called a "lie detector."

Pons An area on the brainstem that acts as a bridge between the medulla and other structures.

Population An entire group of animals, people, or objects belonging to a particular category (for example, all college students or all married women).

Positive correlation A statistical relationship in which increases in one measure are matched by increases in the other (or decreases correspond with decreases).

Positive psychology The study of human strengths, virtues, and effective functioning.

Positive reinforcement Occurs when a response is followed by a reward or other positive event.

Positive relationship A mathematical relationship in which increases in one measure are matched by increases in the other (or decreases correspond with decreases).

Positive self-regard Thinking of oneself as a good, lovable, worthwhile person.

Positive transfer Mastery of one task aids learning or performing another.

Positron emission tomography (PET) An imaging technique that results in a computer-generated image of brain activity, based on glucose consumption in the brain.

Possible self A collection of thoughts, beliefs, feelings, and images concerning the person one could become.

Postconventional moral reasoning Moral thinking based on carefully examined and self-chosen moral principles.

Postpartum depression A mild to moderately severe depression that begins within 3 months following childbirth.

Posttraumatic stress disorder (PTSD) A psychological disturbance lasting more than 1 month following stresses that would produce anxiety in anyone who experienced them.

Power assertion The use of physical punishment or coercion to enforce child discipline.

Precognition The purported ability to accurately predict future events.

Preconscious An area of the mind containing information that can be voluntarily brought to awareness.

Preconventional moral reasoning Moral thinking based on the consequences of one's choices or actions (punishment, reward, or an exchange of favors).

Prediction An ability to accurately forecast behavior.

Prefrontal area (prefrontal cortex) The very front of the frontal lobes; involved in sense of self, reasoning, and planning.

Prejudice A negative emotional attitude held against members of a particular group of people.

Premack principle Any high-frequency response can be used to reinforce a low-frequency response.

Premature ejaculation Ejaculation that consistently occurs before the man and his partner want it to occur.

Preoperational stage Period of intellectual development during which children begin to use language and think symbolically, yet remain intuitive and egocentric in their thought.

Presbyopia (prez-bee-OPE-ee-ah) Farsightedness caused by aging.

Pressure A stressful condition that occurs when a person must meet urgent external demands or expectations.

Primary appraisal Deciding if a situation is relevant to oneself and if it is a threat.

Primary auditory area Part of the temporal lobe where auditory information is first registered in the brain.

Primary emotions According to Robert Plutchik's theory, the most basic emotions are fear, surprise, sadness, disgust, anger, anticipation, joy, and acceptance.

Primary motor area (primary motor cortex) A brain area associated with control of movement.

Primary reinforcers Nonlearned reinforcers; usually those that satisfy physiological needs.

Primary sexual characteristics Sex as defined by the genitals and internal reproductive organs.

Primary somatosensory (SO-mat-oh-SEN-so-ree) **area (primary somatosensory cortex)** A receiving area for body sensations.

Primary visual area The part of occipital lobe that first receives input from the eyes.

Priming Facilitating the retrieval of an implicit memory by using cues to activate hidden memories.

Private self-consciousness Preoccupation with inner feelings, thoughts, and fantasies.

Proactive (pro-AK-tiv) **interference** The tendency for old memories to interfere with the retrieval of newer memories.

Problem-focused coping Directly managing or remedying a stressful or threatening situation.

Procedural memory Long-term memories of conditioned responses and learned skills.

Programmed instruction Any learning format that presents information in small amounts, gives immediate practice, and provides continuous feedback to learners.

Progressive relaxation A method for producing deep relaxation of all parts of the body.

Projection Attributing one's own feelings, shortcomings, or unacceptable impulses to others.

Projective tests Psychological tests making use of ambiguous or unstructured stimuli.

Prosocial behavior Behavior toward others that is helpful, constructive, or altruistic.

Prostate (PROSS-tate) A gland located at the base of the urinary bladder that supplies most of the fluid that makes up semen.

Prototype An ideal model used as a prime example of a particular concept.

Proxemics (prok-SEE-miks) Systematic study of the human use of space, particularly in social settings.

Pseudopsychology (SUE-doe-psychology) Any false and unscientific system of beliefs and practices that is offered as an explanation of behavior.

Psi (sigh) **phenomena** Events that seem to lie outside the realm of accepted scientific laws.

Psyche (sigh-KEY) The mind, mental life, and personality as a whole.

Psychiatric social worker A mental health professional trained to apply social science principles to help patients in clinics and hospitals.

Psychiatrist A medical doctor with additional training in the diagnosis and treatment of mental and emotional disorders.

Psychoactive drug A substance capable of altering attention, memory, judgment, time sense, self-control, mood, or perception.

Psychoanalysis A Freudian therapy that emphasizes the use of free association, dream interpretation, resistances, and transference to uncover unconscious conflicts.

Psychoanalyst A mental health professional (usually a medical doctor) trained to practice psychoanalysis.

Psychoanalytic theory Freudian theory of personality that emphasizes unconscious forces and conflicts.

Psychodrama A therapy in which clients act out personal conflicts and feelings in the presence of others who play supporting roles.

Psychodynamic theory Any theory of behavior that emphasizes internal conflicts, motives, and unconscious forces.

Psychogenic Having psychological origins, rather than physical causes.

Psychokinesis The purported ability to mentally alter or influence objects or events.

Psychological dependence Drug dependence that is based primarily on emotional or psychological needs.

Psychological efficiency Maintenance of good morale, labor relations, employee satisfaction, and similar aspects of work behavior.

Psychological perspective The traditional view that behavior is shaped by psychological processes occurring at the level of the individual.

Psychological situation A situation as it is perceived and interpreted by an individual, not as it exists objectively.

Psychological trauma A psychological injury or shock, such as that caused by violence, abuse, neglect, separation, and so forth.

Psychologist A person highly trained in the methods, factual knowledge, and theories of psychology.

Psychology The scientific study of behavior and mental processes.

Psychology of law Study of the psychological and behavioral dimensions of the legal system.

Psychoneuroimmunology Study of the links among behavior, stress, disease, and the immune system.

Psychopathology The scientific study of mental, emotional, and behavioral disorders; also, abnormal or maladaptive behavior.

Psychophysics Study of the relationship between physical stimuli and the sensations they evoke in a human observer.

Psychosexual stages The oral, anal, phallic, and genital stages, during which various personality traits are formed.

Psychosis A withdrawal from reality marked by hallucinations and delusions, disturbed thought and emotions, and by personality disorganization.

Psychosocial dilemma A conflict between personal impulses and the social world.

Psychosomatic (SIKE-oh-so-MAT-ik) **disorders** Illnesses in which psychological factors contribute to bodily damage or to damaging changes in bodily functioning.

Psychosurgery Any surgical alteration of the brain designed to bring about desirable behavioral or emotional changes.

Psychotherapy Any psychological technique used to facilitate positive changes in a person's personality, behavior, or adjustment.

Psychotic disorder A severe mental disorder characterized by a retreat from reality, by hallucinations and delusions, and by social withdrawal.

PsycINFO A searchable online database that provides brief summaries of the scientific and scholarly literature in psychology.

Puberty The biologically defined period during which a person matures sexually and becomes capable of reproduction.

Public distance Distance at which formal interactions, such as giving a speech, occur (about 12 feet or more from the body).

Public self-consciousness Intense awareness of oneself as a social object.

Punisher Any event that decreases the probability or frequency of responses it follows.

Punishment Any event that follows a response and *decreases* its likelihood of occurring again.

Pupil The opening at the front of the eye through which light passes.

Quality circle An employee discussion group that makes suggestions for improving quality and solving business problems.

Racism Racial prejudice that has become institutionalized (that is, it is reflected in government policy, schools, and so forth) and that is enforced by the existing social power structure.

Random assignment The use of chance (for example, flipping a coin) to assign subjects to experimental and control groups.

Random search strategy Trying possible solutions to a problem in a more or less random order.

Random selection Choosing a sample so that each member of the population has an equal chance of being included in the sample.

Random search strategy Trying possible solutions to a problem in a more or less random order.

Range The difference between the highest and lowest scores in a group of scores.

Rape myths False beliefs about rape that tend to blame the victim and increase the likelihood that some men will think that rape is justified.

Rapid eye movements (REMs) Swift eye movements during sleep.

Rating scale A list of personality traits or aspects of behavior on which a person is rated.

Rational-emotive behavior therapy (REBT) An approach that states that irrational beliefs cause many emotional problems and that such beliefs must be changed or abandoned.

Rationalization Justifying your behavior by giving reasonable and "rational," but false, reasons for it.

Reaction formation Preventing dangerous impulses from being expressed in behavior by exaggerating opposite behavior.

Reaction range The limits environment places on the effects of heredity.

Readiness A condition that exists when maturation has advanced enough to allow the rapid acquisition of a particular skill.

Reality principle Delaying action (or pleasure) until it is appropriate.

Reality testing Obtaining additional information to check on the accuracy of perceptions.

Recall To supply or reproduce memorized information with a minimum of external cues.

Recessive gene A gene whose influence will be expressed only when it is paired with a second recessive gene.

Receptor sites Areas on the surface of neurons and other cells that are sensitive to neurotransmitters or hormones.

Reciprocal inhibition The presence of one emotional state can inhibit the occurrence of another, such as joy preventing fear or anxiety inhibiting pleasure.

Recoding Reorganizing or modifying information to assist storage in memory.

Recognition memory An ability to correctly identify previously learned information.

Rectum The lowest section of the large intestine.

Redintegration (ruh-DIN-tuh-GRAY-shun) Process by which memories are reconstructed or expanded by starting with one memory and then following chains of association to other, related memories.

Reference group Any group that an individual uses as a standard for social comparison.

Referent power Social power gained when one is used as a point of reference by others.

Referred pain Pain that is felt in one part of the body but comes from another.

Reflection In client-centered therapy, the process of rephrasing or repeating thoughts and feelings expressed by clients so they can become aware of what they are saying.

Reflective cognition Style of thinking arising while actively thinking about an experience.

Reflex An innate, automatic response to a stimulus; for example, an eyeblink.

Reflex arc The simplest behavior, in which a stimulus provokes an automatic response.

Refractory period A short period after orgasm during which males are unable to again reach orgasm.

Refusal skills training Program that teaches youths how to resist pressures to begin smoking. (Can also be applied to other drugs and health risks.)

Regression Retreating to an earlier level of development or to earlier, less demanding habits or situations.

Reinforcement Any event that increases the probability that a particular response will occur.

Reinforcement value The subjective value a person attaches to a particular activity or reinforcer.

Relational concept A concept defined by the relationship between features of an object or between an object and its surroundings (for example, "greater than," "lopsided").

Relaxation response The pattern of internal bodily changes that occurs at times of relaxation.

Relearning Learning again something that was previously learned. Used to measure memory of prior learning.

Reliability The ability of a test to yield nearly the same score each time it is given to the same person.

REM behavior disorder A failure of normal muscle paralysis, leading to violent actions during REM sleep.

REM rebound The occurrence of extra rapid eye movement sleep following REM sleep deprivation.

REM sleep Sleep marked by rapid eye movements and a return to stage 1 EEG patterns.

Reminding system Pain based on small nerve fibers; reminds the brain that the body has been injured.

Replicate To reproduce or repeat.

Representative sample A small, randomly selected part of a larger population that accurately reflects characteristics of the whole population.

Representativeness heuristic (hew-RIS-tik) A tendency to select wrong answers because they seem to match pre-existing mental categories.

Repression The unconscious process by which memories, thoughts, or impulses are held out of awareness.

Research method A systematic approach to answering scientific questions.

Research participant bias Changes in the behavior of research participants caused by the unintended influence of their own expectations.

Researcher bias Changes in participants' behavior caused by the unintended influence of a researcher's actions.

Resistance A blockage in the flow of free association; topics the client resists thinking or talking about.

Resolution The fourth phase of sexual response, involving a return to lower levels of sexual tension and arousal.

Respondent reinforcement Reinforcement that occurs when an unconditioned stimulus closely follows a conditioned stimulus.

Response Any muscular action, glandular activity, or other identifiable aspect of behavior.

Response chaining The assembly of separate responses into a series of actions that lead to reinforcement.

Response cost Removal of a positive reinforcer after a response is made.

Resting potential The electrical charge of a neuron at rest.

Restless legs syndrome An irresistible urge to move the legs to relieve sensations of creeping, tingling, prickling, aching, or tension.

Restricted Environmental Stimulation Therapy (REST) A form of sensory deprivation that results in a variety of psychological benefits.

Results The outcome of the investigation is presented. Data may be graphed, summarized in tables, or statistically analyzed.

Reticular (reh-TICK-you-ler) **activating system (RAS)** A part of the reticular formation that activates the cerebral cortex.

Reticular (reh-TICK-you-ler) **formation (RF)** A network within the medulla and brainstem; associated with attention, alertness, and some reflexes.

Retina The light-sensitive layer of cells at the back of the eye.

Retrieval Recovering information from storage in memory.

Retroactive (RET-ro-AK-tiv) **interference** The tendency for new memories to interfere with the retrieval of old memories.

Reward Anything that produces pleasure or satisfaction; a positive reinforcer.

Reward power Social power based on the capacity to reward a person for acting as desired.

Rods Visual receptors for dim light that produce only black and white sensations.

Role conflict Trying to occupy two or more roles that make conflicting demands on behavior.

Role reversal Taking the role of another person to learn how one's own behavior appears from the other person's perspective.

Romantic love Love that is associated with high levels of interpersonal attraction, heightened arousal, mutual absorption, and sexual desire.

Rorschach (ROAR-shock) **Technique** A projective test comprised of ten standardized inkblots.

Rote learning Learning that takes place mechanically, through repetition and memorization, or by learning rules.

Run of luck A statistically unusual outcome (as in getting 5 heads in a row when flipping a coin) that could still occur by chance alone.

Saltatory conduction The process by which nerve impulses conducted down the axons of neurons coated with myelin jump from gap to gap in the myelin layer.

Sample A smaller subpart of a population.

Satisficing Engaging in behavior that achieves a minimum result, rather than maximizing the outcome of that behavior.

Scaffolding The process of adjusting instruction so that it is responsive to a beginner's behavior and supports the beginner's efforts to understand a problem or gain a mental skill.

Scapegoating Blaming a person or a group of people for conditions not of their making.

Scatter diagram A graph that plots the intersection of paired measures; that is, the points at which paired X and Y measures cross.

Schachter's cognitive theory States that emotions occur when physical arousal is labeled or interpreted on the basis of experience and situational cues.

Schedule of reinforcement A rule or plan for determining which responses will be reinforced.

Schizophrenia A psychosis characterized by delusions, hallucinations, apathy, and a "split" between thought and emotion.

Scientific jury selection Using social science principles to choose members of a jury.

Scientific method A form of critical thinking based on careful measurement and controlled observation.

Scientific observation An empirical investigation structured to answer questions about the world in a systematic and intersubjective fashion (observations can be reliably confirmed by multiple observers).

Scrotum (SKROE-tehm) The sac-like pouch that holds the testes.

Seasonal affective disorder (SAD) Depression that occurs only during fall and winter; presumably related to decreased exposure to sunlight.

Secondary appraisal Deciding how to cope with a threat or challenge.

Secondary elaboration Making a dream more logical and complete while remembering it.

Secondary reinforcer A learned reinforcer; often one that gains reinforcing properties by association with a primary reinforcer.

Secondary sexual characteristics Sexual features other than the genitals and reproductive organs—breasts, body shape, facial hair, and so forth.

Secondary traits Traits that are inconsistent or relatively superficial.

Secure attachment A stable and positive emotional bond.

Selective attention Giving priority to a particular incoming sensory message.

Selective perception Perceiving only certain stimuli among a larger array of possibilities.

Self A continuously evolving conception of one's personal identity.

Self archetype An unconscious image representing unity, wholeness, completion, and balance.

Self-actualization The ongoing process of fully developing one's personal potential.

Self-assertion A direct, honest expression of feelings and desires.

Self-concept A person's perception of his or her own personality traits.

Self-disclosure The process of revealing private thoughts, feelings, and one's personal history to others.

Self-efficacy Belief in your capacity to produce a desired result.

Self-esteem Regarding oneself as a worthwhile person; a positive evaluation of oneself.

Self-fulfilling prophecy An expectation that prompts people to act in ways that make the expectation come true.

Self-handicapping Arranging to perform under conditions that usually impair performance, so as to have an excuse for a poor showing.

Self-help group A group of people who share a particular type of problem and provide mutual support to one another.

Self-image Total subjective perception of one's body and personality (another term for self-concept).

Self-managed team A work group that has a high degree of freedom with respect to how it achieves its goals.

Self-recording Self-management based on keeping records of response frequencies.

Self-reference The practice of relating of new information to prior life experience.

Self-reflective SQ4R method An active study-reading technique based on these steps: survey, question, read, recite, reflect, and review.

Self-regulated learning Deliberately self-reflective and active self-guided study.

Self-reinforcement Praising or rewarding oneself for having made a particular response (such as completing a school assignment).

Self-testing Evaluating learning by posing questions to yourself.

Semantic memory A subpart of declarative memory that records impersonal knowledge about the world.

Semantics The study of meanings in words and language.

Seminal vesicles (SEM-in-uhl VES-ih-kuhlz) These two small organs (one on each side of the prostate) supply fluid that becomes part of semen.

Sensate focus A form of therapy that directs a couple's attention to natural sensations of sexual pleasure.

Sensation A sensory impression; also, the process of detecting physical energies with the sensory organs.

Sensitive period During development, a period of increased sensitivity to environmental influences. Also, a time during which certain events must take place for normal development to occur.

Sensitivity group A group experience consisting of exercises designed to increase self-awareness and sensitivity to others.

Sensorimotor stage Stage of intellectual development during which sensory input and motor responses become coordinated.

Sensorineural hearing loss Loss of hearing caused by damage to the inner ear hair cells or auditory nerve.

Sensory adaptation A decrease in sensory response to an unchanging stimulus.

Sensory analysis Separation of sensory information into important elements.

Sensory coding Codes used by the sense organs to transmit information to the brain.

Sensory conflict theory Explains motion sickness as the result of a mismatch between information from vision, the vestibular system, and kinesthesis.

Sensory deprivation (SD) Any major reduction in the amount or variety of sensory stimulation.

Sensory gating Alteration of sensory messages in the spinal cord.

Sensory memory The first stage of memory, which holds an exact record of incoming information for a few seconds or less.

Sensory neuron A nerve cell that carries information from the senses toward the CNS.

Separation anxiety Distress displayed by infants when they are separated from their parents or principal caregivers.

Serial position effect The tendency to make the most errors in remembering the middle items of an ordered list.

Set point (for fat) The proportion of body fat that tends to be maintained by changes in hunger and eating.

Sex One's biological classification as female or male.

Sex drive The strength of one's motivation to engage in sexual behavior.

Sexism Institutionalized prejudice against members of either sex, based solely on their gender.

Sexual and gender identity disorders Any of a wide range of difficulties with sexual identity, deviant sexual behavior, or sexual adjustment.

Sexual aversion Persistent feelings of fear, anxiety, or disgust about engaging in sex.

Sexual masochism Desiring pain and/or humiliation as part of the sex act.

Sexual orientation One's degree of emotional and erotic attraction to members of the same sex, opposite sex, or both sexes.

Sexual sadism Deriving sexual pleasure from inflicting pain and/or humiliation.

Sexual script An unspoken mental plan that defines a "plot," dialogue, and actions expected to take place in a sexual encounter.

Sexually transmitted disease (STD) A disease that is typically passed from one person to the next by intimate physical contact; a venereal disease.

Shape constancy The perceived shape of an object is unaffected by changes in its retinal image.

Shaping Gradually molding responses to a final desired pattern.

Shared leadership (Participative management) A leadership approach that allows employees at all levels to participate in decision making.

Short-term memory (STM) The memory system used to hold small amounts of information for relatively brief time periods.

Shyness A tendency to avoid others plus uneasiness and strain when socializing.

Sidedness A combination of preference for hand, foot, eye, and ear.

Signal In early language development, any behavior, such as touching, vocalizing, gazing, or smiling, that allows nonverbal interaction and turn-taking between parent and child.

Simultaneous color contrast Changes in perceived hue that occur when a colored stimulus is displayed on backgrounds of various colors.

Single-blind experiment An arrangement in which participants remain unaware of whether they are in the experimental group or the control group.

Situational demands Unstated expectations that define desirable or appropriate behavior in various settings and social situations.

Situational determinants External conditions that strongly influence behavior.

Situational judgment test Presenting realistic work situations to applicants in order to observe their skills and reactions.

Situational test Simulating real-life conditions so that a person's reactions may be directly observed.

Size constancy The perceived size of an object remains constant, despite changes in its retinal image.

Size-distance invariance The strict relationship between the distance an object lies from the eyes and the size of its image.

Skin receptors Sensory organs for touch, pressure, pain, cold, and warmth.

Skin senses The senses of touch, pressure, pain, heat, and cold.

Sleep apnea (AP-nee-ah) Repeated interruption of breathing during sleep.

Sleep deprivation Being prevented from getting desired or needed amounts of sleep.

Sleep drunkenness A slow transition to clear consciousness after awakening; sometimes associated with irritable or aggressive behavior.

Sleep hormone A sleep-promoting substance found in the brain and spinal cord.

Sleep patterns The order and timing of daily sleep and waking periods.

Sleep spindles Distinctive bursts of brain-wave activity that indicate a person is asleep.

Sleep stages Levels of sleep identified by brain-wave patterns and behavioral changes.

Sleep terror disorder The repeated occurrence of night terrors that significantly disturb sleep.

Sleep-deprivation psychosis A major disruption of mental and emotional functioning brought about by sleep loss.

Sleep-wake schedule disorder A mismatch between the sleep-wake schedule demanded by a person's bodily rhythm and that demanded by the environment.

Sleepwalking disorder Repeated incidents of leaving bed and walking about while asleep.

Social anxiety A feeling of apprehension in the presence of others.

Social comparison Making judgments about ourselves through comparison with others.

Social competition Rivalry among groups, each of which regards itself as superior to others.

Social development The development of self-awareness, attachment to parents or caregivers, and relationships with other children and adults.

Social dilemma A social situation that tends to provide immediate rewards for actions that will have undesired effects in the long run.

Social distance Distance at which impersonal interaction takes place (about 4 to 12 feet from the body).

Social distance scale A rating of the degree to which a person would be willing to have contact with a member of another group.

Social environment An environment defined by a group of people and their activities or interrelationships (such as a parade, revival meeting, or sports event).

Social exchange Any exchange between two people of attention, information, affection, favors, or the like.

Social exchange theory Theory stating that rewards must exceed costs for relationships to endure.

Social facilitation The tendency to perform better when in the presence of others.

Social influence Changes in a person's behavior induced by the presence or actions of others.

Social learning theory Combines learning principles with cognitive processes, socialization, and modeling to explain behavior.

Social loafing The tendency for people to work less hard when part of a group than when they are solely responsible for their work.

Social motives Learned motives acquired as part of growing up in a particular society or culture.

Social nonconformity Failure to conform to societal norms or the usual minimum standards for social conduct.

Social norms Rules that define acceptable and expected behavior for members of a group.

Social phobia An intense, irrational fear of being observed, evaluated, embarrassed, or humiliated by others in social situations.

Social power The capacity to control, alter, or influence the behavior of another person.

Social psychology The scientific study of how individuals behave, think, and feel in social situations.

Social Readjustment Rating Scale (SRRS) A scale that rates the impact of various life events on the likelihood of illness.

Social reinforcement Praise, attention, approval, and/or affection from others.

Social reinforcer Reinforcement based on receiving attention, approval, or affection from another person.

Social role Expected behavior patterns associated with particular social positions (such as daughter, worker, student).

Social smile Smiling elicited by social stimuli, such as seeing a parent's face.

Social stereotypes Oversimplified images of the traits of individuals who belong to a particular social group.

Social support Close, positive relationships with other people.

Sociocultural perspective The focus on the importance of social and cultural contexts in influencing the behavior of individuals.

Soma (SOH-mah) The main body of a neuron or other cell.

Somatic nervous system (SNS) The system of nerves linking the spinal cord with the body and sense organs.

Somatic pain Pain from the skin, muscles, joints, and tendons.

Somatic therapy Any bodily therapy, such as drug therapy, electroconvulsive therapy, or psychosurgery.

Somatization (som-ah-tuh-ZAY-shun) **disorder** Afflicted persons have numerous physical complaints. Typically, they have consulted many doctors, but no organic cause for their distress can be identified.

Somatoform (so-MAT-oh-form) **disorder** Physical symptoms that mimic disease or injury for which there is no identifiable physical cause.

Somesthetic senses Sensations produced by the skin, muscles, joints, viscera, and organs of balance.

Somnambulism Sleepwalking; occurs during NREM sleep.

Somnambulists (som-NAM-bue-lists) People who sleepwalk; occurs during NREM sleep.

Source traits Basic underlying traits, or dimensions, of personality; each source trait is reflected in a number of surface traits.

Spaced practice A practice schedule that alternates study periods with brief rests.

Specific goal A goal with a clearly defined and measurable outcome.

Specific phobia An intense, irrational fear of specific objects, activities, or situations.

Spinal nerves Major nerves that carry sensory and motor messages in and out of the spinal cord.

"Split-brain" operation Cutting the corpus callosum.

Spontaneous recovery The reappearance of a learned response after its apparent extinction.

Sports psychology Study of the psychological and behavioral dimensions of sports performance.

Squeeze technique A method for inhibiting ejaculation by compressing the tip of the penis.

Stage ESP The simulation of ESP for the purpose of entertainment.

Stage hypnosis Use of hypnosis to entertain; often, merely a simulation of hypnosis for that purpose.

Stage of exhaustion Third stage of the GAS, at which time the body's resources are exhausted and serious health consequences occur.

Stage of resistance Second stage of the GAS, during which bodily adjustments to stress stabilize, but at a high physical cost.

Standard deviation An index of how much a typical score differs from the mean of a group of scores.

State-dependent learning Memory influenced by one's bodily state at the time of learning and at the time of retrieval. Improved memory occurs when the bodily states match.

Statistical abnormality Abnormality defined on the basis of an extreme score on some dimension, such as IQ or anxiety.

Statistical significance The degree to which an event (such as the results of an experiment) is unlikely to have occurred by chance alone.

Status An individual's position in a social structure, especially with respect to power, privilege, or importance.

Status inequalities Differences in the power, prestige, or privileges of two or more persons or groups.

Stereoscopic vision Perception of space and depth caused chiefly by the fact that the eyes receive different images.

Sterilization Medical procedures such as vasectomy or tubal ligation that make a man or a woman infertile.

Stimulant (upper) A substance that increases activity in the body and nervous system.

Stimulus Any physical energy sensed by an organism.

Stimulus control Stimuli present when an operant response is acquired tend to control when and where the response is made.

Stimulus discrimination The learned ability to respond differently to similar stimuli.

Stimulus drives Drives based on needs for exploration, manipulation, curiosity, and stimulation.

Stimulus generalization The tendency to respond to stimuli similar to, but not identical to, a conditioned stimulus.

Stimulus motives Innate needs for stimulation and information.

Storage Holding information in memory for later use.

Stress The mental and physical condition that occurs when a person must adjust or adapt to the environment.

Stress disorder A significant emotional disturbance caused by stresses outside the range of normal human experience.

Stress inoculation Use of positive coping statements to control fear and anxiety.

Stress management The application of behavioral strategies to reduce stress and improve coping skills.

Stress reaction The physical response to stress, consisting mainly of bodily changes related to autonomic nervous system arousal.

Stressor A specific condition or event in the environment that challenges or threatens a person.

Stress-vulnerability model Attributes mental disorder like psychosis to a combination of environmental stress and inherited susceptibility.

Striving for superiority According to Adler, this basic drive propels us toward perfection.

Stroboscopic (strobe-oh-SKOP-ik) **movement** Illusion of movement in which an object is shown in a rapidly changing series of positions.

Structuralism The school of thought concerned with analyzing sensations and personal experience into basic elements.

Style of life The pattern of personality and behavior that defines the pathway each person takes through life.

Subcortex All brain structures below the cerebral cortex.

Subjective experience Reality as it is perceived and interpreted, not as it exists objectively.

Subjective well-being General life satisfaction combined with frequent positive emotions and relatively few negative emotions.

Sublimation (sub-lih-MAY-shun) Working off unmet desires, or unacceptable impulses, in activities that are constructive.

Subliminal perception Perception of a stimulus below the threshold for conscious recognition.

Substance-related disorder Abuse of or dependence on a mood- or behavior-altering drug.

Sudden infant death syndrome (SIDS) The sudden, unexplained death of an apparently healthy infant.

Superego A judge or censor for thoughts and actions.

Superordinate goal A goal that exceeds or overrides all others; a goal that renders other goals relatively less important.

Superstitious behavior A behavior repeated because it seems to produce reinforcement, even though it is actually unnecessary.

Suppression A conscious effort to put something out of mind or to keep it from awareness.

Surface traits The visible or observable traits of one's personality.

Survey method The use of public polling techniques to answer psychological questions.

Surrogate mother A substitute mother (often an inanimate dummy in animal research).

Symbolic prejudice Prejudice that is expressed in disguised fashion.

Symbolization The nonliteral expression of dream content.

Sympathetic branch The part of the ANS that activates the body at times of stress.

Synapse (SIN-aps) The microscopic space between two neurons, over which messages pass.

Syntax Rules for ordering words when forming sentences.

Systematic desensitization A reduction in fear, anxiety, or aversion brought about by planned exposure to aversive stimuli.

Task analysis Breaking complex skills into their subparts.

Taste aversion An active dislike for a particular food.

Taste bud The receptor organ for taste.

Teaching strategy A plan for effective teaching.

Telecommuting An approach to flexible work that involves working from home but using a computer to stay connected to the office throughout the workday.

Telepathy The purported ability to directly know another person's thoughts.

Temperament The physical core of personality, including emotional and perceptual sensitivity, energy levels, typical mood, and so forth.

Temporal lobes Areas that include the sites where hearing registers in the brain.

Tension-release method A procedure for systematically achieving deep relaxation of the body.

Teratogen (teh-RAT-uh-jen) Radiation, a drug, or other substance capable of altering fetal development in nonheritable ways that cause birth defects.

Term schedule A written plan that lists the dates of all major assignments for each of your classes for an entire semester or quarter.

Territorial behavior Any behavior that tends to define a space as one's own or that protects it from intruders.

Territorial markers Objects and other signals whose placement indicates to others the "ownership" or control of a particular area.

Test anxiety High levels of arousal and worry that seriously impair test performance.

Testis (TES-tis, singular; testes, plural) One of the two male reproductive glands; the testes are a source of hormones and sperm.

Testosterone (tes-TOSS-teh-rone) A male sex hormone, secreted mainly by the testes and responsible for the development of many male sexual characteristics.

Thalamus (THAL-uh-mus) A brain structure that relays sensory information to the cerebral cortex.

Thanatologist (THAN-ah-TOL-oh-jist) A specialist who studies emotional and behavioral reactions to death and dying.

Thanatos The death instinct.

Thematic Apperception Test (TAT) A projective test consisting of 20 different scenes and life situations about which respondents make up stories.

Theory A system of ideas designed to interrelate concepts and facts in a way that summarizes existing data and predicts future observations.

Theory X leadership (scientific management) An approach to leadership that emphasizes work efficiency.

Theory Y leadership A leadership style that emphasizes human relations at work and that views people as industrious, responsible, and interested in challenging work.

Therapeutic alliance A caring relationship that unites a therapist and a client in working to solve the client's problems.

Therapy placebo effect Improvement caused not by the actual process of therapy but by a client's expectation that therapy will help.

Thought stopping Use of aversive stimuli to interrupt or prevent upsetting thoughts.

Threshold The point at which a nerve impulse is triggered.

Thyroid gland Endocrine gland that helps regulate the rate of metabolism.

Tip-of-the-tongue (TOT) state The feeling that a memory is available but not quite retrievable.

Token economy A therapeutic program in which desirable behaviors are reinforced with tokens that can be exchanged for goods, services, activities, and privileges.

Token reinforcer A tangible secondary reinforcer such as money, gold stars, poker chips, and the like.

Top-down processing Applying higher level knowledge to rapidly organize sensory information into a meaningful perception.

Tragedy of the commons A social dilemma in which individuals, each acting in his or her immediate self-interest, overuse a scarce group resource.

Trait profile A graph of the scores obtained on several personality traits.

Trait theorist A psychologist interested in classifying, analyzing, and interrelating traits to understand personality.

Trait–situation interaction The influence that external settings or circumstances have on the expression of personality traits.

Tranquilizer A drug that lowers anxiety and reduces tension.

Transducers Devices that convert one kind of energy into another

Transference The tendency of patients to transfer feelings to a therapist that correspond to those the patient had for important persons in his or her past.

Transformation The mental ability to change the shape or form of a substance (such as clay or water) and to perceive that its volume remains the same.

Transformation rules Rules by which a simple declarative sentence may be changed to other voices or forms (past tense, passive voice, and so forth).

Transition period Time span during which a person leaves an existing life pattern behind and moves into a new pattern.

Transsexual A person with a deep conflict between his or her biological sex and preferred psychological and social gender roles.

Transvestic fetishism Achieving sexual arousal by wearing clothing of the opposite sex.

Traumatic stresses Extreme events that cause psychological injury or intense emotional pain.

Trichromatic theory Theory of color vision based on three cone types: red, green, and blue.

Trust versus mistrust A conflict early in life about learning to trust others and the world.

Twin study A comparison of the characteristics of twins who were raised together or separated at birth; used to identify the relative impact of heredity and environment.

Two-way bilingual education A program in which English-speaking children and children with limited English proficiency are taught half the day in English and half in a second language.

Type A personality A personality type with an elevated risk for heart disease; characterized by time urgency, anger, and hostility.

Type B personality All personality types other than Type A; a low-cardiac-risk personality.

Unconditional positive regard An unqualified, unshakable acceptance of another person.

Unconditioned response (UR) An innate reflex response elicited by an unconditioned stimulus.

Unconditioned stimulus (US) A stimulus innately capable of eliciting a response.

Unconscious Contents of the mind that are beyond awareness, especially impulses and desires not directly known to a person.

Uncritical acceptance The tendency to believe generally positive or flattering descriptions of oneself.

Understanding In problem solving, a deeper comprehension of the nature of the problem. In psychology, understanding is achieved when the causes of a behavior can be stated.

Undifferentiated schizophrenia Schizophrenia lacking the specific features of catatonic, disorganized, or paranoid types.

Upward comparison Comparing yourself with a person who ranks higher than you on some dimension.

Urethra (yoo-REE-thra) The tube through which urine drains as it leaves the body. In males, semen also passes through the urethra.

Urinary bladder The sac that collects urine before it is eliminated from the body.

Usability testing The empirical investigation of the ease with which users can learn to use a machine.

Uterus (YOO-ter-us) The pear-shaped muscular organ in which the fetus develops during pregnancy; also known as the womb.

Vagina (vah-JINE-ah) Tube-like structure connecting the external female genitalia with the uterus.

Vaginismus (VAJ-ih-NIS-mus) Muscle spasms of the vagina.

Validity The ability of a test to measure what it purports to measure.

Validity scales Scales that tell whether test scores should be invalidated for lying, inconsistency, or "faking good."

Variable Any condition that changes or can be made to change; a measure, event, or state that may vary.

Variability The tendency for a group of scores to differ in value. Measures of variability indicate the degree to which a group of scores differ from one another.

Variable interval (VI) schedule A reinforcer is given for the first correct response made after a varied amount of time has passed since the last reinforced response. Responses made during the time interval are not reinforced.

Variable ratio (VR) schedule A varied number of correct responses must be made to get a reinforcer. For example, a reinforcer is given after three to seven correct responses; the actual number changes randomly.

Vas deferens (vaz DEH-fur-enz) The duct that carries sperm from the testes to the urethra.

Verbal intelligence Intelligence measured by answering questions involving vocabulary, general information, arithmetic, and other language- or symbol-oriented tasks.

Vestibular senses The senses of balance, position in space, and acceleration.

Vicarious classical conditioning Classical conditioning brought about by observing another person react to a particular stimulus.

Vicarious desensitization A reduction in fear or anxiety that takes place vicariously ("secondhand") when a client watches models perform the feared behavior.

Virtual reality exposure Use of computer-generated images to present fear stimuli. The virtual environment responds to a viewer's head movements and other inputs.

Visceral pain Pain originating in the internal organs.

Visible spectrum The narrow spread of the electromagnetic spectrum to which the eyes are sensitive.

Visual acuity The sharpness of visual perception.

Visual agnosia (ag-KNOW-zyah) Inability to identify seen objects.

Vocational interest test A paper-and-pencil test that assesses a person's interests and matches them to interests found among successful workers in various occupations.

Voyeurism "Peeping," or viewing the genitals of others without their permission.

Waking consciousness A state of clear, organized alertness.

Warning system Pain based on large nerve fibers; warns that bodily damage may be occurring.

Weapons effect The observation that weapons serve as strong cues for aggressive behavior.

Weber's law The just noticeable difference is a constant proportion of the original stimulus intensity.

Weekly time schedule A written plan that allocates time for study, work, and leisure activities during a one-week period.

Wellness A positive state of good health; more than the absence of disease.

Wernicke's (VER-nick-ees) **area** A temporal lobe brain area related to language comprehension.

Wish fulfillment Freudian belief that many dreams express unconscious desires.

Withdrawal of love Withholding affection to enforce child discipline.

Withdrawal symptoms Physical illness and discomfort following the withdrawal of a drug.

Work efficiency Maximum output (productivity) at lowest cost

Working memory Another name for short-term memory, especially when it is used for thinking and problem solving.

World Wide Web (WWW) A system of information "sites" accessible through the Internet.

X chromosome The female chromosome contributed by the mother; produces a female when paired with another X chromosome, and a male when paired with a Y chromosome.

Y chromosome The male chromosome contributed by the father; produces a male when paired with an X chromosome. Fathers may give either an X or a Y chromosome to their offspring.

Yerkes-Dodson law A summary of the relationships among arousal, task complexity, and performance.

You-message Threatening, accusing, bossing, lecturing, or criticizing another person.

Zener cards A deck of 25 cards bearing various symbols and used in early parapsychological research.

Zero correlation The absence of a (linear) mathematical relationship between two measures.

Zone of proximal development Refers to the range of tasks a child cannot yet master alone, but that she or he can accomplish with the guidance of a more capable partner.

z-Score A number that tells how many standard deviations above or below the mean a score is.

Abe, N., Suzuki, M., Mori, E., et al. (2007). Deceiving others: Distinct neural responses of the prefrontal cortex and amygdala in simple fabrication and deception with social interactions. *Journal of Cognitive Neuroscience, 19*(2), 287–295.

Abraham, W. C. (2006). Memory maintenance: The changing nature of neural mechanisms. *Current Directions in Psychological Science, 15*(1), 5–8.

Abrahamse, W., Steg, L., Vlek, C., & Rothengatter, T. (2005). A review of intervention studies aimed at household energy conservation. *Journal of Environmental Psychology, 25*(3), 273–291.

Abrams, D. B., Brown, R., Niaura, R. S., et al. (2003). *The tobacco dependence treatment handbook: A guide to best practices.* New York: Guilford.

Accordino, D. B., Accordino, M. P., & Slaney, R. B. (2000). An investigation of perfectionism, mental health, achievement, and achievement motivation in adolescents. *Psychology in the Schools, 37*(6), 535–545.

ACT Against Violence. (2005a). *Facts related to media violence.* Washington, DC: Adults and Children Together Against Violence. Retrieved October 18, 2006, from http://www.actagainstviolence.com/materials/handouts/FamilyMV1.pdf.

ACT Against Violence. (2005b). *Early violence prevention.* Washington, DC: Adults and Children Together Against Violence. Retrieved October 18, 2006, from http://www.actagainstviolence.com/violprevent/index.html.

Adams, J. (2001). *Conceptual blockbusting* (4th ed.). New York: Basic Books.

Adamson, K. (2004). *Kate's journey: Triumph over adversity.* Redondo Beach, CA: Nosmada Press.

Addis, K. M., & Kahana, M. J. (2004). Decomposing serial learning: What is missing from the learning curve? *Psychonomic Bulletin & Review, 11*(1), 118–174.

Adler, S. A., & Orprecio, J. (2006). The eyes have it: Visual pop-out in infants and adults. *Developmental Science, 9,* 189–206.

Adolphs, R. (2008). Fear, faces, and the human amygdala. *Current Opinion in Neurobiology, 18*(2), 166–172.

Adorno, T. W., Frenkel-Brunswik, E., Levinson, D. J., & Sanford, R. N. (1950). *The authoritarian personality.* New York: Harper.

Advisory Council on the Misuse of Drugs. (2009). *MDMA ('ecstasy'): A review of its harms and classification under the Misuse of Drugs Act 1971.* Retrieved April 10, 2009, from http://drugs.homeoffice.gov.uk/publication-search/acmd/mdma-report?view=Binary.

Afifi, T. O., Brownridge, D. A., Cox, B. J., & Sareen, J. (2006). Physical punishment, childhood abuse and psychiatric disorders. *Child Abuse & Neglect, 30*(10), 1093–1103.

Ahima, R. S., & Osei, S. Y. (2004). Leptin signaling. *Physiology & Behavior, 81,* 223–241.

Ajzen, I. (2005). *Attitudes, personality and behaviour* (2nd ed.). New York: McGraw-Hill.

Åkerstedt, T. (2007). Altered sleep/wake patterns and mental performance. *Physiology & Behavior, 90*(2-3), 209–218.

Albarracín, D., Johnson, B. T., & Zanna, M. P. (Eds.). (2005). *The handbook of attitudes.* Mahwah, NJ: Erlbaum.

Alberti, R., & Emmons, M. (2008). *Your perfect right* (9th ed.). San Luis Obispo, CA: Impact.

Alberto, P. A., & Troutman, A. C. (2009). *Applied behavior analysis for teachers* (8th ed.). Englewood Cliffs, NJ: Prentice Hall.

Alcock, J. E. (2003). Give the null hypothesis a chance: Reasons to remain doubtful about the existence of psi. *Journal of Consciousness Studies, 10*(6-7), 29–50.

Alcock, J. E., Burns, J., & Freeman, A. (2003). *Psi wars: Getting to grips with the paranormal.* Exeter, UK: Imprint Academic Press.

Allen, D., Carlson, D., & Ham, C. (2007). Well-being: New paradigms of wellness-inspiring positive health outcomes and renewing hope. *American Journal of Health Promotion, 21*(3), 1–9.

Allen, K., Blascovich, J., & Mendes, W. B. (2002). Cardiovascular reactivity in the presence of pets, friends, and spouses: The truth about cats and dogs. *Psychosomatic Medicine, 64*(5), 727–739.

Allgower, A., Wardle, J., & Steptoe, A. (2001). Depressive symptoms, social support, and personal health behaviors in young men and women. *Health Psychology, 20*(3), 223–227.

Allik, J. (2000). Available and accessible information in memory and vision. In E. Tulving (Ed.), *Memory, consciousness, and the brain: The Tallinn Conference.* Hove, UK: Psychology Press.

Allport, G. W. (1958). *The nature of prejudice.* Garden City, NY: Anchor Books, Doubleday.

Allport, G. W. (1961). *Pattern and growth in personality.* New York: Holt.

Alsaker, F. D. (1995). Is puberty a critical period for socialization? *Journal of Adolescence, 18*(4), 427–444.

Altemeyer, B. (2004). Highly dominating, highly authoritarian personalities. *Journal of Social Psychology, 144*(4), 421–447.

Altman, L. K. (2002, July 3). AIDS threatens to claim 65M more lives by '20. *Arizona Daily Star,* A7.

Altschuler, G. C. (2001, January 7). Battling the cheats. *The New York Times: Education,* 15.

Alvarado, N. (1994). Empirical validity of the Thematic Apperception Test. *Journal of Personality Assessment, 63*(1), 59–79.

Alvino, J., & the Editors of *Gifted Children Monthly.* (1996). *Parents' guide to raising a gifted child.* New York: Ballantine.

Alwin, D. F., Cohen, R. L., & Newcomb, T. M. (1991). *Political attitudes over the life span: The Bennington women after fifty years.* Madison: University of Wisconsin Press.

Amabile, T., Hadley, C. N., & Kramer, S. J. (2002). Creativity under the gun. *Harvard Business Review, 80*(8), 52–61.

Amato, P. R., & Fowler, F. (2002). Parenting practices, child adjustment, and family diversity. *Journal of Marriage & Family, 64*(3), 703–716.

Ambady, N., & Rosenthal, R. (1993). Half a minute: Predicting teacher evaluations from thin slices of nonverbal behavior and physical attractiveness. *Journal of Personality & Social Psychology, 64,* 431–441.

American Lung Association. (2006). *Smokeless tobacco fact sheet.* Retrieved April 30, 2009, from http://www.lungusa.org/site/c.dvLUK9O0E/b.1694879/k.CFC8/Smokeless_Tobacco_Fact_Sheet.htm.

American Lung Association. (2009). *Secondhand smoke fact sheet.* Retrieved April 20, 2009, from http://www.lungusa.org/site/pp.asp?c=dvLUK9O0E&b=35422.

American Psychiatric Association. (2000). *Diagnostic and statistical manual of mental disorders* (4th ed., text revision). Washington, DC: Author.

American Psychological Association. (2003). Guidelines on multicultural education, training, research, practice, and organizational change for psychologists. *American Psychologist, 58*(5), 377–402.

Ancis, J. R., Chen, Y., & Schultz, D. (2004). Diagnostic challenges and the so-called culture-bound syndromes. In J. R. Ancis (Ed.), *Culturally responsive interventions: Innovative approaches to working with diverse populations.* New York: Brunner-Routledge.

Anderson, C. A. (1989). Temperature and aggression. *Psychological Bulletin, 106,* 74–96.

Anderson, C. A. (2004). An update on the effects of violent video games. *Journal of Adolescence, 27,* 113–122.

Anderson, C. A., & Bushman, B. J. (2001). Effects of violent video games on aggressive behavior, aggressive cognition, aggressive affect, physiological arousal, and prosocial behavior: A meta-analytic review of the scientific literature. *Psychological Science, 12*(5), 353–359.

Anderson, C. A., & Bushman, B. J. (2002). Human aggression. *Annual Review of Psychology, 53*, 27–51.

Anderson, C. A., Anderson, K. B., & Deuser, W. E. (1996). Examining an affective aggression framework. *Personality & Social Psychology Bulletin, 22*(4), 366–376.

Anderson, C. A., Berkowitz, L., Donnerstein, E., et al. (2003). The influence of media violence on youth. *Psychological Science in the Public Interest, 4*(3), 81–110.

Anderson, C. A., Carnagey, N. L., & Eubanks, J. (2003). Exposure to violent media: The effects of songs with violent lyrics on aggressive thoughts and feelings. *Journal of Personality & Social Psychology, 84*(5), 960–971.

Anderson, J. R. (2005). *Cognitive psychology and its implications* (6th ed.). New York: Worth.

Anderson, M. C. (2001). Active forgetting: Evidence for functional inhibition as a source of memory failure. *Journal of Aggression, Maltreatment & Trauma, 4*(2), 185–210.

Anderson, M. C., & Bell, T. (2001). Forgetting our facts: The role of inhibitory processes in the loss of propositional knowledge. *Journal of Experimental Psychology: General, 130*(3), 544–570.

Anderson, M. C., & Green, C. (2001, March 15). Suppressing unwanted memories by executive control. *Nature, 410*, 366–369.

Anderson, M. C., Ochsner, K. N., Kuhl, B., et al. (2004). Neural systems underlying the suppression of unwanted memories. *Science, 303*, 232–235.

Andrasik, F. (2003). Behavioral treatment approaches to chronic headache. *Neurological Sciences, 24*(Suppl. 2), S80–S85.

André, C., Jaber-Filho, J. A., Carvalho, M., et al. (2003). Predictors of recovery following involuntary hospitalization of violent substance abuse patients. *The American Journal on Addictions, 12*(1), 84–89.

Andresen, J. (2000). Meditation meets behavioural medicine: The story of experimental research on meditation. *Journal of Consciousness Studies, 7*(11-12), 17–73.

Andrews, J. D. (1989). Integrating visions of reality. *American Psychologist, 44*(5), 803–817.

Anekonda, T. S. (2006). Resveratrol: A boon for treating Alzheimer's disease? *Brain Research Reviews, 52*(2), 316–326.

Annett, M. (2002). *Handedness and brain asymmetry: The right shift theory.* Hove, UK: Psychology Press.

Annett, M., & Manning, M. (1990). Arithmetic and laterality. *Neuropsychologia, 28*(1), 61–69.

Antle, M. C., & Mistlberger, R. E. (2005). Circadian rhythms. In I. Q. Whishaw & B. Kolb (Eds.), *The behavior of the laboratory rat: A handbook with tests.* London: Oxford.

Antony, M. M. (2004). *10 simple solutions to shyness: How to overcome shyness, social anxiety & fear of public speaking.* Oakland, CA: New Harbinger.

APA (American Psychological Association). (2002). Ethical principles of psychologists and code of conduct. *American Psychologist, 57*, 1060–1073. Retrieved April 21, 2009, from http://www.apa.org/ethics/homepage.html.

APA (American Psychological Association). (2003a). *Demographic shifts in psychology.* American Psychological Association Center for Workplace Studies. Retrieved April 21, 2009, from http://research.apa.org/demoshifts.html.

APA (American Psychological Association). (2003b). *Demographic shifts in psychology.* American Psychological Association Center for Workplace Studies. Retrieved April 21, 2009, from http://research.apa.org/general08.html.

APA (American Psychological Association). (2003c). Guidelines on multicultural education, training, research, practice, and organizational change for psychologists. *American Psychologist, 58*(5), 377–402.

APA (American Psychological Association). (2007). *2007 APA directory survey.* Retrieved April 21, 2009, from http://research.apa.org/profile2007t3.pdf and http://research.apa.org/profile2007t4.pdf.

Arbona, C. B., Osma, J., Garcia-Palacios, A., et al. (2004). Treatment of flying phobia using virtual reality: Data from a 1-year follow-up using a multiple baseline design. *Clinical Psychology & Psychotherapy, 11*(5), 311–323.

Ariely, D., & Wertenbroch, K. (2002). Procrastination, deadlines, and performance: Self-control by precommitment. *Psychological Science, 13*(3), 219–224.

Armeli, S., Gunthert, K. C., & Cohen, L. H. (2001). Stressor appraisals, coping, and post-event outcomes: The dimensionality and antecedents of stress-related growth. *Journal of Social & Clinical Psychology, 20*(3), 366–395.

Arnett, J. J. (2000). Emerging adulthood. *American Psychologist, 55*(5), 469–480.

Arnett, J. J. (2001). Conceptions of the transition to adulthood. *Journal of Adult Development, 8*(2), 133–143.

Arnett, J. J. (2004). *Emerging adulthood: The winding road from late teens through the twenties.* New York: Oxford University Press.

Arnett, J. J., & Galambos, N. L. (Eds.). (2003). *New directions for child and adolescent development: Exploring cultural conceptions of the transition to adulthood.* San Francisco: Jossey-Bass.

Arnett, J. J., & Tanner, J. L. (Eds.). (2006). *Emerging adults in America: Coming of age in the 21st century.* Washington, DC: American Psychological Association.

Aronow, E., Altman Weiss, K., & Reznikoff, M. (2001). *A practical guide to the Thematic Apperception Test: The TAT in clinical practice.* New York: Brunner-Routledge.

Aronson, E. (1969). Some antecedents of interpersonal attraction. In W. J. Arnold & D. Levine (Eds.), *Nebraska symposium on motivation.* Lincoln: University of Nebraska Press.

Aronson, E. (1992). *The social animal.* San Francisco: W. H. Freeman.

Aronson, E. (2008). *The social animal* (10th ed.). New York: Worth.

Aronson, E., Wilson, T. D., & Akert, R. M. (2007). *Social psychology* (6th ed.). Englewood Cliffs, NJ: Prentice Hall.

Arthur, W., & Doverspike, D. (2001). Predicting motor vehicle crash involvement from a personality measure and a driving knowledge test. *Journal of Prevention & Intervention in the Community, 22*(1), 35–42.

Artz, S. (2005). To die for: Violent adolescent girls' search for male attention. In D. J. Pepler, K. C. Madsen, C. D. Webster, & K. S. Levene (Eds.), *The development and treatment of girlhood aggression.* Mahwah, NJ: Erlbaum.

Ary, D. V., Duncan, T. E., Biglan, A., et al. (1999). Development of adolescent problem behavior. *Journal of Abnormal Child Psychology, 27*(2), 141–150.

Asch, S. E. (1956). Studies of independence and conformity: A minority of one against a unanimous majority. *Psychological Monographs, 70* [Whole no. 416].

Ash, D. W., & Holding, D. H. (1990). Backward versus forward chaining in the acquisition of a keyboard skill. *Human Factors, 32*(2), 139–146.

Ashby, F. G., & Maddox, W. T. (2005). Human category learning. *Annual Review of Psychology, 56*, 149–78.

Ashton, M. C. (2007). *Individual differences and personality.* San Diego: Elsevier.

Asmundson, G. J. G., & Taylor, S. (2005). *It's not all in your head.* London: Psychology Press.

Assanand, S., Pinel, J. P. J., & Lehman, D. R. (1998). Personal theories of hunger and eating. *Journal of Applied Social Psychology, 28*(11), 998–1015.

Atkinson, R. C., & Schiffrin, R. M. (1968). Human memory: A proposed system and its control processes. In K. W. Spence & J. T. Spence (Eds.), *The psychology of learning and motivation* (Vol. 2). London: Academic Press.

Aucoin, K. J., Frick, P. J., & Bodin, S. D. (2006). Corporal punishment and child adjustment. *Journal of Applied Developmental Psychology, 27*(6), 527–541.

Avery, D. H., Eder, D. N., Bolte, M. A., et al. (2001). Dawn simulation and bright light in the treatment of SAD. *Biological Psychiatry, 50*(3), 205–216.

Awadallah, N., Vaughan, A., Franco, K., et al. (2005). Munchausen by proxy: A case, chart series, and literature review of older victims. *Child Abuse & Neglect, 29*(8), 931–941.

Ayers, L., Beaton, S., & Hunt, H. (1999). The significance of transpersonal experiences, emotional conflict, and cognitive abilities in creativity. *Empirical Studies of the Arts, 17*(1), 73–82.

Ayllon, T. (1963). Intensive treatment of psychotic behavior by stimulus satiation and food reinforcement. *Behavior Research and Therapy, 1*, 53-61.

Ayllon, T., & Azrin, N. H. (1965). The measurement and reinforcement of behavior of psychotics. *Journal of the Experimental Analysis of Behavior, 8*, 357–383.

Baard, P. P., Deci, E. L., & Ryan, R. M. (2004). Intrinsic need satisfaction: A motivational basis of performance and well-being in two work settings. *Journal of Applied Social Psychology, 34*(10), 2045–2068.

Bachman, J. G., & Johnson, L. D. (1979). The freshmen. *Psychology Today, 13*, 78–87.

Baddeley, A. D. (2003). Working memory: Looking back and looking forward. *Nature Reviews Neuroscience, 4*(10), 829–839.

Baddeley, A., Eysenck, M. W., & Anderson, M. C. (2009). *Memory.* Hove, UK: Psychology Press.

Baer, J. M. (1993). *Creativity and divergent thinking.* Hillsdale, NJ: Erlbaum.

Bailey, C. H., & Kandel, E. R. (2004). Synaptic growth and the persistence of long-term memory: A molecular perspective. In M. S. Gazzaniga (Ed.), *The cognitive neurosciences* (3rd ed.). Cambridge, MA: MIT Press.

Bailey, L. M., & McKeever, W. F. (2004). A large-scale study of handedness and pregnancy/birth risk events: Implications for genetic theories of handedness. *Laterality: Asymmetries of Body, Brain & Cognition, 9*(2), 175–188.

Baillargeon, R. (1991). Reasoning about the height and location of a hidden object in 4.5- and 6.5-month-old infants. *Cognition, 38*(1), 13–42.

Baillargeon, R. (2004). Infants' reasoning about hidden objects: Evidence for event-general and event-specific expectations. *Developmental Science, 7*(4), 391–424.

Baillargeon, R., De Vos, J., & Graber, M. (1989). Location memory in 8-month-old infants in a non-search AB task. *Cognitive Development, 4*, 345–367.

Bain, S. K., & Allin, J. D. (2005). Stanford-Binet Intelligence Scales, Fifth Edition. *Journal of Psychoeducational Assessment, 23*(1), 87–95.

Baker, T. B., Brandon, T. H., & Chassin, L. (2004). Motivational influences on cigarette smoking. *Annual Review of Psychology, 55*, 463–491.

Balk, D. E., Lampe, S., Sharpe, B., et al. (1998). TAT results in a longitudinal study of bereaved college students. *Death Studies, 22*(1), 3–21.

Bandura, A. (1971). *Social learning theory.* New York: General Learning Press.

Bandura, A. (2001). Social cognitive theory: An agentic perspective. *Annual Review of Psychology, 52*, 1–26.

Bandura, A., & Walters, R. (1959). *Adolescent aggression.* New York: Ronald.

Bandura, A., Blanchard, E. B., & Ritter, B. (1969). Relative efficacy of desensitization and modeling approaches for inducing behavioral, affective, and attitudinal changes. *Journal of Personality & Social Psychology, 13*(3), 173–199.

Bandura, A., Ross, D., & Ross, S. A. (1963). Vicarious reinforcement and imitative learning. *Journal of Abnormal and Social Psychology, 67*, 601–607.

Banks, A., & Gartrell, N. K. (1995). Hormones and sexual orientation: A questionable link. *Journal of Homosexuality, 28*(3-4), 247–268.

Barabasz, A. (2000). EEG markers of alert hypnosis. *Sleep & Hypnosis, 2*(4), 164–169.

Barber, T. X. (2000). A deeper understanding of hypnosis: Its secrets, its nature, its essence. *American Journal of Clinical Hypnosis, 42*(3-4), 208–272.

Bard, C., Fleury, M., & Goulet, C. (1994). Relationship between perceptual strategies and response adequacy in sport situations. *International Journal of Sport Psychology, 25*(3), 266–281.

Bargh, J. A., McKenna, K. Y. A., & Fitzsimons, G. M. (2002). Can you see the real me? Activation and expression of the "true self" on the Internet. *Journal of Social Issues, 58*(1), 33–48.

Barkataki, I., Kumari, V., Das, M., et al. (2006). Volumetric structural brain abnormalities in men with schizophrenia or antisocial personality disorder. *Behavioural Brain Research, 169*(2), 239–247.

Barlow, D. H. (2000). Unraveling the mysteries of anxiety and its disorders from the perspective of emotion theory. *American Psychologist, 55*(11), 1247–1263.

Barlow, D. H. (2002). *Anxiety and its disorders* (2nd ed.). New York: Guilford.

Barlow, D. H. (2004). Psychological treatments. *American Psychologist, 59*(9), 869–878.

Barnier, A. J., McConkey, K. M., & Wright, J. (2004). Posthypnotic amnesia for autobiographical episodes: Influencing memory accessibility and quality. *International Journal of Clinical and Experimental Hypnosis, 52*(3), 260–279.

Baron, I. S. (2005). Test review: Wechsler intelligence scale for children (4th ed.). (WISC-IV). *Child Neuropsychology, 11*(5), 471–475.

Baron, R. A., Byrne, D., & Branscombe, N. R. (2007). *Mastering social psychology.* Boston: Pearson/Allyn and Bacon.

Baron, R. A., Byrne, D., & Branscombe, N. R. (2009). *Mastering social psychology* (12th ed.). Boston: Pearson/Allyn and Bacon.

Barrett, D. (1993). The "committee of sleep": A study of dream incubation for problem solving. *Dreaming, 3*(2), 115–122.

Barrett, D., Greenwood, J. G., & McCullagh, J. F. (2006). Kissing laterality and handedness. *Laterality: Asymmetries of Body, Brain & Cognition, 11*(6), 573–579.

Barrick, M. R., Moun, M. K., & Judge, T. A. (2001). Personality and performance at the beginning of the new millennium. *International Journal of Selection & Assessment, 9*(1-2), 9–30.

Barron, F. (1958). The psychology of imagination. *Scientific American, 199*(3), 150–170.

Barrowcliff, A. L., & Haddock, G. (2006). The relationship between command hallucinations and factors of compliance: A critical review of the literature. *Journal of Forensic Psychiatry & Psychology, 17*(2), 266–298.

Bar-Tal, D., & Labin, D. (2001). The effect of a major event on stereotyping: Terrorist attacks in Israel and Israeli adolescents' perceptions of Palestinians, Jordanians and Arabs. *European Journal of Social Psychology, 31*(3), 265–280.

Bartholow, B. D., & Anderson, C. A. (2002). Effects of violent video games on aggressive behavior. *Journal of Experimental Social Psychology, 38*(3), 283–290.

Bartholow, B. D., Bushman, B. J., & Sestir, M. A. (2006). Chronic violent video game exposure and desensitization to violence: Behavioral and event-related brain potential data. *Journal of Experimental Social Psychology, 42*(4), 532–539.

Bartholow, B. D., Sestir, M. A., & Davis, E. B. (2005). Correlates and consequences of exposure to video game violence: Hostile personality, empathy, and aggressive behavior. *Personality & Social Psychology Bulletin, 31*(11), 1573–1586.

Bartram, B. (2006). An examination of perceptions of parental influence on attitudes to language learning. *Educational Research, 48*(2), 211–222.

Basadur, M., Runco, M. A., & Vega, L. A. (2000). Understanding how creative thinking skills, attitudes and behaviors work together. *Journal of Creative Behavior, 34*(2), 77–100.

Basson, R., Brotto, L. A., Laan, E., et al. (2005). Assessment and management of women's sexual dysfunctions: Problematic desire and arousal. *Journal of Sexual Medicine, 2*(3), 291–300.

Bastian, B., & Haslam, N. (2006). Psychological essentialism and stereotype endorsement. *Journal of Experimental Social Psychology, 42*(2), 228–235.

Bath, H. (1996). Everyday discipline or control with care. *Journal of Child & Youth Care, 10*(2), 23–32.

Batson, C. D. (2006). "Not all self-interest after all": Economics of empathy-induced altruism. In D. De Cremer, M. Zeelenberg, & J. K. Murnighan (Eds.), *Social psychology and economics.* Mahwah, NJ: Erlbaum.

Batson, C. D., & Powell, A. A. (2003). Altruism and prosocial behavior. In T. Millon & M. J. Lerner (Eds.), *Handbook of psychology: Personality and social psychology* (Vol. 5). New York: Wiley.

Batterham, R. L., Cohen, M. A., Ellis, S. M., et al. (2003). Inhibition of food intake in obese subjects by peptide YY3–36. *New England Journal of Medicine, 349*, 941–948.

Bauer, J. J., McAdams, D. P., & Pals, J. L. (2008). Narrative identity and eudaimonic well-being. *Journal of Happiness Studies, 9*(1), 81–104.

Baum, A., & Posluszny, D. M. (1999). Health psychology. *Annual Review of Psychology, 50*, 137–163.

Bauman, L. J., Karasz, A., & Hamilton, A. (2007). Understanding failure of condom use intention among adolescents: Completing an intensive preventive intervention. *Journal of Adolescent Research, 22*(3), 248–274.

Baumeister, R. F., & Bushman, B. (2008). *Social psychology and human nature.* Belmont, CA: Cengage Learning/Wadsworth.

Baumeister, R. F., Campbell, J. D., Krueger, J. I., & Vohs, K. D. (2003). Does high self-esteem cause better performance, interpersonal success, happiness, or healthier lifestyles? *Psychological Science in the Public Interest, 4*(1), 1–44.

Baumrind, D. (1991). The influence of parenting style on adolescent competence and substance use. *Journal of Early Adolescence, 11*(1), 56–95.

Baumrind, D. (2005). Patterns of parental authority and adolescent autonomy. In J. Smetana (Ed.), *New directions for child development: Changes in parental authority during adolescence.* San Francisco: Jossey-Bass.

Baumrind, D., Larzelere, R. E., & Cowan, P. A. (2002). Ordinary physical punishment: Is it harmful? *Psychological Bulletin, 128*(4), 580–589.

Bearman, P. S., Moody, J., & Stovel, K. (2004). Chains of affection: The structure of adolescent romantic and sexual networks. *American Journal of Sociology, 110*(1), 44–91.

Beck, A. T. (1991). Cognitive therapy. *American Psychologist, 46*(4), 368–375.

Beck, A. T. (2004). Cognitive patterns in dreams and daydreams. In R. I. Rosner & W. J. Lyddon (Eds.), *Cognitive therapy and dreams.* New York: Springer Publishing.

Beck, A. T., & Greenberg, R. L. (1974). *Coping with depression.* New York: Institute for Rational Living.

Beck, B. L., Koons, S. R., & Milgrim, D. L. (2000). Correlates and consequences of behavioral procrastination. *Journal of Social Behavior & Personality, 15*(5), 3–13.

Beck, J. S. (2002). Beck therapy approach. In M. Hersen & W. H. Sledge (Eds.), *Encyclopedia of psychotherapy.* San Diego: Academic Press.

Beck, R. C. (2004). *Motivation: Theories and principles* (5th ed.). Englewood Cliffs, NJ: Prentice Hall.

Beebe, B., Gerstman, L., Carson, B., et al. (1982). Rhythmic communication in the mother–infant dyad. In M. Davis (Ed.), *Interaction rhythms, periodicity in communicative behavior.* New York: Human Sciences Press.

Beeber, L. S., Chazan-Cohen, R., Squires, J., et al. (2007). The Early Promotion and Intervention Research Consortium (E-PIRC): Five approaches to improving infant/toddler mental health in Early Head Start. *Infant Mental Health Journal, 28*(2), 130–150.

Beersma, D. G. M., & Gordijn, M. C. M. (2007). Circadian control of the sleep–wake cycle. *Physiology & Behavior, 90*(2-3), 190–195.

Behrend, D. A., Beike, D. R., & Lampinen, J. M. (2004). *The self and memory.* Hove, UK: Psychology Press.

Beirne-Smith, M., Patton, J., & Shannon, K. (2006). *Mental retardation: An introduction to intellectual disability* (7th ed.). Englewood Cliffs, NJ: Prentice Hall.

Belenky, G., Wesensten, N. J., Thorne, D. R., et al. (2003). Patterns of performance degradation and restoration during sleep restriction and subsequent recovery: A sleep dose-response study. *Journal of Sleep Research, 12*(1), 1–12.

Bellezza, F. S., Six, L. S., & Phillips, D. S. (1992). A mnemonic for remembering long strings of digits. *Bulletin of the Psychonomic Society, 30*(4), 271–274.

Belsky, J. (1996). Parent, infant, and social-contextual antecedents of father-son attachment security. *Developmental Psychology, 32*(5), 905–913.

Bem, S. L. (1974). The measurement of psychological androgyny. *Journal of Consulting & Clinical Psychology, 42*(2), 155–162.

Bem, S. L. (1975). Androgyny vs. the tight little lives of fluffy women and chesty men. *Psychology Today,* Sept., 58–62.

Bem, S. L. (1981). Gender schema theory. A cognitive account of sex typing. *Psychological Review, 88,* 354–364.

Benbow, C. P. (1986). Physiological correlates of extreme intellectual precocity. *Neuropsychologia, 24*(5), 719–725.

Benjamin, L. T., Jr. (2009). *A history of psychology.* London: Blackwell.

Benloucif, S., Bennett, E. L., & Rosenzweig, M. R. (1995). Norepinephrine and neural plasticity: The effects of xylamine on experience-induced changes in brain weight, memory, and behavior. *Neurobiology of Learning & Memory, 63*(1), 33–42.

Bensafi, M., Zelano, C., Johnson, B., et al. (2004). Olfaction: From sniff to percept. In M. S. Gazzaniga (Ed.), *The cognitive neurosciences* (3rd ed.). Cambridge, MA: MIT Press.

Ben-Shakhar, G., & Dolev, K. (1996). Psychophysiological detection through the guilty knowledge technique: Effect of mental countermeasures. *Journal of Applied Psychology, 81*(3), 273–281.

Bensley, L., & Van Eenwyk, J. (2001). Video games and real-life aggression. *Journal of Adolescent Health, 29*(4), 244–257.

Benson, H. (1977). Systematic hypertension and the relaxation response. *New England Journal of Medicine, 296,* 1152–1156.

Benson, J., Greaves, W., O'Donnell, M., & Taglialatela, J. (2002). Evidence for symbolic language processing in a bonobo (*Pan paniscus*). *Journal of Consciousness Studies, 9*(12), 33–56.

Bergin, A. E. (1991). Values and religious issues in psychotherapy and mental health. *American Psychologist, 46*(4), 394–403.

Berman, S. L., Weems, C. F., & Stickle, T. R. (2006). Existential anxiety in adolescents: Prevalence, structure, association with psychological symptoms and identity development. *Journal of Youth & Adolescence, 35*(3), 303–310.

Bernstein H. J., Beale M. D., Burns C., & Kellner C. H. (1998). Patient attitudes about ECT after treatment. *Psychiatric Annals, 28*(9), 524–527.

Bernthal, M. J. (2003). The effects of professional wrestling viewership on children. *The Sport Journal, 6*(3). Retrieved April 21, 2009, from http://www.thesportjournal.org/article/effect-professional-wrestling-viewership-children.

Berntsen, D., & Thomsen, D. K. (2005). Personal memories for remote historical events: Accuracy and clarity of flashbulb memories related to World War II. *Journal of Experimental Psychology: General, 134*(2), 242–257.

Berry, J. W. (1990). The psychology of acculturation. In R. A. Dienstbier & J. J. Berman (Eds.), *Nebraska Symposium on Motivation 1989: Cross-cultural perspectives, 37.* Lincoln: University of Nebraska Press.

Berry, J. W., Phinney, J. S., Sam, D. L., & Vedder, P. (2005). *Immigrant youth in cultural transition.* Mahwah, NJ: Erlbaum.

Berscheid, E. (2000). Attraction. In A. Kazdin (Ed.), *Encyclopedia of psychology.* Washington, DC: American Psychological Association.

Berscheid, E., & Regan, P. (2005). *The psychology of interpersonal relationships.* Englewood Cliffs, NJ: Prentice Hall.

Bersoff, D. M. (1999). Why good people sometimes do bad things: Motivated reasoning and unethical behavior. *Personality & Social Psychology Bulletin, 25*(1), 28–39.

Bertsch, G. J. (1976). Punishment of consummatory and instrumental behavior: A review. *Psychological Record, 26,* 13–31.

Betancur, C., Velez, A., Cabanieu, G., et al. (1990). Association between left-handedness and allergy: A reappraisal. *Neuropsychologia, 28*(2), 223–227.

Bhushan, B., & Khan, S. M. (2006). Laterality and accident proneness: A study of locomotive drivers. *Laterality: Asymmetries of Body, Brain & Cognition, 11*(5), 395–404.

Bialystok, E., & DePape, A.-M. (2009). Musical expertise, bilingualism, and executive functioning. *Journal of Experimental Psychology: Human Perception & Performance, 35*(2), 565–574.

Binder, J. L. (2004). *Key competencies in brief dynamic psychotherapy: Clinical practice beyond the manual.* New York: Guilford.

Birnbaum, M. H. (2004). Human research and data collection via the Internet. *Annual Review of Psychology, 55,* 803–832.

Bisson, J. I., Ehlers, A., Matthews, R., et al. (2007). Psychological treatments for chronic post-traumatic stress disorder: Systematic review and meta-analysis. *British Journal of Psychiatry, 190*(2), 97–104.

Blackmore, S. (2001). What can the paranormal teach us about consciousness? *Skeptical Inquirer, 25,* 22–27.

Blackmore, S. (2004). *Consciousness: An introduction.* New York: Oxford University Press.

Blackwell, D. L., & Lichter, D. T. (2004). Homogamy among dating, cohabiting, and married couples. *Sociological Quarterly, 45*(4), 719–737.

Blair, K. S., Richell, R. A., Mitchell, D. G. V., et al. (2006). They know the words, but not the music: Affective and semantic priming in individuals with psychopathy. *Biological Psychology, 73*(2), 114–123.

Blakemore, C., & Cooper, G. (1970). Development of the brain depends on the visual environment. *Nature, 228,* 477–478.

Blanchard, D. C., & Blanchard, R. J. (2003). What can animal aggression research tell us about human aggression? *Hormones & Behavior, 44*(3), 171–177.

Blanchard, E. B., Kuhn, E., Rowell, D. L., et al. (2004). Studies of the vicarious traumatization of college students by the September 11th attacks: Effects of proximity, exposure and connectedness. *Behaviour Research & Therapy, 42*(2), 191–205.

Blatner, A. (2006). Current trends in psychodrama. *International Journal of Psychotherapy, 10*(3), 43–53.

Bloch, S. (2006). *Introduction to the psychotherapies* (4th ed.). New York: Oxford University Press.

Blood, A. J., & Zatorre, R. J. (2001). Intensely pleasurable responses to music correlate with activity in brain regions implicated in reward and emotion. *Proceedings National Academy of Sciences, 98*(20) 11818–11823.

Bloom, B. (1985). *Developing talent in young people.* New York: Ballantine.

Bloom, C. M., & Lamkin, D. M. (2006). The Olympian struggle to remember the cranial nerves: Mnemonics and student success. *Teaching of Psychology, 33*(2), 128–129.

Bloom, J. W. (1998). The ethical practice of WebCounseling. *British Journal of Guidance & Counselling, 26*(1), 53–59.

Blunt, A., & Pychyl, T. A. (2005). Project systems of procrastinators: A personal project-analytic and action control perspective. *Personality & Individual Differences, 38*(8), 1771–1780.

Boergers, J., Spirito, A., & Donaldson, D. (1998). Reasons for adolescent suicide attempts. *Journal of the American Academy of Child & Adolescent Psychiatry, 37*(12), 1287–1293.

Bohannon, J. N., & Stanowicz, L. B. (1988). The issue of negative evidence: Adult responses to children's language errors. *Developmental Psychology, 24*(5), 684–689.

Bohbot, V., & Corkin, S. (2007). Posterior parahippocampal place learning in H.M. *Hippocampus, 17*(9), 863–872.

Boivin, D. B., Czeisler, C. A., & Waterhouse, J. W. (1997). Complex interaction of the sleep–wake cycle and circadian phase modulates mood in healthy subjects. *Archives of General Psychiatry, 54*(2), 145–152.

Boldero, J. M., Moretti, M. M., Bell, R. C., & Francis, J. J. (2005). Self-discrepancies and negative affect: A primer on when to look for specificity, and how to find it. *Australian Journal of Psychology, 57*(3), 139–147.

Bonanno, G. A., Papa, A., Lalande, K., et al. (2004). The importance of being flexible. *Psychological Science, 15*(7), 482–487.

Bond, R., & Smith, P. B. (1996). Culture and conformity: A meta-analysis of studies using Asch's (1952, 1956) line judgment task. *Psychological Bulletin, 119*, 111–137.

Bongard, S., al'Absi, M., & Lovallo, W. R. (1998). Interactive effects of trait hostility and anger expression on cardiovascular reactivity in young men. *International Journal of Psychophysiology, 28*(2), 181–191.

Bonham, V., Warshauer-Baker, E., & Collins, F. S. (2005). Race and ethnicity in the genome era: The complexity of the constructs. *American Psychologist, 60*(1), 9–15.

Boniecki, K. A., & Britt, T. W. (2003). Prejudice and the peacekeeper. In T. W. Britt & A. B. Adler (Eds.), *The psychology of the peacekeeper: Lessons from the field. Psychological dimensions to war and peace.* Westport, CT: Praeger.

Bood, S., Sundequist, U., Kjellgren, A., et al. (2006). Eliciting the relaxation response with the help of flotation-REST (Restricted Environmental Stimulation Technique) in patients with stress-related ailments. *International Journal of Stress Management, 13*(2), 154–175.

Booker, J. M., & Hellekson, C. J. (1992). Prevalence of seasonal affective disorder in Alaska. *American Journal of Psychiatry, 149*(9), 1176–1182.

Bootzin, R. R., & Epstein, D. R. (2000). Stimulus control. In K. L. Lich & C. M. Morin (Eds.), *Treatment of late life insomnia.* Thousand Oaks, CA: Sage.

Borlongan, C. V., Sanberg, P. R., & Freeman, T. B. (1999). Neural transplantation for neurodegenerative disorders. *Lancet, 353*(Suppl. 1), S29–30.

Bornstein, M. H., & Tamis-LeMonda, C. S. (2001). Mother–infant interaction. In A. Fogel & G. Bremmer (Eds.), *Blackwell handbook of infant development.* London: Blackwell.

Bornstein, R. F. (1996). Sex differences in dependent personality disorder prevalence rates. *Clinical Psychology: Science & Practice, 3*(1), 1–12.

Borod, J. C., Bloom, R. L., Brickman, A. M., et al. (2002). Emotional processing deficits in individuals with unilateral brain damage. *Applied Neuropsychology, 9*(1), 23–36.

Boskey, E. (2008). *Is oral sex safe sex?* Retrieved May 16, 2009, from http://std.about.com/od/riskfactorsforstds/a/oralsexsafesex.htm.

Bouchard, T. J., Jr. (1983). Twins—nature's twice-told tale. In *Yearbook of science and the future* (pp. 66–81). Chicago: Encyclopedia Britannica.

Bouchard, T. J., Jr. (2004). Genetic influence on human psychological traits: A survey. *Current Directions in Psychological Science, 13*(4), 148–151.

Bouchard, T. J., Jr., Lykken, D. T., McGue, M., et al. (1990). Sources of human psychological differences: The Minnesota study of twins reared apart. *Science, 250*, 223–228.

Bourne, E. J. (2005). *The anxiety & phobia workbook* (4th ed.). Oakland, CA: New Harbinger.

Bovbjerg, D. H., Redd, W. H., Jacobsen, P. B., et al. (1992). An experimental analysis of classically conditioned nausea during cancer chemotherapy. *Psychosomatic Medicine, 54*(6), 623–637.

Bower, G. H. (1981). Mood and memory. *American Psychologist, 36*, 129–148.

Bower, G. H., & Springston, F. (1970). Pauses as recoding points in letter series. *Journal of Experimental Psychology, 83*, 421–430.

Boyle, S. H., Williams, R. B., Mark, D., et al. (2004). Hostility as a predictor of survival in patients with coronary artery disease. *Psychosomatic Medicine, 66*(5), 629–632.

Brach, T. (2003). *Radical acceptance.* New York: Bantam Books.

Bradley, R. H., & Corwyn, R. F. (2002). Socioeconomic status and child development. *Annual Review of Psychology, 53*, 377–399.

Bradley, R., Greene, J., Russ, E., et al. (2005). A multidimensional meta-analysis of psychotherapy for PTSD. *American Journal of Psychiatry, 162*(2), 214–227.

Bradshaw, S. D. (2006). Shyness and difficult relationships: Formation is just the beginning. In D. C. Kirkpatrick, D. S. Duck, & M. K. Foley (Eds.), *Relating difficulty: The processes of constructing and managing difficult interaction.* Mahwah, NJ: Erlbaum.

Brainerd, C. J. (2003). Jean Piaget, learning research, and American education. In B. J. Zimmerman & D. H. Schunk (Eds.), *Educational psychology: A century of contributions.* Mahwah, NJ: Erlbaum.

Bramerson, A., Johansson, L., Ek, L., et al. (2004). Prevalence of olfactory dysfunction: The Skovde population-based study. *Laryngoscope, 114*(4), 733–737.

Brannon, L. (1996). *Gender.* Boston: Allyn & Bacon.

Brannon, L., & Feist, J. (2010). *Health psychology: An introduction to behavior and health* (7th ed.). Belmont, CA: Cengage Learning/Wadsworth.

Bransford, J. D., & McCarrell, N. S. (1977). A sketch of cognitive approach to comprehension: Some thoughts about understanding what it means to comprehend. In P. N. Johnson-Laird & P. C. Wason (Eds.), *Thinking: Readings in cognitive science.* Cambridge, MA: Cambridge University Press.

Braun, A. R., Balkin, T. J., & Herscovitch, P. (1998). Dissociated pattern of activity in visual cortices and their projections during human rapid eye movement sleep. *Science, 279*(5347), 91–95.

Braun, K. A., Ellis, R., & Loftus, E. F. (2002). Make my memory: How advertising can change memories of the past. *Psychology and Marketing, 19*, 1–23.

Braun, S. (2001). Seeking insight by prescription. *Cerebrum, 3*(2), 10–21.

Braun-LaTour, K. A., & LaTour, M. S. (2004). Assessing the long-term impact of a consistent advertising campaign on consumer memory. *Journal of Advertising, 33*(2), 49–61.

Breckler, S. J., Olson, J., & Wiggins, E. (2006). *Social psychology alive.* Belmont, CA: Wadsworth.

Breslau, N., Johnson, E. O., Hiripi, E., & Kessler, R. (2001). Nicotine dependence in the United States. *Archives of General Psychiatry, 58*(9), 810–816.

Bressan, P., & Pizzighello, S. (2008). The attentional cost of inattentional blindness. *Cognition, 106*(1), 370–383.

Bressi, C., Albonetti, S., & Razzoli, E. (1998). "Communication deviance" and schizophrenia. *New Trends in Experimental & Clinical Psychiatry, 14*(1), 33–39.

Bretherton, R., & Orner, R. J. (2004). Positive psychology and psychotherapy: An existential approach. In P. A. Linley & S. Joseph (Eds.), *Positive psychology in practice.* New York: Wiley.

Brewer, K. R., & Wann, D. L. (1998). Observational learning effectiveness as a function of model characteristics. *Social Behavior & Personality, 26*(1), 1–10.

Brewer, N., & Wells, G. L. (2006). The confidence-accuracy relationship in eyewitness identification: Effects of lineup instructions, foil similarity, and target-absent base rates. *Journal of Experimental Psychology: Applied, 12*(1), 11–30.

Briand, L. A., Flagel, S. B., Seeman, P., & Robinson, T. E. (2008). Cocaine self-administration produces a persistent increase in dopamine D2-super (High) receptors. *European Neuropsychopharmacology, 18*(8), 551–556.

Bridges, K. M. B. (1932). Emotional development in early infancy. *Child Development, 3*, 324–334.

Bridges, L. J. (2003). Trust, attachment, and relatedness. In M. H. Bornstein, L. Davidson, C. L. M. Keyes, & K. Moore (Eds.), *Well-being: Positive development across the life course.* Mahwah, NJ: Erlbaum.

Brinton, R. D., & Wang, J. M. (2006). Therapeutic potential of neurogenesis for prevention and recovery from Alzheimer's disease: Allopregnanolone as a proof of concept neurogenic agent. *Current Alzheimer Research, 3*(3), 185–190.

Brock, T. C., & Green, M. C. (Eds.). (2005). *Persuasion: Psychological insights and perspectives* (2nd ed.). Thousand Oaks, CA: Sage.

Brodley, B. T. (2006). Non-directivity in client-centered therapy. *Person-Centered & Experiential Psychotherapies, 5*(1), 36–52.

Brooks, M. (2008, August 20). The power of the placebo effect. *New Scientist, 2670*, 36–39.

Brooks, M. (2009). Rise of the robogeeks. *New Scientist, 2697*, 34–36.

Brooks-Gunn, J., & Warren, M. P. (1988). The psychological significance of secondary sexual characteristics in nine- to eleven-year-old girls. *Child Development, 59*(4), 1061–1069.

Brothen, T., & Wambach, C. (2001). Effective student use of computerized quizzes. *Teaching of Psychology, 28*(4), 292–294.

Brown, A. E., & Jeffcott, H. A., Jr. (1970). *Absolutely mad inventions.* New York: Dover Publications.

Brown, A. M. (1990). Development of visual sensitivity to light and color vision in human infants: A critical review. *Vision Research, 30*(8), 1159–1188.

Brown, A. S. (2004). *The déjà vu experience.* New York: Psychology Press.

Brown, A. S., Cohen, P., Harkavy-Friedman, J., et al. (2001). Prenatal rubella, premorbid abnormalities, and adult schizophrenia. *Biological Psychiatry, 49*(6), 473–486.

Brown, K. W., & Ryan, R. M. (2003). The benefits of being present. *Journal of Personality and Social Psychology, 84*(4), 822–848

Brown, L. M. (2005). *Girlfighting: Betrayal and rejection among girls.* New York: New York University Press.

Brown, P. (1990). The name game. *Journal of Mind and Behavior, 11,* 385–406.

Brown, R. L., Leonard, T., Saunders, L. A., & Papasouiotis, O. (1997). A two-item screening test for alcohol and other drug problems. *Journal of Family Practice, 44*(2), 151–160.

Brown, R., & Kulik, J. (1977). Flashbulb memories. *Cognition, 5,* 73–99.

Brown, R., & McNeill, D. (1966). The "tip of the tongue" phenomenon. *Journal of Verbal Learning & Verbal Behavior, 5*(4), 325–337.

Brown, S. A., Tapert, S. F., Granholm, E., & Delis, D. C. (2000). Neurocognitive functioning of adolescents: Effects of protracted alcohol use. *Alcoholism: Clinical & Experimental Research, 24*(2), 164–171.

Brown, S. G., Roy, E., Rohr, L., & Bryden, P. (2006). Using hand performance measures to predict handedness. *Laterality: Asymmetries of Body, Brain & Cognition, 11*(1), 1–14.

Brown, T. A., & Barlow, D. H. (2007). *Casebook in abnormal psychology* (3rd. ed.). Belmont, CA: Thomson/Wadsworth.

Brown, T. D., Dane, F. C., & Durham, M. D. (1998). Perception of race and ethnicity. *Journal of Social Behavior & Personality, 13*(2), 295–306.

Browne, N., & Keeley, S. (2007). *Asking the right questions: A guide to critical thinking* (8th ed.). Englewood Cliffs, NJ: Prentice-Hall.

Brownell, K. D. (2003). *Food fight.* New York: McGraw-Hill.

Bruch, M. A. (2001). Shyness and social interaction. In R. Crozier & L. Alden (Eds.), *International handbook of social anxiety.* Sussex, England: Wiley.

Bruer, J. T. (2001). A critical and sensitive period primer. In D. B. Bailey, Jr., J. T. Bruer, F. J. Symons, & J. W. Lichtman (Eds.), *Critical thinking about critical periods.* Baltimore, MD: Paul H. Brookes Publishing.

Bruner, J. (1973). *Going beyond the information given.* New York: Norton.

Bruner, J. (1983). *Child's talk.* New York: Norton.

Bryden, P. J., Bruyn, J., & Fletcher, P. (2005). Handedness and health: An examination of the association between different handedness classifications and health disorders. *Laterality: Asymmetries of Body, Brain & Cognition, 10*(5), 429–440.

Buchwald, A. (1965, June 20). Psyching out. *The Washington Post.*

Buckworth, J., Lee, R. E., Regan, G., et al. (2007). Decomposing intrinsic and extrinsic motivation for exercise: Application to stages of motivational readiness. *Psychology of Sport & Exercise, 8*(4), 441–461.

Buddie, A. M. (2004). Alternatives to twelve-step programs. *Journal of Forensic Psychology Practice, 4*(3), 61–70.

Budney, A. J., & Hughes, J. R. (2006). The cannabis withdrawal syndrome. *Current Opinion in Psychiatry, 19*(3), 233–238.

Buehner, M. J., & May, J. (2003). Rethinking temporal contiguity and the judgement of causality: Effects of prior knowledge, experience, and reinforcement procedure. *Quarterly Journal of Experimental Psychology A: Human Experimental Psychology, 56A*(5), 865–890.

Buller, D. J. (2005). *Adapting minds: Evolutionary psychology and the persistent quest for human nature.* Cambridge, MA: MIT Press.

Bunde, J., & Suls, J. (2006). A quantitative analysis of the relationship between the Cook-Medley hostility scale and traditional coronary artery disease risk factors. *Health Psychology, 25*(4), 493–500.

Bunn, G. C. (2007). Spectacular science: The lie detector's ambivalent powers. *History of Psychology, 10*(2), 156–178.

Burchinal, M. R., Roberts, J. E., Riggins, R., et al. (2000). Relating quality of center-based child care to early cognitive and language development longitudinally. *Child Development, 71*(2), 339–357.

Burger, J. M. (2008). *Personality* (7th ed.). Belmont, CA: Cengage Learning/Wadsworth.

Burger, J. M., & Lynn, A. L. (2005). Superstitious behavior among American and Japanese professional baseball players. *Basic & Applied Social Psychology, 27*(1), 71–76.

Burgess, C. A., & Kirsch, I. (1999). Expectancy information as a moderator of the effects of hypnosis on memory. *Contemporary Hypnosis, 16*(1), 22–31.

Burgess, M. C. R., & Weaver, G. E. (2003). Interest and attention in facial recognition. *Perceptual & Motor Skills, 96*(2), 467–480.

Burke, D., Hickie, I., Breakspear, M., & Götz, J. (2007). Possibilities for the prevention and treatment of cognitive impairment and dementia. *British Journal of Psychiatry, 190,* 371–372.

Burlingame, G. M., Fuhriman, A., & Mosier, J. (2003). The differential effectiveness of group psychotherapy: A meta-analytic perspective. *Group Dynamics: Theory, Research, and Practice, 7*(1), 3–12.

Burlingame, G., & Davies, R. (2002). Self-help groups. In M. Hersen & W. H. Sledge (Eds.), *Encyclopedia of psychotherapy.* San Diego: Academic Press.

Burnett, R. C., Medin, D. L., Ross, N. O., & Blok, S. V. (2005). Ideal is typical. *Canadian Journal of Experimental Psychology. Special Issue on 2003 Festschrift for Lee R. Brooks, 59*(1), 3–10.

Burns, D. D., & Persons, J. (1982). Hope and hopelessness: A cognitive approach. In L. E. Abt & I. R. Stuart (Eds.), *The newer therapies: A sourcebook.* New York: Van Nostrand Reinhold.

Burns, T. (2004). *Community mental health teams: A guide to current practices.* New York: Oxford.

Burt, S. A., McGue, M., Carter, L. A., & Iacono, W. G. (2007). The different origins of stability and change in antisocial personality disorder symptoms. *Psychological Medicine, 37*(1), 27–38.

Burton, C. M., & King, L. A. (2004). The health benefits of writing about intensely positive experiences. *Journal of Research in Personality, 38*(2), 150–163.

Burtt, H. E. (1941). An experimental study of early childhood memory: Final report. *Journal of General Psychology, 58,* 435–439.

Bushman, B. J., & Anderson, C. A. (2001). Media violence and the American public. *American Psychologist, 56*(6/7), 477–489.

Bushnell, L. W., Sai, F., & Mullin, L. T. (1989). Neonatal recognition of the mother's face. *British Journal of Developmental Psychology, 7*(1), 3–15.

Bushnell, M. C., Villemure, C., & Duncan, G. H. (2004). Psychophysical and neurophysiological studies of pain modulation by attention. In D. D. Price & M. C. Bushnell (Eds.), *Psychological methods of pain control: Basic science and clinical perspectives.* Seattle, WA: IASP Press.

Buss, D. M. (1985). Human mate selection. *American Scientist, 73*(1), 47–51.

Buss, D. M. (2000). The evolution of happiness. *American Psychologist, 55*(1), 15–23.

Buss, D. M. (2004). *Evolutionary psychology: The new science of the mind* (2nd ed.). Boston: Allyn & Bacon.

Buss, D. M. (2007). The evolution of human mating. *Acta Psychologica Sinica, 39*(3), 502–512.

Butcher, J. N. (2005). *A beginner's guide to the MMPI-2* (2nd ed.). Washington, DC: American Psychological Association.

Butcher, J. N., Mineka, S., & Hooley, J. (2007). *Abnormal psychology and modern life* (13th ed.). Boston: Allyn & Bacon.

Butcher, J. N. (Ed.). (2006). *MMPI-2: A practitioner's guide.* Washington, DC: American Psychological Association.

Butler, J. C. (2000). Personality and emotional correlates of right-wing authoritarianism. *Social Behavior & Personality, 28*(1), 1–14.

Butler, M. G. (2001). *Overcoming social anxiety and shyness: A self-help guide using cognitive behavioral techniques.* New York: New York University Press.

Butler, R. (1954). Curiosity in monkeys. *Scientific American, 190*(18), 70–75.

Byrne, S. M., & McLean, N. J. (2002). The cognitive-behavioral model of bulimia nervosa: A direct evaluation. *International Journal of Eating Disorders, 31,* 17–31.

Cadinu, M., Maass, A., Rosabianca, A., & Kiesner, J. (2005). Why do women underperform under stereotype threat? Evidence for the role of negative thinking. *Psychological Science, 16*(7), 572–578.

Caharel, S., Fiori, N., Bernard, C., et al. (2006). The effects of inversion and eye displacements of familiar and unknown faces on early and late-stage ERPs. *International Journal of Psychophysiology, 62*(1), 141–151.

Cahill, L. (2006). Why sex matters for neuroscience. *Nature Reviews Neuroscience, 7*(6), 477–484.

Cahill, S. P., Carrigan, M. H., & Frueh, B. C. (1999). Does EMDR work? and if so, why? *Journal of Anxiety Disorders, 13*(1-2), 5–33.

Cahn, B. R., & Polich, J. (2006). Meditation states and traits: EEG, ERP, and neuroimaging studies. *Psychological Bulletin, 132*(2), 180–211.

Callahan, C. M. (2006). Giftedness. In G. G. Bear & K. M. Minke (Eds.), *Children's needs III: Development, prevention, and intervention.* Washington, DC: National Association of School Psychologists.

Cameron, J. A., & Trope, Y. (2004). Stereotype-biased search and processing of information about group members. *Social Cognition, 22*(6), 650–672.

Cameron, J., & Pierce, W. D. (2002). *Rewards and intrinsic motivation: Resolving the controversy.* Westport, CT: Bergin & Garvey.

Campbell, L., Campbell, B., & Dickinson, D. (2003). *Teaching and learning through multiple intelligences* (3rd ed.). Boston: Allyn & Bacon.

Canli, T., Desmond, J. E., Zhao, Z., et al. (1998). Hemispheric asymmetry for emotional stimuli detected with fMRI. *Neuroreport, 9*(14) 3233–3239.

Cannon, W. B. (1932). *The wisdom of the body.* New York: Norton.

Cannon, W. B. (1934). Hunger and thirst. In C. Murchinson (Ed.), *Handbook of general experimental psychology.* Worcester, MA: Clark University Press.

Cannon, W. B., & Washburn, A. L. (1912). An explanation of hunger. *American Journal of Physiology, 29,* 444–454.

Caplan, P. J. (1995). *They say you're crazy.* Reading, MA: Addison-Wesley.

Capuzzi, D. (2003). *Approaches to group counseling.* Englewood Cliffs, NJ: Prentice Hall.

Cardoso, S. H. (2000). Our ancient laughing brain. *Cerebrum, 2*(4), 15–30.

Carducci, B. J., & Fields, T. H. (2007). *The shyness workbook for teens.* Champaign, IL: Research Press.

Carlbring, P., Gunnarsdóttir, M., Hedensjö, L., et al. (2007). Treatment of social phobia: Randomised trial of Internet-delivered cognitive-behavioural therapy with telephone support. *British Journal of Psychiatry, 190*(2), 123–128.

Carlson, M., Marcus-Hewhall, A., & Miller, N. (1990). Effects of situational aggression cues: A quantitative review. *Journal of Personality & Social Psychology, 58*(4), 622–633.

Carlson, N. R. (2007). *Physiology of behavior* (9th ed.). Boston: Allyn & Bacon.

Carlson, N. R. (2010). *Physiology of behavior* (10th ed.). Boston: Allyn & Bacon.

Carnagey, N. L., & Anderson, C. A. (2004). Violent video game exposure and aggression: A literature review. *Minerva Psichiatrica, 45*(1), 1–18.

Carney, P. R., Geyer, J. D., & Berry, R. B. (Eds.). (2005). *Clinical sleep disorders.* Philadelphia, PA: Lippincott Williams & Wilkins.

Carney, R. N., & Levin, J. R. (2001). Remembering the names of unfamiliar animals: Keywords as keys to their kingdom. *Applied Cognitive Psychology, 15*(2), 133–143.

Carney, R. N., & Levin, J. R. (2003). Promoting higher-order learning benefits by building lower-order mnemonic connections. *Applied Cognitive Psychology, 17*(5), 563–575.

Carroll, D. W. (2008). *Psychology of language* (5th ed.). Belmont, CA: Cengage Learning/Wadsworth.

Carroll, J. M., & Russell, J. A. (1996). Do facial expressions signal specific emotions? Judging emotion from the face in context. *Journal of Personality & Social Psychology, 70*(2), 205–218.

Carroll, K. M., & Rounsaville, B. J. (2007). W(h)ither empirically supported therapies (ESTS)? Reply to commentaries. *Addiction, 102*(6), 867–869.

Carskadon, M. A., Acebo, C., & Jenni, O. C. (2004). Regulation of adolescent sleep: Implications for behavior. *Annals of the New York Academy of Science, 1021,* 276–291.

Cartwright, D. (2002b). The narcissistic exoskeleton: The defensive organization of the rage-type murderer. *Bulletin of the Menninger Clinic, 66*(1), 1–18.

Cartwright, R., & Lamberg, L. (1992). *Crisis dreaming.* New York: HarperCollins.

Casey, P. (2001). Multiple personality disorder. *Primary Care Psychiatry, 7*(1), 7–11.

Caspi, A., Roberts, B. W., & Shiner, R. L. (2005). Personality development: Stability and change. *Annual Review of Psychology, 56,* 453–484.

Caspi, A., Sugden, K., Moffitt, T. E., et al. (2003). Influence of life stress on depression: Moderation by a polymorphism in the 5-HTT gene. *Science, 301*(5631), 386–389.

Cassady, J. C. (2004). The influence of cognitive test anxiety across the learning–testing cycle. *Learning & Instruction, 14*(6), 569–592.

Castro, J. R., & Rice, K. G. (2003). Perfectionism and ethnicity: Implications for depressive symptoms and self-reported academic achievement. *Cultural Diversity and Ethnic Minority Psychology, 9*(1), 64–78.

Castro, J., Gila, A., Gual, P., et al. (2004). Perfectionism dimensions in children and adolescents with anorexia nervosa. *Journal of Adolescent Health, 35*(5), 392–398.

Catalano, R., Novaco, R., & McConnell, W. (1997). A model of the net effect of job loss on violence. *Journal of Personality & Social Psychology, 72*(6), 1440–1447.

Cattell, R. B. (1965). *The scientific analysis of personality.* Baltimore: Penguin.

Cattell, R. B. (1973, July). Personality pinned down. *Psychology Today,* 40–46.

Cautela, J. R., & Kearney, A. J. (1986). *The covert conditioning handbook.* New York: Springer.

Cavaco, S., Anderson, S. W., Allen, J. S., et al. (2004). The scope of preserved procedural memory in amnesia. *Brain: A Journal of Neurology, 127*(8), 1853–1867.

CDC (Centers for Disease Control and Prevention). (2003). *Deaths, percent of total deaths, and death rates for 15 leading causes of death in 5-year age groups, by race and sex: United States, 2000.* CDC and National Center for Health Statistics, National Vital Statistics System. Downloaded September 20, 2006, from http://www.cdc.gov/nchs/datawh/statab/unpubd/mortabs/lcwk1_10.htm.

CDC (Centers for Disease Control and Prevention). (2005). Annual smoking–attributable mortality, years of potential life lost, and productivity losses: United States, 1997–2001. *Morbidity and Mortality Weekly Report, 54*(25), 625–628.

Chakos, M. H., Alvir, J. M. J., Woerner, M., & Koreen, A. (1996). Incidence and correlates of tardive dyskinesia in first episode of schizophrenia. *Archives of General Psychiatry, 53*(4), 313–319.

Chamberlin, J. (2004, July/August). Survey says: More Americans are seeking mental health treatment. *Monitor on Psychology,* 17.

Chamberlin, J., & Rogers, J. A. (1990). Planning a community-based mental health system. *American Psychologist, 45*(11), 1241–1244.

Chambers, R. A., Taylor, J. R., & Potenza, M. N. (2003). Developmental neurocircuitry of motivation in adolescence: A critical period of addiction vulnerability. *American Journal of Psychiatry, 160*(6), 1041–1052.

Chambless, D. L., & Ollendick, T. H. (2001). Empirically supported psychological interventions. *Annual Review of Psychology, 52,* 685–716.

Chamorro-Premuzic, T., & Furnham, A. (2003). Personality predicts academic performance. *Journal of Research in Personality, 37*(4), 319–338.

Chan, G. C.-K., Hinds, T. R., Impey, S., & Storm, D. R. (1998). Hippocampal neurotoxicity of D-sup-9-tetra-hydrocannabinol. *Journal of Neuroscience, 18*(14), 5322–5332.

Chance, P. (2009). *Learning and behavior* (6th ed.). Belmont, CA: Cengage Learning/Wadsworth.

Chandrashekar, J., Hoon, M. A., Ryba, N. J. P., & Cammann, C. (2006). The receptors and cells for mammalian taste. *Nature, 444*(7117), 288–294.

Chansler, P. A., Swamidass, P. M., & Cammann, C. (2003). Self-managing work teams: An empirical study of group cohesiveness in "natural work groups" at a Harley-Davidson Motor Company plant. *Small Group Research, 34*(1), 101–120.

Chao, R., & Tseng, V. (2002). Parenting of Asians. In M. H. Bornstein (Ed.), *Handbook of parenting* (Vol. 4): *Social conditions and applied parenting* (2nd ed.). Mahwah, NJ: Erlbaum.

Chapman, R. A. (Ed.). (2006). *The clinical use of hypnosis in cognitive behavior therapy: A practitioner's casebook.* New York: Springer Publishing.

Chassin, L., Presson, C. C., Sherman, S. J., & Kim, K. (2003). Historical changes in cigarette smoking and smoking-related beliefs after 2 decades in a midwestern community. *Health Psychology, 22*(4), 347–353.

Chasteen, A. L., Bhattacharyya, S., Horhota, M., et al. (2005). How feelings of stereotype threat influence older adults' memory performance. *Experimental Aging Research, 31*(3), 235–260.

Chaves, J. F. (2000). Hypnosis. In A. Kazdin (Ed.), *Encyclopedia of psychology.* Washington, DC: American Psychological Association.

Cheek, J., & Buss, A. H. (1979). *Scales of shyness, sociability and self-esteem and correlations among them.* Unpublished research, University of Texas. (Cited by Buss, 1980.)

Chen, Z., Lawson, R. B., Gordon, L. R., & McIntosh, B. (1996). Groupthink: Deciding with the leader and the devil. *Psychological Record, 46*(4), 581–590.

Cheng, H., Cao, Y., & Olson, L. (1996). Spinal cord repair in adult paraplegic rats: Partial restoration of hind limb function. *Science, 273*(5274), 510.

Chess, S., & Thomas, A. (1986). *Know your child.* New York: Basic.

Chester, A., & Glass, C. A. (2006). Online counselling: A descriptive analysis of therapy services on the internet. *British Journal of Guidance & Counselling, 34*(2), 145–160.

Cheyne, J. A. (2005). Sleep paralysis episode frequency and number, types, and structure of associated hallucinations. *Journal of Sleep Research, 14*(3), 319–324.

Cheyne, J. A., Rueffer, S. D., & Newby-Clark, I. R. (1999). Hypnagogic and hypnopompic hallucinations during sleep paralysis: Neurological and cultural construction of the night-mare. *Consciousness & Cognition, 8*, 319–337.

Chisolm, T. H., Willott, J. F., & Lister, J. J. (2003). The aging auditory system: Anatomic and physiologic changes and implications for rehabilitation. *International Journal of Audiology, 42*(Suppl. 2), 2S3–2S10.

Chomsky, N. (1975). *Reflections on language.* New York: Pantheon.

Chomsky, N. (1986). *Knowledge of language.* New York: Praeger.

Christakis, N. A., & Fowler, J. H. (2007). The spread of obesity in a large social network over 32 years. *New England Journal of Medicine, 357*(4), 370–379.

Christakis, N. A., & Fowler, J. H. (2008). The collective dynamics of smoking in a large social network. *New England Journal of Medicine, 358*(21), 2249–2258.

Christensen, A., & Jacobson, N. S. (1994). Who (or what) can do psychotherapy. *Psychological Science, 5*(1), 8–14.

Christian, K. M., & Thompson, R. F. (2005). Long-term storage of an associative memory trace in the cerebellum. *Behavioral Neuroscience, 119*(2), 526–537.

Christophersen, E. R., & Mortweet, S. L. (2003). *Parenting that works: Building skills that last a lifetime.* Washington, DC: American Psychological Association.

Chua, H. F., Boland, J. E., & Nisbett, R. E. (2005). Cultural variation in eye movements during scene perception. *Proceedings of the National Academy of Sciences of the United States of America, 102*(35), 12629–12633.

Cialdini, R. B. (2001). *Influence: Science and practice* (4th ed.). Boston: Allyn & Bacon.

Cialdini, R. B., & Goldstein, N. J. (2004). Social influence: Compliance and conformity. *Annual Review of Psychology, 55*, 591–621.

Cialdini, R. B., Reno, R. R., & Kallgren, C. A. (1990). A focus theory of normative conduct: Recycling the concept of norms to reduce littering in public places. *Journal of Personality & Social Psychology, 58*(6), 1015–1026.

Ciarrochi, J., Dean, F. P., & Anderson, S. (2002). Emotional intelligence moderates the relationship between stress and mental health. *Personality & Individual Differences, 32*(2), 197–209.

Cinciripini, P. M., Wetter, D. W., & McClure, J. B. (1997). Scheduled reduced smoking. *Addictive Behaviors, 22*(6), 759–767.

Clapham, M. M. (2001). The effects of affect manipulation and information exposure on divergent thinking. *Creativity Research Journal, 13*(3-4), 335–350.

Clark, D., Boutros, N., & Mendez, M. (2005). *The brain and behavior* (2nd ed.). Cambridge, MA: Cambridge University Press.

Clark, R., Anderson, N. B., Clark, V. R., & Williams, D. R. (1999). Racism as a stressor for African Americans. *American Psychologist, 54*(10), 805–816.

Clayton, N. S., Yu, K. S., & Dickinson, A. (2001). Scrub jays (*Aphelocoma coerulescens*) form integrated memories of the multiple features of caching episodes. *Journal of Experimental Psychology: Animal Behavior Processes, 27*, 17–29.

Cnattingius, S., Signorello, L. B., Annerén, G., et al. (2000). Caffeine intake and the risk of first-trimester spontaneous abortion. *New England Journal of Medicine, 343*(25), 1839–845.

Cochran, G. M., & Harpending, H. (2009). *The 10,000 year explosion.* New York: Basic Books

Cohen, N. L., Waltzman, S. B., & Fisher, S. G. (1993). A prospective, randomized study of cochlear implants. *New England Journal of Medicine, 328*(4), 233–237.

Colangelo, J. J. (2007). Recovered memory debate revisited: Practice implications for mental health counselors. *Journal of Mental Health Counseling, 29*(2), 93–120.

Coles, C. D., & Black, M. M. (2006). Introduction to the special issue. *Journal of Pediatric Psychology. Special Issue: Prenatal Substance Exposure: Impact on Children's Health, Development, School Performance, and Risk Behavior, 31*(1), 1–4.

Colin, A. K., & Moore, K., & West, A. N. (1996). Creativity, oversensitivity, and rate of habituation. *EDRA: Environmental Design Research Association, 20*(4), 423–427.

Collins, A. M., & Quillian, M. R. (1969). Retrieval time from semantic memory. *Journal of Verbal Learning and Verbal Behavior, 8*, 240–247.

Collins, N. L., Cooper, M. L., Albino, A., & Allard, L. (2002). Psychosocial vulnerability from adolescence to adulthood: A prospective study of attachment style differences in relationship functioning and partner choice. *Journal of Personality, 70*(6), 965–1008.

Collins, W. A., & Gunnar, M. R. (1990). Social and personality development. *Annual Review of Psychology, 41*, 387–416.

Collop, N. A. (2005). Obstructive sleep apnea: treatment overview and controversies. In P. R. Carney, J. D. Geyer, & R. B. Berry (Eds.), *Clinical sleep disorders.* Philadelphia, PA: Lippincott Williams & Wilkins.

Comer, R. J. (2005). *Fundamentals of abnormal psychology* (4th ed.). New York: Worth.

Compton, W. C. (2005). *An introduction to positive psychology.* Belmont, CA: Cengage Learning/Wadsworth.

Conway, A. R. A., Cowan, N., & Bunting, M. F. (2001). The cocktail party phenomenon revisited. *Psychonomic Bulletin & Review, 8*(2), 331–335.

Conway, M. A., Cohen, G., & Stanhope, N. (1992). Very long-term memory for knowledge acquired at school and university. *Applied Cognitive Psychology, 6*(6), 467–482.

Coolican, H., Cassidy, T., Dunn, O., Sharp, R., et al. (2007). *Applied psychology* (2nd ed.). London: Hodder Education.

Cooper, J., Mirabile, R., & Scher, S. J. (2005). Actions and attitudes: The theory of cognitive dissonance. In T. C. Brock & M. C. Green (Eds.), *Persuasion: Psychological insights and perspectives* (2nd ed.). Thousand Oaks, CA: Sage.

Cooper, M. J. (2005). Cognitive theory in anorexia nervosa and bulimia nervosa: Progress, development and future directions. *Clinical Psychology Review, 25*(4), 511–531.

Cooper, R. P., Abraham, J., Berman, S., & Staska, M. (1997). The development of infants' preference for motherese. *Infant Behavior and Development, 20*(4), 477–488.

Cooper, S. J. (2008). From Claude Bernard to Walter Cannon: Emergence of the concept of homeostasis. *Appetite, 51*(3), 419–427.

Corballis, M. C. (2002). *From hand to mouth: The origins of language.* Princeton, NJ: Princeton University Press.

Corbin, W. R., & Fromme, K. (2002). Alcohol use and serial monogamy as risks for sexually transmitted diseases in young adults. *Health Psychology, 21*(3), 229–236.

Coren, S. (1992). *The left-hander syndrome.* New York: Free Press.

Coren, S. (1996), *Sleep thieves.* New York: Free Press.

Corey, G. (2008). *Theory and practice of group counseling* (7th ed.). Belmont, CA: Cengage Learning/Wadsworth.

Corkin, S. (2002). What's new with the amnesic patient H.M.? *Nature Reviews Neuroscience, 3,* 153–160.

Cormier, J. F., & Thelen, M. H. (1998). Professional skepticism of multiple personality disorder. *Professional Psychology: Research and Practice, 29*(2), 163–167.

Correa-Chávez, M., Rogoff, B., & Arauz, R. M. (2005). Cultural patterns in attending to two events at once. *Child Development, 76*(3), 664–678.

Corrigan, P. W., & Penn, D. L. (1999). Lessons from social psychology on discrediting psychiatric stigma. *American Psychologist, 54*(9), 765–776.

Corrigan, P. W., & Watson, A. C. (2005). Findings from the National Comorbidity Survey on the frequency of violent behavior in individuals with psychiatric disorders. *Psychiatry Research, 136*(2–3), 153–162.

Corrigan, P. W., Watson, A. C., Gracia, G., et al. (2005). Newspaper stories as measures of structural stigma. *Psychiatric Services, 56*(5), 551–556.

Corsini, R. J. (2001). *Handbook of innovative therapy* (2nd ed.). York: Wiley.

Costa, P. T., Jr., & McCrae, R. R. (2006). Trait and factor theories. In J. C. Thomas, D. L. Segal, & M. Hersen (Eds.), *Comprehensive handbook of personality & psychopathology* (Vol. 1): *Personality and everyday functioning.* New York: Wiley.

Côté, J. E. (2006a). Emerging adulthood as an institutionalized moratorium: Risks and benefits to identity formation. In J. J. Arnett & J. L. Tanner (Eds.), *Emerging adults in America: Coming of age in the 21st century.* Washington, DC: American Psychological Association.

Côté, J. E. (2006b). Identity studies: How close are we to developing a social science of identity? An appraisal of the field. *Identity: An International Journal of Theory & Research, 6,* 3–26.

Côté, J. E., & Levine, C. (2002). *Identity formation, agency, and culture.* Hillsdale, NJ: Erlbaum.

Coursey, R. D., Ward-Alexander, L., & Katz, B. (1990). Cost-effectiveness of providing insurance benefits for posthospital psychiatric halfway house stays. *American Psychologist, 45*(10), 1118–1126.

Court, J. H., & Court, P. C. (2001). Repression: R. I. P. *Australian Journal of Clinical & Experimental Hypnosis, 29*(1), 8–16.

Cowan, N. (2005). *Working memory capacity.* Hove, UK: Psychology Press.

Cowden, C. R. (2005). Worry and its relationship to shyness. *North American Journal of Psychology, 7*(1), 59–69.

Cox, J. J., Reimann, F., Nicholas, A. K., et al. (2006). An SCN9A channelopathy causes congenital inability to experience pain. *Nature, 444,* 894–898.

Craig, L. (2006). Does father care mean fathers share?: A comparison of how mothers and fathers in intact families spend time with children. *Gender & Society, 20*(2), 259–281.

Craig, T. Y., & Kelly, J. R. (1999). Group cohesiveness and creative performance. *Group Dynamics, 3*(4), 243–256.

Craik, F. I. M. (1970). The fate of primary items in free recall. *Journal of Verbal Learning and Verbal Behavior, 9,* 143–148.

Craik, F. I. M., & Bialystok, E. (2005). Intelligence and executive control: Evidence from aging and bilingualism. *Cortex, 41*(2), 222–224.

Crano, W. D. (2000). Milestones in the psychological analysis of social influence. *Group Dynamics: Theory, Research, & Practice, 4*(1), 68–80.

Craske, M. G., Rose, R. D., Lang, A., et al. (2009). Computer-assisted delivery of cognitive behavioral therapy for anxiety disorders in primary-care settings. *Depression & Anxiety, 26*(3), 235–242.

Cravatt, B. F., Prospero-Garcia O., Siuzdak G., et al. (1995). Chemical characterization of a family of brain lipids that induce sleep. *Science, 268*(5216), 1506–1509.

Crawley, S. B., & Sherrod, K. B. (1984). Parent–infant play during the first year of life. *Infant Behavior & Development, 7,* 65–75.

Crencavage, L. M., & Norcross, J. C. (1990). Where are the commonalities among the therapeutic common factors? *Professional Psychology: Research & Practice, 21*(5), 372–378.

Crisp, A., Gowers, S., Joughin, N., et al. (2006). The enduring nature of anorexia nervosa. *European Eating Disorders Review, 14*(3), 147–152.

Crocker, J., & Park, L. E. (2004). The costly pursuit of self-esteem. *Psychological Bulletin, 130*(3), 392–414.

Crooks, R., & Baur, K. (2008). *Our sexuality* (10th ed.). Belmont, CA: Cengage Learning/Wadsworth.

Cropley, A. (2006). In praise of convergent thinking. *Creativity Research Journal, 18,* 391–404.

Crosby, R. A., & Yarber, W. L. (2001). Perceived versus actual knowledge about correct condom use among U.S. adolescents: Results from a national study. *Journal of Adolescent Health, 28*(5), 415–420.

Crown, C. L., Feldstein, S., Jasnow, M. D., et al. (2002). The cross-modal coordination of interpersonal timing. *Journal of Psycholinguistic Research, 31*(1), 1–23.

Crowther, J. H., Sanftner, J., Bonifazi, D. Z., & Shepherd, K. L. (2001). The role of daily hassles in binge eating. *International Journal of Eating Disorders, 29,* 449–454.

Csikszentmihalyi, M. (1997). *Creativity.* New York: HarperCollins.

Csikszentmihalyi, M., Abuhamdeh, S., Nakamura, J. (2005). Flow. In A. J. Elliot & C. S. Dweck (Eds.), *Handbook of competence and motivation.* New York: Guilford.

Cull, W. L., Shaughnessy, J. J., & Zechmeister, E. B. (1996). Expanding understanding of the expanding-pattern-of-retrieval mnemonic. *Journal of Experimental Psychology: Applied, 2*(4) 365–378.

Culver, R., & Ianna, P. (1988). *Astrology: True or false?* Buffalo, NY: Prometheus Books.

Cummings, M. R. (2006) *Human heredity: Principles and issues* (7th ed.). Belmont CA: Wadsworth.

Cummins, D. D. (1995). *The other side of psychology.* New York: St. Martin's.

Curci, A., & Luminet, O. (2006). Follow-up of a cross-national comparison on flashbulb and event memory for the September 11th attacks. *Memory, 14*(3), 329–344.

Czeisler, C. A., Duffy, J. F., Shanahan, T. L., et al. (1999). Stability, precision, and near-24-hour period of the human circadian pacemaker. *Science, 284,* 2177–2181.

Czeisler, C. A., Richardson, G. S., Zimmerman, J. C., et al. (1981). Entrainment of human circadian rhythms by light-dark cycles: A reassessment. *Photochemistry, Photobiology, 34,* 239–247.

Dane, S., & Erzurumluoglu, A. (2003). Sex and handedness differences in eye-hand visual reaction times in handball players. *International Journal of Neuroscience, 113*(7), 923–929.

Daniels, H. (2005). Vygotsky and educational psychology: Some preliminary remarks. *Educational & Child Psychology, 22*(1), 6–17.

Danziger, N., Prkachin, K. M., & Willer, J.-C. (2006). Is pain the price of empathy? The perception of others' pain in patients with congenital insensitivity to pain. *Brain: A Journal of Neurology, 129*(9), 2494–2507.

Darley, J. M. (2000). Bystander phenomenon. In A. E. Kazdin (Ed.), *Encyclopedia of psychology* (Vol. 1). Washington, DC: American Psychological Association.

Darley, J. M., & Latané, B. (1968). Bystander intervention in emergencies: Diffusion of responsibility. *Journal of Personality & Social Psychology, 8*(4), 377–383.

Darling, C. A., Davidson, J. K., & Passarello, L. C. (1992). The mystique of first intercourse among college youth: The role of partners, contraceptive practices, and psychological reactions. *Journal of Youth & Adolescence, 21*(1), 97–117.

Darou, W. S. (1992). Native Canadians and intelligence testing. *Canadian Journal of Counselling, 26*(2), 96–99.

Daruna, J. H. (2004). *Introduction to psychoneuroimmunology.* Amsterdam: Elsevier.

Darwin, C. (1872). *The expression of emotion in man and animals.* Chicago: University of Chicago Press.

Das, J. P. (2000). Mental retardation. In A. Kazdin (Ed.), *Encyclopedia of psychology.* Washington, DC: American Psychological Association.

Dauvilliers, Y., Cervena, K., Carlander, B., et al. (2004). Dissociation in circadian rhythms in a pseudohypersomnia form of fatal familial insomnia. *Neurology, 63*(12), 2416–2418.

Davidovitch, N., & Milgram, R. M. (2006). Creative thinking as a predictor of teacher effectiveness in higher education. *Creativity Research Journal, 18,* 385–390.

Davidson, P. R., & Parker, K. C. H. (2001). Eye movement desensitization and reprocessing (EMDR): A meta-analysis. *Journal of Consulting & Clinical Psychology, 69*(2), 305–316.

Davidson, R. J., Kabat-Zinn, J., Schumacher, J., et al. (2003). Alternations in brain and immune function produced by mindfulness meditation. *Psychosomatic Medicine, 65*(4), 564–570.

Davidson, T. L. (2000). Latent learning. In A. E. Kazdin (Ed.), *Encyclopedia of psychology* (Vol. 4). Washington, DC: American Psychological Association.

Davis, D., & Follette, W. C. (2002). Rethinking the probative value of evidence. *Law & Human Behavior, 26*(2), 133–158.

Davis, M. A. (2009). Understanding the relationship between mood and creativity: A meta-analysis. *Organizational Behavior & Human Decision Processes, 108*(1), 25–38.

Davis, M. R., McMahon, M., & Greenwood, K. M. (2005). The efficacy of mnemonic components of the cognitive interview: Towards a shortened variant for time-critical investigations. *Applied Cognitive Psychology, 19*(1), 75–93.

Davison, G. C., & Neale, J. M. (2006). *Abnormal psychology* (10th ed.). San Francisco: Jossey-Bass.

Day, S., & Schneider, P. L. (2002). Psychotherapy using distance technology. *Journal of Counseling Psychology, 49*(4), 499–503.

de Bono, E. (1992). *Serious creativity.* New York: HarperCollins.

de Jong, P. J., & Muris, P. (2002). Spider phobia. *Journal of Anxiety Disorders, 16*(1), 51–65.

de las Fuentes, C., & Vasquez, M. J. T. (1999). Immigrant adolescent girls of color. In N. G. Johnson, M. C. Roberts, & J. Worell (Eds.), *Beyond appearance.* Washington: American Psychological Association.

de Leon, C. F. M. (2005). Social engagement and successful aging. *European Journal of Ageing, 2*(1), 64–66.

de Rios, M. D., & Grob, C. S. (2005). Editors' introduction: Ayahuasca use in cross-cultural perspective. *Journal of Psychoactive Drugs, 37*(2), 119–121.

Deardorff, J., Hayward, C., Wilson, K. A., et al. (2007). Puberty and gender interact to predict social anxiety symptoms in early adolescence. *Journal of Adolescent Health, 41*(1), 102–104.

Deckers, L. (2005). *Motivation: Biological, psychological, and environmental* (2nd ed.). Boston: Allyn & Bacon.

Deckro, G. R., Ballinger, K. M., Hoyt, M., et al. (2002). The evaluation of a mind/body intervention to reduce psychological distress and perceived stress in college students. *Journal of American College Health, 50*(6), 281–287.

Deeb, S. S. (2004). Molecular genetics of color-vision deficiencies. *Visual Neuroscience, 21*(3), 191–196.

DeGaetano, G. (2005). The impact of media violence on developing minds and hearts. In S. Olfman (Ed.), *Childhood lost: How American culture is failing our kids.* Westport, CT: Praeger Publishers.

Dein, S., & Littlewood, R. (2005). Apocalyptic suicide: From a pathological to an eschatological interpretation. *International Journal of Social Psychiatry, 51*(3), 198–210.

Deinzer, R., Kleineidam, C., Stiller-Winkler, R., et al. (2000). Prolonged reduction of salivary immunoglobulin A (sIgA) after a major academic exam. *Interna-*

tional Journal of Psychophysiology, 37, 219–232.

Delgado, B. M., & Ford, L. (1998). Parental perceptions of child development among low-income Mexican American families. *Journal of Child & Family Studies, 7*(4), 469–481.

Delpero, W. T., O'Neill, H., Casson, E., & Hovis, J. (2005). Aviation-relevent epidemiology of color vision deficiency. *Aviation, Space, & Environmental Medicine, 76*(2), 127–133.

Demos, J. N. (2005). *Getting started with neurofeedback.* New York: Norton.

Denmark, F. L., Rabinowitz, V. C., & Sechzer, J. A. (2005). *Engendering psychology: Women and gender revisited* (2nd ed.). Boston: Allyn & Bacon.

Denollet, J., & Van Heck, G. L. (2001). Psychological risk factors in heart disease. *Journal of Psychosomatic Research, 51*(3), 465–468.

Derlega, V. J., Winstead, B. A., & Jones, W. H. (2005). *Personality: Contemporary theory and research* (3rd ed.). Belmont, CA: Wadsworth.

Deutsch, M. (1993). Educating for a peaceful world. *American Psychologist, 48*(5), 510–517.

Devlin, B., Daniels, M., & Roeder, K. (1997). The heritability of IQ. *Nature, 388*(6641), 468–471.

Devoto, A., Lucidi, F., Violani, C., & Bertini, M. (1999). Effects of different sleep reductions on daytime sleepiness. *Sleep, 22*(3), 336–343.

Di Forti, M., Lappin, J. M., & Murray, R. M. (2007). Risk factors for schizophrenia: All roads lead to dopamine. *European Neuropsychopharmacology, 17*(Suppl. 2), S101–S107.

Di Marzo, V., Goparaju, S. K., Wang, L., et al. (2001). Leptin-regulated endocannabinoids are involved in maintaining food intake. *Nature, 410*(6830), 822–825.

Diano, S., Farr, S. A., Benoit, S. C., et al. (2006). Ghrelin controls hippocampal spine synapse density and memory performance. *Nature Neuroscience, 9,* 381–388.

Dickens, W. T., & Flynn, J. R. (2001). Heritability estimates versus large environmental effects: The IQ paradox resolved. *Psychological Review, 108,* 346–369.

Dickerson, F. B., Tenhula, W. N., & Green-Paden, L. D. (2005). The token economy for schizophrenia: Review of the literature and recommendations for future research. *Schizophrenia Research, 75*(2–3), 405–416.

Dickinson, D. K., & Tabors, P. O. (Eds.). (2001). *Beginning literacy with language.* Baltimore, MD: Paul H. Brookes.

Dick-Niederhauser, A., & Silverman, W. K. (2006). Separation anxiety disorder. In J. E. Fisher & W. T. O'Donohue (Eds.), *Practitioner's guide to evidence-based psychotherapy.* New York: Springer.

Dieterich, S. E., Assel, M. A., Swank, P., et al. (2006). The impact of early maternal verbal scaffolding and child language abilities on later decoding and reading comprehension skills. *Journal of School Psychology, 43*(6), 481–494.

Dinan, T. G. (2001). Stress, depression and cardiovascular disease. *Stress & Health: Journal of the International Society for the Investigation of Stress, 17*(2), 65–66.

Dingus, T. A., Klauer, S. G., Neale, V. L., Petersen, A., et al. (2006). The 100-car naturalistic driving study, Phase II: Results of the 100-car field experiment. *National Highway Traffic Safety Administration Report No.* DOT HS 810 593. Retrieved April 21, 2009, from http://www.nhtsa.gov/staticfiles/DOT/NHTSA/NRD/Multimedia/PDFs/Crash%20Avoidance/Driver%20Distraction/100CarMain.pdf.

Dinkmeyer, D., Sr., McKay, G. D., & Dinkmeyer, D., Jr. (1997). *The parent's handbook.* Circle Pines, MN: American Guidance Service.

Dion, K. L. (2003). Prejudice, racism, and discrimination. In T. Millon & M. J. Lerner (Eds.), *Personality and social psychology. The comprehensive handbook of psychology* (Vol. 5). New York: Wiley.

Dirkzwager, A. J. E., Bramsen, I., & Van Der Ploeg, H. M. (2001). The longitudinal course of posttraumatic stress disorder symptoms among aging military veterans. *Journal of Nervous & Mental Disease, 189*(12), 846–853.

Distin, K. (2006). *Gifted children: A guide for parents and professionals.* London: Jessica Kingsley Publishers.

Dixon, M. J., Smilek, D., & Merikle, P. M. (2004). Not all synaesthetes are created equal: Projector versus associator synaesthetes. *Cognitive, Affective, & Behavioral Neuroscience, 4*(3), 335–343.

Dixon, S. V., Graber, J, A., & Brooks-Gunn, J. (2008). The roles of respect for parental authority and parenting practices in parent-child conflict among African American, Latino, and European American families. *Journal of Family Psychology, 22*(1), 1–10.

Dobelle, W. H. (2000). Artificial vision for the blind by connecting a television camera to the visual cortex. *American Society of Artificial Internal Organs, 46,* 3–9.

Dobson, K. S., Backs-Dermott, G. J., & Dozois, D. J. A. (2000). Cognitive and cognitive-behavioral therapies. In C. R. Snyder & R. E. Ingram (Eds.), *Handbook of psychological change: Psychotherapy processes and practices for the 21st century.* New York: Wiley.

Doidge, N. (1997). Empirical evidence for the efficacy of psychoanalytic psychotherapies and psychoanalysis. *Psychoanalytic Inquiry* (Suppl.), 102–150.

Dollard, J., & Miller, N. E. (1950). *Personality and psychotherapy: An analysis in terms of learning, thinking, and culture.* New York: McGraw-Hill.

Domhoff, G. W. (2001). A new neuro-cognitive theory of dreams. *Dreaming, 11,* 13–33.

Domhoff, G. W. (2003). *The scientific study of dreams: neural networks, cognitive development, and content analysis.* Washington, DC: American Psychological Association.

Domingo, R. A., & Goldstein-Alpern, N. (1999). "What dis?" and other toddler-initiated, expressive language-learning strategies. *Infant-Toddler Intervention, 9*(1), 39–60.

Domjan, M. (2010). *The principles of learning and behavior* (6th ed.). Belmont, CA: Cengage Learning/Wadsworth.

Donate-Bartfield, E., & Passman, R. H. (2004). Relations between children's attachments to their mothers and to security blankets. *Journal of Family Psychology, 18*(3), 453–458.

Dooling, D. J., & Lachman, R. (1971). Effects of comprehension on retention of prose. *Journal of Experimental Psychology, 88,* 216–222.

Doran, S. M., Van Dongen, H. P., & Dinges, D. F. (2001). Sustained attention performance during sleep deprivation. *Archives of Italian Biology, 139,* 253–267.

Dorfman, J., Shames, J., & Kihlstrom, J. F. (1996). Intuition, incubation, & insight. In G. Underwood (Ed.), *Implicit cognition.* New York: Oxford University Press.

Dorman, M. F., & Wilson, B. S. (2004). The design and function of cochlear implants. *American Scientist, 92*(Sept-Oct), 436–445.

Dosher, B. A., & Ma, J. (1998). Output loss or rehearsal loop? *Journal of Experimental Psychology: Learning, Memory, & Cognition, 24*(2), 316–335.

Dougall, A. L., & Baum, A. (2003). Stress, coping, and immune function. In M. Gallagher & R. J. Nelson (Eds.), *Handbook of psychology: Biological psychology* (Vol. 3). New York: John Wiley.

Dougherty, D. D., Baer, L., Cosgrove, G. R., et al. (2002). Prospective long-term follow-up of 44 patients who received cingulotomy for treatment-refractory obsessive-compulsive disorder. *American Journal of Psychiatry, 159*(2), 269–275.

Douvan, E. (1997). Erik Erikson: Critical times, critical theory. *Child Psychiatry & Human Development, 28*(1), 15–21.

Dovidio, J. F., & Gaertner, S. L. (1999). Reducing prejudice: Combating intergroup biases. *Current Directions in Psychological Science, 8*(4), 101–105.

Dovidio, J. F., & Penner, L. A. (2001). Helping and altruism. In M. Hewstone & M. Brewer (Eds.), *Handbook of social psychology.* London: Blackwell.

Dovidio, J. F., Gaertner, S. L., Kawakami, K., & Hodson, G. (2002). Why can't we just get along? *Cultural Diversity and Ethnic Minority Psychology, 8*(2), 88–102.

Dovidio, J. F., Glick, P., & Rudman, L. A. (Eds.). (2005). *On the nature of prejudice: Fifty years after Allport.* Malden, MA: Blackwell.

Dowling, K. W. (2005). The effect of lunar phases on domestic violence incident rates. *Forensic Examiner, 14*(4), 13–18.

Dozois, D. J. A., & Dobson, K. S. (2002). Depression. In M. M. Antony & D. H. Barlow (Eds.), *Handbook of assessment and treatment planning for psychological disorders.* New York: Guilford.

Dozois, D. J. A., & Dobson, K. S. (Eds.). (2004). *The prevention of anxiety and depression: Theory, research, and practice.* Washington, DC: American Psychological Association.

Draguns, J. G., Gielen, U. P., & Fish, J. M. (2004). Approaches to culture, healing, and psychotherapy. In U.P. Gielen, J.M. Fish, & J.G. Draguns (Eds.), *Handbook of Culture, Therapy, and Healing* (pp. 1–9). Mahwah, NJ: Erlbaum.

Drigotas, S. M., Rusbult, C. E., Wieselquist, J., & Whitton, S. W. (1999). Close partner as sculptor of the ideal self: Behavioral affirmation and the Michelangelo phenomenon. *Journal of Personality & Social Psychology, 77*(2), 293–323.

Drolet, G., Dumont, E. C., Gosselin, I., et al. (2001). Role of endogenous opioid system in the regulation of the stress response. *Progress in Neuro-Psychopharmacology & Biological Psychiatry, 25*(4), 729–741.

Druckman, D., & Bjork, R. A. (1994). *Learning, remembering, believing: Enhancing human performance.* Washington, DC: National Academy Press.

Drummond, M., Douglas, J., & Olver, J. (2007). Anosmia after traumatic brain injury: A clinical update. *Brain Impairment, 8*(1), 31–40.

Duclos, S. E., & Laird, J. D. (2001). The deliberate control of emotional experience through control of expressions. *Cognition & Emotion, 15*, 27–56.

Duffy, J. F., & Wright, K. P., Jr. (2005). Entrainment of the human circadian system by light. *Journal of Biological Rhythms, 20*(4), 326–338.

Dulewicz, V., & Higgs, M. (2000). Emotional intelligence. *Journal of Managerial Psychology, 15*(4), 341–372.

Duncan, J. (2005). Frontal lobe function and general intelligence: Why it matters. *Cortex, 41*(2), 215–217.

Duncker, K. (1945). On problem solving. *Psychological Monographs, 58*(270).

Durand, V. M., & Barlow, D. H. (2006). *Essentials of abnormal psychology* (4th ed.). Belmont, CA: Thomson/Wadsworth.

Durand, V. M., & Barlow, D. H. (2010). *Essentials of abnormal psychology* (5th ed.). Belmont, CA: Cengage Learning/Wadsworth.

Durham, M. D., & Dane, F. C. (1999). Juror knowledge of eyewitness behavior. *Journal of Social Behavior & Personality, 14*(2), 299–308.

Durrant, J. E., & Janson, S. (2005). Legal reform, corporal punishment and child abuse: The case of Sweden. *International Review of Victimology, 12*, 139–158.

Dutta, T., & Mandal, M. K. (2005). The relationship of handedness and accidents: A meta-analytical review of findings. *Psychological Studies, 50*(4), 309–316.

Dutton, D., & Aron, A. (1974). Some evidence for heightened sexual attraction under conditions of high anxiety. *Journal of Personality & Social Psychology, 30*, 510–517.

Dywan, J., & Bowers, K. S. (1983). The use of hypnosis to enhance recall. *Science, 222*, 184–185.

Dzokoto, V. A., & Adams, G. (2005). Understanding genital-shrinking epidemics in West Africa: Koro, juju, or mass psychogenic illness? *Culture, Medicine & Psychiatry, 29*(1), 53–78.

Ebbinghaus, H. (1885). *Memory: A contribution to experimental psychology.* Translated by H. A. Ruger & C. E. Bussenius, 1913. New York: New York Teacher's College, Columbia University.

Eckerman, D. A. (1999). Scheduling reinforcement about once a day. *Behavioural Processes, 45*(1-3), 101–114.

Eddy, K. T., Dutra, L., Bradley, R., & Westen, D. (2004). A multidimensional meta-analysis of psychotherapy and pharmacotherapy for obsessive-compulsive disorder. *Clinical Psychology Review, 24*(8), 1011–1030.

Eichenbaum, H., & Fortin, N. J. (2005). Bridging the gap between brain and behavior: Cognitive and neural mechanisms of episodic memory. *Journal of the Experimental Analysis of Behavior, 84*(3), 619–629.

Eidelson, R. J., & Eidelson, J. I. (2003). Dangerous ideas. *American Psychologist, 58*(3), 182–192.

Eifert, G. H., & Lejuez, C. W. (2000). Aversion therapy. In A. E. Kazdin (Ed.), *Encyclopedia of psychology.* Washington, DC: American Psychological Association.

Eimas, P. D., Quinn, P. C., & Cowan, P. (1994). Development of exclusivity in perceptually based categories of young infants. *Journal of Experimental Child Psychology, 58*(3), 418–431.

Eisenberg, N., Valiente, C., Fabes, R. A., et al. (2003). The relations of effortful control and ego control to children's resiliency and social functioning. *Developmental Psychology, 39*(4), 761–776.

Eisler, I., Simic, M., Russell, G. F. M., & Dare, C. (2007). A randomised controlled treatment trial of two forms of family therapy in adolescent anorexia nervosa: A five-year follow-up. *Journal of Child Psychology & Psychiatry, 48*(6), 552–560.

Eisler, J. A., Justice, J. B., Jr., & Neill, D. B. (2004). Individual differences in reward sensitivity: Implications for psychostimulant abuse vulnerability. *North American Journal of Psychology, 6*(3), 527–544.

Ekman, P. (1993). Facial expression and emotion. *American Psychologist, 48*(4), 384–392.

Ekman, P., Levenson, R. W., & Friesen, W. V. (1983). Autonomic nervous system activity distinguishes among emotions. *Science, 223*, 1208–1210.

Elder, P. (2006). *Critical thinking: Learn the tools the best thinkers use.* Englewood Cliffs, NJ: Prentice-Hall.

Eliot, L. (1999). *What's going on in there?* New York: Bantam.

Elli, K. A., & Nathan, P. J. (2001). The pharmacology of human working memory. *International Journal of Neuropsychopharmacology, 4*(3), 299–313.

Ellickson, P. L., Martino, S. C., & Collins, R. L. (2004). Marijuana use from adolescence to young adulthood. *Health Psychology, 23*(3), 299–307.

Elliott, M., & Williams, D. (2003). The client experience of counselling and psychotherapy. *Counselling Psychology Review, 18*(1), 34–38.

Ellis, A. (1979). The practice of rational-emotive therapy. In A. Ellis & J. Whiteley (Eds.), *Theoretical and empirical foundations of rational-emotive therapy.* Monterey, CA: Brooks/Cole.

Ellis, A. (1995). Changing rational-emotive therapy (RET) to rational emotive behavior therapy (REBT). *Journal of Rational-Emotive & Cognitive Behavior Therapy, 13*(2), 85–89.

Ellis, A. (2004). Why rational emotive behavior therapy is the most comprehensive and effective form of behavior therapy. *Journal of Rational-Emotive & Cognitive Behavior Therapy, 22*(2), 85–92.

Emmorey, K., Grabowski, T., McCullough, S., et al. (2003). Neural systems underlying lexical retrieval for sign language. *Neuropsychologia, 41*(1), 85–95.

Emurian, H. H. (2005). Web-based programmed instruction: Evidence of rule-governed learning. *Computers in Human Behavior, 21*(6), 893–915.

Engle, D. E., & Arkowitz, H. (2006). *Ambivalence in psychotherapy: Facilitating readiness to change.* New York: Guilford.

Engler, B. (2009). *Personality theories* (5th ed.). Belmont, CA: Cengage Learning/Wadsworth.

Enns, J. T., & Coren, S. (1995). The box alignment illusion. *Perception & Psychophysics, 57*(8), 1163–1174.

Enns, M. W., Cox, B. J., & Clara, I. P. (2005). Perfectionism and neuroticism: A longitudinal study of specific vulnerability and diathesis-stress models. *Cognitive Therapy & Research, 29*(4), 463–478.

Erickson, C. D., & al-Timimi, N. R. (2001). Providing mental health services to Arab Americans. *Cultural Diversity and Ethnic Minority Psychology, 7*(4), 308–327.

Ericsson, K. A. (2000). How experts attain and maintain superior performance. *Journal of Aging & Physical Activity, 8*(4), 366–372.

Ericsson, K. A., & Charness, N. (1994). Expert performance. *American Psychologist, 49*(8), 725–747.

Ericsson, K. A., & Chase, W. G. (1982). Exceptional memory. *American Scientist, 70*, 607–615.

Ericsson, K. A., Delaney, P. F., Weaver, G., & Mahadevan, R. (2004). Uncovering the structure of a memorist's superior "basic" memory capacity. *Cognitive Psychology, 49*(3), 191–237.

Erikson, E. H. (1963). *Childhood and society.* New York: Norton.

Erlacher, D., & Schredl, M. (2004). Dreams reflecting waking sport activities: A comparison of sport and psychology students. *International Journal of Sport Psychology, 35*(4), 301–308.

Ernst, E. (1994). Is acupuncture effective for pain control? *Journal of Pain & Symptom Management, 9*(2), 72–74.

Eron, L. D. (1987). The development of aggressive behavior from the perspective of a developing behaviorism. *American Psychologist, 42*(5), 435–442.

Eschholz, S., Chiricos, T., & Gertz, M. (2003). Television and fear of crime: Program types, audience traits, and the mediating effect of perceived neighborhood racial composition. *Social Problems, 50*(3), 395–415.

Espie, C. A. (2002). Insomnia. *Annual Review of Psychology, 53*, 215–243.

Esterling, B. A., L'Abate, L., Murray, E. J., & Pennebaker, J. W. (1999). Empirical foundations for writing in prevention and psychotherapy: Mental and physical health outcomes. *Clinical Psychology Review, 19*(1), 79–96.

Ethier, K. A., Kershaw, T., Niccolai, L., et al. (2003). Adolescent women underestimate their susceptibility to sexually transmitted infections. *Sexually Transmitted Infections, 79*, 408–411.

Evardone, M., Alexander, G. M., & Morey, L. C. (2007). Hormones and borderline personality features. *Personality & Individual Differences, 44*(1), 278–287.

Everly, G. S. (2002). Thoughts on peer (paraprofessional) support in the provision of mental health services. *International Journal of Emergency Mental Health, 4*(2), 89–92.

Ewen, R. B. (2003). *An introduction to theories of personality* (6th ed.). Hillsdale, NJ: Lawrence Erlbaum.

Eysenck, H. J. (Ed.). (1981). *A model for personality.* New York: Springer-Verlag.

Eysenck, H. J. (1994). The outcome problem in psychotherapy: What have we learned? *Behaviour Research & Therapy, 32*(5), 477–495.

Fabrega, H., Jr. (2004). Culture and the origins of psychopathology. In U. P. Gielen, J. M. Fish, & J. G. Draguns (Eds.), *Handbook of culture, therapy, and healing.* Mahwah, NJ: Erlbaum.

Fahim, C., Stip, E., Mancini-Marïe, A., et al. (2005). Brain activity during emotionally negative pictures in schizophrenia with and without flat affect: An fMRI study. *Psychiatry Research: Neuroimaging, 140*(1), 1–15.

Fahle, M., & Poggio, T. (Eds.). (2002). *Perceptual learning.* Cambridge, MA: MIT Press.

Fain, G. L. (2003). *Sensory transduction.* Sunderland, MA: Sinauer.

Faith, M. S., Wong, F. Y., & Carpenter, K. M. (1995). Group sensitivity training: Update, meta-analysis, and recommendations. *Journal of Counseling Psychology, 42*(3), 390–399.

Falkowski, C. (2000). *Dangerous drugs.* Center City, MN: Hazelden Information Education.

Farah, M. J. (2004). *Visual agnosia* (2nd ed.). Cambridge, MA: MIT Press.

Farah, M. J. (2006). Prosopagnosia. In M. J. Farah & T. E. Feinberg (Eds.), *Patient-based approaches to cognitive neuroscience* (2nd ed.). Cambridge, MA: MIT Press.

Farb, N. A. S., Segal, Z. V., Mayberg, H., et al. (2007). Attending to the present: Mindfulness meditation reveals distinct neural modes of self-reference. *Social Cognitive & Affective Neuroscience, 2*(4), 313–322.

Farrell, M. J., Zamarripa, F., Shade, R., et al. (2008). Effect of aging on regional cerebral blood flow responses associated with osmotic thirst and its satiation by water drinking: A PET study. *PNAS Proceedings of the National Academy of Sciences of the United States of America, 105*(1), 382–387.

Farrimond, T. (1990). Effect of alcohol on visual constancy values and possible relation to driving performance. *Perceptual & Motor Skills, 70*(1), 291–295.

Farroni, T., Massaccesi, S., Pividori, D., & Johnson, M. H. (2004). Gaze following in newborns. *Infancy, 5*(1), 39–60.

Federal Bureau of Investigation. (2005). *Crime in the United States, 2005.* Washington, DC: Author. Retrieved October 17, 2006, from http://www.fbi.gov/ucr/05cius/.

Feingold, A. (1992). Gender differences in mate selection preferences. *Psychological Bulletin, 111,* 304–341.

Feldman, D. H. (2004). Piaget's stages: The unfinished symphony of cognitive development. *New Ideas in Psychology, 22*(3), 175–231.

Fellous, J.-M., & Ledoux, J. E. (2005). Toward basic principles for emotional processing: What the fearful brain tells the robot. In J.-M. Fellous & M. A. Arbib (Eds.), *Who needs emotions? The brain meets the robot.* New York: Oxford University Press.

Fenn, K. M., Nusbaum, H. C., & Margoliash, D. (2003). Consolidation during sleep of perceptual learning of spoken language. *Nature, 425*(6958), 614–616.

Fenton, G. W. (1998). Neurosurgery for mental disorder. *Irish Journal of Psychological Medicine, 15*(2), 45–48.

Fernald, A. (1989). Intonation and communicative intent in mothers' speech to infants: Is the melody the message? *Child Development, 60*(6), 1497–1510.

Fernald, A., Perfors, A., & Marchman, V. A. (2006). Picking up speed in understanding: Speech processing efficiency and vocabulary growth across the 2nd year. *Developmental Psychology, 42*(1), 98–116.

Féron, F., Perry, C., Cochrane, J., et al. (2005). Autologous olfactory ensheathing cell transplantation in human spinal cord injury. *Brain: A Journal of Neurology, 128*(12), 2951–2960.

Ferrari, J. R., & Scher, S. J. (2000). Toward an understanding of academic and nonacademic tasks procrastinated by students: The use of daily logs. *Psychology in the Schools, 37*(4), 359–366.

Festinger, L. (1957). *A theory of cognitive dissonance.* Evanston, IL: Row Peterson.

Festinger, L., & Carlsmith, J. M. (1959). Cognitive consequences of forced compliance. *Journal of Abnormal & Social Psychology, 58*(2), 203–210.

Ficca, G., & Salzarulo, P. (2004). What in sleep is for memory. *Sleep Medicine, 5,* 225–230.

Field, C. E., Nash, H. M., Handwerk, M. L., & Friman, P. C. (2004). A modification of the token economy for nonresponsive youth in family-style residential care. *Behavior Modification, 28*(3), 438–457.

Fields, R. D. (2007). The shark's electric sense. *Scientific American, 297*(8), 74–81.

Fields, R. M., & Margolin, J. (2001). *Coping with trauma.* Washington, DC: American Psychological Association.

Figueredo, A. J., Sefcek, J. A., & Jones, D. N. (2006). The ideal romantic partner personality. *Personality & Individual Differences, 41*(3), 431–441.

Fink, M. (2000, March–April). Electroshock revisited. *American Scientist, 88,* 162–167.

Fink, M., & Taylor, M. A. (2003). *Catatonia: A clinician's guide to diagnosis and treatment.* London: Cambridge University Press.

Fiore, D., Dimaggio, G., Nicoló, G., et al. (2008). Metacognitive interpersonal therapy in a case of obsessive-compulsive and avoidant personality disorders. *Journal of Clinical Psychology, 64*(2), 168–180.

Fireman, G., Kose, G., & Solomon, M. J. (2003). Self-observation and learning: The effect of watching oneself on problem solving performance. *Cognitive Development, 18*(3), 339–354.

First, M. B., & Pincus, H. A. (2002). The DSM-IV text revision: Rationale and potential impact on clinical practice. *Psychiatric Services, 53,* 288–292.

Fischer, A. H., Manstead, A. S. R., Rodriquez Mosquera, P. M., & van Vianen, A. E. M. (2004). Gender and culture differences in emotion. *Emotion, 4*(1), 87–94.

Fisher, R. P., & Geiselman, R. E. (1987). Enhancing eyewitness memory with the cognitive interview. In M. M. Gruneberg, P. E. Morris, & R. N. Sykes (Eds.), *Practical aspects of memory: Current research and issues.* Chinchester, UK: Wiley.

Fiske, S. T., Cuddy, A. J. C., Glick, P., & Xu, J. (2002). A model of (often mixed) stereotype content. *Journal of Personality & Social Psychology, 82*(6), 878–902.

Flanagan, M. B., May, J. G., & Dobie, T. G. (2004). The role of vection, eye movements and postural instability in the etiology of motion sickness. *Journal of Vestibular Research: Equilibrium & Orientation, 14*(4), 335–346.

Flannery, D. J., Rowe, D. C., & Gulley, B. L. (1993). Impact of pubertal status, timing, and age on adolescent sexual experience and delinquency. *Journal of Adolescent Research, 8*(1), 21–40.

Flavell, J. H. (1992). Cognitive development: Past, present, and future. *Developmental Psychology, 28*(6), 998–1005.

Florida Medical Examiners Commission. (2008). *Drugs identified in deceased persons by Florida Medical Examiners: 2008 Interim report.* Tallahassee, FL: Medical Examiners Commission Staff, Florida Depart-

ment of Law Enforcement. Retrieved April 10, 2009, from http://www.fdle.state.fl.us/Content/getdoc/c75b8a3c-95ea-41d1-96c5-3b00c9c6eeb4/2008InterimReport.aspx.

Flowe, H. D., & Ebbese, E. B. (2007). The effect of lineup member similarity on recognition accuracy in simultaneous and sequential lineups. *Law & Human Behavior, 31*(1), 33–52.

Flynn, J. R. (2007). *What is intelligence? Beyond the Flynn Effect.* New York: Cambridge.

Fobair, P. (1997). Cancer support groups and group therapies. *Journal of Psychosocial Oncology, 15*(3–4), 123–147.

Fochtmann, L. J. (1995). Intractable sneezing as a conversion symptom. *Psychosomatics, 36*(2), 103–112.

Fogel, S. M., Nader, R., Cote, K. A., & Smith, C. T. (2007). Sleep spindles and learning potential. *Behavioral Neuroscience, 121*(1), 1–10.

Folkman, S., & Moskowitz, J. T. (2004). Coping. *Annual Review of Psychology, 55,* 745–774.

Follett, K., & Hess, T. M. (2002). Aging, cognitive complexity, and the fundamental attribution error. *Journals of Gerontology: Series B: Psychological Sciences & Social Sciences, 57B*(4), 312–323.

Fontaine, K. R., Redden, D. T., Wang, C., et al. (2003). Years of life lost due to obesity. *Journal of the American Medical Association, 289,* 187–193.

Fontenelle, D. H. (1989). *How to live with your children.* Tucson, AZ: Fisher Books.

Foo, P., Warren, W. H., Duchon, A., & Tarr, M. J. (2005). Do humans integrate routes into a cognitive map? Map- versus landmark-based navigation of novel shortcuts. *Journal of Experimental Psychology: Learning, Memory, & Cognition, 31*(2), 195–215.

Foot, M., & Koszycki, D. (2004). Gender differences in anxiety-related traits in patients with panic disorder. *Depression & Anxiety, 20*(3), 123–130.

Ford, D. Y., & Moore, J. L. (2006). Being gifted and adolescent: Issues and needs of students of color. In F. A. Dixon & S. M. Moon (Eds.), *The handbook of secondary gifted education.* Waco, TX: Prufrock Press.

Forney, W. S., Forney, J. C., & Crutsinger, C. (2005). Developmental stages of age and moral reasoning as predictors of juvenile delinquents' behavioral intention to steal clothing. *Family & Consumer Sciences Research Journal, 34*(2), 110–126.

Forsyth, J. P., & Savsevitz, J. (2002). Behavior therapy: Historical perspective and overview. In M. Hersen & W. H. Sledge (Eds.), *Encyclopedia of psychotherapy*. San Diego: Academic Press.

Fosse, R., Stickgold, R., & Hobson, J. A. (2001). The mind in REM sleep: Reports of emotional experience. *Sleep: Journal of Sleep & Sleep Disorders Research, 24*(8), 947–955.

Foster, C. A., Witcher, B. S., Campbell, W. K., & Green, J. D. (1998). Arousal and attraction. *Journal of Personality & Social Psychology, 74*(1), 86–101.

Foster, G., & Ysseldyke, J. (1976). Expectancy and halo effects as a result of artificially induced teacher bias. *Contemporary Educational Psychology, 1*, 37–45.

Fowers, B. J., & Davidov, B. J. (2006). The virtue of multiculturalism: Personal transformation, character, and openness to the other. *American Psychologist, 61*(6), 581–594.

Foxhall, K. (2000, January). Suddenly, a big impact on criminal justice. *APA Monitor*, 36–37.

Frank, J. D., & Frank, J. (2004). Therapeutic components shared by all psychotherapies. In A. Freeman, M. J. Mahoney, P. DeVito, & D. Martin (Eds.), *Cognition and psychotherapy* (2nd ed.). New York: Springer.

Franken, R. E. (2007). *Human motivation*. Belmont, CA: Wadsworth.

Franzoi, S. L. (2002). *Social psychology*. New York: McGraw-Hill.

Franzoi, S. L., & Klaiber, J. R. (2007). Body use and reference group impact: With whom do we compare our bodies? *Sex Roles, 56*(3-4), 205–214.

Fraser, C. (2002). Fact and fiction: A clarification of phantom limb phenomena. *British Journal of Occupational Therapy, 65*(6), 256–260.

Fredrickson, B. L. (2003). The value of positive emotions. *American Scientist, 91*, 330–335.

Fredrickson, B. L., & Branigan, C. (2005). Positive emotions broaden the scope of attention and thought-action repertoires. *Cognition & Emotion, 19*(3), 313–332.

Freeman, D., & Garety, P. A. (2004). *Paranoia: the psychology of persecutory delusions*. New York: Routledge.

French, C. C., Fowler, M., McCarthy, K., & Peers, D. (1991). A test of the Barnum effect. *Skeptical Inquirer, 15*(4), 66–72.

French, S. E., Kim, T. E., & Pillado, O. (2006). Ethnic identity, social group membership, and youth violence. In N. G. Guerra & E. P. Smith (Eds.), *Preventing youth violence in a multicultural society*.

Washington, DC: American Psychological Association.

Freud, S. (1900). *The interpretation of dreams*. London: Hogarth.

Freud, S. (1949). *An outline of psychoanalysis*. New York: Norton.

Frey, M. C., & Detterman, D. K. (2004). Scholastic assessment or g? The relationship between the scholastic assessment test and general cognitive ability. *Psychological Science, 15*(6), 373–378.

Fried, P. A., & Smith, A. M. (2001) A literature review of the consequences of prenatal marihuana exposure. *Neurotoxicology & Teratology, 23*(1), 1–11.

Friedman, H. S. (2002). *Health psychology* (2nd ed.). Englewood Cliffs, NJ: Prentice-Hall.

Friedman, L. (2006). What is psychoanalysis? *Psychoanalytic Quarterly, 75*(3), 689–713.

Friedman, L. J. (2004). Erik Erikson on generativity: A biographer's perspective. In E. de St. Aubin, D. P. McAdams, & T.-C. Kim (Eds.), *The generative society: Caring for future generations*. Washington, DC: American Psychological Association.

Friedman, M., & Rosenman, R. H. (1983). *Type A behavior and your heart*. New York: Knopf.

Friedman, R. C., Bucci, W., Christian, C., et al. (1998). Private psychotherapy patients of psychiatrist psychoanalysts. *American Journal of Psychiatry, 155*, 1772–1774.

Fritz, C. O., Morris, P. E., Acton, M., et al. (2007). Comparing and combining retrieval practice and the keyword mnemonic for foreign vocabulary learning. *Applied Cognitive Psychology, 21*(4), 499–526.

Froufe, M., & Schwartz, C. (2001). Subliminal messages for increasing self-esteem: Placebo effect. *Spanish Journal of Psychology, 4*(1), 19–25.

Frydman, M. (1999). Television, aggressiveness and violence. *International Journal of Adolescent Medicine & Health, 11*(3-4), 335–344.

Fukuda, K., & Ishihara, K. (2001). Age-related changes of sleeping pattern during adolescence. *Psychiatry & Clinical Neurosciences, 55*(3), 231–232.

Funder, D. C. (2006). *The personality puzzle* (4th ed.). New York: Norton.

Funk, J. B. (2005). Children's exposure to violent video games and desensitization to violence. *Child & Adolescent Psychiatric Clinics of North America, 14*(3), 387–404.

Furnham, A., Chamorro-Premuzic, T., & Callahan, I. (2003). Does graphology predict personality and intelligence? *Individual Differences Research, 1*(2), 78–94.

Gable, S. L., Reis, H. T., Impett, E., & Asher, F. R. (2004). What do you do when things go right? The intrapersonal and interpersonal benefits of sharing positive events. *Journal of Personality & Social Psychology, 87*, 228–245.

Gabrieli, J. D. E. (1998). Cognitive neuroscience of human memory. *Annual Review of Psychology, 49*, 87–115.

Gadzella, B. M. (1995). Differences in processing information among psychology course grade groups. *Psychological Reports, 77*, 1312–1314.

Gaertner, S. L., Dovidio, J. F., Banker, B. S., et al. (2000). Reducing intergroup conflict: From superordinate goals to decategorization, recategorization, and mutual differentiation. *Group Dynamics, 4*(1), 98–114.

Galambos, N. L., Barker, E. T., & Tilton-Weaver, L. C. (2003). Who gets caught at maturity gap? A study of pseudomature, immature and mature adolescents. *International Journal of Behavioral Development, 27*(3), 253–263.

Galanter, M., Hayden, F., Castañeda, R., & Franco, H. (2005). Group therapy, self-help groups, and network therapy. In R. J. Frances, S. I. Miller, & A. H. Mack (Eds.), *Clinical textbook of addictive disorders* (3rd ed.). New York: Guilford.

Galati, D., Scherer, K. R., & Ricci-Bitti, P. E. (1997). Voluntary facial expression of emotion: Comparing congenitally blind with normally sighted encoders. *Journal of Personality & Social Psychology, 73*(6), 1363–1379.

Galea, S., & Resnick, H. (2005). Post-traumatic stress disorder in the general population after mass terrorist incidents: Considerations about the nature of exposure. *CNS Spectrums, 10*(2), 107–115.

Galea, S., Ahern, J., Resnick, H., et al. (2002). Psychological sequelae of the September 11 terrorist attacks in New York City. *New England Journal of Medicine, 346*(13), 982–987.

Gallagher, S. (2004). Nailing the lie: An interview with Jonathan Cole. *Journal of Consciousness Studies, 11*(2), 3–21.

Ganis, G., Thompson, W. L., & Kosslyn, S. M. (2004). Brain areas underlying visual mental imagery and visual perception: An fMRI study. *Cognitive Brain Research, 20*(2), 226–241.

Ganster, D. C., Fox, M. L., & Dwyer, D. J. (2001). Explaining employees' health care costs: A prospective examination of stressful job demands, personal control, and physiological reactivity. *Journal of Applied Psychology, 86*, 954–964.

Garbarino, S., Beelke, M., Costa, G., et al. (2002). Brain function and effects of shift work: Implications for clinical neuropharmacology. *Neuropsychobiology, 45*, 50–56.

Garbarino, S., Mascialino, B., Penco, M. A., et al. (2004). Professional shift-work drivers who adopt prophylactic naps can reduce the risk of car accidents during night work. *Sleep: Journal of Sleep & Sleep Disorders Research, 27*(7), 1295–1302.

Garcia, E. E. (2008). Bilingual education in the United States. In J. Altarriba & R. R. Heredia (Eds.), *An introduction to bilingualism: Principles and processes*. Mahwah, NJ: Erlbaum.

Gardner, H. (2003, April). *Multiple intelligences after twenty years*. Invited address at meeting of American Educational Research Association. Retrieved May 10, 2009, from http://www.pz.harvard.edu/PIs/HG_MI_after_20_years.pdf.

Gardner, H. (2004). *Frames of mind* (10th anniversary ed.). New York: Basic.

Gardner, R. A., & Gardner, B. T. (1989). *Teaching sign language to chimpanzees*. Albany: State University of New York Press.

Garland, A. F., & Zigler, E. (1993). Adolescent suicide prevention. *American Psychologist, 48*(2), 169–182.

Garlow, S. J., Purselle, D. C., & Heninger, M. (2007). Cocaine and alcohol use preceding suicide in African American and White adolescents. *Journal of Psychiatric Research, 41*(6), 530–536.

Garnets, L. D. (2002) Sexual orientation in perspective. *Cultural Diversity & Ethnic Minority Psychology, 8*, 115–129.

Garnets, L. D., & Kimmel, D. (1991). Lesbian and gay male dimensions in the psychological study of human diversity. *Psychological perspectives on human diversity in America*. Washington, DC: American Psychological Association.

Gass, R. H., & Seiter, J. S. (2007). *Persuasion: Social influence and compliance gaining* (3rd ed.). Boston: Allyn & Bacon.

Gastner, M. T., Shalizi, C. R., & Newman, M. E. J. (2005). Maps and cartograms of the 2004 US presidential election results. *Advances in Complex Systems, 8*(1), 117–123.

Gatchel, R. J., & Oordt, M. S. (2003). Insomnia. In R. J. Gatchel & M. S. Oordt (Eds.), *Clinical health psychology and primary care: Practical advice and clinical guidance for successful collaboration* (pp. 135–148).

Washington, DC: American Psychological Association.

Gates, A. I. (1958). Recitation as a factor in memorizing. In J. Deese (Ed.), *The psychology of learning.* New York: McGraw-Hill.

Gatz, M. (2007). Genetics, dementia, and the elderly. *Current Directions in Psychological Science, 16*(3), 123–127.

Gauquelin, M. (1970). *Astrology and science.* London: Peter Davies.

Gayle, H. (2000). An overview of the global HIV/AIDS epidemic, with a focus on the United States. *AIDS, 14*(Suppl 2), S8–S17.

Gazzaniga, M. S. (1970). *The bisected brain.* New York: Plenum.

Gazzaniga, M. S. (2005). Forty-five years of split-brain research and still going strong. *Nature Reviews Neuroscience, 6*(8), 653–659.

Geary, N. (2004). Endocrine controls of eating: CCK, leptin, and ghrelin. *Physiology & Behavior, 81*(5), 719–733.

Geddes, L. (2008, October 3). Could brain scans ever be safe evidence? *New Scientist, 2676,* 8–9.

Gedo, J. E. (2002). The enduring scientific contributions of Sigmund Freud. *Perspectives in Biology & Medicine, 45,* 200–211.

Gegenfurtner, K. R., & Kiper, D. C. (2003). Color vision. *Annual Review of Neuroscience, 26,* 181–206.

Geiselman, R. E., Fisher, R. P., MacKinnon, D. P., & Holland, H. L. (1986). Eyewitness memory enhancement with the cognitive interview. *American Journal of Psychology, 99,* 385–401.

Geliebter, A., & Aversa, A. (2003). Emotional eating in overweight, normal weight, and underweight individuals. *Eating Behaviors, 3*(4), 341–347.

Genesee, F., Paradis., J., & Crago, M. (2004). *Dual language development and disorders: A handbook on bilingualism and second language learning.* London: Paul Brookes.

George, A. (2006, September 18). Living online: The end of privacy? *New Scientist, 2659,* 50–51.

Georgiades, A., Sherwood, A., Gullette, E. C., et al. (2000). Effects of exercise and weight loss on mental stress-induced cardiovascular responses in individuals with high blood pressure. *Hypertension, 36,* 171–176.

Gerardi, M., Rothbaum, B. O., Ressler, K., et al. (2008). Virtual reality exposure therapy using a virtual Iraq: Case report. *Journal of Traumatic Stress, 21*(2), 209–213.

Germain, A., Krakow, B., Faucher, B., et al. (2004). Increased mastery elements associated with imagery rehearsal treatment for nightmares in sexual assault survivors with PTSD. *Dreaming, 14*(4), 195–206.

German, T. P., & Barrett, H. C. (2005). Functional fixedness in a technologically sparse culture. *Psychological Science, 16*(1), 1–5.

German, T. P., & Defeyter, M. A. (2000). Immunity to functional fixedness in young children. *Psychonomic Bulletin & Review, 7*(4), 707–712.

Gersh, R. D. (1982, June 20). Learning when not to shoot. *Santa Barbara News Press.*

Gershoff, E. T. (2002). Corporal punishment by parents and associated child behaviors and experiences: A meta-analytic and theoretical review. *Psychological Bulletin, 128*(4), 539–579.

Gerwood, J. B. (1998). The legacy of Viktor Frankl. *Psychological Reports, 82*(2), 673–674.

Geschwind, N. (1979). Specializations of the human brain. *Scientific American, 241,* 180–199.

Gever, J. (2009, May 19). APA: Major changes loom for bible of mental health. *MedPage Today.* Retrieved June 21, 2009, from http://www.medpagetoday.com/MeetingCoverage/APA/14270.

Gewirtz, J. C., & Davis, M. (1998). Application of Pavlovian higher-order conditioning to the analysis of the neural substrates of fear conditioning. *Neuropharmacology, 37*(4-5), 453–459.

Giarratano, J. C., & Riley, G. (2005). *Expert systems, principles and programming* (4th ed.). Belmont, CA: Cengage Learning/Wadsworth.

Gibson, E. J., & Walk, R. D. (1960). The "visual cliff." *Scientific American, 202*(4), 67–71.

Gibson, K. R. (2002). Evolution of human intelligence: The roles of brain size and mental construction. *Brain, Behavior & Evolution, 59*(1–2), 10–20.

Gielen, U. P., Draguns, J. G., & Fish, J. M. (2008). Principles of multicultural counseling and therapy: An introduction. In U. P. Gielen, J. G. Draguns, & J. M. Fish (Eds.), *Principles of multicultural counseling and therapy.* New York: Routledge.

Gilbert, P. (2001). *Overcoming depression.* New York: Oxford.

Giliovich, T., Keltner, D., & Nisbett, R. (2005). *Social psychology.* New York: Norton.

Gillespie, C. F., & Nemeroff, C. B. (2007). Corticotropin-releasing factor and the psychobiology of early-life stress. *Current Directions in Psychological Science, 16*(2), 85–89.

Ginet, M., & Py, J. (2001). A technique for enhancing memory in eyewitness testimonies for use by police officers and judicial officials: The cognitive interview. *Travail Humain, 64*(2), 173–191.

Ginott, H. G. (1965). *Between parent and child: New solutions to old problems.* New York: Macmillan.

Ginsberg, D. L. (2006). Fatal agranulocytosis four years after clozapine discontinuation. *Primary Psychiatry, 13*(2), 32–33.

Giummarra, M. J., Gibson, S. J., Georgiou-Karistianis, N., & Bradshaw, J. L. (2007). Central mechanisms in phantom limb perception: The past, present and future. *Brain Research Reviews, 54*(1), 219–232.

Giuseppe, R. (2005). Virtual reality in psychotherapy: Review. *CyberPsychology & Behavior, 8*(3), 220–230. doi:10.1089/cpb.2005.8.220.

Gladwell, M. (2005). *Blink: The power of thinking without thinking.* New York: Little, Brown.

Gleason, J. B. (2005). *The development of language* (6th ed.). Boston: Allyn & Bacon.

Glisky, M. L., Williams, J. M., & Kihlstrom, J. F. (1996). Internal and external mental imagery perspectives and performance on two tasks. *Journal of Sport Behavior, 19*(1), 3–18.

Global Footprint Network. (2009). *Footprint basics: Overview.* Retrieved April 20, 2009, from http://www.footprintnetwork.org/en/index.php/GFN/page/footprint_basics_overview/.

Glueck, J., Ernst, R., & Unger, F. (2002). How creatives define creativity. *Creativity Research Journal, 14*(1), 55–67.

Gobet, F. (2005). Chunking models of expertise: Implications for education. *Applied Cognitive Psychology, 19*(2), 183–204.

Gobet, F., & Simon, H. A. (1996). Recall of random and distorted chess positions: Implications for the theory of expertise. *Memory & Cognition, 24*(4), 493–503.

Godnig, E. C. (2003). Tunnel vision: Its causes & treatment strategies. *Journal of Behavioral Optometry, 14*(4), 95–99.

Goel, V., & Dolan, R. J. (2004). Differential involvement of left prefrontal cortex in inductive and deductive reasoning. *Cognition, 93*(3), 109–121.

Gogate, L. J., Bahrick, L. E., & Watson, J. D. (2000). A study of multimodal motherese: The role of temporal synchrony between verbal labels and gestures. *Child Development, 71*(4), 878–894.

Goldberg, C. (2001). Of prophets, true believers, and terrorists. *The Dana Forum on Brain Science, 3*(3), 21–24.

Goldberg, R. (2006). *Drugs across the spectrum* (5th ed.). Belmont, CA: Cengage Learning/Wadsworth.

Golden, J. (2005). *Message in a bottle: The making of fetal alcohol syndrome.* Cambridge, MA: Harvard University Press.

Goldenberg, H., & Goldenberg, I. (2004). *Family therapy: An overview* (6th ed.). Pacific Grove, CA: Brooks/Cole.

Goldman, H. H. (1998). Deinstitutionalization and community care. *Harvard Review of Psychiatry, 6*(4), 219–222.

Goldstein, E. B. (2008). *Cognitive psychology: Connecting mind, research and everyday experience* (2nd ed.). Belmont, CA: Cengage Learning/Wadsworth.

Goldstein, E. B. (2010). *Sensation and perception* (8th ed.). Belmont, CA: Cengage Learning/Wadsworth.

Goldston, D. B., Molock, S. D., Whitbeck, L. B., et al. (2008). Cultural considerations in adolescent suicide prevention and psychosocial treatment. *American Psychologist, 63*(1), 14–31.

Goleman, D. (1995). *Emotional intelligence.* New York: Bantam.

Gomez, R., & McLaren, S. (2007). The inter-relations of mother and father attachment, self-esteem and aggression during late adolescence. *Aggressive Behavior, 33*(2), 160–169.

Goode, E. (1996). Gender and courtship entitlement: Responses to personal ads. *Sex Roles, 34*(3-4), 141–169.

Goodwin, R. D., Fergusson, D. M., & Horwood, L. J. (2005). Childhood abuse and familial violence and the risk of panic attacks and panic disorder in young adulthood. *Psychological Medicine, 35*(6), 881–890.

Gopnik, A., Meltzoff, A. N., & Kuhl, P. K. (2000). *The scientist in the crib: What early learning tells us about the mind.* New York: HarperCollins.

Gordon, A. K., & Kaplar, M. E. (2002). A new technique for demonstrating the actor-observer bias. *Teaching of Psychology, 29*(4), 301–303.

Gordon, T. (2000). *Parent effectiveness training: The proven program for raising responsible children.* New York: Three Rivers Press.

Gorman, J. M. (1996). *The essential guide to mental health.* New York: St. Martin's Griffin.

Gottlieb, G. (1998). Normally occurring environmental and behavioral influences on gene activity: From central dogma to probabilistic epigenesis. *Psychological Review, 105*(4), 792–802.

Gould, E., & Gross, C. G. (2002). Neurogenesis in adult mammals: Some progress and problems. *Journal of Neuroscience, 22*(3), 619–623.

Grabe, M. (2006). *Integrating technology for meaningful learning.* Boston: Houghton Mifflin.

Grabill, K., Merlo, L., Duke, D., et al. (2008). Assessment of obsessive-compulsive disorder: A review. *Journal of Anxiety Disorders, 22*(1), 1–17.

Grack, C., & Richman, C. L. (1996). Reducing general and specific heterosexism through cooperative contact. *Journal of Psychology & Human Sexuality, 8*(4), 59–68.

Grande, T., Rudolf, G., Oberbracht, C., & Pauli-Magnus, C. (2003). Progressive changes in patients' lives after psychotherapy. *Psychotherapy Research, 13*(1), 43–58.

Grandner, M. A., & Kripke, D. F. (2004). Self-reported sleep complaints with long and short sleep: A nationally representative sample. *Psychosomatic Medicine, 66,* 239–241.

Granrud, C. E. (2004). Visual metacognition and the development of size constancy. In D. T. Levin (Ed.), *Thinking and seeing: Visual metacognition in adults and children.*

Granrud, C. E. (2006). Size constancy in infants: 4-month-olds' responses to physical versus retinal image size. *Journal of Experimental Psychology: Human Perception & Performance, 32*(6), 1398–1404.

Grant, B. F., Hasin, D. S., Stinson, F. S., et al. (2006). The epidemiology of DSM-IV panic disorder and agoraphobia in the United States: Results from the National Epidemiologic Survey on Alcohol and Related Conditions. *Journal of Clinical Psychiatry, 67*(3), 363–374.

Grant, I., Gonzalez, R., Carey, C., & Natarajan, L. (2001, August 13). *Long-term neurocognitive consequences of marijuana.* Paper presented at National Institute on Drug Abuse Workshop on Clinical Consequences of Marijuana, Rockville, MD.

Graves, J. L. (2001). *The emperor's new clothes.* Piscataway, NJ: Rutgers University Press.

Gravetter, F. J., & Wallnau, L. B. (2010). *Statistics for the behavioral sciences* (8th ed.). Belmont, CA: Cengage Learning/Wadsworth.

Gray, J. M., & Wilson, M. A. (2007). A detailed analysis of the reliability and validity of the sensation seeking scale in a UK sample. *Personality & Individual Differences, 42*(4), 641–651.

Greenberg, D. L. (2004). President Bush's false 'flashbulb' memory of 9/11/01. *Applied Cognitive Psychology, 18*(3), 363–370.

Greene, D., & Lepper, M. R. (1974, September). How to turn play into work. *Psychology Today,* 49.

Greenfield, P. M. (1997). You can't take it with you: Why abilities assessments don't cross cultures. *American Psychologist, 52,* 1115–1124.

Greenglass, E. R., Burke, R. J., & Moore, K. A. (2003). Reactions to increased workload: Effects on professional efficacy of nurses. *Applied Psychology: An International Review, 52*(4), 580–597.

Greenwald, R. (2006). Eye movement desensitization and reprocessing with traumatized youth. In N. B. Webb (Ed.), *Working with traumatized youth in child welfare: Social work practice with children and families.* New York: Guilford.

Greenwood, J. G., Greenwood, J. J. D., McCullagh, J. F., et al. (2006). A survey of sidedness in Northern Irish schoolchildren: The interaction of sex, age, and task. *Laterality: Asymmetries of Body, Brain & Cognition, 12*(1), 1–18.

Gregory, R. L. (1990). *Eye and brain: The psychology of seeing.* Princeton, NJ: Princeton University Press.

Gregory, R. L. (2000). Visual illusions. In A. Kazdin (Ed.), *Encyclopedia of psychology.* Washington, DC: American Psychological Association.

Gregory, R. L. (2003). Seeing after blindness. *Nature Neuroscience, 6*(9), 909–910.

Greitemeyer, T. (2009). Effects of songs with prosocial lyrics on prosocial thoughts, affect, and behavior. *Journal of Experimental Social Psychology, 45*(1), 186–190.

Grello, C. M., Welsh, D. P., & Harper, M. S. (2006). No strings attached: The nature of casual sex in college students. *Journal of Sex Research, 43*(3), 255–267.

Griffin, D. R. (1992). *Animal minds.* Chicago: University of Chicago Press.

Griffin, W. A. (2002). Family therapy. In M. Hersen & W. H. Sledge (Eds.), *Encyclopedia of psychotherapy.* San Diego: Academic Press.

Griffin-Fennell, F., & Williams, M. (2006). Examining the complexities of suicidal behavior in the African American community. *Journal of Black Psychology, 32*(3), 303–319.

Grigorenko, E. L. (2005). The inherent complexities of gene–environment interactions. *Journals of Gerontology: Series B: Psychological Sciences & Social Sciences* [Special Research on Environmental Effects in Genetic Studies of Aging], *60B*(1), 53–64.

Grigorenko, E. L., & Sternberg, R. J. (2003). The nature-nurture issue. In A. Slater & G. Bremner (Eds.), *An introduction to developmental psychology.* Malden, MA: Blackwell.

Grobstein, P., & Chow, K. L. (1975). Perceptive field development and individual experience. *Science, 190,* 352–358.

Grubin, D., & Madsen, L. (2005). Lie detection and the polygraph: A historical review. *Journal of Forensic Psychiatry & Psychology, 16*(2), 357–369.

Grunbaum, J. A., Kann, L., Kinchen, S., et al. (2004). Youth Risk Behavior Surveillance: United States, 2003. *Morbidity and Mortality Weekly Report Surveillance Summary, 53*(SS02), 1–96.

Gruner, C. R., & Tighe, M. R. (1995). Semantic differential measurements of connotations of verbal terms and their doublespeak facsimiles in sentence contexts. *Psychological Reports, 77*(3, Pt 1), 778.

Guastello, D. D., & Guastello, S. J. (2003). Androgyny, gender role behavior, and emotional intelligence among college students and their parents. *Sex Roles, 49*(11-12), 663–673.

Guéguen, N. (2002). Status, apparel and touch: Their joint effects on compliance to a request. *North American Journal of Psychology, 4*(2), 279–286.

Guéguen, N., & Pascual, A. (2003). Status and people's tolerance towards an ill-mannered person: A field study. *Journal of Mundane Behavior, 4*(1). Retrieved August 4, 2007, from http://www.mundanebehavior.org/issues/v4n1/gueguen-pascual.htm.

Guéguen, N., Pascual, A., & Dagot, L. (2002). Low-ball and compliance to a request: An application in a field setting. *Psychological Reports, 91*(1), 81–84.

Gullette, D. L., & Lyons, M. A. (2005). Sexual sensation seeking, compulsivity, and HIV risk behaviors in college students. *Journal of Community Health Nursing, 22*(1), 47–60.

Gur, R. E., Cowell, P., Turetsky, B. I., et al. (1998). A follow-up magnetic resonance imaging study of schizophrenia. *Archives of General Psychiatry, 55*(2), 145–152.

Gurung, R. (2010). *Health psychology: A cultural approach* (2nd ed.). Belmont, CA: Cengage Learning/Wadsworth.

Gustavsson, J. P., Weinryb, R. M., Göransson, S., et al. (1997). Stability and predictive ability of personality traits across 9 years. *Personality & Individual Differences, 22*(6), 783–791.

Haas, B. W., Omura, K., Constable, R. T., & Canli, T. (2007). Is automatic emotion regulation associated with agreeableness? A perspective using a social neuroscience approach. *Psychological Science, 18*(2), 130–132.

Haber, R. N. (1969). Eidetic images; with biographical sketches. *Scientific American, 220*(12), 36–44.

Haber, R. N. (1970). How we remember what we see. *Scientific American, 222,* 104–112.

Haber, R. N., & Haber, L. (2000). Eidetic imagery. In A. E. Kazdin (Ed.), *Encyclopedia of psychology* (Vol. 3). Washington, DC: American Psychological Association.

Haddad, S. (2003). Islam and attitudes toward U.S. policy in the Middle East: Evidence from survey research in Lebanon. *Studies in Conflict & Terrorism, 26*(2), 135–154.

Hadwin, A. F., Kirby, J. R., & Woodhouse, R. A. (1999). Individual differences in notetaking, summarization and learning from lectures. *Alberta Journal of Educational Research, 45*(1), 1–17.

Haenschel, C., Vernon, D. J., Dwivedi, P., et al. (2005). Event-related brain potential correlates of human auditory sensory memory-trace formation. *Journal of Neuroscience, 25*(45), 10494–10501.

Hafer, C. L., & Bègue, L. (2005). Experimental research on just-world theory: Problems, developments, and future challenges. *Psychological Bulletin, 131*(1), 128–167.

Haier, R. J., Jung, R. E., Yeo, R. A., et al. (2004). Structural brain variation and general intelligence. *NeuroImage, 23,* 425–433.

Haier, R. J., Siegel, B. V., Nuechterlein, K. H., et al. (1988). Cortical glucose metabolic rate correlates of abstract reasoning and attention studied with positron emission tomography. *Intelligence, 12,* 199–217.

Haier, R. J., White, N. S., & Alkire, M. T. (2003). Individual differences in general intelligence correlate with brain function during nonreasoning tasks. *Intelligence, 31*(5), 429–441.

Halbert, J., Crotty, M., & Cameron, I. D. (2002). Evidence for the optimal management of acute and chronic phantom pain. *Clinical Journal of Pain, 18*(2), 84–92.

Hall, C. (1966). *The meaning of dreams.* New York: McGraw-Hill.

Hall, C. (1974). What people dream about. In R. L. Woods & H. B. Greenhouse (Eds.), *The new world of dreams: An anthology.* New York: Macmillan.

Hall, J. (2006). *What is clinical psychology?* (4th ed.). New York: Oxford University Press.

Hall, N. C., Perry, R. P., Goetz, T., et al. (2007). Attributional retraining and elaborative learning: Improving academic development through writing-based interventions. *Learning & Individual Differences, 17*(3), 280–290.

Hallahan, D. P., & Kauffman, J. M. (2006). *Exceptional learners* (10th ed.). Boston: Allyn & Bacon.

Halpern-Felsher, B. L., Cornell, J., Kropp, R. Y., & Tschann, J. (2005). Oral versus vaginal sex among adolescents: Perceptions, attitudes, and behavior. *Pediatrics, 115,* 845–851.

Hamilton, V. L., & Sanders, J. (1995). Crimes of obedience and conformity in the workplace. *Journal of Social Issues, 51*(3), 67–88.

Hammer, L. B., Grigsby, T. D., & Woods, S. (1998). The conflicting demands of work, family, and school among students at an urban university. *Journal of Psychology, 132*(2), 220–226.

Hancock, P. A., & Ganey, H. C. N. (2003). From the inverted-U to the extended-U: The evolution of a law of psychology. *Journal of Human Performance in Extreme Environments, 7*(1), 5–14.

Handsfield, H. H. (2001). Resurgent sexually transmitted diseases among men who have sex with men. *Medscape Infectious Disease, July.* Retrieved October 2, 2008, from https://profreg.medscape.com/px/getlogin.do?urlCache=aHR0cDovL3d3dy5tZWRzY2FwZS5jb20vdmlld2FydGljbGUvNDA4MzAx

Hanley, S. J., & Abell, S. C. (2002). Maslow and relatedness: Creating an interpersonal model of self-actualization. *Journal of Humanistic Psychology, 42*(4), 37–56.

Hansell, J. H. (2007). *Abnormal psychology: The enduring issues* (2nd ed.). New York: Wiley.

Hansen, C. J., Stevens, L. C., & Coast, J. R. (2001). Exercise duration and mood state. *Health Psychology, 20*(4), 267–275.

Hansen, N. B., Lambert, M. J., & Forman, E. M. (2002). The psychotherapy dose-response effect and its implications for treatment delivery services. *Clinical Psychology: Science & Practice, 9*(3), 329–334.

Hanton, S., Mellalieu, S. D., & Hall, R. (2004). Self-confidence and anxiety interpretation: A qualitative investigation. *Psychology of Sport & Exercise, 5*(4), 477–495.

Hardaway, C. A., & Gregory, K. B. (2005). Fatigue and sleep debt in an operational navy squadron. *International Journal of Aviation Psychology, 15*(2), 157–171.

Harding, D. J., Fox, C., & Mehta, J. D. (2002). Studying rare events through qualitative case studies. *Sociological Methods & Research, 31*(2), 174–217.

Harding, R. W., Morgan, F. H., Indermaur, D., et al. (1998). Road rage and the epidemiology of violence. *Studies on Crime & Crime Prevention, 7*(2), 221–238.

Hare, R. D. (2006). Psychopathy: A clinical and forensic overview. *Psychiatric Clinics of North America, 29*(3), 709–724.

Harker, L., & Keltner, D. (2001). Expressions of positive emotion in women's college yearbook pictures and their relationship to personality and life outcomes across adulthood. *Journal of Personality & Social Psychology, 80*(1), 112–124.

Harlow, H. F., & Harlow, M. K. (1962). Social deprivation in monkeys. *Scientific American, 207,* 136–146.

Harlow, J. M. (1868). Recovery from the passage of an iron bar through the head. *Publications of the Massachusetts Medical Society, 2,* 327–347.

Harm, D. L. (2002). Motion sickness neurophysiology, physiological correlates, and treatment. In K. M. Stanney (Ed.), *Handbook of virtual environments: Design, implementation, and applications.* Hillsdale, NJ: Erlbaum.

Harrigan, J. A. (2006). Proxemics, kinesics, and gaze. In J. A. Harrigan, R. Rosenthal, & K. R. Scherer (Eds.), *The new handbook of methods in nonverbal behavior research.* New York: Oxford University Press.

Harris, C. (2004). The evolution of jealousy. *American Scientist, 92*(Jan-Feb), 62–71.

Harris, J. A., Rushton, J. P., Hampson, E., & Jackson, D. N. (1996). Salivary testosterone and self-report aggressive and pro-social personality characteristics in men and women. *Aggressive Behavior, 22*(5), 321–331.

Harris, J. C. (2003). Pinel delivering the insane. *Archives of General Psychiatry, 60*(6), 552.

Harris, J. R., & Liebert, R. M. (1991). *The child.* Englewood Cliffs, NJ: Prentice Hall.

Harrison, P. J., & Weinberger, D. R. (2005). Schizophrenia genes, gene expression, and neuropathology: On the matter of their convergence. *Molecular Psychiatry, 10*(1), 40–68.

Hart, B., & Risley, T. R. (1999). *The social world of children learning to talk.* Baltimore, MD: Paul H. Brookes.

Hart, D., & Carlo, G. (2005). Moral development in adolescence. *Journal of Research on Adolescence. Special Issue: Moral Development, 15*(3), 223–233.

Hartgens, F., & Kuipers, H. (2004). Effects of androgenic-anabolic steroids in athletes. *Sports Medicine, 34*(8), 513–554.

Hartlep, K. L., & Forsyth, G. A. (2000). The effect of self-reference on learning and retention. *Teaching of Psychology, 27*(4), 269–271.

Hartmann, P., Reuter, M., & Nyborg, H. (2006). The relationship between date of birth and individual differences in personality and general intelligence: A large scale study. *Personality & Individual Differences, 40*(7), 1349–1362.

Harvey, C. A., Curson, D. A., Pantelis, C., & Taylor, J. (1996). Four behavioural syndromes of schizophrenia. *British Journal of Psychiatry, 168*(5), 562–570.

Hashibe, M., Straif, K., Tashkin, D. P., et al. (2005). Epidemiologic review of marijuana use and cancer risk. *Alcohol, 35*(3), 265–275.

Hashimoto, I., Suzuki, A., Kimura, T., et al. (2004). Is there training-dependent reorganization of digit representations in area 3b of string players? *Clinical Neurophysiology, 115*(2), 435–447.

Hauck, F. R., Moore, C. M., Herman, S. M., et al. (2002). The contribution of prone sleeping position to the racial disparity in sudden infant death syndrome. *Pediatrics, 110,* 772–780.

Hawks, J., Wang, E. T., Cochran, G. M., et al. (2007). Recent acceleration of human adaptive evolution. *Proceedings of the National Academy of Sciences, 104*(52), 20753–20758.

Hayne, H., & Rovee-Collier, C. (1995). The organization of reactivated memory in infancy. *Child Development, 66*(3), 893–906.

Heath, R. G. (1963). Electrical self-stimulation of the brain in man. *American Journal of Psychiatry, 120,* 571–577.

Hecht, J. (2007). *The happiness myth: Why what we think is right is wrong.* New York: HarperCollins.

Heimann, M., & Meltzoff, A. N. (1996). Deferred imitation in 9- and 14-month-old infants. *British Journal of Developmental Psychology, 14,* 55–64.

Heinrichs, R. W. (2001). *In search of madness.* New York: Oxford.

Heisel, M. J., Flett, G. L., & Hewitt, P. L. (2003). Social hopelessness and college student suicide ideation. *Archives of Suicide Research, 7*(3), 221–235.

Helgeson, V. S. (2005). *The psychology of gender* (2nd ed.). Englewood Cliffs, NJ: Prentice Hall.

Hellerstein, D. J., Rosenthal, R. N., Pinsker, H., et al. (1998). A randomized prospective study comparing supportive and dynamic therapies. *Journal of Psychotherapy Practice & Research, 7*(4), 261–271.

Hellige, J. B. (1993). *Hemispheric asymmetry.* Cambridge, MA: Harvard University Press.

Helson, R., & Srivastava, S. (2002). Creative and wise people. *Personality & Social Psychology Bulletin, 28*(10), 1430–1440.

Helton, W. S. (2007). Skill in expert dogs. *Journal of Experimental Psychology: Applied, 13*(3), 171–178.

Henderson, N. D. (1982). Human behavior genetics. *Annual Review of Psychology, 33,* 403–440.

Henman, L. D. (2001). Humor as a coping mechanism. *Humor: International Journal of Humor Research, 14*(1), 83–94.

Henningsen, D. D., Henningsen, M. L. M., Eden, J., & Cruz, M. G. (2006). Examining the symptoms of groupthink and retrospective sensemaking. *Small Group Research, 37*(1), 36–64.

Hepper, P. G., Wells, D. L., & Lynch, C. (2005). Prenatal thumb sucking is related to postnatal handedness. *Neuropsychologia, 43*(3), 313–315.

Hergenhahn, B. R. (2009). *An introduction to the history of psychology* (6th ed.). Belmont, CA: Cengage Learning/Wadsworth.

Hergenhahn, B. R., & Olson, M. (2005). *Introduction to the theories of learning* (7th ed.). Englewood Cliffs, NJ: Prentice Hall.

Heriot, S. A., & Pritchard, M. (2004). 'Reciprocal Inhibition as the Main Basis of Psychotherapeutic Effects' by Joseph Wolpe (1954). *Clinical Child Psychology & Psychiatry, 9*(2), 297–307.

Hermann, B., Seidenberg, M., Sears, L., et al. (2004). Cerebellar atrophy in temporal lobe epilepsy affects procedural memory. *Neurology, 63*(11), 2129–2131.

Hernstein, R., & Murray, C. (1994). *The bell curve*. New York: Free Press.

Herrmann, D. J., Yoder, C. Y., Gruneberg, M., & Payne, D. G. (2006). *Applied cognitive psychology: A textbook*. Mahwah, NJ: Erlbaum.

Herxheimer, A., & Waterhouse, J. (2003). The prevention and treatment of jet lag. *British Medical Journal, 326*(7384), 296–297.

Herz, R. S. (2001). Ah sweet skunk! *Cerebrum, 3*(4), 31–47.

Hettich, P. I. (2005). *Connect college to career: Student guide to work and life transition*. Belmont, CA: Cengage Learning/Wadsworth.

Higbee, K. L., Clawson, C., DeLano, L., & Campbell, S. (1990). Using the link mnemonic to remember errands. *Psychological Record, 40*(3), 429–436.

Higgins, S. T., Heil, S. H., & Lussier, J. P. (2004). Clinical implications of reinforcement as a determinant of substance use disorders. *Annual Review of Psychology, 55*, 431–461.

Higham, P. A., & Gerrard, C. (2005). Not all errors are created equal: Metacognition and changing answers on multiple-choice tests. *Canadian Journal of Experimental Psychology, 59*(1), 28–34.

Hilgard, E. R. (1968). *The experience of hypnosis*. New York: Harcourt Brace Jovanovich.

Hilgard, E. R. (1977). *Divided consciousness*. New York: Wiley.

Hilgard, E. R. (1994). Neodissociation theory. In S. J. Lynn & J. W. Rhue (Eds.), *Dissociation: Clinical, theoretical and research perspectives*. New York: Guilford.

Hilsenroth, M. J. (2000). Rorschach test. In A. Kazdin (Ed.), *Encyclopedia of psychology*. Washington, DC: American Psychological Association.

Hinkel, E. (Ed.). (2005). *Handbook of research in second language teaching and learning*. Mahwah, NJ: Erlbaum.

Hinterberger, T., Kübler, A., Kaiser, J., et al. (2003). A brain–computer interface (BCI) for the locked-in: Comparison of different EEG classifications for the thought translation device. *Clinical Neurophysiology, 114*(3), 416–425.

Hintzman, D. L. (2005). Memory strength and recency judgments. *Psychonomic Bulletin & Review, 12*(5), 858–864.

Hirshbein, L., & Sarvananda, S. (2008). History, power, and electricity: American popular magazine accounts of electroconvulsive therapy, 1940–2005. *Journal of the History of the Behavioral Sciences, 44*(1), 1–18.

Hirstein, W. (2005). *Brain fiction: Self-deception and the riddle of confabulation*. Cambridge, MA: MIT Press.

Hobson, J. A. (2000). Dreams: Physiology. In A. Kazdin (Ed.), *Encyclopedia of psychology*. Washington, DC: American Psychological Association.

Hobson, J. A. (2001). *The dream drugstore*. Cambridge, MA: MIT Press.

Hobson, J. A. (2005). Sleep is of the brain, by the brain and for the brain. *Nature, 437*(7063), 1254–1256.

Hobson, J. A., Pace-Schott, E. F., & Stickgold, R. (2000). Dream science 2000. *Behavioral & Brain Sciences, 23*(6), 1019–1035; 1083–1121.

Hochstenbach, J., Mulder, T., van Limbeek, J., et al. (1998). Cognitive decline following stroke: A comprehensive study of cognitive decline following stroke. *Journal of Clinical & Experimental Neuropsychology, 20*(4), 503–517.

Hodapp, R. M. (1994). Mental retardation. *Encyclopedia of human behavior* (Vol. 3). San Diego, CA: Academic Press.

Hodgson, R., & Miller, P. (1982). *Self-watching*. New York: Facts on File.

Hofer, B. K., & Yu, S. L. (2003). Teaching self-regulated learning through a "Learning to Learn" course. *Teaching of Psychology, 30*(1), 30–33.

Hoff, E. (2006). How social contexts support and shape language development. *Developmental Review, 26*(1), 55–88.

Hoff, E., & Tian, C. (2005). Socioeconomic status and cultural influences on language. *Journal of Communication Disorders, 38*(4), 271–278.

Hoffart, A. (2005). Interpersonal therapy for social phobia: Theoretical model and review of the evidence. In M. E. Abelian (Ed.), *Focus on psychotherapy research*. Hauppauge, NY: Nova Science Publishers.

Hoffer, A., & Youngren, V. R. (2004). Is free association still at the core of psychoanalysis? *International Journal of Psychoanalysis, 85*(6), 1489–1492.

Hoffman, H. G., Garcia-Palacios, A., Carlin, A., et al. (2003). Interfaces that heal: Coupling real and virtual objects to treat spider phobia. *International Journal of Human-Computer Interaction, 16*(2), 283–300.

Hogan, E. H., Hornick, B. A., & Bouchoux, A. (2002). Focus on communications: Communicating the message: Clarifying the controversies about caffeine. *Nutrition Today, 37*, 28–35.

Hoge, C. W., Castro, C. A., Messer, S. C., et al. (2004). Combat duty in Iraq and Afghanistan, mental health problems, and barriers to care. *New England Journal of Medicine, 351*(1), 13–22.

Hohwy, J., & Rosenberg, R. (2005). Unusual experiences, reality testing and delusions of alien control. *Mind & Language, 20*(2), 141–162.

Holden, C. (1980, November). Twins reunited. *Science, 80*, 55–59.

Hollon, S. D., Stewart, M. O., & Strunk, D. (2006). Enduring effects for cognitive behavior therapy in the treatment of depression and anxiety. *Annual Review of Psychology, 57*, 285–315.

Holman, E. A., Silver, R. C., Poulin, M., et al. (2008). Terrorism, acute stress, and cardiovascular health: A 3-year national study following the September 11th attacks. *Archives of General Psychiatry, 65*(1), 73–80.

Holmes, J., & Adams, J. W. (2006). Working memory and children's mathematical skills: Implications for mathematical development and mathematics curricula. *Educational Psychology, 26*(3), 339–366.

Holmes, P. S., & Collins, D. J. (2001). The PETTLEP approach to motor imagery: A functional equivalence model for sport psychologists. *Journal of Applied Sport Psychology, 13*(1), 60–83.

Holmes, T. H., & Rahe, R. H. (1967). The social readjustment rating scale. *Journal of Psychosomatic Research, 11*(2), 213–218.

Holtzen, D. W. (2000). Handedness and professional tennis. *International Journal of Neuroscience, 105*(1–4), 101–111.

Holzinger, B., LaBerge, S., & Levitan, L. (2006). Psychophysiological correlates of lucid dreaming. *Dreaming, 16*(2), 88–95.

Honts, C. R., & Alloway, W. R. (2007). Information does not affect the validity of a comparison question test. *Legal & Criminological Psychology, 12*(2), 311–320.

Horgan, J. (2005). The forgotten era of brain chips. *Scientific American, 293*(4), 66–73.

Horn, R. R., Williams, A. M., Scott, M. A., & Hodges, N. J. (2005). Visual search and coordination changes in response to video and point-light demonstrations without KR. *Journal of Motor Behavior, 37*(4), 265–274.

Horne, R. S. C., Andrew, S., Mitchell, K., et al. (2001). Apnoea of prematurity and arousal from sleep. *Early Human Development, 61*(2), 119–133.

Hortman, G. (2003). What do facial expressions convey? *Emotion, 3*(2), 150–166.

Horvath, L. S., Milich, R., Lynam, D., et al. (2004) Sensation seeking and substance use: A cross-lagged panel design. *Individual Differences Research, 2*(3), 175–183.

Hosch, H. M., & Cooper, D. S. (1982). Victimization as a determinant of eyewitness accuracy. *Journal of Applied Psychology, 67*, 649–652.

Houghton, D. P. (2008). Invading and occupying Iraq: Some insights from political psychology. *Peace & Conflict: Journal of Peace Psychology, 14*(2), 169–192.

Howard, A., Pion, G. M., Gottfredson, G. D., et al. (1986). The changing face of American psychology. *American Psychologist, 41*, 1311–1327.

Howard, I. P., & Rogers, B. J. (2001a). *Seeing in depth* (Vol 1): *Basic mechanisms*. Toronto, ON: Porteous.

Howard, I. P., & Rogers, B. J. (2001b). *Seeing in depth* (Vol 2): *Depth perception*. Toronto, ON: Porteous.

Howell, D. C. (2008). *Fundamental statistics for the behavioral sciences* (6th ed.). Belmont, CA: Cengage Learning/Wadsworth.

Howes, C. (1997). Children's experiences in center-based child care as a function of teacher background and adult:child ratio. *Merrill-Palmer Quarterly, 43*(3), 404–425.

Hsia, Y., & Graham, C. H. (1997). Color blindness. In A. Byrne & D. R. Hilbert (Eds.), *Readings on color* (Vol. 2): *The science of color*. Cambridge, MA: MIT Press.

Hubble, M.A., Duncan, B. L., & Miller, S. D. (Eds.). (1999). *The heart and soul of change: What works in therapy*. Washington, DC: American Psychological Association.

Hubel D. H., & Wiesel, W. N. (2005). *Brain & visual perception: The story of a 25-year collaboration*. New York: Oxford University Press.

Hübner, R., & Volberg, G. (2005). The integration of object levels and their content: A theory of global/local processing and related hemispheric differences. *Journal of Experimental Psychology: Human Perception & Performance, 31*(3), 520–541.

Huesmann, L. R., Moise-Titus, J., Podolski, C.-L., & Eron, L. D. (2003). Longitudinal relations between children's exposure to TV violence and their aggressive and violent behavior in young adulthood: 1977–1992. *Developmental Psychology. Special Issue: Violent children, 39*(2), 201–221.

Hughes, J. N., & Hasbrouck, J. E. (1996). Television violence: Implications for violence prevention. *School Psychology Review, 25*(2), 134–151.

Hughes, J. R., Oliveto, A. H., Liguori, A., et al. (1998). Endorsement of DSM-IV dependence criteria among caffeine users. *Drug & Alcohol Dependence, 52*(2), 99–107.

Hughes, M., & Morrison, K., & Asada, K. J. K. (2005). What's love got to do with it? Exploring the impact of maintenance rules, love attitudes, and network support on friends with benefits relationships. *Western Journal of Communication, 69*(1), 49–66.

Huijbregts, S. C., Séguin, J. R., Zelazo, P. D., et al. (2006). Interrelations between maternal smoking during pregnancy, birth weight and sociodemographic factors in the prediction of early cognitive abilities. *Infant & Child Development, 15*(6), 593–607.

Human Rights Watch. (2003). *Ill-equipped: U.S. prisons and offenders with mental illness.* New York: Holt.

Hunt, R. R., & Ellis, H. C. (2004). *Fundamentals of cognitive psychology* (7th ed.). New York: McGraw-Hill.

Hunter, E. (1998). Adolescent attraction to cults. *Adolescence, 33*(131), 709–714.

Hunter, J. P., Katz, J., & Davis, K. D. (2003). The effect of tactile and visual sensory inputs on phantom limb awareness. *Brain, 126*(3), 579–589.

Hutchinson, S. R. (2004). Survey research. In K. deMarrais & S. D. Lapan (Eds.), Foundations for research: *Methods of inquiry in education and the social sciences. Inquiry and pedagogy across diverse contexts.* Mahwah, NJ: Erlbaum.

Hutchinson, S., Lee, L. H. L., Gaab, N., Schlaug, G. (2003). Cerebellar volume of musicians. *Cerebral Cortex, 13*(9), 943–949.

Hyde, J. S. (2004). *Half the human experience: The psychology of women* (6th ed.). Boston: Houghton Mifflin.

Hyde, J. S., & DeLamater, J. D. (2006). *Understanding human sexuality* (9th ed.). New York: McGraw-Hill.

Hyman, R. (1996a). Evaluation of the military's twenty-year program on psychic spying. *Skeptical Inquirer, 20*(2), 21–23.

Hyman, R. (1996b). The evidence for psychic functioning: Claims vs. reality. *Skeptical Inquirer, 20*(2), 24–26.

Hyman, R. (2007). Talking with the dead, communicating with the future and other myths created by cold reading. In S. Della Sala (Ed.), *Tall tales about the mind & brain:*

Separating fact from fiction. New York: Oxford University Press.

Hysenbegasi, A., Hass, S. L., & Rowland, C. R. (2005). The impact of depression on the academic productivity of university students. *Journal of Mental Health Policy & Economics, 8*(3), 145–151.

Iacono, W. G. (2008). Effective policing: Understanding how polygraph tests work and are used. *Criminal Justice & Behavior, 35*(10), 1295–1308.

Ida, Y., & Mandal, M. K. (2003). Cultural differences in side bias: Evidence from Japan and India. *Laterality: Asymmetries of Body, Brain & Cognition, 8*(2), 121–133.

Ingham, A. G., Levinger, G., Graves, J., & Peckham, V. (1974). The Ringelmann effect: Studies of group size and group performance. *Journal of Personality & Social Psychology, 10,* 371–384.

Ingram, V. (2003). Alzheimer's disease. *American Scientist, 91,* 312–321.

Iosif, A., & Ballon, B. (2005). Bad moon rising: The persistent belief in lunar connections to madness. *Canadian Medical Association Journal, 173*(12), 1498–1500.

Iversen, L. (2006). *Speed, Ecstasy, Ritalin: The science of amphetamines.* New York: Oxford University Press.

Izard, C. E. (1977). *Human emotions.* New York: Plenum.

Izard, C. E. (1990). Facial expressions and the regulation of emotions. *Journal of Personality & Social Psychology, 58*(3), 487–498.

Izard, C. E., Fantauzzo, C. A., Castle, J. M., et al. (1995). The ontogeny and significance of infants' facial expressions in the first 9 months of life. *Developmental Psychology, 31*(6), 997–1013.

Jablonski, N. G., & Chaplin, G. (2000). The evolution of human skin coloration. *Journal of Human Evolution, 39*(1), 57–106.

Jackson, S. L. (2008). *Research methods: A modular approach.* Belmont, CA: Cengage Learning/Wadsworth.

Jackson, T., Fritch, A., Nagasaka, T., & Gunderson, J. (2002). Towards explaining the association between shyness and loneliness. *Social Behavior & Personality, 30*(3), 263–270.

Jackson, T., Towson, S., & Narduzzi, K. (1997). Predictors of shyness. *Social Behavior & Personality, 25*(2), 149–154.

Jacob, A., Prasad, S., Boggild, M., & Chandratre, S. (2004). Charles Bonnet syndrome: Elderly people and visual hallucinations. *British Medical Journal, 328*(7455), 1552–1554.

Jacobs, M. (2003). *Sigmund Freud.* Thousand Oaks, CA: Sage.

Jacobs, M. K., Christensen, A., Snibbe, J. R., et al. (2001). A comparison of computer-based versus traditional individual psychotherapy. *Professional Psychology: Research & Practice, 32*(1), 92–96.

Jacobs, S. R., & Dodd, D. K. (2003). Student burnout as a function of personality, social support, and workload. *Journal of College Student Development, 44*(3), 291–303.

Jaeggi, S. M., Buschkuehl, M., Jonides, J., & Perrig, W. J. (2008). Improving fluid intelligence with training on working memory. *Proceedings of the National Academy of Sciences.* Retrieved June 15, 2009, from http://www.pnas.org/content/early/2008/04/25/0801268105.full.pdf+html.

Jaehnig, W., & Miller, M. L. (2007). Feedback types in programmed instruction: A systematic review. *Psychological Record, 57*(2), 219–232.

Jaffe, J., Beatrice, B., Feldstein, S., et al. (2001). Rhythms of dialogue in infancy. *Monographs of the Society for Research in Child Development, 66*(2), vi–131.

Jamison, K. R. (2001). Suicide in the young: An essay. *Cerebrum, 3*(3), 39–42.

Janis, I. L. (1989). *Crucial decisions.* New York: Free Press.

Janssen, S. A., & Arntz, A. (2001). Real-life stress and opioid-mediated analgesia in novice parachute jumpers. *Journal of Psychophysiology, 15*(2), 106–113.

Janus, S. S., & Janus, C. L. (1993). *The Janus report.* New York: Wiley.

Jarvin, L., & Sternberg, R. J. (2003). Alfred Binet's contributions to educational psychology. In B. J. Zimmerman & D. H. Schunk (Eds.), *Educational psychology: A century of contributions.* Mahwah, NJ: Erlbaum.

Jawahar, I. M., Stone, T. H., & Kisamore, J. L. (2007). Role conflict and burnout: The direct and moderating effects of political skill and perceived organizational support on burnout dimensions. *International Journal of Stress Management, 14*(2), 142–159.

Jay, T. B. (2003). *Psychology of language.* Englewood Cliffs, NJ: Prentice Hall.

Jeffery, R. W., & Wing R. R. (2001). The effects of an enhanced exercise program on long-term weight loss. *Obesity Research, 9*(Suppl. 3), O193.

Jenkins, J. G., & Dallenbach, K. M. (1924). Oblivescence during sleep and waking. *American Journal of Psychology, 35,* 605–612.

Jerabek, I., & Standing, L. (1992). Imagined test situations produce contextual memory enhancement. *Perceptual & Motor Skills, 75*(2), 400.

Joffe, R. T. (2006). Is the thyroid still important in major depression? *Journal of Psychiatry & Neuroscience, 31*(6), 367–368.

Johnson, K. E., & Mervis, C. B. (1997). Effects of varying levels of expertise on the basic level of categorization. *Journal of Experimental Psychology: General, 126*(3), 248–277.

Johnson, K. J., & Fredrickson, B. L. (2005). "We all look the same to me": Positive emotions eliminate the own-race bias in face recognition. *Psychological Science, 16*(11), 875–881.

Johnson, S. (2005). *Everything bad is good for you: How today's popular culture is actually making us smarter.* New York: Riverhead.

Johnson, T. J. (2002). College students' self-reported reasons for why drinking games end. *Addictive Behaviors, 27*(1), 145–153.

Johnson, W., Jung, R. E., Colom, R., & Haier, R. J. (2008).Cognitive abilities independent of IQ correlate with regional brain structure. *Intelligence, 36*(1), 18–28.

Jones, E. E., & Nisbett, R. E. (1971). The actor and observer: Divergent perceptions of the causes of behavior. In E. E. Jones, D. E. Kanouse, H. H. Kelley, et al. (Eds.), *Attribution: Perceiving the causes of behavior.* Morristown, NJ: General Learning Press.

Jones, G. V., & Martin, M. (2001). Confirming the X-linked handedness gene as recessive, not additive. *Psychological Review, 108*(4), 811–813.

Jones, L., & Petruzzi, D. C. (1995). Test anxiety: A review of theory and current treatment. *Journal of College Student Psychotherapy, 10*(1), 3–15.

Jones, M. K., & Menzies, R. G. (1998). Danger ideation reduction therapy (DIRT) for obsessive-compulsive washers. *Behaviour Research & Therapy, 36*(10), 959–970.

Jones, R., Yates, W. R., & Zhou, M. (2002). Readmission rates for adjustment disorders: Comparison with other mood disorders. *Journal of Affective Disorders, 71*(1–3), 199–203.

Jones, S. S., & Hong, H.-W. (2001). Onset of voluntary communication: Smiling looks to mother. *Infancy, 2*(3), 353–370.

Jonides, J., Lewis, R. L., Nee, D. E., et al. (2008). The mind and brain of short-term memory. *Annual Review of Psychology, 59,* 193–224.

Jouvet, M. (1999). *The paradox of sleep.* Boston: MIT Press.

Joyce, P., & Sills, C. (2001). *Skills in Gestalt counseling & psychotherapy.* Newbury Park, CA: Sage.

Juliano, L. M., & Griffiths, R. R. (2004). A critical review of caffeine withdrawal: Empirical validation of symptoms and signs, incidence, severity, and associated features. *Psychopharmacology, 176*(1), 1–29.

Julien, R. M. (2005). *A primer of drug action: A comprehensive guide to the actions, uses, and side effects* (10th ed.). New York: Worth.

Jussim, L., & Harber, K. D. (2005). Teacher expectations and self-fulfilling prophecies: Knowns and unknowns, resolved and unresolved controversies. *Personality & Social Psychology Review, 9*(2), 131–155.

Kadosh, R. C, & Henik, A. (2007). Can synaesthesia research inform cognitive science? *Trends in Cognitive Sciences, 11*(4), 177–184.

Kagan, J. (1971). *Change and continuity in infancy.* New York: Wiley.

Kagan, J. (2004). New insights into temperament. *Cerebrum, 6*(1), 51–66.

Kagan, J. (2005). Personality and temperament: Historical perspectives. In M. Rosenbluth, S. H. Kennedy, & R. M. Bagby (Eds.), *Depression and personality: Conceptual and clinical challenges.* Washington, DC: American Psychiatric Publishing.

Kahneman, D. (2003). A perspective on judgment and choice. *American Psychologist, 58*(9), 697–720.

Kahneman, D., & Tversky, A. (1972). Subjective probability: A judgment of representativeness. *Cognitive Psychology, 3,* 430–454.

Kahneman, D., & Tversky, A. (1973). On the psychology of prediction. *Psychological Review, 80,* 237–251.

Kahneman, D., Krueger, A. B., Schkade, D., Schwarz, N., et al. (2004). A survey method for characterizing daily life experience: The day reconstruction method. *Science, 306*(5702), 1776–1780.

Kahneman, D., Slovic, P., & Tversky, A. (1982). *Judgment under uncertainty: Heuristics and biases.* Cambridge, MA: Cambridge University Press.

Kail, R. V., & Cavanaugh, J. C. (2010). *Human development: A life-span view* (5th ed.). Belmont, CA: Cengage Learning/Wadsworth.

Kalat, J. W. (2007). *Biological psychology* (9th ed.). Belmont, CA: Wadsworth.

Kalat, J. W. (2009). *Biological psychology* (10th ed.). Belmont, CA: Cengage Learning/Wadsworth.

Kalat, J. W., & Shiota, M. N. (2007). *Emotion.* Belmont, CA: Wadsworth.

Kallio, S., & Revonsuo, A. (2003). Hypnotic phenomena and altered states of consciousness: A multi-level framework of description and explanation. *Contemporary Hypnosis, 20*(3), 111–164.

Kamimori, G. H., Johnson, D., Thorne, D., & Belenky, G. (2005). Multiple caffeine doses maintain vigilance during early morning operations. *Aviation, Space, & Environmental Medicine, 76*(11), 1046–1050.

Kamin, L. J. (1981). *The intelligence controversy.* New York: Wiley.

Kampman, K. M. (2005). New medications for the treatment of cocaine dependence. *Psychiatry, 2*(12), 44–48.

Kandel, E. R., Schwartz, J. H., & Jessell, T. M. (2003). *Principles of neuroscience* (5th ed.). New York: McGraw-Hill.

Kaplan, P. S. (1998). *The human odyssey.* Pacific Grove, CA: Brooks/Cole.

Kapleau, P. (1966). *The three pillars of Zen.* New York: Harper & Row.

Kapur, S., & Lecrubier, Y. (Eds.) (2003). *Dopamine in the pathophysiology and treatment of schizophrenia: New findings.* Washington, DC: Taylor & Francis.

Karim, A. A., Hinterberger, T., Richter, J., et al. (2006). Neural internet: Web surfing with brain potentials for the completely paralyzed. *Neurorehabilitation & Neural Repair, 20*(4), 508–515.

Karon, B. P., & Widener, A. J. (1997). Repressed memories and World War II: Lest we forget! *Professional Psychology: Research & Practice, 28*(4), 338–340.

Kasser, T., & Ryan, R. M. (1993). A dark side of the American dream: Correlates of financial success as a central life aspiration. *Journal of Personality & Social Psychology, 65*(2), 410–422.

Kasser, T., & Ryan, R. M. (1996). Further examining the American dream: Differential correlates of intrinsic and extrinsic goals. *Personality & Social Psychology Bulletin, 22*(3), 280–287.

Kassin, S. M. (2005). On the psychology of confessions: Does innocence put innocents at risk? *American Psychologist, 60*(3), 215–228.

Kassin, S. M., Fein, S., & Markus, H. R. (2008). *Social psychology* (7th ed.). Boston: Houghton Mifflin.

Kassin, S. M., Tubb, V. A., Hosch, H. M., & Memon, A. (2001). On the "general acceptance" of eyewitness testimony research. *American Psychologist, 56*(5), 405–416.

Kataria, S. (2004). A clinical guide to pediatric sleep: Diagnosis and management of sleep problems. *Journal of Developmental & Behavioral Pediatrics, 25*(2), 132–133.

Katz, P. A. (2003). Racists or tolerant multiculturalists? *American Psychologist, 58*(11), 897–909.

Kaufman, A. S. (2000). Intelligence tests and school psychology: Predicting the future by studying the past. *Psychology in the Schools, 37*(1), 7–16.

Kaufman, L., & Kaufman, J. H. (2000). Explaining the moon illusion. *Proceedings of the National Academy of Sciences, 97*(1), 500–505.

Kawai, K., Sugimoto, K., Nakashima, K., et al. (2000). Leptin as a modulator of sweet taste sensitivities in mice. *Proceedings of the National Academy of Sciences, 97*(20), 11044–11049.

Kawasaki, H., Adolphs, R., Oya, H., et al. (2005). Analysis of single-unit responses to emotional scenes in human ventromedial prefrontal cortex. *Journal of Cognitive Neuroscience, 17*(10), 1509–1518.

Kearney, C. A., Sims, K. E., Pursell, C. R., & Tillotson, C. A. (2003). Separation anxiety disorder in young children: A longitudinal and family analysis. *Journal of Clinical Child & Adolescent Psychology, 32*(4), 593–598.

Kebbell, M. R., & Wagstaff, G. F. (1998). Hypnotic interviewing: The best way to interview eyewitnesses? *Behavioral Sciences & the Law, 16*(1), 115–129.

Keefe, F. J., Abernethy, A. P., & Campbell, L. C. (2005). Psychological approaches to understanding and treating disease-related pain. *Annual Review of Psychology, 56,* 601–630.

Keel, P. K., & Klump, K. L. (2003). Are eating disorders culture-bound syndromes? Implications for conceptualizing their etiology. *Psychological Bulletin, 129*(5), 747–769.

Keller, J. (2002). Blatant stereotype threat and women's math performance. *Sex Roles, 47*(3–4), 193–198.

Keller, M. C., & Young, R. K. (1996). Mate assortment in dating and married couples. *Personality & Individual Differences, 21*(2), 217–221.

Kellermann, A. L., Rivara, F. P., Rushforth, N. B., et al. (1993). Gun ownership as a risk factor for homicide in the home. *New England Journal of Medicine, 329*(15), 1084–1091.

Kelly, I. W. (1999). "Debunking the debunkers": A response to an astrologer's debunking of skeptics. *Skeptical Inquirer,* Nov.-Dec., 37–43.

Kelly, M. P., Strassberg, D. S., & Turner, C. M. (2006). Behavioral assessment of couples' communication in female orgasmic disorder. *Journal of Sex & Marital Therapy, 32*(2), 81–95.

Kempermann, G. (2005). *Adult neurogenesis: Stem cells and neuronal development in the adult brain.* New York: Oxford University Press.

Kendler, K. S., Thornton, L. M., & Prescott, C. A. (2001). Gender differences in the rates of exposure to stressful life events and sensitivity to their depressogenic effects. *American Journal of Psychiatry, 158*(4), 587–593.

Kennaway, D. J., & Wright, H. (2002). Melatonin and circadian rhythms. *Current Topics in Medicinal Chemistry, 2,* 199–209.

Kenneth, M., Carpenter, K. M., & Hasin, D. S. (1998). Reasons for drinking alcohol. *Psychology of Addictive Behaviors, 12*(3), 168–184.

Kensinger, E. A. (2007). Negative emotion enhances memory accuracy: Behavioral and neuroimaging evidence. *Current Directions in Psychological Science, 16*(4), 213–218.

Kernis, M. H., & Goldman, B. M. (2005). Authenticity, social motivation, and psychological adjustment. In J. P. Forgas, K. D. Williams, & S. M. Laham (Eds.), *Social motivation: Conscious and unconscious processes.* New York: Cambridge University Press.

Kety, S. S. (1979). Disorders of the human brain. *Scientific American, 241,* 202–214.

Keysers, C., Xiao, D.-K., Földiák, P., & Perrett, D. I. (2005). Out of sight but not out of mind: The neurophysiology of iconic memory in the superior temporal sulcus. *Cognitive Neuropsychology, 22*(3-4), 316–332.

Kida, T. E. (2006). *Don't believe everything you think.* Buffalo, NY: Prometheus.

Kiecolt-Glaser, J. K., McGuire, L., Robles, T. F., & Glaser, R. (2002). Emotions, morbidity, and mortality. *Annual Review of Psychology, 53,* 83–107.

Kim-Cohen, J., Moffitt, T. E., Caspi, A., & Taylor, A. (2004). Genetic and environmental processes in young children's resilience and vulnerability to socioeconomic deprivation. *Child Development, 75*(3), 651–668.

King, N. J., Muris, P., & Ollendick, T. H. (2005). Childhood fears and phobias: Assessment and treatment. *Child & Adolescent Mental Health, 10*(2), 50–56.

Kingsley, C. H., & Lambert, K. G. (2006). The maternal brain. *Scientific American, 294*(1), 72–79.

Kinnunen, L. H., Moltz, H., Metz, J., & Cooper, M. (2004). Differential brain activation in exclusively homosexual and heterosexual men produced by the selective serotonin reuptake inhibitor, fluoxetine. *Brain Research, 1024*(1-2), 251–254.

Kirby, D. B. (2008). The impact of abstinence and comprehensive sex and STD/HIV education programs on adolescent sexual behavior. *Sexuality Research & Social Policy, 5*(3), 18–27.

Kirsch, I. (2005). The flexible observer and neodissociation theory. *Contemporary Hypnosis, 22*(3), 121–122.

Kirsch, I., & Lynn, S. J. (1995). The altered state of hypnosis. *American Psychologist, 50*(10), 846–858.

Kirsch, I., & Sapirstein, G. (1998). Listening to Prozac but hearing placebo: A meta-analysis of antidepressant medication. *Prevention & Treatment, 1*, art. 0002a. Retrieved May 18, 2007, from http://journals.apa.org/prevention/volume1/pre0010002a.html.

Kirsh, S. J. (2005). *Children, adolescents, and media violence: a critical look at the research.* Newbury Park, CA: Sage.

Kirveskari, E., Salmelin, R., & Hari, R. (2006). Neuromagnetic responses to vowels vs. tones reveal hemispheric lateralization. *Clinical Neurophysiology, 117*(3), 643–648.

Kiser, L. J., Heston, J. D., & Paavola, M. (2006). Day treatment centers/partial hospitalization settings. In T. A. Petti & C. Salguero (Eds.), *Community child & adolescent psychiatry: A manual of clinical practice and consultation.* Washington, DC: American Psychiatric Publishing.

Kisilevsky, B. S., Hains, S. M. J., Jacquet, A.-Y., et al. (2004). Maturation of fetal responses to music. *Developmental Science, 7*(5), 550–559.

Kitayama, S., Markus, H. R., & Kurokawa, M. (2000). Culture, emotion, and well-being: Good feelings in Japan and the United States. *Cognition and emotion, 14*, 93–124.

Klein, B., Richards, J. C., & Austin, D. W. (2006). Efficacy of internet therapy for panic disorder. *Journal of Behavior Therapy & Experimental Psychiatry, 37*(3), 213–238.

Klein, D. W., & Kihlstrom, J. F. (1986). Elaboration, organization, and the self-reference effect in memory. *Journal of Experimental Psychology: General, 115*, 26–38.

Klein, K., & Boals, A. (2001a). The relationship of life event stress and working memory capacity. *Applied Cognitive Psychology, 15*(5), 565–579.

Klein, K., & Boals, A. (2001b). Expressive writing can increase working memory capacity. *Journal of Experimental Psychology: General, 130*(3), 520–533.

Kleinke, C. L., Peterson, T. R., & Rutledge, T. R. (1998). Effects of self-generated facial expressions on mood. *Journal of Personality & Social Psychology, 74*(1), 272–279.

Klohnen, E. C., & Luo, S. (2003). Interpersonal attraction and personality: What is attractive—self similarity, ideal similarity, complementarity or attachment security? *Journal of Personality & Social Psychology, 85*(4), 709–722.

Knaus, W. J., & Ellis, A. (2002). *The procrastination workbook: Your personalized program for breaking free from the patterns that hold you back.* Oakland, CA: New Harbinger Press.

Knoops, K. T. B., de Groot, L. C., Kromhout, D., et al. (2004). Mediterranean diet, lifestyle factors, and 10-year mortality in elderly European men and women. *Journal of the American Medical Association, 292*(12), 1433–1439.

Koch, C. (2004). *The quest for consciousness: A neurobiological approach.* Englewood, CO: Roberts and Co.

Koch, W. H., & Pratarelli, M. E. (2004). Effects of intro/extraversion and sex on social Internet use. *North American Journal of Psychology, 6*(3), 371–382.

Kohlberg, L. (1969). The cognitive-developmental approach to socialization. In A. Goslin (Ed.), *Handbook of socialization theory and research.* Chicago: Rand McNally.

Kohlberg, L. (1981). *Essays on moral development* (Vol. I): *The philosophy of moral development.* San Francisco: Harper.

Kohn, C. S., & Antonuccio, D. O. (2002). Treatment of kleptomania using cognitive and behavioral strategies. *Clinical Case Studies, 1*(1), 25–38.

Köke, A., Schouten, J. S., Lamerichs-Geelen, M. J. H., et al. (2004). Pain reducing effect of three types of transcutaneous electrical nerve stimulation in patients with chronic pain: A randomized cross-over trial. *Pain, 108*(1-2), 36–42.

Kolb, B., & Whishaw, I.Q. (2006). *Introduction to brain and behavior* (2nd ed.). New York: Freeman-Worth.

Kolb, B., Gibb, R., & Gorny, G. (2003). Experience-dependent changes in dendritic arbor and spine density in neocortex vary with age and sex.

Neurobiology of Learning & Memory, 79(1), 1–10.

Kornhaber, M. L., & Gardner, H. (2006). Multiple intelligences: Developments in implementation and theory. In M. A. Constas & R. J. Sternberg (Eds.), *Translating theory and research into educational practice: Developments in content domains, large-scale reform, and intellectual capacity.* Mahwah, NJ: Erlbaum.

Korol, C., Craig, K. D., & Firestone, P. (2003). Dissociative and somatoform disorders. In P. Firestone, & W. L. Marshall (Eds.), *Abnormal psychology: Perspectives* (2nd ed.). Toronto: Prentice Hall.

Kosslyn, S. M. (1983). *Ghosts in the mind's machine.* New York: Norton.

Kosslyn, S. M. (1985, May). Stalking the mental image. *Psychology Today*, 23–28.

Kosslyn, S. M. (2005). Mental images and the brain. *Cognitive Neuropsychology, 22*(3-4), 333–347.

Kosslyn, S. M., Ball, T. M., & Reiser, B. J. (1978). Visual images preserve metric spatial information: Evidence from studies of image scanning. *Journal of Experimental Psychology: Human Perception & Performance, 4*, 47–60.

Kosslyn, S. M., Thompson, W. L., Costantini-Ferrando, M. F., et al. (2000). Hypnotic visual illusion alters color processing in the brain. *American Journal of Psychiatry, 157*(8), 1279–1284.

Kosson, D. S., Suchy, Y., Mayer, A. R., & Libby, J. (2002). Facial affect recognition in criminal psychopaths. *Emotion, 2*(4), 398–411.

Kotkin, M., Daviet, C., & Gurin, J. (1996). The *Consumer Reports* mental health survey. *American Psychologist, 51*(10), 1080–1082.

Kottler, J. A. (2004). *Introduction to therapeutic counseling.* Belmont, CA: Wadsworth.

Kowert, P. A. (2002). Groupthink or deadlock: When do leaders learn from their advisors? *SUNY series on the presidency.* Albany: State University of New York Press.

Kozart, M. F. (2002). Understanding efficacy in psychotherapy. *American Journal of Orthopsychiatry, 72*(2), 217–231.

Krakow, B., & Zadra, A. (2006). Clinical management of chronic nightmares: Imagery rehearsal therapy. *Behavioral Sleep Medicine, 4*(1), 45–70.

Krall, E. A., Garvey, A. J., & Garcia, R. I. (2002). Smoking relapse after 2 years of abstinence: Findings from the VA Normative Aging Study. *Nicotine & Tobacco Research, 4*(1), 95–100.

Krantz, D. S., & McCeney, M. K. (2002). Effects of psychological and social factors on organic disease. *Annual Review of Psychology, 53*, 341–369.

Ksir, C. J., Hart, C. L., & Ray, O. S. (2006). *Drugs, society, and human behavior* (11th ed.). New York: McGraw-Hill.

Kuehner, C. (2003). Gender differences in unipolar depression: An update of epidemiological findings and possible explanations. *Acta Psychiatrica Scandinavica, 108*(3), 163–174.

Kuhl, P. K. (2004). Early language acquisition: Cracking the speech code. *Nature Reviews Neuroscience, 5*(11), 831–841.

Kulik, J., Mahler, H. I. M., & Moore, P. J. (2003). Social comparison affiliation under threat: Effects on recovery from major surgery. In P. Salovey & A. J. Rothman (Eds.), *Social psychology of health: Key readings in social psychology.* New York: Psychology Press.

Kumaran, D., & Maguire, E. A. (2005). The human hippocampus: Cognitive maps or relational memory? *Journal of Neuroscience, 25*(31), 7254–7259.

Kunkel, M. A. (1993). A teaching demonstration involving perceived lunar size. *Teaching of Psychology, 20*(3), 178–180.

LaBar, K. S. (2007). Beyond fear: Emotional memory mechanisms in the human brain. *Current Directions in Psychological Science, 16*(4), 173–177.

LaBar, K. S., & LeDoux, J. E. (2002). Emotional learning circuits in animals and man. In R. J. Davidson, K. R. Scherer, et al. (Eds.), *Handbook of affective sciences.* New York: Oxford University Press.

LaBerge, S. (2000). Lucid dreaming: Evidence and methodology. In F. E. Pace-Schott, M. Solms, M. Blagrove, & S. Harnad (Eds.), *Sleep and dreaming: Scientific advances and reconsiderations.* Cambridge, UK: Cambridge University Press.

Labov, W. (1973). The boundaries of words and their meanings. In C. J. N. Bailey & R. W. Shuy (Eds.), *New ways of analyzing variation in English.* Washington, DC: Georgetown University Press.

LaBrie, R. A., & Shaffer, H. J. (2007). Gambling with adolescent health. *Journal of Adolescent Health, 40*(5), 387–389.

Lacayo, A. (1995). Neurologic and psychiatric complications of cocaine abuse. *Neuropsychiatry, Neuropsychology, & Behavioral Neurology, 8*(1), 53–60.

Lachman, M. E. (2004). Development in midlife. *Annual Review of Psychology, 55,* 305–331.

Lackner, J. R., & DiZio, P. (2005). Vestibular, proprioceptive, and haptic contributions to spatial orientation. *Annual Review of Psychology, 56,* 115–147.

Lamb, M. R., & Yund, E. W. (1996). Spatial frequency and attention. *Perception & Psychophysics, 58*(3), 363–373.

Lambert, M. J., & Cattani-Thompson, K. (1996). Current findings regarding the effectiveness of counseling. *Journal of Counseling & Development, 74*(6), 601–608.

Lambert, M. J., & Ogles, B. M. (2002). The efficacy and effectiveness of psychotherapy. In M. J. Lambert (Ed.), *Handbook of psychotherapy and behavior change* (5th ed.). New York: Wiley.

Lambert, W. E. (1987). The effects of bilingual and bicultural experiences on children's attitudes and social perspectives. In P. Homel, M. Palij, & D. Aaronson (Eds.), *Childhood bilingualism.* Hillsdale, NJ: Erlbaum.

Lance, C. E., LaPointe, J. A., & Stewart, A. M. (1994). A test of the context dependency of three causal models of halo rater error. *Journal of Applied Psychology, 79*(3), 332–340.

Landau, J. D., & Bavaria A. J. (2003). Does deliberate source monitoring reduce students's misconceptions about psychology? *Teaching of Psychology, 30,* 311–314.

Landau, J. D., & Leynes, P. A. (2006). Do explicit memory manipulations affect the memory blocking effect? *American Journal of Psychology, 119*(3), 463–479.

Lane, C. (2009, June 3). The slippery slope of bitterness disorder and other psychiatric diagnoses. *Psychology Today.* Retrieved June 21, 2009, from http://www.psychologytoday.com/blog/side-effects/200906/the-slippery-slope-bitterness-disorder-and-other-psychiatric-diagnoses.

Langer, E. J. (2000). Mindful learning. *Current Directions in Psychological Science, 9,* 220–223.

Langleben, D. D. (2008). Detection of deception with fMRI: Are we there yet? *Legal & Criminological Psychology, 13*(1), 1–9.

Langleben, D. D., Loughead, J. W., Bilker, W. B., et al. (2005). Telling truth from lie in individual subjects with fast event-related fMRI. *Human Brain Mapping, 26*(4), 262–272.

Langone, M. D. (2002). Cults, conversion, science, and harm. *Cultic Studies Review, 1*(2), 178–186.

Larsen, R. J., & Buss, D. M. (2005). *Personality psychology* (2nd ed.). New York: McGraw-Hill.

Larsen, R. J., & Kasimatis, M. (1990). Individual differences in entrainment of mood to the weekly calendar. *Journal of Personality & Social Psychology, 58*(1), 164–171.

Larsen, R. J., & Prizmic, Z. (2004) Affect regulation. In R. Baumeister & K. D. Voohs (Eds.), *Handbook of self-regulation: Research, theory, and applications.* London: Guilford.

Larsson, B., Carlsson, J., Fichtel, Å., & Melin, L. (2005). Relaxation treatment of adolescent headache sufferers: Results from a school-based replication series. *Headache: The Journal of Head & Face Pain, 45*(6), 692–704.

Larsson, J.-O., Larsson, H., & Lichtenstein, P. (2004). Genetic and environmental contributions to stability and change of ADHD symptoms between 8 and 13 years of age: A longitudinal twin study. *Journal of the American Academy of Child & Adolescent Psychiatry, 43*(10), 1267–1275.

Latané, B., Nida, S. A., & Wilson, D. W. (1981). The effects of group size on helping behavior. In J. P. Rushton & R. M. Sorrentino (Eds.), *Altruism and helping behavior: Social, personality and developmental perspectives.* Hillsdale, NJ: Erlbaum.

LaTour, M. S., & Henthorne, T. L. (2003). Nudity and sexual appeals: Understanding the arousal process and advertising response. In T. Reichert & J. Lambioase (Eds.), *Sex in advertising: Perspectives on the erotic appeal.* Mahwah, NJ: Erlbaum.

Lattal, K. A., Reilly, M. P., & Kohn, J. P. (1998). Response persistence under ratio and interval reinforcement schedules. *Journal of the Experimental Analysis of Behavior, 70*(2), 165–183.

Laub, J. H., & Sampson, R. J. (2003). *Shared beginnings, divergent lives: Delinquent boys to age 70.* Cambridge, MA: Harvard University Press.

Laurent, G., Stopfer, M., Friedrich, R. W., et al. (2001). Odor encoding as an active, dynamical process. *Annual Review of Neuroscience, 24,* 263–297.

Laureys, S, & Boly. M. (2007). What is it like to be vegetative or minimally conscious? *Current Opinion in Neurology, 20,* 609–613.

Lavie, P. (2001). Sleep-wake as a biological rhythm. *Annual Review of Psychology, 52,* 277–303.

Lawson, H. M., & Leck, K. (2006). Dynamics of Internet dating. *Social Science Computer Review, 24*(2), 189–208.

Lay, C., & Verkuyten, M. (1999). Ethnic identity and its relation to personal self-esteem. *Journal of Social Psychology, 139*(3), 288–299.

Lazar, S. W. (2005). Mindfulness research. In C. K. Germer, R. D. Siegel, & P. R. Fulton (Eds.), *Mindfulness and psychotherapy.* New York: Guilford.

Lazar, S. W., Bush, G., Gollub, R. L., et al. (2000). Functional brain mapping of the relaxation response and meditation. *Neuroreport, 11*(7), 1581–1585.

Lazarus, R. S. (1991a). Progress on a cognitive-motivational-relational theory of emotion. *American Psychologist, 46*(8), 819–834.

Lazarus, R. S. (1991b). Cognition and motivation in emotion. *American Psychologist, 46*(4), 352–367.

Lazev, A. B., Herzog, T. A., & Brandon, T. H. (1999). Classical conditioning of environmental cues to cigarette smoking. *Experimental & Clinical Psychopharmacology, 7*(1), 56–63.

Leal, M. C., Shin, Y. J., Laborde, M.-L., et al. (2003). Music perception in adult cochlear implant recipients. *Acta Oto-Laryngologica, 123*(7), 826–835.

Leavens, D. A., & Hopkins, W. D. (1998). Intentional communication by chimpanzees. *Developmental Psychology, 34*(5), 813–822.

LeBlanc, G., & Bearison, D. J. (2004). Teaching and learning as a bidirectional activity: Investigating dyadic interactions between child teachers and child learners. *Cognitive Development, 19*(4), 499–515.

LeDoux, J. (1999). The power of emotions. In R. Conlan (Ed.), *States of mind.* New York: Wiley.

LeDoux, J. E. (2000). Emotion circuits in the brain. *Annual Review of Neuroscience, 23,* 155–184.

LeDoux, J. E., & Gorman, J. M. (2001). A call to action: Overcoming anxiety through active coping. *American Journal of Psychiatry. 158*(12), 1953–1955.

Lee, J. M., Ku, J. H., Jang, D. P., et al. (2002). Virtual reality system for treatment of the fear of public speaking using image-based rendering and moving pictures. *CyberPsychology & Behavior, 5*(3), 191–195.

Lee, M., Zimbardo, P. G., & Bertholf, M. (1977, November). Shy murderers. *Psychology Today.*

Leenaars, A. A., Lester, D., & Wenckstern, S. (2005). Coping with: The art and the research. In R. I. Yufit & D. Lester (Eds.), *Assessment, treatment, and prevention of suicidal behavior.* New York: Wiley.

Leeper, R. W. (1935). A study of a neglected portion of the field of learning: The development of sensory organization. *Pedagogical Seminary & Journal of Genetic Psychology, 46,* 41–75.

Lefcourt, H. M. (2003). Humor as a moderator of life stress in adults. In C. E. Schaefer (Ed.), *Play therapy with adults.* New York: Wiley.

Lefebvre, C. D., Marchand, Y., Smith, S. M., & Connolly, J. F. (2007). Determining eyewitness identification accuracy using event-related brain potentials (ERPs). *Psychophysiology, 44*(6), 894–904.

Lefkowitz, E. S., & Zeldow, P. B. (2006). Masculinity and femininity predict optimal mental health: A belated test of the androgyny hypothesis. *Journal of Personality Assessment, 87*(1), 95–101.

Lefrançois, G. R. (2006). *Theories of human learning: What the old woman said* (5th ed.). Belmont, CA: Cengage Learning/Wadsworth.

Lehman, D. R., Chiu, C., & Schaller, M. (2004). Psychology and culture. *Annual Review of Psychology, 55,* 689–714.

Leichtman, M. (2004). Projective tests: The nature of the task. In M. J. Hilsenroth & D. L. Segal (Eds.), *Comprehensive handbook of psychological assessment* (Vol. 2): *Personality assessment.* New York: Wiley.

Lejuez, C. W., Eifert, G. H., Zvolensky, M. J., & Richards, J. B. (2000). Preference between onset predictable and unpredictable administrations of 20% carbon-dioxide-enriched air. *Journal of Experimental Psychology: Applied, 6*(4), 349–358.

Lench, H. C. (2004). Anger management: Diagnostic differences and treatment implications. *Journal of Social & Clinical Psychology, 23*(4), 512–531.

Lenton, A. P., & Bryan, A. (2005). An affair to remember: The role of sexual scripts in perceptions of sexual intent. *Personal Relationships, 12*(4), 483–498.

Lenzenweger, M. F., & Gottesman, I. I. (1994). Schizophrenia. In V. S. Ramachandran (Ed.), *Encyclopedia of human behavior.* San Diego, CA: Academic.

Leor, J., Poole, W. K., & Kloner, R. A. (1996). Sudden cardiac death triggered by earthquake. *The New England Journal of Medicine, 334*(7), 413.

Lepore, F. E. (2002). When seeing is not believing. *Cerebrum, 4*(2), 23–38.

Leslie, K., & Ogilvie, R. (1996). Vestibular dreams: The effect of rocking on dream mentation. *Dreaming: Journal of the Association for the Study of Dreams, 6*(1), 1–16.

Lessow-Hurley, J. (2005). *Foundations of dual language instruction* (4th ed.). Boston: Allyn & Bacon.

Lester, D., & Yang, B. (2005). Regional and time-series studies of suicide in nations of the world. *Archives of Suicide Research, 9*(2), 123–133.

Lettvin, J. Y. (1961). Two remarks on the visual system of the frog. In W. Rosenblith (Ed.), *Sensory communication.* Cambridge, MA: MIT Press.

Levant, R. F. (2001). Men and masculinity. In J. Worell (Ed.), *Encyclopedia of women and gender.* San Diego: Academic Press.

Levant, R. F. (2003). Treating male alexithymia. In L. B. Silverstein & T. J. Goodrich (Eds.), *Feminist family therapy: Empowerment in social context.* Washington, DC: American Psychological Association.

Levant, R. F., Good, G. E., Cook, S. W., et al. (2006). The Normative Male Alexithymia Scale: Measurement of a gender-linked syndrome. *Psychology of Men & Masculinity, 7*(4), 212–224.

LeVay, S. (1993). *The sexual brain.* Cambridge, MA: MIT Press.

LeVay, S., & Valente, S. M. (2006). *Human sexuality* (2nd ed.). Sunderland, MA: Sinauer Associates.

Levenston, G. K., Patrick, C. J., Bradley, M. M., & Lange, P. J. (2000). The psychopath as observer. *Journal of Abnormal Psychology, 109*(3), 373–385.

Levesque, M. J., Steciuk, M., & Ledley, C. (2002). Self-disclosure patterns among well-acquainted individuals. *Social Behavior & Personality, 30*(6), 579–592.

Levi, A. M. (1998). Are defendants guilty if they were chosen in a lineup? *Law & Human Behavior, 22*(4), 389–407.

Levin, B. E. (2006). Metabolic sensing neurons and the control of energy homeostasis. *Physiology & Behavior, 89*(4), 486–489.

Levin, R., & Fireman, G. (2002). Nightmare prevalence, nightmare distress, and self-reported psychological disturbance. *Sleep: Journal of Sleep & Sleep Disorders Research, 25*(2), 205–212.

Levine, M., & Harrison, K. (2004). Media's role in the perpetuation and prevention of negative body image and disordered eating. In J. K. Thompson (Ed.), *Handbook of eating disorders and obesity.* New York: Wiley.

Levitsky, D. A., Nussbaum, M., Halbmaier, C.A., & Mrdjenovic, G. (2003). *The Freshman 15: a model for the study of techniques to curb the 'epidemic' of obesity.* Paper presented at Society for the Study of Ingestive Behavior annual meeting, July 15–19, University of Groningen, Haren, The Netherlands.

Levy, J., & Reid, M. (1976). Cerebral organization. *Science,* 337–339.

Lewandowski, G. W., Jr., Aron, A., & Gee, J. (2007). Personality goes a long way: The malleability of opposite-sex physical attractiveness. *Personal Relationships, 14*(4), 571–585.

Lewchanin, S., & Zubrod, L. A. (2001). Choices in life: A clinical tool for facilitating midlife review. *Journal of Adult Development, 8*(3), 193–196.

Lewis, M. (1995, January-February). Self-conscious emotions. *American Scientist, 83,* 68–78.

Leyendecker, B., Harwood, R. L., Comparini, L., & Yalçinkaya, A. (2005). Socioeconomic status, ethnicity, and parenting. In T. Luster & L. Okagaki (Eds.), *Parenting: An ecological perspective* (2nd ed.). Mahwah, NJ: Erlbaum.

Lichtman, A. H., & Martin, B. R. (2006). Understanding the pharmacology and physiology of cannabis dependence. In R. Roffman & R. S. Stephens (Eds.), *Cannabis dependence. Its nature, consequences and treatment.* New York: Cambridge University Press.

Liddell, S. K. (2003). *Grammar, gesture and meaning in American Sign Language.* Cambridge, MA: Cambridge University Press.

Lilienfeld, S. O. (1999, September/October). Projective measures of personality and psychopathology. *Skeptical Inquirer,* 32–39.

Lilienfeld, S. O., Fowler, K. A., Lohr, J. M., & Lynn, S. (2005). Pseudoscience, nonscience & nonsense in clinical psychology: Dangers and remedies. In R. H. Wright & N. A. Cummings (Eds.), *Destructive trends in mental health: The well-intentioned path to harm* (pp. 187–218). New York: Routledge.

Lindemann, B. (2001). Receptors and transduction in taste. *Nature, 413,* 219–25.

Linden, M., Baumann, K., Rotter, M., & Schippan, B. (2008). Diagnostic criteria and the standardized diagnostic interview for posttraumatic embitterment disorder (PTED). *International Journal of Psychiatry in Clinical Practice, 12*(2), 93–96.

Linden, W. (2005). *Stress management: From basic science to better practice.* Thousand Oaks, CA: Sage.

Linderoth, B., & Foreman, R. D. (2006). Mechanisms of spinal cord stimulation in painful syndromes: Role of animal models. *Pain Medicine, 7*(Suppl. 1), S14–S26.

Lindsay, E. W., Mize, J., & Pettit, G. S. (1997). Differential play patterns of mothers and fathers of sons and daughters. *Sex Roles, 37*(9-10), 643–661.

Lipsey, M. W., & Wilson, D. B. (1993). The efficacy of psychological, educational, and behavioral treatment: Confirmation from meta-analysis. *American Psychologist, 48*(12), 1181–1209.

Liu, X., Matochik, J. A., Cadet, J., & London, E. D. (1998). Smaller volume of prefrontal lobe in polysubstance abusers. *Neuropsychopharmacology, 18*(4), 243–252.

Liu, Y., Gao, J., Liu, H., & Fox, P. T. (2000). The temporal response of the brain after eating revealed by functional MRI. *Nature, 405,* 1058–1062.

Lodi-Smith, J., Geise, A. C., Roberts, B. W., & Robins, R. W. (2009). Narrating personality change. *Journal of Personality & Social Psychology, 96*(3), 679–689.

Loeber, R., & Hay, D. (1997). Key issues in the development of aggression and violence from childhood to early adulthood. *Annual Review of Psychology, 48,* 371–410.

Loehlin, J. C., McCrae, R. R., Costa, P. T., & John, O. (1998). Heritabilities of common and measure-specific components of the Big Five personality factors. *Journal of Research in Personality, 32*(4), 431–453.

Loftus, E. F. (2003a). Make-believe memories. *American Psychologist, 58*(11), 867–873.

Loftus, E. F. (2003b). Memory in Canadian courts of law. *Canadian Psychology, 44*(3), 207–212.

Loftus, E. F., & Bernstein, D. M. (2005). Rich false memories: The royal road to success. In A. F. Healy (Ed.), *Experimental cognitive psychology and its applications.* Washington, DC: American Psychological Association.

Loftus, E. F., & Ketcham, K. (1994). The myth of repressed memory: False memories and allegations of abuse. New York: St. Martin's Press.

Loftus, E., & Palmer, J. C. (1974). Reconstruction of automobile destruction: An example of interaction between language and memory. *Journal of Verbal Learning & Verbal Behavior, 13,* 585–589.

LoLordo, V. M. (2001). Learned helplessness and depression. In M. E. Carroll & J. B. Overmier (Eds.), *Animal research and human health: Advancing human welfare through behavioral science.* Washington, DC: American Psychological Association.

Long, V. O. (1989). Relation of masculinity to self-esteem and self-acceptance in male professionals, college students, and clients. *Journal of Counseling Psychology, 36*(1), 84–87.

López, S. R., & Guarnaccia, P. J. (2000). Cultural psychopathology: Uncovering the social world of mental illness. *Annual Review of Psychology, 51,* 571–598.

Lorenz, K. (1966). *On aggression.* Trans. M. Kerr-Wilson. New York: Harcourt Brace Jovanovich.

Lorenz, K. (1974). *The eight deadly sins of civilized man.* Trans. M. Kerr-Wilson. New York: Harcourt Brace Jovanovich.

Lovaas, O., & Simmons, J. (1969). Manipulation of self-destruction in three retarded children. *Journal of Applied Behavior Analysis, 2*(3), 143–157.

Low, K. G., & Feissner, J. M. (1998). Seasonal affective disorder in college students: Prevalence and latitude. *Journal of American College Health, 47*(3), 135–137.

Lucas, F., & Sclafani, A. (1990). Hyperphagia in rats produced by a mixture of fat and sugar. *Physiology & Behavior, 47*(1), 51–55.

Luchins, D. J., Cooper, A. E., Hanrahan, P., & Rasinski, K. (2004). Psychiatrists' attitudes toward involuntary hospitalization. *Psychiatric Services, 55*(9), 1058–1060.

Lumley, M. A. (2004). Alexithymia, emotional disclosure, and health: A program of research. *Journal of Personality. Special Emotions, Personality, and Health, 72*(6), 1271–1300.

Lundh, L., Berg, B., Johansson, H., et al. (2002). Social anxiety is associated with a negatively distorted perception of one's own voice. *Cognitive Behaviour Therapy, 31*(1), 25–30.

Luppa, M., Heinrich, S., Angermeyer, M. C., et al. (2007). Cost-of-illness studies of depression A systematic review. *Journal of Affective Disorders, 98*(1-2), 29–43.

Luria, A. R. (1968). *The mind of a mnemonist.* New York: Basic Books.

Lustig, C., May, C. P., Hasher, L. (2001). Working memory span and the role of proactive interference. *Journal of Experimental Psychology: General, 130*(2), 199–207.

Luyben, P. D., Hipworth, K., & Pappas, T. (2003). Effects of CAI on the academic performance and attitudes of college students. *Teaching of Psychology, 30*(2), 154–158.

Lykken, D. T. (1998). *A tremor in the blood: Uses and abuses of the lie detector.* New York: Plenum.

Lykken, D. T. (2001). Lie detection. In W. E. Craighead & C. B. Nemeroff (Eds.), *The Corsini encyclopedia of psychology and behavioral science* (3rd ed.). New York: Wiley.

Lynch, K. B., Geller, S. R., & Schmidt, M. G. (2004). Multi-year evaluation of the effectiveness of a resilience-based prevention program for young children. *Journal of Primary Prevention, 24*(3), 335–353.

Lynch, T. R., Robins, C. J., Morse, J. Q., & MorKrause, E. D. (2001). A mediational model relating affect intensity, emotion inhibition, and psychological distress. *Behavior Therapy, 32*(3), 519–536.

Lynn, S. J., & Kirsch, I. (2006). Introduction: Definitions and early history. In S. J. Lynn & I. Kirsch (Eds.), *Essentials of clinical hypnosis: An evidence-based approach.* Washington, DC: American Psychological Association.

Lyons, A. C., & Chamberlain, K. (2006). *Health psychology.* Cambridge, MA: Cambridge University Press.

Lyubomirsky, S., & Tucker, K. L. (1998). Implications of individual differences in subjective happiness for perceiving, interpreting, and thinking about life events. *Motivation & Emotion, 22*(2), 155–186.

Maas, J. (1999). *Power sleep.* New York: HarperCollins.

Mack, A. (2002). Is the visual world a grand illusion? *Journal of Consciousness Studies, 9*(5-6), 102–110.

Mackintosh, N. J. (2003). Pavlov and associationism. *Spanish Journal of Psychology, 6*(2), 177–184.

Macklin, C. B., & McDaniel, M. A. (2005). The bizarreness effect: Dissociation between item and source memory. *Memory, 13*(7), 662–689.

MacLeod, C. M. (2005). The Stroop task in cognitive research. In A. Wenzel & D. C. Rubin (Eds.), *Cognitive methods and their application to clinical research.* Washington, DC: American Psychological Association.

Maddi, S. R. (2006). Hardiness: The courage to grow from stresses. *Journal of Positive Psychology, 1*(3), 160–168.

Maddock, J., & Glanz, K. (2005). The relationship of proximal normative beliefs and global subjective norms to college students' alcohol consumption. *Addictive Behaviors, 30*(2), 315–323.

Maddock. J. E., Laforge, R. G., Rossi, J. S., & O'Hare, T. (2001). The College Alcohol Problems Scale. *Addictive Behaviors, 26,* 385–398.

Maddox, K. B. (2004). Perspectives on racial phenotypicality bias. *Personality & Social Psychology Review, 8*(4), 383–401.

Maguire, E. A., Frackowiak, R. S. J., & Frith, C. D. (1997). Recalling routes around London: Activation of the hippocampus in taxi drivers. *Journal of Neuroscience, 17*(8), 7103.

Maguire, E. A., Valentine, E. R., Wilding, J. M., & Kapur, N. (2003). Routes to remembering: The brains behind superior memory. *Nature Neuroscience, 6*(1), 90–95.

Mah, K., & Binik, Y. M. (2001). The nature of human orgasm: A critical review of major trends. *Clinical Psychology Review, 21*(6), 823–856.

Maheu, M. M., Pulier, M. L., Wilhelm, F. H., et al. (2004). *The mental health professional and the new technologies: A handbook for practice today.* Mahwah, NJ: Lawrence Erlbaum.

Maier, N. R. F. (1949). *Frustration.* New York: McGraw-Hill.

Maier, S. F. (2001). Exposure to the stressor environment prevents the temporal dissipation of behavioral depression/learned helplessness. *Biological Psychiatry, 49*(9), 763–773.

Mailis–Gagnon, A., & Israelson, D. (2005). *Beyond pain: Making the mind–body connection.* Ann Arbor: University of Michigan Press.

Malaspina, D., Reichenberg, A., Weiser, M., et al. (2005). Paternal age and intelligence: Implications for age-related genomic changes in male germ cells. *Psychiatric Genetics, 15*(2), 117–125.

Mamen, M. (2004). *Pampered child syndrome: How to recognize it, how to manage it and how to avoid it.* Carp, ON: Creative Bound.

Manalo, E. (2002). Uses of mnemonics in educational settings: A brief review of selected research. *Psychologia: An International Journal of Psychology in the Orient, 45*(2), 69–79.

Manber, R., Kraemer, H. C., Arnow, B. A., et al. (2008). Faster remission of chronic depression with combined psychotherapy and medication than with each therapy alone. *Journal of Consulting & Clinical Psychology, 76*(3), 459–467.

Mandler, J. M., & McDonough, L. (1998). On developing a knowledge base in infancy. *Developmental Psychology, 34*(6), 1274–1288.

Mangan, M. A. (2004). A phenomenology of problematic sexual behavior occurring in sleep. *Archives of Sexual Behavior, 33*(3), 287–293.

Mangels, J. A., Picton, T. W., & Craik, F. I. M. (2001). Attention and successful episodic encoding: An event-related potential study. *Brain Research, 11,* 77–95.

Manne, S. (2003). Coping and social support. In A. Nezu, C. Nezu, & P. Geller (Eds.), *Handbook of health psychology* (Vol. 9). New York: Wiley.

Manning, R., Levine, M., & Collins, A. (2007). The Kitty Genovese murder and the social psychology of helping: The parable of the 38 witnesses. *American Psychologist, 62*(6), 555–562.

Manschreck, T. C. (1996). Delusional disorder: The recognition and management of paranoia. *Journal of Clinical Psychiatry, 57*(Suppl. 3), 32–38.

Mansouri, A., & Adityanjee. (1995). Delusion of pregnancy in males: A case report and literature review. *Psychopathology, 28*(6), 307–311.

Mantyla, T. (1986). Optimizing cue effectiveness: Recall of 600 incidentally learned words. *Journal of Experimental Psychology: Learning, Memory, & Cognition, 12*(1), 66–71.

Marcus, E. (2002). Psychoanalytic psychotherapy and psychoanalysis: An overview. In M. Hersen & W. H. Sledge (Eds.), *Encyclopedia of psychotherapy.* San Diego: Academic Press.

Margolin, G., & Gordis, E. B. (2000). The effects of family and community violence on children. *Annual Review of Psychology, 51,* 445–479.

Marks, D. F. (2000). *The psychology of the psychic.* Buffalo, NY: Prometheus.

Markus, H. R., & Nurius, P. (1986). Possible selves. *American Psychologist, 41,* 954–969.

Markus, H. R., Uchida, Y., Omoregie, H., et al. (2006). Going for the gold: Models of agency in Japanese and American contexts. *Psychological Science, 17*(2), 103–112.

Marmarosh, C., Holtz, A., & Schottenbauer, M. (2005). Group cohesiveness, group-derived collective self-esteem, group-derived hope, and the well-being of group therapy members. *Group Dynamics: Theory, Research, & Practice, 9*(1), 32–44.

Marshall, R. D., Bryant, R. A., Amsel, L., et al. (2007). The psychology of ongoing threat: Relative risk appraisal, the September 11 attacks, and terrorism-related fears. *American Psychologist, 62*(4), 304–316.

Marsiglia, F. F., Kulis, S., Hecht, M. L., & Sills, S. (2004). Ethnicity and ethnic identity as predictors of drug norms and drug use among preadolescents in the US southwest. *Substance Use & Misuse, 39*(7), 1061–1094.

Martens, R., & Trachet, T. (1998). *Making sense of astrology.* Amherst, MA: Prometheus.

Martin, A. J., & Marsh, H. W. (2003). Fear of failure: Friend or foe? *Australian Psychologist, 38*(1), 31-38.

Martin, C. L., & Fabes, R. A. (2001). The stability and consequences of young children's same-sex peer interactions. *Developmental Psychology, 37*(3), 431–446.

Martin, G., & Pear, J. (2007). *Behavior modification: What it is and how to do it* (8th ed.). Upper Saddle River, NJ: Prentice-Hall.

Martin, L. R., Friedman, H. S., & Schwartz, J. E. (2007). Personality and mortality risk across the life span: The importance of conscientiousness as a biopsychosocial attribute. *Health Psychology, 26*(4), 428–436.

Martin, W. L. B., & Freitas, M. B. (2002). Mean mortality among Brazilian left- and right-handers: Modification or selective elimination. *Laterality, 7*(1), 31–44.

Martinez-Gonzalez, M. A., Gual, P., Lahortiga, F., et al. (2003). Parental factors, mass media influences, and the onset of eating disorders in a prospective population-based cohort. *Pediatrics, 111,* 315–320.

Mashour, G. A., Walker, E. E., & Martuza, R. L. (2005). Psychosurgery: Past, present, and future. *Brain Research Reviews, 48*(3), 409–419.

Masi, G., Mucci, M., & Millepiedi, S. (2001). Separation anxiety disorder in children and adolescents. *CNS Drugs, 15*(2), 93–104.

Maslach, C., Schaufeli, W. B., & Leiter, M. P. (2001). Job burnout. *Annual Review of Psychology, 52,* 397–422.

Maslow, A. (1954). *Motivation and personality.* New York: Harper & Row.

Maslow, A. (1971). *The farther reaches of human nature.* New York: Viking.

Maslow, A. H. (1967). Self-actualization and beyond. In J. F. T. Bugental (Ed.), *Challenges of humanistic psychology.* New York: McGraw–Hill.

Maslow, A. H. (1969). *The psychology of science.* Chicago: Henry Regnery.

Maslow, A. H. (1970). *Motivation and personality.* New York: Harper & Row.

Masse, L. C., & Tremblay, R. E. (1997). Behavior of boys in kindergarten and the onset of substance use during adolescence. *Archives of General Psychiatry, 54*(1), 62–68.

Masten, A. S. (2001). Ordinary magic: Resilience processes in development. *American Psychologist, 56*(3), 227–238.

Masters, J. L., & Holley, L. M. (2006). A glimpse of life at 67: The modified future-self worksheet. *Educational Gerontology, 32*(4), 261–269.

Masters, W. H., & Johnson, V. E. (1966). *Human sexual response.* Boston: Little, Brown.

Masters, W. H., & Johnson, V. E. (1970). *The pleasure bond: A new look at sexuality and commitment.* Boston: Little, Brown.

Masuda, T., Gonzalez, R., Kwan, L., & Nisbett, R. E. (2008). Culture and aesthetic preference: Comparing the attention to context of East Asians and Americans. *Personality & Social Psychology Bulletin, 34*(9), 1260–1275.

Matheny, K. B., Brack, G. L., McCarthy, C. J., Penick, J. M. (1996). The effectiveness of cognitively-based approaches in treating stress-related symptoms. *Psychotherapy, 33*(2), 305–320.

Mather, G. (2008). *Foundations of sensation and perception.* Hove, UK: Psychology Press.

Matossian, M. K. (1982). Ergot and the Salem witchcraft affair. *American Scientist, 70,* 355–357.

Matson, J. L., Sevin, J. A., Fridley D., & Love, S. R. (1990). Increasing spontaneous language in three autistic children. *Journal of Applied Behavior Analysis, 23*(2), 223–227.

Matsumoto, D., & Juang, L. (2008). *Culture and psychology* (4th ed.). Belmont, CA: Cengage Learning/Wadsworth.

Matthews, G., Deary, I. J., & Whiteman, M. C. (2003). *Personality traits* (2nd ed.). New York: Cambridge University Press.

Matthews, P. H., & Matthews, M. S. (2004). Heritage language instruction and giftedness in language minority students: Pathways toward success. *Journal of Secondary Gifted Education, 15*(2), 50–55.

Mayberg, H., Lozano, A., Voon, V., et al. (2005). Deep brain stimulation for treatment-resistant depression. *Neuron, 45*(5), 651–660.

Mayer, J. D. (2005). A tale of two visions: Can a new view of personality help integrate psychology? *American Psychologist, 60*(4), 294–307.

Mayer, J. D., Salovey, P., Caruso, D. R., & Sitarenios, G. (2001). Emotional intelligence as standard intelligence. *Emotion, 1*(3), 232–242.

Mayer, R. E. (1995). *Thinking, problem solving, and cognition.* New York: Freeman.

Mayer, R. E. (2004). Should there be a three-strikes rule against pure discovery learning? *American Psychologist, 59*(1), 14–19.

Mazur, J. E. (2006). *Learning and behavior* (6th ed.). Englewood Cliffs, NJ: Prentice Hall.

McAdams, D. P., & Pals, J. L. (2006). A new Big Five: Fundamental principles for an integrative science of personality. *American Psychologist, 61*(3), 204–217.

McBride, W. J., Murphy, J. M., & Ikemoto, S. (1999). Localization of brain reinforcement mechanisms. *Behavioural Brain Research, 101*(2), 129–152.

McCabe, C., & Rolls, E. T. (2007). Umami: A delicious flavor formed by convergence of taste and olfactory pathways in the human brain. *European Journal of Neuroscience, 25*(6), 1855–1864.

McCabe, M. P., & Ricciardelli, L. A. (2004). Weight and shape concerns of boys and men. In J. K. Thompson (Ed.), *Handbook of eating disorders and obesity.* New York: Wiley.

McCall, W. V., Prudic, J., Olfson, M., & Sackeim, H. (2006). Health-related quality of life following ECT in a large community sample. *Journal of Affective Disorders, 90*(2–3), 269–274.

McCarthy, B. W. (1995). Bridges to sexual desire. *Journal of Sex Education & Therapy, 21*(2), 132–141.

McCarthy, B. W., & Fucito, L. M. (2005). Integrating medication, realistic expectations, and therapeutic interventions in the treatment of male sexual dysfunction. *Journal of Sex & Marital Therapy, 31*(4), 319–328.

McClelland, D. C. (1961). *The achieving society.* New York: Van Nostrand.

McClelland, D. C. (1965). Achievement and entrepreneurship. *Journal of Personality & Social Psychology, 1,* 389–393.

McClelland, D. C. (1975). *Power: The inner experience.* New York: Irvington.

McClelland, D. C. (1994). The knowledge-testing-educational complex strikes back. *American Psychologist, 49*(1), 66–69.

McClelland, D. C., & Cheriff, A. D. (1997). The immunoenhancing effects of humor on secretory IgA and resistance to respiratory infections. *Psychology & Health, 12*(3), 329–344.

McClelland, D. C., & Pilon, D. A. (1983). Sources of adult motives in patterns of parent behavior in early childhood. *Journal of Personality & Social Psychology, 44,* 564–574.

McClelland, J. L., & Rogers, T. T. (2003). The parallel distributed processing approach to semantic cognition. *Nature Reviews Neuroscience, 4*(4), 310–322.

McCluskey, U. (2002). The dynamics of attachment and systems-centered group psychotherapy. *Group Dynamics, 6*(2), 131–142.

McCrae, R. R., & Costa, P. T. (2001). A five-factor theory of personality. In L. A. Pervin & O. P. John (Eds.), *Handbook of personality.* New York: Guilford.

McCrae, R. R., & Terracciano, A. (2005). Universal features of personality traits from the observer's perspective: Data from 50 cultures. *Journal of Personality & Social Psychology, 88*(3), 547–561.

McDaniel, M. A., Maier, S. F., & Einstein, G. O. (2002). "Brain-specific" nutrients: A memory cure? *Psychological Science in the Public Interest, 3*(1), 12–38.

McDermott, R., Johnson, D., Cowden, J., & Rosen, S. (2007). Testosterone and aggression in a simulated crisis game. *Annals of the American Academy of Political and Social Science, 614*(1), 15–33.

McDonald, J. K., Yanchar, S. C., & Osguthorpe, R. (2005). Learning from programmed instruction: Examining implications for modern instructional technology. *Educational Technology Research & Development, 53*(2), 84–98.

McGregor, I., McAdams, D. P., & Little, B. R. (2006). Personal projects, life stories, and happiness: On being true to traits. *Journal of Research in Personality, 40*(5), 551–572.

McGuffin, P., Rijsdijk, F., Andrew, M., et al. (2003). The heritability of bipolar affective disorder and the genetic relationship to unipolar depression. *Archives of General Psychiatry, 60*(5), 497–502.

McIntosh, W. D., Harlow, T. F., & Martin, L. L. (1995). Linkers and nonlinkers: Goal beliefs as a moderator of the effects of everyday hassles on rumination, depression, and physical complaints. *Journal of Applied Social Psychology, 25*(14), 1231-1244.

McKay, A. (2005). Sexuality and substance use: The impact of tobacco, alcohol, and selected recreational drugs on sexual function. *Canadian Journal of Human Sexuality, 14*(1-2), 47–56.

McKeever, L. (2006). Online plagiarism detection services: Saviour or scourge? *Assessment & Evaluation in Higher Education, 31*(2), 155–165.

McKeever, W. F. (2000). A new family handedness sample with findings consistent with X-linked transmission. *British Journal of Psychology, 91*(1), 21–39.

McKeever, W. F., Cerone, L. J., Suter, P. J., & Wu, S. M. (2000). Family size, miscarriage-proneness, and handedness. *Laterality, 5*(2), 111–120.

McKenna, M. W., & Ossoff, E. P. (1998). Age differences in children's comprehension of a popular television program. *Child Study Journal, 28*(1), 52–68.

McKenzie, K., Serfaty, M., & Crawford, M. (2003). Suicide in ethnic minority groups. *British Journal of Psychiatry, 183*(2), 100–101.

McKim, W. A. (2007). *Drugs and behavior* (6th ed.). Englewood Cliffs, NJ: Prentice Hall.

McKone, E., Brewer, J. L., MacPherson, S., et al. (2007). Familiar other-race faces show normal holistic processing and are robust to perceptual stress. *Perception, 36*(2), 244–248.

McLewin, L. A., & Muller, R. T. (2006). Childhood trauma, imaginary companions, and the development of pathological dissociation. *Aggression & Violent Behavior, 11*(5), 531-545.

McLoyd, V. C., & Smith, J. (2002). Physical discipline and behavior problems in African American, European American, and Hispanic children: Emotional support as a moderator. *Journal of Marriage & Family, 64*(1), 40–53.

McMahon, S., & Koltzenburg, M. (2005). *Wall & Melzacks textbook of pain* (5th ed.). London: Churchill Livingstone.

McNally, R. J., & Clancy, S. A. (2005). Sleep paralysis, sexual abuse, and space alien abduction. *Transcultural Psychiatry, 42*(1), 113–122.

McNally, R. J., Clancy, S. A., & Barrett, H. M. (2004). Forgetting trauma? In D. Reisberg & P. Hertel (Eds.), *Memory & emotion.* New York: Oxford University Press.

McNamara, D. S., & Scott, J. L. (2001). Working memory capacity and strategy use. *Memory & Cognition, 29*(1), 10–17.

McRobbie, H., & Hajek, P. (2007). Effects of rapid smoking on postcessation urges to smoke. *Addiction, 102*(3), 483–489.

Medhus, E. (2001). *When the bough breaks: The making of a terrorist.* www.drmedhus.com.

Mehl, M. R., Vazire, S., Ramírez-Esparza, N., et al. (2007). Are women really more talkative than men? *Science, 317*(5834), 82.

Mehrabian, A. (2000). Beyond IQ. *Genetic Social, and General Psychology Monographs, 126,* 133–239.

Meier, P. S., Donmall, M. C., McElduff, P., et al. (2006). The role of the early therapeutic alliance in predicting drug treatment dropout.

Drug & Alcohol Dependence, 83(1), 57–64.

Meltzoff, A. N. (2005). Imitation and other minds: The "Like Me" Hypothesis. In S. Hurley & N. Chater (Eds.), *Perspectives on imitation: From neuroscience to social science* (Vol. 2): *Imitation, human development, and culture.* Cambridge, MA: MIT Press.

Meltzoff, A. N., & Prinz, W. (2002). *The imitative mind: Development, evolution, and brain bases.* Cambridge, MA: Cambridge University Press.

Melzack, R. (1999). From the gate to the neuromatrix. *Pain* [Special issue: A tribute to Patrick D. Wall], *(Suppl. 6),* S121–S126.

Melzack, R., & Katz, J. (2004). The gate control theory: Reaching for the brain. In T. Hadjistavropoulos & K. D. Craig (Eds.), *Pain: Psychological perspectives.* Mahwah, NJ: Erlbaum.

Melzack, R., & Katz, J. (2006). Pain in the 21st century: The neuromatrix and beyond. In G. Young, A. W. Kane, et al. (Eds.), *Psychological knowledge in court: PTSD, pain, and TBI.* New York: Springer.

Melzack, R., & Wall, P. D. (1996). *The challenge of pain.* Harmondsworth, UK: Penguin.

Mendolia, M. (2002). An index of self-regulation of emotion and the study of repression in social contexts that threaten or do not threaten self-concept. *Emotion, 2*(3), 215–232.

Meneses, G. D., & Beerlipalacio, A. (2005). Recycling behavior: A multidimensional approach. *Environment & Behavior, 37*(6), 837–860.

Mercer, J. (2006). *Understanding attachment: Parenting, child care, and emotional development.* Westport, CT: Praeger.

Merens, W., Booij, L., Haffmans, P. M. J., & van der Does, A. J. W. (2008). The effects of experimentally lowered serotonin function on emotional information processing and memory in remitted depressed patients. *Journal of Psychopharmacology, 22*(6), 653–662.

Merhi, O., Faugloire, E., Flanagan, M., et al. (2007). Motion sickness, console video games, and head-mounted displays. *Human Factors, 49*(5), 920–934.

Merritt, J. M., Stickgold, R., Pace-Schott, E., et al. (1994). Emotion profiles in the dreams of men and women. *Consciousness & Cognition, 3*(1), 46–60.

Mesquita, B., & Markus, H. R. (2004). Culture and emotion: Models of agency as sources of cultural variation in emotion. In A. S. R.

Manstead, S. R. Antony, N. Frijda, & A. Fischer (Eds.), *Feelings and emotions: The Amsterdam symposium.* New York: Cambridge University Press.

Messer, S. B., & Kaplan, A. H. (2004). Outcomes and factors related to efficacy of brief psychodynamic therapy. In D. P. Charman (Ed.), *Core processes in brief psychodynamic psychotherapy: Advancing effective practice.* Mahwah, NJ: Lawrence Erlbaum.

Meunier, M., Monfardini, E., & Boussaoud, D. (2007). Learning by observation in rhesus monkeys. *Neurobiology of Learning & Memory, 88*(2), 243–248.

Meyer, G. J., Finn, S. E., Eyde, L. D., et al. (2001). Psychological testing and psychological assessment. *American Psychologist, 56*(2) 128–165.

Meyers, L. (2006). Behind the scenes of the "Dr. Phil" show. *Monitor on Psychology, 37*(9), 63.

Michael, D., & Chen, S. (2006). *Serious games: Games that educate, train, and inform.* Boston, MA: Thomson Course Technology.

Michaels, J. W., Blommel, J. M., Brocato, R. M., et al. (1982). Social facilitation and inhibition in a natural setting. *Replications in Social Psychology, 2,* 21–24.

Michalak, E. E., & Lam, R. W. (2002). Seasonal affective disorder: The latitude hypothesis revisited. *Canadian Journal of Psychiatry, 47*(8), 787–788.

Michalko, M. (1998). *Cracking creativity.* Berkeley, CA: Ten Speed Press.

Michel, C., Caldara, R., & Rossion, B. (2006). Same-race faces are perceived more holistically than other-race faces. *Visual Cognition, 14*(1), 55–73.

Michelangelo, I., Stefania, B., Donatella, P., et al. (2006). Electrocortical effects of MDMA are potentiated by acoustic stimulation in rats. *BMC Neuroscience*, doi 10.1186/1471-2202-7-13. Retrieved April 20, 2009, from http://www.biomedcentral.com/content/pdf/1471-2202-7-13.pdf.

Middaugh, S. J., & Pawlick, K. (2002). Biofeedback and behavioral treatment of persistent pain in the older adult: A review and a study. *Applied Psychophysiology & Biofeedback, 27*(3), 185–202.

Mielke, H. W. (1999, January–February). Lead in the inner cities. *American Scientist, 87,* 62–73.

Milgram, S. (1963). Behavioral study of obedience. *Journal of Abnormal & Social Psychology, 67*(4), 371–378.

Milgram, S. (1965). Some conditions of obedience and disobedience to authority. *Human Relations, 18*(1), 56–76.

Milgram, S., Bickman, L., & Berkowitz, L. (1969). Note on the drawing power of crowds of different size. *Journal of Personality & Social Psychology, 13*(2), 79–82.

Miller, D. T. (2006). *An invitation to social psychology.* Belmont, CA: Wadsworth.

Miller, E. K., & Cohen, J. D. (2001). An integrative theory of prefrontal cortex function. *Annual Review of Neuroscience, 24,* 167–202.

Miller, G. A. (1956). The magical number seven, plus or minus two: Some limits on our capacity for information processing. *Psychological Review, 48,* 337–442.

Miller, G. A. (1999). On knowing a word. *Annual Review of Psychology, 50,* 1–19.

Miller, G. E., Cohen, S., & Ritchey, A. K. (2002). Chronic psychological stress and the regulation of pro-inflammatory cytokines. *Health Psychology, 21*(6), 531–541.

Miller, M. A., & Rahe, R. H. (1997). Life changes scaling for the 1990s. *Journal of Psychosomatic Research, 43*(3), 279–292.

Miller, N. E. (1944). Experimental studies of conflict. In J. McV. Hunt (Ed.), *Personality and the behavior disorders* (Vol. 1). New York: Ronald Press.

Miller, N. E., & Bugelski. R. (1970). The influence of frustration imposed by the in-group on attitudes expressed toward out-groups. In R. I. Evans & R. M. Rozelle (Eds.), *Social psychology in life.* Boston: Allyn & Bacon.

Miller, N., Pedersen, W. C., Earleywine, M., & Pollock, V. E. (2003). A theoretical model of triggered displaced aggression. *Personality & Social Psychology Review, 7*(1), 75–97.

Miller, R., Perlman, D., & Brehm, S. S. (2007). *Intimate relationships* (4th ed.). New York: McGraw-Hill.

Miller, S. J., & Binder, J. L. (2002). The effects of manual-based training on treatment fidelity and outcome. *Psychotherapy: Theory, Research, Practice, Training, 39*(2), 184–198.

Miller, W. R., & Munoz, R. F. (2005). *Controlling your drinking: Tools to make moderation work for you.* New York: Guilford.

Millman, R. B., & Ross, E. J. (2003). Steroid and nutritional supplement use in professional athletes. *American Journal on Addictions, 12*(Suppl 2), S48–S54.

Milne, R., & Bull, R. (2002). Back to basics: A componential analysis of the original cognitive interview

mnemonics with three age groups. *Applied Cognitive Psychology, 16*(7), 743–753.

Milner, B. (1965). Memory disturbance after bilateral hippocampal lesions. In P. Milner & S. Glickman (Eds.), *Cognitive processes and the brain.* Princeton, NJ: Van Nostrand.

Miltenberger, R. G. (2008). *Behavior modification: Principles and procedures* (4th ed.). Belmont, CA: Cengage Learning/Wadsworth.

Miltner, W. H. R., Krieschel, S., Hecht, H., et al. (2004). Eye movements and behavioral responses to threatening and nonthreatening stimuli during visual search in phobic and nonphobic subjects. *Emotion, 4*(4), 323–339.

Milton, J., & Wiseman, R. (1997). *Guidelines for extrasensory perception research.* Hertfordshire, UK: University of Hertfordshire Press.

Milton, J., & Wiseman, R. (1999). A meta-analysis of mass-media tests of extrasensory perception. *British Journal of Psychology, 90*(2), 235–240.

Minda, J. P., & Smith, J. D. (2001). Prototypes in category learning: The effects of category size, category structure, and stimulus complexity. *Journal of Experimental Psychology: Learning, Memory, & Cognition, 27,* 775–799.

Minton, H. L. (2000). Psychology and gender at the turn of the century. *American Psychologist, 55*(6), 613–615.

Miotto, K., Darakjian, J., Basch, J., et al. (2001). Gamma-hydroxybutyric acid: Patterns of use, effects and withdrawal. *American Journal on Addictions, 10*(3), 232–241.

Miranda, R., & Kihlstrom, J. F. (2005). Mood congruence in childhood and recent autobiographical memory. *Cognition & Emotion, 19*(7), 981–998.

Mirsky, A. F., & Duncan, C. C. (2005). Pathophysiology of mental illness: A view from the fourth ventricle. *International Journal of Psychophysiology, 58*(2–3), 162–178.

Mirsky, A. F., Bieliauskas, L. A., French, L. M., et al. (2000). A 39-year followup on the Genain quadruplets. *Schizophrenia Bulletin, 26*(3), 699–708.

Mischel, W. (2004). Toward an integrative science of the person. *Annual Review of Psychology, 55,* 1–22.

Mischel, W., & Shoda, Y. (1998). Reconciling processing dynamics and personality dispositions. *Annual Review of Psychology, 49,* 229–258.

Mischel, W., Shoda, Y., & Smith, R. E. (2004). *Introduction to personality: Toward an integration* (7th ed.). Hoboken, NJ: Wiley.

Mistlberger, R. E. (2005). Circadian regulation of sleep in mammals: Role of the suprachiasmatic nucleus. *Brain Research Reviews, 49*(3), 429–454.

Mitchell, D. (1987). Firewalking cults: Nothing but hot air. *Laser,* Feb., 7–8.

Mitchell, L. A., MacDonald, R. A. R., Knussen, C., et al. (2007). A survey investigation of the effects of music listening on chronic pain. *Psychology of Music, 35*(1), 37–57.

Miyake, A. (2001). Individual differences in working memory. *Journal of Experimental Psychology: General, 130*(2), 163–168.

Moerman, D. E. (2002). The meaning response and the ethics of avoiding placebos. *Evaluation & the Health Professions. Special Recent Advances in Placebo Research, 25*(4), 399–409.

Mogg, K., Bradley, B. P., Hyare, H., & Lee, S. (1998). Selective attention to food-related stimuli in hunger. *Behaviour Research & Therapy, 36*(2), 227–237.

Moghaddam, B. (2002). Stress activation of glutamate neurotransmission in the prefrontal cortex. *Biological Psychiatry, 51*(10), 775–787.

Moghaddam, F. M. (2007). *Multiculturalism and intergroup relations: Psychological implications for democracy in global context.* Washington, DC: American Psychological Association.

Mohr, D. C., Hart, S. L., Julian, L., et al. (2005). Telephone-administered psychotherapy for depression. *Archives of General Psychiatry, 62*(9), 1007–1014.

Mokdad, A. H., Marks, J. S., Stroup, D. F., & Gerberding, J. L. (2004, March 10). Actual causes of death in the United States, 2000. *Journal of the American Medical Association, 291,* 1238–1245.

Mollon, J. D., Pokorny, J., & Knoblauch, K. (2003). *Normal and defective color vision.* New York: Oxford University Press.

Monahan, J., Steadman, H. J., Silver, E., et al. (2001). *Rethinking risk assessment: The MacArthur Study of Mental Disorder and Violence.* New York: Oxford University Press.

Montgomery, P., & Dennis, J. (2004). A systematic review of non-pharmacological therapies for sleep problems in later life. *Sleep Medicine Reviews, 8*(1), 47–62.

Montreal Declaration on Intellectual Disabilities. (2004). Retrieved May 10, 2009, from http://www.mdri.org/mdri-web-2007/pdf/montrealdeclaration.pdf.

Moor, J. (Ed.). (2003). *The Turing test: The elusive standard of artificial intelligence.* London: Kluwer Academic Publishers.

Moore, S. A., & Zoellner, L. A. (2007). Overgeneral autobiographical memory and traumatic events: An evaluative review. *Psychological Bulletin, 133*(3), 419–437.

Moore, T. O. (2001). Testosterone and male behavior: Empirical research with hamsters does not support the use of castration to deter human sexual aggression. *North American Journal of Psychology, 3*(3), 503–520.

Moran, J. M., Macrae, C. N., Heatherton, T. F., et al. (2006). Neuroanatomical evidence for distinct cognitive and affective components of self. *Journal of Cognitive Neuroscience, 18*(9), 1586–1594.

Moras, K. (2002). Research on psychotherapy. In M. Hersen & W. H. Sledge (Eds.), *Encyclopedia of psychotherapy.* San Diego: Academic Press.

Moreno, J. L. (1953). *Who shall survive?* New York: Beacon.

Morgan, J. P. (Ed.). (2005). *Psychology of aggression.* Hauppauge, NY: Nova Science Publishers.

Morgenstern, J., Labouvie, E., McCrady, B. S., et al. (1997). Affiliation with Alcoholics Anonymous after treatment: A study of its therapeutic effects and mechanisms of action. *Journal of Consulting & Clinical Psychology, 65*(5), 768–777.

Morin, A. (2006). Levels of consciousness and self-awareness: A comparison and integration of various neurocognitive views. *Consciousness & Cognition, 15*(2), 358–371.

Morisse, D., Batra, L., Hess, L., & Silverman, R. (1996). A demonstration of a token economy for the real world. *Applied & Preventive Psychology, 5*(1), 41–46.

Moritz, A. P., & Zamchech, N. (1946). Sudden and unexpected deaths of young soldiers. *American Medical Association Archives of Pathology, 42,* 459–494.

Morrison, R. G., & Wallace, B. (2001). Imagery vividness, creativity and the visual arts. *Journal of Mental Imagery, 25*(3-4), 135–152.

Morsella, E., & Krauss, R. M. (2004). The role of gestures in spatial working memory and speech. *American Journal of Psychology, 117*(3), 411–424.

Mosher, W. D., Chandra, C., & Jones, J. (2005). *Sexual behavior and selected health measures: Men and women 15–44 years of age, United States, 2002.* Atlanta: Centers for Disease Control and Prevention. Retrieved August 25, 2006, from http://www.cdc.gov/nchs/data/ad/ad362.pdf.

Most, S. B., Scholl, B. J., Clifford, E. R., & Simons, D. J. (2005). What you see is what you set: Sustained inattentional blindness and the capture of awareness. *Psychological Review, 112*(1), 217–242.

Motivala, S. J., & Irwin, M. R. (2007). Sleep and immunity: Cytokine pathways linking sleep and health outcomes. *Current Directions in Psychological Science, 16*(1), 21–25.

Mundy, A. (2004). Divided we stand. *American Demographics, 26*(5), 26–31.

Munsey, C. (2006, June). RxP legislation made historic progress in Hawaii. *APA Monitor,* 42.

Munsey, C. (2008, February). Frontline psychopharmacology. *APA Monitor,* 56.

Murray, B. (2001, November). A daunting unbelievable experience. *Monitor on Psychology,* 18.

Murray, J. B. (2002). Phencyclidine (PCP): A dangerous drug, but useful in schizophrenia research. *Journal of Psychology, 136*(3), 319–327.

Murray, S. L., Holmes, J. G., & Griffin, D. W. (1996). The self-fulfilling nature of positive illusions in romantic relationships. *Journal of Personality & Social Psychology, 71*(6), 1155–1180.

Murray, S., Holmes, J. G., & Griffin, D. W. (2003). Reflections on the self-fulfilling effects of positive illusions. *Psychological Inquiry, 14*(3-4), 2003, 289–295.

Murrell, A. R., Christoff, K. A., & Henning, K. R. (2007). Characteristics of domestic violence offenders: Associations with childhood exposure to violence. *Journal of Family Violence, 22*(7), 523–532.

Mussen, P. H., Conger, J. J., Kagan, J., & Geiwitz, J. (1979). *Psychological development: A life span approach.* New York: Harper & Row.

Musso, M., Weiller, C., Kiebel, S., et al. (1999). Training-induced brain plasticity in aphasia. *Brain, 122,* 1781–1790.

Mustanski, B. S., Chivers, M. L., & Bailey, J. M. (2002). A critical review of recent biological research on human sexual orientation. *Annual Review of Sex Research, 13,* 89–140.

Myers, H. F., Lesser, I., Rodriguez, N., et al. (2002). Ethnic differences in clinical presentation of depression in adult women. *Cultural Diversity & Ethnic Minority Psychology, 8*(2), 138–156.

Nairne, J. S. (2002). Remembering over the short-term. *Annual Review of Psychology, 53,* 53–81.

Naitoh, P., Kelly, T. L., & Englund, C. E. (1989). *Health effects of sleep deprivation.* U.S. Naval Health Research Center Report, No. 89-46.

Nakamichi, M. (2004). Tool-use and toolmaking by captive, group–living orangutans (*Pongo pygmaeus abelii*) at an artificial termite mound. *Behavioural Processes, 65*(1), 87–93.

Nakamura, J., & Csikszentmihalyi, M. (2003). The motivational sources of creativity as viewed from the paradigm of positive psychology. In L. G. Aspinwall & U. M. Staudinger (Eds.), *A psychology of human strengths: Fundamental questions and future directions for a positive psychology.* Washington, DC: American Psychological Association.

National Academy of Sciences. (2002). *The polygraph and lie detection.* Washington, DC: Author.

National Center for Chronic Disease Prevention and Health Promotion. (2009). *Tobacco use: Targeting the nation's leading killer.* Retrieved April 20, 2009, from http://www.cdc.gov/nccdphp/publications/aag/osh.htm.

National Institute of Child Health and Human Development. (2008). *Sudden infant death syndrome (SIDS).* Retrieved April 20, 2009, from http://www.nichd.nih.gov/health/topics/sudden_infant_death_syndrome.cfm.

National Institute of Mental Health. (2003). *In harm's way: Suicide in America.* Bethesda, MD: Author. Retrieved September 21, 2006, from http://www.nimh.nih.gov/publicat/harmsway.cfm.

National Institute of Mental Health. (2005). *Getting help: Locate services.* Bethesda, MD: Author. Retrieved August 20, 2007, from http://www.nimh.nih.gov/tools/contactus.cfm.

National Institute of Mental Health. (2006a). *Facts about anxiety disorders.* Bethesda, MD: Author. Retrieved July 25, 2007, from http://www.nimh.nih.gov/publicat/anxiety.cfm.

National Institute of Mental Health. (2006b). *The numbers count: Mental disorders in America.* Bethesda, MD: Author. Retrieved July 25, 2007, from http://www.nimh.nih.gov/publicat/numbers.cfm.

National Institute of Neurological Disorders and Stroke. (2007). *Brain basics: Understanding sleep.* Retrieved April 20, 2009, from http://www.ninds.nih.gov/disorders/brain_basics/understanding_sleep.htm.

National Institute on Drug Abuse. (2006). *Tobacco addiction.* Retrieved April 20, 2009, from http://www.nida.nih.gov/PDF/RRTobacco.pdf.

Nau, S. D., & Lichstein, K. L. (2005). Insomnia: Causes and treatments. In P. R. Carney, J. D. Geyer, & R. B. Berry (Eds.), *Clinical sleep disorders*. Philadelphia, PA: Lippincott Williams & Wilkins.

Naveh-Benjamin, M., Guez, J., & Sorek, S. (2007). The effects of divided attention on encoding processes in memory: Mapping the locus of interference. *Canadian Journal of Experimental Psychology, 61*(1), 1–12.

Neath, I., & Surprenant, A. (2003). *Human memory* (2nd ed.). Belmont, CA: Wadsworth.

Needles, D. J., & Abramson, L. Y. (1990). Positive life events, attributional style, and hopefulness: Testing a model of recovery from depression. *Journal of Abnormal Psychology, 99*(2), 156–165.

Nehlig, A. (Ed.). (2004). *Coffee, tea, chocolate, and the brain*. Boca Raton, FL: CRC Press.

Neisser, U., Boodoo, G., Bouchard, T. J., et al. (1996). Intelligence: Knowns & unknowns. *American Psychologist, 51*, 77–101.

Nelson, C. A. (1999). How important are the first 3 years of life? *Applied Developmental Science, 3*(4), 235–238.

Nelson, T. D. (2005). Ageism: Prejudice against our feared future self. *Journal of Social Issues, 61*(2), 207–221.

Nelson, T. D. (2006). *The psychology of prejudice* (2nd ed.). Needham Heights, MA: Allyn and Bacon.

Nemeroff, C. B., Bremner, J. D., Foa, E. B., et al. (2006). Posttraumatic stress disorder: A state-of-the-science review. *Journal of Psychiatric Research, 40*(1), 1–21.

Neter, E., & Ben-Shakhar, G. (1989). The predictive validity of graphological inferences: A meta-analytic approach. *Personality & Individual Differences, 10*(7), 737–745.

Nettle, D. (2005). An evolutionary perspective on the extraversion continuum. *Evolution & Human Behavior, 26*, 363–373.

Nettle, D. (2006). The evolution of personality variation in humans and other animals. *American Psychologist, 61*(6), 622–631.

Nettle, D. (2008, February 9). The personality factor: What makes you unique? *New Scientist, 2642*, 36–39.

Neufeld, R. W. J., Carter, J. R., Nicholson, I. R., & Vollick, D. N. (2003). Schizophrenia. In P. Firestone & W. L. Marshall (Eds.), *Abnormal psychology: Perspectives* (2nd ed.). Toronto: Prentice Hall.

Neumeister, A. (2004). Neurotransmitter depletion and seasonal affective disorder: Relevance for the biologic

effects of light therapy. *Primary Psychiatry. Special Neurotransmitter Depletion, 11*(6), 44–48.

Nevid, J. S., & Greene, B. (2005). *Abnormal psychology in a changing world, media and research update* (5th ed.). Englewood Cliffs, NJ: Prentice Hall.

Newman, A. W., & Thompson, J. W. (2001). The rise and fall of forensic hypnosis in criminal investigation. *Journal of the American Academy of Psychiatry & the Law, 29*(1), 75–84.

Ng, S. H. (2002). Will families support their elders? Answers from across cultures. In T. Nelson (Ed.), *Ageism: Stereotyping and prejudice against older persons*. Cambridge, MA: MIT Press.

Niaura, R., Todaro, J. F., Stroud, L., et al. (2002). Hostility, the metabolic syndrome, and incident coronary heart disease. *Health Psychology, 21*(6), 588–593.

NICHD Early Child Care Reseach Network. (1999). Child outcomes when child care center classes meet recommended standards for quality. *American Journal of Public Health, 89*, 1072–1077.

Nickell, J. (2001). John Edward: Hustling the bereaved. *Skeptical Inquirer*, Nov.-Dec., 19–22.

Nickerson, R. S., & Adams, M. J. (1979). Long-term memory for a common object. *Cognitive Psychology, 11*, 287–307.

Niedzwienska, A. (2004). Metamemory knowledge and the accuracy of flashbulb memories. *Memory, 12*(5), 603–613.

Niehaus, D. J. H., Stein, D. J., Koen, L., et al. (2005). A case of "Ifufunyane": A Xhosa culture-bound syndrome. *Journal of Psychiatric Practice, 11*(6), 411–413.

Nielsen, D. M., & Metha, A. (1994). Parental behavior and adolescent self-esteem in clinical and nonclinical samples. *Adolescence, 29*(115), 525–542.

Nielsen, M., & Dissanayake, C. (2004). Pretend play, mirror self-recognition and imitation: A longitudinal investigation through the second year. *Infant Behavior & Development, 27*(3), 342–365.

Nisbett, R. E. (2005). Heredity, environment, and race differences in IQ: A commentary on Rushton and Jensen (2005). *Psychology, Public Policy, & Law, 11*(2), 302–310.

Nisbett, R. E., & Miyamoto, Y. (2005). The influence of culture: holistic versus analytic perception. *Trends in Cognitive Sciences, 9*(10), 467–473.

Njeri, I. (1991, January 13). Beyond the melting pot. *Los Angeles Times*, E-1, E-8.

Noice, H., & Noice, T. (1999). Long-term retention of theatrical roles. *Memory, 7*(3), 357–382.

Noland, J. S., Singer, L. T., Short, E. J., et al. (2005). Prenatal drug exposure and selective attention in preschoolers. *Neurotoxicology & Teratology, 27*(3), 429–438.

Nolen-Hoeksema, S. (2007). *Abnormal psychology* (4th ed.). New York: McGraw-Hill.

Norcross, J. C., Hedges, M., & Prochaska, J. O. (2002). The face of 2010: A Delphi poll on the future of psychotherapy. *Professional Psychology: Research & Practice, 33*(3), 316–322.

Norem, J. K. (2002). *The positive power of negative thinking: Using defensive pessimism to harness anxiety and perform at your peak*. New York: Basic Books.

Norenzayan, A., & Nisbett, R. E. (2000). Culture and causal cognition. *Current Directions in Psychological Science, 9*, 132–135.

Nori, G. (1998). Glucagon and the control of meal size. In G. P. Smith (Ed.), *Satiation: From gut to brain*. New York: Oxford University Press.

Norlander, T., Bergman, H., & Archer, T. (1998). Effects of flotation rest on creative problem solving and originality. *Journal of Environmental Psychology, 18*(4), 399–408.

Norlander, T., Bergman, H., & Archer, T. (1999). Primary process in competitive archery performance: Effects of flotation REST. *Journal of Applied Sport Psychology, 11*(2), 194–209.

Norman, D. A. (1993). *Things that make us smart*. Menlo Park, CA: Addison-Wesley.

Norris, R. M., & Weinman, J. A. (1996). Psychological change following a long sail training voyage. *Personality & Individual Differences, 21*(2), 189–194.

North, C. S. (1987). *Welcome silence*. New York: Simon & Schuster.

North, C. S., King, R. V., Fowler, R. L., et al. (2008). Psychiatric disorders among transported hurricane evacuees: Acute-phase findings in a large receiving shelter site. *Psychiatric Annals, 38*(2), 104–113.

Northcutt, R. G. (2004). Taste buds: Development and evolution. *Brain, Behavior & Evolution, 64*(3), 198–206.

Norton, P. (2003). *Teaching with technology: Designing opportunities to learn*. Belmont, CA: Wadsworth.

Nosek, B. A., Greenwald, A. G., & Banaji, M. R. (2005). Understanding and using the implicit association test: II. Method variables and construct validity. *Personality &*

Social Psychology Bulletin, 31(2), 166–180.

Nurnberger, J. I., & Zimmerman, J. (1970). Applied analysis of human behaviors: An alternative to conventional motivational inferences and unconscious determination in therapeutic programming. *Behavior Therapy, 1*, 59–69.

Nuttin, B., Cosyns, P., Demeulemeester, H., et al. (1999). Electrical stimulation in anterior limbs of internal capsules in patients with obsessive-compulsive disorder. *The Lancet, 354*(9189), 1526.

O'Conner, T. G., Marvin, R. S., Rutter, M., et al. (2003). Child-parent attachment following early institutional deprivation. *Development & Psychopathology, 15*(1), 19–38.

O'Connor, M. G., Sieggreen, M. A., Bachna, K., et al. (2000). Long-term retention of transient news events. *Journal of the International Neuropsychological Society, 6*(1), 44–51.

O'Craven, K. M., & Kanwisher, N. (2000). Mental imagery of faces and places activates corresponding stimulus-specific brain regions. *Journal of Cognitive Neuroscience, 12*(6), 1013–1023.

O'Keeffe, C., & Wiseman, R. (2005). Testing alleged mediumship: Methods and results. *British Journal of Psychology, 96*(2), 165–179.

O'Leary, E. (2006). Person-centred gestalt therapy. In E. O'Leary & M. Murphy (Eds.), *New approaches to integration in psychotherapy*. New York: Routledge.

O'Neill, B. (2003). *Don't believe everything you read online*. BBC News. Retrieved April 21, 2009, from http://newswww.bbc.net.uk/1/hi/magazine/3151595.stm.

O'Neill, P. (2005) The ethics of problem definition. *Canadian Psychology, 46*, 13–20.

O'Roark, A. M. (2001). Personality assessment, projective methods and a triptych perspective. *Journal of Projective Psychology & Mental Health, 8*(2), 116–126.

Oakley R. (2004). How the mind hurts and heals the body. *American Psychologist, 59*(1), 29–40.

Oakley, D. A., Whitman, L. G., & Halligan, P. W. (2002). Hypnotic imagery as a treatment for phantom limb pain. *Clinical Rehabilitation, 16*(4), 368–377.

Oberauer, K., & Göthe, K. (2006). Dual-task effects in working memory: Interference between two processing tasks, between two memory demands, and between storage and processing. *European Journal of*

Cognitive Psychology, 18(4), 493–519.

Ochoa, J. G., & Pulido, M. (2005). Parasomnias. In P. R. Carney, J. D. Geyer, & R. B. Berry (Eds.), *Clinical sleep disorders.* Philadelphia, PA: Lippincott Williams & Wilkins.

Ogden C. L., Carroll M. D., McDowell M. A., & Flegal K. M. (2007). *Obesity among adults in the United States: No change since 2003–2004.* Hyattsville, MD: National Center for Health Statistics. Retrieved May 3, 2008, from http://www.cdc.gov/nchs/data/databriefs/db01.pdf.

Ogloff, J. R. P. (2006). Psychopathy/antisocial personality disorder conundrum. *Australian & New Zealand Journal of Psychiatry, 40*(6), 519–528.

Ohayon, M. M., Guilleminault, C., & Priest, R. G. (1999). Night terrors, sleepwalking, and confusional arousals in the general population. *Journal of Clinical Psychiatry, 60*(4), 268–276.

Okiishi, J., Lambert, M. J., Nielsen, S. L., & Ogles, B. M. (2003). Waiting for supershrink: An empirical analysis of therapist effects. *Clinical Psychology & Psychotherapy, 10*(6), 361–373.

Olds, M. E., & Fobes, J. L. (1981). The central basis of motivation: Intracranial self-stimulation studies. *Annual Review of Psychology, 32,* 523–574.

Olio, K. A. (2004). The truth about "false memory syndrome". In P. J. Caplan & L. Cosgrove (Eds.), *Bias in psychiatric diagnosis. A project of the association for women in psychology.* Northvale, NJ: Jason Aronson.

Olson, J. M., & Zanna, M. P. (1993). Attitudes and attitude change. *Annual Review of Psychology, 44,* 117–154.

Olson-Buchanan, J. B., & Drasgow, F. (2006). Multimedia situational judgment tests: The medium creates the message. In J. A. Weekley & R. E. Ployhart (Eds.), *Situational judgment tests: Theory, measurement, and application.* Mahwah, NJ: Erlbaum.

Olsson, A., Nearing, K., & Phelps, E. A. (2007). Learning fears by observing others: The neural systems of social fear transmission. *Social Cognitive & Affective Neuroscience, 2*(1), 3–11.

Olsson, P. A. (2007). Group death myths and terror cult groups. *Journal of Psychohistory, 34*(3), 241–254.

Olszewski, P. K., Li, D., Grace, M. K., et al. (2003). Neural basis of orexigenic effects of ghrelin acting within lateral hypothalamus. *Peptides, 24*(4), 597–602.

Onwuegbuzie, A. J. (2000). Academic procrastinators and perfectionistic tendencies among graduate students. *Journal of Social Behavior & Personality, 15*(5), 103–109.

Ooki, S. (2005). Genetic and environmental influences on the handedness and footedness in Japanese twin children. *Twin Research & Human Genetics, 8*(6), 649–656.

Ord, T. J., Martins E. P., Thakur S., et al. (2005). Trends in animal behaviour research (1968–2002): Ethoinformatics and the mining of library databases. *Animal Behaviour, 69*(6), 1399–1413.

Orleans, C. T. (2000). Promoting the maintenance of health behavior change. *Health Psychology, 19*(Suppl. 1), 76–83.

Orleans, C. T., Gruman, J., & Hollendonner, J. K. (1999). Rating our progress in population health promotion: Report card on six behaviors. *American Journal of Health Promotion, 14*(2), 75–82.

Ormay, T. (2006). Cybertherapy: Psychotherapy on the Internet. *International Journal of Psychotherapy, 10*(2), 51–60.

Osgood, C. E. (1952). The nature and measurement of meaning. *Psychological Bulletin, 49,* 197–237.

Oskamp, S., & Schultz, P. W. (2005). *Attitudes and opinions* (3rd ed.). Mahwah, NJ: Erlbaum.

Oster, H. (2005). The repertoire of infant facial expressions: a ontogenetic perspective. In J. Nadel & D. Muir (Eds.), *Emotional development: Recent research advances.* New York: Oxford University Press.

Overmier, J. B., & LoLordo, V. M. (1998). Learned helplessness. In O'Donohue, W. T. (Ed.), *Learning and behavior therapy.* Boston, MA: Allyn & Bacon.

Oyserman, D., Bybee, D., Terry, K., & Hart-Johnson, T. (2004). Possible selves as roadmaps. *Journal of Research in Personality, 38*(2), 130–149.

Page, K. (1999, May 16). The graduate. *Washington Post Magazine, 152,* 18–20.

Page, M. P. A., Madge, A., Cumming, N., et al. (2007). Speech errors and the phonological similarity effect in short-term memory: Evidence suggesting a common locus. *Journal of Memory & Language, 56*(1), 49–64.

Pagnin, D., de Queiroz, V., Pini, S., & Cassano, G. B. (2004). Efficacy of ECT in depression: A meta-analytic review. *Journal of ECT, 20*(1), 13–20.

Palmer, S. E., & Beck, D. M. (2007). The repetition discrimination task: An objective method for studying perceptual grouping. *Perception & Psychophysics, 69*(1), 68–78.

Pals, J. L. (2006). Narrative identity processing of difficult life experiences: Pathways of personality development and positive self-transformation in adulthood. *Journal of Personality, 74*(4), 1079–1110.

Panksepp, J., & Pasqualini, M. S. (2005). The search for the fundamental brain/mind sources of affective experience. In J. Nadel & D. Muir (Eds.), *Emotional development: Recent research advances.* New York: Oxford University Press.

Papanicolaou, A. C. (Ed.) (2006). *The amnesias: A clinical textbook of memory disorders.* New York: Oxford University Press.

Paquette, V., Lévesque, J., Mensour, B., et al. (2003). "Change the mind and you change the brain": Effects of cognitive-behavioral therapy on the neural correlates of spider phobia. *NeuroImage, 18,* 401–409.

Paradis, C. M., Solomon, L. Z., Florer, F., & Thompson, T. (2004). Flashbulb memories of personal events of 9/11 and the day after for a sample of New York City residents. *Psychological Reports, 95*(1), 304–310.

Parke, R. D. (2004). Development in the family. *Annual Review of Psychology, 55,* 365–399.

Parker, A., Ngu, H., & Cassaday, H. J. (2001). Odour and Proustian memory. *Applied Cognitive Psychology, 15*(2), 159–171.

Parker, E. S., Cahill, L., & McGaugh, J. L. (2006). A case of unusual autobiographical remembering. *Neurocase, 12*(1), 35–49.

Parker, J. D. A. (2005). The relevance of emotional intelligence for clinical psychology. In R. Schulze & R. D. Roberts (Eds.), *Emotional intelligence: An international handbook* (pp. 271–287). Ashland, OH: Hogrefe & Huber.

Pascual, A., & Guéguen, N. (2005). Foot-in-the-door and door-in-the-face: A comparative meta-analytic study. *Psychological Reports, 96*(1), 122–128.

Patterson, C. J. (2002). Lesbian and gay parenthood. In M. Bornstein (Ed.), *Handbook of Parenting* (Vol. 3). Mahwah, NJ: Erlbaum.

Paulhus, D. L. (1998). Interpersonal and intrapsychic adaptiveness of trait self-enhancement. *Journal of Personality and Social Psychology, 74*(5), 1197–1208.

Paulsson, T., & Parker, A. (2006). The effects of a two-week reflection-intention training program on lucid dream recall. *Dreaming, 16*(1), 22–35.

Pavlov, I. P. (1927). *Conditioned reflexes.* New York: Dover.

Penfield, W. (1957). Brain's record of past a continuous movie film. *Science News Letter,* April 27, 265.

Penfield, W. (1958). *The excitable cortex in conscious man.* Springfield, IL: Charles C Thomas.

Pennebaker, J. W. (2004). *Writing to heal: A guided journal for recovering from trauma and emotional upheaval.* Oakland, CA: New Harbinger Press.

Pennebaker, J. W., & Chung, C. K. (2007). Expressive writing, emotional upheavals, and health. In H. S. Friedman & R. C. Silver (Eds.), *Foundations of health psychology.* New York: Oxford University Press.

Peplau, L. A. (2003). Human sexuality: How do men and women differ? *Current Directions in Psychological Science, 12*(2), 37–40.

Perin, C. T. (1943). A quantitative investigation of the delay of reinforcement gradient. *Journal of Experimental Psychology, 32,* 37–51.

Perls, F. (1969). *Gestalt therapy verbatim.* Lafayette, CA: Real People Press.

Perreault, S., & Bourhis, R. Y. (1999). Ethnocentrism, social identification, and discrimination. *Personality & Social Psychology Bulletin, 25*(1), 92–103.

Perry, R. P. (2003). Perceived (academic) control and causal thinking in achievement settings. *Canadian Psychology, 44*(4), 312–331.

Perry, R. P., Hladkyj, S., Pekrun, R. H., & Pelletier, S. T. (2001). Academic control and action control in the achievement of college students: A longitudinal field study. *Journal of Educational Psychology, 93*(4), 776–789.

Pervin, L. A., Cervone, D., & John, O. P. (2005). *Personality: Theory and research* (9th ed.). Hoboken, NJ: Wiley.

Pesant, N., & Zadra, A. (2006). Dream content and psychological well-being: A longitudinal study of the continuity hypothesis. *Journal of Clinical Psychology, 62*(1), 111–121.

Pescatello, L. S. (2001). Exercising for health. *Western Journal of Medicine, 174*(2), 114–118.

Peters, W. A. (1971). *A class divided.* Garden City, NY: Doubleday.

Peterson, C., & Vaidya, R. S. (2001). Explanatory style, expectations, and depressive symptoms. *Personality & Individual Differences, 31*(7), 1217–1223.

Peterson, D. R. (2001). Choosing the PsyD. In S. Walfish & A. K. Hess (Eds.), *Succeeding in graduate school: The career guide for psychology students*. Mahwah, NJ: Erlbaum.

Peterson, L. R., & Peterson, M. J. (1959). Short-term retention of individual verbal items. *Journal of Experimental Psychology, 58,* 193–198.

Peterson, S. E. (1992). The cognitive functions of underlining as a study technique. *Reading Research & Instruction, 31*(2), 49–56.

Pett, M. A., & Johnson, M. J. M. (2005). Development and psychometric evaluation of the Revised University Student Hassles Scale. *Educational & Psychological Measurement, 65*(6), 984–1010.

Peverly, S. T., Brobst, K. E., Graham, M., & Shaw, R. (2003). College adults are not good at self-regulation. *Journal of Educational Psychology, 95*(2), 335–346.

Phillips, D. P., Liu, G. C., Kwok, K., et al. (2001). The Hound of the Baskervilles effect: Natural experiment on the influence of psychological stress on timing of death. *British Medical Journal, 323*(7327), 1443–1446.

Piaget, J. (1951, original French, 1945). *The psychology of intelligence*. New York: Norton.

Piaget, J. (1952). *The origins of intelligence in children*. New York: International University Press.

Pickel, K. L., French, T. A., & Betts, J. M. (2003). A cross-modal weapon focus effect: The influence of a weapon's presence on memory for auditory information. *Memory, 11*(3), 277–292.

Piefke, M., Weiss, P., Markowitsch, H., & Fink, G. (2005). Gender differences in the functional neuroanatomy of emotional episodic autobiographical memory. *Human Brain Mapping, 24,* 313–324.

Piek, J. P. (2006). *Infant motor development*. Champaign, IL: Human Kinetics Publishers.

Pierce, W. D., & Cheney, C. D. (2004). *Behavior analysis and learning* (3rd ed.). Mahwah, NJ: Erlbaum.

Pierrehumbert, B., Ramstein, T., Karmaniola, A., et al. (2002). Quality of child care in the preschool years. *International Journal of Behavioral Development, 26*(5), 385–396.

Piliavin, I. M., Rodin, J., & Piliavin, J. A. (1969). Good samaritanism: An underground phenomenon? *Journal of Personality & Social Psychology, 13*(4), 289–299.

Pillow, D. R., Zautra, A. J., & Sandler, I. (1996). Major life events and minor stressors: Identifying mediational links in the stress process. *Journal of Personality & Social Psychology, 70*(2), 381–394.

Pinel, J. P. J., Assanand, S., & Lehman, D. R. (2000). Hunger, eating, and ill health. *American Psychologist, 55*(10), 1105–1116.

Pinker, S., & Jackendoff, R. (2005). The faculty of language: What's special about it? *Cognition, 95*(2), 201–236.

Pizam, A., Jeong, G.-H., Reichel, A., et al. (2004). The relationship between risk-taking, sensation-seeking, and the tourist behavior of young adults: A cross-cultural study. *Journal of Travel Research, 42,* 251–260.

Plassmann, H., O'Doherty, J., Shiv, B., et al. (2008). Marketing actions can modulate neural representations of experienced pleasantness. *Proceedings of the National Academy of Sciences, 105*(3), 1050–1054.

Plazzi, G., Vetrugno, R., Provini, F., & Montagna, P. (2005). Sleepwalking and other ambulatory behaviours during sleep. *Neurological Sciences, 26*(Suppl. 3), s193–s198.

Pliner, P., & Mann, N. (2004). Influence of social norms and palatability on amount consumed and food choice. *Appetite, 42*(2), 227–237.

Plous, S. (2003). *Understanding prejudice and discrimination*. New York: McGraw-Hill.

Plutchik, R. (2003). *Emotions and life: Perspectives from psychology, biology, and evolution*. Washington, DC: American Psychological Association.

Poland, J., & Caplan, P. J. (2004). The deep structure of bias in psychiatric diagnosis. In P. J. Caplan & L. Cosgrove (Eds.), *Bias in psychiatric diagnosis. A project of the Association for Women in Psychology*. Lanham, MD: Jason Aronson.

Polemikos, N., & Papaeliou, C. (2000). Sidedness preference as an index of organization of laterality. *Perceptual & Motor Skills, 91*(3, Pt 2), 1083–1090.

Polivy, J., & Herman, C. P. (2002). Causes of eating disorders. *Annual Review of Psychology, 53,* 187–213.

Pollner, M. (1998). The effects of interviewer gender in mental health interviews. *Journal of Nervous & Mental Disease, 186*(6), 369–373.

Pollock, V. E., Briere, J., Schneider, L., et al. (1990). Childhood antecedents of antisocial behavior. *American Journal of Psychiatry, 147*(10), 1290–1293.

Pomaki, G., Supeli, A., & Verhoeven, C. (2007). Role conflict and health behaviors: Moderating effects on psychological distress and somatic complaints. *Psychology & Health, 22*(3), 317–335.

Pope, H. G., Gruber, A. J., & Yurgelun-Todd, D. (1995). The residual neuropsychological effects of cannabis. *Drug & Alcohol Dependence, 38*(1), 25–34.

Popma, A., Vermeiren, R., Geluk, C., et al. (2007). Cortisol moderates the relationship between testosterone and aggression in delinquent male adolescents. *Biological Psychiatry, 61*(3), 405–411.

Porter, K., Babiker, A. G., Darbyshire, J. H., & Pezzotti, P. (2003). Determinants of survival following HIV-1 seroconversion after the introduction of HAART. *The Lancet, 362,* 1267–1274.

Posada, G., Jacobs, A., Richmond, M. K., et al. (2002). Maternal caregiving and infant security in two cultures. *Developmental Psychology, 38*(1), 67–78.

Powell, A. L., & Thelen, M. H. (1996). Emotions and cognitions associated with bingeing and weight control behavior in bulimia. *Journal of Psychosomatic Research, 40*(3), 317–328.

Powell, D. H. (2004). Behavioral treatment of debilitating test anxiety among medical students. *Journal of Clinical Psychology, 60*(8), 853–865.

Powell, R. A., Symbaluk, D. G., & Honey, P. L. (2009). *Introduction to learning and behavior* (3rd ed.). Belmont, CA: Cengage Learning/Wadsworth.

Preckel, F., Holling, H., & Wiese, M. (2006). Relationship of intelligence and creativity in gifted and nongifted students: An investigation of threshold theory. *Personality & Individual Differences, 40*(1), 159–170.

Premack, A. J., & Premack, D. (1972). Teaching language to an ape. *Scientific American, 227*(4), 92–99.

Premack, D., & Premack, A. J. (1983). *The mind of an ape*. New York: Norton.

Pressley, M. (1987). Are key-word method effects limited to slow presentation rates? An empirically based reply to Hall and Fuson (1986). *Journal of Educational Psychology, 79*(3), 333–335.

Price, M. (2007, February 28). Star-crossed lovers quit West Bank. *BBC News*. Retrieved July 16, 2008, from http://news.bbc.co.uk/2/hi/middle_east/6405799.stm.

Prigerson, H. G., Maciejewski, P.K., & Rosenheck, R. A. (2002). Population attributable fractions of psychiatric disorders and behavioral outcomes associated with combat exposure among US men. *American Journal of Public Health, 92,* 59–63.

Priluck, R., & Till, B. D. (2004). The role of contingency awareness, involvement, and need for cognition in attitude formation. *Journal of the Academy of Marketing Science, 32*(3), 329–344.

Prochaska, J. O., & Norcross, J. C. (2010). *Systems of psychotherapy: A transtheoretical analysis* (7th ed.). Belmont, CA: Cengage Learning/Wadsworth.

Provencher, M. D., Dugas, M. J., & Ladouceur, R. (2004). Efficacy of problem-solving training and cognitive exposure in the treatment of generalized anxiety disorder: A case replication series. *Cognitive & Behavioral Practice, 11*(4), 404–414.

Puca, R. M., & Schmalt, H. (1999). Task enjoyment: A mediator between achievement motives and performance. *Motivation & Emotion, 23*(1), 15–29.

Puentes, J., Knox, D., & Zusman, M. E. (2008). Participants in "friends with benefits" relationships. *College Student Journal, 42*(1), 176–180.

Pychyl, T. A., Lee, J. M., Thibodeau, R., & Blunt, A. (2000). Five days of emotion: An experience sampling study of undergraduate student procrastination. *Journal of Social Behavior & Personality, 15*(5), 239–254.

Quednow, B. B., Jessen, F., Kühn, K.-W., et al. (2006). Memory deficits in abstinent MDMA (ecstasy) users: Neuropsychological evidence of frontal dysfunction. *Journal of Psychopharmacology, 20*(3), 373–384.

Quigley, B. M., & Leonard, K. E. (2000). Alcohol, drugs, and violence. In V. B. Van Hasselt & M. Hersen (Eds.), *Aggression and violence: An introductory text*. Boston: Allyn & Bacon.

Quinn, P. C., Bhatt, R. S., & Hayden, A. (2008). Young infants readily use proximity to organize visual pattern information. *Acta Psychologica, 127*(2), 289–298.

Quinto-Pozos, D. (2008). Sign language contact and interference: ASL and LSM. *Language in Society, 37*(2), 161–189.

Rabius, V., McAlister, A. L., Geiger, A., et al. (2004). Telephone counseling increases cessation rates among young adult smokers. *Health Psychology, 23*(5), 539–541.

Rachman, S. (2004). *Anxiety* (2nd. ed.). New York: Routledge.

Rainville, P. (2004). Pain & emotions. In D. D. Price & M. C. Bushnell (Eds.), *Psychological methods of pain control: Basic science and clinical perspectives.* Seattle, WA: IASP Press.

Ramachandran, V. S. (1995). 2-D or not 2-D—that is the question. In R. Gregory, J. Harris, P. Heard, & D. Rose (Eds.), *The artful eye.* Oxford: Oxford University Press.

Ramsay, M. C., Reynolds, C. R., & Kamphaus, R. W. (2002). *Essentials of behavioral assessment.* New York: Wiley.

Rathus, R., Nevid, J., & Fichner-Rathus, L. (2005). *Human sexuality in a world of diversity* (6th ed.). Boston: Allyn & Bacon.

Rau, H., Bührer, M., & Weitkunat, R. (2003). Biofeedback of R-wave-to-pulse interval normalizes blood pressure. *Applied Psychophysiology and Biofeedback, 28*(1), 37-46.

Rau, P. R. (2005). *Drowsy driver detection and warning system for commercial vehicle drivers: Field operational test design, data analyses, and progress.* National Highway Traffic Safety Administration Paper Number 05-0192. Retrieved April 20, 2009, from http://www-nrd.nhtsa.dot.gov/pdf/nrd-01/esv/esv19/05-0192-W.pdf.

Rau, W., & Durand, A. (2000). The academic ethic and college grades: Does hard work help students to "make the grade"? *Sociology of Education, 73*(1), 19–38.

Raun, K., von Voss, P., & Knudsen, L. B. (2007). Liraglutide, a once-daily human glucagon-like peptide-1 analog, minimizes food intake in severely obese minipigs. *Obesity, 15*(7), 1710–1716.

Reed, J. D., & Bruce, D. (1982). Longitudinal tracking of difficult memory retrievals. *Cognitive Psychology, 14*, 280–300.

Reed, S. K. (2010). *Cognition: Theory and applications* (8th ed.). Belmont, CA: Cengage Learning/Wadsworth.

Reevy, G. M., & Maslach, C. (2001). Use of social support: Gender and personality differences. *Sex Roles, 44*(7-8), 437–459.

Regan, P. C., Levin, L., Sprecher, S., et al. (2000). Partner preferences: What characteristics do men and women desire in their short-term sexual and long-term romantic partners? *Journal of Psychology & Human Sexuality, 12*(3), 1–21.

Reid, M. R., Mackinnon, L. T., & Drummond, P. D. (2001). The effects of stress management on symptoms of upper respiratory tract infection, secretory immunoglobulin A, and mood in young adults. *Journal of Psychosomatic Research, 51*(6), 721–728.

Reid, P. T. (2002). Multicultural psychology. *Cultural Diversity & Ethnic Minority Psychology, 8*(2), 103–114.

Reiff, S. Katkin, E. S., & Friedman, R. (1999). Classical conditioning of the human blood pressure response. *International Journal of Psychophysiology, 34*(2), 135–145.

Reifman, A. S., Larrick, R. P., & Fein, S. (1991). Temper and temperature on the diamond: The heat-aggression relationship in major league baseball. *Personality & Social Psychology Bulletin, 17*(5), 580–585.

Reinberg, A., & Ashkenazi, I. (2008). Internal desynchronization of circadian rhythms and tolerance to shift work. *Chronobiology International, 25*(4), 625–643.

Reisner, A. D. (2006). A case of Munchausen syndrome by proxy with subsequent stalking behavior. *International Journal of Offender Therapy & Comparative Criminology, 50*(3), 245–254.

Reiss, M., Tymnik, G., Koegler, P., et al. (1999). Laterality of hand, foot, eye, and ear in twins. *Laterality, 4*(3), 287–297.

Reiss, S., & Havercamp, S. M. (2005). Motivation in developmental context: A new method for studying self-actualization. *Journal of Humanistic Psychology, 45*(1), 41–53.

Reiterman, T. (1993, April 23). Parallel roads led to Jonestown, Waco. *The Los Angeles Times,* A-24.

Reitman, D., Murphy, M. A., Hupp, S. D. A., & O'Callaghan, P. M. (2004). Behavior change and perceptions of change: Evaluating the effectiveness of a token economy. *Child & Family Behavior Therapy, 26*(2), 17–36.

Renner, M. J., & Mackin, R. S. (1998). A life stress instrument for classroom use. *Teaching of Psychology, 25*(1), 46–48.

Rentfrow, P. J., & Gosling, S. D. (2003). The do re mi's of everyday life: The structure and personality correlates of music preferences. *Journal of Personality & Social Psychology, 84*(6), 1236–1256.

Rentfrow, P. J., & Gosling, S. D. (2007). The content and validity of music-genre stereotypes among college students. *Psychology of Music, 35*(2), 306–326.

Rescorla, R. A. (1987). A Pavlovian analysis of goal-directed behavior. *American Psychologist, 42*, 119–126.

Rescorla, R. A. (2004). Spontaneous recovery. *Learning & Memory, 11*(5), 501–509.

Restak, R. M. (2001). *The secret life of the brain.* New York: The Dana Press.

Rhine, J. B. (1953). *New world of the mind.* New York: Sloane.

Richards, J. M., & Gross, J. J. (2000). Emotion regulation and memory: The cognitive costs of keeping one's cool. *Journal of Personality & Social Psychology, 79*(3), 410–424.

Richardson, D. R., & Green, L. R. (1999). Social sanction and threat explanations on gender effects in direct and indirect aggression. *Aggressive Behavior, 25*, 425–434.

Richmond, L. J. (2004). When spirituality goes awry: Students in cults. *Professional School Counseling, 7*(5), 367–375.

Ridenour, T. A., Maldonado-Molina M., Compton, W. M., et al. (2005). Factors associated with the transition from abuse to dependence among substance abusers: Implications for a measure of addictive liability. *Drug & Alcohol Dependence, 80*(1), 1–14.

Ridings, C. M., & Gefen, D. (2004). Virtual community attraction: Why people hang out online. *Journal of Computer-Mediated Communication, 10*(1). Retrieved July 8, 2009, from http://jcmc.indiana.edu/vol10/issue1/ridings_gefen.html.

Riley, W., Jerome, A., Behar, A., & Zack, S. (2002). Feasibility of computerized scheduled gradual reduction for adolescent smoking cessation. *Substance Use & Misuse, 37*(2), 255–263.

Riquelme, H. (2002). Can people creative in imagery interpret ambiguous figures faster than people less creative in imagery? *Journal of Creative Behavior, 36*(2), 105–116.

Ritter, J. (1998, October 15). Uniforms changing the culture of the nation's classrooms. *USA Today,* 1A, 2A.

Riva, G., & Wiederhold, B. K. (2006). Emerging trends in cybertherapy: Introduction to the special issue. *Psychology Journal, 4*(2), 121–128.

Roberts, B. W., & Mroczek, D. (2008). Personality trait change in adulthood. *Current Directions in Psychological Science, 17*(1), 31–35.

Roberts, B. W., Kuncel, N. R., Shiner, R., et al. (2007). The power of personality: The comparative validity of personality traits, socioeconomic status, and cognitive ability for predicting important life outcomes. *Perspectives on Psychological Science, 2*(4), 313–345.

Roberts, D. F., Foehr, U. G., & Rideout, V. (2005). *Generation M: Media in the lives of 8–18 year-olds.* Kaiser Family Foundation. Retrieved April 21, 2009, from http://www.kff.org/entmedia/7251.cfm.

Roberts, R. E., Phinney, J. S., Masse, L. C., et al. (1999). The structure of ethnic identity of young adolescents from diverse ethnocultural groups. *Journal of Early Adolescence, 19*(3), 301–322.

Roberts, W. A. & Roberts, S. (2002). Two tests of the stuck-in-time hypothesis. *Journal of General Psychology, 129*(4), 415–429.

Roberts, W. A. (2002). Are animals stuck in time? *Psychological Bulletin, 128*(3), 473–489.

Robertson, I. S. (2001). *Problem solving.* Hove, UK: Psychology Press.

Robertson, L. C. & Sagiv, N. (2005). *Synesthesia: Perspectives from cognitive neuroscience.* New York: Oxford.

Robins, R. W., Gosling, S. D., & Craik, K. H. (1998). Psychological science at the crossroads. *American Scientist, 86*(July-Aug.), 310–313.

Robinson, A., & Clinkenbeard, P. R. (1998). Giftedness. *Annual Review of Psychology, 49*, 117–139.

Robinson, B., Frye, E. M., & Bradley, L. J. (1997). Cult affiliation and disaffiliation. *Counseling & Values, 41*(2), 166–173.

Robinson, D. N. (2008). *Consciousness and mental life.* New York: Columbia University Press.

Robinson, T. E., & Berridge, K. C. (2003). Addiction. *Annual Review of Psychology, 54*, 25–53.

Robinson, T. N., Wilde, M. L., Navracruz, L. C., et al. (2001). Effects of reducing children's television and video game use on aggressive behavior. *Archives of Pediatrics & Adolescent Medicine, 155*(1), 17–23.

Robinson-Riegler, B., & McDaniel, M. (1994). Further constraints on the bizarreness effect: Elaboration at encoding. *Memory & Cognition, 22*(6), 702–712.

Rock, A. (2004). *The mind at night: The new science of how and why we dream.* New York: Basic Books.

Rodd, Z. A., Bell, R. L., McQueen, V. K., et al. (2005). Chronic ethanol drinking by alcohol-preferring rats increases the sensitivity of the posterior ventral tegmental area to the reinforcing effects of ethanol. *Alcoholism: Clinical & Experimental Research, 29*(3), 358–366.

Roeckelein, J. E. (2004). *Imagery in psychology: A reference guide.* Westport, CT: Praeger.

Roediger, H. L., & McDermott, K. B. (1995). Creating false memories: Remembering words not presented on lists. *Journal of Experimental Psychology: Learning, Memory, & Cognition, 21*(4), 803–814.

Roediger, H. L., III, & Amir, N., (2005). Implicit memory tasks: Retention without conscious recollection. In A. Wenzel & D. C. Rubin (Eds.), *Cognitive methods and their application to clinical research*. Washington, DC: American Psychological Association.

Roese, N. J., Pennington, G. L., Coleman, J., et al. (2006). Sex differences in regret: All for love or some for lust? *Personality & Social Psychology Bulletin, 32*(6), 770–780.

Rogers, C. R. (1959). A theory of therapy, personality, and interpersonal relationships, as developed in the client-centered framework. In S. Koch (Ed.), *Psychology: A study of a science* (Vol. 3). New York: McGraw-Hill.

Rogers, C. R. (1961). *On becoming a person*. Boston: Houghton Mifflin.

Rogers, S., & Silver, S. M. (2002). Is EMDR an exposure therapy? A review of trauma protocols. *Journal of Clinical Psychology, 58*(1), 43–59.

Rohsenow, D. J., & Smith R. E. (1982). Irrational beliefs as predictors of negative affective states. *Motivation & Emotion, 6*, 299–301.

Roid, G. H. (2003). *Stanford-Binet Intelligence Scales, Fifth Edition, Examiner's Manual*. Itasca, IL: Riverside.

Rolls, E. T. (2008). Top-down control of visual perception: Attention in natural vision. *Perception, 37*(3), 333–354.

Ronningstam, E. (2009). Narcissistic personality disorder: Facing DSM-V. *Psychiatric Annals, 39*, 111–121. Retrieved June 27, 2009, from http://www.psychiatricannalsonline.com/showPdf.asp?rID=37821.

Roos, P. E., & Cohen, L. H. (1987). Sex roles and social support as moderators of life stress adjustment. *Journal of Personality & Social Psychology, 52*, 576–585.

Rosch, E. (1977). Classification of real-world objects: Origins and representations in cognition. In P. N. Johnson-Laird & P. C. Wason (Eds.), *Thinking: Reading in cognitive science*. Cambridge, MA: Cambridge University Press.

Rosen, G., Hugdahl, K., Ersland, L., et al. (2001). Different brain areas activated during imagery of painful and non-painful 'finger movements' in a subject with an amputated arm. *Neurocase, 7*(3), 255–260.

Rosenberg, L. B. (1994, July). *The effect of interocular distance upon depth perception when using stereoscopic displays to perform work within virtual and telepresent environments*. USAF AMRL Technical Report (Wright-Patterson), AL/CF-TR-1994-0052.

Rosenberg, S. S., & Lynch, J. E. (2002). Fritz Perls revisited: A micro-assessment of a live clinical session. *Gestalt Review, 6*(3), 184–202.

Rosenhan, D. L. (1973). On being sane in insane places. *Science, 179*, 250–258.

Rosenkranz, M. A., Jackson, D. C., Dalton, K. M., et al. (2003). Affective style and in vivo immune response: Neurobehavioral mechanisms. *Proceedings of the National Academy of Sciences, 100*, 11148–11152.

Rosenman, R. H., Brand, R. J., Jenkins, C. D., et al. (1975). Coronary heart disease in the Western Collaborative Group Study: Final follow-up experience of 8½ years. *Journal of the American Medical Association, 233*, 872–877.

Rosenthal, R. (1973). The Pygmalion effect lives. *Psychology Today*, Sept., 56–63.

Rosenthal, R. (1994). Science and ethics in conducting, analyzing, and reporting psychological research. *Psychological Science, 5*, 127–134.

Rosenthal, T. L. (1993). To soothe the savage breast. *Behavior Research & Therapy, 31*(5), 439–462.

Rosenthal, T. L., & Rosenthal, R. (1980). *The vicious cycle of stress reaction*. Copyright, Renate & Ted Rosenthal, Stress Management Clinic, Department of Psychiatry, University of Tennessee College of Medicine, Memphis.

Rosenzweig, M. R., Breedlove, S. M., & Watson, N. V. (2004). *Biological psychology: An introduction to behavioral and cognitive neuroscience* (4th ed.). Sunderland, MA: Sinauer Associates.

Rosnow, R. L. (2006). *Writing papers in psychology: A student guide to research papers, essays, proposals, posters, and handouts* (7th ed.). Belmont, CA: Cengage Learning/Wadsworth.

Ross, H. E., & Plug. C. (2002). *The mystery of the moon illusion*. Oxford: Oxford University Press.

Ross, M., Heine, S. J., Wilson, A. E., & Sugimori, S. (2005). Cross-cultural discrepancies in self-appraisals. *Personality & Social Psychology Bulletin, 31*(9), 1175–1188.

Ross, P. E. (2006). The expert mind. *Scientific American, 294*(7), 64–71.

Rothbart, M. K. (2007). Temperament, development, and personality. *Current Directions in Psychological Science, 16*(4), 207–212.

Rothschild, B., & Rand, M. (2006). *Help for the helper: The psychophysiology of compassion fatigue and vicarious trauma*. New York: Norton.

Rotter, J. B., & Hochreich, D. J. (1975). *Personality*. Glenview, IL: Scott, Foresman.

Rowe, B. (2007). *College awareness guide: What students need to know to succeed in college*. Englewood Cliffs, NJ: Prentice Hall.

Rozin, P., Kabnick, K., Pete, E., et al. (2003). The ecology of eating: Smaller portion sizes in France than in the United States help explain the French paradox. *Psychological Science, 14*(5), 450–454.

Rubenstein, C. (2002, July-August). What turns you on? *My Generation*, 55–58.

Rubin, D. C. (1985). The subtle deceiver: Recalling our past. *Psychology Today*, Sept., 38–46.

Rudd, M. D., Joiner, T. E., Jr., & Rajab, M. H. (2001). *Treating suicidal behavior*. New York: Guilford.

Rueckl, J. G., & Galantucci, B. (2005). The locus and time course of long-term morphological priming. *Language & Cognitive Processes, 20*(1), 115–138.

Rummens, J., Beiser, M., & Noh, S. (Eds.). (2003). *Immigration, ethnicity and health*. Toronto: University of Toronto Press.

Runco, M. A. (2003). Idea evaluation, divergent thinking, and creativity. In M. A. Runco (Ed.), *Critical creative processes: Perspectives on creativity research*. Cresskill, NJ: Hampton Press.

Runco, M. A. (2004). Creativity. *Annual Review of Psychology, 55*, 657–687.

Rushton, J. P., & Jensen, A. R. (2005). Thirty years of research on race differences in cognitive ability. *Psychology, Public Policy, & Law, 11*, 235–294.

Russell, S., & Norvig, P. (2003). *Artificial intelligence: A modern approach* (2nd ed.). Englewood Cliffs, NJ: Prentice Hall.

Russo, M. B., Brooks, F. R., Fontenot, J., et al. (1998). Conversion disorder presenting as multiple sclerosis. *Military Medicine, 163*(10), 709–710.

Rutledge, T., & Linden, W. (1998). To eat or not to eat: Affective and physiological mechanisms in the stress-eating relationship. *Journal of Behavioral Medicine, 21*(3), 221–240.

Rutz, C., Bluff, L. A., Weir, A. A. S., & Kacelnik, A. (2007). Video cameras on wild birds. *Science, 318*, 765.

Ruva, C., McEvoy, C., & Bryant, J. B. (2007). Effects of pre-trial publicity and jury deliberation on juror bias and source memory errors. *Applied Cognitive Psychology, 21*(1), 45–67.

Ryan, M. P. (2001). Conceptual models of lecture learning. *Reading Psychology, 22*(4), 289–312.

Ryan, R. M., & Deci, E. L. (2000). Self-determination theory and the facilitation of intrinsic motivation, social development, and well-being. *American Psychologist, 55*, 68–78.

Ryckman, R. M. (2008). *Theories of personality* (9th ed.). Belmont, CA: Cengage Learning/Wadsworth.

Ryff, C. D. (1995). Psychological well-being in adult life. *Current Directions in Psychological Science, 4*(4), 99–104.

Ryff, C. D., & Keyes, C. L. (1995). The structure of psychological well-being revisited. *Journal of Personality & Social Psychology, 69*(4), 719–727.

Ryff, C. D., & Singer, B. (2000). Interpersonal flourishing. *Personality & Social Psychology Review, 4*, 30–44.

Ryff, C. D., Singer, B. H., & Palmersheim, K. A. (2004). Social inequalities in health and well-being: The role of relational and religious protective factors. In O. G. Brim, C. D. Ryff, & R. C. Kessler (Eds.), *How healthy are we?: A national study of well-being at midlife*. Chicago: University of Chicago Press.

Saadeh, W., Rizzo, C. P., & Roberts, D. G. (2002). Spanking. *Clinical Pediatrics, 41*(2), 87–88.

Sackeim, H. A., Haskett, R. F., Mulsant, B. H., et al. (2001). Continuation pharmacotherapy in the prevention of relapse following electroconvulsive therapy. *Journal of the American Medical Association, 285*, 1299–1307.

Sahelian, R. (1998). *5-HTP*. Wakefield, RI: Moyer Bell.

Saksida, L. M., & Wilkie, D. M. (1994). Time-of-day discrimination by pigeons. *Animal Learning & Behavior, 22*, 143–154.

Salamone, J. D. (2007). Functions of mesolimbic dopamine: Changing concepts and shifting paradigms. *Psychopharmacology, 191*(3), 389.

Salmon, P. (2001). Effects of physical exercise on anxiety, depression, and sensitivity to stress: A unifying theory. *Clinical Psychology Review, 21*(1), 33–61.

Salovey, P., & Mayer, J. (1997). *Emotional development and emotional intelligence*. New York: Basic Books.

Salthouse, T. A. (2004). What and when of cognitive aging. *Current Directions in Psychological Science, 13*(4), 140–144.

Sankofa, B. M., Hurley, E. A., Allen, B. A., & Boykin, A. W. (2005). Cultural expression and black students' attitudes toward high achievers. *Journal of Psychology: Interdisciplinary & Applied, 139*(3), 247–259.

Santrock, J. W. (2007). *Child development* (11th ed.). New York: McGraw-Hill.

Santrock, J. W., & Halonen, J. S. (2007). *Connections to college success.* Belmont, CA: Cengage Learning/Wadsworth.

Sarason, I. G., & Sarason, B. R. (2005). *Abnormal psychology* (11th ed.). Englewood Cliffs, NJ: Prentice Hall.

Sateia, M. J., & Nowell, P. D. (2004). Insomnia. *Lancet, 364*(9449), 1959–1973.

Saunders, T., Driskell, J. E., Johnston, J. H., & Salas, E. (1996). The effect of stress inoculation training on anxiety and performance. *Journal of Occupational Health Psychology, 1*(2), 170–186.

Savage-Rumbaugh, S., Sevcik, R. A., Brakke, K. E., et al. (1990). Symbols: Their communicative use, comprehension, and combination by bonobos (*Pan paniscus*). *Advances in Infancy Research, 6,* 221–278.

Saxton, M., Houston-Price, C., & Dawson, N. (2005). The prompt hypothesis: Clarification requests as corrective input for grammatical errors. *Applied Psycholinguistics, 26*(3), 393–414.

Saxvig, I. W., Lundervold, A. J., Gronli, J., et al. (2008). The effect of a REM sleep deprivation procedure on different aspects of memory function in humans. *Psychophysiology, 45*(2), 309–317.

Schachter, S., & Wheeler, L. (1962). Epinephrine, chlorpromazine and amusement. *Journal of Abnormal and Social Psychology, 65,* 121–128.

Schacter, D. L. (1996). *Searching for memory: The brain, the mind, and the past.* New York: Basic Books.

Schacter, D. L. (2000). Memory: Memory systems. In A. Kazdin (Ed.), *Encyclopedia of psychology.* Washington, DC: American Psychological Association.

Schacter, D. L. (2001). *The seven sins of memory.* Boston: Houghton Mifflin.

Schacter, D. L., Norman, K. A., & Koutstaal, W. (1998). The cognitive neuroscience of constructive memory. *Annual Review of Psychology, 49,* 289–318.

Schafer, M., & Crichlow, S. (1996). Antecedents of groupthink: A quantitative study. *Journal of Conflict Resolution, 40*(3), 415–435.

Schaie, K. W. (1994). The course of adult intellectual development. *American Psychologist, 49*(4), 304–313.

Schaie, K. W. (2005). *Developmental influences on adult intelligence: The Seattle longitudinal study.* London: Oxford University Press.

Scheck, B., Neufeld, P., & Dwyer, J. (2000). *Actual innocence.* New York: Doubleday.

Scheinkman, M. (2008). The multilevel approach: A road map for couples therapy. *Family Process, 47*(2), 197–213.

Schenck, C. H., & Mahowald, M. W. (2005). Rapid eye movement and non-REM sleep parasomnias. *Primary Psychiatry, 12*(8), 67–74.

Schick, T., & Vaughn, L. (2001). *How to think about weird things: Critical thinking for a new age.* New York: McGraw-Hill.

Schilling, M. A. (2005). A "smallworld" network model of cognitive insight. *Creativity Research Journal, 17*(2–3), 131–154.

Schiraldi, G. R., & Brown, S. L. (2001). Primary prevention for mental health: Results of an exploratory cognitive-behavioral college course. *Journal of Primary Prevention, 22*(1), 55–67.

Schlaepfer, T. E., Cohen, M. X., Frick, C., et al. (2008). Deep brain stimulation to reward circuitry alleviates anhedonia in refractory major depression. *Neuropsychopharmacology, 33*(2), 368–377.

Schleicher, S. S., & Gilbert, L. A. (2005). Heterosexual dating discourses among college students: Is there still a double standard? *Journal of College Student Psychotherapy, 19*(3), 7–23.

Schlosberg, H. (1954). Three dimensions of emotion. *Psychological Review, 61,* 81–88.

Schmitt, D. P., & Allik, J. (2005). Simultaneous administration of the Rosenberg Self-Esteem Scale in 53 nations: Exploring the universal and culture-specific features of global self-esteem. *Journal of Personality & Social Psychology, 89*(4), 623–642.

Schmolck, H., Buffalo, E. A., & Squire, L. R. (2000). Memory distortions develop over time: Recollections of the O. J. Simpson trial verdict after 15 and 32 months. *Psychological Science, 11*(1), 39–45.

Schneider, K. J. (2002). Humanistic psychotherapy. In M. Hersen & W. H. Sledge (Eds.), *Encyclopedia of psychotherapy.* San Diego: Academic Press.

Schneider, K. J., Bugental, J. F. T., & Pierson, J. F. (2001). Introduction. *The handbook of humanistic psychology.* Thousand Oaks, CA: Sage.

Schneiderman, N., Antoni, M. H., Saab, P. G., & Ironson, G. (2001). Health psychology: Psychological and biobehavioral aspects of chronic disease management. *Annual Review of Psychology, 52,* 555–580.

Schooler, C. (1998) Environmental complexity and the Flynn effect. In U. Neisser (Ed.), *The rising curve: Long-term gains in IQ and related measures.* Washington, DC: American Psychological Association.

Schopp, L. H., Demiris, G., & Glueckauf, R. L. (2006). Rural backwaters or front-runners? Rural telehealth in the vanguard of psychology practice. *Professional Psychology: Research & Practice, 37*(2), 165–173.

Schreiber, E. H., & Schreiber, D. E. (1999). Use of hypnosis with witnesses of vehicular homicide. *Contemporary Hypnosis, 16*(1), 40–44.

Schreiber, F. R. (1973). *Sybil.* Chicago: Regency.

Schroeder, J. E. (1995). Self-concept, social anxiety, and interpersonal perception skills. *Personality & Individual Differences, 19*(6), 955–958.

Schroeder, S. (2008). Stranded in the periphery: The increasing marginalization of smokers. *New England Journal of Medicine, 35*(821), 2284.

Schuel, H., Chang, M. C., Burkman, L. J., et al. (1999) Cannabinoid receptors in sperm. In G. Nahas, K. M. Sutin, D. Harvey, & S. Agurell (Eds.), *Marihuana and medicine.* Totowa, NJ: Humana Press.

Schuetze, P., & Eiden, R. D. (2006). The association between maternal cocaine use during pregnancy and physiological regulation in 4- to 8-week-old infants: An examination of possible mediators and moderators. *Journal of Pediatric Psychology* [Special Issue: Prenatal Substance Exposure: Impact on Children's Health, Development, School Performance, and Risk Behavior], *31*(1), 15–26.

Schultheiss, O. C., Wirth, M. M., & Stanton, S. J. (2004). Effects of affiliation and power motivation arousal on salivary progesterone and testosterone. *Hormones & Behavior, 46*(5), 592–599.

Schultz, D. P., & Schultz, S. E. (2005). *Theories of personality* (8th ed.). Belmont, CA: Wadsworth.

Schultz, D. P., & Schultz, S. E. (2008). *A history of modern psychology* (9th ed.). Belmont, CA: Cengage Learning/Wadsworth.

Schultz, H. T. (2004). Good and bad movie therapy with good and bad outcomes. *The Amplifier: Official Newsletter of APA Division 46, Media Psychology,* Fall/Winter. Retrieved April 21, 2009, from http://www.apa.org/divisions/div46/Amp%20Winter%2005/for%20Website/ampwinter05.html#therapy.

Schum T. R., Kolb, T. M., McAuliffe T. L., et al. (2002). Sequential acquisition of toilet-training skills: A descriptive study of gender and age differences in normal children. *Pediatrics, 3,* e48. Retrieved July 4, 2006, from http://pediatrics.aappublications.org/cgi/content/abstract/109/3/e48.

Schum, T. R., McAuliffe, T. L., Simms, M. D., et al. (2001). Factors associated with toilet training in the 1990s. *Ambulatory Pediatrics, 1*(2), 79–86.

Schuster, M. A., Stein, B. D., Jaycox, L. H., et al. (2001). A national survey of stress reactions after the September 11, 2001, terrorist attacks. *New England Journal of Medicine, 345*(20), 1507–1512.

Schwartz, B. L. (2002). *Tip-of-the-tongue states: Phenomenology, mechanism, and lexical retrieval.* Hillsdale, NJ: Erlbaum.

Schwartz, M. S., & Andrasik, F. (Eds.). (2003). *Biofeedback: A practitioner's guide* (3rd ed.). New York: Guilford.

Schwartz, S. J. (2008). Self and identity in early adolescence: Some reflections and an introduction to the special issue. *Journal of Early Adolescence, 28*(1), 5–15.

Sclafani, A., & Springer, D. (1976). Dietary obesity in adult rats: Similarities to hypothalamic and human obesity syndromes. *Psychology & Behavior, 17,* 461–471.

Scoboria, A., Mazzoni, G., Kirsch, I., & Milling, L. S. (2002). Immediate and persisting effects of misleading questions and hypnosis on memory reports. *Journal of Experimental Psychology: Applied, 8*(1), 26–32.

Scott, J. P., & Ginsburg, B. E. (1994). The Seville statement on violence revisited. *American Psychologist, 49*(10), 849–850.

Scott, L., & O'Hara, M. W. (1993). Self-discrepancies in clinically anxious and depressed university students. *Journal of Abnormal Psychology, 102*(2), 282–287.

Scully, J. A., Tosi, H., & Banning, K. (2000). Life event checklists: Revisiting the Social Readjustment Rating Scale after 30 years. *Educational & Psychological Measurement, 60*(6), 864–876.

Scurfield, R. M. (2002). Commentary about the terrorist acts of September 11, 2001: Posttraumatic reactions and related social and policy issues. *Trauma Violence & Abuse, 3*(1), 3–14.

Searcy, W. A., & Nowicki, S. (2005). *The evolution of animal communication: Reliability and deception in signaling systems.* Princeton, NJ: Princeton University Press.

Seckel, A. (2000). *The art of optical illusions.* London: Carlton Books.

Segerdahl, P., Fields, W., & Savage-Rumbaugh, S. (2005). *Kanzi's primal language: The cultural initiation of primates into language.* New York: Palgrave MacMillan.

Segerstrom, S., & Miller, G. E. (2004). Psychological stress and the human immune system: A meta-analytic study of 30 years of inquiry. *Psychological Bulletin, 130*(4), 601–630.

Seidler, G. H., & Wagner, F. E. (2006). Comparing the efficacy of EMDR and trauma-focused cognitive-behavioral therapy in the treatment of PTSD: A meta-analytic study. *Psychological Medicine, 36*(11), 1515–1522.

Seidman, B. F. (2001, January-February). Medicine wars. *Skeptical Inquirer,* 28–35.

Seitz, A., & Watanabe, T. (2005). A unified model for perceptual learning. *Trends in Cognitive Sciences, 9*(7), 329–334.

Seligman, M. E. P. (1972). For helplessness: Can we immunize the weak? In *Readings in psychology today* (2nd ed.). Del Mar, CA: CRM.

Seligman, M. E. P. (1989). Research in clinical psychology: Why is there so much depression today? In I. S. Cohen (Ed.), *The G. Stanley Hall lecture series* (Vol. 9). Washington, DC: American Psychological Association.

Seligman, M. E. P. (1994). *What you can change and what you can't.* New York: Knopf.

Seligman, M. E. P. (1995). The effectiveness of psychotherapy. *American Psychologist, 50*(12), 965–974.

Seligman, M. E. P. (1998). Why therapy works. *APA Monitor, 29*(12), 2.

Seligman, M. E. P. (2002). *Authentic happiness: Using the new positive psychology to realize your potential for lasting fulfillment.* New York: Free Press/Simon and Schuster.

Seligman, M. E. P., & Csikszentmihalyi, M. (2000). Positive psychology: An introduction. *American Psychologist, 55,* 5–14.

Selye, H. (1976). *The stress of life.* New York: Knopf.

Senécal, C., Julien, E., & Guay, F. (2003). Role conflict and academic procrastination: A self-determination perspective. *European Journal of Social Psychology, 33*(1), 135–145.

Seybolt, D. C., & Wagner, M. K. (1997). Self-reinforcement, gender-role, and sex of participant in prediction of life satisfaction. *Psychological Reports, 81*(2) 519–522.

Seyle, D. C., & Newman, M. L. (2006). A house divided? The psychology of red and blue America. *American Psychologist, 61*(6), 571–580.

Shaffer, D. R., & Kipp, K. (2010). *Developmental psychology: Childhood and adolescence* (8th ed.). Belmont, CA: Cengage Learning/Wadsworth.

Shaffer, J. B., & Galinsky, M. D. (1989). *Models of group therapy.* Englewood Cliffs, NJ: Prentice Hall.

Shafir, E. (1993). Choosing versus rejecting: Why some options are both better and worse than others. *Memory & Cognition, 21,* 546–556.

Shafton, A. (1995). *Dream reader.* Albany: State University of New York Press.

Shapiro, C. M., Trajanovic, N. N., & Fedoroff, J. P. (2003). Sexsomnia: A new parasomnia? *Canadian Journal of Psychiatry, 48*(5), 311–317.

Shapiro, D. A., Barkham, M., Stiles, W. B., et al. (2003). Time is of the essence: A selective review of the fall and rise of brief therapy research. *Psychology & Psychotherapy: Theory, Research & Practice, 76*(3), 211–235.

Shapiro, F. (2001). *Eye movement desensitization and reprocessing: Basic principles, protocols and procedures* (2nd ed.). New York: Guilford.

Shapiro, F., & Forrest, M. S. (2004). *EMDR: The breakthrough therapy for overcoming anxiety, stress, and trauma.* New York: Basic Books.

Shapiro, J. M. (2006). A "memory-jamming" theory of advertising. *Social Science Research Network.* Retrieved May 3, 2009, from http://papers.ssrn.com/sol3/papers.cfm?abstract_id=903474.

Shapiro, S. L., & Walsh, R. (2006). The meeting of meditative disciplines and Western psychology: A mutually enriching dialogue. *American Psychologist, 61*(3), 227–239.

Shapiro-Mendoza, C. K., Kimball, M., Tomashek, K. M., et al. (2009). US infant mortality trends attributable to accidental suffocation and strangulation. *Pediatrics, 123*(2), 533–539.

Sharf, R. S. (2008). *Theories of psychotherapy & counseling: Concepts and cases* (4th ed.). Belmont, CA: Cengage Learning/Wadsworth.

Sharot, T., Martorella, E. A., Delgado, M. R., et al. (2007). How personal experience modulates the neural circuitry of memories of September 11. *PNAS Proceedings of the National Academy of Sciences of the United States of America, 104*(1), 389–394.

Shaywitz, B. A., Shaywitz, S. E., Pugh, K. R., et al. (1995). Sex differences in the functional organization of the brain for language. *Nature, 373,* 607–609.

Sheldon, K. M., Ryan, R. M., Rawsthorne, L. J., & Ilardi, B. (1997). Trait self and true self: Cross-role variation in the Big-Five personality traits and its relations with psychological authenticity and subjective well-being. *Journal of Personality & Social Psychology, 73*(6), 1380–1393.

Shen, J., Botly, L. C. P., Chung, S. A., et al. (2006). Fatigue and shift work. *Journal of Sleep Research, 15*(1), 1–5.

Shepard, R. N. (1975). Form, formation, and transformation of internal representations. In R. L. Solso (Ed.), *Information processing and cognition: The Loyola Symposium.* Hillsdale, NJ: Erlbaum.

Shepherd, G. M. (2006). Smell images and the flavour system in the human brain. *Nature, 444*(7117), 316–321.

Sherif, M., Harvey, O. J., White, B. J., et al. (1961). *Intergroup cooperation and competition: The Robbers Cave experiment.* Norman: University of Oklahoma Press.

Shiffman, S., Scharf, D. M., Shadel, W. G., et al. (2006). Analyzing milestones in smoking cessation: Illustration in a nicotine patch trial in adult smokers. *Journal of Consulting & Clinical Psychology, 74*(2), 276–285.

Shneerson, J. M. (2005). *Sleep medicine: A guide to sleep and its disorders* (2nd ed.). London: Blackwell.

Shurkin, J. N. (1992). *Terman's kids.* Boston: Little, Brown.

Siegel, R. K. (2005). *Intoxication: The universal drive for mind-altering substances.* Rochester, VT: Park Street Press.

Siegler, R. S. (1989). Mechanisms of cognitive development. *Annual Review of Psychology, 40,* 353–379.

Siegler, R. S. (2004). *Children's thinking* (4th ed.). Mahwah, NJ: Erlbaum.

Siegler, R. S., DeLoache, J. S., & Eisenberg, N. (2006). *How children develop* (2nd ed.). New York: Worth.

Siever, L. J., & Koenigsberg, H. W. (2000). The frustrating no-man's-land of borderline personality disorder. *Cerebrum, 2*(4), 85–99.

Sigelman, C. K., & Rider, E. A. (2009). *Life-span human development* (6th ed.). Belmont, CA: Cengage Learning/Wadsworth.

Silver, S. M., Rogers, S., Knipe, J., & Colelli, G. (2005). EMDR therapy following the 9/11 terrorist attacks: A community-based intervention project in New York City. *International Journal of Stress Management, 12*(1), 29–42.

Simeon, D., Guralnik, O., Knutelska, M., & Schmeidler, J. (2002). Personality factors associated with dissociation: Temperament, defenses, and cognitive schemata. *American Journal of Psychiatry, 159,* 489–491.

Simister, J., & Cooper, C. (2005). Thermal stress in the U.S.A.: Effects on violence and on employee behaviour. *Stress & Health, 21,* 3–15.

Simner, M. L., & Goffin, R. D. (2003). A position statement by the international graphonomics society on the use of graphology in personnel selection testing. *International Journal of Testing, 3*(4), 353–364.

Simon, G. E, Ludman, E. J., Tutty, S., et al. (2004). Telephone psychotherapy and telephone care management for primary care patients starting antidepressant treatment. *Journal of the American Medical Association, 292,* 935–942.

Simons, D. J., & Chabris, C. F. (1999). Gorillas in our midst: Sustained inattentional blindness for dynamic events. *Perception, 28,* 1059–1074.

Simons, D. J., & Levin, D. T. (1998). Failure to detect changes to people during a real-world interaction. *Psychonomic Bulletin & Review, 5*(4), 644–649.

Simons, J. S., Dodson, C. S., Bell, D., & Schacter, D. L. (2004). Specific- and partial-source memory: Effects of aging. *Psychology & Aging, 19*(4), 689–694.

Simon-Thomas, E. R., Role, K. O., & Knight, R. T. (2005). Behavioral and electrophysiological evidence of a right hemisphere bias for the influence of negative emotion on higher cognition. *Journal of Cognitive Neuroscience, 17*(3), 518–529.

Simonton, D. K., & Baumeister, R. F. (2005). Positive psychology at the summit. *Review of General Psychology, 9*(2), 99–102.

Simpson, D. D., Joe, G. W., Fletcher, B. W., et al. (1999). A national evaluation of treatment outcomes for cocaine dependence. *Archives of General Psychiatry, 57*(6), 507–514.

Singer, J. D. (2005). Explaining foreign policy: U.S. decision-making and the Persian Gulf War. *Political Psychology, 26*(5), 831–834.

Singer, M. T. (2003). *Cults in our midst: The continuing fight against their hidden menace* (rev. ed.). San Francisco: Jossey-Bass.

Singer, M. T., & Addis, M. E. (1992). Cults, coercion, and contumely. *Cultic Studies Journal, 9*(2), 163–189.

Singleton, J. L., & Newport, E. L. (2004). When learners surpass their models: The acquisition of American Sign Language from inconsistent input. *Cognitive Psychology, 49*(4), 370–407.

Sinha, R., Garcia, M., Paliwal, P., et al. (2006). Stress-induced cocaine craving and hypothalamic-pituitary-adrenal responses are predictive of cocaine relapse outcomes. *Archives of General Psychiatry, 63*(3), 324–331.

Sipos, A., Rasmussen, F., Harrison, G., et al. (2004). Paternal age and schizophrenia: A population based cohort study. *British Medical Journal, 329*(7474), 1070.

Sirkin, M. I. (1990). Cult involvement: A systems approach to assessment and treatment. *Psychotherapy, 27*(1), 116–123.

Skeels, H. M. (1966). Adult status of children with contrasting early life experiences. *Monograph of the Society for Research in Child Development, 31*(3), 105.

Skillsoft. (2006). *IT pros more like to suffer from stress, says new survey.* Retrieved July 6, 2009 from http://www.skillsoft.com/emea/press-releases/archive/2006/19-May-06.asp.

Skinner, B. F. (1938). *The behavior of organisms: An experimental analysis.* New York: Appleton-Century-Crofts.

Skipton, L. H. (1997). The many faces of character. *Consulting Psychology Journal: Practice & Research. 49*(4), 235–245

Slaby, A. E., Garfinkel, B. D., & Garfinkel, L. F. (1994). *No one say my pain.* New York: Norton.

Slater, A., Mattock, A., & Brown, E. (1990). Size constancy at birth: Newborn infants' responses to retinal and real size. *Journal of Experimental Child Psychology, 49*(2), 314–322.

Slater, A., Mattock, A., Brown, E., & Bremner, J. G. (1991). Form perception at birth: Cohen and Younger (1984) revisited. *Journal of Experimental Child Psychology, 51*(3), 395–406.

Sloman, A. (2008). The well-designed young mathematician. *Artifical Intelligence, 172*(18), 2015–2034.

Slot, L. A. B., & Colpaert, F. C. (1999). Recall rendered dependent on an opiate state. *Behavioral Neuroscience, 113*(2), 337–344.

Smedley, A., & Smedley, B. D. (2005). Race as biology is fiction, racism as a social problem is real. *American Psychologist, 60*(1), 16–26.

Smith, A. P. (2005). Caffeine at work. *Human Psychopharmacology: Clinical & Experimental, 20*(6), 441–445.

Smith, A. P., Clark, R., & Gallagher, J. (1999). Breakfast cereal and caffeinated coffee: Effects on working memory, attention, mood and cardiovascular function. *Physiology & Behavior, 67*(1), 9–17.

Smith, C., Carey, S., & Wiser, M. (1985). On differentiation: A case study of the development of the concepts of size, weight, and density. *Cognition, 21*(3), 177–237.

Smith, E., & Delargy, M. (2005). Locked-in syndrome. *British Medical Journal, 330*, 406–409.

Smith, J. L., & Cahusac, P. M. B. (2001). Right-sided asymmetry in sensitivity to tickle. *Laterality, 6*(3), 233–238.

Smith, L. (2002). Piaget's model. In U. Goswami (Ed.), *Blackwell handbook of childhood cognitive development.* Malden, MA: Blackwell.

Smith, M. L., Cottrell, G. W., Gosselin, F., & Schyns, P. G. (2005). Transmitting and decoding facial expressions. *Psychological Science, 16*(3), 184–189.

Smith, T. W., Glazer, K., Ruiz, J. M., & Gallo, L. C. (2004). Hostility, anger, aggressiveness, and coronary heart disease: An interpersonal perspective on personality, emotion, and health. *Journal of Personality. Special Emotions, Personality, & Health, 72*(6), 1217–1270.

Smith, T. W., Ruiz, J. M., & Uchino, B. N. (2004). Mental activation of supportive ties, hostility, and cardiovascular reactivity to laboratory stress in young men and women. *Health Psychology, 23*(5), 476–485.

Smyth, M. M., & Waller, A. (1998). Movement imagery in rock climbing. *Applied Cognitive Psychology, 12*(1), 145–157

Snyder, A., Bahramali, H., Hawker, T., et al. (2006). Savant-like numerosity skills revealed in normal people by magnetic pulses. *Perception, 35*(6), 837–845.

Sobolewski, J. M., & Amato, P. R. (2005). Economic hardship in the family of origin and children's psychological well-being in adulthood. *Journal of Marriage & Family, 67*(1), 141–156.

Soderstrom, M. (2007). Beyond babytalk: Re-evaluating the nature and content of speech input to preverbal infants. *Developmental Review, 27*(4), 501–532.

Solomon, J. L., Marshall, P., & Gardner, H. (2005). Crossing boundaries to generative wisdom: An analysis of professional work. In R. J. Sternberg & J. Jordan (Eds.), *A handbook of wisdom: Psychological perspectives.* New York: Cambridge University Press.

Solowij, N., Stephens, R. S., Roffman, R. A., et al. (2002). Cognitive functioning of long-term heavy cannabis users seeking treatment. *Journal of the American Medical Association, 287*, 1123–1131.

Solso, R. L., MacLin, M. K., & MacLin, O. H. (2008). *Cognitive psychology* (8th ed.). Boston: Allyn and Bacon.

Somberg, D. R., Stone, G., & Claiborn, C. D. (1993). Informed consent: Therapists' beliefs and practices. *Professional Psychology: Research & Practice, 24*(2), 153–159.

Sommers-Flanagan, J., & Sommers-Flanagan, R. (2002). *Clinical interviewing* (3rd ed.). New York: Wiley.

Soussignan, R. (2002). Duchenne smile, emotional experience, and autonomic reactivity: A test of the facial feedback hypothesis. *Emotion, 2*(1), 52–74.

Soyez, V., & Broekaert, E. (2003). How do substance abusers and their significant others experience the re-entry phase of therapeutic community treatment? A qualitative study. *International Journal of Social Welfare, 12*(3), 211–220.

Spalding, K. L., Arner, E., Westermark, P. O., et al. (2008, May 4). Dynamics of fat cell turnover in humans. *Nature,* doi:10.1038/nature06902.

Spano, R. (2005). Potential sources of observer bias in police observational data. *Social Science Research, 34*(3), 591–617.

Spence, S., & David, A. (Eds.). (2004). *Voices in the brain: The cognitive neuropsychiatry of auditory verbal hallucinations.* London: Psychology Press.

Sperry, R. W. (1968). Hemisphere deconnection and unity in conscious awareness. *American Psychologist, 23,* 723–733.

Spiegler, M. D., & Guevremont, D. C. (2003). *Contemporary behavior therapy* (4th ed.). Belmont, CA: Wadsworth.

Spinella, M. (2005). Compulsive behavior in tobacco users. *Addictive Behaviors, 30*(1), 183–186.

Spiro Wagner, P., & Spiro, C. S. (2005). *Divided minds: Twin sisters and their journey through schizophrenia.* New York: St. Martin's Press.

Sporer, S. L. (2001). Recognizing faces of other ethnic groups. *Psychology, Public Policy, and Law, 7*(1), 36–97

Sprecher, S. (1998). Insiders' perspectives on reasons for attraction to a close other. *Social Psychology Quarterly, 61*(4), 287–300.

Springer, S. P., & Deutsch, G. (1998). *Left brain, right brain.* New York: Freeman.

Sprinthall, R. C. (2007). *Basic statistical analysis* (8th ed.). Boston: Allyn & Bacon.

Squire, L. R. (2004). Memory systems of the brain: A brief history and current perspective. *Neurobiology of Learning & Memory, 82,* 171–177.

Sroufe, L. A., Egeland, B., Carlson, E., & Collins, W. A. (2005). Placing early attachment experiences in developmental context: The Minnesota Longitudinal Study. In K. E. Grossmann, K. Grossmann, & E. Waters (Eds.), *Attachment from infancy to adulthood: The major longitudinal studies.* New York: Guilford.

Staemmler, F.-M. (2004). Dialogue and interpretation in Gestalt therapy: Making sense together. *International Gestalt Journal, 27*(2), 33–57.

Stanovich, K. E. (2007). *How to think straight about psychology* (8th ed.). Boston: Allyn & Bacon.

Stapel, D. A., & Marx, D. M. (2007). Distinctiveness is key: How different types of self-other similarity moderate social comparison effects. *Personality & Social Psychology Bulletin, 33*(3), 439–448.

Steele, C. M. (1997). A threat in the air. *American Psychologist, 52*(6), 613–629.

Steele, C. M., & Aronson, J. (1995). Stereotype threat and the intellectual test performance of African Americans. *Journal of Personality & Social Psychology, 69*(5), 797–811.

Steiger, A. (2007). Neurochemical regulation of sleep. *Journal of Psychiatric Research, 41,* 537–552.

Stein, L. M., & Memon, A. (2006). Testing the efficacy of the cognitive interview in a developing country. *Applied Cognitive Psychology, 20*(5), 597–605.

Stein, M. B., & Stein, D. J. (2008). Social anxiety disorder. *Lancet, 371*(9618), 1115–1125.

Stein, M. D., & Friedmann, P. D. (2005). Disturbed sleep and its relationship to alcohol use. *Substance Abuse, 26*(1), 1–13.

Stein, M. I. (1974). *Stimulating creativity* (Vol. 1). New York: Academic.

Stein, M. T., & Ferber, R. (2001). Recent onset of sleepwalking in early adolescence. *Journal of Development, Behavior, and Pediatrics, 22,* S33–S35.

Steinberg, L. (2001). Adolescent development. *Annual Review of Psychology, 52,* 83–110.

Stemler, S. E., & Sternberg, R. J. (2006). Using situational judgment tests to measure practical intelligence. In J. A. Weekley & R. E. Ployhart (Eds.), *Situational judgment tests: Theory, measurement, and application.* Mahwah, NJ: Erlbaum.

Stephens, K., Kiger, L., Karnes, F. A., & Whorton, J. E. (1999). Use of non-verbal measures of intelligence in identification of culturally diverse gifted students in rural areas. *Perceptual & Motor Skills, 88*(3, Pt 1), 793–796.

Stern, S. L., Dhanda, R., & Hazuda, H. P. (2001). Hopelessness predicts mortality in older Mexican and European Americans. *Psychosomatic Medicine, 63*(3), 344–351.

Sternberg, R. J. (1988). *The triangle of love.* New York: Basic.

Sternberg, R. J. (2000). The holy grail of general intelligence. *Science, 289,* 399–401.

Sternberg, R. J. (2001). Is there a heredity–environment paradox? In R. J. Sternberg & E. L. Grigorenko (Eds.), *Environmental effects on cognitive abilities.* Mahwah, NJ: Erlbaum.

Sternberg, R. J. (2004). Culture and intelligence. *American Psychologist, 59*(5), 325–338.

Sternberg, R. J. (2007, Oct. 27). Race and intelligence: Not a case of black and white. *New Scientist, 2627,* 16.

Sternberg, R. J., & Davidson, J. D. (1982). The mind of the puzzler. *Psychology Today,* June, 37–44.

Sternberg, R. J., & Grigorenko, E. L. (2005). Cultural explorations of the nature of intelligence. In A. F. Healy (Ed.), *Experimental cognitive psychology and its applications.* Washington, DC: American Psychological Association.

Sternberg, R. J., & Grigorenko, E. L. (2006). Cultural intelligence and successful intelligence. *Group & Organization Management, 31*(1), 27–39.

Sternberg, R. J., & Lubart, T. I. (1995). *Defying the crowd.* New York: The Free Press.

Sternberg, R. J., Grigorenko, E. L., & Kidd, K. K. (2005). Intelligence, race, and genetics. *American Psychologist, 60*(1), 46–59.

Steuer, F. B., & Hustedt, J. T. (2002). *TV or no TV? A primer on the psychology of television.* Lanham, MD: University Press of America.

Stewart, A. J., & Ostrove, J. M. (1998). Women's personality in middle age. *American Psychologist, 53*(11), 1185–1194.

Stewart-Williams, S. (2004). The placebo puzzle: Putting together the pieces. *Health Psychology, 23*(2), 198–206.

Stickgold, R., & Walker, M. (2004). To sleep, perchance to gain creative insight? *Trends in Cognitive Sciences, 8*(5), 191–192.

Stinson, F. S., Dawson, D. A., Chou, S. P., et al. (2007). The epidemiology of DSM-IV specific phobia in the USA: Result from the National Epidemiologic Survey on Alcohol and Related Conditions. *Psychological Medicine, 37*(7), 1047–1059.

Stipek, D. (2001). *Motivation to learn* (4th ed.). Boston: Allyn & Bacon.

Stöber, J. (2004). Dimensions of test anxiety: Relations to ways of coping with pre-exam anxiety and uncertainty. *Anxiety, Stress & Coping: An International Journal, 17*(3), 213–226.

Stokes, D. M. (2001, May-June). The shrinking filedrawer. *Skeptical Inquirer, 22*–25.

Stokoe, W. C. (2001). *Language in hand: Why sign came before speech.* Washington, DC: Gallaudet University Press.

Stolerman, I. P., & Jarvis, M. J. (1995) The scientific case that nicotine is addictive. *Psychopharmacology, 117*(1), 2–10.

Stone, J., Perry, Z. W., & Darley, J. M. (1997). "White men can't jump." *Basic & Applied Social Psychology, 19*(3), 291–306.

Stoppard, J. M., & McMullen, L. M. (Eds.). (2003). *Situating sadness: Women and depression in social context.* New York: New York University Press.

Strack, F., Martin, L. L., & Stepper, S. (1988). Inhibiting and facilitating conditions of facial expressions: A non-obtrusive test of the facial feedback hypothesis. *Journal of Personality & Social Psychology, 54,* 768–777.

Straneva, P. A., Maixner, W., Light, K. C., et al. (2002). Menstrual cycle, beta-endorphins, and pain sensitivity in premenstrual dysphoric disorder. *Health Psychology, 21*(4), 358–367.

Strange, J. R. (1965). *Abnormal psychology.* New York: McGraw-Hill.

Straub, R. (2006). *Health psychology* (2nd ed.). New York: Worth.

Strayer, D. L., Drews, F. A., & Crouch, D. J. (2006). A comparison of the cell phone driver and the drunk driver. *Human Factors, 48*(2), 381–391.

Strickler, E. M., & Verbalis, J. G. (1988). Hormones and behavior: The biology of thirst and sodium appetite. *American Scientist,* May-June, 261–267.

Stroebe, W., Papies, E. K., & Aarts, H. (2008). From homeostatic to hedonic theories of eating: Self-regulatory failure in food-rich environments. *Applied Psychology: An International Review, 57,* 172–193.

Strongman, K. T. (2003). *The psychology of emotion: From everyday life to theory* (5th ed.). New York: Wiley.

Strote, J., Lee, J. E., & Wechsler, H. (2002). Increasing MDMA use among college students: Results of a national survey. *Journal of Adolescent Health, 30*(1), 64–72.

Strube, M. J. (2005). What did Triplett really find? A contemporary analysis of the first experiment in social psychology. *American Journal of Psychology, 118*(2), 271–286.

Sturges, J. W., & Sturges, L. V. (1998). In vivo systematic desensitization in a single-session treatment of an 11-year old girl's elevator phobia. *Child & Family Behavior Therapy, 20*(4), 55–62.

Stuss, D. T., & Alexander, M. P. (2000). The anatomical basis of affective behavior, emotion and self-awareness: A specific role of the right frontal lobe. In G. Hatano, N. Okada, & H. Tanabe (Eds.), *Affective minds. The 13th Toyota conference.* Amsterdam: Elsevier.

Stuss, D. T., & Knight, R. T. (2002). *Principles of frontal lobe function.* New York: Oxford University Press.

Substance Abuse and Mental Health Services Administration (SAMHSA). (2005). *Overview of Findings from the 2004 National Survey on Drug Use and Health.* Rockville, MD: Office of Applied Studies, NSDUH Series H-27, DHHS Publication No. SMA 05-4061. Retrieved April 20, 2009, from http://www.oas.samhsa.gov/nsduh/2k4nsduh/2k4overview/2k4overview.pdf.

Suedfeld, P., & Borrie, R. A. (1999). Health and therapeutic applications of chamber and flotation restricted environmental stimulation therapy (REST). *Psychology & Health, 14*(3), 545–566.

Sugimoto, K., & Ninomiya, Y. (2005). Introductory remarks on umami research: Candidate receptors and signal transduction mechanisms on umami. *Chemical Senses, 30*(Suppl. 1), i21–i22.

Suinn, R. M. (1975). *Fundamentals of behavior pathology* (2nd ed.). New York: Wiley.

Suinn, R. M. (1999). Scaling the summit: Valuing ethnicity. *APA Monitor* (30, March), 2.

Suinn, R. M. (2001). The terrible twos: Anger and anxiety. *American Psychologist, 56*(1), 27–36.

Sumathipala, A., Siribaddana, S. H., & Bhugra, D. (2004). Culture-bound syndromes: The story of *dhat* syndrome. *British Journal of Psychiatry, 184*(3), 200–209.

Sumerlin, J. R., & Bundrick, C. M. (1996). Brief Index of Self-Actualization: A measure of Maslow's model. *Journal of Social Behavior & Personality, 11*(2), 253–271.

Sunnafrank, M., Ramirez, A., & Metts, S. (2004). At first sight: Persistent relational effects of get-acquainted conversations. *Journal of Social & Personal Relationships, 21*(3), 361–379.

Sutherland, R. J., Lehmann, H., Spanswick, S. C., et al. (2006). Growth points in research on memory and hippocampus. *Canadian Journal of Experimental Psychology, 60*(2), 166–174.

Suzuki, L., & Aronson, J. (2005). The cultural malleability of intelligence and its impact on the racial/ethnic hierarchy. *Psychology, Public Policy, & Law, 11,* 320–327.

Svartdal, F. (2003). Extinction after partial reinforcement: Predicted vs. judged persistence. *Scandinavian Journal of Psychology, 44*(1), 55–64.

Swaak, J., de Jong, T., & van Joolingen, W. R. (2004). The effects of discovery learning and expository instruction on the acquisition of definitional and intuitive knowledge. *Journal of Computer Assisted Learning, 20*(4), 225–234.

Swann, W. B., Jr., Chang-Schneider, C., & Larsen McClarty, K. (2007). Do people's self-views matter? Self-concept and self-esteem in everyday life. *American Psychologist, 62*(2), 84–94.

Synhorst, L. L., Buckley, J. A., Reid, R., et al. (2005). Cross informant agreement of the Behavioral and Emotional Rating Scale-2nd Edition (BERS-2) parent and youth rating scales. *Child & Family Behavior Therapy, 27*(3), 1–11.

Szabo, A. (2003). The acute effects of humor and exercise on mood and anxiety. *Journal of Leisure Research, 35*(2), 152–162.

Talbot, N. L., & Gamble, S. A. (2008). IPT for women with trauma histories in community mental health care. *Journal of Contemporary Psychotherapy, 38*(1), 35–44.

Talbott, J. A. (2004). Deinstitutionalization: Avoiding the disasters of the past. *Psychiatric Services. Special Issue: A Tribute to John A. Talbott, M.D., 55*(10), 1112–1115.

Talley, P. F., Strupp, H. H., & Morey, L. C. (1990). Matchmaking in psychotherapy: Patient-therapist dimensions and their impact on outcome. *Journal of Consulting & Clinical Psychology, 58*(2), 182–188.

Tal-Or, N., & Papirman, Y. (2007). The fundamental attribution error in attributing fictional figures' characteristics to the actors. *Media Psychology, 9*(2), 331–345.

Tamis-LeMonda, C. S., Bornstein, M. H., & Baumwell, L. (2001). Maternal responsiveness and children's achievement of language milestones. *Child Development, 72,* 748–767.

Tamis-LeMonda, C. S., Shannon, J. D., Cabrera, N. J., & Lamb, M. E. (2004). Fathers and mothers at play with their 2- and 3-year-olds: Contributions to language and cognitive development. *Child Development, 75*(6), 1806–1820.

Tanner, J. M. (1973). Growing up. *Scientific American, 229,* 34–43.

Taraban, R., Rynearson, K., & Kerr, M. (2000). College students' academic performance and self-reports of comprehension strategy use. *Reading Psychology, 21*(4), 283–308.

Tardif, T. Z., & Sternberg, R. J. (1988). What do we know about creativity? In R. J. Sternberg (Ed.), *The nature of creativity.* Cambridge, MA: Cambridge University Press.

Taris, T. W., Bakker, A. B., Schaufeli, W. B., et al. (2005). Job control and burnout across occupations. *Psychological Reports, 97*(3), 955–961.

Taub, E. (2004). Harnessing brain plasticity through behavioral techniques to produce new treatments in neurorehabilitation. *American Psychologist, 59*(8), 692–704.

Tausig, M., Michello, J., & Subedi, S. (2004). *A sociology of mental illness* (2nd ed.). Englewood Cliffs, NJ: Prentice Hall.

Tavris, C., & Aronson, E. (2007). *Mistakes were made (but not by me): Why we justify foolish beliefs, bad decisions, and hurtful acts.* New York: Harcourt.

Taylor, G. J., & Taylor-Allan, H. L. (2007). Applying emotional intelligence in understanding and treating physical and psychological disorders: What we have learned from alexithymia. In R. Bar-On, M. J. G. Reuven, et al. (Eds.), *Educating people to be emotionally intelligent.* Westport, CT: Praeger.

Taylor, K. (2004). *Brainwashing: The science of thought control.* New York: Oxford University Press.

Taylor, S. E. (2002). Classical conditioning. In M. Hersen & W. H. Sledge (Eds.), *Encyclopedia of psychotherapy.* San Diego: Academic Press.

Taylor, S. E. (2006). *Health psychology* (6th ed.). New York: McGraw-Hill.

Taylor, S. E., Kemeny, M. E., Reed, G. M., et al. (2000). Psychological resources, positive illusions, and health. *American Psychologist, 55*(1), 99–109.

Taylor, S. E., Lerner, J. S., Sherman, D. K., et al. (2003). Are self-enhancing cognitions associated with healthy or unhealthy biological

profiles? *Journal of Personality & Social Psychology, 85*(4), 605–615.

Taylor-Seehafer, M., & Rew, L. (2000). Risky sexual behavior among adolescent women. *Journal of Social Pediatric Nursing, 5*(1), 15–25.

Tennesen, M. (2007, March 10). Gone today, hear tomorrow. *New Scientist, 2594,* 42–45.

Terman, L. M., & Merrill, M. A. (1937/1960). *Stanford-Binet Intelligence Scale.* Boston: Houghton Mifflin.

Terman, L. M., & Oden, M. (1959). *The gifted group in mid-life* (Vol. 5): *Genetic studies of genius.* Stanford, CA: Stanford University Press.

Terry, C. (2006). History of treatment of people with mental illness. In J. R. Matthews, C. E. Walker, et al. (Eds.), *Your practicum in psychology: A guide for maximizing knowledge and competence.* Washington, DC: American Psychological Association.

Terry, D. J., & Hogg, M. A. (1996). Group norms and the attitude-behavior relationship. *Personality & Social Psychology Bulletin, 22*(8), 776–793.

Tewksbury, R., Higgins, G. E., & Mustaine, E. E. (2008). Binge drinking among college athletes and non-athletes. *Deviant Behavior, 29*(3), 275–293.

Thase, M. E. (2006). Major depressive disorder. In F. Andrasik (Ed.), *Comprehensive handbook of personality and psychopathology* (Vol. 2): *Adult psychopathology.* New York: Wiley.

The Nature Conservancy. (2009). *Carbon footprint calculator.* Retrieved April 20, 2009, from http://www.nature.org/initiatives/climatechange/calculator/.

Thelen, E. (2000). Infancy: Perception and motor development. In A. Kazdin (Ed.), *Encyclopedia of psychology.* Washington, DC: American Psychological Association.

"They'd kill for $1 million." (1991, July 1). *Los Angeles Times,* A8.

Thiessen, E. D., Hill, E. A., & Saffran, J. R. (2005). Infant-directed speech facilitates word segmentation. *Infancy, 7*(1), 53–71.

Thomas, E. M. (2004). *Aggressive behaviour outcomes for young children: Change in parenting environment predicts change in behaviour.* Ottawa, ON: Statistics Canada. Retrieved April 21, 2009, from http://www.statcan.ca/cgi-bin/downpub/listpub.cgi?catno=89-599-MIE2004001.

Thomas, M. (2009). Some needed changes in DSM-V: But what about children? *Clinical Psychology: Science & Practice, 16*(1), 50–53.

Thompson, R. A., & Nelson, C. A. (2001). Developmental science and the media. *American Psychologist, 56*(1), 5–15.

Thompson, R. F. (2005). In search of memory traces. *Annual Review of Psychology, 56,* 1–23.

Tidwell, M. O., Reis, H. T., & Shaver, P. R. (1996). Attachment, attractiveness, and social interaction. *Journal of Personality & Social Psychology, 71*(4), 729–745.

Tierney, S. (2008). Creating communities in cyberspace: Pro-anorexia web sites and social capital. *Journal of Psychiatric & Mental Health Nursing, 15*(4), 340–343.

Till, B. D., & Priluck, R. L. (2000). Stimulus generalization in classical conditioning: An initial investigation and extension. *Psychology & Marketing, 17*(1), 55–72.

Timmerman, C. K., & Kruepke, K. A. (2006). Computer-assisted instruction, media richness, and college student performance. *Communication Education, 55*(1), 73–104.

Timmerman, I. G. H., Emmelkamp, P. M. G., & Sanderman, R. (1998). The effects of a stress-management training program in individuals at risk in the community at large. *Behaviour Research & Therapy, 36*(9), 863–875.

Tipples, J., Atkinson, A. P., & Young, A. W. (2002). The eyebrow frown: A salient social signal. *Emotion, 2*(3), 288–296.

Tobler, N. S., Roona, M. R., Ocshorn, P., et al. (2000). School-based adolescent drug prevention programs: 1998 meta-analysis. *Journal of Primary Prevention, 20,* 275–337.

Tolman, E. C., & Honzik, C. H. (1930). Degrees of hunger, reward and non-reward, and maze performance in rats. *University of California Publications in Psychology, 4,* 21–256.

Tolman, E. C., Ritchie, B. F., & Kalish, D. (1946). Studies in spatial learning: II. Place learning versus response learning. *Journal of Experimental Psychology, 36,* 221–229.

Tomasello, M. (2003). *Constructing a language: A usage-based theory of language acquisition.* Cambridge, MA: Harvard University Press.

Toneatto, T. (2002). Cognitive therapy for problem gambling. *Cognitive & Behavioral Practice, 9*(3), 191–199.

Toneatto, T., Sobell, L. C., Sobell, M. B., & Rubel, E. (1999). Natural recovery from cocaine dependence. *Psychology of Addictive Behaviors, 13*(4), 259–268.

Tononi, G., & Cirelli, C. (2003). Sleep and synaptic homeostasis: A hypothesis. *Brain Research Bulletin, 62*(2), 143–150.

Toro, C. T., & Deakin, J. F. W. (2007). Adult neurogenesis and schizophrenia: A window on abnormal early brain development? *Schizophrenia Research, 90*(1–3), 1–14.

Tourangeau, R. (2004). Survey research and societal change. *Annual Review of Psychology, 55,* 775–801.

Toyota, H., & Kikuchi, Y. (2005). Encoding richness of self-generated elaboration and spacing effects on incidental memory. *Perceptual & Motor Skills, 101*(2), 621–627.

Trainor, L. J., & Desjardins, R. N. (2002). Pitch characteristics of infant-directed speech affect infants' ability to discriminate vowels. *Psychonomic Bulletin & Review, 9*(2), 335–340.

Travis, F., Arenander, A., & DuBois, D. (2004). Psychological and physiological characteristics of a proposed object-referral/self-referral continuum of self-awareness. *Consciousness & Cognition, 13,* 401–420.

Treffert, D. A., & Christensen, C. D. (2005). Inside the mind of a savant. *Scientific American, 293*(6), 108–113.

Trehub, S. E., Unyk, A. M., & Trainor, L. J. (1993a). Adults identify infant–directed music across cultures. *Infant Behavior & Development, 16*(2), 193–211.

Trehub, S. E., Unyk, A. M., & Trainor, L. J. (1993b). Maternal singing in cross-cultural perspective. *Infant Behavior & Development, 16*(3), 285–295.

Triandis, H. C., & Suh, E. M. (2002). Cultural influences on personality. *Annual Review of Psychology, 53,* 133–160.

Trocmé, N., MacLaurin, B., Fallon, B., et al. (2001). *Canadian Incidence Study of Reported Child Abuse and Neglect.* Ottawa, ON: National Clearinghouse on Family Violence. Retrieved April 21, 2009, from http://www.phac-aspc.gc.ca/publicat/cissr-ecirc/.

Troll, L. E., & Skaff, M. M. (1997). Perceived continuity of self in very old age. *Psychology & Aging, 12*(1), 162–169.

Truax, S. R. (1983). Active search, mediation, and the manipulation of cue dimensions: Emotion attribution in the false feedback paradigm. *Motivation & Emotion, 7,* 41–60.

Tsai, G., & Coyle, J. T. (2002). Glutamatergic mechanisms in schizophrenia. *Annual Review of Pharmacology & Toxicology, 42,* 165–179.

Tse, L. (1999). Finding a place to be: Ethnic identity exploration of Asian Americans. *Adolescence, 34*(133), 121–138.

Tugade, M. M., Fredrickson, B. L., & Barrett, L. F. (2004). Psychological resilience and positive emotional granularity: Examining the benefits of positive emotions on coping and health. *Journal of Personality. Special Emotions, Personality, & Health, 72*(6), 1161–1190.

Tulving, E. (1989). Remembering and knowing the past. *American Scientist, 77*(4), 361–367.

Tulving, E. (2002). Episodic memory. *Annual Review of Psychology, 53,* 1–25.

Turiel, E. (2006).Thought, emotions, and social interactional processes in moral development. In M. Killen & J. G. Smetana (Eds.), *Handbook of moral development.* Mahwah, NJ: Erlbaum.

Turkheimer, E., Haley, A., Waldron, M., et al. (2003). Socioeconomic status modifies heritability of IQ in young children. *Psychological Science, 14,* 623–628.

Turner, S. J. M. (1997). The use of the reflective team in a psychodrama therapy group. *International Journal of Action Methods, 50*(1) 17–26.

Tversky, A., & Kahneman, D. (1981). The framing of decisions and the psychology of choice. *Science, 211,* 453–458.

Tversky, A., & Kahneman, D. (1982). Judgments of and by representativeness. In D. Kahneman, P. Slovic, & A. Tversky (Eds.), *Judgment under uncertainty: Heuristics and biases.* Cambridge, MA: Cambridge University Press.

Twenge, J. M., & Campbell, W. K. (2001). Age and birth cohort differences in self-esteem. *Personality & Social Psychology Review, 5*(4), 321–344.

Tye-Murray, N., Spencer, L., & Woodworth, G. G. (1995). Acquisition of speech by children who have prolonged cochlear implant experience. *Journal of Speech & Hearing Research, 38*(2), 327–337.

Tzeng, M. (1992). The effects of socioeconomic heterogamy and changes on marital dissolution for first marriages. *Journal of Marriage & Family, 54*(3), 609–619.

U.S. Bureau of Census. (2007). *Minority population tops 100 million.* New York: U. S. Census Bureau News, CB07-70. Retrieved April 21, 2009, from http://www.census.gov/Press-Release/www/releases/archives/population/010048.html.

U.S. Department of Energy Office of Science. (2005). *About the Human Genome Project.* Washington, DC: Author. Retrieved May 25, 2007, from http://www.ornl.gov/sci/techresources/Human_Genome/project/about.shtml.

U.S. Department of Health and Human Services. (2004). *The health consequences of smoking: A report of the Surgeon General, Executive summary.* Retrieved April 20, 2009, from http://www.cdc.gov/tobacco/data_statistics/sgr/sgr_2004/.

UNAIDS. (2006). *UNAIDS/WHOAIDS epidemic update: December 2006.* New York: United Nations. Retrieved July 27, 2007, from http://www.unaids.org/en/HIV_data/epi2006/default.asp.

Underwood, B. J. (1957). Interference and forgetting. *Psychological Review, 64,* 49–60.

UNESCO. (1990). The Seville statement on violence. *American Psychologist, 45*(10), 1167–1168.

Unsworth, G., & Ward, T. (2001). Video games and aggressive behaviour. *Australian Psychologist, 36*(3), 184–192.

Urbina, S. (2004). *Essentials of psychological testing.* New York: Wiley.

Uziel, L. (2007). Individual differences in the social facilitation effect: A review and meta-analysis. *Journal of Research in Personality, 41*(3), 579–601.

Vaillant, G. E. (2002). *Aging well.* Boston: Little, Brown.

Vaillant, G. E. (2005). Alcoholics Anonymous: Cult or cure? *Australian and New Zealand Journal of Psychiatry, 39*(6), 431–436.

Vaillant, G. E., & Mukamal, K. (2001). Successful aging. *American Journal of Psychiatry, 158*(6), 839–847.

Valins, S. (1966). Cognitive effects of false heart-rate feedback. *Journal of Personality & Social Psychology, 4,* 400–408.

Valins, S. (1967). Emotionality and information concerning internal reactions. *Journal of Personality & Social Psychology, 6,* 458–463.

Vallerand, A. H., Saunders, M. M., & Anthony, M. (2007). Perceptions of control over pain by patients with cancer and their caregivers. *Pain Management Nursing, 8*(2), 55–63.

van der Hart, O., Lierens, R., & Goodwin, J. (1996). Jeanne Fery: A sixteenth-century case of dissociative identity disorder. *Journal of Psychohistory, 24*(1), 18–35.

van Deurzen, E., & Kenward, R. (2005). *Dictionary of existential psychotherapy and counselling.* Thousand Oaks, CA: Sage.

van Dierendonck, D., & Te Nijenhuis, J. (2005). Flotation restricted environmental stimulation therapy (REST) as a stress-management tool: A meta-analysis. *Psychology & Health, 20*(3), 405–412.

van Elst, L. T., Valerius, G., Büchert, M., et al. (2005). Increased prefrontal and hippocampal glutamate concentration in schizophrenia: Evidence from a magnetic resonance spectroscopy study. *Biological Psychiatry, 58*(9), 724–730.

Van Goozen, S. H. M., Cohen-Kettenis, P. T., Gooren, L. J. G., & Frijda, N. H. (1995). Gender differences in behaviour: Activating effects of cross-sex hormones. *Psychoneuroendocrinology, 20*(4) 343–363.

Van Lawick-Goodall, J. (1971). *In the shadow of man.* New York: Houghton Mifflin.

van Rooij, J. J. F. (1994). Introversion–extraversion: Astrology versus psychology. *Personality & Individual Differences, 16*(6), 985–988.

Vandell, D. L. (2004). Early child care: The known and the unknown. *Merrill-Palmer Quarterly* [Special issue: The maturing of the human developmental sciences: Appraising past, present, and prospective agendas], *50*(3), 387–414.

Vasa, R. A., Carlino, A. R., & Pine, D. S. (2006). Pharmacotherapy of depressed children and adolescents: Current issues and potential directions. *Biological Psychiatry, 59*(11), 1021–1028.

Velakoulis, D., & Pantelis, C. (1996). What have we learned from functional imaging studies in schizophrenia? *Australian & New Zealand Journal of Psychiatry, 30*(2), 195–209.

Venezia, M., Messinger, D. S., Thorp, D., & Mundy, P. (2004). The development of anticipatory smiling. *Infancy, 6*(3), 397–406.

Videon, T. M. (2005). Parent–child relations and children's psychological well-being: Do dads matter? *Journal of Family Issues, 26*(1), 55–78.

Viegener, B. J., Perri, M. G., Nezu, A. M., et al. (1990). Effects of an intermittent, low-fat, low-calorie diet in the behavioral treatment of obesity. *Behavior Therapy, 21*(4), 499–509.

Viveros, M. P., Llorente, R., Moreno, E., & Marco, E. M. (2005). Behavioural and neuroendocrine effects of cannabinoids in critical developmental periods. *Behavioural Pharmacology, 16*(5-6), 353–362.

Vogel, E. K., Woodman, G. F., & Luck, S. J. (2006). The time course of consolidation in visual working memory. *Journal of Experimental Psychology: Human Perception & Performance, 32*(6), 1436–1451.

Vogler, R. E., & Bartz, W. R. (1992). *Teenagers and alcohol.* Philadelphia, PA: Charles Press.

Vogler, R. E., Weissbach, T. A., Compton, J. V., & Martin, G. T. (1977). Integrated behavior change techniques for problem drinkers in the community. *Journal of Consulting & Clinical Psychology, 45,* 267–279.

Volkow, N. D., Fowler, J. S., Wang, G.-J., et al. (2007). Dopamine in drug abuse and addiction: Results of imaging studies and treatment implications. *Archives of Neurology, 64*(11), 1575–1579.

Volkow, N. D., Gillespie, H., Mullani, N., & Tancredi, L. (1996). Brain glucose metabolism in chronic marijuana users at baseline and during marijuana intoxication. *Psychiatry Research: Neuroimaging, 67*(1), 29–38.

Volpicelli, J. R., Ulm, R. R., Altenor, A., & Seligman, M. E. P. (1983). Learned mastery in the rat. *Learning & Motivation, 14,* 204–222.

Vygotsky, L. S. (1962). *Thought and language.* Cambridge, MA: MIT Press.

Vygotsky, L. S. (1978). *Mind in society.* Cambridge, MA: Harvard University Press.

Wager, T. D., Rilling, J. K., Smith, E. E., et al. (2004). Placebo-induced changes in fMRI in the anticipation and experience of pain. *Science, 303*(Feb. 20), 1162–1166.

Wagstaff, G., Brunas-Wagstaff, J., Cole, J., & Wheatcroft, J. (2004). New directions in forensic hypnosis: Facilitating memory with a focused meditation technique. *Contemporary Hypnosis, 21*(1), 14–27.

Waid, W. M., & Orne, M. T. (1982, July/August). The physiological detection of deception. *American Scientist, 70,* 402–409.

Wainright, J. L., Russell, S. T., & Patterson, C. J. (2004). Psychosocial adjustment, school outcomes, and romantic relationships of adolescents with same-sex parents. *Child Development, 75*(6), 1886–1898.

Wakefield, J. C. (1992). The concept of mental disorder. *American Psychologist, 47*(3), 373–388.

Wald, J., & Taylor, S. (2000). Efficacy of virtual reality exposure therapy to treat driving phobia. *Journal of Behavior Therapy & Experimental Psychiatry, 31*(3-4), 249–257.

Walker, D. L., & Davis, M. (2008). Role of the extended amygdala in short-duration versus sustained fear: A tribute to Dr. Lennart Heimer. *Brain Structure & Function, 213*(1-2), 29–42.

Walker, E., Kestler, L., Bollini, A., & Hochman, K. M. (2004). Schizophrenia: Etiology and course. *Annual Review of Psychology, 55,* 401–430.

Walker, I., & Crogan, M. (1998). Academic performance, prejudice, and the jigsaw classroom. *Journal of Community & Applied Social Psychology, 8*(6), 381–393

Walker, M. P., & Stickgold, R. (2006). Sleep, memory, and plasticity. *Annual Review of Psychology, 57,* 139–166.

Wallach, M. A., & Kogan, N. (1965). *Modes of thinking in young children.* New York: Holt.

Walton, C. E., Bower, M. L., & Bower, T. G. (1992). Recognition of familiar faces by newborns. *Infant Behavior & Development, 15*(2), 265–269.

Wampold, B. E., Minami T., Tierney, S. C., et al. (2005). The placebo is powerful: Estimating placebo effects in medicine and psychotherapy from randomized clinical trials. *Journal of Clinical Psychology, 61*(7), 835–854.

Wampold, B. E., Mondin, G. W., Moody, M., et al. (1997). A meta-analysis of outcome studies comparing bona fide psychotherapies. *Psychological Bulletin, 122*(3), 203–215.

Wandersman, A., & Florin, P. (2003). Community interventions and effective prevention. *American Psychologist, 58*(6/7), 441–448.

Wang, S. S., & Brownell, K. D. (2005). Public policy and obesity: The need to marry science with advocacy. *Psychiatric Clinics of North America, 28*(1), 235–252.

Ward, C., & Rana-Deuba, A. (1999). Acculturation and adaptation revisited. *Journal of Cross-Cultural Psychology, 30*(4), 422-442.

Ward, J. (2006). *The student's guide to cognitive neuroscience.* Hove, UK: Psychology Press.

Wargo, E. (2007). Understanding the have-knots: The role of stress in just about everything. *APS Observer, 20*(11), 18–23.

Warren, D. J., & Normann, R. A. (2005). Functional reorganization of primary visual cortex induced by electrical stimulation in the cat. *Vision Research, 45,* 551–565.

Waterfield, R. (2002). *Hidden depths: The story of hypnosis.* London: Macmillan.

Watson, D. L., & Tharp, R. G. (2007). *Self-directed behavior* (9th ed.). Belmont, CA: Wadsworth.

Watson, J. B. (1913/1994). Psychology as the behaviorist views it. *Psychological Review, 101*(2), 248–253.

Way, I., van Deusen, K. M., Martin, G., et al. (2004). Vicarious trauma: A comparison of clinicians who treat survivors of sexual abuse and sexual offenders. *Journal of Interpersonal Violence, 19*(1), 49–71.

Wechsler, H., & Wuethrich, B. (2002). *Dying to drink.* Emmaus, PA: Rodale Books.

Wechsler, H., Lee, J. E., Kuo, M., et al. (2002). Trends in college binge drinking during a period of increased prevention efforts. *Journal of American College Health, 50*(5), 203–217.

Wedding, D., & Corsini, R. J. (2005). *Case studies in psychotherapy* (4th ed.). Belmont, CA: Cengage Learning/Wadsworth.

Weekley, J. A., & Jones, C. (1997). Video-based situational testing. *Personnel Psychology, 50*(1), 25–49.

Weems, C. F. (1998). The evaluation of heart rate biofeedback using a multi-element design. *Journal of Behavior Therapy & Experimental Psychiatry, 29*(2), 157–162.

Wehr, T. A., Duncan, W. C., Sher, L., et al. (2001). A circadian signal of change of season in patients with seasonal affective disorder. *Archives of General Psychiatry, 58*(12), 1108–1114.

Weidenhammer, W., Linde, K., Streng, A., et al. (2007). Acupuncture for chronic low back pain in routine care: A multicenter observational study. *Clinical Journal of Pain, 23*(2), 128–135.

Weinberg, R. A. (1989). Intelligence and IQ. *American Psychologist, 44*(2), 98–104.

Weinstein, R. S., Gregory, A., & Strambler, M. J. (2004). Intractable self-fulfilling prophesies. *American Psychologist, 59*(6), 511–520.

Weintraub, M. I. (1983). *Hysterical conversion reactions.* New York: SP Medical & Scientific Books.

Weishaar, M. E. (2006). A cognitive-behavioral approach to suicide risk reduction in crisis intervention. In A. R. Roberts & K. R. Yeager (Eds.), *Foundations of evidence-based social work practice.* New York: Oxford University Press.

Weisskirch, R. S. (2005). Ethnicity and perceptions of being a "typical American" in relationship to ethnic identity development. *International Journal of Intercultural Relations, 29*(3), 355–366.

Weissman, A. M., Jogerst, G. J., & Dawson, J. D. (2003). Community characteristics associated with child abuse in Iowa. *Child Abuse & Neglect, 27*(10), 1145–1159.

Weiten, W. (1998). Pressure, major life events, and psychological symptoms. *Journal of Social Behavior & Personality, 13*(1), 51–68.

Weitzenhoffer, A. M, & Hilgard, E. R. (1959). *Stanford Hypnotic Susceptibility Scale: Forms A and B.* Palo Alto, CA: Consulting Psychologists Press.

Weitzman, E. R. (2004). Poor mental health, depression, and associations with alcohol consumption, harm, and abuse in a national sample of young adults in college. *Journal of Nervous & Mental Disease, 192*(4), 269–277.

Wells, G. L. (2001). Police lineups: Data, theory, and policy. *Psychology, Public Policy, & Law, 7*(4), 791–801.

Wells, G. L., & Olsen, E. A. (2003). Eyewitness testimony. *Annual Review of Psychology, 54,* 277–295.

Wells, G. L., Memon, A., & Penrod, S. D. (2006). Eyewitness evidence: Improving its probative value. *Psychological Science in the Public Interest, 7*(2), 45–75.

Weltzin, T. E., Weisensel, N., Franczyk, D., et al. (2005). Eating disorders in men: Update. *Journal of Men's Health & Gender, 2*(2), 186–193.

Wernet, S. P., Follman, C., Magueja, C., & Moore-Chambers, R. (2003). Building bridges and improving racial harmony: An evaluation of the Bridges Across Racial Polarization Program. In J. J. Stretch, E. M. Burkemper, W. J. Hutchison, & J. Wilson (Eds.), *Practicing social justice.* New York: Haworth Press.

Wertheimer, M. (1959). *Productive thinking.* New York: Harper & Row.

Wesensten, N. J., Belenky, G., Kautz, M. A., et al. (2002). Maintaining alertness and performance during sleep deprivation: Modafinil versus caffeine. *Psychopharmacology, 159*(3), 238–247.

Wessel, I., & Wright, D. B. (Eds.). (2004). *Emotional memory failures.* Hove, UK: Psychology Press.

West, R., & Sohal, T. (2006). Catastrophic pathways to smoking cessation: Findings from national survey. *British Medical Journal, 332*(7539), 458–460.

West, T. G. (1991). *In the mind's eye.* Buffalo, NY: Prometheus.

Westen, D., & Bradley, R. (2005). Empirically supported complexity: Rethinking evidence-based practice in psychotherapy. *Current Directions in Psychological Science, 14*(5), 266–271.

Westrin, Å., & Lam, R. W. (2007a). Seasonal affective disorder: A clinical update. *Annals of Clinical Psychiatry, 19*(4), 239–246.

Westrin, Å., & Lam, R. W. (2007b). Long-term and preventative treatment for seasonal affective disorder. *CNS Drugs, 21*(11), 901–909.

Wethington, E. (2003). Turning points as opportunities for psychological growth. In C. L. M. Keyes & J. Haidt (Eds.), *Flourishing.* Washington, DC: American Psychological Association.

Wethington, E., Kessler, R. C., & Pixley, J. E. (2004). Turning points in adulthood. In O. G. Brim, C. D. Ryff, et al. (Eds.), *How healthy are we? A national study of well-being at midlife.* Chicago: University of Chicago Press.

Wexler, M. N. (1995). Expanding the groupthink explanation to the study of contemporary cults. *Cultic Studies Journal, 12*(1), 49–71.

Whitaker, B. G. (2007). Internet-based attitude assessment: Does gender affect measurement equivalence? *Computers in Human Behavior, 23*(3), 1183–1194.

White, G. L., & Taytroe, L. (2003). Personal problem-solving using dream incubation: Dreaming, relaxation, or waking cognition? *Dreaming, 13*(4), 193–209.

White, J. (2006). *Intelligence, destiny and education: The ideological roots of intelligence testing.* New York: Brunner-Routledge.

Whitehouse, A. J. O., Maybery, M. T., & Durkin, K. (2006). The development of the picture-superiority effect. *British Journal of Developmental Psychology, 24*(4), 767–773.

Whitley, B. E. (1999). Right-wing authoritarianism, social dominance orientation, and prejudice. *Journal of Personality & Social Psychology, 77*(l), 126–134.

Whitton, E. (2003). *Humanistic approach to psychotherapy.* New York: Wiley.

Whyte, G. (2000). Groupthink. In A. E. Kazdin (Ed.), *Encyclopedia of psychology* (Vol. 4). Washington, DC: American Psychological Association.

Widiger, T. A. (2005). Classification and diagnosis: Historical development and contemporary issues. In J. E. Maddux & B. A. Winstead (Eds.), *Psychopathology: Foundations for a contemporary understanding.* Mahwah, NJ: Erlbaum.

Widner, R. L., Jr., Otani, H., & Winkelman, S. E. (2005). Tip-of-the-tongue experiences are not merely strong feeling-of-knowing experiences. *Journal of General Psychology, 132*(4), 392–407.

Wiederhold, B. K., & Wiederhold, M. D. (2005). Acrophobia. In B. K. Wiederhold & M. D. Wiederhold (Eds.), *Virtual reality therapy for* anxiety disorders: *Advances in evaluation and treatment.* Washington, DC: American Psychological Association.

Wiederman, M. W. (2001). Gender differences in sexuality: Perceptions, myths, and realities. *Family Journal-Counseling & Therapy for Couples & Families, 9*(4), 468–471.

Wigfield, A., & Eccles, J. (Eds.). (2002). *Development of achievement motivation.* San Diego, CA: Academic Press.

Wilber, M. K., & Potenza, M. N. (2006). Adolescent gambling: Research and clinical implications. *Psychiatry, 3*(10), 40–46.

Wilder, D. A., Simon, A. F., & Faith, M. (1996). Enhancing the impact of counterstereotypic information. *Journal of Personality & Social Psychology, 71*(2), 276–287.

Wilding, J., & Valentine, E. (1994). Memory champions. *British Journal of Psychology, 85*(2), 231–244.

Wilkinson, D., & Abraham, C. (2004). Constructing an integrated model of the antecedents of adolescent smoking. *British Journal of Health Psychology, 9*(3), 315–333.

Wilkinson, M. (2006). The dreaming mind-brain: A Jungian perspective. *Journal of Analytical Psychology, 51*(1), 43–59.

Willander, J., & Larsson, M. (2006). Smell your way back to childhood: Autobiographical odor memory. *Psychonomic Bulletin & Review, 13*(2), 240–244.

Williams, D. G., & Morris, G. (1996). Crying, weeping or tearfulness in British and Israeli adults. *British Journal of Psychology, 87*(3), 479–505.

Williams, G., Cai, X. J., Elliott, J. C., & Harrold, J. A. (2004). Anabolic neuropeptides. *Physiology & Behavior* [Special issue: Reviews on Ingestive Science], *81*(2), 211–222.

Williams, R. (1989). *The trusting heart: Great news about Type A behavior.* New York: Random House.

Williams, R. B., Barefoot, J. C., & Schneiderman, N. (2003). Psychosocial risk factors for cardiovascular disease: More than one culprit at work. *Journal of the American Medical Association, 290*(16), 2190–2192.

Williams, R. L., & Eggert, A. (2002). Note-taking predictors of test performance. *Teaching of Psychology, 29*(3), 234–237.

Williams, R. L., & Long, J. D. (1991). *Toward a self-managed life style.* Boston: Houghton Mifflin.

Williamson, D. A., Ravussin, E., Wong, M.-L., et al. (2005). Microanalysis of eating behavior of three leptin deficient adults treated with leptin therapy. *Appetite, 45*, 75–80.

Willoughby, T., Wood, E., Desmarais, S., et al. (1997). Mechanisms that facilitate the effectiveness of elaboration strategies. *Journal of Educational Psychology, 89*(4), 682–685.

Wilson, G. L. (2002). *Groups in context: Leadership and participation in small groups* (6th ed.). New York: McGraw-Hill.

Wilson, S. L. (2003). Post-institutionalization: The effects of early deprivation on development of Romanian adoptees. *Child & Adolescent Social Work Journal, 20*(6), 473–483.

Winger, G., Woods, J. H., Galuska, C. M., & Wade-Galuska, T. (2005). Behavioral perspectives on the neuroscience of drug addiction. *Journal of the Experimental Analysis of Behavior, 84*(3), 667–681.

Wingood, G. M., DiClemente, R. J., Bernhardt, J. M., et al. (2003). A prospective study of exposure to rap music videos and African American female adolescents' health. *American Journal of Public Health, 93*, 437–439.

Winner, E. (2003). Creativity and talent. In M. H. Bornstein, L. Davidson, C. L. M. Keyes, & K. Moore (Eds.), *Well-being: Positive development across the life course.* Mahwah, NJ: Erlbaum.

Winstead, B. A., & Sanchez, J. (2005). Gender and psychopathology. In J. E. Maddux & B. A. Winstead (Eds.), *Psychopathology: Foundations for a contemporary understanding.* Mahwah, NJ: Erlbaum.

Wise, R. A., & Safer, M. A. (2004). What US judges know and believe about eyewitness testimony. *Applied Cognitive Psychology, 18*(4), 427–443.

Wiseman, R., & Watt, C. (2006). Belief in psychic ability and the misattribution hypothesis: A qualitative review. *British Journal of Psychology, 97*(3), 323–338.

Witelson, S. F., Beresh, H., & Kigar, D. L. (2006). Intelligence and brain size in 100 postmortem brains: Sex, lateralization and age factors. *Brain: A Journal of Neurology, 129*(2), 386–398.

Witelson, S. F., Kigar, D. L., & Harvey, T. (1999). The exceptional brain of Albert Einstein. *Lancet, 353*, 2149–2153.

Witherington, D. C., Campos, J. J., Anderson, D. I., et al. (2005). Avoidance of heights on the visual cliff in newly walking infants. *Infancy, 7*(3), 285–298.

Withers, N. W., Pulvirenti, L., Koob, G. F., & Gillin, J. C. (1995). Cocaine abuse and dependence. *Journal of Clinical Psychopharmacology, 15*(1), 63–78.

Wixted, J. T. (2004). The psychology and neuroscience of forgetting. *Annual Review of Psychology, 55*, 235–269.

Wixted, J. T. (2005). A theory about why we forget what we once knew. *Current Directions in Psychological Science, 14*(1), 6–9.

Wolf, W. (2009). *"The Obama Effect": Test-taking performance gap virtually eliminated during key moments of Obama's presidential run.* Vanderbilt University News Network. Retrieved May 2, 2009, from http://sitemason.vanderbilt.edu/news/releases/2009/01/21/the-obama-effect-test-taking-performance-gap-virtually-eliminated-during-key-moments-of-obamas-presidential-run.71208.

Wolfe, J. B. (1936). Effectiveness of token rewards for chimpanzees. *Comparative Psychology Monographs, 12*(5), Whole No. 60.

Wolpe, J. (1974). *The practice of behavior therapy* (2nd ed.). New York: Pergamon.

Wolpin, M., Marston, A., Randolph, C., & Clothier, A. (1992). Individual difference correlates of reported lucid dreaming frequency and control. *Journal of Mental Imagery, 16*(3-4), 231–236.

Wong, A. M., Hodges, H., & Horsburgh, K. (2005). Neural stem cell grafts reduce the extent of neuronal damage in a mouse model of global ischaemia. *Brain Research, 1063*(2), 140–150.

Wood, E., & Willoughby, T. (1995). Cognitive strategies for test-taking. In E. Wood, V. Woloshyn, et al. (Eds.), *Cognitive strategy instruction for middle and high schools.* Cambridge, MA: Brookline Books.

Wood, J. M., Nezworski, M. T., Lilienfeld, S. O., & Garb, H. N. (2003). The Rorschach Inkblot test, fortune tellers, and cold reading. *Skeptical Inquirer, 27*(4), 29–33.

Woodhill, B. M., & Samuels, C. A. (2004). Desirable and undesirable androgyny: A prescription for the twenty-first century. *Journal of Gender Studies, 13*(1), 15–28.

Woods, S. C., Schwartz, M. W., Baskin, D. G., & Seeley, R J. (2000). Food intake and the regulation of body weight. *Annual Review of Psychology, 51*, 255–277.

Worthen, J. B., & Marshall, P. H. (1996). Intralist and extralist sources of distinctiveness and the bizarreness effect. *American Journal of Psychology, 109*(2), 239–263.

Wraga, M., Shephard, J. M., Church, J. A., et al. (2005). Imagined rotations of self versus objects: An fMRI study. *Neuropsychologia, 43*(9), 1351–1361.

Wright, J. P., Dietrich, K. N., Ris, M. D., et al. (2008). Association of prenatal and childhood blood lead concentrations with criminal arrests in early adulthood. *PNAS Proceedings of the National Academy of Sciences of the United States of America, 5*(5), e101. doi:10.1371/journal.pmed.0050101. Retrieved August 2, 2009, from http://medicine.plosjournals.org/perlserv/?request=get-document&doi=10.1371%2Fjournal.pmed.0050101.

Wu, C. W. H., & Kaas, J. H. (2002). The effects of long-standing limb loss on anatomical reorganization of the somatosensory afferents in the brainstem and spinal cord. *Somatosensory & Motor Research, 19*(2), 153–163.

Wulf, G., McConnel, N., Gärtner, M., & Schwarz, A. (2002). Enhancing the learning of sport skills through external-focus feedback. *Journal of Motor Behavior, 34*(2), 171–182.

Wyatt, J. W., Posey, A., Welker, W., & Seamonds, C. (1984). Natural levels of similarities between identical twins and between unrelated people. *The Skeptical Inquirer, 9*, 62–66.

Wynne, C. D. L. (2004). The perils of anthropomorphism. *Nature, 428*(6983), 606.

Yahnke, B. H., Sheikh, A. A., & Beckman, H. T. (2003). Imagery and the treatment of phobic disorders. In A. A. Sheikh (Ed.), *Healing images: The role of imagination in health.* Amityville, NY: Baywood Publishing.

Yang, Y., Tang, L., Tong, L., & Liu, H. (2009). Silkworms culture as a source of protein for humans in space. *Advances in Space Research, 43*(2), 1236–1242.

Yarmey, A. D. (2003). Eyewitness identification: Guidelines and recommendations for identification procedures in the United States and in Canada. *Canadian Psychology, 44*(3), 181–189.

Yeh, C. J. (2003). Age, acculturation, cultural adjustment, and mental health symptoms of Chinese, Korean, and Japanese immigrant youths. *Cultural Diversity & Ethnic Minority Psychology, 9*(1), 34–48.

Yip, P. S. F., & Thorburn, J. (2004). Marital status and the risk of suicide: Experience from England and Wales, 1982–1996. *Psychological Reports, 94*(2), 401–407.

Yokota, F., & Thompson, K. M. (2000). Violence in G-rated animated films. *Journal of the American Medical Association, 283*(20), 2716.

Yonas, A., Elieff, C. A., & Arterberry, M. E. (2002). Emergence of sensitivity to pictorial depth cues: Charting development in individual infants. *Infant Behavior & Development. Special Issue: Variability in Infancy, 25*(4), 495–514.

Yoshida, M. (1993). Three-dimensional electrophysiological atlas created by computer mapping of clinical responses elicited on stimulation of human subcortical structures. *Stereotactic & Functional Neurosurgery, 60*(1–3), 127–134.

Yost, W. A. (2007) *Fundamentals of hearing: An introduction* (5th ed.). San Diego, CA: Elsevier.

Young, R. (2005). Neurobiology of savant syndrome. In C. Stough (Ed.), *Neurobiology of exceptionality*. New York: Kluwer Academic Publishers.

Young, S. M., & Pinsky, D. (2006). Narcissism and celebrity. *Journal of Research in Personality, 40*(5), 463–471.

Yuille, J. C., & Daylen, J. (1998). The impact of traumatic events on eyewitness memory. In C. Thompson, D. Herrmann, et al. (Eds.), *Eyewitness memory: Theoretical and applied perspectives*. Mahwah, NJ: Erlbaum.

Zarcadoolas, C., Pleasant, A., & Greer, D. S. (2006). *Advancing health literacy: A framework for understanding and action*. San Francisco: Jossey-Bass.

Zellner, D. A., Harner, D. E., & Adler, R. L. (1989). Effects of eating abnormalities and gender on perceptions of desirable body shape. *Journal of Abnormal Psychology, 98*(1), 93–96.

Zemishlany, Z., Aizenberg, D., & Weizman, A. (2001). Subjective effects of MDMA ("Ecstasy") on human sexual function. *European Psychiatry, 16*(2), 127–130.

Zentall, T. R. (2005). Animals may not be stuck in time. *Learning and Motivation, 36*(2), 208–225.

Zhang R. L., Zhang Z. G., & Chopp, M. (2005). Neurogenesis in the adult ischemic brain: Generation, migration, survival, and restorative therapy. *Neuroscientist, 11*(5), 408–416.

Zimbardo, P. (2007). *The Lucifer Effect: Understanding how good people turn evil*. New York: Random House.

Zimbardo, P. G., Pilkonis, P. A., & Norwood, R. M. (1978). The social disease called shyness. *In Annual editions, personality and adjustment* 78/79. Guilford, CT: Dushkin.

Zohar, D. (1998). An additive model of test anxiety: Role of exam-specific expectations. *Journal of Educational Psychology, 90*, 330–340.

Zola, S. M., & Squire, L. R. (2001). Relationship between magnitude of damage to the hippocampus and impaired recognition in monkeys. *Hippocampus, 11*, 92–98.

Zucker, K. J. & Spitzer, R. L. (2005). Was the Gender Identity Disorder of Childhood Diagnosis introduced into DSM-III as a backdoor maneuver to replace Homosexuality? A historical note. *Journal of Sex & Marital Therapy, 31*(1), 31-42.

Zuckerman, M. (2002). Genetics of sensation seeking. In J. Benjamin, R. P. Ebstein, & R. H. Belmaker (Eds.), *Molecular genetics and the human personality*. Washington, DC: American Psychiatric Publishing.

Zuwerink, J. R., Devine, P. G., Monteith, M. J., & Cook, D. A. (1996). Prejudice toward blacks: With and without compunction? *Basic & Applied Social Psychology, 18*(2), 131–150.

Aarts, H., 349
Abell, S. C., 408
Abernethy, A. P., 199
Abraham, C., 255
Abraham, W. C., 287
Abrahamse, W., 241
Abrams, D. B., 211
Abramson, L. Y., 453
Abuhamdeh, S., 361
Accordino, D. B., 394
Accordino, M. P., 394
Acebo, C., 184
Adams, G., 474
Adams, J., 328, 337
Adams, J. W., 266
Adams, M. 279
Adamson, K., 62
Addis, K. M., 275
Addis, M. E., 565
Adityanjee, 477
Adler, S. A., 133
Adorno, T. W., 574
Afifi, T. O., 250
Ahima, R. S., 349
Aizenberg, D., 209
Ajzen, I., 569, 570
Åkerstedt, T., 186
Akert, R. M., 563
al'Absi, M., 457
Albarracín, D., 568
Alberto, P. A., 240, 249, 251
Albonetti, S., 483
Alcock, J. E., 173,174
Alexander, G. M., 77
Alexander, M. P., 68
Alkire, M. T., 63
Allen, D., 433
Allen, K., 463
Allgower, A., 430
Allik, J., 390
Allin, J. D., 303
Allport, G. W., 392
Alsaker, F. D., 116
Altemeyer, B., 574
Al-Timimi, N. R., 103
Altman, L. K., 435
Altman Weiss, K., 421
Alvarado, N., 421
Alvino, J., 111, 307
Alwin, D. F., 570
Amabile, T., 337
Amato, P. R., 92, 125
Ambady, N., 333
Amir, N., 277
Ancis, J. R., 474
Anderson, C. A., 283, 255, 256, 442, 580,
    581, 582
Anderson, D. I., 291
Anderson, J. R., 6, 325
Anderson, M. C., 256, 265, 270, 272, 283,
    284, 285, 294
Anderson, S., 451
Andrasik, F., 457
André, C., 537

Andresen, J., 201
Andrews, J. D., 532
Anekonda, T. S., 431
Annett, M., 83
Anthony, M., 149
Antle, M. C., 346
Antonuccio, D. O., 518
Antony. M. M., 423, 424
APA, 29, 32, 33
Arauz, R. M., 310
Arbona, C. B., 521
Archer, T., 202
Arenander, A., 201
Ariely, D., 8
Arkowitz, H., 512
Armeli, S., 459
Arnett, J. J., 115
Arntz, A., 57
Aron, A., 551
Aronow, E., 421
Aronson, E., 551, 563, 578, 588
Aronson, J., 312, 575
Arterberry, M. E., 161
Arthur, W., 395
Artz, S., 405
Ary, D. V., 204
Asada, K. J. K., 359
Asch, S. E., 559
Ash, D. W., 291
Ashby, F. G., 317
Ashton, M. C., 395
Asmundson, G. J. G., 456
Assanand, S., 350, 351
Atkinson, R. C., 265
Aucoin, K. J., 250
Austin, D. W., 517
Aversa, A., 350
Avery, D. H., 489
Awadallah, N., 495
Ayers, L., 332
Ayllon, T., 524

Bachman, J. G., 121
Backs-Dermott, G. J., 527
Baddeley, A., 265, 266, 270, 272, 285, 294
Baddeley, A. D., 266
Baer, J. M., 329, 332
Bahrick, L. E., 107
Bailey, C. H., 287
Bailey, J. M., 82, 359
Baillargeon, R., 112
Bain, S. K., 303
Baker, T. B., 210
Balk, D. E., 421
Balkin, T. J., 189
Ballon, B., 48
Banaji, M. R., 587
Bandura, A., 249, 255, 403, 439, 580, 581
Banks, A., 359
Banning, K., 454
Barabasz, A., 197
Barber, T. X., 200
Barefoot, J. C., 458
Bargh, J. A., 552

Barkataki, I., 485
Barker, E. T., 117
Barlow, D. H., 473, 477, 483, 485, 491,
    493, 496, 497, 500, 502, 513, 531
Barnier, A. J., 199
Baron, I. S., 303, 559
Baron, R. A., 550, 588, 559
Barrett, D., 80, 220
Barrett, H. C., 327
Barrett, H. M., 283
Barrett, L. F., 433
Barrick, M. R., 395
Barrowcliff, A. L., 478
Bar-Tal, D., 574
Bartholow, B. D., 256, 582
Bartram, B., 569
Bartz, W. R., 214
Basadur, M., 339
Basson, R., 356
Bastian, B., 318
Bath, H., 127
Batson, C. D., 585
Batterham, R. L., 349
Bauer, J. J., 410
Baum, A., 430, 438
Bauman, L. J., 435
Baumeister, R. F., 31, 390, 550, 568
Baumrind, D., 125, 250
Baumwell, L., 106
Baur, K., 355, 360, 406
Bavaria, A. J., 15
Bearison, D. J., 113, 114
Bearman, P. S., 434
Beaton, S., 332
Beck, A. T., 194, 344, 452
Beck, B. L., 7
Beck, D. M., 157
Beck, J. S., 526, 527
Beckman, H. T., 521
Beeber, L. S., 92
Beerlipalacio, A., 241
Beersma, D. G. M., 346
Bègue, L., 587
Behrend, D. A., 264, 285
Beike, D. R., 264, 285
Beirne-Smith, M., 309
Beiser, M., 455
Belenky, G., 185
Bell, T., 283
Bellezza, F. S., 289
Belsky, J., 100
Bem, S. L., 405
Benbow, C. P., 83
Benloucif, S., 92
Bennett, E. L., 92
Bensafi, M., 145, 146
Ben-Shakhar, G., 20
Bensley, L., 256
Benson, H., 201
Benson, J., 323
Beresh, H., 65
Bergman, H., 202
Berkowitz, L., 558

Berman, S. L., 497
Bernstein, D. M., 284
Bernstein, H. J., 536
Bernthal, M. J., 256
Berntsen, D., 279
Berridge, K. C., 204, 205
Berry, J. W., 455
Berscheid, E., 550, 552
Bersoff, D. M., 401
Bertholf, M., 414
Bertsch, G. J., 249
Betancur, C., 82
Betts, J. M., 176
Bhatt, R. S., 156
Bhushan, B., 82
Bialystok, E., 320
Bickman, L., 558
Binder, J. L., 513, 533
Binik, Y. M., 357
Birnbaum, M. H., 45
Bisson, J. I., 441
Bjork, R. A., 47, 197, 202
Black, M. M., 91
Blackmore, S., 19, 183, 201
Blackwell, D. L., 552
Blair, K. S., 499
Blakemore, C., 134
Blanchard, D. C., 579
Blanchard, E. B., 233
Blanchard, R. J., 579
Blascovich, J., 463
Blatner, A., 530
Bloch, S., 510
Blood, A. J., 75
Bloom, C. M., 295, 297
Bloom, J. W., 517
Blunt, A., 7
Boals, A., 464
Bodin, S. D., 250
Boergers, J., 503
Bohannon, J. N., 105
Bohbot, V., 285
Boldero, J. M., 410
Boly, M., 62
Bond, R., 559
Bongard, S., 457
Bonham, V., 313, 576, 588
Boniecki, K. A., 577
Bood, S., 202
Bootzin, R. R., 192
Borlongan, C. V., 61
Bornstein, M. H., 91, 106
Bornstein, R. F., 500
Borod, J. C., 68
Borrie, R. A., 202
Bouchard, Jr., T. J., 412
Bouchard, T. J., 412
Bouchoux, A., 210
Bourhis, R. Y., 574
Bourne, E. J., 520
Boussaoud, D., 254

Boutros, N., 68
Bovbjerg, D. H., 229
Bower, G. H., 268
Bower, M. L., 95
Bower, T. G., 95
Bowers, K. S., 272
Boyle, S. H., 457
Brach, T., 515
Bradley, L. J., 565
Bradley, R., 531, 533
Bradley, R. H., 92
Bradshaw, S. D., 423
Brainerd, C. J., 111
Bramerson, A., 146
Bramsen, I., 494
Brandon, T. H., 210, 260
Branigan, C. 169
Brannon, L., 400, 429, 453
Branscombe, N. R., 550, 559, 588
Braun, A. R., 189
Braun, K. A., 270
Braun, S., 209
Braun-LaTour, K. A., 271
Breckler, S. J., 555
Breedlove, S. M., 53
Brehm, S. S., 551, 552
Breslau, N., 210
Bressan, P., 151
Bressi, C., 483
Bretherton, R., 515
Brewer, K. R., 254
Brewer, N., 175
Briand, L. A., 56
Bridges, K. M. B., 97
Bridges, L. J., 100
Brinton, R. D., 61
Britt, T. W., 577
Brock, T. C., 570
Brodley, B. T., 514
Broekaert, E., 538
Brooks, M., 305, 456
Brooks-Gunn, J., 103, 115
Brothen, T., 6
Brown, A. M., 95, 500
Brown, A. S., 275, 482
Brown, E., 159
Brown, L. M., 404
Brown, R., 202, 275, 286
Brown, R. L., 205
Brown, S. A., 214
Brown, S. G., 80
Brown, S. L., 465
Brown, T. A., 491, 493, 497, 513
Brown, T. D., 576
Browne, N., 19
Brownell, K. D., 350, 351, 352
Bruce, D., 292
Bruch, M. A., 422
Bruer, J. T., 91
Bruner, J., 2
Bruyn, J., 82
Bryan, A., 358
Bryant, J. B., 271
Bryden, P. J., 82
Buddie, A. M., 215
Budney, A. J., 216
Buehner, M. J., 156
Buffalo, E. A., 286
Bugelski, R., 573
Bugental, J. F. T., 29
Bührer, M., 457
Bull, R., 292
Buller, D. J., 554
Bunde, J., 457
Bundrick, C. M., 408
Bunting, M. F., 151
Burchinal, M. R., 101

Burger, J. M., 236, 388, 415
Burgess, C. A., 198, 272
Burgess, M. C. R., 280
Burke, D., 61
Burke, R. J., 439
Burlingame, G., 544
Burlingame, G. M., 529
Burnett, R. C., 318
Burns, D. D., 526
Burns, J., 173, 174
Burns, T., 538
Burt, S. A., 499
Burton, C. M., 464
Burtt, H. E., 276
Bushman, B., 550, 568
Bushman, B. J., 255, 256, 442, 580, 582
Bushnell, M. C., 149
Buss, A. H., 423
Buss, A., 423
Buss, D. M., 389, 423, 551, 553, 554
Butcher, J. N., 418, 419, 470
Butler, J. C., 574
Butler, M. G., 423, 424
Butler, R., 361
Byrne, D., 550, 588, 559
Byrne, S. M., 354

Cadinu, M., 575
Caharel, S., 170
Cahill, L., 72, 264
Cahill, S. P., 522
Cahn, B. R., 201
Caldara, R., 280
Callahan, C. M., 307
Callahan, I., 20
Cameron, I. D., 152
Cameron, J. A., 587
Cammann, C., 556
Campbell, B., 311
Campbell, L., 311
Campbell, L. C., 199
Campbell, W. K., 390
Cao, Y., 60
Caplan, P. J., 500
Capuzzi, D., 530
Cardoso, S. H., 74
Carducci, B. J., 424
Carlbring, P., 517
Carlino, A. R., 536
Carlo, G., 117
Carlsmith, J. M., 571
Carlson, D., 433
Carlson, N., 581
Carlson, N. R., 55, 71, 74, 76, 148
Carnagey, N. L., 256, 582
Carney, R. N., 294, 295
Carpenter, K. M., 214, 531
Carrigan, M. H., 522
Carroll, D. W., 104, 106, 319
Carroll, K. M., 533
Carskadon, M. A., 184
Cartwright, D., 414
Cartwright, R., 219
Carvalho, M., 537
Casey, P., 494
Caspi, A., 411, 413, 488
Cassaday, H. J., 281
Castro, J., 353
Castro, J. R., 394
Catalano, R., 442
Cattani-Thompson, K., 531
Cattell, R. B., 393
Cautela, J. R., 540, 541
Cavaco, S., 273
Cavanaugh, J. C., 119
Chabris, C. F., 151

Chakos, M. H., 536
Chamberlain, K., 437, 438
Chamberlin, J., 538, 542
Chambers, R. A., 204
Chambless, D. L., 526
Chamorro-Premuzic, T., 20, 389, 395
Chan, G. C.-K., 217
Chance, P., 229, 245, 246
Chandra, C., 356
Chandrashekar, J., 146
Chang-Schneider, C., 389
Chansler, P. A., 556
Chao, R., 103
Chaplin, G., 588
Chapman, R. A., 199
Chase, W. G., 289
Chassin, L., 210, 432
Chaves, J. F., 198
Cheek, J., 423
Chen, S., 242
Chen, Y., 474
Chen, Z., 559
Cheney, C. D., 235
Cheng, H., 60
Cheriff, A. D., 465
Chess, S., 93
Chester, A., 517
Cheyne, J. A., 189
Chiricos, T., 569
Chisolm, T. H., 144
Chiu, C., 32
Chivers, M. L., 359
Chopp, M., 61
Chow, K. L., 134
Christakis, N. A., 432
Christensen, A., 544
Christensen, C. D., 308
Christian, K. M., 74
Christoff, K. A., 255, 581
Christophersen, E. R., 404
Chung, C. K., 464
Cialdini, R. B., 561, 557, 570
Ciarrochi, J., 451
Cinciripini, P. M., 211
Cirelli, C., 188
Claiborn, C. D., 545
Clancy, S. A., 189, 283
Clapham, M. M., 338
Clara, I. P., 394
Clark, D., 68
Clark, R., 293, 441, 576
Clayton, N. S., 245
Clinkenbeard, P. R., 308
Cnattingius, S., 210
Coast, J. R., 462
Cochran, G. M., 91
Cohen, G., 279
Cohen, J. D., 438
Cohen, L. H., 459
Cohen, N. L., 455
Cohen, R. L., 570
Cohen, S., 437
Colangelo, J. J., 284
Coles, C. D., 91
Colin, A. K., 177
Collins, A., 583
Collins, A. M., 272
Collins, F. S., 576, 588
Collins, N. L., 100
Collins, R. L., 216
Collins, W. A., 100
Collop, N. A., 193
Colpaert, F. C., 282
Comer, R. J., 470
Compton, W. C., 31, 510
Conway, A. R. A., 151
Conway, M. A., 279

Coolican, H., 15
Cooper, D. S., 175
Cooper, G., 134
Cooper, J., 571
Cooper, M. J., 352, 354
Cooper, R. P., 107
Cooper, S. J., 345
Corballis, M. C., 321
Corbin, W. R., 435
Coren, S., 80, 82, 83, 166, 164
Corey, G., 529, 531
Corkin, S., 285
Cormier, J. F., 494
Correa-Chávez, M., 310
Corrigan, P. W., 482, 500
Corsini, R. J., 43, 518
Corwyn, R. F., 92
Costa, P. T., 395
Costa, P. T., Jr., 393
Côté, J. E., 116, 117, 121
Coursey, R. D., 538
Court, J. H., 284
Court, P. C., 284
Cowan, N., 151, 269
Cowan, P., 112
Cowan, P. A., 125, 250
Cowden, C. R., 423
Cox, B. J., 394
Cox, J. J., 149
Coyle, J. T., 484
Crago, M., 320
Craig, K. D., 494
Craig, L., 102
Craig, T. Y., 556
Craik, F. I. M., 320
Craik, K. H., 31
Crano, W. D., 558, 560
Craske, M. G., 533
Cravatt, B. F., 186
Crawford, M., 502
Crawley, S. B., 102
Crencavage, L. M., 532
Crichlow, S., 559
Crisp, A., 353
Crocker, J., 125
Crogan, M., 578
Crooks, R., 355, 360, 406
Cropley, A., 329
Crosby, R. A., 435
Crotty, M., 152
Crouch, D. J., 37
Crown, C. L., 106
Crowther, J. H., 455
Crutsinger, C. 118
Csikszentmihalyi, M., 31, 361
Cull, W. L., 293
Culver, R., 21
Cummings, M. R., 89
Cummins, D. D., 586
Curci, A., 285
Czeisler, C. A., 185

Dagot, L., 562
Dane, F. C., 175, 576
Dane, S., 83
Daniels, H., 114
Daniels, M., 312
Danziger, N., 149
Darley, J. M., 17
Darling, C. A., 358
Darou, W. S., 310
Das, J. P., 309
Dauvilliers, Y., 184
Davidov, B. J., 534, 587, 588
Davidovitch, N., 329
Davidson, J. K., 358

Davidson, P. R., 522
Davidson, R. J., 201
Davidson, T. L., 252
Davies, R., 544
Daviet, C., 531
Davis, D., 334
Davis, E. B., 256. 582
Davis, K. D., 152
Davis, M., 232
Davis, M. R., 272
Davison, G. C., 483
Dawson, J. D., 442
Dawson, N., 106
Day, S., 517
Daylen, J., 175
de Jong, P. J., 232
de Jong, T., 253
de las Fuentes, C., 116
de Leon, C. F. M., 123
de Rios, M. D., 184
Deakin, J. F. W., 485
Dean, F. P., 451
Deardorff, J., 115
Deary, I. J., 388, 391
Deckers, L., 345
Deckro, G. R., 201, 462
Deeb, S. S., 139
Defeyter, M. A., 328
DeGaetano, G., 581
Dein, S., 565
Deinzer, R., 438
DeLamater, J. D., 355
Delargy, M., 75
Delgado, B. M., 103
DeLoache, J. S., 94
Delpero, W. T., 139
Demiris, G., 517
Demos, J. N., 457
Denmark, F. L., 32, 404
Dennis, J., 192
Denollet, J., 458
DePape, A.-M., 320
Derlega, V. J., 422
Desjardins, R. N., 107
Detterman, D. K., 305
Deuser, W. E., 580
Deutsch, G., 68, 82, 83
Deutsch, M., 578
Devlin, B., 312
Devoto, A., 194
Dhanda, R., 450
Di Forti, M., 56
Di Marzo, V., 348
Diano, S., 348
Dickens, W. T., 312
Dickerson, F. B., 525
Dickinson, A., 245
Dickinson, D., 311
Dickinson, D. K., 106
Dick-Niederhauser, A., 99
Dieterich, S. E., 114
Dinan, T. G., 458
Dinges, D. F., 184
Dingus, T. A., 41
Dinkmeyer, D., Jr., 124, 127, 128
Dion, K. L., 587
Dirkzwager, A. J. E., 494
Dissanayake, C., 99
Distin, K., 307
Dixon, M. J., 315
Dixon, S. V., 103
DiZio, P., 149
Dobelle, W. H., 134
Dobie, T. G., 150
Dobson, K. S., 488, 527
Doidge, N., 513
Dolan, R. J., 70

Domhoff, G. W., 195, 220
Domingo, R. A., 105
Domjan, M., 244
Donaldson, D., 503
Dooling, D. J., 267
Doran, S. M., 184
Dorfman, J., 338
Dorman, M. F., 144
Dosher, B. A., 281
Dougall, A. L., 438
Dougherty, D. D., 537
Douglas, J., 145, 146
Douvan, E., 116
Doverspike, D., 395
Dowling, K. W., 48
Dozois, D. J. A., 488, 527
Draguns, J. G., 32, 534, 535
Drasgow, F., 417
Drews, F. A., 37
Drigotas, S. M., 411
Drolet, G., 57
Druckman, D., 47, 197, 202
Drummond, M., 145, 146
Drummond, P. D., 438
DuBois, D., 201
Duffy, J. F., 185, 346
Dugas, M. J., 497
Duncan, B. L., 544
Duncan, C. C., 511
Duncan, G. H., 149
Duncan, J., 70
Duncker, K., 325
Durand, A., 8
Durand, V. M., 473, 477, 483, 485, 496,
    500, 502
Durham, M. D., 175, 576
Durkin, K., 276
Dutta, T., 82
Dwyer, D. J., 439
Dwyer, J., 175
Dywan, J., 272
Dzokoto, V. A., 474

Ebbese, E. B., 276
Eckerman, D. A., 245
Eddy, K. T., 531
Eggert, A., 5
Eichenbaum, H., 285
Eidelson, J. I., 574
Eidelson, R. J., 574
Eiden, R. D., 91
Eifert, G. H., 519, 521
Eimas, P. D., 112
Einstein, G. O., 290
Eisenberg, N., 94, 102
Eisler, I., 530
Eisler, J. A., 239
Elder, P., 19, 43
Elieff, C. A., 161
Eliot, L., 107
Elli, K. A., 287
Ellickson, P. L., 216
Elliott, M., 544
Ellis, A., 5, 7, 8, 527
Ellis, H. C., 325
Ellis, R., 270
Emmelkamp, P. M. G., 531
Emmorey, K., 322
Emurian, H. H., 242
Engle, D. E., 512
Engler, B., 388, 389
Englund, C. E., 185
Enns, J. T., 166
Enns, M. W., 394
Epstein, D. R., 192
Erickson, C. D., 103

Ericsson, K. A., 123, 289
Erlacher, D., 196
Ernst, E., 152
Ernst, R., 336
Erzurumluoglu, A., 83
Eschholz, S., 569
Espie, C. A., 191, 192
Esterling, B. A., 464
Ethier, K. A., 434
Eubanks, J., 582
Evardone, M., 77
Everly, G. S., 538
Ewen, R. B., 407
Eysenck, M. W., 264, 270, 272, 285, 294

Fabes, R. A., 405
Fabrega, H., Jr., 471
Fahim, C., 478
Fahle, M., 169
Fain, G. L., 133
Faith, M., 573, 575
Faith, M. S., 530
Falkowski, C., 212
Farah, M. J., 71
Farb, N. A. S., 201
Farrell, M. J., 344
Farrimond, T., 159
Farroni, T., 95
Fedoroff, J. P., 193
Fein, J., 558
Feingold, A., 554
Feissner, J. M., 489
Feist, J., 429, 453
Feldman, D. H., 108, 112
Fellous, J.-M., 75
Fenn, K. M., 184
Fenton, G. W., 537
Ferber, R., 193
Fergusson, D. M., 91
Fernald, A., 105, 107
Féron, F., 60
Ferrari, J. R., 8
Festinger, L., 550, 571
Ficca, G., 187
Fichner-Rathus, L., 359
Field, C. E., 526
Fields, R. M., 441
Fields, T. H., 424
Fields, W., 323
Figueredo, A. J., 552
Fink, M., 481, 536
Fiore, D., 513
Fireman, G., 193, 259
Firestone, P., 494
First, M. B., 472
Fish, J. M., 32, 534, 535
Fisher, R. P., 272, 292
Fisher, S. G., 455
Fiske, S. T., 575
Fitzsimons, G. M., 552
Flanagan, M. B., 150
Flannery, D. J., 115
Flavell, J. H., 109
Fletcher, P., 82
Flett, G. L., 503
Florin, P., 432
Flowe, H. D., 276
Flynn, J. R., 302, 312, 313
Fobair, P., 544
Fobes, J. L., 239
Foehr, U. G., 255
Fogel, S. M., 186
Folkman, S., 439, 440
Follett, K., 557
Follette, W. C., 334
Fontaine, K. R., 429
Fontenelle, D. H., 126, 127

Foo, P., 252
Foot, M., 491
Ford, D. Y., 308
Ford, L., 103
Foreman, R. D., 152
Forman, E. M., 531
Forney, J. C., 118
Forney, W. S., 118
Forrest, M. S., 522
Forsyth, G. A., 2, 269
Forsyth, J. P., 518
Fortin, N. J., 285
Fosse, R., 196
Foster, G., 41
Fowers, B. J., 534, 587, 588
Fowler, F., 125
Fowler, J. H., 432
Fox, C., 43
Fox, M. L., 439
Foxhall, K., 176
Frackowiak, R. S. J., 75
Frank, J., 532
Frank, J. D., 532
Franken, R. E., 343, 344, 354, 361
Franzoi, S. L., 550
Fraser, C., 152
Fredrickson, B. L. 169, 433, 459
Freeman, A., 173, 174, 482
Freeman, T. B., 61
Freitas, M. B., 82
French, C. C., 22
French, S. E., 116
French, T. A., 176
Freud, S., 512
Frey, M. C., 305
Frick, P. J., 250
Fried, P. A., 217
Friedman, H. S., 395, 437
Friedman, L., 513
Friedman, L. J., 121
Friedman, R., 232
Friedman, R. C., 513
Friedmann, P. D., 194
Frith, C. D., 75
Fritz, C. O., 295
Fromme, K., 435
Froufe, M., 184
Frueh, B. C., 522
Frydman, M., 582
Frye, E. M., 565
Fucito, L. M., 359
Fuhriman, A., 529
Fukuda, K., 185
Funder, D. C., 413
Funk, J. B., 256, 582
Furnham, A., 20, 389, 395

Gable, S. L., 463
Gaertner, S. L., 577, 587
Galambos, N. L., 117
Galanter, M., 544
Galantucci, B., 277
Galea, S., 441
Galinsky, M. D., 530
Gallagher, J., 293
Gallagher, S., 148
Gamble, S. A., 513
Ganey, H. C. N., 361, 362
Ganis, G., 316
Ganster, D. C., 439
Garbarino, S., 185, 346
Garcia, E. E., 320
Garcia, R. I., 210
Gardner, B. T., 322
Gardner, H., 311, 355
Gardner, R. A., 322
Garety, P. A., 482

Garfinkel, B. D., 503
Garfinkel, L. F., 503
Garland, A. F., 502
Garlow, S. J., 502
Garnets, L. D., 357, 358, 359
Gartrell, N. K., 359
Garvey, A. J., 210
Gass, R. H., 571
Gastner, M. T., 577
Gatchel, R. J., 457
Gates, A. I., 292
Gatz, M., 478, 479
Gauquelin, M., 21, 22
Gayle, H., 435
Gazzaniga, M. S., 67
Geary, N., 349
Gedo, J. E., 28
Gee, J., 551
Gefen, D., 551
Gegenfurtner, K. R., 138
Geiselman, R. E., 272, 292
Geliebter, A., 350
Genesee, F., 320
George, A., 552
Georgiades, A., 431
Germain, A., 220
German, T. P., 327
Gerrard, C., 9
Gersh, R. D., 418
Gershoff, E. T., 250, 251
Gerwood, J. B., 515
Geschwind, N., 69, 83
Gever, J., 475
Gewirtz, J. C., 232
Giarratano, J. C., 306
Gibb, R., 58
Gibson, E. J., 160
Gibson, K. R., 66
Gielen, U. P., 32, 534, 535
Gilbert, L. A., 358
Gilbert, P., 526
Gilovich, T., 587
Gillespie, C. F., 441
Ginet, M., 272
Ginsberg, D. L., 536
Ginsburg, B. E., 580
Giummarra, M. J., 152
Giuseppe, R., 522
Glanz, K., 215
Glass, C. A., 517
Gleason, J. B., 104
Glick, P., 573
Glisky, M. L., 317
Glueck, J., 336
Glueckauf, R. L., 517
Gobet, F., 269, 289, 326
Godnig, E. C., 138
Goel, V., 70
Goffin, R. D., 20
Gogate, L. J., 107
Goldberg, C., 566
Goldberg, R., 203, 205
Golden, J., 91
Goldenberg, H., 530
Goldenberg, I., 530
Goldman, B. M., 409
Goldman, H. H., 538
Goldstein, E. B., 133, 138, 140, 155, 265,
  267, 269, 270, 301
Goldstein, N. J., 561
Goldstein-Alpern, N., 105
Goldston, D. B., 502, 503
Gomez, R., 100
Goodwin, J., 511
Goodwin, R. D., 91
Gopnik, A., 95, 96, 105, 114

Gordijn, M. C. M., 346
Gordis, E. B., 582
Gordon, A. K., 557
Gore, J. C., 72
Gorman, J. M., 441, 537
Gorny, G., 58
Gosling, S. D., 31, 392
Göthe, K., 266
Gottesman, I. I., 483
Gould, E., 61
Grabe, M., 242
Graber, J, A., 103
Grabill, K., 493
Grack, C., 576
Graham, C. H., 139
Grande, T., 532
Grandner, M. A., 185
Granrud, C. E., 159
Grant, B. F., 492
Grant, I., 217
Graves, J. L., 588
Gravetter, F. J., 594
Gray, J. M., 361
Green, C., 284
Green, L. R., 404
Green, M. C., 570
Greenberg, D. L., 286
Greenberg, R. L., 452
Greene, B., 487
Greenfield, P. M., 310
Greenglass, E. R., 439
Green-Paden, L. D., 525
Greenwald, A. G., 587
Greenwald, R., 522
Greenwood, J. G., 80
Greenwood, K. M., 272
Greer, D. S., 431, 432
Gregory, A., 40
Gregory, K. B., 185
Gregory, R. L., 154, 158, 166
Grello, C. M., 359
Griffin, D. W., 553
Griffin, W. A., 530
Griffin-Fennell, F., 502
Griffiths, R. R., 210
Grigorenko, E. L., 310, 311, 312, 313, 588
Grigsby, T. D., 555
Grob, C. S., 184
Grobstein, P., 134
Gross, C. G., 61
Gruber, A. J., 216
Gruman, J., 430
Grunbaum, J. A., 431
Gruner, C. R., 318
Guarnaccia, P. J., 474
Guastello, D. D., 405, 406
Guastello, S. J., 405, 406
Guay, F., 555
Guéguen, N., 556, 561, 562
Guevremont, D. C., 240, 518, 520, 525
Guez, J., 279
Guilleminault, C., 193
Gullette, D. L., 362
Gunnar, M. R., 100
Gunthert, K. C., 459
Gur, R. E., 485
Gurin, J., 531
Gurung, R., 430, 441, 455
Gustavsson, J. P., 388

Haber, L., 288
Haber, R. N., 276, 288
Haddad, S., 45
Haddock, G., 478
Hadley, C. N., 337
Hadwin, A. F., 290
Haenschel, C., 266

Hafer, C. L., 587
Haier, R. J., 63, 72
Hajek, P., 519
Halbert, J., 152
Hall, C., 196
Hall, J., 497, 526
Hall, N. C., 279
Hallahan, D. P., 307, 308
Halligan, P. W., 199
Halonen, J. S., 1, 5, 290
Halpern-Felsher, B. L., 359
Ham, C., 433
Hamilton, A., 435
Hamilton, V. L., 564
Hammer, L. B., 555
Hancock, P. A., 361, 362
Handsfield, H. H., 435
Hanley, S. J., 408
Hansell, J. H., 471, 473
Hansen, C. J., 462
Hansen, N. B., 531
Harber, K. D., 40
Hardaway, C. A., 185
Harding, D. J., 43
Harding, R. W., 441
Hare, R. D., 499
Hari, R., 81
Harker, L., 389
Harlow, H. F., 252
Harlow, J. M., 43
Harlow, M. K., 252
Harlow, T. F., 452
Harm, D. L., 150
Harpending, H., 91
Harper, M. S., 359
Harris, C., 554
Harris, J. A., 580
Harris, J. C., 511
Harrison, K., 353
Harrison, P. J., 483
Hart, C. L., 204, 216
Hart, D., 117
Hartgens, F., 78
Hartlep, K. L., 2, 269
Hartmann, P., 21
Harvey, T., 66
Hasbrouck, J. E., 582
Hasher, L., 282
Hashibe, M., 217
Hashimoto, I., 69
Hasin, D. S., 214
Haslam, N., 318
Hass, S. L., 451
Hauck, F. R., 194
Havercamp, S. M., 407
Hawks, J., 91
Hayden, A., 156
Hazuda, H. P., 450
Heath, R. G., 239
Hedges, M., 532
Heimann, M., 94
Heinrichs, R. W., 480
Heisel, M. J., 503
Helgeson, V. S., 405
Hellerstein, D. J., 510
Hellige, J. B., 81
Helson, R., 335
Helton, W. S., 236
Henik, A., 315
Heninger, M., 502
Henman, L. D., 465
Henning, K. R., 255, 581
Henningsen, D. D., 559
Henthorne, T. L., 169
Hepper, P. G., 81
Hergenhahn, B. R., 26, 227, 235
Heriot, S. A., 520

Herman, C. P., 352, 353
Hermann, B., 273, 287
Hernstein, R., 312
Herrmann, D. J., 292
Herscovitch, P., 189
Herxheimer, A., 346
Herz, R. S., 146
Herzog, T. A., 260
Hess, T. M., 557
Heston, J. D., 537
Hettich, P. I., 290
Hewitt, P. L., 503
Higbee, K. L., 296
Higgins, S. T., 204
Higham, P. A., 9
Hilgard, E. R., 197, 198
Hill, E. A., 107
Hilsenroth, M. J., 421
Hinkel, E., 320
Hinterberger, T., 76
Hintzman, D. L., 278
Hipworth, K., 242
Hirshbein, L., 536
Hirstein, W., 67
Hobson, J. A., 189, 195, 196, 221
Hochreich, D. J., 402
Hochstenbach, J., 72
Hodges, H., 61
Hofer, B. K., 7
Hoff, E., 105, 106
Hoffart, A., 513
Hoffer, A., 512
Hoffman, H. G., 522
Hogan, E. H., 210
Hoge, C. W., 493
Holden, C., 412
Holding, D. H., 291
Hollendonner, J. K., 430
Holling, H., 307, 330, 332
Hollon, S. D., 526, 527
Holman, E. A., 441
Holmes, J., 266
Holmes, T. H., 453
Holtz, A., 556
Holtzen, D. W., 83
Holzinger, B., 221
Honey, P. L., 226, 246
Hong, H.-W., 97
Honzik, C. H., 252
Hooley, J., 470
Hopkins, W. D., 323
Horgan, J., 56
Horn, R. R., 241
Horne, R. S. C., 194
Hornick, B. A., 210
Horsburgh, K., 61
Horvath, L. S., 362
Horwood, L. J., 91
Hosch, H. M., 175
Houghton, D. P., 559
Houston-Price, C., 106
Howard, A., 531
Howard, I. P., 160, 161
Howell, D. C., 599
Howes, C., 101
Hsia, Y., 139
Hubble, M. A., 544
Hubel, D. H., 133, 134
Hübner, R., 68
Huesmann, L. R., 256, 257, 582
Hughes, J. N., 582
Hughes, J. R., 210, 216
Hughes, M., 359
Huijbregts, S. C., 91
Hunt, H., 332
Hunt, R. R., 325
Hunter, E., 565

Hunter, J. P., 152
Hustedt, J. T., 569
Hutchinson, S., 74
Hutchinson, S. R., 44, 45
Hyde, J. S., 29, 355
Hyman, R., 173, 174
Hysenbegasi, A., 451

Ianna, P., 21
Ida, Y., 82
Ikemoto, S., 239
Ingham, A. G., 558
Ingram, V., 479
Iosif, A., 48
Irwin, M. R., 438
Ishihara, K., 185
Israelson, D., 149
Iversen, L., 207, 208
Izard, C. E., 97

Jaber-Filho, J. A., 537
Jablonski, N. G., 588
Jackendoff, R., 322
Jackson, S. L., 15, 23, 25, 41
Jackson, T., 423
Jacobs, M., 28, 396, 400, 439, 449,
    511
Jacobs, M. K., 533
Jacobson, N. S., 544
Jaeggi, S. M., 313
Jaehnig, W., 241
Jaffe, J., 106
Jamison, K. R., 502, 503
Janis, I. L., 559
Janssen, S. A., 57
Janus, C. L., 356
Janus, S. S., 356
Jarvin, L., 302
Jarvis, M. J., 210
Jawahar, I. M., 555
Jay, T. B., 320
Jeffery, R. W., 351
Jenni, O. C., 184
Jensen, A. R., 312
Jerabek, I., 281
Jessell, T. M., 75
Joffe, R. T., 77
Jogerst, G. J., 442
John, O. P., 404, 414
Johnson, B. T., 568
Johnson, K. E., 317
Johnson, K. J., 169
Johnson, L. D., 121
Johnson, M. J. M., 455
Johnson, S., 312
Johnson, T. J., 215
Johnson, V. E., 356
Johnson, W., 65
Joiner, T. E., Jr., 503
Jones, C., 417
Jones, D. N., 552
Jones, E. E., 557
Jones, G. V., 81
Jones, J., 356
Jones, M. K., 526
Jones, R., 491
Jones, S. S., 97
Jones, W. H., 422
Jonides, J., 266, 269
Jouvet, M., 189
Joyce, P., 515
Juang, L., 588
Judge, T. A., 395
Juliano, L. M., 210
Julien, E., 555
Julien, R. M., 203, 204, 205, 208, 209, 210,
    216, 535

Jussim, L., 40
Justice, J. B., Jr., 239

Kaas, J. H., 152
Kadosh, R. C., 315
Kagan, J., 93
Kahana, M. J., 275
Kahneman, D., 45, 333, 334
Kail, R. V., 119
Kalat, J. W., 53, 63, 74, 77, 88, 204, 412
Kalish, D., 252
Kallgren, C. A., 557
Kallio, S., 197, 198
Kamimori, G. H., 185
Kamin, L. J., 312
Kamphaus, R. W., 417
Kampman, K. M., 209
Kandel, E. R., 75, 287
Kanwisher, N., 316
Kaplan, A. H., 513
Kaplan, P. S., 103, 104
Kaplar, M. E., 557
Kapleau, P., 177
Kapur, N., 483
Karasz, A., 435
Karim, A. A., 76
Karon, B. P., 283
Kassin, S. M., 176, 558
Kataria, S., 193
Katkin, E. S., 232
Katz, B., 538
Katz, J., 151, 152
Katz, P. A., 573
Kauffman, J. M., 308
Kaufman, A. S., 302
Kaufman, J. H., 165
Kaufman, L., 165
Kawai, K., 350
Kawasaki, H., 70
Kearney, A. J., 540, 541
Kearney, C. A., 99
Kebbell, M. R., 272
Keefe, F. J., 199
Keel, P. K., 474
Keeley, S., 19
Keller, J., 575
Keller, M. C., 551
Kellermann, A. L., 581
Kelly, I. W., 21
Kelly, J. R., 556
Kelly, M. P., 417
Kelly, T. L., 185
Keltner, D. 389, 587
Kempermann, G., 61
Kennaway, D. J., 77
Kenneth, M., 214
Kensinger, E. A., 286, 559
Kenward, R., 515
Kernis, M. H., 409
Kerr, M., 3
Kessler, R. C., 122
Ketcham, K., 271, 284
Keyes, C. L., 122
Keysers, C., 265
Khan, S. M., 82
Kida, T. E., 19, 22, 48
Kidd, K. K., 302, 312, 588
Kiecolt-Glaser, J. K., 438, 463
Kigar, D. L., 65, 66
Kihlstrom, J. F., 317, 338
Kikuchi, Y., 269
Kim, T. E., 116
Kim-Cohen, J., 101
Kimmel, D., 357
King, L. A., 464
King, N. J., 232, 233
Kingsley, C. H., 76

Kinnunen, L. H., 359
Kiper, D. C., 138
Kipp, K., 99
Kirby, J. R., 290
Kirsch, I., 40, 197, 198, 272
Kirsh, S. J., 256
Kirveskari, E., 81
Kisamore, J. L., 555
Kiser, L. J., 537
Kisilevsky, B. S., 91
Kitayama, S., 390
Klaiber, J. R., 550
Klein, B., 517
Klein, K., 464
Klohnen, E. C., 554
Klump, K. L., 474
Knaus, W. J., 5, 7, 8
Knight, R. T., 70
Knoblauch, K., 140
Knoops, K. T. B., 431
Knox, D., 359, 434
Koch, C., 183
Koch, W. H., 392
Koenigsberg, H. W., 498
Kohlberg, L., 118
Kohn, C. S., 518
Kohn, J. P., 246
Köke, A., 152
Kolb, B., 58, 75
Koltzenburg, M., 149, 354
Koons, S. R., 7
Kornhaber, M. L., 311
Korol, C., 494
Kose, G., 259
Kosslyn, S. M., 197, 315, 316
Kosson, D. S., 499
Koszycki, D., 491
Kotkin, M., 531
Kottler, J. A., 527, 528, 533
Koutstaal, W., 270
Kowert, P. A., 559
Kozart, M. F., 532
Krakow, B., 193, 220
Krall, E. A., 210
Kramer, S. J., 337
Krantz, D. S., 458
Krauss, R. M., 322
Kripke, D. F., 185
Kruepke, K. A., 242
Ksir, C. J., 204, 216
Kuehner, C., 488
Kuhl, P. K., 95, 96, 105, 114
Kuipers, H., 78
Kulik, J., 286, 550
Kumaran, D., 75
Kurokawa, M., 390

LaBar, K. S., 75, 286
LaBerge, S., 221
Labin, D., 574
LaBrie, R. A., 528
Lacayo, A., 208
Lachman, M. E., 122
Lachman, R., 267
Lackner, J. R., 149
Ladouceur, R., 497
Lam, R. W. 489
Lamberg, L., 219
Lambert, K. G., 76
Lambert, M. J., 531
Lambert, W. E., 587
Lamkin, D. M., 295, 297
Lampinen, J. M., 264, 285
Lance, C. E., 416
Landau, J. D., 15, 281
Lane, C., 475
Langer, E. J., 327

Langleben, D. D., 64
Langone, M. D., 566
LaPointe, J. A., 416
Lappin, J. M., 56
Larsen, R. J., 389, 423
Larsen McClarty, K., 389
Larsson, B., 457
Larsson, M., 273
Larzelere, R. E., 125, 250
Latané, B., 17, 583
LaTour, M. S., 169
Lattal, K. A., 246
Laub, J. H., 499
Laurent, J., 146
Laureys, S., 62
Lavie, P., 184, 186
Lawson, H. M., 551
Lay, C., 390
Lazar, S. W., 201
Lazarus, R. S., 439, 447
Lazev, A. B., 260
Leal, M. C., 144
Leavens, D. A., 323
LeBlanc, G., 113, 114
Leck, K., 551
Lecrubier, Y., 483
Ledley, C., 552
LeDoux, J., 75
LeDoux, J. E., 75, 398, 441
Lee, J. E., 209
Lee, J. M., 522
Lee, M., 414
Leenaars, A. A., 503, 504
Lefcourt, H. M., 465
Lefkowitz, E. S., 406
Lefrançois, G. R., 229, 241, 243, 252, 254
Lehman, D. R., 32, 350, 351
Leichtman, M., 420
Leiter, M. P., 439
Lejuez, C. W., 438, 519, 521
Lench, H. C., 583
Lenton, A. P., 358
Lenzenweger, M. F., 483
Leonard, K. E., 580
Lepore, F. E., 154
Leslie, K., 221
Lessow-Hurley, J., 320
Lester, D., 502, 503, 504
Lettvin, J. Y., 133
Levant, R. F., 405
LeVay, S., 358, 359
Levenston, G. K., 499
Levesque, M. J., 552
Levi, A. M., 175
Levin, B. E., 345
Levin, D. T., 279
Levin, J. R., 294, 295
Levin, R., 193
Levine, C., 121
Levine, M., 353, 583
Levitan, L., 221
Levitsky, D. A., 350
Levy, J., 80
Lewandowski, G. W., Jr., 551
Lewchanin, S., 122
Leyendecker, B., 102, 103
Leynes, P. A., 281
Lichstein, K. L., 191, 192
Lichter, D. T., 552
Lichtman, A. H., 216
Liddell, S. K., 321
Lierens, R., 511
Lilienfeld, S. O., 22, 47, 421
Lindemann, B., 147
Linden, M., 475
Linden, W., 350, 461
Linderoth, B., 152

Lindsay, E. W., 102
Lipsey, M. W., 531
Lister, J. J., 144
Little, B. R., 410
Littlewood, R., 565
Liu, X., 70
Liu, Y., 348
Lodi-Smith, J., 410
Loehlin, J. C., 413
Loftus, E. F., 270, 271, 284
LoLordo, V. M., 450, 451, 488
Long, J. D., 541
Long, V. O., 406
López, S. R., 474
Lovallo, W. R., 457
Low, K. G., 489
Lubart, T. I., 332
Luchins, D. J., 472
Luck, S. J., 285
Luminet, O., 285
Lumley, M. A., 343
Lundh, L., 423
Luo, S., 554
Luppa, M., 430
Luria, A. R., 264
Lustig, C., 282
Luyben, P. D., 242
Lynch, C., 81
Lynch, J. E., 516
Lynch, K. B., 102
Lynn, A. L., 236
Lynn, S. J., 197, 198
Lyons, A. C., 437, 438
Lyons, M. A., 362
Lyubomirsky, S., 459

Ma, J., 281
Maas, J., 185, 192
Maciejewski, P.K., 493
Mack, A., 151
Mackin, R. S., 460
Mackinnon, L. T., 438
Mackintosh, N. J., 227
Macklin, C. B., 6
MacLin, M. K., 325, 326
MacLin, O. H., 325, 326
Maddi, S. R., 459
Maddock, J., 215
Maddock. J. E., 214
Maddox, K. B., 575
Maddox, W. T., 317
Maguire, E. A., 75, 289
Mah, K., 357
Maheu, M. M., 516
Mahler, H. I. M., 550
Mahowald, M. W., 192
Maier, N. R. F., 443
Maier, S. F., 290, 488
Mailis–Gagnon, A., 149
Malaspina, D., 483
Mamen, M., 125
Manalo, E., 294
Manber, R., 536
Mandal, M. K., 82
Mandler, J. M., 95
Mangan, M. A., 193
Mann, N., 350
Manne, S., 463
Manning, M., 83
Manning, R., 583
Manschreck, T. C., 480
Mansouri, A., 477
Mantyla, T., 291
Marchman, V. A., 105
Marcus, E., 512
Marcus-Hewhall, A., 581
Margoliash, D., 184

Margolin, G., 582
Margolin, J., 441
Marks, D. F., 173, 174
Markus, H. R., 390, 558
Marmarosh, C., 556
Marsh, H. W., 452
Marshall, P., 335
Marshall, P. H., 295
Marshall, R. D., 441
Marsiglia, F. F., 116
Martens, R., 21
Martin, A. J., 452
Martin, B. R., 216
Martin, C. L., 405
Martin, G., 233, 258
Martin, L. L., 452
Martin, L. R., 395
Martin, M., 81
Martin, W. L. B., 82
Martinez-Gonzalez, M. A., 353
Martino, S. C., 216
Martuza, R. L., 537
Marx, D. M., 550
Mashour, G. A., 537
Masi, G., 99
Maslach, C., 406, 439
Maslow, A., 407, 408
Maslow, A. H., 408
Masse, L. C., 204
Masten, A. S., 101
Masters, W. H., 356
Masuda, T., 169
Matheny, K. B., 464
Mather, G., 135, 144, 151
Matossian, M. K., 511
Matson, J. L., 235
Matsumoto, D., 588
Matthews, G., 388, 391
Matthews, M. S., 320
Matthews, P. H., 320
Mattock, A., 159
May, C. P., 282
May, J., 156
May, J. G., 150
Mayberg, H., 537
Maybery, M. T., 276
Mayer, R. E., 254, 319
Mazur, J. E., 234, 235, 240
McAdams, D. P., 410
McBride, W. J., 239
McCabe, C., 146
McCabe, M. P., 353
McCall, W. V., 536
McCarthy, B. W., 359
McCeney, M. K., 458
McClelland, D. C., 313, 404, 465
McClelland, J. L., 306
McClure, J. B., 211
McCluskey, U., 529
McConkey, K. M., 199
McConnell, W., 442
McCrae, R. R., 393, 395
McCullagh, J. F., 80
McDaniel, M., 295
McDaniel, M. A., 6, 290
McDermott, K. B., 270
McDermott, R., 580
McDonald, J. K., 242
McDonough, L., 95
McEvoy, C., 271
McGaugh, J. L., 264
McGregor, I., 410
McGuffin, P., 488
McIntosh, W. D., 452
McKay, A., 355
McKay, G. D., 125, 127, 128
McKeever, W. F., 81, 82

McKenna, K. Y. A., 552
McKenna, M. W., 257
McKenzie, K., 502
McKim, W. A., 212, 213
McKone, E., 280
McLaren, S., 100
McLean, N. J., 354
McLewin, L. A., 494
McLoyd, V. C., 125, 250
McMahon, M., 272
McMahon, S., 149, 354
McMullen, L. M., 488
McNally, R. J., 189, 283
McNamara, D. S., 296
McNeill, D., 275
McRobbie, H., 519
Medhus, E., 103
Mehl, M. R., 24
Mehta, J. D., 43
Meier, P. S., 532, 545
Meltzoff, A. N., 94, 95, 96, 105, 114
Melzack, R., 151, 152, 153
Memon, A., 272, 276
Mendes, W. B., 463
Mendez, M., 68
Mendolia, M., 448
Meneses, G. D., 241
Menzies, R. G., 526
Mercer, J., 101
Merens, W., 56
Merikle, P. M., 315
Mervis, C. B., 317
Messer, S. B., 513
Metha, A., 125
Metts, S., 551
Meunier, M., 254
Meyer, G. J., 416, 420
Meyers, L., 516
Michael, D., 242
Michaels, J. W., 558
Michalak, E. E., 489
Michalko, M., 307, 337, 339
Michel, C., 280
Michelangelo, I., 209
Michello, J., 538
Middaugh, S. J., 457
Mielke, H. W., 478
Milgram, R. M., 329
Milgram, S., 563, 558
Milgrim, D. L., 7
Miller, D. T., 550, 583
Miller, E. K., 438
Miller, G. A., 268, 308, 319
Miller, G. E., 437, 438
Miller, M. L., 241
Miller, N., 442, 581
Miller, N. E., 445, 573
Miller, R., 551, 552
Miller, S. D., 544
Miller, S. J., 533
Miller, W. R., 214
Millman, R. B., 78
Milne, R., 292
Miltenberger, R. G., 518, 526
Miltner, W. H. R., 492
Milton, J., 173, 174
Minda, J. P., 318
Mineka, S., 470
Minton, H. L., 29
Miotto, K., 212
Mirabile, R., 571
Mirsky, A. F., 483, 511
Mischel, W., 388, 401, 402, 413, 414
Mistlberger, R. E., 184, 346
Mitchell, K., 48
Mitchell, L. A., 149

Miyake, A., 266
Miyamoto, Y., 169
Mize, J., 102
Mogg, K., 169
Moghaddam, B., 484
Moghaddam, F. M., 586
Mohr, D. C., 517
Mokdad, A. H., 429, 431
Mollon, J. D., 140
Monahan, J., 482
Monfardini, E., 254
Montgomery, P., 192
Moody, J., 434
Moor, J., 305
Moore, J. L., 308
Moore, K., 177
Moore, K. A., 439
Moore, P. J., 550
Moore, S. A., 283
Moore, T. O., 580
Moran, J. M., 70
Moras, K., 531
Morey, L. C., 77, 545
Morgan, J. P., 580, 581
Morgenstern, J., 215
Morin, A., 183
Morisse, D., 526
Morrison, K., 359
Morrison, R. G., 316
Morsella, E., 322
Mortweet, S. L., 404
Mosher, W. D., 356
Mosier, J., 529
Moskowitz, J. T., 439, 440
Most, S. B., 151, 157
Motivala, S. J., 438
Moun, M. K., 395
Mroczek, D., 410, 411
Mucci, M., 99
Mukamal, K., 430
Muller, R. T., 494
Mundy, P., 577
Munoz, R. F., 214
Munsey, C., 35, 543
Muris, P., 232, 233
Murphy, J. M., 239
Murray, B., 350, 351
Murray, C., 312
Murray, J. B., 484
Murray, R. M., 56
Murray, S. L., 553
Murrell, A. R., 255, 581
Mussen, P. H., 105
Musso, M., 58
Mustanski, B. S., 359
Myers, H. F., 488

Nairne, J. S., 269, 281, 282, 287
Naitoh, P., 185
Nakamichi, M., 41
Nakamura, J., 361
Narduzzi, K., 423
Nau, S. D., 191, 192
Naveh-Benjamin, M., 279
Neale, J. M., 483
Nearing, K., 232, 233
Neath, I., 268, 266, 269, 277, 281, 282, 291, 294, 295, 296
Needles, D. J., 453
Nehlig, A., 209
Neill, D. B., 239
Neisser, U., 310, 313
Nelson, C. A., 90, 92
Nelson, T. D., 123, 573
Nemeroff, C. B., 286, 441, 493
Neter, E., 20
Nettle, D., 394, 395, 412

Neufeld, P., 175
Neufeld, R. W. J., 480
Neumeister, A., 489
Nevid, J., 359
Nevid, J. S., 487
Newby-Clark, I. R., 189
Newcomb, T. M., 570
Newman, A. W., 272
Newman, M. E. J., 577
Newport, E. L., 322
Ng, S. H., 123
Ngu, H., 281
Niaura, R., 458
Nickell, J., 22, 47
Nida, S. A., 583
Niedzwienska, A., 286
Niehaus, D. J. H., 534
Nielsen, D. M., 125
Nielsen, M., 99
Ninomiya, Y., 146
Nisbett, R., 587
Nisbett, R. E., 169, 312, 313, 557
Njeri, I., 31, 588
Noh, S., 455
Noland, J. S., 217
Nolen-Hoeksema, S., 473, 487, 500
Norcross, J. C., 510, 513, 532, 544
Norenzayan, A., 169
Nori, G., 348
Norlander, T., 202
Norman, D. A., 2, 4
Norman, K. A., 270
Normann, R. A., 134
North, C. S., 469
Northcutt, R. G., 147
Norton, P., 242
Norvig, P., 305
Norwood, R. M., 423
Nosek, B. A., 587
Novaco, R., 442
Nowell, P. D., 190
Nowicki, S., 322
Nusbaum, H. C., 184
Nuttin, B., 537
Nyborg, H., 21

O'Conner, T. G., 100
O'Connor, M. G., 278
O'Craven, K. M., 316
O'Hara, M. W., 452
O'Keeffe, C., 173
O'Leary, E., 516
O'Neill, B., 46
O'Neill, H., 17
O'Roark, A. M., 421
Oakley, D. A., 199
Oakley, R., 456
Oberauer, K., 266
Ochoa, J. G., 189
Oden, M., 307
Ogden, C. L., 349
Ogilvie, R., 221
Ogles, B. M., 531
Ogloff, J. R. P., 499
Ohayon, M. M., 193
Okiishi, J., 544
Olds, M. E., 239
Olio, K. A., 284
Ollendick, T. H., 232, 233, 526
Olsen, E. A., 175, 176, 276
Olson, J., 555
Olson, J. M., 569, 576, 577
Olson, L., 60
Olson, M., 235
Olson-Buchanan, J. B., 417
Olsson, A., 232, 233
Olsson, P. A., 566

Olszewski, P. K., 348
Olver, J., 145, 146
Onwuegbuzie, A. J., 7
Ooki, S., 81
Oordt, M. S., 457
Ord, T. J., 17
Orleans, C. T., 430, 433
Ormay, T., 516
Orner, R. J., 515
Orprecio, J., 133
Osei, S. Y., 349
Osguthorpe, R., 242
Oskamp, S., 568, 570, 571
Ossoff, E. P., 257
Oster, H., 97
Otani, H., 275
Overmier, J. B., 450
Oyserman, D., 410

Paavola, M., 537
Pace-Schott, E. F., 189
Page, M. P. A., 266
Pagnin, D., 536
Palmer, S. E., 157
Palmersheim, K. A., 122
Pals, J. L., 410
Panksepp, J., 97
Pantelis, C., 485
Papaeliou, C., 83
Papanicolaou, A. C., 284
Papies, E. K., 349
Papirman, Y., 557
Pappas, T., 242
Paquette, V., 58, 102
Paradis, C. M., 286
Paradis, J., 320
Park, L. E., 125
Parke, R. D., 93, 103
Parker, A., 221, 281
Parker, E. S., 264
Parker, K. C. H., 522
Pascual, A., 556, 561, 562
Pasqualini, M. S., 97
Passarello, L. C., 358
Patterson, C. J., 359
Patton, J., 309
Paulhus, D. L., 390
Paulsson, T., 221
Pawlick, K., 457
Pear, J., 258
Penfield, W., 269
Penn, D. L., 500
Pennebaker, J. W., 464
Penner, L. A., 585
Penrod, S. D., 276
Peplau, L. A., 356
Perfors, A., 105
Perlman, D., 551, 552
Perls, F., 220
Perreault, S., 574
Perry, R. P., 5, 450
Persons, J., 526
Pervin, L. A., 404, 414
Pesant, N., 196
Pescatello, L. S., 431
Peters, W. A., 576
Peterson, C., 451
Peterson, D. R., 34
Peterson, L. R., 269
Peterson, M. J., 269
Peterson, S. E., 290
Pett, M. A., 455
Pettit, G. S., 102
Peverly, S. T., 2
Phelps, E. A., 232, 233
Phillips, D. S., 289
Pickel, K. L., 176

Piefke, M., 72
Piek, J. P., 97
Pierce, W. D., 235
Pierrehumbert, B., 101
Pierson, J. F., 29
Piliavin, I. M., 585
Piliavin, J. A., 585
Pilkonis, P. A., 423
Pillado, O., 116
Pillow, D. R., 455
Pilon, D. A., 404
Pincus, H. A., 472
Pine, D. S., 536
Pinel, J. P. J., 350, 351
Pinker, S., 322
Pinsky, D., 498
Pixley, J. E., 122
Pizam, A., 361
Pizzighello, S., 151
Plassmann, H., 168
Plazzi, G., 192
Pleasant, A., 431, 432
Pliner, P., 350
Plous, S., 573
Plug, C., 165
Poggio, T., 169
Pokorny, J., 140
Poland, J., 500
Polemikos, N., 83
Polich, J., 201
Polivy, J., 352, 353
Pollner, M., 416
Pollock, V. E., 499
Pomaki, G., 555
Pope, H. G., 216
Popma, A., 580
Porter, K., 284
Posada, G., 100
Posluszny, D. M., 430
Potenza, M. N., 204, 528
Powell, A. A., 585
Powell, A. L., 353
Powell, R. A., 226, 246
Pratarelli, M. E., 392
Preckel, F., 307, 330, 332
Premack, A. J., 322
Premack, D., 322
Pressley, M., 295
Priest, R. G., 193
Prigerson, H. G., 493
Priluck, R., 230
Priluck, R. L., 231
Prinz, W., 94
Pritchard, M., 520
Prkachin, K. M., 149
Prochaska, J. O., 510, 513, 514, 532, 544
Provencher, M. D., 497
Puentes, J., 359, 434
Pulido, M., 189
Purselle, D. C., 502
Py, J., 272
Pychyl, T. A., 7, 8

Quednow, B. B., 209
Quigley, B. M., 580
Quillian, M. R., 272
Quinn, P. C., 112, 156
Quinto-Pozos, D., 321

Rabinowitz, V. C., 32, 404
Rabius, V., 517
Rachman, S., 490, 496
Rahe, R. H., 453
Rainville, P., 149
Rajab, M. H., 503
Ramirez, A., 551
Ramsay, M. C., 417

Rana-Deuba, A., 455
Rand, M., 233
Rathus, R., 359
Rau, H., 457
Rau, P. R., 185
Rau, W., 8
Raun, K., 348
Ray, O. S., 204, 216
Razzoli, E., 483
Reed, J. D., 292
Reed, S. K., 317, 320
Reevy, G. M., 406
Regan, P., 550, 552
Regan, P. C., 554
Reid, M., 80
Reid, M. R., 438
Reid, P. T., 32
Reiff, S., 232
Reilly, M. P., 246
Reis, H. T., 100
Reisner, A. D., 495
Reiss, M., 81
Reiss, S., 407
Reiterman, T., 565
Reitman, D., 525
Renner, M. J., 460
Reno, R. R., 557
Rentfrow, P. J., 392
Rescorla, R. A., 230
Resnick, H., 441
Restak, R. M., 204
Reuter, M., 21
Revonsuo, A., 197, 198
Rew, L., 434
Reynolds, C. R., 417
Reznikoff, M., 421
Rhine, J. B., 171
Ricciardelli, L. A., 353
Rice, K. G., 394
Richards, J. C., 517
Richardson, D. R., 404
Richman, C. L., 576
Richmond, L. J., 566
Ridenour, T. A., 208
Rideout, V., 255
Rider, E. A., 95, 99
Ridings, C. M., 551
Riley, G., 306
Riley, W., 211
Riquelme, H., 332
Ritchey, A. K., 437
Ritchie, B. F., 252
Riva, G., 517
Rizzo, C. P., 250
Roberts, B. W., 389, 410, 411, 412
Roberts, D. F., 255
Roberts, D. G., 250
Roberts, J. E., 245
Roberts, R. E., 116
Roberts, S., 245
Roberts, W. A., 245
Robertson, I. S., 326
Robertson, L. C., 315
Robins, R. W., 31
Robinson, A., 308
Robinson, B., 565
Robinson, T. E., 183, 204, 205
Robinson, T. N., 583
Robinson-Riegler, B., 295
Rock, A., 187, 189, 219, 512
Rodd, Z. A., 239
Rodin, J., 585
Roeckelein, J. E., 288
Roeder, K., 312
Roediger, H. L., 270
Roediger III, H. L., 277
Roese, N. J., 359

Rogers, B. J., 160, 161
Rogers, C. R., 409, 496
Rogers, J. A., 538
Rogers, S., 522
Rogers, T. T., 306
Rogoff, B., 310
Rohsenow, D. J., 527
Roid, G. H., 302
Rolls, E. T., 146, 158
Ronningstam, E., 475
Rosch, E., 318
Rosen, G., 152
Rosenberg, L. B., 162
Rosenberg, S. S., 516
Rosenhan, D. L., 499
Rosenheck, R. A., 493
Rosenkranz, M. A., 438
Rosenman, R. H., 457
Rosenthal, R., 333
Rosenthal, T. L., 463, 541
Rosenzweig, M. R., 53, 92
Ross, D., 255
Ross, E. J., 78
Ross, H. E., 165
Ross, M., 390
Ross, N. O., 390
Ross, P. E., 317, 326
Ross, S. A., 255
Rossion, B., 280
Rothbart, M. K., 411
Rothschild, B., 233
Rotter, J. B., 402
Rounsaville, B. J., 533
Rowe, B., 5, 9
Rowland, C. R., 451
Rozin, P., 350
Rubenstein, C., 122
Rubin, D. C., 286
Rudd, M. D., 503
Rudman, L. A., 573
Rueckl, J. G., 277
Rueffer, S. D., 189
Ruiz, J. M., 463
Rummens, J., 455
Runco, M. A., 307, 329, 330, 332, 339
Rushton, J. P., 312
Russell, S., 305
Russell, S. T., 359
Russo, M. B., 496
Rutledge, T., 350
Rutz, C., 41
Ruva, C., 271
Ryan, M. P., 5
Ryan, R. M., 202
Ryckman, R. M., 390
Ryff, C. D., 122
Rynearson, K., 3

Saadeh, W., 250
Sackeim, H. A., 536
Safer, M. A., 175
Saffran, J. R., 107
Sagiv, N., 315
Sahelian, R., 192
Saksida, L. M., 245
Salamone, J. D., 56
Salmelin, R., 81
Salmon, P., 461
Salthouse, T. A., 122
Salzarulo, P., 187
Sampson, R. J., 499
Samuels, C. A., 406
Sanberg, P. R., 61
Sanchez, J., 488
Sanderman, R., 531
Sanders, J., 564
Sandler, I., 455

Sankofa, B. M., 313
Santrock, J. W., 1, 5, 102, 290
Sapirstein, G., 40
Sarason, B. R., 501
Sarason, I. G., 501
Sarvananda, S., 536
Sateia, M. J., 190
Saunders, M. M., 149
Saunders, T., 464
Savage-Rumbaugh, S., 323
Savsevitz, J., 518
Saxton, M., 106
Saxvig, I. W., 184, 188
Schacter, D. L., 270, 271, 279, 281, 291
Schafer, M., 559
Schaie, K. W., 123
Schaller, M., 32
Schaufeli, W. B., 439
Scheck, B., 175
Scheinkman, M., 530
Schenck, C. H., 192
Scher, S. J., 8, 571
Schick, T., 20, 174
Schiffrin, R. M., 265
Schilling, M. A., 326
Schiraldi, G. R., 465
Schlaepfer, T. E., 537
Schleicher, S. S., 358
Schmitt, D. P., 390
Schmolck, H., 286
Schneider, K. J., 29, 514
Schneider, P. L., 517
Schneiderman, N., 438, 458
Schooler, C., 313
Schopp, L. H., 517
Schottenbauer, M., 556
Schredl, M., 196
Schreiber, D. E., 272
Schreiber, E. H., 272
Schreiber, F. R., 494
Schroeder, J. E., 423
Schroeder, S., 432
Schuel, H., 217
Schuetze, P., 91
Schultheiss, O. C., 77
Schultz, D., 474
Schultz, D. P., 26, 27, 234, 396, 403
Schultz, H. T., 33
Schultz, P. W., 568, 570, 571
Schultz, S. E., 26, 27, 234, 396, 403
Schum, T. R., 89, 90
Schuster, M. A., 441
Schwartz, B. L., 275
Schwartz, C., 184
Schwartz, J. E., 395
Schwartz, J. H., 75
Schwartz, M. S., 457
Schwartz, S. J., 116
Sclafani, A., 350
Scoboria, A., 272
Scott, J. L., 296
Scott, J. P., 580
Scott, L., 452
Scully, J. A., 454
Scurfield, R. M., 441
Searcy, W. A., 322
Sechzer, J. A., 32, 404
Sefcek, J. A., 552
Segerdahl, P., 323
Segerstrom, S., 438
Seidler, G. H., 522
Seidman, B. F., 40
Seiter, J. S., 571
Seitz, A., 170
Seligman, M. E. P., 31, 358, 450, 488, 532, 543
Selye, H., 437

Senécal, C., 555
Serfaty, M., 502
Sestir, M. A., 256, 582
Seybolt, D. C., 403
Shaffer, D. R., 99
Shaffer, H. J., 528
Shaffer, J. B., 530
Shafir, E., 335
Shafton, A., 189, 194
Shalizi, C. R., 577
Shames, J., 338
Shannon, K., 309
Shapiro, C. M., 193, 531
Shapiro, F., 522
Shapiro, J. M., 271
Shapiro, S. L., 201
Shapiro-Mendoza, C. K., 194
Sharf, R. S., 510, 511
Sharot, T., 285
Shaughnessy, J. J., 293
Shaver, P. R., 100
Shaywitz, B. A., 72
Shaywitz, S. E., 72
Sheikh, A. A., 521
Sheldon, K. M., 409
Shen, J., 346
Shepherd, G. M., 146
Sherif, M., 576
Sherrod, K. B., 102
Shiffman, S., 271
Shiner, R. L., 411, 413
Shneerson, J. M., 190, 192
Shoda, Y., 402, 413
Shurkin, J. N., 307
Siegel, R. K., 183, 184
Siegler, R. S., 94, 112, 338
Siever, L. J., 498
Sigelman, C. K., 95, 99
Sills, C., 515, 516
Silver, S. M., 522
Silverman, W. K., 99
Simeon, D., 494
Simner, M. L., 20
Simon, G. A. F., 573, 575
Simon, G. E., 517
Simon, H. A., 326
Simons, D. J., 151, 279
Simons, J. S., 271
Simonton, D. K., 31
Simpson, D. D., 209
Singer, B., 122
Singer, B. H., 122
Singer, J. D., 559
Singer, M. T., 565
Singleton, J. L., 322
Sinha, R., 209
Sipos, A., 483
Siribaddana, S. H., 474
Sirkin, M. I., 566
Six, L. S., 289
Skeels, H. M., 312
Skinner, B. F., 234
Skipton, L. H., 388
Slaby, A. E., 503
Slaney, R. B., 394
Slater, A., 95, 159
Sloman, A., 305
Slot, L. A. B., 282
Slovic, P., 333
Smedley, A., 588
Smedley, B. D., 588
Smilek, D., 315
Smith, A. M., 217
Smith, A. P., 75, 293
Smith, J., 125, 250
Smith, J. D., 318
Smith, P. B., 559

Smith R. E., 402, 527
Smith, T. W., 458, 463
Snyder, A., 308
Sobolewski, J. M., 92
Soderstrom, M., 107
Sohal, T., 211
Solomon, J. L., 335
Solomon, M. J., 259
Solowij, N., 216
Solso, R. L., 325, 326
Somberg, D. R., 545
Sommers-Flanagan, J., 416
Sommers-Flanagan, R., 416
Sorek, S., 279
Soyez, V., 538
Spalding, K. L., 349
Spano, R., 41
Spencer, L., 144
Sperry, R. W., 67
Spiegler, M. D., 240, 518, 520, 525
Spinella, M., 210
Spirito, A., 503
Spiro, C. S., 412
Spiro Wagner, P., 412
Spitzer, R. L., 475
Sporer, S. L., 169
Sprecher, S., 550
Springer, D., 350
Springer, S. P., 68, 82, 83
Springston, F., 268
Sprinthall, R. C., 602
Squire, L. R., 285, 286, 287
Srivastava, S., 335
Sroufe, L. A., 100
Staemmler, F.-M. 516
Standing, L., 281
Stanhope, N., 279
Stanovich, K. E., 15, 16, 23, 24, 47
Stanowicz, L. B., 100
Stanton, S. J., 77
Stapel, D. A., 550
Steciuk, M., 552
Steele, C. M., 575
Steiger, A., 186, 187
Stein, Dan J., 422
Stein, L. M., 272
Stein, M. B., 422
Stein, M. D., 194
Stein, M. I., 337
Stein, M. T., 193
Steinberg, L., 115
Stemler, S. E., 313
Stephens, K., 310
Steptoe, A., 430
Stern, S. L., 450
Sternberg, R. J., 302, 310, 311, 312, 313, 332, 436, 453, 588
Steuer, F. B., 569
Stevens, L. C., 462
Stewart, A. M., 416
Stewart, M. O., 526, 527
Stewart-Williams, S., 39, 57
Stickgold, R., 188, 189, 196, 220
Stickle, T. R., 497
Stinson, F. S., 492
Stokes, D. M., 174
Stolerman, I. P., 210
Stone, G., 545
Stone, T. H., 555
Stoppard, J. M., 488
Stovel, K., 434
Strambler, M. J., 40
Straneva, P. A., 57
Strange, J. R., 78
Strassberg, D. S., 417
Straub, R., 431
Strayer, D. L., 37

Strickler, E. M., 354
Stroebe, W., 349
Strongman, K. T., 439
Strote, J., 209
Strube, M. J., 558
Strunk, D. 526, 527
Strupp, H. H., 545
Sturges, J. W., 520
Sturges, L. V., 520
Stuss, D. T., 68, 70
Subedi, S., 538
Suedfeld, P., 202
Sugimoto, K., 146
Suh, E. M., 405
Suinn, R. M., 436, 481, 588
Suls, J., 457
Sumathipala, A., 474
Sumerlin, J. R., 408
Sunnafrank, M., 551
Supeli, A., 555
Surprenant, A., 266, 268, 269, 277, 281, 282, 291, 294, 295, 296
Sutherland, R. J., 285
Suzuki, L., 312
Svartdal, F., 243
Swaak, J., 253
Swamidass, P. M., 556
Swann, W. B., Jr., 389
Symbaluk, D. G., 226
Synhorst, L. L., 417
Szabo, A., 465

Tabors, P. O., 106
Talbot, N. L., 513
Talbott, J. A., 538
Talley, P. F., 545
Tal-Or, N., 557
Tamis-LeMonda, C. S., 91, 102, 106
Tanner, J. L., 117
Taraban, R., 3
Tardif, T. Z., 332
Taris, T. W., 438
Taub, E., 61
Tausig, M., 538
Tavris, C., 571
Taylor, J. R., 204
Taylor, K., 564
Taylor, M. A., 481
Taylor, S., 456, 522
Taylor, S. E., 229, 430, 441, 451, 456, 463
Taylor-Seehafer, M., 434
Taytroe, L., 196
Te Nijenhuis, J., 202
Tenhula, W. N., 525
Tennesen, M., 143
Terman, L. M., 307
Terracciano, A., 393
Terry, C., 511
Tharp, R. G., 237, 258, 259, 539, 540, 541, 542
Thase, M. E., 511
Thelen, E., 97
Thelen, M. H., 353, 494
Thiessen, E. D., 107
Thomas, A., 93
Thomas, E. M., 249
Thomas, M., 475
Thompson, J. W., 272
Thompson, K. M., 255
Thompson, R. A., 92
Thompson, R. F., 39, 74
Thompson, W. L., 316
Thomsen, D. K., 279
Thorburn, J., 503
Tian, C., 106
Tidwell, M. O., 100
Tierney, S., 353

Tighe, M. R., 318
Till, B. D., 230, 231
Tilton-Weaver, L. C., 117
Timmerman, C. K., 242
Timmerman, I. G. H., 531
Tobler, N. S., 433
Tolman, E. C., 252
Tomasello, M., 105
Toneatto, T., 204
Tononi, G., 188
Toro, C. T., 485
Tosi, H., 454
Tourangeau, R., 44
Towson, S., 423
Toyota, H., 269
Trachet, T., 21
Trainor, L. J., 107
Trajanovic, N. N., 193
Travis, F., 201
Treffert, D. A., 308
Tremblay, R. E., 204
Triandis, H. C., 405
Trocmé, N., 251
Trope, Y., 587
Troutman, A. C., 240, 249, 251
Tsai, G., 484
Tse, L., 116
Tseng, V., 103
Tucker, K. L., 459
Tugade, M. M., 433
Tulving, E., 273, 274, 287
Turiel, E., 117
Turkheimer, E., 312
Turner, C. M., 417
Turner, S. J. M., 530
Tversky, A., 333, 334
Twenge, J. M., 390
Tye-Murray, N., 144
Tzeng, M., 552

Uchino, B. N., 463
Underwood, B. J., 282
Unger, F., 336
Unsworth, G., 256
Urbina, S., 420
Uziel, L., 558

Vaidya, R. S., 451
Vaillant, G. E., 123, 215, 430
Valente, S. M., 358, 359
Valentine, E., 289
Vallerand, A. H., 149
Van der Hart, O., 511
Van Der Ploeg, H. M., 494
Van Deurzen, E., 515
Van Deusen, K. M., 233
Van Dierendonck, D., 202
Van Dongen, H. P., 184
Van Eenwyk, J., 256
Van Elst, L. T., 484
Van Goozen, S. H. M., 355
Van Heck, G. L., 458
Van Joolingen, W. R., 253
Van Lawick-Goodall, J., 41
Vandell, D. L., 101
Vasa, R. A., 536
Vasquez, M. J. T., 116
Vaughn, L., 20, 174
Vega, L. A., 339
Velakoulis, D., 485
Venezia, M., 97
Verbalis, J. G., 354
Verhoeven, C., 555
Verkuyten, M., 390
Viegener, B. J., 351
Villemure, C., 149
Viveros, M. P., 91

Vogel, E. K., 285
Vogler, R. E., 214
Volberg, G., 68
Volkow, N. D., 57, 217
Volpicelli, J. R., 451

Wager, T. D., 39
Wagner, F. E., 522
Wagner, M. K., 403
Wagstaff, G., 199
Wagstaff, G. F., 272
Wainwright, J. L., 359
Wakefield, J. C., 500
Wald, J., 522
Walk, R. D., 160
Walker, E., 483, 486, 536
Walker, E. E., 537
Walker, I., 578
Walker, M., 220, 482, 483, 485
Walker, M. P., 188
Wall, P. D., 151, 152
Wallace, B., 316
Wallnau, L. B., 594
Walsh, R., 201
Walters, R., 249
Walton, C. E., 95
Waltzman, S. B., 455
Wambach, C., 6
Wampold, B. E., 39, 544
Wandersman, A., 432
Wang, J. M., 61
Wang, S. S., 352
Wann, D. L., 254
Ward, C., 455
Ward, J., 69, 71
Ward, T., 256
Ward-Alexander, L., 538
Wardle, J., 430
Wargo, E., 438
Warren, D. J., 134
Warren, M. P., 115
Warshauer-Baker, E., 576, 588
Watanabe, T., 170
Waterfield, R., 197
Waterhouse, J., 346
Watson, A. C., 482
Watson, D. L., 237, 258, 259, 539, 540, 541, 542
Watson, J. B., 27
Watson, J. D., 107
Watson, N. V., 53
Watt, C., 171, 173
Way, I., 233
Weaver, G. E., 280
Wechsler, H., 209, 214
Wedding, D., 43
Weekley, J. A., 417
Weems, C. F., 457, 497
Wehr, T. A., 489
Weidenhammer, W., 152
Weinberg, R. A., 312
Weinberger, D. R., 483
Weinstein, R. S., 40
Weishaar, M. E., 505
Weisskirch, R. S., 116
Weissman, A. M., 442
Weiten, W., 438
Weitkunat, R., 457
Weitzman, E. R., 452
Weizman, A., 209
Wells, D. L., 81, 175, 176, 276
Welsh, D. P., 359
Weltzin, T. E., 353
Wenckstern, S., 503, 504
Wernet, S. P., 576
Wertenbroch, K., 8
Wertheimer, M., 254

Wesensten, N. J., 209
Wessel, I., 282
West, A. N., 177
West, R., 211
West, T. G., 316
Westen, D., 533
Westrin, Å., 489
Wethington, E., 122
Wetter, D. W., 211
Wexler, M. N., 566
Whishaw, I.Q., 75
Whitaker, B. G., 45
White, G. L., 196
White, J., 309, 313
White, N. S., 63
Whitehouse, A. J. O., 276
Whiteman, M. C., 388, 391
Whitley, B. E., 574
Whitman, L. G., 199
Whitton, E., 514
Whyte, G., 559
Widener, A. J., 283
Widiger, T. A., 500
Widner, R. L., Jr., 275
Wiederhold, B. K., 232, 517, 521
Wiederhold, M. D., 232, 521
Wiederman, M. W., 356
Wiese, M., 307, 330, 332
Wiesel, W. N., 133, 134
Wiggins, E., 555
Wilber, M. K., 528
Wilder, D. A., 573, 575
Wilding, J., 289
Wilkie, D. M., 245
Wilkinson, D., 255
Wilkinson, M., 196
Willander, J., 273
Willer, J.-C., 149
Williams, D., 544
Williams, G., 348, 349
Williams, J. M., 317
Williams, M., 502
Williams, R. B., 158
Williams, R. L., 5, 541
Williamson, D. A., 349
Willott, J. F., 144
Willoughby, T., 9, 269, 296
Wilson, B. S., 144
Wilson, D. B., 531
Wilson, D. W., 583
Wilson, G. L., 333
Wilson, M. A., 361
Wilson, S. L., 92, 100
Wilson, T. D., 563
Wing, R. R., 351
Winger, G., 205
Wingood, G. M., 256
Winkelman, S. E., 275
Winner, E., 307, 332, 336
Winstead, B. A., 422, 488
Wirth, M. M., 77
Wise, R. A., 175
Wiseman, R., 171, 173, 174
Witelson, S. F., 65, 66
Witherington, D. C., 160, 161
Withers, N. W., 208
Wixted, J. T., 283, 285
Wolf, W., 313
Wolfe, J. B., 240
Wolpe, J., 542
Wolpin, M., 221
Wong, A. M., 61
Wong, F. Y., 530
Wood, E., 9
Wood, J. M., 173, 421
Woodhill, B. M., 406
Woodhouse, R. A., 290

Woodman, G. F., 285
Woods, S., 555
Woods, S. C., 348, 350
Woodworth, G. G., 144
Worthen, J. B., 295
Wraga, M., 315
Wright, D. B., 282
Wright, H., 77
Wright, J., 199
Wright, J. P., 478
Wright, K. P., Jr., 185, 346
Wu, C. W. H., 152
Wuethrich, B., 214
Wulf, G., 241
Wyatt, J. W., 412
Wynne, C. D. L., 42

Yahnke, B. H., 521
Yanchar, S. C., 242
Yang, B., 502
Yang, Y., 344
Yarber, W. L., 435
Yarmey, A. D., 175
Yates, W. R., 491
Yeh, C. J., 455
Yip, P. S. F., 503
Yokota, F., 255
Yonas, A., 161
Yoshida, M., 63
Yost, W. A., 142
Young, R., 308
Young, R. K., 551

Young, S. M., 498
Youngren, V. R., 512
Ysseldyke, J., 41
Yu, K. S., 245
Yu, S. L., 7
Yuille, J. C., 175
Yurgelun-Todd, D., 216

Zadra, A., 193, 196, 220
Zanna, M. P., 568, 569, 576, 577
Zarcadoolas, C., 431, 432
Zatorre, R. J., 75
Zautra, A. J., 455
Zechmeister, E. B., 293
Zeldow, P. B., 406

Zemishlany, Z., 209
Zentall, T. R., 245
Zhang, R. L., 61
Zhang, Z. G., 61
Zhou, M., 491
Zigler, E., 502
Zimbardo, P., 564
Zimbardo, P. G., 414, 423
Zoellner, L. A., 283
Zola, S. M., 285, 287
Zubrod, L. A., 122
Zucker, K. J., 475
Zuckerman, M., 361
Zusman, M. E., 359, 434
Zuwerink, J. R., 587

AA. *See* Alcoholics Anonymous
Ablation, 63
Abuse, drug, 203–218. *See also* Drug abuse
Acceptance, uncritical, 21
Accessibility in memory, 281
Accommodation, 108
  visual, 135
Acculturative stress, 455
Acetylcholine, curare blocking, 57
Achievement, need for, 363–364
Acquired immunodeficiency disease, 434–435
Acquired strategy, 325–326
Acquisition, 229–230
Action potential, 53
  neurotransmitters and, 56
Activation-synthesis hypothesis, 195
Active listening, 533
Actor-observer bias, 557
Acuity, visual, 137–138
Acupuncture, 152
Acute stress disorder, 493–494
Adaptation
  dark, 140–141
  sensory, 150–151
Adaptive behavior, 368–369
Addiction
  nicotine, 210
  to tranquilizers, 212
Addictive drug, brain effects of, 204
Adjustment disorder, 490–491
Adolescence, 90
  development in, 115–117
  Erikson's psychosocial tasks in, 121
Adolescent
  disorders diagnosed in, 476
  drug abuse in, 204
Adrenal gland, 78
Adulthood, 90
  Erikson's psychosocial tasks in, 121–123
  transition to, 117
Affectional need, 101
Affiliation, 550–552
African-American
  IQ scores of, 312–313
  prejudice against, 575
African-American parent, 103
Afterimage, 138
After-potential, negative, 55
Age
  chronological, 304
  sleep and, 185
  suicide and, 502
Age regression, 199
Ageism, 123
Aggression, 442, 579–583
  assertiveness vs., 567
  aversive stimulus and, 580–581
  biological factors in, 580
  displaced, 573
  frustration with, 580–582
  instinct and, 579–580
  prevention of, 582–583

punishment and, 249
  televised, 255–257
Aging, 121–123
Agnosia, visual or facial, 71
Agoraphobia, 491–492
AI. *See* Artificial intelligence
Aid, learning, 241–242
Alarm reaction, 437
Alcohol
  abuse of, 213–215
  aversion therapy for, 519
  brain effects of, 204
  comparison with other drugs, 206–207
  fetal effects of, 91
  health and, 431
  suicide and, 503
Alcoholics Anonymous (AA), 215
Alexithymia, 343
Algorithm, 324
All-or-nothing event, 55
All-or-nothing thinking, 526
Alpha wave, 186
Altered state of consciousness (ASC), 183
Alternate response, 259
Alzheimer's disease, 479
Ambivalent attachment, 100
American Psychological Association
  database of, 11
  website of, 12
American Sign Language (ASL), 321
Ames room, 154, 155
Amnesia
  antegrade, 284–285
  dissociative, 494
  retrograde, 284
Amok, 474
Amphetamine
  abuse of, 206–208
  cocaine vs., 208
  comparison with other drugs, 206–207
Amplitude, 142
Amygdala, 75
  emotion and, 370
Amytal, false memory and, 284
Anabolic steroid, 78
Anal stage of development, 396, 399
Anal-expulsive personality, 396
Analogy, creativity and, 338
Anal-retentive personality, 396
Analysis, sensory, 133
Androgen, 77, 78, 355
Androgyny, 405
Anesthesia, glove, 495
Angel dust, 216
Anhedonia, 208
Animal
  language of, 322–323
  naturalistic observation of, 41
  psychology and, 17
Anorexia nervosa, 352–354
ANS. *See* Autonomic nervous system
Antecedent, 226
Anthropomorphic error, 42
Antidepressant, 535

Antipsychotic, 535
Antismoking program, 431–432
Antisocial personality, 498–499
Anxiety. *See also* Anxiety disorder
  definition of, 447
  desensitization for, 520–522
  moral, 396, 398
  neurotic, 396, 398
  separation, 99
  social, 422–424
  test, 362
Anxiety disorder, 473, 490–497
  adjustment disorder and, 490–491
  behavioral theories of, 497
  cognitive theories of, 497
  dissociative, 494
  humanistic-existential theories of, 496–497
  obsessive-compulsive, 493
  panic disorder as, 491–492
  phobic, 492–493
  psychodynamic theories of, 496
  somatoform, 494–496
  stress disorder as, 493–494
  theories of, 496–497
Anxiety reduction hypothesis, 497
Anxiolytic, 535
APA website, 12
Apathy, bystander, 585–586
Aphasia, 69
Aplysia, 287
Apnea, sleep, 193
Apparent-distance hypothesis, 165
Appraisal
  emotional, 378
  of threat, 439–440
Approach-approach conflict, 443–444
Arab-American parent, 103
Arc, reflex, 60
Arousal
  empathic, 585
  levels of, 362
  stress-based, 461
Arousal theory, 361
Artificial hearing, 144
Artificial intelligence (AI), 305–306
ASC. *See* Altered state of consciousness
Asch experiment, 559
ASL. *See* American Sign Language
Assertiveness training, 566–567
Assessment, personality, 415–421
Assimilation, 108
Association, mental health, 543
Association area of cortex, 69
Associative learning, 226
Astigmatism, 136
Astrology, 20–21
Attachment, emotional, 99–100
Attention, selective, 151
Attitude, 568–571
  behavior and, 569–570
  formation of, 569
  persuasion and, 570–571
Attraction, 550–552

Attractiveness, physical, 551
Attribution, 377–378, 557
Auditory area, primary, 71
Authenticity, 515
Authoritarian belief, 574
Authoritarian parent, 101
Authoritative parent, 101–102
Autonomic nervous system (ANS), 59
  emotion and, 370–372, 380
Autonomy vs. shame and doubt, 120
Availability, memory and, 281
Aversion therapy, 519–520
Aversive imagery, 540
Aversive stimulus, 580–581
Avoidance learning, 249
Avoidance-avoidance conflict, 444–445
Avoidant attachment, 100
Avoidant personality disorder, 498
Awareness
  consciousness and, 183
  in Gestalt therapy, 515–516
  levels of, 398
Awareness training, group, 530–531
Axon, 53, 54
  action potential and, 55
Axon terminal, 53, 54

Bad habit, breaking of, 259–260
Barbiturate, 212
  comparison with other drugs, 206–207
  insomnia and, 191
Barnum effect, 22
Barrier to problem solving, 328
Base rate, 334
Basic needs, 366
Basic suggestion effect, 198
Behavior
  adaptive, 368–369
  attitudes and, 569–570
  brain and, 52–86. *See also* Brain
  in childhood, 404
  critical thinking about, 19–20
  endocrine system and, 76–78
  expressive, 405
  health-promoting, 431
  helping, 533
  insomnia and, 192
  instrumental, 405
  maladaptive, 471–472
  naturalistic observation of, 41
  personality and, 402
  in personality development, 403–404
  prosocial, 583–586
  sexual, 355–358
  social, 549–592. *See also* Social behavior
  study of, 15
  superstitious, 236
Behavior disorder, REM, 189
Behavior modification, 518–522
  for stress, 463
Behavior therapy, 518–522
  aversion, 519–520
  desensitization as, 520–522
  self-management using, 539–542

Behavioral assessment, 417
Behavioral contract, 260
Behavioral dieting, 351
Behavioral genetics, 412
Behavioral medicine, 429
Behavioral personality theory, 391, 401
Behavioral risk factor, 429–433
    for HIV/AIDS, 435–436
Behavioral self-management, 258–260
Behavioral signs of stress, 437
Behavioral statistics, 593–603
    correlational, 599–603
    descriptive, 594–598
Behavioral theory, of anxiety disorder, 497
Behaviorism
    practitioners of, 27
    view of, 30
Behavioristic theory
    comparison of, 414
    of personality, 391, 401
Belief
    attitudes and, 569–571
    authoritarian, 574
    just-world, 587
    in rational-emotive behavior therapy,
        527–528
Benzodiazepine
    abuse of, 212–213
    comparison with other drugs, 206–207
Bertinelli, Valerie, 352
Beta wave, 186
Bias
    actor-observer, 557
    gender, 500
    observer, 41
    in research experiment, 39–40
Bilingualism, 320
Binge drinking, 214
Binocular depth cues, 161–162
Biochemical abnormality, in
        schizophrenia, 483–484, 496
Biofeedback, 456–457
Biological factors in aggression, 580
Biological factors in psychological
        disorder, 475
Biological motivation, 345–360
    circadian rhythms and, 345–346
    homeostasis and, 345
    hunger as, 347–354
    pain as, 354–355
    sex as, 355–360
    thirst as, 354
Biological perspective, 30, 31
Biological predisposition, 391
Biological predisposition for language, 105
Biological rhythm, 184
Biopsychologist, 17
Biopsychology, 30, 34
Bipolar disorder, 487
Bisexual, 358
Blind spot, 136–137
Blindness
    color, 139–140
    inattentional, 151
Body language, 376
Body temperature, ecstasy abuse and, 209
Bonding with infant, 91–92
Borderline personality disorder, 498
Bottom-up processing, 155
Brain, 53, 61–62
    cerebral cortex of, 65–72
    in conditioned emotional response, 232
    CT scanning of, 61–62
    direct stimulation of, 239
    emotion and, 369–370
    forebrain of, 74
    gender differences in, 72

growth of, 112
handedness and, 80–81
hindbrain of, 73
hunger and, 347–349
lead poisoning and, 478
limbic system of, 74–75
localizing function of, 62–63
main structures illustrated, 73
memory and, 284–287
MRI scanning of, 62
nervous system and, 58–61
neurons and, 53–58
neuroplasticity of, 58
of newborn, 90
plasticity of, 90
repair of, 60–61
in schizophrenia, 483–484, 485
"split," 67–68
subcortex of, 73–75
Brain damage
    to cerebral hemispheres, 66–67
    lateralization and, 83
    to limbic system, 75
    to occipital lobe, 71
    split-brain operation and, 67
    to temporal lobe, 71
Brain wave, 186–187
Brainstem, 73
Brainstorming, 336–339
Brainwashing, 564–565
Brief psychodynamic therapy, 513
Brightness constancy, 159
Broca's area, 69
Bulimia nervosa, 352–354
Burnout, 439
Bystander effect, 583–584

Caffeine, 209–210
    comparison with other drugs, 206–207
Caffeinism, 210
CAI. See Computer-assisted instruction
Cannon-Bard theory of emotion, 377
Cardiac personality, 457–458
Cardinal trait, 392
Case study, 43–44
Casier, Rodger, 536
Casual sex, 359
    sexually transmitted disease and, 435
Catatonic schizophrenia, 481–482
Causation, 602
    correlation and, 43, 602
Cell
    brain, 61
    effector, 60
    hair, 142
CengageNOW, 11
Central nervous system (CNS), 58–61
    spinal cord and, 59–60
Central tendency, 594–595
Central trait, 392
Cephalocaudal development, 96–97
Cerebellum, function of, 74
Cerebral cortex, 65–72
    frontal lobe of, 69–70
    hemispheres of, 66–68
    memory and, 286–287
    occipital lobe of, 71–72
    parietal lobe of, 70–71
    size of, 65–66
    temporal lobe of, 71
Cerebral hemisphere, 66–68
Chaining, response, 236
Chance, extrasensory perception and, 173
Chance conditioning, 569
Channel, ion, 55
Character, 388
Charles Bonnet syndrome, 156

Chemotherapy, 229
Child
    critical situations of, 404
    disorders diagnosed in, 476
    Erikson's psychosocial tasks and,
        120–121
    media violence and, 581–582
    mentally gifted, 306–308
    sleep and, 185
Child-rearing. See Parenting
Chimp language, 322–323
Chromosome, 88
Chronological age, 304
Cigarette smoking, 210
    aversion therapy for, 519
Circadian rhythm, 345–346
Clairvoyance, 171
Classical conditioning, 231–233
    operant conditioning vs., 234
Cleanliness training, 404
Client-centered therapy, 514–515
Clinical case study of brain function, 62
Clinical method, 43–44, 45
Clinical psychologist, 34
CNS. See Central nervous system
Cocaine, 208–209
Cochlea, 142
Codeine, 206–207
Coding, sensory, 134
Coefficient, correlation, 42, 600–602
Coercion, 564–565
Cognition
    artificial intelligence and, 306
    basic units of thought, 314–315
    experiential, 2
    hot, 334
    by infant, 94–96
    language and, 319–320
    reflective, 2
Cognitive development, 108–114
    Piaget's theory of, 108–112
    Vygotsky's theory of, 113–114
Cognitive disorder, 476
Cognitive dissonance theory, 571
Cognitive interview
    to aid recall, 292
    for obtaining information, 272
Cognitive learning, 226, 252–254
Cognitive map, 252
Cognitive perspective, 30
Cognitive psychologist, 16, 34
Cognitive theory
    of anxiety disorder, 497
    of emotion, 377–378
Cognitive therapy, 526–528
    for depression, 526–527
    rational-emotive behavior, 527–528
Cohesion, 556
College Life Stress Inventory, 460–461
Color, 135
Color blindness, 139–140
Color vision, 138–140
Color weakness, 139–140
Commitment, 552
Common trait, 392
Communication
    early, 106
    in effective parenting, 127–128
Community health campaign, 433
Community mental health center, 538, 543
Community psychologist, 34
Comorbidity, 495
Comparative psychologist, 16, 34
Comparison
    selective, 327
    social, 550
Compensation, 447

Competence, 551
Competition, social, 588
Compliance, 561
Compulsive abuse, 208
Compulsive disorder, 493
Computed tomography (CT), 62
Computer, artificial intelligence and,
        305–306
Computer simulation, 306
Computer-assisted instruction (CAI), 242
Concentrative meditation, 201
Concept, 315
    faulty, 318
    formation of, 317
    Freudian, 396–400
    types of, 317–319
Conceptual rule, 317
Concrete operational stage, 110, 111
Condensation, 219
Conditioned response, 229
    emotional, 232
Conditioned stimulus, 229
Conditioning, 225–251
    change, 569
    classical, 231–233
    counter-, 250
    higher order, 229–230
    operant, 234–246. See also Operant
        conditioning
    partial reinforcement and, 243–246
    punishment in, 248–251
    stimulus control in, 246–247
    vicarious, 233
Conditions of worth, 411
Conduction, saltatory, 56
Conductive hearing loss, 143
Cone, 136–138
    color vision and, 137–139
    dark adaptation and, 140–141
Confidentiality, 535
Conflict
    approach-approach, 443–444
    avoidance-avoidance, 444–445
    Electra, 396, 399
    management of, 445–446
    Oedipus, 396, 399
Conformity, 558–560
Confrontation in existential therapy, 515
Congenital problem, 91
Conjunctive concept, 317
Connector neuron, 60
Connotative meaning, 318
Conscience, 117–118
    in Freudian psychology, 396, 397
Consciousness
    culture and, 184
    drug-altered, 203–218. See also Drug
        abuse
    hypnosis, 197–200
    meditation, 200–201
    positive psychology, 202
    sensory deprivation, 202
    sleep and, 183–196. See also Sleep
Consequences
    in discipline, 127–128
    in learning, 226
Conservation, 110
Consistency
    in discipline, 125
    personality traits and, 413–414
Consolidation, 285
Constancy, perceptual, 158–159
Constructive processing, 270–271
Consumer psychologist, 34
Consummate love, 553
Context, situational, 471
Contingency, 235

Contract, behavioral, 260
Control, 18
    stimulus, 524
Control group, 37
Conventional moral reasoning, 118
Convergence, 161–162
Convergent thinking, 329
Conversation, shyness and, 424
Conversion, cult and, 566
Conversion disorder, 494–495
Coping
    with frustration, 443
    with threat, 440
    with traumatic stress, 441
Coping statement, 464–465
Cornea, 135
Corpus callosum, 66
Correlation, 599–602
    causation and, 43
Correlation coefficient, 600–602
Correlational method, 45
Correlational statistics, 599–602
Correlational study, 42
Cortex, cerebral, 65–72
Corticalization, 66
Cost, response, 238
Counseling psychologist, 34
Counseling skills, 533–535
Counselor, 35
    peer, 544
Counter-conditioning, 250
Counterirritation, 152
Covert sensitization, 540, 541
Crawling, 96–97
Creative personality, 332
Creative thinking, 329–332
Creativity
    brainstorming and, 336–339
    dreams and, 220
    intrinsic motivation and, 367–368
    stages of, 330–332
    tests of, 330
Crimes by mentally ill, 482
Crisis, midlife, 122
Crisis hotline, 543
Crisis intervention, 538
Critical situation, 404
Critical thinking, 2, 19–20
CT. See Computed tomography
Cue
    to break bad habit, 260
    eating, 350
    memory, 291
Cue-dependent forgetting, 281
Cult, 565
Cultural barrier, 328
Cultural psychologist, 17, 34
Cultural relativity, 32, 471
Culturally skilled therapist, 534
Culture
    emotional expression and, 375
    ethnicity and identity, 116
    intelligence and, 309–310
    obesity and, 350
    parenting and, 102–103
    self-esteem and, 390
    therapy and, 534
Culture-bound syndrome, 474
Culture-fair test, 310
Curare, acetylcholine and, 57
Curve
    of forgetting, 278–279
    normal, 597, 598

Dark adaptation, 140–141
Database, PsychINFO, 11
Date rape drug, 212

Day care, effects of, 100–101
Daytime sleepiness, excessive, 184
Death, ecstasy abuse and, 209
Death instinct, 397
Decay, memory, 280–281
Declarative memory, 273
Deductive thought, 329
Deep lesioning, 63
Deep relaxation, 200–201
    in desensitization, 520
Deep sleep, 187
Definition, operational, 24
Deinstitutionalization, 538
Delta wave, 187
Delusional disorder, 477–478
    examples of, 476
    types of, 479–480
Dement, William, 196
Dementia, 478–479
Demonology, 511
Dendrite, 53, 54
    in newborn, 90
Denial, 447
Denotative meaning, 318
Deoxyribonucleic acid, 88, 89
Dependence
    drug, 205
    marijuana, 216
    psychological, 205
Dependent personality, 399, 498
Dependent variable, 37
Depressant, 211–215
    alcohol as, 213–215
    barbiturate, 212
    definition, 203
    tranquilizers as, 212–213
Depression
    cognitive therapy for, 526–527
    coping with, 452–453
    gender and, 488
    learned helplessness and, 451–453
    recognition of, 452
Depressive disorder, 487–489
Deprivation
    development and, 92
    sleep, 184
Depth perception, 160–167
    binocular cues of, 161–162
    monocular cues of, 162–165
    moon illusion and, 165–166
Description, 17
Descriptive statistics, 594–598
Desensitization
    eye movement, 522
    for phobia, 232
    self-directed, 541
    systematic, 520
    vicarious, 521
Determinant, situational, 401–402
Detoxification, 215
Development
    adolescent, 115–117
    cognitive, 108–114. See also Cognitive development
    environmental influences on, 90–93
    Erikson's psychosocial theory of, 119–121
    heredity and, 88–90
    of language, 104–106
    moral, 117–118
    of newborn, 93–98
    parental influences on, 101–104
    Piaget's theory of, 108–113
    social, 99–101
    transition to adulthood, 117
    Vygotsky's theory of, 113–114
Developmental level, 93

Developmental psychologist, 34
Developmental psychology, 88
Developmental tasks, Erikson's, 119–121
Deviation, standard, 596–597
Deviation IQs, 305
De-victimization, 585–586
Dhat, 474
Diagnostic and Statistical Manual of
    Mental Disorders, 472
    categories in, 476
    disorders added and dropped,
        474–475
Diagram, scatter, 599
Diet, health and, 431
Diet diary, 351
Dieting, 350–352
Differences, significant, 603
Digital media, 10–12
Digit-span test, 268
Direct brain stimulation, 239
Direct observation, 416
Directive vs. nondirective therapy, 510
Disability, intellectual, 308–309
Discipline, 125–127
Discovery learning, 252–254
Discrimination, 231, 573
    operant stimulus, 246–247
Disease-prone personality, 430
Dishabituation, 177
Disintegration, personality, 478
Disjunctive concept, 318
Disorganized schizophrenia, 481
Displaced aggression, 442, 573
Displacement, 219
Dissociative amnesia, 494
Dissociative disorder, 474
    identity, 494
Dissociative fugue, 494
Dissociative identity disorder, 494
Disuse, forgetting and, 281
Divergent thinking, 329
Diversity, 29, 586–589
    broad view of, 32
DNA, 88, 89
Dominance, brain, 80–81
Dominant gene, 89
Door-in-the-face effect, 561
Dopamine
    psychoactive drug effects and, 204
    in schizophrenia, 483–484, 486
Double-blind experiment, 38–40
Doubt, autonomy vs., 120
Downers, 211–215. See also Depressant
Dream, 194–196, 218–221
    analysis of, 512
    REM sleep and, 188–189, 194
    remembering, 218–219
    theories about, 194–195
Dream processes, 219
Dream symbol, 195, 512
Drinking, 214–215. See also Alcohol
Drive, episodic, 354
Drug
    neurotransmitters and, 56–57
    teratogenic, 91
Drug abuse
    of alcohol, 213–215
    brain affected by, 204
    comparison of drugs, 206–207
    dependence and, 205
    of hallucinogens, 215–217
    insomnia and, 191
    patterns of, 205
    polydrug, 205
    prevalence of, 203–204
    of sedatives, 211–212
    of stimulants, 206–211

suicide and, 503
    of tranquilizers, 212–213
Drug interaction, 205
Drug therapy, 535–536
Drug tolerance, 205
DSM-IV TR, categories in, 472
Dual process hypothesis of sleep, 187–189
Duck therapy, 509
Dwarfism, 77
Dysthymic disorder, 487

Ear
    hearing and, 142–145
    vestibular system and, 149–150
Early childhood, 90
Eating disorder, 352–354
Ebbinghaus curve, 278–279
Economy, token, 525–526
Ecstasy
    abuse of, 209
    comparison with other drugs, 206–207
ECT. See Electroconvulsive therapy
Education, bilingual, 320
Educational stimulation, 242
EEG. See Electroencephalography
Effective parenting, 124–128
Effector cell, 60
Ego, 396, 397
Ego ideal, 396
Egocentric thought, 109
Ego-defense mechanism, 398
Eidetic imagery, 288
Einstein, Albert, 66
Elaborative encoding, 269, 290
Electra conflict, 396
Electrical stimulation therapy, 536–537
Electroconvulsive therapy (ECT), 285, 536
Electrode
    in brain function study, 62
    implanted, 536–537
Electroencephalography (EEG), 63, 186
Electrostimulation of brain (ESB), 62
Elite performance, 364–365
Elliot, Jane, 576
Ellis, Albert, 527
Embryo, teratogens and, 91
EMDR. See Eye movement
    desensitization
Emergency, defining of, 584
Emotion, 368–383
    brain and, 369–370
    classical conditioning and, 231–233
    connotative meaning and, 318–319
    definition of, 368
    expression of, 374–376
    fight or flight response and, 371
    lie detectors and, 372–373
    memory and, 285–286
    model of, 380
    physiology and, 370
    self-control and, 381–383
    sudden death from, 372
    theories of, 376–380
Emotional appraisal, 378
Emotional attachment, 99
Emotional barrier, 328
Emotional development of infant, 97–98
Emotional eating, 350
Emotional expression, 369
Emotional feelings, 369
Emotional intelligence, 381–383
Emotional response
    conditioned, 232
    limbic system and, 75
Emotional signs of stress, 437
Emotion-focused coping, 440
Empathic arousal, 585

Empathy, 515
Empathy-helping relationship, 585
Empirical evidence, 15
Encoding
    elaborative, 269, 290
    failure of, 279
    of information, 265
    selective, 327
    of short-term memories, 266
Encounter group, 530–531
Endocrine system, 76–78
    in puberty, 115
Endogenous depression, 488
Engineering psychologist, 34
Enrichment of environment, 92
Environment
    in development, 90–93
    intelligence and, 312
    schizophrenia and, 482–483
Environmental psychologist, 34
Epinephrine, 78
Episodic drive, 354
Episodic memory, 274
Equal-status contact, 576
Ergotism, 511
Erikson's psychosocial theory, 119–121
Erogenous zone
    in Freudian theory, 396, 398
    sexual response and, 355–356
Eron, Leonard, 582
Eros, 396, 397
Erotomanic delusional disorder, 479
Error
    anthropomorphic, 42
    fundamental attribution, 557
ESB. See Electrostimulation of brain
Escape from frustration, 442
Escape learning, 249
ESP. See Extrasensory perception
Essay test, 9–10
Estrogen, 355
Estrus, 355
Ethnic differences. See Culture
Ethnicity, identity and, 116
Ethnocentrism, 574
European-American
    IQ scores of, 312–313
    preference in hiring, 575
Evidence gathering, 24
Evolutionary psychology, 17, 553
Excellence, pursuit of, 363–365
Exceptional memory, 287–288
Excessive daytime sleepiness, 184
Excitement phase of sexual response, 357
Exercise
    eating disorder and, 353
    health and, 431
    for insomnia, 192
    for stress, 461–462
Exhaustion, 437
Existential therapy, 515
Existentialism, 496–497
Expectancy, 230, 402–403
    in classical vs. operant conditioning, 234
    perceptual, 168
Experiential cognition, 2
Experiment, 36–40
    Asch, 559
    double-blind, 38–40
    Milgram's obedience, 562–564
    Pavlov's, 228
    in prejudice, 576–578
    single-blind, 39
    variables and groups in, 37–38
Experimental control, 37, 38
Experimental group, 37
Experimental method, 41, 45

Expert, 325–326
Expert system, 306
Explicit memory, 277
Expression of emotion, 369, 374–376
Expressive behavior, 405
External eating cue, 350
Extinction, 230, 523, 524
    of bad habit, 259
    operant, 237
Extracellular thirst, 354
Extraneous variable, 37
Extrasensory perception (ESP), 171–174
Extrinsic motivation, 366–367
Extrovert, 389
Eye, structure of, 135–136
Eye color, 89–90
Eye movement desensitization (EMDR), 522
Eyewitness
    cognitive interview of, 272
    false identification by, 276
    testimony by, 175–178
Eysenck, Hans, 513

Face, infant and, 95–96
Facial agnosia, 71
Facial expression, 374–375
Facial feedback hypothesis, 379–380
Factual information, memory of, 273
Failure, encoding, 279
Fallacy
    gambler's, 528
    of positive instances, 22
False identification, 276
False memory, 272
    recovered memory as, 284
Family factors in psychological disorder, 475
Family therapy, 530
Fantasy as defense mechanism, 447
Fat point of brain, 349
Father, influence of, 102
Faulty concept, 318
Fear
    desensitization for, 520–522
    learned, 232
    limbic system and, 75
Feature detector, 133
Feedback
    facial, 379–380
    as operant reinforcer, 241–242
Feelings, emotional, 369
Female
    emotional expression and, 375–376
    puberty and, 115
Female sexual response, 357–358
Feminine personality
    gender bias and, 500
    traits of, 404–406
Fetal alcohol syndrome, 91
Fetal damage, intellectual disability and, 309
Fetus, teratogens and, 91
FI schedule. See Fixed interval schedule
Fight or flight response, 371
Figure-ground organization, 156–158
Fitness, eating disorder and, 353
Five-factor model of personality, 393–395
Fixation, 327–328
    in Freudian theory, 396, 398–399
Fixed interval (FI) schedule, 245
Fixed ratio (FR) schedule, 244
Fixedness, functional, 327
Flashbulb memory, 286
Flavor, taste and, 146
Flexibility, creativity and, 329
Fluency, creativity and, 329, 330

Fluid reasoning, 303
fMRI. See Functional magnetic resonance imaging
Focusing, visual, 135
Foot-in-the-door effect, 561
Forebrain, function of, 74
Forensic memory, 272
Forensic psychologist, 17, 34
Forgetting, 278–287
    cue-dependent, 281
    curve of, 278–279
Formal operations stage, 110–111
FR schedule. See Fixed ratio schedule
Framing, 334–335
Fraser's spiral, 155
Fraud, extrasensory perception and, 172–173
Free association, 512
Free will, 28
Frequency distribution, 594
Frequency polygon, 594
Frequency theory, 142
Freud, Sigmund, 28, 511
Freudian concepts, 396–400
Frontal lobe, 69
Frustration, 440–443
Frustration-aggression hypothesis, 580–582
Fugue, dissociative, 494
Functional fixedness, 327
Functional magnetic resonance imaging (fMRI), 64
Functional solution, 325
Functionalism, 26
Fundamental attribution error, 557

Gambler's fallacy, 528
Game, video
    effects of, 256–257
    IQ score and, 313
Gamma-hydroxybutyrate, 212
GAS. See General adaptation syndrome
Gate control theory, 152
Gating, sensory, 151–152
Gender
    brain specialization and, 72
    depression and, 488
    emotional expression and, 375–376
    personality and, 404–406
    suicide and, 502
Gender bias, 500
Gender identify disorder, 474
Gender psychologist, 17
Gene, 89
General adaptation syndrome (GAS), 437
General solution, 325
Generalization, stimulus, 230–231
    operant, 246
Generalized anxiety disorder, 491
Generativity, stagnation vs., 121
Genetic disorder, 91
    intellectual disability and, 308–309
Genetics, 88–89
    behavioral, 412
    depression and, 488
    handedness and, 81
    personality and, 411–413
    schizophrenia and, 483
    sexual orientation and, 358–359
Genital stage of development, 396, 399
Genovese, Kitty, 583
Gestalt organizing principles, 156–158
Gestalt psychology, 27–28
Gestural language, 321–322
g-factor, 302
GHB, 212
    comparison with other drugs, 206–207

Ghrelin, 348
Giftedness, 306–308
Gigantism, 77
Gland, 76–78
Glove anesthesia, 495
Glucagon-like peptide-1, 348
Goal
    definition of, 344
    superordinate, 576–577
Goal-setting, 8
Goodall, Jane, 41
Grammar, 320
Grandeur, delusions of, 478
Grandiose delusional disorder, 479
Graphical statistics, 594
Graphology, 20
Group
    conformity and, 560
    reference, 570
    self-help, 544
Group intelligence test, 305
Group prejudice, 573
Group structure, 556–557
Group therapy, 529–531
    individual therapy vs., 510
Groupthink, 559
Growth, sequence of, 90
Growth hormone, 77
Growth needs, 366
Guided imagery, 463
Guilt, initiative vs., 120
Gustation, 145

Habituation, 177
Hair cell, 142
Halfway house, 538
Hallucination, 154, 156
    hypnopompic, 189
    in psychotic disorder, 478
Hallucinogen, 215–217
Halo effect, 416
Handedness, 79–83
Happiness, 459
Hardy personality, 459
Health, stress affecting, 453–465
Health psychology, 429–433
Health-promoting behavior, 431
Hearing, 142–145
Helping behavior, 533
Helplessness, learned, 449–451
Hemisphere, cerebral, 66–68
Heredity. See Genetics
Heroin, 206–207
Heterosexual, casual sex and, 435
Heuristic, 325–326
    representativeness, 333
Hidden observer, 197
Hierarchy, 520
    construction of, 541–542
    of needs, 365–366
    use of, 542
Higher-order conditioning, 229–230
Hilgard, Ernest, 197
Hindbrain, 73
Hippocampus, 75
    memory and, 285
Hispanic parent, 103
Histogram, 594
Histrionic personality, 498
HIV/AIDS, 434–435
Homeostasis, 345
Homosexual, 358–359
Hope, learned helplessness and, 451
Hormone
    behavior and, 76–78
    emotions and, 369
    in puberty, 115

Hospitalization, 537
Hostility, prejudice and, 573
Hot cognition, 334
Hotline, crisis, 543
Hue, 135
Hughes, Howard, 493
Human development, 87–131. *See also*
    Development
Human sexual response, 356–358
Humanism, 28, 407
Humanistic perspective, 30
Humanistic psychology, 28–29
Humanistic theory, 407–411
    comparison of, 414
Humanistic therapy, 514–516
    client-centered, 514–515
    existential, 515
    Gestalt, 515–516
Humanistic-existential approach to
    anxiety disorder, 496–497
Hunger, 347–354
    dieting and, 350–352
    eating disorders, 352–354
    external factors in, 349–350
    internal factors in, 347–349
    memory and, 293
Hyperopia, 136
Hypersomnia, 184
Hyperthermia, ecstasy abuse and, 209
Hypnopompic hallucination, 189
Hypnosis
    reality theory of, 197–199
    stage, 199–200
Hypnotic susceptibility, 198–199
Hypochondriac, 456
Hypochondriasis, 494
Hypothalamus
    function of, 74
    hunger and, 348
Hypothesis
    activation-synthesis, 195
    anxiety reduction, 497
    apparent-distance, 165
    definition of, 23–24
    dual process, of sleep, 187–189
    facial feedback, 379–380
    frustration-aggression, 580–582
    perceptual, 157
Hysteria, 511

Iconic memory, 265–266
Id, 396, 397
Ideal self, 410
Identical twins
    schizophrenia in, 412
    studies using, 311–312
Identification
    as defense mechanism, 447
    false, 276
    gender, 404
Identity, search for, 116
Identity disorder, 474
    dissociative, 494
    role confusion vs., 121
Illness, stress and, 437–438
Illogical thought, 329
Illumination, creativity and, 331
Illusion, 154–155
    moon, 165–167
    Müller-Lyer, 166, 167
    3-D, 162
Image, 315
Imagery
    aversive, 540
    eidetic, 288
    guided, 463
    mental, 315–317

Imagery rehearsal, 193
I-message, 127
Imitation
    gender and, 404
    by infant, 94
    modeling and, 254–255
Immune system, stress and, 437–438
Implanted electrode, 536–537
Implicit memory, 277
Inattentional blindness, 151
Incentive value, 344–345
Incongruence, 409
Incongruent person, 409
Incubation, creativity and, 331, 337–338
Independent variable, 37
Individual vs. group therapy, 510
Individual trait, 392
Individuating information, 587
Inductive thought, 329
Industrial-organizational psychologist, 34
Industry vs. inferiority, 120–121
Inequality, status, 576
Infancy, 90
Infant
    attachment and, 99–100
    cognitive development of, 108, 111–114
    day care for, 100–101
    Erikson's psychosocial tasks and, 120
    language development in, 104–107
    motor development of, 96–97
    parental influences on, 101–104
    perceptual and cognitive development
        of, 94–96
    social development of, 99–101
    sudden death syndrome, 193–194
    temperament of, 93
Inferential statistics, 594, 602–603
Inferiority vs. industry, 120–121
Influence, delusions of, 478
Information
    in operant conditioning, 235
    recalling of, 275
    recognition of, 275–276
    relearning of, 276–277
Information bits or chunks, 268–269
Informational view, 230
In-group, 556
Inheritance. *See* Genetics
Inhibition, reciprocal, 520
Initiative vs. guilt, 120
Injury, spinal cord, 60
Insanity, legal definition of, 472
Insecure-ambivalent attachment, 100
Insecure-avoidant attachment, 100
Insight, 326–327
Insight vs. action therapy, 510
Insomnia, 190–192
Instinct, 579–580
Instruction, programmed, 242
Instrumental behavior, 405
Integrity, despair vs., 121
Intellectual disability, 308–309
Intellectualization, 447
Intelligence, 302–342
    artificial, 305–306
    culture and, 309–310
    defining of, 302
    emotional, 381–383
    environment and, 312
    giftedness and, 306–308
    intellectual disability and, 308–309
    measurement of, 302–303
    multiple, 310–311
    of neonate, 94
    performance, 304
    practical, 313
    race and, 312–313

testing of, 303–305
    verbal, 304
Intelligence quotient, 304–305
    disability and, 308–309
Intelligence test
    culture-fair, 310
    group, 305
    IQ and, 304–305
    of twins, 311–312
    Wechsler, 303–304
Interdependence, mutual, 578
Interference, memory and, 282–283
Internet survey, 44–45
Internet therapist, 517
Interpersonal attraction, 551
Interpersonal psychotherapy, 513
Intervention by bystanders, 583–584
Interview
    cognitive, 272, 292
    personality, 416
Intimacy, 552
    isolation vs., 121
Intracellular thirst, 354
Intracranial self-stimulation, 239
Intrinsic motivation, 366–367
Introspection, 26
Introvert, 389
Intuition, 332–335
Intuitive thought, 109
Ion channel, 55
Isolation as defense mechanism, 447
Izard, Carroll, 97

James, William, 26
James-Lange theory of emotion, 376–377
Jealous type delusional disorder, 480
Jet lag, 346
Jigsaw classroom, 578
Johnson, Virginia, 356–358
Just-world belief, 587

Kaczynski, Theodore, 482
Kanzi's lexigrams, 323
Keyword method, 295
Kinesics, 376
Kinesthetic imagery, 316–317
Kinesthetic sense, 148
Koresh, David, 565
Koro, 474

Labeling, psychiatric, 499–500
Language, 319–324
    acquisition of, 104–105
    age and, 105
    of animals, 322–323
    bilingualism, 320
    definition of, 315
    early communication and, 106
    gestural, 321–322
    parentese, 107
    roots of, 105–106
    structure of, 320–321
Large-group awareness training, 530
Latency in Freudian theory, 396, 399
Latent dream content, 512
Latent learning, 252
Lateral hypothalamus, 348
Lateralization, 83
Law
    of effect, 234
    Yerkes-Dodson, 362
Lazarus, Richard, 378
Lead poisoning, 478
Learned barrier, 328
Learned fear, 232
Learned helplessness, 449–451
Learned motive, 345, 363–365

Learning. *See also* Conditioning
    avoidance, 249
    in behavior therapy, 518–522
    in classical vs. operant conditioning,
        234
    cognitive, 252–254
    conservation and, 241
    escape, 249
    perceptual, 169–171
    self-reflective, 1-3
    social, 581
    state-dependent, 281–282
    types of, 226–227
Learning aid, 241–242
Learning psychologist, 34
Learning theorist, 16
Learning theory of personality, 401–406
Left brain, 67–68
Left-handedness, 79–83
Lens, 135
Leptin, 349
Lesbian, 358–359
Lexigram, Kanzi's, 323
Libido, 396, 397
Lie detector, 372–373
Life event, stress of, 453–454
Life instinct, 397
Life skills training, 432–433
Lifestyle, health and, 430–431
Lifestyle disease, 429–433
Light, wavelength of, 135
Light sleep, 186
Limbic system, 74–75
Linear perspective, 163
Lineup, false identification in, 276
LISAN, 4–5
Listening, 533
Lobes of cerebral cortex, 69–71
Localization
    of brain function, 62
    sensory, 134
Lock and key theory of olfaction, 145
Logical consequences, 127–128
Logical thought, 329
Long-term memory
    brain and, 286–287
    constructive processing of, 270–271
    definition of, 266–267
    forgetting in, 278–287
    organization of, 271–273
    short-term memory and, 267
    types of, 273–274
Love, 552
    triangular theory of, 552–553
    withdrawal of, 125
Low-ball technique, 562
Lucid dreaming, 220–221
Lysergic acid diethylamide, 215–216
    comparison with other drugs, 206–207

Magnetic resonance imaging, 62
Maintenance rehearsal, 269
Major depressive disorder, 487
Major mood disorder, 487
Maladaptive behavior, 471–472
Maladaptive personality pattern, 498
Male
    eating disorder in, 353
    emotional expression and, 375–376
    personality traits of, 404–406
    puberty and, 115
Male sexual response, 357–358
Management technique in discipline, 125
Manifest dream content, 512
Mantra, 201
Marijuana, 216–217
    comparison with other drugs, 206–207

Masculine personality, 404–406
Maslow, Abraham, 28, 407–409
Massed practice, 6, 291
Master gland, 77
Masters, William, 356–358
Mastery training, 451
Mate selection, 553–554
Maternal influences on parenting, 102
Maturation, 89
    sexual, 115
McGraw, Dr. Phil, 516–517
MDMA, abuse of, 209
    comparison with other drugs, 206–207
Mean, 595
Meaning
    connotative, 318–319
    denotative, 319
Mechanical solution, 324
Media
    attitudes and, 569
    digital, 10–12
    modeling and, 255–257
    psychology and, 46–48
    violence and, 581–582
Media guide, parent as, 582–583
Media psychologist, 516–517
Median, 595–596
Mediation, 200–201
Medical psychologist, 34
Medical therapy, 535–538
Meditation, 462
Medulla of brain, 73
Mehl, Mathias, 23–24
Melatonin, 77
Memory
    brain and, 285, 286–287
    definition of, 265
    emotion and, 285–286
    exceptional, 287–288
    explicit and implicit, 277
    false, 272
    hunger and, 293
    improvement of, 290–292
    long-term, 266–267, 269–274
    mnemonics for, 294–297
    of people, 279–280
    photographic, 287–289
    recovered, 284
    repression of, 283–284
    retrieval strategies in, 292–293
    sensory, 265–266
    short-term, 266–269
    sleep and, 293
    stages of, 265–267
    suppression of, 283–284
    working, 303
Memory cue, 291
Memory decay, 280–282
Memory jamming, 271
Memory traces, 280
Mental age, 304
Mental disorder, 471–475. See also
        Psychological disorder
Mental health, positive, 510
Mental health association, 543
Mental health center, community, 538,
        543
Mental hospitalization, 537
Mental image, 288–289
Mental imagery, 315–317
Mental retardation, 308–309
Mental set, 336
Mentally gifted, 306–308
Mercury poisoning, 478
Mescaline, 215–216
    comparison with other drugs, 206–207
Mesmer, Franz, 197

Meta-needs, 366
Methadone, 206–207
Methamphetamine, 207–208
Method
    research, 16
    scientific, 23–25
    study, 1–13
Methylenedioxymethamphetamine
    abuse of, 209
    compared with other drugs, 206–207
Microelectrode, 63
Microsleep, 185
Microstressor, 455
Middle childhood, 90
Midlife crisis, 122
Milestone, developmental, 119–121
Milgram, Stanley, 562–564
Mindblindness, 71
Mindfulness, 202
Mindfulness meditation, 201
Minnesota Multiphasic Personality
        Inventory, 418–420
Mirror technique, 530
Misattribution, 378
Misbehavior, punishment for, 250
Mistrust, 120
MMPI-2 profile, 419
Mnemonic, 6, 294–297
Mode, 596
Model
    of emotion, 380
    five-factor, of personality, 393–395
    of motivation, 344–345
    network, of memory, 272
    stress-vulnerability, 486
Modeling
    imitation in, 254–255
    media and, 255–257
Monocular depth cues, 162–165
Mood, definition of, 369
Mood disorder, 473, 487–490
    examples of, 476
Moon illusion, 165–167
Moral anxiety, 396, 398
Moral development, 117–118
Morpheme, 320
Morphine, 206–207
Mother, influence of, 102
Motherese, 107
Motion sickness, 150
Motivation, 343–368
    biological, 345–360. See also Biological
        motivation
    extrinsic and intrinsic, 366–367
    learned, 363–365
    Maslow's hierarchy of needs and,
        365–366
    model of, 344–345
    stimulus, 361–363
Motor area, primary, 69
Motor development, 96–97
Motor neuron, 60
Müller-Lyer illusion, 166, 167
Multiculturalism, 586–589
Multiple approach-avoidance conflict,
        445
Multiple intelligences, 310–311
Munchausen syndrome, 495
Munchausen syndrome by proxy, 495
Musical personality, 392
Mutual interdependence, 578
Myelin, 59
Myopia, 136
Myth about psychotherapy, 510

Narcissistic personality, 498
Natural consequences, 127

Natural selection, 26
Naturalistic observation, 41–42
    advantages and disadvantages of, 45
Nature vs. nurture, 88–93
Nausea
    chemotherapy and, 229
    sensory conflict and, 150
Need
    affectional, 101
    definition of, 344
    Maslow's hierarchy of, 365–366
    for power, 364
Negative after-potential, 55
Negative emotion, 382
Negative reinforcement, 238
Negative relationship, 600
Negative stereotype, 575
Neglect, spatial, 67
Neonatal period, 90; see also Newborn
Nerve
    optic, 136–137
    spinal, 59–60
Nerve impulse, 53, 55–56
Nervous breakdown, 490–491
Nervous system
    autonomic, 59, 370–372
    parts of, 58–61
    somatic, 59
Network, neural, 57–58
Network model of memory, 272
Neural network, 57–58
Neurilemma, 58
Neurocognitive dream theory, 195
Neurogenesis, 61
Neuron, 53–58
    connector, 60
    motor, 60
    nerve impulse and, 53, 55–56
    neural regulators and, 57
    neurotransmitters of, 56–57
    parts of, 53, 54
    synapses of, 56
Neuropeptide, function of, 57
Neuropeptide Y, 348
Neuroplasticity, 58
Neurosis, 475
Neurotic anxiety, 396, 398
Neurotransmitter
    function of, 56–57
    psychoactive drugs and, 204
Newborn. See also Infant
    brain of, 90
    emotional development of, 97–98
    perceptual and cognitive development
        of, 94–96
Nicotine, 210
    comparison with other drugs,
        206–207
Night terror, 193
Nightmare, 193
Noise-induced hearing loss, 144
Nonassertive behavior, 567
Nonconformity, social, 470–471
Nonexperimental research, 41–46
    clinical method of, 43–44
    correlational studies as, 42
    naturalistic observation as, 41–42
    survey method of, 44–45
Non–rapid eye movement sleep, 187
Nonreinforcement, 523, 524
Norepinephrine, 78
Norm, 556–557
    social, 32
Normal curve, 597, 598
Novice, 325–326
NREM sleep, 187
Nucleus, paraventricular, 348

Nucleus accumbens, 204
Nurture vs. nature, 88–93

Obama effect, 312–313
Obedience, 562–564
Obesity, 349–350
Object permanence stage of development,
        108
Objective test, 9
Observation
    naturalistic, 41–42, 45
    scientific, 15
    in scientific method, 23
Observational learning, 254
Observer, hidden, 197
Observer bias, 41
Observer effect, 41
Obsessive-compulsive disorder, 493, 498
Occipital lobe, 71
Odor, production of, 145–146
Oedipus conflict, 396, 399
Old age, 121–123
Olfaction, 145–147
Open-ended vs. time-limited therapy, 510
Operant conditioning, 234–246
    acquiring response, 234–235
    classical conditioning vs., 234
    definition of, 227
    extinction, 237
    negative reinforcement in, 238
    positive reinforcement in, 234
    punishment in, 238
    reinforcers in, 239–241
    shaping, 237
    timing of reinforcement, 235–236
Operant reinforcer, 234, 239–243
Operant stimulus discrimination,
        246–247
Operant stimulus generalization, 246
Operant therapy, 523–526
Operational definition, 24
Operational stage of development,
        110–111
Opponent-process theory, 138
Optic nerve, 136–137
Oral stage of development, 396, 399
Oral-aggressive personality, 396
Oral-dependent personality, 396
Organ of Corti, 142
Organic mental disorder, 473
Organismic valuing, 411
Organization
    figure-ground, 156–158
    in improving memory, 290
    of memories, 271–273
Organized knowledge, 325–326
Orgasm, 357
Orientation
    creativity and, 330–331
    sexual, 358–359
Originality, creativity and, 329
Otolith, 149
Out group, 556
Overgeneralization, 526
Overlearning, 6, 291
Overly permissive parent, 101

Pain, 148–149
    as biological motive, 354
    endorphins and, 57
Pain disorder, 494
Pain relief, hypnosis and, 199
Panic disorder, 491–492
Paradoxical intention, 192
Paralysis, sleep, 189
Paranoid personality disorder, 498
Paranoid psychosis, 480

Paranoid schizophrenia, 482
Paraprofessional, 538
Parasympathetic branch of nervous
    system, 59, 371
Parasympathetic rebound, 372
Paraventricular nucleus, 348
Parent
    Arab-American, 103
    as media guide, 582–583
Parentese, 107
Parenting
    effective, 124–128
    ethnic differences in, 102–103
    maternal and paternal influences on,
        102
    styles of, 101–102
Parietal lobe, function of, 70–71
Part learning, 290–291
Partial reinforcement, 243–246
Partial reinforcement effect, 243
Passion, 552
Paternal influences on parenting, 102
Pattern
    of personality, 394
    in problem-solving, 326
    sleep, 185–186
Pavlov, Ivan, 227
    experiment of, 228
PCP, 206–207
Peek, Kim, 308
Peer counselor, 544
Percent of variance, 600–601
Perception, 154–178
    bottom-up, 155
    constancies, 158–159
    definition of, 133
    depth, 160–167
    of emotion, 382
    extrasensory, 171–174
    Gestalt principles of, 156–158
    illusions and, 154–155
    by infant, 94–96
    selective, 526
    top-down, 155
Perceptual barrier, 328
Perceptual constancy, 158–159
Perceptual construction, 154
Perceptual expectancy, 168
Perceptual features, 133
Perceptual habit, 170
Perceptual hypothesis, 157
Perceptual learning, 169–171
Perfect negative relationship, 600
Perfect positive relationship, 600
Performance intelligence, 304
Peripheral nervous system (PNS),
    58–59
Peripheral vision, 138
Perls, Fritz, 516
Permanence of memory, 270
Permissive parent, 101
Persecutory delusional disorder,
    478, 480
Personal frustration, 442–443
Personal prejudice, 573
Personality, 387–427
    assessment of, 415–421
    behavior and, 402
    cardiac, 457–458
    creative, 332
    development, 398–400
    disease-prone, 430
    dynamics of, 397–398
    gender and, 404–406
    genetics and, 411–413
    hardy, 459
    humanistic view of, 410–411

key dimensions of, 393–395
learning theories of, 401–406
Maslow's self-actualization theory of,
    407–409
musical, 392
predicting behavior and, 392
prejudiced, 574
psychoanalytic theory of, 396–400
in Rogers' self theory, 409–410
self-concept of, 389–390
situations and, 413–414
theories of, 390–391, 414
type A, 457–458
type B, 457
types of, 389
Personality disintegration, 478
Personality disorder, 474
Personality profile, 21–22
Personality psychologist, 34
Personality questionnaire, 418–420
Personality test
    Minnesota Multiphasic Personality
        Inventory, 418–420
    projective, 420–421
Personality theorist, 16
Personality trait, 388–389
    classification of, 392–393
Person-centered therapy, 514–515
Perspective, linear, 163
Perspective disorder, 499–500
Persuasion, 570–571
PET. See Positron emission tomography
Phallic personality, 396
Phallic stage of development, 396, 399
Pharmacotherapy, 535
Phencyclidine, 215–216
Phenothiazine, 483
Phobia, 232, 492–493
    desensitization for, 520
Phoneme, 320
Phosphene, 134
Photographic memory, 287–289
Photoreceptor, 135
Phototherapy, 489
Physical attractiveness, 551
Physical dependence, 205
Physical signs of stress, 437
Piaget, Jean, 108–113
Pictorial depth cues, 162
Pigment, visual, 138
Pineal gland, 77
Pinel, Philippe, 511
Pitch of sound waves, 142
Pituitary gland, 77
Place theory, 142
Placebo effect, 39
    of therapy, 531
Plateau phase of sexual response, 357
Pleasure principle, 396, 397
PNS. See Peripheral nervous system
Poisoning
    ergot, 511
    lead or mercury, 478
Polydrug abuse, 205
Polygenic characteristics, 89
Polygraph, 372–373
Pons, 73
Population, 602
Position
    serial, 291
    sleep, SIDS and, 193–194
Positive emotion, 382–383
Positive psychology, 31, 202
Positive regard, unconditional, 515
Positive reinforcement, 238, 523
Positive relationship, 600
Positive self-regard, 411

Positron emission tomography (PET),
    63–64
Postconventional moral reasoning, 118
Post-traumatic stress disorder, 493–494
Potential
    action, 53, 55, 56
        negative after-potential, 55
        resting, 53
Poverty, development affected by, 92
Power, need for, 364
Practical intelligence, 313
Practice
    in improving memory, 291–292
    mass, 6
    retrieval, 292
    spaced, 6
Precognition, 171
Preconscious, 396, 398
Preconventional moral reasoning, 118
Prediction, 18
Predisposition, biological, 391
    for language, 105
Prefrontal area, 70
Prejudice, 573–578
    development of, 573
    experiments in, 575–578
    getting rid of, 586–588
    symbolic, 575
Prejudiced personality, 574
Premack, David, 322
Premack principle, 258–259
Premature puberty, 78
Prenatal period, 90
    environmental factors in, 91
Preoperational stage of development,
    109–110, 111
Preparation, creativity and, 330–331
Presbyopia, 136
Pressure, stress causing, 438–439
Prevention
    of aggression, 582–583
    of disease, 431–432
    of suicide, 503–504
Primary appraisal of threat, 439
Primary auditory area, 71
Primary emotion, 369
Primary motor area, 69
Primary reinforcer, 239
Primary somatosensory area, 70–71
Priming of memory, 277
Principle, Premack, 258–259
Private self-consciousness, 423
Proactive interference, 283
Problem-focused coping, 440
Problem-solving, 324–329
    barriers to, 328
    dreams and, 220
    heuristics and, 325–326
    insight and, 326–327
    mechanical solutions, 324–325
    understanding and, 325
Procedural memory, 273
Processing, constructive, 270–271
Procrastination, 7
Professional help, seeking of, 542–545
Profile
    MMPI-2, 419
    personality, 21–22
    trait, 393
Programmed instruction, 242
Progressive relaxation, 462
Projection, 447, 448
Projective personality test, 420–421
Prophecy, self-fulfilling, 587–588
Prosocial behavior, 583–586
Prosser, Inez Beverly, 29
Prototype, 318

Proximodistal development, 97
Pseudopsychology, 20–22
    astrology as, 20–21
    graphology as, 20
    uncritical acceptance and, 21
Psi phenomenon, 171
Psilocybin, 206–207, 215–216
Psyche, 15, 396, 397
Psychiatric labeling, 499–500
Psychiatric social worker, 35
Psychiatrist, 35
PsychINFO, 11
Psychoactive drug, 203. See also Drug
    abuse
Psychoanalysis, 28, 512–513
Psychoanalyst, 35
Psychoanalytic psychology, 28
Psychoanalytic theory, 396–400, 414
Psychodrama, 530
Psychodynamic perspective, 30
Psychodynamic theory, 28
    of anxiety disorder, 496
    dream, 195
    of personality, 390–391, 396–400
Psychokinesis, 171
Psychological changes in emotion, 369
Psychological defense mechanisms,
    447–449
Psychological dependence, 205
Psychological disorder, 469–507
    anxiety-based, 490–497
    core features of, 471–472
    delusional, 479–480
    of mood, 487–490
    paranoid psychosis, 480
    of personality, 498–499
    of perspective, 499–500
    psychosis, 477–479
    risk factors for, 475
    schizophrenia, 480–486
Psychological perspective, 31
Psychological situation, 402
Psychological trauma, 482–483
Psychologist
    media, 516–517
    types of, 16–17, 33–34
Psychology
    animals and, 17
    contemporary views of, 30–32
    defined, 15
    diversity in, 29
    evolutionary, 553
    Gestalt, 27–28
    goals of, 17–18
    health, 429–433
    humanistic, 28
    in media, 46–48
    psychoanalytic, 28
Psychology experiment, 36–40; see also
    Experiment
Psychology Resource Center, 11
Psychoneuroimmunology, 438
Psychopath, 498–499
Psychopathology, 470. See also
    Psychological disorder
Psychosexual stage of development,
    396
Psychosis, paranoid, 480
Psychosocial dilemma, 120
Psychosomatic disorder, 456
Psychosurgery, 537
Psychotherapy, 531–535. See also
    Therapy
    core features of, 532
    counseling skills for, 533–535
    future of, 532–533
    interpersonal, 513

Psychotic disorder, 473
Puberty, 90, 115
Pubescence, 90
Public self-consciousness, 423
Publication of research results, 25
Punisher, 248
Punishment, 248–251
  disadvantages of, 249
  negative reinforcement vs., 238
  operant therapy and, 523
  variables affecting, 248–249
  wise use of, 249–251

Quantitative reasoning, 303
Questionnaire, personality, 418–420

Race, intelligence and, 312–313
Racism, 573, 575
Rain Man, 308
Ramona, Gary, 284
Random assignment, 38
Random search strategy, 325
Random selection, 602
Range, 596
Rape, 212
Rapid eye movement sleep, 187
Rarefaction, 142
Rating scale for personality assessment,
  416
Ratio, variable, 244
Rational-emotive behavior therapy,
  527–528
Rationalization, 447, 448
Reaction
  alarm, 437
  to frustration, 442
  stress, 436
Reaction formation, 447, 448
Readiness, 89–90
Reading, self-reflective, 1–3
Reality, virtual, 521–522
Reality principle, 396
Reality testing, 154–155
Rearing child. *See* Parenting
Reasoning
  fluid, 303
  moral, 118
  quantitative, 303
Rebound
  parasympathetic, 372
  REM, 194
Rebound insomnia, 191–192
Recall, 275
  photogenic memory and, 287–288
  strategies for, 292
Receptor
  in skin, 148
  taste buds as, 147
Recessive gene, 89
Reciprocal influence on development,
  92–93
Reciprocal inhibition, 520
Recognition memory, 275–276
Recovered memory, 284
Recovery, spontaneous, 230
Recruitment for cult, 565–566
Recurring nightmare, 193
Redintegration, 272–273
Reference, delusions of, 478
Reference group, 570
Reflection
  in humanistic therapy, 515
  in psychotherapy, 533
Reflective cognition, 2
Reflex, 226
Reflex arc, 60
Refusal skills training, 432

Regard, unconditional positive, 515
Regression
  age, 199
  as defense mechanism, 447, 448
Rehearsal
  in assertiveness training, 567
  test anxiety and, 363
Rehearsing information, 269
Reinforcement, 226, 525–526
  in classical conditioning, 234
  in operant conditioning, 234,
    235–236
  partial, 243–246
  positive, 238
  self, 403
  self-management and, 258–260
Reinforcer
  operant, 234, 239–243
  secondary, 239–241
  social, 240
  token, 240
Relational concept, 318
Relationship
  empathy-helping, 585
  sexual, 359
  statistical, 599–602
Relative motion, 164
Relativity, cultural, 32
Relaxation
  deep, 200–201
  in desensitization, 520
  for insomnia, 192
  progressive, 462
  test anxiety and, 363
Relaxation response, 201
Relearning, 276–277
Reliability of personality questionnaire,
  418
REM behavior disorder, 189
REM rebound, 194
REM sleep, 187
Remembering, strategies for, 289
Reminding system, pain as, 149
Representative sample, 44, 602
Representativeness heuristic, 333
Repression
  as defense mechanism, 447–448
  of memory, 283–284
Research
  bias in, 38–40
  empirical evidence in, 15–16
  nonexperimental, 41–46
  psychological, 16
  publication of, 25
  scientific method in, 23–25
  specialties in, 16–17
Research method, 16
Resistance, 512
Resolution phase of sexual response,
  357
Respondent reinforcement, 229
Response
  in behaviorism, 27
  definition of, 344
  fight or flight, 371
Response chaining, 236
Response contingent shock, 519
Response cost, 238
Resting potential, 53
Restricted environmental stimulation
    therapy, 202
Reticular activating system, 74
Reticular formation, 74
Retina, 135, 136
  color vision and, 138
  dark adaptation and, 140–141
  rods and cones of, 136–138

Retrieval
  of information, 265
  of memory, failure of, 281–282
Retroactive interference, 282–283
Retrograde amnesia, 284–285
Reversal, role, 530
Reverse vision, 315–316
Rhythm
  biological, 184
  circadian, 345–346
Right brain, 67–68
Right-handedness, 79–83
Risk factor
  behavioral, 429–436
  for violence in schizophrenia, 482
Robot, artificial intelligence and,
    305–306
Rod, 136–138
  dark adaptation and, 140–141
Rogers, Carl
  anxiety disorder and, 496
  client-centered therapy of, 514–515
  personality theory of, 409–410
Rohypnol, 212
Role, social, 555
Role conflict, 555
Role confusion, identity vs., 121
Role reversal, 530
Romantic love, 552
Rorschach technique, 420–421
Rote learning, 252
Rule
  conceptual, 317
  transformation, 320–321
Run of luck, 173

SAD. *See* Seasonal affective disorder
Safe sex, 435
Saltatory conduction, 56
Sample, 602
  representative, 44, 602
Sane hallucinations, 156
Scaffolding, 114
Scale
  rating, 416–417
  validity, 419
Scapegoating, 442
Scatter diagram, 599
Schachter's cognitive theory of emotion,
  377–378
Schedule for partial reinforcement,
  244–246
Schizoid personality disorder, 498
Schizophrenia, 480–486
  brain in, 485
  catatonic, 481–482
  causes of, 482–484, 486
  disorganized, 481
  implications of, 486
  paranoid, 482
  in twin, 412
Schizotypal personality disorder,
  498
School psychologist, 34
Scientific method, 23–25
Scientific observation, 15
Script, sexual, 358
Search strategy, random, 325
Seasonal affective disorder (SAD),
  488–489
Secondary appraisal of threat, 439
Secondary elaboration, 219
Secondary reinforcer, 239–241
Secondary trait, 393
Secondhand conditioning, 233
Secure attachment, 99–100
Selection, random, 602

Selective attention, 151
Selective combination, 327
Selective encoding, 327
Selective perception, 526
Self, 409
  ideal, 410
Self theory, Roger's, 409–410
Self-actualization, 407–409
Self-assertion, 567
Self-awareness in Gestalt therapy,
  515–516
Self-confidence, 365
Self-consciousness, private and public,
  423
Self-control, 381–383
Self-directed desensitization, 541
Self-disclosure, 552
Self-efficacy, 403
Self-esteem, 125
  culture and, 390
Self-fulfilling prophecy, 40, 587–588
Self-help group, 544
Self-image, 409
Self-knowledge, 515
Self-management, 539–542
  behavioral, 258–260
Self-portrait, in psychological disorder,
  473
Self-reference, 2
Self-reflective reading, 1–3
Self-reflective SQ4R method, 2–3
Self-reinforcement, 403
Self-starvation, 352–354
Self-stimulation, intracranial, 239
Self-testing, 6
Seligman, Martin, 449, 451
Semantic memory, 273
Semicircular canal, 149
Senescence, 90
Sensation, definition of, 133
Sensation and perception, 132–181.
    See also Perception; Sensory
    system
Sensation and perception psychologist,
  16, 34
Sensation seeking, 361–362
Sensitive period, 91–92
Sensitivity group, 530–531
Sensitization, covert, 540, 541
Sensorimotor stage of development,
  108, 111
Sensorineural hearing loss, 144
Sensory adaptation, 150–151
Sensory analysis, 133
Sensory change in hypnosis, 199
Sensory coding, 134
Sensory conflict theory, 150
Sensory deprivation, 202
Sensory gating, 151–152
Sensory memory, 265–266
Sensory system, 133–153
  adaptation in, 150–151
  coding by, 134
  hearing, 142–145
  selection by, 133–134
  skin and, 148–149
  smell and taste, 145–147
  vision, 135–141
Separation anxiety, 99
Serial position effect
  definition of, 275
  improving memory and, 291
Set point, 349
Sex, casual, 359, 435
Sex drive, 355
Sex hormone, 77, 78
Sexual abuse, false memory of, 284

Sexual behavior, 355–358
    arousal and, 356
    erogenous zones and, 355–356
Sexual dysfunction, 360, 476
Sexual and gender identity disorder, 474
Sexual maturation, 115
Sexual orientation, 358–359
Sexual relationship, healthy, 359
Sexual response, 356–358
Sexual script, 358
Sexually transmitted disease, 434–436
Shame, autonomy vs., 120
Shape constancy, 159
Shaping, 237, 523
Shapiro, Francine, 522
Shift work, 346
Shock
    in obedience study, 562–564
    response contingent, 519
Short-term memory, 266
    characteristics of, 266
    chunking and, 268–269
    long-term memory and, 267
    rehearsing information and, 269
Shyness, 422–424
Signal in language development, 106
Significant differences, 603
Significant number, 602–603
Similarity, 551–552
Simulation, computer, 306
Singer, Margaret, 565
Single-blind experiment, 39
Situation
    critical, 404
    personality and, 413–414
Situational context, 471
Situational determinant, 401–402
Situational testing, 417–418
Size constancy, 158–159
Skill, social, shyness and, 424
Skill memory, 273
Skinner, B. F., 27
Skinner box, 248
Sleep, 183–196
    dreams and, 194–196
    dual process hypothesis of, 187–189
    insomnia and, 190–192
    memory and, 293
    need for, 184–185
    nightmares and night terrors, 193
    patterns of, 185–186
    sleepwalking and, 192–193
    stages of, 186–187
Sleep apnea, 193
Sleep deprivation, 184
Sleep disorder, examples of, 476
Sleep hormone, stages of, 186
Sleep paralysis, 189
Sleep restriction for insomnia, 192
Sleep spindle, 186
Sleeping pill, withdrawal from, 191
Sleepsex, 193
Sleeptalking, 192–193
Sleepwalking, 192–193
Smell, 145–147
Smile, social, 97
Smoking
    aversion therapy for, 519
    fetus and, 91
    prevention of, 431–432
    quitting of, 211
    risks of, 210–211
SNS. See Somatic nervous system
Social anxiety, 422–424
Social behavior, 549–592
    affiliation and attraction, 550–552
    aggression and, 579–583

assertiveness training, 566–567
    attitudes and, 568–572
    coercion and, 564–566
    compliance as, 561–562
    context of, 555–557
    influences on, 558–560
    liking and loving, 552–554
    multiculturalism and, 586–589
    obedience as, 562–564
    prejudice and, 573–578
    prosocial, 583–586
Social comparison theory, 550
Social competition, 588
Social development of infant, 99–101
Social facilitation, 558
Social factors in psychological disorder, 475
Social influence, 558–560
Social learning theory, 402–403, 581
    comparison of, 414
    of personality, 391
Social loafing, 558
Social motive, 363–364
Social nonconformity, 470–471
Social norm, 32
Social phobia, 492–493
Social psychologist, 17, 34
Social Readjustment Rating Scale (SRRS), 453–454
Social reinforcer, 240
Social role, 555
Social skills, shyness and, 424
Social smile, 97
Social stereotype, 574–576
Social stigma, 500
Social support for stress, 463
Sociocultural perspective, 30, 31–32
Sociocultural theory, Vygotsky's, 113–114
Sociopath, 498–499
Solution
    functional, 325
    general, 325
    insightful, 326–327
    mechanical, 324
Soma, 53, 54
Somatic delusion, 478
Somatic delusional disorder, 480
Somatic nervous system (SNS), 59
Somatic pain, 149
Somatic therapy, 535
Somatization disorder, 494
Somatoform disorder, 473
Somatosensory area, primary, 70–71
Somesthetic sense, 148
Sound, 142–145
Sound wave, 142
Source trait, 393
Spaced practice, 6, 291–292
Spanking, 250
Spatial grammar, 321
Spatial neglect, 67
Specialization, hemispheric, 67–68
Specialty in psychology, 35
Specific goal, 8
Specific phobia, 491–492
Spectrum, visible, 133, 135
Speech, aphasia and, 69
Spinal cord, function of, 59–61
Spindle, sleep, 186
Spiral, Fraser's, 155
Split-brain operation, 67
Spontaneous recovery, 230
Sports, eating disorder and, 353
SQ4R method, 2–3
SRRS. See Social Readjustment Rating Scale

Stage of exhaustion, 437
Stage hypnosis, 199–200
Stage of resistance, 437
Standard deviation, 596–597
Stanford hypnotic susceptibility scale, 199
Stanford-Binet intelligence scales, 302–303
State of consciousness, 182–263. See also Consciousness
State theory of hypnosis, 197
State-dependent learning, 281–282
Statement, coping, 464–465
Statistical abnormality, 470
Statistical significance, 603
Statistics
    correlational, 599–602
    descriptive, 594–598
    inferential, 602–603
Status, 556
Status inequality, 576
Stereocilia, 142
Stereoscopic vision, 161–162
Sternberg's triangular theory of love, 552–553
Steroid, anabolic, 78
Stigma, social, 500
Stimulant, 206–211
    amphetamine, 206–208
    cocaine, 208–209
    definition, 203
    insomnia and, 192
Stimulation
    direct brain, 239
    educational, 242
Stimulus
    aversive, 580–581
    defined, 26
    neutral, 229
    unconditioned, 229
Stimulus control, 524
    for insomnia, 192
    in operant conditioning, 246–247
Stimulus discrimination, 231, 246–247
Stimulus generalization, 230–231, 246
Stimulus motive, 345, 361–363
Storage of information, 265
Strategy
    random search, 325
    for remembering, 289
Strength, hypnosis and, 199
Stress, 436–440
    acculturative, 455
    general adaptation syndrome and, 437
    health and, 453–465
    life events and, 453–454
    management of, 460–465
    meditation for, 201
    traumatic, 441
Stress disorder, 493–494
Stress inoculation, 464
Stress reaction, 436
Stressor, 438
Stress-vulnerability model, 486
Structuralism, 26
Study methods, 1–13
Subcortex, 73–75
Sublimation, 447, 449
Substance-related disorder, 474
Sudden death, emotion causing, 372
Sudden infant death syndrome, 193–194
Suicide, 501–505
Sumner, Francis Cecil, 29
Superego, 396, 397
Superordinate goal, 576–577

Superstitious behavior, 236
Suppression
    of emotion, 380
    of memory, 283–284
Surface trait, 393
Surgery, split-brain, 67
Survey, internet, 44–45
Survey method, 44–45
Susceptibility, hypnotic, 198–199
Susto, 474
Symbol, dream, 195, 512
Symbolic prejudice, 575
Symbolic thought, 109
Symbolization, 219
Sympathetic branch of nervous system, 59, 371
    emotions and, 369
Synapse
    function of, 56
    growth of, 112
    in newborn, 90
Syntax, 320
Systematic desensitization, 520

Taste
    obesity and, 350
    sense of, 145–147
Taste buds, 147
TAT. See Thematic Apperception Test
Telepathy, 171
Telephone therapist, 517
Televised aggression, 255–257
Temperament, 93, 411
Temperature, homeostasis and, 345
Temporal lobe, 71
Temporary insomnia, 190–191
Tension-release method, 521
Teratogen, 91
Terror, night, 193
Test
    of creativity, 330
    intelligence, 310
    situational, 417–418
Test anxiety, 362
Testimony, eyewitness, 175–178
Testosterone, 77, 78
Test-taking, 8–10
Texture gradient, 164
Thalamus, 74
Thanatos, 396, 397
THC, 216
Thematic Apperception Test (TAT), 421
Theorist
    learning, 16
    personality, 16
    trait, 391
Theory
    arousal, 361
    building of, 24
    cognitive dissonance, 571
    definition of, 24
    frequency, 142
    gate control, 152
    humanistic, 407–411
    lock and key, 145
    of love, 553
    opponent-process, 138
    place, 142
    psychodynamic, 28, 390–391, 396–400
    sensory conflict, 150
    social comparison, 550
    social learning, 402–403, 581
    trichromatic, of color vision, 138
Therapeutic alliance, 532
Therapist, culturally skilled, 534

Therapy
  behavior, 518–522
  cognitive, 526–528
  culture and, 534
  drug, 535–536
  electroconvulsive, 536–537
  group, 529–531
  humanistic, 514–516
  media psychologist, 516–517
  medical, 535–538
  operant, 523–526
  placebo effect of, 531
  psychotherapy, 510, 512–513,
    531–535
  by telephone and internet, 517
Thinking. *See also* Cognition; Thought
  all-or-nothing, 526
  convergent, 329
  creative, 329–332
  critical, 2, 19–20
  definition of, 314
  divergent, 329
  language and, 319–320
Thirst, 354
Thought. *See also* Cognition; Thinking
  basic units of, 314–315
  deductive, 329
  egocentric, 109
  illogical, 329
  inductive, 329
  intuitive, 109
  language and, 319–320
  logical, 329
Thought restructuring, 363
Thought stopping, 540–541
Threat, appraisal of, 439–440
Thyroid gland, 77
Time management, 8
Time out, 524
Time-limited psychodynamic therapy,
  513
Tip-of-the-tongue state, 275
Tobacco
  comparison with other drugs,
    206–207
  fetus and, 91
Toilet training, 404
Token economy, 525–526
Token reinforcer, 240
Tolerance

cultural awareness and, 588–589
  drug, 205
Tomography
  computed, 62
  positron emission, 63–64
Tongue, 147
Top-down perception, 168–170
Top-down processing, 155
Touch, 148–149
Training
  assertiveness, 566–567
  large-group awareness, 530
  life skills, 432–433
  mastery, 451
  refusal skills, 432
  toilet, 404
Trait, 391–395
  classification of, 392–393
  personality, 388–389
  situations and, 413–414
  in twins, 412
Trait profile, 393
Trait theorist, 391
Trait theory, 390–391
Tranquilizer, brain effects of, 204
Transducer, 133
Transference, 512
Transformation, 109
Transformation rules, 320–321
Trauma, psychological, 482–483
Traumatic stress, 441
Trepanning (trephining), 511
Triangular theory of love, 552–553
Trichromatic theory of color vision,
  138
Trust vs. mistrust, 120
Twin study
  of intelligence, 311–312
  of personality, 412
Twins
  handedness in, 81
  identical, 88
Twixters, 117
Two-way bilingual education, 320
Type A personality, 457–458

Umami, 146
Unconditional positive regard, 411, 515
Unconditioned stimulus, 229

Unconscious
  in Freudian theory, 396
  in psychoanalytic psychology, 28
  psychotherapy and, 512–513
Unconsciousness, 183
Uncritical acceptance, 21
Understanding, 17
  problem-solving and, 325
Uppers, 206–211. *See also* Stimulant

Validity of personality questionnaire,
  418
Validity scale, 419
Value, incentive, 344–345
Variability, 596–597
Variable ratio (VR) schedule, 245–246
Ventromedial hypothalamus, 348
Verbal intelligence, 304
Verification, creativity and, 331
Vestibular sense, 148
Vibration, hearing and, 142
Vicarious conditioning, 233
Vicarious desensitization, 521
Video game
  effects of, 256–257
  IQ score and, 313
Violence. *See also* Aggression
  media and, 581–582
  schizophrenia and, 482
Virilism, 78
Virtual reality
  exposure to, 521–522
  sensory conflict and, 150
Visceral pain, 148
Visible spectrum, 133
Vision, 135–141
  color, 138–140
  dark adaptation and, 140–141
  eye structure and, 135–136
  of infant, 95
  peripheral, 138
  receptors and, 133
  reverse, 315–316
  rods and cones in, 136–138
  stereoscopic, 161–162
  visible spectrum and, 135
Visual acuity, 137–138
Visual agnosia, 71

Visual image, memory of, 288
Visual perception, 154
Visual-spatial processing, 303
Vogler, Roger, 519
VR schedule. *See* Variable ratio schedule
Vygotsky's sociocultural theory, 113–114

Wain, Louis, 484
Warning signs
  of psychotic disorder, 478
  of suicide, 503
Warning system, pain as, 149
Washburn, Margaret, 29
Watson, John B., 27
Wave, sound, 142
Wavelength of light, 135
Weakness, color, 139–140
Web link, 10–11
Website, psychology, 11–12
Wechsler test, 303–304
Weekly time schedule, 8
Weight loss, 350–352
Weightlessness, 149
Well-being, 202
Wellness, 433
Wernicke's area, 71
Wertheimer, Max, 27
White matter of spinal cord, 59–60
Whole learning, 290–291
Wilf, Andy, 473
Will, free, 28
Wisdom, 335
Withdrawal of love, 125
Withdrawal symptoms, 205
Work
  excessive rewards for, 367
  shift, 346
Working memory, 266, 303
Wundt, Wilhelm, 26

Yerkes-Dodson law, 362
Yo-yo dieting, 351–352
You-message, 127

Zar, 474
Zero relationship, 600
Zone of proximal development, 113
z-Score, 597, 598

To the Student

These cards are a study tool designed to help you better understand essential chapter concepts. The material for each chapter includes survey questions, a visual guide of key topics, and a practice exam consisting of 20 multiple-choice questions per chapter.

Visual Guides

Research has shown that, for some learners, presenting information in a visual format improves retention of material. The visual guides began several years ago with an individual instructor's attempt to give students a study tool in an alterative format that allowed them to review information as they prepared for examinations. Many of you will find the visual guides extremely helpful from the very beginning of your course. For others, you may discover their value as you proceed with your studies.

How do you make use of these visual guides? The Introduction to the main text discusses how to study psychology and explains the SQ4R method (a quick synopsis is also provided here). These visual guides are an integral part of the "S" ("Survey") and two of the "R's" ("Relate" and "Review").

Survey

Even before you survey the chapter, survey the visual guides. A preview like this gives you an overview of what material will be covered and highlights some key concepts that you will want to focus on.

Relate

The visual presentation demonstrates how one key topic relates to another. You may be surprised to see how many concepts are interconnected, and the visual guides provide an overview of these connections. Your long-term retention of the material can be improved by having an understanding of how the material you are studying relates to other material. The material in the visual guides is generally laid out in a top-down, left-to-right format. However, as you will see, the fact that most concepts are interrelated makes the exact layout of no great consequence.

Review

After you have read the chapter and want to test your mastery of the material, use the visual guides for review. At each point along the way, ask yourself:

- How much do I now know about each topic discussed here? What information do I now know that was not included in the visual guide?
- What items would I have added if I had been the creator of the visual guide?
- What questions is my instructor likely to ask about the topics that have been presented?

Some students may find it helpful to make detailed notes directly on the visual guides as they progress through the chapters.

Concept Review

In addition to the Survey Questions and visual guides of key concepts, you will find a chapter quiz consisting of 20 multiple-choice questions in each chapter. You can find additional quizzing and tutorial help at the text companion website, at **www.cengage.com/psychology/coon.**

We hope that you find these visual guides and concept review content a valuable study tool in mastering your course material.

Discovering Psychology and Research Methods

NATURALISTIC OBSERVATION
Active observation of behavior in a *natural setting*

CORRELATIONAL STUDY
A nonexperimental study that measures two or more events that appear to be connected

CLINICAL METHOD
Review *natural events* that have affected an individual or groups. Often uses a case study

SURVEY METHOD
Use of public polling techniques to answer psychological questions

EXPERIMENTAL METHOD
Investigating causes of behavior through controlled experimentation

PSYCHOLOGISTS AT WORK
Not all psychologists work in clinical settings. The American Psychological Association recognizes over 50 special skills or areas of interest.

age fotostock/SuperStock

1. MAKING AN OBSERVATION
Observations prompt psychologists to ask questions and seek answers.

2. DEFINING A PROBLEM
Psychologists then organize those questions in a logical manner.

3. PROPOSING A HYPOTHESIS
The researcher creates a tentative and testable explanation for what has been observed.

4. GATHERING EVIDENCE/ TESTING THE HYPOTHESIS
The hypothesis is tested using a research method.

5. BUILDING A THEORY
Good theories summarize observations, explain them, and guide further research.

6. PUBLISHING RESULTS
Results are published to promote discussion, debate, and replication.

MAJOR PERSPECTIVES
Biological: Seeks to explain our behavior in terms of biological principles such as brain processes, evolution, and genetics

Psychological: Views behavior as the result of psychological processes within each person

Sociocultural: Stresses the impact that social and cultural contexts have on our behavior

PSEUDOPSYCHOLOGIES
Any false and unscientific system of beliefs and practices that is offered as an explanation of behavior

PSYCHOLOGY'S FOUR GOALS
Description: The process of naming and classifying
Understanding: To identify the causes of behaviors
Prediction: To forecast behavior reliably
Control: To alter conditions that influence behavior

SCIENTIFIC METHOD
To conduct their research, psychologists use the scientific method, a form of critical thinking that in its ideal form has six elements.

MEDIA SKEPTICISM
The media is rife with inaccurate information. All information, from whatever source, should be critically evaluated.

CRITICAL THINKING
Critical thinking, an ability to evaluate, compare, analyze, critique, and synthesize information, is central to applying the **scientific method** to psychology.

PSYCHOLOGY
Psychology is the scientific study of **behavior and mental processes.** The professionals who create and apply psychological knowledge are called **psychologists.**

Bettmann/Corbis

concept review for chapter 1

1. When psychologists use information gained from direct observation, they are utilizing _____ evidence.
   a. hard
   b. empirical
   c. naturalistic
   d. direct

2. The four goals of psychology include all of the following *except*:
   a. predict
   b. understand
   c. describe
   d. reflect

3. Who is often considered the "father of psychology"?
   a. Wilhelm Wundt
   b. Jean Piaget
   c. Sigmund Freud
   d. Dennis Coon

4. John B. Watson considered _____ factors to be most influential in an individual's development.
   a. environmental
   b. genetic
   c. unconscious
   d. cultural

5. Psychodynamic theories emphasize _____ and _____.
   a. internal motives, unconscious forces
   b. punishments, reinforcements
   c. thinking, behaviors
   d. potential, ideas

6. A psychologist who utilizes a variety of theoretical perspectives would be considered _____.
   a. undecided
   b. eclectic
   c. humanistic
   d. diverse

7. A _____ is a medical doctor who is trained to affect human behavior at the brain chemical level through the prescription of medications.
   a. psychologist
   b. counselor
   c. psychiatrist
   d. social worker

8. A researcher interested in the dating habits of college students decides to gather information by visiting the local college campus and polling the students concerning their dating experiences. The researcher is using what method of data collection?
   a. naturalistic observation
   b. survey
   c. experiment
   d. case study

9. In an experiment where it is believed that heat causes aggression, a psychologist submits subjects to varying temperatures and then attempts to measure the subjects' aggressive behaviors. In this experiment, heat would be considered the:
   a. independent variable
   b. dependent variable
   c. placebo
   d. controlled variable

10. If data indicated that the more one studied for a test, the higher one's test scores would be, we would say that a _____ correlation existed.
    a. positive
    b. negative
    c. false
    d. underestimated

11. Which of the following is the most accurate definition of the discipline of psychology today?
    a. The scientific study of cognition and emotion
    b. The science of mental processes
    c. The scientific study of mental illness
    d. The science of behavior and mental processes

12. Why can psychology be described as a science?
    a. Psychologists conduct research in laboratories.
    b. Psychologists utilize experiments within controlled settings.
    c. Psychologists provide tests and measures for determining one's level of functioning.
    d. Psychologists attempt to uncover the causes of events by systematically collecting empirical evidence.

13. Which of these correlation coefficients indicates the weakest relationship between two variables?
    a. +.13
    b. -.46
    c. +.76
    d. -.95

14. A researcher considering the issues of respect for a research participant's privacy, dignity, confidentiality, and welfare is addressing the _____ concerns of her research.
    a. moral
    b. ethical
    c. legal
    d. practical

15. Self-actualization refers to:
    a. understanding one's motivations
    b. developing one's fullest potential
    c. a desire to meet one's physiological needs
    d. the process of individualization

16. _____ was the first woman awarded a Ph.D. in psychology.
    a. Margaret Washburn
    b. Mary Calkins
    c. Christine Ladd-Franklin
    d. Laurie Randolph

17. Susan believed that her research on the behavior of dogs was becoming problematic, as some of the dogs were becoming jealous of the attention being given to the other dogs. Susan might not be considering:
    a. species relativity
    b. the anthropomorphic error
    c. egocentrism
    d. introspection

18. In your study, you decided to measure aggression as the number of times your subjects hit a BOBO doll within a 5-minute time frame. In this case you have _____ defined the abstract idea of "aggression."
    a. vaguely
    b. operationally
    c. mistakenly
    d. accurately

19. Experiments attempt to establish a _____ relationship.
    a. cohort
    b. causal
    c. correlational
    d. true

20. Any false and unscientific system of beliefs and practices (such as astrology) that is offered as an explanation of behavior is referred to as a:
    a. superstition
    b. theory
    c. pseudopsychology
    d. scam

Survey Questions

- What is psychology and what are its goals?
- What is critical thinking?
- How does psychology differ from false explanations of behavior?
- How is the scientific method applied in psychological research?
- What are the major specialties in psychology?
- How is an experiment performed?
- How did the field of psychology emerge?
- What are the current perspectives in psychology?
- What is a double-blind experiment?
- What nonexperimental research methods do psychologists use?
- How good is psychological information found in the popular media?

Brain and Behavior

BIOPSYCHOLOGY
The study of the brain, nervous system, and other physical origins of behavior

THE SPINAL CORD
Connects the brain to other parts of the body, but also does some computing on its own, as with reflex arcs

CENTRAL NERVOUS SYSTEM (CNS)
The brain and the spinal column

PERIPHERAL NERVOUS SYSTEM (PNS)
Divided into: The **somatic system**, carrying messages to and from the sense organs and skeletal muscles, and the **autonomic system**, serving the internal organs and glands

ENDOCRINE SYSTEM
Endocrine glands form a second communication system. Chemicals called **hormones** are secreted directly into the bloodstream or lymph system via the endocrine system.

NEURONS
Individual nerve cells

DENDRITES
Neuron fibers that receive incoming messages

THE BRAIN
The brain is the largest center of nerve cell activity. Brain activities and structures are associated with all human capacities.

Courtesy of Richard Haier, University of California, Irvine

BRAIN MAPPING
Researchers make bio-electrical recordings and computer-generated images of brain activity, helping gain insight into how the brain works. Biopsychologists attempt to determine which areas of the brain are responsible for specific behaviors.

CEREBRAL CORTEX
The cerebral cortex consists of two large **hemispheres** covering the upper part of the brain, connected by the **corpus callosum**. The hemispheres are divided into four lobes: **frontal, parietal, temporal,** and **occipital.**

SUBCORTEX
The subcortex consists of the **hindbrain, midbrain,** and lower parts of the **forebrain**. It contains many crucial brain structures necessary for survival.

SOMA
The main body of a neuron or other cell

AXONS
Fibers that carry information away from the soma

AXON TERMINALS
Bulb-shaped structures at the ends of axons that form synapses with the dendrites and somas of other neurons

SYNAPSE
The microscopic space between two neurons, over which messages pass

NEUROTRANSMITTERS
Any chemical released by a neuron that alters activity in other neurons

Presynaptic axon terminal

Synaptic vesicle

Synaptic gap

Neurotransmitter

Receptor site

Postsynaptic dendrite

concept review for chapter 2

1. What are the short, branchlike structures of a neuron that receive signals from other neurons?
   a. axons
   b. dendrites
   c. soma
   d. axon terminals

2. The electrical charge of an inactive neuron is called its:
   a. ion potential
   b. after potential
   c. action potential
   d. resting potential

3. Communication between neurons is:
   a. electrical
   b. chemical
   c. magical
   d. genetic

4. Dopamine, serotonin, and histamine are examples of:
   a. neuropeptides
   b. nerves
   c. neurotransmitters
   d. neural pathways

5. _____ refers to the capacity of our brains to change in response to experience.
   a. Agility
   b. Brain repair
   c. Regeneration
   d. Neuroplasticity

6. Neuropeptides differ from neurotransmitters in that neuropeptides:
   a. do not carry messages
   b. do not regulate the activity in other neurons
   c. are not chemicals found in the brain
   d. are simple compounds

7. Ray is suffering from multiple sclerosis. When his doctor examines a sample of Ray's nerves, what is she likely to find?
   a. reduced growth of axons
   b. reduced production of neurotransmitters
   c. excessive space in his synaptic gaps
   d. degeneration of the myelin sheath

8. Where does the processing of most stimuli/information typically occur?
   a. the brain
   b. the peripheral nervous system
   c. the spinal cord
   d. the dendrites

9. As you write the answers for this quiz, you are most likely using the _____ nervous system to perform this action.
   a. independent
   b. autonomic
   c. somatic
   d. sympathetic

10. The automonic system can be divided into what two branches?
    a. sympathetic and parasympathetic
    b. primary and secondary
    c. CNS and PNS
    d. fight and flight

11. Which division of the nervous system prepares the body for "fight or flight"?
    a. central
    b. somatic
    c. sympathetic
    d. parasympathetic

12. Which of these activities most likely involves activation of the parasympathetic division?
    a. taking an exam
    b. studying for an exam
    c. resting after taking an exam
    d. waiting for a corrected exam to be returned

13. All of the following may be used to provide images of brain function except:
    a. fMRI
    b. EEG
    c. CT Scan
    d. PET scan

14. As demonstrated by PET scans, the brain burns _____ to function.
    a. positrons
    b. salt
    c. neuropeptides
    d. glucose

15. Joel experiences a stroke and subsequently loses the ability to use his right hand. It is most likely that the stroke occurred in his hemispheres.
    a. left hemisphere
    b. corpus callosum
    c. cerebellum
    d. right hemisphere

16. Joshua is watching a football game. Which lobe of his brain is sure to activate as he does this?
    a. parietal
    b. frontal
    c. temporal
    d. occipital

17. Following a head injury, your patient describes a chair as "one of those things you sit in." It is possible that your patient is suffering from:
    a. agnosia
    b. aphasia
    c. reticular formation
    d. apraxia

18. A reflex arc _____.
    a. occurs in the brain
    b. takes place when a stimulus provokes an automatic response
    c. is learned from environmental influences
    d. is voluntary in nature

19. The human growth hormone is released by the _____ gland.
    a. thyroid
    b. pituitary
    c. pineal
    d. adrenal

20. The _____ is the broad band of fibers that connects your brain's two hemispheres.
    a. axon
    b. corpus callosum
    c. cerebellum
    d. cerebral cortex

Survey Questions

- How do neurons operate and communicate?

- What are the major parts of the nervous system?

- How is the brain studied?

- Why is the human cerebral cortex so important and what are its parts?

- What are the major parts of the subcortex?

- Does the glandular system affect behavior?

- In what ways do right- and left-handed individuals differ?

STAGE THEORY

Piaget's **stages** theory of child development provides a valuable map of how children think. Recent studies suggest that children are capable of thought well beyond that observed by Piaget.

SOCIOCULTURAL THEORY

Vygotsky theorizes that a child's mind is shaped by interactions with more competent partners. These partners **scaffold** the child's progress.

DEVELOPMENTAL TASKS

Erik Erikson analyzed a series of challenges (psychosocial dilemmas) that occur across the life span.

TRUST: Trusting others and the world comes from good parental care.

AUTONOMY: Self-control and independence are essential to a sense of self and self-esteem.

INITIATIVE: Learning to make plans and carry them out is necessary for living in the adult world.

INDUSTRY: Achieving goals and being recognized is important to our self-esteem.

IDENTITY: Forming a personal identity is a major task of adolescence.

INTIMACY: Developing the ability to care about others and to share experiences with them.

GENERATIVITY: Being productive and developing an interest in guiding the next generation.

INTEGRITY: Successful lives are based on happiness, purpose, meaning, and integrity.

KOHLBERG'S LEVELS OF MORAL DEVELOPMENT

PRECONVENTIONAL: Based on the consequences of one's choices or actions

CONVENTIONAL: Based on a desire to please others or to follow accepted rules and values

POSTCONVENTIONAL: Based on carefully examined and self-chosen moral principles

MORAL DEVELOPMENT

We acquire values, beliefs, and thinking patterns that guide responsible behavior beginning in childhood and continuing through life.

NATURE VS. NURTURE

Each of us is a product of BOTH genetic heritage (nature) and the environments in which we have lived (nurture).

NEWBORN CAPABILITIES

Newborn babies are able to interact with the world around them. Along with adaptive reflexes to root, suck, and grasp, they can see, hear, smell, taste, and respond to pain and touch.

PARENTING

Parents, as caregivers, play a critical role in development. **Authoritarian**, **permissive**, and **authoritative parenting styles** are associated with different child outcomes.

MATURATION

The physical growth and development of the body, brain, and nervous system is known as maturation.

ADOLESCENCE AND YOUNG ADULTHOOD

Adolescence is a culturally defined period between childhood and adulthood. Humans address many important developmental concerns during this time, including building a consistent **identity**.

LATER ADULTHOOD

Well-being in adulthood is associated with self-acceptance, positive relations with others, autonomy, environmental mastery, life purpose, and personal growth.

OLD AGE

After the late 50s, personal development is complicated by physical aging. The happiest, healthiest older people are optimistic, gracious, and empathetic and have a connection to others.

HUMAN DEVELOPMENT

Developmental Psychology is the study of progressive changes in behavior and abilities from conception to death.

1. What is the study of progressive changes in behaviors and abilities that occur throughout the life span?
   a. gerontology
   b. maturational studies
   c. cognitive psychology
   d. developmental psychology

2. Dr. Worthington believes that people who are intelligent have become so because of their life experiences. Dr. Jakway believes that people are more or less intelligent because of genetic factors. What developmental psychology debate is illustrated by their disagreement?
   a. correlation versus causation
   b. behaviorism versus cognitive
   c. nature versus nurture
   d. longitudinal versus cross-sectional studies

3. How many chromosomes are found in the nucleus of the typical human sex cell (sperm cell and ovum)?
   a. 46 pairs
   b. 23 pairs
   c. Varies
   d. 23

4. A trait controlled by a recessive gene
   a. is always an undesirable trait
   b. may be expressed, depending upon the characteristic it represents (e.g., eye color)
   c. will be expressed regardless of the instructions of the corresponding gene in the other half of the pair
   d. will be expressed only if the instructions of the corresponding gene in the other half of the pair are the same

5. What is widely believed to be the source or origin of temperament?
   a. interaction with one's environment
   b. education and experiences
   c. inborn predispositions for interacting with one's environment
   d. cultural and social norms

6. _____ refers to the sum of all external conditions that affect a person.
   a. Genetics
   b. Environment
   c. Culture
   d. Nature

7. If research demonstrated that a child's brain was more susceptible to the development of close emotional relationships during the first year of life, we would call this time a _____ for attachment.
   a. sensitive period
   b. window of opportunity
   c. critical time
   d. sensitive period

8. Because many of the chemicals in cigarettes can reach a baby during its prenatal development and cause birth defects, smoking is considered a _____.
   a. sensitive period
   b. harmful variable
   c. PCB
   d. teratogen

9. All of the following are types of temperament except:
   a. slow-to-warm-up
   b. extrovert
   c. difficult
   d. easy

10. _____ refers to a lack of normal stimulation, nutrition, comfort, or love.
    a. Enrichment
    b. Abuse
    c. Neglect
    d. Deprivation

11. A person's developmental level is defined by the text as:
    a. an individual's current state of physical, emotional, and intellectual development
    b. the physical and cognitive changes from conception to death
    c. an individual's chronological age divided by his mental age
    d. the scientific study of age-related changes

12. How might you attempt to elicit the rooting reflex in a newborn?
    a. Stroke the newborn's cheek.
    b. Place your finger in the newborn's mouth.
    c. Place your finger in the newborn's hand.
    d. Stroke the bottom of the newborn's foot.

13. According to your text, adaptive reflexes aid infants in _____.
    a. adjustment to their surroundings
    b. survival
    c. neurological development
    d. developmental maturation

14. _____ is a close emotional bond between children and their caregiver(s).
    a. Maturation
    b. Attachment
    c. Connection
    d. Attention

15. Mary Ainsworth identified all of the following classifications of attachment except:
    a. securely attached
    b. securely avoidant
    c. insecure-avoidant
    d. insecure-ambivalent

16. Baumrind classified parents who are high in the areas of control and discipline, yet low in areas such as warmth and affection as _____.
    a. authoritative
    b. authoritarian
    c. permissive
    d. neglectful

17. As you hold your 7-week-old nephew, he begins to make sounds such as "oooh" and "aaah." Developmental psychologists would refer to this type of language as:
    a. babbling
    b. telegraphic speech
    c. cooing
    d. receptive language

18. If you reason that speeding is wrong because it is against the law, Kohlberg would say that you are in the _____ stage of moral development.
    a. preconventional
    b. conventional
    c. postconventional
    d. precontemplative

19. Taking away privileges as a form of punishment would be what style of discipline?
    a. behavior management
    b. power assertion
    c. withdrawal of love
    d. control declaration

20. A little girl sees a butterfly floating across the yard and says to her mother, "Look at the pretty bird!" Piaget would explain the girl's actions as a form of:
    a. accommodation
    b. admiration
    c. deduction
    d. assimilation

Survey Questions

- How do heredity and environment affect development?
- What can newborn babies do?
- Of what significance is a child's emotional bond with adults?
- How important are parenting styles?
- How do children acquire language?
- How do children learn to think?
- Why is the transition from adolescence to adulthood especially challenging?
- How do we develop morals and values?
- What are the typical tasks and dilemmas through the life span?
- What is involved in well-being during later adulthood?
- How do effective parents discipline and communicate with their children?

Sensation and Perception

PERCEPTION
The mental process of organizing sensations into meaningful patterns

SENSATION
A sensory impression; the process of detecting physical energies with the sensory organs

HEARING
Hearing involves an elaborate chain of events in which waves of compression and rarefaction, or vibration in the air, are converted to neural impulses. Hearing collects information from all around the body.

VISION
The visible spectrum (the spread of electromagnetic energies to which the eyes respond) is made up of a narrow range of wavelengths (400–700 nanometers) of electromagnetic radiation.

SOMESTHETIC SENSES
Help us feel and navigate in our environment
Skin senses: Touch (light touch, pressure, pain, cold, and warmth)
Kinesthetic senses: Receptors in muscles and joints that detect body position and movement
Vestibular senses: Receptors in the inner ear for balance, gravity, and acceleration

CHEMICAL SENSES
The senses of smell (olfaction) and taste (gustation) respond to chemical stimulation when small particles of airborne molecules (smell) or food (taste) cause stimulation of receptor sites.

DATA REDUCTION
Only a small part of the sensory information surrounding us actually reaches the brain or registers there. Data from the outside world are reduced so that only the most important information remains.

PERCEPTUAL ORGANIZATION
We unconsciously use the Gestalt principles to organize sensations into meaningful patterns.
Figure-ground: Part of a stimulus appears to stand out as an object (figure) against a less prominent background (ground).
Nearness: Stimuli that are near each other tend to be grouped together.
Similarity: Stimuli that are similar in size, shape, color, or form tend to be grouped together.
Continuity: Complex stimuli tend to be perceived in the simplest form.
Closure: Incomplete figures tend to be completed by our perceptions.
Contiguity: Nearness in time and space often results in a perception that one thing has *caused* another.
Common region: Stimuli found within a common area tend to be perceived as a group, regardless of their similarities to one another.

PERCEPTUAL CONSTANCIES
Size constancy: The perceived size of objects remains constant, despite changes in its retinal image.
Shape constancy: The perceived shape of an object remains unaffected by changes in its retinal image.
Brightness constancy: The apparent brightness of objects remains the same as long as they are illuminated by the same amount of light.

PERCEPTUAL ACCURACY
Perception is greatly affected by expectations, motives, emotions, and learning. The accuracy and objectivity of perceptions can be improved through conscious effort and an awareness of factors that contribute to erroneous perceptions.

DEPTH PERCEPTION
Depth perception (an essential element of our ability to function in the world) is created by **stereoscopic vision**, **muscular cues**, and **pictorial cues**.

VARIED SENSORY LEVELS
Although our senses are continuously active, many sensory events never reach awareness.
Sensory adaptation: A decrease in sensory response to an unchanging stimulus
Selective attention: Giving priority to a particular incoming sensory message
Sensory gating: Alteration of sensory messages in the spinal cord

TRANSDUCTION
Transducers convert one kind of energy into another. Physical stimuli (light, vibration, pressure, touch) or chemical stimuli are converted to neural impulses.

JSC/NASA

Courtesy of Circle Gallery

ANSWER KEY

1. You answer your phone and immediately recognize the voice of your best friend. What process is involved in this recognition?
   a. olfaction
   b. perception
   c. adaptation
   d. sensation

2. Farsightedness due to aging is referred to as:
   a. hyperopia
   b. myopia
   c. presbyopia
   d. astigmatism

3. Which of the following are considered chemical senses?
   a. vision and hearing
   b. smell and taste
   c. somesthetic and kinesthetic
   d. taste and hearing

4. As you move from the bright, colorful movie theater lobby into the darkened theater, your eye transitions from using its _____ to _____.
   a. cones, rods
   b. photo receptors, bars
   c. rods, cones
   d. cones, visual receptors

5. Which sense responds to the energy caused by the rhythmic movement of air molecules?
   a. hearing
   b. taste
   c. vision
   d. smell

6. If you are told by your eye doctor that your vision is 20/40, it means that your visual acuity at _____ feet is the same as an average person's vision at _____ feet.
   a. 40, 20
   b. 20, 60
   c. 20, 40
   d. 60, 20

7. To measure color blindness or weakness, one would likely take the _____ test.
   a. red–green color
   b. WAIS
   c. Visual Receptor
   d. Ishihara

8. While driving at night, you accidentally look into the headlights of an oncoming car. This momentary experience results in the immediate loss of:
   a. light sensitivity
   b. dark adaptation
   c. visual acuity
   d. core adaptation

9. What type of hearing loss can be at least partially compensated by the use of a hearing aid?
   a. conductive hearing loss
   b. noise-induced hearing loss
   c. sensorineural hearing loss
   d. natural hearing loss

10. How would you describe the relationship between odor and taste?
    a. There is no relationship between the two senses.
    b. Both senses enhance each other.
    c. Your ability to smell enhances your ability to taste.
    d. Your ability to taste enhances your ability to smell.

11. What are the five taste sensations described in your text?
    a. rich, sweet, salty, bitter, sour
    b. bitter, umami, hot, cool, salty
    c. brothy, buttery, sweet, sour, bitter
    d. sweet, salty, sour, bitter, umami

12. The somesthetic senses include:
    a. kinesthetic, vestibular, and skin senses
    b. taste, touch, and vision
    c. touch, temperature, and olfaction
    d. the hands and feet

13. The sensory conflict theory states that when _____ sense and the _____ sense do not coincide, nausea may result.
    a. taste, smell
    b. kinesthetic, touch
    c. vestibular, vision
    d. skin, hearing

14. Studies indicate that depth perception is:
    a. learned
    b. inborn
    c. perception of objects as flat surfaces
    d. both (a) and (b)

15. An illusion _____:
    a. is the same as a hallucination
    b. typically accompanies many mental illnesses
    c. is a perceptual misconstruction
    d. is the perception of a sensation without the presence of any external energy

16. The three basic forms of ESP include all of the following except:
    a. clairvoyance
    b. telepathy
    c. psychokinesis
    d. precognition

17. All of the following effects can impair eyewitness perceptions except:
    a. decreased levels of stress
    b. alcohol intoxication
    c. attitudes/expectations
    d. weapon focus

18. The process of acupuncture is an example of:
    a. sensory gating
    b. reality testing
    c. anosmia
    d. a perceptual illusion

19. Smell is to taste as _____ is to _____.
    a. gestation, olfaction
    b. hearing, vision
    c. olfaction, touch
    d. olfaction, gustation

20. Voluntarily focusing on one thing while excluding other sensory messages is an example of.
    a. selective attention
    b. alternating concentration
    c. discriminating awareness
    d. selective exclusion

Survey Questions

- In general, how do sensory systems function?
- How does the visual system function?
- What are the mechanisms of hearing?
- How do the chemical senses operate?
- What are the somesthetic senses?
- Why are we more aware of some sensations than others?
- In general, how do we construct our perceptions?
- How is perception altered by expectations, motives, emotions, and learning?
- How is it possible to see depth and judge distance?
- Is extrasensory perception possible?
- How can I learn to perceive events more accurately?

States of Consciousness

CONSCIOUSNESS

Consciousness consists of all the sensations, perceptions, memories, and feelings we are aware of at any instant. It is based on your own subjective experience. We spend most of our lives in waking consciousness, a state of clear, organized alertness.

ALTERED STATES

Changes in the quality and pattern of mental activity, with shifts in perceptions, emotions, memory, time sense, thinking, feelings of self-control, and suggestibility occur during an *altered state of consciousness* (ASC).

Dennis Coon

MEDITATION / SENSORY DEPRIVATION

Meditation and sensory deprivation are techniques that can be used to focus attention, alter consciousness, reduce stress, and bring about the relaxation response.

Keren Su/China Span/Alamy

SLEEP

Sleep, necessary for our survival, is the most common ASC.

HYPNOSIS

Hypnosis is characterized by narrowed attention and increased openness to suggestion.

DRUG-ALTERED CONSCIOUSNESS

The surest way to alter human consciousness is to administer a **psychoactive drug**. **Physical dependence** (addiction) may result from extended use, and is often accompanied by **drug tolerance**. **Psychological dependence** develops when an individual feels that a drug is necessary to maintain feelings of comfort or well-being.

MEANING IN DREAMS?

The meaning of dreams is still being debated. Three approaches are the **psychodynamic theory**, the **activation-synthesis hypothesis**, and the **neurocognitive dream theory**.

REM AND NON-REM SLEEP

Sleep occurs in two basic states. **Rapid eye movement (REM)** sleep helps us form memories and contributes to general mental effectiveness. REM sleep is generally associated with dreaming. **Non-REM** sleep is generally free of dreams. It consists of 4 stages, ranging from shallow to deep, characterized by different brain wave patterns.

EFFECTS OF SLEEP LOSS

Moderate sleep loss affects vigilance and performance. Sleep deprivation psychosis may result from extended sleep loss. Many highway accidents may be a result of microsleeps.

SLEEP DISORDERS

Sleep disorders include insomnia, sleepwalking, night terrors, narcolepsy, and sleep apnea. Many sleep disorders cause serious health problems.

UPPERS

Stimulant drugs (amphetamines, cocaine, MDMA, caffeine, nicotine) excite the central nervous system but have severe risks.

DOWNERS

Drugs such as alcohol, barbiturates, GHB, and tranquilizers depress central nervous system function.

HALLUCINOGENS

Hallucinogens (LSD, marijuana, peyote) are substances that alter or distort sensory impressions.

1. What term do psychologists use to designate our personal awareness of feelings, sensations, memories, and perceptions?
   a. cognition
   b. unconscious
   c. conscience
   d. consciousness

2. REM sleep refers to:
   a. sleep periods in which a person's eyes move rapidly
   b. sleep periods ranging from stage 1 to stage 4
   c. sleep periods in which night terrors might occur
   d. sleep periods in which only 10 percent of all dreaming occurs

3. Which of the following is classified as a depressant?
   a. cocaine
   b. alcohol
   c. LSD
   d. caffeine

4. Physical exertion during the day may result in one spending more time in _____ sleep.
   a. REM
   b. paradoxical
   c. dreamless NREM
   d. REM rebound

5. Insomnia includes all the following except:
   a. difficulty falling asleep
   b. difficulty staying asleep
   c. difficulty waking up
   d. frequent awakenings

6. Sleep is an example of:
   a. a learned biological rhythm
   b. an altered state of consciousness
   c. an unconscious state
   d. all of the above

7. A _____ is a brief shift in brain activity to the pattern normally recorded during sleep.
   a. microsleep
   b. deprivation
   c. hypersomnia
   d. daydream

8. Sleep deprivation:
   a. can usually be corrected with a good night's sleep
   b. may result in increased concentration and attention
   c. occurs only when one gets less than 4 hours of sleep per night
   d. has no effect on either mood or memory

9. While a person is awake, EEGs reveal small, fast brain waves called _____ waves.
   a. Delta
   b. Alpha
   c. Sigma
   d. Beta

10. The hypnic jerk typically occurs during:
    a. NREM stage 1
    b. NREM stage 2
    c. REM stage 3
    d. REM sleep

11. An individual who suffers from sleep apnea will experience _____.
    a. interrupted breathing while asleep
    b. recurrent nightmares
    c. increased REM sleep
    d. drug-induced insomnia

12. The use of sleeping pills to treat insomnia can result in all of the following except:
    a. increased REM and stage 4 sleep
    b. possible addiction
    c. decreased sleep quality
    d. rebound insomnia

13. SIDS babies:
    a. have an increased arousal reflex
    b. may engage in breath holding
    c. typically exhibit severe health problems
    d. often have a deep, low-pitched cry

14. _____ is often defined as an altered state of consciousness, characterized by narrowed attention and an increased openness to suggestion.
    a. Meditation
    b. Hypnosis
    c. REM sleep
    d. Dissociation

15. Which of the following is not true of hypnosis?
    a. It can be used for pain relief.
    b. It can produce superhuman increases in strength.
    c. It can affect one's sensory perception.
    d. It cannot make a person do something against his or her will.

16. If you focus on the basketball rim prior to shooting a free throw, you may be engaging in:
    a. concentrative meditation
    b. hypnosis
    c. mindfulness meditation
    d. the use of a mantra

17. A truck driver admits that during long night trips, he at times begins to experience difficulty with sustained attention, as well as seeing birds flying at him in his peripheral vision. It is possible that the driver is experiencing these due to:
    a. perceptual restrictions
    b. alcohol intoxication
    c. sensory deprivation
    d. distorted sensations

18. Paul tells you that he begins to shake uncontrollably and feel nauseous when not drinking. He also states that it takes an increasing amount of alcohol to get him drunk. It is possible your friend has developed:
    a. a tendency to binge-drink
    b. alcohol abuse
    c. a psychological dependence
    d. a physical dependence

19. _____ is the tendency to make a dream more logical and to add details when remembering it.
    a. Symbolization
    b. Secondary elaboration
    c. Condensation
    d. Displacement

20. Caleb tells you that he had a dream in which he knew he was dreaming. This would be referred to as a _____.
    a. conscious dream
    b. latent dream
    c. manifest dream
    d. lucid dream

Survey Questions

- What is consciousness?

- What are the effects of sleep loss or changes in sleep patterns?

- Why do we sleep?

- What are some sleep disorders and unusual sleep events?

- Do dreams have meaning?

- What is hypnosis?

- Do meditation and sensory deprivation have any benefits?

- What are the effects of the more commonly used psychoactive drugs?

- How can dreams be used to promote personal understanding?

Conditioning and Learning

UNCONDITIONED RESPONSE (UR)
The involuntary response to an unconditioned stimulus is an unconditioned response.

CONDITIONED STIMULUS (CS)
When the neutral stimulus also begins to elicit a response, it is no longer neutral. It has become a conditioned stimulus.

CONDITIONED RESPONSE (CR)
A learned response elicited by a conditioned stimulus is a conditioned response.

Robert W. Ginn/PhotoEdit

Carleton Ray/Photo Researchers, Inc.

EMOTIONS & CONDITIONING
Phobias are fears that persist when no realistic danger exists. Phobias often begin with *conditioned emotional responses* (CERs).

NEUTRAL STIMULUS (NS)
A neutral stimulus is one that **does not** cause a response. It is repeatedly paired with an unconditioned stimulus.

UNCONDITIONED STIMULUS (US)
An unconditioned stimulus reliably provokes an involuntary response (typically physiological and/or emotional).

POSITIVE REINFORCEMENT
Occurs when a response is followed by a positive event, or **reinforcer.**

NON-REINFORCEMENT
The probability of the behavior being repeated is **decreased** when no reinforcement occurs.

PUNISHMENT
Punishment **decreases** the probability that a behavior will be repeated. **Aversive stimulus** punishment occurs when a physically or psychologically aversive event follows a behavior. **Response cost** punishment occurs when a positive circumstance is removed.

NEGATIVE REINFORCEMENT
Occurs when a response is followed by an end to discomfort or removal of an unpleasant event

REINFORCEMENT
Reinforcement refers to any event that increases the probability that a response will occur again. Responses that are followed by reinforcement become more frequent. Partially reinforced responses are resistant to becoming extinct.

CLASSICAL CONDITIONING
is a fundamental type of learning in which responses are reflexive (involuntary).

COGNITIVE LEARNING
Cognitive learning extends to the use of memory, thinking, problem solving, and use of language. **Cognitive maps** are internal representations of an area that underlie an ability to choose alternate paths to the same goal. **Latent learning** occurs without any obvious reinforcement and remains hidden until reinforcement is provided. **Discovery learning** is based on insight and understanding.

OPERANT CONDITIONING
This type of learning is based on the consequences of voluntary responses.

LEARNING
is a relatively permanent change in behavior due to experience.

concept review for chapter 6

1. Which term describes a relatively permanent change in behavior or the potential to make a response that occurs as a result of experience?
   a. learning
   b. cognition
   c. maturation
   d. perception

2. What must be paired together for classical conditioning to occur?
   a. neutral stimulus and conditioned stimulus
   b. neutral stimulus and unconditioned stimulus
   c. conditioned response and unconditioned response
   d. unconditioned stimulus and conditioned response

3. Repeated presentations of the conditioned stimulus (CS) without the unconditioned stimulus (US) leads to _____.
   a. discrimination
   b. extinction
   c. acquisition
   d. generalization

4. A self-management plan for one's own behavior might include doing all of the following *except*:
   a. rewarding successes
   b. recording progress
   c. establishing goals
   d. maintaining the developed plan, regardless of the progress

5. _____ is any event that decreases the probability that a response will occur or reoccur.
   a. Punishment
   b. Shaping
   c. Intrinsic reinforcement
   d. Reinforcement

6. In operant conditioning, the _____ are the most important elements in the learning process.
   a. consequences
   b. antecedents
   c. societal influences
   d. unconditioned aspects

7. In Pavlov's experiment, initially the bell was the:
   a. unconditioned stimulus
   b. unconditioned response
   c. neutral stimulus
   d. conditioned response

8. The period in conditioning during which a response is reinforced is called:
   a. acquisition
   b. assimilation
   c. extinction
   d. modeling

9. When the NS is followed by the US, _____ may eventually occur.
   a. stimulus generalization
   b. operant conditioning
   c. classical conditioning
   d. latent conditioning

10. The re-emergence of a previously extinguished response is known as:
    a. a stimulus generalization
    b. extinction
    c. an impulsive response
    d. a spontaneous recovery

11. Elizabeth has learned, through classical conditioning, to fear bees. She also has begun to fear houseflies. This illustrates the concept of:
    a. stimulus generalization
    b. spontaneous simplification
    c. instrumental discrimination
    d. observational learning

12. John's emotional reaction to falling off the playground slide has generalized to an irrational fear of heights. This is an example of:
    a. a phobia
    b. observational learning
    c. a neutral stimulus
    d. an unconditioned fear

13. The best way to differentiate operant conditioning from classical conditioning is to decide whether the:
    a. response is voluntary or reflexive in nature
    b. stimulus is conditioned or unconditioned
    c. response is pleasant or unpleasant
    d. antecedent comes before or after the response

14. The process of reinforcing successive or close approximations to a desired behavior is called:
    a. cognitive mapping
    b. molding
    c. fading
    d. shaping

15. Positive reinforcement _____ behavior; negative reinforcement _____ behavior.
    a. increases; increases
    b. increases; decreases
    c. decreases; increases
    d. decreases; decreases

16. Josh gets a commission for every three cars he sells. His payment is on a _____ schedule.
    a. fixed ratio
    b. fixed interval
    c. variable ratio
    d. variable interval

17. Money, affection, and power are all examples of _____ reinforcers.
    a. primary
    b. secondary
    c. principle
    d. tertiary

18. _____ refers to understanding, knowing, anticipating, or otherwise making use of information-rich higher mental processes.
    a. Observational learning
    b. Latent learning
    c. Cognitive learning
    d. Discovery learning

19. Albert Bandura referred to learning through observation and imitation as _____.
    a. rote
    b. modeling
    c. trial-and-error learning
    d. observatory learning

20. All of the following are drawbacks to the use of severe punishments *except*:
    a. Severe punishments encourage escape behaviors.
    b. Severe punishments increase aggressive behaviors.
    c. Severe punishments encourage avoidance behaviors.
    d. Severe punishments increase compliance.

Survey Questions

- What is learning?
- How does classical conditioning occur?
- Does conditioning affect emotions?
- How does operant conditioning occur?
- Are there different kinds of operant reinforcement?
- How are we influenced by patterns of reward?
- What is cognitive learning?
- Does learning occur by imitation?
- How does conditioning apply to everyday problems?
- What does punishment do to behavior?

Memory

MEMORY
Memory is an **active process** for receiving, encoding, storing, organizing, altering, and retrieving information.

FORGETTING
The inability to retrieve information originates in a variety of circumstances.

SENSORY MEMORY (SM)
Sensory organs collect and transmit information to short-term memory, where it is retained for a short period of time. **Selective attention** (focusing on a portion of sensory input) controls what information moves to the next level.

SHORT-TERM MEMORY (STM)
STM is working memory, where we do much of our thinking using small amounts of information for brief periods.

LONG-TERM MEMORY (LTM)
LTM is the large storehouse of relatively permanent, important information.

THREE MEMORY PROCESSES
Encoding: Converting information into a form in which it will be retained in memory
Storage: Holding information in memory for later use
Retrieval: Recovering information from storage in memory

MEMORY LIMITATIONS
Memories are not always accurate. "Flaws" of memory may be adaptive and desirable in most circumstances. We cannot always remember the source of a memory.

IMPROVING MEMORY
Memory can be improved by using feedback, recitation, maintenance rehearsal, and elaborative encoding. Selecting and organizing information, spacing practice, and overlearning material also help memory.

EIDETIC IMAGERY
"Photographic" (eidetic) memory involves the ability to retain a mental image long enough to use it as a source of information.

TYPES OF LONG-TERM MEMORY
Procedural memory: Basic conditioned responses and learned actions
Declarative memory: Stores specific factual information, expressed as words or symbols. It is further broken down into **semantic** and **episodic** memory types.

MNEMONICS
The use of mnemonics can greatly improve immediate memory. It is important to keep in mind the effects of serial position, sleep, review, cues, and elaboration.

ENCODING FAILURE
Failure to store sufficient information to form a useful memory

CUE DEPENDENCY
Many of our memories rely on cues in the environment that must be present again during "remembering." This helps explain state-dependent learning.

PSYCHOLOGICAL MOTIVES
Repression or suppression of information may occur for psychological reasons.

MEMORY DECAY
The fading or weakening of memories. Occurs when trace memories become weaker.

INTERFERENCE
Interference refers to the tendency for new learning to impair retrieval of older memories (retroactive) or old learning to interfere with new memories (proactive).

Nash Photos/Getty Images

1. Which term describes a fleeting mental image that lasts for a few seconds or less?
   a. logo
   b. echoic memory
   c. iconic memory
   d. image

2. Short-term memories are most often stored:
   a. with the sense of smell
   b. for a few seconds or less
   c. as images
   d. phonetically

3. Information that is transferred from short-term memory to long-term memory must be either _____ or _____.
   a. important, meaningful
   b. limited, general
   c. insightful, understood
   d. emphasized, memorized

4. _____ occurs when bits of information are grouped into larger units.
   a. Chunking
   b. Organizing
   c. Generalizing
   d. Maintenance rehearsal

5. _____ is a technique created by Edward Geiselman and Ron Fisher and is used by law enforcement for jogging the memory of eyewitnesses.
   a. Hypnosis
   b. Shaping
   c. The behavioral interview
   d. The cognitive interview

6. As you look through an old photo album, you are flooded with childhood memories. This process is known as _____.
   a. redintegration
   b. constructive processing
   c. cognitive processing
   d. memory networking

7. Basic conditioned responses and learned actions, such as tying your shoe, is an example of _____ memory.
   a. declarative
   b. procedural
   c. semantic
   d. episodic

8. _____ refers to the feeling that a memory is available but not quite retrievable.
   a. Amnesia
   b. Interference
   c. Forgetting
   d. Tip-of-the-tongue

9. If you are trying to prolong a memory by silently repeating it, you are employing a process known as _____ rehearsal.
   a. stimulus
   b. maintenance
   c. elaborative
   d. repetitive

10. The _____ states that when trying to remember a list of items, you are most likely to remember the first and last items, while experiencing the most difficulty recalling the items in the middle of the list.
    a. spontaneous memory effect
    b. short-term memory effect
    c. serial position effect
    d. rote memory effect

11. _____ is an active system that involves encoding, storing, and retrieving information.
    a. Eidetic
    b. Priming
    c. Repression
    d. Memory

12. The three stages of memory *in order* are:
    a. short-term memory, working memory, long-term memory
    b. eidetic memory, sensory memory, long-term memory
    c. sensory memory, short-term memory, long-term memory
    d. short-term memory, sensory memory, long-term memory

13. The storage capacity of long-term memory:
    a. is seven bits of information
    b. may be filled during times of high cognitive activity
    c. is five hundred units of information
    d. is virtually limitless

14. _____ encoding helps link new information to existing memories by concentrating on meaning.
    a. Continual
    b. Massed practice
    c. Maintenance
    d. Elaborative

15. _____ occurs when our brains fill in the gaps in memory with logic, guessing, or new information.
    a. Redintegration
    b. Constructive processing
    c. Eidetic imaging
    d. Consolidation

16. According to state-dependent learning, if one is drinking a caffeinated beverage while studying, it may be most beneficial for memory retrieval to:
    a. drink some of that beverage prior to or during testing
    b. allow time for the body to eliminate the caffeine before taking the test
    c. look at the beverage container while testing
    d. wait at least one day to take the test

17. Multiple-choice questions measure memory through _____.
    a. recognition
    b. recall
    c. relearning
    d. all of the above

18. Eidetic imagery is more common in:
    a. adolescents than in children
    b. children than in adolescents or adults
    c. women than in men
    d. men than in women

19. According to the curve of forgetting, the greatest decline in the amount recalled occurs during:
    a. the first 20 minutes
    b. the second day
    c. the third to sixth days
    d. day 1 to day 30

20. When old information keeps you from learning new information, _____ is occurring.
    a. proactive interference
    b. proactive amnesia
    c. retroactive amnesia
    d. retroactive interference

Survey Questions

- How does memory work?
- What are the features of short-term memory?
- What are the features of long-term memory?
- How is memory measured?
- Why do we forget?
- How does the brain form and store memories?
- What are "photographic" memories?
- How can I improve my memory?
- Are there any tricks to help me with my memory?

Intelligence, Cognition, Language, and Creativity

INTELLIGENCE, COGNITION, LANGUAGE, AND CREATIVITY

How we think, communicate, and solve problems are essential elements of being human.

INTELLIGENCE

A common definition of intelligence is an overall capacity to act purposefully, think rationally, and deal effectively with the environment. The core of intelligence is thought to consist of a small set of general mental abilities (the g-factor).

DEFINING AND MEASURING INTELLIGENCE

Intelligence is operationally defined by intelligence tests that express intelligence in the form of an intelligence quotient (IQ). These tests provide useful but narrow estimates of real-world intelligence and are not universally valid for all cultural groups.

RANGE OF MENTAL ABILITIES

The distribution of IQ scores follows a normal curve, with most people scoring in the mid-range. A very small number of people have exceptionally high IQs (often labeled as gifted or geniuses) or exceptionally low IQs (those with an intellectual disability).

CREATIVE THINKING

Creative thinking involves the typical thinking processes plus: fluency (the ability to generate a large number of responses), flexibility (the ability to shift from one class of possible solutions to another), and originality (the ability to create novel or unusual ideas).

INTUITION

Intuition is quick, impulsive thought that does not make use of clear reasoning. It may provide fast answers, but it can also be misleading and sometimes disastrous.

COGNITION

Thinking (cognition) is influenced by how the information is mentally represented, which can come in the form of images, concepts, and language (symbols). Knowing the pitfalls of intuitive thought can aid in avoiding some common thinking errors.

PROBLEM SOLVING

Problems are solved by acquiring knowledge and developing strategies.

STAGES OF CREATIVE PROBLEM SOLVING

Typically, there are 5 stages: orientation, preparation, incubation, illumination, and verification.

LANGUAGE AND MEANING

Language is a system for encoding and manipulating information. Language carries meaning by combining symbols according to rules (grammar), including word order (syntax). Meaning influences thinking in language. Denotative meaning is the exact, objective, dictionary definition of a word or concept. Connotative meaning is the subjective, personal, or emotional meaning of a word or concept.

IMAGES

Images are mental representations that can be three-dimensional or kinesthetic. Most often, an image is a mental representation that has picture-like qualities; an icon.

CONCEPTS

Concepts are generalized ideas of classes of objects or events; they often make use of prototypes and may be conjunctive or disjunctive.

John Bryson/Sygma/Corbis

Menahem Kahana/AFP/Getty Images

concept review for chapter 8

1. In order to estimate a child's intelligence, we need both the child's _____ and _____.
   a. mental age, test score
   b. developmental level, family history
   c. chronological age, mental age
   d. IQ, emotional functioning

2. A concept's objective, dictionary meaning is its _____ meaning.
   a. denotative
   b. connotative
   c. conjunctive
   d. disjunctive

3. _____ allow events to be encoded into symbols for mental manipulation.
   a. Concepts
   b. Languages
   c. Images
   d. Codes

4. A sudden mental reorganization of a problem that makes the solution obvious is called:
   a. insight
   b. enlightenment
   c. understanding
   d. giftedness

5. Which of the following is *not* one of Howard Gardner's eight types of intelligence?
   a. interpersonal
   b. language
   c. music
   d. performance

6. _____ is the global capacity to act purposely, to think rationally, and to deal effectively with the environment.
   a. Intelligence
   b. Creativity
   c. IQ
   d. Inductive reasoning

7. An operational definition of intelligence is based on the:
   a. procedures used to measure intelligence
   b. individual's general level of functioning
   c. culture in which it is measured
   d. theoretical perspective of the clinician

8. A person allows the problem to "cook" or be contemplated unconsciously during which stage of creative thinking?
   a. verification
   b. preparation
   c. orientation
   d. incubation

9. Which is one of the suggestions given by the text to enhance creativity?
   a. Provide immediate evaluation.
   b. Follow mental sets.
   c. Define the problem specifically.
   d. Seek varied input.

10. The basic units of thought include all of the following *except*:
    a. images
    b. language
    c. cognitions
    d. concepts

11. Mitch considers a robin to be his prime example for the concept *bird*. We would then consider a robin to be a(n) _____.
    a. prototype
    b. model
    c. operational definition
    d. semantic concept

12. If Elizabeth (age 10 years old) has an IQ of 100, we know that she has a:
    a. perfect score on the Wechsler Intelligence Test
    b. test score consistent with other 10 year olds within the standardized sample
    c. mental age below children her same age
    d. mental age above children her same age

13. A mechanical solution is achieved by:
    a. trial and error
    b. a learned set of rules
    c. increased understanding
    d. a. or b.

14. A(n) _____ is a "rule of thumb" that reduces the number of possible solutions.
    a. mnemonic
    b. algorithm
    c. heuristic
    d. lexigram

15. The dividing line between normal intelligence and intellectual disability has been an IQ of approximately:
    a. 80
    b. 70
    c. 60
    d. 50

16. Fluency, flexibility, and originality are all components of:
    a. creative thinking
    b. inductive thinking
    c. imaginative thinking
    d. deductive thinking

17. The inability to see new uses for familiar objects is known as:
    a. representative heuristic
    b. selective framing
    c. unimaginative thinking
    d. functional fixedness

18. A quick, impulsive thought without any clear use of reasoning or logic is referred to as:
    a. intuition
    b. wisdom
    c. framing
    d. instinct

19. While taking a test, you are asked to find the one correct answer to a question. This is an example of _____ thinking.
    a. convergent
    b. divergent
    c. conjunctive
    d. disjunctive

20. _____ thought proceeds from specific facts or observations to general principles.
    a. Inductive
    b. Deductive
    c. Intuitive
    d. Discerning

Survey Questions

- How is human intelligence defined and measured?

- How much does intelligence vary from person to person?

- What is the nature of thought?

- What are concepts?

- In what ways are images related to thinking?

- What is the role of language in thinking?

- What do we know about problem solving?

- What is creative thinking?

- How accurate is intuition?

- What can be done to improve thinking and promote creativity?

Motivation and Emotion

MOTIVATION
Internal processes that sustain, direct, and terminate activities

EMOTION
A state characterized by physiological arousal and changes in facial expression, gestures, posture, and subjective feelings. There are 8 primary emotions: fear, surprise, sadness, disgust, anger, anticipation, joy, and trust.

STIMULUS MOTIVES
These motives express our needs for stimulation and information, such as activity, curiosity, exploration, manipulation, and physical contact. While they appear to be innate, they are not strictly necessary for survival.

LEARNED MOTIVES
These are motives based on learned needs, drives, and goals. Many are related to learned needs for power, affiliation, approval, status, security, and achievement.

BIOLOGICAL MOTIVES
These motives are innate and based on needs that must be met for survival. Biological drives are essential because they maintain **homeostasis**, or bodily equilibrium.

AROUSAL THEORY
An ideal level of bodily arousal will be maintained if possible. Optimal performance usually occurs at moderate levels of arousal. High arousal is best for simple tasks, while lower arousal is best for complex tasks.

SOCIAL MOTIVES
Social motives are learned through socialization and cultural conditioning. Such motives account for much of the diversity of human motivation.

HUNGER AND THIRST
Hunger is a basic physiological need involving a complex interplay among stomach fullness, blood sugar levels, metabolism in the liver, and fat stores in the body.

PAIN
Pain avoidance is an episodic drive rather than a regular daily cycle. Most drives prompt us to **seek** a goal, but pain prompts us to **avoid** discomfort.

SEX
Sex is unlike other biological motives because it is not necessary for individual survival but for the survival of the group. **Sex drive** refers to one's motivation to engage in sexual behavior.

OBESITY
Obesity is the result of internal and external influences, diet, emotions, genetics, and exercise. People with weight problems are prone to overeat when they are anxious, angry, or sad. Radical diets may raise the set point for fat, resulting in **diet-induced obesity**.

EATING DISORDERS
Anorexia nervosa and bulimia nervosa tend to involve conflicts about self-image, self-control, and anxiety. Both disorders are serious and can cause physical damage or death.

SEXUAL RESPONSE
Sexual response can be divided into four phases: (1) excitement, (2) plateau, (3) orgasm, and (4) resolution. Although male and female sexual responses are generally quite similar, the differences that do exist can affect sexual compatibility.

Chad Slattery/Getty Images

Mango Productions/Corbis

THEORIES OF EMOTION
offer different answers to these questions. Prominent views include the James-Lange theory, the Cannon-Bard theory, Schacter's Cognitive Theory, emotional appraisal, and the facial feedback hypothesis.

BODY LANGUAGE
Facial expressions, body gestures, and movements all express feeling. Body positioning can reveal feelings that would normally be concealed.

EMOTIONAL INTELLIGENCE
is the ability to perceive, use, understand, and manage emotions. Being emotionally skilled can make us more flexible, adaptive, and emotionally mature.

PHYSIOLOGY OF EMOTION
Physical changes associated with emotion are caused by adrenaline and by activity in the autonomic nervous system (ANS). The sympathetic branch of the ANS activates the body for emergency action. The parasympathetic branch reverses emotional arousal.

"LIE DETECTORS"
The polygraph measures emotional arousal by monitoring physiological changes in the body. The accuracy of the lie detector can be very low.

1. _____ is defined as the force that acts on or within an organism to initiate, sustain, direct, and terminate behavior.
   a. Emotion
   b. Need
   c. Learning
   d. Motivation

2. Which of the following is the correct sequence of the model of motivation?
   a. drive—need—response—goal attainment
   b. need—drive—response—goal attainment
   c. need—drive—goal attainment—response
   d. drive—need—goal attainment—response

3. The psychological expression known as "thirst" corresponds to which aspect of motivation?
   a. need
   b. drive
   c. goal
   d. goal attainment

4. The value of a goal beyond its ability to fill a need is known as:
   a. motivation value
   b. stimulus value
   c. extra value
   d. incentive value

5. Needs for curiosity, activity, exploration, manipulation, and physical contact are classified as:
   a. learned motives
   b. intrinsic motives
   c. biological motives
   d. stimulus motives

6. The body's optimal level of functioning, or its "steady state," is known as:
   a. incentives
   b. drive reductions
   c. homeostasis
   d. learning

7. "Yo-yo" dieting:
   a. involves repeatedly losing and gaining weight
   b. dramatically increases the body's metabolic rate
   c. makes it easier to lose weight
   d. decreases the risk for heart disease

8. Which of the following is *not* a characteristic of bulimia nervosa?
   a. binge eating
   b. tooth decay, sore throat, and hair loss
   c. use of vomiting, laxatives, or diuretics to lose weight
   d. body weight below 85 percent of normal for one's height and age

9. When there is a loss of water from the fluids found within the cells in a person's body, the person will experience:
   a. intracellular hunger
   b. extracellular thirst
   c. intracellular thirst
   d. hypothalamic dysfunction

10. Sally just finished her aerobics class. She will probably experience a(n) _____ thirst.
    a. extracellular
    b. hypothalamic
    c. intracellular
    d. homeostatic

11. According to the arousal theory:
    a. there are ideal levels of activation for various activities
    b. people become uncomfortable when arousal is too low or too high
    c. most adults vary their activities to keep arousal at moderate levels
    d. all of these are true

12. The inverted U function describes the relationship between:
    a. hunger and thirst
    b. affection and curiosity
    c. arousal and performance
    d. performance and persistence

13. Which of the following is the correct order of Maslow's Hierarchy of Needs from the bottom of the pyramid to the top of the pyramid?
    a. physiological, safety, esteem, love and belonging, self-actualization
    b. self-actualization, esteem, safety, love and belonging, physiological
    c. physiological, safety, love and belonging, esteem, self-actualization
    d. physiological, esteem, love and belonging, safety, self-actualization

14. If Tyrone works on his cars simply because he enjoys it, we would say that this activity is one of _____ motivation.
    a. primary
    b. intrinsic
    c. traditional
    d. incentive

15. According to your text, a polygraph measures:
    a. guilt
    b. general emotional arousal
    c. truth
    d. none of these

16. _____ involves a combination of skills, including self-awareness, empathy, and self-control.
    a. Creative thinking
    b. Emotional intelligence
    c. Kinesic sensitivity
    d. Intuition

17. The sleep-wake cycle would be an example of a:
    a. circadian rhythm
    b. daily cycle
    c. secondary motive
    d. 24-hour measure

18. Needs that must be met for survival are called _____ motives.
    a. biological
    b. learned
    c. questionable
    d. stimulus

19. Which theory asserts that emotional feelings follow bodily arousal?
    a. Cannon–Bard theory
    b. James–Lange theory
    c. Schacter's Cognitive Theory of Emotion
    d. Facial feedback theory

20. _____ is characterized by physiological arousal and changes in facial expressions, gestures, posture, and subjective feelings.
    a. Motivation
    b. Affect
    c. Mood
    d. Emotion

ANSWER KEY

1. d 2. b 3. b 4. d 5. d 6. c 7. a 8. d 9. c 10. a 11. d 12. c 13. c 14. b 15. b 16. b 17. a 18. a 19. b 20. d

Survey Questions

- What is motivation? Are there different types of motives?

- What causes hunger? Overeating? Eating disorders?

- Is there more than one type of thirst?

- In what ways are pain avoidance and the sex drive unusual?

- What are the typical patterns of human sexual response?

- How does arousal relate to motivation?

- What are social motives? Why are they important?

- What happens during emotion?

- What physiological changes underlie emotion? Can "lie detectors" really detect lies?

- How accurately are emotions expressed by the face and "body language"?

- How do psychologists explain emotions?

- What does it mean to have "emotional intelligence"?

SHYNESS

A tendency to avoid others combined with uneasiness and strain when socializing is known as **shyness**. It can be reduced by replacing self-defeating beliefs and by learning social skills.

INTERVIEWS

In an **interview**, direct questioning is used to learn about a person's life history, personality traits, or current mental state. Interviewer bias and misperceptions, along with the halo effect, may lower the accuracy of an interview.

DIRECT OBSERVATION

When used for assessment, **direct observation** (looking at behavior) is a simple extension of this natural interest in "people watching." Misperceptions can be a difficulty, which is why rating scales are sometimes used.

QUESTIONNAIRES

These are paper-and-pencil tests that reveal personality characteristics. Questionnaires are more objective than interviews or observation. A good test must also be **reliable** and **valid**.

PROJECTIVE TESTS

Projective tests seek to uncover deeply hidden or *unconscious* wishes, thoughts, and needs. In a **projective test**, a person is asked to describe an unambiguous stimulus. When you are faced with an unstructured stimulus, you must organize what you see in terms of your own life experiences. These tests have low validity because after a person interprets an ambiguous stimulus, the scorer must interpret the person's (sometimes) ambiguous responses.

HUMANISTIC THEORIES

These theories stress subjective experience, free choice, and **self-actualization**. **Self-image** and evaluation are key components of personality development, and the approach emphasizes positive aspects of human nature.

PERSONALITY TRAITS AND TYPES

A **personality trait** is a stable, enduring quality that a person shows in most situations. A personality type is a style of personality defined by a group of related traits.

FREUD AND PERSONALITY

To Freud, the personality is made up of the **id**, **ego**, and **superego**. **Libido** is the primary energy guiding the personality, which operates on the **unconscious**, **preconscious**, and **conscious levels**. Personality development is a result of a series of psychosexual stages, and fixation at any stage can have a lasting impact on personality.

BEHAVIORAL APPROACHES

These theories focus on the effects of learning, conditioning, and situational influences in the development of personality. **Social Learning Theory** expands this perspective to include thinking, expectations, and other mental processes.

Laura Litterio/Photolibrary

PERSONALITY ASSESSMENT

Psychologists use interviews, observation, questionnaires, and projective tests to assess personality. Each method has strengths and limitations. For this reason, they are often used in combination.

PERSONALITY THEORIES

Psychoanalytic theories: Freudian theory of personality that emphasizes unconscious forces and conflicts

Behavioristic theories: Any model of personality that emphasizes learning and observable behavior

Trait theories attempt to learn what traits make up personality and how they relate to actual behavior.

Humanistic theories stress private, subjective experience and personal growth.

PERSONALITY

Personality refers to a consistent yet unique pattern of thinking, emotions, and behavior. Measures of personality reveal individual differences and help predict future behavior of individuals.

concept review for chapter 10

1. In psychology, the term _____ implies that individual patterns of behavior are both stable and unique.
   a. personality
   b. temperament
   c. character
   d. trait

2. The _____ approach is considered an oversimplified view of human personality.
   a. type
   b. psychoanalytic
   c. behavioral
   d. trait

3. _____ is what we call the evaluation of desirable or undesirable characteristics of personality.
   a. Temperament
   b. Character
   c. Self-concept
   d. Assessment

4. A person with _____ self-esteem is confident, proud, and self-respecting.
   a. high
   b. moderate
   c. low
   d. All of these

5. A stable, enduring quality that a person shows in most situations is considered a:
   a. characteristic
   b. personality type
   c. personality trait
   d. typical trait

6. Traits shared by most members of a culture are referred to as _____ traits.
   a. type
   b. cardinal
   c. individualistic
   d. common

7. All your ideas, perceptions, and feelings about who you are make up your:
   a. ideal self
   b. super-ego
   c. individualized concept
   d. self-concept

8. According to Freud, which part of the personality acts as the judge or moral conscience?
   a. id
   b. ego
   c. superego
   d. conscious self

9. Which of the following is the correct order of Freud's psychosexual stages?
   a. anal, oral, phallic, genital
   b. oral, anal, genital, phallic
   c. oral, anal, phallic, genital
   d. phallic, anal, oral, genital

10. According to Freud, the Oedipus and Electra complexes occur during the:
    a. anal stage
    b. latency period
    c. genital stage
    d. phallic stage

11. Ray tells his daughters that he will always accept them and love them, regardless of what they do or don't do. Ray's daughters have received what Rogers would refer to as:
    a. authoritative parenting
    b. unconditional positive regard
    c. self-actualization
    d. unrestricted regard

12. The tendency to generalize a favorable or unfavorable first impression to an entire personality is known as:
    a. the situational bias effect
    b. the androgynous effect
    c. organismic valuing
    d. the halo effect

13. A person who demonstrates both masculine and feminine traits would be referred to as:
    a. confused
    b. androgynous
    c. self neutral
    d. self-reliant

14. The image a person holds of who he or she would like to be is that person's:
    a. self-image
    b. self-concept
    c. ideal self
    d. imagined self

15. Allport would describe Abraham Lincoln's personality trait of honesty as a(n) _____ trait.
    a. cardinal
    b. central
    c. secondary
    d. objective

16. If a test measures what it purports or claims to measure, psychologists say that the test is:
    a. valid
    b. reliable
    c. accurate
    d. precise

17. One of the best-known and most widely used objective personality tests is the:
    a. Wechsler Adult Personality Test
    b. Myers-Briggs Type Indicator
    c. Minnesota Multiphasic Personality Inventory–2

18. You are asked by a psychologist to describe what you see in a set of inkblots. You are probably taking the:
    a. Cognitive Competency Test
    b. Rorschach Technique
    c. Minnesota Multiphasic Personality Inventory–2
    d. House-Tree-Person

19. Albert Bandura referred to the ability to make a certain outcome occur as:
    a. self-evaluation
    b. self-efficacy
    c. self-reinforcement
    d. self-confidence

20. Historically, Western cultures have encouraged _____ behaviors in boys and _____ behaviors in girls.
    a. expressive, instrumental
    b. instrumental, expressive
    c. relational, aggressive
    d. deterministic, passive

Survey Questions

- How do psychologists use the term *personality?*
- Are some personality traits more basic or important than others?
- How do psychodynamic theories explain personality?
- What do behaviorists and social learning theorists emphasize in personality?
- How do humanistic theories differ from other perspectives?
- How do traits and situations affect personality?
- How do psychologists measure personality?
- What causes shyness? What can be done about it?

Health, Stress, and Coping

HEALTH, STRESS, AND COPING

A variety of personal habits and behavior patterns affect health. How we cope with stress will affect the quality of our lives. Health psychology studies how personal habits and behavior patterns can lead to illness and death or promote health and wellness.

STRESS

Stress is the mental and physical condition that occurs when a person must adjust or adapt to the environment.

A **stressor** is the condition or event in the environment that challenges or threatens a person.

Pressure occurs when a person must meet urgent external demands or expectations.

APPRAISING STRESSORS

Primary appraisal involves deciding if a stressor is relevant or irrelevant (or a threat or challenge).

Secondary appraisal involves assessing our resources and choosing a way to cope with a threat or challenge.

COPING

Our coping is **problem focused** when it is aimed at managing or altering the distressing situation. It is **emotion focused** when we attempt to control our emotional reactions to situations.

MANAGING STRESS

The damaging effects of stress can be reduced with stress management techniques (exercise, meditation, progressive relaxation, modifying ineffective behaviors, and avoiding upsetting thoughts).

LEARNED HELPLESSNESS AND DEPRESSION

Learned helplessness is a **learned inability** to overcome obstacles or to avoid punishment; a learned passivity and inaction to aversive stimuli. Learned helplessness has been used as a model for understanding **depression**. Mastery training acts as an antidote to helplessness.

CONFLICT

Choosing between contradictory needs, desires, motives, or demands involves conflict.

Approach-approach: We must choose between two **desirable** alternatives.

Avoidance-avoidance: We must choose between two **undesirable** alternatives.

Approach-avoidance: A single goal has elements that both attract and repel us.

Double approach-avoidance: Each alternative has both positive and negative qualities.

STRESS AND HEALTH

Long-range susceptibility to accident or illness appears to be related to multiple life changes. **Immediate** psychological and mental health is more closely related to the intensity and severity of daily hassles (microstressors). Intense or prolonged stress may cause damage in the form of psychosomatic disorders, in which psychological factors contribute to bodily damage.

SOURCES OF STRESS

Frustration and conflict are often the origins of stress.

FRUSTRATION

External frustration comes from sources outside the individual that impede progress toward the goal. **Personal frustrations** are based on personal characteristics over which a person perceives that she or he has no control.

REACTIONS TO FRUSTRATION

Persistence, circumvention, escape or withdrawal, and **aggression** are common responses to frustration. Aggression may be **direct** or **displaced**. **Scapegoating** refers to blaming a person or group of people for conditions that they had nothing to do with.

DEFENSE MECHANISMS

A **defense mechanism** (commonly referred to as "ego defense mechanism") is a habitual and often unconscious psychological process used to help us avoid, deny, or distort sources of threat or anxiety, including threats to our self-image.

BEHAVIORAL RISK FACTORS

Behaviors that increase the chances of disease, injury, or early death are **behavioral risk factors.** Wellness is based on minimizing risks and engaging in health-promoting behaviors.

SAFE SEX

Small changes in behavior can almost completely eliminate the health hazard of unsafe sex. Use of condoms, refraining from sex with drug users or other high-risk partners, and reducing the number of partners all reduce the risk of sexually transmitted diseases, including AIDS.

concept review for chapter 11

ANSWER KEY

1. b 2. b 3. c 4. d 5. d 6. b 7. d 8. d 9. a 10. c 11. c 12. c 13. d 14. b 15. c 16. a 17. b 18. a 19. d 20. d

1. The branch of psychology that studies how behavioral principles can be used to prevent illness and promote health is known as:
   a. abnormal psychology
   b. health psychology
   c. developmental psychology
   d. holistic psychology

2. According to your textbook, _____ are those causes of death related to health-damaging personal habits.
   a. stressors
   b. neuroimmune risk factors
   c. lifestyle diseases
   d. none of the above

3. According to the textbook, the primary cause of preventable deaths in the United States is:
   a. obesity
   b. suicide
   c. smoking
   d. alcohol and drug abuse

4. _____ is the mental and physical condition that occurs when we adjust or adapt to the environment.
   a. Frustration
   b. Burnout
   c. Anxiety
   d. Stress

5. Stress is considered more damaging when it is both _____ and _____.
   a. unpredictable, controlled
   b. unpredictable, uncontrollable
   c. predictable, controlled
   d. predictable, uncontrollable

6. The general adaptation syndrome:
   a. consists of three stages
   b. is a series of bodily reactions to prolonged stress
   c. is part of the body's defenses against stress
   d. is all of the above

7. The study of the connections among behavior, stress, disease, and the immune system is called:
   a. health psychology
   b. behavioral medicine
   c. psychoneuroimmunology
   d. secondary appraisal

8. Which type of coping is aimed at managing or altering the distressing situation itself?
   a. task coping
   b. situational stress coping
   c. emotion-focused coping
   d. problem-focused coping

9. In managing the threat of layoffs at his place of employment, Paul first asks himself if the layoffs will affect his job. In doing so, Paul is performing a:
   a. primary appraisal
   b. secondary appraisal
   c. threat assessment
   d. risk assessment

10. The habitual redirection of aggression to some person or group is called:
    a. circumvention
    b. projection
    c. scapegoating
    d. sublimation

11. The easiest conflict to resolve is:
    a. multiple avoidance-avoidance
    b. approach-avoidance
    c. approach-approach
    d. double approach-avoidance

12. When one learns that an obstacle exists, even when it does not, one has developed a:
    a. rationalization
    b. compensatory cognition
    c. learned helplessness
    d. reaction formation

13. When stress causes physical damage to the body in the form of stomach pain, asthma, migraine headaches, hives, or hypertension, the person is experiencing:
    a. a somatoform disorder
    b. hypochondrias
    c. a conversion disorder
    d. a psychosomatic disorder

14. After being told that she was being fired, Glenna told her friend that her supervisor did not really mean what she said and that she was planning on coming back to work the next day. This would be considered an example of the coping mechanism known as _____.
    a. regression
    b. denial
    c. fantasy
    d. projection

15. _____ skills training includes practice in stress reduction, self-protection, decision making, goal setting, self-control, and social skills.
    a. Refusal
    b. Resistance
    c. Life
    d. Health

16. The _____ personality is marked by depression, anxiety, and hostility.
    a. disease-prone
    b. Type B
    c. accident-prone
    d. conflicted

17. All of the following may assist in the management of the bodily reaction of stress except:
    a. meditation
    b. progressive disorganization
    c. exercise
    d. guided imagery

18. _____ is a negative emotional state that occurs when people are prevented from reaching desired goals.
    a. Frustration
    b. Stress
    c. Burnout
    d. Eustress

19. Chris aspires to be a horse jockey; however, at 6 feet 4 inches and 230 pounds, the likelihood of this is doubtful. This would be considered a(n) _____ frustration.
    a. repeated
    b. external
    c. internal
    d. personal

20. One of the most frequent responses to frustration is:
    a. depression
    b. aggression
    c. stress
    d. isolation

Survey Questions

- What is health psychology? How does behavior affect health?
- How can sexually transmitted diseases be prevented?
- What is stress? What factors determine its severity?
- What causes frustration and what are typical reactions to it?
- Are there different types of conflict? How do people react to conflict?
- What are defense mechanisms?
- What do we know about coping with feelings of helplessness and depression?
- How is stress related to health and disease?
- What are the best strategies for managing stress?

Psychological Disorders

PSYCHOLOGICAL DISORDERS

Psychological disorders damage the quality of life, in varying degrees, for many people. Psychological disorders are complex and have multiple causes.

CLASSIFYING MENTAL DISORDERS

The most widely used classification system is the *Diagnostic and Statistical Manual of Mental Disorders*, or DSM (American Psychiatric Association, 2000), which standardizes terminology for mental health workers, organizes mental disorders into categories, provides available statistical data, and establishes criteria to assist mental health workers in making a diagnosis.

WHAT IS NORMAL?

Definitions of normality usually take into account **subjective discomfort, statistical abnormality, social nonconformity,** and **situational context. Maladaptiveness** and **loss of control** are two key elements in judgments of disorders.

ANXIETY-BASED DISORDERS

Anxiety refers to feelings of apprehension, dread, or uneasiness. Anxiety that is out of proportion to a situation may reflect a psychological problem that can cause self-defeating behavior patterns.

TYPES OF ANXIETY-BASED DISORDERS

Psychodynamic: Emphasizes unconscious conflicts as the cause of disabling anxiety

Humanistic-existential: Emphasizes the effects of a faulty self-image

Behaviorist: Emphasizes the effects of previous learning (particularly avoidance learning)

Cognitive: Focuses on distorted thinking, judgment, and attention

MOOD DISORDERS

Mood disorders involve disturbances of mood or emotion. Severe mood disorders may include psychotic features.

CAUSES

Major mood disorders (such as depression) are partially explained by genetic vulnerability and changes in brain chemistry. Loss, anger, learned helplessness, stress, and self-defeating thinking patterns are also important.

Bettmann/Corbis

SUICIDE

People often take their own lives to escape, because of unbearable psychological pain and constriction of options. Suicide can often be prevented by the efforts of family, friends, and mental health professionals.

Darren Robb/Getty Images

PSYCHOTIC DISORDERS

Psychotic disorders, the most severe forms of psychopathology, involve emotional extremes or breaks with reality. Typical psychotic episoces can include **hallucinations, delusions, disturbed communication,** and **personality disintegration.**

PERSONALITY DISORDERS

Personality disorders are deeply ingrained (even beginning in childhood) patterns of behavior that are maladaptive (impair the individual's ability to function adaptively or productively).

SCHIZOPHRENIA

Schizophrenia is a psychosis characterized by delusions, hallucinations, apathy, and a wide difference between thought and emotion. Personality disintegration is often a significant element of schizophrenia. There are four major subtypes: disorganized, catatonic, paranoid, and undifferentiated.

CAUSES

Schizophrenia appears to originate from multiple sources. Explanations include combinations of childhood trauma, environmental stress, an inherited susceptibility, and abnormalities in the brain.

DELUSIONAL DISORDERS

A **delusional disorder** involves a psychosis in which severe delusions are present without the hallucinations; extreme emotional reactions, or personality disintegration found in other psychotic disorders. The main feature of delusional disorders is the presence of firmly held false beliefs.

concept review for chapter 12

1. _____ refers to the scientific study of mental, emotional, and behavioral aspects of disorders and of the disorders themselves.
   a. Psychotic intrusion
   b. Physiology
   c. Psychopathology
   d. Neurology

2. A person with a Ph.D. might be considered abnormal if one were using the measure of
   a. personal discomfort
   b. subjective discomfort
   c. statistical abnormality
   d. social rarity

3. In the United States, psychologists use the _____ to classify and identify mental disorders.
   a. MDIS Manual
   b. WAIS
   c. MMPI-2
   d. DSM

4. If Susan is experiencing hallucinations, delusions, and a retreat from reality, we would suspect that she is suffering from a(n):
   a. mood disorder
   b. anxiety disorder
   c. psychotic disorder
   d. personality disorders

5. Narcissistic, Paranoid, and Dependent are all types of:
   a. sexual disorders
   b. mood disorders
   c. anxiety disorders
   d. personality disorders

6. _____ occur when there are physical symptoms in the absence of any identifiable physical causes.
   a. Stress-related disorders
   b. Somatoform disorders
   c. Dissociative disorders
   d. Personality disorders

7. Temporary psychological amnesia, fugue, and multiple personality are classified as _____ disorders.
   a. dissociative
   b. anxiety
   c. psychotic
   d. somatoform

8. Jon's sexual identity does not match his gender and therefore results in personal discomfort. Jon may be diagnosed with a:
   a. paraphilia
   b. sexual confusion disorder
   c. gender-identity disorder
   d. mood disorder

9. Being insane refers to:
   a. any psychiatric diagnosis
   b. a legal declaration indicating an inability to manage one's own affairs or foresee the consequences of one's actions
   c. a psychiatric diagnosis indicating that an individual is suffering from a severe and persistent mental illness
   d. a requirement for involuntary hospitalization

10. A man who believes that he is the President of the United States (even though he is not) may be suffering from a(n) _____.
    a. illusion
    b. hallucination
    c. contradictory sensation
    d. delusion

11. _____ are imaginary sensations, such as seeing, hearing, or smelling things that don't exist in the real world.
    a. Hallucinations
    b. Delusions
    c. Sensory conflicts
    d. Illusions

12. The belief that psychotic disorders are due to a blend of environmental stress and inherited susceptibility is referred to as the
    a. stress-vulnerability model
    b. dialectic stress model
    c. nature-nurture theory
    d. bio-enviro theory

13. Larry has been suffering from a mild depression for the last 3 years. Larry would probably be diagnosed with:
    a. major depressive disorder
    b. bipolar disorder
    c. cyclothymic disorder
    d. dysthymic disorder

14. _____ refers to a disorder in which one's mood alternates between deep mania and deep depression.
    a. Bipolar I disorder
    b. Bipolar II disorder
    c. Cyclothymia
    d. Manic depressive disorder

15. Intrusive thoughts or images occurring against one's will are referred to as:
    a. fixations
    b. obsessions
    c. compulsions
    d. cognitive coercion

16. Which of the following is true of suicide?
    a. Suicide is the leading cause of death among college students.
    b. With respect to marital status, suicide rates are highest for married individuals.
    c. Women make more attempts at suicide than men.
    d. Suicide rates are lowest for the Native American population.

17. The two core features of abnormality are that it is _____ and results in _____.
    a. maladaptive, loss of control
    b. problematic, an inability to concentrate
    c. permanent, mental illness
    d. uncomfortable, projection

18. Donn is experiencing a significant impairment in psychological functioning. We would say that Donn is suffering from a _____ disorder.
    a. physiological
    b. mental
    c. chronic
    d. psychiatric

19. The text lists all of the following warning signs for an impending suicide attempt except:
    a. depression
    b. personality change
    c. sudden mood swing
    d. increased contact with others

20. A _____ is an intense, irrational fear.
    a. stimulus
    b. phobia
    c. panic disorder
    d. generalized anxiety

Survey Questions

- How is abnormality defined?
- What are the major psychological disorders?
- What is the nature of a delusional disorder?
- What are the general characteristics of psychotic disorders?
- What forms does schizophrenia take? What causes it?
- What are mood disorders? What causes them?
- How do psychologists explain anxiety-based disorders?
- What problems result when a person suffers high levels of anxiety?
- What is a personality disorder?
- Why do people commit suicide? Can suicide be prevented?

Photographers Choice RF/SuperStock

Sodapix/Photolibrary

Therapies

THERAPIES
Psychotherapy facilitates positive changes in personality, behavior, and adjustment.

MEDICAL THERAPIES
The major disorders are treated medically by psychiatrists using drugs, electroconvulsive therapy, or surgery intended to alter the brain (psychosurgery).

ORIGINS OF THERAPY
Evidence exists that stone-age man attempted some form of cure for mental problems. Before the development of modern therapies, superstition dominated attempts to treat psychological problems. More humane treatment began with Pinel in 1793.

HUMANISTIC THERAPIES
Therapies that help clients achieve a deeper understanding of their thoughts, emotions, and behavior.

CLIENT-CENTERED THERAPY
This is a nondirective form of therapy based on insights gained from conscious thoughts and feelings. Unconditional positive regard, empathy, authenticity, and reflection are combined to give the client the chance to solve her or his own problems.

EXISTENTIAL THERAPY
Existential therapy focuses on free will, the human ability to make choices, and taking responsibility for one's choices.

GESTALT THERAPY
Gestalt therapy emphasizes immediate awareness of thoughts and feelings. Its goal is to rebuild thinking, feeling, and acting into connected wholes and to help clients break through emotional blockages.

PSYCHOANALYSIS
The main goal of psychoanalysis is to resolve internal conflicts that lead to emotional suffering. Freud relied on four basic techniques to uncover the unconscious roots of neurosis. Psychoanalysis has become rare due to the large expense and extensive time involved.

DIMENSIONS OF THERAPY
Therapies may treat individuals or groups. They may be directive or nondirective. Some therapists assume an active role, while others focus on clients attaining their own insight into the origins and solutions to their problems.

COGNITIVE THERAPY
Cognitive therapists attempt to correct distorted thinking and/or teach improved coping skills.

BEHAVIOR THERAPY
Behavior therapists assume that people have learned responses that cause problems. Relearning more appropriate behaviors brings about change.

BEHAVIORAL TREATMENTS
Many everyday problems can be dealt with by using behavior therapies' application of the principles of learning: positive reinforcement, punishment, and systematic desensitization.
Aversion therapy: Classical conditioning is used to associate maladaptive behavior with aversive events in order to inhibit undesirable responses.
Desensitization: Gradual adaptation and reciprocal inhibition break the link between fear and particular situations.

SEEKING HELP
Awareness of how to locate services is important. While practical considerations enter into the choice of a therapist, the therapist's personal characteristics are of equal importance.

concept review for chapter 13

1. _____ is any psychological technique used to facilitate positive changes in a person's personality, behavior, or adjustment.
   a. Pharmacotherapy
   b. Directive therapy
   c. Psychotherapy
   d. Positive therapy

2. _____ therapy involves only one client and one therapist.
   a. Action
   b. Group
   c. Nondirective
   d. Individual

3. Josh participates in therapy where he meets with other individuals who are going through similar circumstances and who experience similar problems. This type of therapy would best be described as:
   a. time-limited therapy
   b. insight therapy
   c. action therapy
   d. group therapy

4. Which of the following is considered a possible outcome of psychotherapy?
   a. complete personal transformation
   b. total relief of all life stressors
   c. promotion of personal growth
   d. undoing a person's past history

5. Trepanning involves:
   a. the use of electric shock in order to induce a convulsion within the patient's brain
   b. rewarding close approximations of a desired behavior
   c. the use of psychiatric medications to treat mental illnesses
   d. boring a hole in a person's head to "release evil spirits" or relieve pressure

6. _____ developed the first known formal psychotherapy approximately 110 years ago.
   a. Wündt
   b. Pinel
   c. Rogers
   d. Freud

7. Freud relied on four basic techniques to uncover the unconscious roots of neurosis. They include all of the following except:
   a. analysis of transference
   b. dream analysis
   c. free recall
   d. analysis of resistance

8. Whereas Sigmund Freud focused on unconscious forces, _____ found it more beneficial to explore *conscious* thoughts and feelings.
   a. Carl Rogers
   b. Carl Jung
   c. B. F. Skinner
   d. Jean Piaget

9. A therapist who uses ideas such as "free will" and the human ability to make choices would be considered:
   a. behavioral
   b. confrontational
   c. existential
   d. psychoanalytic

10. Albert Ellis utilized an approach known as _____ to change irrational beliefs that cause emotional problems.
    a. rational-emotive behavior therapy
    b. behavior therapy
    c. aversion therapy
    d. transference

11. The use of electrical currents to induce seizure activity in the brain to alleviate the symptoms of depression is known as:
    a. PET
    b. psychosurgery
    c. psychotherapy
    d. ECT

12. A community mental health (CMH) center is a treatment option typically:
    a. serving the upper class or "private pay" clients
    b. providing long-term treatment and inpatient care
    c. offering a wide range of mental health and psychiatric services
    d. utilizing a partial hospitalization approach

13. Jacob has clients in his therapy group act out their personal conflicts. Jacob is using the technique known as:
    a. psychodrama
    b. role reversal
    c. mirror technique
    d. none of the above

14. By watching his father pet dogs without fear, Todd's fear of dogs gradually began to decrease. This learning would be an example of:
    a. operant conditioning
    b. vicarious desensitization
    c. aversion therapy
    d. systematic desensitization

15. Research on the effectiveness of psychotherapy suggests:
    a. For some people, therapy is tremendously helpful.
    b. For some people, therapy is unsuccessful.
    c. Overall, therapy is effective for more people than not.
    d. All of these

16. Which of the following is *not* an element of positive mental health?
    a. sense of identity
    b. the capacity to forgive self and others
    c. committed and loving personal relations
    d. decreased need for physiological medications

17. _____ refers to any use of classical or operant conditioning to directly alter human behavior.
    a. Behavior modification
    b. Action oriented therapy
    c. Person-centered planning
    d. Stimulus generalization

18. When an alcoholic takes a medication that results in his getting nauseous following the ingestion of alcohol, he is experiencing a(n) _____ therapy.
    a. physiological
    b. cognitive
    c. aversion
    d. reality

19. Whenever Dana begins to think of herself as worthless, she snaps a rubber band worn around her wrist. This technique is known as:
    a. overt desensitization
    b. covert sensitization
    c. aversive behaviorism
    d. thought stopping

20. _____ are nonprofessionals who have learned basic skills of counseling.
    a. Self-help groups
    b. Peer counselors
    c. Social workers
    d. Counselors

ANSWER KEY

1. c   2. d   3. d   4. c   5. d   6. d   7. c   8. a   9. c   10. a   11. d   12. c   13. a   14. b   15. d   16. d   17. a   18. c   19. d   20. b

Survey Questions

- How do psychotherapies differ?
- How did psychotherapy originate?
- Is Freudian psychoanalysis still used?
- What are the major humanistic therapies?
- What is behavior therapy?
- Can therapy be conducted at a distance?
- What role do operant principles play in behavior therapy?
- What do various therapies have in common?
- Can psychotherapy be done with groups of people?
- Can therapy change thoughts and emotions?
- How do psychiatrists treat psychological disorders?
- How are behavioral principles applied to everyday problems? How could a person find professional help?

Social Behavior

Mark Adams/Getty Images

Roy Morsch/Corbis

SOCIAL BEHAVIOR
Social psychology studies how we behave, think, and feel in social situations.

SOCIAL INFLUENCE
When people interact, they almost always affect one another's behavior. Social influence ranges from mild to strong.

MERE PRESENCE
The gentlest form of social influence is mere presence: changing behavior just because other people are nearby.

BYSTANDER APATHY
Unwillingness to offer help during emergencies occurs when bystanders perceive that others are more likely to help (diffusion of responsibility) or when they lack empathy for the victim.

CONFORMITY
The groups of which we are members may prompt us to **conform** (to bring our behavior into agreement or harmony with the norms or behaviors of others in the group). **Sanctions** administered by groups enforce conformity among the members.

MULTICULTURALISM
A recognition and acceptance of human diversity. It gives equal status to different ethnic, racial, and cultural groups. Multicultural harmony can be attained through conscious efforts to be more tolerant of others.

COMPLIANCE
When a person bends to the requests of someone who has little or no authority, he or she is **compliant**. Assertiveness training may help us become more direct and honest in our expression of feelings and desires.

AGGRESSION
Aggression refers to any action carried out with the intention of harming another person. Aggression has many potential causes. The human capacity for aggression is staggering. A variety of theories offer explanations, including ethological, biological, frustration-aggression, and social learning theories.

OBEDIENCE
We **obey** when we change our behavior in direct response to the demands of an authority.

COERCION
Cults and other coercive groups sometimes use **forced attitude change.** Brain-washing requires isolating the target and making her or him dependent on the indoctrinator, who can reward the target for changes in attitudes or behavior.

AFFILIATION
A basic human characteristic, the need to affiliate is based on human desires for approval, support, friendship, and information.

INTERPERSONAL ATTRACTION
Proximity, frequent contact, beauty, competence, and similarity affect interpersonal attraction, the basis for most voluntary social relationships.

ATTITUDES
A learned tendency to respond to people, objects, or institutions in a positive or negative way

FORMING ATTITUDES
Direct contact, interaction with others, group membership, mass media, child-rearing practices, and chance conditioning may all play a role in attitude formation.

LIFE IN SOCIAL GROUPS
Each person is born into an organized society with established values, expectations, and behaviors.

STRUCTURE, COHESION, AND NORMS
Our behaviors within groups are affected by **structure, cohesion,** and **norms.**

PERSUASION
Persuasion is any deliberate attempt to change attitudes or beliefs through information and arguments.

ATTITUDES THAT INJURE
Prejudice is a negative emotional attitude held toward members of a specific social group. Scapegoating, personal experiences, and adherence to group norms are common origins.

1. The area of psychology that studies how individuals behave, think, and feel in social situations is called:
   a. behavioral psychology
   b. social psychology
   c. developmental psychology
   d. humanistic psychology

2. A(n) _____ psychologist might believe that mating-preference differences between genders developed innately, in response to the differing reproductive challenges faced by men and women.
   a. social
   b. cognitive
   c. evolutionary
   d. fundamental

3. Jaime gets cut off on the highway while driving to class. Her first belief is that the person driving the other car was rude and self-absorbed. She does not consider the situational influences that may have affected the driver's actions. Jaime has committed:
   a. self-serving biasing
   b. the fundamental attribution error
   c. actor-observer bias
   d. cognitive reversal

4. When we change our behavior in direct response to the demands of those in authority, we are exhibiting:
   a. obedience
   b. discrimination
   c. compliance
   d. conformity

5. _____ is an urge by decision makers to maintain each other's approval, even at the cost of critical thinking.
   a. Deadlock
   b. The halo effect
   c. Group sanction
   d. Groupthink

6. Stanley Milgram's experiments in which a subject gave varying degrees of shocks to a "learner" demonstrated the effects of the situation on the subject's _____.
   a. obedience
   b. understanding
   c. stress levels
   d. acceptance

7. The car salesperson who only asks you to sit in a car but who later hopes you will take it for a drive and eventually buy it is utilizing the _____ effect.
   a. door-in-the-face
   b. high-ball
   c. foot-in-the-door
   d. low-ball

8. The deliberate attempt to change attitudes or beliefs with information and arguments is called:
   a. social manipulation
   b. social influence
   c. persuasion
   d. compliance

9. Billy paid $120 for a pair of shoes even though he typically believes that he should not pay more than $50 for a pair of shoes. Because of this contradiction in thoughts and behaviors, Billy is experiencing increased anxiety. This anxiety may be a result of what social psychologists refer to as _____.
   a. pessimistic realism
   b. cognitive dissonance
   c. attitude contradiction
   d. groupthink

10. Which best describes stereotypes?
    a. They are oversimplified images of people in various groups.
    b. They are always negative.
    c. They are always positive.
    d. Both a. and b.

11. After Bruce finished his exam, he was compelled to ask others how they had done and what grade they had received. Leon Festinger would refer to Bruce's actions as an example of:
    a. self-serving bias
    b. cultural association
    c. social comparison
    d. humanistic curiosity

12. Which of the following is involved in interpersonal attraction?
    a. physical proximity
    b. similarity
    c. physical attractiveness
    d. all of the above

13. Social psychologists would describe an affection toward another person that lacks passion or a deep commitment as:
    a. liking
    b. loving
    c. companionate care
    d. infatuation

14. _____ are patterns of behavior expected of persons in various social positions.
    a. Cultural affiliations
    b. Values
    c. Personality traits
    d. Social roles

15. Devon considers himself a big Detroit Lions fan and identifies with other Lions fans. He also despises the Chicago Bears and cannot understand why anyone would want to be a fan of that team. For Devon, other Detroit Lions fans would be considered a(n) _____, while Chicago Bears fans would be a(n) _____.
    a. out-group, in-group
    b. social support, social threat
    c. benefit, detriment
    d. in-group, out-group

16. If raising your hand in class prior to asking a question is considered a socially accepted standard of behavior, we would call this activity a _____.
    a. moral
    b. value
    c. norm
    d. limitation

17. The text describes _____ as a mixture of belief and emotion that predisposes a person to respond to other people, objects, or groups in a positive or negative way.
    a. behavior modification
    b. an attitude
    c. personality
    d. affect

18. Prejudice is to discrimination as _____ is to _____.
    a. belief, behavior
    b. cognition, understanding
    c. action, behavior
    d. behavior, understanding

19. _____ implies that the more people likely any one person will be to take responsibility.
    a. Social desensitization
    b. Bystander apathy
    c. Empathic diffusion
    d. Thought stopping

20. Beliefs that imply people get what they deserve are known as _____ beliefs.
    a. self-fulfilling
    b. discriminating
    c. just-deserts
    d. just-world

Survey Questions

- Why do people affiliate? What factors influence interpersonal attraction?
- How does group membership affect our behavior?
- How do psychologists explain human aggression?
- Why are bystanders so often unwilling to help in an emergency?
- How can we promote multiculturalism and social harmony?
- What causes prejudice and intergroup conflict?
- How are attitudes acquired and changed?
- How does self-assertion differ from aggression?
- What have social psychologists learned about social influence?
- How does group membership affect our behavior?

BEHAVIORAL STATISTICS

Statistics allow us to summarize the results of psychological studies and draw valid conclusions about behavior. Statistics bring greater clarity and precision to psychological thought and research.

DESCRIPTIVE STATISTICS

To get a clear picture of how people behave, we often use descriptive statistics to organize and summarize numbers. This allows us to see trends and patterns in the results of psychological investigations.

GRAPHICAL STATISTICS

Graphical statistics present numbers pictorially. Different types of graphs and tables show us the data in an organized manner.

NORMAL CURVE

The normal curve occurs in the form of a bell-shaped distribution, with a large number of scores in the middle, tapering to very few extremely high and low scores. Many psychological variables tend to form a normal curve.

CENTRAL TENDENCY

The tendency for a majority of scores to fall in the midrange of possible values

MEASURES OF CENTRAL TENDENCY

Mean: Calculated by adding a group of scores and then dividing by the total number of scores

Median: Found by arranging scores from the highest to the lowest and selecting the score that falls in the middle

Mode: Found by identifying the most frequently occurring score in a group of scores

VARIABILITY

Knowing the "average" may not be sufficient. Sometimes we need to know the way that average was distributed. Were the scores all close to the average or were they widely dispersed?

Z-SCORE

A number that tells how many standard deviations above or below the mean a score is

STANDARD DEVIATION

An index of how much a typical score differs from the mean of a group of scores

RANGE

The difference between the highest and lowest scores in a group of scores

INFERENTIAL STATISTICS

Some statistical techniques can be used to generalize results from samples to populations, to make decisions, to draw conclusions, and to tell if the results of a study could have occurred by chance.

CAUSATION VS. CORRELATION

Correlation is the existence of a consistent, systematic relationship between two events, measures, or variables. Finding a correlation between two measures does not mean, by definition, that one causes the other. Often two correlated measures are related due to the influence of a third variable.

concept review for appendix

1. Statistics used for decision making, which generalize from small samples and from which one might draw conclusions, are known as _____.
   a. inferential
   b. directive
   c. descriptive
   d. insightful

2. If in figuring test grades for a class you decide to find a "typical score" for the class, you may be looking for:
   a. the mean
   b. the median
   c. the mode
   d. all of the above

3. If instead of a "typical score," you decide it would be more interesting to find how spread out the scores are, you would employ a measure of _____.
   a. central tendency
   b. variability
   c. commonality
   d. inconsistency

4. If Peter has a score on his exam of 130, with the average score for the class being 120, and a standard deviation of 10, his z-score would be _____.
   a. +1.0
   b. +0.1
   c. −1.0
   d. −0.1

5. The distribution of intelligence (IQ scores) within the general population demonstrates a large number of scores in the middle, tapering to very few extremely high and low scores. This distribution could be considered a _____.
   a. normal curve
   b. z-score
   c. standard deviation
   d. standard of regression

6. In Porsha's study of college students' study habits, she has decided to draw her conclusions from a small group of students within her psychology class. She will then apply her findings to college students in general. Porsha is using a _____ for data collection.
   a. random analysis
   b. population
   c. sample
   d. none of the above

7. Tests of _____ provide an estimate of how often experimental results could have occurred by chance alone.
   a. representative transference
   b. correlational coefficients
   c. random assignment
   d. statistical significance

8. If for every bowl of Wheatios cereal eaten each day, your cholesterol dropped five points, we would conclude that:
   a. a perfect positive correlational relationship exists
   b. it is by mere chance, and no relationship exists
   c. a causal relationship exists
   d. a perfect negative correlational relationship exists

9. Causation is _____.
   a. easily proved when using naturalistic observations
   b. a strong correlation
   c. subjective
   d. difficult to prove

10. Graphical statistics include all of the following examples *except:*
    a. frequency polygons
    b. histograms
    c. frequency distributions
    d. frequency diagrams

Survey Questions

• What are descriptive statistics?

• How are correlations used in psychology?

• What are inferential statistics?